FIELDING'S EUROPE 1981

Temple Fielding

Fielding Publications

105 Madison Avenue, New York, N.Y. 10016

In association with William Morrow & Company, Inc.,

Publishers: New York

To my brother,
Captain Dodge Fielding, F. A.
(Philippines, April 30, 1945)
Ever enchanted by travel,
he took the Big Trip with
his usual smile.

Nancy and Temple Fielding

About the FIELDING TEAM

Temple Fielding

A native of New York City who grew up in Stamford, Conn., TEMPLE FIELD-ING has lived with his wife Nancy and son Dodge on the island of Mallorca for more than 25 years.

The idea for *Fielding's* sprang from an orientation booklet Lieutenant (later Major) Fielding—just out of Princeton—was ordered to write for incoming recruits at Fort Bragg. It was so successful that it was adapted by other camps, and over 2 million copies were distributed. Then he was assigned to special intelligence with guerrilla forces in North Africa, and the Balkans, spending several months behind enemy lines in Yugoslavia with Tito.

After the war, FIELDING, by this time a budding foreign correspondent, was working in Europe and found that there was no really practical travel guide available. Nancy suggested that he write his own, using the same highly readable style as in the Fort Bragg manual. And so he did, and so it changed his life and the lives of millions of travelers.

As earlier stated, *Fielding's* was the first revolution in travel guides of this century—the introduction of the practical where-to, what-to, how-to frame-work that avoided what the author calls "the tinsel illusions of Graustarkian fairyland peopled by picturesque native dancers" and also steered clear of the "deadly tedious cathedrals-and-cobblestones" approach of the Baedekers. The inaugural edition in 1948 was such an immediate hit that FIELDING gave up his other writing assignments to devote all his time to annually strengthening this pioneer trailblazer and later to creating and developing the rest of this series.

Glamour job? Not so, says FIELDING. "Only our editors and we can have an inkling of the job's demands upon our legs, digestions, energies, and lives in general. It is ruthless." Last year the team inspected approximately 2100 hotels or pensions, dined in some 700 restaurants, inspected 800 shops, explored at least 350 night spots, and visited hundreds of incidental attractions during their rigorous 5- to-6-month research rounds.

Up to 150,000 words of *Fielding's* are revised or rewritten every year. Al-though the Central Offices are in a neighboring town, much of his writing is done at Villa Fielding, a dazzling white house perched on a mountainside in Mallorca. There he works at an oversize, U-shaped desk painted his favorite color—marine blue—with his only 4-footed "Editorial Assistant," his beloved Golden Labrador Retriever, sprawled at his feet. With a grin, he tells people that Tina and he often hold heated discussions on arcane or esoteric points of syntax.

TEMPLE FIELDING'S 24 foreign decorations or awards for his work include 2 Knight Commanderships and 5 Knighthoods.

Nancy Parker Fielding

Famed international hostess, epicurean cook, imaginative decorator, crossword fiend, and hopelessly soft touch for pets of all shapes and sizes, gifted and glamorous Nancy Fielding lived an unusually happy childhood with her silver-designing family in Newburyport, Mass. After matriculating at Bradford Junior College, Pembroke (Brown University) and Katherine Gibbs, for 2 years she was initiated into her future vocations as an assistant to massively productive author-publisher Fulton Oursler. Several months after she had joined Fulton's sister-in-law as a junior partner in a New York literary agency venture, the boss married and turned over the struggling business to her. So dew-fresh at 23 that the editors fondly dubbed her "Betty Co-Ed with the braids," she sallied forth to build the renamed Nancy Parker Agency into one of the most highly respected authors' representatives in America.

In 1941, through the matchmaking machinations of a *Readers Digest* editor, she met a young Carolina-based Army officer named Temple Fielding and signed him up as the lowest-ranking client on her totem pole. After 5 dates in 2 months they were married. The early pressure following the enormously successful debut of the *Travel Guide* became so overwhelming that in 1950 she took a sabbatical abroad to rescue him. Quickly they became an inseparable team, visiting more than 160 countries together. Co-author of 2 of the annual Fielding books, she is a former columnist for Publishers-Hall Syndicate and foreign correspondent for a number of magazines and newspapers. In addition to numerous other honors and awards, she has been elevated by Spain's government to the rank of Dame of the high Order of Mérito Civil.

Her cookbook collection contains more than 1000 volumes. She also collects perfumes, passionately follows football, baseball, and other sports, plays dangerous poker and kalookie, and produces a continuous parade of utterly useless geegaws in needlepoint.

Joseph A. Raff

Joseph A. Raff, affectionately known as Tio Pepe ("Uncle Joe") in the Fielding circle, first came to Mallorca in 1961 to assist Temple on a complex and difficult one-shot project. Their professional marriage clicked so happily and their friendship rooted so rapidly that within weeks Joe was enlisted as a permanent member of the staff. Today he is the President of Fielding Publications. When not in orbit, the Raffs base themselves at a 350-year-old farmhouse which they have enchantingly reconstructed on a verdant hillside overlooking the ancient Mallorca village of Pollensa and the sea.

Though born in New York, Joe spent most of his younger years in the South. A graduate of the University of North Carolina at Chapel Hill, his further studies in International Relations took him to Indiana, Ohio, and Harvard Universities. Journalism has always been his pursuit. Starting with school papers, he moved to become a Wire Editor of the Associated Press, a reporter for 3 top newspapers in North Carolina, the Automotive Editor for *Sports Illustrated,* and then, after leaping the Atlantic, the Managing Editor of the *Rome Daily American.* It was from the Eternal City that the Fielding travel interests lured him. Indefatigably to maintain the balance between the changing tastes of the Fielding readers and the changing scenes of Europe has long been Joe's vocational lifeblood and Golden Fleece.

Nonprofessionally his joy in sports also keeps him moving. Although Judy has persuaded him to give up auto racing, regularly he descends Europe's fastest ski runs, plays expert tennis, and captains his beloved deepwater Danish sloop.

Dodge Fielding

PEDRO COLL

Dodge Fielding has inhaled and exhaled travel from infancy. After becoming a permanent European resident at the age of 5, his Seven League Boots have spanned more than 31 times Marco Polo's mileage. His present tally of countries, territories, and possessions visited is 92. He speaks 4 languages without accent and 3 others fluently.

Born in New York and matriculated at Dutch, Spanish, and Danish primary schools, he advanced through Massachusetts' Governor Dummer Academy and the World Campus Afloat to a B.A. from Hamilton College in Clinton, New York.

Vocationally and avocationally his background is characteristically in keeping as a Fielding. From childhood he has been immutably wedded to the creative pen. At 10 he composed and bylined 7 of his father's syndicated columns. At 14 he wrote feature interviews in Spanish for 2 Madrid newspapers. At 17 he made his debut with the company in an independent research sweep through 28 cities in 18 nations to provide the information base for the maiden edition of *Fielding's Low-Cost Europe*. As fruit of the comprehensive 7-year training period with Fielding Publications, including a 2-year technical hiatus with an international airline and major travel agency in Manhattan, he added his own perennial to the clan's list of annually revised guidebooks: *Fielding's Favorites, Hotels and Inns, Europe*.

Dodge is the founder and president of the Fielding Corporation, dedicated to the expansion of the group's non-publishing interests in the travel market. Among projects recently concieved and developed by him is the LIVING GUIDE toll-free travel-tip hotline service, the second Fielding-inspired revolution in the industry.

When not on the road or behind his desk, the bon-vivant bachelor can be found on a racquetball court, a karate mat, a reef 100 feet under Caribbean waters, a sandtrap on a golf course, or in the cockpit of a Beechcraft Bonanza.

Judy Raff

Judy Raff came to the Fielding team as a bonus—and what a sage, gracious, scintillating one she is! While Joe was being broken in with Temple in the early sixties, her keen, ever-questing mind became restless for the challenges of new horizons. Nancy and Joe immediately made capital of her sharp eyes, impeccable taste, and unusual intuition by first training her in professionally evaluating the merchandise and fashion worlds for the *Shopping Guide*. From this sphere she progressed rapidly to gathering, weighing, and reporting on every major field of activity covered in all of the Fielding series, splitting her concentration neatly among 3 of its annually-revised volumes. Since 1964 she has been Chief Researcher of the company.

Her U.S. venue is the desert country of the Southwest; the family residence is in Las Vegas. Born in Philadelphia into the broadcasting world, she followed the air waves to New York (where as a child she was a Quiz Kid), to North Carolina (where she handled programming and radio station schedules in the Tar Heel capital), and finally to Europe (where her frequent and arduous cross-continental forays with Joe provide double coverage of their beats). Her education is a nomadic moveable feast provided by the Connecticut College for Women, the University of North Carolina at Chapel Hill, and New York University, where she took a B.A. in history plus graduate courses in art history. Apart from her career with the Fielding clan, Judy has also been active in the fields of architecture, home-living, and magazine redesign.

Like Nancy, she is widely known as an outstanding international hostess. Her chief avocations are the happy pursuit of culinary exotica within the score of nations she regularly visits, zealous tennis, resolute skiing, and crewing aboard the Danish sloop which is the Raffs' beloved second home.

Temple Fielding Travel Award

1981 marks the first occasion that the Temple Fielding Travel Award has been bestowed upon a totally American-oriented organization—illustrating, in our view, that for trailblazers there are no fixed boundaries, and there should be no frontiers except, perhaps, the limits of man's own imagination. Our wide, beauteous, and bountiful country has profited immeasurably from the steadfast and pioneering Greyhound spirit which has swung wide the portals of our republic to welcome visitors from foreign lands. And opening doors means opening minds. Through its program of unlimited travel for low pre-paid fares, a privately motivated people-to-people diplomacy of the most gratifying sort has been solidly constructed. We applaud this achievement as we praise all efforts to broaden understanding. And especially this year do we honor the Greyhound harrier.

The Temple Fielding Travel Award is emblazoned with this simple but potent inscription:

FOR OPENING NEW TRAVEL HORIZONS TO HUMANITY

The Temple Fielding Travel Award is a 64-pound block of sea-green crystal created by distinguished Master Sculptor Vicke Lindstrand at the Kosta manufactory, Sweden.

GREYHOUND

Me To You

(The Confession Box)

This book was the First Revolution in travel guides of the century.

In 1946, before the *Reader's Digest* sent this budding correspondent on a 5-month swing through Europe and Africa, to my dismay only 2 types of touring information—the Baedeker class which measured the monuments and counted the stained-glass windows and the Burton Holmes-Clara Laughlin class which extolled the picturesque native dancers and the sunsets over Ben-Gay Castle.

But sightseeing was not my motivation. At each stop, which would be the decent hotels? Which would have bedbugs? Where could I find the best food and how could I avoid the tourist traps? Which nightclub would show the most? How much should I tip? These and dozens of similar questions were nagging enigmas until I could sweat out their answers the hard way on the spot.

Thus, at the suggestion of my Nancy, I researched and wrote the first comprehensive where-to, what-to, how-to travel companion which concentrated almost exclusively on the hard practicalities of everyday living for the overseas voyager. It was the start of a new school of travel reportage.

Today, 35 years later, we have forged our profession's *Second* Revolution in our toll-free, totally free LIVING GUIDE service exclusively for our readers which is described elsewhere.

Readers are sometimes curious about the backstage operations of this book. Who gathers the information? Who collaborates? Do we travel under our own names? How much freeloading and "compliments of the management" can we squeeze? What kind of a rakeoff do we get from merchants and other businesses we recommend?

Here's a quick glimpse at the inside picture:

First, the name "Fielding" has envolved from a once-upon-a-time one-man band to a generic word involving the most finely honed, smoothly functioning team it has ever been my joy and my privilege to encounter. In 1950 my Nancy sold her New York literary agency to become my first Chief of Staff, researcher, and full-time collaborator abroad. In love, unification in every emotion and endeavor is a miraculous treasure. In 1961 prophetic fate brought us the golden sunlight of Joseph Allen Raff and his lovely, brilliant wife Judy. He has become our President and she our Chief Reseacher. In temperaments, in professional gifts, in ever-sparkling personalities they fit with perfection into the extraordinary special demands which this exacting field requires. Then in 1967 our Marco Polo son Dodge, who had been in intensive training for 7 years, attained the maturity to join hands with Nancy, Judy, Joe, and me, adding his own remarkable aptitude, talents, and background to the clan. He is a dynamo who ideally rounds out the circle. Our Administrative Vice President, Estanislao ("Stan") de la Cruz, whose half-Chinese, half-Spanish bloodline brings out all the grace, loyalty, sparkle, and nobility of both nationalities, with the alert assistance of faithful Jaime Sebastian, has for the 18th year been a tower of strength in running his department and in coordinating the enormous mass of raw material which was ultimately fed into these pages. Our adored New York-based anchor, Eunice Riedel, has long drawn this group's ringing vote as the best Editor in the U.S. publishing industry. She, her competent assistant Wick Sloane, and her X-ray-vision guys and gals continue to dedicate their professional hearts, souls, expertise, and élan to the gargantuan task of keeping on the track of each of the millions of words, spellings, punctuation marks, collations, and other far more technical challenges in the 13 separate volumes produced by our company. In sum, this all-for-all cohesion works out in the very special happy harmony which can be built only through mutual respect, toil, and devotion.

Hundreds of scattered friends and thousands of kind readers have also provided a priceless flow of facts and advice. (If you should write and then not hear from us for months, it's only because we're traveling, we're swamped, and we're so tired at the end of those days that no juice is left for correspondence.)

But the key factor must always be this: The 5 of us have got to remain the *only* ones upon whom the responsibility of this book rests, with me as the final authority. It was often necessary to override other opinions. In this way, a united single level of judgment can be maintained from cover to cover, encouraging you, the reader, to measure your tastes against ours and to make your own uniform adjustment throughout. As a corollary, the sole way to keep this standard alive is for all of those qualified to get out and see those spots for ourselves. Excluding some of Dodge's hideaways, we in the clan have personally covered perhaps 98% of the establishments listed, and, for the rest, it's clear when we haven't.

Third, none of us ever introduces himself or herself until the check has been paid or the work has been done. Our primary obsession is to be accepted as Mr. and Mrs. John Smith, routine American tourists, who apparently speak nothing but English, who are typically easygoing, and who might be somewhat baffled by it all (which is often too true!). Sometimes we lose our little game by being spotted and identified—but the frequency with which we win it, especially after retrudging so much of the same ground time and time again, continues to astound us.

Fourth, this book is 100% independent and 100% clean. The policies to which we have fiercely and totaly adhered for 35 years are far, far tighter than the laudable Code of Ethics of the American Society of Travel Writers. We're proud to say that we've always been faithful to our principles as working reporters—and we're going to stay that way.

Fifth, we pick up our checks wherever we go—often under strenuous protest from the people we write about. In case anyone cares, the ledgers of our 2 companies show that we spent $158,422.24 last year in travel and operating expenses.

Sixth, we work continuously, the calendar round. Our year normally breaks down into 6 months on the road and 6 months of committing to manuscript the new facts and impressions gathered along the way. On a basis of physical fact, with no impertinence or self-assertion, we just haven't come across anyone else in the travel world—author, travel agent, transportation official, or otherwise—who could spare the time or expend the energy and money to visit *personally* even 25% of this number of European facilities.

Seventh, you and we are bound to have violent disagreements at times, due to the necessarily arbitrary structure of this kind of writing. You'll probably call some of our advice fatheaded and many of our conclusions noxious. Only a moron could agree with every sentence on every page—and that's not you, this year's sharp-eyed, travelwise pilgrim! So please regard this book merely as a broad, general tool for your touring pleasure—not as an encyclopedia with all the final answers.

Eighth, sundry skimmers of this opus have accused us of concentrating entirely upon deluxe sites that offer breast of nightingale and liveried footmen as standard equipment. This is nonsense. You'll come across bargains galore in this volume—thousands, thousands, and thousands of them. But if you're a *serious* economizer who seeks ONLY the bottom-budget lodgings and facilities of the Continent, our annually revised paperback, *Fielding's Low-Cost Europe,* has been tailor-made to s-t-r-e-t-c-h every penny of your journey until it hollers. There simply isn't space here to list more tight-economy places than we have already done—so we created this specialized book, now in its 15th voluminously revised and updated annual edition, to blanket these armies of additional entries.

Last, as you will see, we are ruthless in our coverage of clip joints, tourist traps, conniving taxi drivers, hucksters who pay under-the-counter commissions on voyagers' purchases, storekeepers with a special set of prices for U.S. neophytes, and all foreign agencies that deceive or swindle the cheerfully honest North American. In a less venomous way, we're sharply critical of what we believe is a dirty restaurant, a punk hotel, an overpriced merchant, mediocre food, an overrated sightseeing attraction, or any facility which, in our most thoughtful observation, doesn't deliver full value for the traveler's hard-earned dollar. Because nobody wants to read an opinion that his establishment robs the customer or is overrun with bedbugs, this policy has made scores of bitter enemies over the years. Here's the crux: You, our reader, are our *only* consideration in this text. We did not write it for the benefit of hotels, restaurants, airlines, shops, or any other agencies, good or bad. Instead, your protection and your interests are not only paramount to us, but exclusive. Trite as it might sound, your travel happiness is our modest but utterly sincere personal crusade.

Errors, bloopers, boners? With any good fisherman, editor, or author, a few big ones (sometimes horrifyingly big!) are bound to get away—and you'll find them, sure as shooting. If you'll pause to consider the sheer number and bulk of facts in this more than 1,250,000-word treatise on the NOW living patterns of 26 independent nations or key tourist areas, perhaps we'll be forgiven if the occasional but inevitable howler should let you down. As Polydorus said, 2 millenniums ago, "Perfection is unthinkable—except for a beautiful woman." Hence, all we can do is sweat, try like hell, cross our fingers until the knuckles crack, and then brace ourselves our hardest.

This edition which now sits in your hand is the distillation of 35 years of solid work, more than 3-million European miles, countless hours of editorial polishing, and actual field trial by millions upon millions of pilgrims abroad. It has come a long, long way from the slender manuscript we so timidly introduced to the traveler back in '48. Therefore, we're especially happy for the chance to make this offering, by far the best and by far the most useful we've ever produced.

Our fondest hope is that your trip—even if it's in your armchair—gives you half the fun and half the delight that we had with the text of this good-humored companion.

T.H.F.

Europe, the United Kingdom, Ireland . . . Formentor, Mallorca, Balearic Isles.

CURRENCY GUIDE

As we go to press, the value of the dollar on the international money market is as follows. The values are, of course, subject to change, so please consult current rates to determine exact prices.

Austria — $1 = 12.84 schillings	S50 = $3.90	S100 = $7.79
Belgium — $1 = 28.95 francs	FR50 =$1.73	FR100 =$3.45
Denmark — $1 = 5.63 kroner	KR50 = $8.85	KR100 = $17.70
England — $1 = .44 pounds	£50 = $113	£100 = $226
Findland — $1 = 3.71 markaa	MK50 = $13.45	MK100 = $26.90
France — $1 = 4.19 francs	FR50 = $11.90	FR100 = $23.80
Germany — $1 = 1.79 marks	DM50 = $27.85	DM100 = $55.70
Greece — $1 = 41.8 drachmas	DR50 =$1.20	DR100 = $2.44
Ireland — $1 = .48 punts	£50 = $103	£100 = $206

(Note: There is no longer parity between English and Irish currency.)

Italy — $1 = 844 lire	L50 = $.05	L100 = $.08
Liechtenstein — *Uses Swiss francs*		
Luxembourg — *Uses Belgian francs*		
Monaco — *Uses French francs*		
Nethermands — $1 = 1.98 guldens	G50 = $25.15	G100 =$50.31
Norway — $1 = 4.92 kroner	KR50 = $10.50	KR100 = $21
Portugal — $1 = 49.15 escudos	$50 = US$1.01	$100 = US$2.02
Scotland — *Uses English pounds*		
Spain — $1 = 70.35 pesatas	PTS50 = $.71	PTS100 = $1.42
Sweden — $1 = 4.2 kronor	KR50 = $11.90	KR100 = $23.80
Switzerland — $1 = 1.66 francs	FR50 = $30.12	FR100 = $60.24

Through some currencies are quoted to three decimal places and more on international money markets, figures here were rounded off to the second decimal. As three decimals were used in some calculations, however, the one-hundred-unit calculation is not always exactly twice the fifty-unit calculation.

FIELDING'S EUROPE 1981

Contents

Let's Get Ready

THE LIVING GUIDE This innovation—available gratis through the detachable card—could be your single most helpful travel aid in all of the European series of our books.

Now we have leaped beyond the cold confines of the printed page. At your disposal is our Fielding-trained group of warm, knowledgeable, and dedicated human beings who will *care* about you and the success of your trip. At their fingertips is a treasure house of last-minute, Continent-wide information which no publication on the market could possibly furnish due to press deadlines. As our continuous research uncovers day-to-day evolutions, they are pipelined to The Living Guide center to be shared with you.

All we urge is that you tell us where we can send you our toll-free number. As soon as your card has been received, we will immediately forward it in our special Fielding package.

Let's go over your trip, step by step. Some of these preliminaries will be old stuff to you—but use them as a check list. Maybe they'll remind you of something you've forgotten. Or maybe, if we're lucky, you'll pick up a fact or two.

☑ **COSTS** The cost of living varies—and, in every country except Switzerland, the specter of inflation is rampant. You can forget about the "cheap" Europe of yore, with its $5 rooms, $2 meals, and 75¢ drinks, nearly all of which long ago vanished. If you are an *average* vacationer, you can save from 30% to 35% of the total expenditure for your holiday by joining a tour—and, if with your travel agent you will study the field carefully, you'll find a substantial number of excellent ones which will deliver superior value for every cent of your investment as well as a full quota of fun along the way. Because startlingly lower group rates are charged by most hotels for exactly the same rooms (this also applies in most restaurants and other facilities), because the lump transport of the baggage of 30 to 40 people to and from airports and railway stations is a fraction of the same transfers by individuals, and because of a score of similar fiscal benefits built into them, simple economics dictate that they've GOT to be whoppingly less.

You can save duffelbags of money by dining well off the local cuisine rather than selecting chiefly exclusive establishments. We've included the top restaurants in this volume so that you may take your choice, but below the multi-star listings of the Stellar-grade chefs are many, many superb little "sleepers" where you might prefer to be anyway, because here is where you will find the real hometowners tucking in their napkins.

Another way to economize is to live out of the main centers and to romp along on public transportation while you to-and-fro to the bright lights. It is true that rural living is cheaper, but it is *still* rural—and is *that* why you came? Since more Americans travel to Europe to sightsee, museum-hop, shop, and dine (rather than simply to relax in the country), we would urge you to think twice before embracing this mode of cutting back. Consider your motives for the trip and then you decide.

Most expensive as we go to press (subject to changes, of course) are Germany, Switzerland, Norway, Sweden, Finland, Denmark, Belgium, Monaco, France, Luxembourg, and the Netherlands. Second in expensiveness are Austria, the United Kingdom, Italy, and San Marino. Least expensive are Spain, Ireland, Greece, and Portugal.

☑ **PASSPORTS** The passport is the document that seems to combine the best features of the U.S. Constitution, the Message to Garcia, and the Ark of the Covenant. Guard it more carefully than your wallet—or your spouse.

Under the dynamic direction of Norbert J. Krieg, enormous streamlining measures have been wrought by Passport Services. The validity of all touristic passports as of this writing (but subject to change) is 5 years from the date of issue, after which a new one may be obtained. Certain post offices handle the paper work. Ask if yours is one. If you are really in a remote corner and don't fall into one of the categories listed below, your "Application for Passport by Mail," *must* be accompanied by your most recent passport, 2 signed identical photos of your glowing countenance (taken within 6 months of licking the stamps), and a verdant $10. Forward them to your nearest Passport Agency. (Discussions were held recently to alter this procedure, so you'd better check us up on the last-minute status.)

First-timers may not use the mails. They must appear in person before an Agent of the Department of State, a clerk of any federal court or state court of record or a judge or clerk of any probate court who accepts applications, or a postal employee designated by the Postmaster at selected Post Offices. Bring along evidence of citizenship (a certified birth certificate should be submitted as proof of birth in the U.S.), personal identification, those same 2 photos of y-o-u, and that everlovin' $10-bill—plus 4 additional bucks as an execution fee. Others ineligible for postal exchange are (1) anyone who can't provide the most recent passport issued in his or her own name within the past 8 years, (2) any whippersnapper whose earlier travel document was issued before the 18th birthday, (3) any candidate for official or diplomatic papers, or

(4) any supplicant wanderer seeking a wholesale rate for his or her family. Yep, you can wrap up almost the entire brood (minors over 13 must be issued their own), thereby saving a string of individual payments. The rules on this require two 2 × 2-inch photos of the bearer (one of which is placed on page 3) and two "identifiable" photos of the rest of the group (one of which is placed on another page).

Special note to wayfaring brides and new divorcées: The passport-by-mail will be granted only in the name under which the previous passport was recorded. To skirt this one, you can send in an original or certified copy of a court order or marriage certificate showing the name change.

Look in the phone books of New York, Philadelphia, Washington, D.C., Boston, Chicago, Miami, New Orleans, Los Angeles, Seattle, San Francisco, Detroit, Houston, Stamford (Conn.), and Honolulu under United States Government, Department of State, Passport Services. Application forms may be had not only from these offices, but from the 3500 authorized Clerks of Court and post offices across the nation, from your travel agent or international airline.

For those abroad, petitions for new passports must be made _in person_ at the nearest American Embassy or Consulate. Your old, dog-eared, canceled friend will be returned as a souvenir when the new one is issued.

One MUST: Before you go tooling off, be sure to check this vital companion and follow religiously the fine print on the inside covers.

Yet another word of caution: Don't DARE to try to leave America without a _valid_ passport. A number of foreign countries have become so hot under their T-shirts about travelers' increasing demands for entry without valid passports that they are cracking down by holding these truants at the airport or dock and shipping them straight back home by the first available transport. If you're in _genuine_ trouble, nobody can be better friends than Passport Services or the nearest U. S. (or Canadian for Maple Leafers) Embassy or Consulate—but don't try to fool them.

Lost passports? Thanks to another reform, a formerly tedious spool of red tape involving money has been mitigated here. At last an honest American citizen in this miserable predicament may, in an emergency, obtain a temporary one without any fee from the local consulate immediately—in some of them even with a gratis color photo snapped on the spot.

First, _provided that all documents are correctly submitted,_ approximately 2 weeks is the normal maximum issuance. Second, the brochure _Your Trip Abroad_ has been rewritten in a friendly, chatty style; it's free of charge. Third, Passport Services inaugurated the optional use of color pictures, urging voyagers to _"Get a good picture._ The agency welcomes photographs that depict the applicant as a relaxed, smiling person . . ." Fourth, passports are released in 3 versions: (1) a Liberty Bell-ringer in its flag-blue cover, for tourists, with new-hip-pocket-or-purse dimensions and gold lettering—much smaller and more handy than the older size; (2) in-the-red maroon cover, for Government employees traveling on official business; and (3) cloak-and-dagger black cover, for members of the diplomatic service.

Some (rare) photographers will give you a list of each country's picture requirements. It is a wise precaution to get 5 or 6 extra photos; later they might save hours and headaches.

☑ **MEDICAL ADVICE** All European countries have now joined the U.S. in removing requirements for immunization of transatlantic travelers. This entire area, generally speaking, is safe and sound. They have good public health officials, fine doctors, and the latest drugs.

But if you plan to poke through any odd places around the Mediterranean (including *all* of North Africa, the Middle East, the bottom of Italy, and most of the islands)—or if you're heading for deep Africa or Asia—for heaven's sake be brave and let your doctor shoot the works. These hotter lands still crawl with 77 zillion varmints—and nothing is more dismal than hospitalization thousands of miles from home.

Dr. W. Price Fitch of Mamaroneck, N.Y., the internationally famous authority on travel health, recommends a series of immunizations for the latter group of voyagers. The basic ones are typhoid, tetanus-diphtheria, cholera, and a polio booster.

Malaria is still prevalent in some regions, including parts of Yugoslavia and much of Africa, tropical Asia, and the Middle East. Preventive medicine is not only strongly recommended but urged. Some lands require yellow fever inoculation. Certificates are good for 10 years.

Complete information on foreign immunization laws can be obtained from the U.S. Public Health Service. Check your phone book under U.S. Government, Dept. of Health, Education and Welfare.

Please consult your own physician for your specific requirements.

★ **TIPS** For *"turista"* Dr. Fitch suggests only Polymagma or Pepto-Bismol, both nonprescription and both available in tablet form. Take either with strong tea and salt crackers. Diarrhea causes loss of salts and fluids. As tea requires boiling, it will be safe anywhere; it is also mildly constipating, advises the doctor. Entero-Vioform (sometime sold as Mexaform), once a widely used standby, is heavily under fire for allegedly sometimes causing blindness and permanent damage to the brain and central nervous system; it is most definitely not proposed. (Neither is any preparation containing clioquinol, which is sometimes found in drugs abroad.) We recently read an account of a discovery which a Johns Hopkins team claims is the best of them all. It is an antibiotic called Doxycycline (also called doxymycin), of which a single dose each day provides 90% protection. One of its benefits is that it is excreted through the intestines—where the germ is lodged—rather than through the kidneys as are most anti-diarrhea preparations. This should never be taken by children under 9 or by pregnant women. And, as it may cause sensitivity to light, it should be discontinued if unexpected sunburn develops.

Motion sickness? Dr. Fitch states that Meclizine (generic) tablets such as Antivert, Dramamine, and Bonine taken about 2 hours before departure time are often effective. At the onset of nausea, lozenges, suppositories, or injections of Phenergan, Compazine, or Tigan are indicated.

The **handicapped** traveler at last is being given some proper attention. The American Automobile Assoc. (AAA) distributes a guide for such people. Another organization, Society for the Advancement of Travel for the Handicapped, offers further aid; it is located at 26 Court St., Brooklyn, N.Y. 11242, Tel.: (212) 858-5483.

Voyagers who are not fluent linguists might find the booklet *A Foreign Language Guide to Health Care* a reassuring companion. This 95-page publication, the dimensions of a file card, contains translations in English, French, German, Italian and Spanish of common phrases needed to obtain medical assistance and describe symptoms. It is obtainable free by writing to Laurie Allen, Public Relations, Blue Cross and Blue Shield of Michigan, 600 Lafayette East, Detroit 48226.

Special diet? A friendly Iowa reader who could eat only certain foods prepared in special ways had instructions written in detail for the language areas she was to visit; these were shown to waiters along her travel path and she never heard even the slightest growl from a stomach which traveled over 5000 miles of foreign terrain.

If you are diabetic, allergic to penicillin, or have any physical condition that may require emergency care, *please don't fail to turn ahead to "Let's Be European"* for details on the lifesaving diagnostic tags of peerless, nonprofit Medic-Alert. Literally, it might mean your life.

☑ **LUGGAGE**   Our Creative Team has just dredged up all the bags which have been stuffed into odd corners and crannies of our homes over the years.

The only way to test luggage, which of course is one of our functions, is to *use* it—to take it into the field filled with ones neatly packed possessions and then to see what happens. The number we dug up amazes us. The collective total came to 56 pieces that we'd purchased and tried over the past couple of decades—not counting the additional dozen or so which had been lost in Sarawak, stolen in Thebes, busted in Oslo, or heaved out of various hotel windows in rage.

Overheaviness, which steals too many precious pounds from the traveler's free allowance everywhere on European weigh-in scales, is a common bugaboo.

Likewise, cheap featherweight bags from discount houses, supermarkets, or big drugstore outlets are too often a disastrously stupid "economy," a fact we have learned to our disgust and embarrassment. (We challenge any exasperation in the encyclopedia of travel headaches to compare with the shock of that sudden yanked-off handle in the lobby of the London Hilton, the freezing of that tin zipper when 2 minutes are left to catch that plane, that junkily built latch which cascades your dirty dainties over 3 square yards of Zürich railway platform, or that numbing frustration when the moving belt in the air terminal returns that valise with its frame bowed and its thin-skinned fabric flapping with a 6-inch rip.)

Rube Goldberg gimmickry in their interiors is another misery. Many higher-class makers equip their bags with such gadgets as snap-on pouches, accordion-style shirt carriers, "secret" shoe compartments, and/or mechanical devices that "guarantee" to hold the press in your garments. Have you ever found one that *really* works?

Because our continuous surveys keep us up to the minute on what the prospective luggage buyer can find in today's American market, and because only one specialist produces the designs, quality, practicality, and durability in its products that meet our standards on all of these counts, we have decided that it is necessary in this isolated instance to break our no-brand-names policy adopted in 1965 by recommending **Hartmann** for our unrivaled nominee as the leader and pacemaker in the industry.

Early in 1979 my Nancy and I were so intrigued when we saw the bold technical and aesthetic advances in the Hartmann Nouveau Hobo series, which had just been introduced, that we couldn't resist the full set of 7 pieces for professional assessment under fire. The prices were so low for the value that they surprised us. There are 2 touring suitcases and 4 shoulder-strapped carry-ons, all of different sizes, plus a cleverly engineered garment bag and a fold-to-flat "Pancake" which is packable inside with other contents for purchases made en route. The combination of their thin but virtually impenetrable fiberboard frames, their tough washable nylon fisherman's tan packcloth bodies, their trimming in natural unfinished belting leather, their copious zipped pockets on their sides, which are so handy, and their top-grade hardware make them sleek, elegant, rugged, outstandingly light and convenient traveling companions. As a side note, inquiry has revealed that 98% of their construction is by hand. Because all of our numerous trips have different requirements, for the first time in our lives we have been able to choose precisely the pieces needed from this versatile wardrobe.

☑ **MONEY**   At this writing it no longer pays, in most cases, to try to beat other local rates of exchange by outside bank purchases in countries where the currency is strong. The European market nowadays simply is too fickle for safe speculation in sizable amounts. But in parts of Africa or practically anywhere in the Far East, it would help to pick up the maximum amounts you can legally carry across these borders, before your departure from the United States. You can save anywhere from 5% to 50%—extra cash dropped into your lap, for extra fun en route.

All European airports have 24-hour banks where you can exchange dollars or traveler's checks for local currency. (Even so, you should swap the bulk of your bucks at midcity banks, where the rates are usually better.) There are often 2 advantages of the latter over the former. Not only do banks usually pay a bit more for traveler's checks than for bills, but whenever you're ready to buy anything in a store ask first if the merchant will give you a discount for them. *Once abroad, always cash your checks at a bank,* not in your hotel or in a restaurant or shop. The last three's rakeoffs can be rapacious.

Practically speaking, however, many voyagers will not take the time to exchange their money in a foreign bank, preferring instead to absorb sometimes walloping losses for the convenience of an accessible cashier. These people would be much better off turning to Deak-Perera. As the Western Hemisphere's largest retailer of foreign currency, this go-getting outfit offers rates that are approximately within 2% of of the best available overseas (depending on the market, Deak's rate can actually be 2% *better!*). Available are 120 currencies in cash and 12 denominations of traveler's checks. These are there for the asking in any one of three ways: (1) over the counter, at Deak-Perera's 58 offices and airport outlets blanketing 20 cities in the U.S., Canada, Europe, and the Far East; (2) by post, through the company's burgeoning Currency-by-Mail program. Since orders are processed within 24 hours, Deak-Perera guarantees 2-week insured delivery or your money will be refunded— but usually the process takes as little as a week. Minimum orders under this plan are $50 in cash (with a pricey $3.50 handling charge) and $150 in traveler's checks (with a 1% surcharge); (3) by a toll-free call, over Deak's Chicago number (1-800-621-1915). Using this innovative method, one can charge one's Currency-by-Mail pack to one's VISA or Master Charge card. This will be treated as a cash advance by the sponsoring banks, and thus will be subject to a standard interest charge.

In addition to currency exchange, Deak-Perera offers a plethora of helpful hints and other useful travel information. For details, please write Deak's world headquarters at the Deak-Perera Building, 29 Broadway, New York, NY 10006.

A few foreign currencies (subject to change) are mutually "convertible." This means, quite simply, that in exchange for your American traveler's checks within these nations, you may draw any hard monies including our greenbacks. You may also buy traveler's checks valid in francs, marks, or others at foreign-exchange houses in the major cities of the U.S. or Canada, or at most U.S. international airports.

In sum, we find it easiest and wisest to carry about $300 in cash (either in U.S. currency or its foreign equivalent obtained through Deak-Perera) and the balance in (1) traveler's checks, (2) free-market foreign currencies for those countries not party to these currency reforms, and (3) personal checks. Internationally recognized credit cards (American Express, Diners' Club, etc.) have become almost "must" items in these days of volatile currency reforms. Warning: Although legions upon legions of hotels, restaurants, shops, and other establishments abroad will accept at least one of them, some top-line places still turn thumbs down on all.

☑ **CURRENCY AND METRIC CONVERTER** Now for the conversion of foreign money, and a solution—*Fielding's World Currency and Metric Converter*—that instantly translates U.S. and foreign currencies *anywhere in the world,* and is so flexible that it will *never go out of date!* Wherever you go in foreign lands, the man-across-the-counter will smile blandly and mutter, "You owe me 1675 francs," or "29 guilders," or "22,380 lire," or something equally baffling. The poor American traveler, particularly the country-hopping variety, goes into a spin like this: "If 1 escudo is worth 2.75¢, call it 3¢, divide 3 into 878 escudos . . ." and out come the pencil and the shiny little beads of perspiration.

So many readers of this book found themselves stymied that they wrote in to ask for a shortcut, and we've finally come up with a device that does the job with gratifying efficiency.

This pocket-size gadget quickly converts the currency of any country in the world into dollars—or dollars into any foreign currency. Operation of the low-cost *Fielding's World Currency Converter* is simple: You merely set a sliding scale so that the U.S. dollar is aligned with the foreign currency unit —and read across to convert any amount. Because the sliding scale can be set for any exchange rate, floating currencies are no problem. You simply reset the scale as exchange rates change.

As a supplement, on the reverse side you'll find *Fielding's World Metric Converter,* which instantly converts U.S. and metric measurements in the most common categories you'll encounter as a traveler: miles, pounds, ounces, gallons, inches, yards, and temperature.

You should find this red-white-and-blue converter beside the cash register of your local bookshop. If not, ask them to stock it for the convenience of other travelers as well.

☑ **YOUR TRAVEL ARRANGEMENTS** Now let's lay aside all the rich excitement and glamour surrounding your journey—gently, so that we don't bruise or hurt it!—and get down to actual mechanics: By which travel method are you planning to go?

There are 3 choices open to you—as a trailblazer, as a so-called F.I.T., or as a member of an escorted tour. Let's examine each of these carefully, because your decision here might make or break your trip:

As a trailblazer (a term coined for convenience), you'd be 100% on your own. If you already know Europe well—and, most important, *if you nail down and copper-rivet every routing, date, transportation booking, and hotel reservation before your departure from America*—you'll probably have a wonderful holiday, with fun most or all of the way. But if this is your first trip abroad you're almost bound to run into certain headaches, snarls, and disappointments. In Off Season it's relatively easy—but in today's High Season rat race, particularly in the popular tourist spots, the well-meaning but fumbling amateur is often licked before departure. *And* "High Season" has now spread into **early spring** and late autumn!

The F.I.T. category (trade jargon for "Foreign Independent Trip") is ideal for the first-time or unsure new vacationer who wants freedom of movement combined with expert protection. Here's how this works: Merely tell your travel agent where you want to go, how many days you can spare, and how much you can pry out of the piggy bank for the expedition. That's all. When you leave, he'll hand you your complete string of tickets, a tailor-made itinerary that lists dates, times, train numbers, hotels, transfers, the works, and a book of voucher coupons with which you'll "pay" practically every bill you'll encounter. If you wish to have a friendly face greet you at each airport or station and take over your burdens, that's easy too. Naturally, since you're the boss, you'll be booked exactly where and how you specify—and you've a far better chance, especially in High Season, of getting into the most desirable places than you generally have. You'll pay a percentage more if you go as an F.I.T., of course—but you've got professional brains guarding your interests every hour of every day, and the headaches it saves are beyond price.

The character, the caliber, and the spread of the conducted tour field have undergone an enormous change for the better, particularly within the past 2 or 3 years. In former times they were mainly the refuge of older folk with limited budgets and modest earners who wanted to see the most for the least. No longer! With the advent of strikingly lower transatlantic fares, the decline of the purchasing power of the dollar abroad, and the spiraling prices nearly everywhere there, their ranks have now been swelled by multi-thousands of voyagers from the upper-middle-class economic bracket who have taken or are taking advantage of their 30% to 35% savings.

☑ **PICKING YOUR TRAVEL AGENT**   As in all major fields of commerce, the travel-agency business has every type of operator, from superfine to bad.

First in size and in renown are the giants: American Express, Thomas Cook, and AAA World-Wide Travel, Inc. Some carpers feel that (1) their F.I.T. facilities are spotty—excellent in some countries but miserable in others, (2) personalization of their services sometimes suffers gravely because the client is just 1 more name on a roster of thousands, and (3) some (not all) of their charges are steep. On banking matters, the first 2 are so superb that they brook no competition abroad. And not even their severest critic could deny that they're vastly widespread, their integrity is unquestioned, and they're as solid as Mount Everest.

Next in importance and in solidity are the 25 or 30 Old Reliable tour companies—the pacesetters, the Elder Statesmen of this highly complex trade. Most of them are members of a potent regulatory organization called the Creative Tour Operators Association. In any of these you'll find expert guidance, heavy experience, and absolute honesty.

Then comes the backbone and bulk of the field—the small, earnest, hardworking retail agencies in almost every city or town of North America. Maybe it's not as venerable or as big as the Giants or the Old Reliables, but as their local representative it can always call upon them for advice. Most break their backs to add a large helping of happiness to their clients' holidays. With few exceptions, they'll steer you right for standard fees. See this hometown operator first, once you're satisfied that he's not a fly-by-night—because you'll have face-to-face attention, which is always the best.

Finally there are the sharpies, deadbeats, and thieves—fortunately rare. This breed is few in number, but if one of them gets you in his grasp, probabilities are high that this villain will milk you for fantastic charges, ruin your trip, and break your heart.

Let's Be European

Europe is a fascinating checkerboard. Each nation has its own customs, its own quirks. It's just as if between Austin and Amarillo you were to find 3 languages and 3 cultures—each new. (Even Texas isn't *that* different!)

Here are a few generalities for today's traveler. They were learned the hard way—so careful reading is suggested.

☑ **MONEY**   We recommend that your funds be broken down 3 ways: (1) U.S. currency, (2) dollar traveler's checks, and (3) free-market currencies purchased in America or Switzerland. Personal checks are accepted by some shopkeepers, but generally they are very, very hard to cash.

Credit cards? At this writing, the wickedest brawl in the travel industry continues to rage over control of the burgeoning European market. With battle lines still so fluid, we're compelled to abstain from making one overall recommendation. Personally, we use American Express and Diner's Club regularly, and both play helpful roles in our marathon journeyings. Despite tub-thumping advertising claims, no one—repeat, no one—yet offers a "universal" credit card, or anything that remotely approaches it. We have also previously noted that a substantial number of Europe's most distinguished institutions still won't touch any of these fine organizations. Some honor only Eurocard, a venture which, according to them, takes a smaller bite from their exchequers. Visa also is in the economic scenery. Incidentally, if you hold an Amexco card (or if you book through them), you can still receive mail from home at the overseas American Express branches.

If your references are impeccable, your aura is prosperous, and you don't illuminate the lobby with a hula-hula sport shirt, hotel credit managers abroad will sometimes (not always!) accept your personal check. Since $5000 in traveler's checks can cost a fat $50, here's a smart potential saving.

But *some* dollar traveler's checks are a necessity—and you should buy *only* from the biggest of big-name institutions. Dozens of international financial houses are reliable, but you might have the devil's own time proving it to hotelkeepers and department-store managers. The top-line giants are known to most of the little people; there's seldom any question about their validity.

11

For cash transfers, if all goes normally, nothing matches American Express's fast and efficient cable service; in hours, not days, they can and do forward funds to travelers in almost every part of the advanced world—except, possibly, Spain. (Spanish banking laws are so snarled that transfers of U.S. traveler's checks take up to 5 weeks!) Because every foreign or domestic office is staffed by human beings, goofs *do* occur—but these are refreshingly rare.

★ **TIP** When you enter a country, your greenbacks will take care of your expenses until you reach a bank. (Air passengers can almost always convert currencies at airports, but rail trippers aren't always so lucky. Don't change *all* of your lucre at the airport; we've discovered that the midtown banks often offer a better rate.) When you leave a country, a little folding money will handle your breakfast, taxi, porters, and small outgoing expenses. Since traveler's checks come in units of $10 or more, you're not stuck with a fistful of leftover bills.

Leftover European *change* is a far thornier problem. Surplus bills can normally be passed in the next country, but people just sniff at your foreign change. (A blessed and welcome exception is the Banco March in Spain.) Get rid of *all* coins (except souvenirs) before crossing the border.

☑ **CUSTOMS OFFICIALS** Most Customs officials are human beings, even as you and I; a few of them are skunks. None is very fussy with American tourists these days; you might sail through your entire tour through the "Nothing To Declare" gatepaths, if you're lucky, without 1 bag being checked. The speed of your clearance usually depends upon the inspector's state of digestion. Here are some helpful hints:

Be affable and cooperative, but don't be overly conversational. Their sole interest is to get rid of you; if you keep your mouth shut, things will move twice as fast.

Hold your U.S. passport casually in hand—don't flaunt it!—so that the inspector can identify you. (This might sound absurd, but sometimes it's surprisingly helpful.) And speak English solely, *not* a foreign language.

Liquor in your luggage: Break the seals before you get to Customs. In some lands (British Isles excepted) this may get around the import duty. Some countries forbid more than 1. If you have an extra, stick it in the pocket of the topcoat or raincoat that hangs "carelessly" over your arm.

The Common Market nations have upped and standardized travelers' allowances on duty-free items. Now officially they permit 300 cigarettes, 1½ liters of hard liquor (2 "fifth" bottles should pass), 3 liters (¾-gallon) of wine, 1⅓ lbs. of coffee, and ¼ lb. of tea. However, they are seldom closely scanned.

Gifts for European friends: Let Customs assume they're personal belongings (unless you don't mind paying a tax on each item). In any case, make them ask *you* the status of the articles.

U.S. Customs men are astonishingly conscientious and cheerful, considering the fact that 10-thousand of them do the job that it should take 25-thousand to achieve. They have the legal right to examine *every* piece of luggage carried by *every* traveler; generally, however, they'll spot-check your possessions. To save their time (and get you through faster), carry all your European purchases in 1 bag—and don't cheat a penny's worth, because they're experts at snaring fibbers.

Today's duty-free allowance is $300 in *retail* value. (The next $600 in value is taxable at only 10% and yet another $600 worth is allowable at the regular duty rate.) These goods must accompany you personally on your return. Your free importation of wines or booze is 1 quart per person 21 years or over—a monument to the enormous power of the U.S. liquor lobby in Washington. Most states admit more than a quart if a modest duty is paid on the overage; others, such as California, confiscate all extra spirits. (Since beverages, regardless of quantity, are part of your $300 deduction, this damned foolishness has absolutely no bearing on the balance-of-payments question—and the traveler is made the sucker.) Here are a few points to remember: (1) To repeat: *Each individual* is given the maximum amount. You may pool with any member of your family, including infants-in-arms. (2) You may send an unlimited number of under-$25 (fair retail value) gifts from abroad to U.S. friends (more about this below). (3) Most important, European prices are often sufficiently lower so that you can slap down full duty on many of your purchases and *still* save money.

Regarding other regulations, here are some key facts and suggestions: (1) Go easy on those Coronas for the boss or that bubble water for the blonde or blond, because 100 cigars and one quart per person of alcoholic beverages are all you may import without fee (*foreign-made* cigarettes are limited to one carton)—and remember they'll grab your liquor if they think you're going to use it in violation of your local state or county laws. With certain limitations, booze may be "shipped to follow." (2) Foreign fruits, meats, plants, and vegetables are the kiss of death. Because that harmless-looking salami or those shiny grapes or that beautiful little potted shamrock might carry pests which could destroy millions of dollars in livestock, food, forests, or ornamentals, virtually all are confiscated. Most foreign-made eatables are banned unless all ingredients are printed on the label. (3) Your exemptions may include alterations or repairs on anything you originally took abroad; if your car throws a piston or your watch gets a dunking en route, charge off the cost of making them tick again. (4) Antiques 100 years old (exceptions: rugs and carpets made after 1700) are unrestricted. They include furniture, hardware, brass, bronze, marble, terra cotta, porcelain, chinaware, and "any object considered to have artistic value." Be sure to bring certificates of verification, if available. As a side note, insurance coverage may save you endless headaches. We're hearing about more and more cases of dockside theft, particularly of small articles—so this added protection is a bargain at *any* price. (5) Original works of art (*not* copies)—

paintings, drawings, and sculptures of any age—and stamps are duty-free. So are books, prints, lithographs, and maps over 20 years old. (6) Gifts costing less than $25 (or $40 if sent from U.S. island possessions) may be mailed from abroad on a duty-free basis, with no effect on your exemptions. Alcohol, tobacco, and perfume are ineligible. No 1 person may receive more than 1 gift in 1 day; plainly mark the package "Gift—Value Under $25." (7) Certain trademarked articles—especially watches, perfumes, optical goods, musical instruments, and phonograph records—require written permission of the foreign manufacturer or U.S. distributor before they may be cleared intact. (Accordions are especially hairy.) A few well-known manufacturers of cosmetics and beauty products are so stingy that nothing may be imported without their documentary consent. Most companies, however, allow bona fide tourists to bring back at least 1 unit as a souvenir. The way around it? Remove or obliterate the trademark. (8) If you sell some articles within 3 years after importation on a duty-free basis, you'll be fined double the normal quotation. But you *are* permitted to sell anything that was initially purchased for your personal or household use. Original intent is the key factor. (9) Everything in your baggage must be for your personal use or the use of your immediate family, or for gifts; samples and other merchandise will be taxed. (10) Finally, French postcards, egret feathers, ammunition, narcotics, sultry redheads without passports, and various other demoralizing commodities are contraband.

Be especially careful of items made from the skins of crocodile, spotted cat, or other endangered species. The list of God's creatures which are rapidly vanishing from our planet is dismayingly long—too lengthy (and stretching day by day) for us to include here for purposes of up-to-the-minute accuracy. If you're considering this type of purchase, be sure to ask U.S. Customs before departure for a summary of those species which are especially fragile—and please remember that critters that are dispatched in a brutal fashion are also under protection and thus these pelts too can be seized by officials. Arrests for violations are not unknown; moreover, ignorance of the law is, as usual, no excuse.

On the European side, cigarettes are usually what officials look for first— if they look at all. Above the prescribed number, there's a fat duty to be paid. In some cases the excess will be confiscated, or (in England) the levy must be paid on the entire supply. Most wink at a reasonable excess. They *never* wink, however, at drugs so these should never be transported across any frontier. Punishment for drug possession or use can be far in excess of U.S. norms.

If you have 3 or 4 parcels, your inquisitor has been trained to inspect the one wrapped with the greatest care. Likewise, if there is a choice between a bag and an independent package or a case, he will usually examine the latter.

Some officials are straight; some are as crooked as an anteater's nose. Don't play with the Americans, British, Irish, Dutch, Scandinavians, or Swiss.

If the duty is too high, or if you're carrying a taxable item to a 2nd or 3rd country, the Customs will hold it in escrow at the border for your return, without charge—and it's usually safe. One or 2 lands won't do this.

☑ **U. S. CONSULAR SERVICES ABROAD**　To repeat our urgent suggestion, if ever you should encounter serious trouble on your trip—anything from a lost passport to an arrest to death of a companion to a spectrum of other deep crises—communicate *immediately* with the nearest American consular office. Here is a crack corps of highly trained, highly competent, sympathetic men and women whose succor can be literally beyond price. Contrary to popular belief, they are proscribed from extending loans to travelers in financial distress because our Government continues to refuse to allot funds for this purpose—but they are experts with their knowledge of how best to till emergency sources. Although they will give restricted aid in a dispute that could lead to legal or police action, furnish a list of reputable local lawyers, step forward in obtaining adequate legal representation, and try in every possible way to prevent discrimination under foreign law, regulations prohibit them from participating on the *direct* level. If one of our citizens is arrested, they will visit him or her in detention, notify relatives and friends, provide a roster of attorneys, and throw all of their weight in attempting to obtain relief if conditions are inhumane or unhealthy. Here are some of the other duties which the vast majority of this elite perform so well: (1) Assistance in finding appropriate medical services, including English-speaking physicians, in cases of injuries or illnesses. (2) Guidance on how to inform the local police about stolen funds or on how to inform the issuing authorities about missing traveler's checks. (3) The full extension of notary facilities. (4) Help in locating missing Americans. (5) Protection of U.S. voyagers and residents during civil unrest or in natural disasters.

It may be useful to leave behind at home the following direct Washington telephone numbers of the office of Special Consular Services:

• To find missing wanderers about whom there is special concern or to transmit emergency messages: 202-632-9461 or 202-632-3015.

• To transmit funds to your destitute ones on foreign soil when commercial banking facilities are unavailable or to arrange medical evacuation: 202-632-9706 or 202-632-3529.

• For questions about members of your clan who have been arrested and how to get money to them: 202-632-8089 or 202-632-7823.

• For help when an American dies abroad: 202-632-1423 or 202-632-2172.

• For civil judicial inquiries and assistance: 202-632-2400.

• Night and weekend emergency number for all of the above: 202-655-4000. Ask for the Duty Officer.

Please never ask these heavily burdened executives to do the work of travel agencies, information bureaus, or banks, search for missing luggage, settle disputes with hotel managers or shopkeepers, help get work permits, or find jobs. Relative trivialities of this nature would make too great a load for them to handle. Within their larger ken, however, all of us would have to search far and wide to find other friends so capable and generous of themselves in alien climes.

☑ **TIPPING**   Here are 2 important continental practices which baffle most new American visitors: (1) *The bulk of the tip is usually included in the bill,* and (2) *extra tips are usually distributed at checkout time.*

Most hotels and restaurants automatically add a service charge to your statement of from 10% to 20%, depending upon the country. Watch this.

In your hotel the only people customarily tipped *before* the final-hour reckoning are (1) the porter who carries your bags to the room (see individual countries for suggested amounts); (2) the *piccolo, botones,* or *chasseur*—equivalent to the young U.S. bellboy—who brings the occasional message to your door (small change only); (3) the doorman who snags your taxis. Don't shell out to anyone else until you're ready to leave.

On departure from any Deluxe or First-class European hostelry, however, certain *extra* gratuities are *always* expected. Specific recommendations follow, for each land. In general, give the day concierge (Hall Porter) a minimum of $1.50, never less; stretch this to perhaps $7 if your visit has lasted more than a week. (Often the night concierge and he do not pool their tips.) Give the maid some small change (50¢ to $1 per day should do); give the room waiter and the valet slightly more, if you have used them. In the new 1000-room houses now blanketing Europe, you can reduce or even eliminate some tips completely. (If there's a shoeshine machine in the corridor, why throw away money?) Similarly, when concierge desks become peopled by an impersonal battery of 6 to 10 lieutenants, we leave only a token amount; a sizable one would not say "thank you" any better to this faceless throng. In smaller hotels the porter (bellboy) who handles your baggage is usually the man who has shined the shoes you have left by your door (getting rarer every year); he rates 50¢ to $1 when you move in and when you move out. *Never give a concierge a lump sum for distribution to the rest,* because he may keep too much of it for himself; the hotel manager or assistant manager, however, normally may be trusted implicitly as your banker. Second-class or tourist rates are proportionately less.

In restaurants give substantial tips only if your waiter has been unusually attentive. Some local diners let things ride with the service charge on the check. The majority leaves small change on the table.

A good average for miscellaneous services is 15%; if the bill is less than $1, bump it into 20%.

Washroom attendants are always tipped with the smallest coin or coins of the currency; so are theater ushers, except in 1 or 2 countries.

Don't be browbeaten just because you're a tourist. Many Italian and Belgian taxi drivers, for example, have the vicious habit of extracting their own tips before they return your change. They know better. If this happens, demand the full amount, step out of the cab—and tell them to go to hell.

Continental servants are usually 100% better trained, better polished, and more interested in their patrons' welfare than American servants. You'd be surprised what a smile and a pleasant word will do for these excellent people —because not all Europeans treat them as human beings.

Urgent: Wherever you are and whatever you do, always carry a pocketful of assorted small change. Cash a large bill (or 2) each day before setting forth; by always having the EXACT tip on hand, the time and money you'll save will be phenomenal. Please give extra-serious consideration to this suggestion, because we find it one of the most practical in this book.

☑ **LANGUAGE**   In today's Europe language is no barrier. As long as you've got a tongue, 3 or 4 hands, and an active imagination, you'll get along fine.

English is understood in just about every large hotel, restaurant, shop, nightclub, and major sightseeing facility abroad. Only in rural districts should you find any serious difficulties.

Have no fears about going to a linguistically strange country. Plenty of North Americans have been there before to break the ice for you.

★ **TIP**   When you're talking English and Mr. Native is talking Zulu, watch the volume of your voice. If your interlocutor doesn't speak your language, there's a ludicrous tendency on both parts to shout.

☑ **METRIC MEASUREMENT**   The metric system used in every European country (but not extensively in the U.K. and Ireland) is still confusing to most Americans; it won't be soon, because, of course, we are adopting it.

Here are a few translations. Conquer these 5 and you'll get along fine:

A kilometer (pronounced kill-OM-eter by the "mile"-minded British and Irish and KILL-o-meter by the continentals) is roughly 6/10 of a mile. Multiply by 6, knock off 1 decimal point, and you've got it in miles.

A kilo or kilogram (potatoes and onions) is 2.2 pounds.

A meter (dress material) and a liter (gasoline, beer) are both roughly 11/10ths —one of a yard, the other of a quart. There are about 2½ centimeters to 1 inch.

A gram (airmail letters) is very tiny. There are about 28 to the ounce.

If you don't like arithmetic, our handy *Fielding's World Currency and Metric Converter* will instantly convert U.S. and metric measurements in all the above categories, plus temperature.

Now, for those who don't have their copy of our up-to-the-minute, pocketsize *Shopping Guide to Europe*, here are some conversions which might come in handy. Since sizes are not standardized, this is a fairly rough yardstick. Try on the items whenever possible.

Juniors

American		5	7	9	11	13
European		36	38	40	42	44

Women's Clothing

American	6	8	10	12	14	16
European	36	38	40	42	44	46

Women's Shoes

American	4	5	6	7	8	9
European	34	35	36	37	38	39

Children's Dresses and Suits

American	2	4	6	8	10	12
European	40-45	50-55	60-65	70-75	80-85	80-95
English	16-18	20-22	24-26	28-30	32-34	36-38

Men's Sweaters

American	Small	Medium	Large	Extra Large
European	44	46-48	50	52-54
English	34	36-38	40	42-44

Men's Shirts

American	14	14½	15	15½	16	16½	17
European	36	37	38	39	41	42	43

(Men's shirt, hat, pajamas, and suit sizes are identical in U.S. and England.)

Men's Shoes

American	5	6	7	8	9	10	11	12
European	38	39	40	41	42	43	44	45

Last, here's a refresher on how to change Centigrade temperatures into Fahrenheit. The classic method is to take 9/5ths of the *Centigrade* temperature (the reading on European thermometers) and add 32. A much easier way is to double the Centigrade reading, deduct 10%, and add the same 32. Example: Let's imagine that the mercury says 15°. Twice 15 is 30, and 10% of 30 is 3. Taking 3 from 30 leaves 27. Add 32 to 27, and you'll have the Yankee version of 59°. In print it looks complicated—but in practice it's so simple that almost any traveler can do it in his head. Try it and see!

☑ **TRAINS AND PASSES** Eurailpass ("Your-rail-pass") and **Eurail Youthpass** are 2 of the fattest and most rewarding bargains on that continent today. Any *resident* of North, Central, or South America may roam wherever and whenever desired on any continental train (not British; they have a separate Thrift Rail Plan) without further payment except for routine sleeper or *couchette* supplements. This more luxurious plan than its alternate for young people offers 15 days of unlimited *First class* travel for $210, 21 days for $260, 1 month for $320, 2 months for $430, or 3 months for $530. Children under 12 are charged half-fare; those under 4 ride free. Including Trans-Europ Expresses (TEE) and all other extra-fare runs, it is valid on the national railways and many private trains, steamers, and ferry crossings in the following 15 nations: Austria, Belgium, Denmark, Finland, France, Germany (Federal Republic), Greece, Holland, Ireland, Italy, Luxembourg, Norway, Portugal, Spain, Sweden, and Switzerland, as well as on English Channel crossings which link into the continental system. You may choose its continuous usage period during 6 months following its purchase. Anyone under 26 (the limitation to students has been dropped) may opt for the **Eurail Youthpass,** which opens 2 months of unlimited roving in all of the same carriers in *Second class* for a flat $290. Among its other alluring financial benefits is substantial savings on hotel bills by dozing sitting up, spending these nights in an inexpensive *couchette,* or, for slightly more, taking a tourist sleeper. Neither of these arrangements includes reservation fees (strongly urged always and compulsory for berths), meals, refreshments, nor with the latter, fees and supplements required to board certain trains. Both cards are personal and nontransferable, with the penalty of confiscation if another bearer is caught showing them. Your passport must always be produced when requested by conductors, gatemen, and other authorized personnel. Neither is refundable if lost or stolen.

Your Eurailpass, incidentally, is becoming increasingly valuable for **airport-to-downtown rail connections.** Barcelona, Brussels, Dusseldorf, Frankfurt, Paris, Vienna, Amsterdam, Rome and Zürich are now on rails. If you have this card, why pay $15-or-so extra for taxi fare?

VITAL: You must buy it before heading for Europe, because it is not sold abroad. To secure confirmed reservations booked through U.S. agencies is tricky unless application is made long in advance. For further inquiries, see your travel agent or write to Eurailpass at Trains, P.O. Box M, Staten Island, New York 10304. Absolutely Great!

Swiss, Scandinavian, German, French, and Dutch railways are excellent. Spanish, Italian, Portuguese, Belgian, and even some British trains are sometimes terrible. They are ALL overcrowded in High Season, so make your reservations *now* or as soon as you reach Europe.

The aforementioned **Trans-Europ-Express** (TEE) is a high-speed, main-line rocket linking the major cities of 9 nations—Italy, France, Monaco, Holland, Belgium, West Germany, Austria, Switzerland, and Luxembourg. If your destination is within 250 miles, your door-to-door travel time will probably be less than if you bid for airline travel—and at nearly ¼ the cost! Moreover, in winter or foggy periods, rail is far more reliable. The trains are mostly self-propelled diesel units (autorails in France). Tickets are one class only; a 15% to 20% supplement is added unless you have a Eurailpass; air conditioning is standard; cars have smoking and nonsmoking divisions. Average running speed is about 80 mph; as examples of their high-stepping gait, Paris–Brussels is only 2 hours, 22 minutes (3½ hrs. by air *et al.* from midtown-to-midtown), and Paris–Zürich is only 6 hours. Dining facilities are always on hand; frontier formalities have been streamlined to a minimum; conductors and uniformed hostesses or stewards wear TEE insignia and are multilingual. Teleprinter reservations can be made in 15 minutes *if* available—but be safe by requesting them 3 weeks before departure. Here's the greatest step forward in foreign railroading since the Wagons-Lit dining-car people discovered that the Animal Kingdom provides other meats besides veal. Important: Always take your luggage on board with you. If you check it through, it might be put onto a "regular" train and reach your destination much later than you do.

On all other trains abroad make sure *first* that there's a diner. We got stuck again, foolishly, because we neglected to find out that restaurant cars are not carried through the Simplon Tunnel (except on TEE, they never cross borders). Advance knowledge will give you time to improvise your own picnic— much better than the station platform vendors' snacks.

There is no drinking water on European trains. Carry your own bottle if you're a thirsty sort.

When you leave your seat for a meal, put some bulky possession (your spouse, for example?) on the cushion. Otherwise, the first incoming passenger is liable to take over, leaving you the worst place and lousiest view.

Dining cars? Here's the procedure: Usually there are 2 (sometimes 3) separate servings. First the Steward will come to your compartment, learn your time preference, and give you a table-booking slip which must be returned when he greets you in his own domain. Although a few meager à la carte items are available, probably 98% of the customers consume the standard, fixed meal at the standard, fixed price (usually $6.50 to $9). Course after course is served on a 1-shot, universal basis; everybody eats the soup, the veal (1 gets you 10 that it still *is* veal, too!), the salad, the cheese, and the fruit from the same service platters. When the whole car has finished, the cashier presents the check. Almost nobody tips.

Sleeping cars? Wagons-Lits offer 3 First-class and 2 Second-class categories. First class consists of regular 1-berth or 2-berth accommodations, plus "Specials" for shorter runs (20 small single compartments per car). Second class offers the T-2 berthing with 18 double-decked twin compartments per car; these are gradually supplementing the older 3-bunk units. Finally, there's the Second-class *couchette*—a minimum-price 6-seat (or 6-berth) compartment in which passengers may lie down without undressing. These are for the hardy.

If you share your wagon-lit with a stranger, unhappily it'll be a man if you're male or a woman if you're female. (Fascinating booking mistakes sometimes happen, however, to passengers with ambiguous first names such as Sydney,

Evelyn, Clare, Leigh, or Temple.) It's good manners to stand in the outside passageway while he shaves or she dresses.

No portable radios may be played on French, Swiss, and Swedish railways.

When you turn in a ticket, it is sometimes necessary to wait 3 months before you can get your money back. Fantastic red tape, that's all.

Check the date of expiration of your round-trip ticket. On short rides in some countries they expire within 24 hours.

☑ **YOUR OWN CAR**   If you're planning to ship your car across the Atlantic —a punishingly expensive exercise which we urge you to avoid since auto rental agencies abound overseas—we'd recommend 2 standard documents: (1) a valid U.S. Driver's License, and (2) an American International Driving Permit (in nine languages, no longer mandatory but still useful for remote motoring) issued through the AAA. United States license plates may be used for all countries.

Third Party Insurance (Public Liability and Property Damage) is compulsory throughout Europe. *Be sure to get complete coverage*—fire, theft, damage to yourself, the works—*wherever you go on the Continent.* If there's an accident, no matter how trivial, you'll be up to your neck in gendarmes, red tape, and A.D. 1066 legal procedures—and it's the devil to prove that the other fellow is wrong when you have to shout him down in a strange language. Ask the AAA or the agency where you make your purchase.

If there isn't an AAA office nearby, write to *AAA World-Wide Travel,* 8111 Gatehouse Rd., Falls Church, Va. 22047. The Foreign Motoring Service division here is normally very patient and helpful. Although this fine organization has closed all of its overseas offices, your U.S. membership can be extremely valuable abroad because of the reciprocal agreements it has made with its foreign counterparts. When you show your card it is an open sesame to all of the benefits provided by various European clubs, just as those on their rosters can use the AAA gamut when they travel to the United States.

Straight rental of a car in Europe? If this comes as part of your travel agent's package—fine; you're buying his know-how, his service, and your touring convenience. But if you're making your own arrangements independently, *we recommend you wait until you've crossed the Atlantic instead of setting up any advance reservations in the States.* Here is our reasoning:

Every good-size city on the Continent has scads of excellent rental cars, both self-drive and chauffeur-driven. Nobody, but nobody, has a true Europewide chain of auto-hire offices; everybody makes use of a string of local operators. What you're riding isn't a Hertz or Avis or National car, in most cases; it's actually a Schmidt or Delamain, or Angelotti car under a U.S. name.

While we have no special quarrel with this setup, we'd personally prefer the privilege of (1) selecting our own local outfit, (2) examining what we are paying for before agreeing to take it, and (3) making our own deal.

It is our honest opinion that the caliber of their selected firms varies considerably. In some cities we think they're unparalleled, but in others we don't go along. When booked by any U.S. company, however, you get what you get.

No single local outfit can stock every kind of car. Before leaving home, you might *think* you want a Ford or Opel or Simca, but after on-the-spot comparative shopping, that cute little Porsche or that sleek little Fiat might be far closer to your personal taste. Seeing is better.

Prices are supposed to be standard—but they aren't, please believe us. If you do your own talking, particularly in Off Season, you can end up with quotations substantially under the "official" rates.

Therefore, we earnestly believe that your best bet is to walk in cold abroad and strike your own bargains for exactly the car which pleases you most for that section of your tour. A recognized credit card will be a help; today many agents feel that cash deposits are not enough to prevent car thieves from driving off and never returning with the vehicle.

Outright purchase of an auto in Europe, for (1) shipment home, or for (2) eventual resale to the original foreign dealer on the guaranteed repurchase plan? Make sure that your car meets American specifications (California is especially strict) for glass, safety features, emission standards, muffler, and headlights; later conversion can be costly.

There's also a **guaranteed repurchase** scheme in which the agency buys back the vehicle at the termination of your journey, at a price mutually agreed upon in advance. Where the horse trading comes in, of course, is on the repurchase part of any agreement—and that's just routine business. American offices which offer these services are normally reliable and fair-dealing. But since even the best of them are subject to human frailties, we do not assume responsibility for their performance.

While we offer no blanket guarantee, **Auto Europe**, 770 Lexington Ave., N.Y. 10021, seems amply set up for **car purchase**, **rental of vehicles**, and **camper models**. Write directly to Pres. Alex Cecil or phone to its toll-free number, (800) 223-5740, for details. This company pledges extra-special attention for readers of this Guide.

★ **TIPS** At this writing, Americans may drive in any country in Eastern or Western Europe, with one exception—Albania. Motoring in other Iron Curtain lands is complicated; travel by private auto in East Germany is *not* recommended.

With minor exceptions, road signs are standard. There are 3 basic categories: (1) triangular, to indicate danger (intersection, railway crossing, slippery road, etc.), (2) circular, to lay down prohibitions (road closed, 1-way street, no passing, etc.), (3) rectangular, to provide information (garage ahead, telephone ahead, first-aid station ahead, etc.). They are easy to learn.

Gasoline rings up at twice or triple the U.S. price. The fuel crisis created some stalls at first, but later gas flowed abundantly everywhere. In most countries a top speed limit of 110 to 130 kilometers per hour is imposed for freeway traffic with 90 kilometers per hour set for secondary highway runs, and 50 to 60 kph pegged for suburban cruising; almost everywhere these maximums are very seriously enforced to the best of the abilities of the cops. Since the speed limits are not uniform, be sure to ask at each frontier concerning that nation's rules.

Left-hand traffic? Only in Great Britain and Ireland. In all other countries you'll drive as you do at home. (At least that's their hope!)

☑ **OTHER LIFESTYLES** Not everyone plunks his or her suitcase down in a hotel while abroad. In our various national chapters we briefly describe the programs that will expand your economy while broadening your experience. You, of course, have heard of the excellent **parador** and **pousada** systems comprising networks of low-cost inns in Spain and Portugal. France has its **Fédération Nationale des Agents Immobiliers**, where you can find accommodation in a chalet or a villa, and also the **Gîte de France**, which turns on space and hospitality in farmhouses. England has its **Home From Home** collection of rectories, manses, and historic estates where you can become a part of the family for astonishingly low rates. Germany has its **Gast im Schloss** assemblage for those who prefer to hobnob in castles. There is the superb **Relais et Châteaux** organization spotlighting intimate deluxe havens all over Europe and the U.K. Greece, an increasingly popular target, is guaranteeing that you can vacation in a "traditional settlement" that has not been spoiled by rampant tourism.

You can also do your thing on water. **Barge trips** through the Low Countries or through Burgundy, or even a 3-hour boat trip ($15) between Rüdesheim and Coblenz can provide new perspectives of Old World scenery. An innovative group named **Floating Through Europe** (501 Madison Ave., N.Y. 10022, Tel. 212-832-6700) now comes down the ways with a splendid fleet of comfortable hotels that roam for a week along the Thames, pause at exceptional restaurants for onshore dining, and provide nutrition for soul and body while cruising through the loveliness of England. There are ambles along continental canals too—and the prices are river-bottom low when compared with ordinary chartering rates in such high-cost regions.

The point we are making is that the travel horizon is just about as wide as your own vision, so keep your eyes open and your prospects broad.

☑ **ODD FACTS—SOME IMPORTANT!** The American term "First class" becomes "Deluxe" abroad; "First class" is American "Second class."

Wherever you overnight abroad, it's wise to be fire-conscious about your accommodations. Most emphatically, we do not wish to trouble your peace of mind in any way, because you'll find most of the better-grade hotels 100% safe —but once in a million times conflagrations *do* bring disaster. In too many of the less-expensive places, you'll find open stairwells, inflammable furnishings, no fire escapes, or other potential hazards. In these, as a standard practice and small precaution which just might save your life, analyze in advance your possible escape route. If there is none, and if the building should look dangerous, accept only a lower-floor room.

When you register in most European hotels save in Germany, "Joe Jones, Tuscaloosa, U.S.A." won't satisfy that gimlet-eyed clerk. You'll be given a form which is often as long as your arm. Neat trick, if he falls for it: Scrawl your name on the bottom, hand over your passport, and ask *him* to do the work. Sometimes he won't bite, though—so *memorize the number and date of issue of your passport for just such occasions.* In some lands this document will be held overnight at the desk for registration with the local police. If so, pleee-se don't forget to pick it up when you check out!

Be sure to indicate your date of arrival *and* departure when you apply for accommodations abroad. Should you omit the latter, a little man in a large claw-hammer coat might step up, smile apologetically, and bounce you out into the cold, cruel world—routine European practice.

Foreign chambermaids take delight in hiding your pajamas or nightgown under the pillow or actually between the sheets (Scandinavia). But this innocent pastime pales beside the Slipper Game—that ancient major sport of challenging guests to find their slippers on the top closet shelf, in the bedside cabinet which holds the chamber pot, or elsewhere. By dogged diligence and luck, my Nancy and I have managed to bat 1.000 over the years on these contests. Shamefully we must confess, however, that we've lost at least half a dozen sets of nightclothes!

Practically every European hotel has a Grand Panjandrum who is known as the concierge (pronounced "con-see-air-sssh"); in the U.K. and Ireland he is called the Hall Porter. He is the head contact man with the clients—boss of the bellhops, mail clerks, key clerks, nearly everybody on the street-floor service staff except the dining-room-and-bar help. He wears a pair of gold crossed keys ("Clefs d'Or") on his lapels—and he's not to be confused with the striped-pants, pearl-stickpin people at the Reception counter in the lobby. Use him for everything—stamps, outside errands, complaints, reservations for trains, theaters, or restaurants, and, most important of all, questions and advice about what's what in the city. And be sure to tip him when you check out—a minimum of $1.50 per day per couple in Deluxe or First-class houses, and from 50¢ to $1 per day in lesser ones. This tip is pooled for the whole desk (2 to 10 individuals who have served you), and it's cheap at the price. Since setups vary from place to place, it's always safest to ask him what specific areas your gratuity covers. Incidentally, never tip the lofty Reception gents.

Nearly every continental hostelry offers what is called the Pension ("Pahn-see-ahn," not "Pen-shun") Plan, which quotes room and board at one flat daily or weekly rate. It generally breaks down into 3 choices: Full Pension (room and all meals), Demipension (room and 2 meals), and Bed-and-Breakfast. Some innkeepers prefer that you state your choice on registration; some hotels require that you take Full Pension only. *Be sure to find out what is included and what is not included, as soon as you check in*—or you might be paying twice for your lunch or dinner, without being aware of it until they give you the bill.

Watch out for "supplements"—those devilish little sneak-charges which constantly rise to plague the innocent traveler. If you're operating under one of the Pension Plans, for example, most hotels give you the traditional continental breakfast as part of the contract—coffee or tea, toast, jam, butter, and a small pitcher of what is laughingly called cream. This will usually be eaten in your room, because downstairs is often closed. But when the waiter smiles and asks if Madame and Monsieur would like some orange juice, some fruit, some cereal, an egg perhaps?—these are on _your_ bill, not the hotel's. When you sit down to dine, they'll allow you only the dishes-of-the-day—a rigid list —and if you order _anything_ extra, that's socked onto your account, too. If you don't watch these supplements carefully, they can absolutely murder any carefully planned budget.

Almost nowhere abroad will a bellhop appear at Reception to wrassle your luggage. It is normal to separate you from your bags at the entrance—and later to bring them independently up to your room.

Some hotels below Deluxe category do not furnish soap to guests—not poverty or stinginess, but a difference of customs. Try to have your own supply.

The bidet, an institution in European bathrooms, is less known in North America. It's a shallow, kidney-shape porcelain apparatus, which might at first sight be a flat hopper; faucets at one end control the flow and temperature of the water. Our description in earlier editions of this book was so timid and uninformative that it drew a protest from Dr. Kenneth R. Morgan, the Bridgeport, Conn., physician, whose aforementioned _Speaking You English? A Lighthearted Guide to World Travel_ is the most wickedly witty, fun-filled, down-to-earth travel book in which we have ever delighted. Here are the good Doctor's merry but highly useful observations on this subject: "Since the average American looks at it and says, 'What the hell do you do with it?', I propose to explain. Since the average travel writer approaches the subject with such delicacy as to leave the reader in total ignorance, I intend to approach [the bidet] with such vulgarity as to leave no doubt as to its purpose. Its primary use is to wash off your bottom, which, with the strange variety of johns you've been visiting on daytime excursions, probably needs it. In practical use, one fills the little tub with warm water and sits on it facing the wall, a sensation somewhat akin to forgetting to put the seat down before sitting on the john. Europeans probably only do this when stark naked. Ignorant Americans emerge with wet nylons and shoes full of water. The European female or male may subsequently proceed to take a complete sponge bath from ears to toes, either because there is no bathtub or they are too lazy to get into one. The bidets with little fountains in the middle are old-fashioned and are, sad to say, gradually being replaced. Too bad, because they are lots of fun. The spray, if turned full on, goes right up to the ceiling. The technique here is to adjust the spray to a height of about 8 inches or so and allow it to play merrily over your navel. You can also balance a Ping-Pong ball on it; it will stay for hours. As a substitute for an actual douche (American, not French) it is perfectly hopeless, which is why this type of bidet has gone out of style." Anyone for questions?

Pompeii, the Vatican, the Louvre, and other cultural meccas fairly crawl with Roman numerals. If antiquities are your dish, it won't hurt to relearn your MCMLMM's in advance.

Send off all thank-you notes before leaving each city. This will prevent giant-size headaches later, when you've misplaced that damned address.

Dates are written differently in Europe: Our form of 6/30/81, for example, becomes 30/6/81.

Here's an oddity of language, too: Corn (European) is the name for wheat (American), while corn (American) becomes maize abroad.

Carry lots of calling cards—preferably engraved ones, since these are *the* status symbol in the Arrived Set Abroad. Although you may leave a paper trail that would be the envy of Hansel and Gretel, this subtle puff might smooth a VIP path of rose petals and red carpeting for you.

Most restaurants abroad (1) levy a special price for the bread you eat and (2) don't serve drinking water unless specifically requested. At some places (normally either the costliest or cheapest ones) you'll also pay extra for the tablecloth and napkins—the origin of "cover charge."

Store hours are a nuisance. Most shops close at noon and reopen at 2 P.M. —always the period you plan to do your buying. In hot countries such as Spain or Italy, the siesta lasts until 4 or 4:30 P.M., but the doors remain open until 7 P.M. or later. In England, Scandinavia, and other northern climes, however, they go straight through from perhaps 9 A.M. to 5:00 or 5:30.

One institution that nearly always petrifies the overseas visitor is the coeducational toilet room—a facility standard from one end of the Continent to the other. Here's the typical arrangement: One common washroom with washbowls and towels serves all comers. Leading off this, are 2 adjoining cubicles, marked "Men" or "Ladies." Sometimes these booths are separated by a partition which extends only from the knees to the top of the head, with yawning gaps at floor and ceiling level. You'll find this disturbing architecture at topnotch places too! More primitive establishments often offer the Turkish Toilet —2 size-14½ molded concrete feet strategically placed in front of a large hole chopped right through the floor—that's all! And for men, here's one more tidbit: Don't let sudden paralysis freeze the works if a woman attendant should blithely be knitting smack in the center of the men's room. If she can stand it (which she can), just drop a coin in her dish, give her a smile, tip your hat, and relax.

The majority of professional guides in Europe bitterly hate this book and savagely slander its author; once we even received a Death Threat from an anonymous Madrid–Toledo guide. Their rage is based on the fact that for many years we have continued to expose and to campaign against their dirty kickback racket. Here's how they'll try to sting you: This chiseler will ferret out 2nd-rate or 3rd-rate shopkeepers willing to pay a commission (generally 10% to 25%) on suckers who can be persuaded to load up on shoddy, sleazy goods *which have been marked up to cover the guide's rakeoff.* Most bizarre and insulting of all is that many of the "local" goods are production-line-produced elsewhere. Result: They get junk, and they pay from 10% to 25% more for the privilege of being rooked. Remember that _no_ decent, legitimate shop anywhere in Europe would _dream_ of stooping to such shady practice, any more than would Neiman-Marcus or Tiffany; there's one price for everybody. In Paris, Rome, Brussels, Madrid, Nice, Barcelona—yes, even in honest Amsterdam!—this shabby practice flourishes with the tacit knowledge of agency officials. So, (1) _you_ pick the stores, (2) be sure that they're the big ones, and (3) don't let the person talk you into patronizing some quaint little hole-in-the-wall which is "positively the best place in town!" Also, when they curse this book, and pledge on their mother's memory that they've personally watched That Man Fielding accept big bribes from rascally merchants, please reach for a large grain of salt.

The _café filtre,_ that satanic device endorsed by French, Belgian, and other backers of the Perfect Perpetual Motion Principle, has doubtless poleaxed thousands of strangers. Its tiny pot is crowned by a metal gimmick through which the water drips in microscopic droplets, until the supply and you are equally exhausted. Horn-handed veterans speed the process by removing the lid and milking their palm over its top to create additional suction; newcomers are advised to attempt this only with gloves. If time counts, you'll soon find yourself asking the waiter to deliver your demitasse with your soup.

Since lots of metropolitan railway stations abroad are deadends, don't panic when you roll off in the exact opposite direction from your destination.

Many hotel rooms have locks which demand 2 turns of the key instead of one. These must be twisted until both tumblers snap into place (easily audible); if only one is engaged, you have only 50% security against thieves.

For a list of about 200 motels of the European Motel Federation, write to Secretary, E.M.F., Dapplesweg 17, Berne, Switzerland.

Restaurant search while passing through small towns or villages? Silvino Trompetto, the globally esteemed Master Executive Chef of London's illustrious Savoy Hotel, recommends that strangers ask a reputable chemist (drugstore manager), who will probably know the grade of the raw fare and the hygienic conditions of every eating place.

Foreign table etiquette: A Miami Beach reader asks for table tips abroad. Here goes: (1) The man or the host (if it is a party) always leads the way to the table, following the Maître and followed by his guest or guests, including ladies. (2) The fish knife and fish fork are easily recognizable by their distinctive shapes. The former resembles a large butter knife, and the latter has a broad cutting edge on one tine. (3) When you're faced with a multiplicity of knives and forks, always reach for the outside ones, farthest away from the plate. (4) The dessert implements are placed _above_ the plate—not to the sides. (5) The clamplike instrument sometimes presented with asparagus first captures the stalk and is then lifted directly to the mouth. (6) The special pincers for snails are employed to hold the shell firmly while forking out the beastie with the other hand. (7) You might be asked if you prefer your oysters to be served "without beard." The "beard" is the dark circumference surrounding the nugget; most Americans prefer it "with beard." (8) The toothpick is used with abandon abroad. The more discreet diner at least has the grace to manipulate it with his napkin as a screen. When 2 people at the same table are engaged in this comic prophylaxis, it resembles the childhood game of peekaboo. (9) European hand-eating is just about confined to bread. Our American practice of picking up fried chicken with the fingers, peeling fruit Tarzan-style, and touching other comestibles is frowned upon. Continentals almost always use knives and forks.

Foreign theater etiquette: Which way do you face when you try to slither unobtrusively into your center-of-the-row seats? Europeans consider it rude for the latecomer to force them to face YOUR proscenium. They prefer the navel-to-eyeball confrontation. So go in facing the rear of the theater and the citizenry in your row. And who knows? You might even meet the violet eyes of a good-looking and unescorted friend for the rest of the evening!

Shoeshine: Before retiring for the night, ask if it is customary in that particular hostelry to place shoes at your theshold in the hall. (This custom, which used to be universal, is now extinct in Scandinavia and is fast vanishing everywhere else.) If the answer is affirmative, they'll shine 'em free—part of the hotel-service charge (but you must add a small tip when you leave). Not much chance that your neighbor will steal them.

Service: When the telephone-use for room service isn't applicable, press the proper button on the gadget on your bedside table (or on the wall by the entrance). A light will flash outside your door; each button lights its own color, so the waiter and porter won't come when you want the maid. If you can't read the language, there is a clever drawing of each functionary beside his particular button. Sometimes there is a third system: An extra button on the base of the phone which, when pushed, summons the maid.

Bath: If it's down the hall, notify the maid a few minutes in advance. She has to unlock it and clean it up for you. In some countries every time you think of the word "bathtub," you're out another $1-or-so (baths are extra).

Letters: The accordion foldup international air form is available nearly everywhere. Prolific letter writers love 'em because (1) they save up to a third in postage, and (2) they run out of space just after ". . . wish you were here."

Hotel Postage: When you turn over your correspondence to the concierge's lads with instructions that it be airmailed, stand right there until they put on the stamps. Otherwise it might arrive by ordinary postage, with the desk people pocketing the difference. Always stamp postcards yourself, because too many go into the wastebasket. This is a routine petty racket markedly in smaller hotels.

Film: While color film is now available even in most small villages, supplies are often spotty during the summer rush. Take a few rolls of your own as insurance, especially if you are not going to be at any one stop long enough to have European-purchased film processed in Europe. (American developing of foreign negatives often gives blurry results due to differences in chemicals.) Plenty of good black-and-white in all sizes can be found practically everywhere. During these times of skyjack scares, it might be wiser to hand-carry all of your film (stills or even cinema types), since luggage x-raying equipment at international airports can alter the balance of unexposed *and* exposed keepsakes. Carry-on baggage also is subject to radiation damage, so if you see such a device coming up, ask the attendant to physically inspect your cameras and film supplies. If you happen to be gifted with size-56 biceps, lead-laminated pouches by a company called Film Shield are available through some photo-equipment dealers.

Sexy blonde: Take a good look at her these days; she might leave you a souvenir. The venereal rate abroad—as it is at home these days, too—is again a red-alert epidemic. Not only has syphilis made a devastating comeback, but there's a strain of gonorrhea so hardy that it eats penicillin for breakfast. Plenty of willing, gorgeous women in half the cafés and railway station districts in Europe—but it's a chance, nearly always. Gigolos are liable to be infected, too.

Long-distance telephone: Except as specified below, *never make any international or transatlantic calls from your hotel, because you'll pay a surcharge of up to 300% if you do.* For decades it has been common and disgraceful tradition in virtually every hostelry abroad to tack its own "service fee" onto your bill for the casual, simple, normal use of its operator and the instrument. When checkout time comes, travelers are aghast to find that the $8.80 chat with the family in Connecticut has cost them $35.20 or that the $21.55 business talk with their Chicago partner has hooked them for $86.20. Deeply alarmed by this violation against public interest, AT&T's brilliant Executive Vice President Richard R. Hough and forceful Director-Overseas Administration E. E. Carr inaugurated a towering counter-campaign named "Teleplan." In return for huge advertising and public relations expenditures on both sides of the ocean to bring massive new long-distance business to foreign telephone companies, their *quo* for this *quid* is that fair and reasonable maximum supplements be rigidly imposed upon all hotels or other 3rd parties in countrywide prohibitions. Already Ireland, Portugal, Israel, the 72 Hilton hotels in 43 countries, and the giant Trust Houses Forte chain have adopted the "Teleplan" system. Its pioneering by these hostelries marks the first time that honest surcharges in this field have been established in France, Germany and Switzerland, the 3 most notorious offenders in all Western Europe. By the time you read these words, all or some of the vast International, Sheraton, Marriot, and Holiday Inn clusters overseas might so wisely be offering their clients this freedom from such shocking greediness. (You can aid this cause—which will benefit every traveler in the long run—by asking the manager of your hotel if his establishment has accepted the Teleplan program.) Nation by nation AT&T's progressive executives are patiently chopping away to eliminate these cruel excesses. Although Government Post Office ownerships or equipment inadequacies rule out adoption in such lands as France and Italy for the foreseeable future, eventually this team in benevolent Ma Bell may well integrate this project into a quasi-Pan European network and give fantastic savings to permanent or transient international and over-ocean users. If you MUST make an emergency call from your bedroom, there are 2 ways to avoid all extra levies: (1) use your AT&T credit card (no others valid) or (2) reverse the charges. Otherwise, except in the aforementioned locations, pocket the price of a bottle or a magnum of champagne by putting them through at any local telephone center. . . . Almost everywhere you might wander these days in the civilized areas of the Old Continent, you may direct-dial to technically advanced points all over the world. As in North America, toll connections are made almost instantaneously.

Cables: Expensive but dependable, except perhaps in Spain. Telex also is widely available, and it costs much less.

Maps: Not only indispensable after you get there, but timesaving and great fun before you leave. Stateside navigators might wish to send for the catalogue offered by Forsyth Travel Library, P.O. Box 2975, 9154 West 57th St., Shawnee Mission, KS 66201.

Who's Where: Celebrity Service, Inc., brainchild and *opera major* of the inimitable Earl Blackwell, operates full-scale field headquarters in Paris, London, and Rome. If you wish to locate any prominent personality abroad— peripatetic VIP or continental resident—you need only ask the concierge to query these mother hens. For an additional small fee you may subscribe to Ringmaster B's *Celebrity Bulletin,* a daily publication that tells you which film stars, TV luminaries, playwrights, Pulitzer Prize winners, and international socialites are between the sheets in your hotel (but not with whom!).

Office facilities en route: Manpower, Inc., has been set up in more than 325 metropolises on 5 continents. One of its 100-thousand assistants can be found in almost any major European city. Check the local phone books under this name or MAS.

Medical precaution: Medic Alert Foundation renders an invaluable non-profit service to travelers who suffer from any serious medical problem. It furnishes lifesaving emblems of 10-karat gold-filled, of sterling silver, or of stainless steel to be worn around the neck or wrist—or to be hung from a charm bracelet. Should the patient be unable to talk, medical personnel or law-enforcement officials are instantly informed of dangers inherent in standard treatment. The tag carries such warnings as "DIABETIC," "ALLERGIC TO PENICILLIN," "TAKING ANTICOAGULANTS," "WEARING CONTACT LENSES," "NECK BREATHER," or whatever difficulty. It also bears the telephone number of the Medic-Alert headquarters in California to which anyone may call "Collect" from anywhere in the world at any hour of day or night for additional file material about the individual case. For more information about this splendid organization (donations are tax deductible), write to Medic-Alert Foundation International, Turlock, CA 95380.

Austria

No country on the Continent guarantees the footloose wanderer more breath-taking mountains, a larger helping of enchanting beauty, or a warmer welcome from its people. In Vienna, Salzburg, and Innsbruck you'll find the fingerprints, footprints, and bottle prints of migrations of outlanders who have long savored its heady lures; in smaller centers you will experience a sample of living which has remained undisturbed since the days of Franz Josef (well, er, at least since last winter's visit of the Baltimore Ski Club). The popularity of this rollicking republic is romping along at break-the-bank pace. Don't ever confuse Austria with Germany; they're as far apart in customs, attitudes, and culture as are Italy and France.

In winter the ski stations get the big play; in summer, fall, and spring, the cities are aflutter with outlanders. In the capital today, there's scarcely a letup from Maytime until the October rains. The countryside offers a few available kips when cosmopolites are touring the major festivals and fairs, but who wants to spend all his days in the clover? Ironclad hotel reservations, therefore, are an absolute must; *don't go without confirmation!* Despite the whopping national increase of 175 thousand new beds in about a decade (Austrian chamber-*Mädchen* puff up about 600 thousand pillows), she still hasn't enough facilities to cope with the flood of foreign visitors during halcyon days—or even in the fringe seasons. For skiers, the first weekend in January to Easter is the choice period; Christmas, though cold, is also considered High Season on the heights. While Austria traditionally has been known for alpine (downhill) skiing, it now boasts nearly 8000 miles of cross-country trails for Nordic enthusiasts. You may range from such deluxe pleasure domes of sport as the Arlberg's Zürserhof to a simple mode of village living that is comfortable enough for anyone but the fussiest type of traveler, who ought to stick to the largest cities. France is the country in which to parade that mink coat and that new Dior; milady may do the same at Austria's chic resorts or at the music festivals, but in general this is a country where you let down your hair and have fun.

Now, in quick summary, here is our rating of outstanding attractions to the North American traveler:

1. Vienna.

2. The drive over Austria's highest mountain, the Grossglockner, which no visitor should miss. There is a 900-car silo garage at the 8000-foot pass. Pretty little Lienz is an ideal target for overnighting.

3. Salzburg and surroundings.

4. The Austrian Danube cruise (see above), including the Wachau excursion via delightful little Dürnstein and the noted monastery at Melk.

5. The Salzkammergut lake country—Bad Ischl, Bad Aussee, Wolfgangsee, Traunsee, Mondsee, Hallstätter See, Gosausee.

6. Drive, by car or bus, from Bad Aussee through the Gesäuse, the narrowest part of the Enns Valley, and the Salza Valley to Mariazell; from there go via the Seeberg to Graz, branching off at Stainach-Irdning to Schladming-Ramsau, Austriahütte at the foot of the Dachstein Massif, and at Hieflau to Eisenerz with its iron ore deposits.

7. In winter, any of these ski stations: Zürs, Lech, St. Anton am Arlberg, and Stuben; Obergurgl; Hochgurgl, Hochsölden; Igls; Seefeld; Kitzbühel; Zell am See; Saalbach; Badgastein; Hofgastein; the Radstädter Tauern; Mallnitz. Austria is often credited with breeding some of the most daring, the speediest, and the most demanding skiers under God's gray sky, so be sure to pick an address in your appropriate league. If you are an off-trail, deep-powder enthusiast, take a guide or seek detailed directions for the safest areas.

8. For Alpine scenery in summer: Zell am See (cable railway to the Schmittenhöhe and its hotel at 6000 ft.), Salzkammergut lake district near Salzburg, and Badgastein; the Brenner Autobahn in the Tyrol; the Tauern pike from Salzburg to Carinthia; the remarkable Silvretta High Alpine Road and the Hochtannberg Road in Vorarlberg, among the most thrilling mountain highways of Europe. Other outstanding mountain views abound on the Katschberg road (Salzburg—Klagenfurt), the Pötschenpass road (Styria—Upper Austria) and the Wechselbundesstrasse east of the Semmering (Lower Austria—Styria).

9. Winter *and* summer skiing? The Kitzsteinhorn, via the cable car from Kaprun, the cable lift to Zell am See, the glacier at Dachstein, Hintertux and Sölden/Ötztal (both Tyrolian glaciers), or the nearby ice packs at Neustift-Stubaital.

10. Ötztal, Ausserfern, Zillertal, and Achensee, all in the Tyrol.

11. Velden and Pörtschach, both on Wörthersee in Carinthia.

12. The quiet, family-type resorts of Weissensee in Carinthia.

13. The baroque monastery of St. Florian (Bruckner organ) near Linz.

14. Semmering, the mountain health resort 3000 feet up—only a 2-hour drive from Vienna. Bus excursions are operated in season.

15. The Burgenland, 1 hour from Vienna, with its many castles, Neusiedler Lake, Haydn's resting place, and colorful inns with gypsy music.

Pamphlets on these regions are available at the usual sources, notably the Austrian National Tourist Office and the local tourist offices. If Salzburg is one of your goals, the *Official Guide* (published by Karl Gordon Co.) is sold at most newsstands and is more than worth its small charge.

☑ **FESTIVALS** The **Salzburg Festival**, Austria's most famous, is held from the latter part of July to the end of August. The average program includes 8 operas—by Mozart, Strauss, Verdi and others, plus a world première—in 27 performances. Other events: Major orchestra concerts, Mozart chamber opera, instrumental recitals, Mozart matinees, serenades, lieder, ballet and sacred music. While it is on, the visitor will feel as if he had set up a cot next to the Information Booth in Grand Central Station; _don't attempt it without confirmed reservations in advance._ (This holds for the Easter Festival as well.) If you can't find space (as is probable), and if you're sufficiently desperate, write to the Landesreisebüro or the Stadtverkehrsbüro in Salzburg, either of which will try to find a private family with an extra pallet.

Other most illustrious events are the **Vienna Festival** (mid-May to mid-June; a glory of operas, operettas, concerts, and plays), the **Bregenz Festival** (late July to late Aug.; performances on a gigantic floating stage on Lake Constance), and the **Graz Steirischer Herbst Festival** (Oct.; modern music and art exhibits).

Consult the Austrian National Tourist Office for details about these.

☑ **TRANSPORTATION** **Taxis** All modern cars these days. In Vienna's fleet of about 1650 vehicles, roughly 1600 are driven by men and 60 by women. Once we drew a Brünnhilde with a size 17½ collar and muscles more rippling than Ken Norton's; her cowboy driving homogenized us 20 years in 20 yards. But most of the representatives of both genders are courtly, and their prices are still fair.

Unless you're either stony-drunk or desperate, never take a taxi in Salzburg. Although all cabs now have meters, these are the fastest ticking and flipping mechanisms we have ever boggled at in our travels. Absolutely outrageous; strictly for suckers or invalids.

Car Rental Our pick of the crop in _Vienna_ is a small but profoundly conscientious organization called **Erhart Car Hire & Travel**, 25 Zwoelfergasse (out-of-the-way 15th district; tel.: 83-23-22 or his private phone, 86-25-15; Telex 134764). All of our recent capital rounds have been enormously enhanced by its knowledgeable corps of drivers. Furthermore, Proprietor Walther Erhart has volunteered to be a general factotum, consultant, and Dutch uncle to any reader who has problems in his nation or who may be traveling into Eastern Europe. (The 12-hour Erhart whirls to Budapest or to Salzburg are tremendous hits with travelers on brief time allowances). His services are wide, varied, and supremely courteous. He will even romp over the ski zones with special winter-sport holiday packages if you have a large family or small party in tow. You can roll along in a sedan or in a 20-seat Mercedes coach. Airport pickup and delivery of arriving or departing visitors at rates far below the taxi bite (the terminus is almost 1 hour outside the city); multichoice, inexpensive to opulent chauffeur- or self-drive; tantalizing tours to Hungary (2 days, passport and 2 photos required), a full day in the Wachau wine district—you name it and he, his staff, or his fine travel agency in the city will fix it. AND there's that wonderful comfort of a dependable new friend in town who will pull strings to snag you a better hotel room, tickets to the Opera, entry into the always-oversold Spanish Riding School, a babysitter, or help with almost any legitimate and reasonable need. English-speaking pilots, of course. Competitive tariffs; highest recommendation, especially for the pervading brand of Erhart-inspired kindness that envelops this dynamic little company. It also operates a branch in *Salzburg* (10 Dariogasse, tel: 20400). This one is every bit as professionally sound, ethical, and smooth as the alma mater; it does not, however, have self-drive vehicles.

Roads? You'll find many improvements. The impressive Arlberg Tunnel, an engineering marvel, is the most noteworthy and useful, especially for skiers to the region. The chute, which is almost 9 miles long, cuts out the arduous haul over the Pass; the price of admission is just about $10 for a normal car—and less in summer when other options (and roads) are open. The expressway over the Brenner Pass between Innsbruck and Italy is negotiable any time of year—a boon for winter motorists. The Salzburg-Vienna autobahn is not only excellent, but it is one of the most beautiful drives on that part of the globe. The 6-lane highway from Vienna southward reaches just beyond Wiener Neustadt and zips toward Italy via Styria and Carinthia; the link between Innsbruck and Kufstein is finished and functional throughout the year.

Good service stations in practically every city, town, and hamlet. Gas here, as everywhere in Europe, is increasingly expensive.

Trains Most of the international trains are comfortable. The majority have sleepers and dining facilities; all serve drinks. All interior main lines have electric traction, and a number of diesel types chug point-to-point in many areas.

There is a small surcharge on Expresses. The 50% reduction for the Junior Set stops at their 23rd birthday.

The **Austria Ticket** is a useful wrinkle in rod-riding (also includes bus links) which is valid for 9 or 16 days and saves sizable chunks of *geld* from the traveler's pouch. It provides other money-saving favors as well.

And don't forget Austria is included in that remarkable transportation bargain, the "Eurailpass."

☑ **FOOD** Wonderful cuisine with a distinctive approach—most often delicately prepared and graciously served. Each region has its own specialties. Try to work in a sampling of Frittatensuppe (consommé with thinly sliced pancakes in it), Viennese Tafelspitz (boiled beef with a cream and chive mantle plus a side dish of horseradish mixed with applesauce), and Topfenknödel (a sweetish sphere of baked cottage cheese glazed with sugar, wading in a light syrup and plum gravy). For adventure and variety, here's one of the best gastronomic lands we've found.

☑ **DRINKS** Wines are your best bet. Prices average $3.50 to $10 per bottle and $1 to $2.25 for ¼ liter.

While Klosterneuburger is perhaps the best white wine, if you stick to a brand with the equally jaw-cracking name of Gumpoldskirchner (available in most places), you'll always be safe—and very probably pleased. Keep in mind "gum," and "Leopold," and it will stand out on the wine list. Other dependable and sound labels are Kremser, Dürnsteiner, Hohenwarther, and Nussberger. The finest red wine we've ever tasted is

Vöslauer; red wines from Baden are most often superb. From the Wachau district along the Danube, Südbahn and Burgenland pressings win the local medals.

Of the beers, Gösser Bräu is a rich brew made in Styria. It's full-bodied and fine; choice of light or dark. Schwechater is tops in Vienna.

Imported potables are relatively expensive. Bourbon and rye are now amply abundant. Strictly for nickel-plated gullets, there's a local rum which puts life in afternoon tea, a "club whisky" which will lift the hat right off your head, and a schnapps which you'll find still delicately flaked with enamel from the bathtub. If you can take it like Dean Martin, there's also the local plum brandy or slivovitz. Enzian is another brandy, distilled from the roots of the tall curious yellow (not blue) gentian. Locals seem to worship it. Our own very personal verdict: At some indeterminate point between (1) mildly repugnant, (2) actively repulsive, and (3) totally unswallowable. Finally, Bowle is a delicious summer punch made of cognac, white wine, champagne or curaçao, and fresh fruits: served from a bowl at perhaps $1 per glass.

★ **TIPS** When you order a martini, be sure to specify "Beefeater" (cheaper) or "Gordon's"; others which may appear are often best applied to arrest baldness.

Every restaurant, tavern, or bar in the nation must levy a 20% surtax on wines and spirits. Half of this is an alcohol nip while another gulp of 10% is decanted for beverages in general, whether they be coffee, tea, or *milk,* if you please!

☑ **TIPPING** The mysterious word "Trinkgeld" will pop up inevitably during your Austrian journey. It means "tip." Here is a rough guide of the *extra* gratuities which you, as an American, will be expected to give:

Waiter—10% extra (to the man who serves you, not to the headwaiter; in more modest places the Austrian equivalent of two bits is enough); bartender—10% of drinks; maid —10 schillings per night; washroom attendant—2 schillings; taxi driver—10% to 15% of fare; theater usher—5 schillings; doorman—5 schillings; porter and bellboy—5–10 schillings.

If someone gives you extra extra attention with an extra, extra smile, you may wish to bump these up a notch or 2.

☑ **LOCAL RACKETS** A common clip is for your hotel concierge to offer you a so-called cut-rate entry ticket to a night club. It will be printed, for example, "45 schillings," for which you will happily pay 35 schillings. Later, when you arrive at the club, you'll find that your "bargain" is the standard admission fee.

Much too often, ticket purchasing by travelers to Vienna is a classic illustration of caveat emptor. As a preliminary, agency commissions on sales to the opera, sports events, the Spanish Riding School, and other popular events are legally set at a whopping 20%! (Vienna is reckoned to be the most costly city in the world for ducats. Good seats at a top-grade performance garner about $80 for the house.) Almost habitually your hotel or your agency will give you the sob story that "only the most expensive seats are left." (And why not, since their cut is bigger?) Nonsense! At 7 of the 8 major performances we attended during a recent visit, literally scores of satisfactory but less costly seats went begging after we had been told to expect a sellout. Thus, always apply first, in person, at the sales window of the arena, theater, or opera. If *they* tell you that the situation is SRO, *then* retreat to your outside sources, which may be holding admissions up their sleeves. Recently we picked up late tickets at reasonable prices at the Tourist Information desk on the subway level beneath the opera plaza.

If you are certain of your dates the Austrian National Tourist Office (see below) has the musical program for the year and supplies forms for ordering tickets to be picked up in Vienna at the box office; they are held until performance day and can be paid for then. Hallelujah!

In general, the Austrians are forthright and honest people, to whom the trickery of some of their Latin neighbors is completely incomprehensible.

☑ **INFORMATION CENTERS** The Austrians couldn't be nicer. For detailed holiday information on this enticing nation, write, phone, or call in person at the **Austrian National Tourist Office**, 545 Fifth Ave., N.Y. 10017. Its dynamic Director, Dr. Heinz Patzak, has the lore of his native land at his fingertips; you'll find him a gold mine of advice, facts, and guidance.

The home office of this organization is doing an outstanding job. The official **Tourist Information Office** in the capital handles all routine holiday questions. On any extraordinary difficulties or puzzles get in touch with the **Österreichische Fremdenverkehrswerbung** (Austrian National Tourist Office) at Hohenstaufengasse 3–5, Vienna I (tel.: 639671). The knowledgeable and capable Comanagers, Dr. Helmut Zolles and Dkfm. Frank Kübler, are its moving forces. There are 9 **Landesverkehrsämter** (Provincial Tourist Offices), as well as propaganda stations, tourist boards, and spa administrations in Austrian tourist centers. Branches are maintained in 18 foreign capitals.

In local health resorts, ask for the *Kurdirektor;* in other hamlets, try the *Verkehrsamt* (local tourist bureaus).

Special for winter sports: This season 15 mountain resorts will continue their welcoming program titled "American Skiers' Best Friends." In each upland station there will be an official national host who is there to greet foreign visitors, tell them where the snow is best, and generally serve as an amiable Austrian helpmate on their slopes. *Danke vielmals!*

If you are still in the states and trying to decide whether to snap on your boots and head for the hills, you can find out immediately what the slopes are like by picking up the Austrian Snow Phone. Dial (212) 697–8295 around the clock and any day of the week for a recorded report on all major resort conditions.

CITIES

VIENNA Enough to keep the tourist busy for a year.

Sightseeing Your primary targets will probably be (1) a look at the **Ringstrasse,** the famous boulevard circling the city, (2) a ride through the **woods** immortalized by Johann Strauss (pick your tour carefully, because travelers again have complained about ramshackle loudspeaker systems and wheezy guides who droned indistinctly in all 4 languages), (3) for tradition only, a look at the far-from-blue **Danube,** and (4) a peek at the whole picture from the pike's peak of the **Danube Tower,** an 840-foot TV-radio mast (see "Restaurants"). Then you might try (1) a performance at the ultimate glory of this world music capital, the magnificently rebuilt **Opera House** (closed July and Aug.; 200 seats per performance allotted to local travel agents for foreign visitors), (2) the eye-popping **Spanish Riding School** (precision horse-training rehearsals every weekday morning except Mon. for the fabulous full-dress Sun. morning show or Wednesday nightriders; early Mar. to end-June and early Sept. to mid-Dec. only; *book through a travel agency or theater ticket office well ahead and don't miss it!*), (3) the **Theatre an der Wien** (light opera), (4) the venerable **St. Stephen's Cathedral,** (5) **Schönbrunn Palace** (ancient summer castle of the double-eagle monarchy), (6) the **Secular and Ecclesiastical Treasure Rooms in the Hofburg,** where the crown jewels are on opulent display (no English-speaking guides, alas), (7) the **Clock Museum** (near St. Stephen's Cathedral; more than 3000 specimens on silent exhibit—without a single cuckoo in the lot), (8) the house where **Beethoven** wrote his "Heiligenstadt Testament" in 1802 (Probusgasse 6), and (9) the **Imperial** or **Capuchin Crypt.** Then there's the **"Music and Light Around Belvedere Palace"** spectacle (held in German at this famed baroque structure which has played such an important role in the nation's history), concerts in various palaces in summer (consult local tip sheets for when and where), **Auersperg** Palace (which Richard Strauss wrote into *Der Rosenkavalier*), and the splendid Brueghel collection and other *rarae aves* in the **Kunsthistorisches Museum** (Museum of Fine Arts). Plenty of 1st-rate art galleries, other museums, and other Baedeker attractions in and around this center—but remember that music, especially opera and more especially Mozart, is the staff of life to any properly formed Viennese ear. For information *and* reservation of rooms go to Vienna Western Station (Westbahnhof), the Vienna Southern Station (Südbahnhof), the office at the Opera underpass, or Vienna Airport. In addition, during the summer season, you may apply at Purkersdorf, Highway #1, or Inzersdorf, Highway #17, or Praterkai, station for the Danube steamers. Posted conspicuously here and on other main roads leading to the capital are modern information kiosks with official hostesses.

A ride on the Danube? (1) Daily passenger service in summer from the German frontier to Vienna is as popular as ever—and it's a delightful experience to climb aboard at Passau for the 7 A.M. sailing, lunch after the noon stop at Linz, dine in the lingering sunset on the river, and slip into the capital at 7:45 P.M. If this haul is too long for your tastes, the *Stadt Wien,* the *Stadt Passau,* the *Johann Strauss,* and the *Schoenbrunn* may be boarded in the late morning at the railway hub of Linz. Should your car present a problem, a professional chauffeur is on tap to "pilot" it from Passau to Linz or from Passau to Vienna—both at moderate fees. Staterooms available; ample restaurant and bar facilities; modest prices; more beguiling than the Rhine excursion because it's not so cut-and-dried. (2) From Vienna, you may sail up to Linz for a postmidnight arrival and a return the following day in time for a late dinner. (3) Special moonlight cruises (Vienna to Vienna) are sometimes promoted, too. Don't forget that the above services are operated *from May to September only.* (4) Although the Austrian *Theodor Körner* makes occasional cruises downstream (normally it links Vienna and Passau), only the Soviets have a regular run between Vienna and Odessa, docking at such Iron Curtain points as Budapest, Belgrade, Ruse, Giurgiu, and Ismail, with City sightseeing excursions en route. The *Dnjepr* and the *Wolga* ply from Vienna all the way to Yalta, the Black Sea resort. They offer a 13–day round trip to 7 countries. (5) The Austrian hydrofoil *Delphin* and the Hungarian hydrofoil *Siràly* ("Seagull") zip between Vienna, Linz, and Budapest from early May until mid-September; departure and return days vary. For all of the more distant ports, find out whether you'll need a standard or transit visa. And do it early!

VIENNA HOTELS Quick Reference Table

Price categories by national (not U.S.) standards.

EXPENSIVE:

Bristol Kärntner Ring 1. Tel. 529.552; Telex 01/2474; 121 rooms. P. 39
Hilton Am Stadtpark. Tel. 752.652; Telex 07/6799; 620 rooms. P. 40
Imperial Kärntner Ring 16. Tel. 651.765; Telex 01/2630; 160 rooms. P. 39
Intercontinental Johannesgasse 28. Tel. 563.611; Telex 01/1235; 496 rooms. P. 40
Sacher Philharmonikerstr. 4. Tel. 525.575; Telex 01/2520; 123 rooms. P. 39
Krantz-Ambassador Neuer Markl 5. Tel. 527.511; Telex 01/1906; 105 rooms. P. 40
Palais Schwarzenberg Schwarzenbergpl. 9. Tel. 725.125; Telex 07/6124. 34 rooms. P. 40

UPPER MODERATE:

Am Parkring Parkring 12. Tel. 526.524; Telex 01/3420; 65 rooms. P. 41
Am Stephansplatz Stephansplatz 9. Tel. 635.605; Telex 07/4334. 69 rooms. P. 41
Astoria Kärnter Strasse 32. Tel. 526.585; Telex 01/2856. 116 rooms. P.41
Bellevue Althanstrasse 5. Tel. 345.631; Telex 07/4906. 86 rooms. P. 40
Capricorno Schwedensplatz 3–4. Tel. 633.104; Telex 07/5266. 46 rooms. P.41
Clima Favoritenstrasse 12. Tel. 659.605; Telex 01/2699; 31 rooms. P. 41
De France Schottenring 3. Tel. 343.540; Telex 07/4360; 141 rooms. P. 41
Erzherzog Rainer Wiedner Hauptstrasse 27–29. Tel. 654.646; Telex 01/2329; 95 rooms. P. 41
Europa Neuer Markt 3. Tel. 521.594; Telex 01/2292; 100 rooms. P. 40
Kummer Mariahilfer Str. 71a. Tel. 573.695; Telex 01/1417; 108 rooms. P. 41
President Wallgasse 23. Tel. 573.636; Telex 01/2523; 77 rooms. P. 41
Prince Eugen Wiedner Gürtel 14. Tel. 651.741; Telex 01/2483. 106 rooms. P. 41
Regina Rooseveltplatz 15. Tel. 427.681; Telex 07/4700; 127 rooms. P. 41
Royal Singerstrasse 3. Tel. 524.631; Telex 01/2870; 66 rooms. P. 41
Strudlhof Pasteurgasse 1. Tel. 312.522; Telex 07/5256; 48 rooms. P. 41
Tyrol Mariahilfer Str. 15. Tel. 575.415; Telex 01/1885; 35 rooms. P. 41

MODERATE:

Arenberg Strubenring 2. Tel. 521.911; 23 rooms. P. 41
Atlanta Währinger Str. 33. Tel. 421.239; Telex 07/5002; 97 rooms. P. 41
Elite Wipplingerstrasse 32. Tel. 632.518. 30 rooms. P. 41
König von Ungarn Schulerstrasse 10. Tel. 526520; Telex 07/7526. 74 beds. P. 40
Opernring Opernring 11. Tel. 575.518; Telex 01/1359; 35 rooms. P. 41
Schneider Lehárgasse 1. Tel. 577.604; 35 rooms. P. 41

ENVIRONS:

Hütteldorf Youth Hostel Schlossberggasse 8. Tel. 821.501. P. 41
Parkhotel Schönbrunn Hietzinger Hauptstrasse 12–14. Tel. 822.676; Telex 01/2513; 349
rooms. P. 41
Tourotel Kurbadstrasse 8. Tel. 629.211; Telex 01/3361; 256 rooms P. 41

Hotels

The century-old but split-second-fresh **Imperial** is the blue-ribbon choice for the client who wants grandeur, suavity, and action with his million-$ elegance. This beautiful, imposing, 200-room, fully air-conditioned hostelry has now achieved near-perfection in every department. Choice of ultramodern or classic-style rooms, all handsomely decorated; Royal Suites—truly "Royal"— with palatial opulence at a palatial rate; Suite #202–203, considerably less formal and less expensive, is indescribably appealing. Spotless maintenance; flawless taste; Concierge Willi Lache and his minions standouts. Demipension is encouraged at intervals, but the cuisine is extraordinarily delicious. Director Otto Heinke unquestionably deserves Imperial laurels. We regard it as the best hotel in Austria and one of the finest anywhere in the world.

The **Bristol**, sharing the Imperial administration and with similar tariffs, majestically retains a position equal to the above entry but in a style that speaks more of period decor. Its restaurant is *the* after-theater-and-opera gathering spot in the capital. Graciously traditional throughout; well-appointed silk-lined bedchambers where the suites and the singles shine with a special pride; all in all, extremely chic in every element of its decorative scheme. Under the baton of Gerhard Paul, who also conducts the Imperial opera, the orchestration becomes more and more a symphony of delight every year. Highly recommended on every score.

The **Sacher** trades on its global reputation for Old Worldliness. Turn-of-the-century furnishings, high ceilings, oil paintings, and statuary abound; modern touches elsewhere have enhanced its efficiency. Its drawbacks, however, are equally significant. In our judgment, most of its accommodations are painfully small for transatlantic travelers with ample luggage; the house policy of not accepting *any* credit cards seems ill-advised; better soundproofing should be installed on all streetfront units, we again received pushy service during an after-opera meal when the waiters wanted to leave; moreover the cuisine was not up to our former meals here. Undoubtedly here is an aristocrat—of that there's no question; but whether you are lured by its personality depends upon you. We've seen this hotel long enough to be convinced that it is changeless, timeless, and fine in its very own way. Our very own way, however, is different enough to incline us preferentially toward the Imperial and the Bristol with the Sacher chasing closely at their heels. Very special and as the French would say, *"Chacun à son goût."*

The **Hotel Im Palais Schwarzenberg** (Schwarzenbergplatz 9), a charming island of serenity, occupying the right wing of one of Vienna's most beautiful baroque palaces, exudes the feeling that the visitor is ensconced in a provincial mansion. Garden, park, and plaza setting just off the Ringstrasse, 5 minutes from the central whirl; client capacity now at 50; intimate hearthside bar; darkly attractive vaulted dining salon with alfresco meals facing the vast greensward in summer. All 34 rooms have private bath and individual décor, either antique or modern; some units in the chalet extension featuring neat little kitchenettes. Manager Roth is displaying a masterful grasp of town-and-country innkeeping. Although Star Actress Joan Fontaine alleges shocking treatment while staying here during a recent theatrical performance, many other American travelers have found this house to be amiable and excellent.

Vienna claims its very own **Hilton**, a white-structured city in itself that offers 700 latchkeys, a quartet of restaurants (the Prinz Eugen Grill is one of the top spots in town), shops, and—most convenient of all—the main city air terminal smack under its hangar-wide roof. The mayor here is General Manager Rupert Huber. For Hilton buffs this one manifests predictable and familar qualities.

The 14-story, $12,000,000, 500-room **Intercontinental** is an edifice from the impersonal cookie mold that makes guests wonder whether they are in Vienna, Abidjan, Auckland, or Rawalpindi. At last, however, it seems to be warming up here and there. Sleek-modern exterior; quiet but not inconvenient situation near the Wienfluss and Stadtpark; orange-shaded Brasserie for quick meals; excellent, all-you-can-lap-up noon-to-3 P.M. buffet daily; other conveniences. General Manager John Edmair is continuing the company's efforts to give this huge installation more of a human pulse beat. Still more muscle than heart, but very strong indeed in its own particular way.

The **Krantz-Ambassador**, while not advancing, is maintaining its standards. Dual entrances from 2 avenues; twin lobbies; mulberry silk throughout; full air-chilling; handsome, spacious accommodations with comfortable bathrooms; small dining room (for clients only) with superb cuisine; unusually friendly attention.

König von Ungarn is noted for its splendid restaurant in a cozy corner of its interior courtyard. The ancient private house has been newly restructured and seems to have a mandate on quiet luxury.

Europa is another fresh candidate—this one in more contemporary tone with superb modern furnishings and, like the above newcomer, with a first-rate midcity address.

The **Bellevue** is cheaper and correspondingly more modest. Space for 7-score guests, but only 2-score with private bath or shower; décor an uninspired but suitable mixture of modern furnishings, crystal chandeliers, chintz bedpuffs, and frilled lampshades; enclosed garage; interior garden. As one of Vienna's oldest hostelries it provides clean basic shelter.

The 77-room **President** is well groomed by Directress Sylvia Seyrling. Some twins with a 3rd bed; smartly furnished; summer breakfast garden; Nordic dining salon. We prefer this one to the **Strudlhof,** which also is modern and economically priced.

The conveniently-sited, 121-unit **Astoria** recently was restyled; but not to our taste. What we do commend, however, is the space in the bedchambers.

Am Parkring is club-sandwiched on the 11th to 13th floors of a commercial office building. Quiet, viewful units; excellent maintenance overlorded by Manager Ernst Stockinger; tiny singles with half-bathtubs; small, functional, tasteful doubles; cramped luggage space; Lilliputian balconies on the top 2 floors; demipension is mandatory. Modern, utilitarian architecture and motif.

The **Parkhotel Schönbrunn**, facing the palace grounds, can take pride in its lobby, lounges, shops, swimming pool, and a pleasant garden wing. And while it takes pride it also takes tours, in caravan waves! Okay but grimly commercial. The **De France** (slipping again) and the **Prinz Eugen** (7th and 8th floors rear the best) are members of the same corporation. The **Erzherzog Rainer** is coming back to life these days. Special emphasis on its dining facilities; extra-attentive service; renewed public rooms; improved bedchambers. Then come the **Am Stephansplatz** (opposite the cathedral; very nice in its way, and graceful), the **Tyrol** (a perked-up cutie), the **Kummer, Royal** (excellent rooftop solarium; kindhearted people; magnificent views from upper quarters), and the **Clima**. The **Tourotel**, not unlike its sister chain-links elsewhere, adheres to the standard pattern of clean, narrow-dimensioned, moderately priced accommodations, Wienerwald-quality cuisine (same ownership as the restaurant amalgam), and an outlying situation better suited for self-drive motorists than for taxi-borne thrifties. Our thumbs still turn straight down on the **Graben** while they now turn up for the smartly refashioned and most appealing **Regina**, a spacious Old World house that is slightly out of the midcity whirl. For apartment digs lasting 2 weeks or more, try the **Capricorno.**

Pensions? The **Atlanta** is our favorite. Others we find worthy are **Opernring, Elite, Arenburg,** and **Schneider.**

★ **TIP**   **Hütteldorf Youth Hostel,** just outside the capital with a view of the Vienna Woods, is the first of a new series of guesthouses for teenagers. Beds 50 in 8-place dormitories; reasonable meals. The **Pötzleinsdorf Hostel** is also said to be worthy. More on these in *Fielding's Low-Cost Europe.*

Restaurants   Vienna's number one establishment and perhaps the tops in all of Central Europe, in our opinion, is still **The Three Hussars** (Zu Den Drei Husaren, Weihburggasse 4, about a block from the Krantz-Ambassador). Classic atmosphere; topflight international cuisine under the direction of aristocratic Egon von Fodermayer; smooth drinks by Anton; reserve in advance. A famous and delicious feature is the mammoth selection of hors d'oeuvres on rolling carts. *Dinner only;* closed mid-July through August; this charming, sophisticated landmark *can* give you the most distinguished meal in Austria if it puts itself out.

The *rear* room of **Stadtkrug**, directly across the street, offers a grand piano, and 16 candlelit tables in ruby-red Renaissance surroundings with moire tapestries, upholstery, and old paintings. Now serving both lunch and dinner every day of the year; reserve ahead in the Sakristei Room, *ignore the simple entrance segment, and walk straight through to the back.* Attractive it is, and many disciples swear by its cuisine. While our sworn testimonal is not *that* enthusiastic, we do like it and recommend it.

The new **Sirk**, in Art Deco style, is snugly and handsomely located in the Bristol Hotel building, and for our highly considered schillings is one of the best and most attractive buys in the nation—whether at lunch, snacktime, dinner, or after opera. The ground floor evokes an informal mood, while the upstairs seems more appropriate for lingering romantic exchanges. On both levels the service and cuisine are cosmopolitan and cheering. At its moderate price scale, enthusiastically recommended.

The **Belvedere Stöckl** (Prinz-Eugen-Strasse 25) borders the Belvedere Palace gardens on one side and the busy boulevard on the other. Ocher stucco mansion; 15 tables with a long handsome culinary display as its centerpiece attraction; friendly, sophisticated attention; urbane décor employing gold damask, muted colors, and the soft sparkle of well-set *couverts.* For the appearance and gastronomy, the tariffs are quite reasonable for its category.

Certainly some of the most compelling dining for local gourmets is to be enjoyed in a number of the capital's hotel dining rooms. The **Bristol** is high on our list for Old World sparkle, while the **Imperial** is noted for its stately elegance. The expensive Prinz Eugen Grill of the **Hilton** is patrician to its damask-clad core; moreover, it features among the finest cuisine in the entire chain. The **König von Ungarn** is small and select—especially in its presentation of Central European specialties.

Rauchkuchl (Schweglerstrasse 37, about 10 minutes from the center) bills itself as "Vienna's Only Medieval Restaurant"—a cheerful overstatement but not a serious one. Now they have added the baroque Savoyen Rooms upstairs, copied from ancient castles. And true to form at any self-respecting bastion, the "authentic" bar surrounds a swimming pool. A bit of a hoot, but nice.

For local color, the municipally owned, immense **Wiener Rathauskeller** (Rathausplatz, in City Hall) shouldn't be missed. Here's that very rare exception: A government-operated institution that really shines. Four distinctively different dining areas, each a gem in its way, which one should examine before being seated; 2 open for lunch as well as post-7:30 dinner. The cookery is certainly not the most delicate in the world, but for a huge restaurant complex of this type, few can top it. Surprisingly reasonable tariffs; first-quality ingredients; service that was perfection—and friendly, to boot.

The much-discussed **Steinerene Eule**, in a residential backwater of the old midcity, is often recommended by locals, but why we can't fathom. Hideous color clashes of orange, black, teal, and blood-toned floral wallpaper; ugly modern lamps; autumn-hued curtains. We found the cuisine, the service, and the presentation pretentious at almost every turning—and poor to boot. This one is gravely overrated, in our view.

Coq d'Or (Führichgasse 1, around the corner from the Krantz-Ambassador), has tumbled precipitously again in our pecking order. We found medium-price, substandard skilletry not worth even the modest outlay.

Wegenstein (be sure to take a taxi) yields some of the best wild-game platters locally on call. Very small dimensions; definitely "in" among the Hunting Set;

reserve ahead; plan to eat fairly early, because the chef whips off his cap at 10:30 P.M. **Falstaff** (Währingerstrasse 67) is more clownish than it used to be and not so amusing to us as it was in recent years. **Marchfelderhof** (25 minutes out at *Deutsch-Wagram*) is a mixed bag of touristic playfulness. About a dozen halls, dens, crannies, cafés, or caverns; gimmicky but fun with your own throng; lonely for solos.

Kervansaray (Mahlerstrasse) serves Döner Kebab, Yoghurt Sour Yayla, Moussaka, and other Turkish tempters in luxurious surroundings. If you enjoy this cuisine, here's a blue-ribbon candidate. Upstairs there's a fresh-faced seafood restaurant with a refrigerated display counter, brass portholes, greenery, and an upbeat to its table settings. **Ming Court** (Kärntner Strasse) is our Chinese choice. It must be one of the most visually endearing restaurants in Central Europe. Our Sacha Pork, served with puff-bread, sauces, nuts, and greens, was a gastronomic landmark. Not expensive but very deluxe in every respect. **China-Pavillion** (corner of Mariahilfer Strasse—Winkelmannstrasse) is no longer worth the costly taxi ride from the center, in our judgment.

The café and restaurant in **Auersperg Palais,** one of Vienna's masterpieces of baroque architecture, are spectacularly soothing to the eye—but oh, oh, oh, those puffed-up prices! The costs for its indifferently cooked fare seem ludicrously inflated by local criteria. For us, once was *genug,* but perhaps you'll take exception.

The **Lindenkeller** is on the Rotenturmstrasse in the First District; it is excellent. The intimate and charming little **Zum Weissen Rauchfangkehrer** (Weihburggasse 4) is a favorite of actors, artists, and journalists. Classic German décor, tinkling piano, friendly reception, rough service, decent food for the price. Closed Sundays, all of July and August, and many holidays.

The **Paulusstube** (Walfischgasse 7, a 1-minute aria from the opera) is a midtown transplant of a Grinzing *Heuriger* (see below). Handsome façade; shabbily comfortable interior; vaulted ceilings; strolling musicians; friendly but uninspired service; dreary regional dishes. **H. Stiedl's Beerklinik** (Steindelg 4) seats about 350 customers overall, in the amusing cellar or in the Biedermeier restaurant. Open every day of the year; no music; reasonable tabs. The **Griechenbeisl** (Fleischmarkt 11), where the Olde Taverne atmosphere has been laid on with a trowel, is larger, noisier, and poorly ventilated; it is the granddaddy of Viennese dining establishments.

The **Balkan Grill** (Brunnengasse 13, about 15 minutes from the center) is an on-or-off enterprise which, if "on," can be delightful. Restaurant and roofed garden-side terrace; waiters in Bosnian costumes; strolling musicians. Start with a straight-from-the-carafe Barack apricot brandy; order the Serbian hors d'oeuvres first, and then please don't miss the Siskebab à la Jenghiz Khan for 1, 2, or 3 persons. Finally, you'll be given a serving of Turkish paste; tuck a piece between your molars and cheek in the Balkan way, and sip your coffee mumps-style. *Evenings only,* from 6:30 P.M. to 1 A.M.; medium expensive; closed Sunday.

Csardasfürstin is a smaller splash on the goulash circuit. Two levels; off-key gypsy melodizing; cookery featuring Cevapcici (peppery meat patties skewered and served on a flaming rack) and Töltöt Kàposzta (a stuffed cabbage that lost something in the translation). **Feuervogel** (Alserbachstrasse 21) is one of the oldest Russian feederies in town. Painted up in geometric florals; lamps in cookie jars; amiable owner-chef who is proud of his culinary art.

The most dramatic, but hardly the most sparkling, light on the dining horizon stands 820 feet above the capital in the **Danube Tower,** a radio-TV mast which sports a revolving crow's nest. Your tummy can be regulated to twirl at 1 revolution every 52, 39, or 26 minutes, while the city, the river, the Vienna Woods, Schönbrunn Palace, and the profile of the Carpathian Mountains silently glide across your eyeballs. It might unwind and possibly collapse, however, as soon as you start your meal. Every nibble of ours, sad to relate, was uniformly tasteless if not downright wretched—and with taxi fares it's very expensive. It seems to be the inexorable fate of 90% of us visiting firemen to be taken or guided here by hyperzealous Viennese—but if you can feign plague, pyrexia, or lockjaw, PLEASE use ANY excuse to avoid going. A marvelous Tinkertoy for the spirit but not the body.

Sunny weather? Here's a Vienna Woods pilgrimage that's worth every erg of effort: **Fischerhaus,** at the foot of _Hermannskogel,_ is about 30 minutes from the heart of Vienna. Its quality and sophistication are now such that here is really the _only_ recommendable stop for lunch or dinner in the entire area. Small, attractive, redecorated country mansion with terrace; garden for strolling and sniffing the blossoms; dining under a sheltering roof; interesting new downstairs wine museum; fine but not extraordinary view; elaborate menu featuring the specialties of 10 nations. We like especially the Austrian Bauernschmaus ("Farmers' Plate") and the roast duckling. Warmhearted Proprietor M. R. Gura is so understaffed when there's a full house that you might fulminate. Therefore, please _always_ reserve in advance and please _always_ try it either earlier or later than normal—especially on weekends. Better and better.

For summer only **Burg Greifenstein,** in Niederösterreich, a former castle of the Prince of Liechtenstein, is a high-over-the-Danube site reachable by too many steps for elderly or ailing adventurers. Typical enthralling _schloss_-top vistas; adequate service and cuisine. We were fascinated by the arms museum. Youngsters like the Knappenstube, a colorful corner of fun.

Then there's the sylvan **Tyrolean Gardens,** fringing the Gloriet of Schönbrunn Palace. If little ones are in tow, the adjoining zoo is fun.

The Viennese coffee houses, one of Austria's greatest traditions, are fast waning from the onslaught of the brash, Nedick-style café-espresso bars which have crept up from Italy. Worthy old-style survivors are the **Mozart,** the **Landtmann,** and the **Prückel.**

The legendary _Konditoreien_ ("confection shops," for want of a better word) are still rolling along merrily, thanks to Allah. Emperor of this realm—for the time being anyway—remains **Demel** (Kohlmarkt 14), where grateful citizenry have been stuffing themselves cross-eyed since A.D. 1813. In an alleged double cross, the son of Franz Sacher, Metternich's pastry chef, is said to have sold his father's $1,000,000 Sacher Torte recipe to this house. The 25-year _Kriegspiel_ was finally compromised by a court verdict: The hotel may now vend the "Original Sacher Cake," while Demel may purvey simply the "Demel Sacher Cake"! If you enjoy aspics, cookies, salads, sandwiches, cold meats, iced juices, chocolate puffs overflowing with Chantilly, and Viennese coffee (black coffee, sugar, and hot milk stirred into a king-size cup, topped by great blobs of whipped cream), from 30 seconds to 3000 minutes later a countergirl will bring your plate to your tiny table. The service is sweet, but horribly disorganized, especially at peak hours—so go just before noon, if you can. Wickedly expensive; open every day, but poor selection on Sundays; if money is a secondary consideration, recommended with our tongues slapping our chests. **Café Im Haas Haus** vies with Demel, in our view, for having the most maddening service standards in the Austrian republic. Often it wins our trophy for undisputed negligence. Nevertheless, the sweets and meals are excellent, but best of all is the roof-level view of the Dom from the upper floor of this window-lined perch. Forget the human element and buy the sights, the *schlag*, and the coffeecake. Other outstanding examples are **Lehmann** and **Heiner**.

For a more commercial type of operation, pop in at one of the 19 **Aïda** shops. All guarantee tiptop freshness that only a volume operation can turn out at such lowdown tariffs. Ownership by the dynamic Felix Prousek, one of the fastest-rising tycoons in Austria. *Terrific.*

Finally, Vienna is famous for its *Heuriger*—the "new-wine" or "fresh-wine" gardens. The most celebrated of these establishments are in Grinzing, 15 to 25 minutes by taxi. Look for the garland of pine twigs and vine leaves over the door, and bring your own cold meat, butter, cheese, and bread, if you wish to follow the local custom. Or try their old-time specialty, Backhendl, which is very young, milk-fed chicken, breaded in a unique way. Typical, sound examples are **Rode's Heuriger** (Himmelstrasse 4), **Rode's "Alte Haus,"** up the same street at #37 (where we had a delicious meal; go up the small exterior staircase to the timber-and-brick inner sanctum and turn to the right, which is our bid for the snuggest corner), the **Musil**, the **Figlmüller**, the **Backhendlstation** (Grinzingerstrasse 50), **Martinkovits** (Bellevuestrasse 4), and **Reinprecht** (3 entries: Cobenzlgasse 20, 22, and 28, and all nearly always stuffed with tourists). **Hauermandl** offers a garden at its courtyard entrance, a gypsy wagon on its roof (sic), a wine press, 4 rooms, a Kellerstube composed of a long darkened arch, candles that burn as warmly as the friendly waitresses, and delicious farmhouse cookery. About a mile down the hill at Pfarrplatz (you'll need a taxi or car), **Franz Mayer** is in a *cul de sac* sharing nods across the plaza with a charming little chapel. Built around a barnyard close that leads to an attractive windowed hall with community tables where convivial Austrians poise in various stages of ingestion. Very regional and quite good. We'd avoid **Martin Sepp** where to us the cafeteria-style food looked as tired as last month's mackerel. The place itself, however, is so handsome that you might wish to pause for a glass of wine. Locals now feel Grinzing is becoming too touristic; many are moving over to Sievering or Heiligenstadt in the 19th district or to the Brunnergasse in Perchtoldsdorf, about 30 minutes by taxi. The **Spiegelhofer** (Hochstrasse 75) would be our top winery here. All shut down intermittently, whenever the barrels run out; light buffet and wine only except where noted, with no spirits or beer. For even less money, the **Wienerwald** chain (about 500 restaurants in more than 125 European cities, plus 8 in New York) boasts 10 links in the capital. All are slickly rustic, and all turn out unusually savory fare. Quite a money-saver and quite good for its category.

Night Life Moulin Rouge (Walfischgasse 1), is Vienna's most noteworthy purveyor of hides-and-seeks, with most of the hides unpelted. Two-tier circular room with excellent viewing potential; B-gals aplenty; ample strips, magic acts, and similar variety wheezes more-or-less continuously through the evening. On our visit Sandy Schweppes effer-divested herself of apparel intermittently until the house went flat at 6 A.M. If the double-barreled entrance fee doesn't put you into an immediate catatonic state, perhaps your whisky at $8.50 per slug, beer at $5 per mug, or Dom Perignon champagne at $80 per jug will. By contrast, you should pay between $3 and $5.75 per Scotch in most other places, with door charges skittering between zero and $2 per reveler. **Fledermaus** (Spiegelgasse 2) has a low admission nibble. Long, well-ventilated room; 5 alcoves for intimate sipping; danceable combo; friendly atmosphere; large drinks; cabarets in German at 11 P.M. and 2 A.M., which can be dull if one doesn't understand the language; smooth operation. **Eve** (next to the Astoria Hotel) ranks high in the harem. Snuggly ambiance; 2 orchestras; sleek houris eternally disrobing—all in the tradition of chiffon by the bolt. **Queen Anne** (Johannesg. 12) reigns as the sovereign of the disco realm. **Casanova** (Dorotheerg. 6-8) bubbles about its "Erotic Air," which we suppose refers to the atmosphere which is given to salacious pursuits from 9:30 P.M. to the whee hours nightly. Revue-type shows as perceived from theater seats, fancy boxes, or from the bar. For an entry fee ranging from $15 to $20, depending on your proximity to the flesh-and-moans, you can drink or abstain, whichever is desired. **Chez Nous** (Kärntner Strasse 10), a modest entry, in our most charitable view, is one hole we detest with consummate passion. The **Sir Winston Club** is an amusing pub for chitchat, suds, and snacks. **Gerard** draws a nice young following for music and dance. The **New Splendid Bar** (Jasomirgottstrasse 3) is a curiously shaped 3-tier, off-circular room with upbeat music; larger than most and quite attractive; our only carp here is that our later bill, when we dropped in again, illegally carried the music charge on each of our drinks rather than on our first consumption only. **Eden Bar** (Liliengasse 2) is THE perch for chic Viennese night owls. Ho-hum décor; excellent 4-piece combo; no pickups; closed Sundays from May to July and various holidays. Go late. The **Take Five** is a hard-driving disk joint. Twin bars flank the small dance floor; dim lights. So-so. **Atrium** is divided into 4 celler quadrants with 3 bars. Good music and liquids; popular with students. The **Schaukelpferd Bar** (Kegelgasse 30) features stucco walls, wood beams, and fireplace. Nice. **Steckenpferd** (Dorotheergasse) is similar in tone; quiet dance music is the theme. Unusual architecture is a feature of the **Loos Bar** (Kärntner Durchgang near Stephansplatz). On our "never again" roster is the **B.B.-Bar** (adjoining Messe Palace); miserable décor, miserable atmosphere, and miserable patrons.

Elegant tastes? The **Champagne Bar**, a few doors off Kärntner Strasse on Marco d'Aulangasse, serves bubbly refreshment in Art Retro surroundings. Many attractive young executives and their mates clink goblets here. **Ascot**, on Annagasse (also midcity) is more posh in its red velour setting; it also draws a nice crowd, but perhaps a bit older and more amorously inclined. Jazz hounds? **Die Tenne** (Annagasse 3) is a barnlike dance hall. Modest prices; frequently filled with youngsters who would rather dance than eat. The plaid-clad **Scotch-Bar** (Ringstrasse) is also jammed with kids. **Maryland** is a tiny state of mind for similar notes and bars.

Down around navel level come **Casbah** (Naglergasse 23, a good district) and **Café Renz** (Zirkusgasse 50, a dreary section of town). Soberingly ugly house girls (perhaps that's why they give serious scholars a free booklet of cutie photos when they enter); "separates" available. Both are *really* dumps, in our opinion.

Even lower on this circuit's anatomy is **Opium Höhle** (Habsburgergasse 4), a rugged cellar joint advised For Gents Only. Décor faintly reminiscent, to us, of High Chinese Bordello circa the Wan Hong Crooked Period of the Tartar philosophers; adjoining Champagne Room is so much darker that customers are obliged to put aside their newspapers for concentration on more sociable activities, such as games involving digital skills. Go about 11:30 P.M. Interesting as a curiosity only. (Not incidentally in these modern times, its name is a hallucinogenic put-on; the strongest thing we saw being smoked here was a filter-tip Kool.)

Gambling casino? Vienna's **Cercle Wien** is up 1 flight in the Palais Esterházy (Kärntner Strasse)—directly above the Adlmüller shop. Roulette, chemin de fer, and—now—blackjack comprise the play-for-pay; moderate admission. Take your passport.

★ **TIPS**   The nightclub "separate" has a separate meaning here of togetherness. These are small private rooms tucked away in the inner recesses of Viennese hot spots. They are usually available from 2 A.M. to 6 A.M. Amorous roosters select the chickens in the bar. Since John Law forbids doors on these retreats, 3 sets of heavy draw-drapes bar the entries and muffle the groans. The furnishings invariably consist of a small chaise longue, 1 or 2 armless chairs, and a tiny table for the champagne always demanded by the professionally dehydrated babe. Your tab for the champagne is the standard price; the girls hopefully ask for a 1000–schilling fee, but if the evening is lean, the goods can be priced at 500 schillings. Because the nightclub per se is closed, there is little-or-no chance some blundering yokel might mistake a "separate" for the men's room and interrupt the proceedings. This is sex at its most raw and most deep-frozen—worse, most uncomfortable!—level. But it's there, *if* you've just returned from a 3-year fossil hunt in the fastness of Tin-Zaouaten Oasis in the Sahara.

Shopping   Our ★ ★ ★ ★ ★ recommendations are individually noted throughout this section.

Petit point is the first yen of many trippers—and the ★ ★ ★ ★ ★ **J. Jolles Studio** (Fassziehergasse 5, up 1 flight), Grand Prix winner and the largest producer of this item in the world, gets our vote as the leader of the industry. It's a factory, with master painters and more than 1000 home workers. All goods are assembled and sold on the premises—at 10% discount, we might add. The management never authorizes outside representation. In addition to its bottomless supply of petit point articles, gay summer handbags and travel bags, it also features trammed tapestries. Global mailing service with free postage on all purchases; studio open weekdays (not Saturdays) during routine shopping hours. Ask for either Mrs. Lieselotte Illi or Mrs. Christine Zeissl, the friendly co-managers. Highest recommendation.

Jewelry: ★ ★ ★ ★ ★ **A.E. Koechert** (Neuer Markt 15) is worth the time of anyone who likes extraordinarily fine brooches, rings, necklaces, and original creations in the renowned Viennese style. Austrian handwork in precious metals and gems not only has its distinctive flavor, but labor costs are so low that only Portugal can offer such comparatively modest price levels in this magic. Continuously since 1814 this landmark was designated by successive Emperors as Crown Jewelers to the Imperial Court. Gorgeously opulent pieces are available to the millionaire trade, but for travelers like us who haven't much to spend, Koechert also shines with equal brilliance. There's an intangible quality, an ethereal beauty to their pieces, which is impossible for us to describe; all we know is that we love it and that you won't find it elsewhere. Ask for the gentlemanly Mr. Wilfrid, Gotfrid, or Dietrich Koechert. A treasure house.

Regional clothes: **Loden-Plankl** (Michaelerplatz 6) is one of the oldest for typical Tyrolean suits and sweaters; **Tostmann** (Schottengasse) is highly regarded for its dirndls; **Lanz** (Karntnerstrasse 10) is also very good.

Porcelain and glass: ★ ★ ★ ★ ★ **J. & L. Lobmeyr** (Kärntnerstrasse 26) is dead on the bull's eye of distinction with its crystal specialties. In these venerable precincts there is a dazzling display of light radiating from the vast array of gleaming mirrors, as well as from the finest glass tablesets, fixtures, and artistic engravings in both classic and modern designs. There is also a good selection of Herend china from Hungary plus gift articles and other *belles tournures.* Director Harry Rath will be proud to show you their outstanding museum or to tend to your special needs. **Wiener Porzellanfabrik Augarten** (Stock-Im-Eisenplatz 3, Maniahilferstrasse 99, and the Schloss Augarten) has magnificent Spanish Riding School figurines and some knockout dinner settings.

Leather goods: ★ ★ ★ ★ ★ **Mädler GmbH** (Graben 17 and Mariahilferstrasse 24) has dominated the field since this Zurich-based firm expanded to Vienna in 1973. In this illustrious establishment, founded in Leipzig more than 125 years ago and which continues its noble traditions, you will find a sumptuous selection of suitcases, carry-on bags, handbags, briefcases, and scores upon scores of stunning, hard-to-find specialty items. The workmanship is exquisite; the styling has chic and flair; the price range is appealing. We have highest esteem for this classic institution—and we bet you will, too!

Boutique with Viennese handicrafts: **Elfi Müller & Co.** (Kärntnerstrasse 53) is a find for handmade clothing and Austrian mementos. Talented, twinkling Mrs. Müller creates her own designs in enamel, in brass, in wood, and in gold and silver. We also like her *Weinhebers* (Viennese upside-down wine dispensers). Daily shipments to the U.S.; very fair prices. Recommended for many, many years by the American Embassy and by us. **Österreichische Werkstätten** (Kärntnerstrasse 6) also offers a most intersting variety of high-quality wares made by Austrian artisans.

Stag-handled cutlery: **Deckenbacher & Blümner** (Kärntnerstrasse 21–23 and Mariahilferstrasse 70) takes rightful pride in its carving sets, matched sets of knives, and similar items.

Department store: **Steffi** on Kärntnerstrasse, opposite the Ambassador Hotel, sells everything this kind of emporium should, at normal local prices.

Auction: Try, try to go to the enormously intriguing **Dorotheum Auction** if it's operating while you're there. Full details on this fascinating landmark and how best to handle yourself for the greatest fun and greatest bargains (which are often fantastic) are outlined step by step in our *Shopping Guide.*

The city fathers have now set aside malls for pedestrians only which are lined with benches, transplanted trees, and new lighting patterns. These traffic-free islands of serenity in the central district include Kärntnerstrasse (the main shopping street), Graben, Kohlmarket, and Naglergasse; several more are in the outlying precincts. They are a delight.

Please DON'T buy high-duty imported items or the proliferating types of gimcracks such as those marked "Souvenir of Hochland, High in the Edelweiss."

Shopping hours: *Vienna:* Weekdays from 8 or 9 A.M. to 6 P.M.; generally no noon closing; shuttered Saturdays at noon. *Other cities:* 8 to 9 A.M. openings; closing hours variable.

Dedicated shophounds: Space is too tight here for further listings—so consult this year's purse-size edition of *Fielding's Selective Shopping Guide to Europe* for more stores, more details, and more lore.

Other Targets

ANIF   Please refer to "Salzburg."

BADEN   Our first choice for overnighting would be the **Parkhotel** which features a large swimming pool plus health center; the service and cuisnine are outstanding. **Kurhotel Esplanade** is also highly regarded as a cure haven; it too has an excellent swimming pool. The **Herzoghof** is recommended and the **Papst** is blue ribbon (pardon). Another alternative would be the **Clubhotel Schloss Weikersdorf.**

BADGASTEIN's   innkeepers make up some 7000 beds daily in the summer season (cures and medical treatments) and the winter season (skiing), but between mid-October and mid-December, as in most similar resorts, the spooks wear the sheets in this ghost town. Nothing, but nothing, is open. The balconied, 200-room **Parkhotel Bellevue** garners the affluent young and the twinkling old. Completely renewed; lodge-style downstairs bar *the* social nucleus in winter; music nightly by a trio of orchestras; excellent management by smiling, evergreen Proprietor S. J. Wührer. The colorful **Bellevue-Alm** is a chalet pleasure dome 400 meters above the main installation. Accessible by chair lift from below or a morning's ski from the upper slopes; hot lunches, group barbecues, après-ski nuzzling; poolside lounging, or rustic overnighting in its 14 bedchambers. Highly recommended for the spirited. Below this one, the **Kaiserhof,** of ancient vintage, is well maintained and getting better. Luxury standards but the quality of its unquestioned refinement seemed a bit heavy for our taste. The **Habsburgerhof** is said to be noteworthy, but we haven't tried it personally. The **Elisabethpark** has been perked up smartly, enlarged, and given a thermal swimming pool. We certainly were impressed by its sprightly mien on our inspection. Highly recommended. The **Straubinger** is now getting too old-fashioned to suit us. The **Germania** and **Mozart** have been skidding in our estimation. **Haus Hirth** has a distinct sanitarium personality, at least in our eyes. In the budget category, we prefer (1) **Schillerhof** (2) **Sporthotel** (3) **Wildbad** (perhaps now enjoying year-round operation), (4) **Eden**, (5) **Regina**, and (6) **Savoy**. The **Alpenhof** is an economizer's delight. Ownership by (and connected to) the **Parkhotel Bellevue**; lovely situation; guests may use *all* the facilities of its opulent sister. Golden bangles at brass-bed tariffs.

In our estimation, for dining the Grill of the **Parkhotel Bellevue** is the unchallenged leader. The **Straubinger Stüberl** offers a pleasant couplet of rooms, costumed waitresses, and unexciting cookery. For summer motorists, the **Grüner-Baum** is said to be a pleasant outdoor valley haven. In most Austrian ski stations, sporting appetites must be satisfied with your pension-plan hotel fare. Lunches are either picnics on the slopes or obtained through a meal voucher at an upland hut.

For night life, look for it at the **Schafflinger Skialm** (log-cabin motif; full meals and dancing), the **Muhlhäusl** (old tavern setting), the **Park Bellvue**, or at the **Casino Bar** (there's gambling in the **Casino** itself; bring your passport if you're game to play).

BAD HOFGASTEIN This scenic mountain redoubt nestles only about 3 miles north of Badgastein along Route 167. It is reported to be developing handsomely as a comfort-plus resort. Unfortunately, a snowstorm presented us from checking it out on our last alpine foray, but if the praise is accurate, we really missed a honey of a townlet. We won't let *any*thing deter us next round.

BAD ISCHL Overnighters—if they don't choose to pamper their hides in the new spa hotel where stays are generally longer—would probably be most comfortable in the **Post**. Next we cheer the **Goldenes Schiff** and the **Freischütz**.

DORNBIRN The **Park** is the leader for overnighting.

EISENSTADT has the attractive **Drassburg Castle**.

FELDKIRCH The **Alpenrose** is a fine spot for pausing; it's tiny, charming, and very Austrian.

FROHNLEITEN is in the province of Styria and boasts the medieval cliff-hugging **Schloss Rabenstein**, which many travelers applaud—we among them. Golf nearby; located on the main Vienna-Graz line.

GRAZ We would pick the overnight stops in this order: (1) **Daniel**, (2) **Steirerhof**, (3) **Weitzer**, (4) **Parkhotel**.

HOCHGURGL   This is a beautiful upland resort which Alpine lovers admire. For overnighting try the **Hochgurgl**, the **Hochland** or the **Angerer Alm**.

IGLS   See below under "Innsbruck," its next-door neighbor.

INNSBRUCK   For overnighting in big-city comfort, the vastly updated **Europa Tyrol** is tops for sophistication. New entrance and modernized lobby; restyled bar in leather and wood; 80 all-fresh bedchambers. Concierge Klaus Dona is the soul of helpfulness. Ask to see the gorgeous Baroksaal, usually given over to special events and one of the most graceful salons in the nation. For color, antiquity, and charm, the **Goldener Adler**, born in 1390, wins our laurel wreath. Sleekly rustic upstairs dining salon with paisley textiled walls, candles, silk flowers, and raspberry undercloths with white aprons; superb food here with more tavern-style bites and brews in the vaulted cellar restaurant. A quiet retreat and a good one. The **Schwarzer Adler** traces a heritage of more than 4 centuries. Adlerstube with wooden dado, leaded windows, and copperware; antler-festooned Jägerstube for Tyrolean specialties; abundance of artistic touches throughout; only 25 rooms with bath or shower, but oozing with character and unique identity. The **Holiday Inn** is a tall midtown edifice. The bedchambers are the star attractions by far, for comfort, scenic rewards, and modern conveniences. Public sectors are a weakness, in our judgment; the cuisine, if you're lucky, easily can be forgotten. The **Mariabrunn,** 3 miles out, is 1000 feet high on the north slope of the mountain range; exhilarating vista; cellar-sited Kupferstuben in stone and timber (nights only). Adequate. The neighboring balcony-clad **Bellevue,** owned by the same family, is a recent entry with space for 50 nappers. Okay but not truly Belle. The **Grauer Bär** also specializes in package trippers; 147 plain accommodations and 48 baths; almost impossible to get in, unless you bring your charter club, Boy Scout troop, or affinity clause with you. The 30-room **Greif,** with a low bath ratio, is no longer as sparkling as it should be—or was; comparatively lightweight rates. The **Clima**'s bargain-basement taste is not appealing to us. The **Roter Adler** adds one more eagle ("Adler") to your aviary. Not bad for an economizing bird of passage. The **Alpenmotel,** in our judgment, is too remote and too unattractive to be considered. The ever-crowded **Goldener Stern** is a sleeping factory on the Inn River. It's "out" with us, however.

In most choicely sited *Igls* (pronounced "Eagles"), a 10-minute drive above Innsbruck, the **Sporthotel** is just the ticket for the luxury sport buffs. Smooth rusticity; dancing to orchestral lilts nightly; sauna plus hydropathic treatments; pine-and-glass-lined indoor-outdoor pool; another exclusively for summer; free ski lift; individual garages. Comfortable units with bath; demi-suites very appealing. Its Beck family operators also run the nearby **Schlosshotel Igls.** Huge rooms; sumptuous appointments in the finest tradition of highborn Tyrolean life-styles; space for only 30 patricians. Room #36 is perhaps the finest single accommodation in all Austria, in our view; #'s 21 and 25 (one under the conical tower roof) are splendid doubles. The pool and fitness center provide good reason for the recent expansion of the dining facilities. The **Park,** wearing a penthouse swimming pool, is another bucolic hillsider. Glorious setting in a spruced-up pinewood; less costly and more tranquil than the leader; ice rink and 4 ski lifts nearby; 62 spacious bedrooms, most with balcony and 44 with private bath. Lovely for the older or more sedate wanderer.

When hunger strikes, remember that Innsbruck's kitchens churn out nutrition and little else. The most dressed-up evening you'll have will probably be in your own hotel—and as local innkeeping goes, the **Europa Tyrol** is fairly cosmopolitan. **Europastüberl** pans out very worthy vittles. At the latter, the unique Innsbruckersnitzel is topped with cheese; the Tesener Kastanieneis is chestnut ice cream bathed in applesauce. Ummmmm. **Goldener Adler's** fare has picked up notably. Flambé specialties prepared close enough to singe the nap off your funnybone; darkly engaging atmosphere; interesting menu choices; attentive service. The **Schwarzer Adler** is another favorite where the lghts are dim and the gastronomy sparkles. **Bergisel** is simple, savory, and schilling-saving; be sure to try the scintillating strudel.

Among the independents, the **Stiftskeller** is still drawing howls from dissatisfied readers. It rose to the top, slumped, climbed back to number one ranking—and now we opine that it is skidding again. If you'd like to chance it and are adventurous, try the red-hot Paprika Hatschec, a combustible liquid of Hungarian origin with the flash point and chemical characteristics of napalm. Grasp both ears firmly before you sip it, because they'll spin as fast as propellers if you don't. **Stiegelbrau,** our leading candidate a while back, is still atmospheric; the cooking is good, but the selections are very limited. Bierstüberl on one side, exclusively for males; nonsegregated dining facilities across the hall, with a relaxed, comfortable, middle-class patronage; rolls and *blatte* (delicious unleavened bread) automatically appear. **Zipferstuben**, noted for its beer, is a Quaint-y Inn-y built with both eyes cocked on the tourist trade with 5 rooms on 2 floors. Balkan grills the specialty; prices high; cuisine above average; pleasant. The **Palette** provides pizza as the specialty. The **Funzel** is tops for snacks; modern-rustic surroundings. **Tabasco** has a lot of pepper too, but the service burned us up. The town has a **Wienerwald** which is okay for its type. **Weisses Kreuz** once played host to Mozart when he performed for the Empress; we went back once since 1787, and though that was recently, we think we won't be returning for several more centuries.

A café occupies the upper level of the **Bacchus,** and the chic (by Innsbruck standards) **Restaurant-Weinstube** is in the cellar. Because there's an orchestra in the latter they call it a "nightclub"—which it isn't. The cuisine is above average, but the tables are so tiny and the elbowroom so cramped that we find it on the uncomfortable side. Closed Sunday. Students congregate at **Pajazzo** (Meranerstrasse) for beer-drinking, wine-imbibing, and song.

The **Wilder Mann** (4 miles out) is in the beguiling little village of *Lans,* a lovely drive via Igls. You'll find 4 woody rooms here which might have been lifted from a mythical Austrian edition of *House and Garden*. Substantial, appetizing fare that is a lot more refined than you might expect at such a rural address.

After dark, the Keller (cellar, not the terrace) of the **Greifkeller** has crazy Tyrolean ceilings, cow-stall booths, tavern-type bar; tiny dance floor, 2–piece band, occasional entertainment on Saturdays in season; go after 11 P.M. and reserve in advance; this little joint can jump. For the inn crowd, the **Clima**

Hotel has its own Club in the cellar. Cleverly in tune with the tempo. The **Hofgarten,** in the park, has agreeable terrace-dancing in summer and moves into sterile, brash, typical honky-tonk-style quarters in winter. Average but worth a look. The previously mentioned **Palette** is drawing the royal share of young swingers; it's a cellar that's very much in vogue.

Shopping? Well, we found far slimmer pickings than in other centers, but you may disagree.

Regional Tyrolean apparel: Here is one of 2 conspicuous exceptions. **Lodenbaur** (Brixner Strasse 4) is our unequivocal choice. Handsome, urbane Fritz Baur runs this splendid house with keenness, competence, and charm.

Handicrafts: We prefer **Handwerkskunst** on Wilhelm Greilstrasse. **Lanz**, also fine, has opened a branch on the same street.

KITZBÜHEL Falk Volkhart, the Pharaoh of Munich's great Bayerischer Hof, took over the **Zur Tenne** and is creating an upland haven in "alpine deluxe" motif. Space for about 70 in several contiguous pastel-colored houses; 10 rooms with open fires, rich in *gemütlich* atmosphere; sauna; timber-lined grill. Swimming pool is likely for this season. Overall, we like it. The Tyrolean-style, 55-room, 55-bath **Goldener Greif** offers a teensie-weensie, heated-water, interior swimming pool, restaurant, grill, and casino. The painted facade in regional motif is carried out in the tone of this entire house. Very good indeed. The imposing **Grand** has undergone no major changes. The redecorated **Weisses Rössl** boasts 80 units and 40 baths; very well maintained; pleasant atmosphere; tennis court, center-of-town situation. Kindly proprietor Hirnsberger will see to your every comfort. The chalet-style **Reischhof** isn't special. The **Lutzenberg** is another wide-bodied chalet. The public rooms feature open timbers; so does the pool. Not expensive, but you'll need your own transportation—whether in wheel form or on skis. **Schloss Lebenberg,** an overdone, highly polished castle on a hillock 5 minutes from town, offers fancy-schmanzy comfort, a glass-enclosed swimming pool, condominiums by the score for its ever-expanding following of investment settlers, and fairly steep prices. If you are searching for a non-mountainous refined and somewhat formal address, here it is. The **Hirzingerhof** offers far more local flavor, but it too has its share of crystal chandeliers and Parisian décor—just enough to head us back in the direction of the Zur Tenne. Since it is a 10-minute walk from the center, you might want to have a car. **Schlosshotel Münichau,** a 1200-year-old matron meticulously restored by the Goldener Greif directors, brims with flair and vitality. Two miles from the center in pastoral farm country; 50 units, all with bath; attractive dining room plus a 2-story Grill annex and outdoor dining patio for summer meals; same rates as the mother hotel in town. A haven for the let's-get-away-from-it-all traveler. Other candidates a bit closer to the bright lights are the viewful, chalet-style **Maria Theresia** with space for about 200 sporting types and the smaller, contemporary **Jägerwirt**, with its attractive Hallali restaurant and its abundance of south-facing private balconies. The modest **Klausnerhof**, near the station, is our choice among pensions.

LECH, 10 minutes from Zürs am Arlberg, comes up with the (1) **Gasthof Post** (brightly decorated 3-story chalet; extensive antique collection; substantial amenities; ingratiating atmosphere where you might see a queen, a prince, or even a lowly travel writer sipping a crisp Bloody Mary in its convivial nookeries); (2) **Schneider** (across the covered bridge from the frontrunner; razed and rebuilt as one of the slickest mock-ups of rustication we've seen lately; indoor swimming pool; impressive, even dramatically imposing, but somehow too contrived and polished to suit our personal tastes); (3) **Kristberg** (conceived by the legendary Egon Zimmerman who originally put up a tiny house on a tiny knoll; pleasant view; attractive and smashingly successful Egon's Scotch Club with dancing nightly); (4) **Kristiania** (similar in personality to the Kristberg; owned by Othmar Schneider; a traveler's reward if you are seeking pension instead of hotel atmosphere); (5) **Krone** (almost in the belfry of the town chapel; still fairly comfortable, but becoming seedier with advancing age; now a bit campy, in our opinion); (6) **Arlberg**; (7) **Berghof** (a cozy corner for medium-budget travelers). If you don't want the bustle of Lech or the relative isolation of Zürs, then why not try *Oberlech*? It can be reached from the main center by cableway. For us, here is the best of both worlds. The lodgings are all pretty rawboned. **Sonnenburg** seems to be the most sophisticated. About 60% bath ratio; stimulating cookery; friendly people; swimming pool. The **Montana** is noted for its kitchen and the **Goldener Berg** is comfortable. The **Petersboden,** however, is our favorite. Now it has been given a good shakeup with lots of fresh amenities added; today it is a nice little hotel instead of a creaky inn. Handsome firelit lounge in stucco and blond timbers; chummy bar; viewful dining perch; mountain-style bedchambers. Fabulous welcome by Otto Stundner; good vittles by Annie; mecca of scads of celebrities; not for the persnickety, but definitely for dedicated sportsmen and snowbunnies who wish to be in the sun by day and in the quiet of night.

LINZ's **Tourotel** is linked to the convention and concert center, Bruckner Halle. It is just what you might expect. Out on the skirts of town, the **Crest** digs are better for overnighting motorists than for lingerers. We don't advise a pause in this city because it is among the least attractive centers in the nation, sad to say. The **Schwechater Hof** takes pride in its highly regarded restaurant. Its 54 bedchambers are supplied with only 7 baths and 6 showers; a general overhauling has been realized. Old-fashioned, but recommendable for budgeteers. For mealtiming, the **Kremsmünsterer Weinstube,** in the Old Town, has a bar leading to 3 vaulted dining rooms with ancient atmosphere; good regional food, but rather heavy.

MALLNITZ has the **Pension Bellevue** which, if it's 1/12 as good as a friendly wanderer enthuses, then it's the Promised Land.

NEWMARKT Refer to "Salzburg."

OBERLECH Refer to "Lech."

PÖRTSCHACH AM WÖRTHERSEE offers the **Parkhotel**, which is considered by various observers to be one of the better havens in the nation. Others vigorously disagree. It is quietly sited on a 56,200-square-yard promontory, surrounded by the famous flower-bleaches of the region and well-tended parks. Tennis courts; health baths; cozy Weinstube; 25 suites and 147 bedchambers, all with bath, balcony, and unimpaired view. In the same village, **Schloss Seefels**, with more modest facilities and few private baths, is also said to be a tranquil corner for lakeside relaxing.

SAALBACH (1) **Sporthotel**, (2) **Kristall**, and (3) **Saalbacherhof**; all unknown to us personally.

ST. ANTON AM ARLBERG is one of Europe's capitals of winter sport. Here's our rating: (1) **Post**, (2) **Schwarzer Adler**, (3) **Arlberg**. All village hotels are noisy in season.

ST. WOLFGANG **Weisses Rössl** is the world-famous restaurant onto which has been added sleeping space for 100; Easter to mid-October only; no elevator's; # 28 is the choicest.

SALZBURG In addition to the many classic-type attractions such as Mozart's birthplace and the Mozart Museum, do visit the enchanting Salzburg Marionette Theater—probably the best-known company of its kind on the boards today. For kids from 5 to 90—definitely including us! The Salzburg Festspielhaus, like the Vienna State Opera House, ranks at the top in theatrical facilities. This supermodern 7–unit structure contains 2340 seats—none more than 115 feet from that beauty spot on the contralto's chin! Equally interesting to music-lovers are the Palace Concerts, now scheduled for most of the year. Movie fans might give 5 bells to Hans Erhart's **Sound of Music Tour** that reels them over the landmarks of that famous film. And finally, let's not forget the cable car, 9 miles out, which zips up 6170 feet of Alp (the Dürrnberg) in 8 minutes, for a commendably modest price per dizzy head. While in the region you can visit the Hallein Salt Mine, plus the Giant Ice Caves at Werfen (May to Oct.).

This city offers several good hotels—each for a different taste. If charm and local color are your targets, the country-tavern-style **Goldener Hirsch,** which boasts more than 400 years of nubile grace, is small, intimate, and delightful. Since it is in the same administrative linkup as the splendid Imperial and Bristol Hotels of Vienna, smooth management is virtually a guarantee. You'll find more creaks and original tones in the older segment; the newer wing, which almost doubles its capacity, combines Old Goldener Hirsch-flavored garniture with twentieth-century architecture, with nary a squeak to be heard. The numerous behind-the-scenes updatings insure greater convenience and a smooth operation. Ultrakind Concierge Erich Volk; drinks by Kurt Bayer, an amateur musicologist who knows more about Wolfgang than did Frau Mozart. Traditionally the city's number one address for cozy comfort. **Österreichischer Hof**'s renovations are striking. The more conventional wanderer might prefer this one to the above. Glass-front "Panorama" floor with fresh furnishings, private baths, air conditioning, and river view; each unit in its own distinctive décor; all 4 restaurants with waterside frontage, our favorite corner being the Zirblstube; excellent cookery. Over the century mark, but still looking trim and sailing smartly. The **Winkler** remains physically colorful, but it has an extremely commercial air possibly pinned to the fact that it lives and breathes for a travel agency. We imagine that Manager Müller must feel obliged to favor clients sent by the mother company. Even though its administrative reins seem a bit tangled of late, we are still receiving happy tidings from travelers who've paused recently at the **Bristol**. On the spiritual side, we are delighted to report that it retains its famed hospitality, cordiality, and easy homespun graces. On the physical side, the many touchups have given it more èlan. The front billets can be very noisy. Closed in winter. The **Parkhotel Mirabell** is for the ultramodern school; much thought, time, and money went into the construction of this imposing structure, and if you prefer contemporary stylings you'll probably be happy here. Lilliputian rooms; gadgets galore; singles with coffin-size bath and shower; connecting indoor swimming pool; staff eager and smiling. To round out the leaders, the **Kobenzl**, 2500 feet above the city on the Judenbergalpe, is a bargain. The Herzog family (and is each member attractive!) lovingly operate this gorgeously refashioned, spectacularly situated aerie. Spotlessly maintained; heated swimming pool and sauna; renewed panoramic restaurant; proud of its table—and properly so; amiable, wide-angle lodgings and spaced-out bathrooms; annex with sun terrace; glorious new suites overlooking the valley; closed September to April. Chair lift to outskirts of city until 5:30 P.M. but not in bad weather; 10 minutes by car from the center, with 2 daily free runs or independent hire for perhaps $3.50. Except for a few minor nit-picks, here is a heavenly setting run by good people who deserve their success in this unique upland retreat.

Schloss Mönchstein is a splendid, cozy hideaway for a duke, a dentist, an archbishop, or any modern nobleman-and-lady in search of deepdown P & Q. It is not expensive; in fact, we think it is surprisingly low in cost for its palatial-though-homey rewards. Baroness Johanna von Mierka is a gracious hostess; Manager Eggler keeps his towers and gardens in perfect trim; a new chef sets a first-rate table. Functioning from Easter to mid-Oct. A house we've admired for intimacy and comfort for many-a-year; now better than ever.

Haus Ingeborg, about 10 minutes out, is a 4-century-old cutie that oozes Tyrolean grace. Very small, very select, and very much to be recommended to inn-mates with wheels. Open March 1 to October 30.

The others? (1) **Schlosshotel St. Rupert** (55-pillow renovated castle 1½ miles out; lovely gardens; quiet; open Apr.-Oct.), (2) **Fondachhof** (attractive suburban villa; pool; limited menu; for tranquillity lovers), (3) **Schlosswirt** (huge country manse in nearby *Anif;* 20 of its 40 rooms in annex; outstanding cookery; likewise peaceful), (4) **Friesacher** (also in *Anif;* handsome rustic restaurant; book in the main building only), (5) **Kasererhof** (overall taste and startlingly high tariffs here kill it for us), (6) **Europa** (a 15-story eyesore marring the valley profile; to us, grim, commercial, and cold as an Arctic cod). Second class: (1) **Pitter** (bustling with conventions; good for its type; improving steadily), (2) **Auersperg,** (3) **Stieglbräu,** (4) **Kasererbräu,** (5) **Markus Sittikus,** (6) **Zum Hirschen. Weisse Taube** has just been smartly renovated; the people are friendly and the cuisine is warmly recommended. Third class: (1) **Elefant** (pachyderm born in A.D. 1200; inviting ground-floor Stube; 40 clean, nice rooms), (2) **Eibenhaus** (near Friesacher in *Anif;* captivating view in fresh-air surroundings; basic at best), (3) **Blaue Gans** (routine to poor), (4) **Mitteregg** (above the Kobenzl but far below it in quality—that's our opinion; the hospitality lacked sparkle and so did the cookery on our recent visit; strictly for sporting, rawboned budgeteers who want to cash in on a million-dollar vista). Pensions: (1) **Radauer,** (2) **Fürstenweg;** nearly all the better ones are slightly out of town. The **Airport Hotel** is functional and little else.

The lovely **Schloss Fuschl** at *Fuschl,* 15 miles due east, is sailing along better than ever under the able management of Uwe Zeilerbauer. Here's a glorious oasis for the moneyed traveler of taste. Marvelous scenic terrace seating 80; impressive paneled Jägerstube; new bar; Winter Garden; marble swimming pool; 9-hole golf course; automatic bowling alley. Total of 64 rooms and 38 baths; patrician furnishings; swimming, horseback riding, boating, lake or stream fishing. Two romantic suites and a bungalow lakeside; 2 simple hillside guesthouses (one a l-o-n-g hike). PS: If this Schloss is filled, or closed during the mid-April-to-end-October period, drive back to the **Jagdhof,** which flanks the entry road to the aristocratic Fuschl estate. This one is more modest, with a complement of 50 rooms in 2 buildings, the best being in the new annex. Viewful window-lined restaurant plus terrace; outstanding upstairs museum of smoking pipes, guns, and articles of the hunt. Low prices for highland rewards.

When mealtime rolls around, the **Goldener Hirsch** and the **Österreichischer Hof** hotels set the best tables locally.

For elegance among the independents, **Alt Salzburg,** behind the Goldener Hirsch, wins our bouquet of orchids. Arched alleyway entrance flanked by flags of various nations; Frenchy bar just inside; twin inner sancta under brick vaults. Several Italian specialties are spotlighted on the menu but Austrian fare predominates; the latter can be uneven in quality. Service is variable. Highish tabs.

Peterskeller is the traditional showplace if not the pulsing magnet of the tour operators. Never a shrine of gastronomy, its cookery seldom matches the excellence of its wines. Regional dishes only; dim Old World atmosphere; low price tags; supervision by the savvy Benedictine monks who own it. **Schlosswirt,** in the neighboring village of *Anif,* is a favorite of many motorborne trippers (taxis are lethally expensive here). Country manse with cottage specialties; garden dining in summer; very reasonable tabs. This simple place is ably administered by Mr. and Mrs. Graf. **Weinrestaurant Moser** features 3 rooms in solid tones. Vaulted ceilings; amiable staff; substantial local selections only. We now prefer it to the Peterskeller. The loftily sited, modernistic, and viewful **Café Winkler** offers lunch and dinner around the calendar. The **Salzburg Casino** (see later) is its next-door chum atop the Mönchsberg. Although **Weisses Roessl** ("White Horse," at Linzergasse 15) has gone down in the Mouth Department it is still popular. Worth a look if you're looking, but not a bite; the district however, is not for timid types after dark.

Nearby, the **K & K** is modern, clean, fair in price, zestless visually, but highly popular.

Then there's the **Zinnkrug** ("Pewter Pot") on the 4th floor of a building across the street from the Österreichischer Hof. Attractive view over the river and rooftops; overworked minions in regional costume. The chicken in a creamed curry bath was delicious; the gypsy-art grill was pleasant and abundant; the Crêpes Costello might have been pranks by the shades of the Marx Brothers team. Otherwise we enjoyed it.

The **Zum Eulenspiegel** (Hagenauerplatz 2), in the fifteenth-century city gatehouse, has 3 floors, sophisticated tavern-type ambiance, and hungry tourists 6-deep. The jokes and proverbs on the walls are so earthy that we hope your German is academic rather than colloquial. The Proprietor and his staffers are virtuosos at giving the customer the Suave Sell on that extra cocktail, that highest-price item, and that rarest bottle. While it is still passable, we believe that the cuisine and service attitudes have fallen off noticeably.

Festungsrestaurant in the Festung (castle) and **Stieglkeller** (Festungsgasse 10) are more famous for folk dancing (summer only) than for groceries; check your concierge first, because on some evenings nothing happens; the latter spot, designed vaguely like the inside of a beer barrel, is the only place we've ever found where the purple-faced customer climbs 5 flights of stairs to get to the cellar. And when the bus tours roll up, you can forget about receiving service of any kind. The **Augustinerbräustüberl** (Augustinergasse 4), a mammoth, old-fashioned beer hall and chestnut-tree garden which can handle 2000 merrymakers without blowing off the suds, is almost unknown to foreigners. Self-service throughout; cold plates and snacks only; opens daily at 3 P.M.; colorful and amusing, despite the oafs in attendance.

Helbrunn Castle, a costly taxi jaunt from the center, offers practical jokes and squirt tricks with its famous fountains, as well as delicious Châteaubriand and typical Tyrolean folk music. Kids from 5 to 95 love the charming wild-animal preserve on the grounds. **Café Glockenspiel** rings at the Mozartplatz, but the vittles are only passing fair for the passing parade. **G'würzmühl is** slickly rustic in décor and slick enough in its skillet skills. **Weisses Kreuz** has good Balkan dishes—and the irritating feeling that they're rushing the hell out of you.

When the Salzburg sun sets, there's gambling at the plush **Casino** Waaaaay up yonder in the clouds of the Mönchsberg. Handsome furnishings in a handsome building; 1 baccarat and 5 roulette tables; pleasant bar; open from 7 P.M. to 2 A.M. (4 A.M. on weekends) except on Christmas Eve and religious holidays; small entrance fee, from which you are presented a chip to start your play. *Remember to take along your passport, or you won't be admitted.* As a wise Los Angeles physician wryly comments, "If you don't speak fluent German and if you don't quite understand the meaning of the word 'Manque,' take Jimmy the Greek along."

The neighboring **Café Winkler** (not to be confused with the hotel and not under the same ownership), atop the cliff by special elevator, offers year-round revels plus a tiptop restaurant. You'll also discover higher-than-average prices. Fun, scenic, and worth a visit. The **Half Moon** and the **Old Grenadier** are patronized by young discophiles. The **Cocktail Club** has fallen off so dramatically it can no longer be recommended. The **Hexenturm** ("Witches' Tower") in the Elmo Hotel is no longer recommended. **Rendezvous** and **Schubert-Diele** are routine and less-than-routine, respectively. The **Casino Alm,** a few minutes from the center, is a miniature 5–ring circus. Bowling alley; Stadl restaurant; cheerful rustic nightclub. It also offers swimming (day and night), tennis (day and night), minigolf (day), table tennis (day and night), steeplechasing (day), and a surprisingly energetic smile (day and night). Amusing. The **Friesacher**

Stadl in neighboring *Anif* basically is a discothèque; action from 9 P.M. to 4 A.M.; pleasant merrymaking here in a building disguised as an old barn.

Casanova is seedy, 2nd-rate Broadway with Austrian rural overtones; not for us. Finally, if you tire of the noise and smoke and clatter, the wonderful old **Café Bazar** (the coffeehouse opposite Lanz, at the bridge), with marble tables, newspaper racks, and dignity, will give solace and balm to your soul. The venerable **Tomaselli** (Alter Markt) is a popular runner-up.

The sleeping, eating, and carousing done, here are our best bets for shoppers: ★ ★ ★ ★ ★ **Slezak** (Markartplatz 8) lighted its 100th birthday candle in '73. To start, here are star quality and a very wide selection of ladies' handbags; gold-embroidered evening bags and belts; all styles, sizes, and types of leather suitcases; roomy attaché and briefcases; gorgeous sweaters at equal to or lower than English or Scottish tariffs; gloves; unusually fetching souvenirs and accessories. It's a paradise from which to mail gifts to the U.S. Prices? 100% decent. Enchanting Mrs. Dorli Gehmacher and her gentle staff will all charm you with their Austrian sweetness. Unrivaled for taste and old-line integrity.

Lederhosen and leather wearables: ★ ★ ★ ★ **Jahn-Markl** (Residenzplatz 3) always comes up with top-drawer specialties—and thanks to the radiant warmth of friendly Erwin Markl, there's a cozy feeling about this ancient little place. The initial outlay for one of his super-fine, ever-chic suits made of suède, deerskin, or chamois might seem to be dear, but actually here are prime investments because they last for 10 to 12 years *without cleaning!* Giant in craftsmanship and heart of the land!

Regional wear: We're very happy with **Trachten Wenger** (Munzgasse 2). Their versatile assortment of dirndls and their foursquare prices are 2 compelling reasons for our patronage. **Lanz** has a branch at the end of the main bridge.

Handicrafts: **Salzburger Heimatwerk** (Residenzplatz) is the unchallenged leader for this merchandise in the area. As with the aforementioned Slezak, the best word for this shop is "sweet."

Sporting goods: ★ ★ ★ ★ ★ **Dschulnigg** (Griesgasse 8) is a preserve for the aficionado or the expert. In the gun department can be found elegantly fashioned weapons from private homes in Austria or custom-made designs for you. The hunting department features other rifles, shotguns, and equipment for the dogs. The fishing department is a joy for nimrods. Furthermore, the clothing department offers a complete wardrobe of loden, plus accessories in all colors, as well as handknitted vests and walking jackets in boiled wool. Knowledgeable and wise Mr. and Mrs. Helmut Dschulnigg can organize any expedition, be it angling or the chase; write well in advance about hoofed game. *What* a catch!

SCHRUNS   **Kurhotel Montafon** (top-class international spa a skip-and-jump from the Swiss and Liechtenstein frontiers; rich and celebrated clientele; medical supervision). The young **Löwen** recently suffered a fire; we don't know if it is to be rebuilt.

SEEFELD   (1) **Klosterbräu**, (2) **Post** (also on the main square), (3) **Alpenhotel Lamm**. If you like gaming, the **Karwendelhof** houses its own full-blown casino.

STAINACH-IRDNING is the nearest address of **Schloss Pichlarn,** which is large, airy, and far from the personal sort of castle most wayfarers seek for overnighting. The indoor-outdoor pool complex is a dream. Closed November 1 to December 15.

STUBEN is a serious Arlberg ski station. **Hubertushof** would be our pick of the spare harvest.

VELDEN AM WÖRTHERSEE (1) **Schloss Velden** (ownership by the same family who command the famous Three Hussars in Vienna), (2) **Seehotel-Mösslacher-Veldenerhof** (nice vistas; friendly staff; few outlanders; music in the evenings).

WÖRGL is famous for its nearby **Hotel Schloss Itter,** reached by taking the East ("Ost") exit off the autobahn, driving 10 minutes to the village of Itter, and arriving at the end of the hamlet at a hilltop's edge. It's one of the most exciting entries of all architecturally, dating from A.D. 1532. Somewhat remote location; adequate comfort; heated pool; uneven standards; high tabs. The setting is truly postcard country. Closed tight in winter.

YBBS-ON-DANUBE offers the **Weisses Rössl**. Baroque retaurant; Framconian wine cellar with gypsy and Schrammel music; modern; clean; reportedly very pleasent.

ZÜRS AM ARLBERG's leading hotel—and one of the top spots on the European winter sport circuit—is the merrily rich **Zürserhof**. Beautiful appointments in Peasant Baroque; sumptuous wing of suites, all with working fireplaces; a living museum of fine regional furnishings; full range of facilities for skiers; soothing comforts provided by Proprietor Ernst Skardarasy, president of the Austrian Hotel Association; the hitching post of many international notables. Elegant and good. The 70-room **Lorünser,** with more sporting *Gemütlichkeit* and a younger clientele, boasts a permafrost-to-pitched-roof renovation. Its set-meal gastronomy (with options, plus a policy of answering requests for special dishes) is one of the best we've experienced in the alps. The delightful Jochum team, Herbert and Inge, couldn't be nicer. Heaven for sporting types. The **Alpenrose** comes with its own swimming pool and sauna; 2 bars; tea dancing daily plus nightly revels. Somewhat commercial in tone; nevertheless a handsome haven for highlanders. **Edelweiss** is simple, cozy, and bustling. Its *Stubli,* where you should sample the delicious *Backhendl* (fried chicken, Austrian version), is always jammed. The hillbound **Alpenhof,** now grown to 50 units, is infused with the giant-size grace of the owning Thurnherr family. Intimacy is the pivotal word here—with all the comforts of household living, including much of that feeling, too. The village-*centrum* **Albona** seems to be a chalet that just couldn't cease growing. The popular discothèque plus the doin's in the nearby Mara wrap up nearly 99.999% of the nightlife in this sleepy vale. If you're after action and treed landscape, try the next-door townlet of *Lech.*

Belgium

Belgium is a tiny land—but its sinews are huge and its power is enormous. The size of the State of Maryland, here is one of the most densely populated countries in Europe, oozing with a beauty, culture, and elegance that are not seen in thousands of miles of travel elsewhere on Earth's real estate.

The Flemings are the Nawth'n Yankees; the Walloons are the Southern Cuhn'ls; Brussels, like Washington, is just about the only place they'll speak to each other. The language question has been the hottest issue since the Dutch occupation of 1815. About 30 years ago the country was formally divided into 2 linguistic areas—Flanders, where Flemish (or Dutch) is used by about 5 million, and the Walloon section, where French is the official tongue of a minority of 3 million. In the capital, the sole neutral ground, it's often a case of who can speak the loudest. Nowdays, the Belgians are such a busy and prosperous people that most of these differences are put aside.

Since the nation is so small, you'll very likely see most of the monarchy in a brief time span—and much of it will be in bloom if the season is right. Don't think that Holland has a touristic monopoly on blossoms, bulbs, and botany in the Lowlands. You'll probably want to inspect the orchids at **La Hulpe** (see "Brussels"). The Royal Palace at *Laeken* is another worthy target for green thumbs. Furthermore, flower shows exist in *Lochristi* (near Ghent), *Sainte-Marie-sur-Semois*, and at *Spa*, but check on the dates.

Ghent and *Bruges*, under an hour from Brussels on the superhighway, draw the most North Americans. To cover a lot of territory fast (which we don't recommend, since the greater rewards come from lingering), here's a once-over-lightly itinerary which can be comfortably done in 1 highly active day: Start from Brussels at 8:30 A.M. Take the expressway straight to Bruges (ignoring Ghent, which you'll be seeing later). Head for Deleu's attractive pâtisserie on the market square for your coffee break. Have a 35-minute boat ride on a canal, sightsee where you will, and then amble down either the expressway or Route N-10 (distances about even) to Ostend.

Your main target in Ostend, incidentally, should be the **Kursaal**—one of the most modern and efficient gambling casinos in the world. Baccarat, roulette, blackjack, dice, swimming, 2500-seat concert hall, restaurant, nightclub—the works; 50¢ minimum play in the Grand Salle, $1 minimum play in the Sporting Room, and a $600 single play limit in both. Foreigners who bring their passports are admitted to both *salles* on a special 2-day arrangement for $2.50; admission to all else is public. You may be interested in the budgeteer's weekend (not valid in summer) which includes dinner, a hotel room for 1 night, and Sunday-morning breakfast—all for about $40.

If there's time, you might then wish to run out to *Knokke*, Belgium's most chichi seaside resort and site of the World Poetry Biennial, a few miles along the coast to the north. If not, perhaps you'd be happier to head straight for lunch. Either the charming Goedendag at *Lissewege*, 6½ miles from Bruges, or the By Lamme Goedzak at *Damme*, 5 miles from Bruges, or even the economical Siphon, a mile from Damme at *Oostkerke*, is suggested; make advance reservations, for sure. Then climb back on the expressway to *Ghent* for a view of Van Eyck's immortal "Holy Lamb" at the **Cathedral**; follow this with tea at the ramshackle Cour St.-Georges, oldest hotel in the north; the rooms are poor but the dining facilities passable. Those with extra fortitude may want to run out to the **Castle of Laarne** for a peek at its $2,000,000 silver collection, its tapestries, its furniture, and the spook who haunts its grandiose halls. You should be back in Brussels by dinnertime—dogtired but (we hope) reasonably well pleased with your comprehensive excursion.

Another outstanding attraction is the **Grottos of Han**, about 3 hours from the capital in the direction of Luxembourg. The underground streams are interesting, the colors are exquisite, and the rooms are so huge that opera used to be presented in them. Admission is chickenfeed and the train fare is peanuts.

Sound-and-Light *(Son et Lumière)* spectacles glow from May 1 through September 30 in the courtyards of medieval castles at *Bouillon*, *La Roche*, *Ghent*, *Bruges*, *Antwerp*, *Tournai*, and other locations, plus a stunning eye-popper several nights each week in the **Grand' Place** of the capital.

The **Carnival** de *Binche* (pronounced "Bahn-ssh") is worth a 500-mile detour from any set itinerary, if you happen to be in Europe just before Lent. Started by Maximilian in the sixteenth century, the pseudo-Peruvian costumes are fantastically colorful—with ostrich-feather headdresses 4 feet tall. On the climax day, 5000 participants "dance" the grand parade. *Wear your oldest clothes if you go to this*—blue jeans, if possible—because the crowd will kiss you, hit you painlessly with air-filled skin bags, and throw oranges at you, all simultaneously.

For Art and Architecture Addicts: Good King Baudouin threw open the massive doors to dozens of Belgium's most beautiful (and never-before-public) chateaux, including his own palace in Brussels. Court is held for you 9:30 A.M. to 4 P.M. from about July 22 to mid-September. You also might wish to savor rural manors with their priceless treasures. Ticket prices differ; most are in the neighborhood of $2.

For further information on sightseeing, folklore, and other data of interest to the overseas visitor, the official Tourist Office has issued a gem of a booklet called *Belgium*. Written succinctly by ex-newspaperman Jean Gyory, it's of enormous value to every stranger. Available only through its New York office (745 Fifth Ave., zip 10022), and free of charge.

☑ **TRANSPORTATION　Taxis**　Be careful.

Since beginning our annual trek through this country back in '46, we have undergone hassle after hassle with various local drivers. In the capital, or elsewhere in Belgium, you might find courteous and honest hackies—or, alas, you might meet some of the most exasperating and frustrating service personnel you'll ever encounter abroad. The worst of the lot may not return the proper change, insist on inflated tips, and even browbeat and curse their passengers. If your pilot "forgets" to put down the flag on his meter, remind him loudly and instantly.

Incidentally, Belgian taxi fares are among the highest in the world. As one almost criminal example, the 15-minute hop from the airport to the center of Brussels is a preposterous $23, and higher on weekends and at night according to some rogues. The excellent train for the same distance is $1.15! (As baggage handling can be a problem, ask the people at the Welcome Service desk to provide a porter.) Tips are included, *so don't bother with any further voluntary doles,* even though drivers may grumble, whine, or even withhold change.

Trains　Very good nowadays. There's even a car-train that will take your auto from Brussels to Munich, Avignon, St. Raphaël, Villach, and Narbonne for peanut-size outlays.

The 5-day-minimum Tourist Card ("abonnement") is perfect for excursioners. (Five days should be sufficient to cover this little land. but versions of this T-Travel Card now are issued for 10 or 15 days, too.) There is also the wider-ranging Benelux Tourrail plan, which covers 3 nations for 10 days of limitless conveyance. In the capital, an excellent Metro system is now functioning and continues to expand. It is linked to the tram network for added convenience.

Ferry Connections　There's a **Jetfoil** speedster that roars over the waves between Zeebrugge and London. The 200-passenger P & O (Pacific & Orient) vessel skims along at close to 50 mph, linking the 2 cities in close to 3 hours and 45 minutes. It originally boasted a daily run. An additional hydrofoil service flies between Ostend and London in slightly less time. Be sure to check with a travel agent since transportation of this sort is subject to variables in weather and other inhibiting last-minute conditions which could delay or cancel your journey.

☑ **FOOD**　If you can pay the price, you'll get fat fast in Belgium. In its ranking establishments gustatory standards are so high they challenge the best in France. The approach to cuisine, too, is similar. Believe it or not, Filet Américain (an unknown in the U.S.) is Belgian. Locals traditionally down gallons of beer soup each year, delight in eels in green sauce, and ingest mussels in so many disguises that you'd think every citizen in the land automatically rises and falls with the tides.

☑ **DRINKS**　Trappist beer is unique and cheap. There are 2 types: "Double" (the normal variety) and "Triple" (hard to find). Both are different from anything brewed anywhere—vague Coca-Cola overtones; a curiosity. The Rochefort monks produce a 3rd kind from oranges. Other national quaffs (Goud-Ster, Elberg, Artois, Haecht, Gueuze-Lambic, Duke, Ginder Ale *(sic!),* and the like) aren't quite up to Danish or Dutch standards, but they're infinitely superior to that bottled froggy water sold in France. A good 1/3 rd of the nation's 189 breweries bubble in Brabant. The native brew of Brussels is Le Lambic; sipped naturally, it will put a pucker on your kisser that will make you the talk of the harem; many locals add sugar; we suggest about 328 heaping tablespoons per glass. The locals also down Kriek-Lambic, a cherry beverage found only in the oldest taverns. The saturated Belgian is perennially one of the world's heartiest beer drinkers.

As for wine, Belgium's neighbors produce it in Niagaras. Please refer to the "Drinks" sections in other chapters for guidelines on these—and don't forget Luxembourg's bottlings, often the choice of savvy and thrifty Belgian tipplers.

☑ **LOCAL RACKETS**   Leave the clip joints alone. They're expensive—and often dangerous. The B-girls will drink colored water for "cognac"—and when you've spent all your money, they'll move along to the next customer.

Here's one which continues to grow fast: On several side streets leading off the capital's Boulevard Adolphe Max (the main drag through the center), beautifully made-up tootsies in décolleté white dresses frame themselves in picture windows and beckon to passing males with Circean allure. When reuben enters and asks, "How much?", she sweetly murmurs "$70 with a bottle of champagne." (She can be bargained down to $50.) The rotgut is then produced, paid for, and consumed. But before the sucker can take off his coat, she smiles equally sweetly and says "Goodbye!" Should he protest, a heavyweight as muscular as George Foreman will magically appear, sometimes accompanied by a very hungry Alsatian or Doberman. So what sheep ever argues this shearing?

For automotive repairs, go to the dealer who represents whatever you are driving. *Be careful about patronizing the small garages* in Belgium, because often a chiseler will charge you the price of the car to get it out. If you're stuck, make your deal *first,* before allowing them to move one finger on the job.

☑ **INFORMATION CENTERS**   The **Commissariat Général au Tourisme**, 61 rue Marché aux Herbes, Brussels, Tel. 513-90-90, is the official tourist office. Before leaving New York, it might also be wise to check your itinerary with the metropolitan branch, the **Belgian National Tourist Office**, 745 Fifth Avenue. Director Mrs. Frederique Raeymaekers is a walking encyclopedia of travel lore of her nation.

★ **TIPS**   To move around cheaply, pick up a low-cost Tourist Card. This entitles you to 2 days of unlimited tram and bus travel—2 of the least exciting but safest forms of transportation in this taxi-mad, motor-crazed town. Purchase it at the **Tourist Information Brussels**, 61 rue Marché-aux-Herbes (behind the Grand' Place), Tel: 513-89-40.

CITIES

BRUSSELS,   home of more than a million souls, is where you'll probably start. It's the center of government, industry, business, and culture. For some time it had been enjoying the wildest construction boom of any capital in Europe—a Low Country that swiftly became an ultra-High-Riser. It boasts a good airport, 4 railroad stations, a luxurious, clean, and music-fed subway, plenty of excellent hotels, restaurants, movies, and shops.

Sightseeing   After strolling the glorious Grand' Place (where autos are banned), every tourist seems to head for the **Manneken-Pis**—probably because he or she wants to be shocked. It's the famous bronze statue of the boy doing you-know-what; one story goes that a king wanted to immortalize his son in the last position he saw him just before the youngster was accidentally killed. He has been stolen 5 times. A Tokyo newspaper and an Indian prince are among the 80 bemused parties who have donated costumes to cover his nakedness—all of which may be viewed at the Maison du Roi. His miniature in various forms of dress is one of Belgium's most popular souvenirs. Although he may disappoint you, see the "Oldest Citizen of Brussels" anyway, just for the record.

Plenty of cathedrals (Belgium is almost entirely Catholic), including St. Michel. Other standbys are the **King's Palace**, the **Courts of Justice, Théâtre Royal de la Monnaie** with the National Opera plus lavish "Ballet of the XXth Century," and wonderful winter concerts with top-line artists—plus all the museums and art galleries any classicist could wish for. Some of our top choices are the **City Hall** and the **Communal Museums,** both in the Grand' Place, and marvels, the **Belle-Vue** with its 18th- and 19th-century royal collections of furniture and household items, **Erasmus House,** the **Royal Museum of Art and History** (a bit far from the center), the **Atomium** (also somewhat distant, at Heysel), and the **Albert I Library.** Special interests are featured, too, such as the **Horta Museum** (25 rue Américaine), which focuses on architecture and wrought iron, the **National Botanical Gardens** (236 rue Royale, Schaerbeek), the **Lace Museum** (4 rue de la Violette), contained in several restored 17th-century houses, the **Brewers' Museum** (in the cellar at 10 Grand' Place), and the highly inspired **Children's Museum** (32 rue Tenbosch, off Avenue Louise).

The permanent center of Belgian entertainment life is the **Palais des Beaux-Arts,** an underground labyrinth which contains a huge concert hall (3000 seats), several small theaters, a movie house, a king-size exhibition hall for paintings, a restaurant, and headquarters of most of the artistic associations.

For some of the most thrilling Flemish art, go to the richly endowed **Musée d'Art Ancien**, rue de la Régence, near the Beaux-Arts building.

Waterloo Battlefield is not recommended. It is one of the sorriest, poorest tourist sights of Europe. You'll ride a bus or car for a wearisome stretch, and when you get there, ordinary cow pastures and a heap of dirt will greet you. Don't waste your money on this one.

La Hulpe, a Brussels suburb, is famed for its orchids.

BRUSSELS HOTELS Quick Reference Table

Price categories by national (not U.S.) standards.

EXPENSIVE:

Hilton Bd. de Waterloo 38. Tel. 513.88.77; Telex 22744; 373 rooms. P. 67
Hyatt Regency Rue Royale 250. Tel. 219.46.40; Telex 61871; 325 rooms. P. 67
Mayfair Av. Louise 381-383. Tel. 649.98.00; Telex 24821; 100 rooms. P. 68
Royal Windsor Rue Duquesnoy 5-7. Tel. 511.42.15; Telex 62905; 265 rooms. P. 67
Sheraton Place Rogier 3. Tel. 219.34.00; Telex 26887; 500 rooms. P. 66

UPPER MODERATE:

Amigo Rue de l'Amigo 1-3. Tel. 511.59.10; Telex 21618; 183 rooms. P. 67
Atlanta Bd. Adolphe Max 7. Tel. 217.01.20; Telex 21475; 244 rooms. P. 68
Europa Rue de la Loi 107. Tel. 513.78.20; Telex 25121; 245 rooms. P. 68
Metropole Pl. de Brouckère 31. Tel. 217.23.00; Telex 21234; 379 rooms. P. 68

MODERATE:

Brussels Residence Ave. Louise 319. Tel. 648.81.80; Telex 25075; 64 rooms. P. 69
Palace Place Roger 22. Tel. 217.62.00; Telex 21248; 356 rooms. P. 67
President Centre Rue Royale 160. Tel. 219.00.65; Telex 26784; 73 rooms. P. 68
President Nord Bd. A. Max 107. Tel. 219.00.60; 63 rooms. P. 68
Ramada Ch. de Charleroi 38. Tel. 538.91.00; Telex 25539; 202 rooms. P. 68

LOWER MODERATE:

Astoria Rue Royale 103. Tel. 217.62.90; Telex 25040; 110 rooms. P. 69
Siru Place Rogier 1. Tel. 217.75.80; Telex 21722; 101 rooms. P. 69

AIRPORT LODGINGS:

Holiday Inn Holidaystraat 7. Tel. 720.58.65; Telex 24285; 288 rooms. P. 69
Novotel Airport Olmenstr. Tel. 720.58.30; Telex 26751; 163 rooms. P. 69

Hotels Brussels, often called the business office of Europe, is rated among the most expensive cities in the world for the visitor. Fortunately there is a way to cut back on hotel costs and that is to register in one of the older, more venerable establishments rather than in the new ones born and bred primarily for expense-account executives. Since these gracious, spacious dowagers could not compete with the sleek glass and steel 21st-century towers, they have been forced by market pressure to hold the line on tariffs; nevertheless, they still offer lovely traditional-style rooms, personal service, expansive living space, and addresses in the best parts of town. They may not switch on color TV or wake-up consoles in every unit, or have throbbing discothèques and 24-hour coffee shops, but they will provide excellent accommodation, large baths, superb comfort, gilded pilasters, enormous fine tapestries in the lobby, kindhearted minions, and a life-style that is distinctly European—all at a price that is about 25% to 30% below many of the modernists. Superb examples of these are the Palace, the Atlanta, the Amigo, and the Metropole, which form the upper crust, with other lesser candidates described in the following text. Thus, by selecting with care you can save a bundle and have an elegant experience in the bargain.

The **Sheraton** this year shares the top slot with the Hilton. Midcity venue with ample public oases; a fringe benefit of boutiques; gracious lobby; sumptuous Le Comtes de Flandre Grill; Pavillon Coffee Shop, a cocktail lounge, a 1000-car garage—and a lovely glass-bound swimming pool with its own snack bar, sauna, massage parlor, and gymnasium. Generous bedchamber dimensions, some twin units even with 3 beds; yellows, browns, and orange tones in textiles; radio and color TV; small tubs; 33 excellent suites in its Royal Towers with kitchenettes. This plant is physically a stunner.

The high-capacity **Hilton**, re-sparkled with 5 floors attired by Givenchy (who also has a shop here), swings in with such button-poppers as the ruggedly handsome Maison du Boeuf Grill (at treetop level overlooking the Egmont Gardens and the Royal Palace, offering beef flown in from America), the splendid En Plein Ciel ("High in the Sky") Supper Club with outstanding *nouvelle cuisine* and dancing, Le Bar with piano melodizing, cheerful coffee shop, plus one of the finest sauna baths in which we've roasted (see "Tip" under "Nightclubs"). Accommodations color-keyed to rust, blue, and green with interesting mixtures in hues. One entire floor (16th) devoted exclusively to 4 VIP suites, with multiple-connecting bedchambers, kitchenettes; guidance by soft-spoken, sharp-eyed General Manager William Sprokkreeff. This excellent aristocrat now displays more refinement than ever before.

We are becoming increasingly fond of the **Royal Windsor**. There's a darkling cozy richness in all the gathering nooks and a gleaming fresh welcome in the private accomodations. Stately exterior topped by a handsome gabled roof; Victorian-mood mezzanine chophouse; Crocodile discotheque, the top spot in town for wholesome revels; Wellington Pub plus the Waterloo Club for liquids and chitchat; quick-service coffee shop; 265 bedchambers with private bath, hushabye soundproofing (a boon since it is so central), radio, TV (on request), and air conditioning. Though the tariffs may seem exaggeratedly high, they are in line with the competition. What's equally important, the value is there. In winter, incidentally, the Friday-through-Sunday rates are about half of those during the normal business week.

The 325-room **Hyatt Regency** makes a bid for frank modernity, efficiency, and internationality. Lean and linear 10-story edifice; impressive lobby illuminated by hundreds of icicle-like glass tubes suspended from the ceiling; costly appointments in public areas but cool functionality in bedroom schemes; French, Italian, Danish, and American sipping and dining spreads; appealing cocktail lounge. Manager Jan Leenders can be justly proud of this opulent oasis of tranquillity in such a turbulent town. Business travelers probably will find it useful, especially if they are traveling on executive-level expense accounts.

The **Amigo** boasts perhaps the most romantic situation in the city. Step out of its slate-floored lobby and you are in the midst of the most breathtaking assemblage of medieval architecture in existence anywhere on earth: the Grand' Place. It also offers dignified art-filled salons, a cozy vault for a bar, an intimate restaurant in antique Spanish tones *(amigo)*, and almost every room different in size and décor. The staff impressed us as one of the most concerned and most efficient we've encountered in Belgium. If you are a light sleeper, request an inside accommodation. Greatly improved and now recommendable.

The **Palace** is not only one of the best buys for your dollar in Brussels, it is kilometers superior for the visitor who seeks continental rather than Made-in-U.S.A. atmosphere. When its shrewd management found that this Palace simply could not compete with the flashy newcomers in town, it lowered its prices and felt content to offer fine Old World accommodation maintained in perfect trim. The result is a terrific bargain for the vacation traveler. Every wide-angled room with bath and shower, all with radio and TV coming gradually; most units topnotch, but a few clinkers in the stack; attractive park-view restaurant with excellent food; little bar; beauty parlor and barbershop. Try to reserve on the Park, not on the Square. Hardworking, go-getting Manager Robert Ramaekers is kind; he maintains this very sound establishment as 1 of the nation's pacesetters.

The **Atlanta** is also a good value. Its latest wing is a splendid attraction, boosting its room count to 244 and adding a vast shopping enclave plus a Day-Glo rooftop breakfast oasis. Amply appointed throughout for efficient use of its rigid space limitations; all streetside units with acoustic ceilings. Charles Gmür, the veteran Swiss proprietor, deserves salutes for his generous investment in comfort and brightness; here is a friendly and informal stop, especially for those who travel with children.

The moderately refashioned **Ramada** charges almost the same tariffs as the far more luxurious Sheraton for its 200 U.S.-chain-fed accommodations; the exterior strikes us as architecturally boring; inside (sic) there's the Garden Restaurant for light grazing and the Refuge for really donning the feedbag, both of which are brimming with eye appeal. If you like the Ramada life-style in the U.S. of A., then you'll probably feel at home here, but for a similar outlay we'd bid for the Sheraton any day or night.

The totally restyled **Mayfair** beckons with renewed radiance. Quietly modern in tone; bar in brass and rust-color leatherette; small conference facilities; boutique; hairdresser; parking; 100 bedchambers in timeless ambiance. A welcome change which gets our salaams.

While the **Europa's** accouterments boast ample allure and its staff seem to have mastered their jobs, we feel that it is too far from the center for the convenience of shoppers and sightseers. Winning Dukes coffee shop surrounding a fish pond, elegant Beefeater eatery ornately decorated with oil portraits on paneled backdrops; inviting, snugglesome bedrooms featuring rich textiles, dark-wood furniture, and high-grade fittings and garnishment. "Business as usual," could be its credo.

The **Métropole** is a spacious, rambling structure. Since conventions and tour groups are urgently needed to fill its vastness, the fun of the independent wanderer is sometimes a bit dampened. Even so, more than half the rooms and the public precincts have been face lifted. Old in style but becoming younger in spirit by the hour.

The 63-room-and-bath **President Nord** wins our vote for reasonable value at relatively reasonable prices. No restaurant, but pleasant English Bar and snack room; clean, bright atmosphere; cordial staff headed by hardworking Manager A. Formisani. The midtown address is another feather in its sweet little chapeau. Very worthy for the outlay. Its newer running mate, the **President Centre**, reflects the success of the first-termer. The levies are about the same. Our double-barreled recommendation to this pair.

The **Brussels Residence**, also has been doing an outstanding job with its 24 bedrooms and 40 duplex apartments. The décor throughout is so colorful it is almost Scandinavian. Famous grill on ground floor augmented by a Japanese garden and the Aloha Polynesian nightclub; an English pub draped in raspberry velvet and strangely called The Bull; garage; a good buy, provided your architectural tastes are avant-garde.

The **Astoria** is continuing its new Old-World ambiance for the benefit of nostalgic wayfarers who may again enjoy its solid comforts. Especially recommendable to senior travelers.

Young candidates which we don't rank include the 116-room **County House**, with a 20-unit division at the **Airport**, the 70-bedchambered **Diplomat**, and the small **Business**, with only 20 keys.

The **Siru** offers good economy and the attention of personable Director Pierre Halkin; French cuisine in the popular La Gousse d'Ail ("Clove of Garlic") restaurant. The **Arenberg** is a strong challenger now. The **Bedford** (added wing with private baths) fits in about here on our checklist. While very good and reasonable in price, the taste in décor is quixotically torn twixt modernity and traditionalism. Next in line are the **Charlemagne, La Cascade, De France, Central, Residence,** and **Noga.**

Holiday Inn is a welcome addition at the airport. Chandeliered lobby often sharing space with advertising promotions; congress facilities; 2 outdoor tennis courts; enclosed pool; 2 saunas plus biceptual gym. Second-stage Waterloo Tavern, dim but colorfully fitted with toy soldier regimentalia; adjoining Les 9 Provinces restaurant (weekday buffet); bright Café Holiday. All 300 soundproofed rooms with bath, shower, radio, color TV, air cooling, direct-dial phone, and other Space Age gimmickry; excellent w-i-d-e beds with gaily striped spreads. At your service is a shuttle service (request it at the Avis counter in the terminal), plus city hops hourly by minibus from 8 A.M. to midnight. Nearby is the French-bred **Novotel**, its 160 sleepers wrapped around a central swimming pool. Motel space concepts but, like its neighbor, particularly useful for airborne short-timers.

Dedicated budgeteers? Since space limitations prevent additional entries, please consult *Fielding's Low-Cost Europe*, our annually revised paperback, which lists scads more bargain hotels or pensions and money-saving tips for serious economizers. For lesser known centers, consult the Belgian Tourist Bureau's excellent (and imaginatively titled) booklet, "Belgium Hotels." You'll find the addresses, facilities, and prices of every registered hotel or pension in the nation.

Restaurants Villa Lorraine (avenue du Vivier-d'Oie 75) remains a glory for capital diners with no shortage of capital. It is a "must" candidate for anyone's list of romantic lunches or big nights out. Parkland situation bordering the Bois de la Cambre, about 10 minutes by taxi from the center; converted mansion resplendent with deep-pile carpets, rich brocades, and colossal floral decorations; wooden bar with leaded stained-glass doors leading to an open, bower-shaded terrace; sumptuous, even regal, interior dining room with champagne moiré-silk wall coverings, gilt chandeliers and sconces, and a crackling hearth; captivating flower-girt garden patio, glass-lined for dining with nature on inclement days. Sadly but realistically, the prices match the rewards in every way. Very costly, but very, very special indeed. Highly recommended.

Dupont (46 Av. Vital Riethuisen) stands tall not only in the Low Countries but in the highest ranks of *haute cuisine* all across the European tablescape. It is a celebration for the hedonistic senses. Mme. Claude Dupont, also an attraction, greets you at the door of their converted townhouse, which is located about 7 minutes by taxi from the center. There is an immediate impression of spaciousness and grace in the single dining salon. The straw-colored Hessian walls reflect subdued light from shaded sconces; the table coverings are cornflower blue glowing with cut flowers and delicate crystalware; floral displays greet the eye at every turn; the beige-and-brown-patterned banquettes are deeply comfortable; service is kind and impeccable. Chef Claude Dupont inclines his extraordinary talents toward the *nouvelle cuisine*—and it is delicious. Our freshly poached duck liver on a bed of 3 dainty salads and topped with shaved truffle was a masterpiece. So was our partner's mound of *langouste vinaigrette*. The steamed turbot with a light sauce perfumed with leeks was one of the finest preparations of our entire recent rounds, but we also observed meats in pastry shells, game, and desserts that came from the kitchen as gems from Cartier's vaults. A fully composed menu is available for about $35 per diner, but our à la carte dinner for two with the house apéritif (chilled champagne and framboise), a Puilly Fumé, dessert, coffee, and liqueur came to $120 including service and taxes. Closed Mon. and Tues. and from mid-July to August 22. In our view, one of the best on the continent.

The **Parc Savoy** (place Marie-José 9) could almost be considered a miniature Villa Lorraine. Enchanting sylvan setting; flowers bordering the paneled entrance and the patio of the Cercle Privé cocktail lounge; inner Cercle overlooking the greensward; several dining nookeries including the main rotunda, a mirrored alcove ringing one side, and a conservatory-style glassed-in terrace which is extra-extra-charming when the days are halcyon. Specialties run from $14 to $22; a full meal with wine goes for about $55 on the average. (And does it go down smoothly!!!) Exquisite, discerning, and totally aristocratic.

The midtown **Ravenstein** (rue Ravenstein 1) is a wondrous restoration from the fourteenth and fifteenth centuries. Moreover, it was a restaurant even before this century was born. A single hearth-front salon with about 8 tables plus an upper welcoming loge; magnificent crystal chandelier; fine linens; leaded windows; polished beams and wooden dado enhanced by a rouge-and-gold textile wall covering; masterly oil paintings. The cuisine and the service are the perfect complement to its patrician atmosphere. The Soufflé St. Jacques (or with lobster) is especially ambrosial. One of the oldest and finest addresses in the capital. And, of course, blue-ribbon in prices too.

One of the most illustrious and delightful contenders in the plush league traditionally has been **La Maison du Cygne** (Grand' Place 9). It remains as good as ever—and as beautiful. When passing in or out, don't forget to rub the arm of the little Everard t'Serclaes statue in the building's façade and make 3 wishes; it has dispensed good luck since A.D. 1320. Head for the little elevator and ride upstairs, where you'll find paneled walls, luxurious bottle-green banquettes, and a huge rôtisserie grill at one end; 3 sectional divisions lend a feeling of intimacy here.

L'Écailler du Palais Royal (rue Bodenbroek 18, near the Grand Sablon) is a second venture of M. Marcel Kreusch, who is doing such wonders at Villa Lorraine. This one specializes in seafood. Main ground-floor room with green plaid walls, brass sconces, ocean-toned textiles, and a restful oil painting dominating one side; 12-stool counter dominating the other. Upstairs outfitted in burnt orange, brown, and rich polished woods, swinging saloon doors, hurricane lamps, and a handsome painting of a schooner. The shellfish were Atlantic-fresh (oysters are a house pride, with good reason); our grilled Turbot with anchovy butter was one of the most succulent catches we've ever hooked. Closed Sundays and bank holidays.

Bruneau (Av. Broustin 73) is in the same general neighborhood as the previously described Dupont. Both are similar excellent practitioners of the modern arts of gastronomy. This house also features the smiling wife of the owner-chef to mentor you. Single cream-hued room with a small bar at the rear; tiered crystal chandeliers and matching sconces; tables a bit close for intimate conversation; animated atmosphere of affluent young clientele. Two stunning dishes deserve special mention: the filet of sole filled with concentric circles of rose lobster and the mousseline of *loup* topped with caviar on a palette of steamed spinach. Desserts are light, often garnished with exotic fruits; our framboise was presented dramatically surrounded by a compote of cracked ice. Cheers and laurels to the Bruneau clan! Closed Tuesday night and all Wednesday as well as from June 11 to July 18. Superb.

Chez Christopher (5 Place de la Chapelle) faces the entrance of Notre Dame chapel, just below the Grand-Sablon. A lovely restoration of the Belle Époque with blue-gray velour walls offering an attractive patchwork of oil paintings; an ornate bar with a carved-wood tabernacle; bentwood chairs carrying out the fashion trend of its tasteful decorator. The *nouvelle cuisine* also makes abundant claim to tastefulness. Main dishes linger in the $14 region with the overall bite perhaps $55 to $65 per maw. Very attractive, very fashionable, and certainly rewarding if you're having a cost-be-damned occasion. Closed Saturdays and Sundays.

In this district, **Au Vieux St.-Martin**, on the Grand-Sablon #38, is outstanding for typical Belgian fare, sausages, and hardy dishes. If you're not too hungry, go in the evening for snacks.

For elegance, the **Carlton** (boulevard de Waterloo 28) still gets our vote, although some readers recently have begun to demur. Opulently subdued atmosphere; summer garden for lunching or dining; piano lilts after dark. For gastronomes who relish big restaurants, still a reasonably sound candidate.

La Couronne (Grand' Place 28) is chichi, urbane, and expensive. The cookery, however, can be variable. Try for a window seat in summer; avoid the topmost floor always.

Brussels Restaurant (avenue Louise 319) is strong on design. We only wish the chef could do as much for us as the architect does.

Comme Chez Soi (Place Rouppe 23) rates so highly with its loyalists that we wonder at our own bad luck at this revered shrine of gastronomy. Only 12 tables in a narrow, inadequately ventilated room with a center aisle running from the glass-fronted kitchen to its bay-windowed façade of beveled crystal panes. While our spoonings of ham, salmon, and eel mousse were delectable, the specialties of beef filet with truffles and the roasted pigeon were not the cuisine upon which reputations are formed. Our waiter, not really maladroit, forgot one order totally and served our red burgundy so cool that it was undrinkable through most of the meal. Further, our dishes were presented with no more artistry than a blue-plate special in a station restaurant—at a total outlay of $120 for two! Could this candidate be an example of the emperor's new clothes? Perhaps—at least to this gimlet-eyed observer.

We offer top orchids to **La Maison du Seigneur**, 15 minutes out the Chaussée de Tervuren (#189). It is a white brick farmhouse with stables for riders; there's a bar and lounge plus a provincial L-shape dinning room. The cuisine is worthy of any *grand seigneur*—at tabs that jab close to $45 per *tête*. Closed Tuesday.

Seafood? **L'Huitrière** (20 quai aux Briques) cops the title among First-class candidates. (The aforementioned L'Écailler du Palais Royal, if you recall, is a Deluxe entry and is thus more costly.) Main-floor room wood paneled, with inset tiles and enough coffee grinders to send Messrs. Chase & Sanborn into ecstasies; less inspired but more polished upstairs dining salon for overflow traffic (of which there is always plenty). Wild fowl, grills, and other terra firma critters also available, but it would be a pity not to bid for the ocean offerings. Closed Monday; reserve ahead. So g-o-o-d! The same proprietress opened another candidate at nearby *Ganshoren* called **Au Chaudron d'Or**, which dates back to the 17th century. It's good, too, but we prefer the *alma mater* for our shell games.

If L'Huitrière is full, **François**, just a few doors away, is a formidable alternative. Our mussels (we counted 20) on an iced platter was a repast in itself. Moreover, the serving of Turbot Dugleré was so huge that it might have been hacked from a whale. The fried shrimps were a little disappointing. Also popular with locals; also not too costly; also quite recommendable.

Vincent is about as colorful as they come. It is on the narrow rue des Dominicains, just off the even narrower Petite rue des Bouchers in the most shoulder-squeezing quarter of the Old Town. Its wide street-front window is hung with beef and paved with fish. Entry via the kitchen; steamy atmosphere crowded with jocular activity. You won't fall asleep over your meal—and that, good friend, is a gilt-edged guarantee!

Le Londres (rue de l'Ecuyer 23) holds the title as Brussels' most ancient dining establishment. Bright—almost too well watt-ed—cheerful, rectangular room with yellow napery, verdant flora, mirrored walls, and red banquettes; voluminous menu that we feel is outpricing the value on the plate nowadays.

L'Eperon d'Or (rue des Eperonniers 8) specializes in cuddlesome dimensions, brass chandeliers, burgundy tones, and blue-stocking tabulations. Although our wedge of steer is a tender memory, our teeth still rattle at the overall cost. Ouch!

As for *Chinese* cooking, we had agreeable vittles at **Ming's** (rue du Grand Cerf 9–11), a 2-minute totter from the Hilton. To us it resembles a Swiss *Stubli* with Cantonese overtones. **Porte d'Or** (boulevard Adolphe Max 158), is not up to the same chopstick level in our opinion. **Le Mandarin** (rue au Beurre 21) is recommended for its Chinese-Indonesian kitchen.

The typical and delightful **bistros** along Petite rue des Bouchers are kind to budgets. Emphasize the word *Petite* when giving the address to the taxi driver. No great shakes as epicurean palaces, but pleasant bargains. At **Chez Léon's** the Moules au Vin Blanc are sufficiently good and numerous for you to "eat yourself into a coma." **Aux Armes de Bruxelles**, in this same district, fell down on its service and was only fair for cookery on our try.

In **Chez Marius en Provence** (place du Petit Sablon 1), the proprietor seemingly couldn't care less what we ate, and the prices seemed all out of proportion to our investigative eye. Another *Chez* to *Cherchez*? Okay: **Chez Stan's** whomps up championship steaks in a crumbling, darkly nostalgic tavern. Also esteemed are the pot-au-feu and the fried scampi. Two friendly waiters; paper table "cloths"; old-line mien that is simple, honest, and worthy. It's at rue des Dominicains 12. Just opposite, incidentally, **Ogenblik** does pleasant things with piscatorial creations.

Au Bon Vieux Temps (rue Marché-aux-Herbes 12) has a charming, intimate atmosphere. **De Bellemolen**, on the Ghent pike, is another romantic target. It is situated in an old mill. There's also a garden; the cookery on our try seemed lacking in culinary grist.

Game for a small expedition? An assortment of choices, varying in quality:

The famous **Atomium Restaurant** is one of the few unrazed structures from the World's Fair. Zoom by high-speed elevator to the top ball of this fabulous Tinkertoy; get your table on the lower of the 2 levels; be prepared to pay a mint. The view alone is in the megaton range. An experience not to be missed on a clear day.

Out at the hamlet of *Linkebeek,* **Le Café de la Gare** (rue de la Station 90) has a special atmosphere and quite respectable cookery. It's an adventure for Old World buffs.

Barbizon (Welriekendedreef 95) is lovely if you are looking for well-tended natural surroundings and cuisine for the gods. The salmon with watercress is the stuff of dreams, provided you snooze in season.

The colorful **Auberge du Chevalier**, at *Beersel* (7 miles from the heart of Brussels), is a small hunting-lodge-style inn adjoining a moated castle. The cuisine was below average on our incognito visit; it has fairly steep prices. Sit under the big willow on the terrace for your apéritifs, then move inside for vittles. Lovely in sunshine, dull in rain. Important: *Be sure* to get exact road directions from your hotel concierge, because it's a murderous place for any American motorist to find in this Flemish-speaking (not French-speaking) region.

L'Abreuvoir, at place St.-Job in *Uccle*, is moving up strongly. This might be a better alternative. (And if this one's full, try **Brasier** in the same village.)

The **Au Prince d'Orange** (avenue du Prince d'Orange 1, about 5 miles out toward Waterloo) employs an English-country-inn motif. Our enthusiasm for it is waning.

Le Fond'Roy at *Uccle*, 9 miles by car, gives us the impression it has skidded into a slump. Still, the setting is appealing.

Père Mouillard, in *Hoeilaart* (near the Groenendael Station), is a warmly conceived *auberge* with chillingly high tariffs. Neighboring **Pierre Romeyer** better fulfills our requirements. Meats top his list of offerings; the tabs are modest for the quality; the portions are almost massive. Worth the journey.

Dedicated budgeteers? Since we're too bottlenecked here for additional entries, please consult our annually revised paperback, *Fielding's Low-Cost Europe,* which lists scads more bargain dining spots and money-saving tips.

Night Life   In Brussels, most of the pack (not counting the 2 or 3 largest ones) are out-and-out clip joints—bare-bosom floor shows, large orchestras, predatory young ladies at the bar, and champagne at $55 to $110 per bottle—nonvintage at that. This capital, due to its heavy play by lonely businessmen, hasn't run out of the genus known as the B-girl—the type who sips tea while the sucker across the table pays $12 for her "whisky"—but it ain't what it used to be.

In short, Brussels devotes a lot of its energies to bachelorhood (temporary or otherwise), with mechanical fun designed for the outlander. Leave the bulk of your traveler's checks in the hotel, but take along at least $150 if you plan to have a whirl—because it will cost you plenty.

Chez Paul au Gaity (rue Fossé-aux-Loups 18) remains the leader in after-dark entertainment. Always-fresh décor; better than average floor show featuring fast-paced "singles" and plenty of nudity; expensive. Reserve in advance if you want a ringside table. A leading night light for many and many a moon.

Crazystars (rue Crespel 15), near the Hilton, provides a pale replica of Paris's Crazy Horse Saloon. The show is amusing and well mounted by a bevy of leggy beauties. The combo is smooth, the stereo not too loud, the air fresh, and the drinks legitimate. There's less of a variety-show quality here than you'll see at Chez Paul, and frankly, we think the pulchritude is more abundant. **Le Grand Escalier** (rue au Beurre 25) where the *grand* price tags climb a seemingly endless *escalier,* offers fairly good dining with a glittery sequins-and-feathers floorshow at 11 P.M. The 4-plate low-cost dinner is set around $30, with a so-called gastronomic menu about $45 plus wine and service. These are followed by **Show Point** (14 Place Stéphanie) for more of the same.

The **Fashion Club** (avenue Louise) is à la mode this minute with a fad-mad following. High jinks for low tabs; designed for young singles.

Golden Gate, in the Galerie Louise, swings chiefly for the upper *Crustacea* of Brussels' Café society.

Mainly for dancing? **En Plein Ciel** of the Hilton (live orchestra and dinner dancing) and the **Crocodile** of the Royal Windsor (disco music) offer the most respectable venues. **Le Vaudeville** (15 Gal. de la Réine) is another top-grade nightspot.

★ **TIP**   If your dawn comes up like thunder, Dr. Fielding can prescribe no better post-night-owl remedy than a therapeutic descent to the **Hilton** basement's splendid sauna. Soft lighting, soft music, and soft hands applied by 2 massage-specializing lovelies (a blonde or brunette, take your pick), who will gently towel you down as you emerge from the shower. Operating hours: 9 A.M. to 9 P.M. on weekdays, 9 A.M. to 7 P.M. on Saturdays, and 9 A.M. to noon on holidays; closed Christmas and, alas, New Year's Day. Women are accepted by appointment only. The saunas cost about $14 and the massages at least double.

Shopping   Wares are high here, but so is the quality. Our ★ ★ ★ ★ ★ candidates are individually noted.

Lace is the biggest bargain—and it's a racketeer's jungle. *Go alone and unheralded.*

★ ★ ★ ★ ★ **Maria Loix** (rue d'Arenberg 52–54) has been our favorite lace purveyor for more than 30 years. The Loix firm has always been a lighthouse of quality, variety, square prices, and impeccable reliability. Stunning hand-worked lace blouses for less than half U.S. prices (if you can find them in this quality); all sizes of lace-linen tablecloths (napkins to match) in a score of Brussels patterns; bridge cloths and placemats sets; wedding veils in scores of designs and delicate fingertip veils; round, square, oval, or rectangular doilies in all sizes and types of laces; fans, mantillas, butterflies, and other small gift remembrances. Warm, gentle Mme. Georgette and her son, Robert, will find something exciting for *you* in their extensive stocks. During the 3 decades that we have commended this shop, not even one single complaint from anyone has ever been made to us.

Diamonds, charms, jewels, silverware, and gifts: ★ ★ ★ ★ ★ **Wolfers Frères** (ave. Louise 82–84) is as important a Belgian sightseeing attraction as the Grand' Place or the King's Palace. You'll always be warmly welcomed to browse to your heart's content.

Crystal and glassware: Val St. Lambert is gorgeous and it costs a mint. The best outlet in the capital is ★ ★ ★ ★ ★ **Art et Sélection** (83 Marché-aux-Herbes).

Sumptuous and unusual chocolates: **Godiva** (Grand' Place 22, and several other branches) beguiles the senses while tickling one's sweet tooth. Fun, fanciful, and fabulously fattening.

Books: **Smith and Son** (Bd. Adolphe Max) stocks a large selection of hard-cover titles and more than 2000 paperbacks.

A spate of new covered galleries that shelter the walker from inclement weather have been erected. The oldest, built in 1846, is the **Galeries Saint-Hubert** near the Grand' Place. **Rue Neuve** has been closed off as a pedestrian street. Between **Innovation** (the Number One department store) and **Bon Marché** (a rather undistinguished contender), a huge shopping center called **City II** has been inaugurated. At one end of Avenue Louise you'll find **City Gardens**, which takes pride in its surrounding gardens.

Marché-aux-Puces can provide plenty of laughs if you're a bargain hunter. *Always* wrangle until your face is purple. Hours: Sat. from 10 A.M. to 6 P.M. and Sun. from 10 A.M. to 1 P.M. There's a curbside **Bird Market** on Sunday mornings in the Grand' Place.

Shopping hours: The big department stores operate full blast from 9:30 to 6. Other shops often close from 12 to 2 but remain open until 6 or 7. On Fridays almost all of the establishments in the central area remain open until 9.

Things NOT to buy: Shoes, "bargain" Swiss watches, perfume and wine (none commercially produced in the nation).

Dedicated shophounds? Space is too tight here for further listings—so consult this year's purse-size edition of *Fielding's Selective Shopping Guide to Europe for more stores,* more details, and more lore.

Other Targets

ANTWERP is one of the greatest ports on the European continent—yet it's 54 miles from the smell of salt water. The Scheldt River is the answer: 60-thousand barges and 18-thousand ocean ships tie up to the 60 miles of docks every year. In warm weather you can see much of the waterfront by boat. The 6-lane, 2000-foot-long, $62,000,000 John F. Kennedy Tunnel eases train and car traffic under the river; it forms a vital part of the E-3 highway which eventually will link Stockholm with Lisbon. Flemish is the regional language; the **Rubens mansion** (improved in honor of the 400th anniversary of the artist's birth, celebrated in 1977) is a sightseeing must, along with the **Royal Art Gallery** the "**Mad Meg**" (**Mayer van der Bergh**) **Museum**, the 9th-century-old **Steen Castle** housing the **National Maritime Museum**, and the **Plantin More-tus Museum** (patrician house with ancient printing plant); so is the magnificent statue in the Grand Place of the Roman centurion who saved the town, thus providing the legend from which the metropolis took its name. The **Zoo** includes an aquarium in the gardens, a delphinarium, a unique aviary, and a nocturama. Rather commercial atmosphere by day; nightowling that is beginning to ruffle the feathers of the municipal fathers.

There's one sight about halfway between Antwerp and the capital which most visitors miss. This is **Fort Breendonk**, one of the most infamous Nazi concentration camps in Europe. It has been preserved intact as a national museum; even the torture chambers are still there, in all their horror. Some travelers might wish to make a thorough inspection of this grim relic of a dark period of history; personally, it's too heart-tearing for us.

This center's hotel boom is finally bottoming out. Among the contemporary contenders, we'd pick the sleekly elegant, midcity **De Keyser**. It evokes a clean modern air enhanced by quality appurtenances; it is compact but well conceived. The **Eurotel** makes a splash with a good-size swimming pool and a spacious parking lot (important in this traffic-choked anthill). The dining salon is a colorful creation of wood, polished metal, and bright textiles; the café served us (albeit in pleasant surroundings) what was perhaps our most repelling ingestion ever on Belgian soil. Bedrooms are substantial but not inspired. **Crest**, about a mile out on the E-3 pike, greets motorists with several interesting tapestries in its entry hall. Airy Wellington restaurant and coffee shop; chipper Campaign Bar; 5 attractive penthouse suites; more than 300 look-alike chambers stacked in a high-rise configuration. Dedicated conventioneers will feel at home. On the same highway, the 180-room **Quality Inn** is known for its restaurant; it also features a pool and sauna. The **Antwerp Tower** and the **Empire**, both back in town, are appealing. So are the **Theatre** and the **Plaza** if you are seeking a modern mood. In the suburbs, the **Antwerp Docks**, with 80 rooms and 80 beds, has a terrible superhighway location in a complex of dunes and factories; some doubles are passable, but others are totally unrecommendable; huge family-style café on the ground floor. There's a **Novotel** in the harbor district. If you still prefer being out of the city, the totally renovated **Kasteel van Brasschaat** is a semiluxurious country hideaway 15 minutes toward Breda (Netherlands). Lovely converted estate with lakes for boating and swimming, ponds, and arcadian peace; some baronial accommodations with mirrored doors 10-feet high; other disconcerting touches of cheap plastic. Here's the weekend haven of many local G.M. executives. Don't bother with the **Dennenhof Motel** in the same vicinity. Nice outside, but horrid interior, in our opinion.

The **De Keyser Hotel** stokes up enviable cookery at its ovens. The Old Masters segment is ingratiating if you want to dine in formal surroundings. The Paint Pot provides a more casual atmosphere and lighter fare.

Among straight restaurants, **Rôtisserie Cigogne d'Alsace** (Wiegstraat 9) is the unchallenged sachem. Here *is* a charmer. Cozy 10-table, ground-floor dining room with live-trout tank, canopied display case for meats, beamed ceiling, leaded windows, and gaily flowered wallpaper; a spectacular wooden stairway leads to upstairs annex which isn't quite as attractive. Reserve in advance; open all year; top recommendation.

· Another upper-crust address is the tower perch of **Sir Anthony Van Dyck.** It is located at 16 Oude Koornmarkt ("Old Grain Market") in an assemblage of 16th-century buildings called the Vlaaikensgang. The scenery alone makes this one worthwhile, but happily, too, the gastronomy is first-rate. A towering recommendation for this pillar of local culinations.

Vateli (Kipdorprest 50) has the edge over the **Critérium** (De Keyserlei 25) —*nouvelle cuisine* at moderate prices. Good service, atmosphere, and value. The **Heineken Hoek**, on the same street, is great fun for lifting a pre-meal pint or two. Between Sept. 15 and May 15, **La Pérouse** is a luxuriously interesting novelty. It's the dining salon of the *Flandria XVI,* which is moored between these dates at the Flandria Co. dock on the Scheldt River. (In summer the boat makes daily Tourist-class shuttles between Antwerp and Flushing.) Recently refitted wooden deck; interior décor dotted with gay flowers; à la carte menu only; piano music at night; amusing in sunlight or starlight, but not advised during rain, fog, or storms. Closed Monday. The smaller *Flandria XVII* is used for private parties and charters, plus summer toots to Rotterdam. Finally, **Au Gourmet sans Chiqué** (Vestingstraat 3) offers 10 tables, an old-fashioned air, immaculate cleanliness, and an excellent 6-course menu; closed 3 weeks in summer, when Patron Louis T. Verhoeven retreats from his skillets. Pleasant.

Sunny day excursion? Try the **Hôtel du Parc**, between Antwerp and Ghent near the town of *Lokeren*. It's as famous for its food as it is for its architecture. Timber and antique atmosphere; superior cuisine and service; especially captivating on a summer day. In *Boom*, the **Linden Hof** is another veteran to keep in mind.

As for Antwerp's night life, ankle over to Market Square ("Stadswaag") and simply shop around. **L'Abbaye** reveals a sampling of naked flesh. **Sans Souci** is only a few doors away physically and not far behind spiritually. **Whisky-A-Gogo** (just off Grand' Place) is for disks and sips only. **Club 13** (rue Anneessens 13) offers a bar, piano, and singer; lonely males may have luck here finding the better class of pickups. **Nostradamus**, near the Cathedral, has about 25 seats, a bar, a pianist, and casual entertainment from time to time.

To wrap up, there are 2 or 3 joints in the Club 13 area which display photos of performers at their entrances (merely sucker bait, because there's no show), peddle stunningly expensive bad champagne, and condone the most ruthless type of B-girl. The Quartier Latin and the Harbor Area have many small cafés which cater to sailors.

ARDENNES *Bastogne*, way down in the Ardennes Forest, is now officially known as "The Nuts City." General McAuliffe's classic utterance (it was actually a ruder and more pungent word!) is something the nation can't forget. Site of the magnificent Mardasson Monument, dedicated to American troops lost in the Battle of the Bulge. Dull town but fine memorial.

If you're lingering or merely hungry, the century-old, pink-faced **Lebrun** is just about the only show in town. Ardennaise dining room; antlers and a boar's head rampant in its lounge-bar; covered tea garden with climbing plants, aviary, and aquarium. Not great. **Au Luxembourg** would be our next choice. It is located smack on Place McAuliffe.

At nearby *Noirefontaine* (look for Bouillon on the map), **L'Auberge du Moulin Hideux** has been ballyhooed by a baker's dozen of our Belgian brethren—whose only debate is whether it's a charming 13-room hotel with a superb restaurant, or vice-versa. We've oft tilted with this happy windmill and must agree with both opinions. The rose-colored house nestles in a sleepy hollow, offering homey comforts, crackling fires, open beams, and river views through cottage windows. The Lahire and Henrion families have added even more charm with a comfortable glass-lined veranda in the boughs over a brook, fresh furnishings, and a handful of new rooms, some with garden access. The gastronomy, however, remains the chief talking point. We fairly glowed from savoring the mousse of woodcock and Ardennes ham and a Ballotine de Volaille wafer thin and sprinkled with pistachio nuts; one look at the dessert trolley is enough to encourage anyone to embrace obesity for a lifetime. The prices, however, will repeal your hedonistic tendencies and return you safely to ascetic ideals. An experience to be lived.

BRUGES, a medieval city less than 1 hour from the capital, is the favorite of most Americans, including us. If you're in Belgium on Ascension Day, the world-famous Procession of the Holy Blood here should not be missed. The ancient architecture is intact; its intimate fine museums are superb; be sure to see Memling's work at the **Hospital of St. John**; the **Town Hall**, the 13th-century **Cloth Hall** and the **Carillon** are musts; so is the famous **Groeninge Museum**, of course; our favorite churches are the **Notre Dame** and the 10th-century **St. Sauveur**. Handmade lace and the wonderful little local pastries are the industries of greatest interest to the tourist. A pleasant thing to do is to reserve a seat in a little motorboat and laze at random along the canals, which are just about the most romantic settings man and Mother Nature can provide on this planet. It's a delightful town; a visit is highly recommended.

For utter beauty and enchantment of its canal-corner location, nothing here can touch the luxurious **Duc de Bourgogne**, a 9-room hostelry that also is world-famous as a restaurant. The lobby and the dining areas, literally chockablock with paintings, are lovely; the upstairs offers a colorful palette of improvements.

The pert **Holiday Inn** was developed with disarming flair from the assemblage of several ancient houses. The cunning meld of new and old is balm to the travel-weary wayfarer, who also enjoys its swimming pool, its lamp-lit dining room, the bar with medieval weapons, and the garden when the skies are fair. After this one, the **Portinari** is its closest rival in quality. Its 50 rooms, all with bath *or* shower, are neo-Scandinavian in tone; nice dining room and bar; improved cuisine; carpark; breakfast, balky service, sagging beds, and taxes included with the price of the room. The **Europ** again serves naught but the morning repast; it's rather tour-oriented. Only 2 private baths for 37 nervous occupants. **Sablon** has 55 rooms and 28 baths; main structure dates from 1772, with new wing added in '59 (1959, that is!); full or demipension required in season; oppressively old-fashioned. The **Park** is parked in Zand Square, just next to the Holiday Inn, offering 40 rooms with bath, radio, and TV-on-request. Rates are reasonable and the approach is modern. A nice compact little house that is well run. In the village of *Oostkamp* (4 miles out, on the Courtrai road), the **het Schaak** is a worthwhile stop for motorists who prefer a do-it-yourself setup to the more elaborate service of a metropolitan hostelry. The **Lodewijk van Male**, at St. Kruis (Malesteenweg 488), is a bucolic country estate with a river and park at its rear doorstep. The best of its 18 units face a parkland rather than the highway. The cuisine alone is worth a linger.

For dining spots, we've already mentioned the **Duc de Bourgogne** (Huide-vettersplaats 12), which wins honors for atmosphere. It is enchanting to the eye, satisfying to the palate, and not unduly merciless on the wallet; here's a charming lovely canalside oasis. For outright skill at the skillets despite the cost, drive out to the white brick **Weinebrugge**, a few minutes along the pike to Brussels where Owner-Chef Jacques Galens practices his magic with the "new cuisine." He really needs no practice; he's a master. The salon, with open timber beams, peeps through French windows at a bit of greenery; there's a vast open hearth dominating one end of the room; the air is refined; the presentation and service are immaculate Closed Wednesdays and Thursdays. Patrician, with price tags to match. The **Portinari** is pleasant, especially if you're a junky for potted plants; it offers excellent vittles. **Pannenhuis** (Zand-straat 2) is a converted *huis* now panning out a few accommodations and a lot of ooohs-and-aaahs for its cookery. It has the refined air of a country estate. Shoppers like the tempting pâtisserie called **Deleu's** (on market square), which comes up with cold buffet, sandwiches, and light refreshments. There's one country restaurant of unusual aspect which seems to have special appeal to hungry Americans—**By Lamme Goedzak** at *Damme*. Extensive decorative talents were employed in the restoration of these fourteenth-century cellars and this ancient building. The result is a handsome rural tavern, with steaks the specialty. Take route N-67 toward Knokke for 5 miles from the center of Bruges. When you see the "Bezoekt Damme" sign, turn right and cross the bridge into the village, where you'll find this hard-to-locate restaurant; return via the **Bruges–Sluis** canal for more direct motoring and a change of scenery. Closed at odd times, so be sure to make advance reservations. Urbane, highly priced, and pleasant. At *Oostkerke*, a mile away, the **Siphon** pumps up gushers of foodstuffs for a reasonable flow of francs. Old Flemish surroundings; open rôtisserie with crackling meats; waterway specialty of eel in a cream sauce (a bonanza, if you enjoy such dishes). A perfect stop on the economy circuit.

A delightful fair-weather alternative is **Goedendag** in *Lissewege*, 6½ miles from Bruges. White cottage-like structure on Hoogstraat; bar at entrance; large open copper grill; eye-appealing food displays; courteous staff, cuisine positively delicious; tall tariffs. The **Romboudt** and the **Oosthoek**, both within a bivalve's squirt, are also attractive, but they lack that final touch of élan that made us fall for Goedendag.

DAMME   Please refer to "Bruges."

GHENT   now takes a second place to Bruges—at least in our oft-contested opinion. Culture, beauty, and charm abound, of course, and most of the finest edifices are now freshly steam-cleaned, but so many commercial aspects have crept in that much of its color seems to have evaporated. Local chums insist that dedicated antiquarians will be rewarded more profoundly here by ardent searching than by cursory rubbernecking in the more obvious targets.

For accommodation, the clean-lined, modernistic **Europa** wins the day. Moreover, its canalside situation in a residential district near St.-Pieters Station affords much more P & Q than any of the midcity turnstiles. Two-tone brick and glass exterior; broad window-wrapped lounge with warming Persian carpets; ingratiating colonial restaurant; stained glass counterpointing the turn-of-the-century bar. Definitely recommended when the sojourn isn't too long. **Holiday Inn** presented its U. S. passport-to-comfort recently. It is a bit out of the center, beside the turnpike exit from Brussels. While we can recommend the physical plant, we'd suggest that you take your vittles elsewhere. Perhaps at the **Cour St.-Georges** which is suggested only for its Old World restaurant. The hotel itself was founded in A.D. 1228—and when you see it you'll believe it. The **Ascona** tries to be modern, but we found it a bit weary from the effort. The **Carlton** is a drive-inn owned by the Terminus (see below). Not much public space, but passable for pit-stoppers to whom sleep is the main concern. The **Park** unfolds its withered vines to reveal 37 bedrooms. Noisy, midintersection location; basic, in a traditionally moth-eaten way. The station-sited **Terminus** is even more exquisite. Ugh!

For mealtiming, the **Horse Shoe** (Lievekaai 8), in a rustic setting, rings the peg with regularity, except for 30 days beginning July 20 when it's totally unshod and shuttered. Turbot with oysters a house specialty, as is pheasant, but both only in season. Be sure to reserve at this tiny paddock. Next (are you set for a spelling lesson?) our choice is **'t Patijntje**, located at Gordunakaai 94. If you stumble at this mouthful (who doesn't?), retreat to the **Cigogne d'Alsace** at Koningin Astridlaan 155.

KNOKKE-HEIST's   **Sofitel La Réserve** is one of the leading resort hotels in the nation. Situated on the shores of a little lake 200 yards from the sea, it directly faces the Casino. Beautiful interior; 4 tennis courts; swimming pool; fitness center and health clinic to be added; general atmosphere tends toward elegance. **Aquilon** wins orchids for the finest independent kitchen in the region. The prices, not incidentally, are at the high-tide level. The *haute cuisine* is an extra strong point here. Highly recommended.

LIÈGE,   close to the German border, is third in size among Belgian metropoli. Embraced by the Meuse basin, which long ago inspired the masters of Mosan art, today it has become a student center and a springboard to the Ardennes. At night, be sure to see the "Forms and Light" created by reflections of a 175-foot mobile gleaming in the glass face of the Palais des Congrès and in the shimmering surface of the River Meuse. The legendary FN-Browning small arms plant, plus 20 smaller but fine competitors (obtain entrance to some through the local Tourist Office) headquarters here. It has been an armament hub since the Middle Ages. The panorama from the Cointe is particularly worth enjoying. The **Batte Sunday Market** is *formidable* for hagglers and adventurers; go before noon.

An American-born, waterfront **Holiday Inn** (200 units plus heated pool) caters pretty heavily to conference goers since it is located so near to the congress hall. We personally prefer the newer **Ramada Inn** (100 air-conditioned rooms; good cookery), which greatly resembles its sister operation in the capital. The 100-chamber **Post House** is a motel with such added attractions as a pool, a grill, and meeting facilities. The first 2 U.S. imports come on very strong for comfort, efficiency, and convenience. Both are fine additions.

De la Couronne, hard by the station, draws a lot of business clientele. It has been vastly improved, but *still* only rates so-so on our score sheet.

For dining pleasure, **Le Vieux Liège**, sometimes called Maison Havart (41 quai de la Goffe), muses nostalgically on the banks of the Meuse. Strikingly handsome sixteenth-century structure of brick and cross-hatched timbers; 2 floors with candles, brass chandeliers, flowers, tilework, and copperware; extremely inviting rustic milieu; reasonably good cookery which can develop the chills while being run up and down that busy staircase. Costly. **Chêne Madame,** out of the center in Rognac Wood, is an ideal setting for game in the autumn. Other preparations are blue-ribbon too—in a price range that may make you wonder just who's being hunted. We hear praise for the **Orchidée Blanche** and **Chez Septime,** but we've missed both, darn it.

LISSEWEGE   Refer to "Bruges."

NOIREFONTAINE   Refer to "Ardennes."

OOSTKAMP and OOSTKERKE   These are under "Bruges."

OSTEND,   very maritime in feeling, is one of Belgium's most famous seacoast resorts and seafood shrines (one of the very best we've found in the North). It is the summer retreat of thousands of bathers who enjoy its golden sands. On the scenic, speedy superhighway from Brussels, you can stop at Bruges and Ghent, and then breeze up here in practically nothing flat. As previously stated, the Kursaal is among the world's handsomest gambling casinos. Zeebrugge and Knokke-Heist are just up the pike.

For overnighting, everyone now seems to head from the ferry landing straight over to the spanking-fresh **Melinda**. Although it has only 40 units with bath, it is prime for this little port. The restored **Palais des Thermes**, a big seafront bath establishment, is City-owned and privately operated. Several other hotels, among them the 30-room **Bero**, the **Die Prince**, **Strand** and **Prado** as well as the 50-room **Riff** are challengers which provide a cheerful flair, otherwise rare on the coast. In the city, the **Imperial** offers a degree of comfort; rooms ending with "0", "1" or "2" have sea view. The **Ter Streep** ("at the stripe," or the line where the sea stopped centuries ago) copies the Hilton idea of innkeeping down to a modest T. The rebuilt **Westminster**, as well as the **Telstar**, are more "plain," to put it charitably.

When hunger triggers thoughts of pots and pans, we highly recommend that you try this modest house before seeking out fancier digs. **Belgica** is 1 of the perhaps 30 harborfront candidates fighting tooth-and-fin for attention. There's no décor to speak of—but oh, my, what delicious things swim out of that tiny little kitchen! The sole is extraordinary and always sea-fresh. No tricks with fancy recipes; honest fare we are confident you will never forget; hardworking ownership by M. Rottier. Just drive along the port frontage until you come to this house, stop, enter, and prepare yourself for an Atlantic-size treat. Odds are 5 to 1 that you won't be disappointed! Although favorable comments have reached us about the rivaling **Petit Breton**, **Le Vigneron**, **Le Périgord**, **Charles V**, **Lusitania**, and **Prince Albert**, we know where WE'RE going for the next 164 visits to this community.

At *Zeebrugge*, **Le Chalut**, peering at fisherman's wharf through broad windows, is fashionable these days for lunch or dinner. The rich tariffs don't do anything to deny it, either. Waiters in middy blouses; charts on walls; ocean-size choice of briny critters. Our Turbot was as fluffy as a Rinso ad; the muscular tab for a modest lunch took us to the cleaners, too. This one's a question of net worth *vs.* net wares.

Denmark

Don't miss it! Of the 100-odd foreign lands we've visited, Denmark is closest to a 3-ring circus—and closest, too, to our travel hearts.

This mighty midget has something no other nation can quite duplicate. Nothing is bigger, deeper, taller, wider, more spectacular, more rugged, or more awe-inspiring here than anywhere else. Yet for delight and enchantment for the U.S. traveler on holiday, we think that it stands alone, head and shoulders above the rest of the handsome pack.

There are 3 secrets to this extraordinary charm. First is the serene beauty of its rural countryside—cool green forests, tranquil sunny fields, crazy thatched cottages in brilliant whites or soft pastels, endless miles of tidy, eye-soothing scenery straight from a calendar picture. Bisected by running brooks, carpeted with flowers, and dotted with ancient castles on its hilltops, the rolling terrain has a sweet and happy quality of its own.

Second is its gaiety and its polish. Unlike more serious-minded Sweden, more isolated Norway, or more somber Finland, Denmark is so cosmopolitan that it takes its pleasures in a carefree, sophisticated, and urbane way. Paris has traditionally been the amusement and dining capital of Europe; in miniature, Copenhagen offers as much (or possibly more!) brightness and fun.

Third—most important—is its people. Because they laugh at our jokes, look at life with our eyes, share the same robust love for food, drink, sex, speed, gadgets, music, painting, and the other lively arts, Danes are temperamentally closer to Americans than any other Continentals. They are fonder of us than of any other visitors, and their welcome proves it.

This kinship of humor is particularly important. Don't take your *Hamlet* too seriously—because if there's a single Melancholy Dane left, we haven't met him. The practical joke is their special delight—as long as it's harmless. Nothing gives them (or the visitor) more pleasure than a good belly laugh. They're the Pucks of Scandinavia.

Cleanliness is a national fetish. Cockroaches? Bedbugs? Silverfish? Lice? We'll buy you a snaps for every one you find in your hotel or restaurant in Denmark.

Sightseeing Of the attractions in Copenhagen, **Tivoli**, which is more than 130 years young, should be your priority stop. It's incomparable: Central Park, the Botanical Gardens, the Atlantic City Boardwalk, the Flower Show, and a tiny European-style Disneyland rolled into one. The setting and décor are magnificent; the location is smack in the center of Copenhagen. Admission varies between $1.30 and $1.50 depending upon the time of day; prices are halved for children. For this small change you can hear a 54-piece symphony orchestra and Europe's greatest soloists in the stunning Concert Hall. At midnight on certain evenings there are marvelous fireworks; you'll be bowled over by their originality and beauty. Visiting Copenhagen without seeing Tivoli is like visiting Manhattan without seeing Times Square and Rockefeller Center. *Open May 1 to mid-September.*

Behind Tivoli is the renowned **Glyptothek**, outstanding art galleries built, believe it or not, on millions of mugs of beer. Many years ago, the public-spirited Carlsberg brewery endowed a National Foundation for development and furtherance of Danish painting, sculpture, literature, and fine art. Glyptothek is one of the results, and it is a joy to the soul. The totally renewed **National Museum of Fine Arts** is proudly showing its prizes now. It's a thing of beauty. The **Zoological Museum** and the **Music Historical Museum** also tune in on tourists.

The **Little Mermaid**, Denmark's most beloved and most photographed lassie, who had her 65th birthday in '78, looks as fresh, sweet, and charming as she did when the Carlsberg brewery commissioned Edward Eriksen to sculpt her in 1913. She sits and muses at Langelinie Quay, in the port area.

Then, if your taste runs to it, there's **Rosenborg Palace**, with crown jewels and private collections of art, clothing, furniture, and paraphernalia used by Danish kings through many centuries.

And don't forget the **Zoo**, one of the world's best, with more than 700 species of wild animals on 30 well-planned acres of choice ground. This is one of the highest points in Copenhagen; from the big platform you can see Sweden on a clear day. Visited by more than 1½-million people per year; good restaurants; lots of fun.

Another *must* is a **Danish bath**. We don't care where you've been or who has scrubbed you; you've never had anything like it. The once-famous Copenhagen Baths (Badeanstalten København, Studiestraede 63) is now a washed-out copy of its earlier glory, in our view, so today we recommend the Kommunes Varmbadeanstalter (Borgergade 12). The saunas in the Royal Hotel (21st floor), the Sheraton, and Hotel Scandinavia offer fewer facilities in more chic surroundings. At each you will be relieved of any final droplets of perpiration when you are presented with the whopping bill. Long working hours at all three (with the last open even on Sundays); sparklingly clean cubicles and kind personal attention; always be sure to call first for an appointment, because they are much smaller.

At least 8 metropolitan and 5 suburban or rural **sightseeing tours** are now sponsored and operated by all the top travel agencies. Within the capital, their durations vary from 1½ to 2¾ hours, their prices range from $6.50 to twice as much, and the majority are offered during the warmer months only. Among the most popular examples are the Royal Tour (Changing of the Guard cere-mony, the Crown Jewels, Christiansborg Palace, etc.), the World of Tomorrow Tour (Denmark's social institutions in action in everyday life, from kindergart-ens to schools to homes for the aged), and the Industrial Art Tour (visits to the Georg Jensen silversmithy, the porcelain factories, Den Permanente, etc.). The provincial excursions strike out for points as distant as Odense. Starting point for all is the statue of the Lure Horn Blowers in Town Hall Square. For specific dates and details consult the nearest branch of the Danish Tourist Board—or, when you are in the capital, check with the Information Office at Banegårdspladsen 2. Once on the hoof, don't forget to wear your most com-fortable shoes.

For covering Copenhagen by boat, Copenhagen at night, the Carlsberg or Tuborg breweries, North or South Zealand (Zealand is also known as Seeland or Sjaelland), or a ½-dozen other local options, check with The Information Office.

Finally, **hydrofoil boats** now whisk commuters or sightseers between Copenhagen and Malmö (Sweden) in 35 minutes. Hourly departures; informa-tion and tickets from your hotel porter.

In the suburbs of Copenhagen, the **North Zealand circuit** is particularly recommended. *Pièce de résistance* here, of course, is Hamlet's Castle (known to the Danes as **Kronborg Castle**) at **Elsinore**. You'll also see **Frederiksborg Castle**, lovely little lakes and forests, stork nests, fairy-tale cottages in warm pastels, and all sorts of intriguing things.

Louisiana, one of the nation's most modern art galleries, is also north of the capital—20 miles, to be exact, on a private estate at Humlebaek. This creation of philanthropic Knud W. Jensen was opened as a noncommercial locus (de-spite the entrance fee) for the best in Danish and international avant-garde paintings, sculpture, graphic arts, crafts, and design. Now it has incorporated a concert hall, taking its bows several times a year with excellent top-line performers. Everything possible has been done to maintain an atmosphere of natural beauty and of privacy; there are no petty regulations and no uniformed guards; its coffee shop will nourish your mortal coil. At the back of the building there is even a playland for youngsters. A delight to the eyes, to the ears, and to the spirit.

No late June or early July visitor should dream of missing the world-famous **Viking Plays** at the "Viking Town" of **Frederikssund**, 24 miles northwest of Copenhagen. Here is what might be called the Scandinavian Oberammergau, minus religious aspects and plus Hellzapoppin'. All the actors—150 to 200 persons—are townsfolk with either a lot or a little ham in their souls. One universal rule is that they must let their beards grow (though only for the male parts, we must confess). The play takes place in the open air, on a very beautiful stage. The big fighting scenes always give the audience the best thrill (castles are burned down, scoundrels are murdered, and the good always seem to survive). After the performance, everybody gathers in Valhalla, a Viking Guild Hall, where for $9.50 roast chicken and beer are offered and a group of Vikings entertain in various languages. Other Viking pageants are active at *Jels-Rø dding* near Jelling. Again, turn to the Danish Tourist Board for full information.

For a 2- or 3-day ramble by motor coach through the untrammeled charms of rural Denmark, the famous **Fairytale Tours** are an institution. Thousands of Americans have already enjoyed their leisurely progress from Copenhagen through Funen to North Jutland. First-class all the way; English-speaking guide; Tuesday, Wednesday, Friday, and Sunday departures from mid-May to mid-September. There's a 5-day version, which utilizes bus and ferry, and a 2-day Jutland loop by private car; many rushed travelers enjoy the 1-day coach run to Odense on the Hans Christian Andersen Tour. If you can make it over to *Jelling* (near Vejle), be sure to look at Denmark's "birth certificate"—the rune stone erected by Harald Bluetooth in A.D. 940 and dedicated to the ancestors of the present sovereigns. This is also the oldest pictorial representation of Christ as a Viking. The chapel cemetery goes back even further; very recently the floor of the church was excavated and two skeletons surrounded by jewels were found. It was concluded that they were King Gorm and Queen Thyra. There's a small *Kro* (tavern) next to the churchyard for a meal or a coffee break en route.

The spot-of-spots for us, however, is missed by the Fairytale Tour. This is enchanting little *Aerøskøbing*, capital of the tiny island of Aerø, where the houses resemble frosting on a wedding cake, the key to the jail hangs by the door so that everyone may use it, and the fabulous Ships-In-Bottles Museum (also displaying pipes and every Danish stamp ever printed) would make even the Sphinx break into a grin. There are 3 modest hotels in which to lay your noggin. Lately the islanders have been encouraging a plan to make Aerø the "Hong Kong of the North"—a tax-free zone to woo more visitors and shoppers. Some houses and boats now fly their own local flag. Who knows? Before long there may be a Home Rule movement afoot in Lilliput! In earlier years, never in our European travel lives had any village so captivated our hearts. During the principal touristic season, however, the vastly improved train and ferry connections have lured such masses and masses of conducted tours that, while its quaintness has been preserved by governmental edict, the edge of its unique charms has been dulled by this stampede.

Offbeat attractions? (1) For the young-in-heart of any age, a trip to **Legoland** at *Billund* is an Eldorado of vacation fun. The famous Lego toy enterprise has created a miniature wonderland on some 40 thousand square yards of Tiny Tim-like terrain. There are more than 600 buildings, ships, and other structures, surrounded by canals, electric trains, and functioning replicas of urban life; at nightfall, 30-thousand windows light up in the Oz-like dream. As if this weren't enough, there's a real driving school for tots, utilizing electric automobiles and monitored by control towers and traffic lights, and a guiding voice tells the kiddie when he's infracted a law. The streets resemble a shrunken version of your own suburbia. There's a picnic campsite with a feathered Indian chief to oversee the grilling of hot dogs and hamburgers. You'll also find 2 beautiful restaurants—a cafeteria for inexpensive meals or a posh, deep-carpeted dining room. Spotted in the arcade of fine modern buildings adjoining the outdoor exhibits is one of the most entertaining puppet theaters we've ever giggled through. Concurrently, young ladies are enchanted by the collection of 30 doll houses containing authentic antique specimens dating from around 1580 to 1900. In our own childlike excitement, we might have forgotten some other joyful thriller—but go for yourself and see. Open every day from May 1 to September 21 from 10 A.M. to 10 P.M.; $2.60 entrance for grown-ups and half as much for children. By car from Copenhagen it takes about 4½ hours. SAS has put on 4 flights per day in either direction; air taxis make the journey in about an hour (slightly longer than the big birds). The airport is almost beside the Legoland doorstep, so local transportation is no problem. Across the road, the toymakers operate a stunning motel named (appropriately) **Vis-a-Vis**, with attractive dining facilities, making accommodation almost as easy as Little Jack Horner's pie. (P.S. to Mom and Pop: Any Lego toy on display can be ordered here and shipped to the little ones for birthdays, Christmas, or when you wish; the museum-piece dolls can't.) Don't miss it. (2) While in this region, take the roaring side trip to **Vejle Zoo's Lion Park** at *Givskud.* You can stalk around in your own car on an escorted 30-minute photo-safari where 33 tawny cats will wink right in your shutter. The jungle is open daily in summer from 10 A.M. to shortly before sunset. The admission fee is $2.70. (3) Then there are the 1000 sixteenth-century skeletons at the **Cistercian Abbey of Øm**, near Rye (Aarhus is the closest terminal. Doctors may find this engaging because the bones were lifted from the hospital churchyard, providing a link with ancient pathology. Better leave your dog in the car.) (4) Bundgaard's startling statuary in the depths of a chalk mine (ask directions in Rebild for the **Thingbaek Kalkmine**, just off main Highway #10 about 5 minutes north, toward Aalborg).

☑ **BELIEVE IT OR NOT**   You should raise your hat to any Danish friend you see on the street. Men doff their hats to men—a national custom.

When you meet a Danish friend after he has entertained you or been kind to you, your first words should not be "Hello!" or "How are you?" Rigid good manners dictate that your greeting be "Tak for sidst!"—"Thanks for the last time we were together!" As the thankingest people in the world, they also have variations of "Tak" ("Thanks!") for meals, tea, coffee, drinks, the day, the fun, the ride, and just about every human act.

It's unheard of to refuse a Skål. Even if you don't drink, go through the ceremony. Be sure to touch the glass to your lips.

Many Danish women have a taste for cigars and handle them with finesse. Denmark is the only land in Europe which celebrates the Fourth of July on a gigantic scale. At Rebild, a forest-and-heather area, more than 50-thousand U.S.-loving Danes and Danish-Americans gather to hear distinguished speakers and to watch the huge fireworks display at Aalborg. If you're within shooting distance of any part of Scandinavia around this time, don't miss it!

If you'll stand outside Au Coq d'Or restaurant way out toward the curb on H. C. Andersen's boulevard and gaze upward to a famous statue atop a nearby building, you'll share a naughty sight from the far edge of this corner which for years has been a source of merriment to Copenhageners.

☑ **TRANSPORTATION Taxis** Better than they were, but still not plentiful when it rains or at theater time. Usually you must get them by telephone; your hotel porter, or anyone in the store or restaurant you are in will do it for you.

A taxi ride is pretty costly, but it includes an automatic full tip. Even though many drivers now speak English, it's wise to jot down your destination in advance. As a group they're among the most gracious hackies in the world.

Trains and Ferries Pride of the Danes are the *Lyntog,* crack trains which fan out from Copenhagen to the major cities. The *Englaenderen* ("Englishman") Boat Special, fastest and best of all, runs from the capital to Esbjerg (port for England) and back. The service and facilities are excellent—but trains are as crowded as Gimbel's basement, so make your reservations ahead of time. Fares are still a bargain. Incidentally, the overnight ferry between Esbjerg and the British coast was extremely comfortable on our recent voyage.

Most of your local excursions, however, will be made by boat, car or bus; these are the short-hop conveyances in Denmark.

The "Bird Line" project—called "Bee Line" by locals—is the rail-and-superhighway seam from Copenhagen to the southern tip of the archipelago. A train-and-car-ferry handles the 1-hour, 11-mile gusset between Denmark and the West German island of Fehmarn. Smart drivers get advance reservations for their auto, giving them priority when the pickaback train ferries are loaded. From here, a bridge joins the mainland—and you're off running!

The 500 islands of this maritime nation are linked by the cleanest, most efficient, most attractive ferries (many with space for cars) that we have ever encountered. You can also ride the rails, bus routes, or ferry lanes at reduced prices. The "Rover" ticket, a 5-day "Take Five" package of unlimited gamboling, cost about $85 for First-class or close to $65 for Second-class travels. While this ducat is obtainable only in the U. K., a Rover ticket that is good for use during any 5 days in a 17-day span is issued within Denmark; it sells for around $100 in First-class and close to $75 in Second. Both types are splendid bargains for insatiable adventurers.

☑ **FOOD** In France and Belgium the food is most often extraordinary; at the land of the Danes it's most often incomparable. Copenhagen establishments are distinctive as a group and just as memorable as individual beauty spots. Once you've Dined Denmark, you won't easily forget it.

One Danish quirk is their dislike of piquant or sour comestibles. Pickles, garlic, and pungent spices are almost entirely ignored by their cooks. Yet their culinary magic is so great that you'll hardly ever miss them.

This nation, as the rest of Scandinavia, has been hard hit by too much fishing in its coastal waters. For our remarks on how this debacle has affected the herring catch, please see the "Food" section in our Swedish chapter.

As an obvious generality, we feel safe in saying that throughtout this little country restaurants are nearly always good, even the hotdog stands—but they're expensive.

☑ **DRINKS**   Beer, beer, beer—wonderful, rich, foaming beer, everywhere you turn. Danes are among the greatest beer drinkers on earth. In '70, Carlsberg and Tuborg put their heads together in one of the best marriages conceivable. Though now merged commercially, they continue to produce their own delightful formulae. Order either— or both—and you'll see why we consider these the most soothing and delicious brews ever made. The products of the smaller Wiibroe Brewery up in Elsinore are also fine. If you don't like the stronger "Export" (Gold or Silver Cap) grade, there are at least 7 or 8 types to choose from; the dry, pale "Green" Tuborg or "Hof" Carlsberg (never exported) and the Carlsberg bock-style are perennial favorites. Incidentally, you have an open invitation to visit either of these celebrated Copenhagen landmarks; each is twice as big as Radio City, and each offers copious free samples.

Akvavit (snaps) is the national "hard" drink. King of akvavits is the "Aalborg" brand, surpassing all Swedish and Norwegian types. It looks like water, smells like cough medicine, tastes like anisette, and kicks like a broadside of 16-inch naval guns. It's terrific. Drink it *ice-cold* and chase it with beer, as the Danes do—but treat it with proper respect.

Ever try Greenland Sermeq Vodka? Every drop of water in it has been brought to his distillery from the inland ice cap of this island to be blended with alcohol and other ingredients. The glacial ice from which it originates remains as pure as the frozen droplets in the snowflakes that fell in prehistoric times. Among its infusions are rare Arctic plants, handpicked by Greenlanders, which give it its delicate and intriguing taste touch. Not at all incidentally, it makes the most delicious Bloody Mary we have ever tasted. This has met with such enormous success that the Bestle company inaugurated Greenland Kwan Akvavit, which incorporates the same multimillenniums'-old water and other historically curative herbs from this island to produce a more gentle and mild savor than that of the caraway and cumin that are normally employed. Both are unique —and most definitely worth a try.

Peter Heering, formerly called Cherry Heering, is marvelous. Of all the fine liqueurs made today, this ruby elixir happens to be our personal favorite of favorites. It has been a Danish national institution since the first Peter Heering mixed the magic formula in 1818. On only 1 of the country's 500 islands—Zealand—can the dark, rich cherries with their special flavor be found. Debonair cosmopolites Peter Heering IV and Peter Heering V, the present entrepreneurs, ably and skillfully carry on the strict traditions of the business. It is not a cherry cordial, not a cherry drink—but a formula from the Family Heering, unique and delightful. Be sure it's served cold, cold, COLD from the refrigerator. You might also enjoy this company's new mild and golden Christianshavner Snaps, which, unlike other akvavits, is recommended for serving at only a moderately chilly temperature rather than iceberg gelid.

A superduper Danish liqueur specialty has been produced for generations from choice sun-ripened black currants infused with fine West Indian rums. The generic name is "Solbaerrom"—and the brand to be certain to ask for is Bestle. Here's a delectable accompaniment to cheese courses, hot pancakes, apple dumplings, and other sweets. Serve it chilled—and be sure it's Bestle's!

Imported Scotch, rye, bourbon, vodka, and gin are all available—with rum, rye, and bourbon only in the more popular tourist places, because Danes seldom drink them. Because of the brutal taxes, bottled spirits and wines cost considerably more than we pay at home. At bars, the prices alone are enough to produce a mile-wide hangover.

Skål. This is one of the friendliest, most gracious national customs in the world. In Denmark and in all of Scandinavia it is faithfully followed; good manners dictate that you become familiar with the ceremony.

It's a toast, of course—and the rules are rigid. Here's what you do: Wait until somebody gives the signal. Then raise your glass, look the recipient in the eye, nod, and say loudly "Skål" (pronounced "skawl"). Drink bottoms up, never permitting your eyes to waver from the eyes of the recipient. When you finish, raise your glass again and bow slightly; only then can your fixed gaze be lowered.

If you are host, you must "Skål" each of your guests individually at some point during the meal; a guest may "Skål" anyone at any time at any part of the table, with 2 exceptions—the hostess (throughout Scandinavia) and the host (Norway and Sweden). In Denmark you may salute the host with this gesture, because the Danes are less formal than their Nordic brothers, but it is horribly bad manners everywhere to salute the lady. If the party were a large one, she'd be drunk in 10 minutes.

No custom is more heartwarming to the visiting stranger.

☑ **TIPPING**   The best-organized system in Europe. In restaurants the tip is automatically extracted (an extra penny, for example, is often added to the price of a glass of beer). Workers' salaries are so high that the tipping custom virtually has vanished. (Others insist it was removed because it did not insure equal pay for equal work while another segment of society claims it was abandoned because it was considered degrading for service people to depend on the discretion of their clients for their livelihoods. The truth possibly lies equidistant from all of these points.) In dining places any *small* gratuity is entirely at your option, but is generally given *only* if the service has been exceptionally attentive. The same applies for the concierge, floor waiter, and maid; they no longer browbeat the patron, but you might like to leave peanut handouts now and then. The baggage porter gets about 25¢ per suitcase when checking in or on departure, which is included on your bill (but a small additional coin is always appreciated). Taxi drivers are *not* tipped.

One happy thing: You won't find the average Dane with his hand out. Whether you tip him or not, you'll get a warm smile and expert help.

☑ **LOCAL RACKETS** Denmark is a land of honorable, honest people. Of course, the usual flim flams exist among the venally inclined, but their counterparts are common to humanity's heritage everywhere.

☑ **INFORMATION CENTERS** Denmark gives tourists the biggest, heartiest welcome in the continent.

The **Danish Tourist Board** (Danmarks Turistråd), at Banegårdspladsen 2, considered by many to be the most efficient official bureau in tourism today, aids pilgrims by selecting and registering the best of thousands of private homes it has inspected in Copenhagen. Requirements are rigid: Cleanliness, comfort, a telephone, and a separate entrance. If you can't get a hotel reservation in the capital, try the city's Tourist Association (Central Railway Station Kiosk "P") _after_ you arrive. To avoid competition with your travel agent, it will not handle mail reservations—but it guarantees absolutely that you won't be propping up your tired tootsies on a bench in Mutual Park when you climb off that plane or train in Copenhagen. SAS proffers the very same service at Kastrup Airport. These are inexpensive, simple but excellent accommodations.

Erik Palsgaard is the National Tourist Chief. With the experienced help of Director Jørgen Helweg, this network of 15 foreign branches ticks as smoothly as a 21-jewel watch. Incidentally, this organization operates a Complaint Bureau at the headquarters. Since it opened, 90% of the squawks from visitors, no matter how outlandish, have been settled to the satisfaction of these travelers. See any of these goodhearted, good-natured executives if special problems should arise, because they're all there to help you in their very best ways. The 160 domestic offices are autonomous and supply information to tourists as well.

The **Danish Tourist Board** branch in New York is at 75 Rockefeller Plaza, N.Y. 10019; its Director is Steen Løvschal. Your inquiries about his beloved country, whether by letter or in person, are welcomed.

Students seeking inexpensive shelter should write the **Herbergsringen** (Youths Hostels Association), Vesterbrogade 35, DK-1620 Copenhagen V, for knapsacks full of tips. The **Danish Tourist Board** in New York and **Tourist Information** in Copenhagen also are fonts of aid; so is **Use It** at Magstraede 14, DK-1204 Copenhagen K.

CITIES

COPENHAGEN, the 800-year-old city of 7 mayors, _is_ metropolitan Denmark. Pronounce it to rhyme with "Haig & Haig," not "jog" or "bog"; the latter is strictly the German way. More than ¼ of the 5 million national population live and work here. Government, industry, the international airport, the best hotels, restaurants, shops, and amusements are all here. So is one of the finest zoos in Europe. So, too, is the Princess of the harbor, the adored Little Mermaid. You simply _can't_ go to Denmark without seeing this charming, gracious capital.

COPENHAGEN HOTELS Quick Reference Table

Price categories by national (not U.S.) standards.

EXPENSIVE:

d'Angleterre Kongens Nytorv 34. Tel. 120095; Telex 15877; 144 rooms. P. 93
Plaza H. Bernstorffsgade 4. Tel. 149262; Telex 15330; 106 rooms. P. 93

UPPER MODERATE:

Kong Frederik V. Voldgade 25. Tel. 125902; Telex 19702; 127 rooms. P. 94
Opera Tordenskjoldsgade 15. Tel. 121519; Telex 15812; 61 rooms. P. 97
Palace Raadhuspladsen 57. Tel. 144050; Telex 19693; 159 rooms. P. 94
Royal Hammerichsgade 1. Tel. 141412; Telex 27155; 300 rooms. P. 93
Scandinavia Amager Boulevard 70. Tel. 112324; Telex 31330; 537 rooms. P. 93
Sheraton Vester Søgade 6. Tel. 143535; Telex 27450; 474 rooms. P. 95

MODERATE:

Admiral Toldbogade 24. Tel. 118282; Telex 15941; 366 rooms. P. 96
Alexandra H.C. Andersens Bd. 8. Tel. 142200; 65 rooms. P. 96
Astoria Banegardspladsen 4. Tel. 141419; Telex 16319; 90 rooms. P. 96
Codan Sankt Annae Plads 21. Tel. 133400; Telex 15815; 133 rooms. P. 94
Excelsior Colbjørnsensgade 4. Tel. 245085; Telex 15343; 53 rooms. P. 97
Grand Vesterbrogade 9. Tel. 313600; Telex 15343; 108 rooms. P. 97
Imperial Vester Farimagsgade 9. Tel. 128000; Telex 15556; 176 rooms. P. 95
Mercur Vester Farimagsgade 17. Tel. 125711; Telex 19767; 110 rooms. P. 95
71 Nyhavn H. Nyhavn 71. Tel. 118585; Telex 27558; 81 rooms. P. 95
Penta H.C. Andersens Bd. 50. Tel. 126868; Telex 15700; 203 rooms. P. 95
Richmond Vester Farimagsgade 33. Tel. 123366; Telex 19767; 133 rooms. P. 96
Tre Falke H. Falkoner Alle 9. Tel. 198001; Telex 15550; 162 rooms. P. 94
Vestersøhus Vester Søgade 58. Tel. 113870; 59 rooms. P. 97

LOWER MODERATE:

Ascot Studiestraede 57. Tel. 126000; Telex 15730; 57 rooms. P. 97

AIRPORT:

Arthur Frommer Nørre Søgade 11. Tel. 111212; Telex 16512; 53 rooms. P. 97
Bel Air Løjtegardsvej 99. Tel. 513033; Telex 31240; 215 rooms. P. 97
Danhotel Kastruplundgade 15. Tel. 511400; Telex 31111; 272 rooms. P. 97
Globetrotter Engvej 171. Tel. 551433; Telex 31222; 156 rooms. P. 97

ENVIRONS:

Frederiksdal Frederiksdal 360. Tel. 854333; 57 rooms. P. 98
Hvide Hus Strandvejen 111 (Køge). Tel. 03653690; Telex 43501. 130 rooms. P. 98
Marienlyst Helsingor 3000. Tel. 211801; Telex 41116. 160 rooms. P. 97
Marina Vedbaek Strandvej 391. Tel. 02891711; Telex 37217; 106 rooms. P. 98
StoreKro H. Slotsgade 6 (Fredensborg). Tel. 03280047; 38 rooms. P. 98
Trouville Kystvej 20 (Hornbaek). Tel. 03202200; 50 rooms. P. 98
Vinhuset S. Pederskirke Plads 1 (Naestved). Tel. 03720807; 40 rooms. P. 98

Hotels In general, the hotels are admirable—spotless, comfortable—and nearly always offer delicious food. Service is usually cordial, but hoteliers (not unlike their colleagues in other lands) are plagued by staff limitations and untrained personnel. (Overnight shoeshines, as one example, are gone forever, so don't put them in the corridor at bedtime.) _Without meals, but including official increments, a single runs anywhere from about $15 to $88 and a double from about $20 to as high as $130._

The prestigious **d'Angleterre**, a monument for more than 2 centuries, is under the aegis of Britain's Grand Metropolitan innkeepers, which has shown its colors all over the European map. It is also flexing its fiscal muscles in Copenhagen by allocating $3-million for d'Angleterrean updatings, including a fresh facade for the building, improved corridors, brightened lounges and renewed public areas; the glorious Sidewalk Terrace is being remodeled for year-round patronage; 2 complete kitchens are being relocated and modernized. Moreover, each of 150 rooms is being given a $12,000 gift in modernization plus scores of new baths. What remains? To be sure, the fine veteran staff stays intact. Lively, enormously popular Reine Pédauque (see "Restaurants"), where the alluring drawing card is an extra-bountiful fixed price dinner accompanied by all of the excellent Burgundy which the client wishes to drink; the cozy Krinsen, with huge Greenland shrimp and Rhine wine for about $6 as typical lunch offerings; spacious suites and bedrooms with the best-stocked self-defrosting refrigerators on wheels we have ever seen; a galaxy of other luxury amenities. General management by magnetic veteran Eigil Hummelgaard. In elegance, grace, and comfort, the Queen of Danish hostelries.

The **Plaza**, a product of a mighty transformation (it was the modest Terminus, a station hotel) has made its eminently successful bid also on the side of classic traditionalism. What a fine achievement has been wrought by Proprietor Jørgen Tønnesen and his overall Chief of Staff Eggert Møller! The bar, in the form of a serene English private library, is, in our opinions, the most gracious public room we have ever seen in the nation. Adjoining is the deluxe, highly respected Baron of Beef with top-flight cuisine, and nearby the lovely Flora Danica, with 30% to 40% lower prices, has burst into bloom (please turn to "Restaurants"). In this old building, the single remaining weakness is caused by insurmountable architectural obstacles which make the construction of any large suites impossible. Superb.

The 22-story **Royal**, backed by the Scandinavian Airlines System (the town terminal has moved from the hotel to the main station), continues to soar so sweetly that again we are rubbing our eyes. Entirely air-conditioned; magnificent panorama from its Tenno suite, the largest in the capital, where the Emperor of Japan first slept in any hotel; spacious lobby; handsomely redecorated Winter Garden for less expensive fare; Orchid Bar; heavily patronized sauna and massage facilities; 120-car garage. The princely buffet lunch spread in its comfortable main dining room is such an unequaled triumph in its variety, its uniquely Danish artfulness of presentation, and its towering mastery of Scandinavian noontime cuisine that it is a wonder in the world of gastronomy (see "Restaurants"). Thanks to the endless patience, hard work, and wizardry of young General Manager Alberto Kappenberger (helped tirelessly by his beautiful wife, Ruth), we agree with a number of local professional observers who rate it as one of the most smoothly functioning hotels on the Continent.

Swooping out of the wild blue yonder, the sleek **Scandinavia** is almost twice the size of its Royal stepsister. Modernity was born in the Land of Woden; this sky-high streamliner ably reflects its noble heritage. Tranquil but handy off-bridgehead location, a pleasant but longish stroll (or free shuttle) to Tivoli Gardens; trim lobby with equally trim area for well-presented light bites; plush, panoramic 25th-floor restaurant and cocktail lounge; Artillery Bar; discothèque in planning stages; health center with saunas, gymnasium, indoor pool, and expert supervision; shops, including Illums Bolighus and Birger Christensen (open Sun., too!). The comfortable dwelling space is broken down into the following pattern: 4 master suites, 41 junior suites, deluxe doubles, standard duos, singles, and *grand lit* (double-bed spreads for twin or solo occupancy). General Manager Bodo Lemke commands the helm here; Executive Assistant Manager Timothy Whitehead, a personable Englishman, ably unfolded his wings at the Savoy and at Brown's in London; Paul Moen is one of the best Chief Hall Porters in the profession. We are especially impressed by the agreeable, clean-lined décor, the outstanding cuisine, and the almost universal warmth and friendliness of the staff. Here is one of the top luxury addresses in the entire boreal skein.

The **Kong Frederik** was totally and commendably refashioned recently when it brought an adjoining hotel into its own kingdom. Both buildings now reign in a realm of sovereign beauty, although we privately still enjoy a greater love affair with the original edifice. Good location just off Town Hall square; charming lobby and hearth-warmed King's Gallery lined with paintings of all 9 Frederiks; Queens Grill with 20 tables and elegant clublike décor; Queens Pub for informal revels; blissful Roof Garden plus Queens Garden restaurant under red parasóls for summer nutrients and romantic lingerings. All 127 rooms (up from 60) carry the same attractive ambiance but often crowded dimensions with inadequate storage space for luggage; 5 dee-luscious suites nod their "hellos" directly to the penthouse terrace. Manager Jørgen Stampe gives you an excellent value for your kroner in this high-price-hotel nation. A happy stop if you don't hanker for wide-open spaces.

The once proud **Palace** with its excellent midcity location, tumbled down our ladder several years ago; recently it was purchased by the Comfort Hotels group of England. While we are not wildly enthusiastic about this turn of events, it may eventually represent an improvement. Let's wait and see.

The harborside **Codan** has undergone so many architectural and decorative changes that old-timers would have difficulty in recognizing it. Dansk-Bilå, its Swedish owners, have made a revolution here. Now completely air-conditioned; refurbished lobby, lounge, and bar; pleasent 18-table Grill at ground level; sauna; little Coffee Shop at split level. Excepting its 3 large harbor rooms, its 10 duplex suites with circular staircases, and the 3 junior suites — most of them panoramic and of good quality — its other accommodations are shockingly microformed, with bathrooms uncomfortably cramped. Much more modern than it was, but as good?

The **Tre Falke** ("Three Falcons") feathers an attractive, chirpy bank of roosts. Superb indirect lighting; moteless cleanliness; firm, modern beds upholstered in imitation leather; plastic desks that we defy you to discern from wood. Some units are extra-tiny but efficiently arranged (a rooftop water tank prevents altering the vertical superstructure). Tasteful, soothing lobby; intimate dining facilities with superb cuisine at decent tariffs (see "Restaurants"); charming bar; superior service with Chief Concierge Ejvind O. Jensen particularly outstanding; big, big windows but Lilliputian baths; bank; hairdresser; florist; art gallery; large, streamlined convention and exhibition halls; a welcome parking lot directly in front for harried motorists.

The **Imperial** can boast 2 sparkling assets: Director Sonja Mathisen, whose charm, sense of fun, and professional dedication are outstanding in the world of *hôtellerie*, and the justly illustrious sun-umbrellaed Patio, where the fare is superb. There is a bustling, commercial feel to its rather severe lobby. All doubles with bath, toilet, and radio; small and starkly furnished; singles uncomfortable for travelers with transatlantic luggage; no suites available and none contemplated. Not in the top class, but adequate for its purpose.

The **Penta**, formerly the Europa, has been taken over by a British-headquartered consortium of 4 airlines which now operates a chain of 8 others. Estuaryside location; attractive harbor-view Grill with good buffet lunch table at perhaps $14 per head (inferior, however, to larger spread at the Royal); intimate, folksy Flier's Inn Bar from 5 P.M. onward; extensive reconstruction upstairs, with the first 5 floors finished and the remainder soon to be modernized; except for some of the vertical column of "#17" corner accomodations, furnishings hotel-ly in character; all baths and/or showers clean but cramped and poor; heavy group traffic. These once miserable lodgings show a vast improvement.

When the 1000-bed **Sheraton** was born in '73, in our view it was a monumental lemon. Lately the troubleshooters from this alert and savvy chain have descended in a swarm to try to correct the most obvious of its bloopers. Fresh wall-to-wall carpeting; clever re-illumination and other alterations including a bold textile sculpture now warming its formerly austere lobby; pleasant bar adjoining. The King's Court restaurant is indeed inviting; the Felix Brasserie, reworked with raspberry dominant, and manneristic Art Rétro décor; the Penthouse Club is bright lavender and raspberry, with splendid vistas and tea dancing extending into the post-dinner hours. In 74 chambers double beds have replaced the head-to-head or L-positioned studio beds. While there's some distance to go, under General Manager Manfred Nissen, formerly of New York's St. Regis, at last this house is moving forward. Another signal of its progress is that staff morale is much, much higher. Even though we do not happen to agree with the taste of some of these renovations, it is laudably better than it was.

The **71 Nyhavn** (same address and name) bristles with personality. It is a converted "New Harbor" warehouse hard by the docks—an especially desirable mooring for saltier voyagers. The timber-and-stucco interior is the ubiquitous servant of its 1804 construction, ably managed in 1980 fashion by Bente Hjorth. Inn-gratiating atmosphere; kindhearted staff; attractive candle-lit restaurant with appetizing low-cost cuisine; sweet 15-seat bar off lobby; no tubs (only showers) in its grim, cramped baths (again owing to the architectural shoals); small bedchambers in the $66 range; larger viewful junior suites for roughly twice the price. Adequate space is a problem here. Seafarers and seekers of the unusual are normally happy and cozy here.

• The **Mercur** has been taken over and dramatically refurbished by Simon

Spies (pronounced "Spees"), the personable eccentric genius who owns the nation's largest travel agency and Conair airline; he has also purchased the **Richmond** (see directly below). He and Chief of Staff Jørgen Weinold have stirred up an architectural and decorative tempest mainly in its public areas which looked tacky and ill-worn on our latest inspection. The Golden Tournedos Grill, seating 70 and specializing in steaks (but also doubling as a breakfast room), offers the unique bonus of 23-hour service daily and Sunday. Large Baggrunden Bar; shadowy Undergrunden ("Underground") Bar a popular hangout for airline stewardesses and younger folk; spacious outdoor tennis court on the roof of the Mercur Cinema; day-and-night-service bottle shop with beer, wine, liquor, and open sandwiches. Although nearly 100 rooms (many overlooking Vesterport rail station) have been remodeled with new carpets and furniture, too many of them are small; all have private baths and dual-pane windows with transom ventilaters; today's best picks: #'s 205, 206, 218, 616, and 618. While much still must be done to bring this house into the top class, it's now a good practical bet.

The **Richmond** has also undergone a major face-lifting. New façade; new reception area; new lounges; a 100-inch TV in bar (the only one in Europe to their and our knowledge); free interchange breakfast plan with Mercur; 6th floor revivified; warmer and brighter colors being applied. The exciting news here is La Cocotte, which is presided over by a disciple of Paul Bocuse (see "Restaurants"). The excellent local version of smörgåsbord continues to be offered from noon to 2 P.M. This hostelry is moving fastly, too.

The midtown, 65-room **Alexandra** is a cheery corner house that is kept new-penny-bright. Bath and showers now installed in every unit by veteran Manager Preben Christiani; its kips are fresh; only breakfasts are served; the lounge jumps the barrier in an equestrian theme; it is closed December to March as an economy move. Best perches are the spacious 3-window corner doubles; there's a handy garage next door.

The **Copenhagen Admiral** in the bracing dock area overlooking the sea is alleged to be the creation of about 50 SAS pilots as an investment against taxes. This mini-giant of 366 rooms or so-called "suites" impresses us as an architectural nightmare. In the designer's effort to blend rural atmosphere of the 1780's with Danish design of the 1980's, he has placed massive, blond, 200-year-old logs in partitions, in panels, on the ceilings, and even in "trees" in some of the bedchambers—a radical overdose which dominates the entire building. Despite front-desk computerization and its other few advanced installations, from the technical point of view it is a mess, with a grossly inadequate number of tables in its plain-Jane dining room vis-à-vis its head count, no service elevators for transporting baggage, laundry, and breakfasts served upstairs, which are prepared by an outside concessionaire, and other basic variations from the norm which have been ignored in its planning. Many younger people seem to like it, perhaps because its rates—while still high—are somewhat under those of the competition. Not recommended by this book—but perhaps you will disagree.

The almost-half-century-old **Astoria**, a station hotel next to the Grand, has taken a big leap forward. Fetchingly subdued ground floor restaurant; immaculate maintenance; 71 chambers with bath and 19 without, all of them small but livable. Poul Holst, who ran the Hafnia for 25 years, is currently in action here. To us the rate for a standard double with breakfast in season is exorbitant for what it offers.

The **Vestersøhus**, a favorite of many of our Embassy staffers, occupies a lovely old house on the lake which was converted into a 60-room hotel just before WW II. Breakfast-only in 2 small waterside dining rooms with the ambience of a private home; parking space available; most quarters sizable, with ample closet space; 50 twins or convertibles and 30 singles, only about half of which have private plumbing; 6 apartments, some with fully equipped kitchen-dining area, of which #21 is the choicest; tariffs 20% lower in winter; competitively reasonable. Because Director Nilsson maintains such an agreeable homey aura here, it is a sound selection for those who seek a base for a week or a month—particularly families who travel together.

The **Grand** is the leader of a station area trio which includes the **Regina** and the **Excelsior**; experienced Jørgen Thostrup has recently taken them over and made numerous revisions. In the first, the Piano restaurant features (guess what?) 88 keys and a Carvery. It is a rather poor best, mainly because of structural handicaps and the semi-modern austerity throughout its quarters; #170 is handsomely done, but all of the rest impressed us as being subpar. In the Regina the lodgings descend to cubes for singles, the dimensions of which we roughly paced off at 6' x 9'. Overall, we regard this complex as overpriced.

The **Opera** warbles in with 56 dressing-and-undressing rooms. Central situation behind the Royal Theatre; Den Kongelige restaurant on the ground floor; very costly tariffs for the best stalls in the house. Not a prima donna, but to us an unjustifiably high-priced choral voice.

The 57-room-and-bath, midtown **Ascot** has a renewed ground floor and may have added a restaurant by now. Heretofore only breakfast was offered at this converted eighteenth-century address.

The 6-story **Danhotel** resides just 10 minutes by foot from Kastrup Airport. Danish-modern lobby with "Muzak," bank, souvenir shop, cute circular bar, writing area, all of them surrounding a central restaurant. Its 17 "Deluxe" doubles, adequately sized, offer every needed comfort (save for shower curtains in the baths); the "standard" bedrooms are in the "studio" mood, suitable for overnighting but not for fortnighting; 10 additional "family" accommodations sleep 4 on 2 single beds and 2 convertible couches. Winter rates sink by about 30% per category. Quite good for its price levels, in local comparisons. Other Kastrup candidates include the SAS-sponsored **Globetrotter** and the **Bel Air.** They share a similar transient personality. The **Arthur Frommer** hostelry is also appropriate for flocks; more about this one in *Fielding's Low-Cost Europe.*

In the direction of *Elsinore*, not far from the capital, there's the nicely sprawling **Marienlyst** with its spread of 10 suites, 100 doubles, and 50 singles. Vast 500-seat dining room which can be expanded to 1400 *couverts;* recreational "Happyland" open each evening, with pinball machines and other diversions targeted for the 18-to-30-year group; 6 bowling alleys; minicar track with 12 speedsters; basketball court; trap shooting; discothèque for young fry; small stakes roulette wheels, which are the only Government-approved spinneries in Denmark; "Veranda" cafeteria; health studio with 3 saunas; artificial wavemaker swimming pool, with the degree of openings of its slide-away ceiling and fade-away walls controlled by solar intensities. All in all, here's an expensive —and exhausting, if you wish—suburban hideaway.

The **Marina** at *Vedbaek*, just across the Strandvejen and looking to the harbor, is purebred Scandinavian Modern—perhaps too cool for some. Sleek white concrete-and-glass structure; viewful outdoor terrace; bar, counter, and snack corner all connected to the airline-terminal-type dining room; sauna, billiard parlor, and good-size garage. All bedchambers with efficiency baths, radios, telephones, studio beds, sailing-theme photomurals, and crow's-nest balconies; tariffs slightly higher than the Marienlyst, a comparison which seems considerably out of line for the relative value; frequent changes of management in its short life which have been no help to staff morale. Good if you go-go-go for the twenty-first century, but otherwise only so-so-so. As for other popular choices near Copenhagen, the **Frederiksdal** is near *Lyngby*, on a lake 20 minutes northwest of the capital. Appealing in character with its 45 units and well-respected restaurant. Prices are at economy level now—and so may be its service. The sleekly modern, 50-room-and-bath **Trouville** at *Hornbaek,* past Elsinore, now remains open through the 4 seasons; it is known for its kitchen. The **Store-Kro**, near *Fredensborg*, offers several new baths and redecoration of most of its rooms and is once again attracting tourists like clusters of bees. A more modest favorite of ours—virtually unknown to North Americans—is the revivified **Vinhuset** at *Naestved*. Plain but comfortable accommodations; village charm, not city slick; winsomely Danish public rooms; extrasavory food. Paul Rasmussen, the manager, is really doing a job here. *Køge* has the **Hvide Hus**, 7 miles south on E-4 to Rødby; there's also the delightfully revamped **Sonnerup Old Inn**, with its charcoal grill, rôtisserie, and smiling chef ready for a bustling business; our recent peek told us why. Meals only.

Restaurants Let's take a look first at the *hotel dining rooms.* Due to the increased cost of labor and food, these are now frequently your best bet; today's hoteliers often use them as loss leaders in attracting customers.

This year we consider the **Plaza** as the pacesetter of this group. Its enormously fetching 3500-book Library Bar has been previously described in "Hotels." The adjoining dining sections are equally delightful. While its special fish and game segment still remains a "must" on our trip list, the Baron of Beef is a special delight to the senses. Outstanding reception, cuisine, and service; enormous broadside menu; unusually versatile and fine wine list. With prices from 30% to 40% lower, the cornerside Flora Danica is a hit; only Danish food, including sandwiches, is served in this handsome, relaxing, air-conditioned nook. These 3 are notable in all respects.

To repeat our earlier statement about the **Royal**, the princely buffet spread in its oh-so-comfortable main dining room is a wonder in the world of gastronomy. Its choice of 55 different platters, dishes, or baskets is such a triumph in variety, its Danish artfulness of presentation, and its towering mastery of Scandinavian noontime cuisine that it is unique—so much so, in fact, that we selected it as one of the 11 Best Overlooked Sites in the World for the *Book of Lists* by the Irving Wallace family. Stuff yourself happily with all you can savor for about $18 per appetite. The 70-place Snack Bar Grill is for lighter eaters; respectively good fare is also offered in this realm.

The **d'Angleterre** has burst into brilliant bloom with 2 entries which are local epicurean sensations. The Reine Pédauque has been installed in its formerly serene main dining room. In addition to the classic à la carte roster, it features an enormously popular fixed-price menu of 13 appetizers or soups, 13 main dishes, 8 desserts, and every drop of French wine the client wishes to drink—all inclusive at about $35. Evenings only; so jam-packed that on weekends it is booked up to 6 weeks in advance; *reservations mandatory*. The other sparkler is the Krinsen Bistro Bar on one corner, with its own separate entrance. Around 18 small marble-topped tables with restful chairs; cozily decorated; Philosopher's Table for single person occupancy with 2 lamps instead of the customary one; cookery well above average; no bookings accepted. Here is a charming little drop-in oasis for light and reasonable comestibles.

The enclosed patio of the **Imperial**, with its removable roof, sun umbrellas, and fetching mien, also deserves honors; it is so well-liked that during peak hours normally there's a waiting line at its entrance. One famous specialty here is its Gravad Laks (super-delicious slices of fresh salmon marinated in dill); we like it so much that often we eat 2 full portions. Its older waiters serve smoothly and deftly, but some of the apprentices need more tutelage. Recommended with cheers.

While the **Scandinavia's** off-lobby restaurant is pleasant for easy nibbling, the 25th-floor spread (closed on Sunday) deserves kudos for its scenic luncheons and big-nighting; the drinks, the panorama, and the skilletry are superb.

The gifted chef at the **Tre Falke** has laudably upgraded its culinary standards. Charmingly intimate restaurant with cute little summer garden; decent tariffs; now a worthy value.

The Golden Tournedos Grill at the **Mercur**, seating 70 and specializing in steaks, is pleasantly inviting with its slatted wood, well-placed partitions, and paintings of old Danish masters. The most extraordinary feature here is that it continuously runs full blast from 6 A.M. to 5 A.M., closing only one hour daily for the cleanup crew. In the morning a large breakfast buffet (included in the room rates) tempts trencherpeople with juices, eggs, sausages, cheeses, cereals, bread (3 deliveries daily for freshness), and the lot—but if you're hungry for a T-bone, that's fine as well! The **Richmond**, under the same ownership, inaugurated an attractive and unusual rendezvous called La Cocotte. The maestro here in the evening is a disciple of Paul Bocuse. Total of 40 places; black slatted tables from Italy; Swedish Rya white carpets; buffet and coffee section; definitely expensive. A tempting local version of smörgåsbord continues to be served from noon to 2 P.M. Interestingly improved.

The **Kong Frederik's** Queens Grill is a wood-lined charmer with comfortable armchairs and plenty of built-in ease; normally its level is consistently good. The Queens Pub is more taverny in tone, of course. In summer, the Queens Garden, at rooftop level, peaks and peeks among the spires and chimney pots of one of Europe's most enchanting cities. If the sun glows, so will you. The **Østerport** has trimmed its once famous lunch buffet to standard proportions; nonetheless, its all-you-can-eat policy from 12 to 3 for about $9.25 is still a praiseworthy bargain.

With the exception of the **Palace** and the **Opera**, which we do not recommend, the other major hostelries serve adequate but not outstanding fare.

Among the *independents,* the **Anatole** (Gothersgade 35) is still considered the gastronomic nirvana of this roster. Søren Gericke, a dedicated pupil of Paul Bocuse, first brought the lighter, simpler, imaginative nouvelle cuisine to Denmark as the master chef of the Hotel Plaza. Then he totally reconstructed an existing restaurant (the site of a pharmacy in 1802). The result is spectacular. Deliberately muted décor; 14 Portuguese marble-topped tables; soft lighting; elegant simplicity; lovely coffee-liqueur 5-table lounge to rear; 18-item à la carte menu mostly of original creations; unusual presentations on searing hot plates in individual baskets; very expensive, of course fixed-price meals. The demand is so great that reservations should be made at least 3 days in advance. Here is our vote for the number one dining oasis in the city.

The **Kong Hans Kaelder** (sixteenth-century cellar near Magasin du Nord on the Vingårdsstraede) is in dramatic—almost flamboyant—contrast. The open kitchen of this strikingly effective establishment splits its center. The front has a counter with 14 high seats inside the entrance where 9 less costly selections are offered. The rear, under an all-white geometrically aligned 4-arched ceiling, has 8 tables at lunch and 15 at dinner. To the extreme rear is a lovely 2-arched candlelit lounge with a small bar and d-e-e-p cushioned sofas. Significant for such a limited area is the presence of 8 of the chefs and 7 cooks.

Sct. Gertruds Kloster (Hauser Plads 32) is one of the most talked-about restaurants in the city—and most of the chat is favorable. Location in a tranquil little square; library bar with Chesterfield sofas, brass lamps, and marine prints; vast network of cellars (in a restored monastery) illuminated by more than 400 candles—and *no electric lighting anywhere;* mirthful yard-long instruction sheet issued with your cocktail to guide you to and from your table. While the surroundings are highly engaging we found the cuisine and prices too low and too high respectively. If you care more for atmosphere than for gastronomy, you'll probably enjoy it.

L'Alsace (Pistolstraede, through the passageway next to Bee Cee on the Pedestrian Mall) is a shining star in the large complex firmament being developed in Birger Christensen's ancient and splendid hideaway enclave, which used to contain his storehouses. (Bjørn Wiinblad's Fairyland shop is another.) He has torn apart the former Pistolkaelderen from all of its pipes outward to install an utterly charming ambiance with brick walls, benches, prints, an open kitchen, and a new dining terrace in a lovely sequestered courtyard. Simple but highly refined menu with reasonable prices; trout and other fresh water fish a specialty; 48 tables inside and 25 outside; delicious Danish sandwiches at lunch; good wine list; friendly and informal staff; management by English-speaking Franz Stockhammer; open continuously from 11:30 A.M. to 10:30 P.M.; closed Sundays and holidays. Here is a little honey. As an alternate, this dynamic tycoon has also inaugurated the closely neighboring **Bee Cee Café,** which is a delightful money-saver. Accents on herrings, open sandwiches, cheese, and wines; semi self-service; 11:30 A.M. to 5 P.M. only; moderate tabs; very happy for light appetites. **Crank's,** in the same cute-sy district, offers a hoedown of crisp vegetarian ware and health foods.

Egoisten, in the little Hovedvagtsgade street, is a new entry which merits

the attention and respect of cognoscenti. Its fittings, its tiny bar, its 10 tables
and its atmosphere could scarcely be more cozy in the way that can only be
found in this northern land. While the choices are limited, each dish is prepared and presented with a flair. A rewarding find on a medium rather than
budget scale.

The dual **A Hereford Beefstouw** enterprises (Åbenrå 8 and Vesterbrogade
3) specialize in juicy, marble-textured Hereford steaks. No-nonsense ambiance;
clever use of acrylic lighting; a few modern paintings to add splashes of color;
open Mondays through Thursdays from 11:30 to 2 and 5 to 9; closed weekends
at lunchtime. The cost of a T-bone is about $17; by Continental standards the
quality is excellent.

A cheaper candidate in this league is the **Bøf & Ost** ("Beef & Cheese") at
Gråbrodretorv 13. Peter Tholstrup, owner of the Hotel Østerport, is the inspiration behind this venture. Pleasant cellar on a pretty square; 3 connecting
rooms with low ceilings, whitewashed walls, and scrubbed birch tables; extremely popular as a neighborhood drop-in spot for an unelaborate meal or
simply cheese and wine. Our supper was $28 for two. Here is a friendly
elbow-to-elbow atmosphere. Rubbing the nap of its sleeve, incidentally, is the
neighboring **Peder Oxe** in its next-door 18th-century building. Same management; spotlight on a mix-it-yourself salad bar; meats also on call; spacious and
fun.

The **7 Små Hjem** ("7 Small Homes"), at Jernbanegade 4, showed marked
improvement in the quality of its cuisine on our recent visit. For years, this
has been our only major demurrer to this winsomely decorated architectural
jumble of pint-size rooms—one of the most ingratiating interiors of any restaurant we know. You still won't get anything that begins to approach the palate
or tummy satisfaction of more substantial houses, in our opinion, because this
place is frankly and unabashedly designed for the tourist trade rather than for
Danes. But a manful job has been done in injecting more substance into its
former slick-but-hollow, promotion-style fare. A big asset: Drinks are relatively modest in price.

Christian den Tiende (Bredgadde, opposite Sankt Annae Plads) draws some
of the town's most attractive ladies at lunchtime and handsome couples after
dark. Well-mounted wine display at the barside entry; cocktail lounge farther
in; conservatory-style inner salon up a few steps with vine-clad trellis work and
old-time photographs; beautifully prepared and presented set meal for under
$20. The Danish appetizers for casual selection and the cooking which verges
on *nouvelle cuisine* are indeed prizes to be enjoyed. Highly recommended.

The **Langelinie Pavillionen**, in a park-and-seaside setting overlooking
Copenhagen's famous "Little Mermaid," is a few minutes from the center of
town. Its large, modern, glass-concrete-and-wood dining room seating several
hundred guests, on our latest evaluation had perked up considerably; moreover, the cooking was notable by any standards. P.S. to sportsmen: Upstairs
you'll find the lounges and dining room of the Danish Royal Yacht Club,
which is one of the finest sailing anchorages in Europe. Your own local club
card will probably admit you.

Glyptoteket (Stormgade 35), in close proximity to the celebrated sculpture
museum of the same name, is a perennial port-o'-call of visitors.

Brønnum, across from the Opera, is one of the nation's more visually exciting candidates. Behind the bar is an impressive carved altarpiece, the floors are bleached wood, and the tone is white, bright, and *allegre*. The cookery is 100% Danish, with the cost of a meal nudging $25 per person. Cheerful and good.

Heering (Pilestraede 19) is the French-mode chef d'oeuvre of young Thomas Heering, who assembled restaurant, buffet, and takeout facilities under one neat *toit*. Locals are flocking in.

The 13-table **Gilleleje** (Nyhavn 10) is alluringly inviting with its Iranian and African heads, skins and weapons, wooden beaded screens, highly varnished dark tables, and plants. The major drawbacks are that while its tariffs are higher than those of the Hotel d'Angleterre, the quality of our "luxury lunch" impressed us not at all favorably. Open from 11 A.M. to 10 P.M. straight through from Monday through Saturday; closed Sundays and holidays.

Børskaelderen ("Stock Exchange Cellar") is exactly that—sited at the bottom of this handsome ancient building. Its colophon, a top hat, symbolizes what brokers formally wore in the old days. Venerable air; high ceilings and walls with carved panels; bar off entrance; 2 rooms; majestic oversize painting of Christian IV, who directed its building in the early 17th century; open grill; 8 glass-trimmed, brass-rail-topped booths in center rectangle; tiny tables and uncomfortable chairs. Hot meals are served Mon. through Fri. from 11:30 to 11; Sat. 5:30 P.M. to 11 P.M.; closed on Sundays. Historic mien, but food which we rate as indifferent.

Escoffier (Dronningens Tvaergade 43) waxes both generous and jejune. Here's the only place in Scandinavia, to our knowledge, where portions are served in 2 sizes—large if you're hungry, small if you're not. No carpets in its 4 paneled rooms; dark-green leather chairs and wall banquettes; no-nonsense aura; poor ventilation. Proprietor Fritz Petersen's cookbook is dog-eared at the pages describing Gallic sauces and French and Italian oddments. Cuisine so uneven that you should consult the zodiac to decide what to order.

Arne Cohn's (Rørholmsgade 2) is the sole independent kosher restaurant in Copenhagen. Entrance through a bustling butcher shop; small room to one side with exactly 2 tables (a 4-seater and a 2-seater) and counter service; no alcohol served; open 9 A.M. to 5 P.M. Mon. through Thurs.; Fri. from 9 A.M. to 12 P.M. Closed Sat. and Sun. CARE packages available for Shabbath perfect for a Philistine or a Saturday picnic. Recommended—from one Temple to another.

Au Coq d'Or (H.C. Andersen's Boulevard 13) used to be almost universally acclaimed as the undisputed epicurean leader among the nation's dining places. Following the death of its extraordinarily gifted founder-owner and subsequent vicissitudes, all of us on our Creative Team unanimously feel that it has hit the gastronomic and service skids to a degree where we cannot recommend it under any circumstances. How sad we are!

For lovers of splendid Danish sea fare, its still a tossup between **Krogs Fiskerestaurant** (Gammel Strand 38) and **Fiskehuset** (Gammel Strand 34). These next-door institutions both face the docks across the street from where the nation's most famous fisherwomen used to peddle their wares. In the main, more tourists seem to gravitate to the former and more local residents to Fiskehusets. Over the eons we've been fond of Krogs, the specialties of which are lobster salad and filet of sole steamed in white wine; on our latest try, this quiet, unpretentious establishment was again a delight. At Fiskehuset on our latest visit we found the décor renewed but retaining its traditional warm aura, the kitchen totally modernized, the service kind in spirit, and the cookery also superb. Both are surprisingly simple for their piscatorial reputations—and both proudly serve their best fish dishes in the capital.

 Den Sorte Ravn (Nyhavn 14) is down the scale from these twin leaders. Cellar location; only 12 tables; low ceiling and red brick floor; open kitchen; no attempt at special eye-catchers except small, appetizing cheese display at entrance; good food and very friendly people. Not cheap, but what is? Fiskeka-elderen ("Fish Cellar," Ved Stranden 18), downstairs from the large, indiffer-ent Den Gyldne Fortun restaurant, is operated by famous Preben Thykjer, former culinary mentor of the Imperial Hotel plus a number of others, and a member of the Chaine des Rôtisseurs. If there are any tricks in showmanship which he has missed, we didn't find them. Total of 24 slatted wooden booths seating 2 or 4 in its L-shaped room; fishnets draped from beamed ceiling; other maritime gimmicks galore. Except for Sunday lunch and a few holidays, it is open nonstop from 10:30 A.M. to midnight. You might well see more tourists here than residents. Although the cuisine is reported to be uneven, the prices are tops.

 Tivoli Gardens (May to mid-Sept.) has a number of first-class restaurants. If you seek glorious flowers, patios, and delightfully relaxed dining in the open, this marvelous fairyland park can give you a memory which would always remain dear. Our latest evaluation for the first time brings our most enthusias-tic kudos to the handsomely revivified Divan I. When the sun or stars are shining, the air is balmy, and the crowds are reasonable in size, it is heavenly to unkink on its sylvan terrace while lingering over its costly but appetizingly sophisticated fare. Next down our list comes Divan II (also deluxe but not quite as tempting), Belle Terasse (to us pretentious and overpriced, but you might disagree) and Perlen (a bit more moderate). Somewhat lower in cost are the Grøften (perhaps the most Danish of all in personality) and the Balkonen (chintzy all-you-can-eat buffet with carvery option plus à la carte, with medio-cre vittles in an indoor-outdoor combination). The Copenhagen Zoo also offers everything from picnic tables to snack bars to garden consumption for all tastes and price ranges. Nyhavns Faergekro (Nyhavn 5) purports to be the oldest restaurant (1728) in the city. After seeing it and trying it, we'll certainly not fight with this claim.

 Josty (Pileallé 14-A) is a pleasant inside-outside spot. Sprawling converted mansion in a midtown park; several rooms of varying degrees of formality; informal glass-enclosed interior garden for winter munching and hedge row alfresco tables on a summer day; medium tabs; medium-to-poor service; medi-um-to-good cooking. The young fry will love the skittle alley and the woods for romping. Open every day the year round.

 Kommandanten (Ny Adelgade 7) was recommended to us by both General Manager Eigil Hummelgaard and the master chef of the Hotel d'Angleterre, which is directly around the corner from it—and our gratitude is warm for their tip. Sweet family-style coziness is the trump card here, where the wel-come scarcely could be more friendly. Cunningly, regional ambiance; paneled entrance room with 4 tables and elfin bar; small open garden with 3 tables; 10 tables upstairs in 2 beamed rooms; soft taped music; continuous service from 11 A.M. to 12 P.M. except on Sundays and major holidays. Since every dish ordered is individually hand-prepared, such care is taken that its level of national-style offerings including sandwiches is outstanding for any establishment with such realistic tariffs. Flemming Ungermann is the warm-hearted, experienced, English-speaking host. Extra-special for its category.

Kongens Have (Kronprinsessegade 13) is a budget treat at lunchtime on a sunny day—or even for dinner when the weather is balmy. Within its dull building, which looks shabby but is not, there are an open kitchen and 16 tables. Virtually its sole enticing attraction is the open-air garden to the rear, which accommodates 50 different parties. Local-style comestibles are dished or glassed up from 10 A.M. to 10 P.M. every day in the year except 48 hours at Christmastime. Jolly proprietor Ole Bro rightfully draws a heavy and loyal popular trade. Not the best, but very good within its range.

For a whippet-fast, bankroll-painless choice of dishes, **Cheval Blanc** (Mikkel Bryggers Gade 6, behind the Palace Hotel) specializes in light bites, open sandwiches, and grills. Counter in front, plus a lineup of bleached-wood tables; colorful, shrubbed, easy, and inexpensive. Here's a spot to economize after purchasing that white mink jacket from Birger Christensen. Nearby, the **Stedet** (Lavendelstraede 13–15) means "The Place" in Danish. Lightning service; frequent changes of dishes; tiptop quality foodstuffs. Just The Place for shoppers.

Perhaps the best restaurant buy in Copenhagen for lacerated budgets can be found at the **K.A.R.** operation at Frederiksberggade 24. K.A.R. is the local abbreviation for "Women's Alcohol-Free Restaurant"—but for goodness' sake don't let this awful name discourage you from trying this one; it's clean, simple, surprisingly attractive, and serves genuine Danish dishes unobtainable in fancy places. AND it has introduced Tuborg and Carlsberg beers to the "dry" menu of earlier days. *Ave!* We still must try the **Prag** (Amagerbrogade 37), which recently was restyled, and the **Bourgogne** (Dronningens Tvaergade 2).

Due to severely increasing labor problems, *lunch-only* restaurants have now burgeoned into a substantial separate category. Most of these small oases, normally family-run, are open only from 11 A.M. to 2 P.M. or sometimes 4 p.m. from Mondays through Fridays. All are blessedly inexpensive; the majority offer delicious light dishes in the traditional Danish style.

Gammel Strand 46 is both the name and the address of our favorite. Cellar location; about 20 tables; fully licensed for alcohol; no menu; beamingly friendly personnel. Its display case contains some of the most delicious home-made open sandwiches that we have ever found in any public enterprise here; save for the smoked salmon at about $4, all of the others are priced between $2 and $2.50. Nils Sørensen, former Manager of the illustrious Store-Kro near Fredensborg (see later), does such a good job in providing such excellent buys that it is virtually always crowded. It is closed during 3 weeks of July and on Saturdays from June through August. We love it.

In Sankt Annae (Sankt Annae Plads 12) everything you eat, save for the salt and pepper but including the mustard, is homemade. While the accent is essentially on open sandwiches, 2 or 3 warm dishes are featured daily. There are 11 well-lit tables with roses on each. The aura is homey, the food is good, the prices are right, and it is so popular among businessmen that advance reservations are recommended. Open Mondays through Saturdays from 10 to 5; closed Sundays. A sound bet.

Ida Davidsen (St. Kongensgade 70) is operated by the daughter of the proprieter of historic Oskar Davidsen. In this one you will find 10 to 15 warm choices in addition to its sandwiches. Its decorative touch of a salmon-colored band halfway up the walls with the white top used as background for collages of old clippings about the senior establishment is simple but effective. The normal hours are from 10 to 4. Worthy.

Kongens Kaelder ("King's Cellar," Gothersgade 87) consists of 3 small rooms in a charming old basement; the tables with candles and the plants add to its atmosphere. Read the slate menu on one wall, stroll through its very modern kitchen to look over its dishes, and then order at your table. Intimate but rather too crowded when full; hearty food at reasonable tariffs; heavy patronage; open from 11 to 4.

Hos Mathilde (Løngangstraede 39), under the aegis of Mathilde and Palle Clemmensen, tallies 12 tables with red checked cloths. The right-hand side of its menu is comfortably competitive. Sweet.

Ostehjørnet (St. Kongensgade 56) is above a cheese shop. Our light bites here were good.

Slotskaelderen, facing the fish market, has been nicknamed "Hos Karl Kik" for possibly 100 years. Although prime ministers and other illustrious figures have often frequented this most famous establishment in its genre, we were disappointed in the quality of its fare. Perhaps ours was an off-day.

Although several others exist and more are popping up, these are the current pick of the crop.

If you're making the North Zealand "castle" excursion, there are several stops for your noon meal. Our favorite, now that Copenhagen's prestigious Plaza Hotel runs it, is the enchanting, expensive, **Søllerød Kro**, in the village of *Søllerød* (about 25 minutes out of the capital toward Elsinore). Cream-colored seventeenth-century stucco building; thatched roof; a quiet rockbound pond and a tiny church in front; cottage windows and painted doors; a lovely presentation of food that perfectly matches the fairy-tale surroundings. Warmest salutes and recommendations. *Always reserve in advance*. **Store-Kro**, near *Fredensborg*, romps up with a large, semipaneled, gold-pillared room in smooth but coldish international rather than Danish décor. The **Marienlyst** at *Elsinore* is suave, chichi, and international. Now that Torup Kro has burned down, in this same area we are inclined to favor **H. C. Andersen Huset** at *Asserbo*, 24 miles from Copenhagen. While it boasts 150 years in age, it still exudes Mr. Andersen's youthful spirit. **Bregnerød Kro** is another charmer within short commuting distance in the direction of Hillerød. Its red roadside building, with 2 freshly thatched roofs, has offered food and/or lodging to the hungry and/or the weary for more than 3 centuries. Low ceilings with beams and gilded epigrams; green-paneled walls with tastefully painted coffers; intimate illumination by coach lights, 3-unit, red-shaded student lamps, and tapers; casement windows; flowers. The cuisine is good but not spectacular, because it dishes up simple country fare—just that.

Night Life The Danes have a droll sense of humor. They sanction public drinking around the clock—but a citizen reckless enough to take advantage of this broad-mindedness is forced by law to get fresh air at intervals. The Government figures this way: If the customer sits and sits, he might get drunk —but if he is forced by a staggered system of closing times to change places, at some point he's bound to go home.

A total of 100 restaurants or gin mills in Copenhagen (plus a few in Odense, Aarhus, and Aalborg) have been granted special permission to remain open until 5 A.M.—the precise moment, incidentally, when workmen's bars are pulling up their shutters for prebreakfast topers. Most (not all) of the establishments listed below belong to this extra-late group.

Door charges at the better portals toll in at between $2 and $3.50, depending on the night of the week. Scottish libations are decanted for slightly less than the cost of an equivalent quantity of U235. Champagne? Say "gulp" right now and save a small fortune.

The Palmehaven, once the leading contender in the elegance circuit, reconsidered its calling and resumed life as Le Carrousel, then went through yet another self-appraisal and appeared as the Hard Rock, only to switch once again to become **Daddy's Dance Hall** and relocate in the cellar of the giant Palads Cinema complex (with 12 theaters) on Axeltorv. The neonostalgic theme locks onto the Marilyn Monroe and Chuck Berry era, with music drawn from Early Beatlemania. The 2 young, spirited owners often enjoy sellout nights—but for how long? *That's* the question.

The name-rename-game continues apace with the **Valencia,** formerly the Chat Noir, which prior to that was known as none other than the Valencia. (Caramba!) It also has been totally revamped by its proprietor. Improved kitchen to serve here as well as its **Ambassadeur** segment (a scantly used gourmet restaurant); now with striptease and floor show; today's music for today's dancing.

We hear that the **Tordenskjold** is now the city's most distinguished discothèque, but this entry on Kongens Nytorv is still untested by us personally. Sorry.

Raadhus Kaelderen ("Vin og Ølgod"), at Gammeltorv near the site of the Old Town Hall (A.D. 1200), throbs with very special, very Danish zest. Capacity for 400 merrymakers on 3 different levels; separate segments successively devoted to an English pub, a Portuguese *bodega,* a Ratskeller, a Grill-Rôtisserie, and a whopping Main Hall. Emphasis on drinking, snacking, and musical revelry; more frolicking by adults than by teen types; oompah band; songbooks at each place setting; locked-arms singing; "dancing" on the benches whenever the spirit moves. Low prices; active daily from 8 P.M. to 2 A.M. or later. Heaps of hilarity for the fancy-free of all ages. Highly recommended for its delightful, authentic Copenhagen color.

Madame Arthur and the neighboring **Why Not** seem to attract a sexually versatile clientele—and, why not? **Club 10** is for antiques as ancient as 25-or-so. These crocks liked it.

Nimb (also called "Københavner Kroen") used to spell early-evening glamour to the Junior Set. It still features dancing but we're not enthusiastic about it.

In Tivoli Gardens, **Taverna** is the leading light. Among the hotels, the Sheraton's **Penthouse** and the Scandinavia's **Artilleri Bar** are worthy beacons in the night.

Kakadu ("Cockatoo") is peopled by businessmen in 3-button gray flannels and business girls in no-button gowns. The latter invoice the former about $135 per share of their common stock. (Along toward dawn's early light, the price sinks to about $60 across the street at **Maxim**'s, but we consider this place to be too rugged for anyone but Popeye or Clyde Barrow.) Dark, snugglesome, ground-floor hideaway with piano-melodizing, a copper grill, bar, and figures moving languorously in the shadows; upstairs (small entrance fee) with smooth combo; Moorish-arched dance corner; Mitch-Miller-trained bartenders who sip-along with the clients (and don't always hold it as well).

For the more staid businessman on the loose, **Wonderbar** is also well-known for unattached girls in search of companionship. These ladies are older crows compared to the Kakadu chicks, and they charge less for reviewing gents' portfolios. Intimate and cheerful, with pleasant salon furnishings and almost prudishly decorous atmosphere; open until 5 A.M. and occasionally absolutely dead.

Jazzhouse Montmartre, as the name hints, is a modern jazz parlor. Open Tues., Wed., and Thurs. from 8 P.M. to 1 A.M.; Fri. and Sat. from 9 P.M. to 4 A.M. Closed Sun. and Mon. Some of the top names in notes appear on its bandstand. **Trocadero** we wouldn't recommend to anybody with less than the consolidated toughness of the National Hockey League. Even then, we'd still have our doubts. For music buffs, **La Fontaine** (swing and contemporary bars), **Vingaarden** (Dixie and blues to mod-sounds), and **Muskitererne** (New Orleans beats) are the current hot spots, featuring some of the best itinerant U.S. and continental combos. **Cap Horn** in Nyhavn, alas, has become just another discothèque—and not a very good one at that. **Pussy Cat and Bonaparte** (open very late) specialize in youthful revels. **La Cubana** is the loudest pulser for the Teen Team. Ground-floor cluster of 3 bars and numerous pine-paneled alcoves; modern dance band; quieter upstairs lair for steam-heated romantics; rope-swing bar "stools" and barmaids so grateful when you leave a tip that they might ring a cowbell audible in Sweden. Everything up-and-up; fine for the Junior Set. **Café Sommersko**, on Kronprinsensgade, is the public gathering place of the local young people, mainly students.

You'll have kegs of fun in Copenhagen. It's known far and wide as the "Paris of the North"—but that's wrong. For our money, that's as unfair as calling Paris the "Copenhagen of the South."

PORNOtations After a slump had set in, Copenhagen regained her dominance as Scandinavia's sex queen, rivaling even wicked Hamburg. More recently, however, officials shuttered many of the shops and movie haunts—not on morals charges (heavens forbid!) but because many of the operators neglected to pay their taxes or the fees for their licenses. (Paradoxically, some of the biggest specialty houses of nudity now are clothing stores.) A number still exist even on the most exclusive shopping streets, but if anybody has trouble finding one, any taxi driver or concierge can point out their locations.

Some newsstands still groan—even moan—with a surfeit of sizzling salacity, libidinous literature, and cranked-out carnality. English-language directories limn the lusty listings for all of the unblushing bawdiness in the city: film shows, live shows, mixed shows, audience-participation shows, intimate massage services, socially oriented saunas, sex stores-clubs-libraries, even porn beer showing nudes on the labels (from Sweden)—brother, just name your bag and it's in this sensualists' grab bag. If any eyebrows are raised, they might be yours alone.

The Danes themselves regard this exhibitionism with mildly curious amusement—if they regard it at all. But to the visiting outlander they yawn, "If that's what you want, it's here for the asking"—and nobody looks askance.

Shopping   Scores of Americans consider that Denmark offers the most appealing shopping on the Continent. The 20.25% "MOMS" tax is effective on a national scale only *within* the country. Our ★ ★ ★ ★ ★ recommendations are individually noted.

ALL EXPORTED MERCHANDISE is granted a deduction of 16%. Therefore, make arrangements to ship your major purchases direct to your home or, for pickups by you, direct to the airport or other Danish point of exit.

Treasures for the home? Three unique and world-famous establishments follow in alphabetical order:

★ ★ ★ ★ ★ **Den Permanente** (Vesterport Building, with branches in Lyngby Storcenter and in the House of Industry) is the so-called "Permanent Exhibition"—the show, sample, and sales rooms for practically all established firms or individual craftsmen in the nation. Every piece on the spacious, fetchingly decorated floors—each approved by the jury elected by its 250 participants— is Danish. You'll find contemporary furniture designed by a dazzling coalition of the most renowned Grand Masters in the land. In the parade of other products are curtains, cutlery, stoneware dinner service, jewelry, striking ceramics, textile pieces, and a fine arts gallery—everything from $1 mementos to silver flatware to you-name-it. Den Permanente is proud of its wholesale department for foreign retails and its ace shipping department which dispatches all over the world. Managing Director Ivan Engel has superlative expertise in arts and crafts, in administrative complexities, and in easing your buying path. Unique.

★ ★ ★ ★ ★ **Illums Bolighus** (Amagertorv 10, with "Mini-Illums" at the Hotel Scandinavia, Kastrup Airport, and Tivoli—all 3 open late on Saturday and all of Sunday) translates as "Home House." This Center of Modern Design is the closest we've ever found to being *the* dream shop of any American host or hostess. The level of artistry, quality, and technical soundness throughout its 4 sweepingly dramatic, air-conditioned floors is electrifying. True-life displays replace counters. Graceful Danish furniture galore (with guaranteed safe delivery through its flourishing weekly container shipping service to U.S. at a net 40% under U.S. prices); the nation's longest shelves of porcelain, stoneware, and faîence; Fashion Departments; Fur Department; Fauchon gastronomic Boutique; restaurant; art gallery; the famous Wooden Articles Department; Arts and Crafts Department. DON'T MISS the Fairy Tale Department. Fireball Jørgen Basse has an impressive international background and is in taut, zesty, imaginative command.

★ ★ ★ ★ ★ **A/S Lysberg, Hansen & Therp** (Bredgade 3), Purveyors to the

Royal Danish and Royal Swedish Courts, has been Scandinavia's most illustrious Interior Decorating Center for more than 100 years. This block-long landmark has a special contract department for furnishing homes, hotels, restaurants, and embassies all over the world with global tax-free shipment. In its stunning Boutique you will find a large selection of unusual gift creations; for the home there are glorious tablecloths, charmingly original concepts in china, and lots, lots more. Ask for sparkling Mrs. Nova Helbo. Top elegance throughout.

Handblown, handmade glassware: The nation's only producer is **Holmegaard** (Østergade 15), which since 1825 has triumphantly combined craftsmanship with excitingly different ideas. Dozens of free brochures; a glittering wonderland.

★ ★ ★ ★ ★ **A.B. Schou,** and its next-door subsidiary, ★ ★ ★ ★ ★ **Skandinavisk Glas** (Ny Østergade), project a wider attraction because of their greater versatility. The former is the only marketplace in the metropolis for all of the Big 3 Danish porcelain manufacturers; it features Lalique, Lladro, and a flock of other distinguished lines; here is the biggest source for collector's plates. The latter specializes in exquisite crystal from all of the famous Scandinavian glassworks. Their price ranges start very modestly. Be sure to inquire for cordial Manager Kurt Nielsen at Schou or sweet Miss Hanne Christensen at the other. Their mailing list contains the names of more than 30,000 satisfied U.S. clients—so need anyone say more?

Silver: Our leading choice is ★ ★ ★ ★ ★ **Hans Hansens Sølv** (Amagertorv 16) which we regard as the most intimately tasteful silver store in all of Denmark. The design and craftsmanship in this 3rd-generation landmark are perfection, combining the skills of revered masters with the dynamic forms of the sculptor's art. During our painstaking comparison shopping for 5 pieces of similar weight and purity, their entries ran from 8% to 22% under the Georg Jensen prices. Gentle Proprietor Peder Mikkelsen will be your mentor in this treasure trove of temptation.

Furs: More high-grade mink is raised in Denmark than in any other foreign land—and the quality and savings are unbeatable. By far the most eye-gleaming assortment, in our opinion, can be found at the century-old house of ★ ★ ★ ★ ★ **Birger Christensen** (Ostergade 38 and Hotel Scandinavia), Purveyors By Appointment to no less than 3 Royal Courts and to most of the important foreign embassies. They not only offer a reservoir of the largest stocks and widest choices in Europe—but these are sophisticatedly understated and *different.* The inventory is umbrellaed to cover all age and economic groups. The feature here is their world-famous Saga mink in a color galaxy of 20 mutations; there is also a large line of modestly priced Fun Furs. The alert, gifted, and charming Birger Christensen, Jr. has now set up 8 outlets in U.S. centers, 1 in Tokyo, and another in Kuwait! As the only major house in the world to create new collections twice yearly, its fashion shows continue to be smash successes throughout the world. Ask for this instantly likable dynamo in person. Dreamy!

A. C. Bang, across the street, is also chic and highly reputable. However, we still don't think their creations reflect quite the same genius in fashion, styling, and flair as those of the One-And-Only Mr. Christensen.

Exquisite porcelain: Celebrated ★ ★ ★ ★ ★ **Bing & Grøndahl** (Amagertorv

4) traces its root to A.D. 1853 and has Appointments to the Royal Courts of Denmark, Great Britain, and Sweden. This is the pioneer which revolutionized the industry by achieving the final historic breakthrough of the *under*glaze decoration techniques which are amazingly resistant to all kinds of soaps, detergents, and acids. It is impossible to put into words the magic which, in their consummate artistry, they have conveyed to their soaring birds, swimming fishes, friendly dogs, and sweet children in Hans Christian Andersen figurines. Gorgeous porcelain lamps are a late innovation. Up one flight the Dinnerware Department unfolds its lures; more than 100 separate patterns are on display, constituting the largest selection of Bing & Grøndahl dinner services anywhere. In 1979 they inaugurated special tours of their fascinating new factory-museum. Ask for Manager Per Simonsen, who loves his treasures and who is dedicated to his clients.

Royal Copenhagen, a few steps away, is also venerable, highly distinguished, and universally respected. **Frøsig** (Nørrebrogade 9) is a small, crowded center for "seconds" of all leading producers. Please get all of your porcelain while you're on Danish soil, because the markup in North America for exactly the same items is staggering.

Nifty boutiques: ★ ★ ★ ★ **Brodrene Andersen** (Østergade 7–9) has been a stitch in time for well over a century in stylishly attiring the Establishment fraternity—including, we might add, the Royal Danish Court since its more recent princes were in knee pants. Andersen's richly conservative paneled interior exudes masculine character—and so does its debonair clothing. General Manager Jørgen Nexøe-Larsen (3rd generation), your impeccable host, opens a sesame of sartorial treasures—cashmere coats and jackets plus Burberry classics, Danish sweaters and cardigans, and 100% hand-tailored outfits. Also you will find a well-stocked women's department where there are troves of lovely sweaters, skirts, and slacks. Cashmere by the yard from Edinburgh's Harrison can be selected here and sent to you directly from Scotland. In addition to Director Nexøe-Larsen, who would happily solve your problems, Mr. Lund on the ground floor, Mrs. Brandt in the Ladies' Department, and Mr. Hansen and Mr. Gulløv upstairs are also the souls of kindness. Far-and-away the leader.

★ ★ ★ ★ **Bee Cee** (Amagertorv 33 and Hotel Scandinavia) stands for the ubiquitous Birger Christensen—and by now you should know that this name hallmarks q-u-a-l-i-t-y. The spirit throughout is so gay and youthful that the chic buyer of any age finds it irresistibly à la mode. Here are selected Birger Christensen furs, eye-arresting sportswear, casual clothes, accessories and other temptations, plus a line of from-cradle-up male and female Danish hand-knitted sweaters and brad-studded wooden clogs. Manageress Miss Dominique Gandrup and her staff are all the Aee Bee Cee of kindness and fun.

★ ★ ★ ★ **Bjørn Wiinblad's Hus** (Ny Ostergade 11) is a Snow White house full of this world-famous designer's extraordinary, merry ceramics, many of his most celebrated posters, deliciously deft greeting cards, and other inspired creations—all bearing the unique, cunning, instantly recognizable Wiinblad artistry.

"Bits and Pieces" is the English name of **Bee Ting & Sager** (Gronnegade 16)—and in an elfinly charming and amusing way, what could better describe its contents? Fur King Birger Christensen remodeled this small A.D. 1750 house as a catch-all for both practical and zany merchandise—and goodness knows what is in stock from day to day!

Denmark is one of the handiest countries in which to restock your supplies of stateside books and magazines. **Boghallen** (Town Hall Square), **G.E.C. Gad** (Pedestrian Mall), and **Arnold Busck** (Købmagergade) offer the most versatile assemblages in our language.

Last but very far from least, please try not to miss one of the world-famous **"Lunch with the Danes"** which are held every Tuesday, Wednesday, and Thursday at noon from May 1 to Sept. 30 in the rooftop 3 Crowns Restaurant at the Hotel Scandinavia. Experts from Illums Bolighus lay the tables. A specially trained kitchen staff shows the guests the deceptive and interesting art of making typical Danish open-faced sandwiches. Birger Christensen presents his own eye-popping fur fashion show. It is a smash hit which husbands usually enjoy as heartily as do their wives. Advance reservations are strongly urged.

★ **TIPS** The **Gateway Store** in the Free Zone Waiting Room at Kastrup Airport stocks 121 brands of choice liquors and liqueurs and U.S. cigarettes, the _only_ items which are tax-free. Multitudes of other merchandise are available at normal city prices.

Shopping hours: Weekdays generally 9 A.M. to 5:30 P.M.; Saturdays 9 A.M. to 2 P.M.; no noon closings. Many stay open until 7 P.M. on Friday.

Dedicated shophounds? Space is too tight here for further listings—so consult this year's purse-sized edition of _Fielding's Selective Shopping Guide to Europe_ for more stores, more details, and more lore.

Other Targets

AALBORG, magnet of many industrial fairs, manufactures akvavit (the national hard drink)—and is also the most successful Fun Manufacturer on the Jutland Peninsula. The old district dates back to the early sixteenth century and certainly merits a day of exploration.

Among its hotels, the **Phønix** is one of the regions outstanding addresses. It has been continuously operated for more than a century in a building that predates the American Revolution. Colorfully executed and carefully maintained; 141 rooms, 111 of 'em with simple bath or shower; delightful English pub called the Brigaderen; 36-room wing with 100% bath count; eye-soothing green and blue color scheme; radiant heating. The **Hvide Hus** in Kilde Park has grown with dignity. Third-floor heated swimming pool; sauna; shops; tinkling and crackling bar with icy sips by an open fireplace; snack center plus panoramic penthouse grill; 202 rooms in efficiency style, each with private balcony and refrigerator. Modernistic and worthy. If you want to drop your anchor in the harbor, try the 85-room-and-bath **Limfjordshotellet,** a newcomer in the medium-budget fleet. The **Scheelsminde** is a charming motel in an old country house, renowned for its first-rate cuisine. The **Hafnia** and **Park** are both station hotels which are clean, adequate, and routine.

For our first meal in this city, we always head straight to **Faklen** (Jomfru Anegade 21). The building is 300 years old. Cheerful interior in yellow and brown; cunningly illuminated cross-hatched beam ceiling; low, tasteful center partition topped by colorful plants; tartan wall-to-wall carpeting; the waiters sport kilts; candles on every table; 40-place banquet room. We liked this one a lot. The charming **Fyrtøjet**, next door, in rustic style offers well-prepared food at popular prices. Next we'd pick the **Jomfru Ane** or the nearby **Cafeen**, both amply Gallic in tone. **Stygge Krumpen** (Vesteraa) is really sumpin' for fish. **Brix's Gaard** (C. W. Obels Plads) is reported to be "a charming 2-story restaurant in an old merchant's house." Unfortunately we've never met the old merchant himself. For snacks, the **Bistro**, a few doors from the Phønix, or the **Cafeteria Aalborg**, one block from the bridge, should soothe light appetites agreeably. In summer, the splendid view from the **Skydepavillonen** makes this candidate a popular choice among 1st-time visitors.

For revels after gloaming, the **Dancing Palace** spells r-o-m-a-n-c-e for many pairs of local citizens. Also popular are the **Bonaparte,** the **Algier Bar,** and the **Why Not** discothèques. The **Multi Maren,** featuring Danish and international artists, also is a beacon for night owls.

Between *Aalborg* and *Aarhus*, on the Mariager road (not the main highway) above *Randers*, try not to miss the superbly colorful and charming **Hvidsten Kro**. This one is a knockout. A 5-course standard banquet, called "Gudrun's Recipe," has been served in this country inn for elephants' years; the price is remarkably low, and we'll guarantee it'll be one of the unique dining experiences of your travel life. Just ask the sweet, regionally costumed lass who serves your table for the "Recipe" by name, and she'll do the rest. Suggestion: Nibble at *all* offerings until the sausage course comes, because the gargantuan quantity has been known to pop the eardrums of innocent initiates. One of the world's most interesting bets for the price.

AARHUS,   Denmark's second hub, is 1/10 Copenhagen's size. A vacation city, a university city, it boasts a unique open-air museum—a complete medieval town rebuilt with original bricks and timber. It also is proud of its **Tivoli-Friheden**, a park with all kinds of amusements, theater, and music performances. The **Fire Protection Museum** may sound dull, but wait until you boggle over those 60 or more fire engines, some of them manual or horsedrawn and dating back to 1850. Open June to mid-Sept., but closed Mondays. Another attraction is the **Moesgård**, containing prehistoric artifacts; nod "hello" to the **Grauballe Man**, a 2000-year-old resident of the region and still a sparkling conversationalist. The town is as green as an Irish instep, swept by bracelets of sandy beach and punctuated with tall leafy forests. This harbor has perked up commendably in recent times.

In the local hotel marathon, the **Marselis** easily wins the laurels. Outskirts situation in a wooded grove at the lap of the sea; brick exterior carried over into the lobby décor; attractive ceramic art inset along walls and corridors; waterside restaurant with piano melodies counterpointing the beat of the waves; simple but comfortable units with a nautical view through full-length windows; gray or soft-blue fabrics throughout. If peace is your motive, look no farther. Highly recommended. The **Atlantic**, smack in the middle of the busy port, is another high-tide contender. Modern lobby; ground-floor Le Pirate grill; bar plus amusing discothèque called the "9-o'clock train"; viewful 10th-floor spread for dinner dancing; ample garage space. Many doubles with balcony. The ferryboat landing is practically at its doorstep where ships embark for Kalundborg, the rail link to Copenhagen. While the **Royal** has perked up some of its accommodations, it is more noted for its outstanding restaurant. The high-spirited also enjoy its Tordenskjold discothèque. The **Ritz** has become increasingly ritzy and is now recommendable for upper-medium budgets. The dining room and most of the bedchambers have been restyled in a pleasant fashion. The **Ansgar** is more of a family retreat without any special froufrou but with substantial comfort and solid value for your kroner. Many congresses pitch up at the **Scanticon**, which becomes a hotel in summer. There is a restaurant, swimming pool, sauna, plus all of the amenities you would anticipate at a major innkeeping installation. The **Mercur**, in the Viby suburb, occupies the first 3 floors of a college building. The **Three Oaks** offers shade in neighboring Brabrand. Two miles north on Route #10 is the unpretentious **Motel La Tour**.

When hunger strikes, your first inclination should lead you to your hotel dining room—especially if you are booked in any of the above-mentioned leaders. Among the independents you will find a relaxed atmosphere and reasonable international cuisine at **De 4 Årstider**. The **Café Mahler** features intimacy with its French cuisine. *C'est bon ça.* **Barberen** is an inexpensive little shaver incorporating the décor of an antique barbershop, while **Kellers Gård** occupies an old grocery store at Rådhuspladsen. Locals praise the **Windsor Pub** in the Hotel Windsor; it is a sizzling steak restaurant with an all-you-can-eat groaning board at lunchtime.

When darkness falls, comestibles (naturally, of a modest sort), music, and dance are served up at both the **Tropicana** and the **Maritza**.

ANS   is a village 20 minutes southwest of *Viborg* and 15 minutes north of *Silkeborg*. The **Kongensbro Kro** nestles cozily just off the highway intersection, down by the edge of a lovely lake that sparkles about 2 miles southeast of town. Old-style inn restored in the Danish tradition by the proprietary family; forest-green dining room with excellent skillet skills on our feast; cellar-cited tiny pub and TV nook; 32 bedchambers, including a handful of modern units; high bath count boasting plumbing that really works. If you're in the region, make an effort to search out this little gem. We have a hunch you might fall in love with it.

ESBJERG   is best known as the ferry port for England; the harbor itself is quite engaging for salty types. Friends of nature will admire its Fishing and Maritime Museum, its Saltwater Aquarium, and the Seal Basin. **Esbjerg Museum** focuses its scholarly attention on Danish prehistory, while the **Kunstpavillon** concentrates on art of more current times. Students of architecture and interior design shouldn't miss the curious **Saedden Church**, a strange brick structure illuminated inside by 804 suspended lightbulbs. In this *havn,* try your derndest to look pretty for the **Britannia's** reception chief. The facilities are modern, the cookery is delicious (especially the finny fare), and the prices are right. Managing Director Jens Petersen, formerly of the Richmond in Copenhagen, runs a tight ship. If the Britannia is booked solid, you would probably find reasonable shelter at the **Guldager Kro**; the **Ansgar**, a mission inn, is adequate but far from innspiring. **Bang's**? That's a hotel—or so they say. We stayed here and can't believe it. The **Esbjerg** struck us as being equal to it in every visible way; recent word suggests that its future is uncertain. Plan your trip to arrive just before boat time so that you may have the option of moving farther eastward if the Britannia or possibly the Guldager Kro is full.

FREDERIKSHAVN Refer to "Jutland Peninsula" and "A Smattering of Motels" further along.

ISLAND OF FYN *Odense*'s choices are separately listed further along. In *Svendborg*, it's the well-regarded **Svendborg** with 56 rooms and 56 baths. Appetizing food and friendly service; dinner music; very pleasant indeed. Another charmer is the well-regarded **Christiansminde**. At *Nyborg*, don't miss at least a meal, a sip, or a snooze at the waterside **Hesselet**—to us, one of the most charming isles of enchantment in the nation. Two levels, trimly composed of wood, brick, and glass; forested tonsure with an apron of green reaching to the sea; golf course within chipping distance; sauna; sedate library plus a "garden room" for tranquil hours. Ultra-handsome wood-and-glass-lined Tranquebar Grill; costumed Japanese waitresses serving their well-prepared native dishes plus fine Danish cuisine; mulberry tablecloths; hot wet napkins offered before the meal; lovely porcelain by Royal Copenhagen. Both food and attention were superb—the best culinary experience, in fact, of a recent Danish reel. Accommodations sumptuously outfitted with grass-woven wall coverings or textiles, divans, easy chairs, and Oriental art works. The doubles are nice, but the suites are exquisite. Full- or half-pension plan available; prices on the high side aptly suited to the rewards. Could this be the finest resort hostelry on the island? Easily—and perhaps in the entire country, as well. Highest recommendation. The **Nyborg Strand**, nearby, is a bulky relic of a bygone era. Traditional in tone except for a few minor updatings; pool and sauna; a favorite with families and their chillun' for Sunday's lunch out. We've heard stuttering words of restful praise for the highly syllabic **Steensgaard Herregaards Pension** at *Millinge*, which was begun in the fourteenth century and completed as a manor house in the seventeenth (which gives you some idea of the labor problems in Denmark). Said to be a halcyon half-timbered retreat for P & Q. For more of the same, you should sample the cozy **Falsled Kro**. Another worthy tie-up is the **Feriehotel Klinten**. In the northern part of the island, the **Hasmark Strandgård** serves peace and quiet as leading commodities.

GRENÅ is a ferry stop from Hundested (Zealand) and Varberg or Helsingborg (Sweden) 31 miles east of Randers. It is justly proud of a claim to having East Jutland's finest beach. Here, the **Du Nord** comes up with a 100% bath count, good vittles, and good service.

JUTLAND PENINSULA From the German border working north, here is a selection of fair-to-good candidates: **Søgaardhus** ("Stork's Nest House," 7 minutes from *Krusaa*, the German–Danish frontier station) is now just so-so. In this immediate area, the **Am Gränze** and the **Europa**, both on

the German side, are functional. Even the **Krusaagard** and the tiny, tiny
Holdbi Kro, on Danish soil, are more affluent in human warmth than these
2. The latter has just been perked up pertly. At **Abenrå**, about 20 minutes
north of Søgaardhus, the low and linear **White House** is a worthy fjord-stop
on Highway A-10. A couple of miles south of **Haderslev**, the **Syd** should be
considered utilitarian at best. In **Kolding**, the **Saxildhus** is attractive and
immaculate. Excellent restaurant. Worthy on every count. Equally good is the
sparkling **Hotel Kolding**, in midtown, with its appealing cosmopolitan restaurant and the chummy Bacchus Bistro. Solid comfort and good value. Motorists
will probably find the **Motel Tre Roser**, in the city's park, an excellent traveler's rest. Boasting a pool, paths, woods, and ponds, the kids will probably
never get to bed. While in this town, please don't miss the **Geografiske
Have**, a botanical wonderland with specimens from the seedbeds of the globe.
The **Trocadero** appears to be an inn, but it's really a night spot for dancing
and snacks. Just outside **Vejle,** on the brow of a hill overlooking the fjord and
forests, the **Munkebjerg** is one of the best in the region. This former monastic
site is now a low linear retreat for the merry laity. Rough-brick and wood-lined
corridors; window-girt dining room; fireside lounges; dancing to live music;
swimming pool; sauna; hairdresser; comfortable modern-provincial bedchambers, all facing the pines; warmhearted but equally provincial service. We hear
that the culinary efforts are improving. In the town itself, the ii-story, austere
Australia presents a first-rate chef, adequate but uninspired accommodations,
and the often-hopping Kangaroo Pub. One-half mile from **Skanderborg,** the
slick-rustic **Skanderborghus** provides a skandalously beautiful woodland-and-
lake view. It has 43 small rooms, all with toilet plus bath or shower. (Numbers
22, 23, 122, and 123 are corner units with more space). Connected restaurant-
lounge-bar wing as an independent entity, to preserve a modicum of quiet for
sleeping guests (sit at the far end for the best vista); excellent cuisine, presentation, and service; Finnish-type sauna bath; fishing privileges. Inexpensive and
mightily gratifying for a weekend, a week, or an era. In **Ebeltoft**, northeast
of Aarhus off the prime north–south artery, you'll find the **Hvide Hus** (yet
another "White House"). Here is an ultramodern, terrace-lined Arcadia
soughing in a glen several hundred yards from the edge of the Kattegat. Only
53 rooms spread along 4 floors of a long stratiform configuration. Every unit
with bath, all facing the sea and all with private balcony and seating area;
44-inch beds for spacious comfort, painted hessian-covered walls; annex and
4 extra-nice, extra-soul-soothing cottages also available; small bar-nightclub;
nearby stables, sailing port, and 18-hole golf course; 5 minutes' walk to a
not-so-hot beach; sauna; service a bit unseasoned; bales and bales of peace
except for a nostalgic moment each evening (from mid-June to mid-Aug.)
when the town watchman carols the hour as he walks his rounds—and even
that is down in the town. Manager Jorgen Knudsen is its Chief Executive.
Should this happen to be full, the nearby **Motel Vibaek** might be able to take
you; it's also modern and attactive. At the waterside, there's the spawling new
Strand with its half-acre of lobby plus hearth and its minuscule bedchambers.
The latter come with bayfront terrace or balcony, frigobar, bath, radio and the
usual amenities. Water-view dining room; sauna; free golf for guests. It caters
heavily to congresses. In **Randers**, the **Randers** calls itself the "Leaping

Salmon Hotel"—and it's a good catch for the provinces. Considerable updat-ings completed; heated garage; 90 comfortable, traditional units, each with private bath; especially kind direction and staff. No doubt about it, this one has a distinct personality which is enhanced by people who care. The 100-room-and-bath **Kongens Ege** ("Royal Oaks") spreads its limbs in a 16-acre park at the town's edge. A stalwart boasting the sophisticated Bellevue Restau-rant for dinner, a charming tartanesque lunch salon, a hunter's lounge, a discothéque, plus the Algier and the Kings Bars, and a sauna to sweat it all off. Delightful and highly recommended for modernists. At the *Rebild Bakker* turnoff from Highway A-10, 16 miles south of Aalborg, the **Rold Stor-Kro** is a laudable entry. Lovely situation on the fringe of Denmark's largest forest, on the heather of which the Danish-American July 4th celebrations take place annually. Sprawling sun terrace; 2-tier restaurant with oversize windows; snug downstairs bar with TV; children's playroom; most imposing wine cellar in Jutland. All accommodations, most of them with bath and shower, face the wood; a few so-called cabin rooms with double-decker beds are available for students or the Junior Set; the color and eye-appeal of the public quarters are not carried into the sleeping sections. The **Hanstholm** takes its name from its headland setting on the lighthouse cape about 70 miles west of *Aalborg* and 15 miles north of *Thisted*. Perched on a lime rock 125 feet above the North Sea; nearby harbor entrance, Denmark's only year-round ice-free port; game preserve, beach, swimming pool, sauna, and wilderness all in your hip pocket. Long, brick, motel-like structure; lots of wood and warming touches; peaceful views of the dunes; excellent table. Very restful. While we haven't seen it, we're told that the **Madsens** at *Bjerringbro* (south of *Viborg*) is a worthy haven in midtown. At *Nykøbing Mors*, the **Sallingsund Faergekro** is a cozy mooring whose name means the "Ferry Inn"—and so it is.

Other possibilities? At *Billund,* the **Vis-a-Vis** is a very pleasant entry across from the previously described toy town of Legoland. At *Frederikshavn* there's a thatch-roofed charmer in the **Svalereden** for weekend smørrebrøds; this rural delight is a couple of miles south of town. Also refer to "A Smatter-ing of Motels."

In the *Herning* area, the 30-bed **Karup** is a country address. Even though the shelter is modest, the food is mighty satisfying.

ODENSE (Refer also to "Fyn," the island on which it resides; the isle is also written as "Funen" on some maps.) This third city of Denmark is Hans Christian Andersen's hometown; his top hat, his manuscripts, and his trunk, lovingly preserved, rate as high with local burghers as the Holy Grail. There's a festival of Andersen-sational plays and fairy-tale reenactments every summer at **Funen Village**—held in the open air. Kids of all ages build up a head of excitement at the town's **Railway Museum**. In this major port, rich in industry, you may also find King Canute's famous monument in the market square and the A.D. 1090 crypt which contains the ashes of some of Denmark's greatest kings.

Among its hotels, the **Grand** is the grandest. Fine restaurant, popular bar, and cabaret dancing nightly in season. Solid value for your money. **Motel Brasilia**, at the outskirts on the road to Middelfart, is a charmer. Extra-pleasant surroundings enhanced by ducks, swans, and a family of deer as your neighbors; attractive restaurant; #37, a quiet gardenside suite-nik with a refrigerator and a little sitting room. **Motel Odense**, on the Nyborg pike (A8 and A9), is a half-timber farmhouse that is more alluring on the outside than in. Sleeping setup with toe-to-toe bed arrangement; linoleum floors and throw rugs; splash-all showers. The **Windsor** and the **Hans Tausen** are just adequate.

In this town you can eat reasonably well at the dining room of the **Grand**. Among the independents, the **Under Lindetraeet**, opposite the H.C.A. Museum, is perhaps the most distinguished—with corresponding high prices for superior food and service. The **Old Inn** ("Den Gamle Kro") boasts a covered garden in summer; overall, too, it has an interesting atmosphere and excellent fare. An ancient cellar has been tricked out as a cocktail lounge and coffee nook for post-gustatory sipping. The **Ugly Duckling** ("Den Grimme Aelling"), near the H.C.A. House, is a decorative delight. Unthinkably antique building with painted heraldry on the timber and stucco façade; smoky-lantern mien; single room divided by a ceiling-high wine cradle; fresh flowers everywhere. You'll probably enjoy the visual spell it weaves. **Rode7**, **Frank A**, and the **Radhuskaelderen** are all solid medium-budget choices with charm. Out at Funen Village (5 miles), the **Sortebro Kro** is an ancient inn with royal protection; it fairly oozes Danish flavor from every beam and ladle.

RANDERS Refer to "Jutland Peninsula."

REBILD Refer to "Jutland Peninsula."

RIBE Our choice is always the **Dagmar**. Its dining room is a grace note of Old World harmony. Now some bedchambers have been given a dash of New World convenience.

ROSKILDE This town, only 20 miles west of the capital, is one of the oldest in Denmark, its **Cathedral** containing the dust of 38 monarchs! Don't miss the fleet of 5 reconstructed vessels in the **Viking Ship Museum**, 11th-century boats sunk in the fjord to protect the town from attack. **Svogerslev Kro,** 2 miles from the center on A-4, is a 250-year-old thatched-roof tavern; **Club 42** fairly brims with antiquity and charm, too; **Palae Caféen** is for more conventional dining. Something that we find fascinating is the challenging **Lejre Research Center**, 7 miles west of town, where Iron Age houses have been reconstructed and where in summer people live almost exactly as prehistoric families existed in early times.

SILKEBORG The midtown **Dania** is the easy champ. Viewful dining room with delicious cuisine and careful service; Alley Cat Bar meowing from 9 P.M. to 3 A.M.; most units with foot-to-foot twin bed arrangement. Closed Sun. and Mon. Not bad—if you've just had a pedicure. On the outskirts, the **Impala** is located 2 miles northeast on Highway #15; it's fairly new. Cellar pool, sauna, and bar; ornithological theme; 42 rooms, mostly with private bath.

For diners, all roads lead to **La Strada**. Curiously, this small, pleasant town, smack in the center of Jutland, draws gastronomes to sample such specialties as Vol au Vent Pommery, Malay Chicken, Saltimbocca alla Sebastiano, Paella Valenciana, or Bombay Toast. Central location; no view; worth a special detour. The kitchen of the **Hotel Dania** also draws accolades for a job well done. The **Hotel Silkeborgsøerne** at *Laven*, about 15 minutes out, is a heavenly expedition for sunny day or starlit evening. Lovely lakeside situation; spotless napery and kindly attention.

VEJLE   For this "Town in the Mountains" (please excuse a touch of gentle Danish hyperbole), refer to "Jutland Peninsula."

☑ **A SMATTERING OF MOTELS**   If you plan to roam across the several Danish islands by car, you might find this section helpful. Throughout Scandinavia, but especially in Denmark, motor hotels are springing up as thickly as poppies these days—but don't expect North American standards. To Danes, the motel is a simple, functional, convenient roadside stop—for a price. Some offer private toilets and washbasins; some come up with private showers; some even are equipped with private baths. No piped music, no gaudy swimming pools, no fancy balconies for elegant breakfasting—but no $50 tariffs, either. Here's a selected list for the road traveler, some of which we've seen and some of which we've merely heard about:

Approaching Denmark from Germany via the island of *Fehmarn*, the Teuton ferry station of *Puttgarden* offers the basic **Baltic** and the better blue-and-gray **Dansk** (next to the toll gate); on the Danish side is the **Danhotel**; all are efficiency minded.

Island of Zealand, Including Copenhagen Area: There are several, *not* rated in order of attractiveness. **Wittrup Motel**, 20 minutes from the capital on Highway #1 (toward Roskilde, at *Albertslund*). Forty-eight doubles and 8 singles, all with shower and toilet including service; utilitarian rather than fancy. The quieter **BP Motel**, also on Highway #1 near *Roskilde*, 19 miles west of Copenhagen: space for 72 pillow-talkers; 14 units with shower and toilet; restaurant, cafeteria, bar, and lounge. Okay if you don't mind the distance from the doin's. In this district, we hear that the **Lindenborg Kro** at *Gevninge* and the **Prindsen** in *Roskilde* are 2 worthy stops; we haven't checked either. Nor have we parked at the new **Viking**, a half-mile out of Roskilde; it lists 22 doubles with shower and toilet and 7 singles. The **Motel Søvilla**, on the Copenhagen–Gedser highway at kilometer stone #32, has installed baths and toilets in 8 of its 16 doubles; restaurant, lounge, and carports. We haven't inspected the **Risø**, north of *Roskilde,* near the atomic research station (go off A-1, through the town, and 20 minutes into the sticks). At *Falster*, in the south, the **Baltic** is a full-blown hotel but worth noting in this somewhat remote area. Very worthy.

Jutland Peninsula   At *Haderslev*, south of Kolding on E-3, the glass-bound **Haderslev** is a glazed peach for modernists. Agreeable restaurant; very slick. Avoid the Syd. *Aarhus area* : **Motel La Tour**, just north of Aarhus on Highway A-10, has a 20-room-and-bath addition which doubles its capacity. Very pleasant, modern lounge-restaurant-bar with an interior "garden"; a cut above average, but not luxury level. The **Aarslev Kro**, on Highway #15, is a charming half-timber tavern and motel in which you will find ample comfort.

Ebeltoft area: **Motel Lyngsbaek** is a converted farmstead in half-timber style; sea-and-hills views. Beach ½-mile away; all rooms with showers; sound basic comforts in tranquil, no-sound surroundings. *Aalborg area*: Scheelsminde just south of town on Highways E-3 and A-10, rates well above at least 95% of its Danish confreres in appeal. Small restaurant with piano music on weekends; 56 rooms, all with showers, toilets, and washbasins; colorless ambiance in a growing industrial zone, but good carpeting, cleanliness, and comfort; very satisfactory indeed. The **Europa**, farther south at *Svenstrup*, is another possibility; it's only fair but modern. *Frederikshavn area*: The **Jutlandia** commands the port. Public rooms blending modernity and tradition; highly appetizing cuisine on our try; painfully compact accommodations which often follow Scandinavain trends and similar spaceless baths. Very good, especially if you're very little. **Motel Lisboa** has fresh-'n-brite studio-style doubles with toilet, shower, and telephone; we think it has improved notably in its simple clean-lined approach to innkeeping. A restaurant to fill your inner self and Mobil station to fill your tank. **Hoffman's,** in town, has been tastefully styled in the Danish mood. Maritime cocktail lounge expanding into a ruby-toned pub and restaurant; cafeteria; some of its 56 twin bedrooms and 16 singles with brick-lined walls; carpeting throughout; parking facilities for motorists. If you prefer the Suburbs, the **Viking** at *Saeby*, 7 miles south, offers a fresh outdoorsy mien and an expansive sea view. If you're driving north, the 47-room **Skagen**, a wink from the lighthouse, might turn you on. Sport and relaxation are the main themes on those far-flung dunes. In *Kolding*, we've already mentioned the **Tré Roser**.

England

Not all the British are English. The United Kingdom has 4 distinct peoples, about as dissimilar as a horse, a bull, a mule, and a deer. The Scots (say "Scotch" only when you're thirsty!) are geniuses with their hands, sticklers for thrift, conscientious workers who think increasingly about devolution and further separating their economy from that of England's. The Irish are mercurial, whimsical, stubborn, mystical. The Welsh are shrewd, deep, intense, music-prone, hewn from their native granite. We're concerned here with the English.

Great Britain sets its watch to Greenwich Mean Time (GMT), keeping it an hour earlier than continental clocks even in summer when most zones favor farmers with an extra hour of light.

The 55 million people find things pretty crowded on their 93 thousand square miles. Few of the forests remain. There is good farm and grazing land in the south and in parts of Scotland; this is where that renowned fat, tender beef is grown. Rivers and streams abound. The coastline is so tortuous, so full of inlets into which big ships can travel, that no point in Scotland, for example, is more than 60 miles from the sea. If the natural contours weren't that way, we might be living in a far less pleasant world; we can thank this lucky geographic freak for the creation and existence of the British Navy.

Climate? Don't believe the travel posters; on the average it's pretty awful. The Gulf Stream, however, effectively plugs up both ends of the thermometer. It's seldom unbearably hot or unbearably cold, despite common latitude with Labrador and the Baltic States, but its dampness is enough to give chronic rhinitis to Wellington's statue. Remember Browning's classic line, "Oh, to be in England, now that April's there"? For our money, however, June is usually tops. May, September, and October are its next best months; go then if you can possibly arrange it. One asset is the duration of daylight on spring and summer evenings; in Scotland you can often play golf at 10 P.M. Take warm clothing with you whenever you go to these changeable islands—particularly in summer, when you think you need it least!

The charm of the United Kingdom is not in her industrial cities. Go to the moors, the heaths, the dales, and lakes, the hamlets. Run out to Cambridge or Oxford for an excursion (but avoid the latter on the first Mon. and Tues. of Sept., when the annual St. Giles' Fair turns it into a shambles). Try the Shakespeare country in Warwickshire; try Canterbury in Kent, one of the ecclesiastical matrixes of civilization, or Rye and Dorking for simple village charm; try Winchester, the former capital of the realm, for a permeation of history harking back to the Knights of the Round Table; try the 35-mile-square Lake District, a miniature Switzerland in Cumberland, Westmorland, and Lancashire; try the cathedrals and serene stone villages of Gloucestershire; try rugged Cornwall, the Hardy country of Dorset and Wiltshire, Raleigh's Devon, the castles of Snowdonia, the poetic Cotswolds, the Derbyshire peaks, the Yorkshire moors, the Scottish Highlands, the hot springs of Harrogate, the unbelievably broad beaches of Southport, the renowned antiquities in the valleys of the Usk and the Wye. Around every bend in the road you'll find an ever-changing landscape, with customs, dialects, ways of life new to you, but as old to the culture as Chaucer and Malory. London is unique, but skip Birmingham, Liverpool, Manchester, and Leeds. Look for the real England at the roots of her grass.

The single event that everyone tries to witness is the **Changing of the Guard** ceremony which takes place daily in summer (every other day in winter, weather permitting) at Buckingham Palace at 11:30 A.M. If you're *really* hooked, then you also should catch the Horse Guards at Whitehall, where the Mounted Squadron of the Household Cavalry Regiment changes at 11 A.M. on weekdays and an hour earlier on Sunday. Call 246-8041 in London, an official service, for further directions. Times occasionally vary.

Windsor Castle ? Before any excursion here, check *first* as to whether it's open; requirements of the Court usually (but not always) result in the closing of the State Apartments during April and substantial portions of March, May, and June. The Tower of London will be receiving weekdays (9:30 A.M. to 5 P.M.) and on Sunday, beginning around April 1 and running through early October (2 P.M. to 5 P.M.).

Possibly the greatest provincial attractions to travelers are the more than 1000 **castles, homes, and gardens** which have been opened to the public, on payment of a modest fee. The National Trust, a nonofficial, nonprofit body, now owns 200. Of the grand total, 40 are "Great Houses"; the balance consists of stately mansions, country manors, abbeys, and sentimental shrines such as Rudyard Kipling's former residence. Most popular and most outstanding is Woburn Abbey and Zoo Park (42 miles from London, 54 miles from Stratford-upon-Avon) belonging to The Duke of Bedford Trust; 1.5-million guests per year "oh" and "ah" at the 3000 deer, the safariland of African animals, the multimillion-dollar art collection, 3000 acres of enchanting parkland, the model village, the cable car system, the exhibition of 17,000 toy soldiers, the Zoo restaurant, and the splendid antique furnishings of this "Most English of the Palaces." High in popularity is Chatsworth (on the River Derwent 33 miles southeast of Manchester), which is renowned for its magnificent gardens with water effects. The Duke of Norfolk's Arundel (near Brighton), the Duke of Marlborough's Blenheim Palace (8 miles north of Oxford), where Sir Winston Churchill was born, Beaulieu Abbey and Palace House, with a fine vintage-automobile museum (14 miles from Southampton), and the Marquess of Bath's Longleat where 50 African lions roam the ancestral park (24 miles from Bristol) are also favorite tourist targets. The later home of Sir Winston, Chartwell (2 miles from Westerham, in Kent), will undoubtedly become a beloved monument to the history of our own lifetimes. It maintains the flavor of the period between the wars—the happiest years of the great statesman's life. My Lord Montagu's (sic) estate at Beaulieu chugs along on the strength of its Motor Museum, which car buffs love to horn in on. Queen Elizabeth has joined the peerage by opening her 274-room Sandringham House in Norfolk to the public (except from July 21 to Aug. 9, when she is in the residence). Be sure to check whether the day of your visit coincides with the variable schedule at the mansion. If you are seriously interested in touring this circuit, the oversize, exhaustively detailed annual *Historic Houses Castles & Gardens In Great Britain and Ireland* (ABC Historic Publications, London Road, Dunstable, Bedfordshire, England, $2 plus postage) is an absolutely invaluable aid.

What must be the most blue-blooded conference since Runnymede was attended by 600 British dukes, marquesses, earls, and other noblemen who own aristocratic homes in England. Their purpose? To form—please get this—a "trade union" to plan new ways for attracting visitors to their estates. If you wish to overnight in some of these castles or stately homes refer to our comments at the end of our London "Hotels" section further along.

Those interested in modern art should visit the still controversial **Coventry Cathedral**. Designed by Sir Basil Spence, it contains the largest tapesty in the world (the work of Graham Sutherland), sculpture by Sir Jacob Epstein, and stained glass by John Piper. Or, if you can't schedule a pilgrimage to Mecca this year, you can still pay respects to the Holy East by viewing the new **London Central Mosque** plunked—golden dome, minaret and terraces—in stately Regent's Park at the Hanover Gate entrance. By request of local infidels, the *muezzin's* voice, accommodatingly, has been silenced, but inside there's a chandelier from Iraq, carpets from Iran, a pulpit and screens from Egypt, and further wonders from Turkey, Algeria, and Morocco. Just in case you haven't been keeping score over the last 800 years, this is the first major Moslem edifice to be built in Europe since the 13th century (when the Alhambra was begun in Granada).

Canal and river cruising has undergone a renaissance among U.S. visitors. Inland Waterway Holiday Cruises (Preston Brook, Runcorn, Cheshire) and Inland Cruising Co. (The Marina, Braunston, Daventry, Northamptonshire) churn up a wide variey of excursions along much of the country's canal network from midspring to midautumn. Here is about the ultimate in leisurely touring between London and Manchester. Rates are by the week; see your travel agent for bookings, but be sure to nail them down early. For briefer forays, Thames Launches and Thames Motor Boat Co. (London) provide 1-hour, 2-hour, and all-day journeys from Tower Pier to the Tower of London and upstream to Putney, Kew, Richmond, and Hampton Court, plus special 2-hour evening sojourns. Yet another 2½-hour canalization (with lunch) can be had aboard the *Fair Lady* of Camden Lock, Chalk Farm Road, Camden Town. For a more sybaritic approach involving a longer, live-aboard-dine-about experience that combines luxury, enlightenment, and gastronomy, please refer back to "Let's Be European"; there we report on the barges of delight to be had via the **Floating Through Europe** cruises; these include British and Continental ports of call.

The overwhelming sublimity of the little **Chapels Royal** is virtually a secret to all foreign visitors except a relative handful who reside in the Commonwealth. The reason? Unless the tourist dresses conservatively and is quietly mannerly, he or she is not wanted by the vicars and the congregations. As a further illustration, cameras are banned. These gloriously beautiful places of worship are tucked away in a number of the most famous and most historic monuments of the United Kingdom—settings that are incredible to the uninitiated. All are sponsored by the Crown. Some date back to the eleventh or twelfth century. The Sunday services normally start at 11 A.M. The choirs are limited in number but magnificent in voice. Should you wish to attend, you'll find a listing of the locations and the hours in Saturday's better-grade London newspapers. Wear a church-going-type suit or dress (not sports clothes), arrive at least 15 minutes early, and regardless of your religious persuasion you should find it one of the richest experiences of your journey abroad.

Sound and Light spectacles *(Son et Lumière)* have crossed the English Channel from France and caught on fast. So far they have been presented at the Tower of London, Buxton, Canterbury, Carrickfergus Castle, Dover Castle, Eltham Palace, Kenilworth Castle, Greenwich Palace, Cardiff Castle, Gloucester Cathedral, Southwark Cathedral, Ragley Hall, York Minster, and Norwich Cathedral in Norfolk, and Greys Court in Henley-on-Thames; there's also one aboard the *H.M.S. Victory* in Portsmouth, plus others at Pembroke and Stirling Castles; at Winchester, Worcester, and Durham Cathedrals; at Bury St. Edmunds, Hampton Court Palace, Rochester, St. Paul's and Lichfield Cathedrals, and Sherborne and Tewkesbury Abbeys. Consult your nearest British Travel office for last-minute information on the whens and wheres.

The **Chichester Drama Festival** presents stellar performers in an interesting Greek-Elizabethan playhouse. The theater, situated in a 43-acre park, is 62 miles southwest of London. In summer, special trains will whisk you back to Victoria Station by midnight; schedules also geared for matinées; express buses also make the journey; for details consult your hall porter. Tickets average the price of a movie back home; those who hunger for more than the arts may dine at the Theatre Restaurant. The pre-curtain smörgåsbord is said to be excellent, but we've never said skål to this particular table.

Stratford-upon-Avon is a living shrine that no serious Anglophile should miss. (For further information refer to our alphabetical listings further along.) Hardly any do, since during performance weeks (4 programs annually between Mar. and Dec.) and in midsummer it is packed to its rafters with wide-eyed disciples—95% of them Americans. The **Royal Shakespeare Theatre** is, of course, the be-all and end-all of local attractions. If you haven't nailed down your matinee or evening tickets in London beforehand *(which is a virtual "must")*, go immediately to the window in the theater foyer or to the below-mentioned tourist office; sometimes a few last-minute cancellations turn up. Each year the Bard's birthday is commemorated here on April 23. Despite the crush of seething humanity, much of the feeling of Elizabethan times remains in the stucco-and-beam buildings that line its narrow, flower-dotted flagstone streets. Favorite targets in town include Shakespeare's Birthplace, Anne Hathaway's Cottage, The New Place (the poet's retirement home), the adjoining sunken Knott Garden, Hall's Croft, Harvard House, where the university founder lived, and the engaging little Antique Car Museum in midvillage. Excursions into the nearby environs should encompass a visit to Mary Arden's House at Wilmcote, Warwick Castle, Kenilworth, or to such sweet little hamlets as Honington, Temple Grafton, Bourton-on-the-Water, Stanton, Chipping Campden, and those mentioned in our upcoming "Cotswolds" roundup. Hotels and restaurants (see separate sections) run from fair to adequate to promising; almost all, however, are replete with eye-appealing bonuses. Since tourism is this village's chief occupation, *be certain to have your room reservation confirmed in writing.* And if you have any travel problems, shoot arrow-straight for the tourist office (20 Chapel St.). Here is more than a Measure for Measure reward to all who cherish our language and literature.

☑ **TRANSPORTATION** In London, wonderful subways ("undergrounds" or "tubes"); pulsing London (Heathrow) Airport plus ever-expanding Gatwick and Luton to alleviate its raging blood pressure. Incidentally, there's a subway link (carry your own luggage) between Heathrow and Piccadilly Circus (under an hour) with trains leaving to and fro every 4 minutes during peak periods. What a blessing and what a saving! Incidentally, for further economizing, grocery-style baggage carts are available at Heathrow free of charge, but since porters receive a gratuity for their efforts, the carts sometimes "disappear." You'll find squadrons of 'em tucked away in the back of the hall. The Thames makes its friendly way through London's Port, 3000 acres of wharves and docks; the "City" (financial), Westminster (government), the West End (theatrical and shopping), Soho and Chelsea (entertainment and residential), Mayfair (elegant homes and apartments), and many other districts split the metropolis into its components. Write for the value-packed 12-month "Season Ticket to the History of Britain" (£3 at the Department of the Environment, 25 Savile Row, London, S.W. 1) which will admit you to the Tower of London and 649 other eye-poppers in the United Kingdom. Or ask the British Tourist Authority (64 St. James's Street, London, S.W.1A 1NF) for the £7 month-long "Open to View" pass which lowers the drawbridge onto all Department of Environment properties, plus those in the National Trust and about 200 others that are privately owned. Bring your passport. A tour of Britain could be planned around these monuments. If you're economy-minded, there are scads of money-saving programs built around the "Travelpass," the "Rover," or the "Go As You Please" themes which permit you to wander according to your own particular whims aboard a subway, bus, train, or sea ferry for varying lengths of time. Youngsters under 14 roll for less than ½ fare on some schemes.

If you want to move around a lot in many different directions, one tiptop, low-cost suggestion is the **Grey-Green Coach** organization, which operates excellent budget-level bus tours. The vehicles are immaculately maintained; excursions fan out on 2-to-8-day loops touching the historic and scenic heartbeats of the U.K., some even skipping over to the Continent. The packages are too detailed to cover here, but drop a note to the chairman, Henry Ewer, who will send you one of the comprehensive brochures. His address is Grey-Green Coaches Ltd., 53 Stamford Hill London, N16 5TD.

Taxis The quaint, dignified, celebrated horseless carriages long associated with London and other major cities rein nearly alone, offering stately privacy as their proudest product. Passengers are hidden from pedestrians' views as their ancestors were hidden in the cabs of the gaslight era. In our view, they're the finest, most comfortable, best-designed taxis in the world. Rates, however, are sky-rocketing. An average trip in the center of the city runs around $3. For each additional rider above one person, there's an extra charge. All have meters, so look for the flag lever or the light on the roof; if the former is up and the latter is illuminated, the car is for hire.

The minicabs, which for years caused bitterness and violence between their owners and those of the conventional fleets because they had muscled into the Big Boys' domain, are now prohibited from cruising (although many still do). They must operate as "cars for hire," which means that they now can be summoned only by telephone.

If you're traveling between the capital and Heathrow Airport and choose not to utilize the new subway shuttle, legislation now limits the hop to whatever is shown on the meter (it should average about £15). If you should be fleeced on this 14-mile drive, the British Airports Authority wants to be told. The cabbies are so hopping mad about the meter rate, however, that they may suddenly become invisible when they see you emerge from your hotel with a suitcase in one hand and an airline ticket in the other. If you can't find one ranked up at the Airport, buses leave frequently for the city.

★ **TIP** After theater, at rush hours, or when it's raining, you might as well unpack your pogo stick to hop back to your hotel. During the hyper-busy or nocturnal slack periods, London is easily one of the most exasperating metropoli in the world. We have waited literally hours and walked miles in search of hacks. Concierges, we discovered to our surprise, now usually won't bother to telephone for you. Doormen often have as many as 20 customers waiting for them to hail a rover. The *only* suggestions we can offer are (1) hire a car and driver if it's a big night out, (2) do not stray far from the population pockets or theater districts if you hope to get home at a reasonable time, and (3) telephone the Radio Taxi service (272 3030) or Owner Drivers service (286 4848), which might not answer the phone if the cabs are occupied. With public transportation closing down around 12:30 A.M., hundreds of theater-goers are hopelessly stranded in this otherwise sophisticated city every night. Most cabbies simply won't work during the late hours—it's a shocking development.

Trains Because Britain invented railways, it has more track per square mile than any other nation and a station for every 5 miles of line. Most main lines radiate from London, and all are improving these days. Intercity trains—almost all air-conditioned and with a restaurant car plus sleepers on night express runs—are usually fine. In this group are the rockets that can hit 125 mph and can average better than 100 mph flashing across Albion. (These hot-footed speedsters have been sundering the air between the capital and targets such as Bristol, Cardiff, Swansea Plymouth, Penzance, Leeds, Bradford, York, Newcastle, Edinburgh, and Aberdeen. In addition the Advanced Passenger Train, dubbed as the world's most revolutionary iron horse, operates on the London–Glasgow run. It tilts when taking curves at high speed.

If you plan to do a lot of moving around in the U.K., the BritRail Pass will buy 7, 14, 21, or 30 days of unlimited rail travel at bargain rates. Go to the British Railways Offices in New York, Los Angeles, Chicago, Vancouver, or Toronto for details. Remember, please, that these are ONLY for sale in North America. There's also a special BritRail Youth Pass for 7, 21, or 30 days that's even cheaper than the standard version; you've got to be between 14 and 22 to qualify. Again, pick it up BEFORE you leave.

Your big baggage travels separately in the "luggage van"—unless it consists of 1 or 2 normal suitcases, in which case you'll carry it in your compartment. At stations, snag a baggage trolley (porters are becoming as extinct in the U.K. as they are elsewhere). The "open-plan saloon carriage" is most common, although a few "compartment" type coaches are still in use. First-class and Second-class designations remain, with Smoking and Nonsmoking sections. Seats are often bookable in advance on the main circuits; if you see a slip of paper on the back cushion, you're out of luck—unless it's your reservation!

★ **TIPS** Crossing to Ireland on a British Rail vessel used to be a voyage any traveler would yearn to forget. Not long ago, the officials realized this and began to brighten up the fleet. Now the "Sealink" network makes rail, ship, or car connections pleasant, convenient, and economical. It hooks into numerous U.K. destinations as well as into continental gateways.

Brittany Ferries offers a 24-hour car-ferry spin between Plymouth and Santander (Spain) aboard the *Armorique*. While it eliminates your weary wheel hours, it does not save much time or money for Iberia-bound voyagers—and it denies motorists the pleasures of the French countryside and adventures in Gallic cuisine.

The "Motorail" trains (from the special terminals at Kensington) will whisk you and your automobile almost anywhere in the nation (27 separate services and 110,000 car spaces by day and night all year round). There are also Train-Your-Car services from London (avoiding the crowded Exeter bypass) to both Totnes (Devon) and St. Austell (Cornwall), for lazy westbound motorists. All are less expensive than one might think.

A helpmate for the rod-riding wayfarer is BR's timetable, obtainable for about $4 from the Publicity Department, British Railways Board, Melbury House, Melbury Terrace, London, N.W.1, or from bookshops or station kiosks.

Car tips Car-ferrying across the English Channel has become Big Business—and it's mushrooming yearly. There are so many new ships with increased passenger and car capacities and expanded facilities replacing their older sisters that we suggest you consult your travel agent for the very latest tidings. Approximately 1-million automobiles a year are toted between British and continental ports. In peak season, about 70 sailings a day link Britain with France or the Belgian headlands at Ostend. A drive-on-and-off car-ferry service with 3 ships shuttles between Newhaven and Dieppe (103 miles from Paris)— ideal for motorists pointing for southwestern France, Spain, or Portugal. For the connection with Santander (Spain), please see our earlier comment under "Trains." **Normandy Ferries** operates between Rosslare (Ireland) and Le Havre, providing separate hookups between Southampton and Le Havre; **Southern Ferries** weighs anchor with drive-on vessels such as the *Eagle* between Southampton and Lisbon or Tangier. **Hovercraft** now fan out year round between Ramsgate and Calais; you'll be floating on air for a mere 40 minutes; conventional luggers take 3 times longer. Most of these "flying" boats can carry only 36 people, but more recently the *Mountbatten* made its first commando raid from Dover to Boulogne toting 250 S.O.B.'s (souls on board), plus 30 cars. Several more of these ultranoisy, $4,000,000 blowhards also now have taken to the waves. Seaspeed, a division of British Rail, owns the 3 biggest hovercraft in the world, each capable of carrying 400 passengers and 60 vehicles. At peak times there are up to 18 crossings each way every day aboard the *Princess Margaret, Princess Anne,* and *Ingenieur Jean Bertin.* They have terminals at Dover, Calais, and Boulogne. Channel conditions hardly ever bother these skimmers, unless there is unusually heavy weather.

§Conversion to left-side driving and traffic in the British Isles (due to change in the dim and misty future) is a lot trickier than you might think—especially in 90° turns, traffic circles, and passing (oops, "overtaking" is the proper word there!). Gradually, international road-sign symbols are replacing traditional English ones—but for some time, both will be in existence. For the first few hundred miles, most visiting drivers don't dare relax for an instant.

§The Automobile Association and Royal Automobile Club are our candidates for the most alert organizations of their type. Official motorcyclists and service trucks patrol main roads to lend an experienced hand, without charge, to any of the members who may be stalled or in distress. Don't move an inch in Britian without first joining the AA; your card will also be honored in Germany, Scandinavia, Ireland, and the Benelux lands.

§The British gallon is nearly 1/5 larger than the U.S. gallon. Incidentally, this is the only area north of Africa (except perhaps for Gibraltar) where miles are employed instead of kilometers.

§Spot a fast-moving woman driver in your rearview mirror? Slow down! It's likely to be a Scotland Yard bobbette patrolling the highway in a 120-mph sports car. Limits, incidentally, are 70 mph on expressways, 60 mph on 4-laners, 50 mph on 2-lane pikes, and 30 mph in built-up areas. Better wear your seatbelt buckled, too, though the law doesn't require it.

☑ **FOOD** Notably improved over the past decade—and much more variety, too. The fine restaurants offer delectable food; where you'll continue to need your Tums by the gross is in the smaller, cheaper places run by gentle ladies or gentry with palates of Portland stone. Among the constellation of fashionable new stops there is a tendency among chefs to confuse richness with excellence; a surfeit of cream seems to find its unwheyward way into nearly every whip or fold from the kitchen.

Certain items have always been good: Roasts, grills, salmon, Yorkshire ham, Stilton cheese (a favorite for 250 years), and bacon. With an encouraging new interest in food among young housewives and an ever-growing circle of British gourmets, standards are definitely on the rise.

Meal hours are fixed. Breakfast used to be heavy, but now it is comparatively light; lunch is substantial; tea, at 4:30 P.M., is a sacred ritual in every walk of life; dinner, between 7 P.M. and 8:30 P.M., is the biggest repast of all.

★ **TIPS** English oysters are expensive but superb. Imperials (available all of the "R" months) are considered the finest; the larger Colchesters (Oct. to Jan.) are also exquisite. Don't miss them if you're a bivalve fan.

In case you're as baffled by the difference between these so-typical lookalikes as we were, steak-and-kidney *pie* is made with pastry crust, while steak-and-kidney *pudding* ("pud" to the locals) is made with a suet dumpling top which is indigestably deelishus.

Check the prices of all delicacies offered as side dishes. Most are flown in from points as remote as South Africa—so if your maître suggests "a nice piece of melon," for example, it might come from Israel and it might cost $7. Even a portion of humble asparagus might rock you $8.50!

☑ **DRINKS** Please refer to our extensive report in the "London" section further along which is titled "Drinks (plus Pubs and Wine Bars)."

☑ **TIPPING** Railway porters (an endangered species, so you're not too likely to find one) get 15 pence per bag; when there are 3 pieces or more, cut this to 10 pence each. Taxi drivers get 15%, or a minimum of 10 pence. The hotel service charge is included in your bill, but you may wish to give 50 pence to £1 a day extra to the hall porter and your chambermaid; bellboys, doorkeepers, bartenders, and others who give you special attention receive separate consideration, with 10% or a minimum of 10 pence.

☑ **LOCAL RACKETS** Cockney guides can sometimes lie with the artistry of a Munchausen. Any old house is a "castle"; any old street is "where Dickens played as a child." Result: The tourist pays money, but sees and learns nothing. Book only through a reliable agency—or get registered guides through the London Tourist Board.

The occasional taxi driver will offer to "show London to the visitor"—and charge the fee on the meter, which will be astronomical. Don't fall for it; make your arrangements through a reputable company.

Whenever you cash a traveler's check in a hotel, make it a point to inquire *first* about the hotel's percentage on the transaction. If it's too big a bite (it frequently is!), you'll save a chunk by going to the nearest bank. Even more important, don't make international telephone calls from your hotel because of the appalling house rakeoffs which most of them levy. (The Hiltons, Trust Houses Forte, and the Lyngon Arms in Broadway are exceptions since they belong to Teleplan, a program to control phone tariffs.) Either go to the Central Exchange or use your telephone credit-card service (cost: 60¢), which will permit you to charge it to your number.

Guard your wallet carefully in crowds these days—particularly aboard jammed buses or subway ("underground") cars—because pickpocketing is increasing radically. On the transportation scene, often one man will carry on a loud (and distracting) argument with the conductor while his confederate jostles the victim and deftly does the job.

The so-called key swindle is still unlocking portals of woe. This is the vintage con game in which a Soho B-girl or a "hostess" in a 4th-rate booze joint will slip the sucker the alleged key to her apartment, on deposit of perhaps £5 "for good faith." When he arrives at the rendezvous, either it's a phony address or she never shows up. A similar racket was worked recently on a sophisticated bachelor in one of the dingy, sleazy sex-cinema theaters in the Leicester Square area. After showing an innocuous movie, the entrepreneur persuaded 4 fellows in the audience to pay £15 *in advance* to see an "exhibition" a few blocks away. The address turned out to be a vacant lot. When the suckers returned to demand that their money be refunded, the racketeer, then surrounded by bodyguards, smiled benignly and asked, *"WHAT* money?"

Watch railway ticket clerks, who'll mumble about "new fare tables" when you catch them. Bus ticket-sellers are also becoming great palming artists; on our recent month-long London rounds, this writer *never* was given the correct change on any of the numerous bus rides. Know what you gave—and keep your hand extended until all of the proper coins come back.

☑ **INFORMATION CENTERS**   The American offices of the **British Tourist Authority** do outstandingly good work, thanks to U.S. General Manager James T. Turbayne, O.B.E. For his solid achievements, this unusually able and attractive executive has received the decoration of Officer of the Order of the British Empire from Queen Elizabeth—and well merited it was! If the pleasant ladies at his Information Counter at 680 Fifth Ave., N.Y. 10019, or the branch personnel at his Chicago or Los Angeles outlets can't solve your problem, write or call Mr. Turbayne in person.

The Canadian offices are at 151 Bloor St. West, Toronto 5 and Suite 455, 409 Granville St., Vancouver. There are also European branches in Paris, Amsterdam, Brussels, Rome, Madrid, Copenhagen, Stockholm, Zürich, Oslo, and Frankfurt-am-Main.

If you'll pop into the **Tourist Information Centre** at 64/65 St. James's St., or its branches at Victoria Station, SW 1, (near Platform 15), Selfridges or Harrods, or the **Heathrow Travel Centre**, you'll find a veritable font of courtesy and assistance.

CITIES

GREATER LONDON   is a Tale of Two Cities: King's City and Merchants' City. They were invaded by the Romans in A.D. 43, but the story prior to that is still a mystery. She is the grandmother of capitals, almost 8-million strong and 610 miles square, vying with New York and Tokyo as the largest urbanized area in the world.

More and more, her midtown sections profile the rude invasion of steel-and-glass monoliths. The nucleus, obliquely called the Greater London Council, consists of the City of London, Westminster, the Royal Borough of Kensington and Chelsea, and 30 other metropolitan boroughs. London Bridge, which was *truly* falling down, became a tourist attraction some years ago in Arizona's Lake Havasu City. Meanwhile, the mother city has replaced it with a modern 6-lane span.

Despite this frenzy of growth, for ages visitors have thought that London's streets must have been planned by the Mad Hatter or by wandering cows; they wind helter-skelter in 10-thousand directions. But there's beauty about this eccentric old dowager, a sweep to her 5 central parks (St. James's, Green, Hyde, Kensington, and Regent's), a dignity about her Portland-stone buildings, white with weathering or black with soot, and a charm about her pageantry, her pomp, her leisurely Victorian pace. For comments on what to see and how to begin, please refer back to the introduction of this chapter as well as to "Transportation".

Sightseeing Dial 246-8041 or 730-0791, and an official service will give you full details on hours and locations of important London sightseeing events, art exhibitions, theatrical performances, and What's Going On.

There are so many alluring attractions for visitors to this great metropolis that it is impossible to list even the fifty most important ones in the limited pages of this book. Instead, our colleague Margaret Zellers has comprehensively delineated them in *Fielding's Sightseeing Guide to Europe*.

To us, however, there is one which is the best fun of all—not to be missed by *any* pilgrim of *any* age if humanly possible. This is the 45-minute boat ride (80 pence one way or £1.10 round trip) from Tower Pier to the lovely outlying suburban center of nautical Greenwich. All services are operative at 20-minute intervals between April and November. While you glide down the river, you'll be painlessly filled with enchanting facts and tidbits which most native Londoners don't even know. After landing and inspecting the original *Cutty Sark* clipper in drydock, ohing and ahing at the Gypsy Moth Conservatory, admiring the magnificently architected and groomed College grounds, and idling through the charming streets of the town, have lunch at the Trafalgar Tavern, which is directly on the bank, a short skip from where you'll dock. Reserve in advance; delightful ambiance; attempted French-type cuisine; prices highish; Navy-size portions; closed Sunday nights and holidays. You may return either by the way you came or by double-decker bus. What a grand, grand excursion on a sunny day! Nelson's Column and Trafalgar Square, Buckingham Palace, Parliament, Hyde Park, Westminster Abbey, the Tower of London (with the Crown Jewels), the stunning new National Theatre, the Tate, the National Gallery, the Museum of London (free viewing of artifacts from prehistoric to modern times), and Madame Tussaud's wax museum are other targets. There is a marvelous, magic kaleidoscope of literally hundreds more. But what you'll like most is the color of everyday life along these crooked, crazy, sweet little streets.

"Gentleman Guide"? Cambridge and Oxford students, replete with dark suits, bowlers, and carnations, double as tour leaders through **Undergraduate Tours, Ltd.** (6 South Molton St., London W.I), a division of British Tours Ltd. A flock of readers continue to sing their praises. They are selected not only for their knowledge of the country, their personalities, and their background, but also for the quality of their cars—which transport you! Some preplanned itineraries available, but you may always roam whenever and wherever your spirit moves. British Tours also offer "Lilliput Tours" for children. They operate year round. A similar curriculum is offered by the **Take-a-Guide** organization (85 Lower Slone St., London S.W. I, Tel. 730-9144). The latter group even would qualify for graduate work; it handles not only the U.K. but all of Western Europe as well. If you need Stateside advice its New York office is at 19 E. 73rd St. (Tel. 628-4823, or a toll-free 800-223-6450). Another excellent choice would be a **London Taxi Guide**, whose pilots are not only professional drivers but people who have hosting qualifications and unrivalled knowledge of the capital—plus other British distinctions too. Their rates are proper for the ample rewards. The Central Booking Office is at 3 Elystan St., S.W. 3, Tel. 584-3118. Finally, the **Grosvenor Guide Service** (4a William St., S.W. I, Tel. 235-4750), provides an entré to some of the more unusual aspects of Britain and specializes in taking overseas visitors into British country homes.

LONDON HOTELS Quick Reference Table

Price categories by national (not U.S.) standards.

EXPENSIVE:
Athenaeum 116 Piccadilly. Tel. 499.34.64; Telex 261589; 112 rooms. P. 139
Berkeley Wilton Place. Tel. 235.6000; Telex 919252; 152 rooms. P. 135
Claridge's Brook St. Tel. 629.88.60; Telex 21872; 208 rooms. P. 134
Connaught Carlos Place. Tel. 499.70.70; 106 rooms. P. 135
Dorchester Park Lane. Tel. 629.88.88; Telex 261802; 300 rooms. P. 135
Gloucester 4 Harrington Gardens. Tel. 373.60.30; Telex 917505; 539 rooms. P. 140
Hilton 22 Park Lane. Tel. 493.80.00; Telex 24873; 431 rooms. P. 139
Howard Temple Place. Tel. 836.35.55; 111 rooms. P. 143
Inn on the Park Hamilton Place, Park Lane. Tel. 499.08.88; Telex 22771; 228 rooms. P. 137.
Inter-Continental 1 Hamilton Place. Tel. 409.31.31; Telex 25853; 500 rooms. P. 138
Lowndes 19 Lowndes St. Tel. 235.60.20; Telex 919065; 75 rooms. P. 142
Montcalm Great Cumberland Place. Tel. 402.42.88; Telex 28710; 112 rooms. P. 139
Ritz Piccadilly. Tel. 493.81.81; Telex 267200; 100 rooms. P. 136
Savoy The Strand. Tel. 836.43.43; Telex 24234; 500 rooms. P. 134

Sheraton Park Tower 101 Knightsbridge Road. Tel. 235.80.50; Telex 917222. 300 rooms.
P. 137

Westbury New Bond St. Tel. 629.77.55; Telex 24378; 225 rooms. P. 140

UPPER MODERATE:

Blakes 33/35 Roland Gardens. Tel. 370.6701; Telex 21879; 50 rooms. P. 138

Bristol Berkeley St. Tel. 493.82.82; Telex 24561; 190 rooms. P. 141

Brown's Dover St. & Albemarle St. Tel. 493.60.20; Telex 28686; 127 rooms. P. 136

Capital Basil St. Tel. 589.51.71; Telex 919042; 60 rooms. P. 138

Carlton Tower Cadogan Place. Tel. 235.54.11; Telex 21944; 270 rooms. P. 140

Churchill Portman Square. Tel. 486.58.00; Telex 264831; 489 rooms. P. 138

Curzon Stanhope Row, Park Lane. Tel. 493.72.22; Telex 267465; 72 rooms. P. 140

Dukes 35 St. James' Place. Tel. 491.48.40; Telex 28283; 52 rooms. P. 136

Grosvenor House Park Lane. Tel. 499.63.63; Telex 24871; 478 rooms. P. 135

Howard Hotel Temple Pl., Strand. Tel. 836.3555; Telex 268047; 138 rooms. p. 143

Hyde Park Knightsbridge. Tel. 235.20.00; Telex 262057; 182 rooms. P. 136

Kensington Hilton Holland Park Ave. 179. Tel. 603.33.55; Telex 919763; 611 rooms.
P. 143

Kensington Palace De Vere Gardens. Tel. 937.81.21; Telex 262422; 319 rooms. P. 145

Londonderry 19 Old Park Lane. Tel. 493.72.92; Telex 263292; 143 rooms. P. 140

Park Lane Piccadilly. Tel. 499.63.21; Telex 21533; 360 rooms. P. 137

Royal Garden Kensington High St. Tel. 937.80.00; Telex 263151; 442 rooms. P. 140

Royal Lancaster Lancaster Terrace. Tel. 262.67.37; Telex 24822; 435 rooms. P. 140

Royal Westminster Buckingham Palace Rd. Tel. 834.1302; Telex 916821; 130 rooms. p.
147

Stafford St. James's Place. 65 rooms. P. 136

Waldorf Aldwych. Tel. 836.24.00; Telex 24574; 310 rooms. P. 146

MODERATE:

Bedford Southampton Row. Tel. 278.78.71; Telex 263951; 182 rooms. P. 143

Britannia Grosvenor Square. Tel. 629.94.00; Telex 23941; 426 rooms. P. 142

Cavendish Jermyn St. Tel. 930.21.11; Telex 263187; 255 rooms. P. 141

Charing Cross The Strand. Tel. 839.72.82; Telex 261101; 210 rooms. P. 137

Chelsea Holiday Inn Sloane St. Tel. 235.43.77; Telex 919111; 217 rooms. P. 145

Chesterfield 35 Charles St. Tel. 491.26.22; Telex 269394; 120 rooms. P. 144

Cumberland Marble Arch. Tel. 262.12.34; Telex 22215; 880 rooms. P. 146

Cunard 1 Shortlands. Tel. 741.1555; Telex 934539; 640 rooms. P. 144

De Vere 60 Hyde Park Gate. Tel. 373.77.88; Telex 264189; 81 rooms. P. 137

Elizabetta Cromwell Rd. Tel. 370.42.82; Telex 918978; 83 rooms. P. 145

Embassy 150 Bayswater Rd. Tel. 229.12.12; Telex 27727; 193 rooms. P. 146

Europa Grosvenor Square. Tel. 493.12.32; Telex 268101; 274 rooms. P. 143

Hyde Park Towers Inverness Terrace. Tel. 229.94.61; Telex 267465; 110 rooms. P. 146

Imperial Russell Square. Tel. 278.78.71; Telex 263951; 465 rooms. P. 143

Kennedy 43 Cardington St. Tel. 387.44.00; Telex 28250; 317 rooms. P. 143

Ladbroke Chesham Place. Tel. 235.60.40; Telex 919020; 110 rooms. P. 146

Leinster Towers 25 Leinster Gardens. Tel. 262.45.91; Telex 27120; 160 rooms. P. 145

Londoner Welbeck St. Tel. 935.44.42; Telex 22569; 121 rooms. P. 146

Marble Arch Holiday Inn 134 George St. Tel. 723.12.77; Telex 27983; 243 rooms. P. 142

Mayfair Berkeley St. Tel. 629.77.77; Telex 262526; 390 rooms. P. 137

Metropole Edgware Rd. Tel. 402.41.41; Telex 23711; 555 rooms. P. 144
Penta 97 Cromwell Road. Tel. 370.57.57; Telex 919663; 914 rooms; P. 141
Piccadilly Piccadilly. Tel. 734.80.00; Telex 25795; 110 rooms. P. 145
Portman 22 Portman Square. Tel. 486.58.44; Telex 261526; 287 rooms. P. 141
Portobello Stanley Gardens 22. Tel. 727.27.77; 26 rooms. P. 141
President Russell Square. Tel. 278.78.71; Telex 263951; 417 rooms. P. 143
Regent Palace Piccadilly Circus. Tel. 734.70.00; Telex 23740; 1,244 rooms. P. 146
Royal Kensington 380 Kensington High St. Tel. 603.33.33; Telex 22229; 469 rooms.
    P. 142
Royal National Bedford Way. Tel. 278.78.71; Telex 263951; 556 rooms. P. 144
Royal Trafalgar Whitcomb St. Tel. 930.44.77; Telex 24616; 108 rooms. P. 145
St. Ermins Caxton St. Tel. 222.78.88; Telex 917731; 241 rooms. P.147
St. George's Langham Place. Tel. 580.01.11; Telex 27274; 85 rooms. P. 145
Selfridge Orchard St. Tel. 408.20.80; Telex 22361; 296 rooms. P. 141
Strand Palace The Strand. Tel. 836.80.80; Telex 24208; 795 rooms. P. 146
Tower St. Katharines Way. Tel. 481.25.75; Telex 885934; 826 rooms. P. 144
Washington Curzon St. Tel. 499.70.30; Telex 24540; 161 rooms. P. 143
Wilbraham Wilbraham Place, Sloane St. Tel. 730.82.96; 62 rooms. P. 145

LOWER MODERATE:
Averard 10 Lancaster Gate. Tel. 723.88.77; 60 rooms. P. 146
Berners 10 Berners St. Tel. 636.16.29; Telex 25759; 200 rooms. P. 147
Bloomsbury Centre Coram St. Tel. 837.12.00; Telex 22113; 250 rooms. P. 143
Dolphin Square Chichester St. Tel. 834.38.00; 166 rooms. P. 144
Flemings Half Moon St. Tel. 499.29.64; 107 rooms. P. 147
International Cromwell Rd. Tel. 370.42.00; Telex 27260; 424 rooms. P. 146
Mandeville Mandeville Place. Tel. 935.55.99; Telex 269487; 164 rooms. P. 147
Mt. Pleasant Calthorpe St. Tel. 837.97.81; Telex 262542; 479 rooms. P. 147
Mt. Royal Bryanston St. Tel. 629.80.40; Telex 23355; 634 rooms. P. 146
Park Plaza Bayswater Rd. Tel. 262.50.23; Telex 267465; 282 rooms. P. 147
Parkway Inverness Terrace. 80 rooms. P. 147
Post House Bayswater Rd. Tel. 262.44.61; Telex 22667; 176 rooms. P. 146
Regent Centre Carburton St. Tel. 388.23.00; Telex 22453; 350 rooms. P. 143
Ryan Gwynne Place, Kings Cross Rd. Tel. 278.24.80; Telex 27728; 213 rooms.
    P. 146
Stratford Court 350 Oxford St. Tel. 629.74.74; Telex 25971; 136 rooms. P. 147
White House Regent's Park. Tel. 387.12.00; Telex 24111; 586 rooms. P. 144

ENVIRONS:
Astor Lodge St. John's Wood. P. 147
Clive Primrose Hill Rd. Tel. 586.22.33; Telex 22759; 84 rooms. P. 147
Harrington Hall Harrington Gardens. 75 rooms. P. 146
Swiss Cottage Holiday Inn Adamson Rd. Tel. 722.22.81; 297 rooms. P. 142

HEATHROW AIRPORT:
Ariel Hayes, Middlesex. Tel. 759.25.52; Telex 21777; 185 rooms. P.148
Berkeley Arms Cranford. Tel. 897.21.21; Telex 935728; 42 rooms. P. 149
Centre Bath Rd., Longford. Tel. 759.24.00; Telex 934093; 360 rooms. P. 148
Excelsior W. Drayton, Middlesex. Tel. 759.66.11; Telex 24525; 660 rooms. P. 148

Heathrow Tel. 897.63.63; Telex 934660; 680 rooms. P. 147
Heathrow Ambassador London Rd. Tel. 964.4001; Telex 847903; 110 rooms. P. 149
Holiday Inn West Drayton. Tel. 08954.45555; 281 rooms. P. 147
Post House West Drayton. Tel. 759.23.23; Telex 934280; 594 rooms. P. 148
Sheraton Heathrow West Drayton. Tel. 759.24.24; 440 rooms. P. 148
Sheraton Skyline Hayes, Middlesex. Tel. 759.25.35; Telex 934254; 360 rooms. P. 147
Skyway Hayes, Middlesex. Tel. 759.63.11; Telex 23935; 441 rooms. P. 148

GATWICK AIRPORT:
Copthorne Gatwick. Tel. 03425.3001; Telex 95500; 173 rooms. P. 149
Piccadilly P. 149

Hotels For far more comprehensive information on certain British hostelries than space limitations permit here, interested travelers are referred to *Fielding's Favorites: Hotels and Inns, Europe* by Dodge Fielding, our son. The revised edition, in which a total of 300-odd favored possibilities were handpicked from the 4000-plus personally inspected, will be at your bookstore early this year.

In England, declining service; facilities improving, but daily maintenance by untrained or un-caring staffers now slipping dangerously.

In London, a mere single in a posh pad may ring up $60 or so; twin billings bong up to a resounding $130 for bed, breakfast, service, and taxes; make it at least $145 for a small suite or $200 for a large one. Medium-bracket innkeepers charge only about 20% less than their patrician peers, which means that ordinary London lodgings now sock the traveler for about as much as the finest palace-type houses on the Continent. In sum, however, although you'll pay plenty for a latchkey, England offers so much that we'll also bet that your fun will be the merriest in many a year.

Now for our breakdown of the individual hotels. Because of the swelling flood of newcomers, we feel it is not appropriate to rank the Old Guard with the Avant-Garde. We have, therefore, divided our ratings into "Traditional," "Contemporary," and "Assorted" brackets. The candidates surrounding Heathrow Airport and in outlying districts are covered separately toward the end of this section.

TRADITIONAL HOTELS:

Claridge's. There is still tremendous snob appeal in this London home of royalty, rulers, and the famous throughout the world, particularly if Burke's *Landed Gentry* carries your name or if you sport an old-school tie. However, General Manager Lund Hansen has somewhat softened its formerly stiff mien. Crown jewel of the fabulous Savoy Hotels empire; no bar, no dancing; the ultimate in luxury, urbanity, and prices, but aura so autocratic that it's not for the average visitor looking for a home away from home. A gem, at Cartier prices. Better and better.

Savoy. Here, to our minds, is the greatest large hotel of the world, bar none. Five hundred rooms with bath, all instantly convertible into suites; 100 apartments; mini-bar in every room but personal service always available; color TV throughout; vast majority of abodes impeccable, but a scattering of poorly executed "mother-in-law" units allotted to the less fortunate when the house is jam-packed; staff of 1200. Its massive main dining room has just been divided into a lovely off-lobby lounge where tea and other refreshments are served and a cozier new restaurant with dinner dancing facing the river. Savoy Grill in white marble with yew paneling, which some visitors find aesthetically cool; shopping arcade; American Bar; crack Public Relations staff mistress-minded by lively, ever-smiling, Judith Dagworthy. Handsome, effervescent General Manager Claudio Buttafava operates this 7-ring show with commanding flair.

Berkeley. Pronounced "Barkley"; this Savoy Hotels landmark resides on a lovely site edging Hyde Park in the fashionable Belgravia district. We aver that here might be the last truly super-deluxe hotel in the world to be built as a cunningly modernized showcase in the supremely gracious traditional style. At hand are such features as the opulent Lilac Restaurant, the fine-feathered Le Perroquet luncheon salon *cum* nighttime disco (see "Restaurants"), the mellow Bar, the soooo comfy, 68-seat Minema minicinema, the gorgeous penthouse pool with sliding roof, refreshment facilities, and sauna—a galaxy. There are 25 regal suites and 156 knockout doubles; the flawless demisuites among the latter group are our favorites in the house for our personal requirements. Best of all is the fact that General Manager Stefano Sebestiani has one of the finest staffs under any London roof; Chief Hall-Porter Goodberry is among his collection of special prizes. A noble, graceful, remarkably beautiful oasis.

Dorchester. This remains a favorite with thousands of loyalists around the globe. Another massive face-lifting has just been completed. Now diners in both the refurbished Terrace Restaurant (new cleverly raised floor, private drinking oasis, restored skylight, and classical columned gallery) and the relocated, more informal Grill with its own Oyster Bar have an uninterrupted view of Hyde Park. Air conditioning upped to 100%; enlarged lounge areas; Dorchester Bar repolished; elegant shopping arcade. Upstairs, all corridors beautifully redone; bedchambers and baths refashioned; # 618 and # 800 among our pet doubles. The Oliver Messel, Harlequin, and other super-plush suites are regal. Greatest asset of all is its remarkable staff; some are still in service after 45 years. With Managing Director Albert-Jean Ruault, formerly of Paris' prestigious Plaza Athénée, at the helm, we have great admiration for this landmark and its delightful *regum britannicum*.

Connaught. This spell-weaving old-timer couldn't be a more felicitous choice for the traveler in search of comfort and tranquillity in the homespun way—provided, of course, that you live in a palatially homespun mansion. If you desire a spacious room, flawless service, a superior restaurant and grill, a faintly English-Manor-House atmosphere, no orchestras, no dancing, no radio, no TV (except in suites), and quiet British gentility which is nearly Edwardian in tone, here is surely the place for you. Kindly, mannerly, attentive staff, from Head Hall Porter Mannion to Head Barman Tony to the youngest employee; Savoy Hotels, Ltd. ownership, but independent administration. The cuisine in the Grill vies with the most exalted in the capital. Again we couldn't have been happier in what might well be compared in aura to a top-ranking London club. Book l-o-n-g in advance.

Grosvenor House. Virtually everything was swept away and replaced in this house's recent $7,250,000 rejuvenation—excepting the spit-and-polish efficiency of the staff and the somewhat commercial aura of its purposeful functionalism. Two fresh restaurants and the revamped lounges are its proudest button-poppers. We much prefer the colorful decorative schemes on the even-numbered floors, but perhaps you'll disagree. The management is now in the extra-capable hands of young and personable Ray Carroll, who hopes to add even more dash and zip to this imposing establishment. Moving up notably and laudably.

Brown's. Since 1837, this has been one of the most famous hostelries in the British Empire. Manager Bruce Bannister is a staunch guardian of properly maintained traditionalism. Façade recently painted; lobby and public quarters freshened; shortage of staff on our latest visit; mazelike corridors, a result of linking 11 townhouses together to create this composite; older units beautified; 142 rooms and 5 suites; Dover St. chambers quieter during the early morning hours than are those facing Albemarle St.; 70% bath ratio; an overall feeling of slow-motion activity among antebellum furnishings.

The Stafford. This entry is a converted manse tucked away in a little mews. In tone it resembles Brown's and may suit some visitors even more; today it sparkles with a distinctive personality that evokes the flavor of fine English values. Handy location that is quiet, though the house is merely 100 yards from Piccadilly; private-homelike lounge; bustling dining salon; graceful bar (from which, it is vowed, the first martini was exported to the Colonies); classical décor; 65 ample-size units, all with bath; not for bargain hunters. Definitely for the discriminating.

Dukes. This 1908 model has been fitted out to recapture the gaslight-era clatter of horseless carriages over its cobblestone court. Wrought-iron entrance; clubby brown and green lobby; tiny leather bar; St. James's restaurant with moderately priced, reasonably varied menu. Total of 52 tiny fiefs (29 named for illustrious duchies), some of which are in a separate enclave; soft, earth-tone carpeting; bath, telephone, TV, 3-channel radio; suites with fireplaces, fully equipped kitchens, scales, and even electric toothbrushes. Manager Delahayes's crisp staff not only will try to address you by name, Milord, but will stock your castle with fresh flowers, a salver of fruit, and a warmed copy of the *Times.*

Ritz. It recently was taken over by a group that has enhanced its luster while adding sparkle to its marketing approach. Grandly conceived and totally refreshened main floor with pillared corridors, chandeliered lobby, palm-court lounge for tea-timing, and huge, column-lined rotunda dining salon displaying gilded garlands of laurel; many upstairs rooms equally sumptuous and spacious, with satin spreads on brass beds; front units renewed but not restyled, thank goodness; deep-pile flowered carpeting; enormous fixtures in baths that are reminiscent of your rich grandma's house; kind attention by floor personnel who are nearly all old-liners. Below the ground level a posh casino in formal attire has been unveiled; the croupiers are female and wear burgundy velvet gowns; minimum bets are low; there's an attractive independently run restaurant here, too. It's renaissance overall appears to be in full cry—and we like what we see.

Hyde Park. Here you'll find the showcase property in the British capital of the vast Trust Houses Forte chain. Since this fine old Victorian example has been nominated as the flagship hotel, it is receiving more polish than ever before. General Manager Willy Bauer has stripped many walls down to their original marble, restored crystal chandeliers, spread hectares of Persian carpets, added air conditioning to almost all of its 182 rooms, awarded different color schemes to the corridors on each floor, injected far more sophistication into the Hyde Park Grill, re-jiggered the Cavalry Bar, and refurbished scores of accommodations. Whew! Two big pluses are the spaciousness of its living space and its splendid location in the epicenter of the Knightsbridge shopping bonanza.

Park Lane. After deteriorating rather sadly, some of this mainliner's historic urbanity has been recaptured—but only some. Readers either love it or loathe it. Personally, we are no longer among its fans.

Mayfair. There is a busy commercial air about this one augmented by a package-group personality. Still, the accommodations are adequate and amply sized, and the staff are pleasant. The Beachcomber Restaurant and bar add some color; the Candlelight Room doesn't impress us too much. Basically sound and fundamentally agreeable, but there are many others we enjoy more.

Charing Cross. This adjunct to Trafalgar Square couldn't be more central if it tried. Strangely enough, the Charing Cross Station-side rooms are quieter than those fronting on the busy street. Some updatings from *tempus-to-tempus;* 100% bath ratio; 5th and 6th floors clinical but viewful; prices modest for this market and in line with the rewards. For reasonable space in what impresses us as a Formica-lined barn, here 'tis.

De Vere. Our overnight here a while back was a disappointing experience. Manager B. R. Constable wrote us afterwards that many changes would bring new graces to its doorstep. We hope so, but on our 3 follow-up inspections (incognito, of course) we could find spare evidence of what we think we should experience as a fully satisfied customer. Perhaps more updatings are in the pipeline.

CONTEMPORARY HOTELS:

Inn on the Park. Canada's sumptuous bid for the well-heeled wanderer is poised in splendor on a triangle of 14-karat real estate across from the Hilton. Its small but richly appointed lobby has wood paneling, crystal illumination, sandy-beige marble flooring, and a tooled leather table where guests sit, rather than stand, to register. Secluded enclave of shops; mezzanine dining complex composed of the window-lined Four Seasons Restaurant (vast menu at reasonable prices) and bar; the modern-lined Vintage Grill; the pin-lit, rouge-hued bar-lounge. Two sizes of twin-occupancy accommodations with the slightly more expensive billets by far the better ones, Empire furnishings in blue, ocher, or brown schemes; TV's set into stately highboys; single-basin marblesque baths. Its 20 suites vary in motif and mood while their prices are universally stratospheric. Very costly, very appealing to the eye—and especially liked by rich, sophisticated, spirited clientele.

Sheraton Park Tower. Cylindrical, 18-story concrete-and-glass building affording all-around restful views of Hyde Park; penthouse top-of-the-mark suites; wide bay windows; impressive travertine lobby enriched with wood, modern tapestries, orange-textiled furniture, metal sculpture, and cunning illumination; starburst Rotunda bar and lounge with a colossal flower-filled

copper vat as its centerpiece; regally outfitted Le Trianon restaurant, plus
terrace in summer; casino; spring-daubed Le Café Jardin coffee shop in dusty
rose and grass green; underground garage. Managing Director E.
Nicolas Behard has melded solid, proven values with creative new approaches. To
some it may seem flamboyant, or ostentatious, or even overwhelming. We are
betting, however, that most registrants will find the comfort so abundant, the
attention so wholehearted, and the concept so fresh that they will enjoy every
facet of this well-staged production. (See also Sheraton Skyline below.)

The Churchill. This house's Adam-inspired lobby is an immediate indicator
of this era in mass-minded hôtellerie; we were instantly struck by the fact that
as many as 1000 souls can live here at the same time. Its public rooms have
been dressed out for costume roles: The Number Ten Dining Room with
tented eaves and a leopard-spot carpet (a godsend to clumsy waiters); the Bar
surrounded by Japanese murals; the Greenery Coffee Shop dominated by a
tiled niche and a porcelain fountain; and the Regency Lounge (sunken, *mais
oui*). Dynamic General Manager Gordon Webb and kindhearted Reception
Chief Kelegerides have an enormous plant with which to work and they seem
to be pleasing guests by the hundreds—nay, by the thousands.

Blakes. Here is the exact opposite—a small *intime* Victorian hideaway (but
only in structure) on two sides of a residential street that caters chiefly to the
With-It Generation, fashionable communications executives, stunning top-line
models, and youthful upmarket travelers who shun the conventional. The
novel approach is impressive the instant you tumble into its Pacific-island
lobby covered by a colossal garden parasol and dotted with wicker furnishings
which we found more decorative than comfortable. There's a Retro-deco
downstairs restaurant-*cum*-bar, a spotlit lounge, a sauna, and a host of smiling
staff members, often in jeans; across the lane are the "Bosies" and "Benzies"
annexes with additional accretions coming apace. No two nests are alike. Its
tiny baths are often whacky in layout but charming in presentation; there's
color TV in every unit—and frequently there are stereo consoles which must
cost a fortune. Sometimes adequate space is at a premium, but overall there
is such an air of fetching, luxurious Bohemianism at every turn that most
adventurous wanderers will forgive the occasional bruised elbow or overflowing closet. In the mélange of 36 rooms and 14 suites, the rates range from about
$65 for a single to $100 for a double to $275 for the larger apartments. Bizarre,
but excitingly fresh for those who dare to be different.

Capital. Our recent revisit here couldn't have been smoother in comfort,
service, cuisine, and midtown convenience (only a few steps from Harrods).
The restaurant, not particularly strong on eye appeal, has generated a mighty
following of culinary loyalists; we must count ourselves among the chef's
disciples. No real lobby to speak of—merely a Hall Porter's desk and reception
counter; cozy-corner bar; vaguely French bedchamber décor employing blond-
wood furniture and cream-yellow color trends; compact, efficient baths; no
historic or sylvan vistas from any of its 60 windows. Forward-moving, farsighted David Levin is General Manager. For the outlay, we think it is one
of the best buys in the dwelling-space market of Olde London Towne. Warmly
recommended to metropolophiles.

Intercontinental. This one resides in the same convenient hotel cluster as the Hilton, the Inn on the Park, and other top-line contemporary stalwarts. The coolness of its entrance and lobby belie the easy grace, the rich colorations, and the luxurious comfort provided by its bedchambers. Somewhat stuffy Le Soufflé restaurant in dusty-rouge tones; Coffee House for uninspired yet costly snacks and buffet breakfast; viewful 7th-floor discothèque in *art rétro* for sipping and dancing; griddle-hot sauna and cool-off pool; select boutiques with price tags that stunned us; underground parking. The better, costlier units face Hyde Park (with the dual-glaze windows shut, they are quiet); extra-light sleepers may opt for a vistaless courtside address. General Manager Graham Jeffrey possesses professional knowhow, but his corps of chambermaids can be almost woeful in the performance of everyday simple services; Chief Concierge Denicolo is certainly a reliable name on the roster. Big, bustling, and as expensive as the top-liners.

Athenaeum. Our first impression of this patrician was that we were looking at a smaller (100-room) version of our first choice in this category—a sort of Innlet on the Park. A lot of recent funding has provided even more charm. If there can be such a thing as no-nonsense beauty, this Rank-run, first-rank hostelry has it. The renewed restaurant is called "The Restaurant"; the bar is called "The Bar"; the appointments are the finest in quality, bright with floral patterns, and selected for restful color blends. Twins run close to $100 per night here, but if more spacious living is your bidding, the **Athenaeum Apartments** which adjoin—and which are equally tasteful—start at about $475 per week for a double-bedroom spread. The comfort is ample and the savings realized by having your own kitchen can add e-l-a-s-t-i-c to your London budget. Maid service Mon. to Fri.; all hotel facilities available to residents; direct-dial phones; excellent for week-long or lengthier visits. Overall, this house's flexibility and appeal make it very special indeed.

London Hilton. This entry should not be confused with its newer, lowercost, Kensington cousin (see below). Frenzied lobby atmosphere bustling with U.S. colonists, conventioneers, seas of hypertense gumchewers; 4 restaurants, including a handsome roof plateau for dining and supper dancing, and a downstairs Trader Vic's Polynesian thatchery (miserable!); popular Scandinavian Sandwich Shop with Wiinblad porcelains atwinkle; 5 bars, plus the sip-and-dance 007 nightclub; first hotel in England to introduce a computerized, keyless lock system in all rooms; underground parking; every unit with radio and TV plus full-length movies via video cassette; one Y-shape wing houses studio-style accommodations only. In all but a few the décor follows a Eurasian theme; bedchambers are generally large, gracious, comfortable, with thoughtfully executed closet space; well-designed bathrooms. Here, in general, is perhaps the closest version of a "hotel machine" that America could export.

Montcalm. The Loews chain, which also owns the previously described Churchill, recently purchased this 120-room gem. If you have a passion for brown, here is your own true love. Sand, beige, sable, fawn, sorrel, umber, cocoa, chestnut—you'll find them all within these precincts. Well, what's dun is dun. Most of the ground-floor walls are upholstered in suede; furnishings are in leather; even the elevator has kidding around it; baths are carpeted. Suites feature spiral staircases and attractive 1½-story windows; ordinary twins are not spacious, but they are passable if your stay isn't a long one. The cuisine is artfully conceived; the Dial 9 discothèque is an animated hideaway. The staff couldn't be nicer; the service is gracious; we liked it very much.

Westbury. This house does not seem to have changed very much under its new management. More's the pity. A crippling lack of space—the biggest bugaboo in former years—was alleviated by ripping out hundreds of built-in, floor-to-ceiling, room-consuming cupboards and replacing them with slim-line but sufficient-size dressers. The closet areas were rearranged; basic reds, blues, and greens also lend an eye-expanding illusion; the baths remain bruisingly narrow-sided. It is convenient for shopping and theater going, but far from inspirational.

Royal Garden. This 500-room, T-shape giant overlooks Kensington Gardens and Hyde Park. Much of its physical plant is well designed, comfortable, and appealing to the eye, including the revamped Royal Roof and Garden Room dining dens and bar; during our various visits, tour groups have been homing in like swallows returning to you-know-where. So many reports from readers wail about the staff attitudes that once again service remains a big ???.

The Gloucester. What Rank Hotels believed it could do in a small way with the previously mentioned, 100–room Athenaeum, it has repeated with nearly as much style in this grander, splashier, zippy 571-unit star-spangled spectacular. The spatial concepts are so cleverly executed that the untrained observer could scarcely guess that a thousand souls are sharing his address—also a credit to able manager John Chandler. Fresh lobby arcade rising to a mezzanine level; clubby Grill; Hunter's Lodge restaurant; sumptuous lounge; Le Château Wine Bar (upstairs portion with tables; cellar section with counter libations), a very popular fad in present-day London; sauna; hairdressing facilities for men and women. The accommodations, though extremely well equipped, seemed rather spare in dimensions. The prices, however, are in the medium range while the rewards nudge firmly into luxury levels.

Curzon. Tucked into a handy cul-de-sac shouldering the Hilton, this little entry and the **Londonderry**, Park Lane, W.1, which is across the street from the Hilton, used to be excellent bright-eyed tykes which we recommended. Our enthusiasm has declined to a yawn. Now both are quite poor, in our opinion, for their highish tabs.

Royal Lancaster. This 400-room, 18-story entry is another gong-beater for the booming Rank organization. The lobby boasts Hal's Bar; the Beefeater Restaurant has spring-like tones to complement the branch-top vistas from its wide windows; the Mediterranean Café features a lovely centerpiece ceramic tree; the Pub glows with burgundy undertones. The viewful premium bedrooms come with grass-fiber wall coverings, raw-silk spreads, terrific music-news-and-TV consoles, and such thoughtful fillips as fresh flowers in a vase beside the bathtub. Very amiable and able staff; management in the hands of Jonathan Dale-Roberts; excellent parking facilities. Among the gilt-edged peerage in its prices.

Carlton Tower. This 18-story stalwart offers 250 rooms with bath, shower, TV, and radio. Chambers in restful gray, gold, and other soft tones; attractive public areas, including cleverly illuminated lobby, and 2 knockout dining rooms. Ground-floor Rib Room, rich-looking in a ruby haze, serves a diet-busting monolith of roast beef and trimmings for a very reasonable outlay; superb, subdued Chelsea Room. Very worthy in most respects.

The **Bristol**. This 200-unit entry is set only a block from Piccadilly Circus. Clean-lined marble-and-wood reception and foyer; costly and suave white-and-gold Louis XV restaurant; adjoining cream and green cocktail area; convenient underground parking pad; a serious falloff in service and maintenance (not uncommon in today's busy London). Most bedrooms are expansively proportioned (ask for a large unit). Once very good, but now only adequate.

The **Portman**. This British Airways-Intercontinental speedster landed 2 blocks from Marble Arch. A number of reports have reached us that it has just been given a heavy dose of beauty pills to add to its allures—none of which we have yet seen. Particular stress has been laid on the giant steps forward in its cuisine. Captain's Galley providing comestibles around the clock; Rôtisserie Normande offering Gallic fillips in an ambitious menu plus live jazz during Saturday night dinner and Sunday brunch; alfresco terrace; Captain's Bar; hairdresser, barber, boutiques, garage. Accommodations in 2 towers, one with 85 compact solo units, the other with 175 tandems and 16 suites; accoutrements include TV and air cooling plus generously proportioned closets and baths. A rewarding value.

The **Selfridge**. If shopping is your bag, what better shopping bag could you fill but Selfridges'? This one is tucked right into the middle of the famous department store. Handsome wood, glass, and burnished-metal entry and foyer; paneled lounge; cobble-paved Fletcher's Restaurant with a vendor's barrow of garden produce to tempt incomers; charming oaken Stoves Bar recalling the days of Dickens; chipper Victorian Picnic Basket coffee shop open from 7 A.M. to 1 A.M. Its 330 units feature room-wide windows which provide an impression of space when, in fact, little exists. Fitted Empire furniture enhances the clever maximizing of minimum dimensions.

Portobello. This 20-room, 5-suite sweetie is just plain fun. A handsome pair of Victorian homes have been joined in harmonious wedlock by Tim and Cathy Herring, an affable, young, and talented couple. Palms abound, cheer pervades, and good taste is in evidence down to the smallest detail. Its main drawback is in the miniature baths, which really are too small for sultans of ablution. Artfully chic clientele who enjoy its special élan and off-beat personality.

Penta. Almost adjoining the West End Terminal, this jumbo is zooming toward success not only because of the jet thrust from its airline sponsors, but because it is a model of what keen administration, smart budgeting, and shrewd architecture can do. As one simple example, the pictures in the lounge, which people seldom study carefully, are all colorful but inexpensive prints in nice frames, but the chairs in the Pub of Pubs, which you will touch and linger in, are upholstered in the finest polished leather. While the bedrooms are cramped (the brochure is a triumphant illustration of what a wide-angle lens can do for a microscopic subject), the prices are at bedrock level for these cheerful surroundings. On balance, we give it high marks for its unabashed production-line concept.

Cavendish. Speaking of airliners and airlines, here is a 255-unit, "First-class" (not "Deluxe") midtowner that bears a striking resemblance to our own Pan American Building on Park Avenue in Manhattan. Personable Manager

Conal O'Sullivan is a gracious and capable host. Attractive public rooms including the 24-hour Ribblesdale Restaurant, dark-tone Sub Rosa Bar (named after the original Cavendish's famed Rosa Lewis), and mezzanine lounge-bar. All bedchambers with tiny baths, bedside radio and TV controls; limited luggage space; building-wide fresh-air ventilation; round-the-clock laundry at standard town prices (a considerable saving); only continental breakfast or snacks served in the rooms. We prefer nests ending in "21." Its simple, clean-lined efficiency is almost Scandinavian in tone.

Marble Arch Holiday Inn. Since this house is more conveniently sited than its crosstown counterpart (see below), its designers opted for fewer frills as inducement to register; the accent is therefore on functional simplicity. Sedate restaurant; plain-as-plain coffee shop; Tyburn Bar with soft illumination and possibly the most tiddily low-backed chairs on which we've lately tippled; heated pool and sauna gurgling and steaming underground; parking. The 243 pads, all tastefully toned in blue, pink, and beige, come with either 1 or 2 double beds, bath and shower, phone, radio, color TV, individual climate control, and other standard Inn-ovations.

Lowndes. Structurally and decoratively here is one of the more attractive small hotels in London—with the added advantage of having one of the best addresses in the embassy neighborhood of Belgravia. Its previous administration was a disappointment to us but its new brewmaster owners have poured a frothy fresh head on a cup that had gone flat. In the yeasty toast are new curtains, chairs, bed headboards, peignoirs, and buckets of paint. The Chinese Chippendale Bar and the delightful air-conditioned restaurant are added pluses of decorative flair and intimacy. The traditional Adam style predominates—a signature of its elegant heritage. Finally, and happily, recommended.

Britannia. This titan is set back in a brick-lined courtyard directly across from the U.S. Embassy and within walking distance of the major shopping clusters. Two entrances to its handsome structure; Regency-style lobby with adjoining cafeteria-cum-breakfast nook; bar also in flavorful tones; attractive pub for "lifting a few"; discreet shopping gallery. Medium-size soundproofed bedchambers identical throughout, with darkwood furniture, predominantly blue-and-green textiles, radio-TV-clock combo, direct-dial phones, wall-to-wall carpeting, and air conditioning; small bathrooms. The Grand Metropolitan chain has forged a convenient link with this stalwart entry.

Swiss Cottage Holiday Inn. Sorry, but this one is not an Alpine chalet lifted lock, stock, and yodel from Zermatt. Instead it's named after its neighborhood, which nudges suburban Hampstead, a 10-minute subway ride from Piccadilly. Architecture and décor? Arabesque, with persistent use of arches, vaulting, tiles, and carpets. Henry VIII Restaurant, overlooking a garden, tuned more to Aladdin's taste than that of the rotund royalist; attractive King Henry Bar, studded with director's chairs and potted palmery, a short swizzle from the indoor pool; soft-drink and free-ice machines stationed like stoic sentinels on each floor. All 300 chambers duel with the din on 2 main arteries; all sport goatee-sized balconettes and the other standard amenities of these stops. The slightly lower tabs here, versus those of its downtown cousin, can be nullified with the flick of a taxi flag. Moor-or-less too far out in too many ways.

Royal Kensington. This once-proud entry now seems to be skidding, in our opinion. Its far-out location also is not in its favor. No lobby to speak of; squeezed-up reception cabin; Beef Encounter Restaurant; l'Apéritif and Cockpit Bars; Coffee Shop; stylings based upon a fine sensitivity for color and texture, but the housekeeping standards now so scandalous, in our view, that we cannot recommend it until it picks up its socks.

Europa. This 273-room, giant Georgian sentinel is a typical product of modern-day market research. It is designed almost exclusively for tours; furniture and fabrics are precisely the same throughout; living space and staff attention are both in short supply; rates are steepish. All-in-all, no great shakes.

Howard. From its perch on the Strand, this deluxe rehash of an older hostelry overlooks the Thames. Same administration as Lowndes; elegant eighteenth-century décor; 150 bedrooms; penthouse suites; Quai d'Or French restaurant with Temple Bar adjoining; terraced apron of gardens.

Kennedy. Here's a 180-roomer which has some vote-getting awards as well as a few lost precincts that could be serious handicaps. It is convenient to Euston Station, but huddled neglectedly in a metropolitan backwater that we doubt many travelers will like. Okay for its moderate tabs, however.

Imperial. This 461-cell pueblo, adjoining and in the same consortium as the President (see below), won't ever be a worry to the Savoy chain, Entrance cupped in a fountain court; s-p-a-a-a-a-c-i-o-u-s lobby pointing clients to cubicles in 3 wings; mass-production dining room; achingly tiny bedchambers outfitted with what appeared to us to be box-crate furnishings of the cheapest order and unbelievably cramped baths. No, thanks.

President. This 7-story candidate has been spruced up with gold and brown carpeting, fresh wallpaper, and lively curtains; remodeled dining room toned in a salmon-and-moss-green color scheme; quick-service, saw-toothed counter also available. If the bathrooms and elfin tubs are brought up to current standards we'll predict that this President will win a 3rd term.

Bedford. Here's what might be dubbed a 180-room Vice President. Same pattern of its busy-busy carpet; similarly conceived lounge and dining room, but pleasant garden adjoins; minuscule bathrooms with separate toilet; closets much too small. Also routine, except for its friendly staff.

Washington. As an example of mass-production hotel technique, 60% enlarged by a streamlined wing, this one still doesn't come off for us. Neither does the staff, who seemed to prefer being elsewhere.

Bloomsbury Centre. Here's a lackluster commercial pod that occupies part of an office building near Russell Square. In our professional judgment, this dreary number wouldn't be fun for holidaymakers. Its late-blossoming sister operation, the **Regent Centre** near Regent's Park, peeps from its garden with 350 rooms—each cross-pollinated to resemble the original plant.

The 610-room **Kensington Hilton** (way out on Holland Park Ave., near Shepherd's Bush) is offered to Hiltonians at nearly ⅓ off the the deluxe rates of the Park Lane entry. While it is handsomely decorated in richly textured materials, the location is unfortunate because today's taxi fares can push daily expenditures up to top-line levels. If, however, you don't mind using public transport, the subway (tube) and bus stops are practically at your doorstep. Buff brick facade; Nipponese restaurant; weekly medieval feasts planned in the Tudor Tavern; individually adjustable thermostats in all units; likewise refrigerator/bar and color TV.Very well presented; here's a concept which we laud.

Cunard steamed up with bunk space for 1300 mariners moored far out on Talgarth Road. Even though it strains to incorporate a maritime theme, the project is so group oriented that we found nary a trace of personality. The 826-bedchamber **Tower** on St. Katharine's Way reflects all of the charm of the World Trade Center it was meant to complement. Finally, the economy-priced **Metropole**, on Edgware Road near Marble Arch, counts a mere 555 accommodations. The entrance is so awkward for motorists that they would find it much easier to drive only to the back portals. We like the efforts made here to stoke up decorative warmth in the public rooms. The sleepers, however, remain little more than body-size cubicles. The **Royal National** opened its 556 units recently; it functions chiefly for tours. Reasonable prices; reasonable rewards.

ASSORTED HOTELS:

Here is a grab bag that we won't even attempt to classify. Some of its entries are big, some tiny, some new, some with a sprinkling of modernizations, some ancient and flavorful, some downright decrepit. Because of these myriad variables and the added factor of personal taste which would make one house appealing to one traveler and absolutely hideous to another, we will only describe them briefly and let you be the judge. Now let's pull open the strings and see what we've snared. . . . or, what's snared us!

Chesterfield. Here's a youngster with flair. It comprises the union of 2 old houses, incorporating charm, varilevel stair climbing, nice rooms, a Buttery spread with reasonable food buys, and a restaurant that glows with a Regency tradition. Very central.

Dolphin Square. Here, to us at least, is the stop which offers the _very_ best value for the traveler's £ in today's London. A total of 1050 privately leased units are contained in a quadrangle of houses, each named after a British naval personage. Rodney House is the operative nexus and the site for 150 transient accommodations, available by the day, week, or month. Quiet, convenient location; Hall Porter, Reception, Key and Cashier counters; extraordinarily well planned and executed all-purpose shopping arcade; overlooking the heated indoor pool is a pleasant, popular-price restaurant open from 7:30 A.M. to midnight; 2 bars; 8 squash courts; Finnish log saunas; 350-car underground garage; attractive gardens; 26 automatic elevators. One-, 2-, 3-room apartments; 30 so-called Guest Rooms for younger, hardier voyagers (public toilets and tubs). Tabs very low for the market; discounts usually given for stays of a week or more; most accommodations with fully equipped kitchenettes; TV installed upon request for a small additional charge; free maid service 6 days per week (and what a fine, friendly corps they are!). Units ending in "25" are very good, as are the "03's" and "16's". Extra beds or cots can be provided at nominal cost. Here is one enormous advantage: _You can bring along your spouse, and the savings effected in 11 days by both of you in Dolphin Square over your otherwise lonely single in any of London's Deluxe hotels should pay for your companion's scheduled airline transatlantic transportation._

White House. This former apartment-style abode was transformed into a medium-budget hotel. Circular lobby retained but now crammed with kiosks and vitrines; windowless elbow-to-elbow restaurant and viewless coffee shop; sharply angular bar. Of the rooms that had been redecorated by our visit, all reflected a Danish air; each contained a small sitting area, condensed narrow beds, a pair of chairs, a small TV table, and tiny baths. Overall, a bargain spot.

St. George's. Somewhat remote situation, but easily (and economically) within reach of the visceral midsections of the city; split-personality building shared with B.B.C. headquarters; ground-floor entrance; 14th-story lobby; adjoining panoramic Octave Restaurant; bar-lounge combination; all units with truly spectacular townscape vistas through huge full-wall windows. The accommodation we are crazy about is the so-called Bed-Sitting Room, which is enormous and plushly outfitted. Recommended in its upper-medium category.

Elizabetta. This once lovely entry opened its doors in '72 but has aged rapidly since that bright day, we are sad to report. Bustling, relatively far-out location; boxy, 7-tiered exterior; silver slipper-sized bar-lounge; miniaturized restaurant with Middle Eastern cuisine. Recently it changed hands, and our followup inspection was a grave disappointment to us.

The Chelsea Holiday Inn. This 220-unit midtowner features a swimming pool in its courtyard overlooked by the Bohemian Bar and the romantic Papillon Restaurant. All public sectors are of a taste level far above what you might expect from a motel chain. Accommodations are small but fitted with color TV, radio, direct-dial phone, and individually controlled heating and air conditioning; all boast private bath; there are 4 suites. Recent administrative changes should work to its favor. We hope so because basically it's a splendid building with a perfect address.

Wilbraham. This neighbor is older in style but fresh in appearance. Le Beurre Fondue restaurant and the intimate lounges provide their own brand of coziness. Varying assortment of 62 rooms, 34 with bath; substantial and nice as a London town house. Prices are surprisingly low for the reward.

Kensington Palace. This house is still moving up the ladder; the results we've seen are heartening indeed. Lobby tastefully restyled and air-conditioned; coffee shop bubbling from 7 A.M. to 12:30 A.M.; good maintenance; heavy business from conducted tours. About ¼ of its accommodations in dismal studio motif; conventional twins much better by comparison.

Piccadilly. Old-stock, traditional lobby; large, comfortable rooms as British as plum duff; bid for the quieter rear side. Rates? Its bloated price for doubles strikes us as being almost as overstuffed as its sofas. Late reader reports fairly froth with rage about the reception, Hall Porter's desk, and general staff attitudes. These are, however, in tune with the Broadwayesque nature of the plant and its clientele. Far from the dilly-of-the-pick.

Royal Trafalgar. This 110-box bastion is excellently positioned for addicted sightseers—but that's about that, as far as we're concerned. Tiny lobby where we saw throngs almost as dense as Attila's troops; Angus Steak House concession plus Battle of Trafalgar Pub. All rooms seem to have been thoughtfully proportioned so that guests can reach almost anything from dead center; all come with bath, radio, TV, and round-the-clock service. Revamping plans soon may alter it appreciably.

Leinster Towers, a community of several former houses, offers 165 accommodations under one roof. Hodgepodge interior; all units with weensie private baths and ⅔ with cooking facilities; possibly the narrowest beds we've seen since Fort Bragg. Too costly in comparison with its peers.

The Ryan. Because its accent is so strong on group traffic, and since its tabs nudge those of the Holiday Inn at Swiss Cottage, we are compelled to nominate this transplanted Dubliner as a strictly overnight stop.

Strand Palace, Regent Palace. Chrome steel, imitation leather motif. Chillingly sterile a few moons back but their Trust Houses Forte masters are successfully pumping color and life into this pair.

Cumberland. Here is a one-price, glacially commercial house that also has joined the Trust Houses Forte clan. Carvery restaurant, with meats and chef searing in the middle of the room; skull-throbbing public-address system eternally bleating in the lobby; a fat piece of change gives you a depressingly barebones unit with bath. This frenetic ant colony is totally impersonal.

International. Although this 425-compartment jumbo took off in '70, to us it looked as if it might have been hauling cargoes of kangaroos from the Outback for decades. Cavernous marble lobby; Cavalier Room and Cromwell Coffee Shop for pack'em-stack'em feedings; Stuart Bar, a dim water hole; small, modernistic yet seemingly ill-kempt cages while we were there.

Post House, operated by the Trust Houses Forte organization, has completed its expansion with grim results, say we. Too bad, because we once liked it very much. The nearby **Embassy** blends modernisms with period themes in a happy meld of 2 distinct ideas. The medium tariffs and the all-out effort of the staff on our recent visit make us think that foreign envoys will enjoy being in its diplomatic circle. The **Averard** seems to be slipping, in our opinion; mainly for the bargain hunter. **Mt. Royal** is a commercial colossus of 695 identical shoe-boxy cubicles, all with bath, telephone, and radio. An up-only escalator rises from the street to the lobby; functionality on every hand, by the factory load; so-so maintenance; swarming with tour groups. The **Londoner** is less frenetic but just as mercantile. Black and white marble lobby with steel trim, reminiscent of your familiar First National Bank; downstairs Four Seasons restaurant; 125 rooms and baths, all reasonably sized and modern if not worn in tone; 4 suites; front accommodations noisy. The **Waldorf** was renewed in a quasi-Edwardian fashion by its Trust Houses Forte proprietors, who invested $2.5 million recently in refurbishing its 310 rooms and 16 suites. It seemed very expensive for the value; moreover, we're not too fond of the Covent Garden district for residential purposes right yet. The **Ladbroke Belgravia** provides shophounds with excellent fields for the chase. Contemporary lobby with tinted glass, soft lighting and tones of ecru and brown; summery, turquoise Terrace Restaurant with appealing buffet under its cupola at lunchtime; Plum's Bar of the nostalgic P. G. Wodehouse era; striped corridors; contemporary furnishings with traditional accessories. Avoid the small first-floor units. Now one of the better bets in the area. **Harrington Hall**, about 15 minutes from Piccadilly in Harrington Gardens, has a cozy grill, cheery breakfast nook, and attractive basement Chez Cleo French restaurant. All of its 30 singles and 45 doubles with private baths; 2 fair suites; nice staff. Too many recent wails from readers who complained of hammock-like beds and high-crowned prices. No longer the bargain of yore. **Hyde Park Towers** gave its 108 rooms a face-lifting. Restaurant with dancing; coffee shop; commercial but sound. **Parkway** also has a Bayswater address some 10 minutes from Piccadilly. About 80 rooms divided among 3 separate houses; approximately ⅓ with private bath, mostly on the first floor; each bedchamber with radio, telephone, and coin box for individual heating unit. **Park Plaza**, opposite Hyde Park, is an amiable bet for families, provided the children are carefully watched whenever they cross traffic-clogged Bayswater Road. **Mandeville** is a 163-room warren which might bring to your mind a run for captive conducted-tour rabbits. **Stratford Court** could have done with some suds and polish when we saw it. Attractive dining room; 135 bedchambers with private bath; noisy, commercial air in a traditional showcase. The new **Royal Westminster** is only a salute away from Buckingham Palace, along the route for the Changing of the Guard. Utilitarian bedrooms; brick-lined, beamed-ceiling Thatcher's Restaurant with prime vittles.

The **Clive** boasts a medium-size, glass-sheathed structure and a garage. Unless you can find no roof in town or unless you prefer to nest way out here near Euston Station in the suburbs, we think this is too remote. **Astor Lodge** is ½-apartment house; nice staff, but nothing special, in our opinion.

St. Ermin's has been extensively revamped and given baths throughout. We're still not too enthusiastic, but the management seems to be trying to perk it up. **Flemings**, under new ownership, has been completely redone. We hear it is one of the best buys in town today. This is high on our next check list. **Berners** glows low on our burner. **Mt. Pleasant** has a mighty pleasant covey of charming receptionists, but it is so poorly situated in a railway-postal complex that most travelers, we believe, would find it unappealing.

The hotel blips which we pick up on our radar from the fringes of *London Airport* are a boon to flight-weary or strike-bound travelers as transient hole-ups.

The 355-unit **Sheraton Skyline**, is suavely luxurious. Large, tropical-lush, central Carib Patio featuring a fine pool, and a popular, b-i-g Sunday buffet-brunch from 11:00 to 2:00, at about $11 per appetite; Diamond Lil's reincarnated Gold Rush Saloon with honky-tonk ivories and bouncing banjos; Colony Room an Edwardian dine-and-dancer; never-say-dry Café Jardin; excellent maintenance throughout. All traditionally furnished skyliners come with bath and shower, color TV, individually controlled thermostats, and other Age of Apollo instrumentation. This house is for the opulent traveler only. Here is the finest airport hotel we have ever seen in the world.

The **Heathrow**, parked on airport turf, is a sprawling, 4-level, concrete-colored structure hangaring 660 mono-, bi-, and tri-placers. Sweeping lobby-lounge; expansive polar-frosted Rib Room; The Flying Machine and Sir Francis Drake Bars with respective aero-nautical gimmickry; coffee shop; discothèque; indoor pool, bar, and sauna bordered by flowers and fountains. All of its soundproofed chambers provide vivid hues, TV, air conditioning, and kooky, perilous-looking (but absolutely safe) "Bell Captain Bar-lettes" which double as breakfast warmers; units facing the nearest runway are pegged highest. Pilot Allen Deeslam is doing a commendable job.

The **Holiday Inn** architecturally is splayed like a 3-bladed prop; its sister ship is 10 miles away at Slough. Green-and-beige lobby; pale-ish Blue Ribbon feedery revving till 2 A.M.; tan and hearty Beefeater Bar; Satellite Coffee Shop; health center embracing pool, sauna, massagery, gym, and tennis courts; golf links. All 300 units sport smallish but practical baths and showers, the standard entertainment package, floor-to-ceiling panes, and annoying open wardrobes; kids under 12 ride on their parents' ticket.

The **Sheraton-Heathrow** resides on a mile-distant pasture that overlooks an unsightly factory. Low-profile concrete building; protruding blocks suggesting to us a nasty case of architectural hives; cockpit-size lobby in Star Wars Gothic; raised bar; Cranford Restaurant for seafood and grills. The Footlights nightery, staged as a Victorian pub, also offers vittles. In-'n-out swimmery plus steam room; poolside snacks; frequent double-decker bus connection to Knightsbridge. The 440 bedrooms, swathed mostly in purple and maroon, plug into color TV's, radios, electric trouser presses, and bar-lettes; they're passably comfortable, well proportioned, functional, and unfrivolous.

The older **Excelsior**, is still superior for its purpose and still richly priced for its league. About $1 million has just been spent by its Trust Houses Forte pilots to keep this airliner in proper trim. Its coffee shop, pub-style Tavern Bar, brick-bound sunken Rôtisserie, and posh Draitone Manor restaurant are further pluses on its manifest. The last, in opulent post-Victorian décor, exhibits an impressive seafood display as its major culinary attraction. Adjoining this, there's the 8-table "Library" with crystal glasses, superb cookery, and genuine bookery. All 660 of it's small-boned but efficient accommodations have private bath and Jet-Age gadgetry. Moreover, there's a beauty salon, a sauna, car hire service, a heated pool, and ample parking facilities. **Skyway**, has 450 rooms, including 9 suites, all with bath, telephone and TV; facilities nearly always open, with restaurant on 24-hour and Snack Bar on 20-hour basis (our New York-cut sirloin and filet in the former were excellent); heated, floodlit, open-air pool; shopping arcade; flight transportation provided to terminus. The efficient, amiable service standards are a blessing. **Ariel** is a 184-room, doughnut-shape structure. Soundproofed, air-conditioned bedrooms; showers in each bath; TV and radio; free transportation to and from the airport; a specialty restaurant on the homing beam night and day.

The 600-slot **Post House** is practically a self-service sanctuary. Imposing 10-tier house posted on 15 acres; vast lobby bordering on the brash; supermarket carts for transporting your own baggage. Great Britain Grill, Buttery, and Bar all in tribute to I. K. Brunel, the nineteenth-century marine wizard; pool, bank, boutiques, and news kiosk rounding out the public precincts. All cubbies are standardly furnished and are available in 8 color schemes; a continental breakfast will be left *outside* your door; offspring under 16 slumber gratis if they share the parental billet. Low price tags reflect a policy of minimum service. We'd suggest that you file your flight plan well in advance if you expect to land here. The **Centre** is the cheapest of the lot. Its 300 standard quarters and 60 flatlets (bedroom, salon, kitchenette, and bath) are listlessly strung out in a long, low, functional configuration. Simple, brown-carpeted reception; Globetrotter Bar only 800 feet from a runway; lusterless Silver Table restaurant. Look-alike sleepers with gray carpet, rust spreads, radios, phones, adjustable air cooling and reportedly the only triple-glaze panes in or around London. We saw evidence of slipshod maintenance in the wake of heavy tour group traffic.

Coming in on a wing and without a prayer of finding a kip, a sip, and a hot dip? The **Berkeley Arms**, smack in the middle of Cranford, a hamlet 2 miles from touchdown but linked to London by subway, might fill the bill. The charmingly Tudorized inn is attached to a newer slabular structure. Open kitchen with grill; blithe coffee nook in orange and bronze; 4 hefty imbiberies; radiant enclosed garden; ice machines on each floor; automatic alarms in each room; décor somewhat flashy. The distant **Heathrow Ambassador**? We'd rather cuddle in a diplomatic pouch.

At Gatwick Airport, we'd pick the **Copthorne** over the **Piccadilly**, but both should be considered only as emergency hanger space at best. A 444-room **Holiday Inn**, linked to the terminal by a bridge, is expected to open in 1982. This luxury entry will have a pool, squash courts, and sauna.

If you're ever stuck for a place to stay, bookings can be made at the Victoria Station Tourist Information Centre (near platform 15) or the Heathrow Travel Centre. Otherwise, phone the **HOTAC Accommodation Service** (01·451 2311).

Dedicated budgeteers? About 10-dozen stopping places in London are listed and rated in this book. Since there simply isn't space here for additional entries, please consult our annually revised paperback, *Fielding's Low-Cost Europe,* for more bargain hotels, boardinghouses, rock-bottom-cost institutions, and money-saving tips for serious economizers.

★ **TIPS** The **Trust Houses Forte** chain is often your best bet for country lodging. This federation of 880 hostelries scattered all over the U.K. and globally is not luxury class, but you should find comfortable beds, more and more private baths yearly, relatively low tariffs, and adequate fare. Rapid expansion has dulled some of its earlier luster, we think, but basically it is reliable. A company-wide, credit-card plan is operative. Write Trust Houses Forte Ltd., 71/75 Uxbridge Rd., W 5, for full details.

Falcon Inns, which recently joined the Trust Houses Forte flock, also provides some of the best nests in the U.K. Armed with beaks full of capital, this energetic and discriminating outfit has started buying historically or scenically sound hostelries which often have suffered from neglect and then bringing them back to life through careful restoration and expensive decorating.

Restaurants (Plus Country Dining Near London)

In London, Mayfair is chichi and costly; Soho and Chelsea are more theatrical and bohemian in flavor, although the tabs can run plenty high here too. Remember: *Most* major independent restaurants and hotel grillrooms (not hotel dining rooms) are shut tight on Sundays. And remember especially, please, that it's *always* wise to make advance reservations in London, regardless of the place or hour.

Official sources list about 400 so-called quality establishments in the capital. Here is the numbing, leg-wearying Grand Total of more than 200 which we have tried *personally* (unless otherwise indicated)—representing practically every type, style, and price bracket.

For *fashionable dining without dancing*, here are our choices.

Waltons of Walton Street (121 Walton St.) continues to be the choice of the Rolls-Ferrari Set and Foreign High Society. A salon-style champagne bar with smoked mirrors, a hearth, antiques, and rich carpeting now graces an upper tier. The cuisine is judiciously innovative. Breeding shows, too, in the restful décor. Georgian windows overlook the quiet street; a dark inner nook is available for more intimacy (better after theater); the set meals are changed about every 3 weeks as seasonal items come to market. On 7 recent test visits we sampled such inventive creations as a lightly whipped camembert mousse; sole with orange and cream sauce (an eighteenth-century recipe); Veal Paupiettes (thin slices) filled with spinach and smoked ham; a salad of yogurt, mushroom, and celeriac; cream-cheese pie; and a baseball-size melon flavored with cassis. The wines disclose their patrician bearing—and are priced accordingly. Maître Brown projects an imperious yet friendly comic dignity that is straight out of Noel Coward; Manager Rolf Amberge, meanwhile, is continuing to maintain this house's mandate on excellence.

Carrier's (2 Camden Passage, Islington) is a dynamic entry by go-getting North American Robert Carrier whose cookbooks and recipe-card packets are the "in" dishes in many an international home kitchen. His "Take Away" shop, a few doors away in the chic antique quarter called "The Angel," is a distilled toyland for U.S. homemakers or snack-timers. One tier for his "Supper by Candlelight" (4 scrumptious courses served from 10:30 P.M. to 11:15 P.M.); intimate-to-almost-cramped dimensions; 6-table main-floor dining room with plum and fireman-red tablecloths and paisley napkins; green textile-covered walls and deep-sea carpeting; homey white-painted brick; upstairs unit (which we prefer for its bonus of quiet) with flame-red color scheme; a few outdoor tables "greenhoused" with foliage rotating by season; tiny bar and split-level cocktail lounge. Our splendid and continuing feasts couldn't be better in presentation, in concept, and in the basic soundness of an *haute cuisine* enhanced with intelligence and imagination. Be absolutely certain to reserve in advance. Happy recommendation as one of the top gastronomic centers in the metropolis today—and lots of fun too. P.S.—*Out* of the metropolis near Ipswich, you can find yet another dalliance at the Maestro's Hintlesham Hall (see "Country Dining near London").

Cecconi's (5A Burlington Gardens, W1) now seems to be the breathless choice of upper-crusted cognoscenti who require refinement in their surroundings and finesse in their expensive Italian cuisine. The address is one of London's best. Trellis-back chairs with French-blue cushions; fresh-cut flowers; filmy curtained windows along 2 entire lengths of the off-white salon. Elegant simplicity is the keynote. Dignified, warm reception; extremely select but delightfully composed menu; polite attention that is silken suave. If the prices don't disturb you here, then certainly nothing else should. Well accepted and for good reason.

Odin's (27 Devonshire St., W1) is assuredly one of London Town's more beautiful restaurants and one of its most comfortable, too. There are dual segments divided by a walled partition, both hung with exquisite illuminated oils that lend a captivating clublike softness to the atmosphere. These paintings make up the entire element of décor, rising from table level to the ceiling. Our service by liveried waiters was superb. Our gratifying repast for 4 totaled $140; no credit cards are honored, darn it. The same owner operates the adjoining **Langan's Bistro** with a crazy-quilt of gay parasols hanging upside down from the ceiling and fin-de-siècle accoutrements. Here the menu is simpler and lower in cost. See below for our remarks on Langan's Brasserie.

Parkes Restaurant & Mr. Benson's Bar (4 Beauchamp Place) remains an insider among a discreet group of London socialites who know their gastronomy. Messrs. Tom Benson, J. L. Chamberlain, and 3 skilled chef-associates work with imagination and distinction. Cozy dimensions in menu-lined cellar of an old domicile; 21 tables seating 66 lucky clients; no bar, but spirits and extra-fine wines available; jungle of flora. The selections are limited to what the partners find to be the quality shopping bets on that day, but the variety is always extensive. Four-course fixed-price lunch (several choices at each stage) from noon to 3 P.M.; more elaborate fixed-price dinner; Chefs Clarke, Gregori, and Coyle form a triple-threat that's nigh impossible to beat in this towne. Also very expensive. *Nail down that reservation well in advance!*

Mirabelle (56 Curzon St.), dressy and Establishmentarian, bears the reputation of the most sophisticated straight restaurant in Great Britain—but a disturbing number of readers have not been too happy here. Despite these comments, here's one of the most attractive atmospheres to be found anywhere. The air-conditioned, flower-banked, semigarden patio is delightful in rainy or sunny weather. Superior kitchen; fine buffet in summer; clientele of international bluebloods. But remember that it will cost you plenty, and that your welcome may not be as gracious as it could be. Recommended despite these reservations.

Oslo Court (Prince Albert Rd., Regents Park, NW8) occupies one segment of a modest apartment complex of the same name. Though known among relatively few, here is where we enjoyed one of the finest meals sampled on our recent rounds. Only 14 tables set in an Old World atmosphere; delicate porcelain, etched crystal, and silver; pleasant reception and service. The unusual cuisine is based upon Chef Rajko Katnic's wide experience in Croatian and Middle European gastronomy; he is blessed by the warm assistance of wife Megan and daughter June. The duck Bosnaka (with sour cherries), the chicken with cracked wheat, and the quenelles of salmon—to name only a few of his creations—were superb. On top of this, the extensive wine list is fabulous, surely ranking as one of the noteworthy small caves in Europe today. Closed all day Monday and Sunday evening. A gift of—and for—the gods.

Eleven Park Walk (SW10) purloined its straightforward moniker from its swanky address—and a *very* chichi spot it is at This Very Moment GMT. The house is abubble with charming young things in the latest fashions, all escorted by a bedizened host of admiring suitors. It is clearly the haunt for second-magnitude stars, dressed-to-the-nines models, and denizens of the couture cult. The main floor glitters with mirrors on 2 sides, broadening the outlook and providing the perfect backdrop for such overt narcissism. An openwork spiral staircase adds to the tease and the glamour as shapely gams pass up and down. Bright lighting, to see and be seen; ceramic tile floors; loud piped music; adequate but not too careful service. You're invited to lunch, dinner, and on Sundays. Here's a center of the upward moving "In Set."

Ma Cuisine (113 Walton St.) is one of Europe's better choices for French cooking, but since it is so difficult to book a table here, it is pointless to carry it at the forefront of London's dining establishments. Qualitatively, tiny though the precincts may be, it remains in the vanguard. A mere 7 tables; timber-lined wall on one side; burnt-orange textile on the other; brass and copper pans for décor. Warmhearted reception by Lucette, the charming wife of Chef-Proprietor Mouilleron; open weekdays only for lunch and dinner. Our recent repasts have been as delicate as a St.-Tropezian zephyr. As it is so petit, reservations must be made as long as a week or more in advance, but try anyway.

Eatons (49 Elizabeth St., off Ebury St.) is a gem honed to near perfection by the former chef of Inigo Jones (listed elsewhere in this section). A mere 12 tables in 2 cozy adjoining rooms; beige Hessian walls; attractive art; white timber beams. Its modest menu and wine list (the house red is quite nice and reasonably priced) belie the splendid quality produced in the kitchen. Some selections to try: the melon with shrimp and avocado, the salmon blinis, the curry chicken pancakes, the veal scallop, the pork with red cabbage in a pastry shell. For such reliable quality, tariffs are surprisingly reasonable. Closed Sunday; only dinner served on Saturday.

Frederick's, in Camden Passage, is only a few doors away from the previously described Carrier's. After a gustatory slump, it now decidedly is on the rebound. Two unusually attractive dining levels, with the upper one displaying a variety of wines; lower segment, down a few steps, fronted by tall wide windows overlooking a garden patio; white brick walls; slate flooring. We are happy to report that it has achieved that desired status and that it finally is mellowing. Popular and worthy.

Lacy's (26 Whitfield St.) lends excitement to the London culinary scene through the efforts of the hospitable and talented husband-and-wife team Bill Lacy (a childhood protégé of Escoffier) and Margaret Costa (a respected oenologist and frequent contributer to *Gourmet* magazine). Ground-floor reception with restaurant downstairs under white stucco vaults; tile floors, a bit cool to the tootsies; paintings for warmth; fascinating wine list which accents interesting, somewhat remote *crus*; prices moving up in proportion to its mounting success. Here is a champion without pretentions.

Le Gavroche ("The Gamin," 61 Lower Sloane St.) still fails to garner our enthusiasm even though it is considered to be one of London's more important (and expensive) restaurants. Foyer with 2 tables and a floor-to-ceiling wine rack directly behind the bar (a perfect way to sour fine vintages); angular, v-shape room adjoining, with sound-softened ceiling, tobacco-tan walls, ocher banquettes, and 18 tables with shaded candlesticks. The cuisine on our latest repeat performance was still benighted by exaggerated spicing and cloying infusions of superheavy cream. The pretentious pose of our French-speaking maître was a trifle gagging when we consider that he is playing 99% of the time to a monolingual English audience. Here, to us, is a classic example of a restaurant replete with dramatic gimmicks to impress tinsel lovers whose familiarity with high cuisine is at the 5th-grade level. The true gastronome, in our opinion, should strenuously avoid it.

La Croisette (168 Ifield Rd.) recalls a Riviera mood, contrived as it is with service personnel in oystermen's sweatshirts, iced seafood displays, and artwork of the Côte d'Azur. We thought the entrance tatty; it lead down a chipped and scruffy spiral staircase to a miserably ventilated arched cellar.

Extremely cordial reception; immediate offer of an apperitif, gratis; abundant and superior set meal, plus rather expensive wines. It is fairly fashionable at the moment, but we found the close atmosphere uncommodious for true dining pleasure. Perhaps you will have another impression. Closed Mondays and lunch time, except on Sundays. If you prefer à la carte to the fixed-price offerings of La Croisette, the same direction has opened **Le Suquet**, around the corner from Walton's on Draycott Ave. This one is done with open beams, stucco walls, bottle-glass windows, tiny flower bouquets and candlesticks on dark blue cloths; the floors are tiled, the chairs small, the atmosphere Provencal. Waiters in blue sweaters serve better wares, in our opinion, than their colleagues at the alma mater.

For shoppers, the gleaming, amiable **Mes Amis** resides just across the street from Harrods. Inviting bar to right of entry; long dining room to left; mirrored alcove set into a stone niche; green and white upholstery; atmosphere brightened by tubs of illuminated plants, flowers, and candelescence; appetizing small menu of French dishes. Our roasted guinea fowl was superb; so was our partner's platter of grilled sardines, both served with a delicious house white wine. Patron John Parnes produces enough joy to relieve all guilt for having shopped to excess.

Langan's Brasserie (Stratton St., Piccadilly), once the rage in London, left us cooler than a plate of diced cucumbers. Self-conscious decor comprised of bentwood chairs, paper mats over white cloths, and prints on walls. Chiefly French menu with items such as pheasant, quail eggs, and saddle of lamb as perhaps the star attractions. While the dishes we sampled were pleasing, the reception, noise and service were totally punk. And speaking of punks, the nitwits running the bar on our visit could easily qualify as intellectual turnips. Rather chic among midtown executives, but not worth the effort, in our opinion.

La Napoule (8–10 N. Audley St., Grosvenor Sq.) lacks eye appeal but to our palate it approached the quintessence of gastronomic pleasure. Busy, noisy, jovial ambiance; bar at entrance rubbing elbows with the cloakroom activity; long 2-tier room in dull brown; clouded windows on one side, mirrored alcoves on the other, and greenery growing down the middle. The Vichyssoise was perfect; the Quenelles of Smoked Salmon were as light as a dream of minuets; the Scampi Timbale also was so weightless it could have wafted from the kitchen by itself; the duck with mint was bizarre, but essentially good; the sauces were carefully prepared without tricks or gimmickry; the wine list is mammoth. An outstanding meal will clobber your bank balance; of this you can be sure. Strictly for the cognoscenti of the table to whom cost is secondary.

Tiddy Dols Eating House (2 Hertford St., Sheperd Market), named after the legendary eighteenth-century gingerbread man, used to be a delightfully inviting cluster of 6 ancient rooms, 2 bars, and a minstrels' gallery in 9 contiguous domiciles. Sadly some of its charm has been lost in its expansion; the upstairs retains the flavor of yore, but occasionally this is closed; the character of the overslick modern downstairs is blah. Open daily; reserve ahead. Now schizophrenic in its appeal to us, depending on where we are seated.

L'Écu de France (111 Jermyn St.) knows its gastronomy. When you receive that Écu-brand of overbustling but kindly service, we think you will agree that here is one of the leading French restaurants on British soil. Tasteful, lively, not spectacular or chichi; business clientele predominant at lunchtime; large handwritten menus in the Gallic tradition; outstanding vintage wines somewhat overpriced, served by sommeliers in cellarmen's smocks; bar chairs uncomfortably tiny, but dining-room facilities excellent. It is closed for lunch on Saturdays, but open for Sunday dinner. Once more it merits ringing cheers and *santés*.

Also very Gallic in flavor is **Le Bressan** (14 Wrights Lane), where the heavy scarlet damask, satin, and brocade could seem oppressive by daylight and rich by taperlight. Lately it has undergone some redecoration, but the mood of elegance remains. Our reception and service were superb, but the cuisine was variable and perhaps too costly for the rewards. Dinner is best, but plan to bid *adieu* to $100 or so if you arrive in tandem.

Drones (1 Pont St.) boggles our imagination as to why it remains fashionable. The ground-floor room with vines, plants, and its charming stained glass cupola, is a cheerful place to be; the downstairs cell with its dull illumination and Art Retro festoonery is grim, in our opinion. We found the light bites overpriced and wretchedly presented. A dainty spot that thrills us not.

Julie's (137 Portland Rd.), though it remains in the innermost circle of young aristocratic funlovers, has slipped noticeably, in our view. Only the jovial wine bar (with small lunches) is open at midday. Furnishings and décor drawn from various periods of English antiquity; a small forest of potted palms; taped classical music; quite cuddlesome in concept. The food continues to be a sad disappointment; moreover, the tariffs have skyrocketed. While artfully conceived and out of the ordinary, not recommended.

Inigo Jones (14 Garrick St.) is tucked away in a former mission house in the heart of the theatrical district. Look for its entrance beside what appears to be a chapel door but is now the portal of an office building. Impressively handsome interior employing many fine touches left over from its era as a stained-glass factory; bar up front with live harpsichord music nightly; antique-brick walls spotted with illuminated cathedral windows; carved medieval gargoyles which made even *us* look good to our lady companion; tangerine-and-plum linens; cellar den less interesting than the ground level. So-so attention is given by waiters gaily attired in Edwardian waistcoats, ruffled cuffs, skintight trews; reasonably priced. Certainly here's a feast for the hungry eye. Better than tolerable if you don't expect Vitry to prepare your vittles.

Le Carrosse (19-21 Elystan St., S.W.3) has been creating a crossfire of chitchat lately. Textile wall coverings; matching curtains; coach wheels over the doorway; huge centerpiece of dried flowers; yokes and other tack hung here and there; trappings a little shabby; so was our service. The cookery was suprisingly delectable, but because of the dismal location and tacky trim, we are not too enthusiastic.

La Popote (3 Walton St.), to us, at least, goes overboard into the aesthetic seas. A trio of fussy roomettes usually abubble with fastidious people relaxing nervously in its delicate atmosphere. French conservatory ambiance; draped ceiling; candles and flowers on tables; gilt chairs; giltless menu of limited size; sweetie-pie reception and service.

Alonso's (32 Queenstown Rd., S.W.8) is a bit off the beaten path, but the with-it crowd quickly spotted this crazy lair. Childlike watercolors on mat-burgundy walls; dark carpet; inventive, almost playful fixed-price menu that discloses a disdain for culinary convention. Different.

Andrea's (Blacklands Terrace, a backlands alley off King's Road) splits its hearty but unpretentious personality between Italian and French cuisine. Perhaps 16 tables up front plus one typically Latin cranny out back; open wine rack opposite entrance; rainbow of red, yellow, and blue-hued checkered cloths with matching napery; dessert-and-cheese display tray with 4-wheel drive; efficient, friendly staff. We're extremely high on this house's tempting array of easy-on-the-wallet traditional dishes, the gratis Turkish paste offered with coffee, and the welkin of welcomes. Solid through and through.

Old Russia (9 Dean Bradley House, Horseferry Rd.) is a labor of love by Mme. Elena Konstantinovna, who transported all 52 tons of it (only the carpeting is British) from the Far East. The 3 dining rooms recreate the moods of Odessa, Moldavia, and Siberia. If you munch your Marinovanaia Ribba (fish cooked in vegetables) in the last one, please don't be alarmed if you find an old woman sleeping on the mantelpiece—merely a provincial method of keeping warm. When the Proprietress explains her selections, she is proud to point out that some of them are no longer served elsewhere. The white Russian wine (its color, not its politics!) was an interesting change. Two set menus are available including the Zakuski Dinner, a ruble-saving series of Tsar-iffic hors d'oeuvres (try this with one of her 3 specially blended vodkas). Closed Sunday. A Russian Rhapsody.

Barracuda (1D Baker St., off Portman Square), in a suavely styled subterranean setting, just may dish out the most savory Italian delicacies in London. Plush bar to the right of the stairs for prepasta persuasions; catacomb setting; thick carpet; indirect green illumination which Transylvanians would probably adore; discreetly hidden combo alternating with piped melodies; the service was prompt and proper; the tabs have the bite of a hungry Barracuda.

Leith's (92 Kensington Park Rd.), retains its popularity while maturity has mellowed its flair. Multiformed dining segments hewn from a converted apartment in a low-rent district; drab walls; stagecraft lighting. We have just put down our napkins after our very rewarding dinner here. Hors d'oeuvre trolley with so many tempters—a meal in itself; the rest of the set-price menu filled with imaginative and well-prepared dishes. Good.

For *medium-priced dining without dancing*: **Café Royal** (68 Regent St.) is a somewhat scarred veteran. This venerable hangout with the flavor of Delmonico's at the turn of the century still tries, sometimes unsuccessfully, to offer the discriminating diner everything it should. Service leans toward the hurry-hurry school; substantial cuisine often elaborately presented. Be sure to sit in the Grill Room (closed Sun.). **L'Étoile** (30 Charlotte St.) started off nobly when this century was in diapers. How it continues to get better, we'll never understand—but it does. The French-based cuisine is, in fact, more delicate than that of some of the biggest names in Paris. The wines are exquisite and treated with grace and solemnity by one of the finest sommeliers on either side of the Channel. Highly skilled waiters in swallowtail coats; yellow walls ending at a ruby border; red figured carpet. The same clientele keeps coming back delightful year after delightful decade—and so will we. For the medium bracket, here's deluxe gastronomy. Again, highly recommended—and be sure to reserve in advance. **Isola Bella** (15 Frith St.) aims the skillets at chiefly French recipes. Well above average; closed Sundays. **Overtons St. James's** (5 St. James's St.) offers seafood specialties plus a goodly store of grills and meats in modern surroundings. Two floors; excellent oyster bar; noisy; tourist-trammeled; big after-theater trade; snippish, sullen service; closed Sundays. **Vendôme** (20 Dover St.) is also catnip for those with piscatorial palates. Separate counter for bivalve fanciers; eighteenth-century French décor; closed Saturday; pleasant. **La Terrazza** (19 Romilly St.) put on an almost comic display of ill-earned self-importance, amateurish service, and wretched cookery on our very recent try. Double necklace of small rooms in 2 strands (ground level and cellar); tiny tables with elbow-to-elbow relationships among adjoining parties; Italian-born directorial team of Mario and Franco, who also operate the same-style **Tiberio** (see later) and **Mario & Franco's Trattoo** (2 Abingdon Rd.). **White Tower** (1 Percy St.) is a north-of-Soho standby. Two floors eternally busy (and often a 3rd, as well); walls lined with fez-topped braves and decorative plates; superb service; wonderful Dolmades, stuffed eggplant, Moussaka, and other fully developed Levantine delights, plus "retsina" and French wines. We love it. **Frank's Italian Restaurant** (63 Jermyn St.) whips up savory pasta, risotto, and other Latin delicacies for a modest number of lire. Big lunch traffic of clients from the business district; quiet at night; more for good food than for good looks. **Luigi's** (Tavistock St.) is recommended especially as an after-the-final-curtain entry. Reservations a *must;* bid for more ingratiating upstairs perches. **Lugger** (nearby at 147 Strand) likewise sails in with cargoes from The Boot. **Leoni's Quo Vadis** (Dean St.) used to be one of our favorites, but we've gone off it of late. **Marquis** (121A Mount St.) offers a fine presentation of French and Italian dishes (especially the veal and the duck); smart clientele who obviously enjoy its luxury surroundings at medium prices. The small pine-planked quadrant in the rear is chiefly for private parties.

Lafayette (32 King St., St. James's, SW1) harks back to our own Franco-American affiliations when the Colonies were nascent. The cookery is based upon Gallic dishes with an interesting Creole additive from New Orleans. Attractive L-shaped room with brown and black geometric carpeting; hessian walls with prints taken from early Americana; comfortable banquettes; careful, sophisticated attention from the immaculately groomed staff; smallish servings nicely presented. "Lafayette, we are here!"

Montpeliano (13 Montpelier St.) is a fashionable midcity stop these days—when it is so utterly important to be seen in the right places. Frenetic, loud narrow room; crowded tables; some dishes okay, others wretched. Being known here puts you in league with Jupiter and Juno at least, my dear.

Alvaro's (124 King's Rd.), the head of the Chelsea menage not too long ago, now seems vedy old chapeau. Close atmosphere; white walls; plain settings; damnably uncomfortable for long lingering or lounging. Food? Ho-hum—but if you care, you miss the whole point. Alvaro himself left and has opened **I Paparazzi** (54 Dean St.) and **La Famiglia** (7 Langton St.). **Nikitas** (65 Ifield

Rd.) comes on with a ground-level bar, a cellar cell with gold-papered walls, icon fixtures, and dim. lighting. Everyone in our party was disappointed by their cookery, but we all agreed that the wide selection and service of the imported vodkas was excellent. Not for dining, but for imbibing. Other Chelsea chummeries? **Alexander's** (also on King's Rd.) is in the Old Guard of the candlewax-and-gingham gang. It has been so successful that the management now boasts an Alexandrian duet, with the newer branch nearby. Psssssst! . . . **Borgo San Frediano** (62 Fulham Rd.), whispered to be *buonissimo*, we found just plain awful in kitchen skills and service standards on our last try. Though many tout it, we'd prefer to ignore it.

For *English traditional* dining, **Stone's Chop House** (Panton St., off The Haymarket), in our opinion, generally continues as a felicitous exponent of the national art. Handsome décor, warm and delightful, with updated Regency predominant; stone-floor cocktail lounge in black and red leather with hunting motif; wood paneling with windows bordered in stained glass; natural timber pillars; clever soft-sell illumination; lovely mural of a Canaletto harbor scene. The upstairs Domino Lounge leads to the charmingly irregular dinner-only room in brick and tile, with marble statuary; Pebble Bar adjoining booths along the periphery. No fancy French or "International" cuisine here—just English stick-to-the-rib roast grills, "puds," and "Dover Sole that brings tears to the eyes for grief that anything so innocent and tender should have to yield up its life." This quotation was penned by another guidebook scrivener about a century ago. Wonderful old **Simpson's-in-the-Strand** (100 Strand), around the corner from the Savoy, now has fully regained its stride after riding hard on its long and distinguished reputation. We like it today as much as we ever did in its glorious past. Men's Bar in cellar and venerable, paneled, ground-floor restaurant (ladies admitted to latter only Sats.); rich, decorous, comfortable main restaurant up 1 flight (ladies always welcome). It serves almost the same classic dishes as Stone's—and much more gracefully, too. Closed Sunday; mandatory to reserve in advance for lunch; don't forget the custom of tipping your carver. Two oddities: (1) Gentlemen are requested not to smoke their pipes in the dining room, and (2) tea is available but politely discouraged here (Simpson's avows it's for teatime *only*—an hour when its portals are shut). **Rules** (35 Maiden Lane), also a short hike from the Savoy Hotel, presents a charming Edwardian impression of seediness. Creaky, rippled floors; dimensions cramped; friendly welcome. Game, pies, mutton chops, the hearty fare (and feel!) of Old England; no roast beef, but our latest steak was handled with dutiful respect. This ancient landmark, popular for after-theater suppers, is closed Sundays. **The Baron of Beef** (Gutter Lane, Gresham St.) is another retreat where the Aberdeen Angus is deified. Odd-shape, low-ceiling room with stuffy ventilation; décor pleasant but undistinguished; elbow-type tables with sleigh-type seats; service as cheerful and benign as the vases of flowers; very noisy when full. Despite its outstandingly savory beef and extra-courteous attention, not worth the long trek to London's financial district if you're closer to Stone's or the Rib Room (see below). **Cowcross** (6–7 Cowcross St.) is in the center of Smithfield, Europe's largest wholesale meat market—and *that* is exactly why you should order one of its bovine selections. Clublike atmosphere; hunt scenes on walls; wonderful grills; poor desserts; medium prices. The area is fun; so is the meal—if you're not a vegetarian.

If you are herbivorous, try **Crank's** (Marshall St. near Regent St.), where we recently devoured one of the most savory repasts that botany can provide. Juice bar; cafeteria; health-food kiosk; delicious cookery in nice simple surroundings. A welcome change of viands. **Oodles**, on Edgeware Rd., tries to do similar things, but they come off poorly, in our opinion. The **Wig & Pen Club** (229-230 Strand), built in 1625, is the beloved oasis of upper-echelon newsmen from neighboring Fleet Street. Here is the only building on this famous avenue to survive both the Great Fire of London and the subsequent invasion of hungry managing editors and thirsty foreign correspondents. A number of doll-size dining rooms radiate from the 4 crooked flights of stairs; the trispire penthouse roof garden features lobster and other selections in hot weather; 5 bars dispense smiles in season; pine-lined Inns of Court Room for the "hospitality hour." Open until 11 P.M. weekdays except Saturdays until 6 P.M., not at all on Sundays. **The Hunting Lodge** (16 Lower Regent St.) is one of the most ambitious, sumptuous, and elegant projects of the mighty Trust Houses Forte interests. Modern aura, subdued and delightfully pleasant; oak panels, indirect lighting, teak tables, black-leather chairs and banquettes. A dark-brick open grill commands the central focus, producing the mainstays of its now-disappointing British fare. Fascinating menu listing such items as Smoked Bloater, Cottage Pie, and Finnan Haddie; roast beef and steaks (our latest one again was positively wretched) are the noon features, with roast lamb spotlighted at night; both are dispensed from rolling trolleys. Enormous wine cellar—at prices that seem just plain outrageous. Pimm's now has only 1 of its former 4 branches currently in operation: **Ye Olde Dr. Butler's Head** (Mason's Ave.). This institution inspired the famous Pimm's Cups; known the world over. Closed Saturday to Monday. **Guinea Grill Room** (30 Bruton Place) is no longer recommended due to the pushy and almost rude behavior of the foreign-born maîtres who insist on rushing clients through their meals in order to squeeze several seatings out of each lunch or dinner. Entrance is beside a small mountain of raw meat from which you are urged to select your dinner in this heaped carnage (with no indication of price). If you are privileged to be seated in the best section, then you are forced to walk through its kitchen to the inner sanctum where haughty minions will hardly deign to acknowledge your presence. The décor is composed (as far as we could tell) of red-painted pegboard and 1945-style overhead element-heaters with greasy tassel pullcords. The chairs were so scuffed on our visit that we assumed they had participated in the last 20 years of John Wayne movies. All in all, the presumptuousness, the altitudinous tariffs, and the rinky-dink surroundings were *not*—for us, at least —worth the above-average grills from the cuisine.

The **Blue Boar Inn**, on Leicester Square (how more conveniently located could it be?), had lost some of its flair on our latest check. The Jousting Bar, at ground level, is a run-of-the-spigot pub, with nothing to distinguish it from hundreds of its fellows. But down one flight, the venturer finds (1) a candlelit cocktail bar, (2) the Robin Hood Tavern, an optional dining place separated by wrought iron and crossed pikes over its "doorway" from (3) the main restaurant. Medieval English motif with handsome arched ceilings; fat candles for every group; flaming "torchlights" as wall fixtures; artful color blends; perhaps 35 tables; good service. Still popular with its essentially British clientele; convenient to the cluster of first-run movie theaters in this area. **Wilton's** (27 Bury St.), a turn-of-the-century period piece, appeals to well-heeled traditionalists. Although roast beef is *not* the main attraction, it is always available and nearly always excellent. For decades this busy bistro has been famed for its piscatorial splendors, which are now featured less and less but which retain the highest quality. Prices are getting pretty lofty nowdays. **Massey's Chop House** (38 Beauchamp Place) features similar high-protein products, but only a fraction of the atmosphere. Better for dinner than for lunch. The **George and Vulture** (3 Castle Court) is a 2-story, open-grill rough-and-ready chophouse, with ancient, friendly waiters and a near-medieval setting; it claims title as the oldest tavern in existence, founded in A.D. 1175; our salad easily could have dated from the same year; our melon was harder than a tempered cannonball; our steak was rewarding, however. Open for lunch only, Monday through Friday; go before 1 P.M. or after 1:45 P.M., because its regular stockbroker clientele keeps it jammed. Medium prices for no-nonsense cookery; more British than the British; you may have to share a table. Not spectacular, but veddy, veddy Plantagenet. **Mrs. Beeton's Hungry Horse** (196 Fulham Rd.) offers standard fodder at stable tariffs. Simple surroundings in a whitewashed basement rick; fair-withered clientele of Smart Set fillies, stallions, and perhaps a few geldings; pleasant for a long-shot diversion. **Mr. Fogg**, an annex of the previously described Café Royal, permits you to grill your own steak at tableside, leaving the chef free to preside over his salad bowl. The prices are inviting, but the atmosphere is, well . . . Foggy. Very convenient, but short on eye appeal.

For *seafood,* the capital of this salty island has splendid versatility. Our top choice this year is **Poissonnerie de l'Avenue** (82 Sloane Ave., S.W. 7), which certainly must rate as one of the unsung maritime kings in Europe—and with prices so reasonable that you'll be happily surprised. A clublike nookery that grew over 2 oak-paneled floors; rouge carpets; chummy counter service plus numerous tables; specialties chalked onto a blackboard; big, varied menu; beautiful presentation; outstanding quality. This one is generally considered the best catch in London's fish pond; globe-spanner Gerry Herrod tipped us off about it and we're forever grateful to this savvy friend. Top recommendation, but getting a seat will be a problem. Lunchtime is easier than evening. **Scott's** (20 Mount St.) is decked out with raspberry-damask wall coverings, marble columns, Spy prints on white brick, bas-relief panels, and crystal chandeliers. While it remains one of London's leading establishments, the complaints that have reached us lately require that we have another look very soon. **Sheeky's** (29-31 St. Martin's Court) is for the broad-minded. Steamed or grilled seafood only (an oddball lease prohibits frying the fish). Old creaky atmosphere that we love; worn wooden floors; chummy service by waitresses in dental-assistant gowns. The steamed turbot is sinfully delicious; so is the grilled sole. Smack in the theatrical district so very useful to pre-show diners; also serving until 10:45 P.M. A 10-strike for no-frills sea fare. **Cunningham's** (17B Curzon St.) has décor resembling Gaulish Boudoir. The vittles and attention were worth the fishing expedition, but the billings seemed baleen to this Poseidon. We've already described the Riviera-style **La Croisette** as well as its kith, **Le Suquet**, and **La Napoule**. **Wheeler's** (19 Old Compton St.), original link in the chain that includes Vendôme and 5 others, features Dover sole in a wide variety of moods. Our mode left much to be desired, and we were further disgruntled to observe the waiters achatter with each other while patrons pined for pampering. **Carafe** (15 Lowndes St.), now part of the Wheeler's group, offers 14-table intimacy, service that often rankles, so-so cuisine, a clientele of theatrical or business VIPs, and exactly the same menu as its bigger brother we've just mentioned; closed Monday. **Manzi's** (corner Lisle and Leicester Sts., W.C.2) is the oldest maritime den in London; reasonable tabs; grilled sole the specialty; unusually rewarding and money-saving. **Bentley's** (11 Swallow St.) swims in as a firmly fleshed midtown wiggler. Busy ground-floor bar and oyster counter; one-room upstairs restaurant with azalea-red walls hung with paintings; unwatchful disattention by frumpy waitresses; rush-rush atmosphere. Cookery that is almost *too* simple (some would say "bland"); reasonable-to-rich prices. A quality nook—but we won't go out of our way for our next try. **Bill Bentley's** (31 Beauchamp Place), not to be confused with the above, features wine from the copious cave of B-B Himself. Subterranean sherry bar; ground-level pub for sips and nibbles; globe-lit, blue-trimmed upstairs dining area. The herring in heavy cream reaped net profits for our piscatorial speculation; our skewered medallions of turbot, ham, and green peppers, served on a bed of rice and capers, added another dividend. An otherwise pleasant repast was marred only by the sight of waiters gorging themselves on mussels and clams when they weren't attending to the clients. Ah, well . . . a small carp, really. Closed Sunday. Going into heavier poundage, the midtown **Golden Carp** (8A Mount St.) is done up in fishnets, maritime paintings, raw-wood tables, and ship lanterns. Huge portions of better than average cookery; not cheap; quick service; same ownership as the aforementioned Marquis, which makes it a solid bottom feeder.

For *hotel dining*, to select only a handful from the carloads, the cool-toned, yew-tree-and-white-marble **Savoy Grill** is an international legend; while it has had a few detractors of late, scores of serious gourmets maintain that it serves the best-prepared food in the United Kingdom. The **Connaught Grill** is on a par; it may even have a slight edge on the Savoy, depending on personal taste. We like each in its own way, however, so they are neck-and-neck in our ratings. Urbane, cozy atmosphere; impeccable from service to presentation to cuisine. Also especially warranted for after-theater supping. The **Capital** capitalizes on a well deserved reputation for distinguished continental fare. Our Mousseline de Coquille St. Jacques and Carré d'Agneau were nothing short of splendid. Few tables, so reserve ahead; small adjoining lounge; smooth service. Surely one of the finest in today's London. Le Perroquet in the **Berkeley** is the nexus for an excellent luncheon. This handsome, modernistic yet modulated entry, which transforms into a discothèque at night, provides a moderate, low-cost buffet within one of the most decorative and distinguished havens around. Tempting, tasteful, and thrifty. The air-conditioned **Dorchester Grill** is smart for lunch; very social, very urbane; cuisine significantly improved. At **Cla-**

ridge's, the main dining room has been given a shot of adrenalin, plus better lighting, and the chipper little cosmos known as the Causerie has an ample smörgåsbord selection (lunch and dinner this time) including mineral water, wine, or beer. General Manager Hansen is a Dane; he was wise enough to install one of his countrymen as the chef here; now both beam with national pride. Reserve well in advance, even if you are a hotel guest. Our meal in the main restaurant was perfect in every regard, as was our more recent culinary rove at the Causerie. The **Carlton Tower's Rib Room** features red décor and restful lighting; reception, service, and staff attitude eager but sometimes fickle; succulent Prime Angus beef sliced in mammoth slabs. Huge plates that dwarf the foil-baked potato; routine salad; ice water at every table; ventilation on the stuffy side. The **Chelsea Room** is also in this hotel. Personally we find it worlds better than its more famous companion. The staff attention is perfect; the crystal wall panels glisten as does the glassware on the tables; wide windows overlook the lovely park. Our pheasant and our partner's duck were splendid; so were the nicly presented side dishes. Distinguished, but relatively unsung for such outstanding culinary performance. The top-quality and chic **Inn on the Park**'s parking places are mentioned under "Hotels." The **Royal Lancaster**'s Mediterranean Café is one of the best budget moorings on the London shoreline, for our pound of sterling or pounds of flesh. The **Intercontinental**'s Le Soufflé remains a disappointment, albeit an attractive one. The preparations in the Coffee House impressed us as uninspired. The Beachcomber at the **May Fair** is a flash that fizzled into a cornball South Sea Island luau. At the same hotel, but worlds above the low-tide Beachcomber, you'll find patrician dining at the Châteaubriand. The **Hyde Park Grill** and the **St. George's** (viewful penthouse vista) are also well known for their kitchens. The **Ritz** boasts one of the most gorgeous rotunda rooms in Europe; now the gastronomy is coming up, too.

Dining adventures? Perhaps the zaniest meal in London can be found at the Elizabethan Room of the **Gore Hotel** (189 Queen's Gate)—an experience for every visitor (just once). Owner Robin Howard, a scholar and gourmet, has duplicated every detail of a banquet served in the time of Queen Bess and has reproduced the renowned Seven Star Chamber in the basement, where other Olde Worlde flights of fancy take place. Among the dishes you'll be served are Sturgeon or Lobster Pie, Peacock Pâté, Boar's Head Salad, Salmagundi, Good King Henry (wild spinach), Syllabub—all sorts of authentic but odd things, and they're washed down with mead and mulled claret. Wooden plates; 2 old-style table utensils only; clay pipes; straw on the floor; waitresses in Elizabethan costumes who may be pinched at will (or so Mr. Howard says—but please don't take *our* word, because we've never had either the yen or the nerve). Foodwise, you won't dance with enjoyment when you've finished; funwise, however, it's a great experience—to repeat, just once. **Flanagan's** (100 Baker St., 37 St. Martin's Lane, and 11 Kensington High St.), harks back only as far as the Gay Nineties. Sawdust floors; honky-tonk piano; costumed waitresses; beverage posters of the 1800's on the walls; patrons following lyrics printed on the napkins join the community sings. The cookery is indifferent, but in this mesmeric clime, who cares? Beer kegs of joviality 7 days a week until 12:30 A.M. Happily recommended. Pick and choose? **Justin de Blank** (54 Duke St., W.1) is a sort of do-it-yourself delicatessen for the celebrity set. Our quiche was dee-liche! Cute and costly. The **Barbican** (Lee House, London Wall), in the skyrocketing Barbican development, is what might be termed a Caesarean section of the past. Roman highlights in a posh modern setting; top positions held by former Dorchester and Hatchetts personnel; costly à la carte dishes; closed Saturdays, Sundays, and bank holidays; chiefly for expense-account business lunches. There's a viewful restaurant standing over the river in the **Royal Festival Hall**. Midstream in position and in quality, but oh-what-a-location for a variation on Thames.

The **Caviar Bar** (Knightsbridge Green, across from the Scotch House) is fit for a Sultan's budget. Cold-counter, a few tables, blinis, and other snacks for exquisite prices. Sleekly modern and ultraspecial.

Le Cellier du Midi (Church Row in Hampstead) is an outskirts oasis. Dark, snugglesome bracelet of several cellar rooms; candles on rustic plank tables; garlands of garlic hanging from rough walls. No beverage license, so the wines (if you don't bring your own bottle) are imported from a nearby pub. The service is informal, but careful and ever-so-friendly. We richly enjoyed every morsel and moment—and we think you might, too. **Keats** (3-4 Downshire Hill) is another Hampstead address, this one much more expensive and socially ranked. Entry foyer and small salon; nicer ruby-hued inner nook with library, paintings, and dim lights; small dimensions on its Franco-Italian menu. Neighborly service; delicious meats and more complicated dishes on our recent sampling. Attractive but steeply priced for its blue-ribbon patronage.

Now let's look into the *nationalities* grab bag. **Kosher cookery**? **Bloom's** (blossoming at 90 Whitechapel High St.) is a no-nonsense ethnic paradise. Take-out order section and stand-up counters near the entrance where legions of ravenous lunchtime *landsleit* joyously celebrate the glories of pastrami, corned beef, roast beef, chopped liver, tongue, and other inspired deli-cacies; table area with napery as white as a bar mitzvah boy's collar also jammed with midday mavens munching blintzes, gefilte fish, kreplach, and other traditional tempters; health foods such as chicken soup always available. Rituals of the Beth Din and Kashrus Commission are scrupulously (and scrumptiously) observed; rabbi and religious supervisor are on the premises daily (and not just for a snack, either). Second-generation management by Sidney Bloom, the warm and soooo-conscientious son of the 1920 founder, who now sends trucks out for home delivery and stocks the shelves of the best shops in the U.K. with his famous name-brand canned products. Because of the teeming luncheon throngs and the no-reservations policy, we prefer dinner here. Closed Saturdays, of course. Our sincere mazel tov to this, the finest Bloom on the orthodox stem. (Although there's a branch at 130 Golder's Green Rd., we enjoy the original plant a bit more.) **The Widow Applebaum's** (46 S. Molton St.) is a snack and sandwich noshery on a midtown pedestrian mall. (Remember that "Corned beef" becomes "salt beef" in the land of the Picts.) **Spanish savors**? At **Martinez** (Swallow St.) there's a sweet little patio for your pleasure. **East Indian curries** and specialties? The leader now seems to be the rather costly **Shezan** (16-22 Cheval Place), a short walk from Harrods. Ground floor entry; cool lower level with tile floor; brown and beige walls in brick or with textile covering; leather chairs. Excellent service and cuisine. Try **Jamshid** (6 Glendower Place, S. Kensington) for the medium-priced Chicken Curry or the Chicken Dhansak served with Papadams (sun-dried lentil flour bread), and those wonderful Jelibies for dessert. Or try the very much larger and more famous **Veeraswamy's** (99–101 Regent St., with entrance on Swallow St.), which is now directed by R. N. Kapur. Residents often are cynical about this colorfully decorative oldtimer, but year after year we find it provides top value. An Indian friend opined to us, "It suffers from having been the first of its kind in London." **Omar Khayyam** (177 Regent St.) is just plain awful, in this reporter's opinion; unpalatable food; preposterous belly dancing by a pathetic tub-tummied wiggler; clientele of rednecked oglers. The fad for Tandoori now seems to be—and deservedly so—on the tip of every Asian-aimed tongue. This is an overnight marinade of chicken and kebabs baked in a special Indian oven (the "tandoori") and followed by the curry course. **Gaylord** (79 Mortimer St.), a branch of the New Delhi and Bombay trees, is the plushiest exponent of this particular type of cookery. **Agra** (137 Whitfield St.), with a different ambiance but similar cuisine, can pan out Tandoori, curry, and an Indian dessert plus coffee for very reasonable rupees, Sahib. **Italian**? We've already noted quite a few in the foregoing sections, but you might wish to add **La Lupa** (23 Connaught St.) and **Trattoria dei Cacciatori** (in the Old Bond St. area) to your list. The first is in an ornate cellar that could have served as a set in a Cecil B. De Luxe film; the latter is more modestly cast in an atmospheric wood-paneled den. Prices are moderate at both. **Chinese food**? This fever which for several years overwhelmed England is giving way to the rage for so-called Italian-style *trattorie;* nearly all the Cathay ventures are currently moving out from the center. Compared with the Hong Kong or American variety, however, we think them discouragingly 2nd-rate—mainly because the English climate is too windy and too cold to grow the essential greens and vegetables. **Tai Pan** (8 Egerton Garden Mews, S.W. 3), a fairly new trader in Hunan, Peking, and Szechuan Cuisine, is definitely in the big boss league. Downstairs site; carved wood dragon-motif butresses; several intimate booths with slated wood benches overlooking other tables; open daily for lunch and dinner; happy, attentive staff; well-pleased, well-fed clients chop-sticking through over 80 available dishes. If you're one of those who Like It Hot, here's your target. **Fu Tong** (29 Kensington High St.) used to be the best bet in the metropolis, but now we think it has gone off. The celebrated Soho establishment, **Lee Ho Fook,** has a split personality (to match its badly chipped china, no doubt); it is divided into 2 segments. Though the fancy address at 15–16 Gerrard St. wins most of the attention, we've always much preferred the modest and cheaper family nookery just around the corner at 41–43 Wardour St. Look into both, pay your money, and take your choice. (We dislike the branch at 58 Shaftsbury Ave. and don't know the outlet at 4 Macclesfield St.) **Lotus House** (61–69 Edgware Rd., W.2) has soothed that yen of many show-biz types, but as with Fu Tong, we feel it has reached its zenith and may now be descending. **China Garden** (66 Brewer St.), which blossoms under the same Lotus management, greets its guests with unusual Eastern décor; attractive. **Good Friends** (139 Salmon Lane, E.14) , in the tough Limehouse orchard, serves Cantonese dishes at reasonable tariffs. Dull, no-nonsense ambiance; on Sundays, Chinese Embassy personnel jam it tighter than an egg roll. **Kuo Yuan** (259 High Road, Willesden Green, N.W.10) strikes us as one of the best Peking-style contenders in Londontown; book in advance. The **Sailing Junk** (59 Marloes Rd.), which went into a slump, is currently a question mark to us. **Lee Yuan** (40 Earls Court Rd., W.8) gets our favorable nod. So does **Loon Fung's** (37–38 Gerrard St.), where typically no-nonsense décor belies a staggering 127 choices of *Oriental* rather than Chinese-American fare. Piped melodies straight from the pagoda; air conditioning; open noon to 11:30, including Sundays. **Gallery Rendezvous** (55 Beak St., W.1), despite its unlikely name, specializes in northern fare; it is one of our favorites, as is the same-ownership **Dumpling Inn** (15A Gerrard St.), although the staff in the latter seemed to think it was bestowing a favor by serving us. (**Soho Rendezvous** and **Ley On's** are other members of this tong.) **Chelsea Rendezvous** (4 Sydney St.) specializes in Shanghai cuisine at medium-hai prices; mostly it is attended by London's Shang-Hai-Society. **Mr. Chow** (151 Knightsbridge) remains a pacesetter for London's current Trendy Set. A Great Wall exists, in our opinion, between its skilled kitchen staff and its low-powered battery of waiters who, on our visit, seemed grossly deficient not only in basic etiquette, but in the use of the abacus. Henceforth we'll chow elsewhere. **Japanese**? **Saga** (43 S. Molton St.) is a tale first told to us by Oriental specialist Denis McEvoy, the globally known journalist and editor. And what a bewitching story it weaves. Cozy tavern atmosphere with open beams and booths; tables up front and cooking counter farther back; attractive costumed waitresses. Our raw fish (very expensive) platter and tempura were excellent; be sure to sample the Japanese beer. Authenticity is its key feature—and we are grateful to Scholar McEvoy for opening this new portal of discovery to us. The **Masako** (St. Christopher's Place) is in a charming mews amid antique shops and boutiques. Cork walls divided by black enamel beams; red carpets; small stage surrounded by bamboo; excellent sukiyaki, tempura, and many more nipponese creations. Others in this group include **Sushi-Masa, Nanten, Ginnan, Nankin**, and **Hiroko** of the Kensington Hilton. **Turkish delight**? Try **Gallipoli** (Bishopsgate Churchyard, E.C.2), which could fatten any sultan; plush décor; open until 3 A.M.; dancing every night (both Western and belly types); surprisingly authentic, say the eunuchs in the harem. **Viennese**? **Old Vienna** (94 New Bond St., W.1) waxes schmaltzy, with Owner Joszi and his troupe gussied up in lederhosen; group singing to accordionotations; party atmosphere; well worth the outlay if you're feeling not ritzy but fritzy. **French comestibles**? Quite a few already have been covered in previous groupings. The still-growing **Le Français** (259 Fulham Rd., S.W.3) burns hotter than a Languedoc skillet. Proprietorship by a pair of Gauls who do the marketing, whip the sauces, and welcome the patrons. Another "in" spot with Francophiles is **Le Connoisseur** (10 A Golders Green Rd., N.W.11) even though it is "way out" in this bedroom suburb. The recent *gourmet menu* which we studied included 5 courses plus coffee and *petits fours* at the neck-jolting sum of more than $40 per spinning head. Less exalted and less expensive nutrients also available, *mais oui.* **L'Opera** (32 Great Queen St., W.C.2) is only fair, in our opinion. The prices are reasonable and the atmosphere is cheerful, but our cuisine lacked zest. Never, please, *never* let them seat you in the lonely downstairs grotto. The after-theater fun is to be found at ground level. **Imperial settings**? **Villa dei Cesari** (135 Grosvenor Rd., S.W.1) boasts a river view; waiters in centurian garb, and dancing until 2:30 A.M.; closed Monday, but one of the few that features food, music, and dancing on the Sabbath. Very Rome-antic.

Finally, you might brave the rotating restaurant atop the 620-foot **Post Office Tower**, close to Tottenham Court Road. It is revolving 7 days a week for lunch and dinner, and so popular with tourists, businessmen, their out-of-town clients, and "Hey-Martha-Looka-here" rubberneckers that in peak sea-son it's useless even to *hope* to get in without a reservation made 3 days ahead. Poorly arranged circular bar which doesn't properly utilize the spectacular view; one-flight higher to the restaurant. It is set for one revolution every 23 minutes—much too fast, we found, for our digestive comfort. (Others on the Continent creep at closer to one full turn per hour, a pace which is better for the tummy, more romantic, and easier on vertigo sufferers.) The décor screams of tacky institutionality. Three-course table d'hôte; à la carte dinner selections; wretchedly rushed 2-seating system (no leisurely musings here); ludicrously, if not malevolently, expensive for the production-line glop we tried that pre-tended to be *haute cuisine*.

Snacks? Try **The Great American Disaster** (335 Fulham Rd. and 9 Beau-champ Place) where 17—count'em, where 17—different styles of burgers are served. Our thick ½-pounder, shrouded in melted American cheese and ac-companied by French fries and crisp salad, seemed to have had a U.S. passport it was so authentic. Skip the original location, which is hellandgone away; hie to the Beauchamp ("Beecham") Place operation. The latter is a long paneled room lined with step-up booths; the kitchen with its charcoal grill is to the rear; *New York Times* page-one reprints of great American disasters hang balefully on one wall. Since the waiters are young, long-haired, casual, and friendly, and since tapes of pop singers are amplified—but AMPLIFIED—to paralyzing levels, old crocks over 30 are hereby warned. Sirloin steak sandwiches, *deli-cious* cheesecake, "Real American" apple pie (sold out during our visit), banana splits, and hearty milkshakes round out the picture (and probably your tummy, too). Hours are from 11 A.M. to midnight Sunday to Thursday, but until 1 A.M. on Friday and Saturday. Go before 7 or after 10 to avoid the queues (*lines*, mate)—and please remember that, for the category, it's very expensive. Next in order are: **Adam's** (Earls Court Rd.), **Yankee** (newer offering at 22 Brompton Rd. preferable to the original at 26–28 Binney St.), **Burger King** (reigning between Leicester Sq. and Picadilly Circus), and, of course, **McDon-ald's** (Haymarket, Victoria St.) The **Great American Success** isn't, in our opinion. For dessert, try any of the **Dayvilles** ice cream parlors around town. They are sterile to the eye, but the products are excellent.

Roast-beef sandwich? The publike **Running Footman** (corner Charles St. and Berkeley Square) is superduper in this department. The **Square Rigger** (corner Arthur and King William Sts., near London Bridge) has a lunch counter plus 2 small dining nooks; whaling-ship motif; minnow-size tabs; weekdays only; well liked by many. Continental-style espresso bars are a nickel a dozen in today's London; you'll find them all over the city, as a reaction

against rising food prices. Among the better ones are **Cul de Sac** (43 Brompton Rd.) and **Les Enfants Terribles** (93 Dean St.). **Troubadour** (265 Old Brompton Rd.) is not recommended by us. Most of these are not up to U.S. snack-bar standards by a long shot—and relatively costly against the cost of an average full meal in a restaurant—but satisfactory all the same.

High tea at the **Ritz**? Posh, yes. Expensive, no. For a glimpse of the Stately London of yore, drop in between 4 P.M. and 5:30 P.M. at the spacious, gracious, changeless ground-floor lounge of this old-fashioned landmark. Its assorted finger sandwiches are excellent; specify your preferences to your swallow-tail-coated waiter. The average cost is perhaps £3 per person. Gentlemen are required to wear jackets and neckties. If you've reached a certain age and have had a good lunch, this may well serve as your supper.

Footnote: **Covent Garden**, the central London complex which still harbors its renowned Opera House but evacuated its huge flower and produce market, has just burst into blossom with its simultaneous inauguration of 44 restaurants and shops. Since we haven't yet had time to research this area to our satisfaction, our full report will appear in the next edition of this book.

Drinks (Plus Pubs and Wine Bars)   The celebrated Public House —"pub," for short—traditionally has been the heartbeat of England. In the old-timers, there are no jukeboxes, no bustling bartenders, no feelings of haste in your average pub. It's a social center, a place to relax and talk over the latest heavyweight contender, to play darts for a brace of pints. It's wonderful.

But in the pubs, as almost everywhere else, change is in the wind. The British Government is now seriously considering extension of the hour when the jolly publican calls "Time, Gentlemen, Time!" Generally, the saloon doors swing open at 11 A.M. and are fastened shut at 11 P.M. The lawmakers also want to eliminate the 3 P.M. to 5 P.M. closure—a cruel hiatus that parches many a fine British throat. Furthermore, there's a foot-on-the-rail movement to lower the age below 18 for entry into these establishments. All this may be realized by the time you arrive. What already has started, however, fills us with deep regret because it strikes at the very heart of the institution itself: the epidemic growth of the so-called Singing Pub or Entertainment Pub. The classic types (a few listed below) are being overtaken rapidly by these mod-mooded newcomers; within a couple of decades, we fear, the old ones may become extinct. In the capital, **Holsten Bierkeller** (34 Brook St.) is typical of the trend away from quiet conversation and traditional British folkways. In this example, the ambiance is that of a German beer cellar—rowdy, noisy, packed with young swingers, and specializing in Teutonic fare, with an inexpensive 3-course "meal". The **Redcliffe Hotel** (268 Fulham Rd.) asks a cover charge daily except on Mondays and Wednesdays; it features a discothèque (shiver me timbers!). For those who relished the Old England of Yore, these are mournful mutations indeed.

The traditional ones that remain are, like the amoeba, self-divided. On one side you'll find the Public Bar—plain, utilitarian, for drinkers who want no nonsense. On the other side, with a separate entrance, is the Saloon Bar—better decorated, more comfortable, the one you'll probably head for. Prices are usually a trifle higher in the latter. Then, of course, there are 3 styles of classic pubs: City Tavern (spirits and wine featured above draught beers), Gin Palace (typically Victorian if authentic), and Alehouse (plain, ancient, and historic).

As for what to order, there are 3 major British brews: Mild ale ("mild"), a medium-sweet, medium-brown, inexpensive choice which is becoming more rare in Central London; bitter beer ("bitter"), a pale brown, heavier variety; and Burton ("old"), which is deep brown, quite sweet, and richest of all. English drinkers like to mix these basic types to suit their individual preferences. But remember Burton is available September and June only. If you want straight mild ale, *don't* step right up, as one did in the Good Old Days, and ask for a "wallop"; now you might suddenly sprout a cauliflower ear.

Of heroes, England has more than her share. One of them, The Society for the Preservation of Beers from the Wood, is spreading swiftly across the isle. Says Good Banker Arthur Millard, the Chairman, who protests loudest against brews in tin cans: "We are being avalanched with beer drinkers who dislike the sealed dustbin stuff that pubs throw at you nowadays." We, too, join the chorus by lending our hearty bass to "Roll Out the Barrel"!

Beer, gin, rum, and liqueurs are plentiful and good; Scotch is costly. You'll pay £1 for a "small" (Understatement of the Year) and perhaps £2 for a "large" (junior-size) portion in today's London. The bottle price has been nudged up again. Remember, too, that British Scotch is somewhat weaker than ours.

To the average Englishman, ice used to be that strange, transparent, cold-to-the-touch substance upon which the fishmonger chilled his halibut. Now that so many visiting outlanders have insisted that whisky requires the stuff, he'll often go along by dropping 1 small cube—or 2, at the most—into his drink. British beer is customarily served at room temperature (lager is nearly always chilled)—but, as the ever-delightful C. V. R. Thompson wrote before his death, the room is usually so cold that the beer is delicious. We, however, are such barbarians about liking our brews cold, cold, COLD that we order Carlsberg or Tuborg (both Danish) draft whenever we can find them in restaurants—which, to our joy, is now surprisingly often in the larger cities.

★ **TIPS** After-hours, if you order a beer with your meal, the waiter is apt to shake his head righteously and offer you cider instead. Accept the "cider," because more than likely it will be your beer—a "mistake"!

Delicious *English* wine? The versatile cellars of London's luxury **Dorchester Hotel** come up with this phenomenon—Adgestone from the Isle of Wight. Since the vines are ½ German and ½ French, the result is a fresh, clear, interesting product of a Moselle. Please try it! English viticulture gradually is coming to harvest—a very slow process if you consider that the Romans, the Normans, and the British of the Middle Ages had vines growing all over London. Today, Harrods carries a sampling of the 140 products from England's commercial vineyards. Some of the more notable names include Beaulieu, Felsted, Pilton Manor, Hambledon, Kelsale, Hascombe, Cavendish Manor, Lamberhurst, and Chilsdown. And *cheers* to *you,* friend!

★ **WARNING** *Don't drive a car if you have consumed even as little as 2 pints of beer!!* Under the mercilessly stringent provisions of the Road Safety Act, the vehicle operator doesn't have to be drunk to face huge fines, 4 months in the pokey (or both), and loss of his or her license for one year. Suspects are required to take a roadside "Breathalyser" test. There is no recourse for either resident or visitor. The police are tough, too. So ask a teetotaling companion to take over the wheel when you want to live it up—or hie yourself back and forth by taxi, bus, or underground.

P.S. This applies everywhere within the United Kingdom.

As we promised, here are some characteristic pubs (even though a few of these, too, are now trending toward the fashions of Britain's youth cults):

Cockney Pride (Jermyn St.) has been transformed into one of the most "in" houses on the London scene today. Large cellar room colorfully festooned with authentic Victorianisms; old-fashioned horseshoe bar offering such Olde Englande standards as faggots (mincemeat-and-peas pudding), toad-in-the-hole (sausages in batter pudding), shepherd's pie, and many more historic tidbits —all priced at a pittance. Waiters in fancy vests and bowlers; waitresses in long Gay Nineties gowns; player piano tinkling in the background; normal pub hours (from 11 P.M. to midnight you must order food with drink). Very noisy, very crowded, amusing; a fun place for a pint, a snack, or even a meal (if you can stand the din that long). Here's an artful recreation of Good Queen Vickie's day; deservedly popular.

The **Red Lion** (48 Parliament St.), is a favorite with students from Guys Hospital. The Public Bar is on Parliament Street, the Saloon Bar on Derby Gate. Downstairs is best; no darts; ladies welcome. We noted the addition of a piano and vocalist on Sundays, plus an increasing sing-along quality in its atmosphere. It will probably roar even louder soon.

Antelope (Eaton Terrace) is a gem—not too moldy, not too chichi, a gentle introduction to the science of pubbery. Prices higher than average, but *still* low; excellent for a plain, cheerful dinner; one of our favorites.

The **Prospect of Whitby** (57 Wapping Wall), like the Cheshire Cheese (where you should be sure to sit at Samuel Johnson's table) and the previously mentioned George and Vulture (see "Restaurants"), is a tavern drawing huge numbers of tourists rather than a true pub. It has installed a Hawaiian band and a singer—to us, the ultimate abomination in these ancient English surroundings. Hangout of students who are sometimes rowdy. Dock area; rambling, helter-skelter building raised in 1520; Pepys Room for dining; stuffed alligator, human skull, and other oddities suspended over bar. Closed Sunday. **Dirty Dick's** and **The George** also attract droves of rubberneckers.

The **Sherlock Holmes Tavern** (Northumberland St.) is a latecomer in the Whitbread Brewery's series of so-called museum taverns. On the ground floor, you'll find the main bar, a scattering of tables, and, as wall decorations, a fascinating collection of "memorabilia" from his most famous "cases" (a plaster mold of a "paw print" of the hound of the Baskervilles, Detective Lestrade's "handcuffs," the "code" used in the story of the dancing men, etc.); to the side there's a painfully plain little nook for the earnest toper. Upstairs is the Grill, with tapestried wall coverings and white banquettes; to the rear of this section is a glassed-off montage of the famous fictional sitting room shared by the great sleuth and Dr. Watson at "221-B Baker St." Food adequate for pub (not restaurant) level; our tab for 3 was comparatively expensive.

An interesting tour should include a run down to the **Dickens Inn** at the newly developing St Katherine's Docks, near the Tower of London (which lately celebrated its 900th birthday). The quay area stirs merrily with life aboard several Thames barges, a Ferrari-red light ship, and scores of recreation boats. The restaurant is located upstairs in an ancient warehouse that was moved on wheels to this colorful site. About a hundred yards away another entry called **The Captain's Cabin** serves excellent salads and light refreshments. The neighboring **Beefeater** is chiefly for dining and a rather touristic type of cabaret evening.

The **Buccaneer** (Leicester Square) is an imposing example of its namesake. There's a galleon theme floating on a Polynesian undercurrent.

Nag's Head (Covent Garden), now plinking along with folk singers on Sunday evenings, **Samuel Pepys'** (Brooks Wharf, Upper Thames St.), **World's End** (King's Rd.)—the list of names and addresses is long, if you're not too choosy. You'll find them scattered everywhere.

All the above are satisfactory for the dilettante who has come to see a few *other* sights in the nation. But for the serious-minded suds-buff who would make girl scouts out of the ghosts of Brendan Behan, Dylan Thomas, and W. C. Fields, nothing beats the guidance of that camel-bellied specialist of all publicans, Alan Reeve-Jones, author of *London Pubs.* Together with his ever-faithful cast-iron liver, Mr. Reeve-Jones consumed 11 happy years visiting 1500 drinking stations, only to list and to recommend a mere 166. Here are a few of his candidates, but don't stop with these. Track down Mr. R-J's tome and find your own particular pot-o'-gold! Examples: For visual appeal the **Admiral Codrington** (Mossop St.); for film makers, the **Intrepid Fox** (Wardour St.); for doctors, the **Crown** (in Chelsea); for rowing enthusiasts, **The Dove** (Upper Mall); for old-time smugglers, **Anchor** (Bankside, Southmark); for world travelers, the **Fitzroy** (Charlotte St.); for cinema types, **The Victoria** (10 Strathearn Pl.); for experimental theatre, **The King's Head** (the back room at 115 Upper St. in the antique district of Islington); for Egyptologists, the **Museum Tavern** (Great Russell St.); for Members of Parliament, the **St. Stephen's Tavern**, just a skip from Westminster (listen for the bell—a signal that a vote is about to be taken in the Commons). Any thirsty merrymaker will find this a guidebook with a real head on it.

Wine Bars   Gradually these are beginning to supplant the pubs. These colorful oases serve quiches, goulash, cold meats, patés, and cheeses, generally in the range of £2 per platter or less. An overwhelming variety of fair-quality wine is on hand for prices which vary with the quantity you order (pitcher or individual glass); fortified pressings are also on tap. In most cases they function from 11:30 A.M. till 3 P.M., and 5:30 P.M. till 11 P.M.; some remain open later and on Sundays; the hours are extremely variable. Although tipping is not expected in pubs, it is definitely required in wine bars, especially when food is consumed; 10% is considered reasonable. Now let's fill the cup. **Ebury** (139 Ebury St., S.W.1) occupies the ground floor of a converted early Victorian house with walls of dark green wash and cream paint. The salads are excellent. One nice feature: tables can be reserved. **Downs** (5 Downs St., W.1) operates on 2 floors joined by a central spiral staircase. Large bar upstairs with stools; downstairs food counter with inviting display of meats. Candlelit and intimate: convenient to residents of Park Lane and Piccadilly hotels. **Ruby's** (28 Sussex Place, W.2) resides in a quiet backwater opposite the Victoria Tavern—but that's the only thing quiet about it, because as the shades of evening are lowered, its 3 floors are jammed with eager conversationalists. **Jimmie's** (Kensington Church St., W.8) is tucked into the wall of the old Kensington Barracks. Stable atmosphere with dark beams; the aroma of grilled meats permeates the air; vast open fire; guitar music. Fun. **Mother Bunch's** is located under the Arches F and G in Old Sealcoal Lane (EC4) behind Ludgate Circus. The Dickensian flavor is strong; cuisine varies from the simple to the truly luxurious. The **Wine Bar** quite literally *is* a hole-in-the-wall—located in Villiers St. across from Players Theatre. We like its food and its kookiness. **Russkies** (6 Wellington Terrace, Bayswater Road, W.2) is a long cellar combining both Victorian and modern elements. We've already mentioned **Julie's** (see restaurants) and the excellent wine bar in the **Gloucester Hotel. Slaters** (3 Panton St., Highmarket, S.W.1) is a standby for the theater crowd, possibly because of the unusually friendly service. **Motcomb's** (26 Motcomb St., S.W.1) is the sovereign of the fashionable Belgravia district. Thick wall-to-wall carpeting and banquette seating add to the feeling of poshness upstairs. Go to **Swifts** (93–97 Pelham St., S.W. 7) if you are looking for scrubbed wooden floors, an authentic oak bar, an inviting gallery, and sea food specialties. Many North Americans are drawn to the **Cork & Bottle** (44–46 Cranbourn St., W.C.2), which is reached through a garden gate and composed of 2 adjoining cellars. Its New Zealand owner strives to add adventure to the cookery. A good candidate for a pretheater nip. **Penny's Place** (6 King St., Covent Garden, W.C.2) is colorful mainly because of its location, while **Bailey's** (41 North Audley St., W.1) is strongly influenced by its proximity to the U.S. Embassy. **Crawfords** (10–12 Crafords St., W.1) is a candlelit hideaway with soft popular music in the early evening followed by entertainment later on. Half of the premises comprise a restaurant in which tables may be reserved. **The Loose Box** (7 Cheval Place, S.W.7) is popular with the Young Set. We were shocked on our latest visit to see how the prices had taken off. **Fino's Wine Cellar** (123 Mount St., W.1) is approached by a steep staircase beneath its stained glass and wooden canopy. The bar is long and narrow, with small recesses for those who may collapse in obscurity. Very "in" with the advertising world. **The Loose Rein** (221 Kings Road, S.W.3) is a modern spacious basement beneath a wine emporium.

There are more, but this ought to keep your palate dampened for at least a few nights of your English *tastevin*.

Country dining near London All of the following are easy excursions on a sunny day. To us, one of the better sancta, despite its longer-than-average haul, is Robert Carrier's **Hintlesham Hall** in *Hintlesham, Suffolk,* an ancient hamlet near Ipswich and Colchester. This world-renowned culinary authority (see "Restaurants, London") purchased the gone-to-seed Great Hall and its sylvan grounds in 1971. With an emir's ransom he totally restored the mansion and then converted it into a stunningly beautiful landmark. Mr. Carrier's 4-course luncheon (fixed-price choice of perhaps 32 dishes, many original) runs close to £13 (without wine), a sum many antiquarians would gladly pay just for the privilege of viewing the premises. Brandade of Smoked Trout, Chilled Bouillabaisse Salad, Fingers of Sole Rémoulade, Trio of Lamb Chops with Green Butter, Charcoal Grilled Scotch Sirloin with Roquefort Butter, Ragoût of Lamb à la Bourguignonne, and Sorbet au Cassis with Black-

currant Sauce are but random samplings. Debonair Manager Paul Lewis will
offer you the choice of quaffing or savoring in the Long Hall, the Bar, the Blue
Room, the Red Room, the China Room, or the 2-story-high Great Saloon. As
a bonus, "Festival Events"—concerts, recitals, wine-tasting regales, and more
—are held from early June to mid-July. If at all possible, PUL-EEZE ask your
hotel concierge to telephone Mr. Carrier's London namesake restaurant, not
only to find out what's on at Hintlesham Hall, but to make a reservation for
you even if only the culinations are cooking. And while speaking about this
area, in Essex, please do not overlook the possibility of visiting Le Talbooth
and Maison Talbooth which are listed in "Other Targets" under Dedham—
both outstanding in their very special ways. One of the most famous establishments is Gravetye Manor, *East Grinstead*, *Sussex* (30 miles), which is an
impressive Elizabethan mansion (built in 1598) crowning 30 acres of magnificent gardens, woodland, and lake. It reminds us of a British Colonial hotel of
60 years ago—clinging to such typically clublike holdovers as slip-covered
furniture and near Spartan functionality in its handful of accommodations. Its
only bar is maintained exclusively for members. High ceilings; lounge with
overstuffed chairs, sofas, and pukka sahib colonels and their ladies; pleasant
reception and service; discreetly tasteful, even lovely, dining room. Two surprisingly elaborate menus handsomely done, the basic one offering 36 choices
and the smaller offering only savories and sweets. (Both heavily puff Chef
Michael Quinn.) Despite the charm and ambiance here and the mouth-watering bills of fare, the quality of all but one of the dishes we sampled simply did
not measure up to the promise of coming attractions. The cost of an average
meal on our recent visit was $25 to $30 per person without wine. The drive
out is so enchanting, however, and the surroundings are so beautiful, that
despite the drawbacks from our gustatory adventure, we would recommend an
expedition on a sunny day. To get there, take A-22 (the Eastbourne Road);
about 7 miles past Godstone, at the crossroads, turn right on B-2028 to
Turner's Hill. *Advance reservations advised.* Another well-known destination
is The Compleat Angler, at *Marlow*, *Buckinghamshire* (31 miles) with 40
bedrooms and private baths. This opulent inn—with its slick-rustic restaurant
and cheerful bar—which sits beside a peaceful view on the Thames, reaches
a pinnacle of pastoral beauty. Alas, what a pity it is that the staff attention
makes such an unmitigated muck-up of the entire experience. Our own recent
visits have been ruined by slipshod administration; now we have received a
message from our beloved longtime friend, scintillating Joan Fontaine, who
reports "terrible food, indifferent service, and an hour's wait with a reservation
made 4 days in advance!" We couldn't be in fuller agreement with this radiant
film star and authoress. No longer recommended—and what a shame because
it could be one of England's finest. Ye Olde Bell, *Hurley*, *Berkshire* (32 miles;
about ½-hour beyond Northold on M-4), dates from A.D. 1135; for overnighters, 9 rooms and 9 baths. Here's one of the "inn"-spots outside of town, oozing
with lazy charm, fashionable clientele, relaxing ambiance; sound but not top-
London-class fare at top London-class prices; limited selections but a substantial meal; *reserve ahead* here. Happily recommended. The Orchard, *Ruis-
lip*, *Middlesex* (16 miles), is a large, pukka establishment where the dancing
is a gnat's eyelash better than the food and, like the food, is served every night

of the year; Saturday evening it is *black tie only*. Modern mien; immaculate kitchen; drinks served on the umbrella-dotted lawn; in season, gala-night bookings must be made 5 weeks in advance. John Lambourne operates this sophisticated Tudor mansion and continues to offer special warm welcomes to readers of this book.

Other choices are as follows: In *Berkshire,* (a) **Hind's Head** and **Monkey Island** hotels, both in *Bray* (28 miles); the former, operated by Mrs. Kelly, has a terrace and features unabashed English catering competently done; the latter is an eighteenth-century fishing lodge on a tiny island in the Thames. The **Waterside Inn,** in the same village, features more-French-style cuisine—and at nearly Parisian-style tariffs! It, too, overlooks the river; closed Mondays; big rewards for big prices. (b) **Milton Ernest Hall Hotel**, near *Bedford* (45 miles), is a bucolic restoration of the house designed by William Butterfield, the famous Victorian architect. It's also now the 25-hour-a-day hobby of Mr. and Mrs. Harmar-Brown, who hawkeye their chefs and personally select its choice wines. Our great-and-good pals, *Time*'s Chief Photographer Ben Martin and his ravishing actress-wife, Kathryn, say this is a "must" for its glorious décor, cookery, and friendliness. (c) **White Hart** and **French Horn**, both in *Sonning-on-Thames* (36 miles), a captivating rural village; in the former you may enjoy country roast beef while watching the boats skim past, and in the latter (more costly), across the bridge, you'll find an even better river view, but the specialties are more continental and not as appetizing. (d) **Boulter's Inn,** *Maidenhead* (27 miles), has a lovely riverbank situation at Boulter's Lock; 13 rooms and 1 private bath. Direction by Tom Cressy, who also operates the previously mentioned Bridge House Motel at Reigate, resident management by John Moses, who led his own exodus from the same Bridge House; 3-piece combo for dancing nightly. Much improved; now considered by many to be the best suburban target near the capital. (e) The **King's Head** at *Little Marlow* (5 miles from Maidenhead) is still another potential charmer, with Major John Nichols and his wife in command; we missed it on our latest loop. (f) The **Little Angel** in *Remenham* (36 miles) is a cozy and genial retreat across the bridge from Henley; solid, unelaborate cookery; nice clientele; operated by an ex-RAF officer who turned in his wings for this pocket-size seraph. (g) **Skindle's Hotel,** *Maidenhead* (27 miles), once the pick of the area, has skidded so rapidly downhill that our enthusiasm has now completely waned; the old crew has fled, and a gaming room has been installed; no longer the charmer of old. (h) The **Bel and The Dragon** has resided in *Cookham Village* since the reign of Henry V, early in the 15th-century. It is constructed of wattle and daub, with plenty of open beams, signets of age, and cozy warmth. Swiss ownership and management; fair cuisine; medium prices. "Bel," incidentally, is derived from the name of a Babylonian idol. Even if you don't dine here, do stop for a drink in the bar and look around. In *Buckinghamshire,* (a) the **Bell Hotel,** *Aston Clinton* (36 miles), resembles a routine pub; when we tried Gerry Harris' viands some time back, they were quite good—but now we're getting reports that they aren't worth the ride; if you go, always call for advance reservations on weekends. (b) **The Jolly Farmer,** *Chalfont Saint Peter* near Gerrards Cross (23 miles), is a renowned pub which makes to order 401 varieties of sandwiches; top-quality ingredients selected by Proprietors

Tom and Lucille Davies; full menu and wine list; reasonable tariffs; a find. In *Essex,* the **Old Mill** at *Harlow* (25 miles) offers French and English dishes prepared personally by Owner Bronson; not spectacular but good. We've heard nice compliments about **Harlow Hill.** In *Surrey,* (a) **Mayflower Hotel**, *Cobham* (19 miles), is a plushy oasis for the Hungry Man; also nice here is the **Talbot**, which boasts ownership of Nelson's chair. (b) **Whyte Harte**, *Bletchingley* (22 miles), a fourteenth-century inn with old beams, open fireplaces, and better-than-routine vittles supervised by C. H. Mathews. (c) The **Old Bell**, *Oxted* (22 miles), another inn of the same vintage without quite the flavor of the Whyte Harte, but very pleasant all the same. (d) **Onslow Arms**, *West Clandon* near Guildford (about 30 miles), an A.D. 1623 roadside hostelry thick with atmosphere, and mellow with its Free House varieties of beer, ale, and porter. (e) **Great Fosters**, *Egham* (18 miles) features unique 4-centuries-old gardens and 23 guest rooms for lovers of antiquities and service. In *Sussex,* **The Maltravers**, *Arundel* (58 miles) is in the forefront with its gastronomic delights, its furnishings of rare antiques and fine paintings, and its unusual policy, for rural establishments, of staying open until 11 P.M. or after; closed Monday; as good as ever, in our opinion. In *Northamptonshire,* near the border of *Oxfordshire,* **The Cartwright Arms**, *Aynho* near Banbury (62 miles), a famous old coach house that has been renovated; dine in candlelight on mahogany, at the most savory table in the district.

Night Life London's nightscape—as in Paris, New York, Hamburg, and a host of other cities where the moon is better known than the sun—*is one of the fastest-changing in the world.* Entertainment establishments rise and fall so swiftly that even the most up-tonight tip sheets have difficulty keeping *au courant.* Therefore, please do not bet your last tanner on the accuracy of our survey here.

Talk of the Town still wins the brass ring on the metropolitan merry-go-round. Immense stage and music pit, sectionalized into mobile units; one huge, fast show nightly, followed by performances at 11 P.M. of international cabaret stars; 2 oversize, flawlessly integrated orchestras; tables seating a total of 625 have replaced all theater-style chairs. Fixed-price, 3-course dinner for around £19 Monday through Thursday (more on Fri. and Sat.) mandatory for all customers; typical but eatable production-line fare. Open from 8 P.M. to 1:15 A.M.; book in advance for either the balcony or the rear of the main floor for a better view of the spectacles. The Lido in Paris is larger and more elaborate, but for London this Colossal Evening at such reasonable cost is an almost unbelievable phenomenon. If you're a Latin Quarter fan, don't miss it.

The **Royal Roof** of the Royal Garden Hotel gracefully combines sophistication and well-trained minions with a fine flair for theatrics. Beautiful presentation of The Royal Strings, a harmonic blend of 7 violins, a guitar, and an accordion which plays en masse for several numbers, then the musicians individually stroll among the diners while maintaining perfect melodic unison; 20-minute performances at 11 P.M. and midnight. Selective, small menu; matching overpriced wine carte; no admission or cover charge. Here's a lovely, romantic, handholding ambiance, with dim lights, a chic conception, and a wonderful view—BUT pad your wallet, because you can drop a bundle.

Hatchett's Piccadilly is a multilevel, multipurpose caravanserai straight off the drawing boards of the twenty-first century. Stingingly modern main restaurant with silvered walls, steel-braced emerald chairs, and *i*-dot tables so tiny a pair of canaries might feel cramped at feeding time; pale-orange bar that repeats its motif-in-stainless; downstairs discothèque featuring an icy flower theme; mediocre to poor cookery.

Tiberio (22 Queen St., Mayfair) is a touch of La Bella Roma. Peninsular cookery and décor; entrance through a below-stairs tiled bar to a gracious vaulted dining room; low-hanging lamps, 22 pink-clad tables, rush-bottom chairs; nice use of flowers; kitchen shielded by red-tinted glass. Very fine skillet work and service to match; lunch from noon to 3 P.M.; dinner from 7 P.M. to midnight; supper dancing from 11:30 P.M. to 3:30 A.M.; closed Sunday; expensive. An upbeat little swinger that is snatching a lot of business away from the competition. We say *bravissimo!*

Quaglino's (16 Bury St.) served us a pleasant meal and an eveningful of danceable music in the conventional (not modern) mood. Its inner heart glitters with reflections from lovely antique mirrors. Far from cheap, but a fair late-night-out for traditionalists.

La Dolce Notte (55 Jermyn St.) is no longer as sweet as it was. Italian cookery; dancing; a listless lump from the Dolce Vita (Frith St.) sugar bowl.

L'Hirondelle (Swallow St.) is a cellar-bration spot with about 30 tables; floor shows with 5 chorines and a couple of "singles" at 10:30 P.M. and 1 A.M.; dancing until 3:45 A.M. Minimum dinner of 3 routine courses for lofty money; a cover charge appears if you do not order the vittles. Average.

Latin Quarter (13–17 Wardour St., Piccadilly Circus, W.1) exercises a sincere effort to imitate its historic New York namesake—and the price tags more than achieve that noble end. Rectangular chamber; tables set on the sunken floor; Toulouse-Lautrec Bar; wide-angle stage; wide-angle babes frolicking at 11 P.M. and 1 A.M.; dinner dancing to 2 orchestras from 8:30 P.M. until the 3:30 closing.

Élysée (13 Percy St.) is a haven which effuses a Hellenic charm all its own. The décor is routine, but when the crowd is right it's delightfully lively. Big Greek patronage—and what people are merrier?—who richly enjoy the hospitality of host George Karageorgis. Ground floor with 15 tables, a small bar and dance floor, 3 to 4 musicians (*bouzouki* and accordion), and a singing Athena —all imported from Aegean shores. Summer roof garden for nearly 100 midday or evening munchers, some of whom spontaneously leap up to provide impromptu entertainment; hours noon to 3 P.M. and 6:30 P.M. to 3 A.M. Noisy, cheerful, expensive, not at all romantic—but often (not always) hilarious if you bring the right mood. Go late.

Among the hotels, the **Savoy**, the **Inn on the Park** (Vintage Room only), the **Dorchester** (beautiful Terrace Room), the **Hilton**, and **Grosvenor House** all offer the Light Fantastic in their restaurants (separate from their Grills); Claridge's doesn't believe in all that jazz.

Many of the so-called *Membership Clubs* offer extremely attractive facilities for the visitor in search of dining, wining, and excitement. They are organized on a "private" basis to skirt the liquor laws. Local residents must pay nominal annual "dues" of perhaps £3, but travelers with valid foreign passports are usually issued a special card and admitted free.

The "Clubmanship Plan" is a gigantic chowder made up of nearly 400 separate clubs in 57 different cities and stirred into one enormous dining pool. For the full list, from Wales to Tewkesbury, write The Clubman, 5 Avery Rd., W.I.

As for **Les Ambassadeurs** (5 Hamilton Place), there are many surface charms including Le Cercle casino on the top floor with roulette and chemin de fer—but the most tiresome gamble is the process of getting into the joint. Starting way, way back, owner John Mills's quixotic entrance policies alienated so many readers that it fairly turns our stomach. One of them angrily stated, "You are due a round of cheers, because on our bill of £5 or so, three waiters demanded from my confused husband 20% (£1), and then extracted £2 from him. No itemization whatsoever on our bills. J. Mills doesn't think you are so hot—and we don't think he is!" Once again, not recommended to any user of this book—and if any further slanderous nonsense from Mr. Mills or any of his employees reaches our ears, such as his alleged pearl of wisdom that "Fielding will recommend anyone for a free meal," we're going to take a great deal of pleasure in hauling this gentleman to court.

The **Hispaniola Restaurant Ship** is an unimportant splash in the pond. This one is a converted ferry moored Thames-side near the Charing Cross subway station. Tacky entrance; effectively deck-orated; smartly rigged bar; upper level exclusively à la carte; fish is the specialty, and ours was much too saucy for our palate. Open year round. Better for ambiance than for fare.

The **White Elephant** (28 Curzon St.) is still frequented by its allotment of theatrical pashas, business tycoons, and would-be's—but again, speaking personally, we're mystified by whatever mystique draws them here. Brocade-and-velvet Regency with a gilt-complex; bar to the left of entrance; tables so small that one's elbow inadvertently becomes an offensive weapon while dining. Entrance by member introduction (a letter will do); à la carte menu; no entertainment. Mixed French- and Italian-style cuisine; our meal was wretched. We don't think you trekked all the way to Britain to spend your time and hard-earned cash on this type of pachyderm.

The dine-and-dance-until-one-ayem **Wellington Club** (116 Knightsbridge) is a sound bet where you'll have little trouble becoming a Temporary Member. We have recently come from a whirl at the **New Yorker Club** (36 Park Lane) and we were not impressed—except unfavorably. Nix as our picks.

Cabaret and pickups? For early or wee-hours fun and games à la international gin mill, **Churchill's of Bond Street** (160 New Bond St.) is hyperthyroid —and please don't confuse it with the mammoth Churchill Hotel on Portman Sq. Atmosphere just raffish enough to be intriguing; illumination tailor-made for Passive Pitches; 1¼-hour, 40-artist floor shows early, midevening, and late; steep cover charge and drinks at Paris prices (above average U.S. prices). Don't try it unless you expect to spend plenty, because your evening will be *very* expensive. If you're a man and alone, you should have no trouble finding a beautiful and amusing companion, to whom it is gracious to offer a gift as "taxi fare," (£10 to £15 is the going rate) for her conversational company. Dinner begins at 8 P.M. (delay it until about 9:30). If you are an insomniac, breakfasts are always on the house for everyone. Midnight is the best playtime. The **Stork Room** (99 Regent St.) is another tranquilizer for lonesome or amorous gents;

dim, dim lights; hostesses by the platoon; tiny dance floor and cabaret; tariffs very high for values received; "specialized" might be the word for this one. The **New Bagatelle** (Conduit St.) impressed us not a bit. What did we say after our latest play? Nay, nay, NAY!!

★ **WARNING** England's lower, more greedy clip joints are among the worst in the Western World. Law requires nightclubs to display a price list for drinks, forbids overcharging, and bans harpies from the doorways of these establishments, where formerly they attempted to lure customers inside with vague "good time" promises. Operators who break the rules now face stiff penalties. The intent is laudable, but enforcement is dismally lax. So pursue your merriment with care!

Gambling? In the officially approved gaming salons, almost everything goes except pitch-and-toss—a game played by miners which all too quickly can involve staggering sums. No British casino may have more than 2 slot machines (fruit machines, in local parlance). Horses, dogs, football, the gender of an expected royal heir—just name it, and somebody will snap up your wager, but usually in one of England's 2000 licensed betting offices. Better bring cash or traveler's checks, not personal checks, if you plan to play. Some houses are stricter than others about this. Stringent laws now require visitors to register 48 hours in advance at the clubs where they wish to gamble.

CAUTION: *Pick your place carefully, especially if you roll 'em high!*

Meal and spirits services follow the rules governing pubs; hours also can vary with the neighborhood, so it would be wise to check first if you wish to imbibe at gaming tables.

The **Victoria Sporting Club** (150-162 Edgware Rd., W.2), now a Playboy enterprise and the largest contender in the British Isles *or* Europe, might be termed a "gambling factory." Production-belt operation that woos "mass" (*vs.* "class") patronage; 1st floor featuring dice, blackjack, roulette, and chemin de fer; 2nd level offering gin rummy and *kaluki* (13-card rummy); 2 slot machines; restaurant service from lunch to breakfast. This house is cashing in b-i-g. Extremely popular at the F. W. Woolworth—not the Cartier—level.

The **Clermont Club** (44 Berkeley Square)—with 85% of its 5000 disciples from overseas—is known to be chic. It owns the Playboy Club (see below) and its members are permitted to play there; the reverse however, is not the case, as this and Le Cercle (in the previously described Les Ambassadeurs) are ultra-exclusive.

Historic and famous **Crockford's** (16 Carlton House Terrace) is operated by Curzon House (below). Again a high roller and now quite a favorite of backgammon fanciers.

Curzon House Club (Curzon St.) draws about the same type of clientele as Crockford's, and wraps them in a sedate and chilly ambiance. It dwells in the former manse of the 4th Earl Howe, followed by the Duke and Duchess of York (who later became King George VI and Queen Elizabeth). Lavish restaurant with enormous menu and delicious cuisine; Buffet Bar; racing room; choice of blackjack, bridge, poker, *kaluki,* gin rummy, chemin de fer, and roulette; bedrooms available for members' use.

Olympic Casino (79 Queensway) is attractive, but its ultraserious Olympian competitors will scarcely see the change. Packed with gamesters from the Levant; not at all for amateurs; expensive.

Other choices in this group include the **Playboy Club** on Park Lane (a 6-story, 100-bunny warren with eating, drinking, and, yes, even sleeping facilities, plus official playpens for blackjack, chemin de fer, dice, and roulette; very popular and very worthwile for the lone male who likes to look at—touching is taboo—curvacious representatives of the rabbit family); **Charlie Chester Casino** at 12 Archer St. (functioning noon to you-name-it, with roulette, blackjack, and Las Vegas dice); and the **Golden Nugget** at 22 Shaftesbury Avenue (6 types of play). None of these (except the Playboy, which is special,) measures up to the establishments listed above, in our opinion. Still other boxcar candidates where we have yet to roll the dice include **Palm Beach Club** in the old ballroom of the May Fair Hotel (French croupiers); one has opened in the cellar of the **Ritz** (refer back to "Hotels"), where the French Salon features blackjack, American roulette, and punto banco; the busy **Ladbroke Sporting Club**; the **Sportsman** (3 Tottenham Ct. Rd., W.1); the **International Sporting Club** (Berkeley Hotel); the **Knightsbridge Sporting Club** (163 Knightsbridge), which provides French and U.S.-style casinos and free breakfast, and on and on and on.

Discothèques? These, of course, are among the most perishable of all institutions in the entertainment field. They pop up quickly (generally with insufficient investment capital), stay "in" for a short lifetime, and fold up when the "chic" crowd takes its fickle fancies elsewhere.

Burlesque (14 Bruton Place, formerly called Revolution) seemed to be rolling along during our earlier capital rounds. With its combo-notion of recorded and live music, it was also the noisiest. Friday nights come on the jammiest; prices are average. Here is a straight, unpretentious disco which will rivet your eardrums to the back of your chair. **Gullivers** (11 Down St., W1) is more upbeat than its address might suggest. We haven't been to the new **Régine's** yet, but it seems to be as successful as her French enterprises—and probably as expensive, too! The **Embassy** (7 Old Bond St.) and our next entry are both membership haunts, charging around ten bucks a month to enter and bounce. **Tramp's** (Jermyn St.) draws a chic young following. Worth going. **La Valbonne** (62 Kingly St.), with excellent music for dancers, is averred to stage topless waitresses around a swimming pool. **Miranda**, across the street, is popular at lunchtime with well groomed gents from the financial district. **Flicka** (Swallow St.) is still fun.

Among the even more volatile contenders, **Speakeasy** (48 Margaret St.) speaks the easiest. Here's the home of the so-called Wow-Girls, a fractious flummox on the go-go theme. Next comes the **Saddle Room** (1-A Hamilton Mews). Gussied-up tack stall; rustic paneling; main dance floor plus upper tier for the mezzanine peerage; running strong from 10 P.M. to 4 A.M.; better than it was. **Lulu's** (9 Young St.) is aptly sited; very "with it" for "young" devotées of Owner Louis Brown who operates 9 spots *in toto.*

Then there is *Raffles* (287 King's Rd.), with a library complex, open hearths with crackling fires, and Old English décor. **Edelweiss** (19 Oxford St.) is still flowering as an Alpine tavern, attracting all ages and all species for grazing.

Samantha's Psychedelic (3 New Burlington St.) is another scene for cooling it in the nether world. **Le Kilt** (60 Greek St.) is proud of its "Swinging Sounds and Pub Prices".

At least a score of similar places exist, most of them in the same atonal, eardrum-shattering ambiance. We repeat our warning to the dedicated: Since the fad vacillates so rapidly—almost monthly—please do not depend too heavily on these suggestions. Ask your hall porter for a local magazine on London nightlife and consult with him on the sort of revelry you are seeking.

Nudity and Pornography? Almost anything goes—and grows as well. A subculture of shady ways now populates the city's waysides. At present, however, we think the action is more uninhibited, unabashed, and far, far broader (in both senses) in the mammoth concentration of Hamburg's Reeperbahn. London swings with girlishly adolescent hips, but it certainly doesn't swing with either the freedom or the abandon of those St. Pauli *Fraülein*. (Just the playgirls and B-girls there make more than $25,000,000 per year!) Nevertheless, in England there's still a hint of what's meant—and more is on the way.

There are 2 categories of clubs. The 3 mentioned below are among the dwindling strip-and-clip joints, which are fly-by-nighters—most of them easily identified by their jukebox wheeze and their small herd of bovine babes as graceless as heifers. In both categories, the caliber of talent varies from herbivorous, gum-chewing manatee-types (par for the course), to vivacious, chattering monkey-types (the "talkers"), on up to a small handful of exquisite English beauties.

In the "National" spots we list, the ladies wear G-strings right up to that final instant before blackout—then off goes the net—and in the quickest wink you've ever blinked, out go the lights. We've seen butterfly collections that were sexier. All these theaters have music-hall seats and tables for bar service.

The attrition rate among these establishments is so fast and so unpredictable that today's leaders are tomorrow's duds. As we write this, the best by far is still **Raymond Revuebar** (Brewer St.). Entrance fee abolished, but memberships vary with the proximity of your seat to the action—thus a bargain for farsighted voyeurs. ("Life Members" getting the choice perches). These billings all grant admission to a frenetic, jumbo-size lounge, bar, and dance floor. Adjoining is a tier-table, music-hall theater, with fast-moving shows increasingly dominated by singles acts and strippers (5 performances nightly, beginning at 8:20 P.M. and ending with the 1:15 A.M. "Topless" caper), in which the ladies cavort on a raised stage for unimpaired inspection. Best of its type in London; be sure to book in advance; not at all cheap, because you can see a Manhattan musical for the same outlay. Incidentally, Mr. Raymond reopened the celebrated **Windmill Theatre,** and, after a $500,000 tilt with the decorators, he now provides several film shows per nude-filled night.

Casino de Paris Club (5–7 Denman St.) was redecorated as a minitheater with a runway sprinting almost the full length of the aisle. It's one of the few seemingly legitimate places of its type featuring a "continuous" show (breaks of perhaps 20 minutes between each) from 2:30 P.M.—yep, that's "P." M. (!)

—to 10:30 P.M. Excellent choreography; elaborate costumes; sexillated strippers and show girls; all seats about £4. We don't quite agree with the B.B.C. reviewer who stated, "Purists and Puritans may scream, but I thought it great fun"—because we do not find it *this* naughty. We do concur, however, that it can be uplifting for the dedicated girl watcher.

Third on our list is the **Nell Gwynne Club** (Dean St.). Ascend via a Lilliputian elevator and you'll find yourself in its sky-high (for London), refurbished cluster of bar, diminutive theater, and tiny stage. She also caters to the late afternoon gentry; strip from 6 P.M. Worth a peek only as a curiosity.

The Wolfenden Law was designed to end sidewalk soliciting, but Parliament and the police have learned the hard way that You Can't Keep A Bad Girl Down (or is it "Up"?). Frustrated gents to whom taste is no barrier may meet (with less frequency these days) the former pavement pounders by consulting "business cards" on street bulletin boards, or joining various afterdark bus queues which are used as blinds for pickups (if accused of loitering, what better alibi than "I'm whyting for a bus, officer"?).

As in so many parts of today's United States, permissiveness is so great that in Soho, within a 10- to 15-minute walk from Piccadilly Circus, the visitor can find the same style of "bookstores" which sell the hardest-of-hard-core photographs, cartoons, underground magazines, and 8-mm reels of motion-picture film (color and black-and-white).

On a more upbeat note, the flock of *escort agencies* supplying birds-by-the-hour to lone eagles is proliferating. Customers customarily cull newspaper ads or rely on word-of-beak, select their aviary, and then come in to choose their companion from displays of snapshots. At the hour you designate she's at your door, ready to step out. Be sure to check on check-in time, since their very fat fees soar even higher after the bewitching hour. Although a 2 A.M. curfew is standard, it can be stretched if the lady is cooperative. *Bon chance!*

Shopping All goods, regardless of value, may now be purchased by *overseas visitors* without the 15% VAT tax. Because most establishments charge a fee for making the necessary arrangements, it is both sensible and timesaving to pay it in full on all trifling acquisitions.

Our ★ ★ ★ ★ ★ recommendations are individually noted.

Cashmeres, tartans, and materials: Our number one candidate is ★ ★ ★ ★ ★ **W. Bill, Ltd.** (93 New Bond St. and 28 Old Bond St.), the finest woolen specialist we've ever found in the British Isles. This century-old firm was the first to introduce Irish and Welsh tweeds to England. Purest, softest cashmere sweaters; Shetland knitwear with coordinating tweeds; cashmere suitings and coatings; handwoven Harris tweeds; choice worsteds; flannels and tropicals; down mohair throws; tartan cashmere travel rugs; male hats made from its own tweeds by Lock & Co.; large stocks of ready-made jackets for men and tweed skirts and tartan kilts for ladies; many other regional temptations. Personable Brian Bill (4th generation) is your oracle at 28 Old Bond St., while John Milton and Mrs. Oliver will greet you at 93 New Bond St. Don't be fooled by the smallness of their stores, because the stocks are not only gorgeous but copious, and all merchandise is interchangeable between branches within minutes. Far superior, in our personal opinions, to all competitors. Square-shooting, solid, and utterly reliable.

Burberrys rainwear and apparel: Since Thomas Burberry invented his celebrated waterproof cloth around 1856, ★ ★ ★ ★ ★ **Burberrys** (18 Haymarket and 165 Regent St.) has become a familiar name to literally millions of shoppers from Tampa to Tokyo. Here are probably the world's finest weatherproofs under the sun (*and* clouds!). Because the "Burberry Look" has developed into such a highly fashionable rage, you'll find the crowning glories of all: trench coats and overcoats lined in that unmistakable, instantly identifiable Burberry's check, plus a vast assortment of supremely chic Burberry's luggage and umbrellas, a complete floor for ladies' topcoats, as well as a distinguished selection of casuals and knitwear and a forest of tweeds, beautifully soft cashmeres, and camelhairs. A splendid choice of English worsteds, tweeds, tartans, and cashmere is available by the meter. At Haymarket ask for General Manager Mr. Humby; at Regent St., Mr. Auld will be your special mentor. These gentlemen understand North American tastes and will go all out to be helpful (as will all the Burberrys sales staff).

Magnificent leather goods: Fabulous hundred-year-old ★ ★ ★ ★ ★ **Loewe** (25 Old Bond St. and a boutique in the Hilton Hotel) is Spain's revered leather master. This peerless house, with a Royal Court appointment and several international Gold Medals, is proud of its century-old reputation for producing some of the most exquisite works of art in its field anywhere on earth today. All have the finish of precious gems (see "Madrid."). Important bonus: *25% discount on all articles chosen in London and shipped to you from Spain.* Nobody in today's U.K. can touch Loewe's style, workmanship, quality, and flair.

Food delicacies: **Fortnum & Mason** (Piccadilly) is the only store we know where the clerk who fetches your can of tomato soup wears a cutaway coat and striped pants. It used to be one of the greatest centers for comestibles in existence, but now we feel fantastic Fauchon of Paris (see "France") has pulled far ahead as *the* epicurean supply center of the world. Its downstairs restaurant for light lunches is popular and good. There are splendid Food Halls in Harrods and Selfridges department stores.

English perfumes and toiletries: To cross the threshold of 89 Jermyn Street is to take a fascinating step into this empire's history. The ★ ★ ★ ★ ★ **House of Floris**, a family institution established in 1730 and Perfumers to H.M. The Queen, is irresistibly alluring with its heavenly bouquets of rare English flower fragrances set in an unhurried atmosphere of unique Victorian elegance. Their latest essence is an alluringly masculine cologne for men, "Elite." Its newcomer companion for ladies is "Florissa," also available in Spray Cologne, Toilet Water, Concentrated Bath Oil, Toilet Powders, and Soaps. So different —and *so* glorious!

Sporting equipment and sportswear: If you were an Abercrombie & Fitch fan, you'll revel in the overseas twin, **Lillywhites**, the best known and most exciting center of its type abroad.

Men's furnishings: **Hilditch & Key Ltd.** (73 Jermyn St.) is a sturdy, versatile, and reliable old-timer. Even more appealing to our personal tastes are the custom-made and ready-made shirts, blazers, sport coats, and slacks at **Turnbull and Asser**, a few steps away at 71-72 Jermyn St. Why not try both?

Silver or jewelry: It is our most urgent recommendation that you head straight to ★ ★ ★ ★ **Garrard & Co. Ltd.** (112 Regent St.), who are Crown Jewellers to Her Majesty Queen Elizabeth II. The list of British and foreign royalty whose court appointments it holds is a miniature *Almanach de Gotha.* In keeping with its station, this old-line landmark, founded in 1721, offers impeccable standards of design and quality that are universally recognized—plus a reputation for service that is unsurpassed on the globe. And what a Palace of Treasures it is! As three illustrations: The Silver Department, with prices absolutely competitive to the "vaults" and other inferior sources, has a seemingly inexhaustible stock of beautiful flatware and hollowware, both modern and antique. There is a magnificent display of watches and clocks. And the jewels! Here are some of the most elegant gems and other precious objects in the Commonwealth, many designed and fashioned by the same craftsmen who monitor Great Britain's Crown Jewels. Armchair travelers can write for its intriguing catalogues. You'll be welcomed—so browse and be dazzled.

The world's finest furs and the magic of Hermès: Two of the most elegant firms on the international scene have now joined hands to bring to England a regal wedding of the Greats. **Hermès** of Paris and **Birger Christensen** of Copenhagen (see "France" and "Denmark") have jointly opened a stunning showroom in the Time/Life Building (Bond and Bruton Sts.). Both charge the same *export* prices of their own lands—discounts of 10% to 25%. Ask for vibrant John Green or his French wife, Jacquie.

Boutiques: A flood of fresh, provocative young designers has changed the face of traditional British *haute couture.* So many small, chic shops have sprung up that it is impossible to enumerate them in this limited space. See our *Shopping Guide* for more than 3 dozen of our favorites.

Antiques, china, glass, and gift items: The ★ ★ ★ ★ **General Trading Company (Mayfair) Ltd.** (144 Sloane St., Sloane Square) is our happiest British shopping "discovery" in years. This one is a joy, really a joy—the largest retail shop of its kind in the world, occupying elegant headquarters in 4 gracious, spacious, serene, Edwardian mansions. Trashy "fillers" are scorned by Director David Part and his associates. In antiques, English period pieces, china, and *objets d'art* are the specialties. Also on parade are comprehensive displays of modern bone china and fine table glass in quantities; a big and versatile Gift Department of handicrafts, leather work, porcelain cachepots, picnic accessories; a Garden Department; a Soft Furnishings Department with imaginative and tasteful fabrics for contemporary or period decoration, and goodness knows what other lovely items. You will find tempters here from $5 up. Safe shipment is guaranteed to any place on the globe, even to R.T. (Republic of Texas). Be sure to ask for the gentle, delightful Mr. Part in person. Super.

If General Trading shouldn't have what you're hunting for, try famous and fine ★ ★ ★ ★ ★ **Asprey** (165–169 New Bond St.) for anything from an Adam fireplace to a gold swizzle stick.

Books: As most travelers know, ★ ★ ★ ★ ★ **Foyle's** (119–125 Charing Cross Road) is not only the world's biggest bookshop, but it's the most fun. From a teenagers' business started nearly 8 decades ago in the kitchen of their parents' home, the astonishing Foyle brothers expanded to this sprawling jumble of buildings and an inventory of 4-million volumes. While there, we'd suggest that you inquire about the famous monthly Literary Luncheons at the Dorchester, which no U.S. booklover should *think* of missing. Wonderful!

Arrestingly charming stationery, diaries and address books: **Frank Smythson Ltd.** (54 Bond St.), which holds the Royal Warrant of Stationers to Her Majesty the Queen, is a delight. Courtly General Manager Thomas Neale would help you to enjoy your visit.

Finest men's hats and special apparel: Continuously since 1759, there has existed only one top-ranking center in the western world— ★ ★ ★ ★ ★ **James Lock & Co. Ltd.** (6 St. James's St.). The lid of this prize package is the hat —every conceivable male headgear. Be sure to ask for the ever-cordial Messrs. Priest or Brine. The one-and-only.

Shotguns: **Purdey** (57–58 S. Audley St.)—but only if your banker calls you "Mr. Niarchos," because that storied "pair of Purdeys" will set you back at least $16,000. **Holland & Holland**, also remarkable, comes next on the ladder.

Markets: Although the famous **Covent Garden**, covering about 96 acres and bordered by the Strand, Kingsway, High Holborn, and Charing Cross Road, has been reborn, it has retained its former cozy village-type aura. Restaurants, wine bars, shops (such as a kite shop, glassblowing, and trendy boutiques, many unique to London) have mushroomed here. The central area, known as the Piazza, is surrounded by the Market. It claims to be the city's first permanent late-night shopping center, open until 8 P.M. 6 nights a week. The great variety of bazaars for antiques at decent prices are found in the permanent indoor installation. Here the dealers know their business and the competition is keen. There are so many that it is impossible to list them in this limited space. See our *Shopping Guide* for a complete roster.

Where should you bargain? In all holes-in-the-wall which carry second-line merchandise—but never in the topnotch places. Haggle hardest and stand your ground most resolutely in the Markets.

Saddlery, equine equipment, and riding habits: **W. & H. Gidden Ltd.** (15 New Clifford St., New Bond St.), established in 1806, is 7th heaven for the equestrian. Its likable leading expert is Mr. J. Dennett.

Men's made-to-measure: There are so many superb tailors in London that it's hard to make a choice. Among the select houses are **Scherer & Nilsson Ltd.** (33 Old Burlington St.), **Benson, Perry & Whitley** (9 Cork St.), **Hawes & Denman & Goddard** (Sackville St.), **James & James** (11 Old Burlington St.), and **Wyser & Bryant** (45 Maddox St.). Not all the leaders are on the list, again because of lack of room—but here's a good cross section of the standard-bearers.

Prices are a lot cheaper at the London branch of ★ ★ ★ ★ ★ **Angelo of Rome** in the Ritz Arcade (see "Italy"). In the opinions of the 3 male members of this writing team, this institution has long ranked as one of the 2 finest tailors they have ever found in their travels. Now Maestro Angelo is shipping a carefully selected cross section of his latest ready-mades to this northern market. The premises are small, but when you hit it right the assortment is definitely worth investigation. Julian Hurcombe-Blight and John Bradbury will offer you their friendly greetings.

Department stores: **Harrods, Marks & Spencer, Peter Jones, Selfridges, John Lewis & Co., Peter Robinson, D. H. Evans & Co., Bourne & Hollingsworth, Dickens & Jones, Harry Nichols & Co.** Your taxi driver or hall porter can direct you to them. In our opinions, the first 3 are the finest.

Shopper's Reconnaissance: Try either the **Design Centre** (28 Haymarket) or the **Crafts Centre** (43 Earlham St.). The former is a showcase for mass-manufactured goods intended to interest the import-export trades. The latter shows one-of-a-kind pieces of jewelry, pottery, and textiles by artisans who usually work for themselves. Free admission; nothing sold on the premises.

Baggage, parcel or car shipment: Again we have tried **Robert Fisher (Shipping) Ltd.** (32 Lexington St.) in forwarding 5 or 6 crates of miscellaneous personal possessions from this capital to our home in Mallorca. They packed them so beautifully that even their most fragile items arrived in perfect condition.

Shopping hours: London, in general, 9 A.M. to 5:30 P.M. with some Sat. closings at 1 P.M. and others at 5:30 P.M.; large department stores open on a specific weeknight (Thurs. on Oxford St., Wed. at Harrods, etc.); smaller shops in Chelsea, Soho, and similar districts close at 1 P.M. on Thurs., but usually operate all day Sat.; everything shuttered on Sun. except a few delicatessens, food shops (mornings only), and a handful of all-night drugstores ("chemists"). It is advisable to check before setting out.

Dedicated shophounds? Space is too tight here for further listings—so consult the purse-size 25th Anniversary edition of *Fielding's Selective Shopping Guide to Europe* for more stores, more details, and more lore.

Other Targets

Now for our alphabetical rundown of your candidates in the chief cities, towns, and villages on the holiday route. Be sure to see our separate sections on the Cotswolds and the Lake District if you are going into those areas.

ASTON CLINTON is a charming center in Buckinghamshire with one especially fine stop for diners or overnighters. It is composed of a converted complex of stables, malt-houses and a brewery. The eighteenth-century **Bell** chimes on both sides of the A-41 London-Oxford trunk road. Restaurant-*cum*-inn, compleat with courtyard on one flank; rustic brick-and-beam dining salon with bar, banquettes, silver candelabra, and French wine-district maps juxtaposed to Bavarian Chef Jaques Dick's Gallic creations; Pavilion for private parties across the pike. We prefer the 15 rooms surrounding the cobbled court

to the 5 in the main building. The phone number is (Aylesbury) 630252.
Energetic Michael Harris, whose courage and skills we admire, assures guests
of home-style hospitality. Not too far away, at *Chalfont Saint Peter* near
Gerrards Cross, **The Jolly Farmer** is a renowned pub which makes to order
401 varieties of sandwiches. Top-quality ingredients; full menu and wine list;
reasonable tariffs. A jolly choice indeed if the Bell tolls not for thee.

BANBURY   See "The Cotswolds."

BASSENTHWAITE   Refer to "Lake District" in our separate section.

BATH, with just about 85,000 souls, is one of the oldest towns in Somerset,
a quiet region of Southwest England. The **Francis** leads the pack of pillow
stops. Total renewal a short while back; 70 rooms all with private plumbing;
clean and pleasant; friendly staff; spectacularly accoutered restaurant with
cuisine that pales by comparison. Since the front faces a lovely park, but also
borders a noisy street, light sleepers should bid for the back of the house. The
Priory is noted for its culinary glories. It also plays host to overnighters. Small,
intimate, and quality conscious. It was purchased recently by our longtime
friend John Donnithorne, who won such a following with his excellent management of Brown's in London. No major changes are contemplated. The
former owner, John Dupays, has now taken over the luxurious **Hunstrete
House** at nearby *Marksbury* (8 miles along the Bristol pike). It offers a dozen
rooms and the well-known Dupays touch in the kitchen. This game of musical
chairs puts a song on the lips of local diners. **Lansdown Grove**, high in the city,
is tranquil; it sets a fair table, too. **Royal York** is getting a bit fusty, in our
opinion. Some redecorations recently, but still too long in the tooth for us. The
Cliffe, 5 miles out on A-36, is a stone-shelled sweetie; a wonderful site in a quiet
valley; 8 bedrooms and baths; careful supervision by Roy and Freda Donald-
son, its resident proprietors. The **Royal Crescent** has emerged from its ablutions luxuriously restored, so we hear. Other local choices *for dining only*
include the colorful **Hole-in-Wall**, **Popjoys**, **Mario's**, **Lansdown Grove**, and
a 600-year-old pub called **The George** (10 minutes out) with Hanging Judge
Jeffries's gallows and medieval prison tack. In the village of *Limpley
Stoke*, the **Limpley Stoke** is nice but sleepy; the cookery is also pretty good
by suburban standards. The **Northey Arms**, on the A-4, is chiefly a pub, but
its duet of bedchambers are charmers. For a luxury alternative, the tinkling
little **Bell House** at nearby *Sutton Benger* (outside Chippenham) is a delight.
Cozy complement of 17 rooms, ½ with private facilities and many with balconies; each bed with its own rolling table for pajama breakfasts; superior comfort; book away from the roadside for serious snoozing; one of the finest
kitchens away from the gourmet centers of London; not scenic in its locale,
but an excellent rural headquarters for touring Wiltshire and Somerset. Expensive but worthy. The freshly expanded **Manor House**, at the neighboring Dr.
Doolittle village of *Castle Combe*, is a spellbinder. It's only a minute's walk
from the main road; the hamlet, incidentally, has been voted the prettiest
habitat in all of England, and we couldn't agree more fervently, even though
it's virtually trampled by rubberneckers on Sundays and holidays. Lovely

apron of grass edging a stream and murmuring fall, surrounding forests, tiers of flowers; antique shop plus furnishings inside the hotel marked for sale to visitors; superb accommodations, with the best views from #4 or #2; Garden Wing not up to the original edifice. Our recent stay was as peaceful as anything St. Peter could produce because the house is so well insulated from those rubbernecking throngs down in the village. Highly recommended. The **Castle**, on the town square, is also attractive. Lounge ceiling beams so low that one timber is inscribed "Duck—or grouse!" The food here is outstanding and varied, but the living space is more limited than in the Manor. If you have a car, try not to miss this hidden jewel of Britain.

BIRMINGHAM,   with 80 square miles and 1-million people, is the second city of England. The irascible Dr. Johnson found a wife here—no trick for any man, we can assure you, so long as he throws in the promise to take her away from this iron and steel center. Its face is changing radically. However, it remains a Detroit rather than a San Francisco to the traveler.

If you wish to overnight here, the sleekly modern, 9-story, strataform **Albany** resides in the heart of town. Clean, well run, and usually busy; handsome Gun Room downstairs for midday snacks and to while away evenings; bar and adjoining dining room with blue banquettes; 100% air conditioning; 254 rooms, all with radio and duo-pane windows; nicely outfitted baths; 3 penthouse suites; tasteful doubles in the medium-price range; excellent studio singles. This one's a bonanza, considering the competition. The drum-shaped **Strathallan** beats lustily for conference goers; its 170 units are modern, clean, and well outfitted for an overnight kip. We wouldn't care to linger, however. The **Midland** is old-fashioned, creaky, and sprawling. The **Imperial Centre** has an advantage of sharper-eyed sanitation among the traditional candidates—or so it seemed to us. **Plough & Harrow**, with 40 sleeping units, is better for food than for shelter. (Other dining choices might include the **Carosel**, the **Butlington**, or the **Lambert Court**, 3 miles out on Haglex Rd.) The 140-room **Royal Angus** has reasonable twin rates. The **Holiday Inn**-keepers operate a candidate here; it's a welcome addition to this hotel-poor metropolis.

BLANCHLAND We're happily haunted by the **Lord Crewe Arms**, a twelfth-century inn in a ghost village of Durham. Ch-ch-ch-charming.

BOURNEMOUTH The Deluxe-category **Royal Bath** offers a garden situation. Small swimming pool; casino; as clean and fresh as a wind from the Wight. Top recommendation for seaside somnolence, particularly if your quarter faces the water. The **Carlton**, also by Poole Bay and also in the same official bracket, is competitive. No pool, but elevator service down the cliff face to the breakers; dining room plus Causerie; bar; 100 doubles and 20 singles, all with private facilities. Down a notch, **Palace Court** is a pleasant stop for families. Dining salon with adjoining dance quadrant; modern bar; 102 rooms and baths; many couriers' chambers without plumbing; front units with balconies. A sound value. Among the Second-class houses, we like **Highcliff**, **Marsham**, and **Savoy**—in that order. The **Round House** has been a-round only a short time, but long enough for us to get loco-motion sickness at the thought of it.

Cacophonous locale between major roads; piled poker-chip architecture; appropriately named Blandford Restaurant; trio of bars; 100 pastel-toned Late Formica Period boxes. The traffic din and lack of air conditioning mean you choose between ventilation with intonation or modulation with stagnation. Top dining choices include the **South Western Hotel**, **Rancheros**, and **San Marco**. Nearby there are **Harbor Heights** in *Poole*, the **Rose & Crown** in the *New Forest*, and the **Dormy House** at *Ferndown*.

BRIGHTON: The better nests stretch along the beach strip 2 miles from town. Most of these hostelries (1) adhere to the Georgian or Regency periods or (2) entertain a fervent addiction for aluminum, Pullman-car upholstery, and hand-greased velvets. The **Metropole** is possibly now the lone exception. Modern, panoramic Starlit Room 150 feet up, with dancing nightly and boasted *"haute cuisine"* (what else could it be at this altitude?); winter and summer casino; slick Monaco Bar; public children's pool and community beach in front. Complex of 275 modernized units that frankly leave us as cold as a display-case Dover sole; loaded to its gills with conventions in winter. *The* social nucleus of vintage-car buffs and highborne holidaymakers, but inexplicably cheerless to us. The parent company also runs the **Bedford** at the site of the original relic of the same name. This year's model is a functional, neo-Scandinavian 16-decker. The Dickens Bar (after all, he DID stay here and he DID rewrite *Bleak House* here) was the only concession to interest we could find. All 130 units come with bath, radio, and what we rate as icebergs of . . . brrrr. **Royal Albion** is next on the roster. Excellent Albion Grill with open rôtisserie; seafront bar; dour Tudor Bar downstairs; accommodations that are starkly beachy. **Royal Crescent**, on the high road above the cliffs, is our choice among the East Beach hostelries. Here's a lovely perch for sea musings. The **Old Ship** has 122 staterooms; 55 heads; forequarters with small balconies; newer units with less space but much better décor and comfort. Modest but worthy. The **Grand** is a misnomer. At mealtimes, try **La Mascottas**, **Wheeler's Sheridan** (for fish), **Wheeler's Oyster Rooms**, **English's Oyster Bar**, **La Francais**, **Eaton**, or **The French Connection**.

BRISTOL   has a busy, salty atmosphere. If you plan to linger, the **Grand** is the cream of the local sherry cask. Plimsol Bar downstairs, with the sunlight of Jerez on tap; Newmarket Bar, across the street, for snacks in a paddock atmosphere; attractive lounge and adjacent restaurant; handsome Grill; 155 bedchambers; suite #104-105 usually booked by celebrities or wine moguls. Easily the vintage leader. The **Unicorn**, at dockside, takes the honors for modernists; the Rank organization is the guiding force behind this one. All 196 rooms with bath, shower, radio, TV, and phone; Copperfield Cocktail, and Waterfront bars; continental breakfasts served in rooms, but English repasts only in the restaurant. Clean and vitally needed here. The **Royal** struck us as commercial and seedy. **Hawthorne**'s is suggested only for times of dire distress. The **Holiday Inn** should be a boon to this hotel-starved community, as might the **Ladbroke**, or even the **Dragonara**, reportedly backed by the biggest gambling syndicate in the country. For mealtiming, our first choice would be the **Llandoger Trow** followed by **John Harvey's** and the **Chateaubriand**. Out at

Thornbury, Kenneth Bell's 16th-century **Thornbury Castle** is one of the region's proudest gastronomic shrines. Here a meal is an event. Small selection with a leaning toward French cuisine. Open for dinner Tues. through Sat. and on Sundays for lunch.

BROADWAY　See our "Cotswolds" section to follow.

CAMBRIDGE　is, of course, one of the oldest college towns in England and for beauty alone we prefer it to Oxford. The **University Arms** has a depersonalized exterior; building chocked up on stilts, with parking space beneath; dining room facing the Green; 126 units; 82 private baths; host to multitudes of special interest groups. The **Royal Cambridge** has a rotunda lobby; downstairs Western Bar; main floor Royal Bar; plain dining room; barbershop and beauty parlor; parking lot (a blessing in this traffic-choked city); 90 pleasant accommodations. The **Blue Boar,** a midvillage Trust Houses Forte link, is rooting for fatter acorns. Vaulted lobby and attractive lounge; bar staff unruffled by the presence of clients; sedately antique dining room; most accommodations similarly stripped of beauty by stuffing them thickly with vinyl, plastics, ugly bakelite and other synthetics. The **Gonville** may have refurbished 100 new rooms. We'll check soon. The **Cambridgeshire** scores with 100 units plus 18 golf holes. It's touted as a "leisure hotel." Sounds not only needed but a value as well. The **Bath** offers limited amenities but good cuisine. We hear good reports on the **Garden House Hotel.** It has been fully rebuilt and though we haven't seen it personally, friends claim it could be rated tops in the town. For lunch or dinner, we'd first pick the **Coach & Horses** (on the outskirts at *Trumpington*), then the **Turk's Head**, the **Sylder**, or **The Green Man** (across from Coach & Horses). Next would come the **Pagoda** (Oriental, of course), **Arts Theatre**, or **Bistro Italiano**. **Garden House** again is said to be among the leaders, according to local reports.

CANTERBURY　**Slatters** tells the best tale of all for an overnight pilgrimage. Rebuilt in 1963; modernized Forum Restaurant on the foundations of a Roman amphitheater; Founder's room for popular-price vittles; central heating; full carpeting; small bedchambers. Clean and worthy. The **Chaucer**, with 47 rooms and 30 private baths, is surprisingly comfortable. The **County** dates back to the 1500's. Wooden floors; beguiling lobby breakfront; paneled dining room. Fair. **Abbots Barton**, along the Dover road, depressed us; its amenities are basic; its flair is zero. As dining choices are limited try the **Duck Inn** first, then **Slatters** or the **Castle**. The **Flying Horse** at *Boughton Aluph* (11 miles) is not recommended.

CARLISLE　The **Crown and Mitre** reigns supreme at this key hub on the road to Scotland. Coffee Shop for light bites; cranberry-colored Belowstairs Restaurant accurately named and adequately provisioned; Edwardian Peace & Plenty Pub; Jonesian Railway Tavern. All 80 units boast carpeting, TV, and 2-channel radio; 70 sprout sprinklers and tubs. The front singles were minuscule; others, however, were spaciously sized and flairfully outfitted. Deserving of its local crown and modern mitre. The 60-sancta, Victorian **Cumbria** is a serious midtown pretender to the throne since its thorough revamping. About half the units have private bath.

CASTLE COMBE See "Bath".

CHESTER is an engaging town for fans of architecture. The timber-and-stucco houses, covered walks, and balconies are a living national trust. The graciously imposing **Grosvenor** wins the hospitality honors. Smart public rooms; rich leather-padded Arkle Bar; coolish dining salon; 102 comfortable, fully carpeted bedchambers. A giant multilevel garage is available for parking immediately behind the hotel. Recommended. The **Blossoms** is a sound alternative choice. Entrance on the sidestreet façade; downstairs Buttery and coffee shop; public rooms pleasant; corridors refreshened but occasionally serving as the conduits of strong cooking odors; bedchambers inclined toward motelish motivations. The **Queen** wears raiments fitted by her Trust Houses Forte tailors. Facilities? Eighty-two rooms and 70 baths; meal vouchers for other tables in the royal family; definitely not high regency, but a noble effort indeed. The **Curzon**, also in this chain, has just been given a new wardrobe and should be spiffed up for your arrival. Both the **Washington** and the **Westminster** have been modernized in this era; both are small, near the station, have ingratiating bars, and are good bets for budgeteers. For nutrition, try the **Grosvenor**, the **Plantation Inn**, or **Abbot's Well**. Then we'd choose the **Steak House**, the **Kardomah** (for snacks), the **Chanticleer** or the **Courtyard**. Both the **Yen Hong** and **Green Dragon** are Far Eastern in these Chester fields.

COVENTRY is the home of Jaguar cars and Lady Godiva. There's a bombed-out shell of a 5-century-old cathedral and a new one in rose-gray sandstone. Otherwise the town is industrial. The **Leofric** is, to us at least, the only decent stop in town. Modern building with cool functional overtones; 3 restaurants; 2 bars; snack corner; 101 rooms; 75% bath ratio; top-floor units with TV; careful maintenance. Despite its assets, this one gives us the feeling of loitering in a moviehouse lobby. Acceptable but commercial.

DEDHAM Here is a double-barreled treat: Both the **Maison Talbooth** and **Le Talbooth** are under the same proprietarial care and affection of the talented Gerald Milsom—though they are separated by a half-mile of rolling Essex hillside in the Colchester region. The first is a small hotel on the Stratford Rd. with 10 sumptuous Victorian suites looking onto 3 acres of beautifully maintained garden. The second is an ingratiating half-timber, converted mansion dating back to A.D. 1500 that offers superior fare. Two of its enchanting rustic dining rooms peep through leaded windows onto the romantically reflecting Stour River. Construction of beams-and-daub; alfresco drinks or coffee served on the riverside terrace when skies are benign; chummy bar; professional supervision by personable Manager John Benstead. While art followers will recognize the house from Constable's painting of "Dedham Vale," New Englanders will probably be fascinated with this site and the church in Dedham itself, which has Colonial connections. Certainly worth a trip out from London or as a weekend target for tranquillity seekers.

The same Milsom team operates an amusing restaurant down the road called **The Pier** at nearby _Harwich_. Decoratively, it was copied from an American counterpart in Boston. This colorful medium-tab entry, specializing in fish, is in a sprawling maritime edifice that overlooks the salty pilot-boat harbor of one of England's major ports. Don't fail to try it if you are nearby.

DOVER   The **White Cliffs** crests the lot. Seafront porch and glassed-in terrace; 62 rooms in the main building, plus a few more in the annex; 18 private baths; #95 is a nice double. Reasonably good comfort for the cliff dweller. The **Dover Stage**? Candidly, we think it's a horror. It seemed to us that the rooms were designed as cabins for one-night stands, and the whole just slung together. Packed solid during our recent journey. Heartily disrecommended by us as disagreeable to our eyes, ears, nose, and throat. **Holiday Inn** is okay as an overnight stop, but not for long stays, in our opinion.

DURHAM   The 47-room **Royal County** is sweet in its homey fashion. Handsome fifteenth-century staircase; superior cookery for the region; doubles, including breakfast, in the moderate range; thoughtfully equipped, down to that hot-water bottle in your bed. The **Three Tuns**, owned by the same company, is also nicely maintained.

FALMOUTH   Slim pickin's in the town itself, but flanking it is a dual bonanza. **Tresanton**, across the bay in sleepy _St. Mawes_, might have been spirited from the sunny Mediterranean. Three slopeside buildings are partly hidden from the main road. The first contains a reception parlor in granny dress plus several plain rooms; the 2nd, called the Anchorage, harbors Victorian units, including bay-windowed #1, with an almost sensational view of the bay. Then there's the **Avalon** with 19 choice chambers, a rose-covered stone terrace, a homey drawing room, and the partitioned, wicker-chaired, beautifully muraled dining den. In the last, the Chef whomes up Falmouth-style and Gallic Specialties. Super. You may also dine at the **Ship And Castle**. **Meudon**, 12 miles out via a narrow, twisty road, is embraced by breathtaking gardens. Three-hundred-year-old manor house handsomely grafted onto the younger, larger main building; terraced, flora-lined patio; stately lounge crackling cheerily in winter; airy restaurant a pane away from Eden.

FERNDOWN   (8 miles from Bournemouth): **Dormy Hotel**, with a golf course.

FOLKSTONE   Burlington Hotel.

GRASMERE   Refer to our separate Lake District wrap-up further along.

HARROGATE   The **Majestic**—for position and comfort. While the lobby, bar, 2 elevators, and carpets have been renewed, our inside bedchamber seemed to face more tubing than might have been seen at an Apollo launching pad. Pick your room with care and you'll be majestically happy. The **Old Swan**, hatched in 1679, is fun for antiquarians. (Two false fire alarms at 5 AM recently added to our own excitement during our latest check here—without even an apology from the management.) Ancient bar; skylighted Bramham dining room; total of 140 units and 90 baths; 3 suites; book only the newer rooms here. The **Crown** follows this one; the public rooms are very attractive; bedchambers are routine. The 145-room **Cairn** is situated across the garden from Harrogate College. Marble arch-and-pillar lobby; overpowering Ionic dining room; hearthside bar decorated cleverly with textile printing blocks. We also like it more for its public rooms than for its upstairs amenities. Finally, for a lovely daylight excursion or an overnight in the country, we highly recommend a jaunt to the **Devonshire Arms** at *Bolton Abbey*—15 miles across the Yorkshire dales through some of the most glorious countryside in fair Albion. Charming inn with a dozen sleeping quarters and hardly any private plumbing; delicious food and excellent service; cozy dining room overlooking the glistening Wharfe River; friendly rustic atmosphere that any open-hearted traveler would adore for its simple good cheer. After lunch, walk through the back gate and across the meadow to the riverbank; turn left and stroll a ½-mile up to the beautiful ruins of the abbey itself; then return along the highway, where glimpses of the hills and bright water peep through openings in the moss-gathered graystone walls. The prices are extremely moderate, of course. Here is the true pastoral flavor of Olde England—and you will never forget its joy.

HATHERLEIGH,   North Devon: **The George**.

HELMSLEY   The **Black Swan**, a 400-year-old nestler, is the pick of the gaggle in these parts. Nicely scrambled Georgian-Tudor-Moderne cote overlooking the town's market; series of earthy lounges with stone and brick fireplaces and split-rail trimmings; solidly British restaurant with bay windows almost caressing the lawn and garden; 3 bars. Total of 38 nooks, including those in the rear wing; all commonly denominated by ample space, central heating, bathrooms with hot towel racks, TV, radio, and a tea-coffee cooker.

HEREFORD: The **Green Dragon** is the local fire-breather. Eighteenth-century white structure; large dining room paneled in oak that was chopped and planed in 1600; adjoining cocktail cranny; popular ground-floor Offa Bar. All 100 units with full plumbing; #234, the lone suite, a commodious choice.

ILKLEY   **Box Tree** is one of the most talked-about gourmet shrines in England—and almost all the chat is good. Corner residence with cocktail lounge leading past 2 blackamoor statues to the 2 suave inner dining rooms; lots of damask, crystal, and oil paintings; a bit la-di-da for manly types; side dishes more interesting than main selections; perfect service; steep prices but not out of line for the quality; be sure to book in advance.

As long as you're in Yorkshire and if you have a taste for the elegant, be sure to run out to enchanting **Kildwick Hall** (near Keighley, which is about a 15-minute drive from Ilkley). The Graystone Palace is a national trust, so nothing can be altered in its structure. Hence—and this is its only shortcoming, as far as we can see—none of the rooms has a private bath; however, 2 regal segments have been set aside on the dwelling floor, and these are more than adequate for the small number of people who reside under its roof. The

Jacobean Room, with 4-poster bed and canopy, is unreservedly one of the most breathtaking havens in any hostelry anywhere in the world. Several other accomodations are in this style or have an Elizabethan bearing. The dining salon is glorious to the eye but its performance has its ups and downs. Peaceful are the views of gardens designed at the time of William III; and so, too, the dales of Aire which front the castle. For any discriminating traveler this one is the heartbeat of Brontë country and the soul of antiquity.

KENILWORTH   Check further along under "Warwick."

KESWICK   Please refer to our special section on the Lake District further along.

KING'S LYNN   The 3-century-old **Globe** prides itself on its dining facilities: the Apéritif Bar, the Steak Bar (in Routine Rustic, with savory main courses plus light bites), and the Chicken Bar (more uppity, less attractive, and bigger meals). This house is a toper's dream; because it has 9—repeat, 9—bars, there's never the slightest need to get one's feet wet by stepping outside. Its quarters include 49 rooms, 1 suite, and 6 private baths. Amusing in concept. The handsome **Duke's Head**, also on Market Place, comes up with 75 bedchambers, more than half of them lately constructed and with baths. Well run.

LEDSHAM   The best dining bet is at the **Craxton Wood Country Club**.

LEEDS   The **Queen's** belies its 10-story graystone facade which reminds us of a cross between Ataturk's Tomb and the Kremlin Wall. Dignified oval lobby; aloof reception phalanx; split-level, octagonal, and columned Harewood Restaurant; Knave's Coffee House plus 2 bars; sauna and massage cells. The queen of Leeds, but almost agonizingly straight-laced to our shoestring impressions. Next is the **Ladbroke Dragonara**, with another 200 bath-, TV-, and radio-riddled upstairs complex. This one is distinctly "with it," but we'll wait awhile to be sure *we* are. We haven't seen the **Ramada**, a U.S. export. Finally, there's the **Merrion**, about as commercial as Rank can file 'em.

LINCOLN   The **White Hart**, across from the cathedral, offers rich furnishings. Leaded windows; historic lounge in which a conclave of brass hats conceived the first modern fighting tank. Almost all its 60 rooms with carpeted private baths; 12 suites, not including the sumptuous Brownlow Suite (single, double, sitting room, and 2 baths); #36 is our choice of the twins; polished olde inn flavor, above average cuisine, and hospitable air. Very, very good. **Eastgate** is also near the cathedral. Modern in tone; lilac-shaded dining room; adjoining bar and outdoor terrace; Buttery open until 10:30 P.M.; 70 ample-size rooms with bath, radio, individual heating control, and TV for hire; #339 a beguiling treetops double. Totally different ambiance from the White Hart, but agreeable if you prefer twentieth-century appointments.

LIVERPOOL   is England's third city in terms of population. Substitute docks, freighters, and railway tunnels for steel mills, foundries, and lofts, and you have a smaller Birmingham. It, too, is modernizing—but, sad to say, at a far slower pace. If you are pausing for the night, the **Adelphi** is recommendable. Pleasant Grill; attractive French restaurant; well maintained and comfortable. **St. George's**, a Trust Houses Forte fortress, lines up 157 chambers and a like number of baths. The distinctively modernistic **Atlantic Tower**, standing tall near Pier Head at Merseyside, is in the capable managerial hands of Noel O'Neill. Here's a welcome addition to this Liverpudlian pool. So are the **Holiday Inn** on Paradise Street, the centrally sited 100-room **Feathers** (with 2 restaurants and 2 bars), and the 60-unit **Bradford**, also a midtowner. If you don't dine at your hotel's tables, try **Reece's** as an independant candidate.

LUDLOW   The **Feathers** fluffs up a half-timbered facade, a bevy of bedchambers dripping with Shopshire history (and even tubs), and an oak-and-brick restaurant that should take you back to 1565 faster than the Shrewsbury Stage. At *Hopton Castle,* fringing the Clun Forest, the **Lower House Country Lodge** is an intimate hideaway with the personality of a private home. John and Sally Dann are hosts at this restored medieval estate.

LUTON   Charter airline flights often land or start from here. If you are stuck, the 151-room **Strathmore** is a fair choice for clean, modern accommodation.

MANCHESTER   the textile center and fourth city, is connected with the sea by a 36-mile ship canal. Development hurtles ahead in every sector; the air terminal building is an offspring of its booming rebirth pains. Although here is one of the principal centers of political, literary, scientific, and musical advancement, many sightseers find it commercial and unrewarding. Among its hotels the 14-story **Piccadilly** is the undisputed champion of the featherweight lot. Locally, nothing can lay a glove on it. While it is clean, collected, and efficient, it also seems as sterile as a missile center. Circular ramp entrance to a cantilever lobby done in pine-louvered wood, Sicilian white marble, and icelike mosaics; 5 bars (the Plaza and the bale-filled—but not baleful—King Cotton nooks are the pick); dining room; Grill; 24-hour Coffee Shop with miserable service standards and punishing price tabs; 50 doubles and 205 singles (an obvious guidepost to its commercial intent); small bedrooms with nice furnishings and textiles. Very good except for its formidable impersonality. The **Midland** is the oldest in town; still well maintained; highly respected French restaurant. Unfortunately, age is beginning to tattle here. The **Portland**, overlooking Piccadilly Gardens, offers solid traditional shelter in its 220 rooms with bath. The suites are best. The **Grand** lives up to its moniker reasonably well. A fair stop. If the Midland's kitchen doesn't suit you, you might sample the **Café Royal** or the **Gourmet**. Out at the airport, the **Excelsior** has just been given an overall trim by its Trust Houses Forte grooms. Much better it is, too.

MELROSE   Roxburghshire (in Scotland but on the English motoring circuit) boasts the **George & Abbotsford**. The **Leicester Arms** at *Penshurst* looked to us on our checkout as if its furnishings might have been selected from a Green Stamp catalogue. Nix.

MIDHURST   This medieval hamlet, similar to Rye and overrun with equal numbers of summer package tours, is proud of its twin-winged A.D. 1430 and A.D. 1650 **Spread Eagle**. White Tudor facade; skylit entrance; beamed dining room with copper-clad hearth and talon-to-talon tables affording fine views of the courtyard. Trio of bars including the vaulted Coal Hole; a dart room; heavily timbered hunting theme lounge; the Cromwell nook, where The Protector hanged his adversaries. The 20-chamber **Angel** might be heaven for those seeking a more central location, more informality, less deliberate charm, and less pretention than its more famous opponent.

MORETONHAMPSTEAD   **Manor House**, with its incredibly beautiful softly rolling acres of manicured grass and gardens 12 miles from Exeter, is the lord of its well-mannered fief. Iron gate-to-front-door drive fringing the 18-hole golf course; tennis courts; 2 trout streams; rhododendrons, azaleas, willows, and elms galore; long, gray, 3-level stone structure; somewhat austere dining room with white columns, leaded windows, and sound cuisine. Heaven for duffers, anglers, shutterbugs, horticulturists, and dedicated lazybones.

MORETON-IN-MARSH   See our separate section on the Cotswolds.

NEWBRIDGE   The **Rose Revived** is a favorite stop in Oxfordshire, a sweet inn at the junction of the Thames and the Windrush. The kitchen's good, too.

NEWCASTLE-UPON-TYNE   The **Gosforth Park**, overlooking the racecourse, romps over the finish line by at least several lengths. Handsome Brandling Grill; adjoining Silver Ring Bar; 101 bedrooms and 5 suites; double this amount now being readied plus barber and beauty salons, a sauna, boutiques, and a riding school; small baths; radio, remote-control TV. Definitely in our winner's circle, but v-e-r-y expensive. **Five Bridges**, at *Gateshead*, has slipped in the stretch. Increasingly mercantile in tone; décor of the ultramodern mechanical engineer's school; dramatic Bewick's Bar outfitted to resemble the inside of a gearbox; Engine Room public bar; Tynesider Steak Bar; window-lined dining room; shops at street level; public rooms air-conditioned; rooftop parking space (a godsend in this city). The **Royal Station** in midcity offers solid comfort in rather dull surroundings. Public rooms well maintained; cheerful sleeping units. The **County**, in the Gosforth stable, is a mod-lined shooin for its moderate stakes. Its elegant paneled dining salon is especially attractive at night. The 8-story **Swallow** is close on its heels. The **Royal Turk's Head** wears a proud turban; this one, too, runs in the money. There's also a young challenger in the 151-unit **Holiday Inn**. Newcastle is nearly always jammed with business travelers and conventioneers. Be sure your booking is confirmed before arrival. Dining? Most of it is done in the hotel restaurants.

NEW MILTON   **Chewton Glen**, a stately Georgian mansion growing within a sea of flowers 90 miles southwest of London, is now one of the most glorious inns in England. Red brick edifice sprinkled with green shutters; homey lobby; thickly carpeted, book-lined Sun Lounge; Marryat Restaurant with justifiably renowned fare; Garden Room dinery, Cocktail Bar, tennis;

indoor-outdoor swimming pool. The old section snuggles 8 airy attic-type doubles plus others; the Coach House, reached by a covered walkway, contains 2 suites and 6 duplex units slightly lower in cost. The Marryat Suite's big splash is its huge round bathtub for 2, plus a stall shower. There are color TVs throughout the house and many additional sparklers which heighten the luster of this gem. Our only minor carp is that some chambers offer distressingly limited luggage stowage for overseas voyagers. Proprietor Martin Skan, a young dynamo, is working wonders here. Here is virtual perfection at expensive tariffs which merit every single pence. Lovely, lovely, lovely! (Incidentally, if you are making your way between Southampton and London, here is a gracious alternative to England's dismal port city.)

NOTTINGHAM We enjoyed a pause at the **Bridgford**, which has an excellent site on the Trent; bedrooms are small, however. The **Strathdon** offers 67 units, most with shower and about a third with full bath. Functional modernity is the keynote. Sherwood Forest is just down the road apiece.

OTTERBURN's pacesetter (in Northumberland) is the stucco-coated **Percy Arms**, with its pleasant window-lined dining room, 2 bars, and ample comforts. Second, we'd pick **Otterburn Tower**, a converted castle with too few private baths. In nearby *Corbridge*, there's the modest but adequate **Angel Inn**; an angelic host of pipe smokers reads and nods in its lounge. In neighboring *Berwick-on-Tweed*, it's the **King's Arms**, where the death of the lamb to furnish our cutlets we considered a needless atrocity; there's also the **Castle** aside the northern approach to the city.

OXFORD is a traffic choked center mixing higher education with higher blood-pressure readings for motorists. Globe-hopper Denis McEvoy, a former Editor for *Reader's Digest* and visiting lecturer at the Graduate School, tells us that the **Linton Lodge** now is his choice for comfort and Fellowship. If this world-savvy Upperclassman of journalism—a colleague who himself constitutes a current event at any gathering—likes and recommends an establishment, we will go along sight unseen. Next would probably be the **Randolph**. Continual modernizations; dining room plus Ox-in-the-Cellar Buttery; some up-to-date units in plain but passable taste; many Gothic touches; nextdoor garage. **Eastgate** is clean, neat, and small. For budgeteers, the **Tackley**, on High Street, is old-fashioned but sparkling; the **Melville** and the **Isis**, both on Iffley Road, are worthy alternates. Pilgrims on wheels usually aim for the **Excelsior Motor Lodge**, on the outskirts toward Woodstock. It is modern and appealing; best of all, it offers parking space. For dining, the **Elizabeth** and the **Roebuck** lead, but pub crawlers generally enjoy **The Bear**, the **Turf Tavern** or **The Trout Inn** at nearby *Godstow*.

PEMBURY The **Priory** or the sleekly modern **Great Danes** near *Maidstone* with an indoor heated swimming pool are two Kentish winners.

RYE is a bewitching, stone-girt seacoaster that rises above a vast marshland. Overlooking this ancient domain of contrabandists, the **Mermaid** is a masterpiece of feudalism fused with modern provincial comfort. Long stucco-and-timber ivy-clad building topped with chimney pots; oaken dining den; Dr. Syn's Chamber paneled and branded with aphorisms from the Bard of Avon; Giant's Fireplace Bar (look up the flue which was once used by smugglers); tranquil courtyard. Eighteen of the 26 accommodations come fully plumbed; all tend toward the diminutive but are jam-packed with Elizabethan emollients such as 4-poster beds and brassy lamps.

ST. IVES   We recommend **Tregenna Castle** for sports buffs and photographers: tennis, golf, fishing, and boating for the former, and Land's End plus St. Ives harbor for the latter. The 55-unit **St. Ives Bay** underwent revampings which included 2 dining rooms, a new elevator, sauna, and beds; the shower count still is stalled at 1/3rd of the available units; suite #8 crests best for wave watchers. At *Gunnislake*, we take little stock in the **Tavistock**.

SALISBURY   The **White Hart** provides the greatest comfort for your pounds. Woody highlights in bedroom décor; good baths; 25-unit annex. We are still charmed by the original parking lot sign that lists the prices for feeding the horses and washing the carriages. The **Red Lion**, which dates back to the seventeenth century, comes up with a handsome antique dining room, full carpeting, a later wing in which the rooms are smaller than the older ones. Total of 50 units and 30 baths; very nice staff; enjoyable if you're unapprehensive of beamed ceilings and floors which sag with your footsteps. The **Rose & Crown** is a pleasant country town house; its site by the river is peaceful. **King's Arms**, also old-fashioned, has a Tudor façade and a matching interior. The **County Hotel** compiles a curious set of statistics: 32 rooms, 2 private baths, 3 restaurants, and 7—yes, 7—bars. At a tiny hostelry called the **Cathedral** long ago we encountered our first barefoot receptionist (a novitiate, perhaps?). She was better-heeled on our latest look, having gone through 3 changes of ownership and a renovation—the hotel, that is, not the lady. If you prefer the suburbs, why not drive 8 miles farther to the sweet little **Antrobus Arms** at *Amesbury* (near Stonehenge)? Reasonably comfortable inn; inviting bar; oh-so-rustic TV lounge *(sic);* fine restaurant. All 18 bathed accommodations are named for regions; we stayed in the "North Devon," a *grand-lit* double; it was delightful. This one is recommended for country living.

SHEFFIELD   (cutlery, steel) is humdrum to most vacationers but we like its people. Good Yorkshiremen, they—rough, tough, and gruff on the surface but, like purebred bull terriers, gentle as lambs under their bristling exteriors.

SOUTHAMPTON   Crack-off-the-bat, we'd strongly urge that you NOT overnight here. If possible, take a taxi to *Winchester* (13 miles) and book into the **Wessex** (prior reservations advised). For your first or last night in glorious Britain, Winchester (see separate paragraph listed alphabetically) will provide a much more colorful introduction or memory than will this cold, grimy, industrial port. Similarly, we also can recommend the previously mentioned Chewton Glen at New Milton (18 miles). Curiously, the **Skyway** is not near the airport but down by the docks. While its glass-lined Solent Restaurant serves appetizing fish dishes, we dined beside some of the most *mal-de-mer*-provoking oil-painted seascapes we've ever seen. Handsome Habour Bar; penthouse Polynesian deck for snacks and after-dark revels; large car park. The bedchambers could be termed, charitably, as routine, but since the traffic is so heavy at this crossroads, advance reservations are a must. Better for a meal en route than an overnight. The **Dolphin** has been modernized to the scant limits of its antique facilities; 70 rooms and baths; plenty of creaks. The **Polygon,** a large, bulky structure, strikes us as being about as frumpish as a damp wool ulster; some newer units merely passable. The **Royal** is too commercial for our taste. The intimate **Berkeley**, tucked away in the interior of the city, is comfortable and has a commendable table.

STRATFORD-UPON-AVON   The town groans with so many tourist groups that it is difficult today to find a trace of intimate dwelling space anywhere within the immediate limits. For quiet country living nearby, see our comments further along on the Cotswolds. The 260-chamber **Hilton** hunkers discordantly upon 4 acres of carefully Tudored riverside garden. Long, ugly (to us) low structure; Warwick Grill serving up platters which pleased us not; octagonal Actor's Bar; ballroom; parking area. Rooms reasonably proportioned; each offers an individually controlled thermostat, a radio, taped melodies, and a direct-dial phone. The manager must forthwith mor sternlee instructe his troupe according to their separate artes, that they may serve with keener measure and stouter hearts. The venerable **Welcombe**, on Warwick Road, an inconvenient 3 miles outside the village, is the best-known luxury house in the region. Sprawling park surroundings with 18-hole golf course a-building; originally constructed so there would be 1 window for every day of the year (we secretly believe there are as many chimneys, too); 3 suites, 92 rooms, and 81 baths; expensive tariffs. Because of its remoteness, readers have complained of difficulties in securing theater tickets from the busy marketplaces in town. In the center, the **Shakespeare** is much more fun for younger globe-trotters. Charming Tudor architecture replete with gables, open timbers, leaded windows, and hanging flowerpots; gimmicky names for the bar ("Measure For Measure"), the dining room ("As You Like It"), and the bedchambers—all of which bear the title of a play, a poem, or one of the Bard's characters (we can't tell if the bridal suite is "Romeo and Juliet," "A Lover's Complaint," "Much Ado About Nothing," or "Love's Labour's Lost"). **Swan's Nest** is generally modern; comfort in abundance; above-average kitchen. **Alveston Manor**, a Trust Houses Forte interest, has been slipping dangerously, in our view. General Manager Cassini had better light some firecrackers under his go-slow staffers. Fine old main building which contains only the smallest fraction of the complement (and which often is chilly in winter); 100 rooms in newer Charlecote and Warrick wings with simple, almost raw, billets. The **Falcon** is a timber-and-stucco house that reflects the general antiquity of the town; basically sound; reputedly superior cuisine. The Tudor-style **White Swan** has 60 pleasant rooms and few private baths. Imposing **Walton Hall** resides within 68 acres of Dene-side valley and parkland. Its grand house and outbuildings bespeak a heritage of genteel nobility. The interior, while vast and baronial, suffers marginally from a simple amplitude of space which yearns to be warmed up. This is a fairly new project (in its hotel role) so perhaps it will mellow as it matures. Impressive, stately, but still a bit cool. The **Haytor** is more a residence-cum-hotel. Quiet suburban situation (and don't think *that* isn't a joy in this bustling hamlet!). Artistic décor throughout; attractive red map-lined dining room; all bedchambers color-blended down to the linens and blankets; all of the loving touches and pampering amenities of a fine private home The **Red Horse**, where Washington Irving penned his *Sketch Book,* is a polished, modest but praiseworthy budget bet. It is one of the few hotels in Stratford that will accept reservations by telephone instead of by mail. Predictably nice personnel; it knows its task and performs it well. **Ravenhurst** is the choice of many dollarwise travelers; lodging for reasonable prices; many personal attentions; quite satisfactory. Information about the 2 youth hostels in town can be garnered from the local tourist office; charming Mrs. B. G. Browne is a walking (and smiling) encyclopedia of Avon-side news, ticket information, private housing, and transportation (address: 20 Chapel St.).

Many first-timers blindly insist on residing in Stratford while attending the Shakespeare performances or touring the countryside. Seasoned wayfarers with their own transportation more shrewdly avoid the crush of this touristic hub by finding the true Arcadian solace of rural England in the neighboring Cotswolds. The distances are short and cover some of the most inspiring landscape under Merlin's wand. For a minichapter on this region which has such enormous appeal to wanders, please see the comments that follow.

Dining possibilities are extensive in Stratford. Here's how we rate the ones we've sampled: (1) **Giovanni's** (refined continental tone; bar with stools and leather Chesterfield chairs; restaurant with cassis-hue walls and sconces; good quality for average prices), (2) **Marlowe's** (reached via a narrow midtown alley and up a flight of steps; private house of timber and stucco; entry bar plus 2 richly antiquated dining salons; brass chandeliers, plus candles and an open hearth.), (3) **The Dirty Duck** (so named by the extraordinarily charming proprietor of this outstanding drop-in spot in the vicinity as a parody on "The White Swan."), (4) **The Beefeater**, (5) **Mayflower** (this Chinese restaurant overlooks Harvard House through wide windows; simple large room; poor service but very digestible cookery—if you're not from Yale, that is.) Among hotels: (1) **The Welcombe**, (2) **The Hilton**, (3) **The Shakespeare**, (4) **The Falcon**, (5) **The Swan's Nest**. The upstairs restaurant of the **Shakespeare Theatre** opens the curtain on a 4-star steak production for about £5. Be sure to book your table in advance. We haven't boarded the barge that floats in the marina at the edge of the Hilton estate; it could be fun.

STOW-ON-THE-WOLD   Refer to "Cotswolds."

SUNNINGHILL's recently crowned **Royal Berkshire** ascended to its throne smartly; reliable sources already call it a Queen Anne mansion with 5-star standards and tariffs to match. Total of 52 sumptuous chambers, all with color TV and refrigerators; Olympian gamut of sports facilities on its 15 manicured acres. Excellent.

SUTTON BENGER   Refer to "Bath."

SWINDON   Try the **Wiltshire** or the **Post House** for sleeping; the **Old Ship** at nearby *Mere* is known for its galley, not for its cabins.

THETFORD   The unpretentious **Bell** is a blend of the modern and the ancient.

THORNBURY   Refer to "Bristol."

TORQUAY   The **Imperial** was started the year the American Civil War ended. Now part of the Trust Houses Forte empire; reputedly trustworthy restaurant; air conditioning; swimming pool; beauty and barber shops; 2 Imperially supreme saunas. The 45 singles, 110 duos, and 2 suites have a private bath apiece. Sound. Perhaps even more so is the new, sea-fronted **Grand**, which will welcome you with a Regency Restaurant, Caribbean Bar, golf, riding, a pool, sauna, and tennis.

ULLSWATER   Refer to "Lake District" further along.

WALES   Distances are lengthy in this remote region and since town names are so obscure to foreign ears, we are lumping all of our Welsh selections under this single heading for the convenience of motorists. If you range as far as these western hills and littorals, several stops are outstanding, but be sure to consult a detailed map of the area in order to find them. The first is **Gwesty Plas Maenan**, near *Llanrwst*, Gwynedd. (And just for fun, if you haven't swallowed enough syllables by now, you can telephone them at Dolgarrog 049269–232). Here's a 14-room-and-bath country house offering traditional Welsh cuisine and entertainment. It regularly turns on the *Noson Lawen*, evenings of folk singing and clog dancing that form an authentic part of the regional lore. Another choice would be **Plas Glansevin**, a Georgian manor house at *Llangadog* in Dyfed, West Wales. Here again you can sample the specialties of the land, from *cawl* to teas with *Bara Brith*, Welshcakes, and other delicacies produced by Proprietor Wil Rees. Another must for your Welsh rovings is *Portmeirion*, a cottage-laced village on a private peninsula overlooking Cardigan Bay, only a few miles from *Penrhyndeudraeth*—and don't ask us to pronounce that, please! (Okay, if you insist, it sounds vaguely like "penny-headdress," said with a lisp.) The entire complex seems to have been built from an Italian dream sequence. Travelers can cozy themselves into either the hotel or the bungalows. Fireplaces galore; kindness by the shipload; exquisite sea- and landscape vistas; delicious food. The main building and cottages are open from April to early Nov. This is a marvelous retreat for anyone seeking the peace and loveliness of the Welsh byways. An alternative is **Ruthin Castle**, at *Ruthin*, not on the sea. This comfortized fortress specializes in medieval banquets every night except Sunday. The waitresses are in costume; there's folk singing and clog dancing; there's cuisine done in the manner of the Middle Ages; there are tour groups almost scaling the turrets. Surprisingly high living standards, but not too rewarding after the novelty has worn off and the Clwyd

Valley sights have been seen. Friends report pleasant tidings for **Porth Tocyn**, a small inn at *Abersoch* on the Lleyn peninsula; seafood dishes are the chef's specialty; we haven't been out there, however. For more rooms-with-a-view we hear the **Cliff Hotel**, linked to the links at *Gwbert* (near Cardigan) is tops. With few hotels for miles in any direction, be sure to wander with an easy itinerary and firm reservations.

Obviously you'll find scores and scores more. These represent a broadly comprehensive, hand-picked assemblage of the better ones which we've recently either overnighted in or inspected. Half of the fun is in digging up little inns for yourself, to discover that farmers have gathered in the bar for an informal singsong and a few braces of stout. If you wish for other targets write to the **Wales Tourist Board** (you'd tickle their patriotic hearts if you addressed it as the **Bwrdd Croeso Cymru**) at P.O. Box 1, Cardiff, CF1 2XN.

WARWICK　　The **Lord Leycester** offers a tartan Grill, a masculine wood-lined bar, damask-clad corridors, 45 comfortable, fully carpeted rooms, and 6 private baths; its best doubles with plumbing aren't at all expensive, if you can hook one. Not bad. The **Warwick Arms** comes up with passable accommodations. **Saxon Mill**, 10 minutes along Kenilworth Road, is for dining rather than for overnighting; poor and cocky service on our try; famous, but we found it very ordinary; food that edges on being overpriced. **Spencer's West Gate Arms** turns on eye appeal and high quality cuisine for its distinguished following. We're not fond of the **Aylesford** as a dining target. **De Monfort** is modern in concept, if not downright chilly in tone. Look for it in neighboring *Kenilworth*, a short spin from town.

WELLS　　The elfin, 10-room, 5-bath **Crown** takes the throne, but it could easily be unseated by a stalwart sovereign if one were to march in, we'd avow. Legend has it that William Penn once gave a speech standing at one of its windows. The **Star** shines brightest in its Tudor dining room, Grill, and friendly lounges; 22 second-magnitude Star chambers; grand sum of 3 private baths; kindly staff; worthy if you don't hanker for your own plumbing. **Gate House**, the oldest hostelry in this ancient town, is built right into the cathedral walls; the situation is handy for clerics, but it offers only basic amenities. The **Swan** seems Routine Antiquity to our eyes; somewhat molted when compared with the smarter chicks of similar vintage. For dining, please ask about the **Miner's Arms** in neighboring *Priddy*, a Paul Leyton enterprise which is said to be outstanding. Otherwise, the **Gauloise** often does nice things to guinea hen or sea scallops.

WINCHESTER　　As aforementioned, if you are arriving by ship, this town (or, as stated earlier, New Milton) creates a far better first impression of England than does grimy Southampton. The modern-lined, 91-room **Wessex**, built over a Roman well, is the pacesetter for miles around. Situated across the lawn from the world-famous cathedral; twentieth-century architecture which does not clash, odd as it might seem, with the moss-raked edifice; sound restaurant overlooking the hallowed resting places of some of Albion's greatest personages; cozy Buttery for late-hour snacks; well-appointed rooms with blessed space to unkink after shipboard snugness; full bath count. If you reserve in advance and specify details of your arrival (both strongly advised), the hotel will arrange for a car to meet you at the dock. A satisfactory meal may be had here, at the more atmospheric **Elizabethan**, or at the **Royal Hotel**.

WINDERMERE   Please refer to our special Lake District coverage, which you will find further along.

WOODSTOCK   The 750-year-old **Bear**, a short lope from Oxford, rears up as the 4th-oldest inn in Albion. Its 3 structures face the town market, the most ancient comprising a thickly beamed and happily hearthed lounge-bar, a taper-lit dining room further brightened by flowers and mellowed by pewter and brass, and a tally-ho cocktail nook. The adjoining 2-tiered Park Suite annex, enveloping 6 of the 32-den total, is a lazy ursine's delight. The Stable Block, across the courtyard, is another cozy cubby hole.

WORCESTER   Here our overnight pick is the **Gifford** followed by the **Star** and then the **Crown**. The **Raven** quoths well for nearby *Droitwich*—and boasts 18 singles and 30 doubles, 40 of which have small baths. English dishes; fair tariffs that include breakfast.

YORK   The **Royal Station Hotel** chugs in first. Basic comforts in the so-called Grand Tradition; some units with modern teak furniture; front perches which overlook the garden fountain and the Minster. The **Chase** greets guests with a 6-foot-tall saddle at its entrance. (Yorkshire wags claim, "Aye, they've never found a jockey to fit it!"). Ugly pipes on the façade proclaim its introduction to the Age of Indoor Plumbing; central heating; extensive reconstructions which provide smaller bedrooms than in the original building. **Post House** is on the Todcaster Rd. The **Elm Bank** is a living museum of Art Nouveau—one of the finest and most complete collections of the décor of 1897; scholars often come to study it. Should you stay here, however, you might think, as we did, that the chambermaid hasn't popped in since the turn of the century. Total of 55 grim rooms plus 3 more annexed; 24 raw baths or showers; 1 newer floor. If you walk in as a curiosity-seeker, ask to see the fabulous Regency bed in room #44 (for which antiquarians have offered startling sums). Here's a lodgings' oddity we can recommend only if you harbor a driving interest in the culture of this period. The tidy, sparkling **Viking**, a midtown candidate, moors down beside the Ouse River. The backers bankrolling it churned up 106 First-class stalls aimed at conventioneers. Food is not an overwhelming concern with locals if one can judge from the culinary standards we've experienced. Try **Brents** (it's okay) or think westwards toward *Ilkley*.

THE COTSWOLDS   This microdomain is (1) such a charmer and (2) so concentrated that we will consolidate its attractions into this single subchapter. To view its treasures properly an automobile is a necessity. Although the majority of its most intimate corners can be absorbed within 2 or 3 days, lingering for a week brings rich rewards—especially in spring, summer, or autumn.

Broadway is perhaps the most logical springboard from which to plunge. It is only 15 miles from Stratford-upon-Avon, 25 miles or so from Warwick Castle, Kenilworth Castle, Banbury and its cross, Sulgrave Manor (ancestral home of George Washington, where you'll find the original Stars and Stripes), the Duke of Marlborough's Blenheim Palace where Winston Churchill was born, Worcester with its cathedral and its porcelain works, and a host of closer storybook hamlets with poetic names such as Upper and Lower Slaughter, Bourton-on-the-Water (the "Venice of the Cotswolds"), Moreton-in-Marsh, Stow-on-the-Wold, Chipping Campden, and many more. The **Lygon Arms**, in our opinion, is one of the finest inns in England. Aside from a few thickheaded waiters or waitresses, this 400-year-old hostelry is always a pleasure to our senses. With General Manager Kirk Ritchie, dynamic Director Douglas Barrington, a kindhearted and dedicated hotelier, has provided living space for modernists as well as for traditionalists. In its way, the twentieth-century wing is every bit as appealing as is the very room where Cromwell courted the sandman. This house wins our top accolade. The half-timbered and stone **Broadway**, across the main pike, is more modest. Lower rates; amiable family atmosphere; handsome 2-story lounge and adjoining gardens. For dining, **the Hunter's Lodge** is substantial and attractive; then we'd choose the **Lygon Arms** or **Dower House**. At **Banbury**, **Whately Hall** bounds away with local thunder; its downstairs dining room is a special Hall-mark of pride, as is the brick bar room. The building has hosted Benjamin Franklin. Please note that this bustling center is not as quiet as most of the other toyland hideaways. **Moreton-in-Marsh** boasts the **Redesdale Arms** crackling an invitation with its open hearths, the larger chef-blessed **Manor House**, and the slightly commercial **White Hart**. All 3 delight the souls of antique hunters. **Stow-on-the-Wold** 's bid comes from the **Old Farmhouse**, with each of its quintet of bedrooms sweeter than the next. **Unicorn** offers more shelter, but the once revered cuisine is now abysmal, in our opinion. **Bibury** fluffs up the **Swan** for country living and perhaps some trout casting from the banks of the Coln. **Bibury Court** is a fair catch, too. **Burford** tucks the **Lamb Inn** into a cozy corner of the townlet. While tranquillity is present, its fleece could use a little combing now and then. This home lives for teatime—a sip of which we richly enjoyed. **Chipping Campden** chips in with the **Kings Arms**. The village is more appealing than these sheltering arms, but for short stoppers who spend their days out sightseeing, it is more than adequate. Nearby **Sutton Benger** and **Castle Combe**, on the Cotswold fringes, are covered earlier under "Bath." At **Cleeve Hill**, near Cheltenham, the **Malvern View** is a refined cleeveage for golfers, who'll find the links and the Severn Valley a perfect 2 for tee. At **Bourton-on-the-Water** the **Old New Inn** plunks all 24 of its bedchambers on the ground floor. It also is a popular target for its amusing model village, which tickles the fancy of all of us middle-age children. Even the kids like it! **Upper Slaughter** is said to Lord it with **Lords of the Manor**. We'll soon check to see if this really belongs among the peerage.

Don't expect many private baths or Statler-style concepts in any of these hostelries. They are all inns. Most of them date back to the middle fifteenth century. Most of them are operated by good-hearted people who think that you've come to *see* how they live not *change* how they live. The cookery may evoke fond yearnings for a hardboiled egg or a snack from your picnic survival kit, but perhaps this is a good way to start that overdue diet. But one thing is certain: from the *Forest-of-Dean* to *Shipton-under-Wychwood* and from *White Ladies Aston* to *Tintern Abbey*, we'll wager that you'll be as enchanted as we always are by this uniquely colorful loop in the British skein.

LAKE DISTRICT   This is the romantic area in the far north of England, just south of the Scottish frontier. The sylvan hills and lush dales reside within the Cumbrian borders. Rain is common, but coziness and exquisite beauty are guaranteed. The region is a virtual trove of links to the English literature of Wordsworth, Tennyson, Scott, Stevenson, and other titans. The best way to see it is by automobile, stopping 2 or 3 days in the major resorts which we will now describe.

At *Bassenthwaite Lake* near Cockermouth, don't miss a meal or a drink at the unbelievably ancient **Pheasant Inn**, a low beamed-and-stucco white building on highway A-66. The bar is deep brown with antiquity; the dining room is a handsome tavern with open timbers; the rooms are somewhat dinky but satisfactory for short stays.

At the far end of *Ullswater* there are 2 splendid choices which we think are the biggest catches in any of the lakes. The first is **Leeming**, on a hill overlooking the water—its greensward sloping down to a forest of cypress, fir, and pine trees. Exquisite, refined dining room with French blue ceiling and gilt trim; viewful lounges with open fires for cooler days; elegant public rooms; 17 bedchambers, most with private bath; no telephones, but a call system and radio in each unit. Proprietors Mr. and Mrs. Roy Carlsen have polished their young staff to penny brightness; they also make sure that every offering from the kitchen is memorable. Highly recommended. Our second choice is further around Ullswater Lake and closer to the shores, not too far from Pooley Bridge. It is called **Sharrow Bay Country House**, another oasis known for its excellent cuisine. More informal in tone than the Leeming, but nonetheless superb. A cozy hideaway for swimming, boating, and walking in the fells. Total of 26 bedrooms; professional management by Proprietors Francis Coulson and Brian Sack; closed December and January. Not to be missed by any traveler of taste.

In *Grasmere*, if you can accept the haughty attitude of Owner-Manager Reginald Gifford, the small but glowing **Michael's Nook Country House** is perhaps tops in the region. Reservations are an absolute must, and to be privileged to ingest even a morsel in its refined sanctum sanctorum you had better be a resident guest or reserve at least a meal in advance; stragglers are decidedly unwanted here. The 10 rooms are pleasant and rich with touches of Victoriana, especially the baths which are studies in polished brass and nickel. A pompous period piece that is beautifully maintained but of dubious value to well-meaning travelers who might not be greeted warmly here. (If you are turned away, as we were—due to our lack of prescience—they might send you down the pike to an attractive entry called **The Singing Birds**, where we found the cuisine to be utterly repugnant.) At a more plebeian level we would rank

the **Swan**, a comfortable sort of old-shoe hostelry with 35 bedchambers and
11 private baths. Its management by the Trust Houses Forte organization
assures travelers of reasonable shelter. Next comes the **Prince of Wales**, garbed
in regency accoutrements, followed by the **Red Lion**, which provides dens of
no particular distinction.

Keswick **Armathwaite Hall** is one of the most imposing sylvan retreats in
the entire Lake District. Venerable estate 7½ miles out of town, at the north
end of Bassenthwaite Lake; beautiful green apron sloping to the water's edge;
L-shape castle; baronial furnishings; closed November to April. Luxurious but
somewhat austere. **Castle Inn**, a nicely restyled, personally run year-rounder,
is also up at this end of the lake. Crossroads situation; clean, attractive appointments; modest rates. For motorists in search of a cozy 1-night hitching post.
Lodore Swiss, on the outskirts across the road from the lake, generates a
younger, more sprightly aura. Building in gray Borrowdale stone; heated
swimming pool; 2 saunas; 2 gyms with impulse showers; sun lounge; masseuse;
tennis court; dancing twice weekly; film showings; nursery with resident
nanny. Fresh, well-appointed public rooms; modern entrance; bright lounges
(one in avant-garde purple); cheerful bar; waterfront dining salon; La Cascade
Grill; 73 comfortable accommodations and 65 baths. Proprietor England and
his Swiss wife take pride in their well-trained staff and ingratiating house. The
young and the restless (or travelers with children) would probably prefer its
greater informality. The **Keswick** is smack-dab beside the old station *cum*
railroad museum. Lovely manicured garden; 75 bedchambers in a mansion
that is again seeing better days. The repolished **Royal Oak** stays open year
round. Careful Trust Householding; basic but pleasant enough for the quick
bird of passage, especially in its newer nests. The **Skiddaw** is passable for
budgeteers. The **George** reeks with antiquity, among other things; nice people,
however. The **Derwentwater** has an excellent position but an invasion of bus
tours spoils its peace. The **Scafell** attracts many climbers with its new-fangled
"showers" and other modern amenities. The **Borrowdale** has 7 private baths;
it lacks central heating. **Borrowdale Gates** is even more old-fashioned. Nix.

Windermere : The **Belsfield** sprawls scenically over the side of a gardened
knoll. Most of its 85 accommodations boast baths, radios, pants presses, and
other amenities. There's also an indoor pool. Unquestionably the leader. The
Old England has slipped largely because of its convention trafficking, think we.
Nice terrace above the water overlooking the small-boat docks; mixture of
Victorian and Flash Gordon appointments; modern lakefront wing bringing
capacity up to the 100 mark, the latest of which are the best. Nirvana for the
Skruggs Brush Co., Ltd. annual gala. The **Hydro** is big and rambling, but some
Regency touchups have helped; it specializes in group traffic. **St. Martin's**,
across from Old England, is a tiny, clean economy stop. Up at the **Miller Howe
House** the emphasis is on luxury accoutrements and food, food, food and more
food—and Howe! Handsome site, comfortable nesting, but bring along a size
88 belly. *Ambleside*, a midget's skip from Windermere, is one of the most
panoramic vantage points in the Lake District. The **Langdale Chase Hotel** is
stubbornly Victorian in its old-fashioned atmosphere; enough wood carvings
to have kept 100 whittlers busy for 20 years; buckle-bending teas for hikers'
appetites; 36 rooms and 20 baths; the Boathouse, the prime buy, is closed Dec.

8 to Feb. 1. We like the garden and the kindness, but some Pilgrims may find the décor as overpowering as a 3-week holiday in Hagia Sophia. Otherwise warmly recommended. The sprawling **Salutation** is 2nd (many package tours); it is stalked closely by the **White Lion**. **Low Wood**, on the outskirts, is a fair bet for budgeteers; it has been expanded to 141 bedchambers; bid for the newest ones.

☑ **MOTELS**   Popping up as fast as a berserk automatic toaster. All are modern, since investors saw a potential market only within the past few years. The **Watney-Lyon** group is one of the trailblazers, with a gross of operations now and more in blueprint. Samples are at *Epping (Essex)*, *Matford (Devon*, 1½ miles from Exeter on the bypass), *Ower (Hampshire*, on London–Bournemouth road, a convenient stop for Southampton arrivals), *Newingreen* (*Kent*, near Hythe and in easy reach of Dover), and *Frome (Somerset)*. **Trust Houses-Forte Ltd**. has constructed units at *Alveston* (near Bristol), *Chippenham (Wiltshire)*, *Sherborne (Dorset)*, and *Epping (Essex)*., *Norman Cross (Huntingdonshire)*, and *Boroughbridge* (*Yorkshire*, between London and Edinburgh on the Great North Road). At *Plymouth*, the **Holiday Inn** planners have unveiled 224 bedrooms and sited other links at *Leicester* and *Slough-Windsor*, plus the ones that we've already pinpointed. The Forte group has unwrapped the previously mentioned **Excelsior Motor Lodge** and Autogrill 2 miles north of *Oxford*. Then there are the excellent, inn-style **Boulter's Lock** at *Maidenhead* and the equally engaging **Bridge House** at *Reigate*, both under the watchful eye of Tom Cressy, the wayfarers' friend. Finally, just 1½ miles from *London Airport*, the **Master Robert Motel** awaits (ask how it got its name; bet you 10 to 1 you can't guess!) and **Crest** has unveiled a 115-roomer in London (at Wembley Park).

☑ **SPECIAL FACILITIES FOR CHILDREN**   The British Tourist Authority suggests **Childminders** (67 Marlebone High St.). Others include **Universal Aunts** (36 Walpole St.), **Visitors Welcome** (17 Radley Mews), and **Junior Jaunts** (4A William St.). Nanny's rates usually are calculated by the hour and vary according to time of day. **The House on the Hill** (33 Hoop Lane, N.W. 11) and **Walton Day Nursery** (239 Knightsbridge) will take care of toddlers all day long, and the latter by the week. Outside London, **Norland Nursery Training College** (Hungerford, *Berkshire*) will board small fry, and **Holiday Parents** (Petersfield, *Hampshire*) will place them in English homes (temporarily!).

☑ **OVERNIGHT IN A CASTLE OR A COUNTRY HOUSE**   You might query an organization called **Country Homes & Castles** in Great Britain, which lists more than 100 addresses (mostly fine estates rather than historic fortresses). We haven't yet sampled its offerings, but many look worthy. For the photo-filled brochure write to R & I Tours Ltd., 138A Piccadilly, London W.1.

☑ **PRIVATE HOUSES**   Bored with hotels? How about a mansion then, that was constructed before Columbus leapt out of his cradle—or a 15th-century farmhouse with its own swimming pool and tennis court, or a rectory in the Sussex dales? An enterprising group called **Home From Home in England** has pulled together a corps of hospitably minded proprietors who are willing to open their hearths and their hearts to foreign visitors who may wish to bide a while in an English home or enjoy the rich tranquillity of British rural life. There are 6 categories of accommodation varying in price, location, and sumptuousness—but all of them seem unusually rewarding for the outlay. Further description would be too extensive for this volume, but if the idea tickles your sense of adventure you should write for the brochure, which provides photographs and details of the participating houses. Address your request to the above organization at The Old Rectory, Fernhurst, Haslemere, Surrey GU27 2H2, England (Tel.: 0428-53133; Telex: 858623). Here's living abroad—with a very significant difference.

Finland

The word is *sisu*. It doesn't mean "bravura." It doesn't mean "strong-arm toughness." It doesn't mean "steely nerves." It doesn't mean "tenacity." It doesn't even mean "guts."

What it means is ALL of these—tripled in spades.

Sisu is the remarkable combination of courage, stubbornness, and never-say-die which is the remarkable hallmark of the remarkable Finns—occupants of a land called Suomi.

This most northerly Republic in the world—⅓ rd of her anatomy is above the Arctic Circle—sprawls over an area which would hold 16 New Jerseys. Her 60-thousand lakes and 200-thousand islands give her map the strikingly beautiful zigzag venation of blue and white. Most of her terrain is low-lying; some regions are a broken jumble of hillocks, fells, ridges, and hollows, while others are monotonously flat for seemingly endless miles. Prizewinning Danish author Willy Breinholst put it lyrically when he wrote, "70% of her countryside is covered by forests, 30% by lakes, and 100% by skies." To my Nancy, the dominant impression of Finland's spring is pearl-pink and mulberry-blue.

Finland has a population of slightly better than 4.7 million. Most of her 10 cities and 74 towns cling to her coasts. Forestry is the basis of her economy; shipping is her lifeline. Agriculture and industry split the rest of the occupational pie.

Except for the dead of winter, forget about buying a set of Dr. Denton's as your Finnish garb. The Gulf Stream is so benign that in the lower and middle reaches of the nation you may dress as you would for an Ohio February or a Northern California July. In the south there is snow for only about 5 months; in Lapland this stretches to 7 months. And don't bring your skis to Helsinki for that Christmas outing—because it just *ain't* that cool for Yule. The midnight sun is a fascinating phenomenon. In Helsinki, your midsummer days will last 19 hours. At Utsjoki, on the northern tip of Lapland, there is continuous daylight for 73 days.

☑ **SAUNA** A sure way of slapping a Finnish friend in the face is to refuse his or her invitation to a sauna. (Fully one fifth of the population own their

206

own private facilities.) The classic version (you've seen the exported one) takes place in a 2-cubicled log cabin on the shore of the coldest damn lake that could ever possibly quick-freeze Mr. Birdseye's most precious jewels. The stripped participants proceed to a split-level, spruce-lined room. At intervals your host or hostess (mixed saunas, customary among marrieds, are not exactly unknown among unmarrieds) will pitch ladles of cold water over a bed of blast-furnace-heated stones—and the resulting clouds of sizzling steam up to 212° F will poach you scarlet, white, and sapphire. Then the conductor will beat the bejesus out of you with leafy birch branches—"just to start up your circulation." Finally, the party bursts forth, breaks the world's sprint record to the water's edge and pushes aside the larger chunks of ice with their right feet so that they won't fracture their skulls when they dive into the lake.

This variety is murder.

But for the stranger who visits metropolitan climes, the citified version is, by comparison, a sophisticated, gentle, glorious physical experience. Most hotels in the larger centers feature sauna installations so elaborate, handsome, and comfortable that newcomers cannot believe their eyes.

☑ **TRANSPORTATION Taxis** Costly, even for short runs; tipping is not expected, thank goodness. From 11 P.M. to 6 A.M. there is a night supplement of 2 FMK; the same is added all day on Sundays.

★ **TIPS** Three passengers cost more than 2—but only a trifling sum.

Since so few of the drivers speak English, *be sure* to have handy a written slip from your concierge which bears the address of your destination.

Don't grab an airport cab for town; the cost is lethal and bus shuttles run every half hour to the town terminus just behind the Intercontinental Hotel.

Finnair offers a money-saving **Holiday Ticket** to non-Scandinavian tourists, permitting 15 days of unlimited use of all domestic airlanes. Check with your travel agent if interested.

Smoking is prohibited on Finnish domestic flights, part of a national program to discourage the use and promotion of tobacco.

Trains Fair to excellent. The railways offer a galaxy of enticing thrills via the Finnrail Pass, which provides 8 days of travel (train-bus-boat) at astonishingly reasonable prices—a mere $78 for first class and $52 for second class. Finland also now is a member of the Eurailpass program—a real benefit when such great distances are involved.

International Car Ferries This way, getting there is *more* than half the fun. The ships are modern with dining facilities that include sumptuous Nordic buffet tables, conventional meals, grill rooms, or cafeterias. Then there are bars, discos, saunas, pools, barbers, hairdressers, and children's salons. Pullman seats in lounges or cabins are available; most of the latter are spacious enough and amply comfortable, while a few can be cramped.

On the most important *Helsinki-Stockholm* loop, the well-managed Silja Line parades a young fleet of sisters who are twins in all but color. The *Bore Star, Svea, Corona,* and *Wellamo* are their proud names—and lovely they are. In summer their departure is 9

A.M. and arrival 9 P.M., both ways. At other times they take to sea at 6 P.M. and arrive at 9 A.M.

In general the **Viking 5** and **Viking 6** of the Viking Line offer similar amenities. The higher fares are for outside or upper-deck accommodations. The remainder cost less. Bookings can be made on both of these anywhere through American Express.

On the *Helsinki-Travemünde* voyage to and from Germany, the swift **Finnjet** cuts this crossing from the former 2½-day run to 22 hours. Departures are made every second day. There are 2 fare seasons: High and Low. On a per-person scale in High Season, class A is $520 for a single (complete cabin) and $260 each in a double cabin; all of these 156 staterooms come with shower, toilet, and refrigerator, and are outside. Class B is $195 per individual in a double. Class C, with 4 beds squeezed into 4 square meters, is roughly $159 per head. Lounge chairs, available in High Season only, are $110 each. Fares in Low Season—from September through May—are considerably less.

☑ **FOOD** It's finny fare for the Finns. This Far North kitchen puts its heaviest accent on fish dishes. Although a stockyard of meat is always available, the East Arctic version of our Mid-Atlantic adage is still, "A herring a day keeps the doctor away."

Most establishments serve "Night Food" from 12 P.M. until closing time. Among the 2 most popular favorites are an historic concoction amusingly named Jansson's Temptation (a gooey casserole of potatoes, anchovies, onions, cream, and herbs) and Russian-originated Vorschmack (a seemingly outlandish but delicious conglomerate of lamb, herring, mashed potato, cucumber, beet root, sour cream, and garlic).

Try not to miss that glorious midsummer gustatory treat called rapuja (the minisize freshwater crayfish which the Swedes know as kräftor). The waiter will studiously tie you in a paper bib from larynx to pelvis and then pantomime meticulous instructions on how to extract every tender morsel of meat and suck every heavenly drop of nectar from this dill-seasoned-and-decorated crustacean.

The Finnish interpretation of smörgåsbord (see "Food" under "Sweden") is called *voileipäpöytä,* or *pitopöytä* for short(er). In reminiscence, our own tongues shoot out with the alacrity of a New Year's Eve favor when we conjure up the delights of such specialties as Sillisalaatti (herring salad), Smoked Poronliha (reindeer), Kesäkeitto (fresh vegetable soup with milk), Sauna Sausages (munched after *you* bake in the baths), or such "normally" hot dishes as Kalakukko (fish and pork pie with salt-baked potatoes —and if you want your tonsils to last 7450 years after you're interred, just eat the skins of those spuds), Karjalanpiirakat (piping-hot Karelian pastries), Maksalaatikko (liver pudding), Lanttulaatikko (turnip casserole), Punajuuri Salaattia (beetroot salad), and Paistetut Sienet (fried wild mushrooms). The hungry citizenry here normally wash these down with Piimää (buttermilk) or Kalja (nonalcoholic beer); personally, whenever we stare at these 2 beverages, other ideas flow with amazing freedom. Wild game? The most popular candidates include grouse, wild duck, ptarmigan (try it roasted as Riekkopaisti —yum YUM!), venison, and the national favorite, Reindeer tongue (Poron Kieli).

For the perfect finish to your local repast, there are scads of luscious fruit soups made from the wild or cultivated berries of Finland—the lingonberry, cloudberry, brambleberry, bilberry (similar to our huckleberry), and others. These taste gems also garnish pancakes or bejewel the savorful, wondrous, ever-so-tempting Pähkinäkakku (nut cake).

The Finns nourish their bodies while stoking their high spirits, since the majority of Suomi dining spots are what would constitute nightclubs in most other lands. If you have your main meal at midday—and merely nibble and tipple before midnight at places which cater to revelers—your savings will be surprisingly high. Although some offer dancing as early as noon, the more usual opening time is 4:30, with a pause from 7 P.M. to 8 P.M. in all. Some spots feature biweekly Ladies' Dance Nights, when it is customary that only the gals have the option to invite their partners to the floor. Then there are the Mixed Invitation Nights, where total equality between the sexes is maintained in freely approaching strangers. Both are viewed as natural and spontaneous good fun by the participants—not predominantly as preludes to trysts.

☑ **DRINKS** On a recent Saturday morning at 8:30 A.M., 2 Finnish brothers cleared away the remnants of their breakfast and placed 6 quarts of snaps on the table. Two hours later, without a word, they attacked the 2nd jug. At 3:20 P.M., still in total silence, they uncorked number three. When the grandfather clock struck 5 P.M., the younger brother glanced up and said, "Pretty chimes, eh, Urpo?" Urpo scowled fiercely, slammed down his glass, and shouted, "For God's sake, Mikko, are we _talking_ or are we _drinking?_"

The Finns, as a group, are just about the wettest Wets or the dryest Drys we've ever encountered. The polite 2-sherry or 1-whisky sipper is practically unknown, except among the ladies. Like his Swedish cousin, the Finn subscribes to the principle that when a man drinks, he DRINKS.

Prohibition was tried and abolished. In its place, the State formed the alcohol monopoly, "Alkoholiliike" ("Alko" for short, with 25 branches in the capital alone) to centralize control of all intoxicating beverages and to hard-sell the advantages of beer and wine. Its stocks are large and well chosen; its prices range from steep to outlandish—income from the monopoly accounts for 1/6 of Finland's total budget! If you like your weekend tipple, remember that these are open on most weekdays from 10 A.M. to 5 P.M., an hour later on Friday, plus 9 A.M. to 2 P.M. on Saturday.

Authorized hotels and restaurants ladle hooch from noon to 1 A. M. Room service in hotels stops earlier—but please blame the waiters' union, not the barmaid, for this. For teetotalers there are a sizable number of dry hotels, spearheaded by the powerful YMCA chain. Cafés and many restaurants are not granted licenses.

After vodka, Jaloviina (the generic term for snaps) is the Finns' favorite hard likker. There are 5 major types. Pöytäviina and Vaakuna, both distilled WOOD alcohol, are cheap; when you burp after more than 3 ounces, don't be surprised if you should light that gentleman's cigarette 20 feet away. Tähkäviina, made from grain, is costlier and less combustible. Koskenkorva is what might be termed the "standard" snaps of the land; its flavor is reminiscent of Denmark's Aalborg. Finally, Alko's shrewd brainstorm of sponsoring a superior product called "Finnish Dry Vodka" has met with fantastic success both at home and abroad. It offers a far smoother, cleaner, less pungent taste than any of the others, selling for about $12 per jug.

Though soberingly expensive ($25 per ordinary fifth), whisky is popular among the more cosmopolitan inhabitants. Curiously, Finns drink more cognac than do the citizens of any other nation.

Two national liqueurs of consequence present themselves to the connoisseur. Lakka, made from Arctic cloudberries and Mesimarja, distilled from the rare Arctic brambleberry which forms its essence. Costly but delicious. *Don't miss them*—but make certain you get them WELL CHILLED!

Finland boasts 23 major breweries. The aforementioned Mallasjuoma at Lahti is the largest. Helsinki's kingpin is Koff; you may quaff at least 14 other brands here. Turku's Aura is perhaps the third-runner.

Only 3 types of beer are vatted. Pilsner, the lightest, guarantees less than 2.2% alcohol. The most popular choice, "3rd Class" (so named from a taxation gimmick), goes for about the same as its Milwaukee cousins. Strongest and best is "A" ("Atomic"), the export variety. Always order this one, even though it costs a little more.

★ **TIPS** Finnish toasts? *Skol* is the most common; *Hei* ("Hey") is the most friendly, relaxed, and familiar; *Kippis* is the one usually taught to foreigners.

Local law enforces a one-at-a-time clause on the imbiber. Snaps and beer can be mated (with foodstuffs only), but otherwise no 2 glasses of spirits are permitted on your table at the same time (for example, you must finish your Scotch before your cognac can be served). Double drinks are also prohibited—and your waitress is held answerable to the Alko authorities.

Hangover clinics have been opened in Helsinki and 6 other Finnish towns. Signs at their entrances announce "FIRST AID POST FOR HANGOVERS. HOURS: 6:30 A.M. to 8:30 A.M. WEEKDAYS." Ask Your Friendly Concierge for the address of the nearest branch.

Finally, please, please—even if you're DESPERATE—ponder deeply our recommendation to avoid a concoction named Hochmann's. Great balls of lightning! This nuclear explosive, named for the druggist who first compounded it, consists of 96% pure alcohol plus ether. Lapps make this home brew for reindeer roundup time. After castrating the calves with their teeth, they swill Hochmann's (1) as a mouth cleanser, (2) as an antiseptic for the animals, and (3) for the simple purpose of becoming roaring drunk. (We don't object to the alcohol; it's the hors d'oeuvres that kill us.)

☑ **TIPPING** Finland, bless its heart, is one of the least gratuity-conscious nations in the world. Service personnel seemingly could not care less whether you ignore their ministrations or reward them lavishly for their attentions.

As we said before, don't tip your taxi driver. Your concierge should receive a token *only* for special performances—not for his routine functions. Curiously, a doorman gets 2 FM for his modest services, and cloakroom attendants pull down a big 2 FM for just checking your hat and coat. Hotel baggage porters earn 1 FM for every piece they tote. Since it is not Finnish custom to leave your shoes outside your hotel room for polishing, your chambermaid should win at least 2 markkaa for this extra favor—and more for any other exceptional kindnesses.

☑ **LOCAL RACKETS**   Practically none. After exhaustive inquiry among Finnish friends, we finally managed to pin down 2 minor cautions:

In the lowest-class dives, sometimes you won't get the brand of whiskey you order. But it will be _genuine whiskey_ always (never altered, adulterated, or falsified)—because the state-operated Alcohol Monopoly would slice off the proprietor's pouring arm if it weren't. Literally, it can put him in jail.

It is always wise to lock your car, because no law has yet been entered on Finland's law books under which joy-riding kids may be prosecuted.   •

☑ **INFORMATION CENTERS**   Even before you leave home, you can obtain heaps of information and guidance from the **Finland National Tourist Office** (75 Rockefeller Plaza, New York, N.Y. 10010) and from the **Scandinavian National Tourist Offices** (3600 Wilshire Blvd., Los Angeles, Cal. 90010).

First off, the **Finland Travel Bureau**, Kalevankatu 1, Helsinki, is the master organization, guidepost, and Dear Abby for the network. For your average run-of-the-nation puzzlers, simply call on the helpful minions of the FTB who headquarter at Kluuvikatu 8 (3rd floor).

Second, there's an 11-office skein of Travel Information Bureaus in various key cities abroad. If you're a New Yorker, hie yourself to the **Finnish National Tourist Office** (now merged with Denmark, Sweden, and Norway into one central office), Scandinavia House, at 75 Rockefeller Plaza, N.Y. 10019. There is also a joint Scandinavian font at 3600 Wilshire Blvd., Los Angeles, Calif. 90010. Overseas offices are in London, Paris, Copenhagen, Oslo, Stockholm, Amsterdam, Zürich, Hamburg, and Munich.

Third, the cheerful, friendly staff of the live-wire **City Tourist Office**, at Pohjoisesplanadi 19, in Helsinki can be of enormous on-the-scene assistance.

Fourth, most major municipalities provide their own information facilities. Just inquire locally for the City Tourist Office.

CITIES

HELSINKI   (pronounced HELL-sinki, not Hell-SINKI) is still Helsingfors to the founding Swedes. This capital, at the same latitude as Oslo and Leningrad, is the main port, the lodestone for slightly more than a ½ million toilers, and the heartbeat of the land. It is as distinct in character as the other northern capitals.

Its peninsula, flecked by a lovely archipelago, is surrounded on 3 sides by the sea. Architecturally, it's a mishmash of Empire, New York Public Library, Byzantine, and the futuristic fantasies of Aalto, Rewell, and the Siréns; except around the harbor, many visitors feel a distinct overall aura of grimness. At first sight you may not fall in love with this metropolis—but its beauty, ugliness, gaiety, dourness, incredible skein of contrasts and contradictions are guaranteed to leave you with the impression that here is one of the most fascinating hubs of the Western World.

Sightseeing   Our immediate and urgent suggestion would be for you to drop in to see the **City Tourist Office** (Pohjois Esplanaadikatu 19). (In case your taxi driver doesn't get the message, its German name is "Städtisches Fremdenverkehrsamt"—and damned if we can even *spell* the CTO's Finnish name.)

For a starter you might be offered 1½-, 2½-, and 3½-hour *tours by bus* which are run by the municipally-owned **STA** company. Its 2½-hour City Tour operates daily from May 1 to September 30 at 10 A.M., and from June 1 to August 31 at 2 P.M. Both cost about $9. Its 3½-hour Grand Tour, at about $13, goes every day at 11 A.M., and from September 1 to May 31 only on Tuesdays, Thursdays, and Saturdays. Finally, its 1½-hour Nonstop at $5, leaving at 2:45 P.M., gives a lightning view of the center of the metropolis. All of these carry English-speaking guides and cover just about every standard attraction one might wish to visit. The last time we checked, these particular ones originated at Simonkatu 1 (tel: 90 12 200). From the end of June to the end of July similar 2-hour excursions starting at 6 P.M. originate at the Market Square depot. The **Ageba** organization (Passenger Pavilion, South Harbor, tels.: 669–193 and 626–480) also arranges the same types of 2- to 3-hour trips from different departure points and hotels the year round.

For strong-legged sightseers with a cultural bent, this office distributes an excellent brochure which maps the route and gives the background of attractions encountered along the way of the old center of the capital.

Two-hour *boat excursions* from June 5 through August 15 depart from the North Harbor at 11 A.M., 2 P.M., and 6 P.M. If the weather is benign, these are delightful. There are also coastal cruisers from cozy types to Baltic-crossers such as the 1200-passenger car-ferry, *Finlandia.* However, if you should wish to go-it-alone in the capital or in any other major port, "water taxis" of all sizes are available by the hour or day. Go to the end of Aleksanterinkatu, look the craft over, and take your choice. If you're interested, ask the CTO to arrange one for you wherever you wander along the coast or the lakes. The extra fee for an English-speaking guide, also procurable through the CTO, is about $11 per hour. Members of U.S. yacht clubs may share Finnish yacht club privileges nearly everywhere; if you make the proper connections, you can borrow or rent a speedboat this way.

An outstanding target in Helsinki is the **zoo** on Korkeasaari ("High Island"), a ¼-hour ferry ride away or reachable via the new Mutikkamaa Bridge.

You should also get a boot out of the **Open Market**. To find it, just follow the Esplanade down to the base of the harbor near the Palace Hotel. The best time is 7 A.M. until 10 A.M. Here is a colorful cross-sectional slice of Grade-A Finland.

First-timers are often enamored of the special **tram tour** which makes a figure 8 through the heart of the metropolis. The streetcar number is #3-T, and the cost is about 90¢. No guides are supplied, but special pamphlets, printed in several languages, are issued. A good place to start and to finish is the Open Market. You will then be permitted to take any other of its cars or

buses for the rest of the day—absolutely free of charge. (There's also the
10-journey card which rings up roughly $4.)

With the zoo, **Linnanmäki Amusement Park** is the hub's best-liked magnet
for merrymakers. This highest point (270 feet) of the city might be likened, in
a much more modest way, to a smaller Tivoli. Open only on Saturday and
Sunday from early to mid-May, but thenceforth daily except Monday from
May 15 to September 1.

Another recommended excursion is to **Seurasaari**, 10 minutes from the
center on an island connected by a bridge. Awaiting you is a fascinating
collection of authentic Finnish country houses from various provinces, some
of them many centuries old. All have been scouted out on their original sites,
disassembled log by log and nail by nail, and reassembled with love. The guides
are dressed in regional costumes. Folk dancing is featured in season. Here's
the best place of all in which to spend the Midsummer Eve holiday.

Finally, two of the best bets are the CTO's **"Program in Helsinki,"** issued
every 7 days except for bi-weekly publication during two of the winter months,
as well as Pan Am's fine little bulletin, **"This Week in Helsinki."** The latter
is available at all hotels, department stores, and travel agencies.

Starving for the latest news in English? Dial 018 for a taped 24-hour free
service. The 5 P.M. to 6 P.M. evening bulletin is the most complete. Topical
tourist suggestions? Ring 058 for an English synopsis of "Helsinki Today,"
sponsored by the CTO.

In the environs only 6 miles out, you might be staggered by what is probably
the finest modern planned community in the world today—*Tapiola*. About 2
decades ago, the Housing Foundation, a private nonprofit organization, com-
menced the development of 670 virgin acres of lovely sea vistas ringed by
birches and dense pine forests. For outlanders interested in a twenty-first-
century projection of city planning, here is a marvel that can't be found
elsewhere. You can snack at either the viewful Tapiontorni or the Linnunrata
tower cafeteria; the previously mentioned Dipoli, a far-out architectural wonder, exists chiefly for students and conferences.

Hvitträsk, former home and studio of Saarinen, Lindgren, and Gesellius, is
also captivating to architecture buffs. It was one of the earliest serious (and
gracious) attempts to blend structure into landscape. Near the stone and log
complex there's a superb free swimming beach, a sauna, plus a good restaurant.
Connections by bus (platform 55) and taxi are best. The nearest train depot
is *Luoma*—a mile hike unless you can flag down a cab. Open 10 AM to 7 PM.
A charmer!

When the sun is shining, the excursion to *Porvoo* is popular with the
restless. The steamer *J. L. Runeberg* departs Wednesdays, Fridays and weekends from the Helsinki Market Square. You may eat aboard en route, or save
your appetite for the modern (but so-so, sad to say) Crystal Restaurant at the
destination or at the nearby luxury Haikon Kartano Hotel in *Haikko*, where
it moors.

Another lovely SUNday trip is to the Regatta Hotel in **Hanko**. Its only drawback is the 90-mile pull each way. Closer to your Helsinki base is **Aulanko** and neighboring **Hämeenlinna**—and once there, we'll bet you will want to stay several days. A Hotel Aulanko bus shuttles to and from the trains at the Hämeenlinna depot in season. This one's a *special* honey.

The most sought-after regional excursion in Finland is along the so-called Silver Line. Of the many operators, we'd select **Silverline Lake Tour**, which covers the rich south of the nation, with stops at the Hotel Aulanko (the country's leading tourist resort), Tampere (the 2nd largest city), and several other attractions. Highlight is a ½-day cruise by water coach from Aulanko. The duration is 2 days; departures are frequent from early June through late August, and the reasonable price includes transportation, transfers, sightseeing, hotels, meals, English-speaking guide, entrance fees, and tips.

To tie up this Finnish package in bright ribbons, one of the capital's happiest surprises is its **Tourist Ticket** plan that lets you choose your destinations at will and then slices off the normal rates. The lowdown on this economizer, plus the Finnrail Pass (see "Trains"), may be obtained through any Finnish Tourist Board branch, the City Tourist Office of Helsinki, or your own travel agent. Nearly all the circuits are limited to southern and middle Finland; only one touches Rovaniemi, the most northerly terminus. Best liked among foreigners is the 6- to 8-day swing through the southern lake district.

Final admonition, 70 times repeated: The Finnish provinces offer simple, unspoiled, delightful comforts to you—but please never, never, never expect to find the travel amenities of older, less virginal, more cynical lands.

HELSINKI HOTELS Quick Reference Table

Price categories by national (not U.S.) standards.

EXPENSIVE:
Hesperia Mannerheimintie 50. Tel. 441.311; Telex 12-2117; 285 rooms. P. 216
Intercontinental Mannerheimitie 46. Tel. 441.331; Telex 12-2159; 466 rooms. P. 215
Marski Mannerheimintie 10. Tel. (90) 641.717; Telex 12-1240; 162 rooms. P. 215
Merihotelli Hakaniemenranta 4. Tel. 711.455; 87 rooms. P. 215
Hotel President Etelainen Rautatieku 4. Tel. 906.911; Telex 12-1953; 500 rooms. P. 215

UPPER MODERATE:
Helsinki Hallituskatu 12. Tel. 630.701; Telex 12-1022; 85 rooms. P. 216
Klaus Kurki Bulevardi 2. Tel. 602.322; Telex 12-1670; 75 rooms. P. 216
Olympia Lantinen Brahenkatu 2. Tel. 750.801; Telex 12-2101; 100 rooms. P. 216
Palace Etelaranta 10. Tel. (90) 171.114; Telex 12-1570; 58 rooms. P. 216
Seurahuone Kaivokatu 12. Tel. 171.441; Telex 12-2234; 76 rooms. P. 216
Torni Yrjönkatu 26. Tel. 644.611; 100 rooms. P. 216
Vaakuna Asema-aukio 2. Tel. 171.811; Telex 12-1381; 224 rooms. P. 216

MODERATE:
Metro Kaisaniemenkatu 7. Tel. 171.146; 57 rooms. P. 217
Ursula Paasivuorenkatu 1. Tel. 750.311; 46 rooms. P. 216

LOWER MODERATE:
Academica Hietaniemenkatu 14. Tel. (90) 440.171; Telex 12-1444; 226 rooms. P. 216
Hospiz (YMCA) Vuorikatu 176. Tel. 170.481; 141 rooms. P. 216
Perho P. 216
Satakunatalo Lapinrinne 1A. Tel. (90) 647.311; Telex 12-2192; 64 rooms. P. 217

ENVIRONS:
Korpilampi P. 217
Otaniemi P. 217
Tapiola Garden Tapiola. 82 rooms. P. 217
Torppa (Kalastajatorppa) 235 rooms. P. 217

Hotels Although at peak periods space can still be a will-o'-wisp, at last competition has become so keen that your new or spruced-up accommodation will probably please you. The wise voyager is advised _to be sure—especially in summer—to have ALL Finnish hotel reservations confirmed IN ADVANCE._

If you haven't, the **Hotellikeskus** ("Hotel Booking Center") _might_ be able to bail you out. This office is in the Helsinki Railway Station and the telephone is 171133.

Prices vary widely across this land. In the capital, barely adequate singles start at $26, with 2-person rentals going at around $42, and an occasional 3-bed unit available for about $55. Twin accommodations in the top hotels on our list range between $53 and $69, with a few suites bounding up to around $150.

★ **TIPS** It cannot be sufficiently reiterated that hotel staffs could scarcely be warmer, kinder, and sweeter as human beings—but we would lay odds that less than 10% of them know 20 words of English (all put together!).

In Finland, as elsewhere in Scandinavia, do NOT place your shoes outside your door before you retire. Nobody will steal them—BUT, 99.99% of the time nobody will polish them either. Look for shoeshine machines in the corridors.

The **Intercontinental**, now a franchise member of the Finnair-owned chain, faces a sylvan park, conveniently backs on the city airline terminal, opposite the Congress House. Ten-story plant with 186-room extension; lobby face-lifted; red-hued, rooftop Ambassador Club with dance orchestra and bar; excellent saunas and glass-lined pool at the same altitude; Brasserie for pleasant and relatively inexpensive nibbling; standardized bedchambers comfortable but not plush; wide-angle suites. In our opinion, definitely number one in the capital.

While we haven't seen The brand-new 500-room **President**, it has high-quality credentials. Midtown site; ultra-modern decor throughout; 5 restaurants; pool; sauna; nightclub. Let's hope it lives up to its campaign promises.

The youthful **Merihotelli** looms modernistically for seaside meri-makers. It is a fairly long run from midtown, adding to the outlay by gadabout sightseers. Grill-Bar and 300-seat restaurant with green plants galore and a fine panorama; waterfront terrace; Barracuda nightclub in basement; rooftop saunas with plate-glass windows; the best units facing the harbor; 7 suites with accordion door dividers; light but small baths throughout. All in all, here's a very good house.

The **Marski** is in the forefront of the 14 Polar hotels or restaurants in the city. Main bar in lobby corner; copper-ceilinged dining room with dance band until 11:30 P.M.; another vast, restaurant up one flight. Rooms with attractive pastel hues, comfortable furniture, and harmonious aura; all singles convertible to double occupancy. There are the swinging cellar-sited M Club and a thoughtfully planned dining scheme which allows ½-pension guests to eat meals at any of the metropolis' other Polar hostelries or dining places. Still among the best.

The **Hesperia**, adjoining the Intercontinental and officially rated Delùxe, disappointed us sadly on our rounds. Main restaurant plus a Steakhouse and Coffee Corner; subterranean nightclub with submarine atmosphere; a quartet of saunas, a gym and a swimming pool; distinct focus on the "with it" mood throughout; level of maintenance substandard in our eyes. Finally, none of its choicest newer features or colors can possibly compensate to us for its miserably small-dimensioned accommodations. At best, we now rate it as middling (not even fair) for overnighters.

The **Palace** provides a magnificent harbor setting with a lovely sweep of the city and archipelago. Small, unimpressive ground-floor lobby; immense, snack-barish, window-wrapped Grill up one flight and open from 11 A.M. to 11 P.M. except Saturdays; luxurious, popular tenth-floor dining room with red (not blue) ribbon cuisine, and the little American Bar; saunas; charming Finnish-style décor on 9th floor. An excellent mooring.

The midcity **Vaakuna** is enjoying continuing success. Grill open until midnight; penthouse bar and snackery; Scotch Bar; 2 saunas; rich dark-wood singles; grandly modern Presidential Suite; good baths. We like the touches of art in the lodgings and the Sunday movies for children.

The **Helsinki** is owned by the same burgeoning SOK group. In our evaluation, it is a fair but not outstanding choice. If you want its best double, try for a so-called "superior" accommodation. Sirius nightclub open until 3 A.M.; excellent 9th-floor sauna. On the routine side.

The **Olympia**, 10-minute haul from the center, shares the building with the Sport Palace. Pleasant 308-seat dance-restaurant enlivened by multicolored umbrellas hanging from the ceiling; self-service Grill in basement; 2nd-floor bar which we viewed as ugly; pool and sauna; bowling alley; lone concrete tennis court; overcrowded, undersized lobby. Cozy quarters with uptight baths or showers; service almost an unknown quantum. Fair—but only if you speak Finnish and are reasonably self-sustaining.

The **Ursula** is close to the Meri, but without the same glorious waterfront view. Chinesey avant-garde lobby; clinical breakfast room; bedchambers that fairly sparkle with cleanliness and flair; colorful touches of plaids, blues, and orange. Again, fundamentally austere and do-it-yourself, but not at all bad for hard-line budgeteers.

The **Torni**, an old, old-timer, has been partly converted from a wretched relic to a half-refinished enterprise, at which level it apparently will remain. Its galaxy of dining places and oases is unusual, versatile, and interesting. This architectural rabbit warren willingly gets our dining and drinking business—but overnighting? Never.

Although in our view none of the following wins blue ribbons for excellence, here's the way we'd rate the rest of the pack: **Seurahuone** (refreshed while retaining its old style), **Klaus Kurki, Hospiz (YMCA), Perho, Academica,**

Satakuntatalo, and, out of town, the **Otaniemi.** We are not familiar with the Hotel **Uusimaa** or the Hotel **Metro** under their revised ownerships.

In Helsinki's suburbs, the **Torppa** (frequently lengthened to Kalastajatorppa) forms the nidus of what is probably the most imposing and impressive hotel-restaurant complex in Finland. It is 3 miles from midcity—a 15-minute ride by Tram #4 to the end of the line—overlooking a fetchingly serene lake. The original structure is the gloriously beautiful but overrated Kalastajatorppa ("Fisherman's Hut"). Disappointingly small, garish-modern lobby; amiable little sunken bar adjoining; cheerful breakfast-café room to rear; long hike to the Round Room for dining and dancing and the Red Room nightclub; 2 pools; 4 saunas, including the so-called VIP for 10 people; gym, hairdresser, and barber. Massive Presidential Suite plus 9 smaller ones; most bedchambers facing the water, some in the "old" hostelry; all singles front the woods. Overall, here's a laudable addition to knowledgeable innkeeping in the capital area.

The young **Korpilampi** is an 18-mile run each way. Because so patently it was designed for conventioneers rather than for individual travelers, with 4 congress halls and a restaurant for 800, we believe its appeal is moot.

Out at *Tapiola*, the **Tapiola Garden** provides modern compact shelter, a pool, a sauna, and 2 dining decks. The fundamentals are here, but we feel that it's too far from the bright lights.

Restaurants Leading the parade of *independent restaurants without dancing* is **Motti** (Töölöntorinkatu 2). Smooth, soothing, subdued décor; split-level floor plan; comfortable black leather chairs; flowers and lamps softly enhancing the settings. Cuisine excellent, with service to match; all maîtres English-speaking, but menus (and waitresses) in the patois of Finland and Sweden only; 11 A.M. commencement weekdays (noon on Sun.) to 1 A.M. each morn. A tasteful delight in every way. Top recommendation.

White Lady (Mannerheimintie 93) happens to strike us (you might disagree, of course) as one of Motti's closest rivals. About 10 minutes out; windowed-terrace scheme with cascades of ivy; greenery cunningly upstaging the chef for attention; napery whiter than Lapland in March; Musical Department nightly from Mr. Steinway. Extra-savory morsels exquisitely presented; multitude of selections seldom found in Scandinavia; lunch noon to 4 P.M.; dinner 4 P.M. to 7 P.M., with à la carte until 1 A.M.; *closed Saturday and Sunday*. Although still excellent, we did not find it up to the standards of previous visits.

König (Mikonkatu 4, just off the Esplanade, 5 minutes' stroll from the Hotel Marski) is strategically paced by ex-runner Runar ("Pixen") Björklöf, the renowned ½-miler. Today, in strikingly attractive and tasteful contemporary garb, is what used to be a favorite haven of Sibelius and ranking artists of the turn-of-the-century. Charming bar down one flight; excellent cuisine. Try the Pheasant Titania if in season. Probably the most expensive midday (not dinner) stop of all, but an 18-karat joy. ALWAYS booked at peak hours, so reserve in advance.

Havis Amanda (Unioninkatu 23) is widely rated as a contender for the ranking fish and seafood restaurant in the capital. This cellar boasts an ingratiating deluxe tavern ambience. Its prize freshwares are in a counter display at the entrance. Here is expensive but superb cookery in an artful, tasteful setting. Highly recommended.

Savoy (Eteläesplanadi 14), an aerie atop a midtown office building, offers a sophisticated atmosphere highlighted with stress-form plywood furniture designed by Alvar Aalto; white-brick and timber surroundings; brass lamps over flower settings; international cookery intertwined with local fare. We especially liked the Forsmac (minced lamb and herring, served at lunchtime only with a potato baked in salt—but DON'T eat the jacket!). Reserve your chair between noon and 2 P.M. or from 7 P.M. to 10 P.M.

Royal (Esplanaadikatu 2), at the park end of the Swedish Theater, features a lovely alfresco terrace for seasonal munching plus a formal dining room. Beyond this nucleus, facing the greensward and the heart of the city, is the semienclosed, opaque-glass-roofed patio. Cuisine good but not outstanding; service warm; expensive, but delightful under the Arctic sunlight. Half of it turns into the Royal Club in the evening.

Restaurants with dancing at night? **Kappeli** ("Chapel") is a culinary monument near the sea end of the Esplanade, sited on the park which centers this apex boulevard of the city. Pleasantly subdued main establishment in long, high-ceilinged room with windows top to bottom on 3 sides; sizable, lovely open terrace for warm weather consumers; separate café adjoining; Taverna in cellar with lower prices; table d'hôte and à la carte menus at high tariffs. If there is a single landmark restaurant in the nation which virtually every traveled Finn knows, here it is. Sound but not spectacularly fine cuisine in delightfully historic surroundings.

Kalastajatorppa ("Fisherman's Hut"), which we've mentioned previously, is next in national and international fame. Physically it is an epitome of spaciousness and graciousness. However, over a period of many, many years not one of our Creative Team has ever had as much as a satisfactory meal in what is surely one of Finland's most expensive dining establishments—and the latest one was the worst.

Espilä (Fredrikinkatu 56) lures funlovers up a staircase lined with a map of Europe, highlighting beer mugs, national dancers, and everything except the family Maytag. We can't say much for its locally touted hors d'oeuvres or standard lunch, but as a nocturnal choice it can be very lively when gaiety reigns. Operable 7 P.M. to 3 A.M. (Sun. 4 P.M. to midnight), so go early; shows 10 P.M., 11 P.M., and midnight; shuttered Mondays. Swingingest joint in town.

Kaivohuone (Kaivopuisto), or "Well Room," occupies the top of a small knoll in a parkland setting. Unhappily, it still leaves us as cold as a 90-year-old Lapp's libido. Our late light bite was gnashingly costly for the niblets presented to us. With them came the worst cabaret we've witnessed since our last grammar school variety show.

Fennia (Mikonkatu 17) offers a spacious, airy, lozenge-shape salon paneled with compressed seaweed to absorb the din of revelry and painted red to match everything else in the room—including the clients' eyeballs. We don't know the fare, but we *do* like the roominess and aura of this haven. Brief floor shows 10 P.M. and 1 A.M.; rollicks best after 10:30 P.M.; doors part at 7 P.M. and swing shut at 3 A.M.; clusters of finely formed Finnish females (not attached to the house) on tap for a jig and a jug; operative summers. Discounting strictly dancing spots such as Teatteri Grilli or M Club, this is definitely, to our taste, *the* leading light among the cabaret-restaurants.

Adlon (Fabianinkatu 14) sham-facedly says "hello" with a phonyed up medieval mien, a red-brick courtyard, and fake little semicircular balconies around its upper periphery. Through another door is the principal hall in 1920-ish décor. Lunch in the bar Monday through Friday; remains a host until 3 A.M. The bar to starboard is one of the chummiest and most tasteful drinking troughs in Helsinki, in contrast to its big-time emporium.

M Club, downstairs in the Marski Hotel, is usually packed with funloving Jet Setters, Finnish species. Long, narrow basement room; service harassed, haphazard, and perspiring (but cordial); supper snacks available; open every night from 9 P.M. to 4 A.M.. Very active, fashionable, and steep.

Safari Club (Eerikinkatu 14) has an African décor with bamboo walls, a mounted leopard skin, and similar accoutrements; small additional grill where the clients can cook their own steaks. Extremely popular for dancing—but please forget the fare.

Sillankorva (Pitkänsillanranta 3) is another candidate in the Marski ménage. This one, coolishly modern in décor and atmosphere, is extremely popular for evening meals. Businessmen flock here for midday nutrition. But the Suomi concept of dining in a big, brightly illuminated hall that is noisy, bustling, and totally lacking in intimacy somehow doesn't reach our sense of pleasure. While the food and prices are in order, we just can't buy it.

The adjoining **Mobile** is something else. We like it a lot for evening revels. (No one goes here chiefly to dine.)

The **Bellevue** (Rahapajankatu 3) leans toward Russian specialties. Small tables; about 80 seats; intimate aura.

The popular **Arkadia** (Fredrikinkatu 48) is dominated by a highly commercial ambiance. Highly regarded, but not by us.

On our visit, **Ostia** (Hämeentie 33), in one of the modest districts of town, seemed to have corralled every no-necked hick south of St. Nick's capital. We found enough noise to shatter the contents of a large glass factory. If you go, bring your brass knucks and jet-ground-crew earmuffs.

Casino (Kulosaari/Brändö, a 15-minute taxi ride from the center) is presented on the rocks. Magnificent seascape view; rollicking summer bounce. Better order a table in advance; occasional shows presented.

The **Sirius**, in the Helsinki Hotel, creates an enticing atmosphere. Its greatest appeal is to young romantics who are well mannered, well dressed, and well heeled.

In the *miscellaneous category,* **Orfeus** (Yrjönkatu 30) is a tiny cellar with piano titillations after dark. Settings for about 70; baby bar; inexpensive lunch and dinner. Well respected. For Russian calories, hop onto tiny **Troika** first, followed by **Kasakka** or **Saslikki**, all comrades under the same garlic-scented proprietary banner. **Budapest**, in one of the least savory parts of the capital, is chiefly for the younger set. Upstairs mostly for college-age pickups; downstairs restaurant. So-so cookery; ho-hum ambiance. **Esplanaadikappeli** is handy to the flower market; moreover it now blossoms the year around. **Fazer** (Kluuvikatu 3), a sort of English tearoom, is the IN-most cozy corner for— what else?—tea. Light bites, beer, and wine also; mostly for ladies, who love it. There's a newer branch in the City Center, but the original is more our cuppa. As for other candidates, this book does NOT recommend **Vaakuna**, **Elite**, **Pub Angleterre**, **Tullin Puomi**, or the **HOK** to any North American traveler.

In the hotel league, the miniparade of restaurants and bars in the **Torni** merit special attention. All except the large, striking, ground-level American Bar are small and cozy, with garbs ranging from pleasant to extraordinary. Main restaurant standard; Spanish Grill with Iberian kitchen; Balkan Grill featuring kebab, goulash, paprika, and sobbing violins. The twin stars are the 13th-floor, 3-room Panorama Restaurant with 15 tables, a charming aspect, and a grand sweep of the city—and, up a long, old-fashioned circular staircase, the tiny, winsome, 36-seat Artists' Bar. While the quality of all of the fare is not gastronomic and the hotel itself is far from what it should be, this dining labyrinth is normally worth a visit.

The comestibles at the **Intercontinental** are solid but stereotyped. Its showcase is the rooftop Ambassador Club, with dance orchestra, bar, and medium-to-high tariffs. Paradoxically we happen to find more enjoyment in its ground-level Brasserie.

The **Hesperia**? Sorry, but we find the food here routinely uninspiring.

Inexpensive dining? **Chez Marius** (Mikonkatu 1) is so tiny that one Finnish wag quipped, "There's no room for dancing. The idea here is to keep breathing." French cuisine tenderly administered by M. Marius Raichi, formerly of the local film industry and an Oscar-winning personality. No alcohol; *lunch only!!!* Reserve in advance. **Fen Kuan** (Eerikinkatu 14) offers such startling Finno-Ugric delights as Nasi Goreng and Sukiyaki. Not the Oriental recipes to which we Occidentals are accustomed, but nevertheless a sweet-and-sour treat in this northerly clime. Snack-lovers will probably enjoy the coffee shop atmosphere of such chain operations as **Café de Colombia** and **Primula**.

Two excursion points? **Dipoli**, near the Fisherman's Hut, about 3 miles out of town, is popular with the Younger Set. It is owned by the Student Union of the Technological University. Strikingly modern design and decorative concepts; dimly lighted; with-it orchestra; cookery fair to good.

The **Valhalla** ("Old Sea Fortress") occupies part of an eighteenth-century bastion on the archipelago island of Suomenlinna. Short ferry ride from Market Square; hourly departures. Small café for light bites (no lunch in the fort); open from 5 P.M. to 1 A.M., when the straits are navigable; continental cuisine for dinner; dancing within the embrace of its ancient stone walls. *It is open only during the summer.* As a change of pace, worth the trip.

For pickup pickin's, the best hunting grounds in the metropolis are **Espilä**, **Kaivohuone**, and **Fennia**.

Prostitution scarcely exists in Finland. Since there is virtually no discrimination by gender (*e.g.,* 80% of the dentists are women), practically no female needs to solicit to make a living. Whatever exists is done almost exclusively for fun.

In restaurants—not bars or nightclubs—don't be surprised if your eyesight begins to fail in the wee hours, because in most establishments the houselights are blinked 45 minutes before closing. This is your signal to reorder.

Outside the capital, your best bet for dining will probably be your hotel. In most Finnish hostelries, however, full or demipension is not required.

★ **TIPS** Here it pays the toper to review his ABC's. Restaurants with "A" rights are licensed to serve all categories of spirits. Those with "B" classification serve only wines. All "C" category spots limit their libations to lager. These certifications generally parallel their respective price brackets with ceilings imposed by the government.

The separate service charges on your bills add only a soothing 13.5% of your total. Waiters are seldom given more than 50¢. (see "Tipping").

Now for a startler: Most First-class dining establishments open their portals at II A.M. All—except those which also feature nightclubs—have a thriving business by high noon. Standard dinner menus blossom as early as 4 P.M. and wane by 8 P.M. But now the warning: Then, and for the rest of the evening, you must pay those astronomical Finnish prices—everything, of course, on an à la carte basis.

Most menus are printed in the 2 official languages: Finnish and Swedish. A few progressive restaurateurs now add French, English, or German, depending upon their clientele. Incidentally, the lower-case letters "x.à." following the name of a dish mean "2 portions minimum."

Always go late to savor Helsinki night life (except to Espilä, which wraps up the evening at I A.M.). The gear shifts of merriment seldom mesh into overdrive before II P.M.—and from then onward, they're off and racing.

Odd Finnish law: (a) Nobody who shows even a clue of having consumed so much as a teaspoonful of Fletcher's Castoria can be admitted to any night spot—the explanation for the clusters of drunks or semidrunks outside the entrances late in the evening. (b) BUT once inside, practically speaking, there is no limit to the quantities permitted to be swallowed. That is why you'll see these 6-fisted Finnish topers getting ⅞ths embalmed once they reach the inner sanctum.

Shopping Shopping is a delight here. The Finnish eye for form and flair for originality are so exciting that in many creative fields the Finns surpass their northern neighbors. Our ★ ★ ★ ★ ★ candidates are individually noted.

In this metropolis, you might find it expedient to drop in at the **Finnish Design Center** (Kasarmikatu 19) before proceeding to its stores. In its 3 small, rather barren rooms, some of the nation's greatest artists and artisans display their masterpieces. You cannot purchase a single item here—but this nonprofit organization will direct you to any appropriate atelier or retailer to which you have taken a fancy.

Weaving: ★ ★ ★ ★ ★ **Metsovaara** (Mannerheimintie 42, near the Intercontinental) displays beautiful Finnish prints, woven textiles, and other treats. Ask for Mrs. Gronstrand. They also operate a bargain shop with their fabrics at Abrahaminkatu 6. **Vuokko** (Pohjoisesplanadi 25 and Fabianinkatu 12) offers textiles in natural fibers designed by Eskolin-Nurmesniemi for dresses, skirts, and decorating use.

Knockout Finnish jewelry: At ★ ★ ★ ★ ★ **Galerie Björn Weckström** (Fredrikinkatu 24) we flipped when we saw its gloriously conceived and crafted creations. The distinctive style of its Lapponia pieces for men and women combines thousands of years of jewelers' art with the stunningly original, world-famous designs of Björn Weckström, Poul Havgaard, and Juhani Linnovaara. Downstairs can be found their dramatic sculptures in bronze, acrylic, and glass. We rate this house as one of the very finest of its industry in the North. For Arctic gems, it's a tossup between ★ ★ ★ ★ **Kaunis Koru Oy** and ★ ★ ★ ★ **Kaj Erling Oy**, both of which are off the lobby of the Intercontinental Hotel. Unusual and distinguished stocks; competitive prices; spectrolites and other semiprecious stones mined above the Arctic Circle; wide range from inexpensive to fairly costly. **Kalevala Koru** (Keskuskatu 4) specializes in reproductions of ancient Finnish designs in silver and bronze. On its 2nd floor there's a sizable handicrafts section with reindeer-skin rugs, door chimes, rugs, sweaters, and additional lures.

Fashion: Widely heralded **Marimekko** has reduced its operation to only 2 retail outlets: Marimekko Oy (Pohjoisesplanadi 31), the main store in which you will find ready-made clothes and fabrics, and Marimekko (Tunturikatu 1) for seconds.

Crystal, porcelain, and ceramics: In its handsome and r-i-c-h showroom at Pohjoisesplanadi 25, Arabia has combined with Sweden's Rorstrand to form the ★ ★ ★ ★ **Arabia Rorstrand Center**. The former contributes the glass and porcelain and the latter the ceramics. In flair and elegance, it is in the Very First Rank. Costly and lovely.

Strikingly attractive bathwear and sauna equipment: Within the small and charming premises at Mannerheimintie 22–24, the ★ ★ ★ ★ **Sauna-Soppi-Shop** has the biggest collection of sauna-related articles we have ever seen—even including the hot boxes themselves. Its colorful and very fetching ancillary line, which can also be used in the home, at the pool, or on the beach, provides much greater interest to the average visitor. Write to kindly Kaija Rasi for its little pamphlet and price list. Cheers!

Department Store: World-famous **Stockmann** (Aleksanterinkatu) is Finland's largest retail operation—a northern Saks-Field's-Magnin's-Macy's rolled into one. This landmark, with branches in *Tempere, Turku,* and *Pietarsaari,* for more than a century has been a national institution. If you're in a rush you can centralize all of your marketing here, with an English-speaking guide to help you. Its Finnish arts and crafts are especially fine.

Open-air market: From 7 A.M. to 1 P.M., the wonderful **Kauppatori Market Square** at the harbor bristles and bustles with stalls and throngs. You'll find flowers, vegetables, fish, wearing apparel, small articles of furniture, paintings —just name it or spot it, and it's yours. Go early to savor the best of its delightful color.

Things NOT to buy include the following: Imported items, gold, leather goods, and many paper products carry exorbitant price tags. Due to such high-quality standards versus such low production quotas, an increasing supply of cheap "handicrafts" are imported from Japan or Germany—so make sure their source is Finnish before you shell out your beans.

Shopping hours: Weekdays, 8:30 A.M. to 5 P.M. except 8 P.M. on Mon. and Fri.; Sat., 8:30 A.M. to 4 P.M. in winter except 3 P.M. closings in summer.

Dedicated shophounds? Space is too tight here for further listings—so consult the purse-size '81 edition of *Fielding's Selective Shopping Guide to Europe* for more stores, more details, and more lore.

AULANKO,   3 miles from Sibelius' birthplace of Hämeenlinna, is the most glittering sapphire in the bracelet of western lakes. This is a lodestar for the holiday-minded—accessible by car (slightly over an hour on the highway from Helsinki), by train, or by the Silver Line water coach that glides between Hämeenlinna and Tampere. Capital-ists swarm here for its wide range of summer and winter sports activities—as well as p. and q. The **Hotel Aulanko** boasts private baths, a so-so restaurant for 700 clients, a bar, 3 saunas, and a resident orchestra. The **Youth Hostel** at Lake Aulangonjärvi affords more modest shelter for the overflow summer throngs. To gild the lily, there's a daily lake cruise for the restless—restaurant aboard—which touches other nearby beauty ports.

HAIKO   Refer to "Helsinki Sightseeing."

HAMEENLINNA   Refer to "Helsinki Sightseeing."

HANKO,   a sleepy seacoast town, draws the elite to savor its southern summer charms. For overnighters it offers the delightful little **Regatta Hotel**. Since its proprietor owns a TV factory, all of its 34 rooms are equipped with his latest models. Felicitous décor; swimming pool; high but not exorbitant tariffs for the value. Exceptionally good.

JYVÄSKYLÄ   is the northern harbor for the 3-hour hydrofoil cruise up the lake from Lahti. Many structures of this unusually eye-appealing town were blueprinted by the late, globally celebrated Professor Alvar Aalto.

If you wish to linger, the **Rantasipi Laajavuori Hotel** has its limitations. Only fair. The young **Cumulus**, part of a cooperative group, has ordinary, clean, middle-quality standards throughout. Summer-only hostelries include the 84-room **Laajavuoren Kesähotelli** and the 264-unit **Rentukka**. All others here are small, simple, and Spartan.

KEMIJÄRVI   is proud of the 70-room **Suommu**, which boasts a dining room with the Arctic Circle running right through its middle. Handmade furnishings; facilities for winter and summer sports. Since this one is an architectural duplicate of a herdsman's hut, it classifies as a real Lapp-warmer.

KUOPIO   is the touristic capital of the Eastern Lake District. Here is the jumping-off point for the renowned lake excursions. Dominating the settlement is a big hill that is crowned by a tower with a revolving restaurant. Try to visit this center, if you can, in the January Market Days. (The stands in Market Place function year around on weekdays and are fun for visiting, too.) The curious, unique, and legendary Greek Orthodox church and monastery near Kuopio (its museum is in the city proper) is worth a special journey— especially in benign wheather when you can do it by boat.

The region has sparse pickings for the pampered. The **Cumulus** is tops, followed by the **Atlas**. The **Puijonsarvi** is commercial and routine. The **Kalla** and the **Kaupunginhotelli** are lower-ranking also-rans. The **Iso-Valkeinen** is situated just outside the town. A **Polar Hotel** probably will be functioning in time for your hibernation.

LAHTI, a 65-mile inland ride from the capital, was a market crossroads for hundreds of years. Because of its youth, and consequent adaptability, architecturally it is a Design for Tomorrow. One of its key attractions is the twice-daily hydrofoil service up the lake to Jyväskylä. The one-way ride takes 3 hours, and it is so lovely in good weather that it shouldn't be missed.

Among its shelters, the town offers the much improved **Seurahuone**, on its main street. Pleasant restaurant; 120 rooms; worthy. **Valtakulma**, **Mustakissa**, and **Jukola** are our next picks in this heavily traveled but disappointingly hotel-poor community.

LAPLAND The tourist lodestone which radiates the greatest color, magnetism, and fairy-tale fascination is, of course, Lapland. For the comfort-conscious and better-heeled, our top recommendation is the **Lapland North Cape Tour**. This flies you from Helsinki to Rovaniemi (Lapland's gateway; note that the airport's welcoming sign is spelled out in antlers), where you climb aboard a motor coach to strike out almost due north for Enontekiö. From here you proceed still farther north to Alta (how we love this world's-end settlement!) and finally to Ultima Thule—Hammerfest, Norway, the most northerly city in the world. After overnights here and at remote Inari, you are driven back to Rovaniemi, bedded down in the Polar Hotel, and flown back to Helsinki the following morning. This 7-day, 2-country junket departs every Sunday, Monday, and Wednesday from mid-June to mid-August. Highly recommended. Finnair's **Midnight Sun Flight**, which lasts a night and a day, leaves Helsinki every day from early June to early July, visiting Rovaniemi on the Arctic Circle.

For winter sportsmen, the facilities in Lapland are made-to-measure for rawboned pioneers of new slopes and resorts. *Rukatunturi*, a herringbone below the Arctic Circle in eastern Finland, boasts a slalom track, 3 lifts, lights on downhill runs, and the longest jumps in Scandinavia. For experts. *Pallastunturi*, mostly for beginners, provides a special Christmas program, including a gift from Old St. Nick—free skiing instructions. The Finnish Travel Association can fill you in. We've never tried 'em.

OULU, on the west coast about 400 miles due north of Helsinki, is the shopping, trading, medical, and educational matrix for thousands of square miles of hinterland. It draws mainly business traffic.

The fresh **Vaakuna**, while not at all spectacular, is now definitely the number one hotel in the region. The **Tervahovi** is the only other hostelry worth your patronage—at least in our opinion. The **Kauppahotelli** caters more for local tastes. The **Arina** has possibilities but needs a lot of work before they can be exploited.

PALLASTUNTURI   Refer to "Lapland."

PORI,   peaking the isosceles triangle 70 miles above its base of Tampere and Turku, is another west-coast port for the wealthy farming country surrounding it. Very few foreigners pause here, unless $$$$ are involved. If you do wish to bide awhile, try the **Juhana Herttua** ("Duke John"). We hear that this 55-unit house is conveniently situated, pleasantly staffed, and very good. The newer **Cumulus** has come up with 54 rooms with bath or shower, a pool, a sauna, and a cellar restaurant. The **Rantasipi** beckons from the dunes of *Yyteri Beach*, a delightful location for a resort hotel, but its amenities are unknown to us. Its chain, however, is a recommendable one in general. The **Satakunta** and **Otava** are yet 2 other reasons why we must hop out to Pori when the thaws come.

PORVOO   Refer to "Helsinki Sightseeing."

ROVANIEMI,   less than 10 miles below the Artic Circle, is known as the official gateway to Lapland. Still, it's a long way south of the main ranges and camping sites of the Lapps and their reindeer herds. The renovated 350-room **Pohjanhovi** ("Nordic Court") with its river-side site and savory cookery is the leader. The internationally famous **Polar Hotel** is looking more and more well-used. Book as far ahead as possible. The **Motel Ounasvaara** rolls out a jumbo-size restaurant and 38 pedestrian accommodations. You've braked at better. (Sportsmen, incidentally, might be interested in the Polar's 10-person, log-lined **Bear's Den**, a guest lodge 18 miles north on the shores of *Karhujärvi*, which translates as "Bear Lake.") Refer also to "Lapland."

RUKATUNTURI   Refer to "Lapland."

SAVONLINNA   Our lead-off choice is the **Spa Casino** with its modern mien and cure facilities. Then we'd select the vastly refashioned and enlarged **Tott** over the 32-room **Seurahuone**. Their rates are about the same, but neither will call back the wraith of César Ritz bearing a silver salver in homage.

TAMPERE,   109 miles northwest of bottom-situated Helsinki and encompassed by lakes, is 2nd in size. This so-called Pittsburgh of Finland, despite heavy industry, is a green city replete with parks. It's proud of a 1000-seat outdoor auditorium which revolves somewhat less rapidly than a merry-go-round in season only.

The **Polar**, not far from the Summer Theater with its famous revolving auditorium, is geared for the congress rather than the individual trade. The **Tammer**, in town, is much more handily situated. Old-fashioned English colonial ambience; pleasant but not great. **Kaupunginhotelli**, centrally located, has smaller rooms but service on the same friendly par; not exciting but clean and adequate. The renovated **Victoria** is quite a substantial medium-bracket entry. **Hospiz Emmaus**, with 240 rooms, is YMCA-operated and—as usual— as dry as a squeezed and sunbaked salted herring. *All* genders of clients accepted; restaurant absolutely miserable; loaded with cheap tour groups from Eastern-bloc countries; not for any wayfarer who demands his or her amenities.

TAPIOLA   Refer to "Helsinki."

TURKU, a skip and a jump due west of Helsinki, is Finland's cultural center, its oldest city (it was the Finnish capital for 6 centuries), original seat of its tradition-rich A.D. 1640 university, home of its thirteenth-century Cathedral, 9 museums, 3 summer theaters, 2 concert halls, and an important passenger port for Sweden. Shipbuilding, foodstuffs, and ceramics lead its commerce. The Handicraft Museum, one of the few building complexes to survive the great fire of 1827, is especially worth visiting.

The youthful **Marina Palace**, standing on the western bank of the Aura River in the center of the city, is one of the best hotels in the nation, with unusually high standards of quality. Quietly dramatic architecture and furnishings; fully air-conditioned; lounge for drinks or snacks; cellar Submarina nightclub with dancing; window-wrapped Aura Marina Restaurant with live music and terpsichore; Riverside Grill, 41-foot pool, and 4 saunas; open-air Sunmarina Restaurant in summer. Its 12 suites and 164 rooms are tastefully executed in warm colors. The **Ikituuri** teems with so many business people in action, we cannot recommend this one. The venerable **Seurahuone/Societetshuset** has a split Finnish-Swedish official name which in local English nomenclature is "Sausage House." Delightfully cozy bar; excellent cookery with special accent on seafood; thoughtful, warm service; 55 rooms which (if not reconstructed) tend to be larger than the competition's. We think you might like it, too. The **Hamburger Börs** has been extensively remodeled and refurnished. The tasteless, unattractive **Turku** is a pale turkey bustling with conducted tours. The **Ruissalo** is a clean-lined, fresh-faced sea-sider which to us resembles a block of studio apartments. **Domus**, a student dormitory in winter which becomes a 70-room hotel in summer, could scarcely be more basic—but WHAT a bargain! The American Holiday Inn-keepers might now have action here.

France

F or 13 centuries the French have offered the world a puzzling, provocative personality, as multiple and unpredictable as a psychiatric patient. You'll be baffled by the combination of emotion and logic. There's a conflict between generosity and niggardliness, idealism and cynicism, fieriness and apathy, gaiety and shrewdness, which can be found in no other civilized people. If you are able to understand the age-old, mercurial, Gallic temperament, you'll find that this national group can be highly stimulating companions and wonderfully loyal, durable friends, with warmth and hospitality which will overwhelm you.

Our own most recent *tours de France* have been by far the happiest we've personally experienced in years. The people-in-the-street have seemed motivated by amity rather than animosity. We found them phenomenally ready to give of themselves to the stranger from abroad.

April in Paris can be lovely—but August in Paris, except for the howling mobs of foreign tourists, is as dead as last week's lobster soufflé. This is the time of the *congé payé*, when approximately 1¾-million Parisians pack their bags, suntan oil, and mosquito lotion, and swarm from the capital like lemmings to the sea. At the Spanish frontier early last August, motorists sat at their wheels for 5 hours waiting in line to cross the border. French labor unions legalized this paid vacation some years ago. It caught on so successfully that if it weren't for the floodtide of outlanders, the capital would be a semi-ghost-town for 31 days. A feeble effort has been made to stagger the nation's time-off periods, but to date it has met with little success. As you might expect from these quixotic citizens, most agree it's a grand idea—"as long as *you* do it, not me!"

Despite major, laudable, and continuing reforms and streamlining, French bureaucracy and red tape will drive you out of your mind. It's even worse than Darkest Washington. The Government is the top employer, siphoning off an incredible 17% of the total industrial work force and a vast number of civil servants who yawn away their days as official charges. They control ⅓ of all buying and selling within the nation—virtually an economic stranglehold.

Don't ever be foolish enough to set out bravely but alone to redeem a railway ticket, pick up a postage-due package, or fight through any official transaction; before being waved away at 23 windows on 16 different floors, exhaustion and frustration will utterly consume you. If you can't persuade your hotel concierge or some innocent dupe to play patsy for you on administrative chores, it's a lot easier and more sensible to forget them.

Wherever you roam on the Old Continent, the *International Herald Tribune* will be your faithful informant and companion. This cosmopolitan publishing landmark is far zippier, fresher, and more readable than any other English-language newspaper abroad. From Bergen to Lisbon to Athens to Davos to Ruritania, direct your hotel concierge to deliver it to your room daily. To thousands of news-starved wanderers, including us, it's the best penny-for-penny investment in Europe.

☑ **TRANSPORTATION Taxis** At night, when it rains, during meal hours, and at the peak of the rush, Paris' 14,500 taxis are as elusive as ever. From the discovery of the internal combustion engine until a few years ago, cabbies just plain quit as soon as the clock struck lunch or dinner. But now, legally at least, they're supposed to take *you* where you want to go , instead of only in the direction of their garage, mistress, or home. Unhappily, the brutes usually won't, and few additional vehicles seem to be available during these key periods.

There are set fees for the airports (and don't let them charge you for the return leg to the city, which is included in the lump sum), the racetrack, and other suburban destinations, so be sure to check these flat rates to avoid a possible clip.

★ **TIPS** Stay away from large, luxurious taxis without meters which roam the gin-mill areas at night. They'll pry the fillings right out of your teeth!

If the chauffeur who takes you home demands an exorbitant price (very frequent after midnight), here's how to handle him: (1) Note and remember the sum on the meter, (2) give him your sweetest smile, (3) tell him you've got to break a 100-franc note with the hotel cashier, and (4) head straight for the concierge. Then explain the situation to this official and let *him* not only pay the legal amount but also spit in the bandit's eye with your compliments. (Your knowledge of the meter reading is important here, because if the concierge thinks you haven't checked it, *he* might bilk you too!)

Before climbing into any taxi in Paris, be sure that the meter is set at the starting rate (except if you've telephoned for the carriage, of course, when the pickup distance is separate). Otherwise you'll be paying for the last customer's ride in addition to your own. Especially widespread at night.

Don't be startled by the shaggy companion riding beside your driver. Many cabbies now enjoy the fellowship and protection of police dogs to discourage wheelborne criminality.

Trains The French National Railroads (SNCF), a state-controlled network that is 80% electrified, are among the best in Europe. They're also the fastest in the world, *averaging* more than 75 mph over 4250 miles daily, and more than 65 mph over 50-thousand miles. Regular routings also include 125 mph cannonballing along numerous strips of trackage. They link Lyon and Paris with a 185 mph zipper, switch in Geneva and the Savoy region at slightly slower speeds, and add on their extra-comfortable "Corail" service to major French destinations.

If you plan much train travel, take advantage of the Eurailpass, which we've earlier described in detail. France also offers The Vacances Pass for 7, 15, or 30 days at $95, $135, and $200 respectively in Second Class and $150, $200, and $300 in First. This is valid for unlimited rail travel but also provides some rides on the Métro, an airport hop, a museum entry, and free car rental for 1 day.

Fixed meals are served on diners, unspectacular in quality but reasonable in price. You may obtain reservations for 1st, 2nd, or 3rd sitting before departure on the platform in front of the restaurant car, or from the roving steward aboard. You may also be seated without prior arrangements after all reservations holders have been accommodated.

Better still for the budget rider, self-service, cafeteria-style "Cafés à Go-Go" on rails have been introduced. The average price was estimated to be 50% less than a normal repast in the traditional dining car.

There are 3 ways to sleep: Coach, couchette, and *wagon-lit.* The coach is for the birds. The couchette, a French development, offers 6 bunks per unit; you may stretch out but not undress. The *wagon-lit* is the Pullman of Europe; you'll pay for your (1) railroad ticket, (2) berth, (3) reservation, and (4) service tax. It's worth the difference! An improvement on this is the 18-pod (9 uppers, 9 lowers) "T2" car—a cozy his-and-hers arrangement available even with a Second-class rail ticket. The first ones made overnight scoots from Paris to—where else?—the Riviera.

If you are in a hurry to get yourself and your car across the English Channel, please turn to what we have to say about the new giant hovercraft; you'll find it in "Other Targets" under "Calais," one of the principal ports.

Increasingly the French are employing the "turbotrain"—a fan-driven fuselage riding on a cushion of air and directed by a T-shape track. These streakers zip along the Strasbourg–Lyons, Tours–Nantes–Limoges–Bordeaux routes, ultimately to whoosh to Marseille.

Nine separate stations in Paris, spread all over the map. Eliminate the baggage transfer headache by using the *Transit Cloakroom Service,* which connects the 3 main depots. Cost: 2 F for each piece, for pickup on departure at the station cloakroom. Double-check your terminus before consigning your bags, and check again before leaving your hotel.

Redcaps are bluecaps, and are addressed as "porteur." Although there is a fixed fee for each bag, they will *always* expect an extra tip to top it. If your suitcases are too large, they must be deposited in the rack at the end of the car. Make sure they are placed there, and then look again at major stations to be sure no "mistake" is made by a departing passenger.

Tickets are collected after you get off the train. Don't toss yours away, or you may pay double.

Reserve your seat when you purchase your passage. This precaution will cost you about an extra half-dollar (or $1 if you book it in the U.S.), but it's worth $200 not to be forced to fight the mobs.

A package deal called "Service Complet"—tickets, seats, diningcar space, sleeper, hired car, everything but love and beer—is also offered by the railroads. Your travel agent can fix this up for you too.

Except for the Eurailpass, tickets are valid for varying periods from 10 to 30 days. If your trip is postponed, make sure of the expiration date for the return trip to salvage your investment.

Once you buy a ticket, brother, you're stuck. They've never heard of immediate redemption; you'll wait 1 to 3 months for your money—and when you're back in America you'll get it in francs. French bureaucracy again of the most maddening sort.

★ **TIPS** If you prefer wings to rods, you may ride the rails between the Paris-North Station and Charles de Gaulle Airport in 35 minutes; this rail linkup runs every ¼-hour. There is also a rail link between Orly Airport and the Gare d'Orsay (with a stop at Austerlitz station). It runs every 15 to 30 minutes and takes 40 minutes.

Incidentally, while on the subject of airports, at Orly, blue-uniformed baggage handlers of the Elan company tried to extract tips from us on 4 separate arrivals for loading our luggage into the airport–town bus. Don't fall for it because they're already paid very well for operating this concession. But *do* be sure that they put your suitcase inside the bus before it grinds into first gear.

If you wish to fly around the country on a 7-day ($177) or a 2-week ($275) basis, **Air-Inter** sells the service in the USA and issues its "pass" in France. Ask your travel agent how this money-saving scheme works.

☑ **FOOD** Terrific—if you can pay the price. Goodness knows, this will be p-l-e-n-t-y —but in no other place in the world can you eat as well. And this year there are exhilarating changes in the aromatic wind.

The latest—and *what* a boon to the traveler on a budget!—is the rebirth and rapid growth of the *bistro* (see our separate section). Here the chefs reduce the number of selections to only a few well-prepared specialties, feature fixed menus, offer spectacular trays of rillettes, terrines, and other garniture for nibbling, and all at a price that you'd pay for only an appetizer in one of the 3-star establishments. A few gastronomic snobs may sniff scornfully at this trend (catching on like wild *feu* today in Paris), but we'll bet you a *Feuilleté de Homard* that you'll find some of France's most rabid critics waiting patiently in a long line to gain entry to a *bistro* when they can't justify writing off a more expensive meal on their expense accounts.

Girth-conscious chefs are now catering to slimmer waistlines among their svelte patronage. The amazing thing is that flavors remain intense or are even purer than in the classic richer preparations. This year every kitchen sorcerer and saucerer's apprentice will be undercooking at least a few showcase dishes and even serving some viands raw, only mellowed in natural impact by marinades. Strange invaders from the realms of botany and zoology are appearing on the fashionably larger plates (about 2½ inches greater in diameter than customary dinner service), while piscatorial preparations now are being ladled into wide shallow bowls. The trend is to have *everything* created and displayed by the chef, with less emphasis on the theatrical *flambé* flourishes by tableside maîtres. Kitchen kings scour and scout roadside weed patches in quest of fresh savory ingredients for new stews and soups; flour for sauces is no longer chic; specialities of the fifteenth century are being resurrected; and the alternation in color of items on today's colossal-size platters is almost as imperative as the gustation itself.

Women chefs—some of whom have resisted the new wave and scoff at the *innovateurs* by preserving French *cuisine de femme*—are as often on the tip of everyone's tongue as are their fine *beurres blancs* or zesty *pâtés*. Females are being accorded reluctant honors as master cooks in a country where male chauvinism dominates the professional ovens. Though the hesitant, still-feeble movement has only just begun, it is charged with the sort of controversy one might expect in a land that idolizes its nutrients as much as it prizes its womanhood—and from a population that adores debate on *both* of these topics. Anyway that you toss this spring-green salad, gastronomically speaking, France is more exciting today than it has been in many a year.

Truffles from Périgord, saffron from Langres, foie gras from Strasbourg, small duck foie gras or *confits d'oie* from Quercy, mustard from Dijon, mackerel from Nantes, hams from Bayonne, conserves from Normandy, 365 registered cheeses—all are unique. Even flowers are eaten—Tulip Stem Salad in the Eiffel Tower Restaurant (never go tulip picking on a holiday here, because it's a monumental crush!), Lime Blossom Poached Chicken in Lasserre's, Violets Soufflé in the Tour d'Argent, plus acacia-filled fritters and other novelties elsewhere.

If a dish is marked "à la Provençale" or "à la Niçoise," garlic and olive oil will raise their lovely, rugged heads.

Why don't more food writers in North America disclose the hugely important difference between foie gras and paté de foie gras? Because the latter is such a common item on menus, through lack of interest or ignorance, they have kept countless of our discriminating diners in the dark on this canyon of disparity. Of course, foie gras consists of 100% goose livers, often with a central vein or garnish of truffles. This, the real stuff, a Rolls-Royce among delicacies, is expensive even in France but shouldn't be missed. Prices, however, may topple before too long. Recently a way was found to "mass-produce" enlarged livers in these fowl, instead of force-feeding them by hand. A surgical approach destroys the area in the brain that controls hunger. Thus through auto-ingestion, the goose crams itself cockeyed by overindulging. Paté de foie gras (usually listed abroad as "Terrine de la Maison") is an individual house concoction which may contain herbs, nuts, the livers of chickens or other animals, veal, pork, or whatever the chef finds dormant in the kitchen. While the latter can be tasty, there is a vast difference between the two products—and as a loyal French gourmet would cry, "Vive la différence."

Whenever your tab is stamped "Service Not Included," make sure the waiter hasn't surreptitiously added the service charge anyway. Cafés along the Champs-Élysées are especially villainous in this practice.

You'll ask 6 times for a glass of water before you can sell the idea to the waiter. It upsets his stomach to watch you drink it. Many diners stick to the bottled variety. Order Évian if you want the noncarbonated type; Perrier is the classic carbonated one; Vichy, which comes in several types, is equally famous, a bit salty, and somewhat less effervescent. According to our French friends, all of these are therapeutic for everything from pinkeye to clubfeet. Tap water is *l'eau naturelle,* and—with Paris a question mark—it is relatively safe in French metropolises.

Because of a different roasting process, most U.S. travelers feel that French coffee should be used for filling O'Cedar bottles. It's bitter, it's different, but the quality, per se, is as fine as you'll find on the shelves of your gourmet foodshop at home. If your Nescafé runs out (it comes caffeine-free too), you can buy a fresh can at almost any French grocer. But if you don't want to bother about instant coffee, refuse the local offering the moment your gullet will no longer contract, and drink tea, as we do.

Restaurants More than 13,000 in Paris alone, with a fantastic range of specialties and prices. The smaller places may charge $8 to $14 for a delicious fixed-price meal; the larger ones usually run, on the same arrangement, from $18 to $35 per person; if you order à la carte in the Great Establishments, your dinner might go up even to $60 or $90 without pausing for breath.

In Paris, lunchtime customers in the costlier shrines are often businessmen on generous expense accounts. In the country it is still possible to dine well for a reasonable outlay. There are, of course, spectacular contradictions to such a broad statement as exceptionally fine establishments have popped up all over Gaul in recent years. The Lyonnaise and Burgundian regions are especially thick with costly gems. So is the more spotty Riviera, while splendid oases in Brittany and Périgod set magnificent tables for relatively low prices.

A while back inflation squelchers abolished the automatic cover charge (the price you paid for the privilege of eating with a knife, fork, spoon, and table linen) with triumphant political pomp. It was supposed to be replaced with an overall 10% increase—and that was to be the absolute limit. But this "control" is a sorry travesty, because it can never be enforced in a thousand years.

One way to beat the system—sometimes, at least—is to take advantage of the little-publicized *Restaurants de Tourisme* plan. Government-sponsored and promoted through the National Hotel and Restaurant Association, this setup offers a so-called Tourist Menu in every French establishment you're likely to visit; expansion to other Common Market countries is planned. Thus you may enter nearly any restaurant and be fed a full meal, including wine, service, and taxes, for about $4 to $10, depending upon the official category of the institution. In theory you won't be given pressed duck and Haut Brion '61 for this investment, but you will get a substantial and savory repast.

In practice, this scheme has 1 big pitfall: When the foreigner innocently orders the $3.50 dinner, he's all too likely to draw the table by the coal chute, the busboy for his waiter, and the Country Cousin treatment from his soup to his toothpicks. As for the Fielding team, we'd no more stroll into Tour d'Argent, Lasserre, Pyramide, or a similar gastronomic shrine and ask for the "Tourist Menu" than we'd make amorous cries to a wild moose—and we hope you wouldn't. The most common ploy everywhere is to present the à la carte menu without comment, thus forcing the client to ask for the blue-plate special. But if your appetite is on the light side, and you exercise discretion in time and place, it *is* an excellent plan, and it *can* save you a hatful of money. Don't confuse this advice as pertaining to the difference between the Chef's Menu and à la carte. The former *might* be cheaper (it often is), but it is a thoughtful blend of harmonious specialties that is sold for a fixed price. In the new restaurants of the great young chefs, we would recommend this package because it displays the rich spectrum of the cook's talents. Your motivation here, however, should be to broaden your gastronomic experience and pleasure, not specifically to economize.

If you're an August visitor in the capital, *check beforehand* to make certain your place is open. Hundreds of establishments shutter during the 31 days of the *congé payé* ("paid vacation") peak.

Finally—and this is IMPORTANT!!!—never, but *never,* get hooked by knavish taxi drivers (of whom there are many), who tell you the gastronomic shrine you have selected is "closed," "under repairs," or any similar guff. Their game is to steer you to an address where they can collect a commission—which almost certainly will be a joint. If you nail down your reservation in advance, then you're on solid ground to insist the hackie take you there and *only* there. This racket is deplorably prevalent in Paris today.

☑ **DRINKS** Each region proudly offers its own distinctive wine. If you're not particular (or if you're a tried-and-true traveler), much of the time you'll stick to *vin ordinaire,* the routine carafe table wine. It's eminently satisfactory.

Broadly speaking, it's *red* with meat or game, *white* with fish, fowl, oysters, or hors d'oeuvres. If the meat is heavy, gamy, or spicy, Burgundy is usually chosen over Bordeaux. Nowadays, if the Burgundy is a light one or if you are dining in a warm region such as the Rivieria in summer, the house often serves this red wine chilled. Personally we find it a bit put on and oenologically contrary, but each on to his own *goût*.

Never follow a sweet wine by a dry wine, or a heavy wine by a light wine.

Champagne is the only type correctly served through all courses of a meal. Have you ever tried Mumm's Cordon Rosé, the best of the celebrated "pink" varieties? Delicious! Never horrify discerning French by using a swizzle stick—a barbarity to many despite its recent comeback in fad circles; if you don't like its effervescence, take a dry white wine instead. And if the cork pops too loudly, the temperature is wrong; send it back, without delay, for further chilling.

In France's chic restaurants, the house apéritif today often is based on champagne, with an additive such as *cassis* or *framboise* to freshen the flavor—a jovial advance over the older *Kir* (chilled light white wine and cassis).

Add water to your ordinary table wine, if you choose (many people do it)—but never, never, *never* dilute a vintage of character.

When in France, (1) don't fill a wineglass up to its brim (the bouquet is hampered), and (2) leave a few drops at the end, even if they seem too good to waste (you might drink the harmless but unpleasant dregs).

As a result of the new "fast-aging" techniques, wine comes to maturity much earlier than in former times—the whites usually ahead of the reds. The 2 most recent vintages classified as "Exceptionnelle" are '75 and '61, with 66 closely behind; from '61 onward any year to '76 is "Très bonne" except '63, '65, '67,'68, '69, and '72. The "Grand" years of red Burgundy are '61, '64, and '66, with '62, '67, '69, and '76 also choice; avoid '63, '65, '70, '72 and '74, with '73 and '75 being the worst. White Burgundys generally follow the red pattern, save that '64 and '66 are notably poorer.

The top Rhônes are '61, '66, and '70; skip '63, '65, '68, '74, and '76. The Loire produced splendid beverages from '69 through '73, with the exception of '72; '74 also was poor down by that riverside except for Muscadet. For your champagnes, look for a dated bottle, because that is the signal from the producer that it is worthy of being identified by year. It is safer to sip a vintage younger than eight years old or so; beyond that, it can go off to the taste.

Here are our personal favorites among France's leading varieties. These are the very top classification, and they're expensive examples of their types:

Red Burgundy: Romanée-Conti
White Burgundy (dry): Chevalier-Montrachet
Red Bordeaux: Château Haut-Brion
Sauterne (very sweet): Château d'Yquem
Côtes-du-Rhône: Châteauneuf-du-Pape
Alsatian: Gewürztraminer
Rosé: Château Bellet
"Demi" Champagne: Crémant de Cramant

A special word about this last entry: Here is an elixir of great delicacy and rarity made by Mumm, so small in supply that it is sold or given as gifts only to pet restaurant proprietors of this topflight vintner. Halfway between a "full" and a "still" champagne in effervescence, it offers the connoisseur a lovely bouquet and just enough bubbles to add its very distinguishable tang and zest. Our plea: In some deluxe house where you know the *patron* well, sidle up and whisper in his ear—and *hope!*

Among the lower-price red wines, Beaujolais is usually an excellent bet, though fraudulent jugglings are becoming more prevalent in questionable establishments. It should be ordered young. Get either Brouilly, Moulin-à-Vent, Juliénas, Morgon, or Fleurie (the sub-names on the label) if you can. Other old standbys in this range are the less-exalted Bordeaux varieties of St.-Julien, St.-Emilion, Médoc, Pomerol, and St.-Estèphe. Unless you're gilded with gold sovereigns, these should be more than adequate for ordinary dining.

Among inexpensive white wines, Chablis is very tricky, due to minuscule supplies of sound types. If you like your whites dry, as most of us do, Pouilly Blanc Fumé, Pouilly-Fuissé, or Muscadet should do the trick without breaking the bank—and they are *delightful.* What passes for genuine Chavignol in many places today is horrid. But Traminer, from Alsace, still has an affinity for a good filet of sole. Algerian wines are no longer under French control. Consequently, they have swapped their potency (the sugar is vital) for acidity (necessary for aging). "French" table varieties, however, are cut as much as 50% with this African import or "strong" Italian or other "sunny" types; the higher alcohol content (which comes from sugar) is required to satisfy current tastes and pocketbooks. Today more and more bottles of low-grade foreign wines are finding their way onto Gallic grocery-store shelves—and perhaps even into the glass at your bistro's table.

Lasting favorites at tables around the world are:

Anjou	Chambertin (extra fine)
Beaune	Cheval-Blanc (extra fine)
Château Ausone	Corton
Château Lafite (extra fine)	Haut-Bailly
Château Latour (extra fine)	Hermitage
Château Margaux (extra fine)	Meursault
Clos d'Estournel	Pommard
Clos Fourtet	Richebourg (extra fine)

Naturally, this is only skimming the surface. There are scores more.

Order Vouvray or *vin mousseux* (sparkling wine) if you want to save money. Though cheaper than champagne, they have attractive similarities. Reason: The champagne name is patented, and these varieties originate outside the legal district.

Finally—and don't collapse if you see it—France now markets quality wine in *tin cans* (still in test market stage).

Whiskies from Scotland are plentiful. About 60 brands fight for the national market. Gordon-type gin goes for less money, of course (French varieties are awful); the import quota on bourbons and ryes is soaring to the point that the French are considering restoring the Bourbon dynasty.

Traditionally, a good buy always has been cognac, the national "hard" drink, spoken of as *fine* (feen). Lately, however, all of us on the European front have noticed a considerable falloff in quality, even among topline, highpriced brands. Why this might be so, none of us knows, but individually each person on our team has discerned a harshness of bouquet and a diminution of the former smooth mellowness. Delamain (our favorite) and Bisquit (not terribly expensive) both seem to be holding their own; so are a number of fine Armagnacs. But the aristocrats of the field are a puzzle to us nowadays. The people of Normandy are weaned on Calvados, a pungent applejack that can do wondrous things when it's old and warmed. True-blue Normands claim that if sipped between courses it "reams a hole in the belly to make room for more food." Grand Marnier is the standard cordial. Liqueurs such as Bénédictine, Crème de Menthe, Cointreau, Pernod, Crème Yvette, Crème de Cassis, Triple Sec, and Pastis are exclusively French; they are the originals, and all others are imitations or branches of the distilleries (Spain).

Most of the beer is frightful—bitter, watery, with an aftertaste of liver-fed pollywogs —but you'll see a lot of it because it's cheap. Fortunately, some Alsatian types ably contradict this statement. Always ask for "bee-air," because "beer" to the French waiter means "Byrrh," a popular red vermouth-type apéritif. (For serious quaffers of malt-and-hops, a benevolent publican now offers the brews of Gaul, Scandinavia, England, Belgium, Germany, Ireland, Luxembourg, Czechoslovakia, Japan, and several other nations in his recently tapped out brasserie named **Au Général La Fayette**, at 52 rue La Fayette in Paris.) Cocktails are often mixed with thimbles instead of legitimate shot glasses. In most international establishments they're expensive but excellent; in the average provincial hotel or restaurant, however, they're little in demand.

Psssst! Never tell a Frenchman this (he'll either deny it or reply with an uppercut!)

—but over the recent past, border-to-border tastes have been turning to fruit juices (a market increase of 85%) and mineral water (up by 34%). And how is *your* liver, Alphonse?

☑ **TIPPING** Every human being who serves you will proffer a hand with stunning rapidity. You can't beat the Egyptians, French, and Italians. They've got a unique nose for the gratuity. At the movies, if you don't tip, the usherette will probably flash her light into your eyes until you do—normal procedure, and nothing can be done about it! (Besides, her income is based on the alms she garners from you and not on the chicken feed she knocks down as "salary.") There's no use bucking the system. The French don't overtip the French as we do, but their own upper classes get taken too, because that's the tradition.

Hotels add up to 30% in service charges and taxes, depending on class and location. "Restaurants de Tourisme"—most of the better-known places fall into this official category—automatically take a 15% service bite (as previously mentioned, the cover charge has been officially abolished), to which Americans are expected to add another 5% to 7% for the waiter. Where this does not apply (read the bottom of the check), give the waiter 15% to 20%, the checkroom attendant 1 franc, the washroom attendant ½ to 1 franc, and the wine steward (if you use him) 2 francs. Taxi drivers get a franc or two, depending upon the length of the ride; hotel doormen (when calling a taxi) get about the same, ordinarily, and more if they go out in the rain to capture your vehicle.

At the theater you buy your program but you don't have to tip (if you don't mind getting a dirty look). The local residents strongly resent giving anything on top of the purchase price. The above-mentioned usherette gets 50 centimes—rigid custom—and the washroom attendant about equal.

Bartenders expect about 10% on each drink they serve you.

☑ **LOCAL RACKETS** Petty thievery is common. Don't leave *any* valuables in your hotel room; toss your cigarettes in your bag, and lock it. Watch your coat and hat in restaurants. In general, the French are an honest people but the incidence of chicanery, particularly in the cities, is high.

Automobile thievery has risen to shocking proportions. A high-echelon insurance executive, who estimates that more than 2000 cars disappear in Cannes anually, has informed us that his company pays off more theft policies in France than in any other European nation—adding that "In Italy or elsewhere, they more often steal the contents, while here they more often steal the vehicle." Thus, please take the same precautions that you do at home.

The U.S. Consul General has warned that the number of American passports stolen from visitors to Paris will reach record proportions this year. Pickpockets—professional and amateur—congregate most thickly here during the summer traffic peak and concentrate on victims in the crowded subways, train stations, and museums. Since many people carry their airline tickets and travelers' checks in the same folder, the passport makes it easy for the thief to cash them in. This official adds (1) that they should never be placed in hip pockets and (2) that handbags should always be tightly zippered or buckled. By depositing tomorrow's money with the hotel cashier you would always be ahead of the game. Finally, anyone who flashes a big bankroll is asking for trouble in king-sized portions.

Stay out of the disreputable Algerian sections, especially at night. They often mix murder with their larceny.

French hotels and waiters—*even those in the top brackets*—can load your bill more deftly and artistically than can their colleagues in Europe. *Always* demand an itemized bill; *always* check every item and the total.

No matter how dazzling the offer, PLEASE don't change any money on the streets. When *anyone* offers you 6 francs to the dollar, you can be *certain* you're about to be duped. These operators (sometimes aided by eye-popping girls) are so convincing that a Pennsylvania Chief of County Detectives was talked out of a bundle of dollars—and he still doesn't know how it was done.

If your new 5-franc coin feels coarse, just drop it casually on the counter before you accept it. Should it sound flat, ask for another. Silver coins make a clear ring when they're okay.

Don't buy whiskey at "bargain" prices, unless you're sure of the source. It's more likely to be Lipton's Prime Pekoe, or something far less attractive.

Officials have issued warnings to unsuspecting amateur art lovers (and to experts who should know better) that "originals" with phony signatures of Europe's masters are flooding into America.

☑ **INFORMATION CENTERS**   Alain Serieyx is Director of Tourism. A National Tourism Fund to underwrite large-scale facilities is gaining force; under way are a national parks system, a special commission on mountain resorts, a "nautical tourism" program, moves to enliven the "dead" Paris of July and August, a summer program of concerts, theater, and dance called "Festival Estival," and a campaign to promote interest in the charms of less-known rural areas, villages, and hamlets.

For the baffled traveler, the **Office de Tourisme de Paris** can be found at 127 avenue Champs-Élysées.

The City of Paris has set up its own **Information Bureau**, also at 127 avenue Champs-Élysées, linked by Telex to similar centers in other French cities. At your service are an exchange office, accredited representatives of touring agencies, and hotel reservations facilities. Even the Paris Prefecture of Police is in on the hospitality act; foreigners who seek a *permis de séjour* or wish to straighten out an official problem are escorted by gray-uniformed hostesses to pleasantly decorated private offices. *Formidable!* Other tourist information offices are located at the Palais de Congrès, Invalides, Gare du Nord, Gare de l'Est, and Gare de Lyon.

In North America (New York, Chicago, San Francisco, Beverly Hills, and Montreal), the **French Government Tourist Offices** continue their fruitful assistance to the stateside or Canadian visitor. The Canadian Chief is Renée Fromageau. In New York, Jean Roma is the U.S. Director-General for French tourism overall, while George Hern, Jr., is the gifted Director of Public Relations. The expert to consult about planning your trip is Marie-France Baudry, who captains the Information Center on the 6th floor of Rockefeller Center. Here you will also find inquiry desks manned by the French National Railroad, and Air France. Address for information, brochures, and the like: 610 Fifth Ave., New York, N.Y. 10020.

CITIES

PARIS still has such old-time institutions as the Eiffel Tower, fabulous perfumes, Cartier jewels, Fauchon gastronomies, Sorbonne, Folies Bergère, Arc de Triomphe, Notre-Dame, Mona Lisa, and 10-dozen others—plus some shiny new ones, including a lofty crop of controversial high-rise office titans that punctuate (if not dominate) the traditional skyline. Paris boasts 2.6 million people (with 9.2 million counting its close environs), hundreds of hotels, 10 railway stations, 3 airports, 2 heliports, enough art galleries to visit a different one every day of the year, 25 museums, magnificent cuisine, nightclubs galore, charm and local color in many corners. One side of Paris' face remains ancient and grimy, while the other offers sweeping boulevards, broad parks, splendid statuary, and architectural dignity.

To orient yourself, first hop onto a morning or afternoon sightseeing tour on a **Cityrama** double-decker bus. Hourly departures 9 A.M. through 5 P.M., 3-hour duration, phone 260–8430 for details. For about $9.50 you can be guided past the major sights, the ones you've known since grade school: Notre-Dame, Bastille, Conciergerie, Ste.-Chapelle, Sorbonne, Panthéon, Latin Quarter, Montparnasse, Hôtel des Invalides (now with an English version for its *Son et Lumière*— "Sound and Light"), Eiffel Tower, Madeleine, the boulevards, Louvre, Tuileries, Palais de Chaillot, the place de la Concorde, Champs-Élysées, Arc de Triomphe, Sacré-Coeur, Montmartre, and other points. Corny? Certainly—but broad coverage and good fun (1) *if* you can successfully look over, under, or around the 5-inch hearing disks and seat-conduits that block your vision, (2) *if* the sound tapes aren't too worn to be audible (which frequently they are), and (3) *if* that canned voice isn't describing a famous striptease center just as you pass the Chamber of Deputies.

Bird's-eyeing over the city may be yours at Air Paris, Orly Airport, for a swoop over the city or the Châteaux Country; special charters for other nearby regions also are available. If a helicopter suits you better, 4-place choppers make 30-minute rounds at a price that might make your own ears spin like props. Bookings can be made through **Société Hélisab, Auberge de l'hélisation**, Chalon Moulineux, 91740 Pussay (Tel. 495 4379).

For budget trippers, **Paris Transport Company** (RATP) offers a special low-price "Tourist Ticket" valid for unlimited rides, during 7 consecutive days, on any Métro train (subway), metropolitan bus, and certain suburban carriers. On flashing your U.S. passport, you may buy it at various RATP offices in the capital (53 bis quai des Grands-Augustins is one bureau), or before your U.S. departure, at the French National Railroads, 610 Fifth Ave., N.Y. 10020.

Strong-legged wanderers enjoy the **"Rambles in Paris"** walking tours—a series which covers the maximum of interesting places with the minimum of pedestrian effort. Sunday, it's the Île de la Cité and Île St.-Louis; Monday, the Palais Royal, Louvre, and Tuileries; Tuesday, Montmartre; Wednesday, the Bastille and Marais; Thursday, the Latin Quarter; Friday, St.-Germain-des-Prés; and Saturday, wait and see, _chérie!_ Starting time is 3 P.M., at the rendez-vous point for the day; the cost is trifling; telephone 535 2405 between 8 A.M. and 11 A.M. for particulars. Here's the way the inquisitive stranger can _really_ see the City of Light; highly recommended to all who like to stroll.

The **Eiffel Tower**, which sports a "hat"—a big television mast—is perennially the visitor's number one target in France. It was built as a temporary structure for the Paris World's Fair of 1889—not by the man who invented the Tinker Toy, but by the man who designed the Brooklyn Bridge. Open from 10:30 A.M. to 5 P.M. daily; $3.30 admission to top platform, with lower prices for lower platforms; panoramic restaurant (closed Nov. 15 to Easter, due to fog and cold winds that can freeze the hydraulic fluid in the elevator pumps) plus popular grill (operates all year). If someone should sidle up and offer to sell you a "piece" of this structure, don't whistle for the gendarmes. Unlike the Woolworth Building, which has been "sold" to hayseeds since Grandpappy's day, Eiffel Tower stock is traded on the open market. Secret note to gentlemen: Please consult the "Tip" at the end of this section.

Just-for-fun boat tours on the Seine have been Big Business for eons. Entrepreneur Jean Bruel's **"Bateaux Mouches"** fleet includes _La Patache_ (theater, TV, 800 capacity), the _Galiote_ (theater, dance floor, same general facilities), the _Jean-Sébastien Mouche_ (flagship with 300-place restaurant), _Le Coche d'Eau_ (self-service restaurant), and the _Parisien_ (the best cookery of the 5). You have your choice of 2½- or 1¼-hour rides; frequent departures from morning through evening; full of kids before noon, businessmen at lunchtime, tourist mobs in midafternoon, romantics at 5 P.M., and international celebrities after dark; boarding tickets range from around $2 to $5. Meals are served on 12:30 P.M. and 8:30 P.M. voyages, but we thought the cuisine was on about the level of an Albanian army mess hall (for buck privates, that is); we wouldn't pay $4 for the so-called $30 Gourmet Dinner, even at Paris prices. Departures from a Right Bank wharf between Pont des Invalides and Pont de l'Alma; ask your concierge for schedules, or phone 225 9610. **Vedettes Paris-Tour Eiffel** operate small rivercraft at 20-minute intervals from the wharf near the Eiffel Tower. Ninety-minute duration, $2.25 fare, optional visit to historic wine cellars for a little extra. Now paddling is its 5-hour, $25 circuit, which also incorporates lunch or dinner at the restaurant in the Tower. This one and the **Vedettes Pont-Neuf** are not as good for visibility nor are they as comfortable as the "Bateaux Mouches," but they are pleasant all the same. A delightful experience, if you happen to hit a sailing without too many Ladies' SPCA Societies from Ketchikan, Killarney, or Kokomo.

Minicar tours operated by the **"Auto-Mouche"** division provide compact vehicles with taped broadcasts corresponding to prescribed itineraries throughout the city. They even tell you where to find a parking space, which should be recompense enough to warrant *any* rental cost!

A brush with necrology? The world's largest repository of human bones has been unearthed for hardened spirits. The remains of 4-to-5-million souls are stacked along 2700 feet of catacombs near the Place Denfert-Rocherau in Montparnasse. To lend even more spookiness to this macabre nether-netherland, visitors are issued candles for the long gloomy circuit.

A semiprofessional guide service is offered by the municipally operated **Bureau Officiel de Placement des Guides**, 67 rue Pigalle. Specify an English-speaking guide if you don't "parleyvoo." Rates for private English-speaking guides are $40 for a full day (6 hours), $25 for a half day (3 hours). An hourly supplement is $4. Another bet might be the **Association Connaître et Aimer la France**, 400 rue St.-Honoré. Identical idea as London's popular Undergraduate Tours, Ltd.; ½-day Paris rate of about $28; double that for a full day; choice of several out-of-town excursions. We haven't tried this one, but if the lads perform as well as their English counterparts, it should be well worth every franc.

Too many visitors miss the **smaller museums** such as the Cluny (Gothic exterior and medieval collection), the Carnavalet (hodepodge of authentic artifacts of Parisian history), the Gobelins (tapestry), the Rodin (works of the sculptor in a home and garden), the Military (near the Gare des Invalides), the Opéra (part of the famous landmark; separate entrance), the Jacquemart-André (across the street from the Café de la Paix, specializing in Italian Renaissance as well as eighteenth century), the Victor-Hugo (place des Vosges, a relatively untrammeled highpoint), and the Hunting Museum (60 rue des Archives) for city-bound nimrods. For peripatetic philatelists, there's the Musée Postal (exhibits on the history of stamps and how they are made).

The **Louvre** has been rejuvenated inside and outside. The work cost some $20,000,000. Twenty-six new exhibit halls were opened, plus a panoramic sightseeing terrace on the roof of one wing. We are especially fond of the Orangerie, with so many lovely Utrillos, Cézannes, Monets, and other gems set in the atmosphere of a private collector's apartment. Art lovers can replenish lost vitamins at the self-service snack counters not only in the Louvre, but in the Jeu de Paume Museum (Tuileries Gardens), the Museum of Modern Art (13 avenue du Président Wilson), and the Château at Versailles. They may nibble on hors d'oeuvres, cold cuts, cheese, pastries, and the like for about $3. Mona Lisa's smile possibly comes from confidence that even she could cook better. And if these don't destroy your last vestiges of appetite, you might try a visit to Beaubourg's **Georges-Pompidou Art Center**—possibly the most hideous structure ever to be dedicated to the preservation and exhibition of beauty. Unhappily, it probably will stand as an everlasting hymn to modern intestinology—architecture so repugnant to us that it defames France's historic role as an arbiter of taste and erudition. The building notwithstanding, its collections, presentations, and quirky tricks of holding a mirror up to life bring a fresh, bright, and idiosyncratic touch to art appreciation.

Enghien-les-Bains, 20 minutes out, features a spa and a casino where fun-lovers may risk a variety of games of chance. Parklike surroundings, outdoor dining; dancing and scheduled entertainments; thermal baths to soak up that travel fatigue and "ti many martoonis." Season: April 1 to December 31.

Another delight is to take a carriage ride through *St.-Germain-en-Laye*. This forest is one of the most sloth-provoking in Europe, and there is a magnificent, mile-long terrace with a view of the capital when the weather is clear.

Bas-Bréau at *Barbizon* (refer to "Other Targets"), 43 miles out, used to be the home of Robert Louis Stevenson; now it's a cheerful and expensive little hotel-restaurant, the favorite of many film and stage luminaries. Garden; open fireplace for winter; interesting village; happy for lunch or dinner on a sunny day.

There are many other attractions on the outskirts of, or reasonably near, Paris: *Fontainebleau* (François I's palace—now totally renovated—where Napoléon signed his abdication; magnificent forest; see under "Other Targets"), *St.-Cloud* (park and especially good view of Paris), *St.-Denis* (abbey church, tombs of the kings of France), *Chantilly* (horse racing in June-July, château, museum, forest), *Chartres* (lovely drive through the wheat-gold Beauce Plain and across the Eure River to a hillock famed for its impressive cathedral with windows dating from 6 to 7 centuries ago), *Compiègne* (Armistice signed in WW I), *Reims* (world-famous cathedral), and *Château-Thierry* (American battleground, museum). *Versailles* offers a snack bar adjoining the museum. Fountains turned on and admission prices halved on Sundays during the warm months; open 10 A.M. to 5 P.M. every day except Tuesday; remarkably restored theater, with even the eighteenth-century cut-velvet patterns duplicated on hand looms; no heating in winter so climb into your woollies or your flask of Remy Martin. All easily reached by bus, train, or automobile; most offer conducted tours.

RATP, the Paris bus line, operates special ½-day and full-day guided excursions through the Île de France region, with regular departures from place de la Madeleine. It also runs multiday junkets to the Loire Valley Châteaux Country, to Normandy, and to the D-Day beachheads, from late April to the end of October.

★ **FIVE-STAR TIP***** If you're in Paris, steal a day to take the 2½-hour drive over good roads (via Soissons) to *Reims*. By train it's only a 1½-hour zip from the Gare de l'Est. Here, through a very special arrangement between the Mumm champagne moguls and ourselves, you can enjoy one of the tours of your lifetime. As an outgrowth of long and deep personal ties with my Nancy and this author, President René Lalou (who died in '73 in his vigorous 90's) and World Sales Director Georges Prade proposed that a remarkable and unforgettable private welcome be extended to readers of this book. No commissions, kickbacks, or monkey business are involved, naturally—only warm and privileged friendship, as always. The sole hook: Because outsiders must be prevented from horning in on this expensive welcome by Mumm, you *must* show your copy of this book to the authorities there. If you go to Mumm on rue du Champ-de-Mars and ask for Director of the Cellars M. Bernard Geoffroy, you will be given a red-carpet excursion through the premises in which America's most popular champagne (1.5-million bottles annually of the 5-million total sales for the industry) is created, aged, and handled with such love. Hours: 9 A.M. to 11 A.M. and 2 P.M. to 5 P.M., *but no tours on Saturday and Sunday between November 1 and February 28.* Here is the Cordon Rouge and Cordon Rosé of charted exploration into a captivating new realm to most travelers—so please try not to miss this very special opportunity to listen to Mumm's word right from the bottle's mouth. *Santé!*

★ **TIP FOR MEN ONLY** How to impress your *chérie?* Truffles and breast of nightingale at Tour d'Argent? A Jeroboam of Mumm Cordon Rouge? A planeload of posies from Nice? But how unimaginative can you get, chum? Now you can floodlight the skyscraping Eiffel Tower for 1 whole hour as a solo expression of passion for your *amour*—and if *that* doesn't knock her off her heels, you'd better turn in your medals. Notice must be given 48 hours in advance to thee **Service de l'Éclairage Publique** in City Hall any time after October 15 (when this edifice is not illuminated as a standard tourist attraction). The cost? About $100 for a stunt that would make noodle soup out of a blank check at Cartier. Bargain Basement Lotharios may kindle the Arch of Triumph for a piddling $60 an hour and other landmarks for even less. And as we write this, a mischievously wicked (but delightfully delicious) thought occurs to us: Why not telephone *several* of the most luscious *Parisiennes* listed in your little black book, tell each that you are suddenly tied up in a business conference, and that at 9:03½ o'clock, on-the-dot, the tower will burst into radiance as a trifling homage to your love for "her and her alone"? (We'll bet you 50 francs you'll *really* be busy tomorrow night!)

PARIS HOTELS Quick Reference Table

Price categories by national (not U.S.) standards.

EXPENSIVE:

Bristol Faubourg St-Honoré 112. Tel. 2669145; Telex 280961; 200 rooms. P. 247
Crillon Place de la Concorde 10. Tel. 2961081; Telex 290204; 211 rooms. P. 248
George V Av. George V 31. Tel. 7235400; Telex 290776; 315 rooms. P. 248
Hilton Av. Suffren 18. Tel. 2739200; Telex 200955; 470 rooms. P. 249
L'Hôtel Rue des Beaux-Arts 13. Tel. 3252722; Telex 270870; 27 rooms. P. 251
Intercontinental Castiglione 3. Tel. 2603780; Telex 220114; 474 rooms. P. 249
Lancaster Berri 7. Tel. 3599043; Telex 640991; 67 rooms. P. 249
Meurice Rivoli 228. Tel. 2603860; Telex 230673; 160 rooms. P. 247

Plaza-Athénée Av. Montaigne 25. Tel. 3598523; Telex 650092; 213 rooms. P. 247
Prince de Galles Av. George V 33. Tel. 7235511; Telex 280627; 203 rooms. P. 249
Ritz Pl. Vendôme 15. Tel. 2603830; Telex 220262; 162 rooms. P. 248

UPPER MODERATE:
Concorde Lafayette Pte des Ternes. Tel. 7581284; Telex 650892; 975 rooms. P. 250
Grand Scribe 2. Tel. 2603350; Telex 220875; 600 rooms. P.251
Lutetia Bd. Raspail 45. Tel. 5443810; Telex 270424; 288 rooms. P. 255
Méridien Bd. Gouvion-St-Cyr. 81. Tel. 7581230; Telex 290952; 1023 rooms. P. 250
Napoléon Av. Friedland 40. Tel. 2277420; Telex 640609; 140 rooms. P. 252
PLM St.-Jacques Bd. St-Jacques 17. Tel. 5898980; Telex 270740; 812 rooms. P. 250
Raphaël Av. Kléber 17. Tel. 5530770; Telex 610356; 90 rooms. P. 252
Royal Monceau Av. Hoche 35. Tel. 5619800; Telex 650361; 250 rooms. P. 251
Sheraton Cdt-Mouchotte 19. Tel. 2603511; Telex 200135; 964 rooms. P. 254
Westminster Paix 13. Tel. 2615746; Telex 680035; 102 rooms. P. 252

MODERATE:
Ambassador Bd. Haussmann 16. Tel. 2469263; Telex 650912; 300 rooms. P. 254
Bradford St-Philippe-du-Roule 10. Tel. 3592420; 49 rooms. P. 255
Brighton Rue de Rivoli 218. Tel. 2603003. P. 252
California Berri 16. Tel. 3599300; Telex 660634; 170 rooms. P. 254
Castiglione Fg-St-Honoré 40. Tel. 2650750; 100 rooms. P. 254
Cecilia Av. MacMahon 11. Tel. 3803210; 46 rooms. P. 255
Celtic Balzac 6. Tel. 2250925; Telex 290298; 80 rooms. P. 253
Château Frontenac Rue Pierre-Charron 54. Tel. 3593507; Telex 660994; 100 rooms. P. 251
Club Méditerranée Bd. Victor Hugo 58. Tel. 7581100; Telex 610971; 330 rooms. P. 253
Commodore Bd. Haussmann 12. Tel. 7709300; Telex 280601; 180 rooms. P. 252
France et Choiseul St. Honoré. 135 rooms. P. 252
Grand Hotel Littré Littré 9. Tel. 5486771; Telex 270557; 120 rooms. P. 253
Hotel de Castille Cambon 37. Tel. 2615520; 55 rooms. P. 254
Hotel de l'Université Université 22. Tel. 2610939; 26 rooms. P.255
l'Abbaye St. Germain Rue Cassette 10. Tel. 5443811; 45 rooms. P. 251
Lido Passage Madeleine 4. Tel. 2662737; 29 rooms. P. 254
Lotti Castiglione 7. Tel. 2603734; Telex 240066; 129 rooms. P. 252
Madeleine Palace Cambon 8. Tel. 0736144; 116 rooms. P. 254
Madeleine Plaza Pl. Madeleine 33. Tel. 2652063; 50 rooms. P. 254
Nikko Quai Grenelle 61. Tel. 5756262; Telex 260012; 784 rooms. P. 253
Normandy Echelle 7. Tel. 2606108; Telex 670250; 130 rooms. P. 253
Penta Baudin 18. Tel. 7885051; Telex 61499; 494 rooms. P. 254
Régents Rue P. Demours 6. Tel. 7543940; Telex 640127; 39 rooms. P. 256
Résidence du Bois Rue Chalgrin 16. Tel. 5005059; 17 rooms. P. 252
Royal Av. Friedland 33. Tel. 3590814; 280965; 57 rooms. P. 253
St. Simon St. Simon 14. Tel. 5483566. P. 255
San Régis Jean-Goujon 12. Tel. 3594190; 30 rooms. P. 253
Scandinavia Tournon 27. Tel. 6334520; 22 rooms. P. 255
Scribe Scribe 1. Tel. 7420340; Telex 230024; 200 rooms. P. 255
Sofitel Bourbon St-Dominique 32. Tel. 5559180; Telex 250019; 112 rooms. P. 253
Sofitel de Paris Grognet 2. Tel. 6571143; Telex 200432; 635 rooms. P. 253

Suffern La Tour Rue Jean Rey 20. Tel. 5786108; Telex 204459; 400 rooms. P. 252
Terminus St-Lazare Concorde St-Lazare 108. Tel. 2615120; Telex 650442; 335 rooms. P. 254
Vendome Pl. Vendôme 1. Tel. 2603284; Telex 680403; 50 rooms. P. 255
Vernet Vernet 25. Tel. 7201670; Telex 29347; 63 rooms. P. 254
Victoria Palace Blaise-Desgoffe 6. Tel. 5488040; Telex 270557; 120 rooms. P. 253

LOWER MODERATE:
Astor Astorg 11. Tel. 2665656; 140 rooms. P. 255
Bellman François 1er 37. Tel. 3596251; 43 rooms. P. 255
Burgundy Duphot 8. Tel. 2609432; Telex 260717; 90 rooms. P. 255
Cayré Bd. Raspail 4. Tel. 2221082; Telex 270577; 135 rooms. P. 256
Cazaudehore 24 rooms. St. Germain-En-Laye P. 256
Edouard VII Av. Opéra 39. Tel. 2615690; Telex 680217; 95 rooms. P. 255
G. Hotel de Principautes Unis 27 rooms. P. 255
G. H. du Mont-Blanc Huchette 28. Tel. 0336388; 41 rooms. P. 255
Madison Bd. St-Germain 143. Tel. 3265712; 59 rooms. P. 255
Mapotel Pont Royal Montalembert 7. Tel. 5443827; Telex 270113; 76 rooms. P. 256
Masséna Tronchet 16. Tel. 0732560; 30 rooms. P. 256
Montalembert Montalembert 3. Tel. 5486811; 65 rooms. P. 256
Pavillon Henry IV St. Germain-en-Laye. P. 256
Régence Etoile Av. Carnot 24. Tel. 3807560; 38 rooms. P. 255
Regina Pl. des Pyramids 2. Tel. 2603110; Telex 670834; 150 rooms. P. 256
Richmond Helder 11. Tel. 8247527; Telex 290574; 56 rooms. P. 256
Royal St. Honoré Saint Honoré 221. Tel. 2603279; Telex 68429; 82 rooms. P. 255
Tronchet Tronchet 22. P. 256
Vermont Bois-de-Boulogne 11 bis. Tel. 5000497; 29 rooms. P. 256

ENVIRONS:
Trianon Palace-Versailles Bd. de la Reine 1. Tel. 9503412; 145 rooms. P. 256

STUDENT DWELLING:
l'Office du Tourisme Universitaire P. 256
French Cultural Services P. 256

AIRPORT:

ORLY
Air Hôtel Tel. 7260310; 56 rooms. P. 257
Novotel Paris-Bagnolet Tel. (1) 36002010; Telex 670216; 600 rooms. P. 257
Frantel Av. C. Lindbergh 20 (Rungis). Tel. (1) 6773909; Telex 260738; 206 rooms. P. 257
Hilton Orly Aérogares. Tel. 7264000; Telex 842-250621; 388 rooms. P. 256
Holiday Inn Av. Ch. Lindbergh 4 (Rungis). Tel. (1)6872666; Telex 204679; 180 rooms. P. 257
PLM Orly-Aerogare. Tel. (1) 6872337; Telex 204345; 200 rooms. P. 257

ROISSY
Holiday Inn Rue de Paris 54. Tel. 9859611; Telex 695143; 121 rooms. P. 257
Sofitel Charles de Gaulle Airport. Tel. 8622323; Telex 691777; 352 rooms. P. 257

HOTELS For far more comprehensive information on certain French hostelries than space limitations permit here, interested travelers are referred to *Fielding's Favorites: Hotels and Inns, Europe* by our son and teammate, Dodge Fielding. The revised edition, in which a total of 300-odd favored possibilities were handpicked from the 4000-plus personally inspected, will be at your bookstore early this year. Generally speaking, Gallic hotels are now quite good. In the provinces, improvements are now healthy and continuous. Still, don't be surprised if your regional hostelry turns out to be vintage 1893, with hot-and-cold running proprietor complete with seedy vest and toothpick.

All hostelries considered to be worthy of receiving outlanders are classed as *Hôtels de Tourisme.* These are broken down into 5 categories: Deluxe, 4-star, 3-star 2-star, and 1-star. The same applies to the *Relais de Tourisme* (suburban stops) and *Motels de Tourisme* (on major highways). As stated below, price controls cover only the lowest 3 groups. All have been painstakingly reinspected. (One proprietor complained to us that the inspector studied his 46-room establishment for 2½ days and then wrote a 24-page report of its deficiencies.) Therefore, in order to qualify, every physical plant must now conform in every detail to the standards of the rating for which it has reapplied—the ratios of private bathrooms to bedrooms, the presence of adequate breakfast rooms with the specified numbers of seats, the toilets separated by their own individual doors, and scores of similar ukases. Legions of hoteliers frantically —some in panic!—rebuilt and repainted so that they wouldn't be dropped to the next lower category and thus diminish their earnings. This supervision applies to lodging charges only; in "pension" (meal) arrangements, legally the sky is the limit.

Don't forget the requirement of 10% to 15% extra for service charge *(majoration)* and taxes—no matter where you go. Taxes are now included by law in all quotations, but for service and supplements it's still almost a case of "anything goes." The amount depends upon the location and category—*so be certain this total has been calculated in the summation before you sign the register.* It can give you a nasty surprise if you're caught.

The Government has stepped into the travel picture in another way, too. Now French hoteliers can be held liable for the theft of a registrant's possessions—either from the hotel or from the hostelry's parking lot. The law, at least, ought to influence the selection of staff and create better safeguards throughout.

In Paris, tariffs are the same or even higher than those in the larger U.S. cities, despite all Government efforts to hold down the upward spiral. As we've stated, the cost of accommodations has more than tripled within the past decade and the squeeze this year, in seasoned travelers' opinions, is frankly scandalous. Deluxe and First-class establishments set their own charges— which are always as high, naturally, as Old Dobbin Customer will stand without bursting his traces and bolting. One of the biggest dodges is that when space for one is "unavailable," the lone traveler may be charged for double occupancy. *At one extreme, the leaders run perhaps $55 minimum for a single, $75 minimum for a double, and $125 minimum for a suite. At the other, budget vacationers can find scores of tatterdemalion slow-water antiquities around the Étoile, the Opéra, and on the Left Bank for $30 per day—and mighty, mighty* *basic, at that. Between these limits, houses of the "popular" tourist category, such as the Scribe, Commodore, and the like, offer minimum doubles with bath, service, taxes, and breakfast for perhaps $44. Off Season tabs (in the resorts, not in the main centers) can be 10% to 20% lower.*

One caution: When you eat your breakfast in your room (most visitors follow this continental tradition), items such as fruit juice, cereal, eggs, or sausages are not included in the house quotation for the standard coffee or tea *complet.* They cost like the devil and add up fast.

All French Government Tourist Offices have definitive lists of Gallic stopping places everywhere, free of charge. A splendid bet for the less well-heeled vacationer is the *Logis de France Guide*—a roundup of more than 4000 clean, modest country and resort hotels, hand-picked by the **Fédération Nationale des Logis de France**; it's available at this organization's Paris headquarters, 25 rue Jean Mermoz, for $1; although tariffs have edged upward to the average full-pension range of $20 or so, their selections are still generally less expensive than competitive ones. For more opulent tastes, the **Relais et Chateaux** (also nonprofit) offers a superb compilation of perhaps 200 leading French or foreign-owned rural oases—châteaux, manor houses, converted monasteries, and the like—all with well-known restaurants (a few entries are for dining only). Although a handful are substandard, the majority offer dependable quality. What a splendid group it is too! For details drop by the information office at 17 place Vendôme in Paris. King and Queen of the field, however, remain the indispensable **Guide Michelin** and **Guide Kléber-Colombes**, both of which no serious traveler in France should ever be without.

The previously mentioned **City of Paris Tourist Information Bureau**, at 127 avenue Champs Élyseés, will spring to your rescue in emergencies by finding you a room within a 60-mile radius of Cannes, Nice, Marseille, Reims, Lourdes, Strasbourg, Tours, Rouen, Lyon, Vichy, Dijon, Aix-les-Bains, or (of course) the capital. Reservations guaranteed for one night only (this avoids competition with travel agencies); direct connection with Paris Welcome Information Offices at main railway stations, with lovely Hostesses of Paris on tap; Telex network, currency exchange, and similar services; open 9 A.M. to midnight including Sunday. Small fees.

Paris at peak times can be one of the tightest accommodations bottlenecks in Europe. But this squeeze is fast in the process of being not only loosened but virtually eliminated for well stuffed wallets only—*NOT* for lower-spending wanderers. Officially, at least, a massive campaign has been launched to assist responsible professionals through low-interest loans and perhaps grants for the fastest possible proliferation exclusively of 2-star hotels and motels along France's highways—badly needed economy lodgings which will be a godsend to the budget traveler.

★ **TIPS** Prefer an apartment? The 161 real estaters who formed the **Fédération Nationale des Agents Immobiliers** (163 rue St.-Honoré, Paris 1) are girded to attack all the formalities and then plunk you into a chalet, villa or most any other sort of dwelling you select. Though we have never tried this organization, its reputation for reliability and competence is excellent.

Or a farmhouse? Write to **Gîtes de France** which can send you prices, locations, and other particulars on renting an abode in rural Gaul. While we haven't hoed this row, friends who have say it is an enriching, low-cost experience for adventurous types. Address: 34 rue Godot de Mauroy, 75009 Paris.

If you are a traveler of note or if you are trying to locate a VIP who may be in town, direct your S.O.S. to Maggi Nolan, who is the charming Minerva of **Celebrity Service** (7 rue Jean Goujon, Tel. 2250247). This organization combines the best attributes of convenience, skill, and discretion. There's none finer.

In this book's judgment of Parisian hotels, there remains—despite significant administrative changes—essentially a 3-way tie at the top: the Bristol, the Plaza-Athénée, and the Meurice are pounding down the homestretch neck-and-neck-and-neck. On the rail and challenging fast are the Ritz, Crillon, George V, Prince de Galles, and Intercontinental, followed closely by the Hilton and the Lancaster.

The **Bristol**, always a favorite of ours, has, astonishingly, grown even *more* luxurious under its new proprietors (who also operate the prestigious Brenner's Park in Baden-Baden and the sumptuous Hôtel du Cap at Cap d'Antibes). What's more, after spending a fortune here to insure its luster, personable, hard-driving General Manager Peter Spaeth is considering how to invest another ten million dollars on further improvements! Today's visitor will still enjoy the proud, magnificently furnished Bristol of yore, but added to it (and oh-so-discreetly) is a new 28-room wing topped with a covered swimming pool that can be opened in summer for viewing the rooftops of Paris; it is decorated with a *trompe l'oeil* painting of a marine theme. There's a new grill on the ground floor supervised by Master Chef Jean-Paul Bonin, a captivating garden spread over the garage and surrounded by a colonnade of the former cloister; a "Résidence" has been created for longer-staying guests. Rich Gobelin tapestries and splendid paintings; stunning oval dining room; refreshments served in the lounges by 18th-century-clothes-clad butlers; 2 new elevators; air conditioning, automatic telephone system, TV and radio; beauty parlor, barber shop, masseur, and many other services. We are witnessing a 24-carat born-again renaissance of an already superb establishment; it is almost too much for us to believe. (And yet we do!)

For decades the **Plaza-Athénée** has catered with conspicuous success to inconspicuously wealthy travelers, people who have wanted the best in fashionable and reasonably quiet surroundings. Illustrious M. Roland of former Tour d'Argent celebrity now supervises the Very First Rank cuisine; the Régence is known globally for its gastronomy; try the renowned lobster soufflé and you'll see why. While the courtyard restaurant (3 full-time florists!) has now been tailored for year-round operation, its vivid blooms, pools, bridge, free-flying songbirds, gay red parasols, and polka-dotted tablecloths create the impression of Eternal Spring. Every room offers a good bath, an excellently stocked refrigerator, color TV, 4-channel piped music, and news broadcasts in English; the penthouse is composed of 4 supersuites. Cheers, salutes, and salaams to Franco Cozzo and his fine staff for their virtuoso performance!

The **Meurice** has enjoyed a fiesta of renovations that are not just beautiful but are truly magnificent. We are particularly impressed by the crystals, bronzes, gold leaf, marble, and textiles of museum quality incorporated into the noble, high-ceilinged salons, the proportions of which put this house in a peerage with the great palaces of Europe. The 18th-century stylization extends from the portals through the modern adaptations of the corridors and into the gracious, wide-angled accommodations; the latter sometimes are a bit dark for 20th-century pupils. Most of the baths have been renewed; twins all boast separate showers; all accommodations face the park. The kitchen is noted for its cuisine; the Copper Bar evokes a tone of clublike intimacy; there is a beauty salon; there are scores of well-executed features which conspire to provide an aristocratic interlude in the City of Light. Through its New York office (630 Fifth Ave., Tel. 800-223-0333, toll free), reservations can now be made within the United States. A top recommendation for a classic grand hotel.

The **Crillon** has taken such gigantic strides under Director Philippe Roche that it has become a full-fledged member of Paris's élite group, appealing nowadays not just to diplomats but to jet-setters and young strutters and walkers of life. It seems to be growing more frisky in age and approach. Every one of its 210 expanded and refreshed accommodations is *splendissimo*. A cozier Grill and the ultramodern, 2-room Le Concord Bar perform admirably (the latter is radically out of character with its historic image but very nice per se). You'll ride elevators with leather interiors by Hermès; there's also a handsomely keyed-in 3-cabin Telex room; corridors are decked in new attire. While the bedchambers are chipper, bright, and well equipped, they maintain the traditional tone; all baths have been revivified, most of them with thermal taps in tubs and showers, and many in marble; frigobars are in every unit as are color TVs. North Americans (who comprise 75% of its registrations) are fond of the night menu (alas, not around the clock) of cold selections and the he-man breakfasts. Though expensive, this house provides *beaucoup* return for your francs.

The **Ritz** is still the rallying point of the Old Guard. Basically it remains a fine structure with luxurious facilities and an eminently distinguished clientele. Recent changes in ownership have not in any way disturbed its form or content—the Ritz remains immutable. It boasts an unbeatably central location, tons of venerable marble and mellowed woodwork, the ghosts of countless patrician guests. With or in its 50 living rooms and 210 bedchambers you'll now find superefficient baths, 5-channel piped music, and color TV outlets for employment upon request; there's a fine beauty salon and a barbershop; the bar is coming back into a style that faded and is now recovering; perhaps so is the Espadon Grill; a large allocation of funds soon may result in the hotel's general uplifting under Manager Frank Klein. To the delight of its loyal following, who have sworn by it for decades, this monument still qualifies as *A Ritz as Big as a Diamond.*

The **George V** has made such progress structurally and decoratively that it is winning back the tasteful clientele which had drifted away in an earlier epoch. A stroke of architectural genius is manifest in the exquisite floral garden that has been placed behind lobby glass, providing a sensation of springtime even on the darkest days of winter. Les Princes restaurant is handsomely outfitted with royal blue and gold carpeting and flannel curtains that separate the charming windowfront terrace from the interior segment; we'd opt for the veranda tables, but this is personal preference. The entrance passage to the dining room incorporates a stall exhibiting shellfish and other marine fare—

perhaps ironic in a hotel of this category, but nevertheless effective. The bar is restyled with modern crystal chandeliers, matching sconces, and comfortable burgundy booths. The President Suite, at a mere $800 per night, has to reach a bit these days to find a President worthy of it; it is nothing short of awesome. Excellent accommodations of a more modest nature are thoughtfully outfitted; our favorite doubles overlook the tranquil Marble Court. Women may be amused by the Nina Ricci boutique, while gentlemen will be intrigued by the new *caves* where vintage wines may be purchased by the bottle or case. A noteworthy improvement which many affluent travelers will appreciate.

The fine old **Prince de Galles** ("Prince of Wales"), cheek-by-jowl with the George V, has long been a cordial, attractive, and comfortable haven. Now huge sums of money are being pumped into it to provide even further decorative zest. Traditional units have been freshened; there's color TV throughout; the off-lobby English bar is warmly inviting; hair-dressing facilities for men and women complement the princely coiffeur. General Manager Marguerie is the fireman at pump. Two floors per annum completely redone in a 6-year cycle; about 80% of baths with twin washbasins and wallpapered ceilings; corridors particularly fresh, cheerful, and ingeniously colorful; singles with large baths exceptionally appealing; outstanding gastronomy; chic and sheikish Moorish courtyard for terrace dining in summer. Chief Concierge Marc Berthault is a mountain of strength, as were all of the staff we met during our latest visit. An excellent address for midtowners.

The **Intercontinental** can also boast about its central location embracing the original and lovely Garden Court. There's a canopied terrace on one side overlooking a central pond for seasonal outdoor dining; its adjoining lobby is a strikingly attractive mixture of nineteenth-century and Cape Kennedy appurtenances-of-tomorrow. Intimate Rôtisserie Rivoli, curiously shaped with 6 alcoves and seating the grand sum of 180; Le Bistro for lighter biting and libations to music (piped from noon until a pianist comes on from 9 P.M. to 2 A.M.); Bar Rivoli with an after-gloaming harpist; Coffee Shop. Improved service under Manager Jules Prévost, but the high group occupancy steals away some of the sophistication which the plant itself projects. Full air conditioning; double-pane windows for silent-nighting; ample space in rooms with soft-view hues in blue, gray, green, or burnt orange; wall-to-wall carpeting; typically tiny baths; all singles with *grands lits.* Slightly theatrical but basically very sound and recommendable.

The T-shape, II-story **Paris Hilton** features a Tinkertoy called the Eiffel Tower standing in its backyard on the Left Bank. Outlying situation requiring a taxi hop for every midtown errand, shopping jag, or sightseeing jaunt; marvelous vista from Seine-side rooms; dreary claustrophobic view from rear windows, overlooking the Atomic Energy Commission complex; furnishings looking a little tired on our latest inspection. Mélange-happy lobby lined with shops and soon in need of a spiffing up, which we understand it will receive. Convenient 300-car underground garage; 6 refreshment centers (see "Restaurants"); many fundamentally sound features which we anticipate will be given new sparkle and pizazz in the current redecoration spree.

The **Lancaster** is held by London's Savoy Hotels Ltd., the innkeeping chain that includes the golden links of Claridge's, the Berkeley, the Connaught, and, of course, the Savoy. A more perfect commercial marriage can scarcely be visualized, because all parties are on the same wavelength in spoiling the wayfarer with old-fashioned *personalized* attention and satisfaction supreme. Young, winning John Iversen, handsome enough to be a film star, runs the show with subtle command. Most of the rooms are satisfactory but comparatively so small in their dimensions (yet still comfort-plus) that we believe their appeal is greater to ladies than to men; no 2 of them are outfitted alike. All suites have been refashioned; some baths were renewed, a few unsuccessfully; the bar decants for lobby sippers; the chef has perked up cuisine to the point where many business executives appear regularly at lunchtime. While good, we'd like to see even heavier funding for this Lancastrian dowager.

Below the Big 10, the degree varying slightly, is a cluster with fine facilities and distinctive qualities. Let's lead off this next category with a dramatic renewal.

The **Trémoille** is a kid-sister of the neighboring Plaza Athénée, whose dining and other facilities clients here may use. It is a convenient arrangement that combines lower tariffs with extraordinary comfort and abundant luxury. The recent round-house renovation created generous space concepts, highlights of Maytime from the decorators, and graceful traditionalism throughout. A fire crackles in the hearth in winter; a bar with intricately carved panels nods invitingly; a small adjoining restaurant is available for grills and snacks. We were especially fond of units ending in numbers 2, 3, 9, 10, and 12. Quiet, elegant, and highly recommended.

The **Méridien**, with over *1000* latchkeys, is really more of a hotel-city than an inn in the traditional sense. Its lobby, only slightly smaller than the state of Delaware, is dominated by thickets of easy chairs and illuminated by a tubular forest of suspended lamps; a gelid stainless-steel bar chills the nether reaches leading to the cool courtside Clos Longchamps restaurant. Colorful Arlequin Rôtisserie; Japanese Yamoto corner; cellar-sited circular café; night-club—well, you name it and it's probably there. The look-alike bedchambers feature one flank clad in the same carpeting that cloaks the floor; their other facilities include semifitted furniture, radio console and TV, refrigerated bars, baths with space-age tubs and cleverly designed glass splash-plates for showers. This jumbo, largely fueled by Air France financing, is piloted by able Ernst Etter. Basically sound, but with a chillfactor associated purely with the twentieth century.

The **P.L.M. Saint-Jacques** is another Orwellian creation—this one with a mere 812 accommodations. It is handy to the major train stations and the route to Orly Airport (shuttle every ¼-hour), and not too far from Montparnasse. (Our taxi fare to the Étoile totaled nearly $8.50, however.) Impressive cubistic façade; 15 floors of windows angled port and starboard; airy blue-and-white lobby with greenery, a fountain, and drilled steel columns; once again the full panoply of restaurants (including a Japanese one and a Polynesian bar); pentagonal bedchambers in orange, blue, or brown tones; sparrow-size baths with marble-top basins and dip-your-toe tubs. A novel touch is the hotel's credit card system whereby guests charge round-the-house expenditures to a central computer.

The giant **Concorde-Lafayette** connects with the Paris Convention Hall. Its first 2 dozen tiers cater exclusively to groups, with no room service available. The next 8 levels stack up for independent bookings; these come with coral textiles, matched furnishings, brown carpets, and dimensions which seem a shade smaller than those of the above entry. Comfort standards, however, are about the same. General Manager Leclercq's crowning joy is the panoramic penthouse restaurant and bar. Another 1000-room colossus, but segmented in such a clever way that both groupies and soloists share the rewards.

The **Royal Monceau** continues to enjoy a canter toward progress under its new ownership. Lobby festooned with the graceful dignity to match its stately facade; corridors refashioned; all backstage support facilities shaken up or shaken out. This year you'll discover an ingratiating patio-garden restaurant in season, many modernized accommodations and baths (some remain scruffy but are due for updating pronto), carefully prepared cuisine that is not exactly for the budgeteer, kindhearted reception, and cordial attention by a well-trained staff. Very good indeed for its semiaristocratic bearing, but we must wait and see how it develops in new hands.

The **Grand**, despite its convenient central address, seems well on the way to achieving its goal as a convention hotel, serving this function for the Meurice group of which it is a part. The exterior has been brightened with glass and burnished metal. Ceilings have been lowered (but, alas, the prices have moved in the other direction). Careful attention has been accorded to illumination techniques throughout the building. There's the zippier lobby leading to the bar and Café de la Paix, the fresh Pacific Room for quick meals, a refashioned terrace, and much more sparkle. Manager Marcelin is a gentleman who bears the stamp of the true professional. Still, in our view, this must always be a mass-production-belt house with a frigid impersonality.

L'Hôtel (13 rue des Beaux-Arts, on the Left Bank) is dramatically unorthodox. French actor Guy Louis Duboucheron and Texas architect Robin Westbrook spent 27 months transforming the seedy, moldy, 30-room, 3-bath Hôtel Alsace—its only pale distinction that Oscar Wilde died there—into a luxury-class operation of 2 suites, 25 rooms, and 27 baths. To the rear of its Lilliputian lobby its greenhouse-style terrace restaurant presented a tiny fountain, 2 caged monkeys, parrots, drawable curtains under its light-well ceiling, a mass of vines, blue tablecloths, and 2 dirty rugs. The cuisine—which impressed us as substandard—is whoppingly expensive à la carte. The wine card, although versatile, is also overpriced, in our opinion. The bedrooms, each different and some air-conditioned, are all decorated in exquisite taste. The cellar-to-roof drawback here is that all of its dimensions have been telescoped into such super-compactness, including luggage space, that any large-framed guest would find this doll's house uncomfortably cramped. Another conversion job was performed on **l'Abbaye St. Germain,** formerly a convent and later a student dormitory. Interior patio plus garden, with birds aflutter; Art Deco lounge; some of its 45 units overlooking the garden; a few with private terrace entry and breakfast balcony; bath and shower for each accommodation; soft lighting, nice carpeting, colors tending toward teals and browns; no restaurant; intimacy is its chief commodity. The rates are very reasonable for the personalized rewards. **Château Frontenac,** just off the Champs-Elysées, boasts the delightfully cozy, candlelit Salamandre restaurant-*cum*-bar; all 100 units come with TV, radio, minibar, and self-dial phone. We like the modern tapestries, the attractive fresh-faced bedchambers, and the upbeat air of polished professionalism.

The **Raphaël**, 2 blocks from the Arc de Triomphe, exudes understated grace and dignity. Its salons are filled with beautiful oil paintings and its bedrooms evoke the grandeur of a manor house. However, for what is now to us an alarmingly long time, a number of disturbing reader reports have filtered onto our desk, complaining chiefly of a falloff in maintenance which our own eyes confirmed on our very recent stopover. What a pity, because fundamentally this is a charming plant.

La **Résidence du Bois**, also just a totter from the Étoile, is an 18-room hideaway with quietude, luxury, and no fireworks. Operated in a dignified homespun manner; no full restaurant, but light meals available; minimum twins for around $100; 3 suites; one 2-story nest with private entrance; all accommodations tastefully appointed and cheerful; #10 and #23 best for silent siestas. Recommendable on many counts.

The **Lotti** is now under the able guidance of General Manager Jacques Massot. Pleasant bar and grill adjoining the small restaurant; revamped units the best; some garret-style accommodations. An intimate type of house that we like a lot.

The **Brighton** brightens its enviable site on the convenient rue de Rivoli. Traditional rooms with full carpeting, French windows, brass beds, and good illumination; superb maintenance; ample comfort and coziness; #410 an excellent 3-bed corner accommodation; back units quiet. No restaurant, but a spread for breakfast; nice personnel who truly seem to care. It is, in our opinion, just what a small, medium-priced hostelry should be.

As for the 200-room **Suffren La Tour**, sponsored by the French Railways, the accent is on the Suffren. Too much *argent* for too little reward, in our opinion.

The **Hotel France et Choiseul** (across from place Vendôme) is making the most of its near-perfect address. The commercially motivated ownership group bought this veteran, gutted it down to its most basic walls, and then virtually rebuilt the entire structure. Untouched, however, remain its Louis XVI Emperatrice-style foyer, the muraled walls of the main salon, and the courtyard —all ruled inviolable by the French National Art Commission. Upstairs its 135 nests are pretty standard in their somewhat limited elbowroom and their accouterments: Dark brown furniture, dark brown rugs, built-in wardrobes, no pictures (we were told the probable fairytale that they had been spirited away by larcenous guests), and no frills except an outside doorbell, a computerized awakening system, and a minibar. The fresh **Napoleon,** near the Etoile, is much better now in a modernized Regency manner. Looking up (as Bonaparte might) and very well sited. Its restaurant is highly respected generally, but especially (of all things) for its sauerkraut! The Rank-run **Westminster** seemed to us to be blisteringly overpriced for its bedroom talents. The Tudor salon, Bulldog Restaurant and Empire bar, however, are appealing. Now let's dip into the grab-bag of assorted capital hostelries:

The **Commodore**, at a convenient midcity site, used to be a good commercial-style bet. Although the management has cleaned up its lobby and unchipped most of its corridors, we repeatedly saw soiled hand-marks on doors and along the walls. Some frayed carpets have now been replaced or repaired. No longer a bargain.

The **Sofitel-Bourbon** resides at a spiritless address in the feckless VIIe arrondissement. The proof of its modern lobby tasted so weak to our palate that any one of 250 hotels we had inspected directly preceding this one stirred our corpuscles with greater zing. Amiably zesty 40-seat dining room; deep-frozen bar; valiant-to-eye-throbbing color schemes in accommodations; a cocktail shaker of assets and debits in space arrangements, with most dimensions small. The same group operates the 630-unit **Sofitel de Paris.** It is across the *rue* from the capital's Parc des Expositions—which gives you a pretty fair idea of its fair-minded function. Then we have the 32-story, $30,000,000, 800-room, red-toned **Nikko.** Its domain, under the stewardship of Shiro Mikura, is southwest of the Eiffel Tower on the shore of the Seine.

The 75-room-and-bath-or-shower **Celtic**, just off the Étoile, doesn't seem to have lived up to its restyling promises—at least not to our eyes anyway. Our favorite double here is #13. The **Victoria Palace** occupies a silent setting. Friendly reception; equally ingratiating staff; dining room with quality cooking; streetside bar; 3 lounges; well maintained. A solid value for the money.

The **Club Méditerranée**, out of the center, is such an antihotel concept that we couldn't buy it even if we belonged to this worldwide organization. Room service does not even exist; each morning your "breakfast" is delivered through a chute from the corridor—instant coffee plus a thermos of hot water, no less. Regardless of its handy site and successful restaurant, its just not for the likes of us. In fairness, however, a number of readers say they like the attitudes here and the sense of freedom it affords.

The **Grand Hôtel Littré** is in the hands of Proprietor Albert Schmitt (former President of the French Hotels Association) and his charming wife, who also own the Victoria Palace. Since these houses are back-to-back, a hallway connects them, and their tariffs are identical. Before reopening the former, they tore it apart and put it back together again in a commendably clean, fresh, and attractive way. Charming bar; 3-tier lobby; TV room; 2 small but comfortable lounges; sparkling dining room to brighten the visitor's welcome. The chef is rightfully proud of his Gallic *haute cuisine.* All 4 suites and 120 rooms come with adequately spacious private baths. The décor is restful and practical; try to reserve on the courtyard for sun and tranquillity. These good people, including Manager Baer, have now turned this into an excellent bet for the price.

San Regis offers 2 duplex suites, 12 normal suites, and 42 rooms (all with private plumbing), with the better, redecorated units to the rear. Sadly missed is its former restaurant, now converted into a 5-table short-order operation. Not bad, but not good either. The **Normandy** has been invaded by carpenters and plasterers—all 7 floors, all 130 rooms (of which we prefer the "07" series). Ask to see an accommodation before booking if you can, because some are small while others are generous in dimensions. Coming up smartly.

The **Royal Hôtel**, in a tranquil situation near the Étoile, was eminently worth the search. Midget lobby; fresh 6th floor; tour groups never accepted; side-street locations the quietest, despite double windows on the Avenue side; everything spotless. All accommodations we have either stayed in or inspected over the years, while small and costly for the category, have looked pert and have smelled as fresh as a mountain pine grove. Each and every face—from Jean's at reception, Gaston's as Chief Concierge, the housecleaning women's, and amiable, courtly, highly likeable Director André Lebrun's—wears a size-48 smile that should make you glow in response. The **Vernet** is also a 2-minute stroll from the Étoile. Quiet side-street harbor in the *coeur* of Paris; friendly family atmosphere nourished by the Percepied brothers; bar and pleasant restaurant; 63 Gallic bedchambers; only 2 without private bath. **Hôtel de Castiglione** has a grandmotherly ambiance. Smallish lobby; appetizing dining room and handsome tartanesque bar up 1 flight; clean and well illuminated; 110 units, most with private baths. Comfortable. The 29-nest **Lido**, well-scrubbed and polished, offers many thoughtful minutiae. Fairly tranquil considering its proximity to Place de la Madeleine; bright, modern lobby; no restaurant; s-l-o-w elevator; carpeted corridors; large wallpapered bedrooms. Aim high for *les toits de Paris* view.

The **Penta** stands next to the Paris Exhibition Hall at La Défense, about 2 miles west of the Arc de Triomphe. Since here is today's most modern business section in the metropolis or its environs, naturally this venture has been keyed to heavy commercial traffic. The sister operation in London is doing a fine job in its medium category.

The 32-story **Sheraton** is a-bustling on the Left Bank—yes, *Left Bank*—one block from the Montparnasse Railway Station and just above the subway stop. Plastic galore in the lobby but more warmth upstairs; every convention facility imaginable but only 1 bar for 2000 dehydrated palates; no laundry pickup from 10 A.M. Friday until Monday. Surprisingly for such a vast hostelry, the service is good.

Madeleine-Palace (8 rue Cambon) has been zestlessly restyled. Total of 116 accommodations and 110 baths or showers; soiled carpeting throughout on our visit; adjoining King Charles Restaurant in attractive burnt-orange and panels. A mixed bag. The recently expanded **Madeleine-Plaza**, directly on the place de la Madeleine, has pea-pod rooms that glisten. Top floor the most tranquil in this traffic-choked zone; 18 newer units perhaps a few centimeters more spacious. Especially warm greeting for readers of this book from Mlle. Jard, the smiling receptionist. The **Hôtel de Castille** is creaky but comfy.

The **Terminus St.-Lazare-Concorde** should, in our opinion, bring blushes to the cheeks of the otherwise discerning Concorde chain executives whose show-case is the splendid Crillon. This grandpop's-era railway-terminus-style lodging operation, fairly crawling with flockers from other lands during our recent scrutiny, might be viewed as a gimmicked-up Hotel Grand which, as has been intimated, we regard with all the affection we would give a giant bus station. The **Ambassador**, which shoots for the same patronage, offers some bedchambers as grim as a Wagnerian stage, many furnishings as Old-Fashioned as muddled sugar, lemon peel, whisky, and Angostura, plus service either indifferent (especially from the concierge) or dum-dum (from the receptionist); horrid cuisine; cleaned up somewhat on our latest visit. But for its address and highish tabs, we still consider this one an unworthy plenipotentiary. The venerable **California** has been pepped up admirably in all sectors. All 172 units resparkled in Louis XVI style; self-dial phones added plus TV, radio, and mimibar. We are warmly nostalgic about the Eric Hawkins' Corner in its refashioned Golden Gate Bar and adjoining Grill. Better and better.

We remain fond of the **Scandinavia** (2 blocks from the Sorbonne), a historic inn built during the reign of Louis XIII, which features authentic period furnishings and paintings; no elevator; 22 petite rooms and baths with beamed ceilings, velvet curtains, wall-to-wall carpets, elfin beds, and bits of medieval lore; gracious minions, headed by English-speaking Directress Collette Thibault. But—and this is an important "but"—no restaurant, no bar service, no alcohol sold on the premises; breakfast only. They've built a snack bar next door, however. So small and so popular that reservations *must* be nailed down in advance. **Hotel de l'Université**, near St.-Germain-des-Prés, offers ample flair in an old house converted by Mrs. Bergmann. Handsome wrought iron staircase; twelfth-century bar; twentieth-century Club 22 for snacks; wooden beams, vaults, marble, textiles, and stucco blending into a tasteful composite in which no 2 units are the same. Simple furnishings; reasonable prices that vary with the particular accommodation; again, no restaurant. Another Left Banker that we feel is worth the investment. The **Cécilia**, where the kindly manager and wife are putting lots of heart into remodeling, is a friendly but unostentatious port for voyaging families. Exceptionally good for wayfarers who seek a sympathetic house without fancy frills. The **Bradford**, a 5-minute hike from the Champs-Élysées in a quiet backwater, has taken such a dive of late, in our opinion, that it is no longer a worthy choice. Sorry to see it sinking. **Scribe** has retired its plume for a year of restoration.

Vendôme, boasting a situation similar to the Ritz, has been moving ahead manfully. Empire décor plus brass bedsteads; oldish corridors; ample space provided; smilingly helpful staff. We like its slipper-style comfort. The **Madison**, opposite the St.-Germain-des-Prés church, is tops in its vicinity. Fresh lobby; 12 bedchambers revamped each year; front units nicest and largest; okay at best. As for the **Burgundy**, we've received so many reports of dregs in the bottle that we are putting this one on the shelf for a season or so. The **Grand Hotel des Principautes Unies,** facing a half-razed edifice on the Luxembourg Gardens, is far more ingratiating once you are inside. No restaurant but 27 fresh-faced accommodations. Substantial for the outlay.

One of the top bets in the lower priced category is **Régence-Étoile,** so close to the Arc de Triomphe that you'll feel monumentally Gallic. Tiny cubicles that experience merely a nodding acquaintance with the housekeeper, we would guess; 18 cozy-corner bathrooms; breakfast only. A good buy by Parisian standards. **Édouard VII**, next to Brentano's on avenue de l'Opéra, has 90 old but adequate rooms, 80 baths, steel beds, an abundance of stained-glass windows in the upstairs halls, and a bustling impersonal mien; not special. **Royal St.-Honoré** and **Bellman** fall into the routine bracket. Good staffs in all. **Lutetia,** one of the few big hotels on the Left Bank, is favored by French senators from the provinces. Some love it, while others don't appreciate its dated mién. The **Saint-Simon**, also on this *rive,* is chiefly for tranquillity seekers. Family-run pension atmosphere in which no meals are served; no concierge; no elevator; small cellar bar; pleasant for that specialized client who seeks its milieu. **Grand Hôtel du Mont-Blanc**, near Notre-Dame, seems haphazard and far from Grand; not our pony of Pernod. **Astor** (breakfast only) and **Mapotel Pont Royal** are average. The latter is enhanced by Les Antiquaires restaurant. The **Montalembert**, its neighbor, is similar in price but better in *quid pro quo*. Its 65 units with bath or shower recently were refashioned with verve. The leadership shows unusual hospitality and concern for American visitors. Much improved and well managed today. **Cayré** is coming up, too. Now okay for the outlay. **Richmond**, in the 9th arrondissement, is for shelter-seekers only. **Vermont** is even more simple, with no lobby or lounge, meager plumbing facilities, and small sleeping cells. For unfinicky pilgrims only. In the same category and equally inhabitable are the finely honed 23-room-and-bath **Masséna**, the cozy **Tronchet** with 2 atelier units under the eaves, and the patio-sweet **Régent's**; each has distinctive color and charm as well as its particular drawback, but in all 3 your happiness depends on which bedroom you draw. The **Régina** is old, comfy, and clean; here's another candidate for wanderers with large broods. **Pavillon Henry IV**, at St.-Germain-en-Laye (closed Dec. through Feb.) is suburban and lovely for a rest. Nearby there's the **Cazaudehore**, a 24-chamber, charming hostelry which forms a part of the country estate; comfort is princely in La Forestiere segment; the expensive cuisine is superb in the dining portion. Warmly recommended.

At *Versailles,* the beautiful, period-piece **Trianon Palace**, with its classic décor, is not as august as it was. Only 10 rooms renewed recently (and gracefully), with hopes to tackle the remaining 90 soon; 68 baths; much scruffiness visible on this look; savory cuisine and elegant presentation, but, to us at least, bumptious, inept service. For its highborn tariffs, no longer the aristocrat of yore—at least in our opinion.

Student digs? Drop a line to l'**Office du Tourisme Universitaire**, 137 boulevard St.-Michel, and it will send you a list of moderately priced shelters. The **French Cultural Services**, 972 Fifth Ave., New York, N.Y. 10021, which offers a free booklet on summer schools, might also be helpful.

Naturally, there are hundreds more—far too many to attempt to list in this type of book. The ones we've selected, however, are either the best known or the cream of their categories—a wide-ranging cross section of 72 choices. As only 1 example of this vast variety which runs throughout the entire text, why is this book sometimes so absurdly accused of being written for the rich?

Airport lodgings? Aside from those abuilding at Orly, there are 4 major choices. We rate one excellent. The **Orly Hilton** is 20 to 30 minutes from the heart of the city (take a bus to economize); directly across the street from the main terminal building. Modern sawtooth exterior with double windows, soundproofed ceilings and walls, and 100% air conditioning; spacious updated accommodations; 120-unit wing where the Queen-size beds are especially targeted for singles or lovers; totally refurbished lobby; long, wide corridors opening onto 2 lounges, a beauty parlor and barbershop, plus other commercial niches; cunning series of vitrine-like ponds and gardens leading to a separate fuselage containing (1) The re-perked and cheerful coffee shop with light dishes at reasonable tabs (open 6:30 A.M. to 11 P.M. daily), (2) L'Atelier Bar (12-seat counter; tiny dance floor), and (3) La Louisiane Restaurant, an appealingly romantic touch of creole culture and cuisine. Free hotel-terminal shuttle service is offered. If you want to move around a lot while using this house as your base, ask about the Air Inter "France Pass," which will provide you with a French Connection to all Gaul and reduced rates at this hostelry. The staff are now smiling, eager, and helpful. Better and better.

The 3-star, 600-unit **Novotel** is operative overlooking the freeway at a median point between the city and Orly Airport, an $8 to $9 taxi ride or 15 minutes by the Métro to the hub of the urban action. Its high-rise neighborhood is unattractive; bleak, stark efficiency is its bag; tolerable but certainly not happy-making for the pilgrim who seeks a money-saving place of repose. The **Orly P.L.M.**, the airess of its landed big-city sister, makes few pretensions toward luxury. Efficiency and commerce are its prime motivations.

The **Air Hôtel** draws our top scallions. We wouldn't sleep here on a bet. The **Frantel**, looking through lozenge-shape windows upon a roadside heath, is for the fogbound only, in our view. We list it here merely as a convenience, not as a recommendation. **Holiday Inn**-vaded the nearby industrial suburb of Rungis with 180 chambers and opened another 90-room unit at Porte de Versailles.

Curiously, the mammoth Charles de Gaulle Airport at *Roissy* (a hell-and-gone ride for unfortunate passengers who must transfer en route) has only 2 smallish hotels for the weary—**Sofitel** and **Holiday Inn**. After inspecting the pair, we chose the former, which is sited within its confines near the termini —and we found it the better option. Both teem with madding crowds; both are geared for 24-hour operation; both offer free shuttles; save for the above-average Les Valois restaurant in the Sofitel, both are so routine as temporary shelters that they make the Orly Hilton seem palatial. Livable but not lovable.

Restaurants   Among Paris' *expensive indoor* group, it is our conviction that when everything is normal, the **Tour d'Argent** (15 quai de la Tournelle) cannot be surpassed by any restaurant in the world. Stunningly redecorated; penthouse setting over the Seine; brilliant spotlighted vista of Notre-Dame at 9:30 P.M. every night except Monday (paid privately during weekdays); predinner cocktails or postmeal cordials in its cozy, gracious, ground-floor Gastronomic Museum by prearrangement only. Because the presence of more than 20 visitors per day now disbalances the temperature of its wine cellars, you must also apply in advance for candlelit samplings in these romantic surroundings—and please don't forget to give a modest gratuity to the Master of the *Cave*. In addition to its legendary pressed duck (all numbered over many decades), the variety of other specialties is now broad enough to stagger a Lucullus. Wear your best duds; reserve in advance; ask for friendly Director of the Table Jean Joulia or Jacques; we much prefer lunch to dinner here, because the pace is more *lento* and the relaxation is better. Because the aforementioned wine cellars are among the greatest in the world, it is correct dining form to disregard water and to order a vintage wine from Sommelier Christian. If you're host, only your menu will carry prices; none appear on those of your guests. Handsome, debonair, razor-sharp Owner-Author Claude Terrail and his entire staff are to be congratulated for reestablishing their Silver Tower as one of the best-run, most satisfactory epicurean centers in business today. Closed Monday.

Lasserre (17 avenue Franklin-D.-Roosevelt) also has been one of our tip-tip-tip-of-the-top Parisian candidates since '59. For almost 2 decades we have walked in cold annually, always to find a reception which couldn't have been warmer, service which couldn't have been smoother, and cuisine so delicious that our taste buds stood up and sang the "Marseillaise." Sumptuous décor brightened by flowers, greens, and the Maestro's proudest toy—a sliding roof which opens at the touch of a button to admit sunlight or moonbeams; gold-rimmed service plates, silver-necked carafes, antique silver vases, the finest of appointments; chic, sleek international clientele; occasional raffles in which live doves carry the lucky numbers. Please attempt no reservations by mail, because these people aren't set up to cope with their tidal wave of desired advance bookings through correspondence; make them instead by telephone instantly after your arrival on French soil. Closed Sundays and the last 3 weeks of August; always nail down your table ahead of time.

Laurent (41 Av. Gabriel) can provide one of the most refined and altogether entertaining dining experiences in the capital. From the moment you are received with dignity and warmth in its rotunda to the final bow when you are escorted to its elegant portals, everything-but-everything reflects the finesse of *La Belle France.* There are crystal chandeliers, a massive floral centerpiece in its circular dining salon, silver candelabra, and every table with its own flower selections trimmed to perfection; marble pillars glow warmly in the soft light; spacious windows overlook illuminated shrubbery in the surrounding park; discreet live piano music tinkles continuously. Maître Serge Buoso, the soul of kindness, will show you the cornucopial hors d'oeuvre trolley and many of the special platters from the chef. Our very recent repast was a reward in every particular.

Maxim's: Annually since 1960 this book has continued to report that this venerable landmark has remained one of the world's most glittering showcases of *haute couture* and celebrated countenances—but that, in the author's opinion, the cuisine had fallen lamentably short of its reputation. Starting in 1970 this observation was added: "We find it incomprehensible that *Michelin* continues to award its coveted 3rd star to this operation; personally, we would rank it with 2 stars at the most." Eight years later, in 1978, this establishment disappeared entirely from the pages of *Michelin*—according to allegations of restaurant industry sources, at its own request rather than to face the loss of that crucial star. Owner Louis Vaudable is one of the greatest geniuses in public relations whom we have ever met; on the other hand, we cannot classify him as being even remotely close to any of the greatest gastronomic technicians of our acquaintance. If you wish to join the many people who go to these classic precincts principally to see and to be seen, there is scarcely a more chic social milieu in the world which is open to the public. But if you should expect to find culinary standards which match its ambiance, please don't be surprised if you're seriously disappointed by the time it comes to pay that whopping check.

Lucas-Carton (9 place de la Madeleine) embraces the visitor with warm, beautiful, ageless French elegance in food, in spirit, and in ambiance. Nothing has faded from the classic glory of this venerable landmark. Flawlessly maintained décor of dark orange-red banquettes, mirrored walls, sparklingly polished woodwork, and the other ingredients of Gallic tradition; the service, ever-alert (when it is not too crowded), spotlessly clad in well-cut tailcoats (even the young boys); cuisine normally excellent but occasional complaints nowadays are coming to our desk. It is ideally situated for well-heeled shoppers in search of an oasis of calm for their lunch. Open every day.

Taillevent (15 rue Lamennais) has long, long continued to radiate its glories in the Very Very First Rank of Gallic spiritual and atmospheric gastronomic tradition. The *cave* is fantastic; the wine list carries a staggering 502 choices, with 145-thousand bottles to back it up. If you happen to be in town around wine-tasting time (mid-Mar.), try to attend the formal *La Paulée*—a sampling of several dozen new wines; the restaurant closes except to those who wish to engage in this special sport (just ask André Vrinat, who is a Director of France's venerable Academy of Wines). Excellent kitchen; friendly reception; convenient location near Champs-Élysées; high tariffs; closed Sunday; *always* phone beforehand for your table. And, if you can, book here at night, since the Vrinat masters bleed that their high-powered business-executive clients at lunch do not have the time to be served with the attention they so winningly lavish on each guest. Hallelujah!

Concerning the equally noble **Vivarois** (Avenue Victor-Hugo 192), may we be forgiven if we expose, with not the slightest presumption intended, a small ray of pride? When this venture was in its swaddling clothes in 1968, the kind readers who accepted our unusually enthusiastic evaluation from then until 1973 helped it over its rough introductory bumps, when so many French gourmets refused to take it seriously because of their dislike of its nontraditional, clean-lined, modern décor. But 9 seasons back, *Michelin* and *Kléber* both raised it to the top of their respective national categories. Its working proprietors are M. and Mme. Claude Peyrot; certainly he is a virtuoso, a Grand Master of gastronomic genius. Pastel-yellow or sage clothed tables too close together; charcoal-hued banquettes; white Knoll chairs with cushions; 2 avant-garde murals woven by Belgian Monk Dom Robert; beautiful, gleaming, supereficient kitchen. In honor of his years as a pupil at the fabulous Pyramide in Vienne, M. Peyrot now offers Dodine de Canard Truffé à la Façon de Fernand Point—and DO we recommend this to all comers!!! Once our party was extraordinarily fortunate to strike his Le Loup Farci de Quenelle de Brochet as the *plat du jour* during our visit; this marvelous epicurean adventure may be special-ordered a day or so in advance. Charming Mme. Peyrot has a fair command of English. They are closed Saturdays and Sundays and normally from July 15 to September 10. We are ever-grateful to our cherished friend Georges Prade, the world-famous epicure and connoisseur, for steering us here. Always reserve in advance, because the same local gastronomes who used to sniff superciliously at it are now phoning up to 2 weeks ahead for space —and *don't miss it!*

Jacques Cagna (14 rue des Grands-Augustins) is one of our favorite private corners of France, occupying one of the oldest buildings in Paris. The main dining circle is up one flight to a quadrant surrounding the stairwell in which hangs a giant porcelain chandelier with frosted flowered reflectors. Heavy antique timbers; wooden floors; small attentive staff. Our Turbot Farci and the Ray in mustard sauce were splendid examples of the best of France's *nouvelle cuisine*. If you top your meal with a Reine de Saba (a devastatingly delicious chocolate fudgelike cake with English light custard) we can almost guarantee that you will expire from ecstasy and immediately rise to the seventh tier of heaven. Our twin lunch totaled $101 and was one of the most memorable of many a Gallic venture.

Rostang (10 rue Gustave-Flaubert) is one of the brightest lights on the Paris culinary horizon—it is also one of the more attractive *intime* heavens in the city. Lace curtains mantle the arched windows facing the street; brown carpets and textiled walls lend softness to the room; burnt orange colorings yield warmth as do the lovely flowers which abound; quiet music ripples the air. Young chef-owner Michel Rostang produces an amazing panoply of delights. Our sampling of the fresh duck liver in a warm *brioche,* the Petits Chèvres et St. Marcellin Affinés, the Feuilleté de Coquilles St. Jacques, and the sparkling choice of jewel-like desserts were memorable gems from the kitchen. Prices, while high, were certainly reasonable for the superlative gastronomy. Highest accolades.

Chiberta (3 rue Arsène-Houssaye), now totally renewed, lies a few steps off the Etoile. We hear from all quarters of the gastronomic world that young Chef Jean Michel Bedier is continuing the sorcery he formerly conjured up at the old Garin and at Le Camélia in Bougival. With such a splendid backgrounding, all of the praise must be deserved. Inventive dishes with a distinct inclination toward the "new school" of French cooking; expensive and apparently worthy.

Faugeron (52 rue de Longchamp) is the inspired creation of Henri Faugeron, formerly the soul of the bewitching little Les Belles Gourmandes. Splendid, glittering surroundings highlighted by chandeliers and softened by mellow velvet wall coverings; a-thing-of-tomorrow kitchen, even supplied with a bridge from which the chef can observe his crew; spacious floor plan; cuisine that employs the grand as well as the modest in terms of ingredients, e.g., goat cheese, whiting, milt, or calf's liver. In all of the flurry to deify France's *new* wave of culinary masters, it is refreshing to honor a young cook who endorses traditional values and who has the imagination to glorify the simple foods around us. His success is earned and praised. Closed Sat. and Sun.

Lamazère (23 rue de Ponthieu, also close to the Champs-Elysées), a *grand luxe* contender, has entered the scene as what is possibly the most expensive dining establishment in the city today. Owner Lamazère is in love with truffles, foie gras, and cassoulets. So are jillions of others, including us—but, during his 14-year proprietorship of the Proust, his amour extended to experimentation in new blends of these delights. While at least 50 other dishes are always on his card, these are the highest triumphs of his extremely high cuisine. A recent move to encourage late dining seems to be of little interest to the cassoulet, foie gras, and truffle traffic. We found the décor pretentious, the attention urbane, the tariffs astronomical, and the quality aristocratic.

Ledoyen (Carré des Champs-Élysées) occupies a position in the circle of blue bloods, though we personally feel that it may be slipping somewhat. Marvelous park setting (convenient for motorists) and handsome entrance; enclosed terrace dining room banked in rose velvet, with rose-velvet upholstered ceiling beams and star-spangled draped chiffon; large plate-glass windows; sumptuous brocaded sink-in armchairs; low candelabra; ruffled lace mantles over sateen tablecloths; antique silver tureens for flowers; gold service; soft piano lilts filtering through chiffon and chandeliers. A bit precious, very fashionable, and decidedly among the exalted addresses in Paris.

L'Archestrate (84 rue de Varenne, opposite the Rodin Museum) is today one of Paris' gastronomically stylish restaurants. And is it a honey! A small, attractive chamber is the site in which Proprietor-Chef Alain Senderens stirs the magic of his craft. Ocher-tone textile walls; high-back chairs with ruby and gold stripes; matching curtains and carpet; 2 blue-and-white porcelain chandeliers; baronial atmosphere that is in no way austere; flowers almost wherever the eye turns; ingratiating reception. Our merry-go-round began with the customary house gift of a delicious *pipérade*. The party then launched into cream-bathed snails with herbs (but no garlic), a marvelous raspberry-color Sea Bass in red (sic) wine sauce (Bouzy of the Champagne district), and a platter of oh-so-sinfully delectable hot duck livers topped with marble-size apples. Service uneven; expensive price tags (appropriate for its 3rd star in *Michelin*); a totally enjoyable gustatory experience which we hope to repeat for many visits to come. Closed Saturdays, Sundays, and holidays. As the French exclaim—ooo-la-la!

Grand Véfour (17 rue de Beaujolais) is a thing unto itself—and a very expensive thing it is, too. We have met recently with personable veteran Owner Raymond Oliver and find him to be a great showman, a devoted chef, and a gentleman who is always challenging his talent and continually growing, even at a time in life when most men would be deciding idly where to expose their girths to a relaxing sunbelt retirement. In former years we have been sharply critical of this establishment, but our attitude is being reformed by later exposure to improving cuisine and a conviction that while we don't always agree with M. Oliver, he is indeed a conscientious professional. We were especially impressed recently by his truffle soup with its chevroned surface, his unusual lobster plate steeped in a bizarre yet flavorful sweet-garlic bath, and his delicious Pears Grand Véfour. Classic lush décor that is a pinch less than baroque; fine old bas-relief ceilings; interior orientation that might dismay claustrophobes; frequent change of managers. If you are known here, we suspect you will be more warmly welcomed and served than if you are a stranger. Some drawbacks, but generally an exalted house with a mighty capacity to please.

Le Grand Phoenix, or Assiette au Beurre, (11 rue St.-Benoix) is another Raymond Oliver production where young chef Christian Ignace can do marvels with "new" cuisine specials such as lamb's tongue in sauterne or pears in air-light pastry. There's a shambling old atmosphere here that fits the St.-Germain-des-Prés mood. Prices, however, are more in the Right Bank character, with the average dinner spinning up from $35 to $55 *molto presto.* Closed Saturday midday and all Sunday. Excellent.

Le Bellecour (22 rue Surcouf) was first brought to our attention by our former classmate and current globespanner, insurance executive Bill Jadden, who really knows his noodles. How grateful we are to have "found" this sparkler just in the shadow of the Eiffel Tower. A single room with brown carpets, Hessian walls, modern paintings, banquettes, and tables with small lamps and vases of flowers. Our party's samplings of thin-sliced warm sausage on cool salad, of *feuilleté* of asparagus and artichoke, of wild duck, and of frogs' legs were splendid. We credit one notch in our Hickock belt to Mr. Jadden's savvy tip.

Les Armes de Bretagne (108 av. du Maine) is in a neighborhood in the throes of urban renewal, but do not let this dissuade you; inside it is elegance itself. Two sectors, one with sidewalk windows, another in an apse with interior orientation; textiled cognac-color walls; polished blackamoor sconces; art deco paintings; malacca chairs; lace curtains. Courageous Chef André Laurier suggested 2 new-concept creations from his culinary lab; we thoroughly enjoyed the experiments (though we are not sure everyone else will): the first, slivers of raw sea bass marinated in vinaigrette; the second, roast duck in a sauce of pink Chinese peppercorns; both were unique taste experiences. We also were grateful for his Terrine de Turbot à la Mousse de Rascasse—*formidable!* Kindhearted Maître Roland Boyer will lead you amiably through the thickets of the "new" cuisine or consult with you carefully on conventional dishes.

Escargot-Montorgueil (38 rue Montorgueil) seems to be in a slump even while its prices are mounting to numbing heights. Some diners still love it, however. Serene but not plush atmosphere; good attention, as long as you aren't placed in the inadequately staffed upstairs section. Closed Monday and all of August.

In the neighborhood of the Beaubourg, which is also called the Georges Pompidou Center, several restaurants are flourishing as a result of the increased traffic to the district. Certainly one of the most fashionable is La Ciboulette (60 rue Rambuteau). This one also seems to attract some of the most luscious models in the City of Light to its sophisticated tables. The service and cuisine reveal finesse that matches its *fin de siècle* décor. A counter filled with fresh flowers greets you at the entrance; one wall displays a large period poster; main dishes total from $12 to $15. Expensive and oh-so-easy on the eyes —especially if you are male. La Charrette (15 rue Quincampoix) is another much less costly candidate also beside the museum. The establishment appears to be blue-ribbon, but the dishes are surprisingly reasonable. Amusing ground-floor salon with cheerful tables surrounded by movie-director chairs; stone-lined cellar with breathtaking floral displays; extremely pleasant reception and service. Recommended for a modest meal. Across the street is the ever-popular Tour Tour with its assemblage of busy tables tucked into several cramped crannies. Wood ceiling with suspended tasseled lampshades; potted greenery; animated atmosphere but slow service. A 3-course lunch costs about $11— pretty good, if only the food were better. We would advise visiting the restaurant of the museum itself only—and *only*—if you've recently contracted a severe case of lockjaw. It is so grubby and unappetizing that we would not even sip coffee in its precincts.

CUISINE DE FEMME: A woman chef regaled us very recently with masterworks of her fine kitchen. Though the other sex are often the targets of male-chef vilification in the French media, their consummate skill with the skillets will, in our most serious judgment, resist any trivial carping and gender-motivated criticism. Mme. Marie Trama already is bringing fame to her small, rustic, ingratiating Chez Tante Madée (11 rue Dupin). Her Oysters Florentine are superb—almost a meal in themselves. Two tiny rooms separated by a rough-timber divider; stone and brick walls; intimate atmosphere that complements the personalized cooking. For bourgeois platters, Pouzoulou (88 rue de Richelieu) produces unpretentious fare at modest prices. A feminine confrère rules the roosters here. **Chez Allard** (41 rue St.-André-des-Arts) is still so "in" that smart bistro habitués must reserve 2 or 3 days ahead for space. Some reader howls alleging indifferent reception, haughty service, and uninspired cookery. Its 2 formerly tiny, jam-packed rooms have been expanded for the comfort of the identical capacity of diners; there's virtually no décor—but those sauces and that house wine, Bonnesmares! (Our luck has been surpurb.) Fairly steep for the surroundings, but excellent fare prepared by Mme. Allard, who is generally regarded as the top of her professional gender in Paris. Closed Sundays and holidays. A winner. A tiny one but also outstanding (and always booked long in advance) is the lunch-only **Cartet** (62 rue de Malte), which is clad in wood, serving as a perfect sounding board for the oooohs and ahhhs that are inspired by the crab soufflé, the medallions of garlic-scented lamb, or the fig-laden roast duck. Take plenty of time to enjoy this one. Now, for dinner only, try the ultrachic **Olympe** at 8 rue Nicolas-Charlet (15ᵉ). Dominique Nahmias seems to have Tout Paris in her pocket. Alas, it is difficult to climb in with this worshipful throng, but if you can manage a reservation, you won't be disappointed. An oddball entry is **À la Galoche d'Aurillac** (41 rue de Lappe) where typical Auvergne galoshes decorate the ceiling and where you'll find yourself hip deep in the hardy cookery of Nicole Bonnet. Other *"mère"* restaurants which we haven't tried but which we hear are worthy include Georgette Descat's **Lous Landés** (9 rue G.-Saché) with dishes of southwestern France, Germaine Saunière's **Au Cochon d'Or** (31 rue de Jour, near Les Halles and not to be confused with the later-mentioned entry on av. Jean-Jaurés) and **La Bonne Table** (119 blvd. Jean-Jaurés, Clichy), which is overseen by Gisele Berger. Several others exist but these are acknowledged to be the queenly elite for *cuisine de femme*.

Drouant (place Gaillon) splits its personality between a grill (left) and a more formal 2-room dining spread (right). The former harks back to the style of the Twenties; the latter seems a bit stiff with beige marble walls, white linen, and mirrors. We suggest the fish (especially Turbot soufflé) over the meat platters, because our party found all of the hoofware rather plodding. The grill functions daily while the other half relaxes on Saturdays. Okay, but not what it was in former years.

Lapérouse (51 quai des Grands-Augustins—Left Bank) was sold recently and was so grim on our latest inspection that we can no longer suggest it for any discerning traveler.

Nicolas (12 rue de la Fidélité), one of the oldest restaurants in Paris, is owned and operated by our good friend, Julien François, President of France's Restaurateurs, a Commander of the Cordon Bleu, and a Commander of the Légion d'Honneur. As he is the elected spokesman for every dining establishment in the nation, his haven darned well ought to be super—and it is, at astonishingly modest tariffs for such scrumptious fare. Patronage heavily Gallic; always full; smiling invitation to visit the kitchen. The Maestro is ably assisted by his enchanting English-speaking daughter, Mme. Nicole, and her handsome husband, M. Daniel; Maîtres Christian and Maurice also parleyvoo in our parlance. The foie gras is possibly the finest you will ever experience anywhere. (The kitchen prepares about 18 tons of it per year!) Advance booking mandatory; rare bonus of staying open on Sunday (except in July); closed Saturday instead. To us and to countless other devotees, absolutely unbeatable in its category.

Le Train Bleu, which began life as Le Buffet in 1901, changed its name—but it is still in the Gare de Lyon and still one of the dining delights of contemporary as well as nostalgic Paris. Although the sumptuous salons overlook the comings and goings of trains, from this point on its resemblance to any other station restaurant in the world is totally absent. The staircase is a gracious wonder; huge chandeliers hang from gold-leafed ceilings; walls are decorated with carvings; superb woodwork and brassware are abundant.

And before we get off this track, **Le Relais Paris-Est** (in the station at Gare de l'Est) still seems to us to be running out of steam. One of the several points which elicited our disfavor was the flashy, showy, and gimmicky listing of century wines that are completely undrinkable. This is Lesson Number 1 in oenology, and we are frankly puzzled how any knowledgeable diner could be taken in by such an obvious ploy. Not for us, at those prices—and especially with Le Train Bleu (see above) cannonballing down the rails as a competitor.

Les 3 Moutons (63 avenue F. D. Roosevelt) and **Les 3 Limousins** (8 rue de Berri) both specialize in grills—the former on sheep, of course, and the latter on steer. Same shared management; similar trimmings and fixtures; same sort of chuck-wagon attitudes mixed with obvious capital gains for city slickers. Each displays a life-size stuffed representative of its wares—neither of which is nearly so inflated as are the prices, however. Of the pair, we prefer the first. Twin midtowners for rich range rovers.

L'Orangerie (28 rue St.-Louis-en-l'Ile) seems to be getting marginally better. Here is its concept: Select clientele of "SEE-ME!" nabobs; self-generating egotism a pillar as a promotional come-on; more value of late for your greenbacks; somewhat limited choice of main-course and fringe dishes. Rustic trappings in a single chamber 4 yards wide and 20 yards long; candle illumination; timber beams; "spoken" menu with pick of ½-dozen entrées, a dessert, a wine (either open Beaujolais or Bordeaux), and coffee at a fixed price. If you like the juice of this Orangerie, the squeeze is part of the parcel.

Relais Bisson (37 quai Grands-Augustins) currently seems to blow hot or cold—with the emphasis on the latter, we regret to pen. One thing that remains consistent, however, is the bill—thumpingly high. The décor—an Eden of greenery surrounded by beige and orange pastels—is lovely, but nice as it is, it does not make up for the prices we paid for so-so service and only fair cookery.

Chez Albert (122 avenue du Maine) is on the upswing, we are happy to report. Warm reception; attentive service; well-known for its Coquilles St. Jacques plus fish dishes; upper-crust clientele. Deadly serious atmosphere overlorded by the Beaumont family; main room draped in canvas à la sidewalk café; our foursome draped with a franc-heavy wallpaper job which probably was appropriate at today's inflation rate. Don't be lured into the costly trap of ordering the ancient white wines. Closed Mondays and August.

Relais Louis XIII (8 rue des Grands-Augustins) is a colorful, *intime,* stone-and-timber-lined corner of Paris, where the ambiance is soothingly relaxed, the management is strictly professional, and the food is good. The squire of the kitchen, André Marfeuille, presents a limited but tempting selection. Art collection tastefully augmented; air conditioning; salons delightful in their separate ways. Appealing to all of the senses.

Jamin (32 rue de Longchamp) is a treasure—a tiny trove with flowers, coziness, and 14-karat price tags. Increasingly costly, but still drawing an ardent following of devotees; suavely polished; comfortable; delectable omelets embracing shrimp, lobster, sea urchins, truffles, and other exotic dainties; marvelous duck livers. This is one to enjoy if you can afford it.

Here's a midcity quartet which we recently reviewed afresh: **Chez Ramponneau** (21 avenue Marceau), near the Étoile, reflects a tavern air with line-drawn murals, cartwheel fixtures, and an atmosphere that doesn't quite live up to its intent, in our opinion. The billings, however, are exceedingly sincere. The miniscule **La Toque Lorraine** (9 rue de l'Echelle), fringing the Louvre district, is in the able hands of M. and Mme. Michel Thiebaut who redistribute the culinary wealth of Lorraine to lucky Parisians. The coinage in some recipes goes back to the 1750's. The **Pavillon Louis XIV** (8 blvd. St.-Denis) probably is spacious enough to entertain the court of its namesake. It is crowded, lively, and friendly—but not intimate. Closed June through August plus every Tuesday. Average prices for above average quality. **La Bourgogne** (6 avenue Bosquet), peeking up at the Eiffel Tower, sets about 20 tables in an L-configuration, sets partitions between them, and sets flowers upon them. The cuisine seemed very costly for the return, but the heavenly desserts almost make you forgive the cash register. Closed August and Sundays.

Au Vieux Berlin (32 avenue George V), across the street from the George V and Prince de Galles hotels, is delightful for romancers—or even for holding hands with your wife. This urbane, candlelit establishment, with soft piano notes in its background (plus an adjoining snack counter), is a semiofficial German _pied-à-terre_ in Paris. If your palate feels Frenchy, its Gallic yen will be handsomely satisfied—but if it should be your moment for Herring Hausfrau, sausages, potato salad, and draft Löwenbräu, these are also at your command in a flash. Closed Sundays and most holidays. Recommended.

The **Copenhague** (142 avenue Champs-Élysées, part of Denmark House) is moving up dramatically as an exponent of fine Danish fare. Today we think most well-heeled travelers will enjoy its presentation and its skilletcrafts on sight. Bar downstairs; garden dining in summer; urbane atmosphere; good cold buffet in the Copenhagen tradition; excellent wines; prices climbing ominously; licensed and supervised by the Danish Government; open every day; be sure to ask for alert and friendly Maître d'Hôtel René Bernard.

La Marée (1 rue Daru) makes the stylish inner circle—and it is gaining ground steadily with disciples of seafood. Animated atmosphere created by a chic (and often beautiful) clientele; soft glow provided by chapel-glass stained panels and Edwardian globe fixtures on mirrored sconces; split-level construction (we prefer the sunken zone nearer the front); ruby-hue velvet banquettes; fresh flowers on tables; enormous broadside menu; service improved. The prices are in line with its quality and appealing ambiance.

Hostellerie de Nicolas Flamel (51 rue de Montmorency in the 3rd arrondissement, not to be confused with boulevard de Montmorency in the 16th arrondissement) is perhaps the oldest house in town (A.D. 1438). It was once occupied by the alchemist Pernelle. Medieval atmosphere, natch; fixed-price meal (about $35 inclusive)—an advantage, because the client knows in advance how much he will spend. Lunch and dinner served; adequate but not extraordinary cookery; reserve ahead. Worthy.

Chaumière de l'Isle is a very old establishment with a new outlook and renewed vigor. Small, ancient, and now quite good.

Île de France, which toots only on weekends, is moored opposite 32 quai de New-York, between Debilly footbridge and the Pont d'Iéna. This former barge of the Compagnie Générale Transatlantique has been transformed into what might be termed a midstream diner. The galley produces just the fare you might expect from a Gallic interpretation of a Mississippi steamboat. We found it duller than the stern of a paddle-wheeler, but perhaps we cruised in on an off night.

In the *medium-to-moderately-expensive* group, **St. Moritz** (a few steps off the Étoile, adjoining the Royal Hotel) is a handsome contender. Sleek interior highlighted by pale wooden coffers inset with wall plates; colorful, well-appointed décor; cuisine substantial, but not in the Grand category; the *fruits de mer* (seafood) platter a good catch; closed Sunday and all of August.

Coconnas (2 bis place des Vosges) is agreeably situated in an ancient flower market which Louis XII later converted into his personal pavilion. Long, narrow room with 20 wooden tables; simple décor; immaculately clean; special attention to pâtés, a dish called Merlan en Colère ("a whiting biting his own tail"), and Poule au Pot; becoming more and more expensive, unfortunately. Guy is the host. Master Restaurateur Claude Terrail (Tour d'Argent) is the owner. Closed Tuesday.

Rôtisserie de la Reine Pédauque (6 rue de la Pépinière, near Gare St.-Lazare) had faltered quite a bit, but now that it is under new management we must get back for another try. We hear that it is quite good again, however; especially noteworthy are the colorful Terrine de Légumes and the Gratin de Langoustines by Chef Daniel Soret. Probably on the rebound. **Chez Benoit** (20 rue St. Martin) plays its poor little heart out for the ultrapampered Nescafé Society of Paris. Slum-district location which the fad followers find irresistibly with-it; 2 drab rooms; no décor; passable cookery; plenty of smoke. Bah, not for us, but some still find it irresistibly chic. Expensive it is, that's a truth.

Chez Raffatin et Honorine (16 boulevard St.-Germain) in its simple way is once again a celebration for the senses. The small staff really seem to care. Glass-enclosed sidewalk tables; aislelike room hung with sausages and ham; 8-foot buffet serving as one wall; rusticity galore. A friendly spot for relaxation and good value.

D'chez Eux (2 avenue Lowendal), a 2-minute ride from the Hilton, is almost exactly the same since M. and Mme. A. Court followed up their St.-Germain project listed directly above (and which they've since sold) with this even more colorful version. Again, an enclosed sidewalk tonsure; similar kitchen crafts for a somewhat higher $-riddled per-person outlay; shuttered Sunday.

Cochon d'Or (192 avenue Jean-Jaurés) is a rather long ride out to Pont de Pantin—and it shouldn't be mistaken for the previously described Au Cochon d'Or. Several rooms, of which we prefer the 1st-floor salon with mirrored walls and a low ceiling. Our tandem dinner, including wine, came to $63, and we found it unexciting to the point of boredom. Don't go out of your way, but if you are in the neighborhood when starvation strikes it will do.

Bistro Barrière de Clichy (1 rue de Paris), may reside in a dreary suburb (about 20 minutes by car), but the journey is well worth the effort. The scallops in helium-light pastry and the turbot with green lemon are prides of the artful chef; the dessert platter is worthy of space in a Cartier display case.

La Boule d'Or (13 boulevard La Tour-Maubourg) seemed to be the answer to hearty appetites. WOW! Each table was practically swaybacked with nibbling items just to hold you over until the real feed began: pickles, rolls, and chunks of farmhouse butter the size of the Arc de Triomphe and an enormous rillette portion containing at least a pound of meat—merely a starter! Blanquette de Veau designed to quell the hunger pangs of Olympic decathlon champions (we've seldom seen a male in the place who weighed less than 200 lbs.!); desserts from cabbage-size pears in nests of cream and pastry, to towering soufflés, to shells of sweets so tempting that ladies' corsets split asunder at the sight of a passing tray. Just the thing for size-99 tummies.

We wouldn't bother with **Pierre Traiteur** (10 rue de Richelieu) since it is mainly a Gallic businessmen's haunt. Fair skilletry but no joys otherwise, at least to us. Some pretty educated palates, however, disagree with our evaluation on this entry, contending that it provides unusual value for your francs. For you to decide.

Maisonnette Russe (6 rue d'Armaillé) is a moderately priced high-stepper. Dim chamber with faded aristocratic air; antique lamps; maroon velour and leather chairs; 2 boars' heads glaring at diners. Borscht with perhaps half a steer in each bowl; Russian vodka by the iceberg; desserts for dreaming: spun sugar nests and chocolate cake resembling a long ton of chilled fudge. Not for diet watchers; surprisingly rewarding for presentation, cuisine, service, and atmosphere.

Chez les Anges (54 blvd. de Latour-Maubourg) and the **Ambassade d'Auvergne & du Rouergue** (22 rue de Grenier) both exude a pleasant rustic charm. We prefer the former which, unfortunately, runs about 20% higher in its billings. Your profits, however, appear on the platters which we think are perhaps 50% more savory. Both are fun, however.

Paul Chêne (123 rue Lauriston) is à la mode for residents of this silk-stocking neighborhood; Calcuttas of golfers use this as their 19th green. Clean, typical-bistro décor; about 50 couverts; able young chef from Lyon —a recommendation in itself. That ever-savvy Prince of the Mumm champagne domain, Georges Prade, calls its Poule au Pot "intelligently served." In response to this, an equally distinguished and globally renowned gourmet retorted the following to us by mail: "I agree with our friend Georges Prade to say that the Poule au Pot is 'intelligently served,' but I do not agree regarding the quality of the Poule au Pot." Gentlemen, choose your weapons! A winning family house, with careful and honest cooking—*and* a highly controversial Poule au Pot!

Galiote (rue Gamboust) turned on a memorable meal during recent Paris rovings. Three segmented rooms, pleasant but in no way elegant; wood paneling and brass chandeliers; informal but attentive service. Outstanding hors d'oeuvres display; nice wines; full-dress fare in the medium-cost range. Our light veal-chop lunch with _cèpes_ was better than average. Sound.

Le Petit Colombier (42 rue des Acacias) is a bit off the beaten track—a few minutes by taxi beyond the Arc de Triomphe. But if you're wandering in this neighborhood, you might find this small house amiable. Go upstairs for a window table, if available; it has especially good carafe wines. Average check $25 or so; not worth a special pilgrimage, but satisfactory for the price.

Joseph (56 rue Pierre-Charron) is peopled by top French executives and a smart lunch crowd. It is also handy for travelers who stay in either the George V or Prince de Galles hotels. Friendly atmosphere carefully nurtured by owner Patrik Benatar; routine prices; closed Sunday. We've always found them working hard and well.

Auberge de France (1 rue du Mont-Thabor), located between Place Vendôme and the Tuileries, is a seventeenth-century-style entry which also features a _raclette stübli_ in the cellar for Swiss cheese dishes. Manager Ferrié, a former chef schooled by Fauchon, is revealing respectable culinary skills in the classical tradition. Though we haven't sampled either, raptures have been broadcast around the town about the piscatorial Sea-Wolf Ali-Baba and the Musketeer Sherbert. Our recent steerage was superb but our partner's duck was just fair. Worth an experiment.

Lucien (12 rue Sourcouf) is straight Gallic, with mixed French and Yankee colony clientele. Simple ambiance; 8 tables; a nervous, hardworking owner who knows food; with moulés, pheasant, and soufflé on the menu, you should rise to Cloud Nine. Expensive for its setting; reservations a must; closed Monday; sturdy and dependable.

The **Quai d'Orsay** (Left Bank, near rue Fabert) claims many happy disciples. The elbow-to-elbow bistro character is so popular—especially with a young assemblage of chatterers—that bookings must be made a day ahead. The stuffed neck of duck is the stuff of dreams—perhaps not for the _canard,_ but it was for this happy waddler. There's a new 400-seat, moderately priced contender in the former **Gare d'Orsay,** but we haven't tried the food. Grand room with elaborate tracery, red velvet walls, and matching carpets. It could be worth a station stop.

Café de la Paix (12 boulevard Capucines)? This Paris landmark recently was reopened, and—praise to Allah—it remains in the former 19th-century style. The restoration is a joy to any nostalgic Francophile.

For hotel dining, space prohibits a special rundown here, so please refer back to our "Hotels" section where we've tried to describe the more noteworthy tables.

Chez l'Ami Louis, Rôtisserie de la Table du Roy, Aux Lyonnais, and **Michelle** form a quartet over which we are not too enthusiastic even though they have certain admirable points. Service and cookery at Chez l'Ami Louis impressed us as having become careless, if not downright slovenly. Its slum neighborhood might be considered "colorful" by some, but your interests and safety are too much of a concern for us to suggest it. On our last 3 visits, Table du Roy crawled with so many Americans we could shut our eyes and swear we were back in Howard Johnson's. Aux Lyonnais served us delicious scallops in mustard sauce, but the modest surroundings and the immodest prices turned us off; it does evoke a deep-French atmosphere, however. Michelle, we think, has gone off. The last is not **Chez Michel** (10 rue de Belzunce), a specialty bistro where the haute quality matches its haute tariffs.

BISTROS: These are now the rage in Paris due to their vastly improved quality and the reasonable values they offer. The spearhead of this movement is Michel Oliver, son of the redoubtable Raymond Oliver, who for so many years has operated the ultraexpensive Grand Véfour. Oliver *fils* has created uniformity of taste and a remarkably respectable grade of cuisine. The décor borrows extensively from the Belle Époque, with forests of curlicue wood, panels of leaded stained glass, morning-glory lamps, smoked mirrors, bentwood chairs, marble-topped wrought-iron tables, and other beautifully rendered facsimiles of the era assembled by the now-ubiquitous Slavik, a decorator who has taken Paris by *tempête*. Three of Oliver's handiest entries are **Le Bistro de la Gare** (73 Champs Élysées), the neighboring **L'Assiette au Boeuf**, and the **Bistro de la Gare**—another one—(59 Blvd. du Montparnasse). A meal at these can be had for from $8 to $14. If we have any criticism to make it is that the main dish often is not up to the exceptional attractiveness and taste of the first course or the spectacular desserts. Nevertheless, the experience is one of significant reward for the outlay. This must be true because evidence of the booming success is provided by the long lines which form in front of these restaurants at mealtimes. Another interesting candidate is **Le Gros Minet** (1 rue des Prouvaires), located near the garden and esplanade that was Les Halles. Tile floor; zinc counter; ground-floor room plus another small segment through the kitchen and up a narrow spiral staircase over the pantry. Ask the kind proprietor to show you his *cave,* which dates back to 1660. For around $10 you will be regaled with enormous pans and casseroles of terrine, rillette, and salad; then the set meal includes a flank steak *(onglet)* with sauté onions or several other choices of entrée. We found this one outstanding. While the entire district surrounding Les Halles is rebounding with personality and excitement, we were notably unimpressed by that old standby **Pied de Cochon** (6 rue Coquillière), which seems to have drawn every tourist since Pepin the Short. For steaks, no serious beefeater should miss a turn at the tables of **Les Gourmets des Ternes** (Blvd. Courcelles 87) near the Étoile. While the menu lists a stampede of meats, don't fail to have the house's enormous special cut, which is so tender that we almost guarantee it will bring tears to the eyes of any dedicated carnivore. The one room is divided into 2 segments by arches and pillars; it is girdled by smoky mirrors; paper "tablecloths" complete the tone. This one is more expensive than the others, but well worth the effort. Also in the upper category is the well-known **Chope d'Orsay** (10 rue du Bac), where busy, cordial matrons serve up artistic platters to their loyal clientele at a dozen small tables. The salon's ceiling and walls are cloaked in a rich textile; copper skillets blend with old furnishings for warmth; lace curtains drape the streetside windows. The terrine of smoked sturgeon and salmon appears as a delicate pink and white banner; our medallions of scallops in saffron were as lovely to the eye as they were to the palate; and the *baba au rhum* for dessert was a totally sinful escapade. The wine selection is small and not noteworthy, but perhaps this is effected in the interest of economy. An abundant feast will nudge the $33 mark—yet it will be memorable.

In the _inexpensive group,_ **Dominique** (19 rue Bréa), annually updated and refreshed during the month of June when it is closed, is just as satisfactory today as when we first stumbled across it in '46. At the counters near the entrance you can eat nobly for about $17 or so. This includes a choice of soup, _plat du jour,_ cheese, and dessert. For a special treat, we suggest the grilled sturgeon and the blintzes with caviar, borsch à la crème, or Shashlik Karsky. Dining in the intimate room in the rear or upstairs costs more for 4 courses plus a small bottle of wine; à la carte service also is available. Dominique and son Gary always provide a lot for your money, with some excellent Russian specialties and sound French dishes. Recommended for its friendly spirit.

Chez Joséphine (117 rue du Cherche-Midi) couldn't be more typical as a middle-class bistro. Don't expect plush seats or fancy service. The well-known skillets are mastered by Chef Jean Dumonet, who is beloved for his Truffled Andouillettes, his Ballottines, his sweetbreads with morels, and his rabbit in mustard sauce—all for reasonable sums. The heart of France.

Chez Maître Paul (corner of rue M.-le-Prince and rue Casimir Delavigne) is a honey of a little place for economy trippers. The Man Himself does all the cooking, and he features a wine called Bourgueil from his own vineyard in Touraine. Always full—so reserve in advance. Closed Tuesday.

Au Pactole (44 boulevard St.-Germain) draws many businessmen at lunchtime and families in the evening. Enclosed sidewalk terrace; 7-table interior sanctum with gold wallpaper, oil paintings, and flowers; agonizingly slow service on our visit. The set menus are the star attractions here—a 4-course one and a 5-plate spread with more selections available. While the tabs now seem to be rocketing upward, we've noticed an uneven quality in the kitchen of late. Perhaps you'll disagree.

Au Petit Riche (125 rue le Peletier) turns back the mechanism of timelessness to before this century began. If you've got a kink for globes, polished wood, and the décor of saloons in ships that were retired long, long ago, then you may dig this artifact. Go early; on our first attempt they would not serve us at the wicked hour of 9:15 P.M. Closed August as well as Sundays and holidays.

Chez André (53 boulevard St.-Marcel) holds a special attraction for journalists and exquisite mannequins from the couturier precincts which it flanks. (Personally, darned if we can think of a nicer combination.) Paper "tablecloths"; noisy room with old-fashioned partitions; busy enough to encourage early or late arrival by the wisest diners; no reservations taken. Footnote: The gamin stake is delightful.

Le Berthoud (1 rue Valette) is a splendid stop for rubbing the nap off the elbows. It's more engaging than a barrel full of people—and that's just how you'll feel when coffee time rolls around. Fascinating, inexpensive egg dishes bobbling in pools of melted butter or cream or both; Moujik (Russian tasties) worthy of anybody's lip service; gay heaps of salad; wee sausages to lion-share steaks for moderate outlays; calories-be-damned desserts. If you enjoy humanity at close quarters, we think you might relish this community plate.

Vieux Paris (2 rue de l'Abbaye), also on the Left Bank, features Algerian and Middle Eastern fare. You may sample Greek Souvlaki (Shishkebab), Egyptian rice, Arabian Couscous (Wednesday only), and all sorts of exotic preparations. A popular low-cost choice.

The **Bar de Théâtre** (catercorner to the Plaza-Athénée) is a noon and after-theater gossip-and-groceries hangout for young dress designers, high-fashion salesgirls, and models who haven't quite reached the pinnacle. Tiny tables for these tiny appetites; passable fare; fast service; very reasonable tariffs.

Au Beaujolais (19 quai de la Tournelle), across from the famous Tour d'Argent, is ultramodest. Meats hanging from the ceiling; butchers' aprons hanging from the shirt-sleeved waiters; happy bellies hanging from some of the best-fed clients in Paris. About as atmospheric as a pilot's ready room; tantalizing menu; ask for English-speaking Bernard; always reserve in advance. If you must wait for a table, be sure to pass the time with a _Kir_, the house cocktail —white wine with a shot of Cassis. For pure-but-simple eating, this one's tough to beat. Closed Monday and in August. Recommended.

Chez René (around the corner at 14 boulevard St.-Germain) has the same sort of personality. Even noisier (if such a thing is possible) than Au Beaujolais; same prices; similar but less refined cookery; clientele sometimes tacky. You can stuff yourself for about $14, except on Sunday. Bring earplugs.

Chez Marius (30 rue des Fossés-St.-Bernard), taken over by Jacques Chalvet, surges with new energy to upgrade its beloved reputation. Two floors which are as simple as π; mouth-melting Coq au Vin; juicy grills. Extra-savvy Parisian gourmets who can afford much more often dine here and often bring their associates. This haven is easy on the expense account and nice on the palate. It functions every day but Sunday. Sound.

Le Marigny (avenue Marigny, around the corner from the Bristol Hotel) is a simple corner nook for cornering simple cookery. Our latest Coeur de Filet with French fries was particularly savory and modestly priced. For such a high-price district of such a high-price city, here is a budgeteer's find. Recommended.

La Pomme Soufflée (37 bis rue Ponthieu) is designed in the shape of a lollipop, with tables along the stem and a jamup of noisy diners in the "pop" division. Light bites and quick service are the specialties of this busy beehive. Fair, but distressingly cacophonous.

La Quetsch (6 rue Capucines) is a restaurant-delicatessen which once pleased us greatly but now deeply saddens us. Sorry.

Le Boccador (7 rue Boccador, near the Plaza-Athénée) has changed proprietors. It has not, however, changed its mandate on excellence. The value is still there, we are pleased to report.

Le Dahu (10 rue de la Trémoille, very close by) put us off with its cuisine, but it remains a favorite of a certain coterie of the snobbishly inclined. Large cellar dining room; open grill; garlands of garlic, red-check lampshades, cheeses, copperware, beamed ceiling, fruit and vegetable baskets, and other slick-rustic oddments. Attractive, but not for us gastronomically or temperamentally.

Up at Montmartre, there are 2 sparklers that insiders savor: **Les Semailles** (3 rue Steinlen) operated by young Maestro Jouteux (the saddle of lamb with

Kiwi is novel) and **Beauvilliers** (52 rue Lamarck) which issues the special charm and delicate gastronomy of Edouard Carlier. Both highly recommendable and not expensive by local standards.

No other book, not even *Michelin,* or *Kléber,* can begin to tackle the hundreds upon hundreds of good bistros in Paris, so please forgive the necessary omissions of countless worthy examples. The best fun of all is to put on your walking shoes and explore for yourself.

In the *outdoor* group, one of the most attractive places for a summer lunch or dinner, had been **Pré Catelan**, in the Bois de Boulogne—when one of its all-too-frequent business conventions, wedding receptions, or group functions was not overrunning the premises. Because this landmark now caters almost primarily to this patronage, we feel it has lost much of its charm for the independent pilgrim. The cuisine—some of it in the new style—can be interesting since such care is taken with it.

A woodland alternate in the same district, and once the hunting lodge of Napoleon III, is **La Grande Cascade**. It is slightly less costly and creates pleasant conflagrations with its kidneys flambé; this smart house always has a tempting selection of piscatorial preparations. (It runs a seafood restaurant in town, too.) Serious, scenic, and salubrious.

Pavillon Royal (route de Suresnes in the Bois de Boulogne) nibbles at the bank of a sylvan lake; it is making a heartening comeback through the skills of new Chef Jean Guinot. **Samantha** is its nightclub portion.

Auberge du Vert-Galant (42 quai des Orfèvres, Île de la Cité) sits on the bank of the ancient island in the Seine and offers a memorable panorama of the river and the Left Bank. Firmly sustained by lawyers, because it is just a tort's (or tart's) throw from the Palais de Justice. Adequate but not spectacular kitchen actions; high but not exorbitant fees; when the weather is right, not a plaintiff to be found.

La Mère Catherine, another well-known alfresco establishment, is *not* recommended for either its food or its attitudes—at least as we sampled them.

Among the *restaurant curiosities,* **Caviar Kaspia** (17 place de la Madeleine) is beguiling. Above this prominent specialty establishment are 3 tiny rooms à la teashop—but fresh caviar, smoked salmon, smoked trout, smoked eel, and 2 or 3 other delicacies make up its wares. The capacity is similarly limited— a mere 9 tables and munching space at the bar for about 9. Hot borscht is always available. The blinis are the stuff of dreams, and you may choose your own size, grade, and color of the caviar "berry" (trade lingo for "egg"). Chilled French or Alsatian white wines, vodka, and champagne are the only potables. Deft reception and attention by Guy Loup; open weekdays continuously from 9 A.M. to 8:15 P.M.; closed Sunday. A heavenly haven for odd-hour refreshment when your feet and soul are bruised from shopping. One reminder: Don't grow faint when the *patron* presents his neck-snapping bill for "that simple little snack." Caviar is caviar; literally, its cost per ounce is higher than sterling silver nearly anywhere on earth including in Iran and the Soviet Union. Thus your check will be very, very high. As with all delicious morsels in life, the best costs money—whether you marry it or just nibble it. Another jewel shop is **La Maison du Caviar** (21 rue Quentin Bauchar), where an $18 breakfast comprises orange juice or vodka, eggs, toast, a wee ration of caviar, blinis, smoked salmon, and coffee. That nifty package should almost carry you to dinner. It is served between 9:30 and 11:30 A.M.

Au Mouton de Panurge (17 rue de Choiseul) is startlingly pornographic. The takeoff point for the bawdy décor and strange menu is the commemoration of humorist-and-satirist Rabelais; from here, some of the house developments are only vulgar while some are just plain repulsive. The rolls are baked in the shape of a male organ, which also appear as a bottle stopper in the even more organic wine jugs. Others, as well, are right out of the barnyard. Spicy murals; a live sheep which drinks wine; an out-and-out tourist trap in conception and tone, but the new owner seems to be making an effort to improve its overall quality. Still kinky.

Then, let's not forget that famous institution partway up the **Eiffel Tower** by elevator. Glorious panorama of Paris (that's the Hilton, next door); grill open for lunch year round; main restaurant closed November 15 to Easter. The first-floor establishment features headliners of the entertainment world 6 evenings per week (see "Night Life"). Cuisine? On all of our earlier scales it was fully satisfactory—but now more and more complaints from readers have found their ways to our mailbox. Conversely, others whose palates we trust continue to sing its praises in 5X5 enthusiasm. In any case, the setting of this expensive dining place is matchless.

Lefebvre is a hideously shaped floating barge moored at quai Branly. It peers through boggled-eyed tinted glass panels at the river and townscape— much nicer inside than out. France's "new cuisine" comes from the galley; orange salad is a beautiful creation; prices are not too shocking for the novelty of dining afloat (but not under way).

Inside the **Louvre Museum**, there is a self-service restaurant with an outdoor terrace (good weather) overlooking the Carrousel and Tuileries Gardens. Light meals from 10 A.M. to 5 P.M. for as little as $3; drinks and tea to alleviate those hunger pangs and to nurture your search for culture. A 2nd is also operating in another gallery.

Like cheese? The restaurant adjoining **Androuët's Cheese Shop** (41 rue d'Amsterdam, near Gare St.-Lazare) will make you pleasantly cheesy on the cheesiest assortment of dishes and samples in this cheese-loving nation. Marvelous munching if you're as mouselike in tastes as we are. We *adore* this fascinating complex!

For *seafood*, **Le Duc** (243 boulevard Raspail), where we've joyfully taken the hook, line, and sinker, offered the yummiest bait we've snapped at in a long, long time. Its maritime mood is fashioned of 15 flower-decked tables, varnished bulkheads, prints of old ships, brass lamps in gimbals, and hints of its Mediterranean origins. Our iced shellfish platter was so overwhelming in amplitude, arrangement, and variety that it almost constituted a graduate course in oceanography. This should have served as a generous meal by itself. However, our follow-up order of grilled *loup* (rockfish) for 2 was also unforgettable in both eye- and palate-appeal. The service was skilled but busy, the atmosphere was talkative, and the billings are blue-ribbon. Devotees of saltwater fare, however, should not permit themselves to miss it. Outstanding—and that's an understatement.

La Méditerranée (2 place de l'Odéon) became a large brasserie of sorts; it's cool and not at all appealing to us now.

La Coquille (6 rue du Débarcadère), near the Meridieh Hotel, is short on atmosphere, but the cookery is superb for its bistro character. Our billings seemed far too high for our fillings. Otherwise M. Blache and his daughter do a sterling job.

Le Chalut (94 boulevard Batignolles) swims one of the strongest races for the fancier of fine finny fare. Its décor could not be more unattractive and less inspired if it had been designed by a haddock. But oooooooooolaLA, that wondrously huge menu of marine masterpieces—so special, so delectable, and so perfect that gourmets from miles around leap troutlike to get in! Owner Bernardy produces his feasts for high-medium rewards. Pack-jammed, especially on Friday; closed from May 30 to September 1. For the self-chosen few who *really* pamper their palates.

Le Bernardin (35 quai la Tournelle) is a bit of Brittany in the City of light. Chef Le Coze and his comely sister present their sea fare admirably—except Mondays and all of August, when they go fishing.

Prunier (9 rue Duphot) has been absorbed by Le Bernardin's Chef Gilbert Le Coze and his sister Maguy, who has brought the subtle décor of their first establishment to this old Paris landmark. They have also lured back a Parisian following which had abandoned Prunier during its sinking spells of not long ago. Their careful attention to restoring tradition and adding new zest to the cookery is paying off in gustatory dividends which we applaud. Closed Mon.

Rech (62 avenue des Ternes) gradually has slid downward, in our opinions. We now prefer a bright little young sprat called La Pêcherie (24 rue Pierre Lescot) with a white-and-violet theme and a bubbling fountain to greet you. Strong in visual chic.

For *kosher cookery* we like (1) Le Sportif (24 rue Vieille-du-Temple), (2) Eden (36 boulevard Bonne-Nouvelle), (3) Flambaum (37 rue Faubourg-Montmartre; closed Jan. to Apr.), and (4) Henri (9 passage Basfoi). For a quickie bite of gefilte fish (or maybe a corned beef sandwich), try the Goldenberg Delicatessen (7 rue des Rosiers, not far from place des Vosges, or its branch at 69 avenue de Wagram) which stays open 7 days a week from 8 A.M. to midnight. Oy-vay, is *that* good!

For others, here's how we'd pick them in order of desirability: *Spanish:* Chez José, avenue Jean Moulin. *Basque:* Auberge Basque, 51 rue Verneuil, is a touch of the Pyrenees; between dishes, the waiters double as singing guitarists; nobody speaks English, but the atmosphere is so vivacious, who cares? Closed Sundays and July 15 through September 4. *Italian:* (1) Toscana, 7 rue Ponthieu, leaves a good taste on the palate as well as on the spirit, thanks to the skill and kindness of its owner-host; only 10 tables, but each filled with devoted loyalists. (2) Conti, 72 rue Lauriston, also deserves a gastronomic bravo; more and more popular. (3) Peppo (115 avenue de Villiers) dispenses substantial groceries at lower prices. *Russian:* Don't forget Maisonnette Russe and Dominique which we've already written "Da! Da!" about. *Indian:* Annapurna, (32 rue de Berri) curries favor with a multitude of followers. Two small rooms containing 8 tables each; attractive Asian décor; open year round. *Chinese:* China-Town receives our bow for day-to-day Orient-ations. For superluxury,

Tong Yen, (1 bis rue Jean Mermoz) is drawing a heavy trade in expense-account Mandarins who never check the opulent scores from the abacus. Although it does not serve the type of Chinese fare to which we are accustomed in the States, here is unquestionably the leader of this culinary school in Paris. **L'Ambassadeur,** (30 rue de Longchamp) also scores high in the subgum league. _Japanese_: **Miki,** (3 rue d'Artois) appears to be the rising sun in this heaven. **Chez Hanafousa,** (4 passage de la Petite-Boucherie) also glows, especially for its meats. There are now about 50 such ethnic contenders in this city. _Vietnamese:_ **Tan Dinh** (60 rue de Verneuil) is always mentioned first by followers of this cuisine. _Swedish:_ **Relais de Suède,** (125 avenue Champs-Élysées) offers perhaps the only smörgasbord in Paris—reputedly almost as good as any in Sweden. _German:_ **Au Vieux Berlin**, opposite the George V and Prince de Galles hotels, has been previously described. It is _wunderbar! Health foods_ (Yep, in Paris!): **Veggie,** (38 rue de Verneuil) caters to clear-eyed Tarzans, Janes, and assorted bushy-tailed buffs of botany.

Snacks and quick fare? Snack bars and light-lunch places are mushrooming so fast that, in most tourist districts, all the visitor has to do is to wander down the closest boulevard. First and most interesting, famous old **Fauchon** (28 place de la Madeleine) operates a stand-up "Cafeteria" which serves honest-to-goodness Maxwell House coffee (plus French, Italian, Swiss, and Turkish blends), Schlitz beer, superb fresh fruit, various juices, sandwiches, cottage cheese, hot specialties, pastries, and c-r-e-a-m-y ice cream. This appendage to France's most celebrated fancy foods center is a boon to homesick stateside tummies. Recommended with our tongue slapping our chest. A more opulent example to the eye is **Le Drug Store** (133 avenue Champs-Élysées, near Arc de Triomphe) which to our taste can't compare in quality or value. To augment this, a _Wagon-Lits_ movieland version reels in adjoining the busy Place de l'Opéra and there's yet a newer one on the Rond Point. And if you miss that trio of midtown swingers, there's still another branch in St.-Germain-des-Prés.

More typical is **Le Grill-Shop** (67 avenue Champs-Élysées), which is small and bustling and has a clean U.S.-style décor in bright yellow with mirrors. Our order here was for one "Hot Dog sur Toast." But up came one "Super Hot Dog Garni," which consisted of 2 embarrassingly naked and hollow-chested wieners with a plate of potato chips, 2 rolls which any well-groomed American frankfurter would sneer at, and 2 dabs of butter—a total of almost $6, with the coffee—an imitation so pale it couldn't be peddled for 50¢ in a Little League ball park at home. But some of the French-based items being served looked quite appetizing.

For Jehovah's sake, please avoid the huge **Pizza Pino** which glows spectacularly on the Champs-Élysées. Our recent expensive "Pizza Chef" preparation we'd call nothing but a disgusting swill of limp pasta soaking languidly in a polychromatic infusion of runny eggs, tomato broth, and the faintest hint of cheese, the surface charged with some unidentifiable extruded meat that seemed to pose as a distant relative of sausage. One taste and we fled. Ugh!

Jour et Nuit (2 rue de Berri, just off the Champs-Élysées) is open every _jour et nuit;_ it's okay for that last bite before you tuck in.

Le snack has become so popular, in fact, that 1-channel specialists are beginning to pop up. **Chez Aron Fils de Tunis** (19 boulevard Montmartre) spotlights ultrasweet fritters from Africa called Beignet. **Les Écuries Washington** (5 rue Washington) flips oddball-filled *crêpes* or plain old honey-capped flapjacks. **La Boutique à Sandwich** (a totter off the Champs-Élysées on rue du Colisée) builds you-know-whats in 30 different styles. **La Maisonnette du Caviar** (directly across the street) stirs up Russian delights at prices calculated not to hurt any fellow-traveler. The **Bazar** (corner of rue St.-Benoît and rue Guillaume Apollinaire) is an automat-style feedery that is capable of filling 600 mouths at one time. Through its Horn-and-Hardart-type dispensing panels, you can purchase everything from hot cross buns to packaged stockings. Bring a pocketful of coins.

Orly Airport area? In the terminal building, most jetters gobble their calories at the punk drugstore-type counter on the ground floor without ever being aware that the structure also contains the **Trois Soleils**, the **Rôtisserie Le Tournebroche** and a popular-price corner called **Les Horizons**. Infinitely better, in our opinion, is the **Orly Hilton** trio, a 2-minute walk (if you live to dodge the traffic). We like and heartily recommend both its Le Coffee Shop and L'Atelier Bar, the secondary lights in this U.S. oasis. Especially at night, La Louisiane Restaurant represents a romantic bayou attempt to reproduce Olde New Orleans. Cajun-based cuisine which shows imagination and, in some dishes, honors the Crescent City with skillful skilletry. In *Viry Châtillon*, a few miles from Orly, there's the highly regarded **La Daroile**, which is said to be a not-too-costly target with ample charm and the inspired cuisine of Gilbert Druoelle. Our recommendation comes from such a gastronomically high-flying sorce that it is reliable even though we haven't visited it personally. Nor have we touched down at the **Maxim's** hangar at Orly Ouest. Local high-flyers praise it warmly. Charles de Gaulle Airport (utilized almost exclusively for trans-atlantic flights) also provides refueling by Maxim's—and expensive it is! This is a catering affiliate of the city shrine.

Good restaurants in the provinces are as thick as Fido's fleas. To cover them all here is impossible, due to the space limitations; in any case, the wonderful *Guide Michelin* and *Guide Kléber* already list and rate them by the thousands, in the world's most dependable mass surveys. Below are some of the better (or best) tables of France; consult *Michelin* or *Kléber* for more modest selections. Most of these offer cookery at its highest, usually (not always) with prices to match:

Near Paris:

  Bougival (11 miles): (1) **Le Camelia** (blossoming better than ever under the tender tenure of a "new chef" in this national trend, M. Delaveyne; well-known for its garlic-flavored squab and its terrine of woodcock; outstanding meal for $50 or so; selection varied and uniformly excellent; closed Aug. as well as Sun. nights and all Mon.) (2) **Coq Hardi** (once superb, it hit a slump; while some declare that it has regained its former status, personally we still think it is waffling in its quality; its art collection is better than ever, however).

  Chennevières-sur-Marne (11 miles): **Écu de France**.

Louveciennes (10 miles): **L'Auberge du Coeur Volant** (very "in" with the Jet Settlers).

Pontchartrain (24 miles): (1) **L'Aubergade** (run by the president of the chef's Association, Lucien Ogier, a master among masters), (2) **Chez Sam**.

Port-Royal-des-Champs (21 miles): **Chez Denise**.

St.-Germain-en-Laye (15 miles): **Pavillon Henri IV**.

Versailles (14 miles): **Trois Marches** (a splendid table by young Chef Gérard Vie who is destined for a starlit future; perfect for combining with a tour of the palace).

Night Life   You have your choice of a $100 dinner, a watusi, a punk rock warehouse, a sophisticated bar, a 50—count 'em—50-leg show, a strip at 11:30 A.M. or P.M., a prostitute, a gigolo, an "exhibition," a glass of beer, a team of acrobats, or a Mickey Finn. Take your pick, because Paris has them all.

But let's never forget, for one minute here, that some of the most cold-blooded, ruthless poachers of the evening world have set you up as their top-priority target. You're nothing but a big, fat, ripe North American chump who will drink any rotgut with a "champagne" label, applaud any tired old bag sans her usually necessary brassière, and pay a triple king's ransom for the "privilege." Most Parisian cabaret operators are downright vicious toward the suckers who keep them alive—and this includes innocents from Saudi Arabia, England, Holland, Egypt, Zululand, or anywhere. Taxes, steeper than Mont Blanc, contribute materially to this psychology. According to a government official quoted by a U.S.-owned periodical, they're so outrageously discriminatory that these rookeries are *forced* to exploit customers to stay alive—and the police wink at corrupt practices out of sympathy for the owners. Thus while there are notable exceptions, *we make no blanket guarantee whatever* on the spots listed below.

The big brassy places are tourist favorites. Some charge $5 or so admission per person (a flat rate at the door), and most refuse to serve anything but champagne at $18 to $60 per bottle at the tables; if you do manage to ransom a Scotch and soda here, it might fizz in for around $14 per cup. Such beverages on a drink-by-drink basis, however, normally can be had only if you stand at the bar, where each will ring up $8-or-so for the comptroller. All the big ones are out for the indiscriminate spender who won't bother to check the bill.

The **Lido** (116 Bis Champs-Elysées) stages what is probably the most elaborate spectacle on earth today—imaginative, grand, dynamic, and beautiful. It stuns the customers with its ensemble of at least 50 dancers, showgirls, semi-nudes, and headline international acts. In the spacious 1200-seat venue located in the Normandie Cinema Building, the theater-restaurant affords all customers an adequete view of the stage; the slope-away design terminates at a ringside tier that sinks to navel level. Fantasy effects have been introduced by extending mechanical equipment out over the audience—all subtle, surprising, tasteful, a socko hit! Shows at 10:30 and 12:30, so if you want to dine here, too, around 9 P.M. is the best time to go. Here's strictly a dealer's choice as to whether or not this globally famous mecca of dazzle is worth its blue-ribbon investment to you.

The almost equally renowned **Moulin Rouge**, immortalized by Toulouse-

Lautrec and later known for its can-can by generations of wide-eyed spinsters, has been taken over by the Lido. Although the tariffs are just about the same, it is purposely geared to a lower category. Huge, tiered, theaterlike hall; bar atop the pyramid; lavish show with some seminudes. Here again we have the TV "spectacular," with mammary glands the twin features, plus enough feathers and chiffon to bury the Gare du Nord. Old egret to most travelers—except, of course, first-timers.

Le Jardin (avenue Gabriel) flowers with yet another cabaret-theatre setup and a restaurant-auditorium for 700 visitors; shows comprise vignettes familar to Las Vegas habitués. Technically advanced, well costumed, but apparently 101% designed for touristic traffic.

The **Eiffel Tower** adds its gleam to the City of Light with a dinner show in the first-floor restaurant. Supper begins at 8 sharp; the show is at 9:30 P.M., concluding 2 hours later; the elevators stop elevating at midnight, but there is little to let you down in the entire evening of refined relaxation and fun. It goes every night but Sunday. Recommended.

Olympia, a music hall fixture since 1893, has been snatched from the brink of oblivion by its tenacious director, Bruno Coquatrix. The house that hosted such luminaries as Maurice Chevalier and Mistinguette promises to hang on in spite of what it protested as a confiscatory tax situation. We wish it continued success.

The **Crazy Horse Saloon** (12 avenue George V) continues to draw masses of U.S. tourists with wives, U.S. tourists with oo-la-la nonwives, U.S. tourists solo, and U.S. tourists. Contrived, occasionally salacious, sometimes entirely nude striptease, cleverly aided by projected images; thunderously loud musical assists; rapid, knock-'em-back service; your 1st drink at the bar will pour for close to $15; if you are seated at a table the cost will be considerably more; it is open every night year round. Perhaps we're being stuffy or miserly, but at these prices, for what is there, we always have the feeling of being such suckers that the place just doesn't appeal to us. Scads of travelers disagree. If you go, be double-sure to watch your billings and to check your change (especially the folding money).

For the revue type of attraction, the **Folies Bergères,** with its 40 tableaux displaying 1600 costumes, is the most glamorous. (As with all shows in its century-plus history, the title of the latest production contains 13 letters.) **Casino de Paris,** also for outlanders, is runner-up is in this category, but there was some scuttlebutt about the possibility of it closing, so you'd better check once you're in Paris.

Was anyone speaking of a fascinating study called s-x? If so, the "Sexyrama" at small, crowded, ruby-velvet **Sexy** (68 rue Pierre Charron) offers a parade of s-xy-looking dames and oily muscular male escorts on a tiny stage between 10:30 P.M. and 12:30 A.M. nightly. Oh-so-friendly-nuzzling atmosphere; numerous darkened nooks to discuss French economics with yumptious and pleasant B-girls with a marathon state of thirst. This one is stuffed with slack-jawed, bug-eyed gents. Provocative but expensive.

Lucky Strip (4 rue Arsène-Houssaye, a minute from the Étoile) is the type of place where you could take your children—_if_ they happened to be junior delinquents. Bar at entrance; tiered "orchestra" section with armchairs and

tables stair-stepping down to the proscenium; peppery combo zinging from
10:30 P.M. until the last customer weaves out; attractive B-girls who struck us
as more rapacious (at least on our recent visit) than a pack of starving hyenas;
knavery from the fang-tooth barmaid who tried to hide the "official" house
prices from our view. Because of the jackal-jaded attitude encountered by us
we cannot recommend it. Go strictly at your own risk.

The **Fifty-Fifty** (26 rue Fontaine), seems to start its sexes at the 50-50 degree
and then move them up to more complex ratios. This time the house featured
"Les Mini-Boys et Les Mini-Girls"—but we didn't see mini of either, if we
must be specific. The manager impressed us as being almost as scruffy as one
of his well-worn carpets. The area is dangerous. Approach with caution—in
every respect. **Madame Arthur** (75 bis rue des Martyrs, near Sacré-Coeur),
with its horrible orange façade and rococo pillars, draws a number of madames
named Arthur; female impersonators are its feature; don't pinch anything here,
because it might pinch back. **Elle et Lui** (31 rue Vavin) bills itself as "The
sensational Night Club of Montparnasse Where the Woman is 'King'." It
seemed to us to be more elle et elle and lui et lui. Although we heard that for
a time it was operated as a private club, we suspect the only people turned away
might have been those without billfolds or purses. Open every night—unfortunately. The side-by-side **Le Carrousel** struck us as being a perfect study hall
for sociologists and geneticists.

Shéhérazade (3 rue de Liège), a traditionalist, now has gone so commercial
that we no longer applaud it; it is run by the Folies-Bergéres ensemble, incidentally. The service is kind—but at $15 per drink it ought to be almost loving.
(A jug of Chivas sells for a mere $110!) To have your fortune told you must
grease Madame Monika's palm with $25—quite a handout. Its décor is seedy
and overwhelmingly rococo. The cuisine is White Russian, not distinguished
but adequate—and quite costly. It operates 7 nights per week—and "operates"
is the operative word.

The tariffs at **Chez Raspoutine** (58 rue de Bassano), yet another Folies' folly,
are OUTRAGEOUS. Previously we have reported about our own clipping
here—but this was somewhat less gross than the indignity recently suffered by
our esteemed friend and *bon vivant*, Senior Editor Dennis McEvoy of the
Reader's Digest. No entrée was ordered. His bill for 2 blinis with smoked
salmon, 2 cups of borscht, a double soufflé, 2 vodkas, and a bottle of the
cheapest wine on the menu? $153.16!!! Now that he and we have been so brutally
sheared, this joint is on our Black Books forevermore. **Tsarevitch** (1 rue des
Colonels-Renard) is a posh pad for passionate pashas. Doorman who is an
exact duplicate of Harpo Marx à la astrakhan; wall coverings in old gold
damask; mauve-draped ceiling; incarnadine silk tablecloths bearing silver candelabra with red (but White) Russian tapers; a royal Tartar portrait commands
the rich Slavic scene. Cuisine heavy in both quality and cost (only the host sees
those aristocratic menu prices); coffee and champagne (the latter pushed
strongly) served on sterling doilies; friendly professional attention; performers
(some excellent) every 20 minutes throughout the evening; zither, accordion,
and string ensembling between singles' acts. Better, in our opinion, than any
of the above Russian trio. How long it can last at its present tariff level is hard
to say. Recommendable—but check your bill carefully. **Monseigneur** (94 rue

d'Amsterdam) offers high-life violin serenades, high prices, and high controversy as to whether it can survive. Well done, but costly. You can also find
gypsy strings and the Hungarian spirit of yore at **Paprika** (14 rue Chauchat),
especially after midnight; here's fodder as spicy as the name. **Franc-Pinot** (1
quai de Bourbon) shouldn't fool you by its unpretentious entrance. An intimate
seventeenth-century _cave_ in soft mulberry down the narrow staircase which
fairly oozes with character; mirrors, tiers of tables, air conditioning, and an
intermittent floor show from 10:30 P.M. onward, alternating with dancing to
a 3-piece combo; music and dinner commencing at 9 P.M., with supper available until dawn. Hospitality carefully supervised by kindly, young, English-
speaking Yves Sénié. First-timers usually like this one. **Alcazar** (62 rue Maza-
rine) offers a gay-oriented evening to its followers. Turn-of-the-century
atmosphere; singing, jesting waiters; kooky diversions plus a zesty parade of
entertainment. **Michou** (80 rue des Martyrs) does a similar thing in its own
more modest way. **Étoile de Moscou** (6 rue Arsène-Houssaye, near the Étoile),
is a semicircular family-type club with loud singers (a Russian chorus,
maybe?). Hosting by Igor and Vava in this nucleus or in the **Au Stéréo
Club**, a bar and discothèque on the same property; same ownership as Tsarevitch. **Villa d'Este** (a few doors away and also tied in with its neighbor) seemed
to us to draw a cheaper clientele even though they are asked to pay considerably higher tariffs; it's open for the cocktail hour and tea dancing from 4:30 P.M.
on Saturday and Sunday—and always from 9 P.M. until morn. We quaffed but
did not sup. The French cabaret isn't bad. **Topless** (2 rue Coustou) is earning
bra-vos from goggle-eyed gents these evenings. On our swing down this mammary lane a number of males seemed to be doing a good job of pouring their
Martinis down their natty wide lapels as they watched. **Pussy Cat** (22 rue
Quentin Beauchart) makes our back arch. No thanks.

Visit a quarter of this list, and you'll need a new oil well to cover your
checks.

Discothèques? As in London and all of the major continental cities, they wax
and wane with such astonishing rapidity that yesterday's vogue might be
tomorrow's bane. If possible, they are even more volatile than the "traditional"
night spots. Therefore, a number of the following places might well be out of
business by the time of your arrival.

Régine's (74 rue de Ponthieu) is the offspring of the ever-fertile, eternally
verdant Régine, creator of New Jimmy's (see below). A twin outing here could
easily kiss adieu to $300. Entrance down several flights of stairs; mirrored
ceiling; well-faked marble dressing; soft illumination across paneled walls and
potted palms. You may be interested to see the Pop-Art kitchen. Though the
dance _piste_ evokes notions of a sophisticated moonscape, the overall tone is
that of the flapper era. Excellent band; generous and genuine libations; sparkling clientele. We recommend it, but mainly to Middle Eastern émirs with oily
gushers at their gateposts.

The **St. Hilaire** (74 rue de Rennes, not to be confused with the rue Vavin
or rue Geoffroy-St.-Hilaire installations) is a private club; visitors are welcomed, however, by prearrangement with concierges at leading hotels. Restaurant segment directed by Alan Senderens of Archestrate fame (see "Restaurants"); space for 50 diners behind glass-sheathed walls; disco portion in long

narrow room with oval dance floor; open all week, with meals surrendered on Sundays. Nod hello to the silver stork on the staircase for us. Discreet, chic, and another one that is wickedly expensive.

Chez Castel was still very much "in" during our latest visit. It is in a slum quarter grandly and euphemistically named rue de Princesse. Ground-floor waiting room lined with creepy rejects who were praying for enough prominence to earn a table downstairs; same-level cozy grill and fin-de-siècle bar; grubbed-out subterranean pub; canopied entrance where the more esteemed lemurs played, danced, dallied, and imbibed; supper rooms and a relatively serene bar. The best, in our opinion, of this curiously popular species. On the same *rue*, **Le Club d'O** longs for as much traffic. To get it, the portals seem to be open to just about anyone with pocket change. Bizarre-to-eerie interior; curi-form pillars; fiendishly dim illumination; beverages conjured up by clever alchemists. Popular among wizards, sorcerers, nighthawks, and tradesmen in nocturnal bitchcraft? **King's Club** (rue de l'Echaudé), impressed us as being as gussied up as the study of Mad King Ludwig. Wall-to-wall carpets, but not on the floors—on the walls, naturally, where they belong; weirdly shaped lighting fixtures; speakers, or plutonium extractors (God knows which) around the ceiling; a hairy-underarmed, porridge-faced female record spinner in the corner; handsome waiters who bob, weave, double-shuffle, bump, grind, and jerk with the music as they transport your liquids. **New Jimmy's** (125 boulevard Montparnasse) is still popular, but it's no longer a monumental effort to jimmy your way into its sacred precincts. Inside, the aforementioned *Doyenne* of the Dandies, Régine herself, occasionally waddles, slops, and swoops among her chosen people. Dark surroundings that almost sequester the features of its clientele; black-tile décor; black-and-blue patrons contusing on the eensy dance floor while trying to maintain their overconscious chic; jammed with youthful blue bloods whose red corpuscles hover at 102° F. Going down, in our opinion. **Number One** is so *privé* that you'll have to collar a local prince-in-exile to help you storm its social barricades. We did, and found it hardly worth the effort. François-Patrice's *other* **St. Hilaire** (24 rue Vavin) tops the expected facilities with a restaurant terrace. We prefer the hilarity more at the rue de Rennes address (see above). **Abreuvoir St.-Hilaire** (7 rue Geoffroy-St.-Hilaire) serves inexpensive fare in its dining room and reasonable drinks in its bar, with its gyrations confined to its basement. **Le Boeuf sur le Toit** ("The Steer on the Roof"), now operated along the same lines as a student hangout, is highly cliquish. The **Bus Paladium** (6 rue Fontaine) is in the rugged and avaricious Pigalle district, yet it draws mostly young people to its running board. For a time it was shut down for being too noisy. Orchestra; matinées Sundays and holidays. Watch your hat, coat, wallet and—if necessary—your molars. The cellar-sited **Ecossais** surrounds itself in red Scotch plaids, Tiffany lamps, and tinseled ceilings. Upstairs is the Kilt, which is less fashionable. Both serve as pick-up centers for under-25's. **Montparnasse 2000** (28 rue Vavin) makes us yawn well into the next century.

The hottest after-dark fad in the capital this instant is *punk rock* and the leading purveyors of the moment are **La Main Bleue** (Sq. Jean-Jaurès, Montreuil) and **Le Palace** (8 rue du Faubourg Montmartre). Both feature decibel levels that could dwarf mortar practice at Parris Island; both provide vast space for the spaced-out mood; both come on like TV studios with the focus on backstage architecture. If you're funky for punky people, here are the places to find 'em.

Shopping It is important for all visitors to know that an automatic 10%–25% discount (depending on the category of the item) is offered nation-wide by merchants on hard-currency traveler's or foreign personal checks (not banknotes). The buyer must produce his or her passport at the store. If the purchases exceed 400 francs in value (or 690 francs if you are from a Common Market country), you may carry them with you and still receive the discount. Smaller ones are rebated only if shipped abroad. Any currency is now accepted. All of the merchandise accompanied in person must fit into your luggage. Those who leave by train or car must follow specified rail or highway routes, as well as an explicit procedure, to be eligible. The seller may opt between giving the customer the deduction on his premises (thus taking the appreciable risk that the voyager will forget to surrender the forms at the border), or mailing the discount money to the buyer after Customs has returned the forms (thus creating an equally appreciable risk for the foreigner if the shop should be dishonest or if the documents should stray during their peregrinations). This red tape reaches a new height in silliness—but who hates a reduction of up to 1/4th of the entire purchase price?

At last by law, all goods except certain perishable comestibles sold in bulk must display a price tag—a bonus of protection and fair dealing for you and a device for curbing inflation for the government.

Our ★ ★ ★ ★ recommendations are individually noted.

Gloves and scarves: ★ ★ ★ ★ **Denise Francelle** (244 rue de Rivoli) has been our favorite since '46—and she gets better every year. There is room for exactly 5 1/2 customers, and it's always crowded—but her selection is so smart and her prices are so sensible that her vast international clientele couldn't care less. She must have a colossal storage room because in gloves alone she carries all sizes of about 400 different models in each of the popular colors. You'll find Kislav exclusives, children's, plain, fancy, daytime, evening, barbecue—styles for every mood. In addition to scarves, two of her popular specialties are handmade beaded models or attractive Beauvais bags with gloves to match, plus her umbrellas. Problem-solving dividend, even when you're back in the States: For a nominal postage fee, Madame will airmail one pair of gloves per box to your Christmas or Special Occasion designee. And what a sensation they cause when they arrive from Denise Francelle of Paris! Ask for sweet Mlle. Edith. Reliable and excellent.

Leather goods: For the most illustrious artistries in leather in France, please don't miss a look at ★ ★ ★ ★ **Hermès** (24 rue du Faubourg-St.-Honoré). Everything imaginable knockout item is here; most are hand-fashioned on the premises. High price tags for superquality.

Haute Couture: The tariffs in most of the major houses—**Christian Dior**, **Givenchy**, **Yves Saint Laurent**, **Balmain**, **Lanvin**, **Valentino**, **Ungaro**, **Lapidus**, **Laroche**, **Féraud**, and **Courrèges** among them—start in the $1,500 range. But how swiftly they can climb! If you're smart and sharp-eyed, from seeing the collections you can approximate the latest couture look in ready-to-wears at these original establishment's boutiques (or many lesser ones) at less than half of the original prices. If you want to attend some showings, merely call the reception desks at the places desired and invitations should come by return mail. When you arrive, a saleswoman will hand you a program and escort you to your seat. If you're determined to buy on the spot, circle the number of the item on the card. But those tariffs—ouch!

Perfumes: Here's probably the number one bargain in France, because for $20 to $40 you can get brands that sell from $50 to $120 in the States—and in the more costly bracket you can save up to $110 an ounce! Please be warned that in Paris and the tourist centers there are more racketeering and swindling retailers than in any other legitimate industry we have ever found on the Continent. Altered bottles are common. One nearly universal trick is to hard-sell a "house" abomination or another shoddy unknown brand as "outstanding" and to offer a huge "discount" on a tenth-class product which yields a 75%–80% profit. This jungle is rife with frauds, even in many of the large, seemingly respectable houses. Don't let purveyors in *Grasse,* the tourist-choked perfume-flower center on the Riviera, gull you about their products, either. For honesty, dependability, variety, and convenience ★ ★ ★ ★ **Les Trois Quartiers** department store, near Fauchon, is especially recommended.

It should be remembered that *most* of the leaders are "restricted brands" in the U.S. Customs. Whenever this applies, your importation into the States is limited to 1 bottle of the same type *per person.* (In a few brands either the 3-oz. size or 2 bottles are standard.) Direct mail shipment to America is sometimes prohibited. Be sure to check these restrictions before you buy, because excess amounts are automatically confiscated by our Lads in Blue.

For a comprehensive roundup of the newest scents plus our categories and rankings of France's top 51 scents, see our *Shopping Guide.*

Inimitable crystal: After ★ ★ ★ ★ **Baccarat** (30 bis rue de Paradis) had successfully petitioned Louis XV in 1765 for creation of the nation's first official art glass, for over 2 centuries it swept gold medals, grand prizes, and many other awards in virtually every prestigious national or international competition. Its newly renovated showrooms display beautifully the splendor of the galaxy of their wonders. But no one should be mistakenly overawed because it has been patronized for formal State services for kings, presidents, maharajahs, and a host of others. For more simple folks such as you and us who must control our pursestrings, the eye-popping bar decanters, paperweights, wine and liqueur glasses, vases, and animals are all glorious, all reasonable for their exquisite perfection. Don't miss the fascinating museum nurtured by debonair, gifted Chairman Count René de Chambrun, or the 10-minute audio program in English. Refund of 14.96% on all orders over $100; closed Sundays and holidays; factory with retail shop at Baccarat Meurthe & Moselle; branch in N.Y.C. A glittering fairyland.

Gourmet foods, liquors, gifts: If you like to eat, to drink and to savor as much as we do, a walk through famous ★ ★ ★ ★ **Fauchon** (24-26-28 place de Madeleine) should be one of the most fascinating sensory experiences of your shopping life. For 90 years Fauchon has been France's number one center for the gastronome. You'll find the modernized "Kingdom of Foie Gras and Caviar" so cherished for its 10% dividends to outlanders; the *ne plus ultra* Epicure Department; the Liquor Department, where the staff will forward purchases to your embarkation point at 15% below the price tags; the Health Food Department where your favorite tea will be blended. Across the street the "Sweet Corner" has delicious candies (15% discount when shipped). The all-day Cafeteria dispenses American-style refreshments. Fauchon is the world's most glittering Ali Baba's Cave for its national *and* foreign gourmet treasures. Huge mail-order business; flawless service; flawless integrity throughout. Brilliant Owner-Director Edmond Bory should glow with pride. Wonderful!

Lingerie: **Cordelia** (21 rue Cambon) features many items from the Dior line. The female member of this writing team thinks of them as "yummy." The male member of this writing team thinks of them—often. Ask for Mme. Saëz.

Exquisite silk flowers: ★ ★ ★ ★ ★ **Trousselier** (73 boulevard Hausmann) wears the crown as the finest creator of handcrafted artificial flowers in silk anywhere in the world. When we asked how many species they could duplicate, we were told "every one nature produces."

Sexy fragrance: ★ ★ ★ ★ ★ **Charles Blair** (374 rue St.-Honoré) is the benevolent sorcerer who, in 1934, invented what *both* members of this pair—and their legions of friends who have since become addicts—regard as the world's sexiest bath essence. A whole line of other libidinous man-traps has been added, all with this inimitable fragrance—plus for Her a lovely perfume named Medea and for Him a super-cologne labeled For Men. This author is bemused by how fast the latter is "evaporated" by so many drop-in friends who use his private bathroom at home. Mail orders welcomed. A personal, very special "find."

Mixed bag of boutiques: For superb quality at prices which are amazingly low for this capital, ★ ★ ★ ★ ★ **Nicole A** (8 rue Duphot) is a prize. The principal clientele consists of knowledgeable Parisian socialites. As a former top model and wife of Jacques Arpel, she knows this business and she does not close for lunch. Excellent. The French institution of **Lubin** (64 Faubourg-St.-Honoré) features $10 to *haute elegance* gift items. **Roger & Gallet** (62 rue du Faubourg-St.-Honoré) stocks an outstandingly attractive stock of accessories for both genders. **Line Vautrin** (3 rue de l'Université) and **Burma** (16 rue de la Paix plus 2 branches) feature an assortment of costume jewelry and trinkets.

Jewelry and gold objects: ★ ★ ★ ★ ★ **Chaumet** (12 place Vendôme), Crown Jeweler to most of the royal courts of Europe, is so distinctive and vital in its design and creative skills that today there are no French purveyors in the field who, in our fervent opinions, nearly so excitingly lend their artistry and dynamism of this school's contemporary stylings as do Jacques and Pierre Chaumet. Their gems are of the same sovereign quality which this house crafted into Bonaparte's coronation. Although its prices follow international levels, Chaumet provides certain unbeatable financial concessions which bear serious inquiry. Be sure to see their striking bronze and gold collection, their pocket lighters in semiprecious stones, the new-vogue short gold necklaces with colored gems and diamonds, their super-chic Breguet watches, and the marvels they have sculpted and fairy-landed from Baccarat castoff extrusion blocks. Their London branch is at 178 New Bond St. Here is a wonder of wonders.

For equally stunning elegance in an entirely different milieu, the namesake-founder of globally-famous ★ ★ ★ ★ ★ **Ilias Lalaounis** (365 rue St.-Honoré) is

100% responsible for reviving the raging fashion for Greek museum-style pieces (see "Greece"). His brilliant creations and interpretations in 22- and 18-carat gold comprise a dazzling assemblage which is renewed constantly. This genius has arranged unique audio-vision spectacles to enable visitors to learn the history, sources of inspiration, and symbolism of his masterpieces. Ask for charming and friendly Manageress Helene Stylianou.

Internationally renowned ★ ★ ★ ★ ★ **Bulgari** (see "Rome") is now displaying their stunning sparklers at the Hotel Plaza-Athenee (27 Av. Montaigne). Their glories simply cannot be described.

Books: **Brentano's** (37 Av. de l'Opéra), **W.H. Smith & Son** (248 rue de Rivoli), and **Nouveau Quartier Latin** (78 Blvd. St. Michel) are 3 formidable sources so your mind won't starve.

Art galleries: Literally hundreds. Serious devotees should first pick up a current copy of *l'Official des Galeries* (15 rue de Temple), the definitive source of information about which painters and sculptors are being shown where in the whole nation.

Antiques center: **Le Louvre des Antiquaires** (168 rue de Rivoli) is a huge 3-story complex dedicated to the purchase and sale of antiques. This site houses 240 different shops representing many different specialties, plus cafes, restaurants, and exhibition halls. It is open from 11 A.M. to 7 P.M. from Tuesdays to Saturdays.

Auctions: The **Hôtel Drouot Rive Gauche** (Faubourg St. Germain) continues to be the top center of this traditionally regulated industry. (Private auctions are forbidden in France.) Flee to the upstairs Secretariat for English-speaking assistance. Inspection of articles from 10 A.M. to 11 A.M. daily and all day Saturday; sales from 2 P.M. to 6 P.M. Monday through Friday; closed Sunday and all of August.

Department stores: **Trois Quartiers**, **Galeries-Lafayette**, and **Au Printemps** are the leaders. They are so close together that you won't need a taxi to cover them all. **Au Printemps-Nation**, a 5-story branch of the last, has recently opened on Paris' eastern edge. **Bon Marché** on the Left Bank is the biggest and cheapest.

Markets: Most famous is the **Flea Market** ("Marché aux Puces," Porte de Clignancourt). Its teeming, trash-filled streets are overrun by tourists and nationals whose quest for "bargains" is too often illusionary. You'll probably pay more here than you would in a legitimate shop—but it's fun just the same if you've never dickered for those reindeer antlers or busted Louis XIV ear trumpets. Go Saturday, Sunday, or Monday only. (The best time to buy is Sat. morning). **Marché Biron** boasts approximately 250 stands and perhaps the most varied collection of European antiques available today. The **Bird Market** cheeps along on Sunday in the then-bare **Flower Market**. The **Stamp Market** is perforated with philatelic bugs on Thursdays, Sundays, and holidays along avenue Gabriel. The **Paris Shopping Forum** is the underground commercial structure built on the site of Les Halles.

Virtually all of the merchandise we saw in the 80-plus shops at the **Tour-Main-Montparnasse Commercial Center** was so trashy that we regretted making the trek.

Please DON'T buy a dress in any but the leading shops. Fashions are patented for a 2-year period. Also, much of the silk isn't up to former standards. If you must have the French variety, be sure it's "Lyon."

Store hours: Completely screwy. Plush jewelers, dressmakers, hatmakers, and chichi operators close on Saturday but are open on Monday. Food stores do business all day Saturday, but they put up their shutters until 2:30 P.M. on Monday. Department stores stay open all day Saturday and Monday during the summer rush, but close on Monday during the rest of the year. As for the noon hours daily, some of the big fellows work straight through—but the vast majority operate only from 9 A.M. to 12–12:30 P.M. and later from 2 P.M. to 6-or-6:30 P.M.

The **Airport Shops** in the International Zone at Orly, Charles de Gaulle, and Nice? Watch out! Although you might be assured to the contrary, we would bet our shoes that very few items of their merchandise are tax-free.

Dedicated shophounds? Space is too tight here for further listings—so consult this year's purse-size 25th Anniversary edition of *Fielding's Selective Shopping Guide to Europe* for more stores, more details, and more lore.

Other Targets

Because of the overwhelming vast number of destinations for relaxing, dining, sport and sun worship throughout France, we have cut our comments to the marrow so that more of them can be mentioned in the limited space available. Below, in our opinions, are some of the top spots for resting and for gastronomy. For further details see your travel agent or consult the French National Tourist Office. See separate sections below on the French Riviera, Châteaux Country, and Normandy Beachhead.

AIX-EN-PROVENCE   (1) **Cézanne** (tucked into a quiet nook of the mid-city district; lovely paintings in lobby; intimate in concept and not many accommodations, so be sure to book in advance), (2) **Hôtel du Roy René** (good physical plant; grand in approach, but a bit frayed in presentation; nice staff if you drive, empty your car of all valuables for the night if it is parked out front), (3) **Riviera "Le Pigonnet"**. Our top choice for dining would be **Le Charvet** (L-shape-room; terribly hot in warm months; heavy, rich décor; delicious cuisine; small selection; numbingly expensive; closed Mon. and Aug.).

AIX-LES-BAINS   (1) **Splendide et Royal** (unchallenged leader), (2) **Astoria**, (3) **Albion**. All summer season only.

ALBI   Hostellerie Saint-Antoine was our pick of the modest in-town selection. Out of the city, the same administration runs the rustically posh **La Réserve**, which is a polished Tarnside gem.

AMIENS   (1) **Grand**, (2) **Nord-Sud**, (3) **Univers** (no restaurant), (4) **Carlton-Belfort**.

ANTIBES, NICE, CANNES,   etc.: See section on "the French Riviera."

ARLES   **Jules César** is the best of an inferior lot but the cuisine is good. Although barny and quite cool it is adequate. Nothing better exists in this charming town. **Select** (35 blvd. G. Clemenceau) is a blissfully quiet stop, but it has no restaurant. Many guests totter over to the neighboring **Grappe,** which specializes in Arlesien dishes; it also has a few bedchambers.

ASNIÈRES-SUR-NOUÈRE   **Moulin du Maine Brun** (a quiet hideaway crooked into "the elbow of Cognac").

AUCH   **Hotel de France** (in Gascogne). It is especially noted for its cuisine which is masterminded by Chef André Daguin—and which is worth a special detour.

AVALLON   (1) **Poste** (famous provincial inn with 24 rooms and 20 baths; Napoleon snoozed alone in #3—a single with w.c.; glorious comforts in #6, a canopy-bed double; magnificent and costly cuisine; attractive décor; reception much improved; compulsory charges on facilities which are normally optional; closed Dec. to mid-Feb.), (2) **Chapeau Rouge** (routine). If you fail to get a table at the Poste (but you'll be rewarded if you *are* successful), then we'd suggest either the cool **Moulin des Ruats** (1 mile out) or **Relais Fleuri** (2½ miles out) for a meal in the area. (Some readers of late have complained about the reception and service at the Moulin, but we haven't experienced these personally.)

AVIGNON   (1) **Le Prieuré** (a small rural gem, at Villeneuve-les-Avignon; closed Dec. to mid-Feb.), (2) **Europe** (in town; reports of lumpy mattresses on some beds; recommendable kitchen, with an A-plus rating for the roast lamb). At mealtimes try (1) **Hiely,** (2) **Auberge de France.** At *Noves* (7 miles out): **Auberge de Noves.** At *Les Angles* (2 miles): **Ermitage-Meissonnier.**

AVRANCHES   See "Normandy Beachheads."

BARBIZON   Here, along with nearby Fontainebleau (see later), is one of the few short excursion points from Paris. (Versailles is practically the only other major one.) Stevenson wrote his *Forest Notes* here; Millet, Rousseau, and other Barbizons had their studios in the village or regularly visited the fantasy woodlands. The paths among the pines and peculiar, haunting rock formations are enchanting, so don't fail to wear your walking shoes. If you succumb to the spell, the **Hôtellerie du Bas-Bréau** is a fine old timber and stucco structure on the main street where the food is expensive but good and the comfort is ample; service, however, can be spotty. **Auberge de la Dague** is more attractive on the outside than in the interior; rates, however, are reasonable.

BAYEUX   **Lion d'Or** (small, quiet, amiable; extensive renovations and additions completed; ably but modestly run by Manager Jouvin-Bessiere; no reservations held after 8 P.M.; closed Dec. 21 to Jan. 11).

BEAUNE   de la Poste (Chevillot management; superior restaurant specializing in Jambon de Dijon Burgundy with green herbs). The **Central** is more modest but more than adequate. Ask for room 26.

BELFORT Hostellerie du Château (plush period furnishings; delicious food.)

BIARRITZ   (1) **Palais** (municipal ownership; 200 bedrooms, stunning swimming pool with chic cabanas, all luxuries; sumptuous and lethally expensive), (2) **Régina et Golf** (between golf course and sea; closed Oct. through May; good), (3) **Plaza** (midtown situation; the only major hostelry open all year; 20% of its small but comfortable units redecorated each season, on a continuing cycle; not dazzling; kind and efficient administration), (4) **El Mirador** (sweeping sea vistas from front windows; Coq Hardi restaurant at ground level), (5) **Marbella** (modest and reasonable). The 126-room, 3-tiered, **Le Miramar**, by the sea, has just made its debut as a hotel and spa. It features paraffin baths, labs, medical and fitness facilities, 3 indoor plunge pools and an outdoor swimmery, a nightclub, and a ballroom. Loews, its patriarch, manifests various taste levels in its several European projects (Loews in Monte Carlo, the Churchill and Montcalm in London), so we will want to see this luxury house in action before offering any further comment. For student digs, tops is the **Beaulieu**, followed by the **Belvédère**. Still cheaper and offering sweet sheltering arms are the pension-style **Central**, **Monguillot**, and **Washington**. The teenie-tiny **Patio**, open year round, is another cheerful bet for budgeteers. Most of the aforementioned are open in summer only; most insist upon full pension.

Among restaurants in the region, we think that the **Relais de Parme**, at the airport, is one of the best. View of Anglet; modern décor; open all year. In the city, it's (1) **Café de Paris** (aviary entrance, with hearth on one side and Atlantic on the other; friendly but forgetful service; closed in Feb.; expensive; father-and-son Pierre and Robert LaPorte alternate between managing this house and the Relais de Parme), (2) **Rôtisserie Coq Hardi** (glorious command of coast from window tables; listless attention; inconsistent cookery; our Coquilles St. Jacques was superb in taste but microscopic in size), (3) **Le Link** (golf course situation; lunch only; rushed atmosphere; same Café de Paris ownership; closed Feb.).

Down the pike, vaguely north of Pau (about 25 miles), in the department of Landes, the noted monarch of modern chefs, Michel Guérard, practices his alchemy at *Eugénie-les-Bains*, located in the health center known as the **Les Prés d'Eugénie**. For low-caloried masterworks here indeed is a dining shrine. Always reserve in advance, especially if you plan to overnight in the 40-room establishment; closed winters; ovens begin stoking in April. A marvel of inventive new techniques now known universally as *Cuisine Minceur* ("the cuisine of slimness"), which, incidentally, is the title of Chef Guérard's brilliant photo-filled cookbook. (It's available in English, published by William Morrow & Co., Inc.).

BIDART   (Biarritz 4 miles) (1) **Chistera** (no special décor; good dining) and **Relais Franco-Espagnol** (slipping further and further in our ratings).

BORDEAUX   We haven't tried the **Aquitania,** but we think that the PLM chain that runs it generally does a good job in the provinces. Otherwise: (1) **Normandie** (no dining room), (2) **Splendid** (pleasant dining salon and public rooms; yokelesque cellar nightclub; gray-dismal but physically comfortable accommodations), (3) **Grand** (100 units; many recent refreshenings; so-so), (4) **Royal Gascogne** (colorful bedchambers; attractive Old World scheme gone somewhat to seed; only fair), (5) **Terminus,** and (6) **Montré.** Our dining choices run this way: (1) **Chapon Fin** (the table is traditional as well as inventive), (2) **Saint-James** (more of the *nouvelle cuisine* appears here), (3) **Réserve Etche Ona** (5 miles out at L'Alouette), (4) **Toque Blanche,** (5) **Hôtel Splendid.** **Dubern** had slipped badly, in our opinion. Now we hear that it is making a dramatic comeback. We'll be anxious to try it anew. **Château Trompette** has lost its lip, in our opinion.

BOURG-EN-BRESSE   The most hospitable nests are at **Le Logis de Brou**, in our opinions. What you want to do in this town is to dine, so head for (1) **Auberge Bressane** (across from the magnificent sixteenth century Église de Brou, which you should visit by day; excellent Quenelles or chicken in cream sauce with rice; frogs legs okay; earnest family house; substantial meal for 2 about $60 with wine), (2) **Chalet de Brou** (½-mile out in the village of *Brou*, opposite the church; an economy stop). Also see our comments listed under "Perouges."

BREST   (1) **Continental** (2) **Moderne** (no restaurant). Both ho-hum.

CAEN   See "Normandy Beachheads."

CAHORS   Le **Château de Mercuès** (5 miles from the center on a hilltop in the Lot Valley; Deluxe amenities; excellent cuisine; one of the true beauty spots of *La Belle France;* seasonal so check first and book in advance. Be certain to drive over to the wonderful prehistoric caves of **Pech-Merle** near *Cabrerets* which will surely be one of the cultural highlights of your visit to Europe).

CALAIS   (1) **Meurice** (good kitchen, but rooms basic), (2) **Sauvage** (also basic). Skip the rest. In fact, if you want to skip the entire country, Calais is the ferrypoint for the brand-new Naviplane, the world's largest commercial hovercraft, which zips in triangles between here, Boulogne, and Dover carrying 385 passengers and 45 cars. It's one of the quickest hops across the Channel.

CARCASSONNE   (1) **Cité** (interestingly situated in the medieval Old City, high above the "new"; excellent, thoughtful service; ample comfort; open Apr. to Sept. only; the leader), (2) **Terminus** (antebellum and clean; when we saw the 4' 11", 75-lb. maid who had been sent out to wrassle our 2 king-size suitcases, we lugged them up ourselves; passable but not distinguished), (3) **Central** (some urgently needed updatings; still poor. The food? Urp, gag, ugh! We suffered 3 days from 1 meal). Dining, we think, is better at (1) **Logis de**

Trencavel or at (2) Le Maillon Périgourdine. Auter has an attractive atmosphere but grossly unappetizing cuisine; it was the most disappointing meal on a recent trek through France.

CHAGNY This townlet is in the heart of Burgundy and is becoming known throughout the gastronomic world for Lameloise, a small modest hotel in the center of the hamlet with a far-from-modest restaurant. It was here, in fact, that we had our most memorable meal of a recent French research round. The house nobly reflects Burgundian tastes, with open-beam ceilings, magnificent tapestries, wrought-ironwork, arches, vaults, and rich furnishings. The $110 gourmet menu for 2 people is vast. Our $23 repast for one was more than ample for an ordinary appetite. Delicious brochet, slices of duck with grapes, and Bresse chicken; outstanding cheese trolley—and those desserts—eeeiiy-wowww! They are fabulous—especially the *feuilleté* with *fraises* (strawberries). In fact, everything was beautiful to the eye, exciting to the taste, and exquisitely served. Try not to miss this very special precinct of heaven.

CHAMONIX (1) Croix Blanche (midvillage situation that can be noisy; main dining room with copper-and-iron hood drawing sparks up the chimney; "modern" rooms with beds lower than your ski bottoms; "traditional" accommodations better; all units with baths; 4-season operation; nice staff; recommended), (2) Mont-Blanc (charming split-level round-the-hearth dining room; gardenside terrace bar; tennis court; pine-lined bedchambers; attentive direction; a favorite with Americans, with good reason), (3) Carlton (big and old-fashioned; superior personnel; substandard furnishings and comforts), (4). La Sapinière, (5) Les Charmoz, (6) Des Alpes (every room with private bath, but most with shabby carpets and furniture). Down the line in attractiveness come Albert et Milan and Hermitage-Paccard. Au Bon Coin is a dainty little corner with lots of heart plus soothing tabs. If none of these suits your taste, there are approximately 100 others on the immediate and nearby slopes. For cuisine, try (1) Le Royal in the Casino (Park Avenue living-room ambiance; glass-enclosed view of illuminated garden; elegant), (2) Lion d'Or, (3) Le Lutetia, (4) Le Choucas (for snacks), (5)Le Crèperie (for crepes of all types). The best hotel dining is at the Carlton, which has begun to skid.

CHATEAULIN (near Port-Launay): Au Bon Accueil (chiefly for its table salmon and its salmon-fishermen clientele).

CHERBOURG (1) Sofitel (from what we know of miserable existing competition and of other Sofitels, this *has* to be the leading light, even though we have not seen it. Total of 80 rooms, all with bath or shower, radio, and available TV; beach-and-harbor-view dining room; bar; parking area; handy to the car-ferry dock; a modern Messianic miracle for this port). Then (2) Moderne et Terminus, (3) Louvre et Marine, and (4) Grand (no restaurant)—all beyond our pale.

COLMAR (20 minutes north at Illhaeusern) This little corner of the globe has become famous for its leading restaurant run by the Haeberlin brothers.

The beautified **Auberge de l'Ill**, on the banks of the Haut-Rhin, is now one of the top stops in the nation. Cuisine excellent, but heavy in the Sauce Department (remember this is Alsatian fare, not Classic French). Damned good Turbot Soufflé with lobster sauce, Noisettes de Chevreuil, and ice cream; perfect attention from an alert corps of captains and waiters. Closed Tuesday. Summary: Superb for country dining! Prices here, not incidentally, are not punishingly high for the quality—but they're also miles from cheap. In Colmar itself, the much less expensive **Maison des Têtes** provides highly satisfactory fare.

CONDRIEU The Rhône-side **Hotellerie Beau Rivage** is a captivating stop, in spite of the rather industrial aspect of the river at this point. Waterfront terrace; splendid restaurant (try the Quenelles de Brochet, the trout, or the Marmite du Pêcheur); cordial service. If it's available, book room #35, the owner's former apartment, with renaissance furnishings and about an acre of space. Lovely in every regard.

COURCHEVEL (1) **Pralong 2000** (as the name suggests, it's as modern as the day after tomorrow), (2) **Carlina** (pick of the older snow crop; several slalom-pikes ahead of any contenders from yesteryear and with the top chef in town), (3) **Le Lana** and (4) **Grand** (both similar prices but lower quality). We don't know the **Annapurna,** but we hear that it is worthy.

DEAUVILLE and **TROUVILLE** are tête-à-tête resorts linked by a bridge over the Touques River. The former, more patrician, offers all the accouterments of High-Life leisure—yachting, racing, polo, golf, aero-clubbiness, gambling, curling (the outdoor variety, too), a $2,000,000 covered pool for year-round dipping, a wide flower-lined beach, and a budget that headlines some of the world's greatest entertainers. The famous New Brummel nightclub of the Casino, and the ultracozy winter Casino, are all part-and-pleasant-parcel of the night scene. Efforts are being made to stoke the popular image now on a 4-seasonal basis instead of merely in strawberry time. Trouville (see later), a less opulent refuge, has fewer pretensions of gentility and refinement. Parisians, who can make the drive in about 3 hours, crowd both in increasing numbers.

Here's how we rate Deauville's hotels: (1) **Normandy** is one of France's finest. Fronted by tennis courts and sea; Grand Siècle architecture, partially modernized; some rooms in exquisite taste; the only hotel we've visited where the liners in the wastebaskets matched the curtains, chair fabrics, and wallpaper. Young, alert M. Crauffron will receive you gracefully and see to any needs, whims, or comforts. Stratospheric rates. Open all year; terrific for a weekend, even with your own wife. (2) **Royal** is also excellent. (3) **Golf** has a 1st-rate view and extra-good cuisine; it's popular with golfers and the older generation. (4) **Arcades** and (5) **La Fresnave** (seasonal).

Now let's take a look at the local dining spots: (1) The **Casino Grill** for summer, (2) **La Malibran** (Winter Casino) for the colder months, (3) **Ciro's** on the beach promenade for lunch year round. All have Normandy Hotel supervision, the same chef, and high-quality administration by Maître Paul-

Jean. The 1st is big and nobly bred; the 2nd is cozy with its velvet banquettes and deluxe intimacy; the 3rd is a glass-faced beachfront haven for delectable seafood specialties. Down the line: (4) **La Crémaillère** (saloon ambiance, scarlet carpet, wine-cask table, and copperware galore; menu based on the local finny harvests), (5) **Castel Normand**, (6) **Chatham**, (7) **Le Grand Large**, (8) **Golf** (closed in winter). Tops for hotel fare, of course, is the **Normandy**. The **Royal** also good, has Empire furnishings and a cool atmosphere. Finally, be sure to slip on your espadrilles and hike out to the little restaurants along the Touques River for the petite and delicious *crevettes grises*—the best shrimps in all Gaul.

Honfleur (Deauville 9 miles) offers yet another fine possibility which is the **Ferme St.-Siméon**. (*Very* expensive).

DIEPPE (1) **Univers** (Palm Sun. through Nov.), (2) **Aguado** (closed Feb.). We haven't seen the 52-room **La Présidence**, but it could well be the hottest contender on the Dieppe doorstep today; we hope you like it; most readers seem to prefer it to the other offerings locally.

DIGNE **Ermitage Napoléon** (now slipping; no dining room). The 50-room **Paris** is reported to be modest but adequate; they say its fish-specialty restaurant is its strongest point.

DIJON Not so hot. The opening of the 124-room **Frantel** this season may help matters, however. It will offer a heated pool, a restaurant, a bar, and a garden terrace. Next, you might try (1) **La Cloche**, (2) **Chapeau Rouge** (fine table), (3) **Central**, (4) **Ducs de Bourgogne**. If you like red and white running wine in your room, M. Victor Maillard's unique innovation at the **Terminus** should intrigue you. Heading north (3 miles) toward Paris, **Hostellerie Val-Suzon**, at *Val-Suzon*, might be a worthy alternative; its kitchen is respected locally. We detect good vibrations on this one. A late visit to dine at the **Pré aux Clercs et Trois Faisans** was a sad disappointment.

DIVONNE-LES-BAINS Although French, this resort suburb of Geneva (only 20 minutes out) is so closely linked to its Swiss hub that we've given it full coverage under "Switzerland."

DUNKERQUE **Victoria** is *it;* not advised if avoidable.

ÉVIAN-LES-BAINS (1) **La Verniaz et ses Chalets**, (2) **Royal**, (3) **Splendide**, and (4) **Ermitage**. Three-month season. At mealtime, we'd rate them as follows: (1) **La Verniaz**, (2) **Casino** restaurant, (3) **Hôtel Lumina** (one mile out), (4) **Hôtel Royal**.

EZE VILLAGE This most scenic hamlet is nailed to the mountain along the Middle Corniche halfway between Nice and Monaco. It is noteworthy not only for its rich panoramas and stone-lined lanes, but for a restaurant called **Chèvre d'Or**, which is neither the best nor the most expensive establishment which clings to a Riviera cliff. Nothing really matters here except the craggy

earth, the cobalt Mediterranean, and the cornflower sky. You'll probably pay
scant attention to your plate, but if you did, you should find it pleasing too.

FÈRE-EN-TARDENOIS   Hostellerie du Château (about 1½ hours from
Paris and well worth the jaunt).

FONTAINEBLEAU   As an excursion point from Paris, this royal enclave (with Versailles) tops the list. Less than an hour from the bright lights,
it is also a delightful site for weekending and sharing the beauty that so
many French regents enjoyed since the Middle Ages. Few travelers realize it,
but the region offers its own Châteaux Country, with the magnificent, perfectly preserved Vaux le Vicomte as one of the most impressive estates in all
of France only 12 miles away. (Be sure to check opening dates and times.) In
contrast to pomp, there are the forest paths of romantic Barbizon (previously
described) only a few minutes along the highway. If you wish to linger, **L'Aigle Noir** faces the gates to the palace grounds. It offers alfresco dining in
summer, a refined salon for inclement days, very handsome bedchambers,
some with open timbers and textiled walls. Personable Pierre Duvauchelle is
a competent and cordial host. If you are coming only for the day, dine here
rather than at **Chez Arrighi**, where we had a ghastly bout with the vittles.
Try not to miss the quiet majesty of Fontainebleau and the fringe benefits of
the neighboring hamlets.

GRENOBLE   (1) **Park** (automatic temperature controls, automatic elevators, bathroom telephones, and stocked electric refrigerators in all rooms), (2)
Alpotel (in the same administrative range as the Park), (3) **Terminus** (no
restaurant), (4) **Trois Dauphins**, (5) **Savoie**. All except Park and Alpes (and
perhaps Trois Dauphins) uninvitingly commercial; about 40 other ho-hum
hostelries to choose from. About 4 miles out, the **Rostang** is no longer recommended by us. At nearby _Varces_, try Chef Brunet's **Escale**. It seems to be
soaring.

LA BAULE   (1) **Hermitage**, by all means (vast 300-room modernization
program lately completed; 1st-rank management by Gérard Mauger, ably assisted by his lovely wife, both formerly of the famous Château d'Artigny at
Montbazon). Then, (2) **Marie-Louise** (guests may take some meals at the
Hermitage), and (3) **Royal**. This top triumvirate is owned by the same company; all face the sea; all are comfortable. Next come (4) **Cecil**, (5) **Pléiades**
(attractively renewed), (6) **Hélios** (not as stylish, but better food). **Bretagne**, with its downstairs dining room, down-in-the-mouth aspect, and 1850
sanitarium atmosphere, has the best name for a winter stop. We much prefer
to overnight in the modest but cozy **Auberge de la Chaumière,** with its park
setting; 10 minutes from the sea. **Concorde** and **Beau Rivage** are basic; best for
freshmen on senior allowance. In nearby _Pornichet_, the 35-room, garden-
bound **Fleur de Thé** is said to be a particularly pleasant Teahouse of the August
Moon; we haven't sipped its savor, but it sounds salubrious. Farther up the
estuary, at _St. Nazaire_, Le Bretagne offers simple but clean shelter for one-
night wayfarers; definitely not for lingering.

LA MUSE (AVEYRON) Grand Hotel du Rozier et de la Muse (hook a trout from the River Tarn and bask in the sweet lack of pollution).

LE HAVRE Passable but not more. (1) **Normandie** is the choice; 2nd-line. (2) **Celtic** and (3) **États-Unis** have no restaurants and are rugged. We gather from favorable reader reports that **Grand Hôtel de Bordeaux,** also with no restaurant, may be worth trying, but we don't know it personally. When hunger strikes, you might try either **Le Grand Large** or **Monaco**. We are deeply grateful for a missive on our desk which reads, "Since your restaurant suggestions for Le Havre were so negligible, we started to seek one and quite by accident we 3 priests came upon **L'Etable**. . . . It is such a delight: rustic interior and steaks over a wood fire. I thought I'd died and gone to heaven, they were so delicious." Thank you, Father. *Non sibi, sed omnibus.*

LES BAUX The word "sensational" has been grossly overabused by Broadway and Hollywood—but when applied to **Baumanière** the fit is such perfection that we are impelled to use it. For affluent motorists who seek the cream-of-the-cream on the Paris–Riviera run, this relatively small, elegant, high-price oasis is indisputably one of the world's Better Mousetraps. It crowns a rugged, rock-tortured valley less than 2 hours northwest of Marseille. On an unforgettable incognito visit we had Foie Gras Maison, Gigot d'Agneau en Croûte, Banon (a local cheese similar to Stilton), and a bottle of Romanée Conti. It was the happiest investment of that entire tour. (Such a repast today would cost perhaps $60 per person, without figuring in the wine.) Recently we pushed away from another such feast, and it remains the same superlative treat at approximately the same tariff. Gastronomic heaven! Patio service in season, with a lovely sweep of the valley; *cave* of 25 thousand bottles; friendly country staff, tennis club, swimming pool, and horseback riding. The main building has 10 charming regional-style rooms; there's an adjoining annex with a few more, as well as the Cabro d'Or project ½ mile down the slope, with its own dining room and extra-tranquil privacy. Accommodations in the former cost almost double the tariffs of the latter; they're worth it to the well-heeled pilgrim. Our cheers and our bows to M. Thuilier and his extraordinary—yes, "sensational!" —creation.

LILLE (1) The air-conditioned, romantically situated, air-minded, **Novotel** at the airport. (2) The traditional **Royal**. (3) The **Carlton**, which barely makes the Junior Varsity.

LIMOGES The First-class **Royal-Limousin** boasts its Le Renoir restaurant and 76 well-equipped bedchambers. The hands-down champ for miles around.

LOURDES In 1858, 14-year-old Bernadette Soubirous knelt by Massabielle Rock in Lourdes and received the 1st of her 18 visions. Since then, what is probably the 2nd most famous Catholic shrine in existence has sprung up around the site. More than 1-million pilgrims congregate annually at the grotto where the Virgin Mary started the waters flowing during Bernadette's 9th vision.

Transportation to Lourdes has never been easy because of its off-trail setting near the Spanish border. You may make the 555-mile journey from Paris by rail in 9¼ hours, or you may fly in High Season via Air France, Aer Lingus, or a number of other regular and charter carriers. In winter the best connection is from Paris. Flights arrive at Ossun International Airport, about 4 miles out of town.

Unfortunately, the atmosphere of Lourdes has become sickeningly commercial. On our recent loop we saw a sign reading "Visitez Les Grottes de Bethlehem." It was hanging over a Jolly Roger pinball machine in the Snack Bar Parisien. Shoppers gush through the Maison Catholique and the Palais du Rosare—the local market centers of claptrap—to purchase such items as cry-baby Jesus dolls and "l'Apparition" plastic hip-flasks for carrying away the local holy water. (A jigger-type screw-cap on the latter, however, suggests it may also be used for other curatives.) This sort of thing is a shock to the devout, and well it might be. This shrine city has been sadly victimized by opportunistic souvenir-mongers. But for sincerely religious travelers of any faith, Lourdes can be a deeply moving experience, despite the commercial shoddiness of its fringes.

There are approximately 420 hotels in and around the city. Though some are on the expensive side, their quality ranges from low-mediocre to downright-miserable. In most, full pension (room _and_ meals) is either obligatory or pushed as hard as they can push it. Since the restaurants we've tried here are all poor, however, this practice isn't quite as outrageous as it would be in centers with higher gastronomic standards. And, since they know they've got you hooked, you usually must pay _full menu prices for the first 3 days._ After that you qualify for the reduced half- or full-pension rates.

Best of the lukewarm lot, in our opinion, is the **Grand Hôtel de la Grotte**, with meals compulsory. Down the line come **Ambassadeurs** (dripping with souvenir stands), **Impérial**, **Moderne**, (a misnomer if we ever spied one) and **Chapelle et Paro**—all seasonal, some noisy, and none exciting. We hear that the **Hostellerie de l'Astazou** is homey, but we haven't tried it. For budgeteers, a happy report has come in from a friendly reader about the **Windsor;** he liked his accommodations, was delighted by staff attitudes, raved about the cuisine, and called its low, low tariffs "a fantastic value".

★ **TIP**   Frankly, we found the city so crass and repulsive in all its touristic aspects that we were determined to find some small tranquil haven where we could escape from its hurly-burly sideshow. To our relief, on about a 20-minute easy drive into the Pyrénées we found the mountain-hugged ski station of _Cauterets_. It is peacefully embraced in the lowest point of the Lutour Valley and splashed by a dozen waterfalls, the largest being the Cascade de Cerisey. No hotels are outstanding in this snugglesome sylvan retreat, but somehow any of them seemed better than the best in Lourdes. The **Parc** harks the biggest name, but we prefer the **Chalet**—which _looks_ like a chalet. The fresh-faced **Mouré** is very central; it's a skip and a slip to the ski lift. The **Ambassadeurs**, old but improving, boasts the best cuisine in town. As a sign of its provinciality, the rambling, white-stuccoed, red-windowed **Bordeaux**, where we recently placed our sitzmark, advertises Ping-Pong on its stationery—a "first" for us. The **Victoria** is solid yet creaky, as only the French can make 'em. Nice people, however. About 6 miles toward Lourdes, in the village of **Argelès-Gazost**, the **Miramont** and the **Pyrénées** draw the big-city spenders, but **Mon Cottage** would draw little old *moi* —chiefly for its solace. If you want to be reminded of God's majesty up among the cathedral spires of the Hautes-Pyrénées, we believe you'd prefer either of these 2 tiny hermitages to the blare and screech of the major attraction.

LYON resides at the junction of 2 rivers (Rhône and Saône) and 2 worlds (central and northern Europe). This apex between the Alps and Burgundy has been called "the Scotland of France," due to the fogs generated by the confluence of the streams; despite the mists it is alive, thriving, and a vitally stimulating city. Renowned for its silks and its stupendous dining establishments; improved hotels; heavy industry; ever-growing, modernistic Satolas Airport becoming more important almost hourly; proud, clean-lined Sports Palace, containing one of Europe's largest enclosed tracks; huge convention center to keynote its commercial tone; new Métro line; some Roman antiquities, châteaux, cultural attractions, but a way station rather than a primary target for most travelers.

The **Sofitel** unwrapped 200 bedrooms, a superb panoramic restaurant, and 2 bars which we've sampled and thoroughly enjoyed. Director Lucien Chapat is doing a splendid job with this twentieth-century plant. **Frantel**, in a tower which forms part of one of Europe's largest shopping centers, is architecturally exciting but not as comfortable as the Sofitel. A Moroccan-style lobby rises through 8 floors of atrium with hanging gardens cascading from loggias; the blue and teal l'Arc en Ciel restaurant overlooks the city and the Rhône; bedrooms are plainly modern but adequate. Fanciful, as our second-choice hotel. The **Royal**, a giant step down the ladder, would normally come next. However, a Houston reader who spent one "agonizing" night on the floor here (she preferred it to her bed) opines that we are *still* not emphatic enough about the size of that step. After these, there are the **Grand Hôtel et Nouvel** and the **Beaux-Arts** (no restaurant). The business-oriented **Terminus** is in the P.L.M. chain. Fair. A **Ramada** is projected but no date specified; the **Meridien** is far out near the airport; and a **Novotel** (okay for motorists) is located on the *autoroute* approach from Geneva. For outskirters **La Réserve** at nearby **Lissieu** looks dreamy as a manse-in-the-meadow; reportedly**** service and all the accouterments of God's Little Acre.

Paul Bocuse, one of the acknowledged giants of French cuisine, plies his famous trade in a sprawling converted house on the banks of the Saône about 15 minutes by car from Lyon. Entrance via a small garden and a patio displaying a colossal caldron; further access beside glass panels with a view of the kitchen; 2 interior salons, one facing the river; brick-red ceiling with open timbers; tile floor (cold for ladies' feet in winter); candelabra, cut flowers, and plants dotting the rooms. We think that the original restaurant, which is now used for overflow traffic, is the more majestic. There is nothing timid about the maestro's flavorings. His are deliberate culinary statements—without the remoteness or subtleties that are often so faint as to invite puzzled glances from diners who pretend to recognize the savorings. Garlic appears boldly; so does pepper. The chicken in *chemise* (a specialty) nests in a football-size membrane, a masterpiece of presentation. Food is abundant and beautifully served, but for us it lacked the final golden glow which so many critics accord Bocuse cuisine. There is an uneasy mood of commercialism that the sensitive guest might resent: Paul Bocuse postcards, dishes, cookbooks, chocolates, luggage, and automobile stickers (declaring "This is the emblem gourmets will know.")— all of which cause the reflective diner to wonder about his role in this smoothly orchestrated promotional scheme. If visiting such a shrine is important to you, then you can expect to pay $170 per couple including a moderate wine. A very special experience. Personally, we are fonder of the sophisticated precincts of **Alain Chapel**, who provides surprisingly cosmopolitan accommodation and outstanding gastronomy in the dreary nearby hamlet of *Mionnay* (refer to our special entry farther along). After these stellar attractions, we assure you that you also would not be unhappy at the **Nandron**, the **Vettard**, the **Orsi** or the delightful **Mère Brazier**. In addition, we have had good luck in the popular **Léon de Lyon** as well as the smaller **Bourillot**. **La Tour Rose** is also good.

MARSEILLE, the oldest city of France, is 2nd in importance. (New excavations date it back to Grecian times, when it was called "Massalia.") It's the chief port, with heavy Italian influence, routine-to-poor hotels, superb restaurants, Château d'If (Monte Cristo's famous island prison, an interesting 30-minute boat ride away), practically no major monuments except l'Abbaye de St. Victor or the Basilica of Notre-Dame de la Garde, plenty of color, new construction, new Métro now fully functional, a frenetic atmosphere. The ancient harbor town is brightening to make its bid as the principal anchorage for tourists in southern France. The enlarged airport represents a jet-propelled start in this direction. If you succumb to the wooing, be sure to stay out of the Algerian Quarter (rue Ste.-Barbe, rue des Chaneliers, etc.) after dark, because it's one of the most rugged, dangerous slums in the world.

The PLM hotel chain reshaped its **Beauvau** recently. Usually PLM entries are cool but satisfactory. Out at the airport, there's the reasonably priced **Sofitel**, a real buy if you don't mind its distance from town. Many thoughtful fillips for the traveler. **Frantel** has a new 200-unit entry with 2 restaurants not too far from the Old Port. These are generally clean but functional hostelries with a commercial air. We haven't slept at the **Residence Le Petit Nice et Marina Maldorme** but travelers say it is a fine choice. Then we'd rank them this way: (1) **Concorde Prado**, (2) **Grand Hôtel et Noailles** (try to stay in the original Grand Hôtel section), (3) **Splendide**, (4) **Terminus P.L.M.** (private sancta better than public rooms), (5) **L'Arbois**, (6) **Genève**, (7) **Astoria**, (8) **Rome et St.-Pierre**, (9) **Royal St.-Georges**, (10) **Paris**, (11) **Castellane** (perhaps a lucky number for thrifty but tiny voyagers). Otherwise, this port traditionally has offered such limited comfort in lodgings that well-heeled U.S. motorists heretofore have found infinitely greater pleasure in pushing along to wonderful Baumanière at Les Baux (see above) for their overnight stay.

This city is almost universally conceded to be France's foremost seafood center. **Brasserie des Catalans** (6 rue Catalans) angles its spotlight almost exclusively on sea fare. Go here for absolutely the finest bouillabaisse in the region. The service is rough, the décor strictly utilitarian, and there's no view (except for the vision of the chef!). Master of things briny. **Calypso** (3 rue

Catalans) is a neighboring alternate which also banks on the Atlantic for its wares. Expect to spend about $30 per appetite. Delicious. **Jambonde Parme** (67 rue La Palud) offers exceptionally fine Italian fare at considerably lower prices. The **New York** is highly regarded by hungry locals who haunt the Old Port, but the reception we received gave us the feeling we were inconveniencing the staff by spending our money here. Red awning-covered entrance boasting open-air oyster bar to preview coming attractions; chic-but-no-nonsense-atmosphere of hanging iron lamps and damask panels; jam-packed when the meal gong sounds. **Cintra**, next door, offers a crow's-nest peek at the ship's spars from its 1st-floor deck; ground level for snacks only. Best for its panorama. **Au Pescadou**, inland at place Castellane, will give you the greatest shellshock of your culinary lifetime. We counted no less than 54 types and grades of crustaceans at the market-stall entrance; just point your pinkie at any one of them, and it will be yours. Almost anything that swims, frolics, or creeps in the Mediterranean is here. Noisy; rough service; ghastly décor—but, my, what a piscatorial paradise! **Maurice Brun** (18, quai de Rive-Neuve) has been highly recommended.

MEGÈVE Choice of more than 100 establishments with over 2000 accommodations from Christmas to Easter and July through August. The once-famous **Mont d'Arbois**, which brooked no competition for luxury, this season becomes the **Club Hotel**, in which studios and apartments are being sold for yearly occupancy. Our rankings now stack up this way: (1) **Hermitage** (invitingly highborn; small, with wall-to-wall carpets and ceiling-to-floor warmth and charm; 564 units; try for #33, with double exposure and patio; closed May and Nov.), (2) **Mont Blanc** (the heartbeat of midvillage; 2 rollicking horses out front; beaucoup frolicking clients inside; rather expensive for value received), (3) **Mont-Joly** (modernized and expanded; fine perked-up dining room and improved bedchambers; cozy ambiance; seasonal), (4) **Coin du Feu** (same size; no restaurant; very popular; we've never stopped at its hearthside), (5) **Beau Site** (situated below Club Hotel; 30 rooms, extra-savory vittles, low prices; a sweet haven). When it's time to tie on the napkin, here's how we rate the local tables. (1) **Capucin Gourmand** (blessings bestowed on this patrician by that connoisseur of calories, Edmond Bory, the doge of Fauchon in Paris), (2) **Toque Blanche**, (3) **Le Refuge** (one of the finest exclusively seafood restaurants we've sampled recently; small bamboo-clad room bursting with flowers; limited menu but everything flawless; open ski season only), (4) **Viking** (with dancing and a club atmosphere; grills best; expensive; go late), (5) **La Gérentière**, (6) **Mont-Joly Hôtel** (highly respected by the local high life, but our repast was down in the valley, the valley so low).

METZ The biggest news locally is the opening of the new 112-unit **Frantel** near the station. Its 4 Saisons restaurant and La Cervoise Bar are much in favor, too. Then you might try the '62-vintage **Carlton**. Total of 45 rooms and baths; quiet setting; reasonable rates; superior to the **Royal**.

MIONNAY This crossroad, not far from Lyon, certainly is one of France's more unprepossessing corners, but **Alain Chapel**—chef, owner, and institution—has made it justly famous. The 12-room hostelry is hard by the pike, but it is an oasis of exquisite beauty. Roofed entry gate to a small inner court; summer garden with geometric pool; rather formal dining room with sconce lighting, floral sprays, gleaming crystal, and pale yellow tones. Refined accommodations; subtle gilded wallpaper; 15th-century-style doors; full carpeting; the atmosphere of a fine home. The cuisine is celebrated for its inventiveness and luster. All in all, an experience that is elegant, hedonistic, and related in no way at all to its unfortunate assignment to modest Mionnay. Closed Mondays and from Jan. 10 to Feb. 10.

MODANE **Hôtel de France**, midway between Turin and Grenoble, is a handy refuge from Alpine storms; 18 rooms, with one bath to each floor.

MONTARGIS **Auberge des Templiers** (thatched-roof cottage-style dwelling in the tranquil Loiret district).

MONTBARD **Hôtel de la Gare** (the local trout and ham are superb—not to mention the wine!).

MONT-DE-MARSAN (in Landes province) **Le Bois Fleuri** park setting, swimming pool, and tennis; 12 apartments with kitchen and private terrace.

MONTÉLIMAR **Relais de l'Empereur** is the chioce for sleeping and certainly for dining.

MONTPELLIER About 3 miles out on avenue de Lodève, **Les Violettes** is reputed to be the pick of the patch. The centrally sited, 116-room **Frantel** is newer, if you prefer being in town.

MONT-ST.-MICHEL (1) **Mère Poulard** (warm reception by the Heyraud family; excellent cuisine; coming up and up and up), (2) **Du Guesclin** (3) **Terrasses**. All very simple; seasonal only (April. 1 to end-Oct.); the highest decibel-count in rural France; tourists galore. **Auberge St.-Michel** in *Avranches* (13 miles) is a good alternate. Please refer also to our separate section titled "Normandy Beachheads."

MULHOUSE The **Frantel** is about tops in town. None of the other major stops has dining facilities.

NANCY (1) **Grand**, (2) **Thiers**, (3) **Excelsior et d'Angleterre**. All commercial.

NANTES There's not much choice. **Sofitel** is young but spare. **Frantel** is also a chain operation. The **Central** is an antique and probably tops for traditionalists. None will turn on chills of delight.

NANTUA **Hotel de France** (in midtown; traditional and cozy; nice people; abundant menu; don't order house wine, Roussette de Seyssel, as it is green and severe).

NARBONNE Skip it if you can—but if stuck, you'll probably be happiest in the fresh **Novotel** or in **La Résidence**; **Languedoc** is routine. Many are seasonal.

NÎMES (1) **Impérator** is good, and (2) **Cheval Blanc et Arènes** is fair. About 5 miles away, in *Garons,* the **Alexandre** offers only 5 bedchambers in modern dress, yet the cuisine carries on the finest traditions of *la belle France.* It is sited near the airport, but the birds don't fly by night. Closed Aug. 30 until Sept. 15. At the "Ouest" junction of the Paris-Lyon *autoroute*, the **Sofitel**, the **Novotel**, and the **Mercure** all cluster together in a motorists' village. We stayed in the first with its pleasant grill, swimming pool, bar, and amply comfortable bedchambers.

ORBEC (main road Chartres–Verneuil–Deauville, 12 miles southeast of Lisieux) **Au Caneton** (superb fixed-price lunch; fantastic Feuilleté de Langouste and Caneton Grille; excellent wines, especially fine in magnums; don't miss it!).

ORLÉANS After (1) **Ste. Catherine** (run-of-the-grist), plus (2) **Arcades** and (3) **Les Cèdres** (both small, unimpressive, and without restaurants), just spin the wheel. No winners here!

PEROUGES (Cité) If you are in the Lyon district, please reward yourself with a visit to this historic enclave with roots going back to 1167. As it developed, a small medieval hamlet appeared and has been kept in exquisite preserve by its proud residents, by archeologists, and by artists who love it. It takes about a day to absorb the quiet wonders of the village. We heartily recommend a night in the **Ostellerie** operated by the personable Monsieur and Madame George Thibaut. Except for providing obvious comforts, the rooms are unchanged in appearance since the Middle Ages, containing the furniture, pewter, textiles, and accouterments of the period. Across the cobbled courtyard, the restaurant provides an enchanting journey back in time. In cool months, a vast hearth crackles merrily; waitresses in costumes of the era present parchment menus; a giant scroll is your wine list. The cuisine reflects Bressan tastes, and delicious it is. If crowds have not overrun this little morsel of paradise, we think you will have one of the outstanding experiences of your travel days and nights here. Highly recommended, especially in spring and autumn.

PERPIGNAN Pretty dreary. If you must halt, we'd pick them this way: (1) **De France** (on the main drag; enclosed, sidewalk-sited L'Échanson; cheery, solid qualities in many of the bedchambers), (2) **Grand** (higher category, higher tariffs, but lower charm level, in our opinion), (3) **Catalogne** (under the Grand sway; the only air-conditioned hostelry in the city), (4) **Park**, and (5) **Windsor**. If you are heading toward Barcelona (NB: the Spanish frontier closes at midnight in winter), there are many new candidates by the seaside. None will wow you, but you might prefer one of those, at vastly lower tariffs, to this Hicksville, France.

PESSAC-L'ALOUTTE   La Reserve (one of the more rewarding residential pauses in the Bordeaux region).

PLÉVEN   If you do not share our rejection of administrative haughtiness, you might deign to sample the enchanting fifteenth-century **Manoir du Vaumadeuc**. Madame de Pontbriand, its manorly innkeeper, is selective in her clientele and somewhat chary about Americans, in general. Many discriminating French friends praise its voluminous physical charms and superior cuisine, but our discriminations run another course. Sorry, but this one's on you.

POITIERS   The France is the pick of the patch.

PONT-AUDEMER   (Deauville 24 miles) **Auberge Vieux Puits**. We haven't been back here for too long an interval, but one reader reports, "Utter perfection and charm. . . . Dedicated management. . . . Fantastically fine 4-course lunch. . . . The most charming spot on our entire trip. . . ." The duck with cherries is especially recommended.

QUESTEMBERT   Le Bretagne is an establishment of growing importance, but we've never tried it personally. Many say its the best in Brittany.

REIMS   Squalid for a city its size and for the marketplace of the luxury champagne commerce. (1) **De La Paix** (you won't write home about its illustriousness), (2) **Le Bristol** (satisfactory *if* you draw one of its colorful rooms; clean and reasonably priced; nice people; no dining salon), (3) **Grand Hôtel du Nord** (so designed that some of the shower stalls are smack by your pillow), (4) **Continental** (enough globes in its restaurant to recall the Shade of Edward II; otherwise cold and Shade-less). Before spending a night in almost any of these 2nd-run houses, guzzle a gallon of the local bubbly to temper the temples. The 2-story, chilly **Novotel** (2½ miles out) is motelish in feeling. All 125 units set up for 3 people; coin-operated photostat machine in the lobby (why?); shopping center across the pike; grill room surrounding the bar; an air of boredom surrounding everything else. We're told the **Royal Champagne** (20 minutes toward Epernay, at *Champillon*) might be a passable alternate. At nearby *Fère-en-Tardenois*, the **Hostellerie du Château** is a back-country beauty.
   For your nutrients, try them in this order: (1) **Boyer** (among the most esteemed kitchens in all Gaul), (2) **Le Florence** (especially good chicken in champagne sauce and Gratin du Sole), (3) **La Paix** (plain surroundings; substantial cookery at reasonable prices), (4) **La Coupole** (many tour groups; expensive for value; specialty is lobster). At nearby *Epernay*, try the **Hotel Berceaux**.

RENNES   (1) **Du Guesclin** (good food, simple rooms), (2) **Angelina** (without restaurant).

ROANNE   The fabulous and aptly expensive **Troisgros** (Scallope de Saumon or, if that's out of season, Poisson St.-Pierre à l'Oseille; both the culinary

masterworks). It offers a few rooms, but the focus here is on the gastronomy
served up in its deceptively simple paneled salon dotted by nondescript oils and
an illuminated mural of a chef in action. Recipes can be found in *The Nouvelle
Cuisine of Jean & Pierre Troisgros* (Morrow).

ROQUEFORT   Grand Hôtel. At nearby *Charente-Maritime,* Le Soubise
is the gem of female Chef Lilyane Benoit, one of the dynamic pioneers in this
otherwise male-dominated craft. Worth a visit.

ROUEN   (1) **Poste**, (2) **Dieppe,** or (3) **Astrid**, without restaurant, modest
and cheap.

ST.-ÉTIENNE   (1) **Grand**, (2) **France** (no restaurant), (3) **Cheval Noir.**
None inspiring.

ST.-JEAN-DE-LUZ   (1) **Chantaco** (flamingo-colored estate about 10
minutes out; adjoins marsh and golf course; lovely terrace and Spanish garden; tennis; parking; elegant country hideaway that is better than par); (2)
Miramar (hilltop situation looking to sea and pinewood; Basque furnishings; pleasant; most suitable for older peace-seeking pilgrims; nice staff);
(3) **Modern** (big, white, typically French seaside resort hotel; faces water,
with many balconies; some halfhearted improvements; decidedly not Modern). In the town, the **Madison** is a small and cozy house smoothly run by
M. Robert Pateau and his wife. The once-bubbling **Édouard VII** has gone
flat. **Les Motels Basques** (rond-point Ste.-Barbe), resembling a Pueblo village that has seen hard times, is passable at best for motorists; we'd prefer
to make it firmly passable on our itinerary. The petit **Donibane**, on the
outskirts, offers a gleamingly clean but modest hitching post for short-term
budgeteers.

   Our table rankings run this way: (1) **Au Chipiron** (cozy as a *grand lit des
huîtres;* tiny and delectable), (2) **Petit Grill Basque** (also small, with more
emphasis on cookery than surroundings; closed Jan. to mid-Feb.), (3) **Pigeon
Blanc** (we prefer the main rustic room to the annex; only for regional dishes;
best for budgeteers). **Taverne Basque**, next door, has skidded down and down
on our scoresheet. So has **Bar Basque**. **El Bravo,** in the Hotel Madison, is a
valiant contender. Out of the city, the restaurant of the **Hôtel Chantaco** takes
the laurel wreath for elegant dining. Also, don't forget the **Chistera** in neighboring *Bidart*.

ST.-MALO   (1) **France et Châteaubriand** (Apr. through Oct. only), (2)
Central (all year).

ST.-NAZAIRE   Ouch! See *La Baule*—or pause only briefly at Le Bretagne.

SAULIEU   (Avallon 25 miles, and thus also off the prime auto traffic grid):
Côte d'Or is a small hotel with a grand cuisine. Towering Chefs Minot and
Dumaine both have left in turn and now Bernard Loiseau seems to be grasping

the fine traditions here, perhaps even improving on them. Here's a nova in the gastronomic heavens.

STRASBOURG (1) **Terminus-Gruber** (colors that will either delight or fell you; each floor in another hue-and-cry scheme; richly attractive Cour de Rosemont dining room, plus a second restaurant with less charm; very good for avant-garde travelers who like those busy-dizzy-busy decorator shades), (2) **Sofitel's St.-Pierre-le-Jeune** (modernistic structure, suggestive of a better-grade Statler; coolish bar and Le Châteaubriand restaurant; indoor-outdoor patio; underground carpark; 180 rooms, all with bath, radio, telephone, and pastel bed linens; pay-as-you-chill air conditioning; pleasant, but you might as well be lodging in any up-to-date hotel anywhere in the world), (3) **Grand** (extensive renovations; new units smaller and more expensive than more comfortable traditional ones; no restaurant; fair value without oomph), (4) **Maison Rouge** (attractive, fresh Le Chambord restaurant for foie gras goose-stuffers; bad case of the creaks), (5) **Monopole-Métropole** (inviting hunting-lodge dining room its most worthy feature; kindly staff; most bedrooms now halfheartedly renovated, but many remain with makeshift baths and shift-less space). About 4 miles out, at the Rhine frontier bridge between France and Germany, the **Motel du Pont de l'Europe** spans a gap with 100 nests; the adjoining Kronenbourg brasserie, however, is not a favorite nibble nook of ours. Perhaps you'll disagree. Finally, the rapidly lengthening **Novotel** chain has forged a 30-room motel with pool at the Colmar Airport. Among the city's independent restaurants, here's the way we'd rate them: (1) **Au Crocodile**, (2) **Au Gourmet Sans Chique**, (3) **Buerehiesel**, (4) **Valentin Sorg**.

TALLOIRES **Auberge du Père Bise** (outstanding parkside and lakefront inn where the cuisine draws gourmets from all over the Planet Earth; we can recommend several dishes, but that would be a disservice to all of the other wonderful preparations; very costly, but *very*; closed Mar. 1 to Oct. 31).

THOISSEY The 28-room **Chapon Fin** is more alluring for its tables than for its sheltering arms. The St.-Jacques Maison, or the Gratin of crawfish, or the Poularde à la crème aux Morilles are reason enough to make a 100-mile detour.

TOULON The **Frantel** has replaced the former Tour Blanche; about 10 minutes out, it has a stunning situation. Superior restaurant; Le Surcouf Bar; pool, gardens, most units with balcony and sea view. Other hostelries here are not so hot.

TOULOUSE (1) **Frantel-Wilson** (a fairly good link in a nationwide chain), (2) **Concorde** (100 accommodations; also commercial in feeling), (3) **d'Occitinie**, (4) **Mercur-St., Georges,** (no restaurant), (5) **Cie Midi** (6) **Caravelle.**

TOURNUS The **Greuze** is an attractive, long, stone building with stable-style shutters. It is amply comfortable, noted for its cookery, and not unduly expensive.

TOURS See "Châteaux Country."

TROUVILLE (1) **Bellevue** (opposite Casino), (2) **La Résidence** (off the beachfront Promenades des Planches), (3) **La Plage** (faces Casino and best known for its restaurant), (4) **La France** (on blvd. F. Moureaux, overlooking the Touques River), (5) **Chatham** (nearest the beach). None exceptional.

VAL-D'ISÈRE (1) **Grand Parades** (44 rooms of modern mien; better than average cuisine), (2) the slowly fading **Solaise** (Alpine garden setting with ski slopes at the back door; 3-story rustic wooden structure; 45 bedrooms and many private balconies), (3) **Christiania** (50 fresh accommodations; tariffs less than ½ the Solaise tabs; good), (4) **Edelweiss** (superior kitchen, we're told; best for budgeteers). Ski nostalgics will probably enjoy the house of Jean-Claude Killy's father, **La Bergerie**. We've never stemmed the gates here, but it's said to be delightful and cozy. Another house that we are anxious to sample is **Le Kern** run by the ever-smiling Michel Jeanbin and his hospitable wife, Yvette, who do it all as a hobby. Their La Grange restaurant already has one of the best reputations in the highlands. It's small, friendly, and simple, according to reliable voyagers who have snoozed here before we could, the lucky ducks. We don't recommend the **Sofitel** here, but maybe we're contrary.

VALENCE Just south of *Vienne* (see below) there's another world-famous restaurant. It is **Pic**, where the management also offers a few bedrooms for those who linger. Then, a bit outside of *St.-Romain-de-Lerps* (west of the A7, exit Valence Nord or Sud), there's the impressive stone **Château du Besset**, set in a vast park and glowing in elegant 15th-century style. You'll find a pool, tennis, terraces, cuisine of grand repute, and celestial tranquility.

VARETZ **Château de Castel Novel** is a lovely ancient haven with a new annex overlooking the pool. Nice people and excellent cuisine at satisfying prices. If you're near it, stop here.

VÉZELAY **La Poste et le Lion** is a charmer. Then, over at *St.-Père-sous-Vézelay,* **l'Espérance** wins the orchids due to the skilled cooking of Chef Marc Meneau, one of the "greats" in today's French firmament of gastronomy. This inn and restaurant is at the base of the Roman Ste. Madeleine Basilica.

VICHY Dozens, all loaded with holidaying French families. We haven't taken the waters here lately, but we'd judge they line up this way: (1) **Ambassadeurs** (agreeable atmosphere), (2) **Regina**, (3) **Queens**, (4) **Albert Ier** (good Le Patio restaurant). All seasonal.

VIENNE **Pyramide** was once rated as the world's finest. We find its luster fading to a certain degree, but not so its prices; a meal with wine for 2 easily bids farewell to $110 or so. The turbot in champagne is internationally celebrated. Closed Nov. 1 to Dec. 1, Monday nights and all day Tuesday.

VITTEL　The summer-only **Grand** is outstanding, with the **Pavillon Cérès** and **Continental** (both also seasonal) as runners-up.

VONNAS　The **Chez La Mère Blanc** has been in the Blanc family for 4 generations, and once you see it, we'd bet you'll apply for adoption. Most of its fame centers on the dining room: stone floor panels, open timbered ceiling, tapestries, oil paintings, fresh flowers, candle illumination, and a menu that maintains the glory of Ain, where it resides (not far from Macon). If you are aching to pause, look no further. Recent renovations included addition of a swimming pool.

WANTZENAU　(1) **Zimmer** (rustic), (2) **Au Moulin** (open air; closed Tues. and from mid-July to early Aug.).

☑ **FRENCH RIVIERA**　The sunbathed strip of French soil closest to Corsica and North Africa should have been named "The Gold Coast," because of its glittering sheen, its flawlessness, and its 24-karat prices in comparison to lesser Gallic resorts. Instead, from the color of the bordering Mediterranean, it is called Côte d'Azur, the Azure Coast. Brilliant whites, greens, and yellows predominate; the only blues the visitor will find are the sea, the sky, and the figures at the bottom of many of his tabs. (Strangely enough, they are still somewhat less than along the nearby Italian coast.)

Azure or not, you might see red whenever you try to buck the exasperating traffic. From June 20 to September 20 when the vacation recess of France's schools coincides with High Season, the logjam is catastrophic.

Taxis and Car Rentals　Taxi fares on the Riviera are now metered, thank the Good Lord. *What* a change for the better! The best car rental agency we found is **Cannes-Tourisme**, 8 Grand blvd. de Super Cannes. If you telephone 384873, you'll have a fine automobile with an English-speaking driver at your hotel portal in a flash—or you may rent a self-drive vehicle for your roving. Ask for Guy or Roger who form a duet of helpfulness. **Garage Plaza** in *Nice* perhaps tops that list for chauffeur-driven chariots as well as for self-drive vehicles. Then too you'll find the big international agents in both cities (**Avis, Hertz, Europcar,** or **Citer**—the last for Citroëns only) and at Nice airport.

Information Centers　Try either the **Services du Tourisme de la ville de Cannes**, at the Palais des Festivals (on the Croisette), or the **Welcome Information Service** branches in Nice and Cannes. The first offers an Information Desk, an English-speaking staff (including hostesses who have lived in the States), a greeting service (at that hideous Maritime Station, at the rail terminals, and on the autoroute), cruise ship, and other aids. It keeps 2 girls in touch with all hotels and pensions to find space for new arrivals. It's open every day until midnight during this rush season. The 2nd comes up with the same type of aid, plus a helping hand to locate immediate hotel accommodations for stranded travelers. It is connected by Telex to 12 companion bureaus in major cities. Both have absolutely nothing to sell; their only aim is to assist you so that you'll get the best possible impression of the Côte d'Azur.

For your *bookings,* however (the Services du Tourisme makes no reservations for planes, trains, buses, local sightseeing, etc.), we cheerfully recommend 2 top-ranking centers: **Agence Havas** (5 rue Maréchal Foch) and **Agent Cannes** (Maritime Station)—both in Cannes. R. Fleury, mogul of the latter, possesses vast experience, excellent judgment, and a formidable reputation for honesty, patience, and amiability. These gracious people may be depended upon 100%.

ANTIBES is on the main Nice-Cannes line. Nearby there is probably the most famous independent dining establishment of the Côte d'Azur—**La Bonne Auberge**. Today (or tonight) the food is superb, and what makes it even more pleasant is the ambiance, the service, and how it is run. Celebrities the world over are drawn to it as moths to illuminated tapers. Physically this expensive oasis has always been so stunning that we can scarcely wait to get back!

In town, **Les Vieux Murs** fires the biggest gun from its site on a cannon point of the ancient seagirt ramparts. Lovely antique setting as permanent as time itself; stucco walls; arched ceilings; colorful regional interior. Fish soup and Lobster Thermidor are the house prides; it is popular with a savvy set of gastronomes. Very worthy. **L'Oursin** (rue de la République) is also a winner. Fresh, fresh shellfish during the R-months; a good catch. Book ahead to be safe.

The coastal hamlet offers a caravansary of attractions in its eye-popping **La Siesta**. This amusement center (which has also opened a casino), 7 miles from Cannes and 12 miles from Nice, adjoins the highway bridge over the Brague River. Among the facilities are adult Go-Karting, infant Go-Karting, bowling, swimming, water skiing, trampolines, a restaurant, a rôtisserie, a pizzeria, and a nightclub. The main building of this mélange contains such bizarre touches as 3 large bats in a large pansy-ringed cage and wagon-wheel cocktail tales with spokes filled with peppercorns, maize niblets, pine nuts, and a couple of similar products we could not identify. On Saturday nights during the Season it is almost too crowded to move; teen-agers invade in regiments. During the rest of the week, however, it's lively, merry, and patronized by all age groups. At this writing everything except the Go-Karting is shuttered from October till April, but serious consideration is being given to no siestas the year round for anything. Go about 8 P.M.

For lodgings try the **Royal** first, followed by the tiny **Josse**.

BEAULIEU **La Réserve** is a jewel which shimmers more beautifully than ever. Its special atmosphere of intimacy, luxury, and elegance was masterfully preserved through its major reconstruction. Among epicures its world-famous restaurant has long been one of France's most *distingué* landmarks—and now its hotel section matches its superb cuisine. Beguiling lobby; lovely, lovely lounge restyled as a replica of the best reception room in Rome's Farnese Palace; richly appointed bar; beautiful summer patio for alfresco dining when the wind is low; dining salon segmented into 3 parts, with the center portion the private domain of Réserve residents; many balconies; 5 suites and 54 rooms, all with bath and most with fresh, tasteful refurbishing; 2-story annexed "pavilion" with viewless accommodation close to the highway (used mostly for overflow); fully air-conditioned; a Telex board. The large pool area, extending into the bay, incorporates a sun-restaurant, 3 saunas, a massage room, detension hydrotherapy with high-pressure hose, 38 dressing rooms, a bar, and an inside restaurant; this complex is also reserved for the exclusive use of hotel guests. Director Henri Maria maintains a standard which renders this house the virtually unchallenged jewel of the coast. The adjoining, air-conditioned **Métropole**, situated in a 2½-acre, flower-girted park directly bordering the surf, is also proud of its revisions, although they are not as sumptuous as those of the neighboring La Réserve. Entire building freshly repainted; restaurant and bar outfitted in new raiments; bedchambers and baths resparkled and bubble-bright. Professional guidance by veteran Manager Badrutt whose experience is your guarantee of holiday satisfaction. Heated pool, barette, and seaside summer restaurant on a terrace above its rock "beach"; quiet ambiance; traditional furnishings; sumptuous lounges. Very pleasant indeed, but still overshadowed by its great neighbor.

CAGNES-SUR-MER, halfway between Antibes and Nice, is proud of its perky little parimutuel racetrack. It's called Hippodrome de la Côte d'Azur, and it's open from mid-December to mid-March, and during most of July and August (night races only, because of the heat). Cultural touts also praise the neighboring Renoir Museum. Nearby, at the *Biot* turnoff on RN7, you'll find a Marineland splashing with a gay flotilla of flippery fellows. Regular performances begin at 2 P.M. P.S. That background activity is coming from *Sofia Antipolis,* a totally new city being built as an international research center. The **Novotel** is the newest roof for travelers to the area.

CANNES, normally about 25 minutes from Nice via the *autoroute,* is so popular in High Season that it can be uncomfortably overcrowded. There's a magnificent 2nd yacht harbor, called Port Canto, at the eastern extremity of the bay, with 450-car parking lot adjoining; it's connected to a second car park west of these piers by a free bus shuttle service. This auxiliary nautical port-of-sport boasts a clubhouse, heated pool, exhibition hall, card rooms, and bowling facilities—the works. The quay itself—big enough to accommodate 450 pleasure boats—furnishes electricity in 3 voltages, telephone, T.V., running-water connections at each mooring, and guarded access (all night, too) from the shore walks. Take a stroll along the Croisette, the main boulevard that separates the beach from the more lush hotels. Overlooking the city and illuminated at night is the tenth-century Castrum Canoîs with the Museum of Mediterranean Civilization in its dungeon. Smack in the center of town is the original yacht basin, crowned by the Maritime Station; big ships must be reached by lighter, however, because of the harbor's relatively narrow and shallow conformation. Boats run frequently to the Lérins, where the fifth-century Monastery of the Cistercians was St. Patrick's starting point for evangelizing Europe; it is open to women visitors, too. At the Royal Fort on Île Ste-Marguerite, you might like to visit the cell which has inspired stories, plays, and movies by the ream—once occupied, they say, by the Man in the Iron Mask. The beaches surrounding Cannes (summer bathing only) are the best east of St.-Tropez now that tankers have been rerouted to avoid oil spills. (Helicopters resolutely police the coast to shoo the ships away.) The Palais des

Festivals will be reopened next year. There are 3 casinos—the Municipal house
(Nov. 1 to May 31), the Palm Beach (June 1 to Oct. 31; a beauty), and the Casino
des Fleurs (all year). The first may soon be moved into the second when plans
are afoot to build a $100-million hub for gaming, theater, and congresses. Then
you'll find a Sports Palace; an active polo green; 3 golf courses; an annual Film
Festival, automobile *Rallye,* and other events; Super-Cannes, with its spectacular vista; a spate of luxurious hotels; a collection of villas unequaled in France;
a continuous parade of suntanned celebrities; a busy sidewalk trade in sex (of
any inclination); and a gala almost every night. Much more lively and fashionable than metropolitan Nice.

Hotels The Casino-owned **Majestic** has parlayed a $250,000,000 gamble
into a bonanza jackpot. And what a sleek-lined filly she is! The fortune poured
into improving her performance has produced not only some of the finest
accommodations along the Riviera, but comfort and beauty standards that vie
with the best on the Continent. Here are samples of her ground-level innovations: an elegant high-ceiling, marble-clad lobby and reception area; a stylish
dining salon, with garden terrace; a Grill in modern coolish tones; a handsome
teal-blue bar with an antique-auto theme; a crescent-shape, heated seawater
swimming pool in the romantic palm grove (meal service on its aprons); a
beauty parlor and barbershop; an underground parking station. Upstairs, her
units are outfitted with sumptuous creature comforts and costly engineering
details, more of which are being added each happy season. Jacques Bardet, the
dedicated, charming, extraordinarily able General Manager has made a difficult (and to us, wise) decision in concentrating his sizable stake on a series of
limited but painstakingly planned targets. By doing so, he has established a
criterion of taste that has restored the Côte d'Azur to its former glories. Our
highest recommendation—but book your room far, far, far in advance, and
only in the revitalized quarters. The same group undertook the total rebuilding
of the **Montfleury**—and no sooner completed the Herculean task when it sold
the hotel to the Intercontinental chain. It boasts 235 air-conditioned rooms,
3 restaurants, a bar, 10 tennis courts, 2 heated pools, and an ice-skating rink
within the 9-acre hillside estate. Rates are not too steep, but we haven't yet
stayed here so we can't tell you anything about its value.

The **Carlton**, which earlier was in a state of flux, has made significant
advances of late. Today, almost all of the formerly forlorn pockets of feckless-
ness have fled, with numerous freshenings supplanting them, and vastly improved cuisine is now being served, it pleases us to report. Personally, our
favorite haven here would be in the west wing because of the quiet, the lovely
foliage, and the breathtaking vista of the Riviera sunsets. (Please check this out
with the reservations desk first, however, because approval is pending for an
8-story building nearby—and it *could* be right next to your pillow!) A reborn
Stalwart.

The **Grand** provides a set-back garden situation; it was erected by Master
Hotelier Paul Augier of the Negresco interests in Nice. Ultramodern L-shape
structure with all-glass fronts for every accommodation; 90 rooms with seaview terraces; 300 studios and apartments available for long-term rentals. The
bar, snack foyer, and public quarters are a mushroom patch of Saarinen chairs
and white-top tables; the cozy little Grill is best after dusk; it is supervised by

the prestigious Lamour chefs and is excellent. The penthouse has an exotic cluster of 10 demisuites with curtains which separate the beds from the sitting areas; these are absolutely enchanting in twenty-first-century stylizations. The "normal" sleeping chambers have ersatz-leather furnishings, low beds, silk watermark wall coverings and dominant hues of mustard, salmon, lagoon blue, and Formica white; garage, parking space, sun lounge, and private beach are at your command. Hiltonites generally love it. Very good indeed.

Gray d'Albion was taken over by Middle Eastern interests who plan to reopen it for this season. While we haven't seen the refinished product, we can recommend the site. **Le Fouquet's**, with a mere 10 rooms, also has been rebuilt; it gives us the impression of being a deluxe gemstone. **Univers** has been refashioned nicely, adding a restaurant atop its roof and offering half-board to its clients on a noncompulsory basis. Air-conditioned; adequate comfort; very agreeable for the price.

The young **Victoria**, under the same administrative commonweal as the Canberra (see below), is winsome but costly. Gracious overall décor introduced by its English-style lobby; wood-toned bar; captivating garden with a small swimming pool; front units with terraces and striped awnings; flowered carpets; silk bedspreads and padded headboards; baths with basins in alcoves; radio and electrically controlled shutters; no restaurant. It has so much style that we think it will quickly acquire many Victorian vassals within its Gallic realm.

The **Martinez-Concorde**, a property of the state with 15 suites, 400 bedchambers, and 415 baths, is one of France's largest resort havens. Dynamic Manager Michel Dissat has overseen a thorough overhaul, which has rejuvenated this vast establishment. Moreover, the hyper-costly Vergé touch of the Moulin de Mougins (see further along) lends a dash of sparkle to the cuisine. Central situation which streetwalkers seem to find convenient, judging from the curbstone traffic during our stopover; theater-type entrance; snack corner for light bites; outdoor terrace restaurant; very pleasant L'Amiral bar extending to Croisette. Private beach with restaurant, circular bar and water skiing (with or without instruction). Conventions galore during the colder months; a few conducted tours from April to October.

The 60-unit **Savoy** (directly in back of the Carlton, one short block from the waterfront) is set in a lovely little garden. Its squeaky floors, comfortable living dimensions, and old-fashioned furnishings (including brass beds) betray its 4 decades of existence—but its housekeeping is spotless, and eye-appealing fresh paint is nearly everywhere. Just off the side entrance, a flight below the lobby, you will find a little restaurant. In High Season both a 3-day minimum stay and demipension are required. There's a feeling of leisure in this venerable place which appeals to many Quiet Americans—yet the action is less than 5 minutes away. Recommended to the tranquil type of vacationer.

The **Méditerranée**, at the edge of the Old Port and a public beach, has taken beauty pills. The façade has been spiffed up smartly; the lobby has been brightened by a camouflage of flowers and plants. Viewful maritime lounge; amiable outdoor terrace; gay yellow-and-white La Louisiane Restaurant; partially air-conditioned; piped music. Its upstairs has also been refashioned; accommodations are now ample in size, with fresh furnishings and bright ambiance; try to book #312. This corner is very noisy, of course, but so is practically every other bayside site in Cannes. Improved so vastly that the administration merits applause.

The **Canberra**, with its sweet garden and separate parking area, has no restaurant but offers agreeable living. Try to stay on the garden side, because the din from rue Antibes is often disturbing; #104 is the pick of the house. The price range is about the same as that of the Savoy, but it draws a much livelier clientele. Generally satisfactory.

Good accommodations in Cannes at low prices? These are rare birds on these high-flying shores. Perhaps you'll have luck at the **Belle Plage**, about 150 yards off the Plage du Midi (Cannes' other beach). Although you'll probably be asked for a demipension arrangement, you may be able to wrangle a bed-and-breakfast rate if you *both* talk fast. The **Solhotel**, in the same neighborhood, is new and popular. The **Univers**, on the rue du Maréchal Foch, has snapped back to attention with a total refitting. Good solid shelter at a good tarriff. Otherwise, there's the value-packed **Villa Palma**, near the Martinez, and the downtown **Athénée** in a nice plant. The **Mondial** is sinking, in our opinion.

Restaurants The colorful **La Reine Pédauque** (in the center at 4 rue Mar.-Joffre) delighted us with one of the most carefully prepared, graciously served, and gastronomically gratifying meals that we have consumed in many a year along this azure coast. Single room with figured-tile floor; oil paintings; brass and copperware hanging from the ceiling; chairs with cut-velvet upholstery; fresh flowers abounding. The repast is introduced with a gratis offering of tiny hot canapés. Bountiful hors-d'oeuvres cart, sporting even Caviar Niçoise (a ground-olive curiosity); oh-so-heavenly, helium-light Mousseline de Rascasse; butter-soft pepper-filet in either wine or cream sauce; fluffy Ris de Veau in a pastry shell; additional specialties including Langouste Gastronome and Filet d'Agneau en Croûte, which we didn't sample (darn it; there wasn't room!). Chef Dorange and the dedicated little tribe who collectively make this such a delightful culinary outing, deserve Big E's for Efforts Well Done. Surely a leading light within many miles, in our judgment. Closed Mondays and from June 28 to July 19.

Le Festival (55 blvd. Croisette, opposite Palais des Festivals) was taken over by former Parisian interests with Chef Claude Rocher, previously of the capital's Plaza-Athénée, at the stoves. Gay colors; fresh décor; animated, high-decibel atmosphere; choice of sidewalk or interior placement. If the sun is shining and the bikinis are jiggling, enjoy a lazy noonday meal in the open section. If you hit it right, superior.

La Poêle d'Or (23 rue des Etats-Unis) insists on getting better and better. Don't be put off by its décor, which is as plain as an old *soulier*. About a dozen tables; kind and keen attention by Maître Serge Ryembault; noted for its Mousseline of trout and the Bresse chicken in a creamed morille sauce (mushrooms of a very special sort); platters prepared by Proprietor-Chef Chartier, a master of the kitchen who is destined for greater fame. Reasonable prices for splendid gastronomy.

Le Refuge (Quai St. Pierre) is simplicity itself, but the fish selections are superb and the prices are at sea-floor level. Not so at the rising-in-cost **Chez**

Chez Félix (between the Carlton and the Miramar), which is spirited, touristy, and often patronized by the motion-picture people. Closed mid-November to mid-December. The food is only so-so. **Gaston et Gastounette** (6 quai St.-Pierre) ranges from excellent to dreary, depending on how you hit it. Travelers have complained lately of being given the à la carte menu and having to demand the fixed-price card; others squawk about waiters who are marvels at addition (they seem to keep adding, ADDING, and A-D-D-D-D-D-D-I-N-G). Check your bill carefully here. Variable. **Voile au Vent** (17 quai St.-Pierre) sails in with a bar and restaurant, side by side, reached through individual street entrances. Chef Polo conjures up simple magic with his skillets. Frenchy atmosphere; smooth administration by Mme. Ducrot, who provides a warm welcome. One of the best culinary buys in town. The **Laurent** (12 rue Macé) was a happy discovery on a recent Cannery cutup. Laurent and wife Michele minister to diners in the tranquil, antique-cutlery surroundings of their "museum of the table." Moderate tariffs; careful preparations; ingratiating hosts; recommended. The expanded **Blue Bar** in the Palais des Festivals, is almost a carbon copy of Chez Félix—except that it hasn't been discovered by the Jet Set. Lower tabs, slick service; recommendable when we popped in, but a management switch could alter things considerably. **Meridien** (near the Hotel Méditerranée) is a charmer for daydreaming, sea-gazing, and sipping at snack time. A winner in the outdoor league, but the attention can sometimes be strictly low tide.

In the vicinity of the station, a trio of smart bets stand in a cluster on rue 24-Août. These are: **Au Bec Fin, Le Monaco**, and **Bougourne**. All moderately priced; all with respectable wares; all right. **Da Bouttau** (10 rue St.-Antoine) is an atmospherey little retreat where they sketch your order (instead of writing it) on your paper tablecloth and dining check; much of the spark was lost with the death of the owner, because neither the uncle nor the daughter has his zip; rôtisseried chicken is its specialty. Timbered, cozy, colorful room, with lipstick-smeared names covering the walls; guitar and accordion music; other branches in Nice and Évian; cookery good but not stupendous; reserve ahead during summer. **Toque Blanche** (3 rue Lafontaine) has skidded to the point where the quality of its fare matches—and no longer makes up for—its frenetic and haphazard service, in our opinion. Off our list. **Denis** (10 rue de Bône) is a pleasant grill adjoining the Embassy Hotel. This family operation strives to satisfy—and we think that it achieves its purpose amply and for only a moderate quota of funds. Solid. **Vesuvio** (on the Croisette near Hotel Martinez) erupts with pizza poofs. Full of fire and flair; always packed; right for *bastante pasta*. **Le Pingouin** (36 rue Jean-Jaurès) has a laudable table d'hôte. Clean and pleasant; slightly tearoomy in feeling; closed in November. **Le Coq Hardi** (just off quai St.-Pierre) is in the same low price bracket, and it's also cheerful, well scrubbed, and recommendable as a good little "find." **Au Foie Gras**, once a favorite of ours, was been taken over by Britishers Pascal and Freda Cozzolino, who are assisted by their Savoy-trained son George. While not a single friend in Cannes had a kind word to say about it, our own meal, taken from the fixed menu, was remarkably worthwhile for a modest outlay. Busy, elbow-to-elbow ambiance; extremely pleasant family; savory repast from snails to sole to vegetables to dessert. **Le Maschou** (17 bis rue St.-Antoine) has been suggested with enthusiasm by a discriminating reader from Gotham; we're always delighted by his suggestions, so we're looking forward to our first sampling of this one.

Night Life   The **Municipal Casino**, as already mentioned, will transfer its gaming to the Palm Beach Casino both in summer *and* winter while new facilities are being constructed over the next two or three years. **La Chunga** features guitar pickin's from the *pampas;* saddles and tack for décor; high-stirrup society roundup on busy nights; not too expensive, and chic. **St. James**, formerly called the Moulin Rouge Hi-Fi Club, starts perking nightly at 10 P.M., and there's a Sunday Matinée from 4 P.M. to 8 P.M.; striptease, other acts, paper favors; drinks relatively inexpensive, with no cover or minimum. You've seen better. **Maxim's de Cannes** couldn't be more typical of its type. The **Playgirl Club,** formerly called Playboy Club before Chief Surgeon Hugh Hefner altered its gender with a juridical scalpel, is back in business again. If it plays in the same old ways of yore, we'd call it too costly for all but consenting adults. Nix, in our unabashed opinion.

Shopping   In proven big-name perfumes—not junk—**Rimay** (46 rue d'Antibes) offers splendid stocks. The charming M. and Mme. Taillebois are completely truthworthy and ethical in every respect. Here's where we always make our purchase when we're in this area.

CAP D'ANTIBES   is crowned, at the tip of the point, by the famed **Hôtel du Cap** and the **Eden Roc** restaurant. The former, which recently lighted its 100th birthday candle, is a baronial, Second-Empire-style structure that counts among its guests the wealthiest and most ultrachic travelers in the world. Nearly every room in the house has been redone exquisitely; full air conditioning has been installed; the staff-client ratio is an almost unheard of 3 to 1; J. C. Irondelle, the young, gracious, and attractive General Manager, is outstandingly competent. Both du Cap and Eden Roc are open from Easter to late September only. What a glorious place it is! Next in line is the **Résidence du Cap**, sited in 5 acres of garden away from the sea. Its best amenities are a lovely swimming pool with bar, a tennis court, corridors replete with paintings on exhibition, and an Italian patio for breakfast. Its 3 suites and 40 other accommodations, all with private bath, are simply but cheerfully furnished; demipension is obligatory from June 15 to September 15. Mrs. Fay, the owner, is to be commended for making it more and more desirable every year. Clients are received from March to October. Because it is so sedate, it appeals to travelers in search of gentle tranquillity—not to swingers.

CAP MARTIN   The sea-level **Victoria** rules the ripples in a modest pond. Lobby plus main-floor bar, but no restaurant; 32 units with good private bath; 22 with balcony; classical décor highlighted by silks and brocaded walls. Fair value for your franc. The **Alexandra**, with Le Sporting nightclub directly in front, is less prepossessing. Never exposed to the sun—a crucial drawback to most holidaymakers; all units with small loggias; fully air-conditioned and carpeted. Okay in execution, but no rave. **Le Pirate** is the liveliest dinner morring in the vicinity. It executed in phony gypsy-encampment style with a roaring fire, flamenco dancers, bare-chested waiters, and gimmickry galore. Photos of many celebrities line its walls. Rickety structure which impresses us as being a gussied-up nest of packing cases; prices so high that we think they are outrageous; lunch starting at 1 P.M. and dinner from 9 P.M. onward. Cartiers of ultrarich notables still tie up here.

COLLE-SUR-LOUP bows in with the **L'Abbaye Joseph**, a good-size family-operated restaurant which oozes with charm. Historic building; lovely garden terraces; beautiful small chapel decorated by Michel Marie Pulain, the well-known French artist; stalagmites of accumulated candles on rock piles and dividers nearly everywhere one looks. Although lunch is served, it is more pleasant to take dinner on its flower-filled court or in 1 of its 3 interior rooms. Its gay Gallic ambiance in the evening is heightened by a strolling accordionist and guitarist. The atmosphere is happy, the portions are large, and the food is average rather than outstanding. **Toque Blanche**, the next one, is suggestive of a tavern house. Nice little patio with a middling view; semiopen kitchen; about 12 tables; better-than-average wine card for the region. Not special—but not expensive, either. **Les Oliviers**, perhaps 300 yards farther along, serves the most distinguished cuisine in the immediate neighborhood. Big open-air rôtisserie next to an orange tree in the garden; flowers abounding; beautiful open patio (no view); awnings and glass façade protecting its immaculate row of canary-yellow tablecloths; small terrace with another file of tables running along one wall; 4 menus standard; sizable à la carte. To the rear is a pleasant and tranquil 10-room "hôtel" in a separate building. We'd rate this as one of the best establishments in the entire area. Closed from November 15 to December 15.

CROIX VALMER (10 miles from St.-Tropez) has the quiet, clean **Hotel Restaurant Saint-Michel**. Breathtaking view of the Bay of Cavalaire. A discriminating Swiss friend says it offers "excellent bourgeois cuisine." Open April 10 to early October.

GOLFE JUAN The family-run **Chez Tétou** is indisputably outstanding for finny fare. Alfresco terrace with 9 tables; enclosed terrace with about 16 tables; main room unadorned; scrubbed wood tables. Dozen-item seafood menu, with the Sole Meunière and the bouillabaisse especially enjoyable but rather expensive. Friendly, informal atmosphere; open day and night in summer, but only at noon in winter.

GRASSE is just a skip and a jump from both Nice and Cannes. Perfume is supposed to be one of the best buys—but our enthusiasm for some of the much-touted distillations of this region is very much on the dim side. These products all have their virtues and advantages, which are excellent *within the limits of their categories*. But don't let anybody tell you that they're the same as the Big Name brands, because definitely, emphatically, and conclusively, they're NOT!

And don't let them con you, either (as several friends reported last year), that we are any less disgusted by various local pitchmen and pitchwomen and that we have "changed our minds." We are NOT—and we have NOT!

What boobs or rubes do these people take us tourists for? A low-grade moron knows that a dune buggy is *like* a Cadillac, in that it has 4 wheels, an engine, and a chassis; equally, these scents are *like* the others, in that they smell good and add to a woman's allure. But they just aren't in the same league, because the top operators spend thousands of dollars to develop and to protect their own secret masterpieces. Your $5 bill here will bring you exactly $5 worth of merchandise—not $10 or $20, as some sellers are prone to indicate. As 3rd-line gifts for the home folks, samples of these local varieties might do the job, because they're cheap, they're pretty, and nobody can deny that they're French. But the sales practices impress us as being so slippery, misleading, and morally vile that we personally want no truck with them. In the future, we will never touch these lower-quality imitations again.

HAUTS DE CAGNES, in the walled city above Cros-de-Cagnes, has such narrow, hilly streets that even the visitor in the smallest European-made car must scramble up 3 challenging flights of steps to reach **La Cagnard**. Here is a little charmer which commands a splendid view of the valley and a glimpse of the sea. Twelve small and tastefully but simply decorated rooms, all with bath, are available for overnighters. For the strong-legged, worth the climb.

JUAN-LES-PINS and Cap d'Antibes are on the opposite sides of an oyster-shaped peninsula—geographically close, but socially so far apart they barely nod to each other. The former is a vast vacation center on the popular level, with its own Jazz Festival in July. The latter is a more sheltered retreat which caters to the rich. Commodores will now find a better yacht basin than ever before. A 5-star attraction is the Château Grimaldi, the reconstructed medieval fortress filled with Picassos—a *must* for every sightseer. Since parking is difficult here, you'd be wise to leave the car below and to hike to its portals on foot. Perhaps even more interesting is the Escoffier Museum, a few miles inland at *Villeneuve-Loubet*. This shrine to one of France's master chefs also is used as a center of culinary education, technology, research, and historical reference dating back to the fourteenth century. Much of the support for the foundation and reopening of the birthplace of the gastronomic genius came from French chefs living in America.

Belles Rives, open from April to October, is proudest of its seaside situation, its charming beach restaurant with a fabulous built-in vista, and its boating facilities for water skiing or sailing. Splendid terrace; furnishings colorful and attractive; repainted halls; immaculate mien. Now that its rooms have been pepped up, here is a formidable contender. The **Juana** is forging ahead encouragingly. The lobby, stairs, dining room, bar, and all of its refashioned bedrooms have been lately carpeted; the pleasant terrace garden in front has been made even more tempting for lunching or dining; its German clientele seems to be increasing. Hard work which shows happy results. The little **Astoria** stays open all year. Of its 53 rooms, 32 come with bath, 21 come with shower, and only 5 lack balcony. A coffee shop and bar are operative; the use of a nearby private beach is part of your package. While it is modest in its dimensions and décor within its category, the hospitality of Proprietor Virgili Brancaleoni and his sons, Raymond and Marcel, couldn't come straight from their hearts.

LA GAUDE (near Vence): Here the **Hostellerie L'Hermitage** definitely merits a try when hungertime nears. Window-lined dining room overlooking a lovely landscape of farm-girt hills and the valley of the River Cagnes; strawberry linens, tropical plants, and the chirping of caged birds. For a good unpretentious meal in inexpensive arcadian comfort, this spot is hard to beat in the area. Closed November and December. A pacesetter in the nonsumptuous bracket.

Le Mas des Serres is 1½ miles from the village and oh-so-lovely. Enclosing the whole property is a handsome cypress hedge. The twin main buildings form 2 sides of a garden which bursts with flowers and flowering shrubs. Its bedrooms in the converted farmhouse and the long "bungalow" row are all different; named rather than numbered, they are comfortably, tastefully (but not overlavishly) furnished. During the week, there is a good choice of viands; on Sunday, only the all-inclusive menu is available. It is without question the feeling of being *chez soi* that impresses us most here—an ease of living that one would be hard put to find elsewhere. Mme. Marité Saucourt will welcome you with superlative grace. Wonderful!

LA NAPOULE, west of Cannes, is the proud owner of the beautiful and interesting Château de la Napoule Art Foundation. Two large, well-lighted galleries with capacity of up to 100 paintings; guided tours from 3 P.M. to 5 P.M. every day except Tuesday; courtyard recitals during the summer; chamber music concerts and small theatrical performances from time to time. Another interesting development here is the 550-yacht marina. It is aflutter with burgees of discerning skippers from all over the Mediterranean.

LA NAPOULE-PLAGE, 5 miles west of Cannes, offers the **Ermitage du Riou** (swimming and golf). Seafront construction has given this one a backseat location. All rooms are large and comfortable; those on the rear, overlooking the river, are less noisy. A favorite among the mashie-and-putter set.

This settlement has become famous because of **L'Oasis**, one of the nation's leading restaurants and once again paradise for our palates. At last, the reception and staff attention—once with a chill factor uncommon to such a fine establishment—have warmed up notably. Entrance beside a somnolent tree-arched pool; recently restyled and expanded single room with several 2- or 3-table adjuncts radiating from it; flowers, wrought-iron fixtures, and understated provincialism; owned by the Outhier family, who try to give it their all. One absolute must: PLEASE try the Brioche de Foie Gras, in its featherlight disk of pastry. Reserve ahead; closed Tuesday. Great for its glorious cuisine and finally gracious to its clients.

La Brocherie II, at the boat basin, sails in with a lovely vista, failing skilletry, and yachtsman prices. Now we prefer **Le Boucanier**, further along the quai toward the castle. Here's a lovely anchorage for launching or lunching.

MENTON, east of the Monaco enclave, offers as its leader the year-round, 40-room **Napoléon** on the quai Laurenti. Each medium size unit with private bath and loggia; Sun Roof Grill with a commanding view of the Old Town. The **Viking**, under Swedish management and down a notch in price and quality, has 34 units with bath, 20 with their own cooking facilities. Top nightclub in the city (which often makes its early-to-bedders howl about the disturbance); handsome sweep of the Italian Riviera, the mountain, and Cap Martin from its cost-accounted dining salon. The renovated **Prince de Galles** has 65 bedrooms; homey feeling, with down-to-earth comforts. **Vendôme**, an updated old-timer, provides lots of elbowroom, good management, and perhaps the best kitchen in the area. The **Victoria** occupies one floor in an apartment building. Nothing outstanding but not disagreeable—which amply sums up all of Menton's facilities.

This town has a secret. It's **Francine**, located at the port. Some dear friends shared this treasure with us and now we'll pass it along to you. Francine does the cooking; the place is simple but nice; no English is spoken (who cares?); the prices are low for the value. Remember—it's a secret.

MIRAMAR-ESTEREL is blessed by the **St.-Christophe** on its Red-Roc Beach. Same ownership as Paris' San Regis; 5-tier building with 5 front locations per floor; all rooms with terrace; nice pool; Easter to October only. Tranquil isolation.

MOUGINS (a short ride up from Golfe Juan) in the past has attracted the reverent attention of nabobs from miles around because of **Le Moulin de Mougins**. Monsieur Vergé, who today may be spreading himself too thinly among his several interests, is capable of producing cuisine and price tags that are highborn and patrician—attitudes that equally apply to guests and to the way they are welcomed. Lately we have received a sprinkling of complaints suggesting a falloff in quality; nobody, however, complains that the prices are too low. This one is set beside a running stream in the valley below the village. It is composed of a loosely linked bracelet of dining niches, the most desirable being the glass-fronted veranda, which is usually booked by favored customers. The atmosphere of the entire establishment is charmingly esthetic. Tariffs run from wincing, to twitching, to paralyzing. Mme. Vergé oversees the skillets at **l'Amandier**, where a substantial meal is auctioned for about $40 per bib; **Le Bistrot** pans out local specialties for approximately half that figure. **Mas Candille** is pitched more toward its resident homebodies than toward outsiders. Patio dining in summer; fireside munching in chilly weather. Excellent day-to-day skilletcraft, but not a candidate for That Big Night Out. **Le Relais à Mougins** was taken over by André Surmain of Lutèce in New York, a personable chef-patron who also did such a fine job at our island home of Mallorca with his distinctive Foc y Fum. His *étoile* continues to shine at this latest venue. You'll probably enjoy this midvillage contender, which has just won its second star in *Michelin*, thanks to André's skill, talent, and fervent application. Happily, the center has been closed to car traffic, but parking lots dot the perimeter of the main sector.

NICE Its contrast with smaller, more sophisticated Cannes seems sharper every year. Nevertheless, Nice offers acolytes a race track, an opera house, the nearby Matisse Museum, nightclubs, tennis, speedboating, water-skiing, and scores of hotels and restaurants. The Ruhl Casino was outruhled by the Finance Ministry recently, but when fresh capital is staked a new pitboss may throw open its portals. (Since no solution for inaugurating the Palais de la Mediterrannée has been discovered, Nice, for the moment, has no casino at all.) The Promenade des Anglais, extending for miles along the sparkling waterfront, beats Miami Beach's Collins Avenue 40 ways. Recent additions include the Convention and Exposition Hall, the esplanade flanking the Paillon River, a fascinating Museum of Shells (many alive), the Chagall Museum, and a slew of new municipal parking spreads. The Old Port is presently being returned to use by pleasure craft. A new port and a fancy brand-new marina were washed away in a tidal wave (which struck, incidentally, as we were landing at the nearby airport); hopes for rebuilding it have been dashed. Because the beaches are comparatively poor and pebbly (a fact not advertised by the local tourist office), winter is the best season. King Carnival will be burned for the 94th spring season this year on the day before Ash Wednesday, in a spectacle rivaling Mardi Gras. Mid-January to March is the most rewarding time to go, whereas November and early December are the worst. At any period, however, it is wise to stay in the city itself rather than in the noisy airport environs. In recognition of this, all jet traffic has been eliminated between 11 P.M. and 6 A.M.

The **Riviera Airport** (which has, incidentally, a delightful open-air restaurant and restrooms with showers) offers a special shop to passengers bound for any country except France. It's a great place to load up on spirits, at tariffs which can't be touched domestically. But are the perfumes tax-free, as a clerk so blithely assured us, or are they priced the same as in Nice or Cannes? Payments in foreign hard currencies only (no francs).

Hotels The picture boasts an exciting future—and even an impressive present with such imposing names as **Hilton, Sheraton, Holiday Inn,** and **Novotel** on the just-opened or upcoming roster. **Hyatt Regency** has now unveiled its entry; prices range from $62 on up to $450 per night, so the spread for choosing your nest must be generous. While the 200-room **Frantel** now nods hello from the av. Notre-Dame, several more may fling open their portals before these words are read by you, so be sure to have your travel agent keep you posted on exact debut dates. The **Meridien** is another member of this new generation. Sited on hotel row adjoining the Albert Ier Gardens, it provides a heated pool, 2 restaurants, an open-air café, full air conditioning, and the ice-cool chill of a purely commercial institution, almost expressly designed to pack in busloads of sun seekers. (Though restyled and converted in part to nonhotel facilities even within the period of its infancy, it still shares the same edifice as the shuttered Ruhl Casino.) The rates seem quite reasonable.

The **Negresco** remains among the most distinguished stopping places on the coast. The award-winning dining spread is shared by 4 separate sections: (a) The Salon Louis XIV, with its gorgeous antique, Louvre-restored ceiling from the Mancini Castle and a huge white stone fireplace, (b) Le Trianon dining room in Regency décor, (c) an adjoining salon, similar in tone, and (d) the new Le Chantecler, which is already garnering distinctions for its gastronomy. The Salon Royal now gleams in 24-karat gold highlights; it is becoming a gallery of period furniture, sculpture, and paintings. The boutiques and perfume shop have been enlarged and beautified. Revampings underway from lobby to cupolas by Manager Michel Palmer, a hard-driving pro; epoch textiles incorporated into accommodations and many baldachines added to the upholstered beds; air conditioning, music consoles, TV, and minibars throughout; large, handsome, lively bar; French renaissance uniforms for key staffers, including knee breeches for the elevator operators; first-rate concierge in verteran Léon Cinci. Its winningly farsighted, personable, and progressive Maître-President Paul Augier is one of the top hoteliers on the Continent. Now open year round. Head, shoulders, and Napoléonic hat above everything else in town; highest recommendation in Nice.

The **Plaza**, restyled and air-conditioned, features a waterfall in the lounge, off-lobby bar; bedchambers ending with "12" with views of the Albert Ier Gardens and the sea. The comfort and appurtenances of its 12 suites and 160 nests, all with private bath, vary sharply. Its Concierge, M. Del Rocchio, will work hard to please you. Okay, but quite a step down from Negresco's heavenly climes.

The 137-room, 8-story, fully air-conditioned **Splendid** also occupies a town site rather than a beach location. Warmhearted Director Henry Tschann, who was born within its premises, is the 3rd generation of his family to hold its reins (the 4th generation is in the wings); although he operates on friendly agreement with the Sofitel chain, he is the boss, and that's clear. Rooftop swimming (the only pool in the city reserved exclusively for its hotel clients); kiddies' pool and cascade; solarium and sauna; no restaurant, but handsome grill-bar (thus no forced-feeding policy); 40-car garage, barbershop, beauty parlor, bank, and travel agency. Bless 'em, every one! Tastefully modern rooms; soft, restful tone; multichannel radios. Mr. Tschann and his good people provide a lot for your francs in First-class (not Deluxe by intention) returns. We like this one very much, and we recommend it very highly indeed.

The **Park** greets callers with a street-level complex which includes 6 airline desks. Garage to ease midtown parking; garishly dramatic lobby with fireplace, a fountain, and flickering gaslights as eternal lighting; bar; breakfast room now doubling as conference room. Top-floor sleepers under its mansard roof the best bet; others a cocktail of good, fair, and poor. Approximately 60% of the traffic in this house consists of conducted tour groups. The end product is no great shakes, despite all the recent efforts for its resurrection. Generally, however, it is better than passable.

The **Westminster Concorde** is fuddy-duddy in concept, but the location alone accords it several points over other lackluster entries. Updatings may be on the way.

The **West-End**, beautifully situated with one side to the sea and another facing a lovely garden, has employed its share of carpenters, plasterers, and painters over the past half-dozen years. Most bedsteads have been replaced with carved wooden frames; #417 is an exceptionally nice twin; #419 is a commodious triple; units glancing sidewise at the garden or the sea are tranquil and viewful; the back is quiet but bereft of scenery. Considerably more agreeable; a good value in the medium stratum.

The **Atlantic** redid some of its units in plasticy-tacky themes. We'd place it as a toss-up between the very old-timers and the very mods—of neither of which are we too fond.

The **Georges** is almost unbelievably sumptuous for its modest category and bargain-basement costs. Tiny, spotless structure on the hard-to-find rue Henri-Cordier (a few doors from the École Hôtelière); all units with private bath; high-level appointments, including picture windows, chandeliers, crystal sconces, satin spreads, and good furnishings; no restaurant; small lounge. This one is a hobby of a gentleman named Vidal and his English-speaking son, both of whom like doing things right.

Restaurants For dining, **Le Périgord** (7 ave. Georges-Clemenceau) now out-dazzles everything here. Timber-toned dining room; handsome hearth adorned with pewter cups; copperware and carved-wood trim; sweet, tree-shaded patio. Chef-Owner Jean Hebrard, aided by his wife, turns on truffles in pastry shells, smoked goose and duck, Gratin of Sole Filets, and similar delights, with superb Bellet and Château Minuty wines. Two set menus are offered, plus à-la-carte specialties, which of course can jingle up to much more. Although it is quite expensive, we found it worth every centime of our outlay.

Another culinary spellbinder is **L'Ane Rouge**, a seafood tieup that's smack in the port. Sidewalk terrace on the viewful Quai des Deux-Emmanuel, under blue-and-white striped awning; planter boxes; azure tablecloths; polished open beams in 2 rooms. Tears of gratitude may issue from your soul if you order the Moules Farcies, the creamy fish stew called Bourride, and the achingly, sinfully, oh-I-can't-stand-it-it's-so-good homemade chocolate cake. The Vidalot family has created a little gem here that no serious gastronome should miss. If you really want to pamper your palate (while ignoring your budget) do try this one. Since our latest incognito meal here we've heard comments that when it is busy, the staff loses its normal mandate on courtesy. True? We'll try again.

Chez Puget "Le Petit Brouant" (4 bis rue Deloye) is yet another splendid independent dining establishment; prices, however, are now leaping upward at an astonishing rate. Bar at entrance; about 25 tables; handsomely redecorated dining room with Burgundy touches, paintings, plates on walls, and a small fountain—all of them made brilliant with flowers and made charming with Provence paneling circa 1875. Three standard menus are at hand. For an appetizer, try the mouth-melting Dodine de Canard aux Vieille France (duck pâté); then, if a light, low-calorie but savory dish should appeal to you, launch into the delicious Sole Meunière. The service is savvy, kind, and warm; ask for Madame Marie Thérâse, the English-speaking daughter-in-law of the proprietor. Urban location with no view; adjoining outdoor terrace; closed Mondays and all of June.

La Poularde Chez Lucullus (across the street at 9 rue Deloye) might be its closest local contender. Bar near door; L-shape premises with beamed ceiling and Baccarat-rose-colored banquettes; semiopen kitchen to rear; perhaps 15 tables. The culinary level is high; the menu is versatile and interesting; every dish (all different) for our party of 4 was turned out with loving care. However, its illumination is so overbright, its ventilation so inadequate, and its noise level so high when the house is full that we much prefer the serenity and atmosphere (not necessarily the cookery) of Chez Puget.

Chez Don Camillo (5 rue des Ponchettes), serene and comfortable, has placed its 8 round tables so thoughtfully that no one can overhear your private whispers. Smiling welcome and attention; limited menu featuring Italian specialties; veal, veal, and more veal its pride. Our sommelier-waiter, an Italianate Frenchman who couldn't have been kinder, first poured our ½-bottle of wine to both of us without prior tasting by me; then he poured the second ½-bottle into our partially filled glasses. To us, a pleasant but not distinguished hideaway.

St.-Moritz (5 rue du Congrès, adjoining the Casino de la Méditerranée) turns out mouth-watering Swiss specialties; chalet atmosphere that can seem touristy. Excellent cookery.

La Bourride (6 rue de Rivoli) is a tiny, tiny establishment with a capacity for 1 man, 3 small boys, and a dwarf—but it's so well-liked that people queue up on the street to squeeze into it; try to go just before noon, or 1 P.M., 7 P.M. or 8 P.M.

"**Fish Row**" is what we term the cluster of restaurants which line the eastern end of the quai États-Unis, the boulevard along the seafront. Most of them have "terraces" which, for obvious reason, are glass-enclosed. The traffic is so heavy, the road is so high-crowned, and the cars so close that timid souls at their front tables cringe when the Gallic motorized cowboys zip literally within 10 feet of their Salade Niçoise. Proceeding outward from the center, you'll find **Hublet**, **La Maison Rouge**, **Le Scampi** and **Raynaud** (same management and same kitchen; the latter is one of the largest and most popular along the boulevard—railroad-apartment layout; about 70 tables; service forgetful but kind), **Prince's**, **Le Bouée**, **Le Fort**, **Le Marée**, and **La Girelle Royale**. They are pointedly tourist-oriented; their service is too often harried. In our opinion, Raynaud and La Girelle Royale are the picks of this mass-production lot.

Other nocturnal lairs include **La Chunga** (related to the fine little night spot in Cannes; shellfish display outside; discothèque downstairs), **Cave Niçoise**, **La Coquille** (solid medium-bracket stop), the Hotel Westminster's **Il Pozzo** (superb Italian fodder) and **Taverne Bavaroise**.

Snacks and casual libations **Le Tramway** (Lamartine 11) is an amusing novelty which overflows with the local Smart Set—an ancient converted trolley car which used to run between Nice and Marseille. Enterprising Piero Terrot bought it in the boneyard, inserted it intact into the building, and refashioned its interior in a bizarre and entertaining manner. It now contains 7 green-leather booths each for 4 persons, a tiny kitchen, and such appurtenances as street mural photographs on both sides to give the illusion of motion, display ads above, and subway-style handstraps for nervous standees. Normally packed at lunchtime and around 9 P.M.; closed Sundays, holidays, and all of August. Fun.

Le Koudou (on the Promenade, a few steps from Negresco, West-End, and

Westminster) boasts an agreeable terrace with tables; attractively modern ambiance of blond woods and black leather chairs or banquettes; piped music; appetizers, salads, eggs, sandwiches, vast choice of crêpes, ice cream, and all types of beverages available. During High Season it is open from 1 P.M. to midnight 7 days per week; from November 1 to December 1 it is shuttered. So tastefully executed that we like it.

The **Negresco**'s 3-part dining complex is a stellar attraction for well-heeled visitors—and its dramatic La Rotonde is one of Nice's most popular stops for the voyager-in-a-hurry.

Ciel d'Azur at Nice Airport is one of the higher fliers in the local skies. It is a deluxe candidate; a snack bar and medium-priced restaurant are also available in the same flight plan.

About 15 minutes above Nice (by car, not by plane) atop the mountain ridge, you'll find the garden-terraced **Rôtisserie de St. Pancrace**, run by Marccau Teillas, who often cooks for the finest chefs on the coast when they take a day off. It is heaven-scent country (beacuse of its altitude, no doubt); dining under the trees is a sylvan gift; the Royale de Poissons, Sweetbreads en Croute, and duck with morilles must have been handed down to Chef Teillas by the gods themselves. While the cookery is from the welkin, the prices are down to earth considering such extraordinary quality. Go only on a sun-filled day for the fullest rhapsody of the heights.

Night Life   Kick up your kilt at the **Thistle Club** (6 rue Halévy); the French call it "Chez les Ecossais." One of Scotland's whisky giants opened this pure distillate of after-dark sparkle, but now private management has taken over. You'll find tartans everywhere, and a map of the motherland at the entrance delineates the country clans. Spectacularly attractive and tasteful planning and décor, with 3 bars festooning its double-decker motif. Closed Thursday. Recommended with *slainthevas!*

On a par with these, but not in the mainstream of midnight traffic, **La Pignata** in the hills above Nice is a honey for romancers. Dancing, small cabaret, and outdoor restaurant in summer; mini-*corrida* for sun-filled *pica-dores;* open all year, but best in season. **Pizzaiolo**, in the Old Town, is i-t for young fry. Modest show; good music; dinner available; cramped for space, but popular with the tolerant. In neither of these are neckties required, since they are much more informal than metropolitan digs.

The girlie cabarets, in the next category, to us smell the same as their older sisters in Paris—tailor-made for butter-and-egg men with fistfuls of francs and a fine lack of interest in who grabs them. **Brummel** (place Masséna) stands at least a swizzle-stick higher than any other *genus nightclubus in corpore.* The show time seems to be determined by the traffic. Our whisky was uncut, but don't take this for gospel. **Folies Club** (place Masséna) is the largest independent operator; there's dancing from 5 P.M. to 7:30 P.M. and from 9 P.M. to 2:30 a.m. Two shows: 11:30 P.M. and 12:45 A.M., with 10 to 15 performers. Crowded during July, August, holidays, and Carnival time. Tables in tiers; bar-ette to one side; atmosphere reminiscent of the '20s, except for the whisky which tasted legit. **Tcha-Tcha** (rue Masséna) is a cellar-bration gin mill where 45 pairs of dilated pupils strain into Stygian darkness. After a brief singles act every 15 minutes, the lights flicker off and you're again paddling on the Styx. A local sidekick and I—both of us exactly 20-million miles from being Apollos—weren't there 2 minutes before the waiter brought a note in English which read, "Both of you are so devastatingly handsome that I *cannot* resist you. I love handsome Americans! I will come to your table and you will give me champagne, yes?" When we answered that we were naught but simple, humble U.S. journalists whose parsimonious editors (ed.: *sic*!) didn't pay us enough to buy champagne, she abruptly developed the swoons for another devastatingly handsome customer—this one a bald, balloon-bellied, 5′5″ French Hercules with a face like a toad's. And don't thirst for Scotland's best, because our libation never saw dawn over the heather. Plenty of "hostesses" in all of these joints, but remember that here and elsewhere, *the girls are required to stay on the premises until closing time;* so don't let yourself be conned for a string of hideously expensive drinks without keeping this in mind.

Shopping Nice boasts 2 shopping attractions that we find so far superior to all of the similar establishments on the entire Riviera that they are enthusiastically commended to your special attention.

Encompassing the prestigious ★ ★ ★ ★ ★ **Royal Salon of the Hotel Negresco**, in Nice, a National Historical Monument, is its unique cluster of glittering boutiques. These are yet another triumph of Mme. Jeanne Augier, wife of the Negresco's Maître-President. Not only does this grand circle present the creations of the greatest names in French wearables, but it also offers its own personal and exclusive creations specially designed for its *beau monde* international clientele: Open daily from 9 to 7:30; almost entirely duty-free; experienced worldwide shipment. Cheers and salutes!

The other star in this firmament is ★ ★ ★ ★ ★ **La Boutique du Meridien**, up 1 flight in Nice's Hotel Meridien. Under the inspired direction of charming and oh-so-savvy Ms. Sheila Hall, its American owner, this newish cosmos has soared high so fast that it is doubling its clientele every 12 months. The differences between these 2 operations are marked. This draws a younger group. Among the unusual items here is its runaway best-selling collection of designer bathing suits and coordinates for both genders, south-of-France regional specialties, and her gift articles. Open daily. Superb!

ROQUEBRUNE is perched high above Cap Martin, where the **Vistaëro** provides one of the most breathtaking views this side of a NASA space capsule. From one flank you can look down practically every chimney in Monte Carlo; from the other you can see the blue-mist haze of the Italian Riviera. To enhance the panorama, almost every inch of seafront wall space is plate glass —in public rooms as well as in bedchambers. Some complaints, in fact, have trickled in that the eye-filling restaurant charges "50% for the menu and 50% for the sights"—a bargain, we'd say, even if it served grubworms and seaweed (which it doesn't). Colorful mezzanine with chirping birds and a babbling fishpond; quality furnishings; 30 bedrooms, all with bath and balcony; suite #22-23, with its canopied bed, outstandingly attractive; another pair of apartments also very good; pool agurgle for simmertime splashers. We hope you will share our enthusiasm for it. Tiptop. **Au Grand Inquisiteur** STILL makes us Grandly Inquisitive, because when we huffed and puffed our way up to it on May 13, a sign on the door informed us it didn't open for its season until May

15. It is situated on a hillside lane in this lovely tenth-century village, most of which must be penetrated on foot through dipping, soaring, crazily winding footpaths between its buildings. Although this one is billed as an inn, its main function is obviously that of a restaurant. Even if its cuisine should prove indifferent, the fortress-hamlet itself would be worth the excursion. Warning: Cardiac patients, the infirm, or the elderly would be ill-advised to select it, because for them the gradients might prove dangerously steep.

ST.-JEAN-CAP-FERRAT   The Deluxe **La Voile d'Or** ("The Golden Sail") is similar architectually to La Réserve, around the bay at Beaulieu—the work of the same designer. Total of 50 rooms, each with a distinctive decorative theme; bid for a portside unit only if you're feeling affluent; superb marble baths; full air conditioning and soundproofing; excellent waterfront restaurant nuzzling the yacht harbor; excellent beach; pool on a raised garden platform; oodles of beauteous terraces. This one is in the same price bracket as La Réserve; its clientele now leans heavily toward Italian patronage. A smoothly sailing vessel. The nearby **Grand** has been enjoying a Grandiloquent house party in which more than 2 million dollars was allocated for the jamboree. Air conditioning now whispers cool blessings; the swimming pool has been restored and a cable car strung to whisk guests from the hotel to the H_2O; extensive bedroom restoration has been effected, including the addition of a splendid honeymoon suite. The Sun Beach Club incoporates water sports, tennis, and volleyball. A commendable resurgence of spirit, comfort, and hedonism.

ST.-PAUL-DE-VENCE   is the proud custodian of the Maeght Foundation, an art museum-cum-park which alone is worth a transatlantic journey. If you are anywhere on this coast do make an effort to experience this celebration of the senses.

Near the access road to Nice Airport, up in the neighboring mountain range, there's the much heralded, air-conditioned **Mas d'Artigny,** a sister operation to the Château d'Artigny in the Loire Valley at Montbazon. It's a gilt-edged dreamland, too, for romantic types who enjoy being in luxury while off the beaten pathways of the coastal mash. Suites with individual swimming pools and private entrances from your own garden; main pool and terrace on a tier below the lackluster dining salon and lounges; service as lazy as the climate inspires; tennis and 16 acres of hillside for strolling. Taut administration could easily bring this house up to the level to which it aspires.

Many independant lunchers or diners finally tuck themselves behind the napkins at the romantic **Colombe d'Or** ("Golden Dove"). You'll find a warm reception, relaxed patio dining under parasols when the sun is shining, an interior cluster of cozy rooms reflecting slick rusticity, an outstanding collection of paintings, a fine swimming pool, and a magnetic physical allure. The selection is ample, but though the food is served atop a lovely mountain peak it still falls short of *haute cuisine.* The nearby **Vieux Moulin** is ground out with contrived millings from Claude Laurent, "The dangerous man for your figure." We are forced to agree with him. In *Vence* itself, there's the little Hostellerie Lion d'Or which enlarged its name to **Hostellerie et Auberge des**

Seigneurs et du Lion d'Or when it remodeled the upstairs to provide its handful of rooms with baths. Its view is nil—but when we last checked it sometime back, we liked its simple milieu and fare. Fartherest along is the internationally renowned **Le Château du Domaine St. Martin,** which commands an eagle's-eye sweep of the countryside. The lobby is a hodgepodge of needlepoint, cretonne, and brocade; the overall effect is one of a well-intentioned effort which in our eyes simply does not jell. Heart-shape bicarbonatized swimming pool (possibly for indigestion sufferers); well-tended sylvan grounds; tower accommodations for the steady-in-balance; some rooms agreeable; others not so hot. The restaurant-dining room, with 3 sides of glass opening to its stupendous vista, is the main attraction. Its ambiance is lovely; its cookery and service standards are now on par with the finest in the land. Here's a stunning project on a stunning site.

ST.-RAPHAËL's   Continental is nearest the beach. It's noisy and no rave in any sense. **Beau Séjour** is pleasant enough. The **Hôtel au Golf de Vallescure,** 6 miles out, has been thoroughly updated over recent years; it now emits a beckoning glow. Through a series of slipups—both technical and personal—our text has failed to note the many and continuing virtues of this house. On our next coastal romp, we will certainly make a point of trying to stay here as a client. In the meantime, our apologies go to General Manager Percepied, a gentleman who seems to be extra-anxious to please the traveling public.

ST.-TROPEZ merits bravos for not succumbing to the characters who have tried to whittle it down to their level. In winter it's still a sweet little port. In season, however, it crawls with oddballs—especially on weekends. But why not, since it boasts what are probably the finest beaches of the province? At *Port Grimaud,* 3 miles to the southeast, a more residential colony of sun seekers has set up aweigh of life. Topless sunning is legally indulged in especially on the Tahiti or Salins beaches, but an anything-goes-off attitude exists nearly everywhere despite a recent effort by gimlet-eyed police to levy fines on bottomless baskers of both sexes. Unless you are a swinger, you probably won't cotton to it during Pandemonium Time.

The rest of the Azure Coast sparkles with small coastal or mountainside settlements—some unattractive, many overbursting with humanity during the warm months, but most scenically charming.

For lingering, the resort's flashiest bidder is the expensive anti-hotel called **Le Byblos,** slightly below the Citadel, with a distant view of the harbor. Its overall concept strenuously fights against conventional hotel-keeping. Irregular configuration suggesting a casbah mystique; swimming pool in a palm court; dining room ceiling in Persian carpeting; a leopard-skin (genuine) bar; snack facilities for bathing-suited nibblers where the client should rear up on hind legs if they attempt the old racket of trying to overpressure him or her into ordering a huge repast; decorative highlights featuring paisley brocades, gold embroideries, heavy damask, rich mosaics, and hammered brass; numerous raw stone walls and open beams; 59 bedrooms; some split-level suites; baths with brick tiles and wooden panels. The cramped dimensions of some of the accommodations might present a vexing problem to the long-term visitor; early-to-bedders howl that the swingers frolic too noisily under the dome of night. For those who can afford its wincingly high tariffs (no credit cards are accepted), here's a fascinating—perhaps too overwhelming—layout.

La Pinède is another costly but ingratiating San-Trop hideaway. Proprietors M. and Mme. Jean Michel added one wing some time ago consisting of a glass-fronted dining flank and bar plus sleeping facilities, each of the last boasting its own crescent-shape terrace, alcove beds, rheostat illumination, and a coin-operated vibrator-belt machine (1 franc per 3-minute jiggle). At water's edge is a tiny 4-cell tower which many silver-screened cupcakes have used as a retreat; surrounding this is a small private beach. For taste and peace by the shipload, this one should be the stuff of which dreams are made. But we balked strenuously on our layover when we found it was impossible to order anything less than a full meal at lunchtime; nothing à la carte was ever available, in fact. Such shortsighted lack of flexibility in an establishment where the twin rate is equal to or higher than that of the Byblos struck us as sheer folly—especially in a resort where well-tended waistlines are scrutinized by connoisseurs, measured by micrometers, and admired by all. We hope that this offensive, expensive, caloric overglut will have been changed by the time of your arrival. Aside from it, however, here is a blue-ribbon port-o'-call.

L'Ermitage, next to the Byblos, offers the disadvantage of remoteness balanced by the same asset of tranquillity. Only 32 units, many with baths and showers which share the bedroom with you; lots of kooky charm that can be fun for the open-minded. Mr. and Mrs. Jean Bremond (he's an excellent painter) runs their house in such an aggressively personalized manner that many travelers love it (and others abhor it). We happen to like it for its slaphappy-artsy mien. **Mas Bellevue**, about 2 miles out between Tahiti and Salins beaches, is a pink structure overlooking the bay and a tumbling boscage of Mediterranean foliage. Somewhat raw but satisfactory for the let's-get-away-from-it-all traveler. **Lou Troupelen** comes on in similar style. While it is slightly more polished, we are not so fond of its situation. On our investigation, **Tahiti**, at the site of the same name, seemed replete with bare-breasted gals sans sunsuits, and beefcake bruisers. Hardly a discriminating oasis, in our carefully lingering view. The **Coste**, with 30 look-alike bedchambers, is too dreary for our tastes. If you must, bid for the bzack rooms only, which face the bay and sport private balconies. Closed November and December. The **Paris**, operative from April to September, is too noisy for all but the deaf. The **Giraglia** in *Port Grimaud* is moored in a quiet anchorage where no automotive traffic is permitted beyond the gates of this private canal-laced village. Wood-on-stucco construction; maritime décor; tacky undertones but generally amusing in concept and presentation. A bonanza for boating buffs who are seekers of the bizarre. The 50-room **Le Kilal**, at *Grimaud*, is smack in the village with views oriented toward the seaward valley. We haven't yet had an opportunity to meet new Director André Lemoine, but we hope to soon. Gorgeous setting; delightful dining room or patio at poolside; perfect accommodations. Capable backing by the ubiquitous PLM group (usually with more commercial entries than this cozy gem) should assure a happy holiday here.

A stunner in a hilltown showcase. Forget the rest—but don't forget to RE-SERVE IN ADVANCE in all.

For dining, the "in" place at the moment is the **Pizzeria Romana**. Don't let the name fool you because the menu is much more ambitious than its handle implies. Not only is it good, but *everybody* knows it and *everybody* goes. **Da Lolo** also is sometimes judged to be a fashionable stop. Roughhewn sturdy interior clearly in contrast to the fragile squadron of pixilated waiters soaring through the ozone; close atmosphere redolent with Gigot aux 7 Herbes; on our latest try some time back, everything from lamb to our partner's steak to salad apparently floating in the very same sauce. Only open house-wine was available, which we recognized as Spanish (later confirmed by the maître); custard dessert tasted as if it had been put together with a cement mixer. Not over-costly, but not overgood, either. **Les Mouscardins** commands a panoramic situation at end of the port quay. It's busy, bustling, attractive, but not fancy, and expensive. Closed mid-Oct. to Feb. 1. The next challenger is **Auberge des Maures** (4 rue des Lices); also costly; shuttered Nov. to mid-Dec. This one tries to create the atmosphere of a gypsy pad, and it does so in an amusing way. The walls are decked with cast-off items and sentimental knickknacks; the dimensions (except for the portions, which are huge) are cozy; the waitresses are tricked out in regional costumes. Outside there's a dawdle-and-dine, arbor-covered patio which is attractive in season. The special cookery of Provence is its *raison d'être*. Prices trending upward, but well worth the investment for quality and friendly service. It evokes a sense of comin'-through-the-wry.

For casual dining or drinking, there are several resorty hangouts along the waterfront. Each features an awning-covered apron partially exposed to the sun, the stars, and the stares of the passing parade; back of this sits a more interior "exterior" patio; finally comes the inner sanctum itself—a tiny culinary enclave big enough for perhaps 3 tables, a small-boned waiter, and the inevitable bowl of fruit. **L'Escale** is still the harbor master, with a prix fixe docking fee; **Le Girelier** specializes in simple fish plates and matching tariffs; **La Rascasse** isn't bad; neither are **Tante Marie**, **L'Équipage**, and **L'Adventure**; **La Goûtade** *is*—at least we think so after our latest supper here. For drinking only, **Sénéquier** hosts some of the tightest-hipped gals' slacks on the coast. Deep lounge chairs for loafing from sunup to moonrise—or the reverse. The ONLY place to go if you have 14 or 15 hours to kill, plus a cast-iron liver. As for the rest, **La Belle Isnarde** (40 bis rue Allard) is typical of the less-costly digs in town, while the very rich (those who can cough up taxi fare) sometimes venture up to **Fenière**, a garden restaurant near the Citadel, or out to suburban *Grimaud* (**Les Santons** is costly but probably the best restaurant in the area, in the hill town, not in the waterside community of Port Grimaud), *Ramatuelle*, *La Bonne Fontaine*, or *Gassin*. The cuisine at the **Le Byblos Hôtel** is Deluxe—in cost, but less than patrician in savor.

Down on this coast night life becomes formal when the customer wears shoes. **Papagayo**, with orchestra from June to September and stereo in the fringe weeks, has routine décor and no show. On a busy night here, you'll find more shaggy heads than at a conference of Kalahari tribesmen. **Club 55** is the fashion center where planter's hats, hot pants, and *longuette* rags were raging the instant we popped in—and surely became as dated as buttonhooks by dawn. **Esquinade** is a noisy cluster of 3 cellars; records only; for budding gentlemen-to-be who can get by on 2 shaves per week; same ownership as the Megève pop-spot of the same name. **Woom-Woom** was still boom-booming for the small fry on our most recent zoom-zoom through town. **Yeti** appeared an abominable snow-woman when we peeked in—strictly for "the girls" (well groom-groomed). **Les Caves du Roy** has turned on the charm and tuned up an orchestra; it was very much in vogue, at least as of last week. **Le Gorille** is still the stop for that predawn breakfast and early-morning-cap. If these don't fill the bill, try **Café de Paris**, a summer meeting place of the famous, or the other café bars we mentioned earlier.

On the same road, you'll find **Les Collettes**, where Auguste Renoir did his painting from 1908 until his death in 1919. It is now a museum. At nearby *Verrerie de Biot*, the widow of **Fernand Léger** has opened to the public an impressive building which houses more than 200 of this great modern's works. You may wish to study the glass creations here. In the area, you will also find the gemlike **Matisse Chapel** (open Tues. and Thurs. only) and the impressive **Maeght Foundation**, already mentioned, with its splendid collection of mobiles, sculpture, Impressionist mementoes, and abstract paintings.

VILLEFRANCHE-SUR-MER has the fading **Versailles**, a post-debutante smack on the main highway leading up the Corniche. In a topsy-turvy arrangement, the lobby, restaurant, and bar are at road level; an elevator drops you down to your accommodations. About 50 small, functional, rather sterile rooms, all with bath, radio, and individual balcony; small sun terrace with excellent view of the passing hubcaps. Rates which we consider overpriced; ringside at the Indianapolis "500" is a lot more fun.

Among its restaurants, **La Mère Germaine** has climbed back to first rank here. Alfresco terrace-dining for 100 in season is vexingly rushed; hearty Salade Niçoise; bouillabaisse without a smidgen of vitally necessary rouille (saffron-garlic paste) until *you yourself* add and blend it from your personal sidedish; closed November 15 to December 20 and every Wednesday in winter; open for lunch *only* on summer Wednesdays. **Bidou**, formerly Le Potis Chez Veidou, is next, followed by **La Frégate-Chez Irene** and **Le Corsaire**; this trio is also agreeable. But not all the happy possibilities are at harborside. Up on the Grande Corniche, **Le Rustique** (La Ferme St.-Michel) is a charmer for the eye, but now we hear that both service and cuisine have fallen off drastically. Terrace for ruminating or hunting-room interior snugly glass-wrapped; checked cloths; quilted green ceiling; candle beams, piped music, and intimacy. We are told the **Tiki-Club** peddles a pseudo-Tahitian atmosphere and a small hula-hula-type show. Small; reasonably priced; drinks and snacks only.

☑ **CHÂTEAUX COUNTRY**   Renaissance France flourished at the peak of its elegance in this region. Because of its serene beauties and proximity to Paris, kings, courtiers, and courtesans relaxed here in dazzling luxury. Strongholds were built, aristocracy thrived, and culture was unfettered. To this day, linguistic scholars point out, the nation's purest tongue is spoken in the Loire Valley.

The tumbrels of the Reign of Terror swept away the actors of this historic drama, but little of their glorious handwork was despoiled. Still preserved are 46 great castles or mansions.

From June to end-September, 6 châteaux are further embellished with *Son et Lumière* ("Sound and Light") programs. At least 2-dozen others are flood-lit nightly or on weekends for nocturnal excursionists. However, the presenta-tions (except at Chenonceaux and at Blois) are given in French—a pleasure-dampening, needless hardship to thousands of foreign visitors. Most nations offering *Son et Lumière* schedule English-language versions at least once a week; France doesn't generally, and it's a pity.

First off the bat, don't rush. Even to begin to savor its charms, you'll need 3 to 5 days; a week will pay dividends.

Second, it would be helpful to read up as much as possible in advance of your arrival. The Anglicized edition of Michelin's *Châteaux de la Loire* offers the greatest detail of any publication we've found; suggested trips from 1 to 5 days are also outlined. *Châteaux of the Loire,* distributed by England's Auto-mobile Association (Fanum House, New Coventry St., London W.1), strings together a 450-mile itinerary. Michelin's sectional map No. 64 is indispensable to the motorist.

Your key base should be *Tours* or its vicinity, because this central point is less than 25 miles from most of the principal châteaux.

Our candidates for the 4 most interesting structures in this cluster are Chenonceaux, Amboise, Azay-le-Rideau, and Villandry. Cheverny (see below) is in a special category.

Chenonceaux, a breathtakingly graceful castle, straddles the Cher River. Beautiful formal gardens extend from its sides. Within the trussed-arch build-ing are tapestries and other seventeenth century treasures. Although finishing touches weren't applied until 1634, Diane de Poitiers, beloved mistress of Henri II, occupied it nearly 100 years earlier. Many Americans vote this one as their favorite.

Amboise, the burial place of Leonardo da Vinci, is smaller and less spectacu-lar—but hardly less rewarding. At this writing, it offers a spectacle called "The Cradle of the Renaissance," which draws upon music from the fifteenth and sixteenth centuries. Here you may also visit the illuminated terraces, the chapel, and the gardens. **Azay-le-Rideau**, charmingly sited over the Indre River and surrounded by groves, is now a Fine Arts Museum; from the French point of view, this one is possibly the most dramatic of all. **Villandry** is noted for its magnificent 3-tier gardens, as well as for its history; the top level has a 7500-square-yard lake, the middle level formal horticulture, and the bottom level a grandly conceived layout of vegetables!

Cheverny, tucked away at *Loir-et-Cher,* is one of the most perfectly con-ceived and best preserved edifices in the region. It is thriving as an occupied homestead under the aegis of the Marquis de Vibraye. Entry around $1; only ½-dozen rooms open to the public, but these are exquisite; fabulous Hunting Museum dating back through centuries of royal hunts. Don't miss this impos-ing beauty with its tonsure of precisely maintained gardens and parkland.

Others of note include **Chambord** (largest; 40 miles north of Tours), **Lan-geais** (privately owned and lived in; another with a beautifully preserved interior; no Sound and Light; 15 miles), and **Loches** (so medieval that it's an

Olympus for antiquarians and a bore to travelers with no architectural interests; 15 miles). One of the most exciting from the theatrical point of view is **Château du Lude** (32 miles), with a twice-weekly pageant—in season—of 400 characters in costume, prancing horses, boats, dancers, and singers. The oration is in French, *bien sûr!*

From Tours you can visit **Chenonceaux** (19 miles) and **Amboise** (16 miles) in 1 evening. Buses leave the below-mentioned Syndicat d'Initiative at 8:15 or 9 P.M. and return at midnight; the all-inclusive excursion is around $10 per person. Scads of additional bus departures to your choice of other châteaux are available both daytimes and evenings at the Tours railway station; costs vary from $3 to $7, plus entrance fees.

Spot and floodlighting are employed on various occasions at châteaux in the following places: Ainay-le-Vieil; Bourges (the Mansion of Jacques-Coeur and the Cathedral of St.-Étienne here), Châteaubriant; Châteauneuf-sur-Loire; Culan; La Ferté-St.-Aubin; Fontevrault; Gien; Nantes; Sully-sur-Loire; Tours (with musical program); Valençay.

The châteaux which must be seen by daylight are Beauregard, Chaumont, Cheverny, Chinon, Cinq-Mars-la-Pile, Langeais, Lavardin, Luynes, Ménars, Meung-sur-Loire, Montgeoffroy, Moncontour, Montoire, Montreuil-Bellay, Montsoreau, Poncé, Romorantin, St.-Aignan-sur-Cher, Saumur, Talcy, Ussé (inspiration for "The Sleeping Beauty"), Vaux-le-Vicomte, Villandry. We haven't yet unhitched our coach-and-six at the "new" Courtanvaux, the castle of the Duke of Fezensac, scion of the oldest family in France. This 500-year-old, 112-room estate is at Besse-sur-Braye, between Tours and Le Mans.

One *must* stop for newcomers—the earlier, the better!—is the Tours Syndicat d'Initiative, an ultramodern, round, glass-bound facility on place de la Gare. It is linked by Telex to Cannes, Nice, Paris, and 11 other centers, in case your later reservations have gone awry; it will change your money when the banks are closed (Sun., Mon., and after 6 P.M.); it comes up with brochures by the yard and regional information by the bushel. From mid-March to mid-October, this voyager's gold mine is open from 9 A.M. to 9 P.M. (10 P.M. on weekends), with a lunch hour shuttering between 1 P.M. and 2 P.M. Be sure to ask for vivacious, attractive, highly knowledgeable Mme. Tandeau.

Hotels One of the happier aspects of life in the Loire Valley is that you can take your choice, among the top-liners, of a huge château or a little one. Let's start small. The lovingly restored **Château de Marçay**, set in an enchanting estate dating back to the fifteenth century, is only a few minutes from *Chinon* by car. The lounges are intimate and sumptuous, with brass chandeliers, painted beams, rich textiles, and oil paintings; the dining salon is a masterpiece of refined rusticity, featuring a handsome hearth, thick timbers, exquisite table settings, and the finest cuisine we encountered on our most recent gustatory fossick through this sector of France. The service was kind-hearted and impeccable. For quiet country living at its most discriminating level, this gem really glisters.

At the other end of the scale, and certainly even more imposing in its larger, grandiose concept, is the **Château d'Artigny**, which stands watch over the Indre Valley on National Highway No. 10 in *Montbazon* (7 miles from Tours). Here you'll find a twentieth-century entry conceived in pure eighteenth-century style. The site, once the palace of the King's Treasurer, was razed in 1769 and rebuilt over 2 decades beginning in 1912 by the perfumer François Coty, who lavished so much money on his pet avocation that he even installed cold-vaults so that visiting ladies could safely store their furs! Imposing view, especially on the meandering river side; manicured gardens and 50 acres of private woodland, swimming pool, tennis, riding, and fishing; hunting, shooting, golfing, rowing, sport-flying facilities or clubs all within easy reach, and even chamber music ensembles on selected winter evenings. Grand-but-cold entrance hall leading to stately lounges; richly carved library; next-door chapel with 4 exceptionally cozy duplex apartments. Total of 56 extra-spacious bed-chambers; #5, on the river, is fit for royalty (many chiefs-of-state stop here); #31 features a bath that was the former pastry kitchen, and it's one of the nicest on the garden side; don't let them shunt you over to the so-called "pavilion", a down-the-road annex used for overflow bus groups or late arrivals. In general, the cuisine tries hard, but still comes well short of perfection, in our opinion. Manager Alain Rabier has improved the service, but running such a palatial monument indeed must be taxing. Certainly one of the most impressive addresses in the nation.

Domaine de Beauvois, at *Luynes* (9 miles west of Tours), is also owned by the d'Artigny musketeers. Structurally and decoratively it, too, is an architectural paradise. There is, for us at least, more coziness here, but then perhaps you're looking for grandeur. We also noted more careful service and superior cookery here in comparison with the alma mater. Both are recommendable in their respective manorisms.

Château de Beaulieu, at *Joué-les-Tours*, is more modest. This one seems to draw bouquets of orchids and bunches of onions from readers, some of whom love it and others of whom abhor it. Enormous grounds and homey surroundings in a garden setting; swimming pool; tennis courts; alfresco terrace for summer dining; open every day the calender round. *Beau* it is.

Le Choiseul at *Amboise* (15 miles from Tours) has been brought back to life gloriously—both as a gourmet oasis and as an elegant hostelry—by owners, Nicola and Jacqueline Diaferio. This vigorous, spirited, and ever-smiling couple have inspired this house with their own zest and vitality. The dining room, with its captivating view of the river, is especially recommendable for lunch. Better and better.

Le Domaine da la Tortinière, near *Montbazon* (turn left 1 mile toward Tours), is a century-old mansion astride a hill in a sylvan private park. The terrace, shaded by red umbrellas, overlooks the peacefully winding Indre River. The cuisine, once superb, seems to have lost some of its flair of late; the rooms did not give off the sparkle that one might expect and the service, while cordial, was a bit slack.

The **Bon Laboureur et du Château**, at *Chenonceaux*, is a knockout for gustation, but merely functional for overnighting. The tariffs are quite reasonable, too.

Next in preference—for geographic reasons *only*—come the hotels of *Tours*. In general, they're a cheerless, scruffy lot, considering this city's importance as a sightseeing mecca.

The 5-story, 125-room **Meridien** is a link in the chain that has its big-sister operation in the capital. La Crémaillère grill, with alfresco terrace for summer; cookery simply awful on our sampling; adjoining La Bergerie bar; pool and tennis. The site, just off the busy highway, murders any semblance of tranquility, but it is convenient for the caravans of buses that roll in here to disgorge the throngs who arrive in migratory proportions. To us, crass and blatantly commercial.

The **Univers** has at last swallowed 4 or 5 lovely-pills, but it needs to take the rest of the bottle. Complement of 85 pleasant units with bath; #232 spacious and quiet; 42 without bath; 29 recently revamped in Tour-ist style; top-rate singles seemed cruelly expensive for the value; minimum cells are available, however. From New Year's Day until March 15 the restaurant is closed; hungry guests are either left on their own or shuttled over to the Hôtel Métropole.

The group-minded **Métropole** offers 70 bedchambers. Now most accommodations lean toward the Directoire school of decoration. The tavern-style dining salon and bar are clean but uninspired. This hostelry introduced us to what we now call the "Murphy bidet"—a curious streamlined contraption that swings out from its disguised recess in the wall by fingertip control. The **Central** is a recently revitalized vintage landmark. Still no restaurant; almost spotless housekeeping; 45 rooms, 15 baths, and 5 showers; mile-high ceilings; simple but agreeable sleeping quarters. A few baths are conventional, but others have that awful peekaboo, where-are-your-earmuffs-darling, half-partition arrangement. Improved to the point where the French would call it "a proper place." The **Grand**, a station hotel, provides reasonable shelter but chug-chug staffwork. **Bordeaux** has been modernized; ho hum. The **Foch**, with 14 rooms and 2 private baths, is a value for budgeteers. So is **Le Rabelais**, which is okay as a tiny nest. **De l'Europe's** 51 rooms are scrubbed, but that's about all that can be said about them. **Mondial**, over the Buré Restaurant (no connection), is not recommended for U.S. patronage. The **Mayflower** seemed more wretched, and **Le Moderne** is at the bottom of our barrel.

Other stopping places in the Château Country or Loire region, some good and some poor, are as follows:

Angers : **Boule d'Or, Croix de Guerre, Anjou**.
Blois : **Château, Médicis** (the latter 4 miles out, at St.-Denis).
Chambord : **St.-Michel**.
Charité-sur-Loire : **Le Grand Monarque**. .
Chinon : **France, Boule d'Or**.
Gien : **Rivage**.
Loches : **France, Tour St.-Antoine**.
Orléans : **Arcades**.
Saumur : **Budan, Roi René, Hostellerie du Prieuré**.
Valençay : **Espagne**.
Vendôme : **Grand Vendôme, Commerce**.

Restaurants   In the Tours area, **Barrier** directly across the bridge at *St.-Symphorien*, is world famous, but our own recent repast here was a severe disappointment—at a price that can easily jolt a headbone from the neckbone.

We've heard other complaints, too, so we can only caution you from our own findings and from what we've picked up lately from travelers. In fairness, many still swear by M. Barrier and his kitchen magic. Not this reporter, however. Of lesser importance but nevertheless a factor, for our taste the décor simply doesn't jell. There are so many competing elements under such bright illumination that we are put off as soon as we step into the room. Perhaps you will feel otherwise and that this presents no Barrier to overall enjoyment.

For château dining, the previously mentioned **Marçay** would be our pick among the thoroughbreds. **Le Choiseul**, at *Amboise*, and **Domaine de Beauvois**, at *Luynes*, usually are tiptop too, followed by **d'Artigny** for its aristocratic bearing.

Lyonnais (48 rue Nationale, in *Tours* itself) is quite satisfactory if you want to be among the brighter lights of the city. Modern mien, with tile floors which would chill the visitors' bones if they weren't offset by the kindliness of the hostess and the friendliness of the staff; excellent fare, at tariffs considerably lower than those of Barrier. Recommended. **Rôtisserie Tourangelle** (23 rue Commerce), the next contender, has a leisurely, old-fashioned air, shy but eager-to-please personnel, and praiseworthy cookery. **Buré** (street floor of Hotel Mondial) is adequate but routine. **La Trattoria** is fair if you seek a change-of-pasta. **Meridien** makes us gag at the very thought.

Please don't forget the previously mentioned **Bon Laboureur et du Château** at *Chenonceaux*, which is a rustic dream spot with heavenly cuisine. At *Amboise*, the little **Auberge du Mail**, behind the river dike and beyond the center of town, offers less costly menus. Sweet postage-stamp-size patio with 9 red-clothed tables under a grape arbor; plain, clean, no-nonsense interior; Gallic family management. Not plushy but substantial. The riverside **Bellevue** served us a very decent and inexpensive tourist lunch which we enjoyed on a recent stop; simple but nice. The nearby, more-attractive **Lion d'Or** is very appealing if you are not expecting gourmet-level cuisine. We enjoyed our recent lunch here.

The **Château de Pray**, 1½ miles up the river, is a hillside mansion with a spacious front terrace offering a fine view of the Loire. Sixteen rooms in pseudo-Renaissance motif; deluxe food and prices; numerous readers have complained about tabs coming up higher than they bargained for, so be sure to check your bill before payment; closed January 5 through February 10. Elegant and pleasant.

In *Langeais*, the **Duchesse Anne** has a beguiling garden in which a cote of snow-white doves will puff up and preen at the first sign of a paying client; their fantails are so disciplined that we have dark suspicions of managerial sorcery. About 50 tables outside, 20 more in the modern dining room, and large windows between the sites. Savory vittles and engaging atmosphere; see-for-yourself kitchen, where the white caps are in constant flurry. Definitely worth a try. The **Hôtel Hosten**, almost directly across the street, has a less attractive patio adjoining its Charles VIII bar. Piquant; hospitable attention from the owners; coming up steadily.

In *Guécélard*, 10 miles south of Le Mans on Route N-23, **La Botte d'Asperges** is a slender, long-fronted pit stop with a tiny front terrace that provides a panorama of passing cars and trucks and the *Boucherie Charcuterie* across the highway. In the rear, however, there's a sleepy little garden with even sleepier goldfish, where you may drowse over your Noix de Veau.

If you plan a visit to the previously mentioned Château de Cheverny, you can stoke up at the **Hôtel des Trois Marchands.** It is in the heart of the toy village, edging on the church square. It also has skidded to appalling depths, in our opinion, but is now offered as an emergency refueling pit for famished motorists.

Other alternatives of varying magnitude are:

Angers: **Le Vert d'Eau** (closed Fri.), **Hostellerie Château** (6 miles).

Bracieux: **Le Relais**.

Chartre-sur-le-Loir: **France**.

Château-la-Vallière: **Écu**.

Chaumont-sur-Loire: **Hostellerie du Château**.

Les Bezards: **Auberge des Templiers**.

Montoire-sur-le-Loir: **Cheval Rouge**.

Orléans: **Auberge St.-Jacques, Auberge de la Montespan, Jeanne-d'Arc, Aux Canotiers**.

Poitiers: The people here are spoiled rotten, in our opinion, by the migrations of tourists who sate their gluttonous coffers with a supererogation of international shekels. Though old-fashioned, the **Hotel France** was the *only* place where we were greeted with courtesy and where any effort was made on behalf of human decency. For this alone we are grateful.

Final suggestion: During High Season (which now includes May and June), the Châteaux Country is deluged by sightseers of umpteen dozen nationalities. April and September are perhaps the best months, because everything is open but traffic is slightly thinner. Whenever you go, however, try to wrap up ALL your reservations *in advance*.

☑ **NORMANDY BEACHHEADS** In quiet salt breezes blowing softly over St.-Laurent-sur-Mer, you can stand beside the magnificent polychrome plaque which marks the spot where the first wave of U.S. troops doggedly fought their way up the sand banks to achieve what was to become the most planet-shaking mass military movement in the annals of mankind. Below, in serene majesty, lies the full sweep of Omaha Beach and the sun-twinkled waters of the Channel. To the rear is a beautiful chapel, an impressive *rondure* with the names of the fallen, and a trim reception center for pilgrims. To your flank stretches the immaculate greensward and tidy white crosses of the far-flung cemetery, in which 2 Roosevelts are buried beside thousands of their brave comrades.

If you're motoring, strike out first for *Arromanches-les-Bains* (roughly 38 miles from Deauville), strategic center of the British zone of attack and site of the only remaining "Mulberry" artificial harbor. The string of ships deliberately sunk to form the breakwater has been raised, but the mammoth concrete pierheads and a large stranded landing craft remain in its sands. A stretch of highway with telescopes, charts, and listening devices enhances the historic site. Be sure to visit the fascinating Musée du Débarquement (loosely translated as "Invasion Museum"), where battle memorabilia and autographed photos of the commanders are on display, where movies of the fighting taken by combat cameramen are shown frequently during the day, and where an ingenious diorama reconstructs the action on a grand scale. Transatlantic visitors are greeted by ever-kind, English-speaking Antoinette de Berenger.

Then move along to the previously described memorial and cemetery at Omaha Beach in *St.-Laurent-sur-Mer* (perhaps 7 miles). From this U.S. fountainhead, take the several-hundred-yard skip to the seaward road marked St.-Laurent-sur-Mer (par la Côte). This detour, about 1½ miles long, permits you to drive directly along Omaha for a snail's eye view. At the north end you may inspect a small complex of Nazi pillboxes.

The most dramatic terrain of all is Pointe du Hoc (7 miles from central Omaha), where Colonel Rudder's American Rangers stormed its incredibly perilous cliff, seized and held its death-spewing German fortifications for 48 hours in which all but 14 of these heroes were killed or wounded—to find later that they had attacked the wrong promontory!

Utah Beach, about 20 miles farther along, holds little of sightseeing interest today—unless, of course, there are personal reasons for visiting it.

With these stirring battlegrounds behind you, swing down to the base of the peninsula to fabulous Mont-St.-Michel, southeast to Tours and the Châteaux Country of the Loire (see separate section), and then up through Joan of Arc's Orléans (or several alternate routes) to Paris. Distances from point-to-point are short; this entire trip, which can be taken in either direction, of course, should total less than 450 miles—and it's a honey. Whenever you are faced with a choice between a major highway or an off trail by-lane, always take the smaller road. The latter are well paved, and it is on them you will find the essence of the people and the nation.

Hotels and restaurants in Normandy are generally simple and 2nd line. *Caen*'s **Malherbe**, in the center but overlooking a wide prairie, was the pacesetter. Check first to make sure it is in operation by the time of your Norman invasion. The modest **Moderne** offers dining facilities; it is a suitable alternate during this hiatus. The **Metropole** and **Place Royal** come up with breakfast only. The **Gourmet** is said to be okay for budgeteers. For independent dining, **Alcide**, an ivy-covered modern bower, served us a delicate meal at a very reasonable price—considering the high quality of the fare. Outside of a visit to the Abbey, previously we had recommended *Mont-St.-Michel* as a meal stop chiefly, but if you wish to linger, there's been a splendid renaissance at the **Mère Poulard**, with fresh paint, good plumbing, and a massive overhaul. The Heyraud couple who run it perform daily wizardry in the kitchen, and their magic spills over to their welcome. Cheers to them and to it! Closed from October to April. However, the tiny 2nd-place **Du Guesclin** is still too raw. In winter, the 21-room **Mouton Blanc** is almost the only show in town; our hardy and well-cooked fixed-meal consisted of 6 Portuguese oysters, a huge omelet, leg of lamb, beans, potatoes, and apple tart; we haven't room to describe the à la carte choices. Even though here is one of the most astonishing architectural wonders of any civilization, it's so noisy and so glutted with excursionists in season that restful sleep is at a premium. You'll also have to climb by foot to your destination, because no cars are permitted on its narrow steep streets. Be sure not to wander off the causeway over the shoal, especially if you're traveling with children; the tides rise so fast that the sands can be dangerous. Nearby *Avranches* has the little **Auberge St.-Michel**, opposite the statue of General George Patton. This one, however, now seems to be in retreat, according to frontline reports from our scouts. During cold months, the creaky-but-kindly **France et Londres** is worthy only for the sweeter-than-sweet Bertheaume family and staff. **Croix d'Or**, also in the same family but seasonal only, has 17 extra-nice rooms, a 50% bath count, many redecorations, and the finest cuisine of all contenders (especially the hors d'oeuvres and the duckling). **Bellevue**, across from the Auberge St.-Michel, is another possible bet in the modest-shelter category. In *Vire*, the **Cheval Blanc**, fronted by a garden plaza, is the pacesetter, both for its comfort and for its table. In *Bayeux*, the **Lion d'Or** roars about its gay but modest dining room, with a "Mathilde" frieze; simple yet adequate bedchambers; nice personnel; a favorite of our old friends, the international oilcompany pilgrims Charlie and Alice McWilliams, who always use it as a base for their Invasion Coast wanderings. *Lisieux* ? We hear sweet murmurings about the **Espérance**, but we can't verify them from personal experience.

If you happen to be as far east as *Orbec* (13 miles from Lisieux)—or even as far east as Tokyo (6132 miles)—be sure to plan a meal at **Au Caneton,** a heavenly little rustic tempter that makes us drool in retrospect. Proprietor Joseph Ruaux stuffed us fuller—and happier—than a Christmas goose on the morning of Dec. 24. Our repast of Timbale de Langouste (lobster in a succulent port sauce), plain roast duck, cheese, and a mulled, very old Calvados were all the stuff from which culinary dreams are made. We won't tell you more. Just go, and we will accept your supplicant gratitude for the rest of our envious lives. Closed Tuesday and October. Reserve ahead.

When en route to the Châteaux Country (or to the wonderful Benedictine Abbey at *Solesmes*, world famous for its Gregorian chants), try to plan a lunch break—or a night's stay, if time permits—at the **Ricordeau** in *Loué* (3 miles off N-157, about ⅔rds of the way from Laval toward Le Mans). This high-class but not elaborate provincial hotel is worth a detour; its cuisine rates our ardent cheers. Seventeen small, tranquil, and agreeable rooms; high-ceilinged, traditional dining salon; terrific wine cellar (even Romanée-Conti '28 available!).

Germany

The miracle of today's Western Germany must be seen to be believed. Probably no other nation in the history of the world has made such enormous strides in so short a time.

This year's visitor will find every conceivable amenity—luxurious hotels, delicious food, an unrivaled transportation network, and all the pleasures or comforts of meticulously organized tourist facilities. In blue-ribbon havens, he will also see the glimmerings of the broad smile and the warm welcome which hark back to a more gentle era.

☑ **SIGHTSEEING**   Aside from political factors, Berlin is one of the most interesting and rewarding single tourist targets in Germany, in our opinion. More on this under "Cities." Otherwise, in order of popularity, here are the sights which this year's visitor to Germany is most likely to seek out:

1. **Rhine excursions**. The traditional pastimes afloat include the Düsseldorf–Cologne–Mainz runs. Comfortable, modern steamers of the "White Fleet" offer full-day excursions, overnight round trips or inexpensive intermediate voyages. There are also 3- and 4-day cruises aboard the 4-decked *Europa* and similar ships which do the river from Basel to Amsterdam. Unhappily, schedules are not always reliable—so sometimes you may spend longer than you wish in an undesirable port. Ships are modern and quite large for river-boating. If you're making a solo journey, expect to share your cabin with someone (of the same gender, fortunately or unfortunately). Avid sightseers, particularly mature or elderly ones, like these; younger, more volatile ones sometimes find them monotonous and boring. If you're among the latter group, you might consider making the Cologne-Mainz skip aboard the *Rheinpfeil*, a 64-passenger hydrofoil which cruises at 37 mph. Hold onto your hat! Most sailings (or those also linked into the Moselle) are scheduled between March and October, but more runs are being stitched into the winter pattern every year. In some cases, part way may be covered by rail on a combined arrangement.

If you start from Cologne, you may find it much, much wiser to debark at Rüdesheim or Assmannshausen. Low water levels in summer often delay

dockings at the Wiesbaden or Mainz terminals as much as 3 hours. If you want
to be sure of reaching your bed by a decent hour, hop off early and motor down
to your destination. The Philipp Keller service in Frankfurt (see "Transportation," the subsection titled "Buses and Cars") will meet you.

2. **Bavarian castles**, particularly Neuschwanstein, Herrenchiemsee, Linder-
hof, and the Residence Palace at Würzburg. (Check the German Federal
Railways about its combined rail-bus tours during weekends in summer.)
From Munich there's an easy excursion to the Cloister of **Andechs**—first by
subway to Herrsching am Ammersee, then from the exit by bus to your
destination. It's a baroque joy! The neighboring restaurant can fill your mortal
coil while your eyes give feast to your soul. Inexpensive and splendid on a
sunny day.

3. **Churches** and **cathedrals** at Ulm, Würzburg, Munich, Freiburg, Mainz,
Worms, Speyer, Cologne, Bremen, Marburg, Limburg, Regensburg, Trèves,
and Aachen.

4. The **Neckar Valley** and **Heidelberg**.

5. The **Hag** development and "Böttcherstrasse" in Bremen.

6. The **medieval castles** along the Moselle (especially beautiful for driving
or for delightful loafing aboard one of the tiny steamers). The Rhine, Danube,
Ahr, Lahn, Main, and Weser are also studded with ancient fortresses.

7. The "**Black Forest Post**" (from Karlsruhe through the upper Black
Forest to Freiburg), the "Black Forest–Lake Constance Post" (from Freiburg
through the lower Black Forest to Constance), and the "German Alpine Post"
(from Lindau through the Allgäu Alps via Garmisch–Partenkirchen to Berchtesgaden—summer only). These fine bus tours offer dirt-cheap rates, modern
equipment, and magnificent scenery. The "**Romantic Road**" tours (see under
"Other Targets") between Würzburg and Füssen in the Allgäu Alps (also
summer only) and the "**Castle Road**" tours from Mannheim via Heidelberg
and Rothenburg to Nürnberg are outstanding, too.

8. The **motorboat rides** on the Neckar between Heidelberg and Neckar-
steinach, on the Moselle between Coblenz and Cochem, or Trier (summer
only) and other points, and on the Danube between Passau and Linz. Let's not
forget, either, about the slaphappy *plätten* (flat-bottom barges) rides on Sal-
zach, an Inn tributary, and on the Isar.

9. **Bayerischer Wald**, a 30,000-acre national park nestling along the Czech
border near Regen. This first legally designated wilderness in Germany
abounds with wolf, lynx, otter, red deer, bear, beaver, alpine marmot, and 2
rare species of owl (Ural and pygmy). Some captive fauna is available to lazy
shutterbugs.

Hitler's Eagle's Nest, atop Mt. Kehlstein at Berchtesgaden and owned by
the State of Bavaria, receives hordes of tourists. If you make the trek, it will
be for the view alone (when it's a clear day, and often it isn't) because there
are no significant buildings or artifacts. Take the special Bundespost bus up
the safe but hair-raising mountain road to a point 450 feet from the summit.

Then ride the brass-plated elevator through solid rock up to the peak, which if it isn't in a cloud, will provide an Alpine panorama that should leave you breathless. Other Hochland flings? Steeplejacks, free-balloonists, and edelweiss gatherers with greater stomach than your craven correspondent will be pleased to know that more than 100 funiculars and teleferics now await the hardy for conveyance to almost any pinnacle in the land.

Son et Lumière ("Sound and Light") or similar spectacles have caught on big in Germany. One outstanding example is at Schloss Herrenchiemsee, a copy of Versailles Palace on an island in the Chiemsee, about 46 miles down the fast autobahn from Munich. The castle is fully furnished with its original treasures and illuminated by more than 4000 wax candles; chamber music is played; the pools and gardens are on show, but Mad King Louis' (Ludwig II of Bavaria) pornographic pictures are not. Every Saturday evening from May to September; book in advance in American Express, Munich, or you won't get in; arrive before 5:30 P.M., after which the palace tours end for the day; no photography permitted.

On a completely different note is the museum in the crematory of **Dachau** concentration camp, a 45-minute subway and bus ride from Munich, where at least 30-thousand human beings were cremated. Surviving inmates, representing 21 nations, established this monument to atrocity. Documents, orders, and photographs relating to the torture and extermination of prisoners are displayed.

Finally there's the Richard Wagner Festival at Bayreuth during July and August, the Munich Opera Festival during the same period, concerts by the Berliner Philharmonic Orchestra the calendar round and more folk festivals, home festivals, jubilees, fairs, religious events, expositions, congresses, and conventions than anyone can shake a stick at—or attend. Ask the German National Tourist Association or your nearest German National Tourist Office (New York, Chicago, Los Angeles, Montreal) for their excellent programs of these topical events. If you write for tickets, do so by late November; after that, it's often a gamble.

★ **TIPS** Weather forecasts, road conditions, and information on Germany and its people are broadcast in English and 7 other languages during the tourist season over the South German Radio Station in Stuttgart. They are beamed during the musical program from 10 A.M. to 10:45 A.M.

Note for hobbyists, efficiency experts, and industrial spies: Germany's " **Open House** " program flings wide the doors of hundreds of the nation's factories and workshops. If you want to see how your Porsche, Volkswagen, or Mercedes-Benz is glued together, how they sandpaper the lenses of your Zeiss-Ikon camera, or how those trained fork-tongued aardvarks lick the gum on the labels on all those bottles of German beer or wine, here's your chance. The German National Tourist Information Office in New York will provide a long list of the names and addresses of these hospitable companies or ateliers. Naturally, your welcome will be warmer if you'll write ahead and advise them of your arrival date.

☑ **TRANSPORTATION Taxis**   In the larger cities, taxis are fairly plentiful. Lots of new ones, because competition is tough; most are in the Mercedes, Opel, or Datsun size and they're comfortable. They're cheap when compared, for example, with the Swiss or Belgian brotherhood.

Trains   The German Federal Railways surpass almost any other system in Europe today. This year all Intercity services will carry First *and* Second class; even better, they now run every hour in a similar fashion to subway passage; these function on 4 main lines linking 30 major cities over a network of almost 1750 miles. Trains are punctual, clean, and comfortable, and now feature nonsmoking sections similar to those on Lufthansa airliners. DB (for "Deutsche Bundesbahn") sleepers offer individually adjustable air conditioning, broad beds with foam-rubber mattresses, quilts, folding walls, electric razor outlets, shower-baths, and many other innovations; DB diners are efficient and reasonably priced; Trans-Europ-Express and Intercity electric locomotives which can average 125 mph on certain runs are painted a distinctive cream-and-burgundy (others are cream and turquoise). Prides of the line are the *Rheingold,* the *Blauer Enzian,* the *Parsifal,* the *Helvetia,* the *Wilhelm Busch,* the *Porta Westfalica,* the *Münchner Kindl,* the all-sleeper *Komet,* the *Roland,* the *Rheinpfeil,* and the *Gambrinus.* After the network's quick-lunch counters on wheels—buffet units that serve low-cost meals and snacks—became big hits, DB forged out 28 more with lower counters and seats à la U.S. drugstore style. Air-conditioned dining cars are attached to most of these trains today.

Almost all German trackage and switches have undergone the so-called seamless-welding process; the rhythmic clickety-clack of the wheels is a nostalgic memory nearly everywhere.

Tariffs are more than reasonable, by U.S. standards. And don't forget that great travel bargain—the Eurailpass.

First-class is worth the investment. Second-class, usually quite crowded, is cheaper and agreeable. Buy your international railway tickets and railway agency coupons *outside* Germany, because you'll save money. Within the country, many stations now provide computer data print-outs; just punch the key coded with your destination and out pops all the scoop on departure times, connections, arrival and cost.

★ **TIPS**   On most of the better cars (not necessarily the streamlined ones) seats which to the eye are completely ordinary can be lowered like a barber's chair by an ingenious mechanical arrangement.

"Bunk cars" *(Liegewagen)* are available to budgeteers on many intra-German and some international night runs. They're sort of "Economy Pullmans," with no curtains and 3 decks of 6 bunks per compartment; the passenger sleeps (if he can) in his clothes. Far, far better than sitting up, even in those newfangled chairs.

For sufferers of compartment-claustrophobia, full sleepers provide roomier dimensions with wider beds. Air conditioning can be regulated by each individual by use of bunkside knobs.

On medium-short hauls (*e.g.,* Cologne–Frankfurt), the better trains are now beating the airliners' time—airport-to-city coverage considered.

Several fast trains offer continuous telephone service en route and more are getting it.

For tired motorists, piggyback service rides your car along with you between various international and domestic points. These destinations have become so numerous they literally pepper the European map. They require too much space for us to include them here. Please check with your travel agent for the latest details. Sleepers and bunk cars carried; reservations later than one week in advance accepted on space-available basis only; comparatively high prices, varying with bumper-to-bumper measurements.

Luggage problems? Get rid of your heavy pieces by registering them through to your destination; fees are in the flea-bite class. Since most centers offer this service, you can forward your possessions direct to your lodgings by rail and post bus; it costs only a little more than the railway shipping charge. Actually, the most painless method is to turn over all your bags to your hotel porter at check-out time—and he'll forward them direct to your room in your next hotel, probably via the train which you ride. Wonderful for lone ladies or lazy folks like us! A score of depots now feature self-service hand carts, just as in your supermarket, into which you may pile your effects and roll them to the taxi or tram platforms.

Buses and Cars Most long-haul buses, particularly in sightseeing districts, are modern—and gentle to the area in contact with the seat. Many offer adjustable chairs, nonsmoking zones, public-address system, radio loudspeakers, and huge windows for maximum visibility. The German Federal Railways, the German Federal Post, and the German Touring Company all run good ones. If it weren't for the fiendish traffic in most urban centers, this would be a delightful way to cover the country.

Dozens of kind readers have sent rave reports about motor-coach tours of the Bavarian Alps, the Allgäu Alps, the Black Forest roads, and other scenic high spots. Some of them even go to Salzburg and the Tyrol in Austria. These tours are astonishingly cheap; the buses are excellent, service is frequent, and the routes are glorious.

Automobiles to hire? The German Federal Railways inaugurated an admirable service: When the traveler buys his train ticket at any of 130 major stations, for a small returnable deposit he may order a self-drive car to meet him at any of 40 important destinations. (You also can preorder a rental car at the secretarial compartments of TEE and IC trains.) Approved private companies are used locally; rates vary with the type of car, but all are comparatively reasonable; no profits accrue to the railroads. If you shouldn't want to bother with this more generalized facility, we've had complete satisfaction for years from the firm of **Philipp Keller** (Schlossstrasse 32-36) in *Frankfurt am Main*. Our good friend Peter, as Mr. Keller is known, has chauffeur-driven cars with English-speaking drivers—plus a close working affiliation with the best self-drive company in the Frankfurt area. Careful, reputable, thoughtful service; highest recommendation. In *Munich*, we've also had good luck over the years with **Auto-Sixt** (Seitzstrasse 9-11). This efficient outfit, Germany's largest car-hire company, offers more than 400 self-drive or chauffeur-drive vehicles to the motorist—all brand-new or very late models in perhaps a dozen different makes (including a splendid Mercedes 600 with TV, sliding roof, and a constantly replenished cocktail bar). Write to genial Erich or Regina Sixt (both of whom speak fluent English and who offer a special warmth to readers of this book) for further details. **Severin & Luer** is the best we've come across that is rooted in *Hamburg*.

ADAC and AvD, the 2 most important German automobile clubs, offer tour information in most cities. In the ports of Hamburg and Bremerhaven, and at a number of key frontier crossings, they and the German Tourist Association have set up special bureaus to help foreign visitors plan their trips. No charge. There's also a free motorists' aid service for outlanders stranded on the autobahns. Just flag down a red or yellow patrol car or get to one of the telephones set 7 miles apart throughout the network. In the Alps, the ADAC rents snow chains to winter trippers; your small deposit is refunded when you return 'em. Postscript for families: Children under 12 must ride in the back seat, but an exception is made if there is an overflow of offspring.

Motoring? There are oodles of self-service cafeterias on the nation's high-speed autobahns—and more are popping up by the minute. American-style snacks are their stock in trade. Simple, low-price, functional, tummy-filling fare that is a boon to hungry wayfarers.

Like France, Germany has so many hundreds of interesting eating places there simply isn't space to attempt to cover them all here. For information on other centers or villages, consult the local Tourist Offices everywhere.

☑ **FOOD**   First-class restaurant meals currently average $15 to $25 without wine, coffee, and spirits. If you want to do yourself well, with caviar, lobster, Prague ham, or other gustatory delights, your bill may run into the Wild, Wild Blue Yonder. But if you are content to eat in the small, family-type establishments (plenty available; most of them completely satisfactory), your tab should be close to perhaps $10. In country inns you can sometimes have a 3-course feast for as little as $6.

Coffee and tea are higher than in America. There are at least 7 different brews and strengths of coffee, ranging from the insipid, prune-juice-colored Mokka to the popular Kaffee Hag (caffeine-free) to Italian-style Espresso. "Filter," sometimes known as "Karlsbader Kaffee" from the machine in which it's made, is closest to American-style; Double Mokka is grainy and strong. You'll be safest if you always specify your type to the waiter.

National custom dictates that tables be shared by 2 or more parties if the restaurant or nightclub is crowded. Quite often you might find yourself sitting with strangers—fortunately, most of the time in a courteous but remote "please pass the salt" relationship rather than one of compulsory small talk and yak-yak. If you wish to yatter, fine—but if you're tired, they'll generally confine their conversation to their own group.

Contrary to legend (and the myopic standards of some otherwise reliable gourmets), German regional cooking is often light, delicate, and highly inventive.

★ **TIPS**   If in doubt about a good place to eat in a strange town, head for the nearest *Ratskeller*. The word means "council cellar" and it's the place (usually the cellar of the town hall) where in the Middle Ages municipal officials received guests. There is one in most communities; part of the *Ratskeller* is known as the *Ratstrinkstube* (council drinking room). The tradition of quality is stoutly upheld in most of these; some are better than others, but as a whole they are thoroughly dependable.

What to call the waiter? That's an amusing puzzle. Some old-fashioned Germans address him as "Kellner," which means, quite simply and logically, "Waiter." Certain others give a boost to this toiler's ego by shortening "Oberkellner," which means

"Headwaiter," to "Ober"—and spreading this one around to all comers. But now, in these less discriminating times—or more flattering ones (what you will)—nearly everyone expects to be addressed as "Herr Ober"—"Mr. Headwaiter."

☑ **DRINKS** Most connoisseurs (if they weren't born in Burgundy, Bordeaux, or Champagne) agree that Germany makes the finest white wines of the world. With typically Teutonic attention to detail, every bottle of character bears its full pedigree on the label—type, year, district, grower, shipper, and often even the condition of the grape at the picking ("Spätlese" for fully ripe, "Beerenauslese" for overripe, etc.). "Riesling" is a generic term for any wine of the Riesling grape, as opposed to the Sylvan grape. Moselle, Rhine, Ahr, Franconia, Palatinate, and others are named for their specific districts or valleys, although technically they could be called Rieslings. Steinwein is harsh and rough; most visitors prefer others. Hock, derived from "Hochheimer," is erroneously used by many British drinkers as a blanket appellation for all Rhines and similar types; the vineyards for this are actually on the north bank of the Main.

A few Americans seem to be familiar with only one German name—Liebfraumilch. Practically speaking, there are 2 good bottles of this for 10 bad ones, because this banner covers *all* of the output of the Rheinhessen region. Ask for Oppenheimer Schlossberg, Niersteiner Domthal, or Nackenheimer Rotenberg for delicious examples, and forget about most others. Among late offerings, the '76 pressings are among the finest in the lineage.

All sugarless types (often Moselle, Ruwer, Saar) are best when young.

If you're a zillionaire, "Beerenauslese" and "Trockenbeerenauslese" are the topmost rungs of wine quality (see below); they're so difficult to produce and so limited in supply that you'll pay from $45 to $150 per bottle at any fine restaurant (a 1921 vintage brings about $245!). They're categories, not brand names.

If you're a plain millionaire, Schloss Johannisberger is the finest "regular" wine in the land; the best years run up to perhaps $65. Other winners, not as expensive, are Deidesheimer Kieselberg Riesling Auslese, Berncasteler Doctor, and Piesporter Lay. In the medium range, our favorite is Jesuitengarten Riesling Auslese, a Palatinate variety available at Frankfurt's Rheinpfalz Weinstuben (see "Restaurants") at about $2.50 per 3-glass-carafe.

But don't be dazzled or intimidated by those important-sounding names, because starting with the '71 vintages, the government uncorked 3 general classifications for every drop of nectar produced in the country and set official testing numbers for both of the top grades. The categories are: Table wines ("Tafelwein") for the lowliest entries; Quality wines ("Qualitätswein") for the middle-bung brands; and Quality wines with Award ("Qualitätswein mit Prädikat") for the choicest crushings. That last (and best) batch becomes, in ascending order: Kabinett, Spätlese, Auslese, and with the aforementioned Beerenauslese and Trockenbeerenauslese the kings. The penalty for slapping an exalted label on a lower class distillate? Loss of the right to have it tested by the pros, which automatically means condemnation to the cheaper Table wine vine. And please don't be put off, either, by that humble designation. We could tick off at least 8 other European nations that would trade half of their agricultural budgets for the ability to grow German Table grapes.

German "champagne," called "Sekt," is frequently sparkling Rhine or Moselle wine. Remarkable strides have been made in recent years to improve its quality. Today, selected labels of the *brut* types have an urbane and noble character. Mumm Dry (no relative of the French brand of the same name) is an excellent candidate for your white; Henkell Rosé is a delightful pink nectar. (The Henkell cellars in Wiesbaden produce much of their Sekt from French wines, incidentally. This house is famous and excellent.) Many other so-called German champagnes are still cloyingly sweet, less bubbly than their French originals, and repulsive to the knowledgeable international palate.

German beer is as appetizing as ever—and it's about 60¢ to $1 per large mug in the average place. Fritz guzzles almost 256 pints a year; blotter-mouthed Bavarians turn up their steins with an astonishing 353 pints apiece annually with Frankfurt citizens topping even that figure. The choice is vast. There are Helles or Export or simply Ex (light), Pilsner or Pils (light in color but stronger), Dunkles (dark), Weisse (extra light), served in Bavaria chiefly but available elsewhere, the different Berliner Weisse (Berlin wheat-malt specialty which is light and lemony)—more varieties than the tourist can tilt a mug at. The Bockbier season is January to March; this beer is one of the most delicious of all. Best-known brews are those of Munich, Frankfurt, Dortmund, Donaueschingen (Fuerstenberg), Nürnberg (Siechen, Tucher), Würzburg, and Kulmbach. (The last is famous for being frozen into an iceblock which packs a 9% alcoholic punch after the solidification!) As a curiosity, you might like to try a stein of Weihenstephan. This brewery, in Freising, has been running continuously for almost a thousand years; the yeast in your potion first saw the light of day in the eleventh century.

☑ **TIPPING**   In all German hotels there is an automatic service charge of 10% to 15% of the price of the room. Now it is usually lumped into your overall bill rather than itemized separately. For meal service in hotels and restaurants the service bite is 10% to 15%; it no longer must be noted on the overall billing. For drinks most anywhere a separate tax (*Getränkesteuer*) is levied, but it does not often appear on your tab; generally this is 10%, but in Munich and Stuttgart it is 20%; you're still expected to shell out something for the bartender, however.

Tip about what you would in New York. Remember the concierge, maid, washroom attendant, baggage porter, valet, room waiter, and barber, if you use them—all in very small amounts. Forget doormen and theater ushers unless you are feeling expansive, generous, or 3-martini-ish.

☑ **LOCAL RACKETS**   Few rackets are tried on travelers in Germany. Most important is the tendency of unauthorized moneychangers to stick their customers with counterfeit bills.

As usual, long tons of minor swindles and slippery tactics occur in flesh parlors. Accordingly, some of these are described in the "Night Life" sections in the cities which follow.

If you lock your suitcase, leave no valuables unwatched, and try not to look like the

"Man Who Arrived This Morning," you should have no troubles. Most visitors find the Germans honest and straightforward.

☑ **INFORMATION CENTERS** With typical organizational ability and attention to detail, German travel experts set up such an outstanding new holidays program that they put to shame some larger colleagues.

Headquarters and fountainhead of the national and international network is the **German National Tourist Board** (Beethovenstrasse 69, *Frankfurt am Main*). Its General Manager is dynamic young Günther Spazier. Masses of color-illustrated booklets in English, French, German, and 7 other tongues, covering every region of the Federal Republic, are available at the Frankfurt apex or at any of its subordinate offices. These are often an enormous help in the selection of travel goals.

The branches in New York, Chicago, Los Angeles, Montreal, Paris, London, Stockholm, Copenhagen, Amsterdam, Madrid, Brussels, Zürich, Rome, Vienna, Tokyo, Johannesburg, and Rio de Janeiro reflect this efficiency. The New York headquarters is at 630 Fifth Avenue; Manager Herman Krüger will solve your problems in a trice. In Chicago, the GNTO branch is at 104 South Michigan Ave., and the Manager is Ernst Gerth; in Los Angeles, at Broadway Plaza, Suite 1714, 700 S. Flower St., Hans Baumann is now holding the reins; in Montreal at 2 Fundy, P. O. Box 417, Place Bonaventure.

The **German Travel Association** (not to be confused with the official German National Tourist Association, which concerns itself only with promotion outside the homeland) has its own organization to aid the traveler. To date, more than 130 information centers —recognizable by a red plaque with a white *i*—have been accredited by it as worthy of serving the wayfarer. The bulk of these at present are concentrated in the Bavaria, Württemberg, Hesse, and Rhineland districts.

Matriculation at a German university, institute, or professional school? Try the **DAAD** (Deutscher Akademischer Austauschdienst), D-5300 Bad Godesberg, Bonn 2; it's all at their fingertips, from Abaddon Philosophy to Zebra Zoology.

At least 50 feudal palaces and knights' castles have been converted into hotels— Gothic vaults, moats, battlements, ghosts, and all. Some are luxury class, some are plainer—and a teasing selection of them are listed under "Other Targets" further along. The northern Rhineland, the Palatinate, Franconia, Upper Bavaria, Hesse, and Baden-Württemberg are especially thick with them. Too scattered to list all of them here, due to space limitations, but you'll usually find one within shooting distance of most major points of the nation. Great fun for motorists, as a change of pace; try at least one, if only for the experience. Write to **Gast im Schloss**, Geschäftsstelle, Burghotel, D-3526, Trendelburg 1, Germany, for details. The **German National Tourist Board** also will gladly send you a special folder containing a full list plus particulars.

For further data on accommodations (outlying motels for example), consult the local **Tourist Office** in any of the larger cities or towns. They are usually at or near the railway stations, and will gladly try to answer your needs.

Youth hostels? The **German Youth Hostels Association** offers 75 thousand beds in more than 700 branches; some perking-up of accommodations has been done in the hiking areas. A building spree is putting up hostels in or near the larger cities and cultural centers.

Dedicated budgeteers in Frankfurt, Munich, and Berlin? Since we're too bottlenecked here for additional entries in these key hubs, please consult our annually revised paperback, *Fielding's Low-Cost Europe*, which lists scads more bargain hotels or pensions and money-saving tips for serious economizers.

☑ **SHOPPING**   Outbound passengers for foreign destinations are eligible for duty-free, tax-free bargains in liquor, cigarettes, cigars, and French perfumes ONLY at the **Airport Shops** in Frankfurt am Main, Hamburg, Munich, Cologne and Düsseldorf. You won't save a penny on cameras, Rosenthal china, Offenbach leather, or any *German-made* goods, because they're sold here at the same prices as at all German stores.

Our ★ ★ ★ ★ ★ recommendations are individually noted throughout this chapter.

Shopping hours: These have recently been standardized throughout the nation: 9 A.M. to 6:30 P.M. Monday through Friday, 9 A.M. to 2 P.M. on most Saturdays, but from 9 A.M. to 4 P.M. on the first Saturday of every month.

Please DON'T buy: Nonstandard items in spas, resorts, small towns, or villages. Big-city merchants get the break which they pass along to the customer. The 300-day clock is usually so delicate that even dusting might throw it off. Be sure your electrical equipment is designed for 110 volts or a 110/220 combination.

Cameras: For an informative, exclusive, complete section on how best to buy one and what to avoid, consult our purse-size 25th Anniversary Edition of *Fielding's Selective Shopping Guide to Europe.*

CITIES

BERLIN   Let's not stand on that perfunctory ceremony of making Bonn the curtain raiser for this chapter simply because it happens to be the *official* capital (a city that's often accused of having half the population of the Chicago Cemetery and being twice as dead). Berlin is the historic heartbeat of the German nation and the traditional focal point of its soul. Hence, we hope you'll forgive us for not being sticklers for form. ("Bonn" is fully covered under "Other Targets.")

The Black Forest, the Rhine, and probably 50 other localities of today's Germany have greater beauty and more spectacular scenery than Berlin. Yet, political eruptions aside, if we were forced to limit any German tour to a single goal, we'd pick Berlin in a walk.

First, let's get the Big Question out of the way. As we write this, at least, the masters of the Orwellian-termed German Democratic Republic (DDR for short) are still observing the nonagression, nonmolestation multilateral treaty which was signed in '72. West Berlin continues to be trouble-free. In the

Communist-ruled areas, visitors continue to be safe *as long as they stay within the proper boundaries.*

The city is divided into 4 Sectors (don't call them "Zones," because that is the national, not local, term for apportionment). The Western Sectors have a population of 2 million, and the remaining 1.1 million are under Soviet control. Within Free Berlin are 12 districts; since each may exercise its civic pride by naming its own streets; one famous interdistrict thoroughfare has no less than 8 different titles from place to place. The Berliner, always noted for his lightness, gaiety, and rapier wit, is America's best friend in Germany.

East of the Wall, more than 3 decades of 5-year programs reveal approximately 130 thousand apartments. State-operated stores line the main boulevard, a handful of skyscraping hotels have appeared to house the delegations from Minsk to Sinkiang, and there is more stir and bustle than ever before in the postwar era. Hardly a soul, however, has the money to shop in those stores. The hotels are drab even though they are modern. The avenues may be smooth but the few vehicles on them are usually government-owned. Behind these rows of apartment buildings is the gray, frightful carcass of a neglected and helpless society. On a guided tour by sunlight, it seems to represent real achievement. On our own, it was another story. After dark—and foreigners must leave by midnight—it is a dreary, suffocating nightmare. West of the Wall, there's always light, action, fun, progress, and—you will sense it right to the tips of your toes—*freedom.* Nowhere on earth can the difference be felt so dramatically. A few yards from bleakness, one of Europe's most sparkling glass-and-aluminum cities has sprung up in phoenix fashion. Most visitors never realize that this metropolis has now become Germany's largest industrial center; approximately 86% of her wares are exported. It also has a congress center (ICC) to house this city's myriad conventions.

Here, in capsule form, is a quick roundup of pertinent facts for the voyager. Please keep in mind that this information is accurate only up to this book's deadline, subject to later changes. Since conditions could again be volatile despite the treaty, you should check with your travel agent, who can advise you of up-to-the-minute developments:

Travel Documents A valid U.S. passport is all you need. Baggage examination is waived except on commercial merchandise. If you're driving, be sure to have ownership, registration, insurance, and a car identity plaque showing country of origin. Incidentally, youngsters under 16 are not permitted to enter the East without an adult leader or guardian.

Transportation By air is best. It's cheaper, too, than comparable flights to other destinations; ticket prices have been slashed to attract more visitors to the isolated city (see Germany: "Airlines"). Pan Am (using Boeing 727's) and British Airways fly heavy shuttle schedules (almost hourly) to Hanover, Hamburg, Bremen, Cologne/Bonn, Düsseldorf, Stuttgart, Nürnberg, Frankfurt am Main, and Munich. Air France makes a Paris–Berlin–Paris round each day, while BA does the same for London, Manchester, and Glasgow trippers. Now that Tempelhof is being used solely as a U.S. military base, be sure your plane is scheduled to land at the modern, orange-colored Tegel Airport (with a duty-free shop) in the French sector of West Berlin, *not Schoenefeld Airport in the East German Zone* (outside the city); while the Communists have not yet substantially interfered with transients who have made this mistake, you'd be subjected to unfriendly passport controls and forced to pay for the special visa. From Tegel, city bus #9 leaves every 10 minutes and runs right through the center of town with pauses along the route; you can also grab the very same service from metropolitan stops out to the airport.

For U.S. motorists, the Munich–Berlin and the Helmstedt–Marienborn–Berlin autobahns, among others, are authorized 2-way routes at this writing; at the outgoing checkpoints of Warnemünde, Sassnitz, and Zinnwald, fees are collected. The East German stop is at Dreilinden, utilized for the routes between Helmstedt and Marienborn and between Munich, Rudolphstein, and Hirschberg. You're forbidden to stray one inch from them; the Soviet sections are badly maintained. You should have a full tank of gas, despite the fact service stations have opened along this path; they're especially marked; payment *must* be made in West German Deutsche Marks. Hence, our advice is to leave your auto in Hanover, buy a round trip by plane, and take the 40-minute hop to West Berlin. Now available are the DB's flat-rate round trips to Berlin which include Second-class travel on express trains and up to 6 nights in a hotel or pension with breakfast. Buses are also possible, and they're modern.

Taxis and Car Rentals   The city is well accommodated by a 4500-car fleet, mostly composed of comfortable Mercedes diesels; ½ of them are linked to a central exchange by radio-telephone. Drivers are courteous—so nice, in fact, that they consider a tip a gratuity and express their appreciation politely. Here it's really silly to rent a self-drive vehicle, because your area of free movement is peanut-size. If you plan a tour, we'd suggest hiring a taxi or a private chauffeur-driven car. Of the latter, we think the prices are not only outrageous for Germany but high for anywhere in Europe.

Tip for the Tipsy: Drink too much and reluctant to drive? Just telephone 313-40-54 (if you can), and any one of 400 available students (who also will serve as baby sitters) will come to your rescue as chauffeur, crutch, and fellow philosopher. The cost is about $5 per hour; the pickup service works in a matter of minutes.

Sightseeing   Since the Soviets put up their evil Wall-of-China in Berlin, conditions have been so fluid and uncertain that we urge you to consult a travel agent before scrambling off to possible disappointment. Highlights of special interest that are accessible or visible at this moment include the following—and "new" is the operative word as you skim down this paragraph: (1) a circuit of the western side of **The Wall** (your heart will weep, because here is one of the most profoundly moving jolts of anyone's travel life. To try to counter the

shock of viewing this monstrous horror, the East Germans built a wall with
revolving tubing on top to prevent a solid grip when scaling, a whitewashed
surface—because moving targets show up better—and concrete watchtowers
to house and hide machine-gun nests. Surrounding it is a no-man's-land bristling with camouflaged fortifications and obstacles as a replacement for the
propaganda-damaging visible battlements and barbed wire); (2) the repaired,
Red-sentried **Brandenburg Gate**; (3) the **Soviet War Memorial** 300 yards
inside Free Berlin from this Gate—a *Soviet*-controlled and guarded monument
containing stones from the former Reichs Chancellery (called "the Last Plun-
derer" by the wisecracking Berliners), the 2 first T-34 tanks to enter the city,
and masses of phony flowers; (4) the famous **Freedom Bell** (in Schöneberg
Town Hall), which rings for 3 minutes daily at noon; (5) the **Kaiser-Wilhelm
Memorial Church**, around the war ruins of which, after years of debate, a
modern building designed by Professor Egon Eiermann has been raised; popular organ recitals, brief meditation services at 5:30 P.M. and 6 P.M., Monday
through Friday; (6) **Charlottenburg Castle**, reconstructed in the original baroque as the only structure in the Western Sectors which still bears the architectural tradition of the Prussian kingdom; while here, don't miss the Arts
and Handicrafts Museum, the Museum of Pre-and-Proto-history and the
Egyptian Museum housing the 3000-year-old bust of the Egyptian Queen
Nefertiti; (7) **Ethnology Museum** in Dahlem, our bid as the world leader in
this field; nowhere have we seen items so intelligently and engagingly displayed; (8) **Ernst-Reuter-Platz**, named for the late, great burgomaster, where
a 40-jet fountain gives a jazz-ballet effect amid rising modern skyscrapers in
one of Europe's largest traffic circles; (9) the **Congress Hall** in the Tiergarten,
designed by U.S. Architect Hugh A. Stubbins and built from joint funds of the
Benjamin Franklin Foundation and the German Federal Republic; (10) the
Art Gallery at Dahlem, with 600 valuable paintings from the thirteenth to the
eighteenth century; (11) the **Academy of Arts**, built with $2,000,000 con-
tributed by Berlin-born Philadelphian Henry H. Reichhold to house the creative arts (includes theater, studios, and halls); (12) the stupendous **Neue Na-
tionalgalerie** on Potsdamer Str. in the Tiergarten, (13) the **Hansa Quarter**, site
of the '57 International Building Exhibition and transformed into a 1600-
apartment residential section by 54 architects from all over the globe; (14) the
1936 **Olympic Stadium**; (15) the **West Berlin Zoo**, largest in Europe, with 9,500
residents of 1800 species; (16) the **Aquarium**, a superb midtown treat containing
one of the most extensive finny collections on the globe; (17) **Potsdamer Platz**
—the junction of the U.S., British, and Soviet Sectors; and (18) a **Waterway
Tour** on the Havel River and its cozy coves; 6 departures daily in summer
beginning at 9:30 A.M. from Wannsee; refreshment bars aboard. Well worth
hearing is the **Berlin Philharmonic Orchestra** in its dazzling concert hall (next
to the National Galleries) designed by Architect Hans Scharoun. If your visit
corresponds with the dates of the city's Performing Arts Festival, don't miss
these outstanding cultural events at the **Deutsche Oper Berlin**. There are 18

playhouses in the city, including the popular **Freie Volksbühne**. For facts
about the vast flock of other museums (Botanical, History, Childrens', Antiques, Musical, Radio, others) and routine attractions, consult the official
Tourist Office (open from 7:30 A.M. to 10:30 P.M. at Budapester Str., Europa
Center) or inquire at the **Information Center**; the latter, at Hardenbergstr. 20,
now has 22 specialists equipped to answer any questions on recreational,
artistic, or commercial topics—in English, naturally. While at the Tourist
Office, be sure to pick up the free Bummel ("Stroller's") Pass. This handout
contains coupons which entitle the visitor to discounts up to 33⅓% on hosts
of things he or she may do in the city. Valid for 1 full year; a marvelous
guideline for seeing and saving.

Tours to East Berlin   Combined excursions which cover both sides of
the wall take 4 to 5 hours, cost about $17, and offer English-speaking guides.
They originate from the intersection of Kurfürstendamm and Uhlandstrasse;
from the Kaiser-Wilhelm Memorial Church; and from the corner of Meinekes-
trasse at the Kurfürstendamm. The crossover point for foot, car, or bus traffic
is at the junction of Friedrichstrasse and Zimmerstrasse (you may know it as
"Checkpoint Charlie"). We strongly recommend you book onto a circuit that
includes the awesome Pergamon Museum (usually only a ½-hour stop, so try
to get back for a longer browse) and the birch-lined Russian Cemetery. The
loop that highlights the enormous communications tower is a mockery of
Soviet bearish bureaucracy. While the view is magnificent, you'll pay for it
through the admission charge. Only cold meals are served, at a minimum of
close to $9 when we were last there; all comestibles we saw were barely edible;
and, finally—get this—after you've spent _precisely_ 1 hour in the rotating restaurant (it's on a 60-minute cycle), the guards march in and give you the boot.
To employ an irresistible word play, comes the revolution and out you go!
Itineraries usually contain a coffee break so you won't perish from hunger or
thirst en route. Subway entry into the East (watch for the submachine guns
bristling in the abandoned platforms through No Man's Land) may be made
by taking the train from Zoo Station. To enter the Red district you must pay
a visa fee of 5 DM, give over 6.50 DM as the sum you promise to spend while
in this sector, and carry a valid passport (or normal motoring papers, if you
go by car; this adds a 10 DM route tax). We must stress and restress that there
_is_ risk in parting the Iron Curtain with anything less than an organized touring
group. All currency, incidentally, must be declared on entry; all Sovietside
expenditures must also be accounted for on departure.

Other Eastern targets? We experienced a 6-hour spin to neighboring Potsdam by motor coach. On this trip, 2 hours each way were consumed by frontier
formalities and relentless fisheyed surveillance by Russian military martinets.
Passing the time in the halted buses, we witnessed passenger cars being gutted
by suspicious inspectors at the border. The official docket was composed of a
shuffle through Frederik the Great's crumbling Sanssouci Castle (you don
enormous felt slippers so that your shoes won't mar the flooring) and a whisk

through the Tudor-style Cecilienhof Mansion (where the Potsdam Agreement was signed in 1945). Your reward? A slab of tasteless cake and a cup of insipid coffee at the mile-long tables of the Interhotel (meant to be a showcase of Eastern innkeeping, but pathetically 3rd-rate by Western guidelines—at least, so sayeth this *Guide*). If you ever, ever, ever wish to confirm the free-press reports of Red tape, grimness, and bathetic spiritless life beyond the Wall, then this is the tour to snatch. Otherwise, don't be tempted. Dresden, Meissen, and Leipzig also can be absorbed on a 2-day swing, but our pores were too saturated to consider it for 2 seconds. All, incidentally, are relatively inexpensive. The reason is obvious.

Travel Information   The Berlin Tourist Office (Europa Center), directed by the efficient, hardworking, Hans-Jürgen Binek, is outstanding for its aid to the traveler. Offices are maintained at key points to dispense advice, brochures, and every type of assistance to any voyager; there's even a branch at the airport, to greet the visitor as he steps off the plane! Write or contact the dedicated Mr. Binek if any problem should plague you—or, in his absence, ever-helpful, keen-eyed Mr. Karl-Bernhard Ulbrecht is an unusually helpful member of this brilliant staff. They'll go all out to make your stay a happy and comfortable one!

BERLIN HOTELS Quick Reference Table

Price categories by national (not U.S.) standards.

EXPENSIVE:
Intercontinental Budapester Str. 2. Tel. 26.10.81; Telex 0.184.380; 600 rooms. P. 351
Kempinski Kurfürstendamm 27. Tel. 88.10.91; Telex 0.183.553; 335 rooms. P. 351
Steigenberger Ranke-Marburger Strasse. Tel. 215625; Telex 27155; 400 rooms. P. 352

UPPER MODERATE:
Ambassador Bayreuther Str. 42. Tel. 24.01.01; Telex 0.184.259; 119 rooms. P. 352
Excelsior Hardenbergstr. 14. 320 rooms. P. 353
Palace Budapester Str. Tel. 26.20.11; Telex 0.184.825; 180 rooms. P. 352
Park-Zellermayer Meinekestr. 15. Tel. 88.20.51; Telex 0.184.200; 140 rooms. P. 352
Schweizerhof Budapester Str. 21. Tel. 2.69.61; Telex 0.185.501; 400 rooms. P. 352
Seehof Lietzensee-Ufer 11. Tel. 32.10.51; Telex 0.182.943; 77 rooms. P. 353
Sylterhof Kurfürstenstr. 116. Tel. 213.20.01; Telex 0.183.317; 131 rooms. P. 353

MODERATE:
Am Zoo Kurfürstendamm 25. Tel. 88.30.91; Telex 0.183.835; 144 rooms. P. 353
Arosa Lietzenburger Str. 79. Tel. 88.20.11; Telex 0.183.397; 127 rooms. P. 353
Arosa-Airline Kurfürstendamm 68. Tel. 883.40.41; Telex 0.184.705. 70 rooms. P. 354
Berlin Kurfürstenstr. 62. Tel. 26.92.91; Telex 0.184.332; 255 rooms. P. 353
Bremen Bleibtreustr. 25. Tel. 881.40.76; Telex 0.184.892; 48 rooms. P. 353
Crest Güntzestr.; nearing completion; approx. 100 rooms. P. 353
Europäischer Hof Messedamm 10. Tel. 30.20.11; Telex 0.182.882; 189 rooms. P. 353
Hamburg Landgrafenstr. 4. Tel. 26.91.61; Telex 0.184.974; 240 rooms. P. 353

Hervis Stresemannstr. 97. Tel. 261.14.44; Telex 0.184.063; 73 rooms. P. 353
Penta Nürnberger Str. 63. Tel. 88.27.461; Telex 182877 BEPEN; 425 rooms. P. 353
President An der Urania 16. Tel. 213.80.61; Telex 0.184.018; 72 rooms. P. 353
Savoy Fasanenstr. 9. Tel. 31.06.54; Telex 0.184.292; 115 rooms. P. 352
Studio (Am) Kaiserdamm 80. Tel. 30.20.81; Telex 01.82.825; 77 rooms. P. 353
Tourotel Albrechtstr. 2. Tel. 79161; Telex 183545; 220 rooms.

LOWER MODERATE:
Dom Hohenzollerndamm 33. Tel. 87.97.80; 40 rooms. P. 353
Franke Albrecht-Achilles-Str. 57. Tel. 892.10.97; Telex 0.184.857; 75 rooms. P. 354
Lichtburg Paderborner Str. 10. Tel. 891.80.41; Telex 0.184.208; 72 rooms. P. 354
Plaza Knesebeckstr. 63. Tel. 88.20.81; Telex 0.184.181; 132 rooms. P. 353
Savigny Brandenburgische Str. 21. Tel. 881.30.01; Telex 0.184.053; 60 rooms. P. 353
Thober Kurfürstendamm 100. Tel. 324.10.21; 103 rooms. P. 354

ENVIRONS:
Gehrhus Brahmsstr. 4. Tel. 826.20.81; 35 rooms. P. 354
Stössensee Glockenturmstr. 30. Tel. 304.55.95; 45 rooms. P. 354

Hotels Berlin's chambermaids fluff up perhaps 16 thousand pillows. Here is one of the few remaining continental hubs in which one can usually find nonreserved space in High Season; in winter the middle-bracket wayfarer can pull on his nightcap for 20% less than in summer. Generally the quality is outstanding; the newer candidates, however, hew the narrowest line possible when it comes to adequate living space. A common wheeze has it that a pitifully crippled Münchener was seen one morning by his friend, hobbling along the Kurfürstendamm. _"Gott im Himmel!"_ cried the Berliner. "What happened to you? Were you hit by a freight train?" "No," replied the friend from Munich, "I just spent a night in your most modern hotel." Calling them "cramped" would be akin to dismissing the Himalayas as "tall."

The **Kempinski** remains one of Europe's tiptop hotels under the savvy handling of Rudolf Münster, a most personable host. This season you will be greeted by $18-million worth of improvements (almost a new hotel within the old skin—but then, even the facade is new). Restaurant refashioned maintaining Berlin style; air conditioning throughout; new elevators; 5 new suites with terraces; all baths slicked up with marble suits; new carpets, new furniture, and double-glaze windows plus a fortune in behind-the-scene updatings. Superb public areas; outstanding grill; fun-filled bar with dancing; sparkling, oh-zoned jetstream pool and sauna; flawless service. Highest accolades for its big-city concept.

The **Intercontinental** took over the 350-unit Hilton, switched name-plates, and began a program of renewal and fresh construction which will bring the overall room count up to 600. The expansion spree also ties the giant into Berlin's new International Congress Center. While several restaurants, a Bierkeller, pool, sauna, 50 suites, and a shopping arcade are blueprinted, the majority of the revisions are taking place as we write these words; hence any comments on the concept or rendition would be premature for this edition. Our very recent 2 nights in the renewed older section were sufficient to almost guarantee that the new building has _got_ to be better. Check with your travel agent, an Intercontinental office, or Pan Am before departure.

The **Steigenberger** is due to unveil its 7 floors of 400 rooms in time for this year's visitor. Residing in midcity, it is being ballyhooed as a strong contender for the Deluxe traveler. Some efforts by this chain are excellent, while others are blatantly commercial; hence, we prefer a wait-and-see stance to passing on the hearsay.

The **Palace**, sited conveniently in the Europa Center, is thick in the decorator department. Spacious, elegant lobby; adjoining dark-hued bar combining English Establishment with Erstwhile Empire; numerous vitrines recalling images of The Old Curiosity Shop; woody ground-floor grill with open rôtisserie; restaurant up 1 flight-of-fancy to a soft green and rich blue haven; easy access to the nearby public pool and other thermic therapies. Manager Karl Stiehle is laboring overtime to create a Palace of comfort here.

The **Ambassador**, with Director Henze Rachfahl its latest envoy, offers beautiful public rooms, perhaps the most alluring in the metropolis; entrance lounge with spherical copper hearth; captivating canopied dining quarter with deftly prepared but comparatively high-priced culinations; popular bar and grill with quiet patio, flowered chairs, and garden setting; terrace-rimmed Coffee Shop for nibblers; modern penthouse swimming pool with slide-away roof, plus adjoining sauna, massage parlors, and solarium; beauty salon; eye-catching murals in corridors; woody tones throughout; TV with every latchkey. Somewhat expensive, but not unreasonable considering the rewards in color, flair, comfort, and service.

The **Savoy** is an excellent buy for traditionalists. L-A-R-G-E rooms, all with bath and shower and most with twin basins; doubles ending in "10" particularly worthy; casual-style restaurant and bar with snacks available; courteous concierge and reception staffs; management by Mr. Rudigkeit. Very good indeed for Old World seekers.

The quiet, residential-style **Parkhotel Zellermayer** is a delight for nonbusiness types and families seeking a noninstitutional retreat within the frenetic metropolis. Recent expansion program augmented by around-the-calendar updatings; all bedchambers with bath or shower; fine restaurant; friendly snack corner; Jockey Bar; tranquil interior courtyard with babbling fountain; underground garage. If you are so-in-love, ask especially for 1 of the 2 units with a large bed snuggling in a great wicker basket—ooooo, la, la! Here's a cozy nook, if we ever spied one. Warm recommendation for its ingratiating charm.

The **Schweizerhof** struts an imposing stance across the street from the Intercontinental with which it shares top management. It is always so jammed with conventioneers and commercial wayfarers that it added a wing for 350 more occupants, plus the Old Marketplace restaurant with cobblestones, streetlamps, and fountain, Le Mascaron nightspot and bar, a banquet hall, and its very own swimming pool. Handsome lobby; spacious corner-sited breakfast garden; wood-shingled salon; chalet-style Grill with adjoining 3-table Schützenstübli and the Zunftstube extension; Wappen Bar with Swiss heraldry; 2 garages; 100% air-chilled; full range of contemporary trappings from Naugahyde furniture to multichannel radios. If the studio units in the new section seem too small for your brood, 1200 Marks a night will secure the Presidential

Suite. (Parents will appreciate its triple-glazed, bulletproof windows!). Actually, the 7th-floor accommodations are now amply wide-angled. Manager Klaus Stolle is giving this Swiss house Alpine helpings of worthy projects and charm. ·

The new **Excelsior** recently uncorked its 8 sleek layers of modernity on Hardenbergstr. within walking distance of the center; in its fresh shell are several dining areas (including the colorful Peacock with a 25-foot-long breakfast buffet) plus banquet and conference facilities. The accommodations are simple, clean, narrow, and contemporary. **Crest** also crested recently 3 stops by U-Bahn from the main part of town. It is inclined toward motelishness. **Penta** alighted recently with 425 air-conditioned units with minibar, TV and radio, plus a _bierstube,_ a cocktail lounge, restaurants, boutiques and special-interest shops. This chain, linked together through the cooperation of several airlines, delivers outstanding value, flair, and comfort for the moderate billings.

The 5-story **Sylterhof** provides an overall feeling of Frenchiness rather than Germanic heaviness. White, clean-lined restaurant; posh Casino Bar; corridors with handsome bas-relief panels, heavy draperies, and mirrors; colored towels furled in pea-pod-size bathrooms; sleek appointments that are beginning to show some wear. Here's a superior bet for any Man or Woman of the Times. Recommended.

The heart of the **Seehof** seems to us to have sclerotic inner chambers. Blue and white checkerboard façade; enchanting situation with restaurant, lamplit terrace, bar, and covered, glass-lined swimming pool all oriented toward the lovely Lietzensee (town lake); fresh rustic tones cunningly conjured up by its architect owner and his artist wife. It is so thoroughly winning in so many, many ways that we wonder how the designer possibly could have sketched its accommodations in such ridiculously paltry dimensions.

The **Hamburg** is next. Red canopied entrance; large blue-carpeted lounge; nice copper-tone bar; fresh dining salon; quick-meal corner; flowers everywhere for brighteners. Its units also were planned for small-boned trippers.

After the above, our choices would run as follows: **Europäischer Hof** (non-central situation near the bus terminus, but handy to the international exhibitions at the Funkturm and new ICC), **Bremen** (peaking above a filling-station complex, useful midcity site; penthouse breakfast room with open terrace for snacks; no bar or restaurant; 44 of its 48 units earmarked as singles; the other 4 with TV and Frigobar), **Berlin** (dimly lit, brick-lined Grill with delicious cuisine for the outlay; active bar; some units with tiny balconies; fair but not special), **Am Zoo** (Weinkrüger restaurant quite agreeable), **Am Studio** (a study in miniaturism; clean as a surgeon's pinkie; low rates; conscientious management by Günter Wendl), **President** (behind the Sylterhof in an area of urban growth; supermodernistic in structure and efficiency), **Arosa** (appealing, but surely one of the narrowest-gauge hostelries we've ever, ever, ever inspected; for no-hipped striplings exclusively), **Hervis** (a 10-minute stroll from Checkpoint Charlie; ample lebensraum; '68 vintage instrumentation; very kind staff), **Plaza** (140 rooms, all with bath or showers; low tabs in Low Seasons; all in all, pretty slim pickin's), **Savigny** (to our peepers, better for geriatrics than peripatetics), **Dom** (in a fast-fading district; tailor-made for traveling parties and tour packages of foreign origin; not recommended by us), either the

Lichtburg or its sister the Franke (substantial but commercial), and Arosa Airline Hotel (good location but little else; slipping). The rooms at the Thober are no longer tolerable, in our view. The Gehrhus is in a special category, occupying a suburban site about 20 minutes from Action Central in the Grunewald district. Here's a castle structure that recently was brightened up and touched up in a most ingratiating way, revealing the best of its aristocratic origins.

Apartment dwelling? The 12-tier Stössensee, beside its namesake lake and a warbler's chirp from Grunewald's greenery, comes up with 2-score functional but uninspired abodes. Water sports (lake or covered pool), tennis, and sauna close by; adjoining supermarket; spartan lobby; midget bar; limp restaurant-cum-clubroom; somber, linoleum-lined corridors. All units are decorated in the Middle Mundane Modern Mode; #1001, for example, provides orange walls, a beige carpet, tartan chairs and sofa, an indestructible table, a mini-kitchenette, and an alcove sleeping nook. Minimum stay 2 weeks; 40% discount applied to a month or more; buses #92 and #94 routed to the doin's. A fair bet for wallet-watching wanderers.

Restaurants The robust Ritz, a decorously beaded string of 3 small rooms, retains its position as one of the best dining bets in the Divided City. Some of the dishes that surely will dally delightfully with your fancy include the Gordon's Gin Tomato soup, the Blinis, the Scallops in Sweet Basil Broth, and the Rack of Venison. The versatile monarch of the ovens also cooks up a mélange of dishes from all over the globe; Chinese egg rolls, Russian ragout, palm-wine soup served in a ceramic molding of an Oriental girl's head, Indonesian Nasi Goreng—goodness knows what else. Its maintenance has improved notably; service is polite, but waiters tend to push the most expensive dishes. Again, *always* reserve in advance; closed Sunday; very well liked by U.S. wanderers, including this writer. Also in the top bracket is the Maître, French ownership and French chef; 3 salons, of which we prifer the Paris Room in the evening; interesting and varied menu, with prices listed on the host's card only; superb wines in this club center for champagne connoisseurs; unusually attentive service; presentation of match covers with the client's name inscribed in gold; surprisingly reasonable tariffs. Open for lunch and dinner; *always* book your table ahead. *Vive Le Maître!*

In the charm department, top marks—and D-Marks, too!—go to Le Popote, which is quite chic at the moment. Of its 2 cozy roomlets, we prefer the one to the rear. Bar near the entrance; black wooden carnival horses mounted on the coral-colored walls; about 10 obsidian-hued enamel tables; sprays of explosive color in dried-flower arrangements; cuisine imaginative and well presented. We hope its popularity thrives.

A candidate we liked even more, but which is far more modest in concept as well as in price, is the Big Window. Since it is known only by the Berlin cognoscenti, we include its address and phone number: 49 Joachim-Friedrich Str., Tel. 892 58 36—and *be sure to reserve in advance.* The whole shebang is only about 10 yards deep with tables on either side of a center aisle, kitch on the walls, and wonders from the kitchen. The affable proprietor, Ivan, will explain (in English) his native Armenian specialties as well as his own adaptations of them. But please take our rapturous word for it and try the spareribs followed by his Lule Kebab with Lavasch. The latter is composed of seasoned strips of marinated meat grilled inside a large crêpe. Tear off a morsel of the bread, enfold a nibble of lamb, sprinkle on the dust of dried levantine berries, and prepare your taste buds for a culinary treat that you will long remember. The **Tessiner Stuben** and the **Chalet Suisse** both evoke, of course, the muses of Helvetian tummyware. Decoratively, too, the inspiration is reenforced by rough stucco walls, wrought iron, copper pots, garlic garlands, and other touches of Alpine lore. The cookery is substantial though not thrilling. We do recommend this upland pair, but more for atmosphere than for skilletcraft. **Zlata Praha**, one of our beloved Czech-Points which slipped a notch or so, has now pulled itself together and once more wins the esteem of Berliners and this team of travel writers. In fact, we found it better than ever this visit. Two simple chambers; overworked waiters in trim waistcoats and velvet cummerbunds; little English spoken. Slovakian specialties, including Prague Ham in a pastry shell, Pussta Hirtenfleisch (Shepherd's Meat with Dumplings), and Rumpsteak Lecso (with hot peppers); fascinating Sirner Paska dessert (a cheese loaf with a chilled tutti-frutti complex). Try—if you dare—the ultra bitter Pilsner Urquell beer which takes 10 to 15 minutes to draw from the tap (the Slavic toast is "Eschi Shigeria"). **Le Connoisseur** (Wieland Str.) is a noted practitioner of the *nouvelle cuisine,* but we were unable to find time to sample its nouvelty; next time for sure. **Epicure** (Prinz Regenten Str. 53) is a kooky spot with 15,236 unmatched pieces of furniture, laughing young people, and inexpensive good food. **Alexander** with 6 rooms on 2 floors is recommendable for its cozy ambiance, not for its cookery. Front section in traditional dress; middle unit with horseshoe counter for quick feedbagging; back segment in hunting-lodge motif; additional corners for private parties. Highish tabs and lowish cuisine, think we. **Conti-Fischstuben** is a prime catch for seafood anglers; it's rather costly, however. The renovated and newly furnished **Schultheiss Brauhaus**, across from the Kempinski, is a sparkling candidate in the low-price league—especially for such a centrally sited establishment. Terrace entrance invitingly splashed with garden greenery; inner landscape charming. Gargantuan portions for reasonable outlays; he-man steaks presented appetizingly on wooden platters. The formula is winning. So is a South American version off the same grill: the **Churrasco**, an Argentinian harnessmate of similar *ranchos* in Frankfurt, Munich, Hamburg, and Bremen. The penthouse **I-Punkt**, just below the revolving Mercedes Star emblem crowning the Europa Center, is tops for view but not for flavor. Glass-lined ring of scruffy tables; breathtaking vista; sky-high tabs for basement-level cookery, in our opinion; the eyes—not the palate—have it here. In the same building, the Cologne-based Blatzheim interests have sponsored a quintet of caloric consumerism. It consists of (1) the **Edelweiss** (beer-hall atmosphere including an oooompah band), (2) the **Alt-Berlin** (for hometown boosters), (3) the **Europa-Bistro**, (4) the **Europa-Terrassen** (lovely in summer), and (5) the **Twenty-five** (dancing and friendly nibbles). It may seem strange, but after a trial of each, we found the entire package uniformly poor in quality and 2nd-rate in concept and décor. Any resemblance to urbane service seemed purely coincidental. In the same architectural complex, you'll find the **Jade** (with oh-so-feeble stabs at that noble Chinese cuisine), the fine little **English Pub** (for short orders), a

Danish niche (for smørrebrød), and such a multitude of bars and snackeries that they could occupy a month of sampling and fill 100 tummies the size of the *Graf Zeppelin*. The **Holland-Stübl** cooks up nutrients drawn from the traditional Dutch and Indonesian tables. The **Hardy Wine Restaurant** is a veteran from yesteryear. Limited menu but unlimited grape larder; enchanting turn-of-the-century atmosphere; go late when it zings. This one can be fun if you are with a German-speaking group. **Le Bou Bou** rates as a full-scale booboo, in our opinion. It tries to recall an earlier era with modern affectations. We found slaphappy service and larrikin attitudes. In the hotel category, the Grill of the **Kempinski** often dishes out some mighty savory viands (especially those sautéed *scampi*). In the hotel dining room do us—and yourself—a favor by ordering the heavenly Kalbfleischröllchen (tender veal niblets bathed in a Boursin cheese and whipped-spinach sauce). Even Ali MacGraw can't beat *that* for tempting calf. Incidentally, Kempinski's **"Funkturm"** is Berlin's answer to the Eiffel Tower restaurant of Paris; about 150 feet up a steel structure by elevator; magnificent view; definitely worth a visit by everyone, if only for tea or a snack. The same management has opened a second Fair Grounds establishment called **Palais am Funkturm**; mass-production service in a cavernous exhibition hall. The **Berlin Hotel**'s Grill has a mighty reputation locally, but we found the service so totally bumbling as to be downright comic. It can't be beaten for punctured pomposity, even though the rare dish might be above average. The **Four Seasons**, in the same hotel, is cheaper, less presumptuous, but not worthy of special attention. **Huthmacher** is young, crowded, and reminiscent of Schrafft's in tone; big restaurant upstairs with agreeable décor, and bakery-coffee shop downstairs; piano and violin at teatime. **Drei Bären** is coming up rapidly; now particularly well liked for its sidewalk terrace whenever the sunbeams glow. For steaks, **Heinz Holl** hits the steer's eye; flavorful filets (for Germany) on a wooden platter; chummy ambiance for its chic following of devoted patrons; only 6 tables; candles in hurricane lamps; sand-colored banquettes. Your waitress will serve you with taurine grace. The **Hong Kong**, followed by the **Lingnan**, offer the best Chinese cookery in town; neither is a rave by top U.S. standards, according to sinophiles. A merry group of local friends detoured us to the **Lung Fung** instead. Surprisingly, its management found itself short of chopsticks. The last one in the group (yours truly) was handed one solitary stick—a digital trial-by-fire which we defy even our own "Wily Oriental" colleague, Stan de la Cruz, to pull off with aplomb. Clumsily, but with fierce determination, we finally jabbed our way through a mediocre repast. **Alt Nürnberg** is about average.

Among the *Bierstuben,* the **Alt-Berliner Biersalon**, a skip and a jump from the Kempinski, is a baronial beer hall with Yorkville or Milwaukee overtones; sidewalk café; mass-production food and service, with adequate fodder for a moderate investment. Across the *damm,* just opposite, the **Berlin Palast** raises a toast with brew, vittles, live shows, big-name acts, terpsichore, and table telephones, all set in a tableau of Prussian décor. *Quick snack?* Try the ground-floor counter in the **Bilka** department store; full restaurant 1-flight up. The **"Quick"** operation has slowed to a walk; no longer recommended.

Sunny day? Drive out to a lakeside establishment called **Wannsee-Terrassen**, in the Wannsee District (25 minutes and about 24 DM each way by taxi from the center, or 1.50 DM by bus #66); heavenly, open, 3-tiered terrace on a hill, lovely panorama, and mediocre cookery at modest prices; don't miss it, despite its poor kitchen, if the weather is fair. You can have a swim at a sandy beach here, too. Another excursion point for summer is the lakefront, split-log **Blockhaus Nikolskoe** at the Havel, near the frontier. It was built for Tsar Nicholas's visit to Berlin; you can even putt-putt out by ferry in warm months, a good economy move since the taxi ride is quite expensive. Very scenic inside and out, but not as spectacular in the culinary sector. *Weinstuben?* **Habel**, near Am Roseneck is the choice, with **Koelsch** second. We've also heard good things about the **Neumann** (very well liked locally), but we've never emptied glasses here. Don't forget the previously mentioned Hardy, which is a wine house with a difference. *Cafés?* The **Caroussel**, on the boulevard side of the Kempinski, takes the honors; excellent for snacks. The nearby **Pientka** is a happy choice, for young people chiefly. The **Kranzler** is very good; from its perch you can command an excellent view of the Kurfürstendamm and Joachimstaler Strasse. The **Mozart-Terrassen**, on the corner of the K-damm and Leibnizstrasse, is a pleasant reminder of Vienna. **Das Caféhaus** (Kurfürstendamm 234) perks anew in an attractive building dating back to 1901. Large pillared room with moss-green bankettes, brass sconces, and paisley walls; back sector with greenery and more tables; delightfully robust shelves of pastries where you can feel your girth expanding as you merely shop for a goody.

Night Life A plethora. There are about 220 honest-to-no-goodness nighteries in the heart of the city alone. Counting bars and hideaways in the outlying suburbia, approximately 500 owl-ing stations swing. The entrance fees or cover charges hover between $2 and $6, roughly paralleling the cost of a Scotch-and-Soda. As in most after-dark dens, beer is cheap and champagne is hell on the budget.

Among the "In-Set" disco-hubs, the innermost clique gather at **Annabel's**, unrelated to the London shrine of nightlife that bears the same name. Smart crowd; modish music; reasonable prices. Maybe you can pry your way in if it is not a busy status-Saturday night. The very costly (keep a vigil) **Safari** would be the next campsite, followed by **Joy**, mainly for an older assemblage of café society. The **VIP** is gaining ground with young people who are VIPs only to themselves. If you don't hanker for intimacy, the **Metropol** is your spot —with a mere 43,000 square feet of floor space on which to strut your stuff. The footage is the *only* thing square about it, since it swings with about the same wild abandon as Gotham's Studio 54. You'll find a restaurant, movie, music hall, and theater all at the same Nollendorfplatz spread. Disco doin's from Wednesdays through Saturdays; special features on other nights.

The **Keese** bounces up with an intriguingly named gimmick called the "Ball Paradox." When it comes time to dance, guess? Girl picks boy! If you enjoy oddballs, you'll have one here. **Chez Romy Haaq** is currently the SRO gayest blade in town. While the show reflects deviant preferences, the audience is drawn from the general public. So popular that it is difficult to get in, especially on weekends. **Chez Nous** has 2 elaborately decorated rooms with quilted and draped walls and ceilings in the style of what might be called Louis XIV½. You'll find fancy candelabra, a gold grand piano, a bar, and—incongruously—a bright honky-tonk jukebox not quite concealed between the 2 ornate sancta. Think thrice here before reaching for the hand of that beautiful blonde, because "she" might turn out to be a blond; some of the patrons we saw were gay boys attired in exquisitely modish gowns. **Le Clou** tries to get its share of the same traffic, but we think this one should be renamed Le Clip. **Kleist Casino** (fondly labeled "K.C.") also is clad in the gayest of moods. **Wu Wu**, across the street, also woowoos you-know-whowhos. **Trocadero** comes hither with the less modish *belles* of the *belle* -bottomed populace. Incidentally, there are about 55 homosexual clubs in this city. **Big Eden** (Kurfürstendamm at Knesebeckstrasse, and not the same as the next spot we mention) is chiefly for kids; inexpensive; huge dimensions; a 400-speaker stereo unit. **New Eden Saloon** (different building) offers a glass-lined sidewalk café and a spacious interior with ultradim illumination and iron-lung ventilation; 2 midget bars; a sprinkling of B-girls; ear-rending music so raucous it chased us out before show time; intermittent melodies by a 5-piece combo (all of whom are surely deaf by now, poor fellows). Okay, if you bring your earmuffs. **Eden's Discomania** pours drinks for only $2 per quaff, turns on the music, and turns down the lights. **Eierschale** ("Eggshell"), with 2-watt lights and low-cost cokes, crawls with all kinds of characters; the Firestoners, Louisiana Hot Seven, or Spree City Stompers give with everything from Dixie to Slop; man, it jaunts and jactitates. **Coupé 77** remains one of our favorite local watering places. Interior designed as an antique railroad coach; brass lamps, polished woods, quilted leather benches; disk music only; inexpensive drinks. Toots of praise for this little caboose. **Dorett** is an okay corral for show-timing and dancing. **Cabaret** provides a fair strip that should suit some gents to a T-ease. **Big Apple** (this time not from the same paradise) is a center for the Teenie Bopper Set; hot music, cokes, beer—plus enough long hair for a complete camouflage job on the Brandenburg Gate. The **Cheetah** appeals to the avant-est of the avant-garde. A fairly expensive taxi ride from the center to its jungle lair; entrance through a looooooooong and madly painted tunnel; interior resembling a 3-dimensional atomic structure; radar dishes behind the frizzy-headed orchestra; orange toadstool lamps; multilevel pods for nonjiggers; clear-plastic cushioned chairs on lilypad platforms. Loud as sin, of course. Not our earful, but perhaps the kids will love it. The **English Pub**, in the décor you'd expect, is a more sedate station for quaffs and suds. **Chateau** draws a nice following of young people to its semicircular bar. Attractive and inexpensive. The **Hofbräu Haus**, sited near the zoo, is jammed with groups on the weekends; it was said to cater "to Turks, Arabs, and assorted cameldrivers." The **Moon** rises to modern notes only; the chords are no longer live, but on tape or waxing eloquently.

Sobering Facts: The $1,600,000 **Thermen** in the Europa Center should cure any hangover. This grandiose health haven contains a swimming pool, a sauna, Russian and Roman baths, massage parlors, a gym, a medicinal hydrotherapy salon, sun rooms, a beauty parlor, plus summer terraces and a restaurant. An all-day sweat can be had extremely reasonably; its hours are from 10 A.M. to midnight, on Sundays to 9 P.M.

Berlin has its very own **Casino** in the Europa Center rolling from 3 P.M. to 5 A.M. Roulette and blackjack are available, too. Entry is 5 DM.

Porn? Stay away from the live shows as they are often sham acts. Film theaters—myriad in number, vast in choice—charge from 6 to 10 D.M. for about as much pepper as you can take—and are *they* hot stuff. Wow!

Narcotics? We found no permanent drug scene, except perhaps the odd exchange in subway stations. Don't horse around in this league whatever you do.

Play for pay? The most popular rendezvous is now the midriff of Kurfürsten-damm, near Lehniner Platz and Uhlandstrasse. It is most heavily patronized from 11:30 P.M. onward. Mobilized *Mädchens* usually cruise along Strasse des 17 Juni. While the standard fee is about 50 marks, the unknowing visitor is often persuaded to part with a higher figure. In general, the caliber of this group is brassy, coarse, and very, very tough. Other pickups may be found in such places as the **Scotch 13**, **La Strada**, and **Mambo**. Striptease shows in all; clip practices prevailing and often perilous for visitors; B-gals housebound until dawn's early light, but free-lancers usually available RIGHT NOW. We do not advise anyone—repeat, *anyone*—to hit this sometimes-dangerous cir-cuit, so please be warned if you do.

Shopping   The prices of most commodities in West Berlin now corre-spond with those in the rest of Free Germany. In porcelains, **Staatliche Porzel-lan-Manufaktur Berlin** carries the most interesting specialties; its dinner sets are beautiful; go to the factory (Wegelystrasse 1) or salesroom (Kurfürsten-damm 205) for 25% to 50% off on 2nd and 3rd qualities. Optical goods? Wonderful **Söhnges** now has branches at Kurfürstendamm 139, Reichsstrasse 83, Forum Steglitz, and at "Europa Center"; here's a world leader. For depart-ment-store buying, it's a toss-up between Kurfürstendamm's new **Wertheim** and the more traditional **KaDeWe** ("Kaufhaus des Westens"); if you pick the latter, don't miss walking up (not riding up!) at least 3 floors; a local institution. For cutlery, **J. A. Henckels** (see *Frankfurt*) offers a branch at Kurfürsten-damm 33; Mr. Böhm is the local manager. For antiques Keithstrasse is the street, with 12 or 14 shops nearly in a row. For books, **Marga Schoeller Bücherstube** (Knesebeckstrasse 33) and **Kiepert** (Hardenbergstrasse 4-5) are attractive and versatile; you'll find scores of new U.S. titles and reprints.

Other Targets

ASSMANNHAUSEN   This is a convenient cruise stop if you're bound down the *east* bank of the Rhine. The famous old **Krone Hotel-Restaurant** (21 miles from Wiesbaden and 42 miles from Frankfurt am Main) is an en-chanting choice for lunch when sunbeams are dancing on the river. Terrace-dining on the warmer days, under a grapevine "roof"; long, paneled, inside salon with low ceilings and ancient spirits; quite expensive; red-wine specialties are Assmannshäusener and a sparkling burgundy-type called Schäumender Special Roter Cuvée; open mid-March to mid-November. There's so much flavor here that it's worth a short (but not too time-consuming) detour. On the main road beside the stream; you can't miss spotting it from your car.

AUGSBURG, home of the Rennaissance commercial leaders named Fugger, boasts the oldest socialized housing project in the world. If you're an opera lover, don't miss the open-air performances at the famous Rotes

Tor ("Red Gate"). For hotel suggestions here and nearby refer to "Romantic Road."

BADEN-BADEN splashes in with its famous Lichtentaler Allee, Roman baths and thermal ablutions. The 3-story Congress Hall, with its main-floor restaurant and flowering terrace, has been inaugurated at nearby Augusta-platz; the more youthful, jazzed-up casino with a recreational wing, spa gardens, 300-car underground garage, racetrack, and other enticements, is drawing discriminating vacationers. Its "Grand Week" of big-time horse racing (late Aug. to early Sept.) is internationally known. Enthusiastically recommended for rural resort lazing.

And one of the finest addresses in the world to put your feet up (not literally) is the **Brenner's Park**, which is a classic. Rhapsodic location in a sylvan grove with a terraced stream and fountain exchanging sweet babblings; fast and friendly service; lounge music nightly, but most clients are wrapped in the arms of Morpheus long before midnight. To woo a younger following, it has splashed up a breathtakingly attractive, classically Roman indoor swimming pool with a view of the park, a party room, and—but of course—a beauty parlor. Faithful old-timers, however, still clamor so vigorously to get in here that its management has had to establish a 3- to 4-week limit-of-stay for all guests—depending, naturally, on the length of their cure. To relieve some of the pressure, it opened the summer-only adjoining Villa Stephanie with its own dining salon and 20 superb rooms, including 4 extra-comfortable suites. World-famous for its high standards—and deservedly so. The more commercial **Europäischer Hof** is the hub of activity for the swinging affluent set. Just a toss of the dice from the Casino; charming streamside dining room; candle-light dining on weekends; revivified bar with piano lilts until after midnight; low personnel-to-client ratio. Its 60 doubles front the park; 90 singles are to the rear; all now have private bath. Alive and thriving. The faun-colored **Bellevue** has a garden setting, lovely awning-covered balconies, set-back alcoves, and a conflict of heavy Teutonic traditionalism with twentieth-century aluminum extrusions. Coolish bar, potted-palm atmosphere downstairs; 90 rooms and 72 baths; #214-215 is a choice double. Closed from November 1 to early April. This one might appeal more to European tastes than to ours. The **Badischer Hof**, owned by the Europäischer Hof people, is built as a 4-story atrium. Total of 90 attractive modern bedrooms; all units with bath and most equipped with thermal water taps. Sound, but you pay a hefty premium for that special H₂O. **Peter's Bad-Hotel Zum Hirsch** has been in the same family for more than 300 years. Busy location; part of its triangular structure spans a street that cuts an isosceles swath through the courtyard. Inviting reception area, restaurant, bar, and elevator; connecting annex comfortably renovated; Manager Brück knows his innkeeping. Many of its accommodations have private balconies and thermal water taps; all units warmed with original oil paintings; demipension not required in season. The **Atlantic**, on the Oos River (well, rivulet) offers a lovely terrace for dining; all units with rivulet-fronting balconies and a disappointing fustiness. The **Holland** has an indoor pool and exercise parlor, it renovated all its bedchambers, and generally updated itself. For golfing buffs, the lovely First-class **Waldhotel Selighof** is a linkside, chalet-style siren that effuses allure. Magnificent hill-bound, timber-lined course; private swimming pool and tennis courts; improved entrance; brightened breakfast terrace. Since comfort is in its righteous domain, top recommendation for the Sporting Set. The nearby **Golf Hotel** is a sprawling, gable-garbled, and gaunt example of typical old-fashioned resort innkeeping; the later wing is somewhat ameliorative; the indoor swimmery with jet stream, sauna, massage, plus solarium segments, and added private baths (bringing the count up to 100%), may have thawed its cool overall demeanor. Both are about 2½ miles from the center of Baden-Baden and, in their respective categories, a satisfactory Two for Tee.

When it comes to dining in this Old World enclave, the **Brenner's Park Hotel** is classified in the nation's highest gastronomic category by savvy Teutons. Richly elegant décor, not overstressed, in off-white, crystal, and gold; red and flaxen carpeting; flowers in silver vases; sweetly bucolic vistas from dining room or gardenside summer terrace; service that anticipates your slightest whim; cuisine as smooth and gentle as the attention you receive. The auditorium-size **Casino Restaurant** draws crowds in season but no plaudits from us the year around. Instead, within the same building, we prefer the **Mirabelle**, which is linked to the more popular-priced **Boulevard Terrace** as well as to the attractive **Paddock Bar**, with a pianist from 7 to midnight; downstairs is the Club Tavern disco-restaurant. **Stahlbad** (Lichtentaler Strasse 27), a 3-minute walk from the Brenner's Park, provides 2 adjoining rooms tricked out with hanging lamps, copper cake-molds, an emerald-tile fireplace, and gaily painted plates. Menu in German, but a color photo album of the selections is on hand to ease your ordering perplexities. Hard working, white-jacketed-and-capped Owner-Chef Schwank prepares most of the dishes at your tableside— such High German specialties as Sukiyaki, Risi-Bisi, and "Hollywoodsteak." For dessert, please try his half-melted sherbet served in a giant brandy snifter. Theatrical and very, very expensive—but viable and fun if the Mark is no object. The **Baden Wine Cellar** is pleasant for a sip and snack. The **Mandarin**, with both Cantonese and Peking perkings, pans out only fair Oriental fare. We suspect the chef was born a little west of the Yangtze—somewhere between Karlsruhe and Pforzheim, for example. In nearby _Herrenalb_, the **Post Hotel** is a dream. Former twelfth-century monastery; Klosterschänke Grill, with beamed braces in stone and stucco walls or arches; flowers and candles on each table; the bread is served in 2-foot-long baskets. Our consommé, smoked trout with whipped horseradish sauce, and saddle of venison washed down by local wine was a deliciously memorable repast. Not too costly, and _what_ a delight! **Schloss Neuweier** turns on a reasonably good kitchen in an atmosphere of antiquity. At _Oberbeuern_, the **Wald Hotel Fischkultur** is really a trout ranch, so you can guess at the specialty. **Burg Windeck** perches about ½-hour from Baden-Baden above the village of _Bühl_. This rebuilt castle site is a small hostelry and restaurant. Breathtaking vista from wide windows overlooking the vine-draped hills, the rilling Rhine Valley, the cobalt horizon with the peaks of the Vosges Mountains, and the frontiers of France. (That's Strasbourg twinkling in the sunlight.) Regional dishes only; delicious local wines; handsome rustic interior décor ignorable for the panorama. If you should lunch late or on a weekend, there's a fair chance you'll be joined at your table by a clutch of dumpy *Hausfrauen* in bullet hats who clutch their eternal umbrellas. These ladies will examine the entire menu, comment extensively on each item, contemplate as deeply as a Hindu guru, and finally order their "usual," a wedge of whip-creamy cake with a glass of cold water. Their gab will be incessant until sunset or moonrise. They are a sociological fact of life in many German dining rooms—the Vestal Matrons of a Bombazine Goddess. May they never perish! When the sun is glowing and so are you, try to sample the unique flavor of the Black Forest. Ride out to nearby villages in the vineyard country—preferably by any route other than the autobahn. Hamlets such as *Varnhalt* (**Hotel Katzenberger's Adler**), *Umweg* (**Boxbeutel**), and *Neuweier* (the previously mentioned **Schloss, Lamm,** or **Rebenhof**) are just a few of the many oases within a 10-mile radius of Baden-Baden. Don't miss a drive through this region—perhaps a longer excursion down to *Hinterzarten*'s captivating **Hotel Adler**, Here you will savor the peace, the silence, the majesty, and the pastoral loveliness of the romantic *Schwarzwald.*

BARGTEHEIDE   The ancient **Schloss Tremsbüttel** resides on an attractive piece of Schleswig-Holstein. Some rooms in the castle are lovely, others dowdy.

BERCHTESGADEN,   Travelers usually pause only briefly here. If you wander in, the **Geiger** will probably register the loudest beeps on your counter, even though its skillets are only mildly atomic. Our steak dinners produced sighs from contented waistlines; 70 beds available for overnighters. This town, for our money, is a brass-plated tourist trap.

BONN,   possibly Europe's least exciting capital, now stretches out into several suburban hamlets. Its population was more than doubled by its absorption of 10 adjoining communities, pushing up the headcount to 300-thousand. It boasts Poppelsdorf Palace, the Rhenish Land Museum, the versatile Zoological Research Institute and Museum, and Beethoven as its most famous son—but the streets (on which $150,000,000 are finally being spent) are a rat race. Such a frenetic and impersonal atmosphere pervades that we'll take central Detroit anytime. An incredible number of cars jam its streets en route to other destinations; 36 times per day, 3 railway crossings halt traffic for an average of 20 minutes each hour. (To relieve this maddening congestion a *2nd* bridge across the Rhine is now operative, thank goodness); 36 thousand vehicles per day funnel through and clog the Koblenzer Gate along the main north-south link between Cologne and Coblenz. And if this isn't enough, rain falls on its unfortunate inhabitants 162 days per year! Acknowledging that some visitors may want (or have) to stay here, the Steigenberger hotel chain (Frankfurter Hof and a peck of others) opened its sleeping factory in the aggressively ugly City Center—a crassful, classless urban subdivision which reflects far more haste than taste. Although the massive **Steigenberger** functions as an efficient institution, it performs with so little inspiration that it was a letdown to us. Passably interesting vista from the 18th-floor Ambassador Restaurant (where the window tables are usually reserved for diplomats); adjoining bar and **neighboring swimming** pool; Atrium Coffee Shop a tepid and listless decorative blend; a megalopolis of boutiques, kiosks, and service facilities skirting the ground level. Spacious studio singles—a trademark of German hostelries where the solitary executive roams interminably in homeless tangents; light, well-furnished, mod-school doubles, especially roomy in the corner accommodations; the twins ending in "23" are best. While nothing is overtly offensive here, our impression is one of consuming boredom. The **Königshof**, more traditional in tone, shoulders the riverbank. Adequate shelter and no more. The midvillage **Stern** is sternly cold. The midtown **Schlosspark** is small and clean; it boasts a swimming pool that might be described in the same way. In the diplomatic enclave of *Bad Godesberg*, a mile or so along "Embassy Row," the **Rheinhotel Dreesen** has a beautiful riverscape command but a lead-heavy air. The redecorated **Rheinland** offers 50 bedrooms with private bath; another routine hatrack. The **Eden** is fair, but the 80-room-and-bath **Arera** is choicer. The **Parkhotel Zum Kurfürsten**, at *Frankenthal* on the Bonn–Strasbourg highway, got high but well-spent marks from an Austrian reader who raves about its "food, service, and exceptional standards." For additional Bonn-*mots,* please look to our remarks on nearby Cologne—to our palate, a sweeter bonbon any day or night. At *Königswinter*, the modest, town-owned **Düsseldorfer Hof** is open the calendar round. Director Dieter Schäfer knows his *Hofs.*

Im Alten Hut (Meckenheimer Strasse 27) is generally considered to be Bonn's leading restaurant. Plenty of atmosphere; medium-expensive; evenings only; closed Sunday. The **Hansa am Kaiserplatz** (Kaiserplatz 18) is our 2nd choice; international cuisine; not very special. **Salvator** (Sürststrasse) wins the beer mug for typical German fare. **Em Höttche** is headed by a brewery. Main square situation with main-line cookery. The viewful salon aloft the **Steigenberger Hotel** in the Bonn Center can be fun when it offers one of its frequent "gastronomic weeks." Otherwise it's pretty routine. **Am Tulpenfeld**, nearby, seemed better for day-in-night-out cookery. In neighboring *Bad Godesberg*, **Maternus** is the popular and cost-be-damned rendezvous of the diplomatic set. Very worthy, if price is neither object nor objection.

After dark, most night owls fly to **Eve**. Brass stools; electrified "kerosene" lamps; copper dance floor; an ancient bicycle hanging from the ceiling; these and other curios form the décor. Supper available, recorded music only. You won't weep if you miss it. The **Carlton** is another one that doesn't turn us on. Why not drop in at the **Steigenberger Hotel** for a nip or drive over to Cologne if insomnia strikes and if there's an itch that *really* needs scratching?

BREMEN,   the 2nd-largest seaport, is a typical *Hanse* (medieval merchants' union) city. Fine Ratskeller, marketplace, golf course, 600-year-old City Hall statue of Roland, and a rather gnu zoo, and the tavern-studded Schnoor district for sipping, shopping, or browsing.

If you've got wheels and want to drive to your hotel, the **Park** is majestically situated on 500 acres of Hanseatic real estate, fronted by a small lake and backed by a prairie-size lawn. Just 5 minutes from the station, but celestially quiet; 100 rooms and a trio of suites on the Paul Bunyan scale; dancing nightly in the Halali Bar; the thinking is so lavish there's even a special alfresco "Hund Bar" to furnish tidbits to your dogs. Unquestionably the leader, and a beautiful one. Next, the **Crest** probably offers the most comfort. The drawback here, however, is that it is out of the city heartbeat, so once again a car would be required. **Columbus**, in a century-old shell, offers an appealing lobby plus a few updatings; 170 tiny units with 110 baths; 2 restaurants and bar; very commercial; The next-door **Zur Post**, darker than its neighbor, is adequate but nothing more. **Overseas**, in the same category, is smack in the center and oh-so-noisy. The latter rents many accommodations with 3 beds; mostly for families or the *ménage à trois*.

Diners often like the **Essig Haus**, with its venerable Hanseatic woodwork; ownership by the Parkhotel. **Schnoor 2**, which takes its name from its address, is extremely well regarded by Bremen-and-women; 400-year-old gabled house in snazzy rustic tones; certainly tops in eye appeal, with cookery just a chef's pinch less savory than Essig Haus. **Belgrad**, a skip away at Schnoor 12, specializes in gypsy music and atmosphere; open for lunch and then until 2 A.M. The **Balkan Grill**, at Am Herzogenkamp 32, in the suburb of *Horn*, repeats the same kitchen, the same hours, the same music, the same ambiance —and, oh yes, the same management. Also take a peek or a nibble at the historic and good **Ratskeller**, where the Faust legend is said to have been originated centuries ago. The **Alt-Bremen**, recalling the city from 1750 to 1850, sounds touristy, but it could be fun. Too much bustle and commerce in this metropolis for truly comfortable dining leisure.

BREMERHAVEN, 45 miles north, offers the **Nordsee** with 85 rooms and nearly a full bath count. Stark lobby in functional simplicity; cheerful breakfast quarter filled with greenery; men's bar; large clean doubles. A better-than-average buy for skippers who dock at eventide. **Naber**, a cut lower, comes up with rou-teeny roomery. The less-attractive **Metropole** completes the roundup.

CELLE Refer to "Hanover."

COBLENZ The best of a modest lot is the **Hohenstaufen** for overnighting.

COCHEM The **Alte Thorschenke** is a sweet little inn by the river with an excellent wine restaurant. The **Germania** offers a grander atmosphere and the **Brixiade** is more modernistic. Pick your room carefully in this town if you are a light sleeper. Road traffic can raise a horrendous din.

COLOGNE's modern midtown towers contrast dramatically with its beautifully preserved Cathedral, a magnificent structure, the largest Gothic building in the world. The big draws otherwise are the stunning theater-opera house, the playhouse, the Roman Germanistic Museum surrounding the Dionysus Mosaic, plus a splendid gem display, and Phantasialand, the local answer to the Disney realms. Inquire at the city's Tourist Office about the "Meet-the-People Teas" (5 P.M., except Sat., Sun., and holidays), which are opening many homes to foreign visitors. Tickets for this hospitality service, plus free eau de Cologne (the real thing), city guides, maps, and color slides, are also available at the Hotel Excelsior Ernst, a 2-minute skip from the tourist headquarters.

The City's foremost address for overnighting, by the way, is the stately and famous **Excelsior Ernst**, facing the Cathedral square. Continual updating campaigns; appealing polished-wood, oh-so-richly elegant Hanse Stuben grill, one of the nicest rooms in all Germany; lobby also in Hanseatic tones; every bedchamber refashioned. Antebellum décor; cozy twins and nice apartments; frenetic atmosphere; on the commercial side, but smoothly managed. Concierge Brehm is the perfect man to answer 4711 of your Cologne questions. An aristocratic contender. Pan-Am's **Intercontinental** globespanner has established itself as the local leader for modernists. Wood-pillared lobby glowing with globe lamps and cushy accoutrements; savvy front-desk team; ground-floor Brasserie and Interview Imbibery dispensing succulent Thüringer sausage and potent martinis, respectively and respectfully; vistaful rooftop Belvedere Restaurant and Bar with terpsichore on tap; pool, solarium, sun terrace, and sizzling sauna; bevy of boutiques; subterranean parking quarters. Recommendable.

The **Dom**, Dom-inated by hardworking Proprietor-Director Edgar Lührs, remains one of the better traditional hostelries in the region. In this traffic-occluded town, its 650-car underground garage, with direct entry to the hotel, comes as a blessing to anyone on wheels. Cheery restaurant; pleasant summer terrace; spacious accommodations, all with radio; TV on request; excellent direct-dial telephone installation; corner-sited #105, #206, and #306 pick of the litter. Excellent location but cool-natured staff. The **Mondial** caters especially to motorists and tour groups. Ground-floor garage topped by 150 units, each with bath and shower; some larger quarters available; overall functionality, but rates rather steep for the high level of chill. The **Senats-Hotel**, in a noisy location, boasts 70 fully carpeted rooms with floor-to-ceiling windows, 70 baths with curtain partitions, a dining room, and simple amenities. The **Europa** would be a decent hole-up if only someone would read the riot act to at least ½ of its personnel. The **Ramada** is located out at the industrial community of *Leverkusen*; the plant is fine but unless business required that we locate out here we'd prefer to be in Cologne. **Atlantic**, associated with the Europa, serves breakfast only; its sister relationship is enough to make us fly its coop. **Breslauer Hof**, near the station, is a diminutive little dandy. **Berlin** is not recommended. The **Adria**, at Hohe Pforte (which you might never find) in the midtown area, is a satisfactory economy stop. Modern, but so tight in dimensions you'll feel more snug than a knackwurst in a frankfurter roll. The **Regent** is too far into the outskirts to bother about. The **Crest** is out there, too; motorists are its bag.

When mealtime strikes, the Hanse Stuben in the **Excelsior Ernst** is easily our choice as the most elegant spot. The cuisine more than matches the glorious setting. Among the independents, **Die Bastei** is so spectacular it shouldn't be missed. Elevated, glassed-in, ¾-circle building jutting out almost into the waters of the Rhine; split-level dining; French, Belgian, Swiss, Austrian, and German specialties, all identified on the menu by national license-plate markings ("CH" for Switzerland, etc.); tea music through the gloaming, dinner chords from 7:30 P.M. to 10 P.M., and dance melodies thereafter; vastly improved service and culinations on our latest foray; steep tariffs. A must for its revitalized skilletry, unusual architecture, and striking Rhine view.

Wolff's Wine House, in a less glamorous urban location; is as strong on cuisine but weaker on vista. Uninteresting, windowless composite of 2 poorly ventilated rooms. Peppy service (when it finally comes!); menu in German only. **Le Pot-Flambé,** to go into reverse again, is better for eye appeal than for palate satisfaction. Entrance enhanced by a wooden-trough cattle-fountain; barn décor with sausage-hung wooden beams, Swiss farmhouse lanterns, red napery, and drip-draped waxed bottles for candle illumination; wine served in crockery drinking pitchers. Highly embroidered busboys; zither-plucked melodies; food heavily seasoned and undistinguished. The **Schweizer Stube** brews up a similar ambiance and very little Swiss bliss from the kitchen. The twin-room **Balkan Grill,** one link in a chain, comes up with a superior brand of national cookery. Trout tank at entrance; wood paneling; brass chandelier; Adriatic patterns on linens; generally informal air. Our Grill-Teller (composed of Cevapcici, Raznijici, and other native meats) and our partner's Djuwetsch (pork with paprika, rice, onions, tomatoes, and herbs) were very good indeed, and the portions were piled almost as high as a Dinaric Alp; other novel touches were the Balkan salad and the Yugoslavian red wine. Surprisingly inexpensive; recommended. **Weinhaus im Walfisch,** the choice of many U.S. service families, offers 2 floors and tavernish, 2-fisted cookery. Built in 1750, it has been a restaurant continuously since 1837. For local color, the **Früh** (to the rear of the Dom-Hotel) or the **Päffgen** couldn't be more characteristic; waiters in dark-blue shirts; no tablecloths, no fripperies; crowded with _Herren_ and _Hausfrauen_ drinking wine or special Cologne beer, and gossiping like mad; go to either for a sausage, a beer, and to watch the locals unwind. **Im Hahnen** is a slightly more refined version of this ilk. **Alt Köln,** next to the Excelsior Ernst, slaps on Old Cologne in 4711 predictable ways. Aromatic of spit-roasted bantams; fun if your tastes run to corny; poor service; chicken-feed prices. A mixed grill. (On the other flank of the same hostelry, you'll find an American-bred **McDonald**'s.) **Treppchen** ("Little Staircase") of the Hotel Europa is a charming wine cellar for sipping and snacks; music but no dancing; closed Wednesday; late afternoon or evening only; not quite up to its former glories. These are the best in their respective leagues, in our opinion. Travelwise friend Kurt Luhn sends us words of praise for the outskirting **Gaststätte Marienbild.** His observations are so keen that we pass this entry along to you unhesitatingly. We're anxious to try it, too. A resident of this city, moreover, now advises us that we have committed a sin of omission by failing to list an inn called **Altenberger Hof,** east of town in the Bergischer hills. We'd never heard of it or even of the "famous Altenberger Dom" which it apparently faces. So live and learn. Out at _Köln-Mergeim_ the **Golderner Pflug** is said to whip up commendable French cuisine in a private house. More for evening than for midday.

Cologne's leading nightspot for the young executive set is **Big Ben**—at this point in time, that is. **Love Story** also tells a similar tale. For lone males, **Kokett** takes a cupcake. Intimate as the inside of a Turk's tent; draped walls; mirrored panels; drumhead dance pad. Sex-elating strips and good whiskey. **Chez Nous** offers _vous_ about 12 tables backed by a tiny bar, short "shows" every 20 minutes, shorter but untampered-with libations, and comparatively bundled-up B-girls. Okay for snorting, but not for serious cavorting. **Goldener**

Spiegel reflects a boudoir mood. Tiny bar at entrance; larger one farther back; candlelight and frilly wrought-ironwork; well-wrought bar girls who were not predatory on our swing; smooth trio for dancing; snuggling in the Frenchy booths at the periphery. In the same neighborhood, nighthawks can also wing in at **Westminster**. **Play Boy**, **Black Horse** and **P-7** spin for discothèque-niks.

CONSTANCE The comfortable, cloistered **Insel** is a former monastery; it is highly recommendable. So is the **Bayerischer Hof** at the nearby island resort of *Lindau*.

DUISBURG The town proudly lends its name to the 135-room **Duisburger Hof** where each unit has built-in personality, a large bath, king-size beds, and flawless service. This one is a link in the lengthening Steigenberger chain.

DÜSSELDORF is Germany's center of *haute couture;* beautiful clothes (on beautiful mannequins). It is also one of the world's more expensive cities. The main street, called "Kö," runs along a lovely waterway; many hotels; good restaurants, Benrath Castle, scads of churches and art galleries, a modern 4-story apartment-style bordello with 228 "tenants" and 8000 "visitors" a day, cosmopolitan citizens, and handsome environs, one of which includes the $5,000,000 Minidomm, elf-size scaledowns of world-famous architectural wonders from Gothic cathedrals to Kennedy Airport (open daily from 9 A.M. to 11 P.M.; between Düsseldorf and Mülheim). Both the **Hilton** and the **Intercontinental** open their shiny portals in an outskirting commercial subdivision. Due to their remoteness, we'll evaluate these ultracontemporary houses at the end of this roundup. For traditionalists—as opposed to modernists—nothing in the city proper can beat the totally refreshed **Breidenbacher Hof**, a classic that is smoothly run by Renate Linsenmeyer. This one, from cellar to roof, is a little jewel. Elegant reception and lobby salon; bar-lounge with wood paneling, black leather and pastoral paintings; marvelous, cozy Eck ("corner") restaurant in Art Deco, with beaded lamps, salmon textiles, iced-glass partitions, and imaginative selections on a small menu. Fine concierge and staff; grill-lounge as easy on the optic nerves as it is on the tummy, with VSOP cognac walls and fine Italian mahogany furniture; quartet of gorgeous suites; many little touches so many German houses lack. The **Park-Hotel** has a lobby that's usually achatter with businessmen; dining room enriched with wood carvings; Étoile Bar. All bedrooms with adequate furnishings, full carpeting and good baths; streetside units just soundproofed. Coolish, but eminently satisfactory. The **Savoy** is First-class rather than Deluxe. Restaurant with adjoining bar; all 95 units on the small side except for a few corner doubles with wraparound windows and ample space. Stereotyped. The **Esplanade** is in the same category and under the Savoy banner. Quieter situation; similar to the Savoy in most aspects of its insti-Teutonic atmosphere; heated indoor swimming pool available to guests at no extra charge (a privilege shared by the next-door **Atlantik**, which is lower priced and might be a worthy bet for budgeteers); sauna (supplement added); woody restaurant-cum-grill; grandmotherly breakfast quarter. As solid as a Deutsche Mark, but just about as passionless to the touch. The **Börsen**, a breakfast-only hostelry, is in the same chain; it employs the same decorator, but it thrills us even less. The **Eden** flowers with 90 small but fresh-faced pods, and 70 private baths. We are especially fond of #264, a corner double with roco-collaborations. The **Uebachs** attracts an older clientele of loyal German wayfarers. We like its overall feeling of cleanliness and puffy-pillow snap.

Now for our outlying stalwarts: The 12-story, 383-room, fully air-conditioned **Hilton** took root adjacent to the Congress Hall. Expansive off-lobby shopping gallery; sauna; health center; beauty parlor; swimming pool; thumpingly expensive turn-of-the-century San Francisco Restaurant; coffee shop; 1890 Night Club in burgundy velvet, happily a-jiggle with luscious costumed hostesses; inviting Düssel Bar for quiet libations; bedchambers poured from the familiar cookie mold; typically narrowlined baths. A carnival tone but passable.

The neighboring **Intercontinental** discloses cleverly conceived public rooms highlighting an Old Rhenish motif in the ground-floor dining and sipping segments; ultimate finesse reflected in the penthouse Belle Epoque restaurant and bar, where the cost of its Champagne Dinner, a special feature, was enough to levitate our own roof; fanciful appointments which to us sputter disappointingly; expensively outfitted accommodations; more space than is at the Hilton, but not employed to its best advantage; excellent concierge; snail-pace room service. It has basically the same upper-level tariffs and structural facilities as its peer, but we don't find it quite as appealing in our overall estimate. Perhaps you'll disagree.

Ramada now has joined the fray with a muscular entry across the river from the city. Taverny public rooms; English country-life feeling which provides a dark nesting quality; bed-roosts rather compact; medium price range. The nearby **Penta** has similar tariffs, but overall we find it cool and institutional. Its leading features include the restaurant and bar as well as the pool and sauna.

Further out, the **Schloss Hotel Hugenpoet**, a 25-minute ride along the pike to Essen, dates back to before the fifteenth century. Local citizens venture here for weekend repasts, wedding parties, and strolls around its historic frog ponds. Only 25 antique rooms, most with private bath; #28, a single, featuring a 300-year-old bed; #27, the bridal chamber, boasting newer springs and a softer mattress (thank heavens!); spooky corridors. We enjoyed our meal in the ancient castle dining hall. Out at the airport, the **Wartburg** will shelter you in perfunctory fashion if you are fogged in. We hear that the **Park** in the suburban town of *Witten* is new and appealing, but we haven't had a chance to test it personally as yet.

Now let's enjoy some table talk. The Eck in the **Breidenbacher Hof** would be our choice for any daytime meal, while the grill is nicer for evening. The **Hilton**'s San Francisco Room impresses us as offering more show than value. The neighboring **Intercontinental** leans (natch) to continental cuisine at its penthouse restaurant. Again, costly for the rewards. Among the independents, the prize easily goes to the wickedly cost-be-damned **Orangerie**, with red textile walls, candle sconces, mirrored coach lamps and orchard color intonations. Only the host receives the prices on his menu, so if you notice a transfixed glaze on his eyes and the beginnings of paralysis setting in, you'll know why.

Perfect service; superb French cuisine; very stylish, but oh those tabs! Next in the fleet comes **Bateau Ivre** ("Tipsy Ship"), at Kurzestrasse ii, in the Old Town—a 5-minute swagger from the Breidenbacher Hof. Gangway entrance; Maritime Bar; impressive nautical interior with polished-wood bulkheads, portholes, riveted supports, canvas and lapstreak topsides, carpeted deck, a brass binnacle, a telescope, and a holdful of salty lore; gob-ishly overworked but seaworthy waiters in navy-and-orange middy blouses; leather seats; candlescent tones. Reserve well in advance. Closed Sunday. **Walliser Stuben**, centrally located, struck us as gimmicky and lethally expensive for the return in nutrients. Doorway bar leading to 3 chalet-style rooms; split-timber and stucco walls; Blue Ox cowbells; alcohol lamplighting; enormous 12-page menu and rather poor wine card. **Zum Schiffchen** is the Real McCoy for local flavor; big regional menu; no tablecloths; home town beer a feature; simple, inexpensive, unelaborate, and a good value for budgeteers. The Düsseldorf water table is such that historically this city has never had a cellar restaurant *("Ratskeller");* this is the closest thing to it here. Back in the Old City, the **Schneider-Wibbel-Stuben** is a sound up-one-flight operation for fish specialties, sausages, and beer. **Zum Kurfürst**'s cookery impressed us not. **"M & F"** is large, bustling, noisy—a beehive of upper-bracket office people and toilers-in-a-hurry; not for the tranquil or peace loving. **Schnellenburg**, about 15 minutes from the center, sprawls handsomely on the bank of the Rhine; modern, country-inn atmosphere; watch the boats putt-putt by as you sit on its terrace; the cuisine would be tops if the chef would use his herb-shelf more liberally. A delight, *if* you pick your weather.

Düsseldorf's more finely feathered night owls generally alight, become a-lit, and trip a light-fantastic evening at the **Breidenbacher Hof** where the redoubtable **Régine** has established a nicely polished foothold. This is followed by the **Hilton's** 1890 Club. Slightly older fowl and slower of wing usually perch at the Belle Epoque of the **Intercontinental**. The migrations of additional afterdark revelers have their choice of about 50 so-called dancing-bars—small drop-ins with glib bar girls who pour the drinks (often from tampered stocks), hostesses who cannot leave before 5 A.M., dim lights, postage-stamp dance floors, and music of sorts. Their vogue changes from year to year. **Salome** and **Queen**, jointly owned, specialize in luscious dehydrated B-girls, elegant dimness, and white-hot price tags. Be careful. Disco-haunts include the **Barcelona** (a Wild West saloon ambiance, plus a loooong bar), the **Lord Nelson** (nautical rig; snacks and light meals from the galley), and the **Big Apple** (youthful and green). **Rio-Rita** is on the comeback trail—but there's still a long, long trail a-winding. **Kokette** is small, *intime,* slick, and coquettish; sexy loners on a lily-pad stage; whisky crudely cut—and at a surgeon's billing per slice; teeming with attractive yum-yums. **Klamotte** is replete with baubles, bangles, and beady-eyed babes. A rough spot. We'd prefer to court those same kicks with **Erotica**—that is, if we'd already finished reading the last issue of the *Plumbers' Quarterly.* **Klein Paris** would serve almost the same function. **Black Bottom** is for dancing; bottom drawer, in our opinion. **Das Kommödchen** is amusing for topical humor, all of it in German, *natürlich.* **Fatty's Atelier** is deep, narrow, and lamplit; fun for a sip, but nothing more. **Charley's**, the **Old Fashioned**, and **Bonbonnière** are bars within an olive's throw of each other;

all are respectable *if* you respect their normal quota of sucker tactics and other perils. **New Orleans** (for dancing) and **Der Pferdestall** (for nuzzling) are both owned by the stylish, high-quality Bateau Ivre; they are okay. The niches along Hunsrückstrasse near the corner of Bolkerstrasse are mostly for late late libations and sweepup operations after the evening is spent—and so are you.

ESSEN   is a railroad hub, an iron and steel community, a virtual Krupp fief. It is also the home of a well-stocked art museum, and it borders Gruga Park, the so-called Garden Spot of the Ruhr. The good burghers of this thriving center have built flower-lined pedestrian malls, spread out carpets of attractive urban esplanades dotted with trees, and sprinkled glass façades everywhere to reflect the remnants of proud medieval steeples and gables. Still not for the everyday tourist, but highly engaging and improving year by year.

ETTLINGEN   The handsomely sophisticated **Erbprinz** is worthy as a lunch stop or for overnight on the route between Frankfurt and Munich.

FRANKFURT AM MAIN   is pretty impersonal—except for the beauty of the Römer and the fun to be had sipping *appelwoi* (apple wine) in the colorful taverns of Sachsenhausen, the most ancient district of this modern metropolis. Overall you might not like it as much as other cities (it has never been a particular favorite of tourists). But it is the transportation hub, the banking center, the leading Trade Fair center, and the home of one of Europe's busiest jumbo jetports—so there's a good chance you'll spend at least one night in this bustling hive of 700-thousand. One dazzler is a rotating restaurant perched 332 feet up the world's tallest silo. Another is its 1085-foot TV tower, the highest building in the Federal Republic; it also sports a revolving dining platform. A third is the Opera House. Theater, concerts, Goethe's house, outstanding zoo, a full range of hotels, fine restaurants, tempting shopping, a "Welcome Service" for motorists, a host-and-hostess fillip for bewildered sightseers. The Rhine Main airport terminus is replete with the latest facilities and trimmings. Escalators convey passengers to platforms for trains which whisk them to the Central Station in 11 minutes.

Hotels   But while this city is one of Germany's key spots for visitors, its hotels are geared for the commercial traveler rather than the tourist. (The Schlosshotel Kronberg is a notable exception; see further along, please.) In this strongbox of more than 1000 banks, 80% of its transients are on missions of commerce, and the remaining 20% are merely changing planes or waiting to go elsewhere. As a result, you're more likely to find a cool, businesslike approach than a warm welcome. Also, during busy periods, it is common Frankfurt practice to overbook, even when reservations are confirmed and the bills prepaid. Reception personnel, moreover, have the infuriating gall to confess receipt of the advanced money which they will return to the supplicant, while at the same time bumping him from the registry and not offering to help locate substitute accommodation. Readers—especially conventioneers—have sent us properly outraged bleats concerning chiefly the Intercontinental and the Plaza for this particular offense, but anyone would be naive to think it stops at these two portals alone.

Our personal choice for overnighting is the **Frankfurter Hof**, which has been gladdened and spiffed and polished from portal to portal. The keen new manager, tall and personable Fred Eggert, has done almost all that is possible to create an atmosphere of robust vigor. Old Frankfurt cellar restaurant (called the "Stubb") with vaulted ceilings. Charming Restaurant Français in Empire II and rich emerald tones; spacious wicker-and-wood Grill with iron firebacks; Apéritif Bar, with squat leather easy chairs; handsome Lipizzaner Bar which may undergo further updatings soon; cuisine in every segment distinctive and rewarding. Bedchambers now with hush-the-traffic windows; good parking facilities; color TV. Service attitudes professional and cordial yet often rushed. Still a busy-busy-busy beehive, but very fine indeed.

The **Hessischer Hof** is smaller, more sedate, and less colorful. Mixture of older and newer rooms in varying segments; so-so service; thoroughfare situation, with extra-ply windows to shut out the noises. Cellar bar for romantic couples; zestless dining room; tiny summer café; winter garden with sliding roof; bedchambers roomy and uncozy, with ample closet space; large baths. Now quite recommendable.

The air-conditioned, 21-story **Intercontinental** commands an ideal site beside the Main River. On an adjoining plot, there's a newer 20-floor, 300-unit annex; this addition—connected to its alma mater by a tunnel and an escalator—jostles the overall room count up to more than 800 accommodations with exactly the same narrow dimensions and routine décor; it also boasts a swimming pool. The refashioned Rôtisserie is richly garbed in wood and brocade. The ground-level bar and breakfast room have been re-formed amiably. A Wine Room, off the Brasserie, is a novel cup. The annex restaurant and shops are going full steam ahead under the direction of Guy Frey. An institution, but a good one.

The **Gravenbruch Kempinski** has been a charmingly cozy nook which is expanding grandly into a 350-room hostelry through a $16-million building spree. Two-story pavilions, tennis courts, and swimming pools have been introduced, but Manager Gunter Haug protests that every effort is being made to maintain its former mandate on tranquillity. A tavern, grill, and dining room are all-new creations; bedchambers vary widely in style, but most are outfitted with traditional English furnishings. One mild disadvantage is that it is located 15 minutes from the heart of the city—a short hop from the airport and only a few seconds off the north-south autobahn intersection called Frankfurter Kreuz (a handy pull-off for motorists). Pleasant man-made lakeside site; ground-floor units with direct access to the gardens; 2nd-floor duos with balconies. An excellent choice for wheelborne families, especially if it lives up to its promises for preserving the peace.

The towering, glassy **Plaza** is located across from the Messe (fair grounds); hence, it is a major asset to exhibitors. Canadian Pacific is the host; luxury is the category (but we'd guess you'd never know it); service is almost as appalling as the shockingly low level of house maintenance—and at prices that crack the whip at more than $90 per night! On top of these unforgiveable sins, the bedroom design loses sight of the fact that some travelers may arrive with luggage and may wish to distribute their contents into generous drawer space. Woeful is our personal reaction overall.

The 2-part **Park** greets guests with a handsome entrance; dining room ideal for business tête-à-têtes; superb cuisine and overall service standards; late-model glass-and-stone wing in linear form; every fresh unit with private bath or shower; currently so popular that the reception desk turns away as many as 30 or 40 potential clients a day. Agreeable, but not luxurious. The **Savoy** is a bright addition with lots of hospitality fixin's: Sauna, pool, open grill, attractive bar, nightclub, and restaurant, plus the able direction of Ernst Bloemers. For its moderate tabs, very sound, even if the living space is limited.

The **Airport Hotel**, with 350 units, is backed by the Steigenberger people (owners of the Frankfurter Hof). The hospital-modern, 10-story, Y-shape structure jets in with a full bath count, air conditioning, soundproofing, a large pool under a glass dome for all-season splashing, a sauna, a nightclub, a coffee shop, and a country-club grill plus a conventional restaurant. Exceptionally well done for its particular type. The 9-story, S-shape, air-conditioned, 560-room **Sheraton**, even closer to the terminal, is linked to it by a pedestrian bridge. There are a pool, a sauna, 3 restaurants, the Red Baron nightery, parking for 7000 (sic) cars, a subway station beneath you (10 minutes to town) and a first-rate concierge in dynamic Eric Plant. Cool, big, but efficient. A 312-pit **Esso** station is here as well as 2 **Holiday Inns** (the Frankfurt entry is country-kilometers better than the one out in the boonies of Sulzbach); America has exported a **Ramada** to the airport district, and a reasonably nice commercial house called the **Arabella** resides in the industrial suburb of **Niederrad**.

Next is the peaceful, well-run **National**. Manager Steier is as easygoing—yet as efficient—as the domain he commands. Pleasant restaurant; bedchambers modernized in a thoughtful way; most suitable for the maturer wayfarer.

The **Baseler Hof**, the **Hamburger Hof**, and the **Savigny** are off our list.

The 95-room **Monopol-Metropole**, hard by the station and in the Excelsior roundhouse, has been chugging along at a sprightly clip—and its carloads of improvements show. The **Excelsior** has been busy gulping down its charm pills; trouble is, they haven't worked.

The **Continental** is pretty good in a traditional mood. The **Savoy** is more modern in tone and is equally pleasing, depending on your taste. The **Wiesbaden** is fair in a modest way.

The little **Hotel am Zoo** (across from the Zoo garden) is clean, bright, and okay for small-boned travelers; somewhat expensive. **Württemberger Hof**, with 16 added singles and baths, is less costly, but less comfortable; students might like it. **Haus Marina** offers 27 rooms with small bathrooms; breakfast only; quiet situation and good-humored ambiance; not bad for the price if some much needed retouchings are effected soon. In the meantime, the **Diana**, in the same league, might be a cozier nest. The **West End** and the **Hübner** also are pleasant tykes. The **Luxor** and the **Jaguar** are contenders in Second-class; the latter seems to have more spring to its gait. The **Westfälinger Hof** is chiefly for the merchant trade; the back rooms are quieter. The **Palace**, **Rex**, and **Gloria**, also in this category, are commercial, commercial—oo-la-la, are they commercial; no place for Guidesters, in our opinion.

For limousine motorists and golfers, the **Schlosshotel Kronberg** is a knock-out on the Carriage Trade Circuit. It's 10 miles (about 25 minutes) from the center of Frankfurt at *Kronberg*, seat of the Hesse Empire and the baronial headquarters of the proprietor, the Prince of Hesse. (His ancestors once conquered Frankfurt.) After its recent fortune-consuming restoration and expansion, the Schloss is better than ever before—a dream come true, managed with professional élan by Klaus' Fischer. (Avoid the top floor if you hanker for antiquity.) This original Tudor castle of Empress Friedrich III, the eldest daughter of Queen Victoria, still retains its grand terrace, its priceless tapestries, its art masterpieces (Titian and Holbein paintings in the dining room), and its beautiful furnishings which so deftly have been combined with up-to-the-minute amenities. Strange as it may seem, prices are lower here than at the top-line institutional hotels in the city, offsetting to a degree the cost of taxi links to town. Exquisite—a heritage preserved. The nearby **Viktoria** is a less expensive carpark for buckboarders seeking a Kronberg address but simpler shelter. Total of 30 starkly modern, unadorned bedchambers; golfing privileges, so duffers can dig their divots with the Kronberg Klan. Fair for the fairways, but only so-so at the 19th hole. **Kurhotel Sonnenhof** is at nearby **Könegstein**, a fine home with a swimming pool, large viewful lounges, and traditional furnishings both in the main house and in the newer wing. Of its 2 excellent restaurants, we are fondest of one with cream-colored wood panels inset with Delft platters, pewterware, and chandeliers suspended from a coffered ceiling. Prices are moderate considering the rewards of space and tranquillity. Perfect for families with a car.

Restaurants　For color and atmosphere mellowed by centuries of time, dozens of candles, and the music of accordion, guitar, and violin, the **Brückenkeller** (Schützenstrasse 6) is fun. Every stop on the console has been pulled to romanticize this medieval-type cellar with its fine arched ceilings; 20 tables banked in 3 tiers; large, elaborately carved wine barrel; harried service of good-but-not-great food. An entertaining evening and an enriching experience for 2 might total $60—and it would be worth every pfennig. **Adolff** (Hochstrasse 27) is tiny, select, and thunderingly expensive; nevertheless the cuisine is memorable. Paisley wall coverings; a halfdozen tables mainly set in booths; refinement is the keynote of its portly chef-patron who sells his fine wares at about $17 per main dish. Petit and pleasant.

Now, why not cross the river and go over to the old quarter of **Sachsenhausen**, where the **apple wine taverns** offer their special flavor and revelry? There are many scattered around, so the custom is to roam from one to another taking small dishes at each. Our favorite is **Klaane Sachsehäuser** (Neuerwall 11), where our party delighted in the Schneegestöber ("snow flurry") of camembert-like cheese mixed with chopped onion, and the Ripchen, a smoked pork chop. Community tables; singing as the mood commands; lots of laughter and jovial fraternizing. But more on this further along. (We included this one here just to tease your appetite with the unconventional.)

Börsen Keller, across from the stock market ("börse") could be considered Frankfurt's nearest equivalent of a *rathauskeller,* as local food writers boast —and with justifiable pride. Low brick arches, cleverly partitioned sectors, soft lighting, cordial and genteel service of regional preparations. Worth a visit. **Walliser Stuben**, in the underpass at Theater Platz 2, is dark, woody, and very agreeable once you are inside. The rough walls and textiles of the Valais evoke a cozy Swiss charm. The Helvetian food is straightforward and good. **Erno's Bistro** (Liebigstr. 15) is a highly appreciated French contender with gastronomic tendencies toward *nouvelle cuisine*. **Heyland** (Kaiserhofstr. 7) mixes game (in season) with its commendable catch of sea fare. Several small rooms are linked by traditional taste, Old World décor, a cheerful patronage, and gustatory flavor. Very central and useful. **Gastronomie da Claudio** (Zum Jurgenstr. 10) is excellent for Italian pannings, but it's about 10 minutes by taxi from the center. Two simple sancta; raffia lamps; choice chiantis; exceptional pasta. *Buono!* The **Mövenpick** (Opernplatz 2) continues to sizzle as the hottest skillet among local socialites—with tariffs to match. Cuddlesome personality but snail-pace attention; about 400 seats in several sections (including a "Quick-Pick"); soft lighting and pink napery that melds with the copper highlights. Its adjoining Café Opera invites fair-weather small talk on a wide garden-fronted terrace. Still another link has been forged at a shopping center 4 miles from midtown. This one is called **Rôtisserie Baron de la Mouette**. Same foodstuffs, very nicely presented among wood-slat walls and apple-red textiles.

Perhaps the best nutrients in this city today can be digested in **hotel dining** rooms; we have always found them consistent, at least—and that, in itself, is something. For a well-prepared novelty, be sure not to miss the Old Frankfurt (or "Stubb") in the cellar of the **Frankfurter Hof**. Vitrines in white stucco walls displaying artifacts; each corner different in personality, yet melding nicely into a harmonious whole. Friendly reception by a smiling hostess in period attire; open kitchen where only a portion of the dishes are prepared; ambiance of congenial vitality rather than stuporous dignity. The cookery is not to be confused with that of sophisticated gustatory shrines; it is almost cottage fare in its straightforward hardiness, and it is good. Several of the hostesses speak English. This one is a highlight for the city and a "must" for any venturesome visitor. On the same premises you'll find the chic Restaurant Français for international cuisine and the he-man Grill (Maine lobsters flown in regularly); both are highly touted by local taste-makers. We've also snatched a snack at the comfortable Apéritif Bar, and it was delicious. The **Intercontinental Hotel** provides perhaps the city's richest mood in its lovely, river-view Rôtisserie—a delight to the aesthetic senses. For light bites and sipping, we like the Brasserie, the Wine Room, and the Oyster Bar. Its Sunday buffet has almost become a ritual among Frankfurters. The **Gravenbruch**, outside of town, is a delight; it has been injected with renewed vigor by its Kempinski masters. The **Parkhotel** boasts a good kitchen; the hors d'oeuvres merit a blue ribbon.

Down by the riverside, the **Park**, in front of the Intercontinental Hotel, now makes the biggest waves in the China Seas. Excellent oriental cookery in kooky occidental surroundings that somehow never got converted when the previous tenants checked out. **Peking**, opposite the Frankfurter Hof and often touted by its concierge as a good Chinese eatery, impressed us as being a pet promotion project of modern Maoists. We were sitting Cantonese Ducks for this one. Not recommended. We found the **Asia** reasonable for curry; our abalone with Chinese mushrooms was excellent; otherwise you've got a choice of about 250 items. In aforementioned Sachsenhausen Borough, across the Main, nonacrophobics may dine in **Henninger**'s rotating **Tower Restaurant** mounted on a 396-foot-high circular structure. Wow! You may sit and stuff while 360° of landscape passes before your eyes in the course of an hour. We've recently come from a meal in the more expensive Panorama tier where, upon careful consideration we gladly would serve our chef with what we think he possibly most deserves—defenestration! For budgeteers, it offers the twirling **Drehscheibe** circle which orbits in the opposite direction to the Panorama ring. If you don't mind dining miserably and expensively in a slow-motion centrifuge, you'll probably be awed by this impressive turn of events. Still not impressed? The newer **Skyline Tower** (Wilhelm-Epsteinstr.) roars on up to 1000 feet in altitude, revolves at the same speed, and easily outdistances its runty colleague in the race for miserable cookery. There seems to be an inverse ratio here between height and quality. The midtown **Schwarzer Stern** (Kalbächer Gasse 8) offers hardy fare in the earthy surroundings of a decorator's barn. Timber-and-stucco walls in both downstairs snackery and 2nd-story dining room; trimmings of pewterware, copper knickknacks, grain flails, and a wine press; regional cooking (and language) only; appetizing nutrients and mountainous servings. If you aren't stung by the crush of busy-bee diners in this little hive, the value for your marks should be returned. **San Remo** is an attractive Italian restaurant in midcity. Good theater but routine cookery. **Faust**, below the Opera, is colorful but gastronomically unexciting. **Taverne** is downright poor in our judgment.

Now—as promised—back to the typical *Apfelweinstuben* ("Apple wine rooms"). **Grauer Bock**, on the other side of the river, is another neighborhood tavern to end neighborhood taverns: Wooden tables, grimy floors, smoky walls, pretzel vendors, great color and animation; hot dogs, sauerkraut, beer, sandwiches, and a redoubtable affair called "Handkäs mit Musik"—"Handkäs" being the cheese, with vinegar, oil, paprika, onions, and kümmel combined on top to make the "Musik." BROTHER! The smaller **Gemaltes Haus** ("Painted House") is another fine example of this school. Among the equally typical wine restaurants, **Rheinpfalz Weinstuben-Hahnhof** has a sweet terrace and a Palatinate-rural-inn ambiance of scrubbed tables and woodcarvings; you can have an excellent dinner with delectable Forster Jesuitengarten Riesling Auslese; thoroughly enjoyable on a balmy summer's night; central location. **Stadt Wien**, formerly called Pfälzer Weinstube (at the Cathedral), and **Bacchus** are also attractive, but Rheinpfalz has them all licked. **Casa Nova** (Stresemannallee 38), while you are in this district, is a good name to have on your list; it specializes in Italian calories which are among the best in town.

For light refreshments, **Café Hauptwache** has a modern production-line restaurant facing the esplanade on its lower floor and a marvelous coffee and pastry parlor at ground level. Go to the latter for extraheavy calories and a peek at the painted figures on the walls. A sweetie.

If the sun is shining and transportation is at hand, the best luncheon expedition one can make in the area is the drive to the former castle of Empress Friedrich III—the **Schlosshotel Kronberg** (see "Hotels"). Gorgeous 200-foot open terrace for dining; expensive; so relaxing it's a *must* for anyone who can do it. The taxi price, unhappily, is robbery. Open all year. The happiest "discovery" of one of our recent local huntings was **Gutsschänke Neuhof**, 20 minutes out at the settlement of **Neuhof**. Self-contained farming village at work continuously since 1499; locally harvested and husbanded flora and fauna; packaged products sold at the Alte Backstube outbuilding (sausages, dairy goods, sweets, nuts, wines, plus some touristy craft items). Restaurant in the handsome half-timber manor house; 2 floors of compartmentalized dining rooms; outdoor terrace for summer daydreaming; warm, cozy atmosphere; flowers on every table; attentive waiters in cranberry waistcoats. Be sure to reserve well in advance here, because savvy Frankfurters love this one with a passion. Tops for its type. Next most amusing is the **Tennis Bar** (restaurant) in the Kurpark at **Bad Homburg**. Covered porch, same prices as Kronberg, select menu, snail-like service; closeup view of the courts and players; closed Mondays from November through April. Between Frankfurt and Kronberg, there's **Bad Soden** for an outdoor tea stop or light terrace-dining. Pleasant, but a straw hut compared to the Schloss. The **Unterschweinstiege** at the Airport Hotel is a beauty for grill buffs; it has just been freshened and expanded for indoor-outdoor dining. A well dominates the rustic interior; the garden and trees are Sylvan in summer; on Sundays from noon to 3 P.M. there's an all-you-can eat buffet for under $10. And for families, there is a supervisor for children's games in fields or playroom.

Night Life Locally the jernts are known as *"Nepp"* (a loose translation of "clip," which has been adopted universally throughout Germany), so take it from there as to what you can expect. Even a number of the finest hubs have gone so predatory that if you are not careful, they'll peck your eyes from their sockets. **Imperial** still has the biggest name. A short chug from the station, in the nightlife district; scarlet velvet semicircle with banquettes and picture-gallery booths; full head of steam at 10:30 P.M.; only clusters of bored, yawning males on our latest sleepwalk; anything's likely to appear, from jigglers to jugglers; waitresses in short skirts and lo-o-o-ong necklines. When it comes time to pay the bill, caution is advised. **Europa Cabaret** offers a spacious interior; happy atmosphere in Frenchy tones; ro-busty show; tantalizing strips. A wee tot of whisky rings up an eye-popping tab. The red-hued Europa Bar is its cozier downstairs nook with booths on one side and a counter on the other. Not bad, if the Frankfurt-by-Night tours don't usurp the fun. The **Casino de Paris** lies in wait with an alcove-lined main room fully equipped with tiger-toothed babes. Entrance gouge from a jerk who apparently can't count and obviously had convinced himself that our change should be short; the stairway from this portal leads to a convenient hotel above; whisky costs are outrageous. Sorry, but we detest this dive. **BB Club**, a longish taxi ride from the center, is infinitely better for persuasive exchanges. Arcade décor with small balcony; tiny band cooing sweet nothings; friendly bar and reasonable tariffs. Pleasant as a hideaway. **Black Jack**, the draw of the deck for under-21 disco-types, can easily be trumped—if you'll excuse the mixed metaphor. For fun and sophistication, **St. John's** would evoke almost any intimate confession. This pub-style hermitage was canonized for candlelight worshipers and TV-escapists; smiling redeemers sit comfortably at a horseshoe bar with built-in piano, or at low cocktail tables with dwarf-size captain's chairs. Pretty waitresses in tartans; white-painted brick wall; woody touches; fireplace crackling during cold months; fine ventilation; dartboard usually in use by males throwing for drinks. St. John himself, a topnotch showman, takes to the mike, cues the piano, and belts out tuneful swing-songs at ½-hour intervals. Delicious snacks and light meals are available at reasonable tithings. **Jimmy's Bar**, downstairs in the Hessischer Hof Hotel, is another pleasant dewdrop-inn for liquids and chitchat. **Taverna Bar** decants a rather distinguished atmosphere. Cellar situation in an office building; excellent orchestra enhanced by harp strains; tile dance floor; yellow and black striped banquettes; good drinks; well ventilated and clean; no shows. Could be romantic if you bring your own companion. **Swing Bar** is slightly better than routine—but very slightly. **Pik Dame** specializes in lesbian acts and other more pathetic charades. Skip the next-door **Riz**, 'cause 't'ain't Rizy and it is risky. **Erotica** also will murder your faith in the Boy Scout Oath. **Ellis Elliot** has such poor talent that it has become to us an economy-size disappointment. For jazz, the **Kneipe** (near the Frankfurter Hof) does it best; some great sounds are created here. Then come the narrow little **Jazzhaus** and the neighboring **Jazz Keller**—all of them in midcity. For pickups, the **Café Express** turns on the steam at its central Kaiserstrasse address. If it's a quick belt you're after, ankle over one block from the station to the **Lili Franz Bar**, **New York City Bar**, **Kasino Bar**, **Cocett Bar**, or several dozen more to quell that raging thirst. Never, incidentally, rendezvous at the **Rendezvous Bar**. The **Star Cabaret** shines in a similar magnitude, but the next-door **Sex Theatre** is fair enough for raw, no-nonsense overdoses of gut-and-creaky grinds. **Dr. Müller's**, with several midtown sites, purveys porn to the masses. It is possibly the most reliable spot of all for unknotting any kinks, too.

An unsavory sample of many a Frankfurter's night life can be encountered on the selected streets where "taxi girls" ply their winsome trade (there are no meters in the vehicles, however!). Kaiserstrasse and Taunusstrasse are 2 of the busiest lovers' lanes that traffic in this rolling sport. The Mossellestrasse and Elbestrasse also are reasonably safe; these areas are policed to some degree. At ALL costs, avoid the shanties in the so-called Gypsy Court.

Shopping   For shopping here, one of the first places we always head for is that wonderful **J. A. Henckels**, now in 7 more German hubs, plus others outside the country. Almost no one disputes that the pert "Twins," trademark and colophon of this giant since 1731, symbolize the world's finest cutlery, bar none.

Rosenthal: **Studio Haus Gilbert** (Friedenstrasse 10, next to Frankfurter Hof Hotel) is our local magnet for this most famous of German china. Ask for Mr. Peter Klötzer.

Cameras and optical devices: **Foto-Koch** (Kaiserstrasse 26, Am Dornbusch, and Frankfurt Airport) is by far the best in this area. Good variety; solid reputation; 1-day film processing. Director Mühler (Kaiserstrasse headquarters) would happily help you with your problems.

FREIBURG   The **Colombi** offers 7 floors of comfortable modernity and better than average cookery. The **Stadt Freiburg** is functional but okay.

FÜSSEN   Refer to "Romantic Road."

GARMISCH-PARTENKIRCHEN, is an Alpine resort with strong tourist appeal and backup facilities sprouting everywhere—so much so, in fact, that much of its charm is swiftly vanishing. Magnificent panorama of the German and Austrian Alps; bracing climate; restyled casino; winter sports galore, with ski runs and lifts, bobsledding, cable cars, a glass-lined public swimming pool, and much more. Take the train for a short roll out to Eibsee, then whistle up the 12-minute cable ride to the 9730-foot crown of Zugspitze Mountain; it's an eyeful you'll never forget.

The **Alpina** reveals an alp's-worth of high-fashion hotel baubles in a low-profile, stucco-and-wood, chalet-style building. Exquisite garden and pool area; inviting public rooms; 40 Deluxe bedchambers; superior cuisine on our try. The **Post** in the Partenkirchen part is also excellent, especially for its luxurious hunting lodge flavor. The expanded **Wittelsbach** is wiggling with renewed vigor. Newer south-side wing with balconies, bringing the overall total to 56 units, all with bath or shower; indoor swimming pool; eye-rejoicing flower garden. Solid and recommendable. The **Riessersee**, 2 miles from the center, commands a lovely hilltop view of the valley. Large sprawling structure; tennis courts, minigolf, sauna and thermal water treatments; attractive public rooms; about ½ its 100 units have private bath. Pleasant for rural relaxation. The 300-year-old **Clausing's Posthotel**, back in the Garmisch segment, attracts chiefly a European clientele. If you are looking for that Old World atmosphere with scarcely a Colonist in sight, you'll most likely find it here. **Golf Sonnenbichl** is more modest and more rural. The excellent eyeful from its frontside balconied rooms, the viewful Blue Restaurant, the Zirbelstube for highland hilarity and yodeling, and its Delft-style bar are all pluses. Managing-Proprietor Georg Bader is making things gooder every year. Closed October 1 to December 20. The **Partenkirchener Hof** is rich in alpine personality, and it boasts one of the best tables in the valley for the medium budget. The **Obermühle** makes a splash with its indoor pool. The 45-room **Garmischer Hof**, a breakfast-only hostelry, has had many improvements; approximately ⅓ of its units have private bath. The **Neu-Werdenfels** also provides reasonably good shelter for budget travelers. Outstanding pensions are (1) **Leiner**, (2) **Schell**, (3) **Flora** (expanded to semihotel proportions), and (4) the young **Gästehaus Georgenhof**. More? Take your pick of the other 172 hotels, inns, pensions, and guest houses—and *viel Glück!*

Want to get away from it all? Atop the 9730-foot Zugspitze, masons in crampons have constructed the miraculous **Hotel Schneefernerhaus**, with its lovely winter garden overlooking the top of the world. Basic accommodations for ski buffs, scenic buffs, and yeti; a wonder of engineering. If you travel in the uplands in spring, please be extra-cautious of the snow-cliffs above you. (As skiers know, the greatest danger comes after a rain that freezes and is followed by snowfall; the ice below serves as a death-dealing sliding board to chute tons of new surface snow down the slopes when even a slight noise or a ½-degree change of temperature breaks the pack.) On the Austrian side, a few yards away, the 50-bed **Alpenhotel der Tiroler** may be another candidate. If this one is functioning, both are accessible via the cog-rail route or the bone-chilling cable-car ride to the summit. High life at low tariffs—but please *do* be careful **in spring!**

HAMBURG, with approximately 2-million population, is Western Germany's first seaport and largest city. It spins a 890-foot-tall TV spindle that has a rotating restaurant. Next, it will proudly welcome the airs and airesses of the Soaring Seventies with its Holstenfeld Airport—a project so mammoth it vies with the Dallas-Ft. Worth complex. Dine in the famous Ratsweinkeller, stroll through Planten un Blomen Park, shop along Alster Lake, visit one of Germany's largest collections of fine paintings at the Art Gallery (50 showrooms!), take a whirl through that naked, rowdy Reeperbahn night district, ride a steamer to Blankenese on the Elbe River, or to the war-famous island of Helgoland, see Hagenbeck's renowned zoo with its Troparium to display its apes, snakes, crocodiles, and other exotic critters in natural surroundings—and you'll come home with happy memories for the rocking chair.

Hotels Among its fine hotels, the high-tide **Atlantic** exchanges nightly reflections across the lake with the Vier Jahreszeiten (see below). It is completely comfortable and elegant; it is also the center of The Action from sunup to cock's crow. Its Poseidon is tall, amiable Karl Walterspiel—a master of innkeeping, cuisine, and, judging from his ability to lever D-Marks for improvements, he is certainly one of the industry's top fundraisers. The results are vast and sparkling. As you enter, the lobby is a gracious restoration of the Atlantic of 1909—and a pleasure to behold. You'll find Die Brücke restaurant for quick meals, the Edwardian-modern Rendez-vous Bar with piano music, a dining room with orchestrated dinner dancing, a superb grill in the care of Grand Chef Wolfgang Paulmann, air conditioning in all public quadrants, an indoor pool-massage-sauna complex, and 105 rooms and some glorious suites (the "Hanseatic" is a sailor's dream) freshly turned out and furnished anew. A 3-story garage adjoins; excellent concierge team; an entire revamping of every behind-the-scene facility that is so dramatic that entire new hotels have been constructed for less money. An urbane beautifully run colossus that we highly recommend.

The exquisite, lakefront **Vier Jahreszeiten** is a salubrious choice for the discriminating voyager who prefers subtle tapers to bright lights. This patrician is a dreamy haven for tranquility seekers. Its 200 units offer 200 baths and showers (many with colorful tile mosaics); some small but nicely decorated singles, some luxurious and spacious single-suites or alcove-twins, and some viewless inside units; all public rooms newly air conditioned. Excellent cuisine; delightfully serene grill with open hearth; dining room beautified; charming hand-holders' bar adjoining the sleepy-looking dance-bar which has music from 9 P.M. to 2 A.M. The Condi Café features split-level lunching and a candy shop on the ground floor. The new Simbari Bar, with its own small loft, is an artistic and cozy corner which adds a discreet zest to the house. Personable Director Gert Prantner is young, inventive, and highly capable. The 2 radiant Haerlin daughters also lend grace notes to this joyful composition: Anne conducts hotel matters, while Thekla usually adds her sweetness to the Candy Corner. Again we give this one our fond long-standing plaudits of praise.

The stately **Intercontinental** resides a bit farther down the same lakeshore, fronted by a few trees along the residential drive. The 9th-floor Fontenay Grill is one of Hamburg's high spots—both physically and gastronomically. The nautically inspired Hulk Brasserie is so popular that a reservation is a must nearly any time. While the Hansa Kogge bar is refined, the hardy Bierstube is far more fun for easy chitchat and casual imbibing. Attractive glass-lined pool; spacious suites; colorful but somewhat narrow-lined twin units. In general, probably one of the more suave candidates in the Interconti family.

The 32-tier **Plaza**—spliced neatly into the municipal convention center—boasts of being the Federal Republic's highest hostelry. Canadian Pacific now runs this show which is plainly a massive commercial enterprise. Beige slab-ular structure with tinted windows; escalator ushering ticket holders to its marble bijou lobby; brick-and-board regional Vierlander Stuben; tapestried English Grille; nautical Galleon Bar; Blue Satellite discothèque; glass-sheathed sauna and pool; battery of boutiques; garage. Its cloying peppermint-striped corridors lead to 570 look-alike units; most are cookie-mold-standard doubles or twins; all are powdered in variations of brown and white accented by red or yellow; the boxy coffee tables, plastic chairs, globe lamps, and abstract paintings remind us of a Creative Playthings school. Air conditioning, direct-dial phones, remote-control lighting, 5-channel radios, and color TV are standard; the windowsills are a tall 4 feet above carpet level; the wake-up-your-eyes bathrooms—wowee!—are jazzed up in silver, white, and yellow patterned wallpaper. Sassy. Modern.

The **Prem** is a renovated mansion made prem-and-proper through many recent improvements. The entrance and lobby, with its adjoining paneled bar, broadened and perked up smartly; corridors repainted; excellent cookery; warm service; parking lot and individual garages unveiled; all units brightened. We thoroughly enjoyed a 4-night stay in #14, a good-size Louis XV-style double facing the placid garden. Very nice indeed. The neighboring **Bellevue** boasts 85 bedchambers and an 85% bath ratio. The **Berlin**, a Y-shape structure, is convenient for motorists who weary near the autobahn junction of Bremen and Lübeck-Kiel. Overall, it's tasteful and well maintained; the run-of-the-mill doubles are small and cluttered. The oval restaurant is O-kay but not inspiring; the underground garage parks 100 cars. The **Crest Motel** in the *"City North"* district is styled for the year 2000. Superb physical facilities, but weak in service and culinary points. The **Parkhochhaus** is another candidate designed for motorists on the go-go circuit. Handsome restaurant in Swedish modern is open until 2 A.M.; gay yellow breakfast room with balcony; spotlessly clean; efficiency-type doubles with shower or full bath; 14 nests with private balconies; garage space for all guests. We admire its hardworking administration and its conscientious efforts to please. The **Falck**, more for motel types than for city lovers, also leans to Scandinavian simplicity, but what it reveals in starkness it fails to recover in personality. The 135-room **Ambassador** struts in with a swimming pool, a sauna, a happily plaid-clad dining room, and a rustic bar. The tiny bedchambers in this converted office building are its chief handicap. Non-central and only fair. The **Reichshof**, a station hotel, has smartened itself up while retaining very pleasant period décor. We like it now. The **Europäischer Hof** also comes up with a brightened yet stolidly traditional personality; 500 rooms with a high proportion of singles; groups use it a lot, but value is here. The **Oper** and the more modest **Norddeutscher Hof** are appealing in the budget bracket. We wouldn't bother with either the **Pacific** or the **Motel Hamburg**. Ugh. The **Royal**, near the Atlantic, is for students, serious budge-

teers, or self-abnegating eremites. The **Alsterhof** has 80 varying accommodations, 2 so-called penthouse suites (possibly because one gets that pent-up
feeling in them), and 21 of the most minuscule baths outside a U-boat; #211
and #212, among the latest batch of improved units, are exceptions, with twin
basins and adequate tubs. Maintenance is picking up. We're happy to say that
this one's now right for the price.

Pensions? **Zeyn** (Rothenbaumchaussee 177), across from the Funkturm, is
tuned in on hospitality. These simple householders are kindly and most helpful. Clean; only 1 room with bath. **Marlyta**, across the way, is smaller but also
amiable. As for other pensions, it's a good general rule to steer clear of the
station and the St. Pauli areas because of their heavier-than-average patronage
by prostitutes.

Restaurants When it comes to dining out, the baronial **Ratsweinkeller**, pride of the municipality, is one of the best of its type in Germany.
Elaborate, dignified and cosmopolitan atmosphere; service careful and prompt
for such a large establishment. Try its Nordsee-Steinbutt Gekocht mit Zerlass-
ener Butter if you're a jet-propelled turbot-fan. For serious (and expensive)
gastronomy, **Landhaus Scherrer**, a $7 taxi ride from the center, is a low house
facing the Elbe; it features 2 rooms of which we prefer the pale green salon
dominated by a large Kokoschka painting. Dishes—and marvelously light they
are—appear exquisitely under silver bells. The music is baroque; a rehboam
of Pauillac costs $1250, with German wines ranging down to $15. You'll never
suffer heartburn here, but the host might achieve heart failure when billtime
rolls around. Wonderful, but $$$$$$! **Wein-Restaurant J. H. C. Ehmke** is
good but not grand; some vegetables are insipid; better for sea-faring than
steer-age; closed Sundays. Nice sampling of the Old World. **W. Schümann's
Austernkeller** ("Oyster Cellar"), Jungfernstieg 34, is a page out of the memoirs
of Kaiser Wilhelm. Ground-floor situation belies its subterranean title; photos
of celebrities so elegantly bearded they would challenge Commander White-
head; high-backed booths and chairs; stained-glass touches; 7 private dining
roomettes with closable door for business conferences or monkey-business
conferees; bustling but friendly attention. For skilletry we prefer this one to
Ehmke. Recommended. **Jacob**, 20 minutes out at *Hamburg-Nienstedten*, is
a riverbank mansion that served its first guest on April 1, 1791. Now it wears
a fresh wardrobe and is viewful and fetching when it is warm enough to dine
on its terrace. At other times we prefer **Landhaus Dill** which is across the
roadway and better skilled at handling pots and pans. The hilltop **Süll-
berg**, in nearby *Blankenese*, might be another worthy alternative. **L'Auberge
Francaise** is a meticulously operated Gallic entry where Owner Jacques Lem-
ercier and Chef Matias Therry try to create the best of France in northern
Germany—even to shopping twice weekly in the Paris markets! Locals lavish
praise upon their efforts, but our own judgment is more tempered. Decora-
tively it is pleasant but not elaborate; *nouvelle cuisine* is the main thrust from
the kitchen; wines are *only* French. Expensive? Well, what do you think of $100
per twosome? **Le Canard** is another quacker from Gaul—a smidgen bigger,
also with the latest fashion in French cuisine, also on the costly side—but
worthwhile if you hanker for *la belle France*. **Bavaria Blick** is a split-level,
glass-lined aerie topping the St. Pauli Brewery. Suave reception for its prosper-

ous clientele; 25 flower-clad tables; dishes as appealing to the eye as to the palate; the house pride is its finny fare; coffee comes up with a snooker of double-rich whipped cream; it seems to improve every time we go. Don't forget to ask your waiter for binoculars, to put yourself right on the bridge of that freighter piloting up the Elbe. The **Uberseebrücke** (auf der Uberpromenade) almost could be its twin. Situated adjacent to the river; tall, wide windows on 3 sides; 101-item menu; child's plate "For Our Little Guests" at less than half the adult billings (but what boy could eat with all of those boats passing right under his nose?); exquisite presentation and culinary performance, but portions too large for most North American midriffs. Costly but definitely rewarding. **Riper** (Grosse Reichenstrasse 56) is an amusing old-time establishment where the Hamburg Card Playing Society meets nightly. Family ownership since the first cut of the deck; "hot pots" and typical local fare for penny-ante prices; again, big portions; fun as a change of pace. **Panorama**, appropriately perched in a penthouse, comes next. Care for the address? Get set: It's Glockengiesserwall Ecke Ferdinandtor 1 im Kunsthaus, Hamburg 1. Whew! Simple glass-bound nest overlooking the Alster, the boats, cars, trains, and Hamburgers below; illumination by pods of long plastic icicles; padded cupcake-shape chairs and placemats on tables; bustling café-type service and cookery that was surprisingly good; eel soup is a specialty, and it is deeeeel-ishous. The daytime is best in summer; evenings are nicest in winter. A recommendable lookout— *if* you spend a working day memorizing its name and site. In the same vicinity, **Alsterpavillon**, the large semicircular building with the sprawling sidewalk café and tiers of terraces over the lake, is so central and so obvious that most visitors at least see it in passing; plush dining room upstairs, tearoom downstairs, snacks in the open; attractive and good. **Fischereihafen-Restaurant**, on a quay overlooking the busy Norder Elbe waterway, has excellent salmon, sole, and other fruit of the sea. Reserve in advance, especially at lunch when businessmen wiggle in; go upstairs; quite expensive; don't order lobster or crab, because the tab will kill you. **Alsterschiff**, a small ship permanently anchored in the Inner Lake (center of town), offers 11 tables in the tiny cabin for dining afloat; amusing experience, but the galley's not the best. **Schiffer Börse**, opposite the station, is one of the most impressively tricked out maritime hideaways we've ever moored in. The grub is not all that good, but see it even if you only invest in a beer or a glass of wine. Very salty in a well-hoked-up and ancient Hanseatic fashion. **Coelln** is famous for its oysters (expensive!) during the winter months. **Mühlenkamper Fährhaus** (Osterbekstrasse 1, a few minutes out from the center) again and again has served us perfectly splendid gastronomy. Our latest sampling was so superior in every respect that we are convinced this is one of the best dining spots in the North. Atmosphere almost homey in execution; padded red-leather booths for sink-in comfort; oil paintings, brass chandeliers, and warm wood paneling; excellent-to-extraordinary service masterminded by all Hillersheims plus Maître Otto, a real pro. While there are several rooms upstairs, we prefer the main level for coziness and action. Delicious slivers of smoked salmon and sturgeon were delivered on individual wooden platters and garnished with fresh salad tidbits. Our sweet-and-sour goose was so tender, flavorful, and handsomely presented that we still go into a roc-style flap when we think of it. We also purloined a slice of our partner's lamb with chive and cream sauce (and nearly had an arm chopped off in the process); it was so succulent that we bow to her aggressiveness. Our Raspberry Romanoff (a Hamburg specialty of smooth, tart gelatin folded in cream) was a dessert fit for the czars. Nothing faltered. **Peter Lembcke** (Holzdamm 49) is another diet-buster that turns out irresistible calories for Hamburg's cognoscenti. Here is a 2nd example of the "secret" corners which too often resist international fame; it is, however, well known and loved by discriminating locals. Proprietor-Chef Karl Krause oversees his domain, his skillets, and his guests while wandering broodingly in a floor-length laboratory technician's gown. Godawful fittings which constitute no décor at all; worn, tattered, and utterly charmless surroundings in a creaky town house; only a 3-minute waddle from the Atlantic Hotel; poor ventilation; such fine old-fashioned Teutonic cuisine that none of these obvious shortcomings really matter. For our money, the steaks have no peer anywhere in the city. The prices are surprisingly modest. **Blockhouse** (Dorotheenstrasse is one location, but there are 6 others now) is named for Herr Block, its beefeating proprietor. Attractive interiors, usually rustic in nature; Western-style steaks; good baked potatoes and salads; young waitresses who struggle valiantly and vainly, yet sweetly, with the English language. **Franziskaner**, around the corner from the Vier Jahreszeiten, is a sound budget bet for local vittles. Heavily wooded den with moss banquettes, beige walls, and brassy bar; spotlessly clean; fleet-footed service. Nürnberger sausages over sauerkraut go fastest here. **Churrasco** (Ferdinandstrasse 61) is an Argentine steak-out that will probably make you wish you'd stayed down on the pampas. Some in this chain are okay, but this'un ain't for us'ns. The **Finland Restaurant** in Finland House is very much in the swim these days. Its very highly regarded for its buffet table—and with ample reason. So is **Kon Tiki** in the Hotel Norge, where for a set price voyagers can stuff down a raft of ship's stores. Keep sailing back for seconds or thirds at no extra charge; beverages are separate. **Zillertal** is the leading *Bierstube*—only fair—and **Münchener Hofbräuhaus** is pretty vulgar and unappealing; the latter has convenient hours, however, because it dishes out light bites and soup until 3 A.M. We haven't sampled the new 300-seat **Orpheus**, which reportedly serves jazz, folklore, and frolic with its comestibles. For snacks, try the spotlessly modern "**K.B**," chain, a self-service operation, or **Edelweiss**, where the quality is usually excellent. Among the hotels, the **Atlantic**, the Fontnay Grill of the **Intercontinental**, and the **Vier Jahreszeiten** duel in mortal combat for a *touché;* we'd give the edge to the mood you are in at the time you dine, because each is distinctive and outstanding for gastronomy. The **Parkhochhaus** is inexpensive and cheerful, but passable only for its à la carte selections.

Like so many other German metropolises, Hamburg has its own TV tower *cum* revolving restaurant, dubbed the **Fernsehturm**, which places rather poorly in our ratings. Lower-level cafeteria with formica tables; toptier dining ring with color-keyed booths set on a moving floor; stationary bar at the axis. The whip cracks for dinner at 6:30 sharp; then the herd stampedes in like bulls thundering through the streets of Pamplona. Its management seemingly prefers to work tightly packed grazers rather than strays; therefore they loaded up communal boards even when tables stood empty elsewhere.

Night Life It continues to be our conviction that, for the most rugged, down-to-bare-facts night life, Hamburg holds the diamond-studded G-string over any other European metropolis by at least 6 bumps and 24 grinds. The Reeperbahn and its sidestreets are brilliant from dusk to dawn with the neon enticements of dozens of girlie-joints. Some of the flesh marts, with elaborate cabarets and slick décors, are sufficiently respectable for family trade. Others, however, are for men only—and that means *for men only.* In these, generally 3 to 12 "artistes" perform solo or in tandem in the seminude or nude and to the outer limits of human imagination.

The local alphabet begins and ends with B—not only for the regiments of B-girls who quaff so-called double-gin fizzes at a 10-spot each (it's the most expensive drink), but also because the area is the B-all and end-all of organized eroticism. Sex Unabashed permeates the atmosphere.

In this twilight zone, 3000 of the 13 thousand residents are prostitutes. Then there are the local shills, pimps, strippers, and associated tradesmen. Despite continuing pronunciamentos, mobster elements remain snugly in the saddle. Although the cleanup crusade initiated by reputable operators and supported by such influential newspapers as *Bild-Zeitung* has begun to make inroads, much of this area still is NOT safe for visitors.

If you'll stick to the places recommended below, your wallet and your molars *should* be safe (no blanket guarantees by us). The best fun, of course, is to make the rounds of as many as possible, with 1 drink and 15 minutes in each. As a rule, there's an $8 to $10 entry fee (if there's a show), another 2 bits for your coat check (never tip here); Scotch (much of it falsified) runs up to $10 per slug. *But don't wander elsewhere under any circumstances.*

PS for budgeteers: A rash of porno cinema halls now sweep the city. The shows are varied, long, cheap, and even more revealing (if possible) than much of the live action on stage in the cabarets. Ask locally for the flick of the moment.

Among the smaller strip depots, **Colibri** (Grosse Freiheit 34) is absolute tops. One of the few offering live music; coveys of girls who have earned their major-sports'-letter "B" in the professional leagues. One excessively well-endowed barmaid actually offers an uddermost private part for the boggle-eyed gentleman to kiss (a new nightclub high or low, depending upon how one regards such brazenry). Jammed with lone males; continuous show; young, accomplished, good-looking strippers who work up their amorous themes with partners of all persuasions; unmonkeyed-with whisky; beer plus schnapps for reasonable tabs (a mandatory combination not sold separately). Should you have trouble getting in, because of its popular appeal, tell Albert, the tall bumper-faced bouncer at the door (whose heart is gold), that you "read Fielding's." For some unfathomable reason he will bend over backward to slip you in. **Salambo**, across the street, has it all—including what's happening on the banquette beside you. It's not for the timid, and it certainly has to be the most uninhibited community of carnality since Sodom. **Erotica**, next door, is one of those which we've mentioned that deals in free-reelers. "Blue" films; beer the most popular beverage; no entry fee; as raw as they come. **Travesti**, next to Colibri, lights up a small stage with the top transvestite acts in the city. Strangely enough, they can be more tasteful than many of the other performances. Don't go if you're human enough to know pathos, however. **Safari** offers an expandable interior glazed by a colossal onstage sun; iridescent flora on the ceiling; starboard bar with unbroken view of the action; disturbingly handsome bar girls. Good spirits; good shows; swinging for the broadminded. **Tabu** drums up a pleasantly cozy mien, but its whisky comes in sampler bottles with their seals already broken; the product is just what you'll think it is—or worse! Tabu on our score sheet. For pickups, connoisseurs usually consider that **Mehrer Café** stocks the choicest and safest dainties; the admission fee is about $7, which may be used to buy a Coke; the going rate for those other sweets, during our reportorial shopping, was 80 DM or so as the "gift" to the lady; the hotel room rents for about half that outlay, and the normal check-out time is 2 hours after initial entry. **Lausen**, with no show, is also for pickups. **Atlantis** has become a porn shop —and wow, what a stock! The **Barcelona** features a cabaret in which it would be difficult for even a gynecologist to distinguish between the señoritas and the señores. A spot named **Kesse** bounces out its so-called Ball Paradox nightly. **Koenigin** has become a disk spinner. **Zillestal**, a beer garden, also taps out terpsichore; wives are tolerated (even if not always by their spouses). **Moonlight** during our visit was loaded with transvestites, odd sexes, and nonsexes; here was one of the dirtiest, rottenest, most tasteless shows we've ever seen anywhere, anytime. On one loop, we heard that a trio of Japanese visitors was zapped $820 for 45 minutes of drinking. If true, that's either one helluva thirst or one helluva condemnation. We won't say which. Ugh! **Pulverfuss** also is bent toward transvestites. The **X-Club** is working its way backward through the alphabet; now it earns straight "A's" for what it is. A ½-dozen strippers; intimate ambiance; relatively honest; worth a peekaboo. **Maxim**'s functions as a western-style pub. Locals have commented to us that it's *alles Käse* or "all cheese" (low German slang for "it stinks"); we don't know, however, from our own sniffer. **Petite Fleur**? Please, please stay far away from this Little Flower.

In many cases, the syndicates have hired jail-hardened scum to take over in areas being threatened with extinction by cleanup patrols and by the city's responsible citizenry. One fulcrum is the infamous, eye-popping Herbertstrasse, a 1-block street just off the main drag, where harlots sit in showcase windows facing the sidewalks. Here the prostitutes ask about $45 per encounter. Another is the Fish Market district, where the scales fall even lower for a squalid catch. Frequently their milieu is the back seat of a car. These areas are as riddled with peril as they are with disease.

To combat them with an officially supervised competitor, private sources have erected a $1,000,000 play-for-pay mill on the Reeperbahn. Dubbed the Eros Center, it provides "office space" for 136 pros. The U-shape structure was thoughtfully conceived: A "contact courtyard" with infrared heating for winter solicitation, an underground garage, a beauty parlor, 9 R-&-R rooms (where only the ladies may meet), and comfortable apartments equipped with kitchens. In these confines, rates nip from $30 to $50 for a short meeting; full-night lingerings are not encouraged. At the adjoining ground-floor snack bar of the Café Mira, the toll is about $65 per hour; the turnabout for a full nocturn (negotiable here and *not* discouraged) soars into the $250 range.

Extensive precautions are taken to insure sanitation, including regular check-ups by doctors.

As for run-of-the-Hun streetwalkers, please, PLEASE avoid ALL contact with these babes—the dregs of the port. Remember always that none of the bar or taxi girls in the St. Pauli area may leave before the doors close—and that's 4 A.M. or later. Final stop for 'most everybody is **Blauer Peter**, *open from 4 A.M. to 10 A.M. only;* no show; 5-piece combo for dancing; all kinds of light food and all materials for that nightcap; very pleasant.

Gambling? You'll find roulette, baccarat, blackjack, and slot machines at the Casino in *Hittfeld*, about ½-hour by car or by train. Tables open at 2 P.M. daily. *Glück und Glas wie bald bricht das!*

HANOVER, basically an attractive mercantile mart, boasts a marvelous jam-free street system—but where do people go? In the State Opera and the Herrenhausen Park and Palace, however, you'll find 1st-quality music and theater. Out at *Hodenhagen*, there's also a wildlife park with numerous residents of Serengeti shivering under the weak northern sun.

Among the city's hotels, the 8-story, 300-unit **Intercontinental** is, for the moment anyway, a golden turret of this global network; it rates—with us, at least—among the top modern-style hostelries on the Continent. Ideal situation, with the City Hall (magnificently illuminated at night), town lake, and shopping center almost at your doorstep; orange-canopied entrance beside a pool and fountain; glittery lobby warmed by rosewood panels and glamorous movie-TV stars who make this their offstage greenroom; Calenberger Bar with candlelight, red-leather trim, rich appointments, a terrific combo, and perfectly concocted drinks; dancing every night but Monday. Delicious cuisine in the dramatically decorated Prinz Tavern (lunch and dinner), the open-rôtisseried Grill segment, the cheerful Brasserie (6 A.M. to 11 P.M.), and the chummy, rustic *Bierstube* (snacks and suds from noon to midnight); pastry shop; 300-car garage; office space for transients; curvilinear secretaries available for executive suite-niks. The sleeping accommodations contain so many agrémens we can't even begin to describe them. One carp: The baths are much too cramped. Otherwise, enthusiastically recommended. The 220-room **Kastens Hotel and Luisenhof**, with a lobby as frigid as a bathhouse foyer, has been hit hard by its uncontended competitor. Attractive wood, copper, and brick grill, where you can watch your steaks sizzle; air-conditioned; traditional bedrooms. While reasonable shelter is offered, it's not even a light jab on the biceps of the champ. Within the city, this is followed, successively, by the **Grand Hotel Mussmann** with its fresh restaurant and Tessiner Bar, and the **Europäischer Hof**. Outside of town, the **Esso** motel is superb in its category, except in 2 departments. Pleasant Bristol Grill, plus a coffee shop; summer terrace overlooking an enchanting deer park; each well-made unit with balcony and solid first-class comfort; low rates for high standards. We found the service wretched, and the food was on a par with what you might find in any Esso filling station in the States. What a shame, in face of its many assets! **Parkhotel-Motel Kronsberg** (yep, that's its true name) features a restaurant with 5 dining rooms plus a *Bierstube,* each one contributing mightily to the aroma of sauerkraut that was so redolent from portals to penthouse when we walked in. Well furnished and color-accented; slightly more expensive than the Esso; not bad as a 2nd choice if you have a heavy cold. Our recent fly-in to the airport-sited **Holiday Inn** left us wondering why we didn't book on the next flight out. One of the weaker outlets of this empire, in our estimation. About 25 miles northeast, at the medieval village of *Celle*, the **Parkhotel Fürstenhof** would seem to be a boreal dream if one can believe the publicity material. We plan to take a look at Manager Brühl's seventeenth-century baroque mansion and dwelling-annex very soon.

In our opinion, the finest dining spot is the **Intercontinental**'s Prinz Tavern, with cozy clusters of booths plus open tables, crackling grill, wood paneling, painted screens, pewter service plates, handsome ceramics, and waiters in good-looking Lower Saxony costumes. Its Brasserie is ideal for coffee shop habitués. The woody *Bierstube* wins the cup for suds and snacking. Light bites are also available in that wonderful Calenberger Bar. The attractive **Wichmann** (about 10 minutes along the Hildesheimer pike) could be a paradise—if only the chef knew his *assiette* from his aspic. From any aspect, gastronomically our saddle of hare could scarcely have been more clumsily dismounted (poor thing, it must have died miserably); our sauce was ghastly; our wine was foul; our service was bumbling. What a shame, because this thatched-roof farmer's cottage, with cozy individual rooms, candlelight, and a pleasant ambiance, could be a sparkler in the right hands. Perhaps you'll have better luck—but somehow we doubt it. **La Bonne Auberge** is the leading independent choice in midcity. Straw-covered booths with checkered tablecloths and storm lamps; saddles, copper fixin's, and stableware set the scene; waitresses in Basque costumes. A board with 35 hors d'oeuvres selections greets the newcomer; handsome presentation of appetizing fodder; fair prices. A good little hitching post. The **Dubrovnik**, on the Hotel Europa's 5th floor, is a splendid choice for Balkan fare. With fixin's so fine and tabs so low, here's a buy for the adventurous diner. **Herrenhaüser**, 2 blocks from the Intercontinental, bespeaks easygoing neighborliness from 5:30 P.M. until 5 A.M. Small counter up front; plain tables and chairs at the rear; wallpaper possibly dating back to the heyday of Bismark. Since most selections tend to fall into the *wurst* family, no normal repast edges past $8.50. Marginal. If you have 20 seconds to pronounce it, **Brauereigaststaetten** is 20 minutes out the main pike to Bremen. This atmospheric choice is located in a suburban brewery; the skillets know only the most toothsome samplings of regional fare. Not costly. Recommended highly for its type. Insomniacs' delight? **Am Kamin** serves grills and frills around the clock.'

Sophisticates of the after-dark scene don their dandiest duds and shoot straight for the **Calenberger Bar** of the Intercontinental. Cabaret addicts usually prefer **Eve** first (pickups available, but house girls chained to the bar stools until 5 A.M.), **Pigalle** second, and **Jenseits** third (former showman Jens behind the bar periodically breaks into song-and-joke sessions for the happy throng). **Ex** is the leading dance oasis and discothèque. Glass-bulb décor; fascinating vitrine with a montage of musical instruments; plaid bar; rouge carpets; quite nice. **Pendel**, across the street, is under the same ownership; it has an interesting clock theme, which unfortunately seems to be running down. The **Journal** wins our cup for strictly quaffing; it's a 2nd home for newspapermen or writers who happen to be in town. **Löwenbräu** shouldn't be missed by seekers of local color; typically Germanic; sudsy to its core. Avoid all street-walkers in this city, chaps. They ply through the Steintor area at from $50 to $100 per car-hop. These babes too often work in cahoots with strong-arm gangmen who poise in the shadows until the strategic moment, and then the ponce will pounce.

HEIDELBERG ("Heather Hill"), scene of *The Student Prince,* is a sad example of what happens to a glorious, tailor-made sightseeing target when it is overrun by hordes of rubberneckers. It boasts an enchanting situation astride a riverbank, the world's largest wine barrel (58 thousand gallons), Karzer Prison for obstreperous fifteenth-century students of its celebrated university, the Lion Gate, undergraduate dueling clubs (now revived), and the 127-foot TV tower (observation platform open to the public). It is also the seat of the U.S. European Army Headquarters, with 25-thousand bored soldiers housed in a suburban area. Please beware of the trolley cars here; the streets are so narrow they practically cannonball down the sidewalks. Heidelberg is guilty of nothing except an excess of beauty and historic charm; the only thing wrong with it is the rabble of Japanese, French, Italian, Belgian, Scandinavian, Indian, Greek, North American, Latin American, and Hottentot tourists who spoil it in Season. But in good weather during the slowest months—*wunderbar!*

Number one among hotels is the **Europäischer Hof** (sometimes called "Europe"). It makes continuous updatings in the most tasteful of traditional Germanic themes. Its latest bauble is a 33-room wing with shops, conference salons, and a cellar garage. Total of more than 120 units; terrace-dining (with huge windows that vanish into the floor at a button's touch), or upgraded Kurfürstenstube Grill (local specialties and beguiling color); attractive bar. So fine in every department that we're always anxious to return. Congratulations to Managing Proprietor Ernst von Kretschmann for such a smooth, well-integrated expansion and beautification program! **Park-Hotel Haarlass**, out of town overlooking the Neckar, has zoomed up in our esteem as a result of the enormous refashionings wrought here. Lovely window-lined restaurant apart from main building; viewful bar; all accommodations restyled; all with baths; carpets, wallpaper, oil paintings in superb frames; cordial staff. Medium prices reflect heavy group trade. Coming up zestily. **Stiftsmühle**, on the same river, has a much better basic plant, but, alas, it seems to us to be riding on its laurels. Baronial in tone but the aristocracy appears to be fading. Too bad because it could be a winner. Both of these require a car for ease in mobility. The **Schrieder** is a mélange of large, medium, and small bedchambers, some good, some fair, and some poor. The **Ritter**, which planted its first cornerstone in 1592, is growing newer by the moment. Shucks! Except for the restaurant, almost every speck of its once-rich antiquity has been erased. Very central, and now very ordinary. **Neckar**, on the waterside in the city, is an awkward building dappled with bright modern hues and functional furniture. Four doubles and 2 baths added, bringing the total to 34 rooms, 14 with plumbing; décor ranging from fair to substandard; breakfast only. The blue-tile **Kurfürst** offers 47 clean but spare bedrooms, 11 baths, 8 showers, and slaphappy service that discloses unpolished management and a poorly trained staff. Very limited. **Crest** operates a 68-room motel here. Cocktail lounge, 2 restaurants, ample space, and tip-top quality throughout. Incidentally, a **Holiday Inn** is out at nearby **Walldorf**. And, at **Ludwigshafen-Heidelberg**, the U.S.-bred **Ramada** organization has uncorked some competition.

At mealtimes, the versatile facilities and fine cookery in the perked up Kurfürstenstube of the **Europäischer Hof** top them all. The **Ritter** comes up with above-average vittles and authentic Old German surroundings. The suit of armor which we almost mistook for the maître has now been removed, possibly to save other reubens from making the same mistake. Two adjoining rooms; blossoms on each table; English menu; informal ambiance; inexpensive. Sound, but not what one might call thrilling. The **Museum Restaurant** is a delight. Entry through large portals that face a court and a sylvan park beyond; interior with heavy beams supported by carved tree trunks; 2 rooms separated by red granite pillars and ancient arches; windows with stained-glass inserts; bronze chandeliers. The menu is enticing, the service sound, and the prices in the medium bracket. In every way, we enjoyed it. **Molkenkur**, reachable by car or tiny funicular, has a magnificent mountainside 100-foot terrace, well *above* the Schloss; 3 rows of tables and glorious view; attractive inside dining room; expensive and they try hard; a worthy bet, especially in good weather. (The Castle is closed to the public.) As you might expect, tourists often swarm the precincts. **Königstuhl**, way-way-way up at the mountaintop TV tower, broadcasts only so-so-so cookery—BUT that nonvideo view is worth those coaxial impulses in your tummy. **Schinderhannes**, on Theaterstrasse, is fun as a wine restaurant; it is open only for dinner and late revels. For light bites, there are miles of spaghetti factories and endless rounds of pizzerias along the Hauptstrasse in the center of town. **Haarlass Terrace**, across the river, is lovely when the sun shines but often choked with bus crowds. **Kupferkanne** is agreeable; **Goldener Hecht**, at the corner of the Old Bridge, is old, colorful, and a favorite among artists and students (they proudly informed us that Goethe *nearly* spent a night here!). **Perkeo**, once a favorite, is no longer recommended. As for the highly publicized student taverns, the **Red Ox** has the greatest fame, but we found its food miserable, its service glacial, and its atmosphere commercially touristy; try **Seppl**, which seems a far more authentic mirror of undergraduate life—but remember that these places are strictly for sightseers except during the school terms.

HERRENALB 12 miles from Baden-Baden and into the fringing wineland of the Black Forest, offers the rugged-but-refined **Post Hotel**, which has quietly played host to tranquillity seekers from the late Duke of Windsor to the Maharaja of Baroda. Ideal for a pastoral excursion or a restorative holiday. Cuisine that vies with some of the best we have ever tasted in Germany; pleasant but not overdone décor, touched up with rich antiques; cozy twelfth-century Klosterschränke Grill, with beams, stucco, and stone; 2 dining rooms and garden sipping nook; bar; heated pool; 50 comfortable units, most with shower and/or bath. Proprietor Mönch is its courtly Boniface. Here is an isle of bucolic calm where the value of peace is understood to its very core.

HINTERZARTEN, in the Black Forest, offers the **Adler**, which steals the loving cup as one of the beauty queens of Germany. Glorious parkland and flower-girt setting; glass-enclosed swimming pool for year-round dipping; tennis, minigolf, *boccia* court, water sports on Lake Titisee, ice skating, curling rink, toboggan run, nearby ski lifts and golf course; baronial appointments; sumptuouscomfort; owned by the Riesterer family since 1446; only 13 miles from Freiburg; an arcadia of *Hochschwarzwaldian* peace.

KAISERLAUTERN The **President** wins our vote for modernists.

KARLSRUHE If you pause here, the **Park** is worthy; so is the **Schwarzwald** out at *Karlsruhe-Rüppurr*.

KASSEL The **Schlosshotel Wilhelmshöhe** is sited 4 miles up toward the last Kaiser's castle. Though cheerless, it offers 61 balconied rooms, 50 baths or showers, patio dancing and dining in summer, and a distinct proclivity for entertaining conventioneers. Mototists may opt for the 155-pillowed **Holiday Inn** near the east exit of the autobahn.

LÜBECK, "Queen of the Hanse," is so rich in monuments, antiquities, paintings, and antique salt-storage houses that it's a great favorite of serious-minded voyagers—and *Travemünde*, the neighboring Baltic resort, balances the ledger by offering a gambling casino and plenty of excitement in summer to the frivolous. *Kiel*, nearby, was the marine host for the sailing contests of the Olympics. Worth a visit, particularly by old salts. In Lübeck, our overnight choice would be the fresh **Lysia** beside the Trave River. The **Burgstubel** (new with an antique façade) and the more rural **Kaiserhof** are good bets too, as is the **Oller Kotten**, located in the Old Town. **Schabbelhaus**, the last word in Town House refinement and grace, is enchanting as a lunching and dining target. It is an ancient mansion with tall windows, massive beams, perfect service, and delicious cuisine. It's not destructive to the budget, either. Another stunner is the **Haus der Schiffergesellschaft**, which dates back to the dawn of Hanseatic maritime activity. The décor is authentic; dining is at communal tables; ships' models hang from the timbered ceiling—as do 3-tiered brass chandeliers with candles that are illuminated at dusk. A delight.

MAINZ The **Hilton**, ably managed by Eric Moerscher, is by far the leading hotel locally. Open V-shape structure nipping at the banks of the Rhine; adjacent to the 3000-capacity Rheingoldhalle congress center. Specialty restaurant suggestive of a steamer (overlooking the Rhine too); brick-walled Weinstube; Bierstube; cocktail lounge; full air conditioning; garage; car rental facility; beauty parlor; barbershop. All 251 rooms with limited stretch-out space. Nevertheless, it's tops. The **Mainzer Hof**, long one of our least favorite retreats, drops into the 2nd slot. A bit more style has been introduced; the people are nicer now, too. It's sound, solid, and basic, but we can't get very excited by it. The **Europahotel** is a good value for the price. Total of 69 rooms, all with balcony or loggia, bath, TV outlets, radio, dumbwaiter (guests order by pneumatic tube), and other modern appurtenances, including accommodations for Bozo; 5 doubles named and decorated in the styles of the 5 continents; 3

separate dining spots, one of them now a grill; 200 yards from the railway station.

MANNHEIM   There are 2 choices known to us here, both good: The **Mannheimer Hof** (183 units, 160 baths, 2 bowling alleys) and the **Wartburg Hospiz**.

MUNICH,   the Bavarian capital, is the southern apex of industry, commerce, U.S. soldiery, and at least 1 foreign visitor for each 1 of the 1⅓-million permanent population. The typical Bavarian is a better host than the typical northerner; his beer steins are bigger and his smiles are broader. In addition, here's the number one art center; the celebrated **"Pinakothek"** with its magnificent collection of 7000 German, Florentine, Venetian, Dutch, Flemish, and other fourteenth to eighteenth-century masters flowers from May to October each year; in the **Haus der Kunst** there are additional works belonging to the Bavarian State Art Collection. **Residenzmuseum** (historic crowns, tiaras, and treasures of royalty) and adjoining Schatzkammer (perfectly preserved ancient theater) are so fabulous that no wanderer should miss them. There are a **Beer Museum**, the "Museum of Blooming Nonsense" (**Valentin-Musäum**), the 80-thousand-seat **Olympic Stadium**, and the 951-foot **IVA television tower** with a spiraling elevator and a neighboring 100-foot "Space station," plus a pavilion. The glitteringly reconstructed **State Opera House** is an acoustically perfect 6-tier showcase resembling the original *belle époque* marvel of 3 decades ago. The theaters, the **Zeiss Planetarium**, and other cultural attractions are outstanding. So are the fabled Oktoberfest (late Sept. through early Oct.) and the Fasching (Jan. and Feb.). The local adage states that the former is for beer and laughs, while the latter is for sex and Sekt (German "champagne"). Need proof? (1) The peak annual birthrate is during September and October, precisely 9 months after the January-February revels. (2) Besides, who feels like making Oktoberfest love after consuming 3.3-million quarts of beer and 760 thousand weenies? Three times each year the Auer Dult sales on the Mariahilfsplatz keep bargain-seekers hopping at the local version of Paris' Flea Market. Plenty of good restaurants and bright lights the calendar round, too. You'll probably want to stay here as long as you can.

    Hotels   If you do plan a pause, the **Bayerischer Hof** is a zillion-dollar champion that keeps improving with age. Here is the very last of the most illustrious hotels in the world which for 3 generations has been family owned and totally operated with love in almost unique personal dedication. Brightest baubles include a Trader Vic's restaurant (noteworthy for drinks, décor, and now quality cuisine), an 850-capacity festival hall, the Tirolian Stube adjoining the Palais Keller for local atmosphere and short-order regional cookery, a 200-ton sliding-roofed swimming pool, a health center with adjoining bar, 2 separate "his" and "her" saunas, a solarium, and the Grill with its garden-terrace. All corridors have been recarpeted and all units on the (rear) Prannerstr. side have been thoroughly remade. If perfection is your order of the day, try the adjoining Palais Montgelas, an elegant classic serving as sort of a Bavarian cousin to the Waldorf Towers. The tariffs there are only slightly more than in the main building, but from private receptionist to golden bathroom taps, everything here is even more patrician. Both personally and professionally, we are hopelessly in love with #43, a one-of-a-kind atelier which brought us such joy during our recent stay. In the cellar there's the finest and liveliest nightclub in Bavaria for 200. If money's no object, Suites #328-329 and #428-429 in the original structure offer a gold *double* bathtub, piped music in the bathroom, a fine bar in the sitting room, and wide-angle comfort; #705 and #770 are rustic renditions of the same sweet song, with open fireplaces, stereos, and tonight's-the-night terraces. As if this weren't enough, there's now a kilometer-long Mercedes-600 limousine parked at your front door for special airport shuttles, weddings, special events, or private hire. Costly revampings behind the scenes also contribute toward an improvement in quicker and more tightly controlled room service in this vast establishment. Concierges Stoess and Freytag are outstandingly warm, kind, and efficient. Owner Falk Volkhart merits kudos for his zingingly spirited supervision and for creating out of a bombed-out shell containing 30 rooms a Xanadu which now boasts 430 immaculate accommodations. A triumph of love and devotion.

The splendid and fashionable **Vier Jahreszeiten**, a stalwart of the Old Guard, today easily shares the Munich throne. It is a beauty that radiates nobility, hospitality, and good taste. The entrance is a glistering introduction in glass and buffed bronze; the reception and concierge desks are broad, handsome, and efficient; the lobby provides 2 tiers of wood-paneled Edwardian charm; carpets everywhere are fresh, deep, and colorful. The white-and-gold Walterspeil restaurant is *the* focal point of the area's gastronomy. To one side is the intimate English bar serving soft dance melodies with sips and sups; on the other flank is the Eck ("Corner"), a window-lined nookery that has become famous for its Friday-Saturday buffets; the rooftop pool and sun terrace offer breakfast, lunch and the very same panorama provided by the ultraplush Presidential Suite. Other fillips include the sauna, massage center, hairdressing salons, elevators, and a 2-level underground garage. Though every bedchamber was totally remade, key pieces of the finest older furniture were retained for tradition's sake. Concierges Jakob Pfanzelt and Peter Kruppel are only 2 of the superb staff members whom Manager Mass a-masses at his willing command. Recommended any winter, summer, spring, or autumn. Our all-out congratulations to the Four Seasonal team!

The **Continental** is sumptuous too. Spacious lounges; glorious azure-tiled winter roof garden bursting with flowers; 2 small outdoor parks for summer dining; corridors (some skylighted) with Gothic antiques worthy of the world's finest museums. Handsome popular Conti Grill with 2000-year-old fountain; cuisine which many residents and travelers praise but which we've found mediocre on our several tries. We are especially fond of its late-model courtside demisuites outfitted in rich textiles, elegantly etched mirror panels and sixteenth-century oil paintings. Proprietor Billig, who has spent both a fortune and a lifetime collecting these treasures, spared absolutely not one pfennig in cultivating this tasteful setting. Likable Manager Staschik ably commands his decorous silk-stocking realm—but staff problems are his Cross to Bear, just as they are throughout topflight German hoteleries. The attractions far, far outweigh the debits in this normally fine establishment.

Holiday Inn, a 3-part giant in the Schwabing district, leaped into the fray swinging a cluster of 400 door keys. Its trio of buildings contains rather limited but colorful space for 600; all of the singles have been decked out with double beds. Modernistic interior; lobby and reception in the central edifice; handsome Old Munich Bar under brick arches; dining salon, grill, and coffee shop; Yellow Submarine nightclub; beverage and ice machines on the various floors; swimming pool. Moderate prices that we believe will draw many pilgrims to its rather remote portals.

The 500-unit **Hilton**, sited near the English Gardens and thus also a fair fling from midtown, reveals a lobby possessing all the charms to our eyes, at least, of a bank lounge. Ground-floor Asian cookery; dimly viewful roof restaurant with dinner dancing; Marco Polo Bar moored nearby; year-round swimmery plus sauna. Although every accommodation is well outfitted, we found them as short on decorative flair, quality furnishings, and warmth as they were long on gadgetry. Bus service (for a fee) to and from the airport every 90 minutes. So-so.

In this hotel pennant race, we are sorry to report that the outskirting **Sheraton** shows significant promise of striking out—at least in the considered opinion of these scouts who not only have watched it from the bleachers but have faced it from a home-plate field box. To our disappointment, the reception and concierge desks have balked almost every time we've watched them pitch; the snack bar and restaurant bunt well but are far from being gastronomic sluggers; the silver-foiled Vibraphon nightspot we diagnose as an easy victim of the inside curve; lucky line drives were registered by the pool, sauna, and massage center; the shoeshine and ice machines in the corridors of such a high-priced stadium seemed to us to be far more appropriate in dugout-style facilities. Our hatbox double was worthy of a farm club, and our bathroom—well, we'd send it to the showers, too. On our renewed table of statistics, we'd give it a lowly .110 batting average.

The 250-room **Eden-Wolff** boasts a fine plant that we feel is being neglected through poor maintenance. Wood-lined lobby, lounge, and adjoining trellis-work bar; ski-lodge dining room with knotty timbers, stone arch, and Brueghel mural; colorful yet rapidly fading sleeping quarters, many featuring alcove beds; garage. The station-sited **Bundesbahn** continues to win our Silver Medals for Old World Charm and Modern Comfort. All chambers soundproofed and air-cooled; immaculate maintenance; #507, just under the joists, double-teams for pleasant dreams. Although the **Excelsior** is also hard by the train terminal, it is a surprising island of quiet. Contemporary Christmas-card lobby in wood and stained glass; appealing Sankt Hubertus restaurant in 3 tiers and hunting motif; 100 spotless units, including penthouse suites, encircling a peaceful courtyard; some sancta cheery and others dull. A decent value. The air-conditioned **Königshof** offers an attractive and unusual colorama; lovely mezzanine restaurant called the Terrassen, with a sophisticated mood and superior cuisine; cozy hideaway bar at rear of lobby; bid for the 5th-floor rooms—huge windows, piped music, and a maze of convenience-gadgetry. The sparkling **Ambassador** offers 62 little studios with the beds, only 28 of which are doubles, partitioned off by drapes; private baths and kitchenettes throughout; TV and radio in every room; Persian rugs atop wall-to-wall monotone carpets to raise the BTUs on the personality scale. Comfortable and functional for families with children. The low-cost, 600-unit **Penta**, a sister to the airline consortium hostelries of the same name in London and Paris, is functional. Happily, the subway (S-Bahn) stops at its door on Rosenheimer Platz.

The 150-room **Arabella**, in a satellite suburb that's a costly taxi ride from the bright lights, is—like the Sheraton, its neighbor—probably too remote for the average North American merrymaker and shopper. The **Morizet**, even newer and colorfully cloaked in Frenchy tones, is only as distant as Schwabing; it's a much more rewarding choice in many ways. We are especially fond of the Basco wine room and its Parisianne Restaurant. The nearby **International** seemed too aggressively mod-minded to suit us. The 400-bed **Palace** is another outskirter, this one on the route to Garmisch. Most suitable for 2-suitors. **Esso** fuels up 155 capsules that are air-conditioned and Bavarian-modern in style.

The **Deutscher Kaiser**, a toot from the railroad station, is commercial and clean; 180 rooms and 110 baths within its 18 stories; reserve high for wide-window eyefuls and silence. **Drei Löwen** ("Three Lions") is a favorite of well-bred Bavarian gentry who visit the metropolis. Two attractive dining rooms; cheery retreats. Recommended for its warmhearted personnel and matching clientele. The pink-faced **Amba** hosts numerous tour packages within its 90-room shell. The **Platzl**, opposite the beer-weary Hofbräuhaus, is most definitely not recommended. The **Ariston** serves breakfast only. The **Palace** is far from the action. The **Metropol** is stiff, dour, and institutional; icy-cold lobby halfheartedly brightened by tropical flora; routine bedchambers. The **Stachus**, **Esplanade**, and **Luitpold** strike us as being grim, grimmer, and grimmest—in that order. Last, and we think in many respects least, is the boxy **Tourotel**. Distant location in an industrial forest of smokestacks; plasticky reception and lobby; Naugahyde-and-formica restaurant and bar; pool and sauna. While the kind staff remains the big plus here, in our opinion the minuses have it.

Restaurants Munich offers a wide and exciting variety of dining haunts. **Aubergine** is plainly sensational if quality is your object and price is not. Chef Eckart Witzigmann has created a haven of modernistic beauty with *nouvelle cuisine* to match. There are a few windowside tables plus an inner alcove, all in white with brushed aluminum paneling, a curious blend of Empire and Star Trek styles. Reception and service are perfection; a gourmet menu of vast variety and whispy lightness totals about $60; à la carte will come to nearly the same for a third the number of dishes. The city is rightly proud of this splendid contender. **Tantris**, a practitioner of similar gastronomy, is nearly as spectacular. Modular futuristic construction; orange and red color scheme; walls and ceilings carpeted; planter boxes, and tall floral displays; thoughtful yet peculiar illumination in keeping with its challenging architecture. The food too, is graciously constructed with prices a smidgen below Aubergine's. Superb, and enthusiastically recommended. **Boettner** (Theatinerstr. 8), another fine choice, offers only 9 tables in rear of a small wine and gourmet-item shop; pleasant but not ornate atmosphere; close attention by staff who *care;* shuttered on Sundays; very expensive but worth every pfennig. Be certain to make your advance reservation in this extraordinary nook. For the most fun along with overwhelming variety and sparkling culinations, the **Käfer Schänke** (Schumannstrasse/Prince Regentstrasse) is the Barnum & Bailey and

Bulgari of Munich gastronomy. Its enormous success springs largely from its quality. This one grew out of (and above) a patrician delicacy shop. Most of the tempters for first courses and appetizers are displayed in cafeteria-style chilling cabinets. Diners are invited to take their plate and select from the dozens of handsomely presented salads, gelatins, timbales, pâtés, croûtes, cold-cut tidbits, treasures of the briny, and a trove of other 14-carrot nibbles; pick as much or as little as your appetite or diet dictates; the staff keeps a running record for your billing. Later a flock of waiters serves the main dishes, beverages, cheeses, sweets or other platters at your table or at rustic counters. The atmosphere is gay with laughter and bustling with activity. We enjoyed our repast as much as any informal feast we've experienced in Germany in many a year. Now, returning to the silk-stocking precincts, the dining room of the **Vier Jahreszeiten** unquestionably retains its high repute. Excellent soft music is rendered with the comestibles in the intimate bar annex. The Friday-Saturday buffets in the Eck ("Corner") of the lovely dining salon are becoming famous with German epicures. The overall supervision remains under the legendary Walterspiel wand, a name that has become synonymous with fine fare throughout this neck of the *Wald*. The **Bayerischer Hof** rafts ashore with its Trader Vic's, which is keeping the jungle drums busy beating out exciting drinks, delicious Polynesian fixin's, and amiable professional service; the traditional favorite here has always been the Grill. The latter, with an intimate Stube, has substantial cookery, nightly zither melodies, and competent management. **Zur Kanne** (Maximilianstrasse 36), while deservedly popular for both lunch and dinner, is most chic when it becomes an after-theater rendezvous for the opera group; 6 small rooms linked by twilight illumination, enchantment, and tranquillity; subdued chintz banquettes and walls doodled with cartoons, photos, and programs; excellent wine-restaurant menu. We like this one a lot. The romantic little **Bazaar** (40 Bauerstr.), a dimly glowing Ottoman nook, is caparisoned with striped banquettes, perforated brass lamps, and a tucked-away bar for extra-private weavers of mystic spells, potions, and charms. You'll be soothed by such taped Byzantine hits as "I Wish I Was In Love Again" and "My Heart Belongs to Daddy"; our recently repeated Turkish delight consisted of 2 gigantic succulent porterhouse steaks (the specialty), 2 delicious salads, a bottle of French wine, and 2 Irish coffees; all were memorable. **Romanoff** (Bauerstrasse 2) marches in as another costly but quality-minded aristocrat. Friendly atmosphere configured into an L-form; bar at the L's elbow; gas lamps; one raised tier of banquettes; tempting selection of blinis, borscht, main dishes, and side nibbles from the Old Country, plus vodka served in a block of ice. Although local friends report that the waiters often can be snippish, our meal was a pleasure in every respect. **Datscha** (Kaiserstrasse) is a poor-mouth attempt to copy high-Steppeing cookery, in our opinion. The décor is wonderfully cozy, but the service, presentation, preparation, and general lack of finesse were enough to put us off henceforth and forevermore. **La Cave** (Maximilianstrasse) now seems to have lost some of its fad-rage status. Entrance via a copper-plated chute; stairway handrail made from a musket; cellar cells under vaulted ceiling; candles on tables; warm service; food miserably presented and matchingly prepared on our try; ear-stabbing music that never let up throughout the course of that long, agonizing, fretful feed.

For other stakeouts, we must tie up at steak houses **Ochs'n Willi** and **Ochs'n Sepp**, which are also reputed to mix up a nightly mess of old-fashioned Oklahoma spareribs. This same group runs the **Beim Haberer** local-style wine cellar, the modern **Spatenhaus**, and **Max 2** for snacks in a *fin de siècle* setting. For medium-price dining, **Goldene Stadt** (Oberanger 44) whipped up one of the best meals of a recent teutonic trot—including those sampled at restaurants of infinitely higher cost and fame. Four adjoining rooms; main segment adorned with a photomural of the bridge over the Moldau in central Prague; beautiful and respectful reception, the like of which one seldom experiences in this timeless era; careful service by German-speaking waiters. The Slavic and local dishes are all prepared by highly skilled Dušan Hubácek, the white-smocked owner-chef. Be sure to top off his feast with a shot of Barack offered in a stovepipe glass. Here is our top rating as the finest Czech-point this side of the Iron Curtain. **Humplmayr** has impressed us for many years as being uneven, an observation which we've long reported. Recently we hit such a flagrant off day that we were not only disappointed but dismayed. While it can still come up with exceptionally fine meals at costly tariffs when everyone is pulling together, what we found this time was such vivid lack of consistency that our former high esteem for this landmark has markedly diminished.

Next to the ranking Ratskeller (see below), the **Peterhof Gaststätten** complex (Marienplatz) is our pick for good, solid, inexpensive Bavarian fare—far outshining Donisel or the numerous other family-frequented places which dot this central area. Two-floor Peterhof from ground level in clean-lined regional décor and with plenty of space between its tables and big booths; basement Peterskeller for beer and oompah band between 5 and 12:30; slightly more costly Hock Café on 5th floor with lovely view of the square and of the historic moving figures in the Town Hall which enchant big crowds at 11 A.M. and 5 P.M.; both restaurants open continuously from 9 A.M. to midnight. Salt of the earth. The **Ratskeller** is a splendid example of its genre. It's big, of course, and the food is regional, solid, and tasty. Low vaults; low prices; high value. **Gaststätte Drei Rosen** is clean-lined, cheerful, and also large. But it is well partitioned, cozy, and conducive to pleasant dining. Be sure to dine upstairs. **Kuenstlerhaus** has been taken over by the fast-expanding **Mövenpick** interests; it conforms to the usual Swiss-bred pattern of this network. **Schwarzwälder**, also now part of a chain, is superb; **Bei Milan** is pleasant; so are the artist-and-film hangouts of **Kasak** and **Haxenbauer**, **Csarda Piroschka**, a Hungarian cellar beneath the Haus der Kunst (Art Museum), is about as gimmick-ridden as they come—but enjoyable if your mood is right. Walls dripping with painted florals; menus presented in wooden toy houses; cymbal-throbbing gypsy melodies by a high-strung court of costumed musicians; very kind reception; busy but attentive service; cookery that is strictly from Hunger-y. Popular among first-timers—just once. **Walliser Stuben** (Leopoldstrasse), a Swiss Valais cave, is very attractive; garden-dining in summer; no lunch; bowling alley; straight from Zermatt, and fun. The midcity **Chesa Ruegg** (behind the Vier Jahreszeiten) comes up with another ladle of Helvetia: beamed ceiling, copper pans, and pottery; small sidewalk terrace and moderate tabs. **Mifune** (Ismaninger Strasse 136) is run in conjunction with the local Japanese tourist office. Attractive Oriental flavored (and fragranced) décor;

longish bar; large counter service section with Nipponese bell-shaped grills for the Steak Teppanyaki specialty; 2 western dens with about 7 tables; tea room for ceremonial purposes. Two suggestions: Either reserve 1 of the 3 Japanese salons (4 to 8 persons), leave your shoes at its entrance, sit on the floor, and order from the kimono-clad waitresses the special 5-course lunch or dinner menu at $33; or try the delicious à la carte Makunouchi, a red lacquered, covered, compartmented picnic box which contains rice topped by onions, fish, steak, shrimp, pork, egg flan, 4 different types of salads, and pickles. Hours: 11:30 to 2 and 6 to midnight the calendar around, except on Mondays when Mifune rests.

Alois Dallmayr is reminiscent of Paris' fabulous Fauchon but considerably larger. On the vast ground floor is one of the world's most distinguished food centers with a staggering variety of German and imported delicacies including an aromatic coffee department, a tea department, a marvelous selection of cheeses, fish, hams, vegetables, pastries—name your yum-yum. Upstairs is a 4-room skein of charming light-bite restaurants. Adjoining is a very distinguished gift boutique. The food is expensive but superb. *The* sophisticates of Munich patronize this establishment, as well they should. **Kreutzkamm**, near the Bayerischerhof on Maffeistrasse, is an excellent *Konditorei* for nibblings; it is open the whole shopping day. Homemade desserts and candies are main features. Also chic clientele, but more out-of-towners. The tripartite **Café Luitpold** (Briennerstrasse 11) is a splendid midtown oasis for all pocketbooks. Its divisions are the café section, the grill with counter seating, and the pâtisserie-confection shop. Fast service, good food, and lip-smacking snacks; ask for the handsome young Manager, Mr. Pollman. Highly recommended. Italian fixin's? **Galleria** (Sparkassenstrasse across from Haxenbauer) is a narrow, white, stucco, real-life *galleria* hung with a movable feast of paintings and carved polychromatic carriage yokes. Six candle-topped tables and chamber music contribute to the air of unhurried refinement; perhaps 12 pastas and half as many entrées. **Picadore** and **Circus**, both rolling along on Occamstrasse, pizzas for sidewalk revelers and budgeteering nighthawks. The **Conti Grill** of the Hotel Continental is loaded with rustic charm, but our meat a while back was tougher than Batman's bicep. Maybe what we need is a new dentist.

Sightseeing thrill? Head out to the 951-foot **Olympia Tower**, a TV spike looming over the site of the Olympic Games and an enormous ice rink. From its upper tiers the Alps (65 miles away) are easily visible on a clear day. Small entrance fee; ground-floor Atrium Restaurant with wood panels, suspended "gas" lamps, and a chicken-roost wall decoration (the poultry-minded Wienerwald chain operates the food interests here); rocket-thrust ascent via the fastest elevator in Europe (you might swallow your tummy as you rise 7 meters per second); revolving 3-speed, 32-table panoramic dining ring that is breathtaking; stationary snack bar; upper-level observation deck, plus a children's platform still higher (with low but thick walls to prevent parental coronaries when the little ones venture near the edge). Cuisine typical of the Wienerwald kitchens: savory in a few simple dishes, bland in many others, inexpensive, and 1st-rate quality in ingredients, presentation, and handling. For about $6 by taxi, pennies by tram (#3 or #7), or special bus from the station, this is a *must* for any first-timer to Munich. If it's a glaring or bright day, be sure to bring sunglasses for your fullest enjoyment.

For beer gardens or beer cellars in the city proper, **Mathaeser Beer City** bills itself as the "largest beer-tavern in the world." The open-air garden upstairs normally operates during the 3 warmest months. Concerts in main section at 10:30 to 4 and from 4:30 to 12 with a bigger band; open every day except December 24; good hearty food. For an atmosphere-filled and gratifyingly inexpensive meal, **Nürnberger Bratwurstglorkl**, opposite the Dom, should be mentioned. The dumplings, as well as the wursts, are triumphs. **Platzl**, opposite the Hofbräuhaus and a few steps from the Vier Jahreszeiten, might be called a Bavarian Music Hall; a lively show (in German) goes on throughout your dinner every day of the week. Also clean, also sound cookery, also typical. **Löwenbräukeller**, a gigantic building and garden, can handle 8000 customers at a sitting; strictly mass production for local workers of modest means; 2nd-rate in food, service, atmosphere, and feel. **Augustiner-Keller** offers kegs of action in summer and a bunged-out zero in winter. The internationally renowned **Hofbräuhaus**, which has a capacity for 7000 tipplers, seems to have been the target for every tourist since Genghis Khan. There was roughhouse tussling on 2 recent pop-ins, but these altercations usually are directed onto the street where police haul away the combatants. Have a drink, a peek, and a listen to the oooom-pah band. If you do it just once, that's enough.

Wine restaurant? Try the modest **Weinstadl** (Burgstrasse 5), an Old City tavern virtually unchanged since the day it opened more than 5 centuries ago. Here is Munich's most ancient house, the site where town scribes scratched out the first municipal records at long wooden tables. Main floor plus cellar; vaulted ceilings of brick and mortar; nothing fancy and nothing pretended; heavy play from local clientele of blue-collar workers; open daily from 10 A.M. to midnight. Fun as a change of pace.

Outskirts? On a summer evening the **Forsthaus Wörnbrunn**, in the Grünwald forest, is said to promote friendly persuasions with a salubrious setting and pleasant dining. We haven't had the pleasure of anyone's company here yet, but we're anxious to do so soon.

There's one custom that's a *must* in Bavaria—especially in Munich. According to local legend, Weisswürste, the renowned white sausage, must be consumed "before the church bells ring." So that the belfries won't take offense, everyone ritualistically winds up the evening's toot by stuffing his own casing with this specialty. A typical Würste-house is **Donisl** (across from City Hall), where they serve 373 miles of this blanched-veal delight on a slow morning. You'll S-link home—happily!

Night Life Munich has quite a variety of night spots. Our number one choice is the subterranean lode of the **Hotel Bayerischer Hof**. Split-level gem with the bar and wraparound tables mounted high and a dance circle below; brick and timber décor; central heating by some of the hottest bands on the Continent; appetizing snacks and good honest drinks; steady clientele of the prettiest natives and most discerning night wanderers from afar. Tops in Bavaria. The **Hilton** features pana-romantics and dancing on its 15th floor. Also in hotel circles, the Holiday Inn's **Yellow Submarine** packs a lot of firepower. Don't flinch when a shark swims by your porthole. Our independent nominee is **Eve**, a sophisticated lady who is tastefully ornamented. Continuous show beginning at 11:30 P.M.; the inevitable door snip; at tables, the house policy requires a bottle of champagne (expensive to astronomical) or a ½-bottle of whisky; individual drinks grudgingly served at bar; teetotalers find themselves in the squeezer, with orange juice at nectar price levels per cup (and it's been cut!). Without straining a whit, your eyes normally can't miss a clutch of one-dozen Grade-A B-girls. **Ba-ba-lu**, in Schwabing, draws the Smart Young Set, plus a heavy Italian patronage; electrified and electrifying combo turned on at top volume; no cabaret; you, the client, do the performing. The nearby **Big Apple** pulls in the same youth market; its core is more seedy, however. **Käuzchen** takes us back to the bearcat-and-raccoon-coat days. Parisian ambiance woven through 2 adjoining garret-style rooms; color-paned skylight; dark, cozy, and informal; one of the liltingest Memphis jazz bands we've ever eared (the man on that licorice stick was blowing pure candy). The neighboring **Scotch Kneipe** scotched us as a woody, airless den hacked out in zestless log manorisms; not our lodge, but quite popular. **Die Spritz'n** is even smaller, closer, and thus "with it" tonight. Nibbles available at both. **Capt'n Cook** ran a trimmer ship, say we. The skipper is plastered-in-Paris on the main deck; polished interior and polished passenger list; a cargo of pleasure. **Gaslight Club**, a 50-yard stagger from Ba-ba-lu, struck us as one of the better examples of the city's teen-type discothèques. Wooden sawtooth ceiling; twin plank bars; excellent spirits tumbled into a hefty tumbler. Smart, gay, and popular—but almost exclusively for youngbloods. **Nachteule** is also chiefly for those who haven't begun to vote. **Schwabylon**, a multicolored mechanical colossus of a fun factory, resides next to the Holiday Inn. Look for this wildly painted "aircraft carrier superstructure"—but then _who could miss it?_ Wow! **Gisela** is fun for a more senior following. **Bongo** drums up a tropical never-never-land atmosphere. If whisky is your sauce, you must hike up at 1 of its 4—count 'em, 4—bars staffed by native houris; if you want to glim the show, a bottle of wine is SOP; 2 dance floors; intermittent entertainment. Also one of the best of its league in Germany. **Intermezzo** is popular with a young crowd. Small show that's a sizzler; our beverage was served from an overworked Haig & Haig bottle; smooth band; aging ladies of the evening. Take pocket change, because the barmaid made it clear she considers it a mortal sin to break big bills. **P-1** has a charming atmosphere, except the cocktail lounge still looked moth-eaten. Inner sanctum with timber and oil paintings. **Cin-Cin**, near the Four Seasons, is pleasant, too. Circular bar, semicircular booths, no circular women, but very sleek, chic Executive Setters and slim German Pointers. A cozy niche for swanky-panky. Some of the student hangouts in Schwabing, Munich's "Little Montmartre," are amusing and colorful; typical examples are **Heuboden**, a tramcar known as the **Subway**, **Siegesgarten**, and **Badewanne**. **Hängematte** is so heavy and so grimly joyous it's not for Americans; miserable ventilation too. **Lola Montez**, across from the Hofbräuhaus, seemed routine. **Domicile** is the hottest and coolest stop for jazz. **Jack's Bar** and the **Moulin Rouge** are not recommended by us. **Citta 2000** comprises restaurants, shops, bowling lanes, a discothèque—almost anything except a much-needed clinic for ruptured eardrums. The theme, in our opinion, is pure claptrap, whether it be musical, sartorial, visual, or gustatory.

The prostitutes parade along Landsberger Strasse, near the outskirts of the city, and Josephspitalstrasse, where they must remain in doorways or passages to avoid arrest for "streetwalking." From $50 to $85 is the customary fee (not counting, of course, the medical treatment which usually follows). Anyone who touches this group is a con-genital idiot and imbecile. Hausfrauen? In our advanced age of technological nomenclature, the most famous name in the local trade is **Mex Haus** (112 Hohenzollernstrasse). The state winks at its hygienically (we hear) useful function. No credit cards accepted. P.S. When it was inaugurated, its name was Imex Haus, but shortly afterward it changed its moniker because of a complaint from a corporation that bore the same title. (We can imagine the peculiar customer mail *that* company undoubtedly received!)

Shopping   Europe's largest underground shopping center swung into action in '72 beneath the Stachus, Munich's main square.

Cameras and accessories: ★ ★ ★ ★ ★ **Kohlroser** (Maffeistrasse 14) is our favorite camera shop in southern Germany—not only because the stock is so extensive, but also because Mr. Kohlroser and assistants Mr. Schindler and Mr. Schuermann are so honest, so kindly, and so interested in doing the best possible job for each client. They refund the turnover tax of about 9% through the Tax Free Shop Organization after the customs declaration form is returned. Every camera in the shop is guaranteed for a minimum of 12 months, even if shipped. On their shelves you'll find an extensive assortment of the absolute latest models of cameras, movie cameras, binoculars, opera glasses, Zoom lenses for German and Japanese cameras, automatic slide projections, flea-size electronic computer flash units, and goodness knows what else. Furthermore, the house provides 2-day service on Ektachrome. Superb stocks, superb values—but the most important asset around Kohlroser's is that wonderfully gentle and sweet spirit of theirs. For more than a quarter of a century, we have adored the joys of what they have and the joys of them. A shutterbug's heaven!

Porcelain and ceramics: In the spacious, beautifully decorated ★ ★ ★ ★ ★ **Rosenthal** (Theatinerstrasse 8) you will find the complete collections of the Rosenthal "3 C's"—china, crystal and cutlery—as well as the best in tablewares and housewares, the Rosenthal Studio-Line products, the "Classic Rosenthal" dinner sets, and the vast Hummel collection with its beautiful gift items. Prices? An astonishing 50% *average* saving against the same merchandise at home. They do a huge export and mail order business. Ask for the dashing private pilot and porcelain expert, Dr. Hans Zoellner. None better. **Nymphenburg** (Odeonplatz 1) is Rosenthal's only German rival for Cadillac-class porcelains. Also exquisite.

Leather goods and travel aids: It's **Plaschke** (Brienner Strasse 11, a few steps from Kohlroser) which has steadily built up a sterling reputation in individually designed-and-crafted luggage.

Jeweler: **Hans R. Rothmüller** (Briennerstrasse) is the most distinguished here—with the most distinguished price tags, too.

Food delicacies: **Feinkost Kafer** and **Alois Dallmayr** (Dienerstrasse 14–15) offer so many, many goodies to tantalize your lucky, lucky 5 senses that we won't even begin to encourage you on the path of sin here.

Handicrafts: **Wallach** (Residenzstrasse 3) has 2 floors packed to the rafters with them, as well as a basement bulging with antiques.

Optics: ★ ★ ★ ★ ★ **Söhnges** (Briennerstrasse 7 and Kaufingerstrasse 34) is one of the 2 or 3 top optical complexes in the world today. This reporter has bought at least a dozen pairs of contact lenses here over many years. All have been super.

Furniture: **Deutsche Werkstätten** (Briennerstrasse 54) is the marketplace of many independent Bavarian artisans, with its accent on furniture, fabrics, lamps, and wooden paintings.

There is no **Flea Market** in Munich. The so-called **Farmer's Market** (Auer Dult) runs its frenzied course 3 times per year—early April, early August, and October 15 to 23. It's a huge rummage sale which is such fun that we urge you don't miss it if you're there when it's in such happy action.

NÜRNBERG   is a charming example of the once-moated medieval metropolis. Its walls, towers, and ancient landmarks have been almost completely restored (one tower stands 1000 feet tall beaming TV pictures thoughout the area); the impressive **Kaiserburg** (Imperial Palace) dominates the local landscape, but without the "Iron Maiden" and other historic instruments of torture; the kids love the **Grimms' Witch Cottage** at the castle entrance (totally covered with eatable gingerbread at yuletide); the **Meistersingerhalle** is handsome. Dürer's 5-century-old dwelling, and the St. Lorenz and St. Sebaldus churches are the most popular sights.

As for its hotels, the **Grand** is still the Old Guard leader. Now 130 baths for 160 bedrooms; cocktail lounge; Walliser Kanne restaurant created from a dismantled Swiss chalet; private 60-car garage. The vivacious **Carlton** is almost the same size. Richly attractive emerald restaurant enhanced by a burgundy carpet and wrought-iron fixtures; headwaiters in tails; handsome tartan bar and black executive chairs under a gold ceiling; amiable doubles; modern suites. More active wayfarers will probably prefer this one to the Grand. Very good. **Am Sterntor**'s public rooms and corridors seem dreary while the bedchambers are contrastingly fresh and cheery. The **Victoria**'s exterior and downstairs, on the other hand, belie what you'll find when you open your bedroom door: heavy, dismal, grim cells. **Kaiserhof** impressed us as being too rickety for its stiff tariffs. **Am Ring**, situated in the eye of an intersecting traffic hurricane, is bright, clean, and satisfactory; breakfast only. **Reichshof** evokes a commercial feel, with furniture that looks as if it were borrowed from a nightclub. Personally, if we had wheels and were only passing through, we'd pick the **Crest Motel** in a jiffy or a jitney. Handy site for road-runners near the exit to the Berlin–Munich and Frankfurt–Nürnberg autobahns; 6 stories containing a specialty restaurant, the Puppengrill for international fare, the Oldtimer Bar, and 92 bedrooms or suites, each with bath or shower, telephone, and radio. Fill 'er up?

When we speak of food in this town, let us lead off with our first choice of THE place to avoid: The famous **Goldenes Posthorn**. This self-appointed temple of gastronomy claims to be both the oldest wine cellar in Germany (A.D. 1498) and very nearly the finest restaurant on both hemispheres. With as much charity as we can muster, let us simply impart that our views hardly coincide with those of its management. Pure fun and authentic local color? We adore the **Bratwurst-Herzle**. Community tables; standard pewter plate, heart-shape platter of fingerling sausages, sauerkraut and horseradish (about a buck), beer, cheese—and that's all; always packed. In the same category, **Schranke, Bratwurst-Häusle**, and **Bärle** are also worthy but offer less flair. The **Spi-tal**, spanning the river on 2 giant arches, is a typical wine restaurant that dishes up typically awesome German proportions. **Nassauer Keller** has better cook-ery.

When Nürnberg's night shadows fall and masculine temperatures rise, **Chérie** is the most popular root of their fever; they quaff costly libations to see women who don't even wear clothes, poor things. **Erotica** follows suit in this suitless art. Many similar spots line Luitpoldstrasse, if anyone is a glutton for torture.

The leading candidate among its hotels is still the ancient **Alois Lang**. Quiet situation enhanced by a no-tour-group policy (rare in this frenetic hive); 51 rooms; all units with private balcony and most with bath; carpeting through-out. Its 3 dining rooms serve up savory vittles. Manager Ranges is trying extra-hard to please Americans—and he seems to be doing it, day-after-day. Recommended as a pleasant but unfancy hitching post. The **Wolf** offers more charm in its bedchambers (especially the top-floor Bavarian rooms), but its central situation and busy-busy public areas give it a somewhat commercial feel. Flowers and colorful touches everywhere; prices lower than the leader; very good value. **Alte Post** comes up with cheery accommodations but a very low bath count. **Böld** plays host to battalions of G.I.'s during ski season; not bad for the basic-minded sportsman. The **Wittelsbach** turns over more tou-rists, it seems, than does Mr. Cook. Going bach-ward Wittel-by-Wittel. In neighboring *Ettal*, also in Oberbayern, the barnish **Ludwig der Bayer** has a big name locally, but to us it seems as cold as a penguin's pinfeather; if you burrow into its icebergs, take the newer wing only.

PUTTGARDEN This is on the island of Fehmarn (auto route to Den-mark). The **Dansk** or the **Baltic**, 10 minutes south of the toll gates, are passable. Over the border at *Rodby Havn*, you have the clean **Danhotel** or the **Motel Rodby Havn**.

RAVENSBURG Our favorite stop here is the 14-story **Europa**, perhaps because of its Alpine lake view from the roof garden.

REGENSBURG Refer to the nearby "Romantic Road," which follows.

ROMANTIC ROAD First off, here is a smattering of its history. What you seek, of course, is preserved obsolescence. You'll discover exactly that. This fascinating route was a vital and thriving lifeline during the Middle Ages, when a military link between fortresses was imperative for survival. The word "Hof," which is suffixed to the names of so many modern German hotels, literally derives from the walled and safe "courtyard" where travelers could rest while passing from stronghold to stronghold. Initially, they slept in their carriages or under their horses. Soon drink was provided. Later food was served. Finally overnight shelters were constructed. When the wars ended and transportation lanes were shifted, these great installations became super-annuated. Not until recent times did historic interest regenerate their unique touristic allure.

Now to the practical side. Even though the authentic Romantic Way begins in the Würzburg environs, we'd suggest you spend your first night in either *Mainz* (the Hilton is a far cry from a "Hof") or in *Wiesbaden* (where accommodations are better than anything you'll find en route, with the exception of Rothenburg ob der Tauber). If you insist upon *Würzburg*, however, we'd recommend the old-fashioned **Lämmle** (convenient, because it's beside the Market Square), the much better **Erbachshof** (4 miles out of town; good food; a bit costly), or even the **Grundmühle** (about the same distance from the center; converted mill in a lovely valley; also outstanding cuisine for the region). *Bad Mergentheim* is no longer lauded as a scenic attraction; today it's more famous as a spa, with the top watering spot the modernistic **Viktoria**. Now zip through *Weikersheim* and *Creglingen* to *Rothenburg ob der Tauber* for the best and most exciting overnight of the entire loop. This antique sparkler is the gem of the bracelet, so we urge that you concentrate most of your time, calories, and shut-eye here. As for hotels, we'd rate them as follows: (1) **Eisenhut** (this famous "Iron Hat" offers a stunning terrace-restaurant over the Tauber, an expanded dining room and an added wing; 2 adjoining buildings recently purchased and 1-unit façade extended; some ac-commodations perked up, but still flairless in the older sections; room #102 is praised as one of the *most* "romantic" on the entire "road" by one gallant knight of the nightscape; much improved cuisine that can be inconsistent; a surfeit of haughty staffers; very high tabs), (2) **Goldener Hirsch** (superb view; lower rates and a special greeting for 1st-and-2nd honeymooners; some newer units with baths; Blue Terrace dining room in Louis XVI mood; very good; very friendly), (3) the colorful 13-unit **Adam** (*Weinstube;* far better bedcham-bers than the older ones in the Eisenhut at twice the bite), and (4) the cozy 30-room **Markusturm** (group-minded in season). Moving on through *Feucht-wangen* to *Dinkelsbühl*, the **Goldene Rose** has been reperfumed petal by petal and is now quite recommendable; the next-door **Deutsches Haus** is passable at best; the little **Palmengarten**, though without a restaurant, is better as an alternate choice for sleeping. *Nördlingen* is nörd for lingering, and *Donauwörth* is nau worthwhile; both should be daylight pauses only. In *Augsburg*, the most august is the **Drei Mohren** ("Three Moors"); the **Lamm** baaaas up to our 2nd slot; the **Alpen** peaks in for show money. None will really wow you. In *Landsberg*, the once-pleasant **Goggl** is slipping. In *Regens-burg* (off "The Romantic Road" but in the same district), the **Avia** flies away with the prize; it's a pipit. *Rottenbuch*, *Wies*, *Steingaden* and world-renowned *Schwangau* strike us as being miserable for creature comforts, but thrilling for rubbernecking. Wayfarers may bunk at the **Hirsch** in nearby *Füssen*, which boasts 50 rooms, 10 baths, a listless restaurant, and a cozy country-style *Stube* for beer, wine, and trencherman fare. Frankly, if we were heading this way for the purpose of seeing the Neuschwanstein and Hohensch-wangau castles, we'd opt for either the road-hugged, tiny **Lisl und Jägerhaus** or the 40-room **Müller** at the base of the path leading up to the summits. The latter recently renewed; some chambers attractively finished in pinewood; snack bar; tavern; not bad if you can sweet-talk private plumbing from the reception people.

RÜDESHEIM This Rhine port is filled with so many booze-soaked revelers in season and such clatter otherwise that we'd advise river cruisers to avoid overnighting here; skit up to Assmannshausen instead.

STUTTGART takes pride in its pleasant location, mineral springs, eye-popping 692-foot Fernsehturm (TV tower) restaurant, German Antiques Fair, Liederhalle for concerts, an art collection acquired from Norwegian shipping executive Ragnar Moltzau, "Sunny" (the performing chimp at the Wilhelma Zoo and Botanical Gardens), and such important factories as Daimler-Benz, Porsche, Kodak-Germany, and Bosch-Germany. Literally translated, the name of the city is "Stud Farm"—a term most servicemen stationed here would call euphemistic. Too many industrial plants and too much commerce; not very exciting for touring humans—*or* stallions.

The 8-story **Am Schlossgarten** is an asset of innkeeping to this Detroit of Germany. Its courteous service and friendly atmosphere are fostered by Manager Bachstein. Good cuisine in its glass-lined dining salon or parkside sun terrace; Swabian tavern with paneled, leather-ceilinged bar; 125 rooms adequate for short stays; small "efficiency" baths; no full suites; pleasant, angular construction with nice touches of wood. Worthy, especially for the staff kindness. The **Graf Zeppelin**, is operated by the ubiquitous Steigenberger chain which has now strengthened this link with an expansion program. Longer-term visitors may find larger accommodations here, plus a goodly supply of suites; double windows; excellent air-conditioning system; refinished Zeppelin-Stüble restaurant; rejiggered bar with handsome wood paneling; an indoor swimming pool plus a sauna. A Zeppelin that is definitely flying high, wide, and handsome. **Parkhotel**, 10 minutes out in Villaberg Park, offers 85 bedrooms, 54 baths, and generally bathetic styling. The surroundings are restful except when the tours pour in. This one *could* shine, but it would take about a million marks to polish it. The 100-unit **Royal** has donned some fresh raiments. Pleasant suites, with #117 our choice of the crop; poor vistas throughout; TV available on request. Pick only the newer nests here. **Schloss Solitude** is a 15-minute scoot from town via the highway that periodically becomes the world-famous sports-car racing course. Its main function (except to coddle Porsche-bred nostalgics who rally out to whip through a few gears) is to serve as a nexus for scores of weddings, meetings, and back-slapping reunions. Complement of 37 rooms, 4 baths, and 13 showers; 2 suites; small restaurant; kitchen off the lobby. While there are a few commendable facets here, it is too remote and hushaby for most lively trippers—unless "I do!" or "I don't!" are on the tip of your tongue. Neither the **Ketterer** (groups galore from Europe's backwaters) nor the **Reichsbahn** (adjoining the station and noisy) will ever put London's Savoy out of business. The **Airport Hotel** glides in with a cargo of flair in its soft-toned, window-lined dining room, its adjoining bar, and the mod-mooded lobby. All 128 rooms with bath, radio, beds with vibrators, and telephone; bus and even a helicopter service for the Stuttgart environs. Public areas are air-conditioned, but bedchambers are only sound-proofed. Simple but ample for short-haulers. Within sight, the 200-unit **Hotel Stuttgart International** raises its proud head just off Highway 27 at **Möhringen**, 5 minutes from the airport and a fairly expensive taxi hop from the center of town. Dining facilities include a cafeteria, breakfast room, banquet hall, Swiss feedery, rooftop aerie, garden nutrition nook, and a ground-floor nightclub; there are also a pool, sauna, bowling lanes, underground garage, beauty parlor, bank, doctor, dentist, and a travel agency. Superb furnishings in all bedrooms, demisuites, and full apartments. Very well appointed. An outstanding candidate for anyone wishing to be away from mid-city.

By day or by night, the **Fernsehturm** (TV tower) is a sensation—for view, not for gastronomy. Atop a hill, it's a 692-foot-high needle which impales a tapered aluminum and glass "cork" at the 558-foot level—and this cork is a 4-story restaurant, TV transmission point, observation platform, kitchen, and wine cellar. The elevator takes 35 seconds to get up there! Lunch moderately priced; dinner more expensive; food decidedly not the main feature here. Back in the city proper, we've always been addicted to the colorful and charming **Alte Post**. If you're neither an eagle nor a landlubber, perhaps **Lukullus** might titillate your fancy. This floating restaurant is a converted excursion liner moored on the Neckar at **Stuttgart-Bad Cannstatt**. Capacity for more than 500 passengers—er, diners; meals served on several deck levels, with special accommodations for winter rigors; Schifferstube ("Skipper's Bar") up forward with lantern fixtures and other rigging. As for the galley, sorry, mates, we're completely at sea. The **Scheffelstuben** (Haussmannstrasse 5) and the rustic-style **Waldhotel Schatten** (near the Solitude race course) are under the same managerial aegis. The latter offers a substantial and inexpensive Sunday buffet. The **Schwabenbräu** was tapped out by a brewery. Typical food of the region (plus suds, of course). A **Mövenpick**, with its woodlined Rôtisserie Baron de la Mouette, sizzles on the Kleiner Schlossplatz. This Swiss chain knows its vittles. **Traube**, about 5 minutes from the airport, is described by one jovial reader as "Black Forest baroque" in décor. Superb gastronomy; extensive wine selection (and well treated, too); lots of country-style atmosphere to spur on the appetite. We think you'll like it, but be sure to phone first to reserve a table.

TRIBERG The **Park Wehrle** is a rich hearty, German colonial establishment in the hands of the same family since 1707. Excellent cuisine, too, from those talented hands!

ULM The **Bundesbahnhotel** is a recommendable contemporary address if you plan to spend a night.

WIESBADEN is a scenic spa and an excellent springboard for your Romantic Road-running. **Nassauer Hof** now leads the list, having enjoyed so many updatings and so much re-sparkling in recent months. Topping the button-poppers is the new deluxe Die Ente vom Lehel restaurant with exceptional duck specialties and other high-flying German dishes. Die Pfanne focuses it culinary spotlight on regional and Alsatian cookery at moderate prices. Enormous input achieved recently by friendly Manager John Van Daalen; superb hall-portering by keen Heino Reichard; bar with copper hearth; pool and sauna. Everyone knows his or her assignment to perfection and performs it deftly, properly, and cheerfully. Warmly recommended. Bright feathers in the cap of the handsome **Schwarzer Bock** include the Le Capricorne French Restaurant (with nearly a ½-acre of priceless fifteenth-century wood carvings), and a newer wing boasting 30 rooms and 10 suites. Classic, tasteful atmosphere; lovely 5th-floor roof garden with grill, Chinese tearoom, restaurant, sundeck, and cocktail terrace; fizzy indoor swimming pool filled with sparkling water from local springs; minimum rooms very small, but each has 2 washbasins in its bathroom and other urbane touches. Substantial and tasteful.

The Intercontinental chain has linked up its 168-room, medium-budget **Forum**. Heated pool; restaurant; buffet breakfast; lounge and bar. Too cool for the vacationer, in our view. The **Blum**, though noisy, again seems to be satisfying a number of readers this year; very popular coffee shop and mezzanine restaurant; nothing special, but reasonably worthy. The **Park** offers a diverse bag of bedrooms along with a generally commodious atmosphere. The 100-room, 50-bath **Taunus** is thumbs down to us. The pleasantly situated **Klee** comes up with 50 kips, all with private bath; breakfast is the only meal; no bar; #34 with 2 balconies and a gay mien is a good buy. Rather informal. The **Grüner Wald**, another Second-class hostelry, has grown too creaky for all but the sparest of budgets. Passable at best. The midtown **Badhaus Bären**, even with its modernization and pool, is overpriced for the value, say we. The aged **Goldenes Ross und Goldene Kette** is a dandy dip for penny-pinchers; no private baths, but a fine spa facility with one of the oldest thermal taps in the city; rock-bottom prices. Good for what ails you—especially if your aches are in your wallet. The **Eden** and the **Sabini**? Never. Finally, in the outskirts at *Östrich*, the ancient and colorful **Schwan** is one of the nation's best-known country inns; set-back Rhine-side location with enchanting view; savory regional cookery; friendly service. Ask for room #27 (with 7 riverview windows) or #21 (cute as a dollhouse); both sunny; operated by the Winkel-Wenckstern family since A.D. 1628; ideal for tranquillity; legendary for its wines; open March 1 to December 1 only. Be sure not to confuse it with the one in *Erbach*, which is 4 miles closer to Wiesbaden, because it's nowhere nearly as Sch-wanderful. The road-clinched, castle-hotel **Reinhartshausen**, in the same riverside neighborhood, was a disappointment to us. As one example of its bizarre motif, the Teutonic vaulted cellar restaurant was filled with good old Rheingau Scottish tartans. If you're stuck, ask for room #100; the terrace adjoining it is the size of a tennis court. We've seen better.

Food-conscious local citizens praise the renowned **Mutter Engel**—a hollow bruit, as far as we're concerned. There are 2 sancta of no decorative significance, one with clay-color walls and the other in green; the waiters were far too busy with bookwork, preening, and self-importance to serve the worthy offerings of the able chef. Basically sound, if some lion tamer would snap the whip at those cats in black. We much prefer the circular grill room at the **Nassauer Hof** or the pepped-up cuisine of the **Schwarzer Bock**. **Am Kamin** bases its reputation chiefly on steaks. **Müller's Weinstube** toasts visitors only in the evenings. The **Mövenpick** is across from the Casino; it's okay for medium-priced dining in this high-priced town. **Lessing Stuben** and **Pfeffermühle** are local in style and typical in cookery. **Yuen's China-Restaurant** is a converted beer hall gone Cantonese.

Among this town's modest night clubs, the leader is the prim and proper **Park**; afternoon openings with magic acts and jugglers, then growing riper as the day grows older. **Intermezzo** spotlights buff-tone strippers. **Parisiana Bar** comes up with revues and booze, but little to amuse.

Greece

Here, with Rome, is 1 of the 2 glittering, shimmering fountainheads of our Western Civilization. Jounce along the pulsing streets of its ancient capital: The golden shadow of Pericles is beside you. Climb the marblecapped Acropolis: You are standing beneath the pillars of mankind's Democracy. Look out to the Aegean: You are smelling the salty sea-swept drifts of early commerce. Watch a pair of brighteyed urchins running out their private marathon: You are experiencing the visible echo of the first Olympic Games, more than 27 centuries ago. At your feet, a white-robed thespian dons a tragic mask, then abruptly shifts to comedy. On your left, Socrates praises "the love of wisdom" —philosophy. On your right gathers a coterie of poets, musicians, architects, astronomers, painters, soldiers, lawyers, doctors, politicians, mathematicians. These were the seeds that germinated in the Plains of Attica and enriched the world. This is Greece. Never mind the origin of your own ancestors. You, with us, share the spirit, the soul, and the treasures of Hellenic heritage.

But to everyone's alarm, over the past 3 years a new blight has been causing the core of this Golden Apple to molder. This was the sudden incredible stampede of foreign travelers—6-million in '79 in a country of 9-million, with a 15% annual increase of the former—who are bursting the seams of her capital from April through October and overinundating the most glorious sites in her hinterlands and on her islands. The combination of its rising but still comparatively reasonable costs, its climate, its towering historical cultural heritage, and its people—the greatest natural resource of all—is fast destroying her formerly tranquil environment of repose. Americans predominate, followed sucessively by Yugoslavs, Germans, British, and French; the ranks of other nationalities are further swelled by a continuously grinding mill of conducted tours from Rumania, Hungary, Bulgaria, and other satellite countries. Hotels in the popular centers are continuously jammed to their cornices. Road traffic in Athens and its environs will continue to be a Dantean nightmare. As one illustration which was particularly dismaying, on a recent trip we counted more than 100 sightseeing buses parked along the narrow country road to the gate of the Temple of Apollo, which meant that roughly 5,000 tourists were simultaneously ant-ing on the rocks of this monument. As we predicted in last year's

edition of this book, motivated by greed the majority of hoteliers have jumped
their rates around 20% for the coming season. The situation has become so
intolerable that even the Finance Minister has expressed fears that the influx
has grown too quickly. With his head in the clouds, he stated that "Measures
might have to be taken to put a break (on it) *when it reaches 8 million in 3
or 4 years*" (italics ours). Wow! More practically, a tourist board spokesman
announced that this organization's new strategy of "quality tourism" has been
initiated. The official said that prices are being raised significantly to discourage lower-income voyagers. One said but inescapable fact is obvious: The
authorities now have no choice except to move radically and fast to prevent
this holidaymakers' former paradise from being ruined as a vacation magnet.

☑ **TRANSPORTATION** Several sleek, comfort-plus ferries operate between
Brindisi (Italy) and Patras. Stops at Corfu and Igoumenitsa; facilities ranging from
airplane-type seats to Deluxe cabins for both day and overnight sojourns; drive-on-
drive-off gangways; space for 150 or more cars; running once every day of the week
the year around and more frequently in summer. Additional routings reach Patras
from Ancona. There is also piggyback railway service for autos through Italy, a
sleeper-bus hookup between Naples and Brindisi in summer, and a viewful coastal
highway at the threshold to Greece. The scenic drive now between Patras and the
capital takes a mere 3 hours.

Taxis Scarce—normally so absent that they should be considered an endangered
species. Even chauffeur-driven cars are rare. Drivers are poor, they don't know where
they're going, and they're far from cordial. Space is so short that passengers often double
up and share a hack together. The best place in Athens we found to hail a taxi is at the
Hilton Hotel. Not once on our latest rounds did we find a driver who immediately knew
an address—even when it was written out in Greek letters. Time after time we ran into
utter confusion, so to allay at least a smidgen of the annoyance, check with your
concierge first.

Due to the acute gas shortage, taxi fares have more than tripled within a short span
of months. Now the minimum ride is Drs. 40; every time the meter clicks it is Drs. 10
per jump. Thanks to the National Tourist Office, a driver who overcharges and is
reported often loses his license. Now he is both more careful and more sly as a result
—so *you* be wary, too!

Legally and theoretically you, as the original passenger, may give the driver your
permission to share the cab with one or more persons and then to split the cost on a
mutual basis. In reality, however, nearly all of these petty chiselers charge each individual or party the full fare. When this happens, *please don't tip him 1 lepta!*

Airline A description of Olympic, the national carrier, is found in the "Air
Travel" chapter.

Caution: Except at airports, all of the airline offices in the nation operate from 8 A.M.
to 6 P.M. only—and they put down their shutters on all Sundays and holidays. Strange!

Trains Greece is now a member of the moneysaving **Eurailpass** system. The
service is improving generally, but it's still spotty in quality. The international expresses

through Yugoslavia to Zürich, Paris, Ostend, Germany, or other European points are comfortable. There is good diesel railcoach service from Athens to Corinth, Olympia, Nauplia, Tripolis, Levadia, Larissa and Salonika. The roadbed to the Peloponnesus is narrow-gauge and rooted in a foundation of Jell-O. Travel by car (but be sure to read the "Hired Cars" warning below) or by bus if you can; the Pullman-coach buses are royal chariots by comparison. If you must take a train, *stick to First-class.*

Hired Cars and Motoring If you wish to drive yourself, the best rental agency we found is Hellascars, with its vast fleet of well-maintained vehicles. Next we'd choose Hertz or Avis. Chauffeur-driven cars in Athens are one of the sorriest examples of legalized hijacking we've encountered anywhere in our wanderings. The iron fist of the Greek Government should bring down the wrath of outraged justice upon these wretches. Book your vehicle *only through one of the recognized and reputable travel agencies in Athens,* such as **Hellenic Tours**, 3 Stadium St., where Mr. Nelson Melamed is director. With the sound guidance of this veteran expert and his staff, you will at least know the established price beforehand. They have kindly offered to serve as special watchdogs for readers of this book. As a footnote, allegedly through the pressures of the taxi unions only about 60 are available in the capital at this writing—and *none,* as far as we know, can be found except in the metropolis. For excursions in the hinterlands, your only solution is to resort to an ordinary cab. Be sure to fix the price before you set out!

If you plan to motor extensively in this land, it is strongly recommended that you join ELPA, the Greek Automobile and Touring Club. There is a registration fee of less than $10 plus a charge of about $20 per year. This worthy organization is similar to the British AA. Among other services, it gives road assistance, legal advice if needed, and discounts on various gas coupons *outside* the country.

From 5 a.m. on Saturdays to 5 a.m. on Mondays, all vehicles can be operated only on alternate weekends, depending on whether the license plate ends in an even or an odd number. Rented cars, which bear a bold striped sticker on their windshields, as well as vehicles with foreign registrations, are immune from this restriction. When any violator is caught, the penalties are severe—the balance of these two days in jail until the courts open on Monday and/or fines up to $2,700.

★ **TIPS** The traffic which clogs the capital's narrow streets and its environs is simply indescribable. There is no way to believe it except to see it.

Roads are not Greece's greatest selling point. On the mainland they are often rutted, washed out, snow-blocked, or mud-drenched. On the islands they frequently seem to vanish entirely. The nation's 2 major highways run from Patras to Athens (limited access and a lovely 3-hour run) and from the capital north to Thessaloniki. The toll pike leading into Athens is very short, only 2 lanes wide in many places, and so poorly engineered as to be especially dangerous on rainy nights.

Don't start any motoring journey after dark. The countryside is so desolate that if a breakdown occurs you could be stranded till dawn. Trucks also begin their long hauls in the evenings; the major arteries are so clogged with them that they're almost sclerotic. Greek drivers—all too many new to the game—do not share our respect for the eyes of oncoming drivers; even buses and trucks contribute in this innocent discourtesy. (On one recently completed 66-mile hitch, we spent more than 2 1/2 hours behind our wheel, due only to the dangers encountered from headlight-blindness.) It's a question of inexperience, not inconsideration.

☑ **FOOD**   When the Greeks try to cook like Frenchmen the results are usually disappointing if not disastrous. When they cook like Greeks they turn out interesting fare. In general, however, to most outsiders, the national culinary level is an adventure.

Regional dishes worth trying are Dolmades (grape leaves stuffed with meat, rice, onion, and seasonings); Souvlakia (a succulent facsimile of shish kebab, consisting of lamb, tomatoes, and peppers roasted on a spit); Moussaka (chopped meat baked with potato, veal, eggplant, tomato sauce, cheese, eggs, and spices); the magnificent red mullet, finest in the 7 seas; kalamaraki (tenderized squid); octopus (so delicious it tastes like chicken-lobster); and the local langouste (clawless crayfish). These are merely samples; there's a large choice of other specialties. Incidentally, to us, Greek ice cream in general (not always) nearly vies with Italian ice cream, which is our favorite on the Continent.

We stumbled across one of our happiest food discoveries some years back. It's called Peïnerli, and it's a "sandwich" of crisp, succulent pizza dough shaped like a Viking ship containing your choice of fillers: cheese and tomato sauce, chopped meat and cheese, chopped meat and egg, ham and cheese, ham and egg, sausage and egg, fried egg and ground meat only. When it comes piping hot to the table, mix the fillers on the "deck" so they soak into the underside of the crust. Then eat the center out, and finally polish off the whole. **Y Pighi Eleftheriatis** ("The Source") at ***Drossia***, 14 miles northeast of Athens, is the original creator and king of this dish. Here is an absolutely TERRIFIC treat—a happy drive for lunch on a benign day, very reasonable in price, and 102% worth the trip! Personally, we love everything about it and find it amazing that each successive yearly visit seems better than the last one! Since the success of "The Source," many less skillful imitators have sprung up in or around Drossia; for a switch, we tried a crowded pavilion-restaurant called the **Small Pines**. it was a big disappointment.

Not recommended is a little number called Kokoretsi (sometimes spelled Cocoretzi), which is mushy intestines stuffed with liver, *very* fresh kidneys, and innards, half-baked by an apathetic fire. Because it's often as high as a vulture, with a monstrously hideous aroma, we've turned kelly green on no less than 7 separate occasions over the years while trying to force it down; it happens to be the only recognized dish we've ever sampled anywhere that we simply couldn't stomach before the 8th try.

Meal hours are generally from 7 P.M. to 10 P.M. for dinner. As in Egypt, Spain, or Portugal, the later the hour, the larger the crowd.

Fruits, melons, and vegetables which grow in the ground should always be washed. In the larger centers, restaurateurs generally do this before serving such food. Don't worry about it in the good places in Athens, but when you buy them yourself or eat them in villages, this precaution must be taken.

★ **TIP**   Whenever you tackle the flavorful little Greek clams called Thalassina, always squeeze a drop of lemon juice over each one before downing it; *if it doesn't wiggle when the juice hits it, leave it alone!*

☑ **DRINKS**   Practically everything is available in unlimited quantities—from Scotch to blends to bourbons to you name it—at prices that are pretty palatable, too. Brandy is the national hard drink; Metaxa, sharply sweet, is the most popular; Camba, far drier and smoother, is the closest contender. Ouzo, bless its jaunty heart, is the national apéritif; it is a thaumaturge's cross between French Pernod, Javanese arrack, and Turkish raki, with a faint licorice flavor. Order Sans Rival brand (its superiority to all others is notable); mix it with water plus lots, lots, lots and lots of ice; then when you sit and sip in that healing Greek sun, zip one errant thought our way. No Greek whisky is made, but Greek vermouth is quite drinkable. So is Greek beer, which is mighty refreshing on a hot summer's day; try "Fix" or "Alpha"—2 popular brews. Amstel, the Dutch beer, also is sudsing over the local market; it is made locally, not imported. Henninger beer has appeared, too.

Order your wine *aretsinto* ("without resin"), or your mouth will pucker so much you'll think you've eaten a basket of persimmons. In Homeric times the Greeks smeared the linings of their wine barrels with pine sap, a crude preservative. Over the centuries the people grew to like the turpentine flavor, and today's vintages are therefore deliberately resinated. But to the neophyte they taste like a blend of nail polish remover and deck enamel. Greek wine is properly poured from a brass mug; nowadays you'll also find it served in aluminum replicas. In *tavernas,* the protocol is to half-fill your cup, especially when quaffing the resinated ones. If you specify that you want *aretsinto,* they'll always find an unprocessed bottle of the same brand for you.

If we were asked to choose 3 wines in this land—1 red, 1 white, and 1 rosé—to the exclusion of all others, here's what we'd pick:

> For the red—Boutari Grande Reserve
> For the white—Domaine Port-Carras Blanc-de-Blanc
> For the rosé—Santa Laura

Among dry-to-medium white wines, Elissar, Cava Kamba, Pallini, St. Helena, Demestica, King, and Minos are also especially favored. In a Solomonic court decision, the former King Minos brand, which came in either white-and-dry or red-and-medium, is now known as King and Minos respectively. Cava Boutari and Caviros reds (Burgundy-type) are heavyish but sound; both are good complements to extra-spicy or garlicky dishes. Montenero is another popular cup. From Rhodes, Chevalier de Rhodes is quite passable. Mavrodaphni and Samos, sweet to very sweet, are favorites of the ladies. Outside this select group, Hellenic wines are almost without exception 2nd-rate to foreign tastes.

True to form in this land of straight brandy and ouzo, the cocktails are lethal except in the tourist-oriented hotels and restaurants.

☑ **TIPPING**   In luxury or First-class restaurants, although the 12% service charge is now included, add 5% on the *plate* for the waiter or maître and small change on the *table* for the busboys. In your hotel, give at least $3 to the concierge, $2 to the maid, and 30¢ per bag to the baggage porter. For special attention of any kind, raise the scale accordingly.

☑ **LOCAL RACKETS**   The one that blackened our eye on recent trips still riles us —the chauffeur-driven car gouge, which we've already described under "Transportation" (Hired Cars and Motoring). Also in Athens there has been a major influx of touts who approach foreigners of both genders on the street, shake hands as effusively as if they had been bosom pals for life, and then smooth-talk the suckers into 3rd-or-4th-rate shops (furs, especially). The Greek people as a whole are extraordinarily honest and decent. They bargain ardently (less ardently, however, than their Eastern neighbors), but once their word is given, it is their bond.

☑ **INFORMATION CENTERS**   The U.S. fountainhead for tourist information is the **National Tourist Organization of Greece**, 601 Fifth Ave., New York, N.Y., 10017. Your next best bet is to write to the Office of the Secretary-General, **Greek National Tourist Organization**, Stadium St., Athens.

For actual travel *arrangements* (ticket, sightseeing, excursions, and the like), for more than 3 decades we've continued to have perfect luck with **Hellenic Tours**, 3 Stadium St., Athens. Director Nelson Malamed couldn't be kinder, nicer, or more efficient, and we recommend this company heartily and unreservedly.

CITIES

ATHENS   (Athinai) with its port of Piraeus (Peiraieus) is the largest, with more than 3.5 million people; as we mentioned, here's the birthplace and heart of Greek culture, a *must* for all visitors. Millions of gallons of paint have been used in sprucing it up; Constitution Square, Omonia Square, and other landmarks have been revamped; 5 additional public plazas have been opened; the Plaka district has been illuminated by lamps, another fillip of charm. Mount Lycabettus, its looming central hill, now has a cable railway zooming through a 225-yard tunnel which whisks sightseers from Plutarchou and Aristippou Sts. to its crown in 2 minutes. Up top, a restaurant and snack bar operate at full blast. The combination of explosively increased prosperity and the aforementioned colossal new tourist stampede, however, brought along 4 noxious handmaidens which are often concomitants of this pattern. First has been the appalling traffic jams. Second has been the gross overcrowding of its historical attractions; the Parthenon of the Acropolis, for example, has had to be closed off to the public because too many feet were wearing out its floor. Third and fourth are the facts that virtually overnight Athens has succumbed to the highest pollution and noise indices of any capital in Western Europe.

Sightseeing   Classic attractions in or near the center include the **National Archaeological Museum** (priceless ancient treasures), **Enaki Museum** (more modern Greek and Levantine displays), the interesting **Museum of War Souvenirs**, the **Byzantine Museum**, the **Ghennadios Library** (Byzantine books, manuscripts, and art objects)—plus scads of world-famous ruins such as the **Acropolis** with its off-limits **Parthenon**, **Hadrian's Arch of Triumph**, the **Temple of Zeus**, the **Theater of Dionysus**, the **Stoa of Attalus**, the **Agora**, and others.

The **Acropolis,** of course, is by far the most popular antiquity. Because the sun can often be searing on your climb, it is strongly suggested that you tackle this early; it opens at 7:30 A.M. Its caryatids have been moved indoors to the **Acropolis Museum** and replaced at the **Erechtheion Temple** by modern copies. There is no entrance fee on Thursdays and Sundays; student cards bring a reduced rate. *Son et Lumière* ("Sound and Light") spectacles are presented the year round. New wiring has been installed. More than 500 varicolored floodlights play over the sights for 45 minutes per performance, accompanied by a musical score and a dialogue. Go on any night to the Hill of Pnyx at 9 P.M. for the English version, which is narrated by John Gielgud. Tickets cost about $3, but students are admitted for less. Please take a jacket.

The majority of museums are closed 1 day a week, normally on Mondays or Tuesdays.

The summertime concerts by the **Athens State Orchestra** or ancient drama performances in the **Herodes Atticus Theater** at the base of the Acropolis are wonderful. The combination of romantic antiquities and starlit nights is unforgettable. The municipality has brought further cultural stature by sponsoring its International Festival, which presents such groups as the Bolshoi Ballet, Covent Garden productions and similar tip-top and tip-toe performers.

Changing of the Guard at the Tomb of the Unknown Soldier is spectacularly colorful; Sunday morning only at 11 A.M. is the big ceremony, but every hour on the hour you may witness the less-glamorous starch.

The **Zappion Gardens** are renowned for art shows, held at intervals throughout the year.

Folk dancing takes place under the stars nightly from May to October, weather permitting, at the theater on the west flank of the Philopappus hill, across the Acropolis. Matinees on Wednesday and Sunday.

More than a dozen **trailer camps** or **tenting sites** have been set up in various rural areas. Check the Automobile and Touring Club of Greece for further information.

★ **TIPS** Most newspaper kiosks, hotel desks, and travel bureaus carry what might be called Greek *Cue* magazines; *The Week in Athens* and the monthly edition of *The Athenian* are tops. They're in English and invaluable.

ATHENS HOTELS Quick Reference Table

Price categories by national (not U.S.) standards.

Expensive:
Athenaeum Inter-Continental Constitution Square. 174 rooms. P. 417
Grand Bretagne Constitution Square 1. Tel. 323.02.51; Telex 21-5346; 450 rooms. P. 416
Hilton Sofias Ave. 46. Tel. 720.201-9; Telex 21-5808; 518 rooms. P. 416

King George Constitution Square. Tel. 323.06.51; Telex 21-5396; 150 rooms. P. 417
Meridien Constitution Square. 174 rooms. P. 417

Upper Moderate:
Acropole Palace Patission St. 51. Tel. 522.38.51; Telex 21-5909; 170 rooms. P. 421
Amalia Amalias Ave. 10. Tel. 323.73.01; Telex 21-5161; 97 rooms. P. 419
Astor Kar. Servias St. 16. Tel. 322.49.71; Telex 21-4018; 133 rooms. P. 420
Athenee Palace Kalokotroni Sq. 1. Tel. 323.07.91; Telex 21-6188; 160 rooms. P. 417
Athens Chandris Syngrou Ave. 385. Tel. 941.48.24; Telex 21-8112; 368 rooms. P. 419
Attica Palace Kar. Servias St. 6. Tel. 322.30.06; Telex 21-5909; 78 rooms. P. 419
Caravel Alexandrou Ave. 2. Tel. 790.721; Telex 21-4401; 471 rooms. P. 419
Divani-Zafolia Palace Parthenonos St. 19–25. Tel. 922.91.53; Telex 21-8306; 193 rooms. P. 418
Electra Hermou St. 5. Tel. 323.21.04; Telex 21-6896; 110 rooms. P. 420
Electra Palace Nikodimou St. 18. Tel. 324.14.01; Telex 21-6896; 120 rooms. P. 420
Esperia Palace Stadiou St. 22. Tel. 323.80.00; Telex 21-5773; 185 rooms. P. 419
Golden Age Michalakopoulou St. 57. Tel. 740. 861; Telex 21-9292; 122 rooms. P. 421
Herodion Rovertou Galli 4. Tel. 923.68.32; Telex 21-9423; 90 rooms. P. 418
Holiday Inn Michalakopoulou St. 50. Tel. 710.001; Telex 21-88703; 200 rooms. P. 418
King Minos Piraeus St. 1. Tel. 523.11.11; Telex 21-5339; 178 rooms. P. 419
King's Palace Panepistimiou Ave. 4. Tel. 362.32.31; Telex 21-5067; 219 rooms. P. 418
Olympic Palace Philellinon St. 16. Tel. 323.76.11; Telex 21-5178; 96 rooms. P. 419
Park Alexandras Av. 10. Tel. 883.27.10; Telex 21-4748; 146 rooms. P. 418
President Kifissias Ave. 42. Tel. 692.46.00; Telex 21-8585; 513 rooms. P. 420
Royal Olympic Diakou St. 28. Tel. 922.64.11; Telex 21-5753; 335 rooms. P. 417
St. George Lycabettus Kleomenous St. 2. Tel. 790.710; Telex 21-4253; 154 rooms. P. 418

Moderate:
Alfa Chalkokondyli St. 17. Tel. 522.12.53; Telex 21-5067; 88 rooms. P. 421
Arethusa Metropoleos & Nikis Sts. Tel. 322.94.31; Telex 31-6882; 88 rooms. P. 420
Athens Gate Syngrou Ave. 10. Tel. 923.83.02; Telex 21-4202; 106 rooms. P. 421
Diomia Diomias St. 5. Tel. 323.80.34; 71 rooms. P. 421
Dorian Inn Piraeus St. 15. Tel. 523.97.82; Telex 21-4779; 146 rooms. P. 420
Galaxy Academias St. 22. Tel. 363.28.31; Telex 21-5077; 118 rooms. P. 420
Ilisia Michalakopoulou St. 25. Tel. 744.051; Telex 21-4924; 69 rooms. P. 421
Lycabette Valaoritou St. 6. Tel. 363.35.14; 39 rooms. P. 422
Minerva Athens Stadium St. 3. Tel. 323.09.15; Telex 21-5838; 50 rooms. P. 421
Stanley Odysseus St. 1. Tel. 522.00.11; Telex 21-6550; 351 rooms. P. 420
Titania Panepistimiou Ave. 52. Tel. 360.96.11; Telex 21-4673; 396 rooms. P. 420
Xenophon Acharnon St. 340. Tel. 202.03.10; Telex 21-5294; 186 rooms. P. 422

Lower Moderate:
Achillion Ag. Konstantinou St. 32. Tel. 523.09.71; 56 rooms. P. 421
Atlantic Patission St. 35. Tel. 523.53.61; Telex 21-5723; 158 rooms. P. 421
Hermes Apollonos St. 19. Tel. 323.55.14; 45 rooms. P. 422
Imperial Metropoleos St. 46. Tel. 322.76.17; 21 rooms. P. 422
Marmara Chalkokondyli St. 14. Tel. 362.63.62; Telex 21-6047; 140 rooms. P. 421
Omonia Omonia Sq. Tel. 523.72.12; 275 rooms. P. 421

Pythagorion Ag. Konstantinou St. 28. Tel. 524.28.11; 56 rooms. P. 421
Sirene Lagoumitzi St. 15. Tel.922.93.10; 103 rooms. P. 421

Hotels As has been stated earlier, the crucial question is whether or not the important hotels in all categories will again jump their rates this year. We urge that you check this either with your travel agent or with our Living Guide before making any solid plans.

Operational cycles in the Greek world of hôtellerie continue to be shorter than those of any other nation in these pages save for Spain. Well into the postwar years the lodgings from border to border were comparatively miserable—Spartan, tasteless, and depressingly old-hat. As the touristic boom continued to swell during the late '50s and '60s—a small one by 1979 figures—a host of entrepreneurs seeking the quick buck threw up hosts of junky buildings with trashy, low-level beds, sparse furnishings, bare walls, cubbyhole rooms, and a woeful absence of concern for the scrub brush and the dust cloth. Please be warned that many, many of these still remain.

The recent thundering stampede of visitors has provoked a regression of high-standard hotelkeeping on a national scale. While several dozen exceptions continue their laudable forward progress, speaking in general, the attitude of the main body of hoteliers seems to be "Why should I spend the money to replace those carpets, repaint those accommodations or restore that faulty plumbing when I'm always so full, full, *full?*" So it's a case expressed by the old Cockney expression: "Yer takes yer chances 'ere 'n 'opes"—but we'll try our best to guide you, sometimes unsuccessfully, through these vast thickets of choices.

At this writing there are—or will be by summer—6 deluxe hotels in the capital. Nearly all of them differ markedly in their architectural and decorative themes.

The **Athens Hilton** is commandingly situated on a knoll facing the Royal Palace and the Parthenon, about 5 minutes by taxi from the heart of town near the U.S. Embassy. Here in our opinions, is one of the most beautiful, graceful, and comfortable houses in this vast international chain. The concept is grand and the line is clean. Expansive lobby; 500 good-size units with balconies and handsome black Carrara baths; suites of varying dimensions; native fabrics and warm colors. Completely air-conditioned; 75-table regional-style Taverna Ta Nissia downstairs which we wouldn't miss while in this city for all the pastry in France; attractive and informal pizzeria; 24-hour Byzantine Café for back-home soda-fountain snacks; Pan Bar for daytime libations; Top-of-the-Mark-type garden restaurant; Galaxy roof nightclub with sliding ceiling and inside-outside dancing; swimming pool and adjoining bar; shops galore. Try to book on the rear of the upper floors for less noise or to their front facing the Acropolis for its fine panorama. Warm, delightfully personable, keenly efficient R. O. Richenbacher, its General Manager, is an outstanding administrator. This is in the best tradition of an *American*-style hostelry which has been deftly augmented by a Hellenic patina in atmosphere.

The **Grande Bretagne**, frequently the choice of traditionalists, has been an internationally famous landmark for generations. Its far-flung clientele affectionately call it the "G.B." Virtually every nook and cranny of this majestically imposing old building has been completely modernized. Also 100% air-conditioned; enormous, high-ceilinged lobby and lounges warmed up with acres of tapestry; chic, silken-suave bar for delightful relaxing; lovely dining room; double-glazed windows throughout; prize chambers the 6th-level terraced perches overlooking Constitution Square; concierge staff renowned for its friendliness and savvy. A super-opulent Presidential Suite with its dining room seating 14. Another attraction is its fresh and boomingly popular GB Corner in 3 tiers with wood and leather décor which dispenses excellent snacks, meals, and drinks continuously from 10 A.M. to 2 A.M. In sum, here for your pleasure is the leading *Greek*-style hotel in the nation, thanks to the whirlwind energies and talents of its dynamic owner, Pericles Petracopoulos.

The adjoining **King George** is still a treasure trove of *objets d'art,* among which are the more than 500 paintings by prominent Greek artists that are scattered through its premises. The cuisine, especially in its penthouse Tudor Hall, is still eminent by local standards. The rooms still retain their special cachet. Physically the plant is still elegant. But during this latest stay we found a decline in service standards that deeply shocked us. In our opinions Proprietor Socrates Calcanis, the young heir of this longtime institution, has permitted it to slide downward a significant degree—and we won't check in again until he has demonstrated a much firmer grasp on its reins.

The **Meridien**, a few steps farther along, is reported to have 174 pleasant abodes, a pool, at least 2 restaurants, a disco, sizable convention and banquet facilities, and numerous other attractions. It opened after our latest Athenian rounds.

So did the $80-million **Athenaeum Inter-Continental**, a very ambitious project which contains 1,200 beds. Its location on Syngrou Ave., more than a mile from the center, is unfortunate. It opens this fall.

The **Astir Palace**, catty-corner from Constitution Square opposite the Grand Bretagne, hopes to open its doors late this spring. The overall track record of the Astir chain is such that we have the feeling that this will be a good one.

Down one grade, the **Royal Olympic**, located across from the Temple of Zeus (or Jupiter, if you're a Roman), has our vote as the pacesetter of the "A" category. Nothing has been too great a challenge to cordial, dedicated Proprietor Sake Papademetriou in his victorious crusade to expand it step by step from a small and modest inn to its status of respect and importance on the local hotel landscape today. Room count of 335, including 5 major suites and 5 demi-suites; pool; Coffee Shop which doubles as a poolside barbecue; convention hall; ballroom; the first automatic computer phone system in Greece. The cuisine in the darkly handsome medieval Templar Grill is generally not too distinguished. Whisper-soft, individually controlled air conditioning plus double-glazed windows as noise shields; pleasant oh-ing and ah-ing at Mt. Lycabettus and the Stadium; upper floor peeks at the Acropolis. Bedchambers with full carpets; multichannel consoles for music and radio; well-appointed baths. Enthusiastically recommended because of its never-ending parade of improvements.

The **Athenee Palace** offers decent, reasonably pleasant facilities. About 150 medium-size, clean, bright, carpetless bedchambers, all with small (or minuscule) bathrooms and some with balconies; slipcovers used extensively but always crisp and fresh; noisy on the Stadium Street side; 2nd-floor restaurant and tiny bar; popular among Japanese tour groups. Entrepreneur Spiros Damingos has just spent a lot of money in upgrading its sleeping quarters. We commend him for his devotion to this faithful old standby.

The **King's Palace** is now disturbingly bustling and commercial. Excellent location which makes it an amendment to Constitution Square; June-to-October roof garden with broad sweep and solarium but no pool; 150 better twins; other accommodations small and spiritless; all with bath or shower and piped music; all s-s-s-soundproofed against street clangor; quiet but viewless units on the Parliament side; air conditioning. Okay for its heavy business trade but only so-so for vacationers.

To us the recently unveiled **Holiday Inn** (50 Michalakopoulou St., back of the Hilton) is an abortive hybrid. Instead of erecting one of its own standard structures, this company purchased an uncompleted 6-story hotel building and undertook the almost impossible task of changing its interior arrangements to conform with its chain-wide specifications. Big, sterile ground floor with the faint ambiance of a casino; 24-hour Coffee Shop and tatty bar adjoining; first basement with small Bistro Grec Taverna, a hairdresser, and a disco; second basement with 16 bowling lanes, a snack nook, and screaming rock music; rooms with TV, radio, air conditioning, and 2 double beds in the twin accommodations. We believe that this variegated patchup is so outrageously overpriced for such a sleeping factory that it is most definitely not recommended by these reporters.

The 90-room **Herodion** is sited on the lower slopes of the Acropolis. Splendid sweep from the upper 2 tiers to the rear; bright accommodations which complement the charm of the public rooms. Many travelers like it. The **Divani Zafolia Palace**, nearby, also appears to be winning friends. Extensive use of marble; merry colors employed in textiles and pigments; remnants of the ancient Themistoclean Wall and its cellar (you are invited to take a look); *taverna* plus conventional restaurant; attractive public areas; swimming pool. The upper bedchambers offer excellent panoramics, but their closets, which resemble gymnasium lockers, are almost too short for anyone bigger than Mickey Rooney. Pretty good, but not for lanky travelers.

High over the city in the Kolonaki residential enclave sits the majestically modern, 150-room **St. George Lycabettus**. Except for the wretchedly serious handicap of transport (taxis are very sparse here and you cannot drive to the entrance), it is a lovely retreat. Two-tiered rooftop pool; appending terraces with snack tables; L-shape lobby with many gracious touches; lower-level restaurant with appetizing color blends; intimate grill, plus a coffee shop that is a knockout for design and rendition; attractive Tony's Bar; bank, shop, hairdresser, and barber; garage (a car is useful). The suites are striking; the normal twins are clean lined and charming but somewhat short on space for this category; the singles are neat and adequate. A splendid choice if you can tolerate the problem of long waits for cabs.

The 150-unit **Park** is a neat package that unfortunately is situated at an inconvenient distance from midtown, facing the Gardens of Areas. It disappointed us even further to see such a fine basic plant so neglected by its housekeepers. There's a penthouse pool, bar, and sun deck; again a pizzeria; a tartan lounge, restaurant, coffee shop, and well-appointed bedchambers with prices that vary with the desirability of the views. With more managerial zip it could have a chance; as it is, we'd prefer to give it a miss.

The **Amalia** resides one block from Constitution Square. It offers 98 fairly cramped rooms, all with bath or shower; individually controlled air conditioning; large windows; furnishings subdue-hued. Suite #603–4 nestles nicely in a corner; the lobby impressed us as being colder than a polar bear's toenail; the dining room and bar seem like hidden afterthoughts. Your free-lance reservations might be troublesome, because group bids, of which there are many, receive A-plus priority.

The **Olympic Palace**, with its central and increasingly raucous site, opened in '59, but periodic refreshenings keep it pert. All 100 units come with bath or shower and wall-to-wall woofing-and-warping, radio, telephone, terrace, and air conditioning; the public rooms are charming. We are especially fond of #608, a viewful double. Reminiscent of the Amalia and deserving of the same ranking even though rates run about 20% lower.

King Minos is under new aegis, a sovereign who may add a plus or two. Clean structural scheme highlighted cleverly by marble and wood; indirect illumination; 100% air-conditioned; beauty parlor and barbershop; 5-stool bar; next-door lounge with ornamental birdcage; balconies on all front units; reasonable tabs for reasonable living space.

The **Esperia Palace**, a vassal under the King's Palace-Alfa scepter, shows continued improvement, although at certain peak periods we've had to crane our long necks over tour groups to see it. Ingratiating Athineos Restaurant and cafeteria; large parquet-floor lounge; library and card room; blithe little bar. All its 185 zestlessly wallpapered accommodations with veranda and private bath, mostly with squat-down tubs; all 3/4-bed singles (often sold for doubles) are for Gulliver's travels, but not yours; air-conditioned. The 2 upper floors (8th and 9th) are singles exclusively. Try to get a high perch for the view and to avoid the traffic din. Worthy for its drachmae. **Attica Palace** has an ideal address and a so-so oft-crowded downstairs. Pencil-thin aluminum-and-glass structure in central location; 100 loooong and narrow rooms with baths and showers; simple, long lobby up one flight. Noisy, but now much improved in its housekeeping standards.

We would never understand in 100 years how the 520-unit **Caravel**, a large triangular edifice near the Hilton, was classified as deluxe by official government inspectors. Good grief! Prairie-size lobby frequently ajam with chattering mobs awaiting their room numbers or tour leaders; air conditioning; rooftop pool; sauna; 2 bars, a 24-hour cafeteria, a pizzeria, and a *taverna;* convention halls. While some of its physical facilities have a certain amount of merit, the food that we were presented was so abominable and the service—*what* service? —we encountered was so incredibly slovenly and inattentive that we wouldn't commend this one at those tariff levels to Lucifer himself. No thanks—ever again.

These same sentiments—with which you may disagree—apply to the **Athens Chandris**. It is situated far out by the racecourse and planetarium. There are

390 chambers and 22 suites, a penthouse pool, a coffee shop, a dining salon, and all of the facilities one would expect in a project of this size. But again the meal we tasted but could not stomach and the surliness of the employees we encountered soured our pleasure in this enterprise.

The **Astor** contains 133 efficient rooms. All offer bath, terrace, and air conditioning. Functional lobby and pleasant bar adjoining; cheerful rooftop restaurant open until midnight; conventional baths totaling 35%; other 65% (a nice one is #710) featuring 2-step tubs which will give you the feeling you're Rodin's *Thinker*. Manager Dimitrios Kokkeas provides golden value for silver coins. This same group inaugurated the 500-room **President**, not too far from the U.S. Embassy. All 530 rooms with balcony; rooftop swimming pool. Somehow the various elements don't jibe, in our opinion. A 1-term President at best.

The 350-unit **Stanley** is unabashedly aimed at package tourism. Sited on Karaiskaki Square with a pleasant greensward at its front door, it is too far from the hub of the city for most hikers to hoof it to the center. Attractive public rooms; top marks for the rooftop pool, solarium, and relaxing zone; lower scores for the utilitarian bedchambers; premium accommodations air chilled. **Dorian Inn** is another contender tailored for conducted tours. Three main columns mark its 13-story triangular ground plan, again with a swimmery at penthouse level. All 150 rooms and 30 suites air-conditioned; restaurant, grill, bar, shop, the usual bag of tricks with few surprises.

The extra-clean, 110-room high-voltage **Electra** crackles with a full bath count, full air conditioning, 1/2 of its bedchambers facing inside; and a restaurant plus cafeteria. Thomas Sviriades, former Chief Receptionist of the Athénée Palace, is one of its owners. The cheeriness in décor, the finger-lickin' savor of its cookery, the perfect midtown situation for active travelers, the try-harder attitude of management and staff, and the low rates all meld to make this one a prize in the Athenian grab bag. Morning, noon, and night become this Electra.

The same Producer uncorked the **Electra Palace** up in the Plaka district. In addition to similar décor and similar bedchambers, he unhatched 150 feebly air-conditioned units all with private bath, a rooftop Eden overlooking the Acropolis, a garage, and a swimming pool.

Arethusa comes up with a viewful roof garden, an inviting mezzanine cafeteria, and 87 quiet panel-windowed bedchambers with modern light-wood furnishings, radios, and individual air conditioning. Ask for any nest ending in "01" or "08"; while these are in the same moderate price range as the standard twins, they provide an extra dividend in scenery and space.

The massive 800-pillow **Titania** is frigid in the most gelid context of a sleeping factory. It has all the basic ingredients—except warmth, in our opinions. Ghastly lobby with better rooms than you would think from a first glance at this building, and a very amiable staff. There's also an attractive roof bar. Parking in this area provokes elephantine headaches.

The **Galaxy** fills its spiral nebula with a wood-lined lobby, marble elevator bank, a mezzanine bar plus snack counter, a glass-lined but viewless restaurant, full-space air conditioning, a myriad of lounges and cozy corners, and a 108-room firmament twinkling with satellite efficiency. A stellar attraction for 4th-magnitude budgets.

The **Acropole Palace**, despite its Deluxe classification, caters almost exclusively to conducted-tour bookings and airline crews. Improved lobby; brightened public rooms; big bedchambers that seem rather gloomy to our eyes. Its chief assets are its A-plus table and a staff that seeks to please.

The **Sirene**, though a mile or so from the metropolitan fulcrum, is not very *sirene,* in our opinion. In fact, we found it very, very noisy. The tone is characteristically modern throughout, with its finest feature the pool and snackery on its 7th plateau. The price is not too high, but then neither are the rewards.

How the 10-story, 400-bunked **Ambassadeur** achieved its First-class rank is a diplomatic mystery to these traveling envoys.

Marmara ("Marble Palace"), another link in the King's Palace-Alfa chain, is a good 10 minutes from midtown but still noisy. Blue-ceilinged lobby in white stonework enhanced by tearoom gallery; zipless bar; attractive dining room; fine modern kitchen. Of its 140 small units, 40 have no private facilities.

The **Diomia** resides on a quiet, narrow lane about one block off Constitution Square. Two floors have been added to the original 71 units; all of its vaguely Danish-modern rooms have bath or shower and a little terrace; 50% are air-conditioned. Scandinavian-style lobby and minibar; airy dining salon; Snack Bar-Drink Bar a split level below the ground floor. We were pleased to see honest-to-goodness rugs and honest-to-goodness pictures in the bedchambers, warm touches provided by Director Manos which are almost nonexistent among its confreres. On the other hand, we are becoming highly alarmed by the number of complaints we have been receiving concerning day-to-night maintenance here. Let's hope that it's only a temporary situation.

At the **Athens Gate** the front units provide Olympian views of the Temple of Zeus. Ground-level public space limited, but plans include utilization of the 360° views from the rooftop; cookery said to be worthy; friendly service; clean. The 120-unit **Golden Age**, not far from the Hilton, struck us as being poorly conceived, with a stark lobby and a somber mien. Excessively small doubles; appealing cellar *taverna;* a mixture of pluses and minuses, with the emphasis on the latter. Not far away, the **Ilisia**, with 85 rooms, impressed us as being run-down, beat-up, and flawed-out.

The **Atlantic** rattles 145 doorkeys. Bath or shower with every unit, and some now air-chilled; commercial and noisy; preponderance of conducted groups; cramped space; strictly functional; sparsely furnished. **Achillion** is reasonably well heeled, but we strongly suspect its mattresses are stuffed with prime-grade Greek marble. Although its situation is unattractive, this one is superior to most of its classification. **Alfa** has 98 accommodations, 1/2 with baths and 1/2 with showers. It also provides a restaurant, a bar, and a cocktail lounge; here is another under the King's Palace baton. Better downstairs than in the sleepers. The **Minerva Athens**, across from the King George, occupies the top 3 floors of an office building. All 60 rooms have bath. It caters in good part to a heavy traffic of local businessmen. In other countries, all of these would be considered Grade-C rather than Grade-A or B houses.

The 275-room, Class-C **Omonia** boasts a full bath-or-shower count but not much else to lift your spirits. The neighboring 56-room **Pythagorion** has much more heart, in our opinion—and for almost the same outlay. Well run by

Proprietor-Travel Agent John Stephanidis. A money saver. **Lycabette**, on a quiet street, comes up with 50 rooms, 15 of which are loners, all with shower or bath.· Air-cooled throughout; chummy bar; nice lounge; well furnished; radio in every nest. Not bad—and happy for medium budgeteers. **Hermes**, on Apollonos Street, has unveiled 45 plain and inexpensive accommodations. Heaven-scent roof garden for summer dining; full pension plan pushed during peak periods. **Imperial** has no lobby—but it does have 21 chambers and an owner who is said to be especially hospitable. The **Xenophon**, on the N-1 highway north of town, is chiefly for motorists.

Suburban settings? The **Astir Palace** was constructed to lure shipowners, yachtsmen, and sybarites of all callings. Long, linear, modernistic structure standing majestically above the *Vouliagmeni* shóres (15 miles from Athens); one façade flanked by a harbor for pleasure craft and the other by golden sand; handsome waterside Club House with restaurant, snack bar, and recreational facilities; new 360-bed hillside tier with its own pool, café, and lounges; 2 other pools for indoor-outdoor splashing; Glyfada golf course 5 miles away. The hotel segment has an elegant classic-style restaurant, a rustic plank-ceilinged grill-cum-nightclub, 2 bars, terraces, balconies, and luxurious fresh-looking appointments. The 69 summer bungalows sprinkled below the hotel have been gracefully re-A-stirred. In winter we would prefer the main buildings. Advance reservations *an absolute must,* since some bookings are made a year ahead. One detriment is the noise factor from its proximity to the airport. Overall, our cheers and salutes to this elegant cluster.

Astir Bungalows at *Glyfada Beach*, 10 minutes closer to town but under the screaming jet approaches to the airport, is operated by the same company. It's more village-like in concept. Hillside perch dotted with 100 one-room chalets, 7 two-room, and 7 three-room villas, all with private bath or shower, refrigerator, wide flower-girt terraces, and central heating. Bigger units cozied-up with working fireplaces; room service; Asteria Tavern for let's-go-out diners; 3 other restaurants or cocktail and snack bars; both rocky and sandy beaches at the bottom of the grassy slopes; pool and imbibery freshly a-bubble. Recommended for families or more thrifty travelers. The **Apollon Palace**, even nearer to town than the Astir Palace, has 300 units that to us suggest prefabrication. Officially it is Deluxe, but we'd label it High First-class. All doubles of standard dimensions; good baths; furnishings pleasant but not striking.

The gigantic resort complex to be called **Sun Palace** has been plagued with such problems (financial? construction?) that its inauguration date has been repeatedly postponed year after year. We will make a full reinspection and report as soon as it swings into action.

Not far away, a slightly less expensive venture has been taking shape under the name of **Cape Sounion Beach**, a First-class dream of Takis Karadontis, president of both the Greek and Athens Hotel Associations, and his radiant sister Ket. The panorama is plainly glorious; there's a huge pool beside the remains of a 2000-year-old silver mine; a 7-sided glass-enclosed bar adjoins its delightful restaurant; another dining salon plus a *taverna* also are available. When finally completed, it will comprise 400 rooms and 400 bungalows— virtually a village in itself. This one shows excellent promise.

The **Xenia** had plummeted to great depths before it was taken over by the National Tourist Office. Because of its situation on one of the most breathtaking headlands on this enchanting coast, it could be a marvelous money-mill. Personally, we much prefer its spacious beachside cottage accommodations to the cramped main-building lodgings. Most of the amenities are here for a tiptop holiday at reasonable prices. **Blue Spell**, closer to town, didn't bind us much. At the **Eden Beach** in _Saronis_ (30 miles out), pick only a front chamber because the rear cubicles struck us as awful. The beds that we tested certainly didn't spring from any Eden we've visited, either. Austere seems to be this Adam's word for it. We haven't yet stopped at the new 220-room **PLM Porto Heli** in the district from which it takes its name (35 miles from Epidaurus with ferry connections to Athens). It is said to have a private beach, a swimming pool, and 2 restaurants. We'll see it soon.

Then there's the **Motel Belvedere Park** with its 80 one-room bungalows, all with shower and bath and varying somewhat in quality. This one is open all year, is directed by the amiable Mr. Papadopoulos, and comes up with a fresh wing, a penthouse luxury restaurant, a basement grill and bar, 2 swimming pools, and a lovely vista. Bed and breakfast only. Relaxing.

Restaurants Don't look for dining elegance in Greece; in routine establishments you're liable to find paper tablecloths, paper napkins, startlingly junky furnishings in comparison to those in other Western European lands, and panting waiters who'll toss successive courses at you as fast as Chinese Ping-Pong balls.

Except in the most sophisticated establishments, it is a national custom for patrons nonchalantly to saunter directly into kitchens to select their fish or to examine the other comestibles before giving their orders to the waiter. Similarly, many _tavernas_ have counters, often in the rear, where all of their main wares are displayed so that their menus can be ignored. To neophytes some of the concoctions in these pans or on these platters look poisonous—but you might be surprised how good even the most evil-looking ones taste!

Menus generally carry 2 columns of figures. One is the price set by the management. The other is the total when the taxes are included. As an example, a Barbecued Half Chicken with trimmings might be listed in the first at 199 drachmas and in the second at 235 drachmas.

No traveler to Athens who enjoys maritime fare should be deprived of visiting the enormously colorful and delightful lineup of restaurants at the crescent-shape base for fishing boats in _Mikrolimano_ ("Small Port") across town near the harbor for private yachts. Almost all these moorings are still simple and unspoiled. In benign weather, go first across the street from the establishment of your choice to the awninged concrete strip directly over the water, to select your table. Then recross the boulevard, enter its front door, and select by the piece your shellfish (as many and as varied as you wish) from the aproned Poseidon in charge of this specialty. Next ask the proprietor to open the trove of stainless-steel drawers where the catches of the day lie in pristine freshness. Watch his scales as he weighs your picks; if he charges more than the Government-regulated 500 drachmae per kilo (2.2 lbs.), he's cheating you. Ask for Greek peasant salad on the side; garlic fans should bid for the piquant and unusual Skordalia sauce. Finally, head back to your table on the quai, order a Sans Rival Ouzo, ice, and water—and bask in peace and joy until the business of addressing the meal commands your attention. They are equally pleasant by day and by night. In the latter case, there's little activity until 9:30.

Along this non-Cannery Row, our favorite is **Paragadia**, where our latest delicious lunch for 5 also was delightfully easy on the budget. **Zephiros** repeatedly has turned on high-tide comestibles for our fishing parties; the shell game here is especially deft and cunningly presented. **Aglamair** is so refined it even offers piano music; we prefer the rougher stops but perhaps your taste is different. **Kokkini Varka** ("The Red Boat") is much less polished, but still a winner. The balance, navigating from the southwest and moving northeast along this short avenue are **Mourayo, Prassina Trehandiria, Kamnires, Kanaris, Kymata, Kranai, Kailanis, Semiramis, Trata, Poseidonos, Kavos** and **Zorba's** (of course)—most of them good. Stroll down the line and choose for yourself. When the skies are clear, the thermometer is kind, and the place is right, here can be one of the most joyful experiences on your entire European itinerary.

Among the much more expensive and soigné institutions, **Dionysos**, at the foot of the Acropolis, is almost as important as the Parthenon to the tourist trade. Despite the drawbacks which you might or might not encounter, it is worth a visit, if only to dwell upon the 3000-year-old architectural vista. And how agreeable it is to watch the Sound and Light spectacles flickering on the historic next-door mountain as you dine! About 30 tables and alfresco terraces upstairs (best view); more below for snacks and libations; heavy-ish and sometimes greasy international cuisine. Most of the time we enjoy it a lot. Evenings it is nearly always jammed, so reserve well in advance; open 8 A.M. to 2 A.M. The newer, slightly less chic branch on Mt. Lycabettus also provides a feast for the hungry eye. (We recommend this Mt. Pentelicus view at lunchtime and the main restaurant's sea wonders after sunset.) Again the staff attitudes are often cool, but this seems minor compared to the glories surrounding you. A *must* for free-spending wayfarers.

For good reason, **Yerofinika** (10 Pindarou St.) has become just about the Hottest Thing in Town Tonight. Fortunately, our beloved Greek friend who was the host had the foresight to book well ahead, because when we entered there was a standing queue of about 30 and when we left its ranks had swollen even more. Entry through a narrow alley; 2-tier dining room with sun terrace on one side; delicatessen-style display case stretching the entire length of a wall with a dazzling galaxy of viands; cheerful and bustling mien; hearty, gregarious proprietor who circulates to welcome his guests; also expensive by Hellenic standards. Excellent on every count.

The **Nine Plus Nine** (Platia Stadiou) is also highly à la mode. *Dinner only* is served, and it revels into the darkling hours in its disco sector. Charming understated ambiance employing bentwood chairs, an Ecuador of greenery, intimate dimensions, and laudable cuisine; again ask your concierge to nail down your table in advance. A favorite of many cosmopolites.

The **Athens Hilton** presents formal or informal nutrition, depending on your whim. Its Taverna Ta Nissia has all of its 8 cylinders purring. As we commented in the "Hotels" section, none of our team would dream of missing this star whenever we're in this metropolis. The adjoining Pizzeria is a sturdy

dispenser of this classic Italian snack. It is open from 7:30 P.M. to 2 A.M. only.
Don't forget the **GB Corner**, which is also described in "Hotels." Darned
good!

Tudor Hall, the penthouse oasis crowning the King George Hotel, offers a
glamorous setting. Baronial 2-story room softly illuminated and richly paneled; solid bank of windows on one side and tiny terrace on the other;
courteous attention on our most recent incognito try. Grill at one end which
is strikingly different but equally tasteful in its décor; the white-capped chef
here pits his Greek-style specialties against the international cuisine of his
adjoining competitor; it is open at lunch and dinner 365 days per year. In both,
you will find high culinary standards plus a magnificent panorama of the
rooftops, Acropolis, and floodlit Parthenon.

The **Templar Grill** in the Royal Olympic has its lesser attractions—this time
at ground level. We've never seen it crowded, although we are told that it is
rising in Athens' social circles. Lip service? Could be, because our own dining
experience here has not been too favorable.

Vladimir (12 Aristodimou St.), perched on a steep hillside a short climb
from the Hilton, offers a curious but tempting mélange of Russian, Greek,
French, and Oriental specialties. To our surprise, even "American Hamburger" is offered as a main course. Terrace munching in rear garden during the warm months; immaculate kitchen; pleasant ambiance; on the
costly side for Greece.

For straight fare in more typical surroundings, **Facyo** occupies premises
at 5 Efroniou St., also near the Hilton. The famous Kyrios Facyo, its
aproned Turkish host, beams in avuncular radiance to bring happiness to
his clients. About 18 tables in a simply furnished square room; refrigerated
display counters backed by shelves of bottles running the entire length of
the right side; choose your appetizers from these cases; hot dishes in adjoining segment. Unelaborate but fun. Closed Sun.

Papakia (5 Iridanou St.) means "The Duckling"—and its fowl deeds to us
are dismal cookery of late and declining service standards.

Try **Maxim** instead; it's in Kolonaki—an old mansion with seating for 250.
It is suave in atmosphere, soothed by taped melodies, and features terrace
dining in summer.

Three Brothers (7 Elpidos St.) is a fraternal import from Corfu. Nondescript, smokefilled front room chuckling gaily with lively parties of food-savvy
Greeks; passageway with bustling kitchen on the left; 14,926,344-calorie showcase of comestibles on the right (pick your share before sitting down); garden-
like sanctum to the rear containing perfectly awful seacoast paintings, lanterns,
and maritime riggings. No English spoken; fish plates especially fresh and well
prepared; not at all fancy; no fancy tariffs either. A winner in its fraternity.

Tabula, about 10 minutes by foot from the U.S. Embassy, yearns to be the
leader among the young In Set. The move was a fortunate one because the
cookery is better and it still has eye appeal. Its garden dining is pleasant under
summer skies.

The **Steak Room** (4 Aeginitou St.) also is a short walk from the Hilton in
the direction of the U.S. Embassy. Small narrow den with a busy bar to the
left; pine ceiling; modern copper lamps; blue carpet; pink and green linens; only

12 tables. The most expensive cuts of steer, though often tough, are reasonably priced and come with trimmings. Not bad.

Down the line, **Zonar's** (9 Venizelou Ave.) is a coffee shop, confectionery, tearoom, bar, and restaurant combined in a single operation under the Dionysos aegis. Hot in summer; average in quality; popular with trippers. **Floca** continues to uphold its good reputation. Café-restaurant aura; by local standards, prices on the high side. **Élysée** is a below-decks fastness with brick pillars, wrought iron chandeliers, green rush-bottomed chairs, and mediocre cookery on our night. The street-level snack-and-pack shop works around the clock.

Corfu appeals more to the stomach than to the eye; this one is simple, spotless, reasonable, and enormously popular. If you don't mind the rush-rush atmosphere, it can fill that tummy as satisfactorily as many far more costly addresses. **Delphi** (13 Nikis St.) is a midcity favorite among businessmen because of luscious lunches, tiny tabs, and ΦΑΣΤ service. The front segment is rustic in aura while the rearward enclave seeks to appear more refined. (It barely makes it.) The **Stagecoach** (6 Loukianou St.) aims to recreate them thar places like Laramie, Cheyenne, Laredo, Dodge City and such. Does a fittin' job, too, it does. Purty fine steaks, burgers, and chili through them swingin' doors. Easy on the moneybelt, too! So is **Kentrikon**, which is behind the Hotel Athenee Palace. Our lunch was unusually satisfactory for this low-cost category and its staff was smilingly efficient.

Now—would you be interested in experiencing one of the most unusual and fascinating meals of our travel lives? This is served at the little grocery-shop-restaurant called **Vassilena** (corner of Etolikon and Vitolion Sts., port of Piraeus, 20 minutes from the heart of Athens). About 14 tables in a clean but simple room with wine bottles and canned tomatoes on shelves. No menu is offered; you merely sit down and your waiter will start the 1-price, no-choice parade of 18 heavenly dishes which will take you 2 1/2 hours to consume. Price of this gargantuan repast, including coffee and all the open wine you can pour down? Less than the cost of one fine bottle if you were at home! We've touted this dark horse so heavily since 1957 that you might have to wait in line behind other adventurous readers. _Dinner only;_ closed every Sunday; reserve in advance. Please don't be detoured by the ridiculous deceit evinced by the people at any Concierge's desk. Since the restaurant is too small to give them a cut of your business, their attitude is easily explained—but don't YOU swallow this nonsense.

For a less exotic but border-to-border change of atmosphere and diet, every traveler should pay at least one visit to a typical Greek _taverna._ (Ta Nissia in the Hilton is much too urbane to be classed as such.) These famous institutions, most of which operate on a cold-weather basis _only,_ feature rôtisserie-type grills, hearty masculine menus, wine from huge barrels, folk music that is often deafening, and informal, family-style hospitality. Within the city (not the environs), most do not serve lunch; evening is the time to go. Probably the most elaborate is **Palia Athina** (4 Flessa St.). Reslicked rustic décor; orchestra and dancing; vague aura of a transplanted German _Bierstube;_ outdoor frolics adjoining during summer. **Steki tou Yanni** (1 Trias St.) is a perpetual favorite —with good reason. Motif—if we can call it that—trending toward a shambling stew of reed mats, bamboo fixtures, pastel-washed stucco, eclectic odds-and-endless ends; clangorous, busy, and stuffy; leather-lunged singers backed up by guitarists; hustling service. Here, unless you make an emphatic point of ordering just what you desire, a huge, multicourse, set meal will appear automatically. We like it, for its type. **Xinou** (4 Geronta St.) gave us several of the best repasts of our very recent Plaka parades. To the eye, it's a tumbled-down shack divided vaguely into 3 rooms and a tree-covered patio. To the palate, it was a happy surprise. Plank ceilings; exposed pipes; coal stoves; the inevitable cretonne curtains; genre paintings on cracking walls. Its trio of musicians wander from room to room playing folk melodies with expressionless visages. If you're not persnickety, we think you'll take to it as much as we did. Very inexpensive for the rewards. **Taverna Ambrosia**, in the same district, strums up interesting cookery and live guitar music. **O Yeros tou Moria** is no longer recommended, chiefly because of the frequent tiffs in the district in which it resides; the food also has gone down in quality, we think. **La Bussola** for Italian fare, **Psaropoulos** for fish and **George's** for steaks are bettable bets in the Glyfada district, about 9 miles from town. **Belle Maison** (Victoria Sq.), appeals to locals chiefly; they come to hear the guitar pickin's and to dine on its finger-lickin' vittles. **Erotokritos**, in the Plaka, is another popular target, as is **Bacchus Taverna**, which offers a small show in its ancient nook of the Acropolis. **Kritiku** (24 Mnissikleous St.), in 4 rooms, is an escape from the sidewalk cracklings of Shishkebab. Along this same street there are more kebab joints than you can shake a shish at.

A few Frenchies? **L'Abreuvoir** and **Je Reviens** (51 and 49 Xenokratous St.) are next-door neighbors up in the Kolonaki district. While the cuisine is high-level in both year round, we prefer their summer wiles at parkside tables. You also might like **Le Foyer**, near the Caravel Hotel, with its international menu and its Retro live music. **Bagatelle**, opposite the Hilton, is rather expensive.

Game for game? Shoot arrow-straight for the modest, galleried, shoplike **Zafiris** (4 Thespidos St.). Top your boar, pheasant, partridge, or luscious pigeon with a dessert of quince jelly or a pool of golden honey flecked with walnut chips. Good hunting!

Turkish tempters? The previously described **Facyo** (5 Efroniou St.) is the top of the fez. **Bosphorus, Maxim**, and **Yerofinika** are others.

Pagoda (2 Bouscou St.) and **Mr. Yung's** (3 Lamahou St.) adhere to that Oriental proverb: "Spare the rib and spoil the customer." Both offer a wide array of platters. The former is part of a chain; while we've also sampled its link in Nairobi, we can assure you it is not worth the effort to try its sister entries in Beirut and Nicosia. The latter is more appealing to the eye, but its treatment of Eastern cuisine impressed us as being . . . well, bizarre. **Michiko** (27 Kydathineon St.) in a Plaka mansion, pans out Japanese dainties plus continental fare. None will cause you to worship their ancestors.

Lunch or dinner excursions to the suburbs? Our top favorite—one which we make it a point never to miss—is to **Y Pighi Eleftheriatis** ("The Source") at *Drossia*, 14 miles northeast of the capital. (Please turn back to the "Food" section, in which its magnificent Peïnerli, a 32nd cousin of pizza, is described in detail.) **Isabela**, 11 miles out at *Voula,* we don't find as good as it was under the former management. **Psaropolou**, facing the sea at *Glyfada*, is a handsome kettle of fish. Entrance terrace dotted with flowers; glass-lined, modern dining room; expensive for the region, but worth the angling. We're told that **Mooring**, in the Vouliagmeni marina, also serves up a wide variety of superb sea specialties at moor or less reasonable prices. *In all suburban tavernas, (1) drink wine or beer only, and (2) scrutinize the ceremony of weighing your fish to see that YOU aren't the critter being hooked.*

La Belle Hellene, in *Kifisia* (on the way to the mountain in Politea), nestles on a slope. Spacious patio with pines and a trout pool; covered terrace; stone and glass-lined dining room; floor-to-ceiling copper hearth; flame-lit lanterns on tables; small selection; friendly service; fair cuisine. High tariffs, but pleasant enough in good climate. These Alleghenies of Atticus also come up with **Blue Pine Farm**—yup, Blue Pine Farm—which is known for its hillbilly-Xerxes steaks. It is rustic and deservedly popular. Always reserve ahead. For tip-top tavern cooking and harmonious guitar music, **Myrtia**, near the Stadium, is another winner, but in winter only.

Kira Maria, in the suburb of *Halandri*, tugs at the girthstrings as ardently as it pulls at the heartstrings. The surroundings are as alluring as are the mouthwatering Souvlakia and other charcoal specialities. Very recommendable for adventurers.

The coffee-bar business is percolating vigorously. A potful have bubbled up, some of which serve griddle sandwiches. One of the better blends is **Brazilian**, located in the Arcade at 3 Stadium St. You might try **American Bar and Restaurant** in Constitution Square; it's owned by a Greek-American who knows which side his burger is broiled on.

Dedicated budgeteers? Since we're too bottlenecked here for additional entries, please consult our annually revised paperback, *Fielding's Low-Cost Europe*, which lists scads and scads of other bargain dining spots and money-saving tips for serious economizers.

Night Life   In 1979 the government crippled a Greek way of life which has been vibrant for 2,000 years by decreeing an "entertainment curfew" at 2 A.M. Conservation of energy was its stated basis. Now every restaurant, nightclub, disco, and *taverna* in the nation must close at this unprecedented time or face fines of up to the equivalent of $30,000. As a result, prohibition-type speakeasies are springing up in cellars and even on rooftops of buildings in all major cities. When the managements are compelled to order their customers off their premises, there is a mass exodus to these clandestine drinking havens. As reported by Chris Eliou in the *International Herald Tribune*, the result is that tourists on a limited budget in the capital are now roaming the streets in the early hours of the morning clutching bottles of retsina and ouzo purchased in desperation before this witching hour. Come the revolution—and how the populace *hates* it!

Ever try a *bouzouki?* The devil-may-care custom of breaking cheap saucers when the excitement reached a climax has risen from the simple and inexpensive merriment of yore to a startlingly expensive pastime. First, the customer has no trouble in spending up to $40 per person for the dinner. Second, the crockery and the small baskets of flowers which are thrown are purchased by the piece—and the cost of the latter averages from $35 to $40 per unit. Here's why these places draw such a large proportion of the local patronage among young spendthrifts and the *nouveaux riches*. If you go, please sit well away from the stage or protect your eyes from flying fragments. The heavy action generally starts after midnight. **Fantis**, in the Plaka district, is fair, but we can't really forgive the management for spoofing up the evening with electronic musical assists. Our meal was routine-to-poor. One dancer carried a table clenched between his teeth—more tender, we'll wager, than our beefsteak. **Dilina**, at distant *Glyfada*, ranks in the top league at the moment. A kind reader from Lunenburg, Mass., sent us such an outraged report on **Kalokerinos** (10 Kekropos St.) that we gave it a special reinspection on a recent visit. In our view, her summary was understatement. We haven't been sheared in such a clip joint for quite a while. This one is not recommended under any circumstances. You might cotton to the cabaret at **Mostrou** (Mnissikleous St.), also in the Plaka district, which pulls at the strings of many an Athenian heart with its own show backed by the national folk music; we like this professional operation. Others in the dervish whirl include the popular **Palia Athina** (4 Fleesa St.) and **Plakiotiko Saloni** (15 Dedalou St.); both feature Greek cabaret. **Erotokritos** (1 Erotokritou St.) romps in with long floor shows of a national character; it draws a consistent following. We hear that **Jimmy's Cooking** (at the steps of Lycabettus on Loukiano St.) is fun in summer when tables nuzzle the curbside. Owner James spent much of his career cooking in the USA. Go to any of these for drinks (or if you can stand the snacks!) around 12:30.

As is the case with most night spots, they rise and fall rapidly—frequently disappearing altogether while we are rushing to get this perishable research fodder printed, bound up, and onto the bookseller's shelves. Athenian nighteries seem to be particularly fickle, so for your up-to-the-instant convenience and fun we're going to list the top *bouzouki* players and singers currently in vogue. If you can pinpoint where they are at the moment of your visit (with the help of some local tip-sheet or your concierge), we think you could derive heaps of musical lore in the shortest time. They are as follows: Bithikotsis, Hadji, Poulopoulos, Voskopoulos, Marinella, Moschóliou, Kokotas, Mitsakis, Tsitsanis, and Zabetas—and they're generally considered to be the Carusos of the troupe.

The continuing popularity of the taverns has caused a nightclub debacle of major proportions. Of today's scepter bearers, **Galaxy** is one of the frontrunners. Big time entertainment nightly; high but value-filled tabs; nearly always crowded. Be sure to reserve ahead. **Fantasia** is a lesser light. **Copacabana**, on Constitution Square, produces the biggest floor show of all. It's sort of a Levantine version of any gin mill or bump-and-grind emporium one might find in any big city. The geography changes, but the game's the same. **Athinea** offers winter-only dancing at 6 Venizelou Ave.; in summer it gallops to an enchanting open-air site at the racecourse. No cover charge; no cabaret; passable vittles; dinner reservations mandatory.

Discothèques? Platters spin at the **Galaxy** of the Hilton. **Nine Muses, Nine Plus Nine**, and the **Stardust** wrap up the disc 'n dance scene.

Lonely and masculine? **Las Vegas, Maxim, Flamingo, Flamenco**, or **Minuet** —call it what you wish!—is next to the Olympic Airways office on the main square (as we write these words, we have the hollow vision of its sign painter slapping out still another name-change); here's the most pleasant pickup spot, if you don't mind that 2 A.M. deadline until your companion is permitted to leave. Small show; one 30-day padlocking by the authorities for alleged over-charging; nothing special, but best-scrubbed of its type. **Mimosa** (5 Ionos St.) couldn't be more routine. Earlier in the evening (7:30 P.M. onward), **Apotsou** (University St.), **Number 17** (17 Voukourestiou St.), **Orphanides** (7 Venizelou Ave.), and **Zonar's** (9 Venizelou Ave.) are the best frequented spots for C_2H_5OH addicts. Most of this lot can be deadly dreary and zzzzzzip-less.

A spin on the wheel of fortune? At **Mount Parnes**, 3500 feet above Athens and 25 miles north of it, private interests have taken over the Greek National Tourist Office's 5-story fizzle. This modern Phoenix, has now risen from its ashes in the form of a posh gambling casino. The cuisine is above average, the accommodations are comfortable, and for gamesters it can be an excellent target for an evening, a weekend, or the "full-house" treatment.

★ **TIPS** Practically every elaborate night spot in Athens requires its bar girls to stay until closing. Don't let them sucker you into buying extra drinks on the promise they'll sneak out earlier, because they can't.

Motorized prostitution, with taxi-girls in the true sense of the word, is still rolling on the Athens afterdark scene. Around midnight they pop out of cruising cabs and inveigle lone pedestrians to a bit of l'amour on wheels. Despite increased police surveillance, plenty of strangers are trapped-and-robbed on this pitch, so don't be tempted.

Shopping The shops covered below were all standing at their listed addresses during our very recent rounds. However, midtown Athens is in such a turmoil that there might be a sudden relocation or two before your arrival. Our ★ ★ ★ ★ recommendations are individually noted.

Handwoven ladies' clothes and regional crafts: ★ ★ ★ ★ **Levantis** (3 Nikis St.) is one of *the* most soundly established quality places. Elias Levantis, an alumnus of Saks Fifth Avenue and 13 years of U.S. expertise, designs all of the beautifully color-blended fabrics and models which comprise his exclusive 104-piece collection. Each item is individually named. Recently he has added a selection of gay washable cottons and outfits in a variety of prints. He will custom-make in American sizes your choices of ensembles within 48 hours (if necessary) at his standard prices. Also on hand are his famous adjustable gold belts, his uniquely created kombaloi ("worry beads"), plus other carefully selected temptations. *Don't miss it!* **Kori** (13 Mitripleos St.) has expensive peasant-type garb for the younger group. The **National Welfare Fund** (24a Voukourestiou St., plus boutique in the Hilton) offers lovely needlepoint, woven or Persian rugs, pillowcases, and other well-chosen items. All worth a stop.

Gold jewelry: Full honors for today's spectacular planet-wide renaissance of spectacular Greek gold jewelry in the international best-dressed set belong to one single genius— ★ ★ ★ ★ **Ilias Lalaounis**. His headquarters are at 6 Panepistimiou Ave., with others at 12 Voukourestious St., Athens Hilton, Tower of Athens, G.B. Hotel, *Mykonos, Corfu, Rhodes, Zürich, St. Moritz, Geneva* and others from *Paris* (see "France") to the *Virgin Islands*. His con-temporary creations and interpretations—responsible for reviving the again-raging fashion for museum-style pieces which have enchanted ladies in the days (and nights) of Helen of Troy—comprise a vast galaxy of 18- and 22-carat gold treasures. The classical and Minoan-Mycenaean periods predominate, with their emphasis on lions, serpents, and other talismans of Ancient Greece; a second line of 11th-century Byzantine reproductions captivate more ornate feminine taste; his latest are 3 complete creations using movement as the theme. Prices? They are amazingly low for such purity of craftsmanship in this metal. Here's Lady Luck, if we ever saw it! For unusual regional-style rings and other less electrically striking jewelry, you might try **Voulgaridis** (6 Voukourestiou St). **Gold Coin** (17 Stadium St.) has been renowned for its exquisite trove of reproductions of the coinage of the Greece of antiquity which are made up as decorative individual pieces—completely different from the massive Ilias Lalaounis New Wave.

Sterling creations: The ★ ★ ★ ★ **4 Lamda** ("Tower of Athens") is another showcase for the ever-rich, ever-versatile talents of Mr. Lalaounis—but it owes its name, spirit, and stimulation to his daughters Katerina, Dimitra, Maria, and Joanna. Inspired and inspiring.

Icons and antiques: Jet-setters and shipping heiresses flock to the knowledge-able **Constantine Haritakis** (Valaoritou 7). His shop is small but his friend-ships are global in extent. Ask for ebullient "Mr. Talkis" in person.

Extraordinary rugs: ★ ★ ★ ★ **A. Karamichos & Co.** (3 Mitropoleos St., up one flight) for at least 400 years (probably 1000!) has crafted *flokati*—gorgeous, fluffy, 100% virgin wool floor coverings. It is officially classified by the government-sponsored National Organization of Hellenic Handi-crafts as their Number One creator in the nation. Sold by weight—which provides a measure of their purity—these top-line Karamichos carpets are handloomed to last a lifetime. Bred in water, visibly they improve with both washing and wear. Mr. Karamichos is so justly proud of these crea-tions that, as far as we have learned, here is the sole dealer in the land who gives a money-back guarantee. These handwoven beauties are sold ex-clusively here; the extra-thick category ("Karamichos Anniversary Flokati") is the Rolls-Royce of the art. If miracles could happen, Karami-chos is the only place we would know where they just *might* produce a magic flying carpet if we were sufficiently serious!

Furs: Should you not be thoroughly conversant with their subtleties, they can be terribly tricky to buy in this land. The leading house is 4-generation-old **J.A. Sistovaris & Sons, Inc.** (14 Voulis St., 4 Hermou St., and 9 Panepistimiou St.). But caution, please.

Greek souvenirs, paintings, handcraft: ★ ★ ★ ★ **A. Martin's Attika Gift-shops** (Air France Building, 4 Kar. Servias St.) is the largest institution of its type in the nation. Over 2,000 different items can be found on its premises. You can pick between a $2 wine glass or a $850 handwoven Minoan-style carpet (mailing and packing included). The Art Corner boasts one of the most impres-sive and versatile displays of bas-relief copper work and contemporary paint-ings that can be found in Greece today. Genial Proprietor Fred Martin, his lovely wife Litsa, and their 2 hardworking sons Taki and Tom use as the motto of this fine, 10,000% reliable house "You are not a customer, but a guest." And they mean it!

Flea Market: Pandrossou St. is the start of its Athens equivalent. Good fun for the shophound, if you strike it right.

Reading matter: **Eleftheroudakis** (Nikis St.) carries a mouthwatering supply of American and English books, originals and reprints. **Pandelides** (11 Amerikis St.) is also versatile and worthy.

Department stores: The **Minion** (Patissia St.), **Lambropoulos Bros.** (Aeolou and Stadium Sts.) and the **Athénée** (Stadium St.) are the national pacesetters. None of these appeals to us.

Things NOT to buy: Beware of the regiments of "soovineer joints"; shoddy inexpensive ready-made dresses or suits; all imported merchandise except books, regardless of category, because of their high duties. In '77 a heavy luxury tax applicable to all *residents* was imposed on perfumes, furs, jewelry, tape recorders, cameras, alcohol, and bills in Class A restaurants. This does NOT apply to foreign visitors on store-bought items such as jewelry, although the ante has been raised on wines, spirits, and Class A meals.

Shopping Hours: These were switched recently in an experimental move by the government so that they vary on alternate days. Currently on Mon., Wed., and Sat. they are from 8:30 to 2:30 only, closing down in the afternoons. On Tues., Thurs., and Fri. they operate from 8:30 to 1:30 and 5:30 to 8:30. Because this awkward system might well be temporary, please check upon your arrival.

Dedicated shophounds? Space is too tight here for further listings—so consult this year's purse-size, 25th Anniversary edition of *Fielding's Selective Shopping Guide to Europe* for more stores, more details, and more lore.

Other Targets

You really haven't seen Greece unless you've visited the islands. No 2 are alike. They are scattered in their infinite variety from the Ionian to Aegean Seas, and Crete rises from the Mediterranean.

Although the larger islands are available by air as well as by sea, we recommend hands down that you, the discerning traveler, don your dark glasses with your widest-brim hat and head for a ship (be it cruise or chartered). *If you proceed with utmost caution in the selection of your vessel,* here can be one of the most heavenly experiences of your entire journey. See "Yacht Charters" and "Aegean Cruises" sections later in this segment.

Now for an alphabetical rundown of some of the better known tourist hubs on the Peloponnesus and in the surrounding seas. To avoid confusion, villages and towns on the Greek Islands are not listed here but are included in our overall island reports.

CAPE SOUNION Refer to Athens "Hotels" under "Suburban Settings" and "Sounion."

CORFU Here's a little charmer measuring 48 by 20½ miles and boasting 150-thousand residents—1/5 of them in the city proper. The usual sea connection is from Piraeus via Corinth to Kerkyra; by air, Olympic links it to the capital with daily flights. Motoring from Athens is arduous work. If you think your'e seeing green spots before your eyes, you are, because this isle sprouts more than 4 million olive trees. (The color-blind might note in advance that the bigger species bear oranges!) Olive oil, the only industry that challenges tourism, has finally lost its lead against the mushrooming facilities for the traveler. Here is a floral paradise—the principal garden spot, in fact, of Greece. This is due chiefly to the abundance of rich soil and many little soft raindrops. The gentle atmosphere is scented by wildly rampant natural blossoms—wisteria, jasmine, dahlias, camellias, mimosa—Ferdinand's bullheaven! The airport has been enlarged, but it still could use another notch or 2 in its belt; a few jets swoop in on international runs.

The Italy-Greece car ferries almost certainly will call again this year, from 3 to 7 days per week, depending upon the time of year. These leave from Brindisi and Ancona, with some cruise schedules to and from Venice. Patras (Greece) also handles a lot of Corfu's traffic. Smaller craft make daily runs to and from the Greek mainland. Generally, this sea-blessed community is more *mañana*-prone than Mallorca; it trails its Balearic rival's construction explosion by about a decade. *Corfu*, its capital and main port, has no commercial fishing interests whatever. The best swimming can be found at the Yacht Club. *Dassia* (4 miles) splashes up next. *Paleokastritsa* (40 minutes) is packed with bathers; *Ermones* is pebbly; *Sidari* has sand, but it's an hour's drive; *Kanoni* (2 miles) is rocky and not too appealing. *Mon Repos*, in the town itself, isn't worth the effort.

Hotels   The recently unveiled **Corfu Hilton**, sited in *Kanoni* on a seaside plateau with a splendid panorama, is 2 1/2 miles from this center. Its principle facilities consist of a 231-unit curvilinear main building and 3 independent clusters of tiered "bungalows" with a total of 51 accommodations in various configurations. Bright, airy colors and lots of ceiling-to-floor glass; every structure 100% air-conditioned; sophisticated-rustic Eptanissa Grill where guests can optionally prepare their own barbeques; overgarish Kefi Bar with international entertainment; alfresco dancing in summer; good outdoor pool adjoining the gaily hued Poolside Restaurant with snacks, salads, seafood, steaks—and yes, even a soda fountain—its specialties in season; heated indoor pool; health club with full equipment; uncrowded beach with snack bar and a variety of water sports. You'll also find 2 tennis courts where white clothing is required, 4 bowling alleys, a 75-car garage, spacious conference and banquet rooms, a beauty parlor, a barber shop, and a shuttle bus to and from the hub. One highly unusual amenity is its around-the-clock room service. General Manager Bernard Brack tautly runs his impressive and excellent domain.

The deluxe **Corfu Palace**, with its beautiful garden setting in the capital of this nation's most northerly isle, has just been taken over at this writing by principals unknown to us. Since we can't give you a report on whether the loveliness of this house and its sister operation, the **Miramare Beach complex** (in the suburbs one hour from the city), will continue to be maintained or will slide downward under its new management, we must wait until their progress or deterioration unfolds. Sorry.

The **Astir Palace**, 6 miles from Corfu town at *Komeno Bay*, is a major offshoot of the Astir chain. Here is a hotel and "bungalow" complex which is nested on a headland overlooking the waves. A total of 600 beds are offered in the self-styled VIP suites, twins and singles of the dominant edifice, as well as in the banks of the outlying structures. Completely air-conditioned; Feakes

Restaurant for the European mode of cuisine; Taverna Nafiska for Greek cookery and music; 2 unremarkable bars; Kyklopes Disco which we did not see; 1 pool and so-so beach. While it's not bad, we think that these big-time entrepreneurs have done considerably better elsewhere.

The launching of the **San Stefano** is of special interest to discriminating voyagers because it is backed and operated by one of the most savvy groups in European hôtellerie—the Gauer chain, which is headquartered in Bern. Whatever these Swiss experts do, they do right. This one has 630 beds, partly in the main building and partly in bungalows bordering the beach. We look forward to seeing it in action. On the northwest coast 9 miles from the city, they also operate the **Emones Beach**. Gorgeous site on a small mountain; golf links on one flank, pebble beach on another; spectacular pool with terrace and snackery overlooking this precinct of paradise; tennis court; inside-outside dining; 2 bars; lounge dominated by a massive pewter hearth; 30 air-conditioned rooms in main unit plus clusters of bungalows in 14 tiers blanketing the hillside. Jean-Pierre Wütschert is its capable pilot. A gem among Greek resorts which we salute.

Back in the city, the plaza-sited **Cavalieri** now seems to be on the upswing again, with extensive amenities added. Still not large but with a special personality. It is just the opposite of the huge hotel village at *Nissaki*, which was taken over by the **Club Méditerranée** group; naturally, its function is specialized. Beyond this one is the colorful **Nissaki Beach**, which is approached down a steep lane from above the hotel. Appealing *taverna;* active bar; pebble beach; pool; unspoiled site for romantic holidaymakers. **Corcyra Beach Hotel** perches bright and white on a slope above *Gouvia Bay* (5 miles from Corfu); it faces the tiny islet of Vidos and St. George's Chapel on the promontory. Entrance beside a filling station to a stairstep main building; 20 bedchambers in the central complex; more than 100 bungalows; swimming pool plus 2 beaches. Simple, clean, not at all expensive. **Castello Corfu**, converted from a private villa, offers a 30-room main building and a 26-room annex. Ownership by Emil Bouas, one of the most genial, obliging, and conscientious Bonifaces on the isle; most accommodations with bath; entrance via a narrow, winding lane; no pool but swimming club about a mile away. A restful haven. The **Kanoni**, one mile south of Corfu and just below the airline flight path, is a horizontal slab containing a restaurant-by-pool, 150 bedchambers (mostly twins) with balconies, cold-air-by-button, telephones, and baths. Adequate, if unoriginal. **Astor-Corfu** (not an Astir project) is on the noisy main street of the port. Dreary lobby; drearier rooms; only 50% private-bath count; beds so lumpy they'd fascinate holidaying phrenologists; chilly reception. Not recommended. For emergency use only, the **Swiss** and **Splendid** are dinky, with no private plumbing; Third class. The **Marbella Beach**, 12 miles south of town, is composed of 64 Moorish-style apartments, plus a huge main building, a discothèque-in-a-cave, and other dazzlers. The **Messonghi** is a large, unimaginative edifice wrapped around 462 sterile rooms; boringly traditional lobby; beach that only a shipwrecked Noel Coward could be grateful for. We weren't excited by it—or in it—or even around it. The neighboring, 4-story **Delfinia** is fair in its comforts, but it's as groupy as a Cherokee Conclave. The **Eagli** was refeathered not long ago; we don't like its site. The smaller **Oasis** is crassly commercial;

it has a better location. Across the island, you'll find the **Mega** and the **Costa** in *Ypsos*; there are 2 tyke-size hostelries at *Zephyros*. The **Grand**, 10 miles west of the capital at *Glyfada* is one of the safest Corfu bets if you yearn for solitude and natural beauty. You'll find 210 air-cooled rooms, suites and apartments, each with its own bath, phone, and radio. At *Kondokali*, the First-class **Palace** is young and worthy; at *Dassia*, the **Chandris** offers both hotel and bungalow-downing; the **Kerkyra Golf** takes its name from its location; you'll probably enjoy it if you want to avoid crowds.

Restaurants (1) **La Lucciola**, (an ancient inn en route to *Paleokastritsa* with good Italian cookery), (2) **Moulin Vert** (in town; French and Greek specialties), (3) **Tripa** (*taverna* in an old country house at Cynopiastes), (4) **The Rock** (fabulous bay situation; disco activity, too), (5) **Xenia Paleokastritsa** (excellent seafare), (6) **Dionyssos** (Greek and international skillets).

Night Life The **Achilleion Casino** has brought a shaft of moonlight to the otherwise dreary afterdark situation. Within this Pompeiian-style oasis renovated to the toss of $1,000,000, you'll find roulette, baccarat, and boule; Entrepreneur Baron Hartman von Richthofen, the only surviving brother of the famous Red Baron of WW I, has older marbles spinning at Baden-Baden. Gaming rooms, nightclub, restaurant, and snack bar open from 5 P.M. to 2 A.M.; park and museum available from 9 A.M. to 1 P.M.; operates year round. Here are 3 straight passes by Lady Luck for Corfu, and a giant step for the farsighted oracles behind Greek tourism. **Bora-Bora** and **Koukouvaia** both feature disco dancing between the new port and *Kondokali*. **Nouveau** does a similar thing in the town.

Shopping The "Hurry-Hurry-Hurry!" class of tourist junk is predominant. Olive-wood bowls and canes made by prisoners make curious souvenirs. **Peroulis Brothers**, Esplanade, has a representative mélange of this merchandise; they also market filigree work, bracelets, and Venetian-style wares. Small silver boats bearing Corfu's heraldry and handwrought gold rings symbolizing the 7 Ionian Islands are available here, as well as at **Tantis Anthony** and **Ionas Spiros**. Finally, for connoisseurs of the truly exotic, we recommend the island pride—delicious preserved kumquats and the sweet, strange, interesting kumquat liqueur—almost unknown in other parts of the world.

CORINTH You can drive here from Athens in about 1 1/4 hours. The ancient ruins are splendid and the crossover at the Corinth Canal is an important junction for travelers. The town itself is not inspiring.

CRETE Except for Athens and its three neighboring one-day excursion targets of *Delphi*, the *Apollo Coast Road to Cape Sounion* and the *Peloponnesus*, here is suddenly the greatest magnet for foreign visitors to the nation. Scandinavians, Germans, and British are the vanguard of the frenetic army of invaders, in that order. Although individual voyagers swarm here in profusion, they are overwhelmingly outnumbered by tour groups.

Here are some thumbnail gleanings: *Geography?* The outline of this largest of the Greek islands is vaguely reminiscent of a running deer without legs. It is 160 miles long but never more than 36 miles wide. Its variegated terrain ranges from beaches and plains to rolling foothills to the rugged mountains of up to more than 8,000 feet which form its central spine. It's on the same latitude as Tripoli in North Africa. *Population?* About 460,000. *Climate?* So beneficent that its planners are striving to transform it into the principal market garden of Europe. As one example, the average yield of 1,100 square yards of land is 15 tons of magnificent tomatoes per 40 days from roots to shipping boxes. The winds are too strong for commercial quantities of bananas. *Industry?* Olive oil, wine, nuts, citrus fruit, dairying, and small mineral workings. At this point of development, raisins are the main export. *Culture?* Western civilization was born here about 3,000 B.C. when the Minoans migrated from Asia Minor. Through causes still unknown to archaeologists or historians, this great power mysteriously vanished 1,600 years later. Since then it has been occupied by the Dorian Greeks, the Romans, the Genoese, the Venetians, the Turks, England, France, Russia, Italy, Germany, and other rulers. The influence of its Venetian occupiers is strongly evident today. *Connections?* Between an assortment of ports on Crete and various points on the mainland or other islands, there are several daily all-Economy **Olympic** flights plus more than a dozen ferries, the majority of them in "B" and "C" grades with 3 or 4 classes. Early reservations are strongly advised. *Wines?* Because it was so blazingly hot during our latest nonstop rounds we stuck exclusively to **Dilanda Minos**, a delightful, very palatable and deliciously cooling white bottling which is an old friend. Thus, through our selfishness, with apologies we can give you no other up-to-date suggestions on Cretan varieties.

Cities and towns? **Iraklion** ("Heraklion" in English, with its name changed from Candia in 1823), the capital and principal port with 100,000 residents, is the hub of its wheel. It is so sleazy, strident, and graceless that we loathe this center. Because tourism is just *too* good in this sellers' market (there are 70 travel agencies and 85 rent-a-car offices), with very rare exceptions its facilities are dismayingly crummy. Almost in their entirety vacationers from other shores regard it as a jump-off point for greener pastures; only the cheapest and poorest conducted groups use it as their base. As a curiosity, more sidewalk cafés are clustered around Eleftheria ("Freedom") Square than in any other municipality that we've ever seen.

Worthwhile sightseeing targets are limited to the absolutely splendid **Archaeological Museum**, the **Historical Museum**, and the nearby world-famous ruins of the **Palace of Knosos**. (The official spelling has dropped one "s.")

With one exception, the hotels run the gamut from production-belt mediocrity to wretched. The 4-storied **Galaxy** (67 Dimocratias Ave.), which is rated Class B by the government, to us far outstrips its 2 Class A competitors. This U-shaped building on stilts was erected around a polyangular pool. Strikingly different multi-leveled lobby; dining room with one wall an aquarium; 2 roof gardens; coffee bar; big pastry shop; total of 144 rooms with shower and 28 with bath, all simply decorated, small, functional, and with individual terrace. The general effect is modern, fresh in color and calm in ambiance. We find the **Atlantis**, traditionally the pacesetter of this miserable roster, a depressing machine without a trace of spirit or flare. Lobby stark and unattractive; rooftop pool which would surprise us if you would want to use it; cynically impersonal staff to whom the clients seem to be numbers instead of persons; rooms and balconies clean, no more than technically adequate in furnishings, with atrociously thin walls. So commercial, so sterile, so uncaring about its faceless guests that it was a joy to check out. The 150-unit **Astoria Capsist**, on the main square, goes it one better in the air conditioning of its chambers. Otherwise we found that even more dreary. The 90-room, C grade **El Greco**, just off a small square a few blocks from the seafront, serves breakfast only. Small, amiable lobby backed by a little garden; friendly bar-let adjoining. Here's an unusually satisfactory family operation for this low-priced category.

Restaurants? Good ones suffer from the same paucity. **Le Safari** (150 Leoforis Knosou, less than 2 miles from the center on Knosos Rd.) is owned and operated by a repatriated Greek who sold his bistro in France to return. Costly décor with jungle motif; 18 stuffed animals in corner glass cases ranging from lioness to tiger down to a sweet little dik-dik; immaculate kitchen; kind and fast service; 21 tables on main floor and 11 on mezzanine. Extremely well-cooked and presented repast on our night; portions as heroic as Hercules; open for lunch and dinner every day the year round except on Good Friday. It starts late, in the national tradition. A vernal oasis in a culinary desert. **Belle Hélène**, 7 miles out past the Hotel Arina Sand, has long been one of the best-known eating places here. Smallish building; covered open terrace with 14 tables and wine barrel; divided 2-room interior with Minoan murals and blue-and-white checkered table cloths topped by red ones; careful sanitation; good regional-style cuisine. Worthy if you have your own transport, but we believe that the high cost of a taxi is too great an investment. *Tavernas,* overwhelmingly the favorite of Mr. and Mrs. Average Citizen, are as common as popcorn in U.S. amusement parks. None we have tried in these precincts has ever impressed us as outstanding or even different in any significant way. Ho hum . . . As a small cross section, the **S. Renata** is particularly popular; the **Kallithea** and **Aretoussa** feature local music; **Ariadni**, **Zorbas**, and **Stamna** lean more heavily toward the national idiom. Nightlife? The so-called nightlife here adds up to a fat goose egg. If you absolutely must, try the **Eleven**, **Africa**, or for *bouzouki,* **Alkyon**. Shopping? Tourist junk is rampant. **Zacharopoulos** in the Knosos Palace is worth exploring for jewelry and handicrafts. **Helen Kastrinojianni**, opposite the Iraklion Museum, also features local handiwork plus attractive woven fabrics. **Midas**, on Freedom Square, displays some gold and silver table pieces and picture frames of excellent quality. **Ariane** has two stores. We found the larger selection of *bijouterie* and shells at its Morozini Square headquarters. Information? Young Smraryanakis Evangelos at the **Greek National Tourist Office** is tops as an official source. Otherwise write to or visit the **Creta Travel Bureau** at 25th August St. They will plan your tour, whistle up a self-drive car and in general be your genial guide.

The only other city of importance is *Hania* ("Canae" in English), which is 85 miles due west and about one-half the size of Iraklion. Except for a far lesser flood of foreign visitors, in atmosphere and facilities it rather closely resembles its larger sister. The listless **Kydon** is its only Class A hostelry. Among the 7 Class B entries the little **Doma** gets our vote as the overall leader in attractiveness. This neoclassical mansion facing the water, with 29 rooms and showers, has been redone so charmingly that it is a gem among zircons. All of the 9 Class C and numerous Class D and E houses which we have inspected are plain Janes. Restaurants? The most colorful are those around the old harbor that are crowded with habitués on summer evenings. There is a large, unadorned café in the Public Gardens. One of the most unusual dining places we've found in Greece is the **Aposperida**, in a restored Venetian structure on Kondylaki. Among those which feature music and dancing with their fare are **Prasini Paparouna** ("Green Poppy") on King George St. and **Honolulu** on Venizelou St. **Neraida**, **Nykterida**, and **Asteria** add the bonus of views in this category. None of these is anything to write home about. Sightseeing? No magnets of any special distinction. Shopping? Even a more threadbare assembly than in the capital. In sum, to us a visit here is wasted time.

Ag. Nikolaos ("St. Nicholas" in English and often spelled "Ayios Nikolaos" in Greek) is a delightful port town 44 miles east of Iraklion. Although its overnight accommodations are Spartan (the **Hotel Hermes** is the best of a sorry lot), its restaurants, *tavernas*, and discos are a lodestone in season for vacationers from complexes which dot the hills of its environs. The best place to eat is the **Cretan Restaurant**, in our opinions; next down our list come **Vassilis**, **Trata**, **Pharos**, **Rififi**, and **Limni**. Why not scout around to find your own preference? Normally there is a lovely air of languor here, particularly on sun-drenched days.

Sleepy *Ierapetra*, which is a Dullsville, is the only habitation of any size worth mentioning on the island that is south of the long ribbon which runs the full length of the north coast.

As doubtless you have gathered from the above, wise pilgrims flee the twin cities as fast as they can shake their dust to settle into a colony on a beach. A string of huge, totally self-sustaining resort factories has sprung up which cater exclusively to vacationers. Perhaps 95% of their patronage is conducted tours. Most of them operate in season only. Curiously but incorrectly, the majority of them seem to have used the same interior decorators, including the pervasive Cretan-style theme. Common to most are such features as air conditioning, 1 or more swimming pools with snack bars, cocktail bars, one or more big restaurants with buffet lunches, a *taverna*, a coffee shop, a TV and card room, a hairdresser, a news kiosk, one or more boutiques, piped music, a disco, a sauna, tennis courts, mini-golf, sailboats, pedal boats, riding, bowling alleys, table tennis, billiards, a children's playground, "bungalows," and other facilities which give them the scope of all-inclusive mini-villages built for pleasure. Not at all incidentally, it is important to realize the difference between bungalows and "bungalows." The former are individual or semi-individual detached structures of which you will find only a few here. The latter are tiered clusters of rooms, often in 2-storied buildings, which accommodate 20 or 30 parties in what are actually annexes. These are normally more expensive than the lodgings within the main edifice. Don't expect to find high cuisine, vintage wines, or the soaring butterfly colors of summer gossamer gowns anywhere, because total informality universally reigns 24 hours per day.

The Electra Chain's **Creta Beach**, about 3 miles from Iraklion, is situated in a different direction from the aforementioned seaside belt. Small central apex; 141 units all in "bungalows" which are depressingly basic; not for most North American travelers.

The center of the action along this highway starts just below the *Iraklion Airport* and extends almost 50 miles along the North coast to *Elounda*. We have just thoroughly inspected every complex on it. Here are our observations: There are 2 deluxe settlements which are head, collar, and shoulders above the rest. These are the **Elounda Beach** and the **Astir Palace Elounda**. There is a possibility that the **Yarizina**, which will be inaugurated this year by the Minos Beach proprietors, might add a third to this roster. Among the lower-priced group the **Creta Maris** is tops. Details on these follow.

The **Marina** is close to the city. Large, stark, functional lobby with 7 separate desks for tour group information; spacious restaurant down one flight opening to a large pool; indifferent beach and big adjoining play area; many of the facilities at hand typical of these operations. Our overall impression? So-so.

The **Arina Sand**, 5 1/2 miles out near the village of *Kokini Hani*, has 83 chambers and suites in its main building plus a complex of 141 accommodations in "bungalows" of up to 3 stories. Although its beach is poor, it's lively and well-maintained. We like it for what it is.

Creta Beach ("The Massive"), a 12-mile run at *Limin Mensonissou* has been laid out as a Cretan village. This 1200-bed compound, with a staff of 400 and 11 beautifully landscaped gardens, is one of the largest hostelries in the nation. The 360 nests in its simple but colorful bungalows (not "bungalows") with large verandas are the choicest. The range of its facilities for its clients is enormous. Its poor European-style cuisine is balanced by its Greek culinary offerings. Despite its size, clients can easily find privacy if desired within its friendly, relaxed and discreet precincts. Our highest recommendation in Class A.

Reports have reached us that the **Ikaros Village** at *Malia*, 15 miles out, will again be rented to a German travel organization this year. Whether or not this will be true is possibly moot, because we'd rate it very low among its competition.

The construction pattern of **Kernos Beach**, also near *Malia*, is diametrically opposed to standard planning, with its center of activities adjoining the beach rather than the reception area. This requires a great deal of unnecessary walking. Although its installations are passable, both of these reporters felt a total lack of T.L.C. in its cold and impersonal ambiance. No thanks.

Mirabello Village, 30 miles from the capital, is close to the lovely little seaside town of *Ag. Nikolaos*. This one struck us as being so old-fashioned, commercial, and unappealing that we say Nope.

Minos Beach, a 44-mile drive, is on the skirt of a bay within walking distance of *Ag. Nikolaos*. Inaugurated in '61 as the granddaddy of them all, the years have taken such a toll that in our opinions it no longer merits its deluxe official rating. Beautiful setting; seedy lobby; 106 twin-bedded bungalows with showers and porches; 2 beaches; clean and threadbare. This once-fine old house has lapsed into a weary old shoe. It's no wonder that its owners instead of trying to revivify this are opening the opulent 300-bed **Yarizina** across the bay.

The fully air-conditioned **Elounda Beach** near *Elounda*, 5 miles beyond Ag. Nikolaos via a spectacularly scenic route, is a knockout. In '73 it was awarded 1st prize by the Greek National Tourist Organization for its design and concept. Lovely setting on a promontory above 2 semicircular beaches; main building spacious, attractive, and spotlessly maintained; masterful settings directly below of individual bungalows and a big pool cunningly landscaped among carob trees; replica of a Greek mini-village with a sweet blue-and-white chapel, an art gallery, a *taverna,* a café, boutiques, a hairdresser, a newsstand, and more; open-air cinema with English-language films; a plethora of other joys. No tour groups are accepted in season. Personally, if we were to choose any hotel on this island for a restful vacation (what's that?), this would be *it.* Expensive, but more than worth every drachma.

The setting and comforts of the nearby **Astir Palace** come reasonably close to those of the Elounda Beach, without equaling them. Here's another luxury hotel and bungalow resort on 20 acres which stands sentinel over 2 sandy beaches and a small cove. In or around its tastefully blended green area at its base are a main pool, a children's pool, an enclosed heated pool, a *taverna,* a bar, a beauty salon, boutiques, and 2 floodlit tennis courts. One of its most popular drawing cards is the staggering daily 52-platter lunch-buffet. This government-owned chain has pulled out all of its stops here and it is expanding them. Also costly and superb in every regard.

On the other side of the north coast's road between Iraklion and Hania, the only operation worth a mention is the giant **Capsis Beach** at *Rithymna*, about 45 minutes from the former. A long and variegated cluster of "bungalows" descends a gentle hillside to the huge, V-shaped nexus which is on a narrow peninsula with sea scenes on both sides. Almost every imaginable amenity described earlier can be found here. We do not cotton to the establishment for two reasons: First, it's so colossal that the feeling of individual attention seemed discouragingly lacking. Second, it has grown so quickly by such leaps and such bounds that some of its construction impressed us as jerry-built. Not our glass of ouzo at all.

To sum up the Big Picture, it is easy to understand how the natural wonders and the man-made allures of this fifth largest island in the Mediterranean have so quickly made Crete the rage among middle-and-lower income pilgrims to this ancient and gracious nation.

DELOS   Refer to Mykonos "Excursions by Sea."

DELPHI   This classic sightseeing target, 105 miles from Athens, draws countless excursionists—and well it should, because were it not for the teeming mobs that overswarm this target, few travel rewards in Greece could be richer. A now-abuilding cultural and spiritual center also may bring even further crusades of pilgrims and scholars to its majestic heights in the very near future.

Transportation   CHAT offers a bus tour from the capital; the loop includes lunch; the ride is 4 hours each way. Key Tours, the cooperative enterprise of Athens travel agencies, also provides worthy packages aboard air-conditioned coaches. Private operators base their tariffs on the number of passengers—and prices are positively cutthroat. For one person, the rate is plainly outrageous; for 5 occupants the split fee is merely paralyzing—for a simple one-day outing! There are magnificent vistas peppering this road; all buses pause frequently for picturetaking. Many visitors prefer to drive themselves at a leisurely pace and hire a guide when they arrive. The highway itself is not the best.

Points en route The **Monastery of St. Luke** boasts a trove of outstanding eleventh-century mosaaics. *Levadhia*, 1 1/4 hours out, comes up with a striking panorama of Mt. Parnassus and the Thebes Plain. Its principal restaurant, featuring the usual specialties plus peasant bread and beer, is unattractive. For sunny-day lunching, we much prefer the charming little establishment at Falling Water, on the edge of town. Its scads of rug shops should be completely avoided. *Arahova*, 6 miles before Delphia, nestles in a hillside; most of its homes are in Turkish style.

Sights The **Oracle**, **Museum**, and **Theater**—the why-and-wherefore of your trip, of course—are in the near suburbs of Delphi. On full-moon nights, scads of Athenians run up here to see the lovely phenomenon of moon beams on the ravine and the lower plain containing 9 million (!) olive trees. The reflections are such that it is impossible to discern where the land ends and the Gulf and Corinth begin. If you go, be sure to book a seafront room, of course. The settlement itself has 2000 permanent residents and is perched at an altitude of 2132 feet.

Hotels The 100-room **Amalia** garners the local laurel wreath. Modernistic, wood-stone-and-glass-lined lobby, almost Danish in concept; lounge, dining room, and bar; efficient, color-toned bedchambers; air conditioning; small but light baths. Viewful, youthful, and you-ful. The **Xenia**, run by Spiros J. Damigos, offers a dining room with a wide terrace. Fresh lounge; 45 rooms, all with bath and a view of the gulf; door numbers on tiles with flower patterns, a sweet touch; 4-story ranch-design construction; simple but tasteful. Down a peg, with identical rates, is **Vouzas**. Situated on the main thoroughfare; 60 units with 60 baths or showers; many outsiders with private terraces; roof restaurant with glorious sweep of the mountainscape; management by John Vouzas. Also good, but not quite up to the leaders. **Hermes** and **Baronos** are side-by-side; good vistas from both; okay. The **Parnassus** and **Pythia** are fair. **Castalia** is more frentic and less inviting; we found it smelly as well. Avoid all other lodgings in this area, because they're unlivable. The **Youth Hostel** is more fun than comfort—but, as old Plato said so gloomily, "If you've got youth, then who the hell cares?"

Restaurants The **Amalia**, the **Xenia**, and the **Vouzas**, plus the 2 tourist pavilions (Mr. Damigos has the **Belvedere**), are open all day; tea, sandwiches, and beer are served in the latter.

Shopping Most seriously we advise that you buy *absolutely nothing* either en route or at the destination. The merchants are so cynically tourist-oriented that generally the quality is shoddy and the prices are much higher than those in Athens.

DROSSIA Refer to "Food" and Athens "Restaurants."

EPIDAURUS The world famous Drama Festival draws as many as 50,000 visitors each year in June and July. Greek theater at its purest; marvelous acoustics; top caliber stars. We also enjoy this stop while on the Argolis tour, which includes Corinth and Mycenae.

GLYFADA   Refer to Athens "Hotels" and "Restaurants."

HYDRA   Here is a beachless, almost bare rock which seems to serve as the regional bohemia. If that's your taste, you might enjoy it.

KIFISIA   Refer to Athens.

MISTRA   The Byzantine mosaics are at the root of its only fame—and amply deserving of it too.

MYCENAE   Here the **Lion Gate** and the **Tombs of the Kings** are the big attractions. This playground of Agamemnon reached its high point in the thirteenth century B.C. The marvelous excavations are a compulsory lure to any student of antiquity. If you are traveling independently, please be *certain* to aviod the **Ifigena** restaurant on the highway a couple of miles east of these proximate relics, as well as all others in the area which are inferior even to this massive culinary factory for tour groups. Drive further along to either of the infinitely superior **Xenia Hotels** in *Naupalia*.

MYKONOS   This dazzling white islet in the Cyclades is tourist-conscious —but not quite spoiled. (To cite a charming example which amused us, the ancient bus that grinds up from the port to the town boasts a placard over the driver's seat proclaiming that your 10¢ fare can be charged to your Diner's Club credit card.) Aside from its topographical attractions and its 300 tiny churches (you may see 3 individual chapels side-by-side-by-side), it is most famous for its pet pelicans—Peter and 2 or 3 cronies who back up his Satchel-mouthed Highness as spares. Long, long ago the original bird, who flew in from the unknown, was credited as the Talisman who relieved the islanders' financial woes. Just as Gibraltans pin their faith on their lucky Barbary Apes, the Mykonos folk believe they will prosper as long as a pelican is in residence to freeload on the community. *Area?* 32.5 square miles. *Population?* About 10-thousand. *Terrain?* Largely rocky. *Climate?* Usually windy but sunny. *Industries?* Fisheries and tourism. *Towns?* **Mykonos**, a small, charming village clustered in the center of a bowl-shape bay, is the only important one. *Beaches?* Excellent. The swimming is wonderful. *Things to see?* Practically nothing—and nearly everything. It is a town to stroll through. Since the roads are poor and they go almost nowhere, it stands to reason that there is practically no motor traffic. Greek Easter is nothing short of spectacular here. Don't be alarmed when you see the outdoor services at midnight, with boys tippling in the belfries ready to haul on the bell cords, skyrockets going off, and the magnificently robed priest calling out "Christ is Risen!" while parishioners try to toss lighted firecrackers under his skirts. (Most of the explosives, not all, are wrapped in rope to prevent injury.) Then come processions, incense, plenty of imbibing throughout the holiday weekend, and so much lamb to eat that you'll think your hide is coming up in white fleecy tufts.
   Hotels   No recent changes. Since officials are worried about insufficient water supplies, an embargo was imposed on new construction. Thus what was, is—and probably will be for a long time to come. The **Xenia** is our favorite

of the mini crop. It is on a promontory overlooking a bay, a picket line of windmills, and the white-on-white townlet of Mykonos. Comfortable, motel-like accommodations; abundant and sometimes even appetizing cookery; extremely nice people who run it. The **Leto**, owned by the same company, nibbles at the edge of the main tour boat and fishing harbor, so bathing here is not the best. Its uninspired décor leaves us cold. The **Aphrodite**, about a 30-minute bus jog-and-jostle across to the desolate end of the island, maintains a romantic lonely vigil over some of the most breathtaking sea-and-landscapes in the Cyclades. Two beaches enfolding twin coves; 110 so-called "bungalows" which, in fact, are joined in one stair-step structure; all with bath and balcony facing the waves; swimming pool; tennis; ample recreation hubs for the groups to which it seems to cater; careless service, as might be expected in so remote a clime. The solitude is the thing here—good or bad. Shoppers will find it too far from town; peaceniks will probably love it.

Restaurants   The hotels will likely require that you have breakfast and one other meal with them. We pecked with the pet pelicans at both **Alefkandra** and **Fouskis**. Though the regional cookery was good at both, we prefer the former because of its sea view and beguiling, sail-covered open plaza. Every turn in the land seems to have a café, so never fear starvation.

Night Life   The very air lilts with Greek music wafting with forlorn softness from the myriad bars. The best places to weep or fall in love with its infatuating melodies are at the **Mykonos**. It has a rush ceiling (the only thing hurried about it) dancing, and someone is normally on hand to give informal instruction in the *bouzouki*. Next come the **Montparnasse** (go to the back room for more meaningful hand-holding), the **7 Seas** (near the harbor and strong on atmosphere), and **Meltemia** (quite a nice spot; close supervision by Managing Proprietor Vassiliou; house policy is to discourage gay assemblies under this roof). The **Remezzo** leads the discothèque file. It specializes in fluid sedations for the more sedate set, plus heavy breathing, sighs, and sips on its incredibly beautiful harborside patio. The **9 Muses** is much more of a swinger; it's recommendable for old married couples who are enjoying their 2nd week anniversary. Because lots more await, the fun is to wander and discover.

Excursions by sea   The most popular is the 1/2-hour voyage on stout fishing launches over to the small island of **Delos** with its famous museum, its extensive ruins, its mosaics, and its famous stone lions. Quickie trips can be had for peanuts, leaving at 9 A.M. from the main harbor and returning from the rocky uninhabited archaeological sites by lunchtime. *Other sightseeing?* Walking, drinking ouzo in the port, and viewing the **Archaeological Museum** plus **Mykonos Folklore Museum** overlooking the dock.

Shopping   Fabulous **Lalaounis** has a jewelry branch here. **Yannis Travassaros** turns lovely handwoven textiles into dresses and other items of feminine desire. The **Present Shop** weaves a tale of local blouses, jerkins, and yummy lump-knit sweaters. The **Mykonos Art Shop** purveys some of the better quality souvenirs on the island. Prices are low by U.S. standards; please bargain.

Mykonos is unique. Since the aforementioned water shortage has placed a governor on its growth, it offers the rare mixture of rewards that so many vacationers seek but seldom find in combination: sun, sea, and relative solitude. Clever, those pelicans!

NAUPLIA   Here to us is the most lustrous gem among all of the towns in the Peloponnesus. Although it's a l-o-n-g haul for a 1-day excursion from Athens, legions of foreign travelers take it in stride. Wise planners of this journey start very early, comb the principal inland sightseeing classics during the morning, have a late lunch and possibly a short siesta, and then return via the new and spectacular coastal highway. This lovely little port is the most southerly settlement of importance on what is technically the Greek mainland. (Actually this province is an island which is connected only by a single bridge at Corinth.) Both of the air-conditioned **Xénia Hotels**, one somewhat newer than the other, are sited high on a hill which blesses them with glorious panoramas over the harbor and sea. The lower one, with sound cuisine and comfortable rooms, is Class A. The upper one, in the luxury category, is more striking and elaborate. It has 55 bedchambers in its main building and 54 "bungalows" in 2 connecting double-story annexes. The exhilarating indoor-outdoor restaurant is 2 levels below the entrance. They are excellent for that afternoon nap or as overnight nests, with the most attractive facilities we have found on this land-mass.

OLYMPIA   Once it was thronged by visitors from every cranny of the ancient world who came to participate in or to view the original Olympic games. The Olympiads were devoted not only to athletic contests, because poetry and prose readings, lectures, philosophical debates, and musical and dramatic competitions were also held. While the **Stadium**, of course, is the main focal point, the **Museum** is one of the most important in the nation. Sculptures of the pediments of the Temple of Zeus, Paionios' "Victory" statue, and the statue of Hermes by Praxiteles are among its many masterpieces. Superseding its then-seedy lodgings, the 150-unit, Class A, air-conditioned **Hotel Amalia** opened its doors in '79. Greek and European-style fare without much flair; open-air bar; swimming pool; intimate tea room; convention hall for 350; smallish but comfortable quarters. Although we'd rate its amenities below those of both of the aforementioned Xenias in Nauplia, here is indeed a welcome addition.

PATRAS   You're most likely to catch this rather uninteresting port only in passing, since virtually its only role of importance is to act as the fulcrum between the routes by land or by sea to and from western Greece.

PORTO CARRAS,   near Thessaloniki, is the name of both a place and a resort created by shipowner John Carras. It was due to open after our latest coastal loop, and the scuttlebutt is that it will be huge, lovely, and deluxe. We'll pop in soon for a check.

PORTO HELI   Refer to Athens "Hotels" under "Suburban Settings."

RHODES   The "Isle of Roses" now has more tourist beds than Athens. (Astonishing, but true!) Yet the parade of hotels cheek-by-jowl has not seriously affected the basic charm of the capital or its environs. Battalions of buses? Yes. Regiments of new lodgings? Yes. Alien hordes of migratory invaders? Yes. But these have not made serious dents on the island's historic radiance. *Location?* Largest of the Dodecanese Islands, roughly 16 miles off the Turkish coast and 280 air miles southeast of Athens. *Size?* 54 by 27 miles, shaped like an ocarina. *Population?* Nearly 70 thousand. *Cities?* *Rhodes* proper, with 30-thousand people, is the capital and the only important settlement. *Lindos*, a whitewashed village with its own Acropolis, is about an hour away. In fair weather this charming coastal hamlet is a *must* for sightseers despite the increasing influx of this century's worst examples of so-called architecture—visual pollution. *Connections?* From *Athens* (Piraeus): Overnight boat service which stops at other islands en route—simple and pretty rugged; from Athens airport 50 weekly Olympic Airways flights which take a little over an hour; from other islands thrice per week. Caution: In peak periods, traffic is so heavy that normally you will be asked to show your confirmed return ticket before Olympic will permit you to board in Athens. A 600-yard runway extension enables larger airliners to fly in and out; an entire new air facility called Paradise is now functioning 10 miles from the capital. Although these efforts are calculated to relieve the pressure, we anticipate only greater congestion as the jet-boom zooms. *People?* Lovely; very clean and overwhelmingly kind. With the influx of tourism, avarice and graspiness have raised their inevitable heads. *Best season?* Late spring or early fall. Summer is fine when the breezes blow, but when they don't, it can be hot; winter is comparatively mild, but some spells are unpleasant; prices from November through February in many hostelries have been slashed 50% as a spur to Off Season tourism.

Hotels With its vast new wing, the 100% air-conditioned **Grand Hotel Astir Palace** bows welcome to nearly 800 courtiers, all of whom may make their individual splashes in any of the 3 swimming pools, including 1 indoors for cooler months. Oases of snacking corners and alfresco lounges; 2 restaurants with nearby cocktail bars, popular self-service snack bar; English pub; Isabella nightclub; casino for year-round gambols from 9:30 P.M. to 2 A.M. Some units with verandas facing gardens and pools; other seafront accommodations slightly more expensive; winter reductions about 50%. The situation is its primary asset. The **Dionysos** is probably next. This also-superbly-sited youngster consists of 2 separate air-conditioned buildings, tennis courts, minigolf, and 3 swimming pools. The first structure, in the deluxe category, is limited to suites which offer a 2-bed room and bath, a sitting room, a kitchenette with refrigerator, and a big veranda also with a magnificent view of the sea. There is a garden cocktail bar plus an adjoining snack installation featuring regional specialities. The second structure is a complex which embraces the main dining room, the main bar, a cinema, a lecture hall, and a nightclub. The accommodations here, down one peg in the "A" category, are conventional in pattern but not in décor; refrigerators throughout are a thoughtful touch. Satisfactory in its bracket. The **Miramare Beach**, an ambitious project 3 miles from the city on the airport road, offers a central edifice, 152 1- and 2-storied bungalows and a bevy of 2-bedroom deluxe cottages. Beachfront ambiance in a lovely setting; swimming pool; international cuisine with Greek specialties; windsurfing; tennis; minigolf. Not imposing but homey and friendly; particularly good for traveling families. The faded **Des Roses** is due to be uprooted and replanted by gardeners from the Bank of Greece, which owns it. Blossom time is unknown.

The young 11-story **Rodos Bay** looms up as one of the loftier buildings on the island, allegedly 30 feet higher than the vanished Colossus of Rhodian legend. (*Of course* you remember that this ancient statue was 100.206 feet tall!) Sited 2 miles out toward the airport, this entry fronts the beach from a slight rise. Rooftop saltwater pool; bar and restaurant sharing a twinkling tableau of southwest Turkey; cookery that's easy to forget (service can be forgetful, too); shops, tennis, minigolf, and sauna; *taverna;* nightclub; cavernous, granite-girt lobby punctuated by wooden beams and paved with gray marble; 28 relatively spartan but air-cooled bungalows; 35 split-level suites; 175 bedchambers with white stucco walls, pastel-tiled decking, telephones, baths or showers. Our favorites are the high-ceilinged duplexes on the 5th level. Heavy group traffic. The **Belvedere** is back in the middle of town. Biggish structure with an austere sense of modernity; 165 rooms, all with bath or shower; the fronts have terraces looking seaward, but the backs peer onto a truck route. The food to us was inedible. Despite the nice pool and tennis court, we'd call it a noisy bunker. The midcity **Mediterranean** was awash with cheapjack groups and redolent with petroleum odors on our visit. Very pleasant sidewalk terrace but otherwise too commercial and crass for our taste. This same organization has unveiled its neighboring **Rodos Palace Resort Complex** consisting of a deluxe tower hotel for 800 plus chalet accommodation for nearly as many. The Maurice Bailey décor makes handsome use of marble and panels, with ample space and the clever employment of trickling water to add a note of solace. Cheer-packed grill, huge restaurant, colorful nightclub, pink coffee shop, shops also for shopping. We think this one shows real sticking power. The sleek **Oceanis**, with a relaxed composure, is sited out near the Miramare. Inviting swimming pool; fair public rooms; air conditioning; well-appointed bedchambers. If you prefer a noncentral address (across the highway from the breakers), this is it. The youthful **Metropolitan Capsis**, across from the Dionysos, is an imposing structure. Roof garden, pool, sauna, and gym; seaview rooms with air conditioning; food and service geared to the throngs of tour registrants who roll in as waves to the shore. The vastly widened **Golden Beach** peers furtively at Mt. Filerimos across a narrow strand of sand. Modern, sawtoothed structure perfectly complemented by enough athletic paraphernalia to sponsor its own Olympic games; bath, telephone, and radio for every registrant. The **Cactus**, **Sirabas**, and **Ibiscus** line up side by side by side, revealing equal proclivities for provoking our professional boredom. The young **Chevaliers Palace** may lack an apostrophe, but it offers a chivalrous, air-conditioned welcome to some 300 pilgrims and sun worshippers. Decoratively, it jousts merrily with its own image: flags, armor, chain mail, and other hokum of ages gone by. **Imperial** is almost viewless. The **Marie**? New-y, but phooey. **Thermai** bubbles in its own sylvan park. So-so. The **Plaza** is pleasant but hardly a Ritz. The **Park**'s best feature is its nightclub. **Spartalis** eschews the obligatory pension policy. The 3rd floor, claiming the finest rooms, is vintage '61; not all accommodations have bath or shower. **Olympic** has 46 small rooms. Front units with terraces; baths just a bit more spacious than bassinets; one block from the sea; gaudy lobby. **Cairo Palace**'s III rooms have baths or showers (13 singles excepted); the

restaurant and main hall are brashly redecorated. The **Soleil** comes up with
93 units, 41 baths, one newer wing, and a garden restaurant; it has finally roused
itself sufficiently to add curtains to its windows. Many Class C hotels have
sprung up; they're so basic they're scarcely worth mentioning. In the mountains, 30 miles distant, there is one choice—the **Elaphos**. No swimming pool
and way-the-hell-and-gone up on a Grecian Alp.

Restaurants Most hotels impose a full-pension plan, but a few independents have had the courage to serve the more adventurous public.
Kon-Tiki, moored at the extension of a marina which overlooks a small bay,
is the tightest little ship on the horizon, in this salt's opinion. All the nautical
trimmings come with this one: Hurricane lamps, tarpaulins, ship's tackle, and
the fetching charm of a cozy bark. Excellent regional cuisine, among the best
we've had in Rhodes; sparkling cleanliness; friendly crew; reasonable tabs. Our
pick of the fleet. **Oscar** is also above average. **Alexis** is for seafood stalkers,
while **Casa Castellana** caters to steak hounds. **Deluca** gave us wretched regional fare in something less than a hospital-clean atmosphere. The **Farm
House**, a 3-minute walk from the Grand Hotel, is recommendable. Bamboo
trappings; sea-vista terrace in summer; open-kitchen hearthside in winter.
Inexpensive, simple, and good. **Aira Mare** and **Maison Fleuri** rank high in the
luxury category; the former is Greek, the latter French. **Kaliva** is a cutie by
the bay. **Elli** is so-so for snacks. As for local *tavernas,* the colorful **Vrachos**
huddles by the shore; it is haunted by burly sailor lads and assorted toughies.
Arapaki is a worthy alternate. The **Yachting Club** sails in with alfresco service;
forthright, unglamorous cuisine; fine view. The **Park Rodini**, 2 miles from the
center, comes up with music occasionally; agreeable for dancing; not too bad
for a late bite and a nuzzle. Several **cafés** line the New Market; all are dirty
and 3rd-class to our eyes. **Peristeri** is emphatically not recommended.

Night Life Nearly all of the Deluxe and First-class hotels have nightclubs that function from time to time. The **Miramare** spotlights dancing in the
bar. **Rhodes By Night**, near the Miramare, is a gimmicky mock-fortress structure offering dining, dancing, cabaret, and no-seaview portholes. Summer
patio; clean; festivities from 8 P.M. until the last Socratic barfly crawls out; open
all year. Best of the circuit. Café-bars *(kafenion)* are popular, especially in the
Old Town. In the New Town **Aketon** is tops, followed by **Trianon** and
Lindos.

Sightseeing The site of one of the Seven Wonders of the World, the
Colossus of Rhodes, which once straddled the harbor and which was destroyed
by an earthquake in 224 B.C. (a group of sculptors and archaeologists plan to
erect an aluminum replica of the original); a 1-hour tour of the ramparts and
defenses of the **Old Town** (a *must* for every visitor), built by the Crusaders;
the magnificent medieval **walled city** of the Knights Hospitalers of St. John
of Jerusalem (today the Knights of Malta), with its castles, palaces, and
fairy-tale ruins; the **Archaeological Museum** and the **Palace of the Grand
Masters**; the **Thermal Springs of Callithea**, 6 miles out, with Moorish architecture, a grotto restaurant, a spring house, 3 kinds of beneficial waters, and
a challenging array of 120—count 'em 120—toilets; the splendid cellar **Aquarium** with an amazing variety of rays, moray eels, turtles, brilliant starfish, and
local sea denizens in a series of tanks; the somewhat overrated **Valley of**

Butterflies at Petaloudes, 15 miles out, where clouds of pinkish-gray beauties rise by the thousands as you walk along the little cascades (season only). The young-in-legs may pedal about the capital on a rented bike. And for other types of sightseers, we've read that a nudist colony for 500 bare-skin buffs was undraped in the coastal region opposite the airport from the capital. Its announcement blithely stated, "The accommodations will consist of huts for two, planned so that the erection and placement takes into consideration the local topography and vegetation." Anyone for landscape gardening? Finally, try not to miss a drive out to **Lindos**, an hour from your metropolitan doorstep. This ancient, lime-washed, seacoast village is nestled in a rugged meander of an age-old ravine. Park your car in the town square and take the 20-minute hike up the footpath to the cliff-high fortress and the quietly eroding sandstone Acropolis. The awe-inspiring vistas of the sapphire water, the cubistic white-on-white jumble of houses, the fishing harbor, the still lagoon in a bracelet of volcanic rock, and the far-ranging sweep of a golden sandy beach, are breathtaking. If you pack a picnic lunch, nibble and daydream on the flower-covered slopes below the ramparts; you will be much happier than if you had dined at the handful of rawboned *tavernas* in the town. On the way down, take the path leading to the small but gemlike Byzantine chapel. Be sure to give a moderate tip to the 212-year-old woman who explains in perfect Greek just what every statue, painting, niche, and curlicue means (to her, not to you, unless you speak the language). If you *must* overnight, the **Pallas** and **Electra** boardinghouses are just about the only pads available; neither will bring fond memories of your nights at the Ritz. The drive back is over the same good but narrow route.

   Shopping   For that marvelous Rhodes pottery and handicrafts, try **Icaros** first; retail store at 1 Museum Square, factory 1 1/2 miles on the outskirts, and the leader of the industry. **Frarakis** (7 Museum St.) is probably the 2nd-best choice; same prices as Icaros, and some different specialties. **Papanikitas** (corner of Museum Square and Street of the Knights) is also good for similar things. For costume jewelry, try **George Stavrianakis** (2 shops—Hippocrates Square and 21 Ethnarchis Macarios St.). Or for more costly items, **Lalos Louizidis** (French St. at the New Market), **Skiathitis** Bros. (just below Cairo Palace Hotel), and **Demetrius Anghelou** (Museum Square) are the best in the city. For embroidery, **Arapoudis** offers a collection of needlepoint, blouses, bridge sets, and children's local costumes. In general, we're very disappointed by what shopkeepers offer in Rhodes. Too much of it is sucker bait for the mass tourist trade.

   Things Not to Buy   A gigolo—of any size, shape, shade, or flavor. The Rhodes Rogue's Gallery is alive with more slippery critters than can be found in the Bronx Zoo's Reptile House. These Lotharios, this island's indigenous vipers, encourage women to ply them with expensive talismans for their favors; then they seek kickbacks from some of the sleazier brand of shopkeepers. Even worse, they have been known to blackmail their naïve nymphs after they have returned to hearth and home. The mayor asserts that a lass can usually recognize them by their English, German, or Swedish vocabularies which inevitably stress and restress, "I love you!"

Further Data Write or get in touch with the Director of Tourism, Rhodes; his office will send you a boatload of brochures and handle your travel puzzles.

Take a look at Rhodes; you won't be sorry. It's a delightful off-trail adventure for the inquisitive or the peace-seeking voyager.

SALONIKA We haven't been up here in ages. Ever since the buddings of foreign tourism in 1949, except for business people and a relative scattering of independents, North American visitors have targeted en masse on Athens, the excursions in its environs, and the islands, virtually ignoring this destination, which is 418 miles from the capital. This second most populous city is on the Aegean at the middle of the nation, only 30 miles from the Yugoslav border. More than 700,000 residents; key railway junction; fevered port in continuous motion; heaps of modern buildings, many of them commercial; myriads of Byzantine churches, mosaics and tombs; the chapel where St. Paul once preached; the jumping-off base for disciples of the sun who are pointed toward *Chalkidiki* and of culture buffs bound for *Philippi* (near Cavalla) or *Pella*, where Alexander the Great was born. Since we haven't inspected its hotels and restaurants for too long, we will refrain from commenting on them in these pages.

Now strong signs are appearing that at last Salonika is being "discovered." Hence, high on our list of priorities is a full and fresh report which will appear in our next edition.

SARONIS Refer to Athens.

SOUNION Take the drive out from Athens to see it even if you don't stay. If you're here at sunrise or sunset, you might be sufficiently lucky to be blessed with one of the most inspiring moments of your lifetime. The gleaming white marble of the **Temple of Poseidon** was the first vision of the Cape seen by mariners navigating from the Eastern markets, the Dardanelles, and the Aegean archipelago. It's lonely, it's silent, and its beauty is—well, "awesome" just doesn't half describe it.

SPARTA Above the plains of the modern but dull town, the **Temples of Athena and Artemis**, as well as the **Circus**, rise against the snow-banked crags of Taiyetos. You may also inspect a worthwhile museum in midvillage; a number of Byzantine churches and palaces, and a fortress built by the Franks.

THESSALONIKI See Salonica.

☑ **YACHT CHARTERS** This has become such a snake pit of racketeering, misrepresentation, and undelivered promises that we throw up our hands and advise an entirely different approach from our previous one. After careful research for past editions of this book, we selected and recommended individual yachts for vacation cruising. To our shame and regret, it was a mistake simply because this field of activity has become too volatile. Excluding the crooks who promise the world and deliver disastrous heartaches, owners change so frequently and crews gypsy so constantly from boat to boat that our prior counsel has spoiled the holidays of 2 families among our readers. Our feelings of guilt are so profound that never, never again will we repeat this procedure.

The ONLY way around today's dilemma, in our opinions, is to seek the guidance of a completely honorable, impartial, and candid expert who is a recognized authority and who is constantly on the scene to keep up-to-the-minute with its changes. Providently, we have found a paragon in Souren Jenazian, the recently retired Greek Director of T.W.A. who has been our closest friend in the nation for more than 30 years. As an additional hobby to keep him occupied, Mr. Jenazian has volunteered to help any *Fielding's* follower on any problem in his now-favorite area. He will accept no fees. We would trust this ever-kind, ever-generous gentleman with our lives. Hence, if you wish information on this subject, please feel free to write to him at 63 Vyzantiou St., Nea Smyrni, Athens. He'd love it!

☑ **AEGEAN CRUISES** Since 1-to-14-day trips are available, plus special weekend jaunts, which should you choose? Every ship's officer and ship's social hostess with whom we've ever discussed this question corroborates our own conviction that the longer the Aegean voyage, the greater the rewards. When a sizable group of strangers is thrown together, only the fastest workers aboard are given enough time in a weekend or even in 4 days to sort out the fellow-passengers whose companionship beckons with the greatest fun. Therefore, following proper selection of your vessel and your stateroom, our most urgent recommendation is that you live it up at sea for one full week.

Next, as of now but subject to change, these itineraries, which begin and end at the Athens port-suburb of Piraeus, are virtually standard. The 3-day wanderer will probably head to Delos, Mykonos, Rhodes, Crete, and Santorini. The 4-day sailor is almost sure of stopping at Crete, Rhodes, Santorini, Kusadasi (Ephesus), Patmos, and Mykonos. The 7-day pilgrim is even more certain—but not 100%—to disembark at Crete, Santorini, Rhodes, Kusadasi, Istanbul, Alexandria, Delos, and Mykonos. (Generally if Alexandria is on the list, then Istanbul and Kusadasi are off it and vice versa.)

Next, depending upon your option, any day can be sailing day. Departures are usually scheduled for late afternoon or early evening. Long voyages weigh anchor between late morning and late afternoon. Current capacities vary between 200 and 750 berths. No company runs these cruises between the end of October and the middle of March. Most operators start later and end earlier.

For details and reservations on all of the vessels listed below, please consult splendidly efficient, all-knowing **Hellenic Tours**, 3 Stadium St., Athens, or your travel agent.

Last, on all of the good ones, you can expect to find stabilizers, full air conditioning, ample lounges, at least 2 bars, poor-to-fair institutional-style cuisine, a ship's hospital supervised by a doctor, a swimming pool (perhaps 5 postage stamps in breadth), a beauty parlor, a cinema, a sundeck (too often cruelly cramped), trap shooting, a nightclub with orchestra, and piped music. A few offer such extras as elevator, laundry service, telephones in the staterooms (the *Jason* and a couple of others feature a 10-button system throughout), a sauna, and a small gymnasium.

However, barring the meager handful of costliest deluxe accommodations, you can also *count* on the fact that the miniaturization of your stateroom will dismay and disappoint you at first sight. This is why we beseech you to heed this special word of counsel: *Pare down your wardrobe to its absolute minimum before climbing up that gangplank,* because the storage space allotted to each routine excursionist is so sparse that it is absurd. Any good-natured hotelier in Athens would be happy to store your excess while you're afloat, either free of charge or for a trifling fee.

In all the ships which have earned our approval, *generally* you will find clean quarters, decent service, adequate but not opulent comfort, and tariffs commensurate with value received. But let's be mountain-brook-clear in stressing the word "generally," because the lack of consistency in the quality of these cruises—usually excellent but occasionally execrable—has given serious grounds for many complaints to these reporters.

The Sun Line has unveiled the reigning Queen of the Aegean, the 700-passenger *Stella Solaris.* Inside she has become an opulently lavish floating hotel with altered stateroom dimensions, a rich stem-to-stern décor, and just about every amenity possible to imagine. She breaks the waves smoothly on the 7-day circuit in summer and brings happiness to Caribbean trippers in winter. For big-ship buffs, what a honey she is! We are equally fond of the tasteful and dignified *Stella Oceanis,* which roams the waters of the Mid-Med and the Aegean. Talk about dreamboats—these 2 have it. The even newer *Oceanus,* a 500-passenger, 11,000-ton competitor from Epirotiki Lines, cast off her wraps in '79. Full air conditioning; 230 cabins with private plumbing; pool; discothèque; shopping gallery; hospital unit. Her maiden lanes took her on 3- and 4-day prances around Mykonos, Rhodes, Crete, and Santorini.

The *Constellation* carries the Commodore's flag of the K Lines. Total of 200 outside cabins with private facilities; 1 complete deck of play areas; 2 pools; disco; movie theater; full air conditioning; more. She plies the 7-day loop to Istanbul. We've not yet trod her planks, but advance reports indicate that she's good.

The same applies to the *City of Mykonos,* which Cycladic Cruises will place in Aegean service this spring. This one will also make the same 7-day swing to Turkey. We'll be interested in reports on her quality.

The *Atlas,* formerly the comely *Ryndam,* is now the Epirotiki flagship. She, too, has been renovated almost totally. Her public rooms reflect the outstanding talents of Maurice Bailey—and there are many happy surprises, including such extras as a heated inside swimming pool (not counting the big one in the sun), a cinema, and a fastness of open deck space. Nearly all of her cabins are relatively spacious vis-à-vis much of her competition. Very sound, too.

The 4800-ton *Aquarius* has taken to the 7-day seaway, covering 11 ports including Turkey on her itinerary. Again designer Maurice Bailey conceived her interior garb. She has a swimming pool and nightclub, plus an intimacy evoked by her somewhat small capacity (280 voyagers). We haven't gone with her yet, but she is a popular lady who is known for good service.

The *Galaxy* is slightly smaller. You'll find her spinning in 3- and 4-day orbits in her cool, steady, and sleek way. Especially amiable crew.

The *Golden Odyssey* will again spin her yarn this season. Built by Danes and managed by the Royal Cruise Line, this creation of modern shipbuilding art is already being touted as one of the finest ladies to take to sea. She roams in 12-day circuits, and from initial reports, we'd guess she'll be a very popular gal indeed.

The sea-green *Jason,* who hastens for the Epirotiki Line, continues her love affair with Turkey on the conventional 7-day run. She is imaginative in her ambiance and versatile in her facilities. If you can afford her best, the Castor and Polux suites on Apollo Deck are worth the extra investment. Next best are staterooms #A-1 to #A-6, equipped with tubs. Try #P-7 to #P-22 on D Deck for a less costly but satisfactory buy. We'd avoid E Deck (named "Nereus Deck" by the PR-minded owners) as we'd avoid sleeping in a birdhouse. For this one-week cruise, she's high among the pacesetters.

Lower on our tide line comes the *Kentavros* (K Lines). Despite her ancient age of about 3 decades, she still skims at her normal 16 knots. Her work zone has been switched to the northern Aegean out of Thessaloniki and running to Istanbul. She's a popular ship.

The *Atlantis* (a sister to the *Jason* and the *Stella Oceanis*) and the *Illyria* (converted by her Blue Aegean Sea Line skippers) are on the 3-to-4-day circuits. Both are recommendable. So is the Sun Line's *Stella Maris,* which is not too large and boasts excellent food and service on these half-week voyages. Similarly we hear favorable comments on the *City of Andros* though we haven't boarded her for a 4-day spin.

The *Poseidon* (Greek name) or *Neptune* (Latin name), the same ship that goes on 4-day swings, is another we haven't tried personally. We have had several complaints recently alleging that this line juggles reservations and cabins to better suit its load factors. True?

The 23,000-ton *Navarino,* formerly the *Gripsholm,* once again carries old-world nostalgia into new ports of call this season. Though we haven't made an inspection since her latest transformation, readers have praised her highly.

The *Saronic Star* is our prime choice for one-day cruises from Piraeus to Aegina, Hydra, and Poros. Also very good are the *Meltemi II* and the *City of Hydra.* The *Hermes* zips out to the same isles under the Epirotiki burgee. Rates are amazingly low, including lunch, for a sailing day that dawns at 8:30 A.M. and ends at 7 P.M. *No scheduled ship unlisted above is recommended this year.*

Ireland

Ever heard of an entrancing, beguiling, little nation named Poblacht na hÉireann? Pronounce it *"Pub*lockt nah *Hair-* un," but call it the "Republic of Ireland" if you don't speak Gaelic. The country is free from English interference, economically and otherwise; this is a subject best left alone when there's an Irishman around. It's an island, of course, smaller than Pennsylvania but larger than South Carolina; you could drop its entire area into Lake Superior.

One-sixth of the seagirt—Northern Ireland, in the northeast—is also taboo as a conversational subject. Orangemen of Belfast heartily reciprocate this mutual distrust and suspicion. It's as different from the rest of Ireland as Morocco from Milwaukee, particularly since the tragic and bloody civil war erupted there to make it currently risky for residents and travelers alike. The majority of the populace of Antrim, Derry, and the northeastern counties is Protestant; in the Republic, 95% of the people are Catholic.

The Emerald Isle is a good name for it. See for yourself as you wing over the countryside. The fields are so green you might imagine you're wearing tinted glasses. The climate is mild, and to call it "moist" is like calling the Sahara Desert "dry." The summers are cool (50°–60°) and the winters are gentle (40°–50°). A bored newspaper editor with a sense of humor once ran this banner headline in August: "76° HEAT WAVE SWEEPS COUNTRY—THOUSANDS PROSTRATED!"

Here is the sod on which to relax. As *Time* stated so pungently, "The Irish have always cultivated the art of living, and they still have time and space for the slow perusal of race horses, the thoughtful consumption of stout, and the weighty disputation in rich, foamy periods that make English English seem like verbal porridge. . . . Ireland has in abundance the qualities that often seem to be disappearing elsewhere: kindliness, an unruly individualism, lack of snobbery, ease, style, and, above all, sly humor." National awareness of the value of foreign tourism hit the Man in the Street only recently, and the revolution since this awakening has been one of the most startling and gratifying developments we've ever witnessed in travel. The fine Irish air is laced today with the sweet aroma of touristic success—a dollar-green that enhances their own lovely shade of Kelly. And coupled with this trend, the traveler finds that his dollar is threaded with spools of elastic. Dublin today—not to mention the even cheaper rural Irish targets—can provide one of the lowest-cost holidays in Europe. But if you want floor shows, superhighways, strip joints, recreation directors, subways, nightclubs, and the frenzied, taut scurrying of the mass-produced American vacation, here still isn't your answer. Ireland will offer you a good chair and invite you to enjoy what John Burroughs once called "the Beautiful Foolishness of Things." Should you be after medicine for overtired nerves—a gentle peace in simple surroundings with a people so warm you'll be on first-name terms in 5 minutes—this is your Arcadia, your Hesperides, your long-sought haven.

☑ **SHANNON INTERNATIONAL AIRPORT**   Shannon is the airport and Limerick is the town. Transit passengers generally have time to refuel in its outstanding restaurant, to polish off a quickie at its friendly bar (amazingly low prices), and, *if not bound for Dublin or domestic points,* to load up with tax-free spirits, U.S. cigarettes, French perfumes, Swiss watches, English pewter, Irish linens, and other goodies at the Tax Free Airport Store. This one makes all other tax-free operations in all other European or U.K. airports look sick. The Souvenirs Department, with ¼-million customers annually, does a turnover Macy's would envy; the Mail Order Department has been set up for Americans who cannot travel to Europe but who wish to share the soothing cost advantages. Write Manager Dick Scott, Shannon Mail Order Service, Shannon International Airport, Ireland, for the fine low-cost catalogue. Absolutely reliable; money-back guarantees promptly honored. WHAT a bonanza for Christmas worriers—and who isn't?

Airport moguls and the C.I.E. bus interests have pooled resources to offer a delightful 24-hour "Medieval Tour" for international wanderers—a worthy and interesting stopover en route in either direction across the Atlantic. A highly sophisticated reader wrote to us, "I expected this to be the usual mechanical, touristy, gimmicky bore—but it was so fresh that I had a *lovely* time!" The all-expense fee of about $58 per person includes hotel room, transportation, and the usual—plus a colorful fifteenth-century banquet in the Great Hall of Bunratty Castle, during which a "Lord and Lady" are elected. Transients may enjoy the dinner, if space is available.

Adjoining this monument, the reconstructed Irish village complex called Bunratty Folk Village has 6 cottages, a forge, and a souvenir and craft shop to the rear. Within a few steps is **Durty Nelly's**, which first started as a pub more than a century ago. After careful restoration and expansion in the late 1960's, it has 4 rooms with stone walls, sawdusted floors, and 2 peat fireplaces. Typically light food is served inexpensively at all licensed hours. Its friendly atmosphere and convincing authenticity make it definitely worth a stop-in for drinks before the banquet. While here, please don't miss the unusually fetching fashions for both genders at the **Bunratty Cottage Shop** opposite the Castle.

It is the loving creation of Designer Vonnie Reynolds, whose poise, polish, and charm warmly complement the wealth of her talent. While her own inspired styles are featured, you can also find a wide range of tweed and knit suits by Jimmy Hourihan, and beautiful pure-cotton crocheted blouses and other wearables pleasantly displayed in a cottage atmosphere. Branch in Killarney's **Hotel Europe**. Highly recommended.

An interesting tour is a **cruise on the Tinarana**, which chuffs from June until September. Departures from Killaloe at 3 P.M. daily; $4 per adult and half that for children. Morning and evening trips may be arranged only if 40 or more people book; in practice this normally trims it down to weekends in summer. Further information may be had from Cormacruisers, Killaloe. Also, a number of attractions (castles, prehistoric lake dwellings, ring forts, and museums) reflecting the natural history and culture of the area can be absorbed painlessly on day tours by coach from Limerick City; check the Tourist Office in O'Connell St. for details.

Eye-popping evidence of the country's economic resurgence greets you right inside the gateposts. Shannon Development Co. has attracted an impressive industrial complex to the once stark and barren sandspit adjoining the runways. Stop to see it. It's exhilarating to witness pioneer spirit and Celtic muscle in action.

Weathered-in passengers may take the 2- to 3-minute walk from the terminus to the **Shannon International Hotel**—but we hope that they don't. Tycoon Bernard P. McDonough, who also owns Dromoland Castle and Clare Inn (see "Limerick") has transformed this once-pleasant stop into what amounts in essence to a training school for these other two establishments. On our latest revisit, we found that a so-called Building Supervisor (actually a glorified maintenance man) had replaced the manager, that the upkeep was poor, that the tariffs were higher in low and mid-season than in the Shannon Shamrock, that guests were required to take their main meals at the airport, and that the level of comfort and service had deteriorated too seriously for us to find it even barely acceptable. If you should stay here, be certain to rely on your own alarm clock for awakening, because a number of travelers have told us that their morning calls which they had left at the desk were completely ignored. Sad, sad, sad. On the other side of the coin, **Fitzpatrick's Shannon Shamrock Inn** has zoomed up in appointments and administrative savvy at missile speed. When taken over by this gentleman and his equally enterprising wife who have conquered an even bigger challenge in the Fitzpatrick Castle at Killiney (see "Dublin"), it was bare, gimmicky, and tastelessly modern in tone. Now, while still on the somewhat plain side, it is attractive and immaculate. Pleasant dining room flanked by enclosed pool with a view of Bunratty Castle; fetching bar; sauna and massage; courtesy £1 shuttle to airport; ice machines; among its 83 accommodations with bath, the 8 end rooms (4 in atelier style) are very much worth the £2 difference if you're splurging a bit. The others are designed in conventional studio style. Manager Michael Rice and Assistant Manageress Miss Geraldine Butler are warm, efficient, and on top of its smallest details. Their personnel are kind and well trained. Tariffs jump by almost 50% from winters to summers. To us, here is definitely the No. 1 standard hostelry in the entire area.

☑ **SIGHTSEEING** In the countryside, the drive through the extreme south-west of the nation (*Bantry–Ballylicky–Kenmare* and around the legendary "Ring of Kerry" to *Killarney* or the nearby *Dingle Bay*) is particularly stirring, beautiful, and worth adventuring. The L54 *coastal* road up to *Ballyvaughan* (County Clare) is even more breathtaking. You will thrill to a parade of glorious seascapes and landscapes in wild and unforgettably impressive terrain. Remember, however, that most of the hotels in this area are closed during Off-Season.

And while in Killarney, don't miss the extraordinary excursion up the mountain road to "Ladies View" and "Moll's Gap." If you don't use your own car or take a conducted bus tour, you may proceed by jaunting cart, pony trap, or pony-*back* (if you're out of your orangutan mind) up, in, out and around, to the upper lake. Here a mediocre but filling picnic lunch may await you. Your return may then be made by big comfortable rowboats, with 4 brawny oarsmen pulling you down the 14-mile channel through the 3 lakes. This is a 6-hour trip. We took ours the easy way, by self-drive automobile. Also in Killarney, **Muckross House Folk Museum** is well worth a visit.

Tralee, County Kerry, is the base of **Siamsa, the National Folk Theatre**, where the traditions of the countryside—the thatching, weaving, butter-churning, story-telling—are brought alive through mime, music, song, and dance.

The *Naomh Eanna,* a handsome little steamer, handles the Aran run all year round and is ably assisted by *The Galway Bay* from June 1 to mid-September. Arrival and departure times are such that you will have to spend 2 nights in Galway. The *Naomh Eanna* trip takes about 2 1/2 hours to the main island and after a stay of approximately 1 1/2 hours (depending on tides) returns via the other islands, taking about 5 hours. *The Galway Bay* calls on the main island and returns on a direct route, taking about 2 1/2 hours each way. If you can't spare that much time, regularly scheduled 20-minute flights zip out of Galway; they're very reasonably priced. Distressingly, however, a growing percentage of the traditionally independent and ingrowing people here have become surly and greedy in their receptions of visitors. This now spoils a lot of fun of yore.

For amateur sailors the appeal of a relatively new and utterly delightful vacation option is rightfully escalating in eye-popping proportions. Today more than 300 "rent-a-boat" flotillas are available for self-operated cruises of the Shannon River, where you can get away from it all by enjoying the peace, quiet, and scenery of one of the world's most unpolluted and beautiful freshwater streams where all commercial traffic is banned. Before launching you'll be briefed on handling and navigation. Easily spotted signs mark its channels and rescue craft are on patrol. Periodically the river broadens into serene loughs (lakes). At night you tie up at a village of your choice and spend the evening quietly, often enjoying the amenities of the local pub or visiting with the friendly rural folk. All standard craft are available. One class, for example, sleeps 6 in 3 private cabins, has 2 heads, a shower, a refrigerator, and a stove, plus plenty of living and sunning space. Among the 10 or 12 agencies in this field, the largest are Emerald Star Ltd. (104 St. James's Gate, Dublin 8) and Cormacruisers (Killaloe, County Clare). Sheer heaven for tranquillity seeking, nautically inclined adventurers! If you don't care to take the helm yourself, there are river circuits aboard tour boats; the 2-hour Shannon Candlelight loop including a meal in Athlone at the Jolly Mariner is one example.

Perhaps the most famous single tourist landmark is **Blarney Castle**, near the city of **Cork** (75 miles from Shannon, 160 miles from Dublin). If you kiss the stone (admission now about $1; children half price), be sure the man holding your feet is sober—as ours wasn't.

☑ **TRANSPORTATION**   Several fleets of radio-contact cabs: **Blue Cabs**, tel. 76IIII; **Metro Taxis**, tel. 683333; **National Cabs**, tel. 772222; **VIP Taxis**, tel. 783333. In addition, the **independents**, recognizing competition, have perked up their cars and services and even have a central telephone of their own: 766666. Call any of these and you may expect to have a metered taxi within 10 minutes, regardless of where you are.

The Irish take a casual view generally regarding firm car rental reservations. In other words don't count too heavily on driving away on the day you booked your wheels.

Jaunting cars (the Irish "dogcart," a one-horse affair) are lots of fun. In Killarney, as one example, there are a multitude of tours that range in price from $15 to $30 for 4 people. **Bicycles** cost perhaps $4 per day, a fine investment. But the most exotic transportation available has got to be the **Gypsy Caravan**, a horse-drawn trailer capable of accommodating 4 persons. These brightly painted wagons are equipped with foam-rubber berths, a bottled-gas stove, heat, light, sheets, and blankets—and they're all yours for between $200 and $250 per week, depending on the time of year. You don't even need to know one end of the beastie from the other, because they'll cheerfully give you free lessons in harnessing and driving—something which you should accept as insurance against mishaps. Check the Irish Tourist Office for details.

Short-run trains are showing great improvement. The majority of the **Irish Railways'** local lines are now dieselized. Among the blue-ribbon runs, the *Enterprise Express* and the *Dublin-Cork Express* are outstanding. On the former, we had the most delightful train ride of one European circuit. The breakfast was a joy—piping hot scones, ham finger-sandwiches, fluffy cake, generous servings of coffee, and other ttemptations; the schedule was nonstop.

On hinterland hauls, the Irish Railways are still a far cry from their Swiss confreres. For a quiet trip ride First-class; for fun unrefined, ride Second.

Ireland has joined the Eurailpass system; connections from Rosslare in the southeast to Cherbourg and Le Havre by ships of the Irish Continental Line.

Long-distance **bus** hauls—and some of the newer short-haul links—are as modern and speedy as our Greyhound routes. But when you climb aboard the average rural Irish bus, prepare yourself for An Experience. Many of them are primitive, most are crowded, most pick up passengers every 42 feet—but you'll get a kick out of your ride, and you'll probably arrive on time. The friendliness and banter are worth the price of admission.

The **C.I.E.** (35 Lower Abbey St., Tel.: 300777), a big-time organization with large and comfortable vehicles, many of them diesels, operates (1) a wide choice of full- and half-day tours from the Central Bus Station; (2) 6-day round-robin tours; (3) a so-called Super Deluxe 6-day swing through the south in summer; (4) other 2- to 12-day offerings to various parts of the country. Railroading is also possible, linking up with a bus or jaunting car along the circular route. Americans are so fond of these C.I.E. excursions they're sold out long in advance; book early to insure your space.

☑ FOOD AND RESTAURANTS

Irish cuisine is superb—so long as it involves grills, roast beef, steaks, salmon, or simple dishes. We're sad to report, however, that neither fancier fare nor vegetables are as well cooked or well presented as in the more food-conscious of European lands.

Odd Tidbits Department, Culinary Division: In the counties (not cities, generally), the man of the sod prefers his roast beef stone dead; if you like yours rare, specifically ask if they have it "underdone" when you order. As in Finland, normally tea is brewed in improper metal pots and nowhere could we find a tea strainer (don't these hardy folk have use for 'em?). Insomniacs will be cheered to know Sanka is available—and it makes magnificent Irish Coffee. Incidentally, this happy brew never tastes as wondrous in any other country, and why, we don't know. The same holds true for Guinness. Mashed potatoes are called "creamed potatoes"; paper napkins pop up even in some of the most elegant establishments. Milk is rich, plentiful, and pasteurized; soda fountains are dubbed "cafés" or "milk bars."

☑ PUBS

The pub lunch is burgeoning in popularity. It is eminently practical because the fare is light and the service is fast.

On a nationwide basis they initially operate from 10:30 A.M. to 11 P.M. in winter and 11:30 P.M. in summer. In Dublin, Cork, Waterford, and Limerick they shutter from 2:30 P.M. to 3:30 P.M. daily—a hiatus irreverently known as "the Holy Hour." On Sundays Irish elbows bend from 12:30 to 2 and from 4 P.M. to 10 P.M. Public service in the entire country is bone dry on Christmas Day and Good Friday. St. Patrick's Day used to call for special foxiness because the only whiskey openly sold anywhere was in the annual Ballsbridge Dog Show. They're still talking about the chap who looked up from his glass, focused both bloodshot eyes on his surroundings, and growled in exasperation, "What stupid eejit let all these *demmed* dogs into this respectable pub?" Today John Law regards St. Patrick's Day as any other Sunday.

As in England, the venerable color, serenity, and neighborliness of Irish pubs are fast vanishing. Less and less are they companionable gathering places for a pint, a quiet chat, and a game of darts. Explosively, these old-style havens are undergoing a revolutionary change in character to become what are called "Singing Pubs."

Younger people are the majority who frequent this mutation. Generally speaking, the middle-aged and the elderly continue to maintain their loyalty to the traditional-style establishments.

☑ **DRINKS** As in Finland, the divisions concerning alcohol are radical. At one extreme, you'll find an exceptionally large percentage of heavy topers. At the other, the Pioneer Society, a fiercely dedicated temperance organization, has enlisted legions upon legions of the population; its male members may be spotted by its distinctive insignia worn as lapel buttons. Visit after visit, we are surprised to find so many fanatically vehement Drys in the nation where strangers are addressed perhaps faster and more frequently than in any other by the hospitable phrase, "D'ye want a drink?"

A taste of Irish whiskey is a must for drinkers. (One of its greatest salesmen was Brendan Behan, author of *The Hostage* and *The Quare Fellow*, plays which must have been written in Pot Still ink.) No potatoes at all; it's triple-distilled from barley (Scotch is merely twice distilled!). Put $1.50 on the bar, ask for "a half one," and up will come this unique, potent, and healing libation.

A consortium called Irish Distillers Group now produces all of this category of spirits in the country, despite the continuing competition between individual brands. John Jameson's (Holinshed's "Sovereign Liquor At Its Finest"), John Power's ("Enjoy That Gold Label"), D. E. Williams at Tullamore ("Give Every Man His Dew"), and Cork's, makers of Paddy ("Will 'oo have a Paddy?") means your host is a true blue Cork man. Bushmill's Black Label, a long-aged premium offering, is extra-full-bodied, peat-smoky, and heavier than most. Many people, including us, regard it as the best of all; the oldest licensed distillery in the world, its birth certificate is dated A.D. 1608! Crock 'O Gold is our least favorite brand.

After a lapse of more than a decade, distillers of an illegal firewater called "poteen" have reentered the scene, en masse to beat the stiff new taxes which make this country one of the most expensive in Europe for drinkers. The standard price of a bottle of this bootleg liquor is less than half the rate of legal purchases.

Scotch is plentiful; Canadian Club is obtainable in the better bars. Sparkling water is cheap by the split.

Generally speaking, however, the average Irish toper is not a natural consumer of hard booze. He is a devotee of stout—a dark, very rich, very special beer. This dedication is so important that the price of the pint is chronically a dominant issue in political elections. Guinness comes in both bottle and draught. This brewery landmark, on which the original Arthur Guinness took a 9,000-year lease, has merely another 8,780 years to go before expiration; the same yeast strains have been continuously under cultivation and in use since its founding. The brewery stands on 60 acres, the largest in Europe. Visitors are welcome any time between 10 A.M. and 3 P.M. from Monday through Friday to see a film of its operations and sample the product. Murphy's stout is particularly popular in the Cork area. It is a bit lighter and sweeter than Guinness. Many Americans take these diluted with beer or ale; "Black Velvet" (50% champagne and 50% stout) holds vast appeal.

Beer flows in Niagaras, of course. The Harp brand twangs a tangy note. In your sweetest Irish tenor, warble for an extra-cold one. Otherwise it will be served to you at skin temperature.

Virtually from coast to coast, wines are limited in selection, secondary in quality, and poor in handling and presentation. Due to the heavy influx today of German visitors and residents, the white grape is now beginning to apppear in greater quantity, but it is not distinguished.

If you should be puzzled by a beverage listed as "Black Wine," as we were, it is a somewhat repellent mixture of lemon pop and an inferior red wine.

Irish coffee (also known as Gaelic coffee) is one of the pleasantest beverages possible to sample. To make it, add a jigger of Irish whiskey to ⅔rds of a glass of steaming black coffee; add sugar to taste; float thick, rich cream on the top without stirring, and sip slowly. It's wonderful. Just ask for it by name, and the waiter will bring you pure bliss in a glass.

For your after-dinner liqueur, Irish Mist is to Ireland what Drambuie is to Scotland. Interesting and different; increasingly popular. Bailey's Irish Cream is a new liqueur composed of the native elixir and rich squeezings from Elsie the cow.

★ **WARNING** *Don't drive a car if you have consumed even as little as 2 pints of beer!* As in the United Kingdom, the police have cracked down mercilessly by applying the roadside "Breathalyser" test to anyone they suspect. If the crystals in the plastic bag turn green (even that 2nd pint will do it for some people), the offender will face fines up to $1000 or 6 months in the pokey (or both). There is no recourse for either resident or visitor.

Ice for your nip? Plentiful in the cities, of course—but if you should ask for it deep in the countryside, your sweet rustic waitress is liable to say, "Shure and where would I find *that* at this time of the year?"

☑ **TIPPING**   In many hotels and restaurants a 10%–15% service charge is added in lieu of gratuities and no additional outlay is expected. Tipping is not customary in pubs and never in movies, theaters, shops, or stores. Ten pence is usual for taxi drivers for a normal ride and at least 20p should be given for anything greater; 10p to 20p is okay for porters and 10p for your cloakroom attendant.

☑ **INFORMATION CENTERS**   One master organization runs the show—**Bord Fáilte Éireann**. Director-General Joe Malone, a fireball, is its helmsman. Since the income from tourism makes such a significant contribution to the Irish economy, it is understandably persnickety about safeguarding its unspoiled scenic charms. Its "Tidy Towns" competition is doing just that; derelict sites are being cleared, and roadside gardens are sprouting everywhere. The **Information Offices** (14 Upper O'Connell St. and 51 Dawson St.) courteously handle your itinerary problems, distribute reading material, and answer routine inquiries on anything from sports to theatrical events.

A "**Meet-the-Irish**" program enables visitors to meet people with like interests and to be invited into their homes. By writing to your nearest Irish Tourist office and stating your name, address, profession, hobbies, and age group along with the dates and places where you would like to have introductions, everything will be set up for you on arrival. But be sure to make application not less than one month in advance.

If your trip is still in the planning stage, touch base with the **Irish Tourist Office** at either 590 Fifth Ave., N.Y. 10036; 230 N. Michigan Ave., Chicago; 681 Market St., San Francisco; 510 W. 6th St., Los Angeles; 69 Yonge St., Toronto.

An indispensable item to carry along is the thin-lined guidebook, *Ireland—Hotels and Guesthouses,* which you can obtain free from the **Irish Tourist Offices**. More than 400 listings!

CITIES

DUBLIN, first, foremost, and always. The world's 2nd largest brewery, widest main street, oldest Chamber of Commerce, tattler of tallest tales—and courtliest people. Settled by Danes in A.D. 852, it's the size of Seattle, with over ½ million people; quaint and colorful, it's a fascinating blend of bustling metropolis and dusty one-horse town. Here's a city that's as warm and engaging as her people. Museums, gorgeous parks, dance halls, movies, a million things to see—don't miss Dublin, if you can possibly get there. Her airport, once a sleepy bump on the heath, is atingle with activity as a result of improvements to accommodate large jets. Aer Lingus-Irish Airlines runs a 45-minute shuttle service from here to Shannon, and it also flies direct to various cities in England and on the Continent.

Sightseeing The National Theatre houses the famous 625-seat **Abbey Theatre** and the 157-place **Peacock Theatre**. Morning tours may be arranged through the Press Officer and bookings through the box office. The revitalized **Gate Theatre**, sired in 1928, specializes in an international and classical repertory not included in the Abbey playbills. Then, to skim the surface, you'll also find the **Hugh Lane Municipal Art Gallery** (now proudly showing the Lane impressionist paintings), the **National Gallery** in Merrion Square (partially endowed by George Bernard Shaw), the newly opened 12th-century **Malahide Castle** (period rooms with Irish furniture and paintings, plus the adjoining abbey ruins), the **Chester Beatty Library** (really a repository of Middle and Far Eastern artifacts), **St. Stephen's Green**, Georgian **Merrion Square**, **Phoenix Park**, **Guinness's**, the **James Joyce Museum** (appropriately sited in the Martello Tower in suburban Sandycove, where Joyce lived), the "Crusader's Corpse" in **St. Michan's Church**, the *Book of Kells* and the new Douglas Hyde Gallery in **Trinity College**—the city is full of wonderful things.

DUBLIN HOTELS Quick Reference Table

Price categories by national (not U.S.) standards.

EXPENSIVE:
Berkeley Court Lansdowne Rd. Ballsbridge Tel. 601711; Telex 5517; 200 rooms. P. 463

UPPER MODERATE:
Bloom's Anglesea St. Tel. 715622; 86 rooms. P. 465
Burlington Upper Leeson St. Tel. 785711; Telex 5517; 420 rooms. P. 464
Gresham Upper O'Connell St. 20. Tel. 746881; Telex 5308; 208 rooms. P. 464

Jury's Pembroke Rd. Ballsbridge. Tel. 767511; Telex 5304; 314 rooms. P. 464
Royal Hibernian Dawson St. 46. Tel. 772991; Telex 5220; 93 rooms. P. 464
Royal Dublin Upper O'Connell St. Tel. 749351; Telex 4288; 110 rooms. P. 465
Sachs Morehampton Rd. 21. Tel. 680995; Telex 31667; 20 rooms. P. 464
Shelbourne St. Stephen's Green 27. Tel. 766471; Telex 5184; 166 rooms. P. 463

MODERATE:

Central Exchequer St. 2. Tel. 778341; Telex 30880; 80 rooms. P. 465
Skylon Upper Drumcondra Rd. Tel. 379121; Telex 5517; 88 rooms. P. 465
Tara Tower Merrion Rd. Tel. 694666; Telex 5517; 84 rooms. P. 465

LOWER MODERATE:

Buswells Molesworth 25. Tel. 764013; 53 rooms. P. 465
Clarence Wellington Quay. Tel. 776178; 70 rooms. P. 465

ENVIRONS:

Fitzpatrick Castle Killiney Hill Rd. Tel. 851533; Telex 30353; 48 rooms. P. 466
Grand Malahide. Tel. 450633; 52 rooms. P. 467
Green Isle Clondalkin. Tel. 593406; Telex 5517; 56 rooms. P. 466
Montrose Stillorgan Rd. Tel. 693311; Telex 5517; 190 rooms. P. 466
Royal Marine Marine Rd. Tel. 801911; 115 rooms. P. 466

AIRPORT:

Crofton Airport Swords Rd. 9. Tel. 370111; Telex 31334; 125 rooms. P. 466
International Tel. 379211; Telex 5184; 142 rooms. P. 465

Hotels For far more comprehensive information on certain hostelries than space limitations permit here, travelers to the Emerald Isle are referred to the annually revised *Fielding's Favorites: Hotels and Inns, Europe* by Dodge Fielding. Among other discoveries they will find descriptions of his picks among the 24 members of the Irish Country Houses & Restaurants Association —rural establishments which are small, colorful, charming, and Hibernian to their cores. Its latest edition, in which a total of 350-odd favored possibilities were handpicked from the 4000-plus personally inspected, will be at your bookstore early this year.

It's a sad fact that temperamentally the Irish—like Americans—aren't built to be first-rate hotelkeepers. You may disagree violently with this statement, but we doubt it. In the handful of leading international houses, you still should find top-grade attention although the touristic in-rush is gradually manifesting obvious strains even at this level; in the rest, organization is improving, but it's most often on the slaphappy side. Staff people everywhere, despite professional shortcomings, have hearts of pure gold; *always*—repeat, *always*—treat them as friends rather than servants, because they can tie you up in knots if they feel you're unduly lordly, snooty, or arrogant.

An ingenious twist is the **Rent-An-Irish-Cottage** program which was launched by the Shannon Development Company (turn back to "Shannon International Airport"). Twelve units made their '69 debuts in *Ballyvaughan* (County Clare); 13 became operative in *Corofin* (County Clare) almost immediately afterward; a total of 117 dot the rural resort map. These thatched-roof houses, extremely simple in execution and in furnishings, embody the flavor of a small, traditional farmhouse. Each is complete with half-door and open peat-burning hearth, traditional furnishings, all-electric kitchen, central heating and all modern conveniences. Cottage types A and B sleep 8 and 7 persons, respectively, and prices range from $100 per week to $275 per week, depending on time of year. Types C and D sleep 6 and 5, respectively, and the range is $100 to $260 per week. The minimum rental must be for 7 nights (or weekends in off seasons); extra days are charged pro rata. The costs of food, drink, utilities, linens (other than bed clothing), and cleaning woman are not included. Although this is a far cry from opulent living, we wonder where else 8 individuals can find such a vacation for such a modest outlay.

To assure yourself of a hot bath in many of the older hotels here, you may require (1) clairvoyance, (2) flexibility, and (3) dexterity. The first will enable you to divine when the water is warm enough, the second to bathe at precisely the hours you do not wish to, and the third to leap gazelle-like out of the shower when the hot changes to cold or warm to scalding (rare!).

The Irish Tourist Board issued a list of over 100 stopping places which furnish baby-sitting service up to midnight for about $3 per hour. Since most already offer a 10% to 33⅓% discount for children under 10 years of age, this supervision of the Dr. Denton members of your party is a built-in bonus.

A "room only" charge—sans the customary breakfast inclusion—has been agreed to by 483 proprietors. A number of them have also dropped the tradition of multiplying the single rate by 2 to determine the double rate; these now offer a realistic concession.

Law requires that tariff sheets be displayed either at or close to all Reception Desks.

Dedicated budgeteers? Since we're too bottlenecked here for additional entries, please consult our annually revised paperback, *Fielding's Low-Cost Europe,* which lists scads more bargain spots and money-saving tips for serious economizers.

Dublin's luxury pacesetter is the new **Berkeley Court**, set amid 3 acres of gardens. The site of the 8-story edifice is on Lansdowne Road in the fashionable Ballsbridge district. Communication is so efficient between this suburb and midtown that its location will not represent an inconvenience to your Irish reel. Gourmet restaurant plus grill; cocktail bar and lounge; indoor swimming pool; saunas; hairdressing facilities; boutiques; in-and-outside parking. Sprinkled among its 200 elegant bedchambers is a handsome complement of suites. Undoubtedly this will be the new flagship of the expanding Doyle fleet, which also operates the local Burlington, Montrose, Tara Tower, Skylon, and Green Isle hotels. Certainly a splendid contribution to the capital's innkeeping scene.

The stately **Shelbourne** is the home of the nation's literati, the hunt-shoot-and-fish country squires, and the touring cosmopolites; here also seems to be the after-hours rendezvous of Everybody who is Anybody for "a jar before the waif." Authors from Thackeray to Elizabeth Bowen have fondly sung its praises in their books; the Constitution of the Irish Free State was framed within its venerable walls. A project to revamp 50 bedrooms was undertaken to raise their level of comfort despite architectural roadblocks that are occasionally insurmountable. It has an L-shaped, air-conditioned restaurant, a high-in-the-stirrups, neo-rustic Saddle Room spotlighting 3 separate ribs of beef (rare, medium, and well done), and a handsome Grill Bar with a long chummy counter and 12 tables. Newer 6-story wing; 14 suites; high ceilings throughout; parking lot for 50 cars. Its Georgian facade commands a splendid view of St. Stephen's Green.

The downward slide which we felt that the century-old, once-great **Gresham** had taken anguished us. It has gone through 2 changes of ownership recently, both of them undistinguished in our view, as far as hôtellerie is concerned. Now we can report that major renovations are currently underway and extensive redecoration is the order of the day. As usual, however, we must personally overnight here before we can properly rank the house and its panoply of services and facilities.

The 420-room **Burlington** seeks to blend traditional décor with modern comfort. Vast improvements have recently taken place. Airy lobby with busy adjoining bar and popular lounge; ground-floor Sussex Room, its premier restaurant; roof-top salon candlelit at night, which is a first-class Carvery with after-dark taped music and dancing; Grill-cum-coffee shop; old Dublin Pub in today's raiments; indoor pool with President Bar, sauna, and massage; partly closed parking space a big bonus to motorists. The accommodations provide space, light, and efficiency, but very little inspiration. All over it swings, but in a peculiarly sedate Irish manner.

The **Royal Hibernian** was built more than 200 years ago. Under its present ownership by the Trust Houses Forte group, this clipper is smartly outfitted and sailing sweetly again. The entrance, lounge, and dining rooms are gay and bright; there are a splendid kitchen and many renovated bedchambers. The Lafayette Restaurant features an expensive menu and sound cuisine, with varying regions of Gallic gastronomy highlighted on Saturday nights in winter; the Bianconi Grill-Bar seats 55 *bons vivants,* with snacks, wine, and beer available; the freshly turned, mod-style Rôtisserie accents more expensive grills and is targeted for the young executive clientele; the Buttery Bar continues to draw the fashionable. Much better and steadily improving.

The 21-room **Sachs** is quite a long drive from the center. It has gained a reputation for chicness which we believe is somewhat exaggerated. Because one Regency house and 5 adjoining Georgian houses in a row were connected, it is replete with short stairways and crinkum-crankum corridors. Cozy bar off small lobby, in which lunch is served 6 days weekly; pleasant restaurant; expensive menu. Nearly all quarters adequately decorated but, like the baths, uncomfortably elfin; wall-to-wall carpets everywhere. In actuality, however, it is too small to be of much consequence in the existing hotel scene.

Jury's is clearly a 20th-century efficiency hotel. Cluttered, baby-spotlighted, busy-busy lobby with piped music, an awkwardly architected raised lounge, and a notably intrusive airline counter; extremely attractive Dubliner Bar in pseudo-antique Irish motif; routine but adequate Embassy Grill; smashingly successful Coffee Dock snack bar (open from 6 A.M. to 4:30 A.M. except Sunday when it snoozes from 11 P.M. until Monday morning); hairdresser and barber. The Pavilion houses the Kish fish restaurant, a pyramidal bar, a lounge, a swimming pool, a hot whirlpool massage unit, a children's zone, all set amid waterfalls, rocks, and greenery; a conference center also has been inn-corporated. Total of 315 well-kept units divided almost equally between studio types and conventional doubles; 2 large suites with bar, kitchen, TV, sitting room, and standard bedchamber; tiny bathrooms throughout. This hostelry makes no pretense to be what it is not. Very good for what it tries to be.

The 110-room-and-bath **Royal Dublin**, opposite the Gresham, greets guests with a lobby painting of Sitric, the Viking king, and "raths" (plans) of fortresses in sandstone and pebble. Its Oyster Bar features bivalves shipped fresh from Galway Bay each dawn in season. Cool-tinged yet appealing grill, bar, and dining room; underground carpark; gray brick corridors; front units with balconette-bay windows; velvet headboards; matching curtains; emerald carpets; radios, telephones, and thermal shower taps; inviting Queen Gormley suite.

Bloom's Hotel, where the old Jury's used to stand, was named after Leopold Bloom, hero of Joyce's *Ulysses.* All rooms with bath, radio, and color TV; popular restaurant and Molly Bloom Bar. It is said to be a Best Seller. We'll inspect it on our next visit.

Although the **Skylon**, about 10 minutes by car from both the airport and the center, sprang on the scene not long ago, it's due for another growing spree soon. It is a sister operation to the Tara Tower, the Montrose, and the Green Isle (see below). Low, rather extensive lobby with simple furnishings, piped music, and buried baby spotlights in an acoustic ceiling; bizarre hodgepodge bar-lounge with 13 swingable stools; intimate but clashing 007 Bar; Grill-Bar with counter and tables, featuring low-price fare; fetching dining room with Cecil King murals and well-planned illumination; beauty parlor; sauna. Its 88 keys unlock 88 rooms which are identical, with orange-striped wall-to-wall carpets and matching curtains, adequate but not spacious dimensions, terribly cramped baths, and insufficient storage space. We'd judge it as run-of-the-mill —but, comparatively speaking, not bad for the price.

Tara Tower, described to us by a bellhop as having "an evocative name for the Irish," refers to a hallowed spot in County Meath, 20 miles northwest of Dublin, which was the capital of the Celtic Empire and the site from which St. Patrick began his evangelizing mission in the fifth century. This newcomer could almost serve as a carbon copy of the Skylon. We were attracted by its grill with ship's lantern illumination, the shingle-roofed counter for lighter biting, and the purple dining room with globes and flowers. Pick a high waterfront unit; we'd judge it might render evocative moments for you, too— Irish or not.

The totally restyled **Central**, which used to seem an epitome of dullness to us, is at last brightening up laudably. Grill plus Foxes' Restaurant downstairs; lobby and bar fairly cheerful; bedchambers remade in a commodious way. Now we think it is much, much better.

The **Clarence** is rated "A" by the Tourist Board inspectors—but we wonder how in heaven's name it deserves it. Or as James Joyce might have opined: "?Htiw hcihw dne fo eht tebahpla od uoy esoppus yeht nageb"

Buswells is a mixed bag—and not the most glamorous one, at that. Georgian bar which hints more of a Chatham County (Ga.) courthouse; raspberry-and-white dining room; mélange of sleeping themes; baths that—no, that couldn't be a ring in the tub, or could it? Our lack of enthusiasm is Pullman-Bus size.

The 150-room **International** at the airport, a Trust Houses Forte enterprise, strikes us as being a dud. We would venture that the same architect created its dark-brown exterior as well as its interior decoration since both in this 2-storied structure are heavily chunky. Because the lobby is a maze of very tall-backed banquettes which face inward, the effect is reminiscent of entering a walled city. The bedrooms evoked the same reaction. The bar is large, utilitarian, and charmless, in our opinion. Only in the coffee bar and the restaurant did we feel any warmth. At best we'd call this a 1-overnight convenience.

After our latest inspection of the **Crofton "Airport" Hotel** we recommend that it be resolutely avoided.

On the outskirts you'll find the popular **Royal Marine Hotel** at *Dun Laoghaire* ("Done Leery"), on a harbor 6 miles south of the capital. Here's a viable candidate for pilgrims taking the 3-hour car-ferry hop to Holyhead. It is a gingerbread structure (vintage 1865) with high ceilings. On one recent Marine patrol, a lounge had been refurbished, a cute little Edwardian bar added, and 48 extra twin-bed units, all with private bath and shower have now followed suit. The Gay Nineties Charcoal grill offers excellent food, pleasant ambiance, and good service at reasonable prices; 5 acres of lawns and flowers; boating, swimming, yachting, sailing, golf, tennis, racing, hunting, and dancing; pick your weather carefully here. More popular with visitors from within the British Isles and conference clans than with Yankee colonists. Anthony McClafferty, its engaging manager, will give you a fine Irish welcome.

The **Fitzpatrick Castle** at Killiney, 9 miles out, is reported to be so extraordinarily delightful that we can scarcely wait to visit it. From its lavish 26-color-picture brochure which has just reached us it is easy to ascertain that here is a super operation. Imposingly spacious private residence dating back to 1741 which has been reconstructed and redecorated by Paddy Fitzpatrick and his wife Eithne; 9 acres of ground overlooking Dublin Bay; candlelit Victorian dining room; cheerful Castle Grill numerous bars and coffee shop; fine inside pool; squash court; tennis; minigolf. The samples portrayed of the 50 bedrooms and 3 executive suites, all with baths, are imaginatively and suavely furnished; many of them have four-posters. This is the couple who have accomplished such a splendid resurrection of the Shannon Shamrock near Limerick (see later). Our top priority for our next visit to the Emerald Isle. **Montrose**, in the *Stillorgan* residential district, offers a vast panoply of sleeping combinations that can accommodate almost anything from an eremite to a Ringling Brothers troupe. Every unit with coin-operated TV and central heat; Belfield Grill for light appetites, open noon to midnight; noisy restaurant; huge bar; 2 saunas; hairdresser and gift-shop-newsstand-book-counter; parking lot. Practical— especially if you happen to have a family à la Brigham Young's. The same organization guides the **Green Isle**, beside the Naas Road just off the Shannon turnpike 4 miles from the center. Its lodgings are split into 32 in its main building and 34 in its so-called motel section. Modern, often frenetic lobby blaring with public address announcements and staffed by flocks of pretty colleens with emerald minis and shamrock brooches; fresh dining room with oversize windows; cookery routine; lobby bar a nothing; 1200-seat ballroom with international cabaret on Saturday night. Most of the motel units have 2 conventional beds and 2 studios—far too snug for 4 adults. Not our dish, because (1) it is too far from the action and (2) it's clean but too impersonal and sterile to seduce us. The **Grand** at _Malahide_, a 10-mile skip, has been decorated and enlarged. We didn't make the trek, because so many Dublin reports were discouraging.

Restaurants The Shelbourne has divided its dining facilities in thirds: One link is the Saddle Room, featuring pine paneling, a beamed ceiling, and an open grill; rib beef is carved (lunch and dinner, in 3 separate degrees: stunned, medium, and crispy). The Grill-Bar adjoining, for light bites and theatergoers' fare, is also engaging; 12 tables, counter with stools, good colors, reasonable prices. The 3rd section retains the conventional atmosphere, with Paul Hogarth illustrations and 3 handsome chandeliers. More expensive tabs; table d'hôte or à la carte selections. A new bar was decanted more recently; snacks are available here. All are air-conditioned. All are good.

The Lafayette Restaurant at the **Royal Hibernian** is fine. Though its high-style furnishings and overbright illumination do not happen to appeal to us, the quality of its cookery is, for Ireland, at gastronomic level. This relatively costly rendezvous stages Gallic dinners drawn from varying regional special-ties on Saturday nights in winter; its Bianconi Grill-Bar comes up with lighter and more reasonable comestibles; the excellent rôtisserie falls between these extremes. For day-in-night-out dining, we would pick the last as one of the most rewarding corners of culinary excellence and consistency in the city. Nothing fancy, but darned good for quality, price, and atmosphere.

The **Hotel Sachs** is attracting socialites and what we would term in North America as expense-account diners. There is a cunningly partitioned bar ad-joining its small lobby in which lunch is served daily except Sunday. The gracious 17-table restaurant is in the Regency mode with banquettes and white trim. Both are costly and fashionable. The **Berkeley Court** and the new Kish (for fish) at **Jury's** Pavilion are already well respected among locals and outlanders. The fare at the **Burlington** and the **Royal Dublin** is adequate but not outstanding. The dish-clattering, fast-food **Hunting Lodge** at the **Gresham** is so routine that it will be a long time before we go back for more.

Le Bistro (facing Christchurch Cathedral) features luxury French-type cui-sine prepared by an Italian chef. Following the advice of _Gourmet_ magazine we tried its Escalopes de Veau Florentine—sautéed veal scallops in cream and wine sauce on a bed of spinach, as well as 2 other specialties. The only thing we didn't like was the noise of its somewhat intrusive taped music. Verdict? Excellent.

The Celtic Mews (109a Lr. Baggot St.) is a sound independent. Host Joe Gray is warmly hospitable and he can produce savory and interesting meals. Ground-floor lounge with attic room for dining; wooden floors; candle illumi-nation. Ours was an altogether enjoyable experience. Highly recommended. **Snaffles** (Leeson St.) is now perhaps even better in the gustatory department. Cellar location; 2 rooms with oil paintings, Chippendale chairs, Persian car-pets, and a glow of mellowness. Our party's raw plaice and mousse, plus game paté, kidneys with mustard, and piquant tongue, were superb. The wines are expensive but choice and well maintained. Very good indeed. **Buck Wha-ley's**, a neighbor, tries to do a similar job, but we think it fails.

The **Soup Bowl** (2 Molesworth Place) is inconspicuously cupboarded behind its single red door. Cathy and Peter Powry are the prime movers at this one. Downstairs there are 3 tables in a living room ambiance with a fireplace and a large refrigerator; 10 more tables are up one flight; service is rather informal. Dinner only is served (8 P.M. to midnight); it is closed Sunday; be sure to reserve in advance. This *potage* is recommended for what it is.

A pleasant expedition is a ramble through the zoo at **Phoenix Park** and an inexpensive meal in its lovely setting of lawns and flowering shrubs; worth the trip when the sun is out. **Barnardo's** (19 Lincoln Place) is an Italian specialist with a bleak décor but appetizing dishes; reasonable. The **Golden Orient** (Leeson St.) is just the place for adventurers who'd enjoy exploring genuine Pakistani cookery. The Tandoori Rooms downstairs are said to be rewarding.

Pot Pourri (32 Parliament St.) is especially noted for its limited but unusually original first courses including Camembert Frit and croutons with mushrooms in a cream sauce with a chicken liver flamed with sherry as its crown. Your outlay will be relatively moderate, including that for the better-than-passable carafe wine. Warm and pleasant.

The **Lord Edward** (23 Christchurch Place) is rightfully known for its fine fresh seafood. A small lunch is served in its bar, which is up one flight. Above this is the restaurant which contains only 10 tables. Dark wood predominates in this atmospheric veteran, with odd chairs, wall plates, and prints of Lord Edward grace-noting its charm. No meat is served and the tariffs are medium. As an incidental tip, because commercial fishing is inactive on weekends, Monday is not the best time to patronize this or any of its counterparts. The staff here is unusually kind. Recommended.

For a light lunch, the Buttery in the **Royal Hibernian** is recommended. The manager was granted special permission by London's Berkeley to duplicate the décor of the internationally famous original. The previously mentioned **Coffee Dock** snack bar at **Jury's** is tremendously popular. Total of 80 seats; muralled walls featuring ships of all ages; fast service and decent prices. What a convenience! The **Berni Inn** is a promoter of olde-fashioned atmosphere with its grills; this is part of a chain. **Bewley's Coffee Café Ltd.** has 3 branches in the capital. They are well liked coffee and tea houses for sandwiches, cakes, and candies to consume on or off the premises. **Murph's** serves a bountiful assortment of sandwiches and salads—and that's it. The premises are no-nonsense and the fare is appetizing at reasonable prices. The variety and efficiency are reminiscent of a good counter establishment in North America. Normally it is filled to the scuppers at lunchtime. In their new precincts at Bachelor's Walk hot meals are provided.

The Iron Curtain has been drawn back behind the **Grey Door** on Pembroke Street. There is said to be an entente cordiale of Russian and Finnish fare. It takes high priority on our next Dublin mission.

Shopper's Special? Try **Le Savoir Faire** in Switzer's department store for high quality at low cost; both a fixed menu and à la carte are available. For even tighter budgets it also operates a cafeteria on the same floor.

Pocket-size excursions? In nearby *Stillorgan*, a residential suburb, the **Beaufield Mews** offers antiques and nutrition to pilgrims who hunger for a quiet haven similar to our own popular northeastern Red Barns, White Turkeys, or Spinning Wheels. Softly illuminated converted stable; 2-or-3-choice menu nightly; operative 7 P.M. to 10 P.M., but never for lunch, Sundays, bank holidays, or Christmas and Easter weeks. Oodles of charm. In *Howth*, a sweet little fishing village only 20 minutes north of midcity, the **Abbey Tavern** draws raves from almost every quarter. Old-style tavern to which a restaurant has been added; good cookery composed mostly of shellfish; other landed specialties also on tap; ballad-belting troubadours entertain nightly in the barnlike room to the rear. James Scott-Lennon is the proprietor. Corny in general and often too crowded. There's a more refined sort of seafood restaurant called the **King Sitric** (named for the famous ninth-century Viking sovereign of Dublin) around the corner on East Pier that's touted for its fresh net-work. White facade looking to the harbor; upstairs bar done out preciously in florals and ruby; cheery sea-level restaurant with waiters in black tie. Both of these anchorages can be reached by bus from town. By taxi, the ride is perhaps $9.50. The Sutton House recently was promoted to **Sutton Castle** under the reign of a new lord; we haven't sampled the change. Near *Sandyford*, a 6½-mile junket into the mountainscape, **Lamb Doyles Roadhouse** provides a glorious view of the city and surrounding hills. Starkly modern structure with granite blocks, sheets of glass, panels of pine, and a purple and blue ambiance; lunch from 1 P.M. to 3 P.M.; dinner plus dancing from 7 P.M. to 11 P.M.; culinary standards only so-so. At **Roundwood Inn**, the management and some of the staff are German. We bristled a bit when they tried to hurry our meal to accommodate the next sitting. Another debit was that it was not as clean as it might be while we were there. Our reaction was nix. We prefer the **Glenview Hotel** near *Bray*. For seasiding, *Dun Laoghaire* offers the gray and white **Mirabeau** facing the harbor (a neat house with superior kitchen crafts), **na Mara** (a converted railway station and specializing in seafood), and **Trudi's** (1920's décor and an unusual but tempting menu including delicious orange and carrot soup). This town makes an excellent excursion point for old or young salts. One run we really enjoy is the skip out to seaside *Malahide*, where **Johnny's** does its magic. Johnny and Eileen Oppermann are the Merlin-class magicians—and what a culinary show you'll receive! Downstairs hideaway in a Georgian town house; brick and stone walls; crackling fire; spluttering candles; peeking views of the open kitchen and busy, smiling Chef Johnny. The menu is small but truly select. Frankly, we love it. Closed Sunday and Monday. Out at *Killiney*, **Rolland** is the creation of Henri Rolland whose father, Pierre, cooked for palates named Kennedy, Nixon, de Gaulle, and MacMillan. The word is out that it is attractive not only to the eye, but to the taste as well. We'll try it next time in County Dublin. We've had excellent word concerning **Barberstown Castle** at *Straffan*, said to be "on the horsy outskirts of Dublin, with outstanding cuisine and enjoying its popularity with local gentry at cocktail and dinner hours." Here's one to check very soon.

Pubs Among the new genus in the capital, **Gulliver's Inn** (67 New St.) was launched to celebrate Jonathan Swift, who was the dean in St. Patrick's, just around the corner. Red velvet cushions; only slightly cacophonic solos by guitars and other instruments; terrible ventilation. Except for its lack of dancing and psychedelic lights, it could be a disco. Probably the costliest—and perhaps the noisiest—in the city. **Leinster Inn**, in the Harp Complex of restaurants and bars at the end of O'Connell Bridge, is a honey. Its delicious seafood specialities won the 1976 Award in the National Bar/Food Competition. In its handsomely decorated triangular room, there are 9 stools at its counter and 6 small marble-topped tables. The savory food and the friendly service obviously well merit this kudo. Our favorite in the **Mooney's** chain is on Parnell St. around the corner from the Royal Dublin. This one is colorful and cheerful in the modern mode, with a 15-stool bar; perhaps 7 tiny tables within each of 3 banquettes, and overloud piped music. Its limited offerings include steak-and-kidney pie and cottage pie, with a small selection of sandwiches, salads, and desserts which are unfancy but big and filling. Go from 12 to 12:30 before the crowd descends in force. **Slattery's Terenure House** (Terenure Rd.) consists of 3 sections in a large building. The first is a ground floor lounge-bar which could be mistaken for an expanded version of a typical Irish hotel installation. The 2nd is a spartan ground-floor bar for the serious male toper. The 3rd is its *pièce de résistance:* An upstairs cabaret-bar (small admission charge) which holds 400 revelers. Stage and orchestra; electric organ; lone singers or small groups airing their adenoids in tandem; public address system twisted up to its maximum. Friday and Saturday are its only scheduled nights of operation. It is one million miles from the classic milieu for elbow-bending. **William Searson** (42 Upper Baggot St.) is a suavely decorated contemporary complex of 3 bars with lounges; while 2 are modern, the Public Bar is done in fake turn-of-the-century. Crowded by students; known for the fights (now less frequent) on its premises. In atmosphere, here could be a cocktail lounge in any American city. **Bartley Dunne** (Mercer St.) offers an unusually versatile selection of booze drawn from its wines-and-spirits shop adjoining. Dim lighting; candles on tables; piped music (softly so, for a change); 2 arched, cozy, corner rooms to rear which encourage romance. Also popular among the Junior Set.

Classic types? The **Bailey** (Duke St.), for decades one of the city's most celebrated haunts of the literati, fell into disrepute a few years back, but now, thank goodness, it has been pleasantly revived. Ground-floor bar and diner; inner Fish Bar with leather booths, slat-faced walls, and delicious sea delicacies; upstairs U-shape salon, again wood lined and touched up with old mirrors and hanging plants. The air of conviviality is manifestly inviting; so is the splendid quality of its foodstuffs. Richly recommended for blue-ribbon pubbery. **Davy Byrnes** (Duke St.) draws more than its share of Intelligent Young Dolls and Very Earnest Young Authors. **Stag's Head** (1 Dame Court) weaves its musical spells among stuffed namesakes, old clocks, stained glass, and surroundings which seem best in semidarkness. **Patrick Conway** (Parnell St.), with its panels and semi-partitions, is authentically old-school Hibernian. Ham cooked in red wine plus the ubiquitous steak-and-kidney pie are its best-known specialties. Typical charm in somewhat faded surroundings. The **Toby Jug** (South King St. next to Gaiety Theatre) has a small, amiable lounge-bar in front and Public Bar at the rear. As in Conway's, its patrons can *talk* in this typically plain milieu. **Neary's** (Chatham St.), with a tiny cocktail bar on one side, is also friendly and unpretentious; it is reminiscent of a U.S. corner tavern. **McDaid's** (Harry St. off Grafton) doesn't seem as amusing as it used to be. **Peter's Pub** is dullsville, in our opinion. **Jerry Dwyers**, the pungent but far from hygienic center on Moore St. in the street market district, attracts playboys.

Shopping   As in a number of countries abroad, the VAT system deeply permeates the economic lives of the citizenry. The version here requires that you pay from 10% to 20% extra on all purchases if used within its borders. To avoid this levy, either arrange delivery to your departing aircraft or ship, or forward them unaccompanied straight to your home. For mail-order, of course, no VAT problem exists.

Tweeds are the best buy in the nation—gorgeous handwoven 100%-wool Donegals. *Don't miss them.* Ready-made sport jackets for men are surprisingly reasonable and made-to-your-measure examples run only slightly higher. You can get the "Irish hacking cut" (which we prefer in the rougher materials) or the straighter lines of the conventional "American" concept (which will be more Irish than Yankee). Ladies normally go mad at the bargains in piece goods; every inch is handloomed. Be sure to buy a sufficient quantity, because once a run is exhausted it can seldom be duplicated.

There are 2 specialists whose standing, merit, and reliability are so equal in every respect that we have to list them alphabetically: ★ ★ ★ ★ ★ **Kevin & Howlin Ltd.** (31 Nassau St.) and ★ ★ ★ ★ ★ **O'Beirne & Fitzgibbon Ltd.** (14–15 Upper O'Connell St.). We'd suggest that you look at both in order to find exactly the pattern, color, and texture which best strike your fancy. Three choices are offered: (1) Made-to-measure sport jackets, suits, slacks, and other wearables (the required period varies according to season), (2) ready-mades (suits, jackets, and topcoats in tweed), and (3) materials straight from the bolt in single or double width, for adaptation by your own tailor or dressmaker. These tweeds run from large, bold hounds-tooth checks which can be seen (and heard!) 23 miles away to soft, subtle hues so gently blended that a magnifying glass is necessary for full appreciation of their intertwinings. Many of the dyes are made from local berries grown in the farmyards; much of it spun in country cottages by gnarled oldsters who learned their skills a half-century ago or more. You will also find Irish sweaters of pure wool, tweed hats and caps (some to match the jackets and suits), and tweed ties. Sara and Noel Kevin, a charming mother-and-son team, will welcome you with heartwarming Irish friendliness and grace to the former. Twinkly-eyed Patrick and Tony O'Beirne are your gentle bonifaces in their house (which does an enormous mail-order business in America). Generally speaking, prices fall within the same limits in both institutions. Don't miss these supervalues, because here's the only stop on your trip where they exist.

Your own coat of arms in decorative heraldry: **Mullins of Dublin Ltd.** (36 Upper O'Connell St.) has long been a world leader in this field. Catalogue; major mail-order facilities with guaranteed delivery. Manager Peter Kelly and Connell Gallagher are your mentors here.

Handwoven, hand-knit, or hand-fashioned wearables: ★ ★ ★ ★ ★ **Irish Cottage Industries Ltd.** (44 Dawson St.) was established a half-century ago to encourage ancient Irish crafts. You'll find glorious ladies' lightweight tweeds individually designed and dyed in special I.C.I. hues, chic purses, gossamer-weight blouses, tams, scarves, stoles, shawls, hats, mittens, tweed placemats, and a vast range of Aran knitwear. For men there are tweed jackets, hats, caps, Aran sweaters, cardigans, and gnat-weight ties. Please give cheers from us to Co-Directors Kevin and John Cassidy. Truly fine.

Antiques, bric-a-brac, and silver: **Butler** (Bachelor's Walk) has 3 different showrooms and they're all good in their own ways. Other leading choices are **The Fine Arts Showroom** (South Anne St.) for a splendid collection of early Georgian Irish and English silver, plus quality furniture, paintings, jewlery, and porcelain, **Weldon** (55 Clarendon St.), **Dooly** (Dawson St.), **Louis Wine** (Grafton St.), and **Naylor** (Liffey St.). If none of these proves fruitful, roam at random along Bachelor's Walk and Ormond Quay. They say one can even occasionally find a Godhram here—an ancient Irish instrument which we ignoramuses wouldn't recognize were we to stumble across one.

Haute Couture: **Ib Jorgensen's** showroom (24 Fitzwilliam Sq.) and boutique (Molesworth St.) are foci of considerable interest in the industry. **Anna Livia** (32 Dawson St.) caters to the more athletic Country Club Set; **Thomas Wolfangel** (99 Lower Baggot Street) offers fashionable designs and well-cut day suits and dresses. It's potluck at tiny **Florry Carthy** (Pembroke St.) which comes up now and then with the odd item that is deliciously easy on the pocketbook.

Bookbinder: ★ ★ ★ ★ ★ **John F. Newman and Son Ltd.** (Belvedere Court, which is very difficult to find) is a joy for the aficionado. These craftsmen work on Governmental gifts and invitations, valuable first editions, old manuscripts, special presentation books, and other *rara avises.* There is a large range of bindings and especially handmade papers for endpapers. Mail orders are welcomed. Fine—and a find!

Department stores: Historic **Switzer & Co. Ltd.** (Grafton St.) and **Brown, Thomas & Co.** are almost directly across the street from each other. Both are excellent.

Souvenirs as such are either very, very good or horrid.

Shopping hours: In the capital, generally from 9 A.M. to 5:30 P.M. In some parts of the country, 1 P.M. closings are made on Wednesday or Thursday.

Dedicated shophounds: Space is too tight here for further listings—so consult our purse-size, 25th Anniversary edition of *Fielding's Selective Shopping Guide to Europe* for more stores, more details, and more lore.

Other Targets

ACHILL (County Mayo, extreme West) offers the Grade-B **Achill Head**, which after a decline now seems to be bouncing back. The **Great Western** lies at the entrance of Achill Island. Now that it is under new management, we hear that it may be a worthy alternate.

ADARE (County Limerick, 10 miles southwest of Limerick City) prides itself on the famous little **Dunraven Arms**. Within striking distance of Shannon Airport; décor of antiques, soft colors, and serene character; pleasant dining room with cuisine we found mediocre for its category; Long Bar swarming with families including small fry on summer weekends; ramps for wheelchairs; all of its 22 rooms and 15 baths unfancy but spotless in maintenance. While we felt on our latest visit that most definitely it has slipped, enough charm still remains to make it worth a stop.

ATHLONE (County Westmeath, halfway between Dublin and Galway on the main road): The **Shamrock Lodge** has changed hands recently; we're losing our enthusiasm for it. Small, clean rooms with 8 private baths; so-so lunch stop en route to Ashford Castle. The **Prince of Wales**, in an easier-to-find central location, has been demolished, rebuilt, and redecorated—yet in the process its 49 nests were afforded a mere 10 baths and no elevator was stitched in. Not our version of farsighted innkeeping.

BALLYNAHINCH (County Galway): **Ballynahinch Castle** is smaller than its more famous neighbor, Ashford Castle, but from the sportsman's point of view it's even better. Excellent salmon and trout fishing, both river and lake. Recently acquired by a syndicate of wealthy American sportsmen who have no intention of spoiling the fun of its loyal clientele. Accommodations fair, at best. The nearby **Zetland Arms**, was built on a cost-no-object basis by the Guinness family and is one of the most luxuriously decorated fishing hotels in the nation. It is centered in more than 10-thousand acres of bog, lake, and estuary landscape for rough shoots and angling. Managing Director Edwards has created a very exclusive anglers' lodge for today's Izaak Waltons.

BALLYVAUGHAN (Country Clare): **Gregan's Castle Hotel**, 4 miles from this coastal hamlet on the Lisdoonvarna road, is seemingly hell-and-gone from everywhere—but actually it is in beautiful country only 30 miles around the bay from Galway. (If you are proceeding northward, be sure, *double sure*, not to miss the glorious coastal drive along L54, one of the most magnificent ocean panoramas in the nation.) In no way is this country inn a "castle." Sited on a slight promontory, with a sweeping view of the countryside down to the distant bay; Corkscrew Bar, Tudor-style dining room and 2 lounges; 16 rooms, 12 with private bath, all named for Irish towns or counties instead of numbered. There's a cozy air about the house; now we hear many renovations have been effected while food and service have perked up too.

BANTRY (County Cork, extreme southwest) has the **Ballylickey House,** situated in wild terrain for visitors who wish to relax. Not Deluxe, but adequately substantial. We haven't seen it, but a friendly American who resides in Ireland suggests the **West Lodge**.

BUNDORAN (County Donegal, northwest coast): The **Great Southern** chain has sold its namesake house here and the new administration has renamed it **The Great Northern**. Approximately 130 acres of treeless "parkland" bordering a small sand beach and rocky shoals; large, Victorian building serenely surrounded by an 18-hole championship golf course (free to guests); heated seawater pool; tennis court; putting green; lobby and lounge completely updated. Its 96 bedchambers and baths are an Irish mulligan of good and poor; if you're a duo, try to maneuver yourselves into #115; although many of its accommodations are cramped and unappealing, all are clean. Not a crown jewel—but darned good for this isolated simple resort. The **Hamilton** (Main St.) recently underwent alterations, but we haven't seen the changes. The **Central** (also Main St.) has applied scattered cosmetics to its weary mien, and a more efficient fire-prevention system has been installed. Nonetheless, we would take no delight in sleeping here.

CAHIR (pronounced "care," County Tipperary) **Cahir House** is not bad for a brief stay. Its rural-style welcome is warming and its restaurant amiable. There are 3 private baths for its 20 rooms. Our only cavil concerning this simple lodging is that it can be noisy. **Kilcoran Lodge Hotel** is 5 miles outward toward Cork. This one also radiates a happy family atmosphere. It has been spruced up considerably. Homey furnishings; spotlessly kept; flowers throughout; #10 our pick; try for your reservation in the shooting lodge from which it was converted, rather than in either wing. Better than its mate.

CARRICKMACROSS (County Monaghan), despite its globally famous lace, has never picked up the stitches in its hotel-keeping. The best known is the **Nuremore**, which makes us shudder in reminiscence. We hear it has made some changes of late, but we'll have to see 'em to believe 'em. **Markey's Pub**, on the central drag, is said to be a better dining choice, notably for its inexpensive grills; in our opinion, it would have to labor awfully hard to be worse. **Shirley Arms**, nearby, is in the "C" category. How we bleed for the poor wretches whose bosses send them to buy the products of this center!

CASHEL (County Tipperary, roughly ⅔ along the Dublin–Cork highway): **Cashel Palace** is a converted eighteenth-century bishop's manse. Substantial appointments; popular with equestrians; Derby Kitchen Grill-Restaurant with very uneven standards; adjoining Derby Bar; soul-soothing gardens and lawns; 20 rooms and 20 baths, all attractively done; #2, #7, and #1 are own favorites, in that order. Reserve early. Except for its up-and-down cookery, our warm salutes. **Longfield House** is for special tastes. A country inn is what we'd call it.

Chez Hans, in a converted church, is said to provide choice meals for wanderers in this domain. Irish critics number it among the better bets in the country for culinary performance. The glass-lined **Cashel Kings** (formerly the Cashel Inn) archly commands a winning perch from out of town. It is cool and simple in a modern mood and more than ample for motoring transients. The view of the distant mist-cloaked Rock of Cashel (medieval abbey and cathedral) is enchanting.

CASTLEBAR (County Mayo) is a town we are always happy to pass through at the maximum speed limit. **Breaffy House**, about 2 miles out, was almost completely rebuilt after a fire; it now runs a bath for every unit. We're told that this mansion is quite comfortable and worthy for a breaffy stopover. The central **Travelers Friend Hotel** is no friend of this traveler. You can sleep much, much more comfortably elsewhere. For dining, try **La Petite France** on Castle St.

COBH (County Cork) Skip it.

CONG (County Mayo): **Ashford Castle** gets our vote as clearly the Number 1 hotel in Ireland today. It is dramatically sited on the shores of Lough Corrib. Its turreted walls and its baronial furnishings, including incredible 3-dimensional paintings, are straight out of the pages of a fairytale book. This captivating leader, a 4-hour drive from Dublin directly across the island to this former home of the Guinness family, was rather recently acquired by an Irish consortium headed by John A. Mulcahy, an American. He, his razor-keen son, and his associates then gave it a no-limit financial infusion to eliminate all of the creakier old segments and to raise it to its current state of glories. Rory Murphy is doing an excellent job as its General Manager. If we were given the choice of roosting in peace, comfort, and happiness anywhere in the nation, we would choose this wonder first, without a second of hesitation. Closed for 2 months in winter. Our highest and warmest recommendation throughout.

CORK, the size of Schenectady, is 2nd in importance in the nation. It's on the River Lee, way down south; Blarney Castle is 6 miles from the center. Cork Airport serves an increasing tourist traffic to the Southern Counties. Because of its lusterless mien, heavy industries, lowgrade hotels and restaurants, and maddeningly narrow, complex, traffic-choked bridges and streets, here is our least favorite center on the Emerald Isle. Its citizens, however—Corkers to their core—radiate a special vitality that you'll adore. The small-boat harbor of **Crosshaven**, around the river's bend nearby, is much more scenic and tranquil for overnighting. (See below.)

The major town bobs up with a meager fishnet of attractive hotels—with 2 conspicuous exceptions. **Arbutus Lodge** indubitably leads the uninspired parade, with Jury's more effective in its quarters but far less so in its comestibles. The former is a converted house that overlooks from its hillside site the industrial muscle of the city below—best seen from its totally revivified Gallery Bar in cheerful brown and gold, as well as from the accommodations directly above. This colorful oasis, with an elaborate pub-type ambiance and open terrace service in summer, offers light fare. In its famous dining room such superb cuisine—much of it seasoned from its galaxy of spices grown in its own versatile herb garden—regularly wins prestigious gastronomic awards. As one sample of its magic skilletry, we strongly commend the drisheen with creamed tansy sauce—tansy being a plant which thrives only in the Cork area and to our knowledge nowhere else in the world. The wine list offers 145 choices. Sean and Mary Ryan, assisted by the elder son Declan and his wife Patsy, are the prime movers. After we inspected its accommodations, the father smilingly made the true comment that "Our good rooms are good and our bad rooms half-price." Unassailably, here's one of the greatest kitchens in the land. The 96-room **Jury's**, has improved vastly. Pleasant airy location a few minutes from the center; lobby refit; attractive bar-lounge with brushed velvet banquettes and tartan rug framed in a "window" setting with piano 5 nights a week; Vintage Room for elegant dining; cozy 12-table Coffee Dock restaurant for à la carte; U-shaped 2-storied banks of refurbished units in 2 styles—¾-bed twins with a studio-couch to accommodate 3 very close relatives and impersonal, utilitarian singles; compact mini-baths; floor-to-ceiling windows; free cots for Young Fry. The service is attentive, kind, and willing. Good. The **Silver Springs**, also a short haul along the Dublin highway from the nexus, is a 7-tier, waffled structure of contemporary design. Modern lobby with Danish-style illumination; spectacular blue and white hexagonal dining room with large panes for its river view; Blarney Bar directly underneath, also hexagonal and also attractive; big carpark. All sleeping quarters quintagonal in shape to offer maximum vistas; dimensions on the small side; baths tiny and now newly tiled; new carpets throughout. Improving. The **Imperial**, on the main street, and the **Metropole** both have dressed up their foyers and lounges, and added or refreshened their dining facilities to a significant degree. On the outskirts, the German-run **Cork Airport Motel** occupies 4 acres of a treeless hillside with a wonderful view. Postage-stamp lobby with glass-sided 10-table dining room adjoining and bar to rear; air-conditioned; central heating; piped music. Its 20 sleeping quarters, all standard, are Lilliputian, with trickle showers. The boldly lettered sign "No charge for Children, but nominal charge for cot in same room" swiveled our neck in a ludicrous double-take. Far, far, far from U.S. motel standards, but passable as a one-night shelter. **Ashbourne House** at *Glounthaune*, 6 miles along the Waterford road, is a converted private mansion which comes up with 24 rooms with bath, and good cookery. Atmospherically, however, we don't think most North Americans would find themselves fond of it. Our dining choices in town would be either the **Arbutus Lodge** or the recently opened **Lovett's** at Gregg's Cross. The **Grand Hotel** at *Crosshaven*, 12 miles from Cork, really would be our preferential port if we were to pause anywhere in the Cork environs. Coastal setting beside what claims to be "the oldest yacht club in the world" (Commodore Denis Doyle owns the hostelry; yachtsmen often rag him by calling it the Royal Doyle); starkly white, angular, 25-unit Victorian edifice; elegant entrance and dining room with rose carpets and moss walls; air-conditioned bar swathed in Williamsburg blue and white; bar overlooking modern indoor pool; hairdresser and barber. All chambers chat-up telephones, radios, and TV's; the majority draw baths; most scan Cork estuary and the river harbor; 2 suites are extra-inviting. Manager Michael Doran and Assistant Joe Ryan run a tight ship which we personally find delightful.

DONEGAL (County Donegal) has second-rate contenders. Neither the **Central** nor the **National** impressed us one whit. The neighboring **Rathmullan House** in *Rathmullan* is a different story. This old mansion has lovely grounds, a clutch of separate chalets, friendly attention, and culinary preparations so worthy that it is a member of the Relais de Campagne. The caliber of the 41 rooms, of which 38 have bath, varies tremendously. The beachside **Sand House** in *Rossnowlagh* takes second honors in this region.

DUNDALK (County Louth, directly south of the Northern Ireland border on the coastal highway) has 3 possibilities, none of them outstanding. The **Fairways**, a few miles to the south, would have our option here. Lounge with sweet little fireplace; large, bright dining room; small garden to the rear; 45 tiny units, 27 with bath. The upkeep is not what it might be; when we made our inspection, it could have benefited from a generous application of Air Sweetener. Nonetheless, it's better than passable. **Ballymascanlon House**, about 4 miles down a side road north of the center, is enchanting from its exterior. Its long, winding entrance of prize-winning lawns and gardens, its small watering pond for cows, and its steeds wandering in their green pastures whet the appetite for its handsome structure. Some of the furnishings and art exhibited were made available through the Arts Council of Ireland. The same people also operate the **Imperial** in Dundalk.

ENNIS (County Clare; about 20 miles north of Shannon Airport): The **Old Ground** is a charmer. Its venerable interior has been smartened up radically. Mellowness of lobby typified by its well-rubbed grandfather clock and other serene antiques; lovely rose-hue, wallpapered dining room; Poets' Corner Bar with its slate floor, copper, ceramic casks, and old prints infinitely preferable to its brasher modern beverage rendezvous; 63 rooms with bath, all redone and fresh; our preference, the older section; top-grade direction by Manager Richard Oldfield. Highly suitable in comfort, in staff morale, and in tone. The 77-unit **West County Inn** has been given new paintwork and a face-lifting; there's a canopy over the entrance, and walks have been carved through the beautified gardens. Large, large lobby; Grill and banqueting facilities; every accommodation with bath, radio, and adequate storage space; all very clean; abundant staff friendliness. Coming up smartly.

GALWAY is the capital of western Ireland, a city of consequence but nevertheless, an unprepossessing center. An effort is being exerted to add some additional cultural notes to those voiced melodically each night at the King's Head Pub (gratis), but so far mainly students are involved and facilities are spare.

Its lodgings would never send the late César Ritz into raptures. (Perhaps this is the biggest understatement in these Irish evaluations.) The **Great Southern** is far and away the local leader. Among its refurbishings is the Claddagh aerie complex—a Top-of-the-Mark-style installation which incorporates a penthouse restaurant, cocktail bar, swimming pool, and sauna. Irish entertainment is presented in season. Not great by international standards, but pleasantly viable. The 100-room **Galway Ryan** is on the Limerick highway perhaps a mile east of the center. Dramatic space-age main building, centered by white-brick, orange-chaired cockpit which is its sunken lounge; red-carpeted, purple-walled, white-chaired dining room divisible with sliding panel; tasteful low-ceilinged bar; piped music. The 115-unit **Corrib Great Southern**, a relatively new star in the Great Southern cross, now glimmers in the local heavens. All accommodations with private bath; pool and sauna. The **Flannery Inn Motel**, about 400 yards south of the Galway Ryan, greets guests with a TV set fitted into the stone wall directly above the lobby fireplace, plum-colored lounge chairs, and a huge gilt-framed picture of a floating swan. To call it functional would be a gratuitous gilding of this chilly lily pond. The beach resort area of *Salthill*—only minutes from the center—might be summed up in 3 words: A cleaner Blackpool. The **Warwick**, with 50 rooms and 28 baths, is the best of the scruffy lot. The **Rio, Banba,** the ever-expanding **Ardilaun House**, and its 29 other lodgings are not geared for North American vacationers unless they enjoy being pushed around by seething mobs, or unless they are in dire financial distress.

GLENBEIGH (County Kerry), our favorite village on the Ring of Kerry, has 2 little treasures. The **Towers** is internationally famous for its cuisine which is masterminded by jovial Ernest Evans. Simon, one son, also handles the skillets, and another has been in training at the exalted Troisgros in Roanne, a shrine of gastronomy in France. This intimate, family-style haven is predominantly a center for sportsmen; one-week fishing or rough shooting parties including all living costs, gillies or guides, and all expenses except drinks, laundry, and tips, come to roughly $425 per person. On Friday and Saturday nights especially, its guests often simultaneously play its piano and sing in its bar, even including the local Bishop! Here is a fine Irish country hotel —simple, friendly in its welcome, and with personnel enchanting in their solicitude. The **Glenbeigh**, with its riot of flowers which catch the passerby's eyes, is a lovely 1½-century-old mansion which holds greater appeal for the ladies. Not only do its lobby and lounge also burst with blooms, but its shining brass, bright-yellow-upholstered furniture, and chuckling peat fire during colder days provide a cheerful welcome. With its large bay window overlooking the fine garden and lawns on the side, the dining room is a delight. The same loving attention has been lavished on the bedchambers; although some are quite small, all are different and all are attractively decorated. The senior Mrs. Evans is a warm gentlewoman who patently adores her home and her clientele. Miss Flannery is her kindhearted assistant. Almost without exception, the guests are as friendly as the staff. The charges are virtually identical in both. Highly recommended for pilgrims in search of beauty and serenity.

KENMARE (County Kerry): Modernists should opt for either the expanding **Kenmare Bay** or **Riversdale House**. Traditionalists would probably be happier in the **Great Southern**.

KILKENNY, about 1½ hours from Dublin on the Cork road, presents the **New Park** as a pleasant stopping spot for visitors to the city's castle and craft center. Set on the edge of rich meadows and a lawn dotted by oaks, this modern entry is very well run and genuinely inviting.

KILLARNEY AND ENVIRONS (County Kerry): **Dunloe Castle**, 9 miles out on the *Gap of Dunloe*, offers the greatest luxury and snob appeal of the region—but, in our opinion, in an uncomfortably self-conscious manner. It is not a castle; the original rooms were razed to make way for a totally modern 3-building complex with a magnificent sweep of the countryside. The large separate building opposite its entrance is its convention hall, the center of its many congresses; there's also a swimming pool, a sauna, and a hairdressing parlor. Burnished modern lobby; vast dining room seating 180; pleasant little grill adjoining; 12-stool, 4-table bar nicely done; spacious lounge up one flight. We prefer the so-called old wing, because of the warring colors in the "new." This 141-bedchamber, 8-suite extravaganza is operated by the same German entrepreneurs who run the Hotel Europe (see below); a large segment of its staff has been recruited from their fatherland. (One guest wrote us that she "had to look out the window to be sure I was in Killarney and not Kiel.") Far better for our own personal tastes is the spellbinding, richly viewful, ever-friendly **Aghadoe Heights Hotel**, about a mile toward Tralee. Its hilltop setting offers a 360° sweep of the lakes and countryside—wow, WHAT a glorious situation! Rooftop restaurant and cocktail bar to take maximum advantage of its unique panorama; 46 rooms with bath, all on the smallish side; proprietorship by Louis O'Hara, former General Manager of the Great Southern (see below). The cuisine, the warmhearted Hibernian attention and graceful service, the sink-in modern comfort, and the enrapturing solace of those fairyland hills and silvered lakes beckon our spirits so completely that we can hardly wait to return. We loved it—and we think you will too. The **Europe** is the harnessmate of Dunloe Castle. Stark, nearly treeless lakeside location, about 3½ miles from town; 3 dining salons, swimming pool near the boathouse; sauna; 8 suites and 168 rooms, all with bath or shower; bowling alley; Killarney Golf Course adjacent; fishing rights; adjoining bungalows not a part of its complex; enormous, well-used parade ground for trotting out the vast stable of horses. The bone in our throat here is that its tariffs seem inflated for the return in value. Here's a typical late-model city-slick hotel, the prototype of which can be found in dozens of booming international centers. Satisfactory for wayfarers who seek efficiency at high prices with sparse charm or character. The ancient, urban **Great Southern** in town, but yet with a new golf course at its doorstep, has been given massive plastic surgery—so successfully that the patient is now much more beautiful than she ever was. The ornate, flavorful lobby, with its high ceilings, masses of filigree, and mélange of furniture, is as Celtic as a leprechaun. There's the new Walton Room for serious gastronomy; Irish cabaret has been introduced from May to Oct.; the bar is called The Punch Bowl; the huge, white dining room with its dome center overlooks green, green lawns; stunning heated indoor pool and sauna for both genders in a separate building. A handful of extra accommodations have been created, and all of its so-tired rooms have been given the Benzedrine of central heating and redecoration in the style of the fresh wing. Busy, busy, busy—but oodles of flavor. **The Torc** (meaning "Boar Mountain") is a cool motel-style structure just out of the city on the Cork highway. Modern-as-next-week main building; hollow-square interior containing reception at entrance, bar to rear, dining room on other side and broad corridor, all enclosed by floor-to-ceiling glass. Piped music; live entertainment 4 times per week; heated pool; sauna; delicious food for its reasonable tabs. The adjoining bedrooms section displays better taste than the competitive Ryan's houses, but its luggage space and baths are inadequate for overseas guests. Okay for solo trippers or for couples, but a brannigan is virtually guaranteed when more adults are squeezed in. The 168-unit **Killarney Ryan** is a few hundred yards farther along the same road. Open-plan central block with reception, small bar, and lounge seating 100, shamrock-green dining room seating 200; piped music; Telex; occasional evening entertainment in Season. A no-nonsense value for the bargain hunter. The sprawling **Castlerosse**, on the Kenmare Estate 1½ miles along the lake, is a frequent choice of golfers since an excellent 36-hole circuit is only a club-head away. Far from fancy, but ample comfort for the dedicated sportsman. Manageress Miss Elizabeth McCarthy is a sweet, friendly hostess. Swimming pool; tennis; games room; bountiful table of salmon, meats, and homegrown vegetables; car service available. Its 40 bedrooms, including 3 oddly-designed "duplex suites," all have baths which are utilitarian but little more. Pleasant in the simple country style. **White Gates**, a cozy guesthouse on Muckross Road, is big on warm half-timbered charm and small on its tabulations. A winsome nest. The **International** has been overhauled extensively, but we haven't seen the finished product. The **Three Lakes**, 500 yards from the railway station, was launched only a while back, but its maintenance was so slack to our eye that its inauguration could well have taken place in the early fifties. Gloomy modern lobby and lounge; boxy 2-sided bar also leading to lounge; unappealing dining room; drab cookery; carpark under the building. All its chambers are studio-style, with the beds in opposite corners; appended are tiny, sque-e-e-ze-in baths without showers. It is also jammed to its rafters by groups during busy months. Very poor, say we. The **Cahernane**, perhaps one mile along the Muckross road, occupies a 100-acre park through which there is a long driveway to the century-old converted mansion. Today it boasts 35 refitted bedrooms and 30 baths; fine staircase, fireplace, and other antiques in its lobby, plus the amiable Cellar Bar with its handsome vaulted ceiling. A tennis court, stables, and a 9-hole golf course have been added, with more goodies due. Getting better every hour. The **Lake**, 2 miles toward Muckross, is another rebuilt mansion—this one very badly executed, in our judgment. It offers a lovely view of the lake to the rear—but, as far as we're concerned, that's it. The **Muckross**, 10 minutes from Killarney in the hamlet of the same name, borders the highway as closely as is possible. We found it to be clean, but lifeless, and we wouldn't advise it on a bet.

KINSALE (County Cork) now offers the elfin **Monastery** as its prime candidate. Despite its location facing a wooded valley away from the port, there is an excellent view, especially of the sunset at the dinner hour. It is tautly run by Owner Dick Burmby and his clan. The big limitation here is that it has only 19 accommodations and 2 private baths. The **Abbey**, another old mansion with inland scenery, is family-run with care and affection. Notable here is its home-cooked fare. Its 18 units are well tended in the old-fashioned style. So comfy in its intimacy that this is a minor find. Next in line is the Trust Houses Forte's 59-room, 38-bath **Acton's**, an eighteenth-century building with small dimensions, undistinguished furnishings, and a gardenette plus a heated outdoor swimming pool. We wouldn't write home about it. Nor would we this year about the **Trident**, which was sold by the same organization to a Dutch businessman. In our observations, it has dropped so notably in its food, service, and other facilities that it sorely needs more knowledge of professional hotel administration. Not recommended.

LEENANE (County Galway): The **Leenane**, on the outskirts, overlooks Killary Bay and the slopes of a handsome *pin* ("mountain"). Large, gracious lounge with comfortable brown chairs, grand piano, and fireplace; pert Killary Bar; simply furnished rooms in modern Irish with small storage space, cramped baths, and rather austere accouterments. Pleasant for a peaceful overnight or for a brief interlude of fishing and swimming at its nearby beaches. Season: Easter to October 1.

LETTERKENNY (County Donegal): There's the 56-room, 56-bath **Ballyraine** which is not very old; reports about this house are favorable. We are told it is sited ¼-mile from town in a park setting, it is modern in execution, and its rooms are small. **Gallaghers**, in the center of the village, has 20 chambers and 3 baths; here is emergency shelter only.

LIMERICK   (County Limerick): Please also consult the section at the beginning of this chapter on "Shannon International Airport" before deciding to stay in this center, because we think almost all of its hostelries are mediocre in quality. (The outskirters, described at the end of this city, are joyous exceptions.) The 96-unit **Jury's** leads the local pack of hobbled runners. Riverside situation; courtly stablemate of the Cork filly and the larger Dublin hotel; carbon copy of the former, with the same U-shape layout and central service building housing undistinguished restaurant, routine hideaway bar, and lounge. Chambermaid service and overall staff lassitude seem to be the areas drawing most howls. In any case, its accommodations are unarguably the choicest to be found in this busy junction. The 7-story, 36-room, 36-bath **Royal George**, on the main street, completed a major reconstruction job recently. Small lobby with smartly turned-out Hall Porter; dining facilities freshly restyled; tiny, amusing Buccaneer Bar at street level; routine main bar up one flight. Bunkers a standard 12'x 12' in dimensions, which is obviously too snugglesome except for honeymooners; judicious employment of colors almost throughout. Ask for a corner room overlooking the river. Still a long way from great—but an enormous renaissance. The budget-oriented **Ardhu Ryan** draws our 3rd-place ranking—a significant illustration of the paucity of attractive shelter here. This complex is sited in an 8-acre park on the outskirts beside the airport highway. Because of the juxtaposition of hyper-moderna with Victoriana, maintenance appears to be slipshod when, in fact, it is satisfactory for the category. A good money-saver for the thinner-walleted traveler. **Cruises Royal Hotel**, in the center, is a moonshot from being Royal. Although a few revivifications have been applied in the public areas, its rooms are ultramini, with screamingly rippled, clashing carpets. The newer 59-room **Glentworth** is a better bet in this bracket. For the moment anyway, it is fresh and bubble-bright, with a renewed foyer, lounge, bar, and restaurant.

Along the _Dublin-Limerick road_, the pickin's are very poor. In the **Parkway Inn Motel**, the reception flanks one side of the entrance and the lounge-bar the other. Its units are cramped and, in our opinion, sleazy in appointments. The **Woodfield House**, with 25 spartan units and 18 baths, draws not even feeble enthusiasm from us. Although its downstairs is rather cheery, the incredible clutter of antique and pseudo-antique bric-a-brac entirely puts us off. The only favorable observation we can make is that it is clean. This same administration owns **Clifden Guesthouse**, which perhaps is better. For emergency pit-stops, motorists might consider the **Two-Mile Motor Inn** or the **Green Hills**. While both are basic, we feel that we'd blow fewer gaskets in the former. **Hanrattys**, just off the main street, is too scruffy for our tastes.

Dromoland Castle, near _Newmarket-on-Fergus_, is an 8-mile skip-and-jump from the airport and is considered to be in the Limerick area. This baronial fief was purchased in '63 by aforementioned American Midas McDonough, who spent $3,000,000 to take it apart and to put it back together again. Grandiose park setting; 9-hole golf course; tennis court; fishing and shooting facilities; 2 lovely lounges; cozy main bar; a second downstairs with one or two instrumentalists in summer. Our humdrum meal for 2 with a bottle of unexceptional wine came to more than $60 without tips; on a prior visit one entrée—at these prices, mind you, and from a total choice of just 3—was *corned beef and cabbage!* The majority of its 67 bedchambers and 67 baths are spacious; a few mother-in-law rooms are uncomfortably small; avoid #11 and #12 at all costs. We repeat and repeat that its tariffs are moon-high—but for prosperous travelers who like their comfort in theatrically dramatic surroundings, here is one of Ireland's very few answers. The **Clare Inn**, a few hundred yards down the highway on a corner of the Dromoland estate, was launched in '68 by Mr. McDonough as supposedly "a less costly option." Nevertheless, our twin bill for a very recent overnight, breakfast, and our bland lunch reads out at over $80 in the Off Season! Hilltop situation; white building reminiscent of high-class motel; more subdued décor by the same firm; golf course privilege, fishing, and other facilities of its sister house extended to all guests. Small but pleasant reception area; panoramic bar in tartan (where you'll be asked to have a sandwich and/or soup for lunch if you arrive in fringe seasons); dining room with wild purple-and-rouge circus colorations; serene lounge and solarium in light greens and whites. Its 121 bedchambers in 4 different color schemes are large and handsomely furnished, and have walls so thin that you should ask for an isolated room if one is available. This venture depends heavily on high-bracket tour groups. A commercialized Dromoland Castle, without the fanfare—and priced way, way up in the fluffy clouds, too. The 133-room **Limerick Inn** is a worthy alternative. Six tall arches on the façade; stone and glass central entrance; floral decorative themes; ample living space; red-damask bar; apple-green restaurant with ginger-jar décor on the walls; basket-weave wool carpets; a high level of cheer everywhere. The **Bunratty Hotel**, directly opposite the castle on a small hilltop, is due for unveiling soon. Roger Perret, the owner of Durty Nelly's, bought it, promptly built in a pub, and then went to work on the bedchambers, none of which we've seen.

LOUISBURGH (County Mayo): Unfortunately, your main chance seems to be at the **Old Head**. Seafaring readers will know our meaning when we write that in our opinion, it lives up to its name in a number of ways. Not recommended.

MULLINGAR (County Westmeath) offers the **Greville Arms**, which is reported to be modest, clean, and good; it also boasts a brand-new dining room. For idlers who wish to break the 4-hour drive between Galway and Dublin, here's apparently a satisfactory stop. The town's commercial—but the fly-casting is great at Lough Ennel.

OUGHTERARD (County Galway; 17 miles northeast of Galway city, directly across the lake from Ashford Castle at Cong) is a sweet hamlet with perhaps 500 inhabitants. The 33-room gardenfronted **Sweeney's** steals the cupcake in this village. It fairly oozes charm, conviviality, and tasteful homeyness. Two-century-old lounges; lawnside dining salon; tiny elevator; laced from cranny to nook with brassware, oil paintings, and highly polished hospitality.

A cutie that is almost irresistible. The **Connemara Gateway Motor Inn,** operated by the Trust Houses Forte chain, is infinitely more commercial in tone. Modern, elongated structure of gray paneled concrete about a mile from the center, sited on 48 acres of lawns and pastoral land, with a view of Lough Corrib in the distance; functional lobby; lounge-bar just reformed with greater intimacy the keynote; color-toned Grill open from noon to 10:30 P.M.; heated swimming pool brightened by umbrellas and complemented by a snack bar; putting green; croquet. All 48 twin-bed, green and yellow, studio-type units come with bath, clip shower (telephone style), electric kettle, coffee, tea, sugar, and 2 cups. It is open from Easter to October 1 only. The expanded **Egan's Lake Hotel,** where the action is, is not on the water but smack in the center of the settlement. Beguiling Mrs. Egan is normally on hand here, because Mr. Egan, who is an auctioneer, likes to follow the races. Although it is a hodgepodge in architecture and in furnishings, the copper and brass shine and the blue-flowered carpeting is cheerful. The aroma of beer faintly permeates the premises. Fishermen generally find this a happy haven. Sportsmen also frequently bunk in at the 18-room-and-bath **Corrib Hotel**, managed by Martin Maguire. At nearby _Clifden,_ we hear that **Abbey House** owned by Paul and June Hughes, is similar to sweet little Sweeney's. That makes us doubly sorry to have missed it.

PARKNASILLA (County Kerry; roughly 35 miles from Killarney and 15 miles from Kenmare) has another **Great Southern** hotel that sits in a 200-acre park on the shores of an island-dotted Atlantic fjord. Lush subtropical vegetation nurtured by the Gulf Stream, which hits the coast at this point; azure cove with sweeping view of the bay, fronting rock-clad beach with patches of sand, and a toy wharf with its tiny boathouse; tennis, golf, deep-sea fishing, shooting, pony trekking, boating, water skiing, swimming in the cove or in the glasslined pool; sauna; revamped bar; quiet and pleasant Manager Brendan Maher has spread new carpets, moved the reception, built a new lounge, spruced up furnishings, and provided all rooms with private bath. We rate this high on the Ring of Kerry for tranquil lazing in the region. Not far away at Tahilla Cove is a charming little guesthouse; limited accommodations; satisfactory food. Incidentally, at nearby _Sneem_, we hear that the **Blue Bull** is an ambitious restaurant effort that combines top quality cookery with a literary atmosphere. All the chat is good, so it might be worth a try.

PORT-NA-BLAGH (north tip of County Donegal at the top of Ireland), a once-charming seaside resort with a sandy beach and polar-bear water, seems to be losing much of its attractiveness. Its resort hotels, led by the **Port-na-Blagh** and **Shandon**, now draw mostly British visitors—many of them families with children at hyperactive ages. Never have we been able to find better than a barely passable meal here.

ROSAPENNA (near Port-na-Blagh): The rebuilt **Rosapenna Hotel**, former estate of the Earl of Leitrim, provides 40 bedrooms and 40 baths. Set in a commanding position between Sheephaven and Mulroy Bays, on some of the most forlorn acreage in Ireland; 18-hole golf course just outside the door; 3-mile sandy beach; fishing, tennis, shooting, sailing, and pony trekking available. Season: March to October.

ROSSNOWLAGH (also in the northwest): The 40-room **Sand House** resides in a quiet cove surrounded by a 2-mile-long beach. A former fishing hutch, it now offers golf, swimming, pony trekking, homemade bread and vittles of the country. Tabs run about $27 per person per night; it functions from March to October.

SLIGO (County Sligo): The **Innisfree** is a reformed Victorian-type relic which has been perked up modestly with new carpets and some replaced furnishings. Still, we believe a lot of money and effort will be required to bring it up to its one-time glories. The **Silver Swan**, inaugurated next to Hyde Bridge in the center, offers the soothing and pleasant sound of rushing waters on 2 sides. Air-conditioned lobby in clashing modern colors, with rugs woven with sufficient ships' wheels to equip a miniflotilla; horseshoe-shape bar; 2 carparks; some food smells where they shouldn't be during our late afternoon inspection. Total of 24 small rooms and 16 baths or showers; immaculately clean when we went through them. Quite good, but certainly not worth seeking out. The **Yeats Country Ryan** is 5½ miles out at *Rosses Point*, overlooking the bay. It is 200 yards from the County Sligo Golf Club (one of the best courses in the nation); guest cards are available to all clients. A fine beach (arctic-temperature ocean!) is a 5-minute walk from its doors. Lobby and lounge with cream and white brick walls plus red and brown carpeting; dining room in original Yeats House; bar attractively blended to conform with the modernity of the housing wing. Another good buy for the thrifty traveler. **Ballincar House** is on a tangent to *Rosses Point*, perhaps 2 miles from the city. It is sited on a tranquil park. Recent touch-ups have now given this country house a certain sylvan charm, although in sum it is in no way outstanding. The **Sligo Park Hotel** occupies a 7-acre chunk of scenic Irish turf. The grand design is that of a motel, while it offers the facilities of a first-class hotel. There are 60 rooms, 60 baths, central heating, a restaurant serving reportedly good cuisine, 2 bars, and a number of interesting amenities.

TIPPERARY (County Tipperary): Yes, it's a long, long way . . . but to us not worth it when you reach this colorless farming town. The **Royal** is clean, and its food smelled country-good. However, when we saw the royally rung-sprung chairs and the shrieking varieties of pinks on its ground floor, we were discouraged from parking here. It has 20 rooms and 2 baths. We are told that **Aherlow House** and **The Glen** in the *Glen of Aherlow* are worthy stopping places, but so far this woodsman has missed them.

TRALEE (County Kerry) has most of its appeal on the fringes of the town itself. Its beauty is in its name and in its famed "Rose" of song. Intimate, sylvan **Ballyseede Castle**, on a 30-acre estate, houses a mere 13 rooms beneath its crenels. Its new owners however, plan a 30-unit extension very soon. Most come with private bath; the dining room is sunlit; the bar is felicitously red; the bridal suite features a canopied bed; all bay-windowed bedchambers are named, not numbered. Perhaps we're wrong, but we strongly sense a basic problem here: Despite the fact that it seems to have everything going for it, we feel that this operation simply does not click. The amenities are so good that this is a pity. The **Mount Brandon** is employed by tour conductors as a sleeping factory. Its 162 small rooms with toilets and showers, tiny closets, and tiny baths demonstrated such inexcusably careless maintenance that we were openly dismayed. **Benners**, on the main street, bespeaks its 1¼ century of careful use. Sweet entrance with shining copper, plus peat fire burning in winter; neighborly bar to the right; old-fashioned lounge to the left; 50 grandfatherly rooms; 18 private baths. Clean, plain, friendly, and very Irish. Out on the Killarney road a few minutes by car, the modernistic **Earl of Desmond** commands an eyeful treasure of land, sea, and sky. Inside it is merely utilitarian, so we'd use it only as a touring base.

TRAMORE (County Waterford) has the completely rebuilt **Grand**, a substantial veteran near the sea which is beloved by local vacationers.

WATERFORD (County Waterford): The **Ardree** ("High King") sits high across the river with a sweep of the port. This massive modern structure contains a restaurant and Grill, an amiable bar, and efficiency-style bedchambers which could scarcely be more impersonal. Its competition comprises the **Tower** and **Dooley's**, both of which are said to be okay; we haven't seen them.

WATERVILLE (County Kerry), a fishermen's paradise, boasts the superdeluxe **Waterville Lake**. This inspired enterprise is handsomely situated on the shores of island-studded Lough Currane. American John A. Mulcahy, who has also lifted the aforementioned Ashford Castle (Cong) to the top, established this as a wonderfully superb sporting shelter, but whether it continues under his masterful aegis seems to be a moot point, according to local rumor, which suggests that it might change hands in the near future. Since we could not confirm this, you should check on its status before planning a holiday here. When Mr. Mulcahy moved in, he also acquired the famous Butler's Pool nearby, where one canny Irishman says the salmon have to jostle for position. The sumptuousness both inside and out is a feast for the eyes. Bedchambers are look-alikes, but of its pair of suites we prefer #2 to #1. Unquestionably among the nation's finest. The promontory which you can see from here is uneasy host to the links- and loughside **Reenroe**, an awkward, commercial structure that also belongs in the Mulcahy net. We found it big and cold, with a personality that oppugns the lovely lay of the land. In the village, **Butler Arms**, a tiny nest for sportsmen, would be our choice of the modest candidates that line the single trail along the shore.

WESTPORT (County Mayo): The **Westport Woods**, owned (appropriately) by Mr. John Woods, is located ½ mile from the center on the Castlebar road. Its split-level, crucifix-shape, ultramodern structure contains a restaurant, quick-service Grill, bar, and 56 twin-bedded units with bath, radio, and central heating. It's both efficient and comfortable. On the nearby **Westport**

House Estate, there is a zoo which attracts many of its guests; salmon fishing and equitation are available nearby.

WEXFORD   (County Wexford): Here the **Talbot** is building a name for its seafare, vegetables, and lodgings. You can work off the nutrients in the leisure center composed of a heated pool, squash courts, and saunas; there are also a games room, a solarium, and a hairdresser. Boxy, 6-story structure; carpeted, partitionable lounge; shopping arcade; spacious dining salon and adjoining patio; pine-paneled Pike Room Snackery; cozy cocktail cranny in mustard and green, Bedchambers, in a modern mode, come with phones, radios, and (praise be!) central heating; most have a diminutive bath. Next there's **Whites**, a mixture of new and old in a half-timbered coaching inn. Perhaps 13 miles out in *Rosslare*, **Kelly's Strand Hotel** is an especially popular target for traveling families with children. Its accouterments are simple; a golf course is across the way; there's an indoor pool; food is said to be above average. Energetic Liam Griffin is revamping the **Rosslare** in what is reported to be a favorable fashion. We'll be happy to inspect it soon.

Italy

The twentieth-century Italian is one of the *oldest* men on the face of the earth. He has seen everything. Before and since the founding of Rome, Etruscans, Greeks, Roman emperors, Carthaginians, Gauls, Normans, Lombards, Saracens, Spaniards, French, Austrians, Germans, and a few others have pushed him around. Centuries of continual crises have made him a moral and political realist, with a hedonistic reverence for good music, good wine, good love, and the pure pleasures of the senses.

His climate is as diverse as his landscape. Along the Italian Riviera, it's subtropical, similar to upper (not lower!) Florida at its most delightful. Around Sicily and the southern coast, you'll bask in typical Mediterranean surroundings. The Adriatic side is cooler than its western twin. The Po Basin, across the North, has seasonal extremes, and is periodically plagued by serious inundations. Around Rome, Naples, Pescara, Bari, and Taranto, conditions are fairly pleasant throughout the year. But keep out of the high Apennines and Alps from September to May, unless you've got skis. April to October are the best tourist months; at other times, "Sunny Italy" often just "ain't."

The people are just as sharply divided, too. Rome–Pescara might be designated as the Italian Mason-Dixon line. Broadly speaking (obviously there are armies of exceptions), the North is far more advanced than the South. Farms are tidier, streets are cleaner, schools are everywhere; Giovanni Doe is a better-dressed, better-educated man. He is taller and more slender than his deep-Mediterranean brother; generally he has a more stable temperament.

By comparison, Southern Italy, along with Sicily, Sardinia, and the lesser islands, is culturally and economically barren. It is officially called the *Mezzogiorno* ("noon" is the literal translation, but its application in this arcane geographical usage is, instead, "half"). Today's boom in land reclamation, transportation improvements, hotel construction, and added commercial responsibility is enormous. But agriculture still predominates. This Southern Sig. Doe retains more of the traditional Mediterranean features—but, curiously enough, you'll see scores of blond, blue-eyed Sicilians who are throwbacks to the Norman conquest of Roger I in A.D. 1060.

But if this sun-kissed nation presents apparent ethnic differences from its topmost shiny button in the north down to the southernmost tip of the Boot and beyond to seagirt Sicily, these are magnified 50 times over when all of its peoples, their parties, their guilds, their unions, their industries, their special flairs, and their proud regional egos come into kaleidoscopic focus in the capital. Leadership of such a divergent land—each segment with such a will of its own—is a near impossibility. Strikes of overwhelming magnitude— averaging 1 a day over the last 5 years or more—and bewildering impact have become a way of life to a shocking degree.

This is a guidebook and nothing more. We never have—and never will— take sides or pontificate on matters of internal policy, whether we personally condone or disagree. Nevertheless, as travel writers we are duty-bound to apprise our readers of the conditions they can expect to find and how these may add to or detract from their traveling pleasure.

We beseech you, therefore, to take a good long look at the day-to-day news bulletins and be alerted to these ever-threatening roadblocks to holiday fun. We entreat you to formulate your plans with wisdom and foresight, keeping in close touch with the international information media and the responsible judgment of your most alert and friendly travel agent.

Conversely, set aside any fears you might harbor about terrorists and kid- nappers. To our knowledge, not one single holiday visitor has ever been mo- lested by these swine whose elaborate plots are directed against far bigger game —Italian politicians or extremely rich Italian tycoons. Purse snatchings and the like? As you will read in "Local Rackets," these petty harassments are rife —but actual physical violence is markedly less than in New York City.

Finally, if you do decide to tuck this scenically glorious Garden of Eden into your itinerary, here is one thoughtful bonus: In Rome, you can simply pick up a telephone and ask a dial-a-strike service just what is going to happen. Will mail be delivered? Will trains run? Will planes fly? The number is 85-85-45. A perfect solution—if there isn't a phone strike!

Three independent domains, each with its separate leader, laws, diplomats, and other governmental facilities, function within the borders of Italy—the Vatican, the Sovereign Military Order of Malta, and the Republic of San Marino.

Patriarch of the **Vatican** is the Polish-born Supreme Pontiff, John Paul II. His papal state of 108 acres and 890 people operates under extraterritorial rights; as spiritual head of the Catholic Church, he is responsible only to his tenets, his followers, and himself. Italian law guarantees him a yearly indem- nity of approximately $700,000, a sum which remains unclaimed and unpaid; under the Lateran Pact, Italy also awards a fixed stipend to every parish priest in the land. But not all of their financial relationships, unfortunately, are this harmonious. The flag is white and yellow, charged with crossed keys and triple tiara. A complete coinage is struck every year; examine your change in Rome for Pius XII coins, because the early ones are already becoming collectors' items. (For further information on the Vatican, turn to "Other Targets.")

The **Sovereign Military Order of Malta** (does the term "Knights of Malta" sound familiar?), with headquarters on via Condotti, and a villa—its demesne —on Aventine Hill in Rome, sends its own ambassadors to many Catholic countries, issues its own "SMOM" license plates, and performs many other functions of separate statehood. Its total population is 40—but it maintains a national air force of 50 planes! The nation now boasts its own stamps, which are prized by many collectors. It is smaller than Vatican City, but potent both ecclesiastically and politically.

In thumbnail form here are some jottings about **San Marino,** the world's oldest and smallest republic, which on September 3 will celebrate its 1680th birthday. *Location?* Only 23.4 square miles of real estate in the Apennines, entirely surrounded by Italian soil, 20 minutes by car from Rimini and the Adriatic Sea via the Autostrada. The District of Columbia is 3 times as large. *Altitude?* More than 2200 feet, with a glorious view as far as the Venice lagoon and Yugoslavian coast when the sky is clear. *Population?* About 19 thousand (its out-of-country citizenry is even more voluminous—22 thousand). *Industries?* Postage stamps, fingernail varnish, furniture, and tourism. *Public debt or unemployment?* Zero. *Armed Services?* There's a standing army of 180 stalwarts—but because it's such a peaceful nation, sometimes they sit. The republic's Grand Council also ratified a pledge not to acquire nuclear weapons. *Number of foreign tourists?* Roughly a million non-Italian sightseers per year; 2,500,000 if you include their Latin neighbors; in High Season, between July 15 and August 15, approximately 10 thousand per day (but as many as 80 thousand have arrived within 12 hours). *Odd facts?* (1) Every U.S. President since Linclon has been made an honorary citizen of this land. (2) The magnificent aqueduct, plus the lovely circular fountain below Government House, were a gift from the U.S.A. (could these be from some honorary citizen?). (3) Though landlocked, San Marino has arranged a toehold of Adriatic beach at **Riccione**—15 miles by your car's odometer, but almost 2 hours distant on a busy Sunday afternoon in August. (4) The Casino, closed as a gambling hall, functions as an occasional dance center or sports arena. (5) The cost of running such a vast Government keeps soaring, with practically no end in sight. The heads of state, 2 Captains Regent, receive $9.60 per diem for the upkeep of their uniforms and for ceremonial pocket money. In a fit of jealous pique, both the Grand and the General Councilmen have begun a campaign to garner $6.40 per session in salaries. Italy has stepped in to award the republic $3.4 million each year for not becoming a tax haven or a gambling enclave. (6) In July, don't miss the biggest, most colorful national contest of all—the crossbow championship. *Currency?* Italian lire. On request you may buy San Marino's copper, silver, and gold coins, which are minted for collectors. *Language?* Italian. *Connections from Rimini?* In addition to the high-speed Autostrada, ordinary buses, and special excursions, there's a 5-flight-daily helicopter in summer only. The Funivia terminus is also a cable-car stop. *Formalities at Border?* Absolutely none; no passport or credentials demanded, but they'll sell you a souvenir visa on request—*if* you find a customs official.

Visit these autonomies, if you can. It'll be hard to realize you're in self-supporting, self-governing foreign nations and not in Italy.

☑ **TRANSPORTATION Taxis** The same old story: Scant when you want 'em and dozens when you don't. In every major center—especially during the late-afternoon-early-evening rush hours as well as whenever it rains—the street traffic moves incredibly slowly and remains incredibly chaotic. To avoid being stranded until you're wild with frustration, find out about bus routes that will drop you close to your hotel. While most of the cabs are late models, a few could be relics of Garibaldi's march across Sicily (1860).

The fares are jumping so fast and so often that sometimes a legitimate boost is correctly added before the meters can be adjusted to tally it—usually 100 or 150 lire per ride. To avoid being conned (which nears attempted standard practice), be certain to look for the *official* notice which by law must be prominently displayed.

Important: *From 10* P.M. *to 6* A.M., *there is an extra charge per vehicle* (not per passenger). Some of the drivers would steal the pennies from a dead man's eyes—and their deliberate abuse of this surcharge is one of the most commonly practiced rackets of Italy. They'll argue, wheedle, bluster, and practically burst into tears—but just remember that when they play you for a sucker in this manner, you should simply hand them what's right and then tell them to buzz off. If things get really bad, demand they drive you to the nearest police station *(Questura,* pronounced "Kwes-too-rah," or to the Distretto di Polizia); 99% of the time this will shut them up instantly.

Equally important: *Be sure the meter is correctly set at the beginning of the ride* (particularly in Rome and a few other metropolises). Otherwise, especially in the via Veneto and piazza di Spagna areas, you might get stuck with the last rider's fare on top of your own.

Unless your driver is extraordinarily patient or kind, 15% should be his maximum tip.

Private Car with interpreter-driver in Rome? Our foremost treasure in this field for many happy years has been an ever-faithful, ever-alert, ever-warm friend and factotum, **Dino Presciutti**, who for more than 2 decades has devotedly served Angelo Bettoja, president of the Rome Hotel Association and proprietor of the famous Bettoja hotel chain, and his illustrious late father before him as the number-one escort and courier for their VIP guests. A range of Mercedes lead off his sizable stable. He personally or his associates may be engaged by you *well ahead of time* for any driving requirements for any length of time in Italy or throughout Europe. You may write to him c/o the Hotel Mediterraneo or telephone to him there or at his home (557-4367). His English is impeccable, his manner is gentle, and his driving is superb. We adore him. Another gem we have used often when Dino has been on tour is **Alessandro Coti-Zelati** at Vía Noto 25, 00182 Rome. Your concierge may also reach him at 786-332 or 786-42840.

Trains A king-size headache for everybody.

The State Railways is unable to cope with the traffic volume and existing equipment is being overworked beyond the limits of safety. One major—repeat major—factor in swelling the virtually standard mob-scene nightmare is the countless thousands, thousands, thousands, and more thousands of free passes which Europe's most befuddled bureaucracy has passed out lavishly as if they were advertising throwaways distributed on a city sidewalk. In near-panic at this state of affairs, the Government earmarked funds for the modernization of rolling stock, track beds, and other hardware. Two-fifths is being invested in the South, where conditions are most critical of all. A high-speed link between Rome and Florence has undergone initial testing, with the goal set at 150 mph eventually. The tariff scale remains among the lowest in Europe.

Your best chance of getting a seat is in First-class. *Make sure of it by reserving in advance, whenever reservations are possible.* If you have no reservations, and if you are leaving from the point where the train is made up or cars are being added, plan to arrive at the station 30 minutes before departure time, to assure yourself of a space when the gates are opened for entry. Rome, Milan, Turin, and Venice are almost always terminal points. In Second-class, there's an excellent chance you'll stand. First is definitely worth the difference. The so-called Lusso, with armchairs, is available on the 6-hour Rome–Milan *Settebello* ("Seven Times Beautiful"). Restaurant service at your seat may be had on *La Freccia della Laguna* ("The Arrow of the Lagoon"), between Rome, Florence, Bologna, and Venice, and on the Rome–Genoa–Turin Express as well. The Rome-Florence route time is being halved and trips down to Lecce in the "heel" are being shortened by 85 mph speeds. Good swift service also exists between the capital and Naples.

Some of the single-compartment sleepers are the best around. The cheapest sleeping accommodation is called the *Carrozze Cuccette* (pronounced "Cah-ROT-zay Coo-CHET-tay")—ordinary coaches fixed up with bunks. Again—be certain to reserve them beforehand.

You may save money by buying a Tourist Ticket (valid for 8, 15, 21, or 30 days and permitting advance seat reservation), a "circular" ticket (a minimum of 600 miles within 60 days), or a "group" ticket (minimum of 4). And don't forget to check into the Eurailpass.

☑ **FOOD** Discounting the North, where rice is king, the average Italian exists on bread and pasta, the latter a word for which there is no literal translation. From the basic ingredient—wheat flour—spring dozens of variations: Ravioli (rectangular), fettuccine (ribbon-like), lasagne (flat), farfalle (butterflies), conchiglie (shells), ziti (large macaronis)m, and many others. Food authorities may squabble with this iconoclasm, but officially, at least, spaghetti is *not* pasta; it is classified as *grano duro* or "hard wheat." You may even run into the square—yep, *square*—spaghetti. It's called Spaghetti alla Chitarra; order it "con Pecorino," a stronger grated cheese than the usual Parmesan. We think it's a delicious variation on a belly-busting theme. Most pastas (pizza is usually considered to be a snack) are served in gargantuan portions; after a dinner plate of this "appetizer," the visitor seldom can find room for the meat, potatoes, vegetables, salad, and dessert that follow. (See "Tips" further along.)

Italian white truffles are the most scrumptious in the world—infinitely superior to the coarser black variety grown in France. Specially trained dogs are used in Alba, south of Turin, the global capital of this delicacy, to sniff out their earthen hiding places and to root them up. Like caviar, if eaten in quantity over several days, they are said to have an aphrodisiac effect. Some medical authorities such as Ole Doc Joe Raff go so far as to claim they have a sexually therapeutic power; he states that one of the early symptoms of loss of amorous prowess is   *

Risotto is marvelous. It has innumerable versions. The basis is towel-rubbed rice, simmered in bouillon or chicken broth until the kernels are dark and tasty. With this are mixed mushrooms, peppers, onions, saffron, butter, and cheese; veal, chicken, pork, lobster, beef. Other ingredients can then be added. Risotto alla Milanese is perhaps the most famous; we personally prefer the illegitimate brother of this simpler dish, the one with chunks of chicken, asparagus, browned onions, tomatoes, and peas, similar to Arroz con Pollo.

Polénta is a staple of the North. It's a cornmeal porridge, white or yellow, so heavy in texture that it stands up by itself. It isn't particularly interesting in taste, but it comes into its own when used to mop up a rich gravy. Don't order it in a First-class restaurant, however, or the waiter will probably throw you out! Incidentally, northern cooking leans heavily on butter; the prime ingredient throughout the South is oil.

Prosciutto, dark spicy local ham served in wafer-thin slices, is an excellent cocktail appetizer. It's wonderful with fresh figs or a slice of melon—but be sure to order it "crudo" (raw), or they might serve it "cotto" (cooked).

Other specialities worth trying are Scampi alla Griglia (grilled crawfish resembling large grilled shrimp), sea crab cocktail (eat the delicate "coral" separately), Carpaccio (heavenly paper-thin slices of raw sirloin spiced with ground pepper and dashed with oil and vinegar), Cannelloni (pasta stuffed with pâté or other meats and baked in cheese and tomato sauce), Minestrone (delicious multivegetable soup with regional variations of added pasta, rice, etc.), Pollo alla Diavola (called "deviled chicken," but actually broiled with herbs), Scaloppine San Giorgio (veal stuffed with ham, cheese, and mushrooms), Pansoti con Salsa di Noce (a Genoese specialty of pasta with a walnut filling), and that king of desserts, Gâteau Saint-Honoré, purely Italian, despite its French name.

Oh—let's not forget that extraordinary Venetian crab, either. Listed as La Granservola, it's a lobster-size crawfish with tiny claws and a huge, meaty body. The favorite way to serve it is in the shell, reinforced with piquant seasonings. Venice is the center; summer is the season; try any good seafood restaurant for a succulent sample.

★ **TIPS** Stick to bottled water in rural or village areas of Italy. (In the larger cities, tap water is pure.) Popular sparkling brands are San Pellegrino and Crodo; Fiuggi is the best bet without gas (said to be *the* remedy for kidney stones—and just ask your physician what he thinks of THIS claim!); the almost-flat San Gemini, recommended by local physicians for bellyaches, is sold in pharmacies but not in bars.

Italian ice cream is now the best in Europe. It's safe in all big cities, because it has been pasteurized.

*Failing eyesight. (We're glad to see that you recovered it.)

You may order half *(mezzo)* portions of spaghetti and similar pasta dishes—a useful gimmick for survival.

Scandals involving adulterated foods have raised the ire of authorities and consumers all the way down the Boot. Cheese made with dirt and banana peels, butter processed from donkey fats, spaghetti paste pressed from rotten eggs, pig fodder baked into loaves of bread, and even nastier rackets have been uncovered. The Government instigated a nationwide crackdown, with raids, confiscations, and shutdown orders (Rome's airport catering service was a recent one), followed by internationally publicized civil and criminal trials.

If you don't outsmart 'em, Italian waiters will try to heap 24 courses on your table in 7 minutes flat. Your best Oneupmanship for this game is to order a single dish at a time—ONLY. Then you can enjoy piping-hot food throughout your meal—and drive them up the wall in frustration.

There are good restaurants in every city. Even the hamlets usually have at least one oasis where you'll find cuisine of high quality. Don't be startled by the down-to-earth simplicity which you'll find in many of them; with surprisingly few exceptions, the Italian entrepreneur concentrates on food rather than on fancy decorations.

Prices? Leaping lasagne and zooming ziti! As at home, the scale in the metropoli generally pole vaults over that in rural centers. However, posh resort stops often charge the same as their city-slick cousins. *Cafeteria-style trays pan out in the $2.75 range. Conventional fodder in the bulk of establishments listed below goes for $8 to $14, including house wine and tip. The star performers twinkle modestly at close to $18, glitter more noticeably at around $22, and sparkle openly for about $37. For hard-bitten budgeteers, a pizza is the most convenient and universal answer; it cuts from $1 a wedge to the same outlay for the entire π, depending on where you munch it. A bottle of respectable wine decants from $2.75 to $10. In doubtful feederies, be sure to check your bills carefully against the menu.*

Finally, roadside dining places of quality are making their appearance in Italy. As a result, excursionists or motorists can dine well without making unnecessary detours into city centers.

Meal hours: In Rome and the South, breakfast, 7 A.M. to 9 A.M.; lunch, 1 P.M. to 3 P.M.; tea, late in the afternoon; dinner, 9:30 P.M. to 11 P.M.—and a midnight snack, usually in the nearest pizzeria. From Rome northward, dinner is often earlier.

☑ **DRINKS**   Grappa, vermouth, and brandy are the national hard drinks. Grappa, popular in the North, is a raw, harsh, high-proof beverage made from the leftovers of the ordinary distillation process; it is considered horrid by most visitors, including us. By the terms of a Franco-Italian treaty, the brandy may no longer be called "cognac"; normally, it's as nectareous as Listerine. Vecchia Romagna and René Briand are the only brands we can recommend. To anyone who likes his Gordon's or Beefeater's, the gin is a magic carpet to the Al Capone days. Cocktails get progressively worse, province by province, from the Swiss border to Sicily. Local whiskies lift the hair straight off the drinker's pate, but some of the liqueurs (notably Strega and Aurum) are extremely palatable. One "discovery" which delights most visitors is Sambuca *(anisette)* when it is served _con mosche_ (with "flies," which are floating coffee beans); delicious! Curiosity, The Power of Advertising Dept.: Hannun and Blumberg's _Brandies and Liqueurs of the World_ (Doubleday, 1976) states, "Galliano is probably as well known in the United States as Bénédictine." Although it was first compounded in Livorno around 1900, just _try_ to find this good product in the next Italian bar or bars you enter! Oceans of imported spirits are freely available; good Scotch runs anywhere from $11 to $16 per bottle.

Italy is a wine country. She has moved ahead of France as the largest producer in the world, even though the Gauls still drink more on a per capita basis; she dedicates 55% of her farmland to the glories of the grape. There are not many quality vintages, though, compared with France, Spain, and Germany; table wines are the specialty. But the prices! Top-drawer bottlings come to perhaps $11 or $14; everyday "cooking" varieties are yours for a fast $2. For special treasures, however, you can pay a miniransom. On a personal note, for more than 30 years we tried without success to run down the rare and legendary Brunello di Montalcino, which a number of otherwise authoritative oenologists in our library flatly call "the most expensive wine in the world." (It isn't. Certain nonancient Burgundies and Trockenbeerenausleses run considerably higher.) In '76 a cherished and generous Roman friend drew from his private cellar to end our quest. Price? $40. But you _could_ pay as much as $500 for an 1888 Biondi-Santi, a robust Tuscan red!

Vinofeiters, who turn out 300-million gallons annually of adulterated or false wines, are a big headache despite recent crackdowns. Ingredients run the gamut from water, sugar, denatured alcohol, apple juice, potato juice, turnip juice, dried fig paste, curry, glycerine, or other chemical and coloring products—many of which are barred by law from human consumption. One of the most repulsive gimmicks is the use of ox blood —yes, ox blood—for the tinting of ruby-red. It sounds like a lot of trouble for a small profit, but the manufacturing costs are 1/5th of those of the true grape essence.

But something is finally being done about it. In addition to punitive court actions, the Government has readied a classification system similar to France's _appellation contrôlée._ Its regulations encompass geography, altitude, soil, humidity, color, acid content, and additives. Under these new labeling controls, "aged" means more than 2 years old and "reserve" signifies an elder citizen of 3 years or more. Only about 15% of vineyards in France come under the controlled-name status—and the same will be true here. Thus if you stick to the officially classified labels _only,_ you'll know what's inside the bottle. If you don't, does a potion of ox blood bother your sensitivities?

If we were forced to drink 3 normally priced wines in Italy—one red, one white, and one rosé—to the exclusion of all others, here's what we'd pick:

> For the red—Valpolicella (Bolla)
> For the white—Soave Bertani
> For the rosé—Bolla

Bardolino (a red from Verona), Verdicchio (a white from the Adriatic slopes), and Rosatello (a rosé) are excellent alternatives; many prefer these, in fact, to the trio which we've selected as a matter of personal taste. Barolo, a rich ruby pressing from the

Piedmont, is especially complementary to pecorino and other strong cheeses. The Lambrusco from Emilia and the Ricciotto from Verona are sparkling reds worthy of attention. Chianti, for us, is too harsh, too rough, and too acid for any dish containing less than 12 oz. of olive oil per person; perhaps you'll disagree. Antinori, however, is an excellent label in this category, and Villa Antinori is the top of the line (with the château depicted on the label). All but one of the Italian rosés, including Bertolli and Rosatello, are downright poor when compared to the products of southern France. The exception is Bolla, made by peeling the grapes before fermentation; the bottle is identified by an attached plastic rose, and this brand is delicious. Sparkling Asti Spumante is the closest facsimile to champagne; the dry types can be forced down pleasantly, but the sweet ones are so cloying they might make you shudder. Booby prize in this department goes to the so-called Moscato of San Marino, popular along the Rimini Riviera; it is the most repulsive wine we have ever tasted.

For an apéritif, often we choose a delicious elixir called Rosso Antico, which is spreading in fame with deserved rapidity up and down the Boot. It's sweeter and more gentle than Campari. Sip it _on the rocks,_ not at pouring temperature. You might also wish to try either a Carpano "Punt e Mes" (characteristic bitter vermouth which we happen to find a delight) or a Cinzano (pronounced chin-ZAN-O) with soda, ice, and lemon peel on a hot day; they're national favorites which many travelers also adore. Or, if you really want to be European, ask for an "Americano"—sweet vermouth, bitter Campari, a dash of soda, and a lemon peel. If you like tart things, you'll probably find this refreshing.

★ **TIP** The best tonic in the world for overeating, flatulence, gas pains, picking yourself up off the floor when you've mixed oysters and bananas—practically any stomach ailment up to chilblains or ulcers—is an Italian bitters called Fernet Branca. The taste is horrible, but the effect is atomic. This hideous black liquid can save your digestion and your temper. Try any bar; it's less than soda pop.

☑ **TIPPING**   Aside from the hotels and restaurants, a nearly general 10%.

Hotels automatically add 18% to your bill for a "service charge." This is sometimes a racket, because the employees who have helped you don't always see it, despite union laws which insist that they must. Give the concierge from $1 per day extra and small amounts in person to your maid, baggage porter, room waiter, and valet, if you use them. At sit-down cafés, the tabs _always_ include service, but many villains stamp the required _Servizio Compreso_ so lightly it's almost illegible. In restaurants, a flat 15% is added to the bill; give your waiter half of the service charge in addition, never exceeding 800 lire.

Always tip everybody for small services, because Italians consider it gainfully earned income.

☑ **LOCAL RACKETS**   Restaurant checks are sometimes padded; smaller hotels will make "mistakes" on telephone calls you never made. A blight growing by skips and leaps is the rigged tabulating machines at the cashiers' desks of hotels, including various large and so-called respectable houses. Your statement printed in IBM-type figures will be meticulously itemized, often correctly—but the total will be hundreds or thousands of lire higher than the sum reached through pencil and paper. Add up every single item on every tab, wherever you go in Italy—and check your change everywhere, especially at Fiumicino Airport.

Pickpockets are very common. Whenever you walk through an Italian train to the dining car, keep one arm over your wallet; these light-fingered gentry are so prevalent in the crowded corridors of Second-class coaches that the police have set up patrols on international expresses. Now we hear that sleeping cars are being invaded, doors quietly unlocked, travelers sprayed with a chemical that drugs them senseless, and their passports, jewelry, and money whisked from the compartment as they snooze away the miles and the night. Watch yourself in trams, buses, elevators, ticket lines, and all other crammed places such as at tourist attractions or at sightseeing targets (the Colosseum area is especially notorious; also please be extra careful anywhere in the port city of Brindisi). And, ladies, now more than ever, beware of the "friendly" little caress. Fleet-footed swains often work in pairs—one for the pinch on the bottom and the other, simultaneously, to pinch the purse. The flattered ego is their fattest asset, so be girdled against all surprise touchings, no matter how gentle.

It is hard to believe, but, officially at least, there is a new law on the books stating that hoteliers, restaurateurs, or other custodians of public places must pay guests for all stolen articles belonging to the visitors which were left behind in their hotel, in cloakrooms, or in other reception areas. (Just try to prove you left it—and then try to collect!).

The so-called motor-mafia is turning car thefts into a flourishing business. During one 2-month period, around 12,000 vehicles were spirited away—many to end up in the Middle East after being given quick re-paints and new chassis numbers. There are said to be mobile workshops that turn out duplicate keys in a flash. You're marked if you have a Mercedes Benz marque. It's on the "most wanted list."

There's an Italian talent for doing almost anything aboard a motorscooter. The 2-wheeled bandit zips up, hooks the handbag in a flash from the lady's arm, and scampers away through traffic. Your 2 best countermoves: (1) Follow age-old etiquette by letting the gentleman walk on the curbside or (2) go to your nearest elephant store and get a giant rubber band for a shoulder strap.

Beware of counterfeit lire. If there's a distinguishable watermark (star in a circle) on the 500-lire or 1000-lire note, or if it is noticeable on the left end of the 500 or 10,000 note, you are generally safe; to date, they haven't succeeded in forging this imprint. Traveler's checks have again become of keen interest to underground printers; recently a multimillion-dollar flummox was uncovered, with American Express as the victim.

As author Cele Wohl once put it, whenever you're approached by street Arabs to change your dollars into lire, "Say NO in loud English. It's the same in Italian." Exchange swindles sting lots of innocent travelers.

Another clever dodge is worked on motorists. Thieves ice-pick one tire of a parked car loaded with luggage. When the owner removes his possessions to lighten it and get at the spare, he is likely to line them up on the curb or shoulder. Quick as a flash, he has one less piece of baggage—and it's always the little one—the jewel box, briefcase, or handbag with traveler's checks in it.

Many filling station attendants will race to check your engine oil and tell you your sump needs 1 or 2 liters. Don't buy it! Wait a couple of minutes with the motor off for the oil to settle; then make sure he shoves the dipstick down the full distance. Examine the mark yourself, and watch the boy carefully so he won't wipe a false line onto the rod. Also hawk-eye that counter on gasoline tanks, so you won't be paying for more than you get.

The "gold watch" con game is back, too. If anybody asks you to "hold" 2 or 3 watches as "security" for a few moments, run for the nearest cop.

A well-traveled journalist told us of one they tried to pull on him in Naples: The menu switch. He ordered from one card, checked his bill, protested it—and was promptly shown a *second* menu, with a different scale of prices! When in this area and uncertain about any restaurant, require that they leave the original on your table.

We've also heard of a twentieth-century deception from our dear friend Captain Robert Mitchell, U.S.N., who with his lovely wife, Liz, discovered the ultimate ploy in this Italian bay-city marketplace. Since Neapolitan housewives often determine the freshness of the fish on the open stands by the luster of the eyes, some very shrewd mongers are now plopping drops of Murine into the peepers of yesterday's (or prior) catches. This world-famous cardiologist noted in his diagnosis: "They sure do sparkle, too!" Thank you, Doctor!

Look out for scalpers at La Scala in Milan. They hang around the opera house on evenings or matinee days when performances are sold out—usually demanding double or triple the box-office prices. The correct prices for all categories of seating are listed on bill-boards in front of the theater. Once inside, be wary of the ushers. (They wear great necklaces of gold medallions). A favorite stunt is to sell foreigners a program just before curtain time—and then scoot to another balcony with the change from their big bills. A colleague from one of the other tiers then replaces him, after effecting the same bilk.

Finally, just across the frontier near Lake Como, the Swiss hamlet of Chiasso nods sleepily in the Alpine sun. It has a mere 7000 inhabitants. So why does it need 15 major banking houses? To handle the $900,000,000 that illegally flows out of Italy each year, of course. The smuggling of lire to greener economic pastures is a big business here and in several similar borderline confederacies. Italians are looking for more profits and greater security than they can find at home. Although this seems to be lessening as we go to press, the savvy Swiss are still cashing in royally and so is Wall Street—at least that's how the rumor goes.

Every country has crooks; Italy suffers far more than most (perhaps the highest incidence of guile in the Western World)—but the majority remain upright, responsible, God-fearing people.

☑ **INFORMATION CENTERS**   The national tourist office is called "ENIT." In New York, it is listed as the **Italian Government Travel Office**, 630 Fifth Avenue, N.Y. 10020. Dr. Emilio Tommasi mans the helm.

American Express and Cook's are weak in Italy, in our opinion (you might stoutly disagree). Their banking services are unparalleled, but we don't feel they're doing the *travel* job for which they have been famous for so many decades.

From intimate experience year after year and place after place as routine clients, our admiration and enthusiasm for the famous **Compagnia Italiana Turismo (CIT)** knows no bounds. We've used them annually since 1950, and they're so extraordinarily good they continue to amaze us. Normally, huge corporations such as this semiofficial giant (60 offices in Italy and 26 in foreign cities) have no business being so efficient, pleasant, and personalized. Here is most definitely the number one operator on the Continent.

No matter who you are, what budget you have, or how you plan to go, our sincere recommendation is this: Place at least the Italian section of your journey in the hands of CIT. You may work with them direct, through any of their branches, or through the offices listed below—or you may instruct your travel agent to turn over this portion to them, at no additional cost to anybody (they'll act as his European representative). In return, we'll practically guarantee they'll make your trip happier.

In addition to excellent facilities for _all_ classes of independent travelers, CIT offers hundreds of guided tours to any point in the country and to most of the Continent. For local excursions (Amalfi Drive, Vesuvius, night life of Rome, and dozens of others), they're versatile, dependable, and inexpensive. The 60 CIT branches scattered all over the Italian map give the voyager an almost instantaneous service network for any problems which might pop up to plague him en route. Foreign offices are also excellent.

Most of their guided tours are booked via SITA, the affiliated bus company created to supply deluxe bus transportation for the tourist. Most of their fleet is made up of fine, easy-riding "Roadmasters"—specially designed 36-seaters with a bar, a public-address system, individual reading lights, 2 drivers, a hostess, and the last word in cruising luxury. Tickets are valid for 60 days; you may climb on or off at your fancy, because stopovers are unlimited. You are seldom deposited at a station or terminal; wherever local laws permit curbside unloading, they'll go straight to your hotel. You'll always be stimulated by a ride on SITA—and it will give you a happy inside look at the country. It goes just about everywhere. For self-drive automobiles, no other reliable agency is more reasonable (see "Cars").

If you want further information about CIT or SITA, ask your travel agent. If he doesn't happen to have the specific things you need, a letter to Dr. E. Refice, General Manager, CIT, Rag. R. Rajata, Commercial Manager, CIT, or Ing. G. Garassino, President, CIT, piazza della Republica, Rome, should bring an immediate answer. These gentlemen are energetic, progressive, tops in their specialities. In Naples, perhaps the most noisomely difficult city in Western Europe to traverse, we never move without the peerless help of encyclopedically knowledgeable and incisive Branch Manager Dr. Amabile Fazi and CIT Guide-Interpreter Joseph Laudato, both of whom have saved us untold time and money for more than 25 years. In our opinion, at least, CIT is the finest big outfit in Europe to fend off travel headaches.

CITIES

ROME (Roma) is said to have been founded in 753 B.C., when Romulus, son of the god Mars, yoked a bullock and a heifer to a plowshare, marked out a boundary, and built a wall. Be that as it may, the city has at least 2500 years of unparalleled cultural accomplishment. Larger than Philadelphia, it now totes up close to 3 million *Romani.* Most impressive of all is the **Colosseum,** which has been crumbling at such an alarming rate that in late '72 its entrance was barred by the City Fathers—but later partly reopened. Among the other leading landmarks are the **Pantheon,** the **Arch of Titus,** the **Arch of Constantine.** You'll find an easy grace, too, along the streets, in the buildings, everywhere, which only centuries of polite concourse can bring. But downtown congestion now is so incredibly bad that the city was moved to ban all vehicles from 5 of its main piazzas. The Traffic Commissioner has sealed off a whopping 25 acres in the Trevi Fountain district for pedestrians (hotel guests, residents, and employees excepted). Plenty of good hotels, nightclubs, and dining places (the top ones expensive even for Americans); a bustling railway terminus; excellent shops; enough churches and antiquities to wear out the Baedeker family. Fiumicino, otherwise known as Leonardo da Vinci Airport, in the heart of the coastal fog belt 45 to 90 minutes and a $14 to $20 taxi ride from the metropolis, is still possibly the most poorly planned and most frustratingly inefficient major international terminus in Europe; its new floor with 7 main exits and automated baggage delivery does little to alleviate the built-in chaos; avoid lunching or dining here at all costs (the airport caterer had been shuttered on a charge that "fecal matter" appeared in the nutrients); a tax-free shop for tobacco and liquor is operated. Among the better attractions are the **St. Sebastian** or **St. Calixtus Catacombs** (a New York-to-Chicago taxi ride from the center), the **Cappuccini Chapel** (walls and furniture of human bones), the **Borghese Art Gallery,** and the **Palazzo Venezia** (Mussolini's famous balcony). For about 25¢ the city-circling streetcars, now labeled "30," will each give you the same fast-whirling grand tour of the city without a guide; board and leave as you wish (the Colosseum is a convenient starting point); set out around 10 A.M. or 5 P.M., because otherwise the 4 daily rush-hour mobs will shred you into vermicelli.

ROME HOTELS Quick Reference Table

Price categories by national (not U.S.) standards.

EXPENSIVE:
Cavalieri Hilton Via Cadiolo 101. Tel. 3151; Telex 610296; 400 rooms. P. 504
Eden Via Ludovisi 49. Tel. 480.551; Telex 61567; 120 rooms. P. 502
Excelsior Via Vittorio Veneto 125. Tel. 489.031; Telex 61232; 374 rooms. P. 503
Grand Via V.E. Orlando 3. Tel. 489.011; Telex 61210; 221 rooms. P. 502
Hassler Trinita dei Monti 6. Tel. 678.26.51; Telex 61208; 120 rooms. P. 503
Parco dei Principi Via Frescobaldi 5. Tel. 841.071; Telex 61517; 203 rooms. P. 505

UPPER MODERATE:
Albani Via Adda 41. Tel. 84991; Telex 612414; 205 units. P. 506
Bernini Bristol Piazza Barberini 23. Tel. 463.051; Telex 61554; 128 rooms. P. 504
Borromini Via Lisbona 7. Tel. 841321; Telex 690485; 90 rooms. P. 506
Cicerone Via Cicerone 55. Tel. 3576; Telex 680514; 250 rooms. P. 506

De La Ville Via Sistina 69. Tel. 688.941; 197 rooms. P. 505
Flora Via V. Veneto 191. Tel. 462.151; Telex 68494; 200 rooms. P. 503
Leonardo Da Vinci Via dei Gracchi 324. Tel. 382.091; Telex 62182; 264 rooms. P. 507
Londra & Cargill Sallustio 19. Tel. 473871; Telex 690412; 105 rooms. P. 507
Lord Byron Via G. de Notaris 5. Tel. 805.541; Telex 62217; 50 rooms. P. 508
Mediterraneo Via Cavour 15. Tel. 464.051; Telex 610556; 350 rooms. P. 504
Palazzo Degli Ambasciatori Via V. Veneto 70. Tel. 480.451; Telex 61241; 152 rooms. P. 503
Quirinale V. Nazionale 7. Tel. 489.101; Telex 61332; 190 rooms. P. 505
Savoia Via Ludovisi 15. Tel. 487.141; Telex 62339; 111 rooms. P. 510
Victoria Via Campania 41. Tel. 480.052; Telex 61212; 110 rooms. P. 507

MODERATE:
Anglo-Americano Via 4 Fontane 12. Tel. 462.572; Telex 68118; 115 rooms. P. 511
Boston Via Lombardia 47. Tel. 475.15.69; Telex 60136; 120 rooms. P. 509
Cardinal Via Giulia 62. Tel. 654.51.75; 68 rooms. P. 508
Carriage Via delle Carrozze 36. Tel. 679.51.66; 25 rooms. P. 508
Claridge Viale Liegi 62. Tel. 868.556; Telex 61340; 200 rooms. P. 510
Colosseum Via Sforza 10. Tel. 475.12.28; Telex 62151; 45 rooms. P. 511
Commodore Via Torino 1. Tel. 475.15.15; 65 rooms. P. 510
Degli Aranci Via Barnaba Oriani 11. Tel. 870.202; 42 rooms. P. 511
Eliseo Via Porta Pinciana 30. Tel. 460.556; Telex 61693; 60 rooms. P. 509
Fleming Piazza Monteleone de Spoleto 20. Tel. 3276741; 280 rooms. P. 507
Forum Via Tor de Conti 25. Tel. 679.24.46; Telex 68252; 83 rooms. P. 508
Giulio Cesare Via degli Scipioni 287. Tel. 310.244; 65 rooms. P. 511
Grande Albergo Plaza Via del Corso 126. Tel. 679.77.51; 207 rooms. P. 512
Gregoriana Via Gregoriana 18. Tel. 679.42.69; 19 rooms. P. 506
Jolly Corso d'Italia 1. Tel. 8495; Telex 60134; 200 rooms. P. 505
Lloyd Via Alessandria 110/a. Tel. 862.977; 48 rooms. P. 510
Majestic Via Veneto 50. Tel. 486.841; 100 rooms. P. 511
Massimo D'Azeglio Via Cavour 18. Tel. 460.646; Telex 610556; 230 rooms. P. 506
Métropole Via Principe Amedeo 3. Tel. 475.14.41; 285 rooms. P. 510
Michelangelo Via Stazione S. Pietro 14. Tel. 631.251; 200 rooms. P. 510
Midas Palace Via Aurelia 8. Tel. 6506; Telex 68414; 360 rooms. P. 509
Napoleon Piazza Vittorio Emanuele 105. Tel. 737.646; 100 rooms. P. 509
Panama Via Salaria 336. Tel. 862.558; 42 rooms. P. 510
Park Via A. Morelli 5. Tel. 870.184; Telex 61693; 27 rooms. P. 509
President Via Emanuele Filiberto 175. Tel. 757.83.41; Telex 62192; 149 rooms. P. 508
Regina Carlton Via Vittorio Veneto 72. Tel. 478.841; 134 rooms. P. 511
Residence Palace Via Archimede 69. Tel. 878.341; Telex 60132; 191 rooms. P. 509
Ritz Piazza Euclide 43. Tel. 803.751; Telex 61570; 350 rooms. P. 509
Sitea Via V. Emanuele Orlando 90. Tel. 481.047; Telex 614163; 40 rooms. P. 507
Tiziano Corso V. Emanuele 110. Tel. 655.087; 50 rooms. P. 511
Villa Pamphili Via della Nocetta 105. Tel. 5862; 255 rooms. P. 509
Visconti Palace Via F. Cesi 37. Tel. 3684; Telex 68407; 246 rooms. P. 509

LOWER MODERATE:
Atlantico Via Cavour 23. Tel. 485.951; Telex 610556; 83 rooms. P. 511
Bellavista Milton Via d. Porta Pinciana 16/a. Tel. 475.15.24; 52 rooms. P. 512

Columbus Via della Concilizaione 33. Tel. 564.874; 100 rooms. P. 511
Garden Roxy Piazza Bartolomeo Gastaldi 4. Tel. 803.041; 55 rooms. P. 512
Hermitage Via Eugenio Vajna 12. Tel. 804.241; 100 rooms. P. 512
Home in Rome Via Corsica 4. Tel. 865.598; 18 rooms. P. 512
Hotel dei Congressi Viale Shakespeare 29. Tel. 596.021; 96 rooms. P. 512
La Residenza Via Emilia 22. Tel. 480.640; 27 rooms. P. 510
Medici Via Flavia 96. Tel. 487.370; Telex 60092; 68 rooms. P. 512
Mondial Via Torino 127. Tel. 480.941; Telex 79294; 75 rooms. P. 512
Nord Via G. Amendola 3. Tel. 465.441; Telex 610556; 156 rooms. P. 512
Orsini Via Virginio Orsini 4. Tel. 312.829; 10 rooms. P. 512
Palatino 213 rooms. P. 512
Rivoli Via Taramelli 7. Tel. 878.140; 50 rooms. P. 512
San Giorgio Via G. Amendola 61. Tel. 475.13.41; Telex 610556; 186 rooms. P. 510
Santa Elisabetta Via Veneto 146. Tel. 475.88.37; 10 rooms. P. 512
Texas Via Firenze 47. Tel. 484.846; 40 rooms. P. 512
Universo Via Principe Amedeo 5. Tel. 475.05.42; Telex 61342; 206 rooms. P. 512
Villa delle Rose Via Vicenza 5. Tel. 495.17.88; 29 rooms. P. 512
Villa Le Terraze Via Morgagni 5. Tel. 858.525. P. 512

ENVIRONS:
Béla Motel Via Cassia. 40 rooms. P. 512
Consul Via Aurelia. P. 512
Motel AGIP Via Aurelia. P. 512
Raganelli Via Aurelia. P. 512
Roma St. Peters Holiday Inn Near Fiumicino Airport. P. 508
Villa Florio Frascati-Grottaferrata. 20 rooms. P. 513

Hotels For far more comprehensive information on certain hostelries than space limitations permit here, interested travelers are referred to the annually revised edition of _Fielding's Favorites: Hotels and Inns, Europe_ by our vastly traveled son and teammate, Dodge Fielding.

Italy tucks in a mighty host of sleepyheads per night. Since the previously mentioned waves of strikes continue to fuel inflation, there's no telling at this writing when, if ever, they will taper off. So-called inclusive billings often fail to include minizaps for sales taxes, service charges, special regional assessments, and such "extras" as cooling your epidermis in summer, warming it in winter, and keeping it clean year round (if you use the tub or shower down the corridor). Therefore, please never trust "official" quotations; they are most often only the start. _Always demand that hoteliers give you the total rate including all supplements before agreeing to sign the register._

Concurrently, many places have sharply jacked up the prices of amenities such as drinks, laundry, and room service items. Your so-called "Continental Breakfast" of a small pot of miserable coffee, 2 rolls, and modest dollops of jam and butter now might go from $2 to $3.50 per person. Hence, do as the nationals do by stepping out to the nearest espresso bar for a savory cappuccino and 2 pieces of fluffy pastry. The cost should be far less.

In summer, a good double room in Rome will cost $40 to $65; 2 people can live in comparative opulence at the finest hotel for _$65 to $95;_ expenses in tourist centers (including taxes upon taxes, service charges, extra charges, and the endless, endless *tipping) remain murderous.* In the small nontourist villages and during Low Season, of course, dwelling space will cost a lot less.

The obligatory pension plan still exists across Italy's hotelscape. Many of the nation's finest and most imposing hostelries engage in this practice of forcing clients to pay for either 2 or 3 of their daily meals as an automatic part of the rental arrangement. Others, due to rising labor costs, are striving to reduce staff and thereby are seeking to close their kitchens and dining rooms. Always ask whether meals are included.

First a serious warning: Please don't be gulled by the local concierges—some of them, sad to say, in top-ranking hostelries—who are so strongly pushing the 1-day Rome–Naples–Sorrento–Rome sightseeing excursions. Usually they depart at 7 A.M. and return at midnight, when the poor limp fish are spooned out of the vehicles. During this 17-hour marathon, only perhaps 3½ hours are passed on terra firma. Result: The victims absorb almost nothing of the character of the stopovers and are zombies during the debilitating hangover which long lingers. Greed is the motivating factor behind this high-pressure salesmanship, because the tour operators pay commissions of up to 50%. If you're in a tearing hurry for an infinitely more rewarding glimpse of these southern attractions, here's how to do it in the fastest and best way: Ride a morning TEE or *rapido* to Naples and check into a hotel. Take a round-trip afternoon bus excursion to Vesuvius and Sorrento. Reasonably early the next morning, board a hydrofoil (preferred) or conventional ship to Capri and/or Ischia; on certain days there are direct sea connections between these 2 island resorts. Then, in the late afternoon, glide back to Rome on another TEE or *rapido.* If your mandatory checkout time should interfere, store your baggage downstairs while you're finishing up your explorations. Fatigue? Normal. Coverage, comfort, and enjoyment? No comparison!

Here is how we found the hotels on our exhaustive re-inspections:

The **Grand**, 100% air-conditioned, is the home of diplomats, dignitaries, and lovers of top traditional European hotelkeeping; urbane, spacious, and luxurious, it is the capital showcase of the CIGA chain. Each floor boasts an exotic Chinese-style nest with red lacquer and bamboo trim. There are 18 regular suites and 16 lately unveiled junior suites beguilingly turned out in golds and yellows, with rose fabrics and rice-paper walls. Royal, and Queen superposh suites reexalted; some extra-modern units added; piped music, TV, and refrigerators now operative in all of its accommodations. Health Club with sauna, massage, barbering, and beauty-parlor facilities; lobby and reception area leading to lovely Le Rallye bar and grill; off-lobby Pavillon in garden-conservatory style, with both liquid and light solid refreshments; pasta-oriented Le Maschere Restaurant ("The Masks") evoking the fantasy of an operatic stage setting with soft guitar strummings and candlelit intimacy. It is silkenly operated by capable, distinguished Director Antonio del Balzo. Highest recommendation for this Grand old landmark.

The beautiful **Eden**, which lit its 90th birthday candle in '79, reveals not even the most minuscule trace of its age today. It commands a central situation atop a small ridge, with the added bonus that it overlooks the Villa Borghese and the Pincio Gardens. Smartly designed entrance; tasteful lobby; lovely skylit lounge in soft dewy hues adjoining library; suave, 2-tier breakfast room, the latest automatic phone network. Its crowning glory for other meals is the penthouse terrace and bar with its marvelous, vista-rich sweep of the city, with romantic illumination, sliding windows designed to disappear vertically, and cascading bowers of greenery and flowers; it is closed Sat., Sun. and all of August. The cuisine is far above average; Silvio, the famous Chief Barman, is an international institution. Since it is located on a very noisy corner, *all windows* have been double glazed successfully to muffle the traffic sounds, and the 100% air-conditioning system is purring. Here's an almost paradisial Eden that serves its tempting apple—sans viper—to its rightfully loyal throng of modern Adams and their elegant Eves. Enthusiastically recommended.

The **Hassler**, favorite of so many Social Registerites and unobtrusively rich travelers, is expertly run by American Proprietress-Directress Carmen Wirth and skilled, ever-kind Nadio Benedetti, who is the General Manager of both this and the now-Wirth-owned Quirinale (see below); together they carry on its noble traditions. Its register reads like a catalogue of royalty, heads of state, and men-of-the-moment on almost any day of the year. The subtle homeyness here is hard to duplicate anywhere in the city. It offers a wonderful roof garden, a sweet new bar with large adjoining lounge, a soothingly delightful reading room in soft greens, extra-smooth service, and, for our money, the best location in Rome (atop the Spanish Steps). Magnificent view from the upper floors; full air conditioning; all front units restyled; many widened by clever architectural techniques and built-in furnishings; hand-painted murals added to some walls; #103 fit for a king—at the very least; freshly wood-paneled #610 also outstanding; #303–304 our favorite, with lovely terrace, cozy ambiance, and a bird's-eye sweep of the center. Recommended with cheers.

The **Excelsior**, CIGA-owned cornerstone of via Veneto, is Rome's Community Center for well-heeled movie moguls, cloak-and-suiters, bet-a-thousand horse players, on-the-make nobility, and flashily attired fingersnappers who want action NOW. Celebrated ground-floor bar by Jansen of Paris; savory food; soundproof double windows wherever you peek; enlarged baths, including twin basins, separate nonskid tub and shower rooms; immaculate maintenance; very expensive; resident direction by lively Giuliano Corsi. The only handicap here—a matter which has nothing to do with either the excellent administration or the quality of its facilities—is the brash, sloppily dressed, loudmouthed type of transient junketeer who has singled out the Excelsior as his Roman Domain.

At long, long last, the conveniently sited **Flora** is on the march again. After nearly a decade of sad decay, this establishment has finally pulled up its socks in a quiet but gratifying way. To widen its appeal, it chose to drop from the Luxury to the First-class groupment. All of the public rooms and all of the bedchambers which we were shown (about 30 of them on 4 different floors) have been face-lifted. Genteel aura; satisfactory overall maintenance; gracious welcome; cuisine pleasant but not memorable. All of the bedrooms have high ceilings, quasi-portable-unit air conditioning, plenty of closet space, and lots of Lebensraum. Better than we've seen it in many a season.

The **Palazzo degli Ambasciatori** ("The Palace of the Ambassadors") is also on the jump, but the fiscal nutrients here have not been quite so manifest. All corridors renewed; more than 70% of the bedchambers restyled, many heavily endowed with synthetic materials; 4th floor the latest to receive cosmetics; very good baths; 2 fine suites; #214 the most imposing; elsewhere pockets of old-fashioned furniture; air conditioning throughout. Since most clients prefer to dine out, the grill has become a snack bar. Congratulations to friendly Managing-Proprietor Aldo Della Casa, but we wish he would loosen up his purse strings on some niggling little aspects of his hotel management.

The **Cavalieri Hilton**? This 400-room, air conditioned, fully balconied hostelry facing the Vatican and the Alban hills is an 8-layer-cake structure which adds dazzle to the Latin scene. Sited in a 15-acre park atop Monte Mario, it is about 15 minutes from Via Veneto by the Giuseppe Mazzini route and about 30 minutes by the Piazza Espagna-Piazza Popolo-via Flaminia route. (Please insist that your taxi use the former.) Extensive gardens; large, impersonal lobby in Italianate boldness; adjoining cocktail lounge; penthouse 90-seat La Pergola restaurant with bar and dinner dancing where advance reservations are advised; new, informal, colorful Trattoria del Cavalieri which is a delight; spacious pool now fitted with detachable cover for year-round splashing, plus one junior brother; sauna; mammoth convention facilities for banquets for up to 2,000; frequent free bus shuttle service to the center of the city. All of the sleeping quarters are graceful, unusually spacious, tasteful, and outstandingly comfortable, with numerous thoughtful touches. We congratulate General Manager Giovanni Gerodetti and the upper echelon of the Hilton International Corporation for this dramatic upswing.

For the typical U.S. visitor to the Eternal City, a splendid candidate is the **Mediterraneo**. It is not as luxurious as our pacesetting pack, but the management shows such alert interest in North American tastes and preferences, the rooms are so clean, and the staff is so friendly that most wanderers seem to feel at home here. This enterprise is the star of the largest family-controlled hotel empire in Europe. Behind its tremendous success is Angelo Bettoja (pronounced Bet-toy-yah), the president of the Rome Hotel Association whose beautiful wife is American. One block from both the central railway station and the airline terminus; 120-car garage—and *what* an asset that is here; 100% private bath count; entire floors redone, with new carpets, and upholstery phased in. This dynamic organization gobbled up the adjoining Hotel Urbe, which was razed and rebuilt to make this Rome's second largest hostelry; the upper 2 levels of this 5-story wing contain only compact apartment accommodations, each with a private kitchenette. You'll find greater lushness and plushness elsewhere, but not quite the same friendly attitude. The entire staff, from veteran Manager Giancarlo Bellavite, through the excellent Concierge team of Neri Martano and Dino Annibaldi, right down the line, they all do their best to honor the Bettoja slogan, "Every Guest Is a VIP"—and please believe that after decades of hard research travel our team has learned enough to spot almost instantly the difference in the comparatively few places where we are known as reporters from the treatment accorded to virtually *"Every* Guest!"

The **Bernini Bristol** lately seems to have lost some of its head of steam. The earlier upliftings now are becoming dated. The restaurant overlooking the famous Bernini Fountain was closed during our visit; a new Grill should now be ready. Full air conditioning; refrigerators in all bedchambers; most rooms small; more space and flair in units ending in "o6" and "o7"; 75% in contemporary décor; double windows installed wherever needed; clientele a mix of tour followers and independents. What it lacks, in our opinion today, is a dash of inspiration.

Since the early 1960s the **Hotel Quirinale** and the connecting Rome Opera House have been imposing landmarks in the Eternal City. As the years passed this former stopping place of The Greats lost its elegance and went to seed. Recently it was purchased by Owner-Directress Carmen Wirth of the aforementioned Hassler—and what a revolution has already taken place! To date her company has spent more than $2 million in its restoration, with an equal amount earmarked for further restoration and refurbishing. The lobby, the rest of the public domain, and many of the other segments have been rebuilt and warmed with gay colors. The spacious, open patio-garden is a beautiful oasis with alfresco dining and its own bar. Overlooking this, is a charming restaurant in the reopened corridor to the artists' entrance of the Opera. This house, officially rated as Superior First Class, is fully air-conditioned. Its 200 rooms, all with bath, are still mixed in their quality and appeal at this stage of the improvement program; some are cheerful and perky while others are routine and tasteless. Young, handsome, dynamic Peter and Roberto Wirth, the sons of the titleholder, are as bright as new pennies. With the help of General Manager Alberto Zampi, they are successfully transforming this hostelry from a gloomy, old-fashioned, dull dowager to such a lady of spirit that it is even attracting a host of young clients. Hats off to this remarkable regeneration!

The 200-unit **de la Ville**, a First-class-category house atop the Spanish Steps next to the Hassler, boasts an ideal address. When Britain's Grand Metropolitan chain took it over, a new restaurant, 50 additional chambers, and many other amenities were added. Quiet lobby, uncluttered and uncommercial; calm Patio Bar; 2 dining areas; air conditioning; most lodgings with TV, radio, direct dial phones and private baths. Despite its physical attractions, when we returned on our latest swing it was dismaying to find that the personnel were simply murdering this establishment for us. The concierge was inexcusably gruff, the reception showed Arctic chill, and the maids and waiters whom we encountered were sour. It makes us almost weep for the expensive renovations that this company has invested to lure guests. Until there is a turnaround in client attention with at least basic civility the order of the day, we are staying far, far away.

The youthful **Jolly**, fringing the Gardens, is to our eyes such a hideous architectural blight it astonishes us that Roman authorities ever permitted it to be built within the glorious Borghese enclave. Iron and concrete exterior that more closely resembles a modernistic factory than a hotel on one of the capital's prime parcels of real estate; bronze-tinted windows; subterranean lobby, bar, and dining spread; 200 units in the twenty-first-century mood, all with a goodly supply of formica veneer, a microscopic bath and shower, a music console, a TV, and double-glaze windows. The balconied treetop accommodations are heaven-sent abodes of tranquillity. The service standards and cuisine in this backyard of princes are typically Jolly—the antonym of the name. (It has one of the lowest staff-to client ratios in the city for its category.)

The 210-room **Parco dei Principi** is perfectly located near the Aviary of the

Borghese Gardens, an 8-minute stroll from via Veneto. Aesthetically, however, our tastes just don't happen to jibe with those of Manager Mario Frassinetti, or with some of his loyal clients. Unattractive cluttered façade that struck us as downright ugly-duckling; standardized interior; frigid lobby; clinical bar; enormous downstairs dining rooms for everyday patronage or for ceremonial occasions; air conditioning; skinny hear-through walls; spindly, modernistic, creaky furniture; 18 showrooms for seminars, fashion shows, and other money-spinners. A rustic snack bar and cabanas are snuggling next to its handsome irregular-shape outdoor pool. Since the Deluxe rating and price scale the ambitious proprietor wrangled for this one did not make a Deluxe hotel, it has now been designated as First class.

The First-class **Borromini** (via Lisbona 7) is a few minutes from the action in a residential zone. Cheerful, softly lit, peaceful lobby in dark blue and orange; no restaurant; snack facilities from noon to 6:30 which carry over to main bar from 10 P.M. to midnight; garage. In addition to 5 suites, there are 85 dark-blue doubles with wall-to-wall carpeting, Frigobars, cramped bathrooms and no bedspreads. Above average.

The **Albani** (via Adda 41), in a sedate area a short stroll from via Veneto, overlooks the Villa Albani park and gardens. Formerly a large private mansion, it has been radically converted into a Superior First-class hostelry. Unusually gracious lobby in light green and strawberry; handsome adjoining bar under a fine cupola of stained glass; down-one-flight restaurant; engaging self-service breakfast room; disco in season. Group of 11 mini-suites in 7th-floor penthouse "attic"; 55 2-room apartments with bath, kitchenette, Frigobar, TV, and other amenities; 69 doubles. This bright and spotless establishment is carefully administered by General Manager Vito Tine. Strikingly different and highly satisfactory.

The **Gregoriana** (via Gregoriana 18, just below the Hassler) is a little gem. It's a beloved magnet for Italian fashion designers and models. Completely air conditioned; virtually no lobby; intimate bar; no restaurant; breakfasts served in bedchambers; apartment across the street for shows. Its 20 petit nests, 14 with bath and 7 with shower, are lettered rather than numbered. Their wall-to-wall rugs and white-painted bamboo furniture are highlighted by the same vividly hued accents in their curtains, bedspreads, and towels. The maintenance is superb. Here's an elfin, fun-filled inn for travelers to whom these special surroundings appeal.

The 250-room air-conditioned **Cicerone**, at via Cicerone 55 in a relatively quiet district near the Vatican, is a strong candidate as the leading First-class Inferior (an official grading) hotel in the city. Angular lobby in brown and yellow; subdued ambiance; large coffee shop seating 250 open from 6:30 A.M. to noon; light fare available in American bar during the afternoon and evening. Both conference rooms with capacity for 90; compact and agreeable bedchambers with small bath, Frigobar, and thoughtful touches such as shower caps, shoeshine cloths, and more but with inadequate storage space; garage. Many high quality tours stop here. General Manager Angelo Manzi runs it tautly. Commercial? Yes—but it's good.

For those who look for extra value for less money, we warmly recommend the **Massimo d'Azeglio**, opposite the Mediterraneo near the station. This is the

Number Two of the aforementioned Bettoja chain. All 300 comfortable but unfancy rooms with private baths or showers; fully air-conditioned; double windows to s-s-s-s-s-s-sh street exposures, but some facets still noisy; modern lobby; bar-ette; serene, cozy, attractive dining room with cuisine which is just plain *terrific* (top, top quality at decent prices). For category and tariff, we just don't know anything in the capital that can better it.

The 105-unit **Londra & Cargill** (Sallustio 18, 2½ blocks from via Veneto) reminds us of the Little Girl With the Curl. On the ground floor its muted-modern lobby in white and heather green, its adjoining 20-table restaurant with freshly white-grilled walls, canary cloths, and coordinated carpeting, and its subtle pinpoint spotlight ceiling illumination are all stunning. Upstairs, however, the burnt oranges and greens are so screaming that they knocked us for a loop. For Latin rather than most North American tastes.

The **Fleming** (piazza Monteleone di Spoleto 20, way out beyond the Olympic Village), the largest Second-class hotel in Rome, so strongly impresses us as cold, impersonal, and mechanically tour-oriented that we cannot commend it in any way.

The **Leonardo da Vinci**, an artfully conceived modern-lined stunner, in some ways is aptly named. On its ground-floor walls hang more than $1,000,000 worth of fine paintings. Noncommercial, nonurban situation on the murmur-quiet via dei Gracchi; entrance flanked by awning-covered terraces for sipping and alfresco chatting; restaurant, grill, and bar; underground garage; 264 rooms, all with bath or shower plus refrigerators with packaged snacks; more units in blueprint. Accommodations generously equipped with 6-channel radios, Venetian fixtures, excellent furniture, tile flooring, double windows, and 100% air conditioning; superb taste throughout; management by Luigi Richard; very heavy play by groups. A fine plant with lots of potential.

The **Victoria** occupies a sedate but convenient location overlooking Borghese Gardens, around the corner from via Veneto. Very attractive clientele of professors, musicians, artists (and even a humble travel author or 2); 115 rooms with 115 baths; optional air conditioning up to 90%; some accommodations lovely and some more simple; radios that tune in to English broadcasting; colorful roof-garden for sunbathing and sipping; French-tone restaurant in soft ocher, white, and Trianon gray; breakfast segment with damask-sheathed walls; superb concierge desk manned by the ever-friendly team of Gino, Nino, and Tony. Swiss-owned by Alberto H. Wirth; resident management by Hans Hürlimann, another product of the excellent Helvetian innkeeping tradition. Mr. Wirth is a splendid host.

Sitea (opposite the Grand Hotel at via Vittorio Emanuele Orlando 90) is a Second-class hostelry with unmistakably First-class comfort. Its progress has been so laudable that, without jack-rabbiting its prices unfairly or unduly, it now vies with the big fellows in more respects than simply value for money. New foyer; delightfully pleasant little dining room, bar, and lounges, all tasteful and immaculate; savory snacks; helpful Alvaro at the desk; parking garage. Its greatest asset is the extraordinary friendly, personalized welcome and care which warm-hearted Gianni (Johnny) DeLuca and his effervescent wife Shirley extend with such grace and sincerity. Tops in its class.

Here, like the previously covered Gregoriana, are 2 more unusual mini-lodgings:

The graceful **Carriage** perhaps cruises as smoothly as any house of its category in the capital. Antiques, chandeliers, mirrors, brocades, and thick carpets adorn its foyer-style lobby, ornate salon, and TV lounge. This candidate has no restaurant and almost no other public amenities. However, its irreverent bar was formerly an altar in a seventeenth-century Sicilian church, and 2 panels on the wall come from an eighteenth-century library. All bedrooms come with bath, telephone, radio, floral wallpaper, combination bed-table-bar wagons, and curious triangularly shaped corner wardrobes. Fuchsia-tone #36 wins our prize among our twins, while rooftop #47, with its wraparound terrace, is a splendid single for the price. Your most powerful yearn here—stronger in daylight than in night—would probably be for soundproofing. Proprietor-Manager Clemente Giuili and his English-speaking son, Elio, have instilled in their hard-working staff the same kindness with which they greet every guest.

If a little voice tells you that the unappealing neo-Victorian building in front of you *can't* be the **Lord Byron**, please don't listen, for as soon as you step across the threshold you will realize instantly that you have come to the right place. You will hardly believe that you are in the same house. Lobby soothed by soft music; handsome appointments and American Bar; 9-table Le Jardin restaurant, which could be a set from an Antonioni masterpiece: glossy white walls warmed by pastel rose broadloom and cream-colored furniture. Although this Parioli-sited hostelry is a hefty hike from the via Condotti and some of Rome's sights, it is a short stroll to the Villa Borghese gardens and the via Veneto. We are particularly drawn to the tranquility and the parking space (!) here. We also like the personal attention devoted to guests by genial, hardworking Manager-Proprietor Amedeo Ottaviani and his courteous minions.

The **President**, near St. John Lateran Basilica, in the past steered a reasonable platform to its group-minded electorate. La Hacienda restaurant with woven tablecloths, Andalusian paintings, Tiffany-style lamps, and a nibble nook devoted to authentic Castilian pizza; woody bar; colonial breakfast room; 170 bedchambers, 50% with bath, 50% with shower; 100% air-conditioned; 5-channel radio; somewhat spindly furniture. Now we feel that its owner is not spending enough and that for this reason it has somewhat deteriorated.

The **Forum**, named for the Imperial Forum which it overlooks, is tucked into a small restored *palazzo*. Intimate, pleasant, wall-to-wall carpeted lobby; neo-Edwardian décor; air-conditioned; double windows for sssssilence; tasteful little roof-garden restaurant; interior dining salon for rain-outs; agreeably furnished bedchambers. Very appealing, but its eensie-weensie rooms and baths and its offbeat location could be detractions to all but midget archaeologists.

The **Cardinal** began life circa A.D. 1400. Recently it finished a massive renovation which we regard as a bad conversion job. When combined with its unsavory location and the miserable service attitudes we encountered on our latest visit, we now think nix for this one.

To us the '72-vintage **Roma-St. Peter's Holiday Inn Hotel**, despite its half-hearted regional style splashes here and there, looks, sounds, and smells typical of just about any of the larger Holiday Inns anywhere in America. In general we'd call it as Italian as Mom's apple pie; when we look at its facilities and guests, are we in Rome or Chicago or Sioux City or Topeka or where? Its hillside address on the access road to Fiumicino carries a modest scenic advantage and a major practical disadvantage. While its view is pleasant but not half what we'd hoped to find, it is so far from the center through traffic that we think of this establishment as being hell-and-gone in the outskirts—even though the brochure misleadingly claims that it's a 10-minute journey. (Could this figure have been based on driving conditions at midnight?)

The 60-room **Eliseo** is located just off the top of via Veneto. Small entrance lobby; adjoining bar; expanded roof-garden restaurant; copper-sheathed rôtisserie. Clean but dreary, in our view; all narrow-gauge units with bath and peignoir; air conditioning on request; some accommodations with small individual balconies. Okay, provided you draw one of the prime units rather than the several mother-in-law rooms. This same company operates the **Park**, a less expensive, 30-room-and-bath establishment in Parioli. Though quite a distance from the doin's, there's ample parking space for motorists, free bus service to town (the Eliseo's doorstep, to be exact), and the added bonus that all bed-chambers face on a sleepy private garden.

The buff-colored, 250-room **Visconti Palace** provides comfortable modernistic shelter, trim uplifting décor, a roof garden (gone to seed on our visit) and an overall mien that would seem to attract conducted tours. (Their rates certainly favor this trade.) Under its new French PLM owners we came away with the impresssion that its former standards have slipped. The rooms are still okay, but the abrupt Reception people and the other staffers we met this time brought us up short. Its restaurant has been closed. So-so but not no-no. **Villa Pamphili**, about the same size, has a location convenient to the Vatican; otherwise it is too far out of the shopping center to suit us. Huge pool; 2 tennis courts; terrace dining plus main restaurant; fair amenities. **Midas Palace,** is somewhat bigger but similar in concept since the same firm also designed the Pamphili. It, too, boasts a large swimming pool. Not bad if you prefer lounging to gadflying around the town. Many groups.

The restyled, air-chilled **Boston**, almost in the shade of the Borghese bowers, is a mixture of Beacon Hill nabobery and baked-bean basics. Seventh-floor units with terraces, the aristocrats of the Back Bay Society; other accommodations so stark that iced codfish cartons would seem warm to us by comparison; interior dining room; woody bar. Overpriced, in our judgment, for its poorer bedchambers, but a fair value for the better nests.

The **Ritz** in the Parioli district, has inn-corporated the adjacent **Sporting** inn-to its corpus. Reports have it that the room count is now 350 and that a heavy modernization program has been principally directed to the rather small-boned acquisition which used to cater to low-spending tour packs from Bremen to Brest. We'll check-inn on it soon.

This time the nearby **Residence Palace** tingled our antennae as a deteriorating abode. In addition, the clientele we saw in this First-class house was Second- or Third-class in their appearance and mien. Sad.

Napoleon, a 10-minute walk from the station, has a piazza location in full view of a public market. All 100 units with bath or shower and "Massage Boy" bed vibrators; about half with radio; 40 singles; 2 tiny suites per floor; full air conditioning; tasteful traditional décor. Pleasant.

The **Michelangelo**, a few steps from the Basilica of St. Peter and the Vatican border, offers a fading modern tone and an ultra-efficiency motif. Scuff marks wherever we peeped; 100% artificially cooled; 200 rooms with dark "interior" full baths or showers; many chambers with floor-length glass doors or windows, but 50% with individual balconies; no spreads on beds; linoleum floors. We think that it badly needs a lot of fresh upkeeping.

The **Commodore** boasts 70 bedrooms with bath or shower, a sprinkling of balconies, sitting rooms, air conditioning, bright and clean appointments, quality furnishings, a helpful staff kindling a friendly/atmosphere, and a central setting. Demipension is not demanded. Pleasant as a midtown haven.

The **Savoia** recently was given a partial overhaul, but the results still leave us ice-ice-cold. Even the once-popular "Pub" now seems threadbare and shabby to us. Despite its fine location bordering via Veneto, we turn thumbs down.

The **Claridge**, on a tramline in the Parioli district, offers 200 air-conditioned, wallpapered rooms, all with bath or shower. Small, rugless, severely modern décor that seems a bit pinchpenny in its rendition; high ratio of tiny individual terraces; chipper dining salon with patio for outdoor ruminations; efficient and friendly concierge and reception staffs; about 15 minutes from the center. Pretty good, despite the increasing aura of commercialism we detected.

The **Metropole** is another semifrigid lady to us. Air conditioning and double windows throughout; modern, plastic-chaired lobby, about as sterile as the inside of a Band-Aid box; lounge music nightly to raise the BTUs; uninspired rooms; monotonous bare floors broken only by tiny bedside rugs; institutional dining room. To its official First-class rating, we'd still say ho-hum.

La Residenza, a few steps off the via Veneto at via Emilia 22, is a 3-star "discovery." It has only 27 rooms, most with bath but all with quiet homespun charm; #25, #35, #51, and #55 are all sweet havens. Snack service only; off-lobby bar; extra-kind Concierge Gustavo. Manager Maisano is trying hard. Here's a darned good decently priced stop, with one of the most convenient (and even quiet!) locations in the Eternal City.

The **Panama** is okay now but it soon may require redredging to remove the silt of bygone years. Also tranquil and also as cozy as the back seat of a Fiat; colorful lobby; attractive restaurant, bar, and downstairs grill; parking area plus a small garage; 42 small, zestless rooms and 40 baths or showers, most overlooking a shady little garden; #101 the largest double; service unusually good for its informal style.

The **San Giorgio**, number 3 in the Bettoja Group, underwent exhaustive renovations. Lobby and restaurant connection with the Massimo d'Azeglio; 200 rooms with baths, 25% of which are fresh; air-conditioned throughout; double windows for quiet; 2 modern automatic elevators; bar with handsome Roman murals; lovely breakfast nook; all immaculate, and all modestly but amply furnished. Here's an excellent midtowner that has come up in price as it has risen in value.

The 60-unit **Lloyd** has a handsome exterior with orange-awning trim, a pleasant, amiable atmosphere, and an efficient English-speaking concierge. Small lobby with adjoining bar; most bedchambers large, but many lack warm décor; bath or shower with most rooms; some of the marble flooring badly chipped. Worthy for lire-minded wanderers.

It is disappointing to state that the **Regina Carlton's** recent refitting program is, in our opinions, a flop. We believe that it still leans too heavily on its wonderfully convenient via Veneto site.

Tiziano, former palace of Cardinal Pacelli (Pope Pius XII), has a noisy location and a mixed bag of airline-terminal and traditional trappings. Beautiful ancient stairwell; much needed new silver-and-crystal décor in lobby; some updatings; in general, furnishings not to our taste—and that would include those schoolhouse water fountains in the hallways; 52 high-ceiling units, almost all with bath or shower. If sleep comes hard, we'd advise an inside accommodation. Adequate.

The **Degli Aranci**, in a quiet residential district, offers its dining terrace suspended in an orange bower. Improved lobby and bars; 47 rooms with 80% bath count. The better accommodations can be plucked with private balconies for the same price as the lesser ones. Young, dynamic Manager Franco Apruzzese is doing a first-rate job in making this little tree a pick of the orchard.

The **Colosseum** offers a nice lobby, a slick-rustic lounge, a handsome breakfast corner, and 50 bedrooms with shower; the units are decorated in Castilian moods; each seems smaller than a Spanish fly. We fear space is so limited you might have to leave your extra socks or nighties downstairs. In addition, too many reports about its "surly, shabby service" (to quote their essence) and its "bus-tour mob scenes" have spoiled our enthusiasm.

The **Giulio Cesare** provides a splendid view of the Vatican and the Borghese from its roof garden. In addition to the successful refurbishment of its salons and many of its bedchambers (both somewhat on the overdelicate side), the service and cuisine have improved notably. Avoid its basement lodgings. While Owner Vincent Pandolfi has retired from its managership, he still keeps a close eye on this operation. Here is an example of how a routine hotel can be upgraded drastically through sound planning, hard work, and dedication.

Anglo-Americano winks hello with an electric-eye door. The lobby has midnight-blue, textiled walls, plus lots of leather and wood. Upstairs the bedchambers and baths are so narrow that we'd bet you'd find it easier to squeeze between the hyphen in its name.

The **Columbus**, in the shadow of St. Peter's and Vatican-owned, was once a convent. Its 115 rooms, 60 with bath or shower, are painfully impersonal, with furnishings that amplify their sterility; in doubles we prefer #345 or #221. Well maintained; a favorite journey's end for religious pilgrimages or tours from all over the world. For the ecclesiastically inclined only.

The **Majestic**, on via Veneto, comes up with a charming outdoor terrace for summer meals. But inside, the beauty fades; 105 units with private bath (14 singles without); clean but darkish atmosphere; puffy old chairs; similar clientele; air conditioning on request. Not for the young-at-heart.

The **Atlantico**, joined to the aforementioned Mediterraneo, has the advantages of Bettoja administration, full air conditioning, and a kindly staff. Its decorative features and general ambiance are geared to the European guest.

The classic **Grande Albergo Plaza**, on the busy Corso (around the corner from the deluxe shopping oases of via Condotti), has changed only a whit, structurally or in décor, since it opened more than a century ago. Many tour groups; adequate maintenance; wall-to-wall air conditioning; 240 rooms and 200 private baths. We'd call it intriguing for some but loathsome for others. This one must be on you.

Mondial has a chilly modernistic lobby, air conditioning in its restaurant and in a scattering of bedchambers, and an overall cast of stark functionality. The big exception to this motif is its warmhearted and ingratiating concierge. Sparkling clean and well maintained but totally without flair; nail down an outside room. Okay but austere.

The **Hermitage** has an unlived-in feeling in its 46 singles, 35 doubles, and 19 suites, all with private bath and air conditioning. It's spacious enough, but the violent color contrasts of flaming roses and poisonous cretonnes are eye-racking. Heavy, stiff furniture; poorly engineered illumination; maintenance a bit down; amateurish execution throughout, though there's a wondrous view from the top floors. One good gimmick is the free self-drive service in a bantam Fiat for any guest who signs the demipension pledge, with a radial limit of 18 miles from Rome proper and a daily allowance of 30 miles. But with traffic so congested, we wonder if you can make it back by mealtime? The **Garden Roxy**, with pleasant terraces and an open-air restaurant in which we find the fare execrable, is continuing to go to seed, in our estimation. It is an alternate accommodation for religious pilgrimages. Still on the Roxies this year. The **Hotel dei Congressi**, near the World Exhibition, is used for—you guessed it —congresses.

Other Roman recommendations? The Bettoja-owned **Nord** tops this list with air-conditioned public rooms, a 70% bath count, and soothing tariffs that are attracting additional new flocks of dollarwise North American sparrows. **Palatino**, on the other wing, asks golden goose eggs for roosts which seem to us to be furnished in Modern Mediocre. Groups galore. **Medici** appeals in all ways but location. **Universo** comes on big, cold, and functional, while the **Moderno** seems traditional, noisy, and costly. **Rivoli** is routine. **Villa delle Rose** literally is a thorn in these travelers' sides.

Pensions? **Orsini** (via Virginio Orsini 4) leads this budget category. Quiet setting; immaculate garden and parking area; cared for care-essingly by the Mainoldis. **Home in Rome** (via Corsica 4) offers 14 rooms and half that number of baths on 2 clean floors of an apartment house. **Texas** (via Firenze 47) dispenses Lone Star-sized comforts at Rhode Island rates, including flavorful vittles and magnificent martinis. *Reserve well in advance for any of these.* **Villa Le Terrazze** and **Santa Elisabetta** don't impress us at all. **Bellavista Milton** can never be *Paradise Regained. Fielding's Low-Cost Europe* lists dozens more in the budget category.

Motorists? **Motel AGIP**, actually a 272-bed hotel 8 miles out on the via Aurelia, wins our rally as one of the most impressive operations of its type on the Continent. You also can place your money on **Raganelli**, about 500 yards away, and on the **Consul**, along the same route. **Béla Motel**, 10 miles out on via Cassia, has a pool, restaurant, bar, and 40 adequate units that are well priced for their value.

Villa Florio, a converted private mansion near the Frascati–Grottaferrata junction (perhaps 40 minutes out), used to be highly fashionable for country dining. Twenty tile-floored, cretonney rooms are also offered to travelers in search of serenity. Swimming pool; citified-rustic. Now the clientele is disturbingly mixed and the prices seem too high for what it offers.

Restaurants First, here is a perfectly wonderful discovery for North American gourmets of both genders who would enjoy a 5-day exploration in the heart of great Italian cuisine. In 1976, beautiful, radiant, Georgia-born Jo Bettoja and equally talented Anna Maria Cornetto-Bourlot combined their expertise to open **Lo Scaldavivande** ("Dish and Cover") **Cookery Club** as what they then thought would be a modest hobby. But it caught fire so fast and so spectacularly that in 1979, following James Beard in '77 and Julia Child in '78, Mrs. Bettoja was chosen as the featured speaker at the annual, ultra-exclusive U.S. Food Writers' Convention. Their curriculum has been expanded to include 12 staggered courses in Italian and 2 (perhaps 3) in English which run from September through May at the normal rate of 1 each per month. There are 4 mornings of intensive and fascinating lessons that start with the art of making perfect pasta by hand and work up through a galaxy of elegant entrées, sauces, desserts, and pastries, many of them from secret aristocratic recipes. Everything is tasted by these small, individually treated groups, accompanied by wines from the cellars of Mrs. Bettoja's husband, who is the President of the Rome Hotel Association and the owner of the largest privately held chain in the nation. Unusual sightseeing to off-trail places is optional on 2 afternoons. On the 5th day the pupils are given a special showing of the 16th-century **Caprarola Palace** en route to Monte Venere in *Romano*, where they are hosted for a super lunch at the glorious hunting villa of the Bettojas and presented with their diplomas. If interested you must enroll early, because the School is often fully booked 6 months in advance. Further information on this sensationally successful enterprise may be obtained at via Flaminia Vecchia 573/L in Rome or from E & M Associates, 655 Madison Avenue, New York, N. Y. 10021.

The capital has everything for every pocketbook and taste. We have again fanned out to eat ourselves cross-eyed through the heart of its galaxy from gastronomy shrines to sleazy spaghetti slingers. Now that we have lumbered away from the last tables of this marathon and compared notes over triple Alka Seltzers, here are our evaluations of this year's culinary scene, with Peninsula-wide differences open for your disagreement:

For *international* fare, in descending order of preference our top kudos go to the quartet of Sans Souci, El Toulá, La Graticola del Jackie O' and St. Andrews.

In atmosphere, quality, variety and s-m-o-o-t-h-l-y polished service, **Sans Souci** (via Sicilia 20) has so steadily and unwaveringly continued to climb the poles of sophistication and savvy that we regard it without qualification as the reigning monarch. Convenient site a few steps from via Veneto; inspired ownership by Bruno Borghese; cunning, softly illuminated little bar in separate room at entrance; necklace of split-level nooks and crannies fetchingly strung with their walls in green, yellow, and white tapestries and their banquettes in handsome light leather; melodizing by singer-pianist with guitarist. Comprehensive, original menu offering outstandingly savory national and international dishes; equally laudable high-priced wines and other libations; splendidly trained service personnel; fleets of alluring tableside carts; cascades of flambé fireworks; dressy clientele; *dinner only* that should ring in at about $45, each with a good wine. Maîtres Danilo Vianello and Giancarlo Schianchi and Sommelier Nino are on top of your pleasure every second. Open every day of the week but closed and *sans souci* in August; always reserve in advance. Here, in our opinion, is absolutely *the* brass ring on the Roman merry-go-round—but you can well expect to pay, as in El Toulà directly following, up to 100% more than in almost any other dining oasis in the Eternal City. Worth it? We think "yes" only for those to whom money is secondary.

El Toulà (via della Lupa 29) is a link in the chain that boasts colorful hideaways in Cortina and on the Costa Smeralda. It exudes a mellowed élan of tranquility and *haute cuisine* which attracts the quiet, burnished, old-moneyed aristocrats as its major clients. Here's a moss-green nookery where the walls are covered with velvet and the carpet is earth-hued; there are vegetables and flowers on the tiny tables; at night everything would dissolve in an instant if illumination were not by candles. Our heaven-sent Tagliatelle and South Tyrolean Sondbichilar white wine made us grateful for our chosen profession; moreover the final summation came as an additional blessing, it was so low by comparison with billings in other top-rank establishments in this and other capitals. The dominant theme here is subtle seduction. If that certain someone shares your mood, you'll probably love it, him or her, and everything in sight. Very, *very* chic, very, very good, and again up to double the tariffs of all local competition except Sans Souci.

La Graticola del Jackie O' (via Boncompagni 11, ½-block from via Veneto) consists of complementary twins. "The Grill," down one flight, is an elaborate, plushly decorated restaurant, while Jackie O' is a glittering ground-floor disco-nightclub. For the moment (but for how long?) it is the leading Italian showcase for theatrical personalities, gold-disk rock stars and other self-styled Beautiful People who come to see and to be seen. The manager told us that Mrs. Onassis has granted permission for the use of her name; we couldn't see if his fingers were crossed. Impressive canopy-corridored entrance; winding staircase to large, quietly voguish, segmented premises in tavern motif; immaculate open kitchen and king-size grill firing to greet clients as they step inside; cunning adjoining bar. Our bill for our light dinners was almost $25 per appetite, but it could have run a lot higher with more costly choices. Go late, late, late—not before 10:30 ever—and reserve in advance; closed July 25 to August 25, but otherwise in action 7 days per week; *dinner only*. Enjoy!

The smaller, more intimate, more reasonably priced **St. Andrews** (via Lazio 22/A, also ½-block from via Veneto) is in major contrast to the above trio. This little siren has the comfortable, cozy milieu of a select private club. Bar at entrance; 2 adjoining rooms; paneled walls with tasteful modern paintings artfully placed; subtle to dark illumination; deft, sophisticated client attention; limited but carefully chosen menu; good wine list. Its tariffs are suprisingly low for its stature. Also *dinner only* from 8 P.M. to 1 A.M.; also go late; closed Monday. Director Turriziani with Barmen Vittorio and Stefano administer it as urbanely as if they were wearing silk gloves. A benison for weary wayfarers who wish to relax, to talk, and even to hold hands.

George's (via Marche 7) is an old standby. Gallic rather than Italian in tone; satin-lined ceilings; lamps and flowers on tables; lovely garden terrace; smooth dinner music; attention sharply honed. It is still popular among its midtown loyalists; there's a gourmet food shop lip-smack beside the canopied entrance. What puts our hair up is its tariffs. A moderate lunch can casually wave *ciao* to $75—up to 50% higher than virtually all of its professional confrerers except the even more expensive Sans Souci and El Toulà. If we wished to splurge *big*, certainly we would choose them instead of it. Usually closed from August 10 to September 10.

Hosteria dell'Orso (via di Monte Brianzo 93), for more than three decades the unchallenged dining and/or dancing rendezvous has lost its crown and deteriorated heartbreakingly. It occupies Dante's fourteenth-century home, an official National Monument. Piano Bar, with a pianist and 2 guitarists; princely Borgia Room with its lapis lazuli pillars and gold utensils; La Cabala now merely a noisy, thumping discothèque. How sad we are!

For *Italian* fare, our numbers 1, 2, 3, 4, and 5 rankings go, with tongues slapping our chest, to **Cesarina** (via Piemonte 109–115). Here is one of Italy's greatest exponents of national cookery and since 1961 our favorite regional culinary pilgrimage in the Eternal City. Each visit reconfirms this happy verdict for us. Mamma Cesarina, a smiling Powerful Katrinka, drew acclaim for her Bologna establishment until she found communist interference intolerable and packed off to Rome. Now you'll probably see her standing in her immaculate open kitchen, pounding the pasta while waving instructions to the staff with her busy, muscular arms. Her cookery superb; noisy after 1:30 or 9 P.M., so go earlier if you prefer its more tranquil moods; ask for Maître Ivo (rhymes with "heave-ho"), whose smile and whose English are cheering. Be *sure* to try a tiny cup (not bowl) of Mamma's heavenly Passatelli first, followed by the tri-plate—bite-size samplings of 3 different types of pasta called Misto Cesarina—while sipping her Albana white wine from the North. After this, nibble her oh-so-delicious Giambella, a featherlight lemon-flavored cake dipped in the Albana before application to your soul. Beef Tartare aficionados normally bask with her Carpaccio—paper-thin slices of filet mignon with the perfectly complementary dressing and seasoning. We offer salaams and salutes to every department. Closed in August and each Sun.

Now for the grab bag of the lesser plums and prunes. Good hunting!

There are 2 famous **Alfredo's**. The first is **Alfredo alla Scrofa** (via della Scrofa 104). This operation impresses us as highly overpriced and distinctly tourist-happy, with cuisine which we thought was definitely substandard, and with tip-hungry musicians who panhandled from table to table in a very bold way. To lure visitors, just about every gimmick on the list seems to be there, including the corny hamming with the spoons when they mix the Fettuccine (the quality of which now also seems to us on the decline). The illumination is overbright, the noise level can be deafening, and the harem-scarem "service" we suffered on our recent round was straight out of a Chaplin scenario. Then there's the simple **l'Original Alfredo** in Trastevere, a so-so *trattoria* which is completely different in tone. Our repeat test meal here recently seemed to be below 2nd-rate and once again our tab contained a well-rounded clip. It boils down to this: Try alla Scrofa if you want action and pictures of movie stars; the service we have found is sometimes abominable. Try Trastevere for low-grade Italian fare at cheaper prices, particularly on a summer's night.

Girarrosto Toscano (via Campania 2), right off via Veneto facing the Borghese's ponderous battlements, has become one of the more fashionable, and likewise costly, dining spots in town. Subterranean setting; 2 bright and cheery sancta with open rôtisserie near entrance; stucco vaulted ceiling; blond wood banquettes for perhaps 150 munchers; wine bottles ringing the room; waiters sometimes overefficient. The antipasto, presented on a massive platter, is a meal in itself; the meat-filled tortellini were excellent; so was our inch-thick Florentine steak (but remember, please, that the price of the steerage gets beefier in direct proportion to its weight). It is shuttered on Wednesday. Our toast to Host Martini for his happily blended Tuscan cocktail.

Osteria St. Ana (via della Penna 68) still radiates debutante grace. Cellar site with steps leading past a food display; long semidivided room (we prefer the pink-toned right side); paintings and sculpture adorning the stucco walls; white furniture. Our ravioli was served in a huge porridge bowl; our grilled quail was fair game; after the repast, a house *digestif* was offered free of charge. Maître Elio told us it was a composition of—hold your breath—Crème de Cacao, Tio Pepe sherry, French cognac, and Grand Marnier, floated with whipped cream and garnished with a cherry. (Horrible as it sounds, we were floored to find it *delicious!*) Closed Sunday.

Al Fogher ("The Forge," via Tevere 13/6), styled as a tasteful country home, seems to have skidded of late. We can't recommend it for the nonce.

Domus Aurea (Giardini al Colle Oppio), rambling across a small hill over-looking the Coliseum, is similar in concept. Inviting open terrace for 150 diners, many of them from bus groups; air-conditioned interior salon; music nightly; sparkling kitchen producing so-so to ho-hum cookery. Easily accessible to midtown sightseers and panoRomantically rewarding. We like it, especially when our eyes are hungrier than our tummies.

Passetto (piazza Zanardelli 14) is a standby of the Old Guard. Kind reception; warmhearted professional attention; boat-shape rolling cart containing shellfish and crustacean appetizers in nests of shaved ice; high quality ingredients; knowledgeable preparation. Should we have any quibble other than its variability, it would be that for some palates the cuisine might seem unusually bland by comparison with the usually sharper Italian flavorings.

Papa Giulio (19 via Giulia), the stable of a fifteenth-century palace that is now a national museum, offers more eye appeal than palate satisfaction. This Brobdingnagian manger is tricked out in Pompeian-red burlap and aqua blue; a great fireplace commands one sector. Since the main dishes we tried were poor, in our opinions, the frills mean little when one is being socked for the full castastrophe—socked hard, too! Sorry, not our Papa any more.

The "31" Al Vicario (via Uffici del Vicario 31) has been handsomely revitalized by its Doney-chain owners. Four attractive rooms in beige and white; comfortable banquettes; thick carpets; rich textiles in salmon and complementing pastels; Picasso, Marini, and other modern-art treasures on the walls;

outdoor patio dining during warm months; closed August. This one is a genuine asset to refinement in Roman culinary circles.

The **White Elephant** (via Aurora 27) is just that. In décor, it is rich. Victorian bar; dining room in Regency ambiance; little gaslit nightclub downstairs. Our 3 latest rechecks revealed that old pachyderms *can* forget—cookery skills, at least.

The old-fashioned **Ranieri** (via Mario dei Fiori 26) has been a citadel of Italian comestibles since 1843. Until recently, its atmosphere was almost *too* mellow and its tempo *too* lento; now this serenity has vanished—especially at lunch. This is one of the few worthy dining places within easy walking distance of the Spanish Steps. Dedicated to sound cuisine and again to be respected.

Mastrostefano is diagonally across from its famous 3-step neighbor (see below); nowadays we think it is overated and overpriced. Extensive 2-part terrace with rows of parasoled tables; one interior room; abuzz with many North Americans. Not so hot now, in our opinions.

Tre Scalini (piazza Navona 28) is named for the "Three Steps" which were immortalized by Garibaldi. Since all but walking traffic has been banned from this large and lovely square, it is a delight on a beautiful day or evening to sit under the awnings of the sidewalk "terrace" here and contemplate the magnificence of the Bernini Fountains. Our latest meal was passable but presented and served so listlessly that the full-scale pleasure of earlier times was greatly diminished. The allure of the setting remains, however, so why not just pause here for coffee or a dish of its famous ice-cream? Now only *Due Scalini* on our scoresheet. The **4 Fiumi**, a similar setup directly next door, does not excite us too much, either. Perhaps the floods of tourists in this pedestrian hub of Rome have dampened the local service standards.

Capriccio (via Liguria 38) has sunk so low, in our view, that a return bout could only be a *capriccio.* Sad.

Da Bolognese (piazza del Popolo) is a favorite meeting place of lovely budding movie stars, gal painters, and gals in the Creative Arts. Their choice is well founded, because the cuisine is superb, the personnel are warm, and while the house isn't opulent in any respect, the prices are right. Closed every Monday, willy-nilly; open the other 313 days of the year. Best in good weather on the terrace. Now—*please don't take dessert, coffee, or liqueurs here.* Move next door to the expensive, highly à la mode **Pasticceria Rosati**, find places on its large sidewalk terrace, and take your pick from its vast variety of homemade pastries, candies, other sweets of many types, or its versatile assortment of alcoholic and nonalcoholic beverages. On a sunny day it is heavenly to laze here almost within the shadows of the Bernini Fountain, the Ramsete Obelisk, and the 2 beautiful churches on Valadier Square, with the Borghese Gardens directly above.

Il Matriciano (via del Gracchi 51–57) is replacing Da Bolognese for some, but *never* for us. Remote outlying location with no scenic charms; sidewalk dining; superswift and cheerful attention. Our latest lunch, 3rd-rate in every regard, totaled $14.80 per head including tip—and the capper came when they again presented us with an incorrect bill.

L'Eau Vive (via Monterone 85) is blessed by the French religious order of

Working Missionaries of The Immaculate Virgin of the Poor, which has missions from Paris and Brussels all the way to the Congo and the Orient. The good sisters first stripped the walls of the 2 high-ceiling rooms of all appurtenances and then repainted them in pleasant but starkly plain horizontal bands of olive green, whitish green pastel, and brown. As a result, the only warm color touches remaining are the red tablecloths and the small flowers at their center. The "maître d'hotel," the "chef," and all of the "waitresses" are nuns. Petit bourgeois clientele; spotlessly clean; piped music; inexpensive tariffs; tipping prohibited. Although this kindly hardworking group tries very hard, it is painful to report that the overall result is amateurish and our cuisine (entirely based on the French kitchen) was not very successful; a few readers report better luck. How sincerely we wish we could recommend this labor of love!

Sabatini (vicolo Santa Maria 18) is one of the two most popular trattorias on the Trastevere banks—deservedly so again after its recent slump under different management. Largish hedged terrace on piazza Santa Maria; front door facing a handsome open grill glowing with charred wood and sizzling with roasts, chops, fish, and fowl; interior hall with leaded windows and 3 enormous ancient timbers supporting a raftered ceiling; aging walls topped by a rich but fading painted molding. Large staff of casual but friendly waiters; good rough fare with a wide variety of offerings; prices low to medium. This one is once more fun-filled and rewarding. **Galeassi**, with a similar outdoor-indoor layout but a bit smaller, faces the same *piazza*. It has its host of loyal adherents, too—and its tariffs are slightly lower. Our verdict? A tossup.

Giggi Fazi (via Lucullo) has become so variable in our several recent tests —ranging roughly between passable and unsatisfactory—that we've lost our enthusiasm for it.

La Tana del Grillo ("The Cricket's Nest"), on Salita del Grillo, is said to evoke cries of "jiminy crickets!" around Trajan's Forum these days. It offers Bolognese dishes for the first reel of cinematic personalities. We can't wait to hop by for a meal.

La Fontanella (largo Fontanella Borghese 86) is brightened by a mosaic in medieval motif; this "Little Fountain" is not glamorous, but clean, attractive, and substantial. The Tuscan house specialty is truffles. Some disturbing ripples have flowed in from travelers about the waiters being cocky. Our latest recheck did not reveal this, but we were not as satisfied with the cookery as we had been in former years.

La Capricciosa (largo dei Lombardi 8) is a sound, budget-level *trattoria* for serious feeders. No bar; 3 clean dining rooms and one basement corner in modern tone; open 9 A.M. till after 2 A.M. every day of the year. The food is good, the ladles are generous, and the prices are right.

Taverna Flavia (via Flavia 9) lines its walls with photos of celebrated clients while lining its clients with celebrated cookery. Simple interior of several interlocking rooms; bottle-green color scheme; generally folksy service; incessantly rising tariffs. Our recent samplings of pasta, White Truffles, Grilled Scampi, Sautéed Brains with a light garlic flavor, and the house wine were all above average. Again, there was a small error on our bill, but it was corrected instantly when we objected; be sure to practice your own arithmetic on your check. Here's a chummy reeler we think you might agree is worth a run.

Da Meo Patacca!!! (piazza dei Mercanti 30, in Trastevere) characteristically labels itself with 3 exclamation points. It couldn't be more shamelessly contrived for the visitors' trade—but it's great fun if you're in the mood. Even nontouring Italians flock in for the frolic and foodstuffs. The ground floor might be a Hollywood producer's concept of a converted Sicilian barn. It has been hung with great necklaces of onions, peppers, and dried corn, and stuffed with such gimmicks as ox yokes, a hand organ, a wine cart, copper peasantware, and other objects known as "picturesque." (Incidentally, we so loathe this overworked adjective that here, presented between quotation marks, is the only time you will suffer it in this book.) Rôtisserie grill and kitchen at one end; gadget-filled cellar down narrow stairway; large open summer terrace on one side. If you'll stick to Antipasto Misto, a double T-bone steak, fruit or cheese, an iced bottle of Verdicchio rosato (rosé), and coffee, you will dine decently for not excessive money; these are the best of its specialties. The proprietors are waiters who pooled to buy it from the American originator. Go at night, because at lunch it is often overrun by conducted tours; you won't escape the loud music by costumed performers (who seem never to be offstage) or by tip-fevered troubadours at your elbow. Very noisy, admittedly 100% cornball—but right now it's one of the most popular tourist meccas in the capital.

The **Da Ciceruacchio**, just in front, is also under the consortium key. Prison-lore motif, derived from its use as an Austrian hoosegow during the Risorgimento; bungling reception on our incognito revisit, keyed to the bus groups which thunder in rather than to individual clients who reserve in advance; overtly clippy musicians who had the gall to put 1000-lire banknotes on their guitars as a tip lure; surroundings so tatty and food so poor that it's simply not for us—ever, ever, ever again.

L'Etichetta (piazza Nicosia) is a fresh fish find we hooked. Its buffet table buckled under dozens of denizens from the deep. Fat goldfish eyed us scornfully as we feasted on Gran Fritto Misto di Pesce and French rosé. Relatively undiscovered, which is a pity since it deserves a school of followers.

Coq d'Or (via Flaminia Vecchia 493, about a 10-minute taxi ride beyond Olympic Village) is a golden rooster that crows more and more for battery clientele. Its barnyard is in a 300-year-old palace. Main-floor bar dominated by gracious stone chimney; tabby-hued velvet walls; pliant leather stools; guitar lilts; upstairs dining room under a lovely painted rotunda; garden view through tower windows; several nooks for friendly persuasions; piano melodizing continued through dinner. For tranquilizing, here's almost a must on the suburban nightscape—if the waves of visitors don't break the spell.

La Csarda (via Magnanapoli 6) is a hearty haven if you hunger for Hungarian vittles and violins. **Il Buco** (via Sant'Ignazio 8) has delicious Tuscan steaks; no longer inexpensive but recommendable. **Al Girarrosto Fiorentino** (via Sicilia 44-48) is another Tuscany import; no decorative zing, but tempting kitchen offerings and ultrakind personnel. **La Vigna dei Cardinali** (piazzale Ponte Milvio 34) offered our party a garden in front, a fireplace in a vaulted room, dark timbers, a 22-dish antipasto of so-so quality, poor client attention, and an error on our tab. Nope, not for us.

Angelino a Tormargana (piazza Margana), which we didn't revisit on our latest rounds, has now provoked such strong critical assessments to us that we entirely withdraw our recommendation until we can again make our customary incognito inspection.

In the low lire league, our number one favorite in Rome since 1950 has been **Scoglio di Frisio** (via Merulana 256). *(Please doublecheck its location after your arrival, because plans are well advanced on its shift to larger premises.)* It gets better every year. The Frisio's "Rock" motif is expressed in rough papier-mâché boulders which project from the walls as from the interior of a cave; fishnets, Bowery Art Shop murals, and stalactites pull hard against one another in polychromatic contrast. But whether you're a spelunker, a troglodyte, a fisherman, or an ordinary wanderer, we think the pizza (special oven hot in evenings only), the spaghetti with clam sauce, the filet of sole with peas, mushrooms, and olives (ask for "alla Frisio") are a dream. Many Vatican disciples bring American pilgrims here; Notre Dame alumni can often be found in a genial huddle. Neapolitan atmosphere; go for dinner, not lunch. Patron Augusto Rossi is an extraordinarily warm, gentle, and kind host to North Americans, whom he adores (and all of our team adore *him!*); handsome, smiling Maître Attilio has been his personable and efficient chief of staff for more than 20 years. What a bargain! Recommended with our tongues hanging out. Closed Monday.

Piperno a Monte Cenci (via Monte Cenci 9), a nonkosher pride of the Jewish-Italian ghetto of the Eternal City, has been famous since 1844 as The Artichoke Capital of the World; its specialty comes in Jewish style only (opened, flattened, and sautéed in some deliciously secret fashion). Operated by a vigorous and competent young couple who have improved it so dramatically that now at nearly every meal the house is full. Friendly, noisy, and bustling; old-fashioned furnishings; closed last half of August and various holidays; wine and beer only. **Giggetto** (portico d'Ottavia) is also said to be a winner when it comes to artichokes, as well as Scampi Gratinée, Canneloni, and its antipasto spread; ask for Olindo. **Giovanni** (via Marche) is better than ever in both culinations and atmospherics. Genial service, high spirits, well-prepared offerings, and medium tariffs. Verdict: Agreeable, but run-of-the-mill. **Al Circo Massimo** (via dei Cerchi 53) is about the same. L-shape room; cheeses, pots, and garlic suspended from rafters; bottle-glass windows; chummy atmosphere. Our fresh fish and quail were fair enough. **Tientsin** (via Capo le Case 55) has Chinese vittles which reasonably—but only reasonably —closely resemble American-Oriental. The décor is a perfectly horrid aqua-hued Cathay nightmare, highlighted by an internally illuminated pillar resembling a mammoth Chungking barber pole. Prices that won't hurt that yen, plus a 100-item menu of Eastern goodies. Recommended for the hungry whose vision ranges from 20/400 to 20/625.

The **Wiener Bierhaus** (via della Croce 22) is rated by aficionados of Bratwurst, Kaiserfleisch, Wiener Schnitzel, and similar specialties as one of the best beer halls in town, but after our latest revisit we're going to go for the ham hocks and that's about it. **Old Vienna** (via degli Artisti 25, about 200 yards from the Excelsior Hotel) has become a zestless pizza parlor, a turn which **good** Austrian burghers might well deplore.

Tempio d'Agrippa (pizza della Rotonda 14) is not recommended to Attila the Hun or any contemporary invader of this land. Our food was dreadful, our service worse, and our rotund bill topped a fiasco we still think is outrageous.

Among the *trattorie*, **Al Chianti** (via Ancona 17), also known as "Ernesto & Mario," has a Tuscan ambiance, with about 14 Lilliputian tables in Italian-rustic. Its motif employs enough raffia, straw, and flotsam to titillate the heart of Trader Vic. The substantial viands lose some of their savor under the high-pressure rush-act of the waiters. Nice tone for the price range. For the down-to-basic-earth Roman atmosphere, **Romolo** (via di Porta Settimiana 8 in Trastevere) is still popular among local socialities. Clean; big garden which once belonged to La Fornarina ("The Bakery Girl"), who was Raphael's mistress; sound food; low, low tariffs. **Cesaretto** (via Cesare Beccaria 3) is a workman's favorite; primitive but spotless; delicious spaghetti, Roman baby lamb, a complete meal with wine or beer for about the price of a movie. Nino speaks good English. Very, very plain, but tops for its class. **Da Mario** (via della Vite 64A) comes up with one room, one waiter, and wonderful Tuscan cuisine; clean, inexpensive, and so crowded our elbows are still contused. **Augustea** (via della Frezza 5) offers 2 plant-lined rooms, a free fish dish to start, a good meal in the middle, and a gratis liqueur at the end. Seafood is the mainstay; closed Monday.

Even worthier is **L'Albanese** (via dei Serpenti 148), an unsung candidate we stumbled across while searching hungrily for a place to eat. No English is spoken, but they must have been double-jointed from the way they bent over backward to communicate. Although there are hundreds of similar places in the city, here's a pleasant, no-fireworks example when you forget your guide-book. Closed Sundays.

Something different? **Ambasciata d'Abruzzo** (via Pietro Tacchini 26), up in the Parioli district, provided us with one of the most fun-filled and tummy-filling experiences of a recent Italian circuit. It was crammed to the rafters with laughing locals, a jovial proprietor, and his staff who kept bellowing, "Mangi, mangi, mangi!" ("Eat, eat, eat!") and similar encouragements. Even as the host carries platters to his patronage, he spoons free bites to other clients along his happy route. The moment you sit down, a basket with 17 types of sausage is placed on your table, plus a cutting board, bread, cheese, and knives. Then you are given a stack of plates and told to take anything (and as much) as you want from the terraces of antipasto; we counted 35 different preparations on our visit, and were they ever delicious! Serious gourmands then go on to roasts, fowl, trout, and a menu so long that our vision blurred just glancing at it. Absolutely imperative to reserve in advance, especially on a Saturday after-noon. The entrance, incidentally, is so narrow that you may squeeze in, but if you "Mangi, mangi, mangi!" as the man says, we'd bet you won't be able to squeeze out.

Snacks? Unfortunately there are NO truly authentic American-style nibble nooks available in the entire capital even though there are some attempts toward it. **California** (via Bissolati) is superb for light bites even though its offerings are 99 + % Italian. It sports attractive raiments; the shaded sidewalk café is especially alluring. Our hamburger (ask for it between bread!) and ham sandwich were quite good in flavor but European in presentation and absurdly high in price for this market. Other tariffs that we studied also seemed exorbitant for the fare. Still, for quality it's the best, in our opinion. The **Piccadilly** (piazza Barberini) is a 1250-seat magnum opus which has grouped a snack bar, a cafeteria, 2 restaurants, an English-style pub, and a shop into a single complex. Sadly, its Old Glory-fications of our home-style cookery draw halfmasted praise from us. Foreigners don't seem to go. God save us, there's a **Wimpy** on via Veneto. The **Luau** (via Sardegna 34) is still in a state of flux.

Additional dining places of character are **La Cisterna in Trastevere** (via della Cisterna 13), which has facinating murals, miserable (to us) cookery, and psychologically impervious waiters in eighteenth-century livery, and **Andrea** (via Sardegna 26–28, a block behind the Flora Hotel), which should give you ample satisfaction at medium-to-high prices. **Nini** (via Borgognona 11) is *not* recommended.

Sunny day or starlit night? When "summer treads on heels of spring," the wise traveler follows the Roman custom of escaping to the suburbs for dining and entertainment. **Villa Florio** (see the final portion of "Hotels, Rome"), about 40 minutes from the capital near the Frascati-Grottaferrata junction, is beautifully executed as a country mansion with swimming pool ringed by tables, but it is now so expensive and the crowd is so mixed that we're no longer fond of it. But one we *are* fond of in the immediate vicinity is **Tuscolo** (via Anagnina 241, in Grottaferrata). Its dynastic proprietors are the Blasi tribe, who all pitch in to make this former pasta shop a roaring success as a restaurant. Now matured into 5 individual kitchens, 6 dining rooms, and 3 summer terraces, with the capacity of stuffing 500 tummies at 1 sitting. Open from 11 A.M. until well after midnight; closed Fridays; tykes under every 2nd foot; frequent weddings, confirmations, and other celebrations (most of them, probably, within the Blasi population). Good wholesome homegrown food, and good wholesome fun. **Il Fungo**, in the suburb of E.U.R. about 35 minutes from the Colosseum, features mushrooms on its menu. Perfectly situated in a watertank of Mussolini's former fair grounds; cuisine so-so in savor, but so-so-SOOO high in cost.

Ferrantelli (via Claudio 7) in *Ostia* should happily satisfy the hunger pangs of visitors to the archaeological ruins of nearby Ostia Antica. Good seafood, but no sea view.

Gina in *Fiumicino*, up the strand 1 mile from Ostia, is reported to be excellent. We went for a summer Sunday lunch (heaven help us, because ½-million people were swarming in the area!), but the place was too packed to get in. It is said to have its own fishing boat, the whole catch of which is used exclusively for its patrons. If you really want to go where the action is, head directly for the quayside restaurants of Fiumicino port. Among its prize catches are said to be **Bastianelli al Centro** and **Bastianelli al Molo**. If you have an extra severe case of sea fever, then the small fishing village and beach resort of *Fregene* might be the right prescription. A lot of the Rome film people soak up sun and calories here. All the eateries are ranged along the beach and have cabanas. We hear that **da Mastino** is in with the In-crowd as of this moment.

L'Escargot (out at Appia Antica 46 with a Roman address of Umiltà 34–35) has a farmhouse atmosphere. Timber ceiling strung with hams and salamis;

calico napery and country lamps; fireplace; about 15 tables; photos of film notables and not-so-notables line the walls. Good but unspectacular food; such hospitable service that the client feels cheerfully relaxed; reasonable prices. **Hostaria L'Archeologia** (139 via Appia Antica) is similar in tone. Cattle-shed restaurant with garden in the back; slow but kindly service; excellent fettuccine with foie gras. A sleepy family place that is amiable if you seek relaxation and a simple value. **La Fattoria**, at the approaches to *Fiumicino*, is a happy little tip for dawdlesome air travelers. It offers especially nice garden dining in summer; the inside restaurant draped with sausages, hams, and the like. If your flight departure is delayed, this quiet corner might be just the spot to soothe those jet-frazzled nerves and to rescue you from those horrid restaurants in the terminus itself. **Casale**, at the 10-kilometer marker on via Flaminia, is a just-barely-converted peasant farm still replete with oil lamps, nestling ducks, and haystacks. No sign at entrance; service in barnyard alfresco setting or in 3 ancient storerooms; beamed ceilings and drying corn, peppers, garlic, and onions comprise the unwhitewashed décor. Large grill for roasting chickens or ½-lambs; large self-service antipasto table. A dude's delight. Others of note are **San Callisto**, via Appia Antica 220 (traditional oasis on the old Appian Way), **Trattoria Pancrazio**, near *Campo dei Fiori* (a cave in the Teatro dei Pompeii excavations, always cool on blistering days)—plus, of course, Santa Maria in Trastevere. **Piccolo Mondo** (via Aurora 39-B) also very central, promotes a celebrity reputation, but—an odd but legitimate question—were all of the clips and photos on the walls given by visitors to these precincts? Exceptionally considerate service and a star-rating reception. Amusing if you like crowds. **Checchino**, in the slaughterhouse district of *Testaccio*, is said to be interesting for meats. It's at the foot of a hill made from the rubble of Roman bricks and has some connection with the Academy of Italian Cuisine. Please excuse our vagueness on details since we didn't get by to test it; we are only mentioning it because this one sounded so curious to us. We'll become beefeaters very soon.

And let's not forget the ubiquitous cafés—an important part of the Roman scene, since professional and social lines are often drawn on the customer's choice of hangout. Americans swarm to the area so aptly christened "The Beach"—a name which has stuck as hard as the chewing gum under its sidewalk chairs. This is table-lined via Veneto, home or next-door neighbor of the U.S. Embassy and Consulate, the Excelsior, "the Ambassadors," and Flora hotels (among many). **Caffè Doney**, delight of tourists from Milwaukee, Madras, Manila, and Manchester since the Jurassic Age of travel, has undergone a curious phenomenon: Local celebrities and in-the-swim folk seem to be staying away in droves. We much, much prefer **Harry's Bar**, a 2-minute walk up and across the street to its farthest corner opposite the Hotel Flora. It has no connection with namesakes in other Italian hubs. The awninged sidewalk portion extends one full block. Inside is its comfortable clublike bar featuring platters of splendid appetizers called Tartina, as well as sandwiches on call; the dining room is quiet and elegant. Complete meals with good table wine in the $9 to $11 range served during normal hours; open for drop-in drinks and snacks from 10:30 A.M. to perhaps 2 A.M.; closed Sunday. To us this leaves all of the rest along "The Beach" way below the neap-tide marker; others prefer

Doney's, Cafe de Paris, or Rosatti's, so you pays your money and takes your choice!

Downtown, **Caffè Greco** (via Condotti 86) is historically the revered haunt of painters, sculptors, authors, and people of the arts; Mark Twain liked it so much that you'll find his statue enshrined in this ancient building, now a national monument. **Babington** (piazza di Spagna 23) is beloved by the British; it dispenses passable but miles from remarkable muffins and scones. There are dozens of interesting cafés—each with its distinctive clientele and aura.

Hotels? For elegant luxury lunching or dining, we're specially impressed by **Le Maschere**, that colorful delight in the Grand—a masterpiece of subtle theatrical lighting, live guitar serenades, melodic fountains, silky-smooth service, and truly fabulous pasta creations (38 types in all!). Our recent feast of Bresaola (dried beef appetizer), Pennette alla Boscaiola (a woodland wonder), and Maccaruni di Segni al Prosciutto (a style of fettuccine, not to be confused with macaroni) was sheer, unadulterated heaven. There's a pizza for every day of the week; black tie is requested for the galas each Friday. It's marvelous. We are also very fond of the brilliantly revivified panoramic Roof Garden at the **Eden**. For the maximum yield per lira to entice and charm the taste buds, the **Massimo d'Azeglio** has all the rest buffaloed. (You might disagree, of course, with this personal evaluation.) It is cozy, intimate, and cheerful; it will give you a superb meal in the classic Italian way. The house blue ribbons are won by its Sole Pirata (prepared with ham and black truffles), its Filet Mignon with Mustard Sauce, its Rigatoni Villa d'Este, and its Taglierini d'Azeglio. If you're still drooling, just wait until you try those pastries! No Roman candles or glamour, but if it's only food you're after, here's mouth-watering fare. For scenery, the winter-only roof at the **Hassler** provides excellent offerings in lovely surroundings. The **Excelsior** has improved notably; it's now fine.

Night Life The Italian nightclub usually blooms for about 6 months, and then dies of creeping boredom. Except for certain landmarks, the places which are crowded today might be boarding up their doors tomorrow—so take at least a part of the following with a grain of salt.

In the capital, avoid as you would hungry cobras nearly all of the wee-hour self-termed "glamour" spots clustered in the famous via Veneto area. With a handful of exceptions, a couple of which are listed below, they are grimy, garish, badly ventilated, dimly lit clip joints in which some of the sharpies on hand would pry the gold from their own grandmother's teeth if Granny were suddenly to become immobile.

The previously mentioned **Jackie O'** (via Boncompagni 11, less than a block from via Veneto) is the most ostentatious dazzler. The best description we find for this is the single exclamation, "WOW!" Ground floor above La Graticola (see "Restaurants"); large room with walls and ceilings in shiny black plastic plus mirrors almost anywhere one double-looks; ultramodern tables and trimmings; small bar plus bandstand for 4 musicians; whisky around $10 per cup all-in, with no cover charge; go very, very late. The with-it cinema, theatre, and rock-music, Big Name, Big Talk, Big I'm-Impressing-Everybody Set finds it Heaven Number Six; to us it is so super-ultra-overwhelmingly-blindingly spectacular (and loud!) that please give us cheese, radishes, and The Glenfiddich in bed.

La Clef (via Marche 13, also near via Veneto), designed, built, and operated by tycoon Bruno Borghese of Sans Souci fame (see "Restaurants"), is the most elegant late-night drop-in oasis in the Eternal City. Here you will find a chic, cozy hand-holding rendezvous in a richly modern and discreet milieu. Subdued strains of a singer-pianist from 10 to 12; rock with dancing from 12 to 1; disco gyrations from 1 to 3:30; cover charge and first drink about $10.50; subsequent drinks about $6; open end of September to end of June only. So skillfully conceived that the top of the night-owl society love it and flock here.

La Cabala (via de Monte Brianzo 93), which used to be the most beautiful and fashionable after-dark rendezvous in Italy and beyond, has been turned into a not-very-special disco. *Porca miseria*!

L'Arciliuto (piazza Monte Vecchio 5) is the love nest created by the re- nowned musician, Enzo Samaritani. His romantic den is tucked in a former studio of Raffaello. (Please note the great artist's fresco plastered into the arch just inside the entrance—a priceless windfall which Sig. Samaritani discovered through private research.) The inner structure has been left almost exactly as originally designed by the sixteenth-century Maestro. Vaulted ceiling; sienna-colored walls mellowed by flickering tapers; beige carpets; provincial wood-work. Comfortable leather chairs and divans for sipping, listening, and be-tween-song conversing; lutes and rare stringed instruments forming the decorative motif; piano for intermission tinkling or for accompanying the proprietor as he strums, chants, or softly whispers the melodies of Calabria, Sicily, and other provinces of his musical land. Excellent and expensive drinks; canapés available; suave service; honest accounting. Be sure to get *exact* direc-tions before you set out, because it's in a hard-to-find, tiny courtyard about 3 minutes' walk from Passetto restaurant. If you wish to reserve a table (it is small), telephone 65-94-19. Warm endorsement for seekers of that tranquil evening.

Scarabocchio (piazza dei Ponziani 8) has capitalized on its living-room structure. Angular bar; ring of chairback stools around the piano occupying one corner and most of the spotlighting; divans kneeling at squat tables; illuminated glass floor for dancing; subtle lighting; an audience that works strenuously at getting with it.

Capriccio (via Liguria 38) is down in the depths of the restaurant of the same name. The bar at the entrance is stretched into a giant fishhook; the display-mezzanine resembles a Steuben casement; through the arches is the inner sanctum of red and gold. Small dance floor kept busy by a peppery band; popcorn-patrician patronage. In our opinion, the insurmountable obstacle is that it lacks truly deluxe flair and charm in décor (see above). Just so-so.

Club 84 (via Emilia 84) is still plugged into the elegance circuit. High voltage prices; year-round operation; L-shape, raucous, close, and intimate; small band; no cabaret; companions available but not graspy; slide projections of resort scenes. A nice spot that is honest.

Gattopardo (via Mario dei Fiore 95A) mixes nutrients with its nightwork. Restaurant plus orchestra and its Piper Show; not too costly by local stan-dards. This "Leopard's" lair is targeted to younger nimrods. Did we smell pot in the air? No—that couldn't be, now could it?

The highly advertised **Fascination** was handcuffed by the police sometime back after a fascinating shoot-em-up. It was given a reprieve and changed its name to **Chez Maxim**; that closed as well, and a new cabaret, **Il Carlino**, appeared, perhaps to replace the moniker with yet another. But no matter what it might be called this year, we'd exert extreme wariness. **La Tour Hassan** (via dei Serviti 28) is said to be an Arabian-style citadel offering worldwide slave-market companionship (Lonely Male Dept.), plus a highly touted floor show. Since we haven't yet hung our burnous here, we don't know how hard it might try to milk us itinerant camels from the open spaces of North America. Nothing would surprise us. The **1001**? One-thousand-and-one times, no.

To round out the nightscape, **Dave's** (in the Hotel Savoia) is a second-rate celebrity ringsider for winter sippers, and **Il Club** (piazza San Lorenzo in Lucina) is a disco-whip cracked by a Neopolitan maestro.

During the warm months, "**Brigadoon**" (about 8 miles along via Aurelia, not far from the big AGIP Motel) is the pacesetter in the alfresco circuit. Name bands and recording artists; First-class rather than Deluxe; in-and-outdoor dinner dancing; small cabaret; relatively medium tabs and lower middle-class patronage. Balmy weather fun for the Non-U. The **Bagaglino** (via Due Macelli 75), is not for the average outlander any more, because comedy and satire in the Italian language have become its features.

The **Mini Club** (via Emilia 48) functions on 2 floors with 2 separate bars and 2 independent coveys of pickups. This tiny microversion of the aforementioned Club 84 could use a bit more grooming, but its tariff levels run ⅓ to ½ of those at the pacesetters. No cover charge, no minimum, no stay-until-3-A.M.-policy.

Tonight's version of *la dolce vita* can be found—at fancy prices—at **Scacco Matto** ("Checkmate"), off the arty Piazza del Popolo. The address is via Ferdinando di Savoia 6. Mostly for the young.

Piper Club, far out at via Tagliamento 9, now features discothèque-nology only, having sent its show over to the previously mentioned Gattopardo. The hostesses attend to a more mature and conservative clientele than in former years. Still, quite a number of young people pipe in. First drink at $8; searching for an identity; not our bag but to each his own special thing.

Medical services Italian doctors are renowned throughout Europe for their excellence. The better ones are as modern in techniques and practices as your good family physician or surgeon at home; complete stocks of American, English, Swiss, German, and local medicines are available in profusion. We were tremendously impressed by the thoroughness, efficiency, and skill with which Dr. Salvatore Mannino tackled assorted ailments of ours. We cannot embarrass Dr. Mannino by directly recommending his service to readers, because this would be a breach of his professional ethics; we can only say that if we should ever pick up anything from a hangnail to yaws in the Eternal City, he's 100% our man. New York-trained, he speaks perfect English. His office is via Lisbona 9; his phone is 84 48 712. Another topliner is the Yankee-born internist, Dr. Frank Silvestri. You'll find this personable stateside-schooled specialist, plus 3 of his English-speaking Italian colleagues, at the American Medical Center, via Ludovisi 36 (phone 464-143 or 485-706).

All-night drugstores throughout Italy carry either an illuminated red cross or the word *Farmacia* in red. Many U.S. pharmaceuticals (manufactured in Italy) are available.

Mail Services: We suppose that *somewhere* in the world there might be a mail carrier that is as total a disaster as the Italian Postal Service; based on our own dismal experience, however, we doubt it. Hard-pressed citizens and savvy visitors use commercial couriers such as Rome's **Missori and Tavani** (viale M. Gelsomini 14) to deliver anything of importance. If you have absolutely no recourse but to use it, please *be sure* to register your letter or package before affixing the stamps. Keep a duplicate, if possible. Better still, save the item and drop it into the first mailbox you spot that is not on Italian soil.

Shopping Before proceeding further, here are warnings to all friends of this book which we hope will save them from being bilked:

Every major tourist center in the nation is now plagued by armies of "steerers." If any well-dressed, charming, suave man or woman of *any* nationality strikes up a conversation with you anywhere and then smoothly suggests that you go with either while he or she picks up a purchase, be measured for a fitting, or similar dodge—BE ON YOUR GUARD IMMEDIATELY. There is at least a 98% chance that they are "shills" whose game is to sucker innocent travelers into dishonest establishments which give them a commission on everything that their victims can be high-pressured into buying.

Be careful when you buy tortoiseshell objects. And be *certain* the item is made from a type which can be legally imported into the U.S. as well as into your state, because many objects are made from endangered species which would be confiscated. The genuine article is always uniformly opaque.

For further tips on shady practices, please turn to the "Local Rackets" section.

In spite of these hustlers, Italy is a wonderland for the shopper.

Our ★ ★ ★ ★ recommendations are individually noted.

Men's and ladies' clothes of various kinds: ★ ★ ★ ★ **Brioni** (via Barberini 79) is a pacesetter for the North American male who wants the best. It collaborates directly with top textile manufacturers in producing exclusive Brioni silk, wool, cotton, and linen designs, creates a complete parallel line of shoes, ties, and accessories to blend with the colors and stylings of its models, and influences world style trends. This establishment is Italy's oldest and most famous High Fashion center for men. If you want to be conservative, brilliant Gaetano Savini-Brioni will make you très soigné, but if you really want to knock them out, choose one of their stunning black silk dinner coats or other custom-made beauties which are their badge and their seal. As a warm gesture of our 30 years of friendship, the founder-owner wants to give any *Fielding's* reader who buys 3 of his marvelous original silk ties a 4th one as his personal present. *Ave!* Normal 3-to-4 day delivery on custom garments; ask for the gentlemanly General Manager Dr. Ettore Perrone-Brioni or our special chum, Edwin Mula. The adjoining Ladies' Boutique, run by the Maestro's daughter, Gigliola, will keep your gal busy, happy, and in mischief. Super-super.

★ ★ ★ ★ **Angelo** (via Bissolati 34/36, a branch at piazza Trinità dei Monti 17-A, and another in London) is equally magnificent. Handsome, talented, magnetic Angelo Vittucci with his similarly gifted and personable partners, Aldo Uggeri and Carlo Illari, made an instantaneous success when they opened this elegant house in 1963. And with their taste, imagination, and own special magic, how well they deserve it! Gorgeous handworked suitings in silks, worsteds, tropicals and others; unique foulard linings; additional full line of chic ready-made suits at lower prices; all haberdashery imaginable; finished delivery in 3-to-4 days. Also just as stupendous.

In this same luxury bracket, **Cucci**, **Caraceni**, and **Cifonelli** are all master cutters, too—but Brioni and Angelo have American-style savvy. Move warily among the smaller, less famous, less costly cutters, because they are all too apt to victimize you. Our closets are stuffed with single-purchase trial suits so butchered that we wouldn't wear them to a chihuahua fight. In all custom-made garments, always, *always* find time for 3 fittings. A minimum of 2 fittings normally does not work.

There are dozens upon dozens of boutiques throughout the capital. ★ ★ ★ ★ ★ **La Mendola** (piazza Trinità dei Monti 15) is our candidate as THE champion. It was founded by Mike La Mendola and the beloved late Jack Savage. Mike's winning personality and design genius spark its vast array of elegant exclusives at price levels for all budgets, at least 50% below chic U.S. resort tariffs. Two of his most famous specialties are the trademarked La Mendola prints on uncrushable lightweight silk and wool jersey, silk chiffon-Georgette and crepes in day dresses and suits, cocktail and evening wear, year-round cruise wear, play and travel clothes, and his ingenious "magic dress" of pure silk jersey which can be worn short or long, at your whim—and, without wrinkling, can be sent home in an airmail envelope! All of these exhibit that inspired La Mendola dash. Extra affection is lavished on difficult figures. His frequent fashion shows have taken him worldwide. His staff is thoroughly experienced in international shipping. Ask for Mr. Mike or Mme. Anne (his Gal Friday)—and enjoy. Terrific!

For knitwear our choices are **Laura Aponte** (via Gesu e Maria 10), **Trico** (via delle Carozze), and **Julian de Ville** (via Veneto 183).

Valentino, **Princess Irene Galitzine**, **Fontana**, **Mila Schon**, **Lancetti**, **Riva**, **Tiziani**, and **Albini** have the most exalted reputations currently in the *haute couture* scene. **Capucci**, **André Lange**, **Balestra**, and **Antonio de Luca** are rising. In this top group you'll be rocked an Arabian Princess' fortune. **Emilio Pucci** is *the* designer for blouses and slacks. **Fantasia** has lovely accessories at high tariffs. **Roberta**, of Venice fame (piazza di Spagna 30), is superb for its gorgeous but very expensive handbags, luggage, and coordinated wearables.

Leather: **Gucci** (via dei Condotti 21) is indisputably the most plush. Its 2-floor premises are rich and its stocks are elegant, but we think that its excellent—sometimes superb—merchandise is grossly overpriced. Perhaps you'll disagree. **Leandro** (via Sistina 21) is Gucci's most serious challenger. **Fendi** (via Borgognona 36A, 36B, 41) is a more down-to-earth candidate, as is **L. Righini** (via dei Condotti 76). **Tivoli Leathers** (via San Martino della Battaglia 60-66) is also fine.

Jewelry and objets d'art: ★ ★ ★ ★ ★ **Bulgari** (via Condotti 10) is one of the most famous treasure houses in the world. On one hand, you will find *the* Thousand and One Nights in jewels—creations of such dazzling beauty that not even the legendary Scheherazade could find the proper words to describe their magnificence to King Shahriyar. On the other hand, shoppers of our bracket meet a vast selection of things that are within almost everybody's price range—all in the exquisite Bulgari taste. Profusely displayed are unique collections of diamonds, rubies, emeralds, sapphires, and superb pearls; the biggest private assemblage of English and continental antique silver in Europe; very rare antique Chinese jades and hard stones; Renaissance jewelry and 16th-century rock crystals; fantastically crafted, historic, one-of-a-kind boxes and watches—enough prizes to dizzy even the most experienced connoisseur. You will be greeted with traditional warmth, patience, and expertise by 3rd-generation Gianni, Paolo, or Nicola Bulgari. There are aristocratic branches in New York, Geneva, Monte Carlo and Paris. They would be happy even if you wish only to look—and we envy your dreams!

Gloves: We've long believed that the small, old-line specialist, ★ ★ ★ ★ ★ **Catello d'Auria** (via Due Macelli 55), does the best job on the Italian Peninsula. All that the d'Auria family has cared about since 1894 is making finer gloves than any other craftsmen. They have succeeded.

Religious articles: ★ ★ ★ ★ ★ **Al Pellegrino Cattolico** (via di Porta Angelica 83) offers complete stocks for the devout. They will have your rosaries blessed by the Pope and delivered to your hotel at no extra fee. Honest, 100% dependable, and fine; none better.

Unusual treasures for the home: ★ ★ ★ ★ **Bottega Danese** (via della Scrofa 96) is THE Danish shop in Rome—small, sweet, intimate, with lovingly selected tempters from Scandinavia at prices dramatically lower than in the North. Here you will find elegant porcelains, hand made sterling silver, characteristically-styled household items in teak, strikingly unique knitwear from the Faroe Islands and Iceland, typically droll gifts, traditional Christmas plates the year around and many, many more enchantments. Co-owners Mogens Lykkeberg and Ole Bang will welcome you with Danish smiles. What fun this is to browse—and to buy!

Cameos, coral, and related items: ★ ★ ★ ★ ★ **Giovanni Apa Co.** (piazza Navona 26–27 and branch on the Tiburtina Road to Tivoli; see "Excursion to Pompeii") is the world's finest specialist. Both these shops are operated by the manly sons of this famous family. Incomparable.

Strikingly charming Italian pottery and handicrafts: In '73 ★ ★ ★ ★ ★ **Bella Copia** (via dei Coronari 8) was launched by attractive Americans Joan and Kellogg Smith to bring together a wide selection of Italian handicrafts normally not found outside of their border-to-border local regions. Featured here are hand-painted creations of 40 independent potters, multicolored majolica articles, other objects in traditional hill-town patterns, signed Annarosa creations, Florentine and Faenza Chinese Carnation or Dog Rose plates, handmade wooden kitchen utensils, marble candlesticks, cotton and woolen handweavings, and much more. Happily different; highly recommended.

Silks and other materials by the yard: **Galtrucco** (via del Tritone 14) has everything. Fine.

Shoes: For ladies, ★ ★ ★ ★ **Lily of Florence** (via Lombardia 38; see "Florence") is the exclusive purveyor of the famous Amalfi line. Mrs. Power, herself an American, is the gracious and warm-hearted director of this branch. For men, ★ ★ ★ ★ **Samo** (via Veneto 189, via del Tritone 204 and via Sistina 106) is the fleetest and most graceful runner in Italian footwear.

Art Galleries: **Gallerias Schneider**, owned and operated by Americans, handles some of the top Italian painters. **L'Obelisco**, **Barcaccia**, and **Il Camino** are well known. There are more than 50 salons in the capital.

Books: **The Lion Bookshop** (via del Babuino 181) has large stocks of reading matter—or try the **American Book Shop** (via delle Vite 57), which is also versatile.

Drugs, cosmetics, and toiletries: **Lepetit Farmacia** (corso Umberto 417) has the largest American and English assortment in the capital.

Antiques: Via Giulia is a good street for general hunting. Via dei Coronari and via Cola di Rienzo are the lower-price centers. Piazza Fontanello Borghese also offers jewelry. Watch out for counterfeits.

Flea Market: Also be careful! This operates on Sundays from 6 A.M. to midafternoon; it is a tourist trap to end all tourist traps. If you absolutely *must* see it, go very, very early, as the dealers do, bargain fiercely, and try to take along an Italian friend to protect your interests. Completely avoid all "genuine Etruscan" articles, because they're fakes.

Please DON'T buy: Sheffield "antiques" or "old paintings" or "jewelry" in small establishments, phony "Made in Switzerland" watches from street vendors, *any* glass items on the island of Murano, or imported perfume (lethal duties).

Shopping hours: There are so many local variations that it's wise to check first with the concierge of your hotel. Wherever the *sesta* (siesta) custom is observed (Rome, Naples, the South), most stores are open from 9 A.M. to 1 P.M. and from 4 P.M. to 7 or 8 P.M. Everything is open at 3 P.M. in Milan, Turin, Genoa, and Bologna.

Dedicated shophounds: Space is too limited here for further listings—so please consult the purse-size, 25th Anniversary edition of *Fielding's Selective Shopping Guide to Europe* for more stores, more details, and more lore throughout the nation.

Other Targets

ABANO   For overnighting, the **Orologio**, with 2 swimming pools and a private park, is the gong-ringer for first place. The **Trieste** would come next, followed in a lower category by the fresh **Savoia**, the **Columbia**, and **Bristol**.

AGRIGENTO   It's (1) **Jolly**, (2) **Della Valle** (air-conditioned; amateurish management; fierce cookery).

ALASSIO   Try the **Mediterraneo** first, then the **Alfieri**.

AMALFI   an important maritime republic during the Middle Ages, is also the target of dozens of daily bus tours from Naples, which pause here for refreshment on the spectacular (but not too difficult) coastal drive between Salerno and Sorrento. Small, increasingly inviting village; handsome yet modest hotels; definitely worth a visit or even a stopover.

If you do pause, the **Santa Caterina** evokes sighs with a patio 150 feet above the sea. Redecorated units for 90 guests in the main building, plus accommodations for 30 more in villas spotted along the lemon grove slopes. Balconies for all; elevators to the beach plus rippling swimmery; well-prepared food with vegetables grown on the premises; service as crisp as the lettuce. The 50-sancta **Luna Convento** also rises proudly above the coastline; you'll find a lift from the street to the hotel, a pool, a fresh dining room and terrace, a summer-only nightclub and a notable kitchen. The **Cappuccini-Convento**, by far the most famous (a marble plaque here recalls the visit of "Enrico Wadsworth Longfellow"), has a fantastic setting in a twelfth-century monastery, but some time ago we found the administration so uninspired, the food so tasteless, the rooms so unattractively furnished, and the atmosphere so brashly geared for tourism that we did not care to overnight here. The **Pensione Sole** is a clean, quiet, family-run house with a bounty of comforts for its extra-low tariffs. A fine buy for the money. The **Excelsior** at *Porgerola*, a twisty 15 minutes up, teeters viewfully above the town. If awards are ever given for tranquillity, this one should win a Peace Prize. First-class category; modern ambiance in a sawtooth layout; all 90 seafront units have bath; most have private terrace. The Second-class **Residence** is no longer recommended. **Caleidoscopio**, about 2 miles from the center, overlooks (but is not on) the sea. Every room with bath or shower; all front accommodations with balconies; large pool; substantial cuisine; a happy choice, in a modest way, for travelers who seek calm. The well-situated **Miramalfi** is budget class, with a good building but mediocre food and service; it, too, has a concrete-lined swimmin' hole. Staircase construction with ample parking space at the uppermost rung; outstanding view. The First-category **Saraceno** courts posh pashas from its perch just below the highway at *Conca dei Marini*. Here's a cliff-hugging structure linked by mirrored elevator to a private beach and jammed-crammed with gimmickry. Whitewashed lobby and lounges; more Middle Eastern memorabilia than Suleiman the Magnificent's tomb; vaulted restaurant-grill with tiled floor; gilt cave-dwelling bar; lower-level pool and mini-chapel. In addition to the so-called "Royal Apartment," there are 60 adequately sized doubles with showers, chilled air, TV's, Frigo-bars, more Arabesque accouterments, and waterfront terraces. The nearby Second-class **Belvue**, a 5-minute drive toward Positano, is a fair roadside spot —if you don't face that noisy roadside. It offers only 24 bedchambers; each with balcony, terrace, and bath or shower. Its bright, hard-working manager is doing a commendable job in converting this former pension into a full-blown resort hostelry. Good news for money-savers.

The best food in this town can be had at the **Luna**, in our judgment. **Santa Caterina** would be next. **Cappuccini** has the most spectacular panorama, but the cookery curled our hair into neat little rows of granny knots. **La Marinella**, on the beach, is the relaxed Poseidon for seafood specialties, since the operators net their own catch for the skillets; it has ocean-floor-level prices, too. **Ciccio**, **Cielo e Mare**, **Lo Smeraldino**, **Lido Azzurro**, and **Flavio Gioria** are additional possibilities.

AOSTA offers no luxury nests. **Europe**, the most modern, tops our list. Next comes **Couronne et Poste**, followed by the chalet-style **Valle d' Aosta** The Rank organization of England must have completed its new entry by now; we're anxious to rank it. All are for serious skiers.

ARENZANO, that pleasant little fishing village 13 miles west of Genoa, boasts the First-class **Residenza Punta San Martino**, which sits high on St.

Martin's Cape, with 2 pools, 9 holes of golf, tennis, restaurant, and nightclub. Despite these attractions, it is not suggested as a stopover for North Americans.

ARGENTARIO   region? See Port'Ercole for **Il Pellicano**.

ASOLO   Refer to "Venice."

ASSISI   is a wonderful little place—for about half a day, if you're average. That's enough time to admire the renowned Basilica of St. Francis, to be wooed fleetingly by its Romanesque romanticisms, and to drink in the view of the plains below. If you'd like a scholarly and pleasant guide, the brothers at the San Damiano Convent are beloved by many Americans; no charge, of course —just alms to the church, which are voluntary. Except for these, what you've got are substandard hotels, approximately 100 tourist-junk shops, and approximately 1000 other excursionists. Pretty overrated for lengthy lingering, but ideal for a passing flirtation. If you do sleep over, the **Subasio** has the eyeful, but the air-conditioned **Umbra** has the best rooms; **Windsor Savoia** and **Giotto** are both passable. All are chilly in the cool months due to their high altitude and low heating standards. **Hotel Giotto** is the culinary choice followed closely by the **Umbria**. **Subasio Hotel** gives indifferent fixed meals or à la carte, but there's a magnificent vista; you'll find lots of bus excursionists. **La Taverna dell'Arco** is the pick of independents. **Bibo** is tops for snacks.

BARI,   founded by the Illyrians and civilized by the Greeks, is the chief port and commercial mart on Italy's heel; next to Naples, it's the most important Peninsular city in the South. The crypt of St. Nicholas, patron saint of gift-giving and the inspiration of Santa Claus, is here (his symbol of 3 brass balls was later purloined by pawnbrokers). Leading attraction is the famous Levant Fair (18 days around mid-Sept.); otherwise it offers fair swimming, a few antiquities, below-average hotels and restaurants, and little of interest.

Skip it if you can and try for shelter at one of the coastal resorts farther south. This center is busy, jammed, and dirty. The **Palace** has 150 air-cooled rooms, all with bath or shower and most with terrace; back-alley location off the main traffic artery; garage. The best of a very poor lot. In a lower category, the **Grand & Oriente**, the **Victor**, the **Leon d'Oro**, and the **Windsor Residence** all reflect degrees of modernity or renovation. The Second-class **La Baia**, at nearby *Palese*, is chiefly a luncheon excursion point, but it should be considered as a worthy alternative. Private garden and beach; comfortable enough. All others not recommended. If you have time to drive 35 miles to *Alberobello* (halfway to Brindisi), you might enjoy **dei Trulli**. Thirty rooms in 20 unique, conical buildings called *truli;* some accommodations with fireplaces and living rooms; swimming pool. This entire village of beehive-shape structures has been deemed a national monument.

For dining, the pick of the midtowners are the **Mediovale La Taberna** and **La Vecchia Bari**. Suburban choices, however, have more appeal to us. **Adriatico**, featuring sea denizens, has improved; we like it, but wonder why a piscatorial house in a Catholic country is shuttered on Fridays. **Grotto**

Regina, at Torre Mare, is okay for mingling with the local chichis and hes. We've had good reports on **Marc Aurelio a Mare**, a 5-mile coastal drive to Palese; fish and barbeques are its specialties. **La Pignata**, back in town, also serves finny fare of renown. Both **La Taverna** and **Taverna Verde** have fallen from our grace; no longer recommended.

BELLAGIO   counts as one of its hospitality treasures the 100-room **Grand Hotel Villa Serbelloni**, a national monument that has operated as a hostelry since 1872, residing today in an enclave of land belonging to the Rockefeller Foundation. Lakeview terrace flanked by palm trees in its park; small sandy *lido* plus a heated pool; main salon with frescoed ceilings, parquet floor, and working fireplace; spectacular garden vista from the restaurant; outstanding kitchen with superb wines. Venetian and Florentine bedchambers come with home-style comfort; about half boast waterfront reflections; only 4 feature balconies. Personally we prefer the north wing, especially suite #160, a corner choice. Proprietors Rudy Bucher and his wife keep this expensive pearl gleaming from April to October annually—so sparkling, in fact, that it is fit for a doge.

BOLOGNA,   boasting about 500-thousand residents, has long had a Communist government; some call it "the buckle in the country's Red Belt". It is better known as the seat of the oldest university in the world (the word "university" was invented here) and the richest, highest-caloried fodder of the nation. Busy, no-nonsense atmosphere; more than 20 miles of arcaded walks; leaning towers; splendid palaces designed by such masters as Palladio and da Vignola; 10 museums with treasures from Etruscan to modern times; National Gallery with works by 56 great painters, including Raphael's "St. Cecilia"; villa and mausoleum of Guglielmo Marconi. "Baloney" originated in Bologna; if you'd like to sample the original article, ask for Mortadella. Incidentally, if you arrive by train, be certain to take the West (Ouest) exit—NOT the East (Est). There are no taxis at the latter. Est is very remote, requiring the time and money of a 15-minute trek plus a wasted tip to the porter.

Among hotels, the city leads off its parade with the Deluxe **Royal Carlton**, located near the station. Manager Piero Moderna, a cherished friend who for years ran the Florence Excelsior like a dream, now is at the helm of this young and highly stylish cruiser. It couldn't have a better skipper and you couldn't be in better hands. The taste overall is an exquisite meld of modernity and tradition, with every comfort available and every convenience provided. Well run kitchen; excellent cave with the accent on Italian vintages; superb Royal Grill that is truly regal; handsome American bar backed by a breakfast room. Total of 250 bedchambers including 22 suites; colors varying from powder blue to cognac to olive green to salmon; extravagant artwork on which millions were spent by newspaper magnate Attilio Monti. Easily Bologna's leading light. Slightly dimmer is the lower-wattage **Internazionale**, a 2-part structure dating from the sixteenth century and 1972. Of its 140 units more than half are singles; both of these Monti hostelries come with ample garage space —an important factor in this cluttered town. Well below these comes the **Residence Elite**, which started life in 1973 as an apartment house and has undergone a beneficial conversion for the traveler. Many suites, some with kitchenettes; charming restaurant with bottles in vitrines for décor; copious buffet popular with Bolognese. An elite treat. The **Garden** has an out-of-center situation, about 5 minutes by taxi from the city's heart; ocher-hued stucco building; glass-enclosed ground-floor portico surrounding a spacious greenery-filled courtyard (obviously the seed of its name); air conditioning on request; garage with service attendants. All 83 soundproofed bedchambers with radio and telephone; furnishings inclined to be rather spindly copies of provincial styles; functional but small baths, some with showers only. Recommended. The **Jolly**, facing the rail station, is more commercial in tone. Chilly ambiance; 2 dining rooms; spacious lounges; 200 units, all with bath; fully air-conditioned. Always booked solid by visiting salesmen, so be sure to nail down your reservation. **Milano-Excelsior**, also opposite the station, gets better every year. Shiny, dirt-free throughout; 109 bedrooms, all with radio, telephone, and bath; 6 very pleasant suites; double windows on the front side; amiable personnel who aim to please. This house owns the neighboring 108-room **Alexander**, also a solid value at an even lower tab. The Second-class **Roma**, which we'd place in a higher category, is a budgeteer's delight, particularly since it was partially renovated. Midtown situation, one block off the central piazza; hotel bus service to and from the station; covered parking area; intimate public rooms; 91 units, all with telephone and many with large private terrace; 55 baths or showers. Replete with good cheer and kindness. **Crest**, on the outskirts near the congress center, offers 164 clean and cheerfully simple shelters. All's here for a pleasant repose. Dropping to Third-class, the 17-room **Kennedy** is out of the center, but it is air-conditioned. We're told that **Tre Vecchi's** 92 cells are superior for its class, but as much has not been said about the service in its dining room. The **Fiera** is young but unexciting. The **Academia** is about the same. The **Cristallo**? Never in a thousand years for this wayfaring stranger. The **Palace** is clean but too decrepit to consider. Other bottom-barrel choices are **San Donato**, **Nettuno**, and **Europa**.

Bologna is properly famous for its kitchens. **Al Pappagallo** (the "Parrot") is known from Zagreb to Zamboanga for its rich, ounce-manufacturing fare. Don't let its nonfancy mien deceive you for 2 seconds, because here, IF you hit it right, can be a happy experience. Unfortunately, this author and a host of readers have been hitting it notably wrong these days. Our latest meal was —to be charitable—even more ordinary than any of our previous repasts. Despite this teetering, its reputation is weighty and its cookery is _so_ right whenever it is right. Closed Mondays.

Resteria Luciano (via Nazario Sauro 19), infinitely more steady in its skillet-craft, is pushing Al Pappagallo mercilessly. On one recent circuit (incognito, as usual), this elf-size gem dished up one of the finest meals in that area. Please don't expect physical charm and eye appeal, because they are negligible. Two very plain rooms behind the kitchen; all 12 tables occupied almost exclusively by local citizenry; walls lined with Luciano's cooking diplomas and awards; no English spoken. Start with his heavenly Manicaretto Garisenda (green pasta roll with lightly smoked ham and a grated Parmesan cheese garnish), and finish with his yumptious Merengo di Ponteassieve (an aerated and iced meringue dessert). Cheers and salutes to this splendid little gastronomic haven. **Nello**

(via Montegrappa2), sometimes known only by its street name, is composed of 3 levels, each with its own personality (we prefer the vaulted cellar with wine cradles and hanging meats); slow-footed but quick-tongued service which tends to push the house specialties—with good reason, since these are the best by far; now expensive; more than adequate for better than average regional dining. **Tre Vecchi** has moved to near the fairgrounds; it remains worthy, with medium-low prices. **Don Rodrigo** (via della Zecca) features international cookery. It is popular with after-theater and post-operatic calorie hunters, as is **Don Quijote**. **Tre Galli d'Oro** ("Three Golden Cocks") and **Nerina** (behind Hotel Roma) come next. **Diana** is highpriced for Second class. For quality at lower cost, try **Al Contoncino** or **Antico Brunetti**. **Château Bellevue** is for summer excursionists. About 15 minutes from the city, up the San Luca funicular; good vista and soothing ambiance on a nice day, but the pot-and-pan-man needs a few more lessons. **Fagiano** (via Calcavinazzi 2) is typical and cheap.

BOLZANO's upland valley offers the aging **Park Laurins** as the choicest for overnighting. This one is smack-dab in the middle of town, but it is peacefully embraced by tall shade trees and a somnolent garden with a private swimming pool. Improved refurnishings in many of its 120 accommodations and 4 suites; lovely terraces for breakfasting or bucolic lounging; open Easter to October 1. If you opt for silence and the amenities of 1910, look no further. The faster-paced **Grifone**, under the same management and with the same rates, draws a livelier clientele. Three restaurants plus a large, coolish bar; 140 unfancy units and 65 baths; garniture in Tyrolean Baroque and Biedermeier. Tops for the young in heart. The flamboyant **Alpi** boasts 120 bedchambers— each with bath or shower. Ceramic-and-marble lobby, somewhat cramped dimensions; air conditioning. The **Scala** has taken admirable steps toward modernizing; the **Luna** also is in a new phase. The **Citta** may delude you by its attractive public rooms—but our love affair with this house stops right there. Seldom do we see such poorly maintained, dismal, and totally depressing "first-line" bedrooms; only the restaurant's passable pasta keeps this one's head above water.

At dinnertime, the leader is the handsomely inviting Grill of the **Hotel Grifone**, which is intimate, colorful, and international in its appeal. Among the independents, **Wienerwald** is a link in the low-price ubiquitous European chain of the same name. The **da Cesare** is pretty good for regional platters. **Vesuvio** fires up crispy pizza; so does **Veruschka**. The **Caterpillar** wiggles up on the outskirts and it's worth a visit.

BORDIGHERA (San Remo region) offers the **Grand del Mare** with its unusual structure. To take advantage of the sea and to avoid highway disturbances, the hotel plus the pool area and surrounding park were jacked up onto struts while the land was filled in beneath. Entrance via an underground parking apron with open _pluvium;_ stunning modernistic pool, with white metallic lily pads for diving or sunning; private beach; conservatory with 50-yard glass wall that rises or falls away to open air at the flick of a switch; 2 restaurants; Charleston nightclub with poolside portholes; 3-part bar; one wing of private apartments; 80 seafront rooms with modern or traditional decor (we prefer the latter). What a honey of a twenty-first-century hostelry this is! Please say hello to Manager Luigi Scianda (for 16 years at the Grand in Rome).

BRINDISI,   the ferry takeoff point for Greece, is an important but woefully inadequate, dregs-ridden crossroads for motorists. If you've prepurchased your ferry passage—and we beg you to do this—plan to arrive only before departure time and overnight either aboard or almost anywhere else up or down the pike. This hub is a blotch on the touristic map. Your choice here is between the **Internazionale** (on the sea) with 85 silo-stark, old rooms, all with bath or shower, or the even less appealing, centrally located **Jolly**. The others are Third-class and recommended only for Marine boot-camp aspirants. Please continue to watch out for pickpockets, dope peddlers, and flimflam artists. They run rampant on the streets, in the ticket agency lines, and at the port. We personally experienced an unsuccessful jostling by a light-fingered team of woman and 9-year-old son. We also witnessed other attempts here. Watch your car, too!

Bring your own picnic basket to this disgusting town—and we're not kidding. Everything we found here was either wretched in quality or served in such seemingly unsanitary surroundings that we settled for a boiled egg and bottled beer. Should hunger overcome you, the dining room of the **Hotel Internazionale** is probably the best option of the scruffy lot. If you're heading for Greece on one of the sleek overnight ferries, you may be able to dine in one of the clean, bright cafeterias or relatively posh saloons aboard. Be extra-careful, however, because we presumably paid for vittles on one tub and received nothing—nor was there even food service for independent travelers. The oily-tongued ticket agents who clog the port area might promise champagne and nightingales' tongues flambé; we would have been satisfied with even a crust of bread and nonrancid butter on our miserable voyage.

CAMPO CARLO MAGNO,   in the Dolomites, offers the restful altitudinous **Golf Hotel**—with what else but a golf course! Ski lifts and everything for outdoor types; rustic lumber-lined dining room for hungry types; peaceful wood-paneled bedrooms for sleepy types. It's almost always filled at Christmas and the first 3 weeks in August by year-ahead enthusiasts. This luxuriously rebuilt chalet-style nook high, high in the hills, is fetching.

CAPRI   is the Jekyll and Hyde of Italian resorts. In summer it has become a cheap, flamboyant hive swarming with sexual partners of myriad persuasions, phony Bohemians, and off-the-record weekenders. Saturation point is reached around August 15, the midsummer holiday of Ferragosto, when a procession carrying a figure of the Madonna parades through the little central piazza. Off Season, however, it is as lovely as it ever was. Blue Grotto; funicular from main port to main village; chair lift to mountain peak; from May 1 to September 30, private cars banned from the tiny isle (fines for disobeying this rule can hop from $80 to $800); taxis and buses available throughout the year; one small, so-so beach at Marina Piccola; fast hydrofoil service (30 minutes) which skims atop the waves from Naples to Capri and returns in half the time of the less expensive—but much more crowded—regular service. In spring or fall you might love it; in summer, Elba (to the north) is a far better bet.

For those who linger, Capri captures many aristocratic hearts with the centrally located **Quisisana**, which never diminishes in its mandate for excellence. Its management is taking giant strides to maintain or better its amenities. Lobby, enlarged and refashioned Colombaia Restaurant, handsome English bar (with live music), nightclub, heated swimming pool, kitchen, shops. Bid for the seafront units only; the back ones face the boisterously noisy footpath just off the town square. Here is solid, old-style, cool-tempered luxury at its tastefully zestful best. A tip of our *cappèllo* to Sig. Dante Cattaruzza, to the supremely helpful Concierge Vicenzo Russo, and to all the staffers who keep this ship sailing so very smoothly.

For perhaps a younger, amorous clientele, the elegant little **Punta Tragara** could qualify as a honeymoon capital of the West. The burnt-ocher, villa-style hideaway was designed by Le Corbusier in 1927 and converted into a hotel in '73; a prohibition against animals and children under 12 insures tranquillity. Graceful seaview thermal pool and salt water bath on cliff; adjoining bar and dining room; unusual, whimsical sunning tiers; Taverna disco-quarter for guests only; sumptuous interiors even though life is oriented to one of the most breathtaking stretches of Mediterranean coast one can find; glorious comfort-laden bedrooms and suites. Overall, here is a sneak preview of what paradise must be like—provided you've come with the right Adam or Eve. Open Easter until October 15. A delight!

The **Luna** also beams with honors. Marvelous view of the Faraglioni cliff on the seaside and L-curving for a townscape panorama along the other shank; one of the quietest sites of any Capri hostelry; entrance via a 100-yard vine-covered path bordered by cascades of blossoms; full air conditioning; swimming pool. Top First-class (not Deluxe) category: 58 rooms; extra-good plumbing in all the better accommodations; somewhat clashy Italian provincial furnishings; generally more space than most new hotels can boast in this pinchpenny era; same Vuotto family ownership as the cozy little La Pineta and Flora (see below). Director Aldo Strina, its original architect and the owner's son-in-law, operates this Capri-ccio. Recommended. The face-lifted **Tiberio Palace** commands a wonderful vista at one of the most convenient perches on the island; traditionally sound cuisine which we hope Proprietor Avino, a Neapolitan industrialist who enjoys this hosting as a sideline, will maintain; full-time direction by Anthony Ferraro. A revivified restaurant and bar; a sizzling grill-*pizzeria;* spick-and-span furniture throughout; air conditioning, radio, and TV. **La Palma** stands in stacked-arcade fashion. Alfresco terrace for sipping and sunning; sauna-solarium complex; wide corridors; superb maintenance. All 80 amply proportioned chambers provide air conditioning, bath or shower, balcony, and Frigobar. Good and even getting better. The **Regina Cristina**, despite the attractive pool it shares with the Villa San Felice, seemed to us once more on our latest revisit to be marking time. Present total of 48 bedchambers, all with showers; 27 with terraces; high decibel level; furniture either tiki or taki. Although one of our twin beds was comfortable, the other felt as though it might have been bought surplus from the Naples Flea Market.

In a lower category, **La Pineta** is a sweetie. Excellent rooms, some even handsomer than those in the Quisisana; heaven-sent privacy; superb view from the heart of a pinewood facing the sea; lovely pool area with sauna and bar, just right for lunch, surrounded by 1- or 3-bedroom units; breakfast on your terrace (or in the nibble-nook if, saints forbid, it should be raining); beach strip at Marina Piccola with cabanas, provision for water sports and lunching facilities at Gloria's Ristorante delle Sirene. Migrations of notables have hidden away here, for very good reason. Young, alert Manager Costanzo is the attentive host. The sky-blue **Flora** is just as nice, with exactly the same medium rates—but it's a smidgen more formal. Both prime for tranquillity and comfort. **Scalinatella** resides next to La Pineta. It's just as melodic as the sound of its name. With the latest additions, it now embraces 12 suites with terrace, Frigobar, and safe, 16 doubles, 3 singles, air conditioning, no restaurant, an oooolala garden, a bar, a wide lobby, and the careful attention of Mario Morgano and his sons, Enrico and Nicole. For romancers only. **La Residencia**, next to the Regina Cristina, comes up with a floorload of late-model pads, plus the original 54 older rooms, 36 private baths, 16 balconies, traditional décor, and Mother Nature outside your window at her most exquisite. If you are maneuvered into the **La Romantica** annex, be sure to demand a front accommodation. Sound. The midvillage **Gatto Bianco**, with many added terraces, is a mélange of conventional and supermodern decorative concepts. Colorful, but becoming flagrant—especially in its psychedelic nightclub called Splash.

Villa delle Syrene, in our revised opinion, is a borderline First-class hotel. New floor with 4 suites, large terraces, and simple décor; lounge with lemon-grove vista; 20 rooms in neighboring annex; clean, attractive, recommendable. We are not so fond, however, of the **Bellavista**, a sister operation which we found dull by comparison. **Semiramis** is cheerful, bright, and dependable. The pension **Villa Margherita**, with a lovely quiet garden at its entrance, a neat little lobby, and some excellent rooms with terrace and bath is an odds-on choice as a residence house; which serves breakfast only. The enlarged and updated **Pensione Esperia** has sensible rates and is good for the bracket. If you're watching the budget closely, **Villa Oreste** taps out 15 bedchambers and simple comfort for the price. So does the equally tiny **La Pazziele** with its splendid garden and thoughtful touches. **Florida** and **Floridiana** are hives for economy package tours. Nix. **Vittoria Pagano** is inexpensive and, for us, looks it in every way. Finally, the **Pensione Terminus** is a Third-class, pocket-size bargain if you don't mind parking at a busy, noisy midcenter address. It's run by the deAngelis family who own the popular La Campannina Restaurant downstairs.

The **Europa Palace**, in *Anacapri*, has a metropolitan rather than resort-type atmosphere. Modernity that somehow seems out of step with the eternal beauty of Mother Nature; panoramic roof garden with bar service; Sans Souci nightclub; tennis court; swimming pool. Foremost in comfort rather than charm—but be sure, sure, *sure* to demand exactly the type of bedchamber you want, since some readers have been sorely disappointed by casual reservations policies. **Caesar Augustus**, on a cliff 1000 feet above the sea, offers one of the most spectacular vistas we've found in any European hotel—and little else, in our most serious professional opinion. You may rightfully disagree with us, but our impression continues to be distinctly unfavorable. How sad, because it could be a stunner. The group-minded **San Michele**, almost across the road, has modern furnishings, a fabulous terrace, and the same disadvantage of this suburban location. A bus stop on the Anacapri-Capri route is immediately outside, however, and this transportation is easy, cheap, and frequent. Even though this resort is geographically more elevated than the town, it's still quite a comedown spiritually. Don't bother with any of the port-sited offerings at *Marina Grande*; they're ideal for sardine fishermen.

When you tuck in your bib, the island's most famed establishment is **La Canzone del Mare**, a chichi beach club at the foot of a cliff adjoining a small beach. Magnificent location; pool; bar; now lunch only; very, very swank, and very, very lovely. But that food, for those prices—ouch! We chuckled at our ridiculously skimpy portions—but we stopped laughing fast when they handed us that tab. If you're poor and famished, you can find the same scenery for 50% less money at attractive little **Da Pietro** (also known as "Gloria's," for the titled Englishwoman who runs it) a short distance down the shore. Check first because it might have shuttered; if it is still functioning you're likely to find much better food these days than in a neighboring high-price spot called **Da Vincenzo delle Sirene**, so don't let yourself confuse them. All closed tight in winter.

Please refer back to the hotel section above for the **Punta Tragara** restaurant, such an enchanting spot that it is a wonder anyone can swallow. Nothing on Capri can touch it for elegance and plushness. The glorious 6-table terrace is Paradise South. Very costly; be sure to reserve.

La Capannina (via delle Botteghe 15) draws the island's top palms and salaams from our old-time, loyal, discriminating friends, Rose and Mortimer Sachs of Palm Beach, Florida. On a 4-week stay, they zeroed in for "at least 40 of our 60 meals." Here's their description: "The 3 charming, tiny inside dining rooms are lovely, and the patio is beautiful. The kitchen is the best equipped of any local restaurant. The house wine, from their own vineyards, is excellent. The prices, while not inexpensive, are competitive." Since then we've come from repeated table tests here and find the Sachs' report 105% correct. Lira-for-lira this is our candidate for top value on the island. Closed Thursday and 4 months in winter.

Ai Faraglioni, on the footpath called via Camerelle, is variable. Scenic, vedy-vedy social, immaculate, pleasant terraces for people watching; far less enjoyable this time than it was on previous incognito samplings. **Da Gemma**, perhaps 50 steps up the arch-covered footpath from the Central Plaza, is the artists' and writers' favorite. There are 2 sections, one a year-round tavern and the other a seasonal patio; the former comprises a series of rooms enclosing an open, sunken kitchen. With Grottino (opposite side of the plaza) and La Capannina, Da Gemma vies for the most delicious regional cookery to be found on Capri. **O'Saraceno** made us feel claustrophobic—a totally unnecessary sensation in this isle of open vistas and space. The garden of the **Quisisana** is particularly attractive at night; for indoor munchers, its French restaurant has been lovingly done over in elegant tones. Much improved. **Casina delle Rose**, with its Taverna now operating during the evening, is coming up again under its improved management; check your bill to make certain no discrepancies exist with listed menu prices. **Grotto Verde,** near the funicular base in the port, is strongly *caprese*—rough but fun, with excellent typical cookery and reasonable tabs. If you don't expect anything but simplicity and honest fare, you'll probably enjoy it. Closed Mondays. **La Pigna,** below the taxi rank off the main piazza, is a family operation which has everything going for it except the cookery. Shame on the chef, say we. **Fontanella,** below the Hotel Punta Tragara, is very chic. Regrettably, only lunch is served. Among the outdoor cafés most frequented at the cocktail hour, the **Caffé Caso** seems to draw the intelligentsia of the island while the **Gran Cafe Town and Country** attracts merely the affluent; **Piccolo Bar** is more for every *uomo.* **Tiberio,** which resides in the cellar of a local church is considered by many to be a tourist trap—perhaps just right, however, for a trappist tour.

Shopping Most shops offer the same merchandise and the same high prices as Naples—with 7 laudable and conspicuous exceptions.

Sea Gull (via Roma 25) was just plain terrific before its very recent change of ownership—as it might well be today. We haven't inspected it since.

A happy and special sparkler of which we're fond is **La Campanina** (Discesa Quinisana 18, a minute down from the square). The inspired original designs in chains, brooches, rings, earrings, bracelets, necklaces, charms, and other wantables grace the small, elegant, trend-setting shop.

La Parisienne (on the square), featuring Livio di Simone's inspired appeal, is the acknowledged fashion arbiter for ladies.

The other 4 stops we like are **Oriane** (via Camerelle, adjoining Hotel Quisisana), operated by an attractive English lass, Mrs. Anne Gargiullo, for handmade Capri silk and high-style boutique items; **Canfora** (opposite the Quisisana) for sandals; **Yves Dupris** (via Camerelle), with its men's shop across the street from its women's shop, for further boutique selections; and nearby **Chantal,** for chic clothes for Him.

For reasons we consider sufficient, the well-known **Mariorita Shop** in *Anacapri* is NOT recommended by this book.

CASERTA is mainly used as a midway point for filling midriffs. In this calling, **Massa da Peppino** is a yummy choice for grills and regional pickings except on Monday. Out on the Capua-Naples main auto expressway, the **Autostrada Pavesi** has a good-quality air-conditioned restaurant. It's a godsend for the motorist in a hurry. **La Bomboniera** is only so-so.

CATANIA is one of the main stopping places in eastern Sicily, at the foot of Mt. Etna. If you wish to pause, the **Excelsior Grand** avoids the city's commercialism. Fully air-conditioned, when it works (you'll pay for it regardless!); somewhat gaudy neo-Italian rooms now with piped melodies; high prices for the region. The **Central Palace** is central, but 'tain't no palace. Air-conditioned; open all year; noisy locale; rather amateurish concierge and slipshod maintenance on our recent peek. If you absolutely *must,* the split-level apartments with kitchenettes are the pick of the dismal pack. The 160-unit **Jolly** is busy-busy with tour groups; the **Costa** is simple. We haven't seen the **Baia Verde**, a youthful seasider a few miles out of town with a swimming pool and air cooling. At least this rocky coast is nice. The **Plaja** is passable for strict economists. The **AGIP Motel**, at the Taormina road exit at Ognina, offers 45 rooms, all with shower. Miserable maintenance; restaurant; bar; garage. All of these are mediocre or worse by international standards. Neighboring *Laveno* offers nothing except the ferry.

If hunger pangs develop, **La Tavernetta**, with its moderate tabs, has been perked up brightly. Modern structure plus alfresco terrace beside the sea. **Costazzurra**, near by, is reasonably sound. The **Alba**? One friend advises, "Simply ignore that it exists." Okay, done. **Forte Apache** dishes out local grub in a mock fortress; its chief hits bull's-eyes with his culinary arrows; here's a chuck wagon that's on the move. **Texas**, left of the entry to the Bellini Gardens, is a fairly international spot with elegant outfitting and Dallas-style prices.

CERNOBBIO (LAKE COMO) is the seat of the world-famous **Villa d'Este**. Built in A.D. 1568 as a private residence for Cardinal Tolomeo Gallio and later occupied by the Dowager Empress of Russia, the Princess of Wales, the Princess Torlonia, and other notables, it has been operated as a hotel since 1873. About 110 ultraposh rooms in the main building; 51 magnificently comfortized ones in the neighboring annex; a quartet of junior suites plus many upgraded standard units; kitchens re-spiced; terrace restaurant; glorious setting; 6 tennis courts and 1 for squash; nearby 18-hole golf course; heated pool with 2-style saunas and gym; outdoor restaurant for bathers; private beach; horses available; slot-car track; nightclub plus discothèque; woody grill in the Sporting Club for informal meals; open early-April to late-October. One of the aristocrats of Italy and priced accordingly. The **Regina Olga** is geographically in the same league, but that's where the similarity stops with a jolt.

COMO, of course, is the pivotal town of the Italian Lake District. In this lovely center, a highly inviting medium-priced stop is the **Barchetta Excelsior**. Piazza location facing the water; modern building; sidewalk café; 57 sky-bright functional rooms, all with cramped baths or showers; very clean and now quite a good buy. **San Gottardo** has perked up some of its appurtenances; it's large, spotless, and so-so. The First-echelon **Como**, sited in the center, is said to be a sound bet for those who don't like too much Como-tion. **Metropole Suisse** is rising, even though it's Second-class. On the road to Villa d'Este, in a wretchedly noisy location, the **Villa Fiori** has been converted from a private home. Peninsular décor; passing-fair now, but long country miles to go. As for the Second-category **Continental**, to date our reader reports have not been encouraging.

When pangs of hunger begin to gnaw, first a warning: The **Funicolare Restaurant**, at the foot of the funicular, is NOT recommended by this book —but definitely, oh so definitely. In the town itself we're partial to the restaurant of the **Barchetta Excelsior** (closed Thurs.), as well as to **Da Celestino** and **Imbarcadero**. A fascinating excursion can be had to **Locanda**, on the island of *Comacina*, which boasts romantic origins back to the early twelfth century. It is located across from the village of Sala Comacina, 20 minutes by road from

Villa d'Este; athletic diners also can row in from Sporano or an oarsman can do the muscle work for you for a small fee. An abundant and flavorful fixed-price menu totals approximately $28 per person. The high point of the meal (only performed when the restaurant is full) is the Fire Rite—a bit of amiable hocus-pocus involving tinkling bells, flaming coffee, and a public taste test of the brew by a supposed virgin. While the *espresso* concoction might enjoy the flambé process, clients themselves are prohibited from smoking throughout all meals as house policy. Closed Tuesday. **Le Tout Paris**, at *Sala Comacina*, is said to be better than satisfactory for cuisine at prices that run anywhere from 30% to 40% under those of Locanda. Closed Wednesday. In *Rogaro*, the 12-table **Veluu** is recommended by 2 local connoisseurs who tell us that it is one of the most attractive, chic, and well-run oases in the area. Sited on the ground floor of Villa Antonini, the dining room overlooks Lake Como from atop its own peninsula. Accessible only by car; closed January. Sounds exceptional. The **Vapore Torno**, 15 minutes out at *Torno*, is another pacesetter for the region (Apr. to Sept. only). **Da Pizzi** offers 2 dining places—an expensive one, open summer only, and a small, typical one, open all year; we prefer the cookery in the little brother, even though it's less costly and less fancy. The **Negri** in *Pusiano*, 9 miles from Como on the Lecco highway, features freshly caught perch with risotto; this one is very cheap, simple, and good. We've already mentioned **Villa Serbelloni** at *Bellagio*.

Here one buys silk, silk, silk, and more silk by the sail-length. Two landmarks vie for the leadership: Proprietor Ercole Moretti of **Seterie Moretti** (via Garibaldi 69) is assisted by 10 designers in the creation of his specialty of strikingly original prints; each pattern is limited to a maximum output of 10 pieces. Proprietoress Giovanna Rainoldi and her nephew Antonio of **Rainoldi** offer wearables at their piazza Cavor headquarters, plus bolt silks, sheets, and linens at their other two branches. Since the tariffs in both are virtually at wholesale levels, identical purchases cost appreciably more in almost any other retailer shop in Italy. Recommended.

In summary, the Italian Lake District is a skein of pros and cons. The overall pattern gives us, at least, the impression that it is *still* somewhat overrated. The scenery can be glorious, with Garda the largest and most enchanting lake, followed by Maggiore and Como. But offsetting panoramas of dramatic mountains, peaceful shorelines, and cool blue waters are a number of drawbacks. Many of these waters are now so polluted that swimming is banned. The roads —narrow and serpentine—aren't built to accommodate the armadas of trucks, scooters, and pleasure vehicles that snarl them in summer. Nearly all its hotels are either as old hat as Grandpa's boater or as claptrappy modern as a $10-down Florida real estate development. The general quality of its restaurants runs from routine to mediocre to poor. The weather is benign for too few months, with the fringe seasons spoiled by unpredictable periods of cold and rain. *Gardone* is an excellent base of operations for Garda, because from here excursions or steamer trips can be made to *Desenzano, Sirmione, Malcesine*, up the Brenta Mountains in the Dolomites, and several other interesting alternatives. *Stresa* is the traditional hub (with Locarno, Switzerland) for *Maggiore*, and *Como* is a convenient starting point for *Bellagio, Menaggio*, and Villa Carlotta.

CORTINA D'AMPEZZO boasts the palatial **Miramonti Majestic**. It is sited in an outskirts situation surrounded by a golf course, ski lifts, tennis facilities, ice and curling rinks, a swimming pool, and the well-tempered chords of a dance band after sunset. Extensive modernizations; ground floor totally restyled; ambitious revampings of its 200 spacious accommodations, most with balcony and many with regadgeted baths; open mid-December to March, and June to September. Very good indeed. The **Cristallo Palace** is another fine choice. Except for a golf course, it has all the recreational features of the Miramonti. Complement of 110 rooms and 105 baths; most units with Tyrolean décor and painted florals; 90% with private balcony; operative December 20 to March 15 and June 15 to September 15. Cigahotels recently aquired this property and plan to improve the facilities. At present its not as chichi as the pacemaker, but in many ways warmer and more friendly. Down in the thick of the action, the **Savoia** is a merry address. Its 2 buildings, connected by a tunnel under the main street, confer the title as Cortina's biggest hostelry. Lively and gaily traditional. The **Corona**—picked by many discriminating wanderers—simply did not demonstrate the flair of a professional hotel operation to our experienced noses. Its patrons, the Rimoldi brothers, have filled it with $1,280,000 worth of contemporary paintings—many of which seemed as abstract as the current management. Chalet-style exterior; 64 rooms; 40 with bath or shower. Perhaps you will crown this Corona with more accolades than we did; personally, we found it as cold as a Dolomite icicle on New Year's Eve. The midvillage **de la Poste** has been rebuilt after its disastrous fire of 1975. **Europa**, under Cristallo Palace aegis, remains open all year. Rooms about as tight as the inside of a ski boot; good food in its below-stairs restaurant. A bit commercial in tone. **Splendid Venezia**, just a few doors away, is a smart buy if you can snatch one of its back-corner doubles with balcony. Fine for its category. The chalet-style **Menardi** should be ranked in a higher official status, but the owner prefers it to remain a quiet "sleeper" value at budget rates. Renewed dining room; 38 units in main house plus 10 in the annex; added furnishings and many resplashed baths; spotless maintenance; savory vittles (so we're told). **Ampezzo** is another bargain, despite its growing age.

El **Toulà**, about 15 minutes toward *Pocol*, is a favorite of Smart Set diners. Checkered table napery; darkness in tone; lightness in cuisine. **El Camineto**, a little farther along (turn right before *Pocol*, is smaller, also chichi, and also worthy. So is the family-run **Beppe Sello** for regional skilletry. **Al Foghèr** isn't what it used to be. **Ra Stua** also has slipped.

ELBA, which Virgil called "The Generous Island," was Napoléon's home prior to his famous 100 days—and we wish it could be ours for 1000. To travelers in the know and in search of tranquillity rather than frenzy, it already has replaced Capri; the boom is zooming; the vanguard of trippers carry the banners of Sweden and Germany to its shores. Simple, primitive, unspoiled; glorious mountains, shimmering olive-toned landscape, breathtaking beaches; only 8 small towns, a dozen small villages, and a scattering of hamlets on this 30-mile home of 32 thousand people; hotels, restaurants, and night life limited but adequate; excellent, zippy 30-minute hydrofoil service between Piombino and Portoferraio 15 times per day, plus numerous regular ferry luggers; daily

High Season link with Leghorn via the Isle of Capraia; excursions (100 minutes) to Corsica from mid-June onward; Aertaxi planes to and from the mainland; scenic route, reminiscent of the Amalfi Drive. Health addicts oink
around in therapeutic mud baths at the Terme of San Giovanni. For the
panorama of a lifetime, take the rope-railway *("cabinovia")* from Marciana to
the 3100-foot peak of Monte Capanne. Nearby is the uninhabited rock known
as Monte Cristo, the islet where the fabulous "Count" created by Alexandre
Dumas found his buried treasure.

Among the hotels, **Del Golfo**, 20 minutes from the port at *Procchio*, wins
many hearts. Beach location with taxis readily available; 95 small- to medium-
size accommodations in 6 different buildings; the nicest in the main structure
and in the "New Villa." Some split-level duplex apartments for families or
single Texans; 2 tennis courts; extra-nice L-shape pool above beach; splendid
kitchen. Energetic Director Ernesto Nagy will be your friendly and thoughtful
host. The **Désirée**, tucked around the neighboring cove, has similar architecture but a less dramatic view. Pleasant décor; private beach and cabanas;
handsome garden; alfresco dining in season; very clean. Most of its 60 good-
size rooms come with shower or bath and balcony. A rewarding Second-class
stop for budget-conscious pilgrims. The **Renée** is only so-so, in our opinion.
La Perla is directly on the noisy highway. The **Hermitage** at *Biodola* on a
woodland inlet is ready-made for honeymooners. Ranch-style building; expansive dining-terrace overlooking the swimming pool and beach; accomodations
in 12 varisize bungalow units (#98 is best if you've brought your Junior
Patrol). The biggest drawback here is lack of adequate room service. A winner
if you enjoy total privacy. **Darsena**, facing the dock in *Portoferraio*, is reasonably comfortable. Every room with private bath and telephone; every front
room with private terrace; medium bracket. The **Massimo**, in the same vicinity, is immediately opposite the ferry landing and subject to all the busyness
therewith. All 60 old-fashioned rooms with toilet and shower; only for overnighting. Open all year. The 62-room-and-shower **Residence** now rents small
apartments only; it has a noisy location. The **Picchiaie Residence** (no relation)
comes up with bungalow-down comforts in 51 rooms; baths number 31; there
are also tennis and a swimming pool. At *Magazzini*, 10 minutes away, the
L-shape **Fabricia** provides a soothing bay view from its olive-grove situation.
Pleasant pool; tennis court; hypermodern décor; animated Italian clientele
mostly. Recommended only if you *parla Italiano*. At *Marina di Campo*,
Marina 2 is on its hilltop. Quiet sealess views; 80 balconied rooms; all amenities including a refrigerator in the bedchamber; dining indoors, on a patio, or
beside the pool; nightclub and sauna. Quite a tranquil haven. Not far away,
Iselba features separate beach-house cabins with individual terraces. Pine-
grove setting fronting a wide strand; 65 units (12 apartments); 2 villas annexes;
open mid-May to mid-October; agreeable. Nearby, the 75-unit **Villa Ottone**
is set in its own park, with a 22-room colony of bungalows fringing the
woodlands. Private pebble beach; tennis; glass-lined dining room; richly decorated bar; somewhat used in feeling, but adequate. The beach and sites are
dreamy but the quality, in our opinion, is poor at both the Second-class
Bahia, and the 119-unit (80% with bath) **Lacona** in Cavoli. The **Elba International**, initially called the Eurotel, in *Capoliveri*, near *Porto Az-*

zurro, has escaped us to date. The Second-class **Garden** on the gulf at _Schiopparello_ has a sublimely quiet setting on a dark-sand beach, but its serenity is often strained by too many tour groups. The former tiny-tot **Pension Valle Verde**, above the Désirée at _Marciana Procchio_, calls itself a hotel, but a rose by any other. . . . Not for plucking by this gardener. The **Grotte of Paradise**, across Portoferraio Bay, a rebuilt villa with a maze of cabins and other outbuildings, is pretty basic. _All or nearly all these are closed from roughly October to May;_ during a recent winter, the only lodgings we could find were at the tiny **Ape Elbana**, which we now like somewhat better, but not much.

Too long ago, we folded our napkins after a gastronomic waddle through this island. Here's what our taste buds told us then—and undoubtedly much has changed in today's wild touristic merry-go-round: (1) **Hotel del Golfo** in _Procchio_, where the chef knew his trade. Barbecue and grills on the beach from June 20 to September 20; excellent Bistecca alla Fiorentina; pizzeria sideline. (2) **La Sirene** in _Portoferraio_ for solid cookery of the family, by the family, and for you; no-monkey-business décor. (3) The **Hermitage** in _Biodola_. (4) **La Marinella** for finny critters and lobster. (5) The seaside **Zi Rosa** at _Portoferraio_, a gem among pizzerie. Other choices are **Kon-Tiki, La Triglia,** and **Iselba** in _Marina di Campo,_ and **Ape Elbana** or **Taverna Giamaica,** both in _Portoferraio_. **Giappone,** on the square, is Third-class; typical and simple. _Most of these establishments are closed in winter._ Incidentally, the **Hotel Centrale** in Piombino (mainland port for Elba excursionists) is decently adequate, if you stick to fish, pasta, and cheese.

FIESOLE   This is included in our report on Florence which follows.

FLORENCE   is the Athens of Italy. Renovations and an aura of freshness have brightened her aspect immeasurably. The metropolis is aburst with works of art bearing such signatures as Fra Angelico, Michelangelo, Botticelli, Donatello, Ghiberti, Cellini, and Leonardo da Vinci. There are Giotto's historic **Bell Tower;** the shop-lined **Ponte Vecchio;** the **opera house;** the **Medici Chapel;** the fractured **Brunelleschi dome** (lately protected from traffic vibrations), the **National Art Museum;** the **Uffizi** (which is supposed to be enlarged, with auto traffic now banned in this vicinity on an experimental basis) and **Pitti Palaces** (2 of civilization's most fabulous centers of art); the **Strozzi Palace** (magnificent courtyard); the **National Library;** the renovated **San Marco Gallery** (Fra Angelico frescoes); the **Bargello Museum** (cameos, ivories, della Robbias), just about everything for travelers with a sense of the beautiful. It is situated in the heart of a chain of lovely hills; some Americans rate it as the pleasantest place in Italy. This center, too, is suffering from traffic headaches; now autos are or will be banned from certain central districts. If you like your painting, architecture, churches, and tombs—and if you don't mind the fact that every 2nd person you stumble across is a visitor (stumble _over_, too, since many of the youngsters now seem to live on the streets)— Florence is highly recommended, even though too many of her inhabitants are so _tired_ of being hosts that their welcome is perfunctory and unsmiling.

  Hotels   In a 2-way tie for the number one Deluxe ranking come the Excelsior and the Savoy. This duet is so neck-and-neck that your preference depends largely on your personal taste. Then we follow up with other stellar selections in this better-than-average hotel oasis.

The **Excelsior** has emerged from her major overhaul in sparking radiance. Her premises now boast suites among the loveliest in Europe, each outside charmer with its own massive penthouse terrace overlooking the Arno or a townscape of gloriously untouched antiquity; the cozy Belvedere Junior-Suite one of the sweetest corners imaginable; Donatello Bar with the split personality of bar, paneled nook, and hearthside room; wonderful rooftop patio for sipping and dining; enchanting and viewful barbeque area; excellent concierge desk lorded by Carlo Mori. Manager Paolo Biscioni runs this 5-star show with vigor and savvy. Catering to so many North American independents and fancy tour-group clients, its cuisine and its atmosphere reflect an awareness of heavy U.S. and Canadian patronage.

The 100-room **Savoy** still shares top honors with the Excelsior. Midtown *palazzo*; high-ceiling corridors; spacious dimensions; wall-to-wall carpeting; walnut, mahogany, or painted Venetian-style furnishings; liberal scattering of antiques and ancient chandeliers to augment the traditional atmosphere; bar and dining room rather heavy and old-fashioned; some of the sparkle of its recent renovation now beginning to fade ever-so-slightly. Hardworking Director Vittorio Spicciani keeps this house in trim as a unique period piece in Italian architecture. Chief Concierge Joseph is a perfect St. Peter to wayfarers from abroad. Recommended with respect, confidence, and cheers.

The marble-entranced **Villa Cora** is situated in a park above the town; there are a fine dinner-only restaurant (flanked by a pool), a tavern, and 56 fully-bathed accommodations which are very beautifully furnished. The frescoed ceilings and public sancta are marvels of their time and a joy to observe. The concierge is one of the city's finest; the earnest manager has taught the staff to smile a bit more often and generally has improved the already excellent standards of his villa.

The **Villa Medici**, always a house of distinctive physical charm, once-again boasts deluxe-level service standards to match its eloquent architectural and decorative graces. Air-conditioned; lobby glowing with fresh flowers; restaurant smoothly and gracefully managed; more than 100 comfortable quarters all with bath or shower; captivatingly landscaped street-level pool and garden with buffet lunch served. The back rooms and 7 penthouse perches, each dubbed and patterned after flora, command the best view and most tasteful décor. Manager Manlio Giardi is an amiable professional who has a building worthy of any modern-day Medici. Here is an establishment that deserves a top rating.

In First-class, the **Jolly** maintains a firm footing at the entrance to Cascine Park. Unquestionably, the reasonable tariffs and contemporary luxury amenities give it a special demand status; its once-dubious future now looks a lot brighter under the management of Sig. Graziano. Spectacular, modernistic lobby; glorious 6th-floor roof garden for alfresco apértifs, backed by 2 glass-fronted interior restaurants and bars for service year round; open-air 7th-floor pool and sun terrace; austere main dining room with open spit and a chef under the tallest cap in Tuscany. All 145 units with bath, air conditioning, piped music; 32 good-size front doubles with balcony, alcove, bathroom, and lavatory. As a guideline for preference when booking, the 3rd-floor units are modernistic in décor, while all other levels are traditional. The **Lungarno** is a beauty—and it's even more appealing since its rates have been trimmed slightly. Its extra-choice situation beside the Arno, a few steps from the Ponte Vecchio, possibly makes it the most expensive real estate anywhere on the river. Original 40 rooms extended to 70; 22 suites, including one atop the thirteenth-century stone tower; some excellent balconied riverfront units; back rooms disgracefully small, as are many other pockets of this miniminded house; cozy bar but no restaurant. Very colorful, tasteful, and comfortable.

The air-conditioned **Kraft** seems to be waiting—perhaps impatiently—for a visit from the carpenters, painters, and textile Kraftsmen who don't appear to have paid their calls in far too long. Roof terrace with panoramic view and swimming pool; fair dining salon; all rooms with bath and shower. Though quiet in location, we wish that those workmen would start raising a little dust and perk the place up again. The hypermodernistic 140-room **Michelangelo** goes all out to say it is with it, *really* with it! Corridor floors, walls, even doors, are carpeted in the same gray-brown woof that cloaks the bedrooms; beds have sleek striped spreads; prints provide color; all in all it is a creature of its time —from small baths to a plenitude of panache. **Park Palace** is lord of its hilltop. Total of 21 units in main building and 9 in the annex; private baths and air conditioning throughout; swimming pool; downstairs Taverna restaurant and bar adjoining. While each ingredient is attractive, it doesn't seem to jell as a whole. You may prefer this at lunch rather than for overnight. The **Minerva**, very central and with a pleasant piazza in front, comes up with 85 doubles with bath and 35 with shower. Modern lobby; attractive restaurant with glassed-in garden; new coffee shop due; air-conditioned; topside pool; interior wall surfacing of harsh and dismal marble-dust gesso; front units more spacious but noisy; newer wing, overlooking a quiet cloister, with cell-size sleeping quarters. Overall verdict? Fair. The extensively revamped **Astoria** has been taking lovely pills. Now the lobby has been reshuffled, the capacity boosted to 90 rooms and 90 baths, air conditioning has been installed throughout, and independent garage facilities have been arranged. The palatial breakfast room is one of the most spectacular one can imagine. (Instead of "Breakfast at Tiffany's," it reminds us of "Eggs Benedict in the Sistine Chapel.") The **Plaza Lucchesi**, up the Arno near Santa Croce Church, has an entrance in glass and brass. Overall perk-up in maintenance; cordiality from every staffer we encountered. Getting better. The **Anglo-Americano**, under the helmsmanship of Manager Bandinelli, was whoooooshed through by a construction hurricane. Modern elevator; 40 floral-tile baths (almost a full ratio now); 35 rooms refurnished; beds in gold leaf or white; serene. More a made-over homestead than a metropolitan hotel. The **Capitol** is on a busy-busy street. Glass-and-steel block-style architecture; cellar restaurant with ugly muslin ceiling; heavy use of plastic wall sheathing; modern lounge; air-conditioned throughout; 60 doubles and 30 singles; all with bath or shower and most too small for our taste. Nice staff; popular among conducted tours. Satisfactory. **Aerhotel Baglioni** is now partially piloted by Alitalia, which has fluffed its wings in the process and aimed its appeal to flocks of groupies who swarm over in such numbers. The **Majestic** is also infatuated by group movements in the touristic field. You'll need wheels to reach the **Monginevro**, which is way-the-hell-and-gone into the industrial sticks. Window-lined 10th-floor restaurant; full air conditioning; 91 units including 3 suites; all units with small bars; fronts with private balconies; linoleum flooring with throw rugs; Second-class price tags.

The fully air-chilled **Continental** is more tastefully tailored for its price than is its Luncarno sister across the river. One of the most romantic little twelfth-century tower suites in Christendom; roof garden plus bar and breakfast room; no dining facilities; plunked smack in the center of the city's worst traffic snarl. Not bad for pedestrians and the slightly deaf. The 71-room **Augustus** nestles beside its *sorella,* tucked slightly off the main drag. Again, no restaurant; sunken, Nordic-style modern bar under a gently arched white ceiling; self-control air conditioning (which aids as well in sound proofing); singles with showers; all twins with baths. **Londra**, inspired by the Minerva prophets, reshaped its main floor, bar, and public sanctuaries. The **Principe** is just adequate. Arno-sited; 24 rooms with bath; centrally air-conditioned. The **Umbria**, with its shady garden and air of sedate solitude, is a tranquil oasis. The **Columbus** is so far out along the Arno that a car is an absolute must—unless you can tolerate a long taxi ride every time you hop into the center. Attractive public areas; downstairs dining pit, plus window-lined breakfast and snack corner; multilevel bar; 105 air-conditioned bedchambers and 72 private baths. One room we inspected was so bone-crushingly narrow it was just plain ludicrous. (When we stepped into the lavatory, our guide said proudly, "Here's one with a shower!" We asked, "Where?" Our companion replied. "Why, you're standing under it!") Okay, if you don't mind the tedious hike from the doin's and if you pick your nest carefully.

Here's how we score the rest of the pack: **Hotel de la Ville**, indeed convenient to the major sightseeing attractions (and nice, as well); **Ritz**, a perky youngster with chilled air but no restaurant; **Della Signoria**, satisfactory for bed and breakfast, and **Berchielli**, a remodeled *palazzo* with 84 charming rooms which mostly go pipeless. **Bonciani, Adriatico**, and **David** are not recommended.

Pensions? Our top laurels go to the lovely little **Hermitage** (Vicolo Marzio 1, at the bridgehead of the Ponte Vecchio) and to the demure **Mona Lisa** (Borgo Pinti 27). The former boasts a roof garden over 18 pleasant rooms and the latter is a fourteenth-century palace with as much charm as tradition. Both require full board. **Beacci** (via Tornabuoni 3) occupies 3 floors over an art gallery; it's quite comfortable. **Centrale** (via dei Conti 3) is clean and agreeable. **Villa Villoresi** (colonnata di Sesto Fiorentino, near the Florence exit of the Autostrada del Sole) is good for lengthy stays, but inconvenient for trippers-in-a hurry because it's 3 miles out; Countess Villoresi and her radiant daughter, Cristina, take great pride in their ancient homestead. **Villa Carlotta** (via Michele di Lando 3) perches on a hard-to-find hilltop; this hideaway is ideal for creative types who yearn to-get-away-from-it-all. **Villa Belvedere**, the leader of the smaller houses and 10 minutes from the center, offers a fine view of the city. The Perotto team (she is the daughter of the late owner) run this haven smoothly. Their pride-and-joy's air-conditioned 30 rooms all boast baths; try for #26 or #36. The pool is an added bonus; half pension is required; it is closed December through February. Here is an especially sanquine choice for those seeking a friendly welcome, reasonable tariffs, and tranquillity. **Park San Domenico** nestles in a cypress forest toward *Fiesole*. Baronial appointments a bit faded but still in the Grand Tradition; 19 rooms with baths; one in which a Czar of Russia is said to have slumbered. Manager Franco Codacci aims to please.

After a short decline, **Villa La Massa**, the Deluxe country-estate-type hotel in neighboring *Candeli*, has now regained many of its earlier assets. The rooms are comfortable, immaculate, and tastefully furnished, due to the efforts of Owner Maria Broggini. Expanded dining salon; 2 improved kitchens; sleekly rustic, blue-clad-and-gold-gilt, October-to-May La Cave nightclub for cellar-brations; touch-ups numerous and well done. There's a tiny pool, and anglers can borrow the gardener's pole for compleat relaxation on the Arno banks. We pray that it continues its special mandate on halcyon days. The best route to reach it is by the Viale Europa, not the Lungarno.

At *Fiesole*, 4 miles out of town, overlooking the Florentine valley, **Villa San Michele** is lord of its hillside. This one is a tastefully converted fifteenth-century monastery originally designed by Michelangelo. Splendid panorama; a guest book that boasts more blue blood than the registry for a royal corona-tion. Its 23 bedrooms, all with bath and all former cells, have been lavishly and comfortably outfitted for distinctly nonhirsuted disciples. Gentle, urbane Lucien Tessier and his sparkling Irish wife, Máire, are a charming and capable host-and-hostess team. Open March 20 to November 1. Here is a Deluxe bell ringer (sweetly muffled, of course).

Restaurants   This Tuscan center boasts numerous worthwhile mid-dle-bracket restaurants—but she has surprisingly few sophisticated tables for a city of her breeding and patrician flair. **Oliviero** (via delle Terme 51R) now comes closest to satisfying that need; it still falls far short, how-ever, of many oases in the capital. Three-room string of nooks, the first containing a bar and melodious piano tinkler and the next pair for calories only; flamingo-hued cloths on extra-tiny tables; matching banquettes; greengage textiled walls; coffered ceilings. Our steak was too well educated to retain any real flavor of beef, but our partner's Delizie de Vitella Mode du Chef (shaved veal in a delicate sauce of cream, parsley, a touch of gar-lic, and champagne) was succulent; the Tuscan house wine is superb. Very attentive service. Substantial, miles from cheap, and moderately elegant, but not a true aristocrat in any sense.

The **Sabatini** (via Panzani 41) seems to be bounding back under the inspired direction of Proprietor Angelo Schiari. The interior has always been an attrac-tive, busy, rambling affair, and now that the cookery has been restored to its former glory, we are happy to recommend it on that score as well. Expect to pay a bundle, but at last the rewards are worth the outlay.

Buca Lapi (via del Trebbio 1) is the classic choice of visiting firemen. Cellar décor; travel-poster motif; 22 individual table lamps hanging from ceiling; indifferent cookery on our tries; in our estimate, too tourist-slick and expensive for anybody except first-timers.

Doney (via Tornabuoni 11), a 2-part restaurant, bar, pastry shop, take-away counter, and tearoom complex all in the same building, is so beloved by U.S.

trippers that there are few Italians normally visible; good cookery and good drinks.

Harry's Bar (lungarno Amerigo Vespucci 22R) is a Florentine landmark; it's only a long olive-pit throw from the Excelsior. Still small, still intimate, still cozy. The waiters are now all Harry's since they bought the original out; happily they have maintained their mandate on quality. Animated, cosmopolitan, fun. Closed Sundays and December 20 to January 15.

For hotel dining, the **Excelsior's** Chef Alzetta is especially gifted in his private preparations of chicken, Spaghetti alla Matriciana, and rice with truffles. The **Aerhotel Baglioni Roof**, lovely on a summer night, caters heavily now to packaged groups.

Back to the independents again, **Bordino** (via Stracciatella 9R) is a gladsome hideaway peeping under richly bold stone and stucco vaults, beckoning with soft illumination, and displaying appetizing and artistic culinary spreads on a central table. Ceramics, wrought-iron, banners, and cooking utensils deck the walls. It is so Tuscan down to its toenails that it is built right into the foundations of the town in a square that nudges the Ponte Vecchio. Regional cuisine; outstanding red wine; closed July, also Sunday and Monday for lunch. Highly appealing for color, antiquity and value. **Giovacchino** (via dei Tosinghi 34R) is noted for its roasts. Self-service downstairs; dancing on the upper level; so-so cookery, in our opinion. The similar-sounding **Giovannino** (Borgognissanti 93R) served us a listless lunch again recently. Still low on our poll. For the economy-minded, **Buca Mario** (piazza Ottaviani 16) should give you a good dinner for low tabs. Three rooms in cellar; clean, attractive, and plain; heavy local trade; increasingly popular with our nationals. As Bucas go, we prefer this one to the aforementioned Buca Lapi. **Nandina** (piazza Santa Trinitá), a simple spot, has recently changed hands, so we must nip back for another test. The downstairs **Buca dell' Orafo** ("Goldsmith"), tucked in behind the Ponte Vecchio, is a family *trattoria* with savory cookery. It has continued to improve to the point that it is now frequented by the elite of Tuscany and their guests. Only a dozen tables; no décor; specialties include Stracciatella alla Buccia di Limone, Petti di Pollo, Bistecca alla Fiorentina, Bollito, and Stracotto. An amiable choice. **Sostanza,** behind the Excelsior at via del Porcellana, is a highly touted *trattoria* among Florentines. Rough, amusing atmosphere; go noonish for lunch or at 7 P.M. or 10 P.M. for dinner, to avoid the peak of the throng; otherwise it's frenzy in Firenze. Best bets were the breast of chicken, local beefsteak that is enormous and vegetable soup. A popular stop. **Le Cantine**, in Palazzo Pucci, has had a change in management; we'll check in again soon. **Sherwood** (via Torta 7) sits you in huge blossom booths that climb up, up, and awaaay, like Jack's beanstalk, while the waiters bee-buzz in and out. Youngsters seem to enjoy its nectar. **La Loggia**, at piazzale Michelangelo, is a municipally owned century-old former art gallery. Its dramatic hillside site commands a 180 ° panorama of the city. Alfresco terrace lunching or dining among portico columns or an open patio bordered by stone balustrade; about 90 tables; pleasant, small glassed-in restaurant for wintertime. As a capricious little fillip, you may ride by carriage to this happy spot via the American Express Night Tour. Enchanting—*if* a surfeit of tour groups doesn't spoil the atmosphere. Have the appetite of a ravenous panther? The stomach of a hippo?

The second revolution

A WHOLE NEW DIMENSION IN TRAVEL INFORMATION
A TOLL-FREE TRAVEL HOTLINE

How the Living Guide Works

1. Fill in this postage-free card and mail it to us.
2. We will send you a toll-free telephone number.
3. You may call this toll-free number to ask personal travel questions and get from our experts the latest day-to-day updatings our research has uncovered since this guide went to press.
4. This service is *absolutely free*. The Living Guide center is not a travel agency that makes reservations or itineraries. It does not sell anything. Here is simply our way of extending our help beyond the pages of this guidebook to help you have a wonderful trip.

The Fielding Team

MAIL THE POSTAGE-FREE CARD TODAY!

This offer is good through December 31, 1989, and only in the continental United States. Please allow 3 weeks for delivery.

The Fielding Corporation
Main Street, Madison, Wisconsin

Call us Free!

THE
LIVING
GUIDE

**TOLL
FREE**

HOT LINE

This is your passport to the Living Guide.
This offer good only in continental United States.

BUSINESS REPLY CARD

FIRST CLASS · PERMIT NO. 7334 · NEW YORK, N.Y. 10001

POSTAGE WILL BE PAID BY ADDRESSEE

The Fielding Corporation
415 West Main Street
Madison, WI 53791

Head straight for **Otello** (near the station). A barrage of howitzers couldn't be noisier—but that Big Gun in the kitchen couldn't possibly mow you down with a more walloping charge of fodder. Even the pepper mills are 5-feet tall! Sit in the hut-style room and wear your Paul Bunyan earmuffs. It won't be the best meal you've ever devoured, and far from the cheapest, but we'll bet you a wheel of Gorgonzola it'll probably be the biggest. Goshen for a glutton. **Al Girarrosto** (9/10 piazza Santa Maria Novella) specializes in wild bore, venison, pheasant, and other forest denizens in season, plus a variety of saddle-broken grills. Frustrated anglers may point a pinkie at the live trout tank in the window and be sure of a satisfying catch. Two pleasant but routinely decorated floors; painting exhibits which are changed fortnightly; in summer, sometimes more comfortable to dine in the cellar nook rather than outside. If you're game for game, draw a bead on this one. **La Bussola**, near the Straw Market, offers back-room seclusion, deft service, and inspired Lasagne alla Ferrarese amid photos of strippers and other "personalities of the world." Open midday and 6 P.M. to 2 A.M.; closed Monday; very easy on the wallet. **Al Campidoglio** (via del Campidoglio 8R) *can* have fine vittles and service to match. But when it's crowded, it's a different story: hurry-hurry, busy-busy, gobble-gobble, brrrrp-brrrrp, damn-damn. **G. Nuti** (via Borgo San Lorenzo 24N) is a tiny pizza sanctuary where the pasta pleases. Perfect for a bite or a nip. The **Da Zi Rosa** (via Fossi 12) is a modest haven where niblets are more of an attraction than its heartier choices. Nice people, but the portions we had were so tiny our female companion joked she would slip her lunch into her compact and save it for a snack later. We found few clients—yet the telephone was so busy on our visit it sounded like a direct line to Hialeah. **Camillo** (borgo San Jacopo 57-59R) is again one of our favorite *trattorias*. Throngs of visiting U.S. buyers continue to pour in here by the score to feast on Owner Bruno's delicate software. The food is still delicious—about that there's no question—and, at last, the client is being given kinder attention than of yore. Very recommendable for its high-quality cuisine. **Mamma Gina**, a few doors away, was taken over by 3 former Sabatini waiters recently and totally redecorated; they revised its kitchen toward the provision of grills. We like it even more now than before. The flairful **Ringo's Bar**, on the same street (19R), is costly but popular for its chef's salad served in a jumbo goblet. Nice on a warm day. **Paoli**, set in a palace, is on the comeback trail. **Villa La Massa** (see "Hotels"), on the outskirts, should dish you up a well-presented meal, if it's an "on" day with the mercurial chef and crew; a happy renaissance. **Pub George & Dragon** (borgo Santissimi Apostoli 33R) comes up with succulent snack selections in cozy Victorian surroundings. Sandwiches at the bar at all hours; upstairs for heavier nibblings; increasingly popular with a seemingly pixilated following of gay young men; ownership by Savino Pinchiorri and his bubbly, extra-friendly, French-born Anna; closed Monday. **Da Dino** is noted for its wines; we were not impressed by the grubby surroundings and mediocre cookery, however. **Celestino** is intimate, inexpensive, and worthy as a purveyor of Florentine platters. Closed Tuesdays. **13 Gobbi** ("13 Hunchbacks") performs in the Hungarian way—and does it well, too. Chinese chow? **Fior di Loto** unwraps its fortune cookies in 5 locations in the city. **Giacosa** is a shopper's pause bang in the heartbeat of midcity. Expresso, cakes, ices, and sore feet are what you'll

find. At *Fiesole*, an art center and hill town a few miles distant, **Mario**, on the main square, served the best fare locally. It's very inexpensive; the view (why you came) does not exist. We prefer the upstairs dining room in winter and the courtyard garden in summer. **Aurora**, nearby, is okay if you can sit outside and gaze along the Arno valley; the interior dining cell is a downright horror, in our opinion. The **Blu Bar** faces the same direction; it's salubrious for sipping. Don't bother with **Il Mulinaccio**, a chuck-wagon-style poser that can be chucked out as far as we're concerned; big show, little value. We're told that **Cave de Maiano** just before Fiesole is a worthwhile den, but time was so short on our latest round that we never climbed into this grotto. Please check locally.

Night Life The city's darkling hours are darkling even more; nightclubs are sparser and sparser in this city. **Moulin Rouge**, on the outskirts along the river (a long taxi ride), can be pleasant during the chillier times. Draped ceiling with inset light boxes; bar with adjoining dance floor; comfortable banquettes and well-padded easy chairs; many good-looking ladies also well-padded and also easy; show that's strictly from The Gong Show. When the charitable waiter noticed we couldn't stomach the house's chemistry, he quietly (without even being asked) spirited it away and spirited back genuine *spiritus frumenti.* Very good—but we'd trust that bartender less than the *Peking People's Daily.* **Full Up** currently is the fullest straight discothèque. Comfortable and highly agreeable for its type. The **Jolly Club**, near the bridgehead of the Ponte Vecchio, comes up with a ceramic-lined entrance and tile-sided youngsters who jig hip-to-hip in jam-packed joviality. Fun for the striplings. So is the now-snapped-up **Red Garter**, which is mostly for beer and teen revels. It's a perfect nest for youthful night hawks with extra-tight elastic in their own little garters—the ones around their wallets. The **River Club** retains its loyal oarsmen. Liquid fuel is the be-all of its being. **Arcadia** lifts spirits with its piano bar, cabaret, and disco doin's. Closed August 1 to September 15. The winter-only **Mach II** has become a membership club. Don't fret about exclusive entry policies, because if American Express will change your greenbacks into lire, we'd almost guarantee you'll qualify as an exalted card-carrier. **Al Pozzo di Beatrice** is a cozy cellar hive swarming with Bee-girls who hungrily buzz for honey in any sugar-daddy's sack. Its dark interior is bathed in a crimson haze; its colorful flooring and its huge pillar are the dominant decorative features. Open nightly at 10 P.M.; also open at 5 P.M. on holidays for tea-dancing—bags provided by the house. Be careful. **Pintor's** is no longer full of beans. Closed mid-June to mid-September; not recommended.

Shopping *Ladies' shoes:* ★ ★ ★ ★ **Lily of Florence** (borgo San Jacopo 20) is one of the best bets—and bargains—within 7 leagues of the Arno. This shop is the sole distributor of world-famous Amalfi designs; the dressier "Lily of Florence" line is also featured, as well as Switzerland's celebrated Bally assemblage for men. All U.S. sizes; tariffs which run 30% to 50% less than those you'd pay back home. Mrs. Power is concentrating on her Rome branch (see "Rome"); her son Lynn, his wife Rosemary, and her daughter Maria will welcome you with grace. Terrific!

Knitwear and silk dresses: ★ ★ ★ ★ **Sonya** (Lungarno Acciaioli 26R) is a

sparkling bijou which is the highly successful creation and namesake of a bright, gay, young, enormously talented Californian. The most glorious of her specialties is knits, in which she's a champion. All of these as well as her wools, silks, cottons, linens, and certain accessories are designed and manufactured through her own virtuosity; when you buy here you'll automatically get wholesale prices with which nobody else can begin to compete. Smart Men's Dept. with jackets, ties, and more. Ask for this radiantly vivacious lady; her love of people is a joy. Not to be missed. /

Romei is also a knockout. Here you will find exclusives of famed Mirsa, Marquesa Di Gresy, and De Parisini silk-dress lines. In addition, there are beguiling assortments of wool-knit models, costume dresses and coats, lovely silk-knit dresses, gay matching silk print scarves and elegant handbags. Mr. Romei has a sense of the subtle, indefinable Italian magic—that special stamp which is instantly recognizable by connoisseurs and patricians of stylistic flair at any gathering place of international society. Ask for blonde and beautiful Mrs. Victoria Romei. High fashion wow!

Extraordinary gifts for friends (or yourself): ★ ★ ★ ★ **Balatresi** (Lungarno Acciaioli 22 R) is so fascinatingly different that no one should fail to visit here. Lots of their treasures are 1-of-a-kind. Head first for their eye-popping alabaster collection, all created by skilled craftsmen exclusively for them. Also importantly featured are magnificent pieces in hard stones such as malachite, lapis lazuli, rodonite, and other specimens, as well as exquisite enamelware including the famous Fabergé reproductions. The crown jewels of their vast array are the gorgeous original works of art which are sold only here, such as those created by the last of the great Florentine mosaicists alive today— Maestro Marco Tacconi. Three more honest human beings than gentle, friendly Proprietor Umberto Balatresi, his lovely wife Giovanna, and his quietly engaging sister Daniela do not exist. As a bonus, these dedicated experts take delight in giving geology lessons on whatever objects intrigue their customers. Safe shipment is made to anywhere in the world; their guarantee is their sacred bond. Hats in the air!

Majolica ceramics and Italian handicrafts: **Soc. A. Menegatti & Co.** (via Tornabuoni 77–79) and **S.E.L.A.N.** (via Porta Rossa 107–113R) offer good browsing.

High-fashion leather: ★ ★ ★ ★ **John F.** (Lungarno Corsini 2)—both the venerable family firm and its personable entrepreneur—win this sweepstakes in a walk. Here in its section of a historic *palazzo* is a small, happily intimate, and convivial reserve of a broad and ultrafashionable range of handbags, attaché cases, leather coats and jackets exclusively made for this shop, as well as small leather articles and a trove of other wantables. The craftsmanship is superb—and all merchandise is at 1/3 of their U.S. and Canadian prices! Please see John F. What buys!

Silver: **Ugo Bellini** and **Peruzzi Bros.** both have tempting stocks.

Embroideries: **Mamma Galassi** (via Calimals 25R) is versatile and inexpensive; here's an especially good bet. As a second choice, the **Rifredi School of Embroidery** (via Carlo Bini 29), run by 2 nice gals, is a 10-minute ride from town.

Galleries: **Masini** usually offers the best selection of paintings at reasonable tariffs. Handsome salons on the Lungarno Corsini; excellent reputation. We also like **Arno** (via della Vigna Nuova 73).

Antiques: **Via de' Fossi** (cheaper) and **via Maggio** are the best streets—but take care!

Markets: The charming **"New" Market** (Porta Rossa and Santa Maria) and the **San Lorenzo "Central" Market** are good for strolling and casual buying. The rather poor **Flea Market** (Piazza Ciompi) operates from Monday through Saturday.

GENOA (Genova) is perhaps the least publicized and visited center in the country—a pity from the standpoint of the traveler, because it is colorful. We don't know why this old port is so neglected by holiday seekers. It became a jet-blown twentieth-century air-harbor as well when it constructed a huge platform over the water named (what else?) the Christopher Columbus Airport. Medium-range planes offer regular connections with London, Rome, and Milan, plus the Italian islands. Something also has been done about highway routes to the south; long tunnels hewn at unbelievable cost now make the approach easier. Fellow countrymen cite the Genoese as generous and friendly away from home, but niggardly and remote within their own borders. We haven't found this so, but we do agree with the charge that they lack the sartorial chic and glamour of the more cosmopolitan Milanese or sophisticated Roman.

The port can be proud of the **Colombia**—classic, comfortable, and though expensive for this city, the lowest rates of any Deluxe hotel in Italy. This CIGA-operated house's major improvements, include the wood-paneled, extra-comfortable, maritime bar, the extensive front-bedroom renovations, self-regulating air conditioning in all accommodations, restyled bathrooms which bring the plumbing ratio up to 1-to-1, many late-sprouting balconies, 100 Frigo-bars, and a dining room with some of the finest ladlings in the region (please try the local specialty: Trenette Avvantaggiate al Pesto). Coupon-clippers should reserve #208–209, the so-called Ambassador's Suite; our pick of the twins is #111. Director Piero Coloru, merry and enormously efficient, is on the go ceaselessly to tighten up and improve this house. He has virtually no competition in the city. The **Savoy-Majestic** is the front-runner's nearest challenger. Director Mauro Placido has reshaped most of the bedrooms, renewed the kitchen, refashioned the lobby, lounge, and bar, and generally spruced it up. He has also been working assiduously on the adjoining **Londra Continentale**. This one, too, is coming along smartly. The **Plaza-Corvetto**, centrally but quietly situated, provides appealing shelter with a small hint of luxury. Total of 100 renewed and attractive bedchambers, most with air cooling; 86 baths; bar and parking area. The **Eliseo** seems to us to be slipping in quality while creeping up in price. On the main piazza, the **Bristol** is a living period piece; the baths on the 2nd floor, for example, could be in a showcase of Italian design crafts; they are so dated, but so beautiful. Public rooms vary between tasteful opulence and gaudy neon color schemes in plastic textiles; its 6-person white Formica elevator must have been built for a dozen Goliaths; it's the biggest we've seen outside of the *U.S.S. Enterprise.* If you enjoy indoor

tennis, push aside the easy chair in room #244 and you should have just about enough space. The **Park**, a dimestore-rococo villa on the corso Italia just across the road from the sea, is usually packed to the scuppers with sailors. Almost impossible to find a berth. The **City** is strictly functional; numbers ending in 23 or 28 are the better bets. Below these, we really can't recommend any. But for emergency use only, here are notations from our meanderings: The cold and dark **Milano-Terminus**, with 1/2-dozen updated rooms, is fair —or let's even say poor. **Aquila & Reale**, near the Colombia-Excelsior, would provide our roof only if the waterfront wharves were filled and no space remained in the bus station. We have seen dentists' waiting rooms with jollier-looking sad sacks than the ones we spied in this lounge. Never. **Italia-Minerva?** Nix. Best pensions are (1) **Simonini** (via Balbi) and (2) **La Principessa** (via Fieschi, in the "Small Skyscraper"); both are noisy, but both can be recommended. Unless you know someone with a warehouse full of insecticides, better avoid the flop joints along the portside via Gramsci. If you check into one of these seamen's digs, you might come home with more itches than Fido.

Your best dining bet is the **Colombia Hotel.** Yumptious regional specialties, plus a wide range of international dishes; set menu tariffs approximately the same as its rivals'—but far, far more savory. Among the independents, two seem to steal the thunder, and both are operated by the Giacomo Oliveri clan. The first is called **Da Giacomo** (Corso Italia 1); the second is **Aladino** (via Ettore Vernazza 8). Both modern, slightly above average in price, well above average in quality, and featuring careful attention by a friendly staff. The latter entry is a smidgen more chic than the former, but not by much. **Pichin** (vico Parmigiani 6) is typical of the locale. Don't be led to the first small room at the right; be sure to march across the hall and past the kitchen into the larger quarters opposite the entrance, where you will find about 25 tables. Up a few steps is a cozier nook. Worthy grills and roll-cart barbecues; wonderful Capricious Salad; appetizing fruit and vegetable displays; à la carte only; becoming rather expensive. Simple—but still a solid value. **Margherita da Zeffirino** (via XX Settembre 20) still draws the local cognoscenti. Some prefer the upstairs section, which offers live music; personally, we opt for the plain and rustic downstairs feedery. Vast open-for-the-eye wildlife refrigerator at entrance; yawning tile oven where the game sizzles gamely; boar, venison, or other season-only choices aboard a rolling "hot counter" to serve you at tableside. If your smile is contagious, bustling young Proprietor Luciano might send over a glass of Prunella at the end of your meal. Thumpingly expensive, but very good. **Olivo** (piazza Raibetta 15) is large and straightforward in its Genoese fare—but now, sadly, it seems to be plunging downhill. Closed Thursday. **Mario** (via Conservatori del Mare 332) is a *trattoria* in the same tradition. Virtually no décor; cookery on the heavy side; dull but recommendable. The spacious **Alfredo El Cucciolo** (via San Vincenzo) features a Tuscan kitchen and tabs that strike us as inflated for the return. **Selvatico**, on the seafront Corso Italia, plays its several tiers to a chic glowing audience who crowd it year round. The blame is usually aimed at Pappardelle alla Boscaiola, delicate fresh pasta with mushrooms and cream. What a yum-yum! **Della Santa** (via Indoratori 1) extends a double blessing: the husband (Prince Borromeo's former chef) is at the skillets and the wife is at your elbow; limited menu of

international selections; slow service; closed Mondays; better and better and better. **Justino's Gran Grotto** (11R via Fiume) is strictly for the traveler who must count and double count every penny; too·dismal to please most merrymaking pilgrims, despite the adequate quality of its wares. **Taverna del Mille**, in the Sturla district, is amusing as a change of pacers. Former stable; décor of saddles, tack, wagon-wheel fixtures, stone walls, and muskets; wine flagons and cups with the names of Garibaldi's G.I.'s; a dozen tables inside, plus an alfresco terrace for warm-weather dining; delicious Triada (3 types of pasta). Saddlebags of fun on our last visit, but later comers now say nay. **Caprice**, on the promenade, remains unspectacular but solid. Good. On a sunny day, a 20-minute excursion to **Boccadasse** (literally: "Mouth of the City") is especially recommended; here are the last remnants of an ancient fishermen's village, over a small cove. **Italia** (toward **Nervi**) offers 2 waterside levels, sweeping panoramic windows to soak up grand vistas of the Mediterranean, and assorted maritime effects. Some of its best effects will appear after you've sampled its seafood antipasto or its risotto. Ummmmm. Many romantic-minded couples steal away from the city's gaze to goo-goo-eye here. Pleasant. Another fair-weather charmer is **La Rocca** at the mountaintop village of **San Rocca di Camogli**, a 1/2-hour drive toward Rapallo (turn right from Ruta before entering the tunnel). Magnificent view from 3 drinking-dining terraces; chic clientele who continue to come, despite the generally slipshod administration; medium-to-high tabs; reserve in advance during peak season; 9 A.M. to midnight; closed January and February. Fetching when the heavens are blue. At **Nervi**, **Re Artu** is said to serve masterful platters from its Franco-Italian cookbook. We'll pop in next trip.

   Shopping? Except for one superspecial bet we have found it distinctly below average here. Extraordinary **A Alioto** (via Ippolito D'Aste 7–5) is the king of handmade fashion jewelry of many varieties. Nothing we've ever seen in Florence or the rest of Italy can begin to touch his craftsmanship in this line. Everything originally designed; stunning bracelets, necklaces, brooches, earrings, chains, charms, and more in both classic and modern, each bearing his own unique flair. Private 3rd-floor studio-apartment (#5) with door marked "A. Testa"; difficult to find, but not to be missed under any circumstances.

GIGLIO the island facing Argentario, offers the First-class **Campese** with a glorious 1/2-mile sandy beach. Packet boat transportation to-and-fro once daily; inviting, if silence is your meat. Back on the mainland, Porto Santo Stéfano offers the **Filippo II**, the best of an indifferent lot; the stone-faced **Don Pedro** isn't much either. **Calamoresca** comes up with 45 units and tubs, a pool, and a movie theater. Local chums award this nominee an Oscar; we'll preview it soon. For budgeteers, **Villa Letizia** (toward the "Pelican" at **Port'Ercole** is a beguiling 12-room pension with a private beach and lip-smacking vittles. In the same general vicinity, but northward along the Grosseto pike, the terracotta **La Corte del Butteri** at **Fonte-Blanda** (10 miles from Orbettello) is a rancho by the sea. Waterside restaurant; Tuscan cowboy bunkhouses in 2 stories; busy atmosphere, similar to an attractive motel on U.S. #1.

GROSSETO The most alluring target in this area is slightly to the north-west at beautiful *Punta Ala*, where you'll find the sea-girt *Gallia Palace*. Here the scenery has much in common with the land-and-waterscape around Port-'Ercole to the south. Architecturally and spiritually, everything is orientated toward the great outdoors—although the great indoors is unusually felicitous, too. Elba is just 10 miles to the west.

ISCHIA, less than 2 hours by ship from Naples or 1/2-hour by hydrofoil, is attractive, faddish, and a favorite of well-heeled pilgrims from many lands (particularly West Germans) for its health spas and sunshine. It's a volcanic island, where outcroppings of lava and pines abound; in character, atmosphere, and feel, it bears little or no resemblance to neighboring Capri. Its 3-wheel minitaxis are an amusing oddity—slow, noisy, but charging 50% or less of the standard vehicles' fares. Prices surprisingly high; scenically, less dramatic than Capri; spiritually, less enchanting than Elba: *never* go out of season, since the slothfulness is disturbed only by the buzzzzzz of a softly snoring volcano. Higher each year on our pleasure chart.

The enchanting **Regina Isabella** complex, 5 miles from Porto d'Ischia at Lacco Ameno, is indeed a *Hôtel de Grande Classe International* which trium-phantly merits its membership in the ultraselective Prestige et Tradition Groupment to which it has been elected. Three separate units connect along the shore of a lovely bay. The nexus is the Queen Isabelle, with 118 rooms and 118 baths, a beautiful indoor-outdoor dining-room-terrace (jackets and ties required at dinner), 2 fine pools (one s-o-o-o charmingly blended into a shaded grove with a natural islet of flowers and greenery in its center), a soothingly elegant décor featuring a plethora of the most stunning tiles we've ever seen in any hostelry anywhere, a gayly umbrella-ed beach, a solarium, 2 TV rooms, a garage, a hairdressing salon and a barbershop, sumptuous cuisine, and lots, lots more. The 2nd link in the chain is the elaborate, computerized **Therme Regina Isabella e Santa Restituta**, the famous thermal baths for physical reinvigoration. Then come the sea-bordered pool and the Sporting Terrace, an urbane and enticing oasis which offers a luxurious buffet at lunchtime. Still farther along, perched atop a cliff perhaps 100 feet high, is the **Sporting Hotel**—15 suites only which command the premium tariffs. Individual water-skiing or participation in a special school; sailing; speedboating; golf driving range; minigolf; Mediterranean bowling; interchangeable meal plan with 4 other establishments. Handsome, vibrant General Manager Harald L. Sellner de-serves congratulatory salutes for its patrician, immaculate mien, its ball-bear-ing organization, and its ever-courteous staff. Closed from mid- or late October to mid- or late April. Superb! The First-class **La Reginella** is situated on the town square in Lacco Ameno; it has the same ownership as the above-men-tioned Regina Isabella, but is lower in official category—with a corresponding drop in tariffs, of course. In the Port, **Excelsior** seems to have made a big comeback. Private bathing beach; comfortable; clean; excellent physical plant; nice pool. Now *the* choice within the town limits. The **Moresco**, across the street and on the beach, comes next. Moorish-style construction; charming gardens and ambiance punctuated with gay touches of color; swimming pool;

cozy bar and public rooms far more ingratiating than the brash modernity of its bedchambers; 56 spotless units with baths and balconies or terraces; chilly management. Older travelers may like this one more than do the youngbloods. The portside **Aragona Palace** evokes our most vehement NO. Life begins here at 1 A.M.. For insomniacs only. **Grand Hotel Punta Molino**, in the curve of the bay facing the Aragonian castle, is a worthy alternate. Sweet gardens; small beach; good pool; routine bedchambers. Under the professional direction of Giorgio Stacchini, the **Jolly** has taken on a decidedly upbeat character. Total of 220 nests; comfortable fittings in simple surroundings; TV, radio, and Frigo-bar; grounds well landscaped; swimming pool that's covered and heated for colder months. The **Elma** resides in its own park at *Casamicciola*, with 65 seaview rooms divided among 4 distinct but interlocked blocks. Large pool; tennis court; thermal bath area (for guests) with doctor and nurses; bar with piano player; films. Superb value, in our opinion. The *Parco Aurora* has a fine location on the beach; it converted a neighboring villa into an annex; its accommodations, however, must have been designed for the smaller, less-obese offspring of dwarfs, because they're claustrophobic. The **Cristallo Palace**, about 5 minutes along the road toward Lacco Ameno, offers 85 rooms—most with baths, and all with balcony or terrace. Pleasant split-level patios for dining and sunning; nice seaview but noisy locale; screaming cretonne and plastics to make your eyeballs bounce. The nearby beach is not recommended for swimming; take the bus service to San Montano, where lunch is available. In Second class, the **Miramare e Castello** faces the castle from its sandy location. Renewed some time back; open March-October only; coming up in every sense. The **Regina Palace** and the **Floridiana** are also in this category; the latter has a "thermal" swimming pool. The **Ischia**, on a strip of seashore, is the bailiwick of an Italo-American *signora*. Simple, no-frills accommodations; 32 units, most with plumbing—and wow! One room at which we winced had pink walls, green doors, and a yellow bath. Okay for colorblind budgeteers. The best pension, in a walk, is **La Villarosa**. Modern building in the port; antique décor; kindly staff; only viewful rooms on 3rd and 4th floors. The **San Pietro** pension, atop a promontory, is wonderfully situated; it was totally renovated a while back—and badly needed. The **Santa Caterina**, at *Forio* on the west coast, also boasts a lovely location; a car is a must for beach or town hopping.

Ischia's highest quality cuisine is dispensed in the lovely outdoor-indoor terrace restaurant of the luxury **Hotel Reina Isabella**; an excellent buffet lunch is daily offered to sunseekers in its informal adjoining **Sporting Terrace**. Both are fondly recommended. **San Montano** at San Montano Beach is the number one independent oasis for the visitor; nothing on the island except the Reina Isabella can touch this waterside restaurant, which draws the cream of the yachting trade. Open-air ambiance; the green tagliatelle and Mediterranean "lobster" terrific; tariffs on the expensive side. Take your bathing suit, pick your weather, and your lunch should be a happy one. **La Lampara** we disliked, because the prices seemed steep and the choice of eatables limited; not for us, despite its attractive setting. The little **Duilio**, almost next door, is 50% cheaper, and the seafood is delicious. Very primitive, with service that couldn't be more confused; fun nevertheless, if you're in the mood. The portside **Il**

Porticciuolo specializes in piscatorial picken's. **Romantica** has slipped somewhat, according to our local rumormonger. We don't know it personally, however. **Da Michele**, a wooden shack and wooden platform directly on the beach, offers bathing-suit dining in summer only. Food? The customers stuff the bikinis better than the chef stuffs the Cannelloni. **Di Massa** is *Ponté d'Ischia*'s best bet. Two excursions for a sunny-day lunch: **Trattoria Terre di Fuoco** above *Citara Beach* (20 minutes from the Port) has unpretentious but viewful terrace dining, with volcano smoke curling about your toes; the specialty is rabbit, but fortunately there is also a selection of heftier critters. **O Padrone do Mare** is *Lacco Ameno*'s leading seafood emporium; we prefer the platters to the people here, however. The southside village of *Sant' Angelo* is renowned for its thermal baths in natural rock formations; 2 lava-grain beaches flank the causeway; the sand is so hot the ravenous can literally fry an egg on it (the ravenous with good teeth, that is); many German tour troups. **Pensione La Palma** might be a good stop here, but arrange your table and your menu in advance. Awning-covered terrace; beach and sea panorama; peaceful. Finally, this terrain is famous for its wine; friendly imbibing is the next-to-principal sport. Of the whites, we'd suggest D'Ambra Vini, the stronger Biancolella or Forastera. Among the reds, Pede E'Palumbo ("Pigeon Foot") is the choicest of the coop.

Shopping? The **Dominique** chain (6 stores) carries outstanding boutique items at stiff quotations; **Filippo** (on the main street) is also expensive and fine for men's and women's slacks. The flock of others on corso Vittoria Colomare "import" their wares from Florence, Sorrento, and other mainland hubs. Sadly, this island has no significant specialty.

LAGO D'ORTA is a lovely sightseeing drive, but we've found nothing recommendable for an overnight stay.

MALCESINE offers shelter at the **Malcesine**, on the water's edge; now you might encounter poor quality beds and cookery, so we're told.

MARATEA is on the coast about 115 miles below Salerno. The **Santavenere** is a long white redoubt in a sylvan setting overlooking the sea on 3 sides. Old-fashioned stylings with modern appointments; 44 units, half with sea view; medium-size pool; pebbled beach; cordial staff. While the drinks were excellent, the food, though graciously served, was just so-so. Excellent for seekers of solitude. Open late May to late August.

MENAGGIO, the little town about an hour from Como, is proud of its **Grand Hotel Victoria**. This one is tricked out with turn-of-the-century spaciousness, a lovely lake vista, 100 old-style rooms and 53 private baths with reluctant plumbing. We don't like the **Grand Hotel e Menaggio**; it's starkly old hat and cheap tour groupy. The modernized Second-category **Bellavista** might be the pick of the lot; we haven't seen it since its renovation.

MERANO offers the **Bristol** as its leading hotel in a combination of Milanese-modern and traditional styling. Here's the GRAND s-p-a-c-e concept in

everything. Manager Hugo Dibiasi places a heavy accent on comfort and clean-line luxury. All 150 rooms and 20 suites with bath or shower; 80% with private balcony; rooftop garden solarium and blue-tiled heated pool; thermal baths; season from early April to late October. By miles the choicest in the Alto Adige region. The dated but well-maintained **Palace** has a fine location, giant indoor and outdoor pools, lovely gardens, and a fair degree of attractions, many coming from its kitchen. The **Ritz** is now moving up and is recommendable. The contemporary **Eurotel**, open all year, is typical of the production-line variety of latter-day budget shelters. Our "normal" double (with space-saving Murphy beds) boasted no less than 52 panels, drawers, or sliding shelves, which amusingly made us feel we were sleeping in the inner coffer of a Chinese puzzle box. **Mirabella**, in a residential setting, is also operative all year. Converted family mansion with thermal waters; somewhat grim public rooms; low bath ratio. Its attractive exterior does not follow through into the interior. The modernized **Bavaria** is quiet; it is said to serve good cookery too. The **Emma** is hostess almost exclusively to groups. Of the later crop, **Meranerhof** has recently moved up to first category; solid fare. The **Mignon** is not bad, either; it's also noted for its outstanding kitchen. The **Irma**, out in Maia Alta, is quite pleasant in a slightly lower bracket.

When the meal gong sounds, Merano offers little, because most hotels require full pension. **Andrea** is intimate and regional. **Forsterbräu** is a beer hall for budget pockets; it is *very* popular (they are also served who only stand and wait). Be sure to sample the Bauer Speck here—a thin-sliced Tyrolean-cured meat that is sheer delight. **Villa Eden**, on the outskirts, is said to provide "refined" cuisine amid parkland greenery.

MESSINA has a fair shake of new or improved accommodations, lavish portions of squalor, ravenous wolf packs of mosquitoes, and a chronic shortage of mosquito netting. Here's a gem of a city—to miss.

MILAN (Milano) is second in size in Italy, with 1 3/4 million people. Primarily commercial, with a non-Latin aura of hustle and bustle, it is the financial and industrial center of the nation, boasting 37% of all Italian businesses; with less than 1/25 of the country's population, it accounts for 1/5 of all wages and pays 24% of the national tax bill. Urbanity and sophistication are at their highest next to Rome; here is one of the most advanced cities in Europe, intellectually and technically—and, according to late surveys, also one of the most expensive. It's in the heart of Lombardy, up north near Switzerland; Como, Maggiore, and other Italian lakes are only a hop, skip, and jump away. The **Duomo**, most famous landmark on the upper half of the Peninsula, concentrates 2300 statues and some of the world's finest stained glass in 2 treasure-filled acres. The **Brera Gallery** sets off its paintings with a unique display technique which delights the spectator. The **Poldi Pezzoli Gallery**, tiny but choice, is the cultural contribution of an unselfish private citizen; Botticelli's "Virgin" and a priceless collection of procelains are found here. The air-conditioned Rinascente Department Store is one of the most modern establishments of its kind in Europe. Then, of course, there are Leonardo da Vinci's soon-to-be restored "**Last Supper**" (at an awarded cost of $1.2 million), **La**

Scala opera (don't miss its museum, open daily at specified times and during all performance intermissions), the **Museum of Modern Design** in the **Sforza Castle**, and a host of other high points.

Hotels Among its numerous fine hotels, there's a rich air of discrimination surrounding the **Principe e Savoia**. Exquisitely rebuilt and redecorated, this aristocrat takes the crown as one of Europe's top Deluxe addresses. Loaded with antiques and ankle-deep carpeting; stunning ceiling-height-marble bathrooms, with 2-entrance split facilities and telephones; electrically raised Venetian blinds for all floor-length, wall-wide picture windows; 100% air-conditioned; handsome, intimate My Grill; adjoining enclosed terrace-garden; finely hewn bar extended into a conservatory style nookery. The modern annex is quite different in tone but many guests prefer it to the traditional main address. Some switchboard inefficency has been reported. Area Manager Roberto Bucciarelli ably guides this house and the other CIGA properties in this city. The **Palace**, once considered almost outlandish by us in its striking modernity, has been warmed up so handsomely that it is now becoming one of our favorite Milanese choices. Color schemes rehued to curry, brown, cranberry, and beige; architecture inspired by 3 different virtuosi in the field; 75% of the house renewed; lighting fixtures often hideous but gradually being replaced; nicely prepared and presented cuisine in the Venetian style. Now restful and recommendable. The 335-unit **Hilton** extends a hearty welcome to contemporary travelers. General Manager Ricardo Damiani works 25 hours per day to make things run as smoothly as Italian silk. Delightful Trattoria da Pepi at mezzanine level; Music Club at penthouse height, with dancing from 9 P.M. to 2 A.M.; off-lobby London Bar, nursery. Twin units somewhat cramped but extra-brightly decorated; attractive furnishings; radio, TV, massage vibrators. For those who can afford the walloping tabs, it's a lovely stop, but our general impression is that most vacationers might find it too costly for the rewards. The **Excelsior Gallia** has put on some additional raiments. Now 100% air-conditioned; 280 rooms and 260 baths, all ample in size, adequate in comfort, and clean. The renewed 5th and 6th floors are best, in our opinion, as well as a few units in the older wing. There's a predominance of business registrants over holidaymakers. Red-blooded males will rocket straight up the walls at the soft, sultry voice purring the floor numbers through the automatic speakers in the elevators. Same rates as the leader; good, but not *that* good—except for the sexy elevators we shuffled around in for 6 or 7 hours one recent afternoon. The young **Plaza** serves breakfast only, but its accommodations are among the nicest in the city. Futuristic, cantilevered lobby; heavy use of chrome and glass; semicircular bar; angular construction; interesting colors. A bit odd but we like it. The 200-room **Jolly President** mixes Empire highlights with an egg-crate ceiling in its lobby and lounge. Air-conditioned; small chambers with floor-to-ceiling windows; competently run in a commercial way. **Michelangelo** has set up its modern easel near the tracks and is highly touted by local *dilettanti*. The revitalized **Duomo** shines in spots—but the trick will be to find those spots. The duplex suites and "VIP rooms" would be our choices, so ask for these first and then request that they show you around if some other accommodation is desired. Manager Ghirardi has brought this one up a long way, with more to go. The 150-room, glass-and-concrete **Nasco** is

a product of our modern times, rendered smoothly in a chipper meld of Italo-Scandinavian concepts. Bar-lounge that doubles as a foyer; spring-green breakfast room; 7 color schemes; snug accommodations, but good ones. A lively candidate with numerous virtues. **Carlton Hotel Senato** offers 80 cramped but efficient bedchambers, all with bath, shower, stocked refrigerator, and micro-TV sets; facial tissues, shoeshiner, silent valet, scales, and other functional gimmicks; garage, restaurant, and bar. Mercantile but convenient. The **Cavour** comes up with a nice lobby, 100 appealing but smallish rooms, and 73 private baths. Choose your location on the courtyard side away from the clattering street; you'll find a tub with every room, radiant heating here and there, and modest features in general. The **Leonardo da Vinci**, 20 minutes out on the Bruzzano pike, offers 320 extra-spacious hotel rooms plus 1000 wide-angled apartments. (Minimum stay in the latter is a month.) Indoor pool, 8 tennis courts, 2 saunas, 2 restaurants, 4 bars, disco nook, shopping arcade, hairdresser—actually, it is a hamlet unto itself. The free shuttle to town 24 times a day is a boon if you don't wish to drive.

More Milanese morsels? **De la Ville** boasts 93 baths for 104 breezy nests; it is soundproofed and sound for medium budgets. The **Andreola,** a toot from the station, has been refashioned in up-to-the-era stylings. The nearby **Splendido** has done the same. **Francia Europa** seems to be on the wane, in our poll. No thanks. **Windsor** is a regal choice for its class. **Marino alla Scala** waits in the wings of the opera stage; here's an untempermental coloratura with a kind and helpful manager. **Manin**'s claim to fame are the Colombo brothers who own it and try to greet every guest by name; garden dining, air cooling, Telex, and proximity to the city's zoo are its fringe benefits. **Cavalieri** refashioned many of its units—but oh, those retailored prices! A bit too *cavalieri* to suit us. The stylishly updated **Touring** does a far better job for the outlay, in our view. The service and the accommodations now show perk and pride. The same can be said for the **Sporting,** which is coached by dynamic Manager Brera. Superb value at medium cost. A penchant for pensions? **Casa Svizzera** (via San Raffaele 3) was reprogrammed with 75 units, 75 baths or showers, and 75 climate-control thermostats, but we still find it humdrum.

If you are a bird of passage, you might wish to wing in at one of the no-nonsense flyway perches in the Milan air space, either the **Aerotel Executive** by the airport or at the **Aerotel Fieramilano**, across from the fairgrounds. Both have clean lines and limited but adequate living space for transients. Sadly, the management changes here are about as frequent as the departure listings on the airport information board, so the quality at both does suffer.

Restaurants In Milan, today's visiting gourmet will be rewarded with a triumvirate of stellar dining establishments plus a sparkling diadem of lesser lights. Crowning the trio is **Gualtiero Marchesi** (Via Bovesin De la Riva 9) which is simultaneously the most modern, elegant, and most expensive restaurant in this most expensive Italian city. If you worship at the shrines of such French chefs as the Troisgros, Guérard, Chapel, and Bocuse, then you will probably find this Italian version of the *nouvelle cuisine* equally exalted in its genre. The interior also reflects the avant-garde tendencies even down to the handsome sculptures that decorate each table. If you don't choose one of the house's special wines (with which the cellar is very well stocked) a superb

repast is likely to cost at least $60. Closed Sundays and Mondays at noon. In terms of intimacy, we have fallen hopelessly for **Scaletta** (Piazzale Stazione di Porta Genova). There is a mood of exclusivity and *richesse* here which evokes faint stirrings of romance in dim places—just the nookery where two Beautiful People might meet for a private tête-à-tête. The cuisine is a happy blend of Franco-Italian mastery, and the billings run slightly more than half of those at Gualtiero Marchesi. It is shuttered on Sundays and Mondays. Delightfully suave. **Romani** (Via Trebazio 3) completes the trio of todays leaders. This one is a favorite nip-inn for the city's top executives. Though traditionally outfitted, there is an air of vital animation that belies the sedate interior. Undeniably this is prompted by so many disciples expressing satisfaction over the superb culinations, the splendid amiable service, and the surprisingly moderate prices. Incidentally, if you have a sweet tooth, the overwhelmingly caloric dessert trolley could probably make a millionaire of your dentist. Like most major centers of gastronomy in the metropolis, this one too rests on the sabbath. Of the old line conventional roosts, **Savini** remains the chosen rendezvous of La Scala artists. Slightly formal atmosphere; happy little bar; too-bright illumination; a landmark operation by the Pozzi family, papa Angelo and son Renaldo, who speak good English. Closed Sunday. **El Toulá** is friendly and often peopled with chic Milanese society. Location behind La Scala in the city's "Wall Street" district; spacious; gracious décor; advance reservation suggested, especially during the opera season. **Giannino** (via Amatore Sciesa 8) now gives us the feeling that it has gone off a bit—possibly because it seems to cater so heavily these days to touristic traffic. Several modern dining rooms; glassed-in kitchen; initial reception sometimes lax, but table service usually (not always) attentive and thoughtful. We hope it will pull up. **St. Andrews** (via Sant' Andrea) is a First-category entry that is beloved by locals. Mock-wood ambiance; central hearth the main decorative feature; bookcases on walls; leather chairs and love seats around low tables; subtle lighting from overhanging hooded lamps; rust carpets; lime-green textiles; profession-proud waiters in formal attire. The cookery was much better than average; it was much costlier than average, too. Our severest complaint, however, involves its deafening music that blares through the sound system. This cacophony forced us to abandon our meal and escape to a quieter retreat. What a pity; this could be a gem.

La Nos ("The Walnut," at Via Amedei 2 in old Milan) is "camp" in concept, but in our most serious view, the novelty wore off through 3 recent changes of management. Diners walk up some stairs to find 2 main sections and 2 smaller nooks. Whirring fans; suspended Tiffany-style lamps; a church pulpit used as a bottle rack; a menu in the shape of a walnut tree—all in all, Grandma's rummage sale décor that just doesn't click. Minstrels who look as if they've been wandering since Justinian's court play softly and pleasantly. We could ramble on but why bother? Closed Sunday and August. Special, but not with us.

Le Quattro Stagioni (the Four Seasons), about 20 minutes along the Autostrada, is a pleasant expedition on a sunny day or starlight night. Open-air dining in an attractive garden with fountain; kidney-shape tables; immaculate glassed-in kitchen; medium-lofty tabs. Try Pollo alla Creta, an herb-soaked

bird of paradise; finish off with its La Grappe cheese from the Savoie—and sigh with bliss. A favorite for upper-crust Milanese family outings. **Giggi Fazi**, the Roman entrepreneur, has 2 places in the area—on piazza Risorgimento in the city, and a summer branch at via Lodovico Il Moro 167-169 in *Ronchetto delle Rane*—both disappointingly inferior to his original in the capital. The metropolitan one is big, bustling, and barren, with friendly waiters who ride you to decide what to order NOW—and, when it comes, to eat it NOW. Dancing under bare-bulb lighting; just so-so NOW. The suburban one has been rebuilt and renamed **El Ronchett**. Neither is our platter of pasta. Yet another outskirter is **La Cupola d'Oro** at *Binasco*, a half-hour along the pike to Pavia (free pickup from hotels in central Milan). It features a music hall show plus dinner and and dancing.

Alfio (via Senato 31) is a honey that seems to get sweeter with each new buzz in our repollination flight. Midway down the entrance stairs you spy a huge open freezer shelf, overhung with garlands of fruits and vegetables and groaning with a magnificently colorful, diversified antipasto exhibit. The cuisine is excellent; the specialties are antipasti and fish, but a huge menu boasts almost everything that grows or wiggles; the prices are medium. We've been fond of this house for many years.

Taverna del Gran Sasso (pizzale Principessa Clotilde 8) looks like the warehouse on the MGM studio lot marked: "Storage #67, Italian Restaurant Scenery." And has it got it—*mamma mia!* Your eyeballs are poked by wagon wheels, garlic strands, corn clusters, brass pots, wine jugs, cheese wedges, cattle yokes, oaken barrels, sausage, hams, chickens, salamis, ceramics, breads, even a sewing machine—plus checkered tableclothes, natch. The dishes are chiefly from the Abruzzi province. We must confess we did not eat here; we merely stepped into the room and let our pores feed us by osmosis. Perhaps that's the way to do it?

Il Canneto, sometimes called Osteria del Vecchio Canneto (via Soferino 56), is the seafood version of Gran Sasso; it's under the same décor-happy ownership. Greetings to all comers with a foghorn and ship's whistle; cellar site; huge room decked with brass musical instruments, an ocean-liner's anchor, sails, a winch, and fathoms of chain; singing waiters in shipwreck costume; leviathan 16-course meal for a white bait price tag. The only items not from the briny deep are the pasta, the fruit, the wine, and the bib tucked under your proliferating chins. Not dressy.

The **Biffi**, which we liked reasonably well, is a modern adaptation of an Edwardian snackery; it's plugged into a subterranean music hall.

Famed and fine orchestra conductor David Blum waves his baton for **Boeucc Flavio** (piazza Belgioioso). We'll give this one a sounding on our own tuning forks soon. Thanks for the upbeat tip, Maestro!

Venturesome? Then don't miss **Scoffone Bottega del Vino** (via Victor Hugo 4), one of the most ancient wine houses in Italy. Scrumptious hot and cold dishes are available at a do-it-yourself counter or in a more modern cafeteria-style dining room in the rear. We much prefer the front segment with its painted walls and ceiling, black dado, wrought-iron chandeliers, and earthy atmosphere. Our bottle of Barolo, slices of cold suckling pig, pickled vegetables, and floating mozzarella (it should come in its whey when it is properly

kept and served) were admirable straightforward fare. Prices are low; the quality is high. Hundreds of varieties of native wines await experimenting oenologists. Very plain—but just plain wonderful for what it is.

Hotel dining? The My Grill of the **Principe e Savoia** is a stunner. The adjoining L'Etoile is perfect for lighter cozy nibbles. The Rib Room of the **Hilton** sizzles with roast beef for penthouse rancheros. Its next-door Music Club is a danceable top spot for the evening. The **Palace Hotel Roof**, open May through October, is so up-to-date it might have been designed by Raymond Loewy; lovely terrace and view. We like it. The **Cavalieri** also has a pleasant roof garden in season.

Cheap, colorful Milanese restaurants? Very few, to our knowledge; the city is too busy and too industrial to support them. One simple, smooth, well-run pizzeria which makes our taste buds stand up and whistle is **Santa Lucia** (via San Pietro all'Orto 3). Walls flanked with perhaps 100 photos of film, opera, and entertainment personalities; open kitchen aft; immaculate surroundings. Nobody we saw spoke English. Fine for wallet-watchers, with low-priced spaghetti (various sauces), pizza, prosciutto, and salami in the buck-and-under league; dramatically mixed clientele, from sable to mink to let-out lapin; here's the Sardi's of Milan. Operates nonstop from 9 A.M. to 3 A.M. Highly recommended. As a budget bet in summer, the Italo-Austrian-rustic **Donlisander Birreria**, at via Manzoni 12A (patio with umbrellas but no grass or trees) is growing lower in quality and higher in price, to this observer's eye. The **Foyer**, on via Verdi, is said to be good for post-operatic suppers, but we missed it.

Now for a gathering of *trattorias,* each distinctive in its manner, which we think are tops in their particular category: Don't be put off by the entrance at the **Cucina delle Langhe** (corso Como 6), which is a discouraging approach to the truly outstanding Piemontese tables within. This hardy cooking is genuine; the prices are honest as well. **Osteria dei Binari** (via Tortona 1) also features cookery from the Piedmont as well as *emiliano* preparations. Artists, journalists, and jet-setters now occupy the places where a century ago travelers paused to change horses. A "with it" spot—but never on Sundays or midday either. **Osteria Via Prê** (via Casale 4) presents such an unabashedly phony fish-house interior that you can easily forgive the decorator—if only out of a sense of humor. You could overlook a lot more once you have dived into the typically Genovese dishes, felt satisfaction with every morsel, and received a bill so low that you might blink with wonder. Closed Mondays; very moderate in price; very commendable for value. **Torre Di Pisa** (via Mercato 26) inclines one block from the Brera Academy, which used to be the center of Milan's red-light district. Today the area is respectable, the "Tower of Pisa" having become a popular rendezvous for advertising people and fashion models. There is a smattering of up-market bohemia here which seems to attract many swinging singles. And, oh yes, the food? That's okay, too. **Alfredo-Gran San Bernardo** (via Borgese 14) specializes in, of all things, Milanese dishes. It's plain to look at but easy to take otherwise. An outstanding meal, perfectly served, will lighten your budget by perhaps $15. The last 2 are shuttered on Sundays. **Bagutta** (via Bagutta 14) also plays host to the artistic community; better for mood than for food. **La Tampa da Antonio** (via Laghetto 3), similar

in tone, is not recommended. **Al Ciovassino**, via Ciovassino 5, down a small alley 300 yards from La Scala, dishes out hardy, belly-filling fare at soothing prices. As yet undiscovered by the hordes; closed Sunday. We hear that **Cascina Mirasole**, about 20 minutes from midcity, is good for typical cuisine; it is situated in a 17th century abbey. **Collina Pistoiese** (via Amedei 1) is one station where the local soccer teams swallow hardy nutrients. It greets you with an entrance crammed with antipasto; then come 4 rooms, wooden arches, paintings, engravings, and a final scrimmage with excellent regional cuisine and house wine, all for very moderate tabs. Closed Friday. Recommended. **Vecchia Osteria del Laghetto**, in the ghetto at via Festa del Perdono 1, is a handsome, rustic haven for game. **La Pantera**, at #12 on the same row, was a dismal, miserable, nauseating failure on every score when we sampled it. Not recommended by us no matter how heavily touted it may be locally or in the international press. Least expensive of all are the **Alemagna** snack bars, several of which are sprinkled through the city; they're clean, fast, and money-saving.

Night Life After dark, top honors for *summer* operation go to **Rendez-Vous**. Garden ambiance, with tables both inside and alfresco; good cabaret (for Milan!); dancing nightly; high-grade attention to cuisine and service; frankly expensive by national standards. Unrivaled during the warm months. Female pickups are often available. For *winter* shenanigans, **Astoria** (piazza Santa Maria Beltrade 2) is currently the most elegant. Rich, large, and brightly illuminated; entertainment and lively orchestra; tiny "music fee" but robust booze bill; companions frequently easy to find; closed June through August, when the staff migrates en masse to Nord-Est in Santa Margherita. **Caprice** (via Borgogna 5) takes the second tinsel-sprinkled popsicle. Longish room in varying reds, with bar at one end and dance floor at the other; dim lights; small show; house girls; closed summers; hard on the pocketbook, but not bad. **Maxim** (Galleria Manzoni) offers coral-velvet banquettes, double-candle lamps on tables, dancing, a modest cabaret, hostesses on tap, and lower beverage charges than those at Caprice. Closed summers, too. **Charlie Max** (via Marconi 2) woos young marrieds with exceptional nightclub cuisine, danceable orchestrations, and sane price tags. Recommendable for couples. **Number One** (via Annunciata) is the *numero uno* disco-hub at this instant; it's *very* costly. For number two, we'd draw on **Bang-Bang** (via Molino delle Armi), followed by the **Old Fashion** in the Park. **Nepentha** (near Plaza Hotel) has drawn outraged complaints from readers who dislike its sharp sell and supposed barnyard treatment. Black lacquer and Chinese red ambiance; table-side whisky service at tabs that trim the plumage of fine-feathered night owls; cagelike dimensions. **Santa Tecla**, behind the Royal Palace, demonstrates its jazz interests through myriad record jackets on its walls. **Sans Souci** seems to have gone down; it is not recommended.

Shopping In this city the shops are closed on Monday mornings.

Jesurum (via Monte Napoleone 14) has an enticing selection of dentelle and an exciting collection of shore fashions. Turn to "Venice" for more details.

Fabulous and famous **Roberta** (also see "Venice") operates a gorgeous branch at Pietro Verri 7. She has remodeled a quaint old stable and filled it with antique treasures to set off her vast and unique merchandise—including her deelightful innovation—her SQUARE umbrella. Tops.

Galtrucco (via San Gregorio 29), on the central piazza near the Cathedral, is the combined Saks-Bergdorf-Macy for yard goods. Branch in Rome.

Baratta (via Monforte 2) dresses the lion's share of the most elegant men and women who patronize La Scala. Here's the only combined male-and-female custom-cut wearables house we've ever run across. Also branch in Rome.

La Rinascente, the big department store, is at via San Rafael 2 on Piazza Duomo.

Second-rate flea market; The **Fiera di Semigallia** (via Calatafini) every Sat. morning. Haggle your hardest!

Via Monte Napoleone is the local peak of chic. If you'll start on its lower end and stroll through the short pedestrian mall of via delle Spigna, and then cut back down via Manzoni, this U-shape trek will show you the choicest galaxy of merchandise in this center.

MODENA has a useful address for a meal stop. A friendly Ontario physician recommends the spotlessly antiseptic **Real-Fini**, which is under the TLC of Dr. Fini, M.D. Food and service come in for equal praise—and our Canadian correspondent enthusiastically prescribes his colleague's *spiritus* Rx elixir retorted from local nuts (be sure to sample this liquor, he pleads).

MONTECATINI, 25 miles from Florence, catches much of the overflow when Florentine hotels are overbooked. To us it seems to be waning for North American pleasure seekers, but local hoteliers are making a valiant effort to reverse this tendency. The waters are famous for their beneficial effects on the liver. Within the immediate area are over 300 square miles of parks and gardens which tend to keep things cool during the hottest months.

It's **Grand Hotel e La Pace**, known as "La Patch-eh" to its international clientele, is slipping, we think, despite genial Proprietor Innocenti's heavy infusions of lire and love. Total of 170 rooms, 170 baths; pool; April to October only. The **President**, we are happy to report, is a delight now that Director Italo Cinini has wrought such charming wonders of intimacy. The predominant color is palm green—fresh, happy, modern, and totally inviting. **Croce di Malta**, next down the line, has been extensively face-lifted. Very good, too; April to November season. The April to October **Bella Vista Palace e Golf**, is smaller, but its reputation is comparable. Cordial reception and atmosphere; extra-worthy cuisine. **Tamerici & Principe** is one of the smartest addresses in the area between April and November. The **Ambasciatori** (formerly Cristallo Bonacchi) has changed hands and demeanor; it now has top-to-bottom air conditioning, a swimmery, and spring-sprung thermal bath. Sounds interesting. The **Nizza e Suisse** has been thoroughly remodeled and boosted up to First class. If you don't like these, there's a choice of more than 50 others in what has been facetiously called "Italy's Beachless Summer Miami Beach."

The resort's 3 feederies of distinction are the **Casa Rossa** (route to Montecatini Alto), **Pietre Cavate** (in town, but with a panoramic view), and **Le Panteraie** (via delle Panteraie). The last is a short hop from the center, in a scenic area. Swimming pool, dancing, solid fare, very agreeable in season; open May to October, and December to February only; recommended. A moderate

price Tuscan house called **San Francisco** is said to be quite good. Lunch only; top service; ask locally for directions. Ditto for **Tettuccio**.

NAPLES (Napoli), the nation's 3rd city, continues to draw our strong mixture of irritation and pity. With all her exquisite natural assets, this oppidum could be THE gemstone in the Tyrrhenian tiara, THE true mermaid of the majestic Italian coastline. Instead, gangsters have almost paralyzed her. The arteries which feed the metropolis contain holes in which an entire vehicle can disappear. Exploding sewers pockmark the terrain so that in some districts it bears a resemblance to Swiss cheese. Scores of people have been killed or injured, and several hundred have been forced to flee their homes in recent years because of these gaping rifts. The barricades surrounding them are untended, the lanterns are stolen, the wood is whisked away to be burned—resulting in mantraps which remain open for months on end. Considered Italy's filthiest city, the streets are littered with tons of uncollected garbage due to corruption in the Sanitation Department. Up to 15,000 people peddle contraband cigarettes on its sidewalks. When cars are stolen, frequently a parking lot attendant can retrieve them within hours—for a small sum. The taxi drivers, porters, boatmen, almost the entire skein of personnel who greet the vacationer have now gotten into the act. Vast armies of migrants, including us, are finding it no fun anymore. These baneful evils, combined with the demise of all scheduled transatlantic passenger shipping, have slid stopover tourism into such a downward spiral that today there is only one truly fine hotel and not a single truly fine restaurant except at this hotel. The airport is a horror. It has deteriorated into a transient way station en route to or from its booming nearby island and mainland resorts. (Incidentally, please *never* be conned into the wretched one-day Rome–Naples–Sorrento–Rome bus excursions which are being so heavily touted by many concierges in the Eternal City; turn to the Rome section in "Hotels" for the inside facts about these nightmares.) Her attractions include **Vesuvius** (take the CIT excursion at 2 P.M. daily, from piazza Municipio 70, by bus and chair lift, straight to the top), the new digs at nearby **Oplontis**, one of the world's most magnificent bays, the **Castel Sant'Elmo** and the former **monastery of San Martino**, the **San Carlo Opera House**, 499 churches—a score of wonders, if one could only see them in peace. As a passing point for excursions to Pompeii, Capri, Ischia, Sorrento, Amalfi, and other places, it is vital; because of this trim-the-sucker attitude toward her visitors, however, to us it is a case of "See Naples and Drop Dead."

Hotels   The **Excelsior**, operated by CIGA and directed by Sig. Sandro Pace, is so far ahead of other hotels here that no other house is in any way competitive with it. From the tallest eaves to the deepest wine cellar, it is a Koh-i-noor diamond which glitters dazzlingly over what has become virtually a derelict wasteland of hosteleries. Most of this plant has been exquisitely refurnished. About 60 bedchambers plus several sitting rooms and lounges redesigned by the famous Stigler (see CIGA hotels in Venice); all lodgings have been renewed in classic elegance; there are soundproof double windows on all sides; doubles #19 and #20 are first among equals. The cuisine in the redecorated restaurant is sumptuous; the service is flawless. Chief Concierge Cavotti and Maître Contiero are star professionals. This operation reflects solidity,

tradition, and sound management. Here's the *only* quality stop of the city—and it's even getting better. The **Royal**, also facing the bay, is gold and blue and glass; the clientele is very mixed, with heavy occupancy by NATO forces in winter; its nonofficial patrons are often alarmingly sleazy. Warm-weather penthouse pool; cramped dimensions. A mass hostelry which packs 'em in and out at tariffs considerably lower than those of the Excelsior. The **Vesuvio** is air-conditioned. Tons of plastic and Formica; range of lodgings from Archaic to Zesty; tabs pegged at about half those of the leader. **Santa Lucia**, next to the Excelsior, has given herself a general puffup since her takeover by the Royal interests. Sleeping lockers to the rear too barnacled for this old salt; bayside #47 the best double stop. Becalmed. **Ambassador's Palace**, now also called **Ambassador's Jolly Hotel** under its new ownership, is proudly called the *Grattacielo* ("Skyscraper"), and it will provide an altogether heebie-jeebie, knee-knocking sensation when the bay-borne winds make the edifice sway in the breeze. It occupies the 16th to 30th floors of an office building, with a separate entrance. Undoubtedly Manager Ezio Zucchi will be sprinkling magic throughout this lanky, 280-room (all with sea view) hostelry now that a fat and Jolly bankroll is his to play with. The **Mediterraneo** is another large, stream-lined, air-conditioned skyscraper. Every room with bath or shower; most with bright tiled floors and sticky plastics; shoddy appointments and linens; 50-car underground garage; glorious panoramic roof, featuring a restaurant-sun terrace complex which is no great shakes in the food department. A longtime chum warned us that the bar pulled a no-menu racket that prices your sandwich and drink at whatever the public will bear. Much too commercial and soulless for our liking. The **Majestic**, centrally located, offers a lovely view from the top 2 floors, a white marblesque lobby, and 120 rooms with bath or shower. Air cooled; further chilling by Northern European tour groups; now breakfast only. Fair at best. The century-old **Parker's Hotel**, above the city, has a passel of charms. Seaview location not far from center; 100-car garage added; cookery far more appetizing. We like the distinctive #414 as a normal double or the split-level #211 for 2 women or 2 men (beds separated). Old-fashioned but superior to most of its younger colleagues. The **Britannique**, once part of Parker's, shares its vista with this veteran. Rated as Second class, its 91 rooms are fair; 57 have bath or shower; #344 is a good double. Both cater heavily and successfully to wholesale package occupancy. Young wayfarers seem to enjoy the Second-category **Stadio**, near the San Paolo Stadium and municipal pool. Wardship by the clergy not restrictive in any sense. We think the **Domitiana**, on the same cinder track, is better, but both are too far out for most older shoppers or sightseers. The **San Germano**, in the same official class, is far along the pike toward the NATO base. Capacity of 83 rooms, 43 baths, and 40 showers; viands above average; routinely modern; except for its distance, a value for your lire. The **Rex**, around the corner from the Excelsior, must have the kindest owners in the city. Why else would they rent rooms by the hour? For bargain hunters on wheels, the 100-bed **Motel AGIP** has rolled in on the outskirts.

Restaurants The late Ian Fleming, debonair creator of Secret Agent James Bond, said in one of his last books, "The American travel writer, Fielding, summed up Neapolitan cuisine: 'It runs,' he wrote, 'from high medio-

cre to just plain lousy.' I cannot improve on that." Back then we were compli-
mented that this famous gastronome and cosmopolite agreed with our premise
that no major city in Italy offered a larger percentage of dirtier, sloppier, or
more disappointing restaurants vis-a-vis good ones. Now we regret to report
that the culinary picture is even darker. Another contributing factor is that its
numerous private clubs provide savory full meals for modest tariffs.

The most consistently dependable choice for lunch or for dinner in the entire
region is the Hotel Excelsior. All of the rigidly top-quality cookery, service,
and hygienic standards maintained throughout the great CIGA chain are
scrupulously observed here, with the consequence that the fare is uniformly
excellent. Because Naples is the birthplace of the pizza, you'll find it on this
menu—and *is* it delicious!?! The **Ambassadors' Palace** and the **Mediterraneo**
offer superior views but we've found their viands sometimes villainous. The
rest of the hotel pack have run-of-the-mill kitchens at best and abominable ones
at worst.

La Sacrestia (via Orazio 116), choicely positioned on a hillside 15 minutes
from the center, draws bevies of smartly attired sophisti-cats. Alcoved main
dining room in neo-Baroque décor; more intimate subterranean chamber with
tiny bar; outside terrace for viewing the crescent-shape metropolis while sampling the Assaggi ("Mixed Pastas to Test"); dignified but not warm service.
Our muted vote as the leading independent.

While **Cantinone** (via San Pasquale 56, at via dei Mille) is liked by locals,
we find it only so-so. Handsome décor featuring a colossal open grill and all
the paraphernalia of Italian Rustic gimmickry; Pompeian-rouge and Capri-
blue linens; rush-bottomed chairs; waiters in red and azure minismocks; appetizing selection of meats; wild goat the roast specialty. Service so rapid we'd
bet you could get a minute-steak in 30-seconds flat—too fast, in fact. It's not
a gastronomic shrine by any means.

Galeone is up, up, up, on Posillipo where it has become a favorite meeting
perch among middle and top echelon businessmen. Lovely situation; vittles
good but not distinguished; service alert. A medium-high flier.

The **Tiffany** (via Petrarca), too, is a steep taxi climb from midcity. It's also
a steep ride back—and seldom have we squandered taxi fare so foolishly. Never
again—not dinner, not lunch, not even breakfast here for us.

Da Ciro (via Santa Brigida 71–74) impressed us most recently as being in
a decline. It was a sad disappointment this time.

Il Girarrosto (Fratelli Imperatore di via Scarlatti 180) is a tiny food shop
with an even tinier restaurant attached. Very informal; excellent for snackery-
smackery; Wednesday is its day off.

La Quercia ("The Oak"), on vicolo della Quercia near piazza Dante, is a
favorite among princes, potentates, and the pasta peerage; it continues to draw
favorable reports; no imported liquors are available in this *trattoria.* It's also
locked up on Wednesday.

Giuseppone a Mare (discesa Capo Posillipo), on the sea perhaps 10 minutes
from the center in the vicinity of Masaniello, is relaxing on a sunny day.
Extra-fresh fish every day; average meal up to $25 per person. Specialties of
oysters and shellfish, vended from table to table by a blue-sweatered *ostricaro,*
or "oysterman"; on the simple side in furnishings; open terrace; clean, bustling,

busy; pizza a dream; not much English spoken; don't go on Wednesday. Add up your bill here before paying. The **Pizzicato** (piazza Municipio) serves allegedly American-style refreshments, with pizza the feature upstairs; when we saw it, however, its cavernous premises were so grubby that they'd have taken away our appetite if their food already hadn't. We rate it as abominable.

Salvatore (Riviera di Chiaia 91) greets guests with a glassed-in sidewalk segment; behind that is a small vaulted room; both are heavily patronized luncheon nooks for neighborhood office workers. There's strolling entertainment by the Geriatric Brothers, who offer witty ditties in the local *lingua.* Fair to middling.

D'Angelo (15 minutes by taxi up the Vomero) couldn't be more gimmicky if it tried for the next 500 years. Glorious view, open terrace, good pizza—but such tourist-trap stridence leaves us not only stone cold but frozen stiff. Closed Tuesday. Our most unfavorite type of restaurant. **Le Arcate** (nearly next door at via Aniello Falcone 249), also large and barnlike, now exudes more zing. A discothèque contributes to its youthful appeal. In this production-belt category, better geared for first-timers; also inactive on Tuesday.

In the Santa Lucia Basin (marine cove opposite the Excelsior and Vesuvio Hotels), except on Wednesday, **La Bersagliera** is still an unabashed tourist-hooker—but, regardless of this drawback, it is now definitely worth a visit. The waterside terrace is a delight, despite its pushy waiters. Spotlessly clean, enormous kitchen, which you may inspect; fresh sea denizens on our try—so newly plucked from the Mediterranean they could shed an indignant sneer your way. Prices are on the high side, in line with the brutal official tariffs on piscatorial gastronomy around the shores of this coastal nation. Although it is sited in Naples' nucleus of huckster hideaways, this one seems to be king of the sea. **Transatlantico** was redecorated some time ago—or "resurrected" would be more accurate. The fabulous refashioning reportedly consumed all of $2000! Lots o fresh paint, awnings on the terrace, some brand-new light bulbs—what next? The locale is bewitching, but we've never been fond of its staff attitudes. As for the rest of them, we're fed up with the dirt, sham, the surly personnel, and the feeling of being clipped which always seems to come when we dine along this row.

Damiani, a hopping pizza emporium 9 miles up the Domiziana Route toward Rome, has facilities for swimming (day or night), including 250 cabanas; restaurant of sorts plus bar; dancing on weekends; much frequented by U.S. officers and families in season; jumping on our visit.

A 'O Re Burlone, above Gaeta Bay, comes on with a strong tourist-oriented, gimmick-riddled personality. Inevitably the show, show, show, and more show is the thing. Some outlanders find it highly appealing; personally, we happen to regard it as a hoked-up trumpery, an opinion with which you might well disagree.

Night Life After-dark attractions are generally honky-tonk and murderously expensive here. The **Vesuvio Roof Garden** in the Hotel Vesuvio is the only truly noteworthy evening oasis in the city—and this one functions only in the summer. **Pacuvio**, at a good site up on Orazio, is a solid, respectable, family-type establishment. Dinner from 9 P.M. until the cabaret begins at II; short breaks until I A.M.; regional fare that is well above average. The only

difficulty is that unless you understand the Italian spoken in the show, you'd probably be bored. Very agreeable otherwise. **Shaker** pours its beverages at half the price except on Thursday, when it's inoperative. Basically,.it is a modern, amiable bar and cocktail lounge. Meals are also available. Not bad. Sportive gentlemen on the loose might find their pleasures (*and* their initial steps toward bankruptcy) in an amazing establishment called the **Antony Cabaret** (via Nazario Sauro, one block from the Excelsior); we use the word "amazing" because we have the feeling that the proprietor could wax fat on the profits of a total of 6 customers per night. Loaded with gobs when the 6th Fleet is in port; watch your wallet; watch your teeth. Obviously, we dislike this one with a passion. The **Snake Pit** (via Vittorio Emanuele 39) is *truly* rugged, especially when the U.S. fleet is in. Plenty of women, plenty of action, plenty of lowdown color; closed Monday. Except for serving us bum whisky from a quality bottle for our 2nd (not first) drink, this place seems to be on the level, but watch out for shady or downright crooked practices in other Neapolitan dives. Mickey Finns, pickpockets, and "rolling" are common.

Shopping This impecunious hub has essentially limited pickings.

Try **Roberta** (via Calabritto 9, described at length in the "Venice" section) for top couture items displayed over 2 floors of elegant Neapolitan real estate; **Mario Valentino** (next door at #10) for fashionable shoes and bags; the **Ricciardi Boutique** (across the street at #15) which exclusively purveys the Micmac, Christian Aujard, and Aqualo lines; **Alinari** (a few doors down) for prints; **Spatarella** (at #1) for bargain purses; or **L'Angolo** (piazza dei Martiri 36) for attractive and unusual gift items. **M. Tramontano** (via Chiaia) has a big choice of brooches and buckles, plus more than 125-thousand different buttons. *Cameos;* Buy *all* your cameos at Apa (see section on Pompeii) instead of in the city.

The **Flea Markets** in the main are wretchedly junky and *loaded* with pickpockets as well as crooked peddlers.

OMEGNA, at the head of Lake d'Orta, is a hideous steel-and-umbrella-manufacturing center.

PADUA is not too exciting, but if you do overnight here the commercial-minded **Plaza** is a substantial bet. It would be followed by the **Europa**, the centrally sited **Leon Bianco** (with a good restaurant), the **Monaco, Biri**, and the **Grande Italia. Villa Altichiero**, west of town off the *autostrada,* is said to be atmospheric and comfortable. Among the dining choices, try **Le Padovanelle**, on the outskirts, **Dotto**, and **Isola di Caprera**, in that order—but without much advance enthusiasm for any.

PALERMO is Italy's 6th city and Sicily's largest center; the lion's share of commerce, however, is concentrated around *Catania*, on the East Coast. Labeled by its promoters "The Golden Shell," it has some pleasant aspects including Moslem ruins, Norman traces, and baroque beginnings—but better-grade vacationing facilities are so limited that it's not worth a special journey. A weekly ferry service to Gela, Catania, and the island of Malta slices the wavelets. Overnight car-ferry connections with Naples (and other more distant

points) are excellent aboard the vessels of either the Canguro or Tirrenia lines. Both services run clean, comfortable ships that can save 2 full days of driving over the desolate hills of southern Italy.

The residential **Grand Hotel Villa Igiea**, in its own back-o-town park by the sea, is a shining oasis in this hotel-poor region. It's rambling, aged, and cool —a traveler's reward. Seawater swimming pool; 100% air-conditioned; erratic service accentuated on a recent visit by one of the most irritating concierges we've ever encountered. The **Jolly**, severed from the sea by a wide avenue, nonetheless gets blasted by highway noise ALL NIGHT L-O-N-G. It's still better than much of the competition—especially if you're a heavy sleeper. The **Grande Hotel & delle Palma**, owned by the Villa Igiea, is a fair choice despite the fact that it's showing its age virtually everywhere. Midcity situation in the throbbing eye of the 4-wheel hurricane; overweening institutionality despite some recent renovations; air-cooling now cooing a Grandiose sigh of welcome relief; clean but zestless bedchambers; generally inviting baths with colorful tiles—almost the *only* touch of hue-someness in the barnlike joint. If you stop, please ask to see the modest little corner where Wagner composed *Parsifal.* This stadium-size hideaway is far from inspiring. The **Mediterraneo**, **Ponte**, and **Metropole** are barely acceptable. **Mondello Palace Hotel**, 7 1/2 miles from the center, is Italian-modern in tone. First category; 70 rooms, baths, and showers, many with terraces; swimming; summer dancing; mini-golf; garden; March through November. The **Sole** is worthy in Second class; so is the **Splendid La Torre** in *Mondello*. A Motel AGIP offers 200 clean beds at a bargain. At **Terrasini**, about 20 miles west along the coast, you'll find the **Cittá del Mare Hotel-Village**. All rooms have shower, terrace, and sea view; we're told that enough bars, restaurants, sports, and entertainment facilities are in high gear to make you think about a vacation after your vacation. The capper is said to be an astonishing architectural oddity: A toboggan run of 10 slides connecting 3 pools that finally empties the adventurous into the deep. We can't wait to try it.

The most distinguished tables in the big city are set at **Gourmand's** (via Libertà). Mod-minded setting; L-shape chamber; sound-suppressing cork paneling; thick carpeting; silver-hued swivel lamps reminiscent of beauty-parlor hair driers; fresh flowers everywhere; adroit service; steep but value-received tabs. Spaghetti alla Gourmand's, with mozzarella blended into the sauce, is a savory selection; so are many of the fish dishes as well as game in season. **Villa Igiea's** kitchen crew and service personnel still seem to be snapping to attention. The Great Hall atmosphere still constitutes a pleasant setting, and with the staff morale higher we are pleased to put it back on the "recommended" list. **La Caprice** (via Cavour 42–44) is chic and so are the tariffs. Bright yellow décor; small bar by the entrance; canopied rear patio; smart. The **Charleston** (piazzale Ungheria) is a similar flapper that has been dancing up the rankings. Now considered by many to be tops in town. (This one migrates to Mondello when the weather warms.) **La Stipa** (via Cavour 97, a block from the waterfront) is a brick-lined den divided into 4 small segments by arches; it is also one of the few truly fine, yet inexpensive, restaurants on Sicily. Antipasto selections are made from the buckling table in the rear. These may be followed by a superb Involtini (veal wrapped around mozzarella, ham, bread crumbs,

and parsley), filet in cream sauce with prosciutto and mushrooms, or the house specialty: Spaghetti Frutta di Mare (spaghetti laced with savory sea-morsels and cooked piping hot in a bag). Unusually friendly service and memorable culinations. Closed Wednesday. **Al Gabbiano**, on the water at *Mondello*, caps them all for finny fare. Nice outdoor terrace for sun-day-excursionists or weekly cooing moonshiners. **Gambero Rosso**, nearby, is similar. In town, we'd pick the rusticky **Osteria Marinera**, only a toot from the ferry port. **La Botte**, in *Monreale*, is said to be worthy. **Al Fico d'India**, in the center of Palermo, is not, but NOT, in our opinion.

Shoppers might like to try **Salvatore Barraja** (same street) for variety items; **La Botteguccia** (piazza Ungheria) for boutique specialties, and **Eugenia Patella** (corso Vittorio Emanuele 474) for fine antiques. The **Daneu** branch (corso Vittorio Emanuele 452) accents antiques rather than the handicrafts of its Taormina headquarters. Via Maqueda, via Roma, and via Ruggero Settimo are the buyer's best stamping grounds.

PALLANZA, on Lake Como, has the First-class **Grand-Majestic** which occupies a noisy roadside site; in our view, here's an old dowager who needs paint pots and nourishing cream by the gallon. Season only.

PARMA is pretty cheesy. The **Park Hotel Stendhal**, in the city, has a cheerful bar-lounge, a restaurant with appetizing cuisine, and 45 units with bath. **Palace Maria Luigia** is said to be fresh and a first-rate First-classer with a well-run dining room.

PERUGIA, like Assisi, draws such a flood of excursionists that its reception is noticeably jaded and mechanical. This ancient hill town is the site of the University for Foreigners, where scads of homesick scholars learn their basic Italian. The Collegio del Cambio has some fine frescoes, the National Gallery has some famous paintings, and the panorama of the valley is lovely.

In hotel circles, the **Brufani** maintains a gimpy lead over a still more slow-footed field. Old, Old, Old World flavor; still renewing its rooms; central situation. Fair. The newer **Excelsior Lilli**, on an outlying hump of roadside terrain, is okay for desperate motorists who prefer modernity. The **Grifone**, of a similar ilk, would come next, but we're not overjoyed with either, although the last has been completely air-cooled and supposedly pepped up. The little **La Rosetta**, down the street from the Brufani, is a lot cheaper and it now provides many renewed units. **Della Posta** and **Dei Priori** are both breakfast only.

The best dining bets are at the **Brufani** and the small, less-expensive **La Rosetta**. We're particularly fond of the high-quality service and sound regional fare of the latter, and our latest check rekindled the longtime romance; a number of readers are just as unfond of the former, which cocks a markedly greater commercial eye toward its numerous banquets and receptions. The **Bibo** is popular; the **Excelsior Lilli** and the **Grifone** are especially interesting for their typical local wines for a reasonable outlay.

PISA, except for its legendary Leaning Tower, venerable Duomo, baptistery, and exquisite Gothic church by Nicola Pisano, is practically a zero for most tourists. June *(Giugno Pisano)* is best, when *Il Gioco del Ponte* (tug-of-war on the bridge) and other pageantry bring it alive.

For determined lingerers, **Dei Cavalieri** is Neo-Italian-Modern, with 102 air-conditioned rooms, 102 respigoted baths, a bright-red American bar, and a redecorated restaurant. Now that it is being managed by CIGA, the improvements have been legion; Italy's prestige hotel chain has given this house a considerable boost in quality—something which was notably missing in Pisa. The **Duomo**, almost at the foot of the Leaning Tower, has 90 air-conditioned rooms, 90 baths, cuisine which is poor, a viewful roof terrace, avant-garde furnishings, and good drinks. First-class (not Deluxe); fair accommodations at reasonable prices. The **Nettuno** is roomy but gloomy. The **Royal Victoria**, although it retains the furniture used by Queen Victoria when she stayed here, is light-years from regal. If it's summer, and if you wish to escape the crush of this tourist-gagged city, the **Golf** at *Tirrenia* (on the coast, 10 miles from the steps of the Tower) might be an answer to your vacation prayers. Pine grove situation just a mashie shot from the sea; adjoining golf course, tennis, swimming pool, and full resort amenities; modern tone with ornate fillips; all 100 units with bath, balcony, and air conditioning. Better than the sweltering hives of midtown. Also for motorists, the **California Motor Inn** was launched at Kilometre 338 of the via Aurelia National Highway—about one mile from the city. It consists of a cluster of 9 villas, each with 6 rooms plus a restaurant and neon lighting à la jukebox; we haven't tried it, but some who have say they've been disappointed.

When it comes to comestibles, Pisa fare leans to the unglamorous, even at the **Hotel dei Cavalieri** and the **Hotel Duomo**. We've been able to find only one surefire candidate in this area: the **Nettuno** at *Viareggio*, 15 minutes out by car. Harbor location; semiopen kitchen; top quality dining; on the expensive side for Italy. Well worth the ride. **Margherita** offers reasonable pasta dishes.

POMPEII   Many visitors breeze in to ramble in an archaeological stupor all morning, hoping to pause for a decent meal at midday. Until recently, we'd rather have lunched on Ken-L-Ration and Octagon soap than chance another crack at the **Ristorante Turistico**, opposite the entrance to the ruins—but reports indicate it has improved. Fervent prayers for (1) its success, if it has, and (2) *ÿou*, if it hasn't. We are told **Tiberio** is better. The former closes on Tuesday; the latter is open the week around.

The highway from and to Rome is loaded with souvenir shops and cameo vendors, most of which are not only second-rate but trashy. Only 2 places, as far as we know, offer top-class stocks and are reliable. While **M. & G. Donadio** is the largest and oldest, with a good reputation, the price tags here alarmed us—much too high, in our strictly personal opinion, to recommend it to our bargain-loving readers. For more than 25 years we've been convinced that the **Giovanni Apa Co.**, at Torre del Greco, is head, shoulders, and carving awl above all competition. This venerable house, more than a century in business, is primarily a factory-wholesaler. This, plus the fact the Apas personally go

direct to sources in the 4 corners of the world to buy their own corals accounts for their low tariffs. Silver-mounted brooches and pendants in exclusive (and heavenly) pink-and-white; large, prime cameo or intaglio (reverse-carved) cuff links; coral or cameo earrings. Lovely ladies' and men's semiprecious stones and rings (topazes, amethysts, and monster aquamarines). Beloved Patriarch Giovanni Apa is still the spry Grand Vizier; Giovanni Jr., Maurizio, Luciano, Ricardo, and Mario Jr., sons of the brother-founders, are brilliantly carrying this monument to new heights. Branches in *Rome* (piazza Navona 26–27), and in *Tivoli* (main square). Highest recommendation.

PORT'ERCOLE   is a quiet harbor of *snobismo* on the Argentario promotory opposite Orbetello, 103 miles north of Rome toward Grosseto). The village itself isn't much; its few hostelries are often inconvenienced by an inadequate water supply. As a nesting spot, **Il Pellicano** is a beak full of charm. Seaside location; Pompeiian-red manor house with a glorious patio for sipping and munching; novel pool; 18 original rooms, plus 5 cottages and an 8-unit annex; fine, highly polished rusticity cooled by full air conditioning; high, high all-inclusive tariffs. There's an air of elegant hominess which we think any well-heeled, social-conscious, and peace-loving traveler would adore.

Our pick of the restaurants in the area is **Egisto** in neighboring *Orbetello* for its well-above-average Peninsular cookery. Next, in the Porto itself, we'd call it a toss-up between **Tonino al Porto** and **La Fontanina**, neither of which is spectacular. The seafood-oriented **Argentario** is beloved by locals.

PORTOFINO   has one of the dreamiest natural settings—a tiny, cliff-lined harbor of unsurpassing charm and intimacy, over which broods a castle and the Splendido Hotel. It's about 75 minutes by road from Genoa. Spring and fall are the best times to go; in summer it's often akin to Times Square, so crowded that the excursionists, the gays, and the souvenir vendors nearly trip over one another along the quay. A *must* to visit—but pick your season.

Splendido, perched on a mountainside, offers one of Europe's most gracious vistas. A pool is splashing for your pleasure. Total of 80 units, 69 with small bath or shower; fresh carpeting and plastering throughout; first-floor accommodations the biggest; only 4 inside rooms; fine, rich appointments almost everywhere, but some beds are indeed sag-sacks. Structurally and from a landscaping point of view it's glorious; its human approach, which we have damned so roundly for so many years, has been flip-flopped for the better. We hope the management will keep up the improved attention to hospitality and plant. The smaller **Nazionale**, in the village, is entirely refitted. Now expanded to 56 rooms and 56 baths; simple, Second class, agreeable, and friendly; parking at an inconvenient distance; noisy in season. The poorly situated **San Giorgio** is under the same direction, but that seems to be where the similarity ends. Not recommended. The **Piccolo**, the only remaining choice, is tiny; facilities are perhaps too regional for the average North American.

Il Pitosforo holds the lead for dining candidates. Situation farthest out on the bayfront; 2 stories above street level, with a small interior restaurant, a 20-table, semiopen terrace, and a lovely view; service friendly; menu regional and substantial; very costly by local standards. Bianco Secco Portofino wine,

dry and agreeable with an amusing label. Best in the village. The **Nazionale**
is tailored for tourists, but skillfully so. Terrace dining 20 yards from bay,
smack in the center of things; better-than-average food; also expensive for the
area. The **Splendido Hotel** cuisine is Deluxe again in every respect, and its
setting is magnificent. Our recent lunch was excellent from soup, to service,
to Saltimbocca. **Delfino**, around the bay between Nazionale and Il Pitosforo,
has a modern kitchen, a plain décor, and a celebrity-starred clientele. Seafood
a specialty; far from cheap; cookery fair rather than outstanding. **La Gritta**
is a Turkish-style bar replete with sports-car-height chairs, cushions, and
diners in blue jeans; it's only for special tastes.

POSITANO, in the opinion of many, is the star attraction of the Amalfi
Drive and of the entire area near Naples. The houses of this highly paintable
village climb straight down the mountainside, like mountain goats; so will you,
every time you go for a swim in the sea. (Happily, many hotels now boast
pools.) If you're planning an overnight in this region, it's a sensible stop.

One of the nicest spots of all is the rock-ribbed, vine-clad **San Pietro**, girt
by flowers, aproned by sea, and showered with love by Proprietor Attanasio
and Manager Cinque. This canon takes its name from the chapel on its cliffside.
Pool and tennis court just unveiled; private beach; plant-lined restaurant with
2 grills and a pizza oven; exquisite taste in its clean-lined accommodations;
floral displays rampant; balconies and terraces cushioned by bougainvillaea.
Though it is officially rated First-class (and so priced, too!), the standards
handily tip it over into the Deluxe bin as far as we're concerned. A dream spot
—but not from mid-Nov. until Easter when it shutters. **Le Sirenuse** also clings
to a hillside, with 7 floors staggered in staircase fashion, and with the main
entrance on the 4th. All living quarters facing the sea; door keys featuring a
mermaid suffering a severe bellyache; *taverna* and barbecue sizzling brightly;
private steps to the waves. Very colorful to the eye and to the spirit. **Villa
Franca**, down the scale, has a similar personality. All of these are intimate and
oriented toward vacationers rather than transients. The **Royal**, a First-class
entry, is not directly on the briny but its 5 levels offer an excellent vista.
Seven-minute walk from the center, with bus service available; elevator; 50
unadorned rooms, all with bath or shower and private balcony, radio, telephone; some units enlarged and modernized; nice pool. **Miramare** has a superb
position over the sea, with a full panorama to the south; enchanting restaurant;
15 rooms with bath, in 2 buildings; glassed-in goldfish swim merrily in some
of the bathroom windows while you bathe; facilities simple but adequate; good
but not outstanding, except for the magnificent location; be prepared to climb
steps until your ears turn cartwheels. The **Poseidon** has an off-beach setting,
with an 11-room addition facing the Gulf of Salerno. Good parking space; fair
cuisine; English-speaking staff; coming up strongly. The newer Second-category **Posa-Posa** is also away from the waves; it is very noisy. The quieter
Montemare, with the same breathtaking sea view as the Miramare, is Second
class, clean, and unpretentious; there are 15 rooms with bath or shower. **Pensione Conca d'Oro** garners 31 cheers for its 31 rooms with bath. A budget bet
and a good one. On the beach, the **Covo dei Saraceni** sails away with salutes.
Also Second-class; convenient for bathing; pleasant. Low man on the local

totem pole is the **Savoia**, with a heavy Italian trade. Motorists might like it because they can park in the little square nearby.

Buca di Bacco still is, and seems to be ever, the favorite among restaurants. Better than ever. Discounting the local white wine, the **Hotel Sirenuse** sets a savory spread—but it costs and costs. **Taverna del Leone**, just past the Hotel San Pietro, keeps pounding pleasing pizzas till 2 A.M. **Tre Sorelle** is another pie-eyed protagonist. **Chez Black** and **Santa Caterina** get honorable mention from local chums; we were too wracked with ricotta to slice our way into either.

PUGLIANO   The Third-class **Ercolano** at the Funicular Station is useful for Vesuvius excursionists. Renovated but still primitive; improved cuisine; wonderful view.

PUNTA ALA   Refer to "Grosseto".

RAGUSA   Here's our short list for overnighting: (1) **San Giovanni** (bed and breakfast only), (2) **Jonio** (more cosmopolitan), (3) **Mediterraneo**.

RAITO,   that alluring cliffside village 2 1/2 miles from Salerno up the Corniche from the main Amalfi Drive, boasts the First-class **Raito** which is tip of this top. Good kitchen; recommended. The nearby **Lloyd's Baia** is also said to be a worthwhile stop, particularly since Lloyd modernized his premises.

RAPALLO,   a short hop from Genoa, is on the blatant side when the summer legions descend to shatter its days and nights. It's a typically crowded 2nd-rate oasis, closer to the taste of Europeans than Americans.

Our first choice among its hotels is the **Bristol**, 2 miles out along the Gulf of Tigullio. Sweeping reconditioning undertaken, but furnishings still suffer from cretonne-itis; fresh 5th floor with 7 small cozy suites and kitchenettes; baths throughout; traditional atmosphere with moquettes in all accommodations; large seawater pool with direct elevator service (the automatic type) from building; private beach; spacious terraces; open-air restaurant; in the hands of Andrea Costa, better and better. **Aerotel** is a 50-room apartment house that rents by the day, week, or month. Appealing restaurant; bar; pool; gardens; excellent for its type. **Savoia** reminds us of an old crone with too much makeup; although seriously in need of a face-lifting, it is still popular with the nationals. **Europa** is also skidding. **Moderne et Royal** is now the leading hostelry in the so-called Superior Second class. The **Riviera**, with private balconies on its 4th floor and a total renovation job a while back, comes next in this category. **Astoria** boasts a glass-fronted entrance and not much more. **Bel Soggiorno**, on the coast, offers barely reasonable value to families. While the **Miramare** is a winner for food, it lacks spice in the bedroom stew. Thoughtful, nice people who run its basic plant very well indeed. With a generous bank loan, this could be one of the better bets in town. The **Eurotel** is air-conditioned. All rooms with balcony overlooking the deep blue; pool; garage. For pensions, try (1) **Bandoni** and (2) **Mignon-Posta**.

For independent dining, there's the air-conditioned, fern-lined **Da Fausto**

(piazza Nuova Posta). Arbor-styled booths for garden effect; the movie stars' favorite; expensive. Ask for Signorina Rosana, Fausto's English-speaking daughter, who is usually on hand. The sea-sited **Sibelius** rolls in with coffee, tea, snacks, and some of the chicest clientele on the coast; a few readers aver that it may be slipping. **Rosa Bianca** is wilting, too, according to our on-the-spot sources. **Tigullio's Rocks**, uphill between Rapallo and Chiavari, has a striking view of Tigullio Gulf; it's popular. Pizzeria-type stops are a good alternative in this town, since none of the above places is gastronomically significant.

RAVELLO is above Amalfi, and it is almost as attractive—one of the more popular (and crowded) targets, in fact, on the Peninsula. Its Villa Rufolo gardens are famed (here Wagner was purportedly inspired to compose *Lohengrin*), its Hotel Caruso and Hotel Palumbo are agreeable, and its wines are well regarded by Italian connoisseurs (a viewpoint we personally cannot share).

The village, 1000 feet above the sea, offers 2 better stopping places and each is recommendable. **Palumbo**, a twelfth-century palace, has 40 units in the main building plus 2 annexes, respectively rated in Categories I and II. Handsome, whitehaired Swiss Director Vuilleumier runs this house very well. Daring color schemes; 20 private baths; rooms identified by the colored tilework as well as numbers; #28, #32, and #34 offer stunning 3-directional panoramas and plenty of breathing space. **Caruso Belvedere**, a converted castle, has an enchanting garden and terraces, 26 old-fashioned rooms (some with fireplaces), and pure serenity. The 3 Caruso brethren are its friendly proprietors (one makes the house wine); even friendlier are the scrumptious Crespelle alla Caruso (ham and cheese filled crepes) and chocolate soufflé. The **Rufolo**, with exquisite gardens, is more modest. The 25-unit **Graal** is a Third-category sweetheart. If you can tolerate a tiny room with an elfin bath, you will be rewarded with the same eye-popping view as is offered by the 2 leaders—but at only about half the tariff. Owner Oliviero Palumbo makes the wine, his wife Anna makes the food, and 2 of their 6 children make the beds. Open the year round for thrifty wanderers with acumen. **Parsifal**, next to the C-B, is the leading pension. Thanks to the Patron Saint of Tired Travelers, a road now wiggles directly up to this highland enclave.

The feederies here are almost entirely limited to the innkeepers' kitchens. Disgraceful!

RAVENNA, halfway between Venice and Ancona, is a culture seeker's paradise—historically and artistically, one of the outstanding smaller sites of the Western world. No other city can compete with its wealth of Byzantine architecture or its unique mosaics. Ecclesiastical treasures; Dante's tomb; Theodoric's tomb; a scholar's heaven. Giant ENI rubber-and-fertilizer plant; indifferent hotels, limited touring facilities; 6 miles from the sea on the Corsini Canal. Not for the fun-lover, but The Pearly Gates if you're serious-minded.

Its hotel honors go to the modern, central **Bisanzio**, with its rather gaudy décor but extra-sweet personnel for this tourist town and a superior restaurant. Second is the **Jolly**, which is also basic and sound. The **Argentario**, with 34 Class II piped chambers, may rank 3rd if what we hear is true.

RIMINI, on the Adriatic coast east of Florence, might be called the Atlantic City of Italy. Strictly a resort, May to September only: Jump-off spot for easy excursions to Ravenna and San Marino; fair restaurants and nightclubs; the Malatestian Temple and the well-packed bikinis the most remarkable attractions.

Now this hub is bloated by more than 60 thousand beds in nearly 1600 hotels and pensions, which run the gamut from gilded, silk-draped fourposters to Italian Boy Scout camp cots. The glutting continues apace. Warning: Since a serious water shortage has developed, we urgently suggest you select your shelter from the choices which follow. (The houses we list either maintain sizable water reserves or have special pumps for emergency dry spells; waterless periods usually occur in summer just before noon and last until well after dinnertime. An aqueduct plus an improved sewage system have been installed, but still there may be pockets which do not benefit from this essential element.) The **Grand** is the lone Deluxe offering. Here is a creaky personification of the fast-vanishing hotel tradition for which it is named. Tennis courts; private beach; hot-and-cold showers in bathing cabanas; lovely dining terrace; dancing in garden as well as in the cellar Lady Godiva nightclub; gorgeously furnished with fading appointments; full of art treasures; lower early-season rates at a good buy; expensive later and worth it. This pacesetter is managed by Director Arpesella who is experimenting with winter operation as well as High Summerizations. We wish him *buona fortuna.* In First class, the starkly modern **Ambasciatori**, with every balconied room facing the sea, rules the roost. Private tract of Adriatic shoreline, plus spacious rooftop solarium; American Bar; cookery that is reported to be noteworthy (we've not tried it); piano lilts at lunch and dinner. Its 75 spare-size accommodations heavily accent glass; substantial but strictly basic comfort. The **Excelsior-Savoia** provides more bedroom space; insist on reservations in only the newer wing here, because the original section is far less agreeable. Arresting twentieth-century décor, reminiscent of the better designs of Miami Beach; push-buttons like crazy; indifferent cuisine; mannerly clientele; satisfactory. A newer one called **Bellevue** (What! Not "Bella Vista"?) is said to be the *bella* of Kennedy Square; 66 First-class rooms; 66 baths; air conditioning. Might be a winner. The beachside **Imperiale** comes up with 60 rooms, 100% bath-and-shower ratio, and a glass-wrapped, Top-of-the-Mark dining perch that is panoromantic by starlight. Still along the shore, the **Sporting**, with its red and yellow exterior, is now one of the better bets. Rooftop solarium plus waterside cabanas; sound amenities; attractive to the eye; pleasant for Sporting types—indoor or outdoor. Management could be improved, say we. The **Corallo,** this one with a blue and pink skin, has turned into a gaudy corral, in our opinion. Perhaps the management has perked things up. Moving inland, the highly touted, 6-story **Abarth**, formerly called Palatino Imperatore, occupies a pine grove residential address several hundred yards from the Adriatic. Institutional and gelid to the marrow; 90 rooms, all with baths and balconies that stare directly onto the balconies of neighboring hotels and apartments. The **Atlantico**, again a fair trot from the sand fleas, offers a vast and viewful penthouse dining room; almost exclusively patronized by package migrations of charter groups from the North and East; little chance of fun for the loner. **Waldorf** towers up as the most modern inn

in the area. A solid First-class choice. Other recent additions, all fair but none sparkling, include the **Amati, Baltimora, Adriaqueen** (wonderful name but sinking fast), and **Metropol**. Of the Second-class shore havens, **Kursaal** leads the pack. With the same ownership and similar architecture as the Ambasciatori, this hostelry offers a waterfront dining salon; all accommodations are canted toward the breakers; it has 2 dozen private cabanas. Very good value. The **National** comes up with solid resort-style amenities and reasonable tariffs; the food we're told is dull. The **Internazionale** is a "show" horse in the Ambasciatori stable. The **de Londres** is so-so, though recently modernized. The 40-room **Mocambo**, once in First-class, has been recategorized; formerly nothing special—and now even less. **Milano île de France** is a comfortable little budget bargain; here's the only stop along the Strand that stays open all seasons. The **Giulio Cesare** is blessed with an excellent situation and a compact, efficient plant. In-town shelter can be had year round at (1) the **Palace** (hotel-school management, clean basic appurtenances, friendly English-speaking staff) and (2) the **Napoleon** (room and breakfast only). **Biancamano**, a Second-class entry, is charming, and its plant is unusually good. The big bugaboo here is its absolutely horrible service. Unless otherwise noted, _all the above are closed from October to March or April._ If you land in this area after nightfall or out of season, it is safer to stick it out in Rimini rather than push on to San Marino, where most choices are duds.

Food? The dining room of the **Grand Hotel** is its only Deluxe oasis. **Chez Vous**, nearby, is about the best independent _chez_ in this sea-side district—but "best" being a relative word, we'd call it only slightly better than fair. In the city, **Vecchia Rimini** is the top choice, mostly for Adriatic fauna. L-shape room broken up by venetian-blind partitions; prices high for this unpretentious corner, but substantial quality and wide range are offered; ask for Giovanni. **Da Bruno** (corso Umberto I 79) has a small terrace; inside, the walls crawl with the most jaundiced painted fish, lobsters, and fruit which ever turned this diner biliousgreen by osmosis; beyond the immaculate kitchen, in the alley, an ancient bag at least 110 years old mumbles and mutters as she grills real fish over a battery of charcoal-filled buckets; they're a masterpiece of cookery, a delight to the palate, especially the _misto_ (mixed) plate; little-to-no English is spoken. **Da Nello** is plain and also maritime. **Artists Tavern** is a boon for travelers who don't speak or read even their own language. No menu—just picture album into which you point your pinkie at your entrée. It consists of an open patio plus a grocery-lined inner sanctum. The chef might be a sculptor, but he certainly isn't an artist when it comes to gastronomy. The prices, not incidentally, are way, way, waaaay too weighty for the featherweight rewards, in our opinion. **Nord Ouest-Club Nautico** (a pert little sailing center) is the pick-o-the-port for salty types. **Belvedere** (a 200-yard walk to the end of the pier) is another favorite mooring for brows that have borne more corporate tax problems than yachting caps; it conjures up visions of a Levantine Atlantic City to our naughty-cal peepers.

RIVA DEL GARDE   nestles on the north shore of Lake Garda, a reasonable haul from Trento or Brescia. A discriminating lady from New York's capital trilled the praises of the **du-Lac-et-du-Parc**—and, from its eye-popping

brochure, well she might. First-class (not Deluxe); large, old-fashioned but renovated headquarters in wooded park; 200 rooms, mostly with bath; 40 bungalows; pool; tennis; private beach; much more. Her comments: "For serenity seekers, beautiful, charming, perfect in every way—and not too expensive." Warmest thanks, kind friend!

SAINT-VINCENT is the winter and summer resort in the Aosta region but the frenetic building boom now seems to be shattering its former tranquillity. Here the Deluxe **Billia** rules the roost. The staff, however, seem to be blasé nowadays, perhaps due to the influx of group traffic which doesn't demand snap and polish. Popular nightclub featured; one of Italy's best casinos connected by direct passageway.

SALERNO, key feederpoint on the *autostrada,* offers the **Grand Diana Splendid** as a resting point. It is a small skyscraper with an attractive roof restaurant and a modern ambiance. Much better than it was. The second-place **Jolly**, on the seaside, is a fair bet; all units have bath or shower and air conditioning. Okay. Don't bother with any of the others unless the 200-room **Sheraton** has opened. Inquire with your travel agent or nearest Sheraton rep., who can provide last-minute details.

SAN FELICE CIRCEO in summer represents Rome's most exclusive escape hatch. The **Maga Circe** is the Old Reliable, with only 38 rooms. The **Neanderthal**, which has 57, is seasonal. The newer **Punta Rossa**, built into the cliffside, counts 25 bungalows with 45 chambers, each with private bath. There's a pool at this very restful haven.

SAN REMO, 9 miles from the French border toward Nice, will still cost you plenty, but its sophistication has gone stale. Those once-resplendent trappings of leisure—casino, race track, golf course, and luxury hotels—now seem static and moth-eaten, because other resorts have pushed forward while this one has marked time. The top drawing card is still the annual Song Festival (late Jan.), but even here, political logrolling has driven away top talent. *Ospedaletti,* 3 miles away, is startlingly cheaper.

This resort, moreover, has become hotel poor. The century-old **Royal**, long the Queen, offers comfort but not luxury. Lovely vista with terraces, flower beds, tables, and pool marching down toward the sea. Total of 15 suites and 130 bedchambers, nearly all with handsome marble baths (those dozens of corridor cupboards disguise the plumbing facilities); newer accommodations furnished in Italian-modern that is skimpy and garish; old ones antique but in less harsh ambiance. The **Savoia** now ranks as a *very* poor second. Grubby, spare furnishings for the price and category; small pool; North European tours rush in where others may fear to tread; closed October and November. In First-class, the **Miramare** commands a viewful seaside and palm-garden domain. Some units even better than some Deluxe nests, at a frond of the price; 70 rooms, including its *dépendance* in the greenery; recommendable kitchen; cordial staff; closed end-September to December 20. Very good for the outlay. The imposing white-faced **Astoria**, across the avenue from the water, is less

tasteful in décor; singles are the better bets here. The **Londra**, pick of many quick-rich Italians, displayed to our eyes gaudy flamboyance coupled with broken walls, cracked baseboards, and furniture suggestive of a hoochy-cooch act in a 2-bit flesh parlor. Not for us—at least, in a hotel. The **Residence** we can live without. **Grand Hotel des Anglais** was renewed, but we're still not sold on it. The central **Europa** is clean, commercial, and nice for what it is—which is "adequate." Here is a careful operation by an old-fashioned hotelier who knows his trade. The bright-white **Victoria-Roma** is fairly appealing; there is easy parking in front. The **Park** is not recommended. **Garisanda** is a well-sited pension. We'd far rather push along to the **Grand del Mare** near *Bordighera* than stay in this withering city. Otherwise, on Cape Nero, between *San Remo* and *Ospedaletti*, the very modern **Rocce del Capo** has another beautiful view and another swimming pool. Private beach, nightclub, and restaurant; very Italian resorty in tone, with possibilities of so-so fun in season.

Food? The stately dining room of the gambling **Casino** will give you a seat over the Gulf; the **Royal**, with its Murano-glass ceiling and bouquet fixtures, will serve you more distinguished viands. Dancing in both. If you're after a savory regional meal at a more modest price, try **Au Rendez-Vous** (corso Matteotti 90). **La Lanterna** faces town from a bend in a quay. Middling view of the harbor and the walls of a medieval jail; natural wood interior; front terrace for fair-weather munching; our recent bill concealed 2 chisels; the cookery now seems oriented strictly for routine tourist traffic. Better by leagues is the **Caravella**, 2/3 of it in the waters. Wonderful maritime vista; tanks for selecting your tearful meal; be sure to try the fruit-of-the-sea cocktail which is prepared at tableside. Very good, but pretty steep tariffs. **Pesce d'Oro** (corso Cavallotti 174) is about 2 miles toward Genoa on the via Aurelia route. No atmosphere; no view; snail-like service and whalelike tariffs for what you get. Ho-hum. At **Castel Doria**, the food is savory when the chef is in the mood, but at other times you'll take your chances. **U Nostromú** specializes in seafood; it's dull. The **Capo Pino** at surf's edge is a bustling aboriginal warren. Entrance from the top; restaurant and bar, in terra-cotta red, 2 levels below the road; pool and terrace by the shore. Finally, minutes before the Ventimiglia frontier crossing, you'll come across 2 possibilities. One is an unusually attractive oasis named **La Mortola**. Simple modern décor; terrace with view of bay; seafood specialties; whopping selection of perhaps 60 hors d'oeuvres (a meal in itself); friendly, accomplished service; open daily from 8 A.M. to 1 A.M., but closed all of June and July; across the road is the 22-room Hotel Eden, under the same management. The other is **Gino** at *Piani di Vallecrosia*, which we've never tried.

SAN MARINO.   Refer to our comments on this separate republic in the introduction of this chapter.

SANTA MARGHERITA   has smart hotels worthy of such a glittering resort, an interesting fish market and a pleasant situation on the water. It is booming today—perhaps because it can accommodate more visitors than lovely, neighboring Portofino.

For Classic Conservatives, the **Imperiale** offers a rococo turn-of-the-century

building, a lushly refurbished décor in the Grand Tradition, a private park and gardens, a vista of Tigullio Bay, an open-air restaurant, and a courteous staff. For Hilton buffs, the **Park Hotel Suisse** has arresting angular architecture of the ultramodern school, self-control air conditioning, a twisted-torso-shape seawater pool, and electric-bright color contrasts throughout. Roster of 75 smallish rooms, all with bath or shower; bay view and quiet hillside situation; interior and alfresco dining or imbibing; charcoal grill. You'll either like it or loathe it, depending upon your receptivity to its progressive ambiance. For Middle Grounders, the **Miramare**, on the beach, is a middle-age structure which has been modernized in a pleasant way under the guiding hand of Manager Paolo Biscioni. Traditional tone retained but brightened; baths in expensive *imported* opaline marble (why this was done in marble-rich Italy we'll never comprehend—but they are lovely); gardenside quietest in summer (important, since there's no air conditioning). Charming, intimate Shangrila winter nightclub, plus the waterside Barracuda for summer-izations; our recent meal here again was one of the finest of that Italian circuit—*but* one of the most expensive. At half the outlay, the **Continental** cops all honors as one of the select bargain paradises along this stretch of coast. Wonderful perch nesting cozily in a park of southerly-exposed flora and palm; romantic private beach; open terrace for breakfast and dinner; simple dining room; 64 good-size bedchambers, including the expanded annex, all with private bath and seafront balcony. Operative year round. The Continental-owned **Regina Elena** is almost as good, but it is more modern and it lacks the marvelous situation of the Continental. Glass-lined dining room under a geodesic dome; double-plate glass doors on all bedroom balconies. Superb for the category. The **Laurin**, down a notch, operates under the Park Suisse aegis. It has been to the beauty parlor and now twinkles. The **Metropole**, while sound in basic amenities, is better geared to European tastes than to our own. Fair. **La Vela** ("The Sail") pulls well. The **Tiguillio**, inside the city, is okay for budgeteers or for seaside vacationers who hate the sea.

Food? The port's top independent kitchen is **Dei Pescatori**, on the fringe of the yacht harbor. It's long and narrow, with no outdoor service; fish, of course, is the specialty. **Nanni**, also harborside, is very popular with the boating crowd; we must drop our hook here soon. We'll also look in on the waterfront **La Posada**, recommended by thoughtful Atlanta readers. For hotel dining, the **Miramare** has one of the better chefs of the nation—but you'll pay plenty for his wares. There is also a summer nightclub restaurant of renown: **Capo di Nord-Est**, which is one mile out, and which is romantic for handholding. Seaside location, dancing, intermittent entertainment; pleasant, but more famous for its atmosphere than for its food. **Helios**, a flamingo-pink structure on the water, has a good vista and nice terrace, but Escoffier never presided here. The little Second-class **Taverna Brigantino** is nautical, simple, on the pagan side, and cheap.

SANTA SEVERA (main road to Pisa, 32 miles from Rome), the **Maremonti**, a private residence transformed into an inn. Private beach; not luxurious and not expensive; good simple rest spot near the capital.

SARDINIA's most alluring siren for the International Beautiful People set is the breathtakingly savage, beautifully sea-lapped *Costa Smeralda*, a 30-mile necklace of wild, lonely, *ponète*-blown coves whose principal landlord is the dedicated, hardworking Aga Khan. A number of average, non-Italian-speaking North Americans are disappointed here because they feel that they simply do not fit in with the glamorous denizens and glittering hangers-on of this picture-postcard milieu—and their point about its snobbism is well taken. Along this glorious villa-specked littoral—more extensive, incidentally, than the entire Belgian seaboard—are no less than 80 powder-white, gemlike beaches. It's a land of twisted cork trees, soughing pines, and glistening juniper, with a boscage of rosemary that scents the Mediterranean sailor's wind. The angular mountains are of granite and basalt. The vales are dotted with nuraghi (prehistoric fortress-shape structures). Its primitive inhabitants speak a Low Latin, with dialect overtones of ancient Genoese, Lybian, Phoenician, Spanish, and Carthaginian. The inlets and quiet corners along this row are far too numerous to mention; a typical one has been described accurately as "a Pacific bay on a Brittany coast." There are 5 hotels of varying categories, co-crowned by the Aga Khan's magnificent Cala di Volpe and the equally luxurious cottage-style Pitrizza. Cuisine? Much of it is about as exciting as a hangnail. The local fare, based ponderously on pasta, is even worse. The yacht basin at *Porto Cervo* is one of the best, most expensive, and most scenic in the western world; the local marina, skipper's club, and nucleus of cozy-corner night spots swing with international celebrities, as well as with Everyday Jet Setters who wing in or cruise over from the nearby thickets of Rome. Winter, when only one hotel stays open to date, can be as lonely as a doxy at a Mississippi revival —bringing just enough rawness to evoke avid interest in timetables. The easiest way is aboard His Highness' sleek, constantly expanding, turboprop airline, Alisarda, which calls regularly at Rome, Nice, and Milan from the home base, *Olbia*. Alitalia zips in daily from Milan and Rome to *Alghero* and *Cagliari*. The latter is hopelessly far away; the pull from the former is a tediously long ride. British Airways has a London link with Alghero. Passenger and car ferries steam 4 times a day in summer from the port of Rome (Civitavecchia) to Olbia and the adjoining *Golfo di Aranci*. A loop with Genoa is also possible aboard the *Canguro Rosso,* the so-called Red Kangaroo that hops with its pouchful of passengers between the north of Italy and Sardinia. We've recently bounded off on one of these vessels and recommend each ship in the Kangaroo fleet heartily. Genoese luggers drop anchor at both Olbia and *Porto Torres*. (The latter is about 80 miles from your hotel.) As islands go, the land of the Sards is so vast that if you head to this northeastern chip of emerald paradise, don't plan to land anywhere else but Olbia. When you alight, we think you'll agree that here is one of the most exquisite shorelines in Europe.

Among the Aga Khan's hotels, his pride is the glamorously rustic, **Cala di Volpe**, which nestles almost village-style by the sands of a glorious bay. His Highness gave French Master Architect Jacques Couelle a blank check to build anything he desired. This genius made one try, disliked what he did, destroyed the first structure, and began anew. To guarantee every detail would be "perfectly imperfect," Couelle supervised the laying of paving stones that do not

quite join, braiding the cane so it does not appear uniform, processing the walls so they seem aged by the centuries. He "rusted," then "stopped" the oxidation of wrought iron. Bleaching, chipping, dusting, beating—he employed a trillion techniques to meld this composite into a creation of the highest form of distilled structural art, a place in which to live, to love, and to relax. Surrounding the pueblo enclave is a toy harbor. Here you will find hotel boats bobbing at their moorings, tennis courts, a huge glittering olympic swimming pool, and a parcel of what might be called beach-lets. Entrance across a bamboo-covered footbridge to a timber-toned lobby; main restaurant and bar under giant wooden beams and plaited stalks, both overlooking the teal waters and the 100-yard long pier; 44 rooms in the older segment, each in different dress (bid for these since the newer wing is only so-so and can be hotter). Rates surpass Deluxe standards almost anywhere in Italy—but, because of its relative isolation, the frolicking nightlife, and the fun-filled ambiance of play-filled luxury, a pair of pilgrims could easily work through $225 per day, including normal meals (not caviar, plover's eggs, and the like). There's one all-encompassing word for this Eden —*fabulous!* **The Pitrizza**, also owned by the Aga Khan, is in the same Deluxe category. This one is nearer to the coastal heartbeat of **Porto Cervo**, a 10-minute panoramic ramble by car. Although it is more private in concept—a 1/2-dozen 4-to-8 person bungalows—it is equally glorious, equally comfortable, with the opulence of a potentate's diadem. Each yard-thick roof of the villas and main building has been given a rich blanket of soil, an independent irrigation system, and a magnificent assortment of Mediterranean flowering plants and shrubs. The pool, hewn from native cobble, first flows through hillside pockets and then cascades over a rocky weir into the sea. Central clubhouse with restaurant, bar, and coveside terrace; candlelight dinners twice weekly; dancing a regular feature; all chalets with air conditioning plus working fireplaces; individual patios under vine-draped, raw-wood lattices; stable-type doors; agrestic Sardinian handicrafts; colorful, nature-toned décor. A splendid 18-hole golf course designed by Trent Jones is teed up. The vastly restyled Rank-run, 100-room **Romazzino** has moved up to the Deluxe bracket. It commands what we believe is the most scenic site of all—a hillside perch above a bay twinkling with salt-and-pepper islands. Every unit with seaview balcony and air conditioning; North Wing best; modern lobby and lounge with ceramic "trees"; Juniper Bar; dining salon; beachside "Wooden Leg" barbecue hutch; Alfonso's Pizzeria; private boat dock; hairdresser and barber; free baby-sitter service; Sunfish sailboats for rent; full range of water-sport facilities; newspaper kiosk and a few shops. Its generally spacious bedchambers have colorful tile floors and raffia carpets. Selected antique furnishings mixed with contemporary comfort-insurers; baths, showers, and individual peignoirs; private balconies; single bedsteads from a nunnery. This regally priced haven is better suited to animated young folk than to older Grand Tour peace-seekers. The fully air-conditioned expanded **Cervo**, smack in the center of the port, is the nucleus of the social, boating, and nightlife whirl. It is the only area in the close-knit community that stays open year round, encompassing a marina, a swimming and barbecue area, restaurant, bar, supermarket, equestrian club, shopping arcade, plaza for star-sprinkled galas, real estate agency, post and telegraph office, and ultra-exclusive Yacht

Club. Simpler accommodations than Cala di Volpe and Pitrizza; correspondingly lower tariffs; same administrative aegis; more than adequate comfort; convivial people; usually full in season—and with good reason. The nearby 80-room **Luci di la Muntagna**, with its distant view of Corsica, also hops with carefree abandon. Architecture that suggests it came out of a plaster-of-Paris mold; active floating jetty for sport boats (6 for rent by guests); good beach with free deck chairs and umbrellas; restaurant; rooftop solarium; swinging discothèque; all units with bath or shower; narrow dimensions; 5 pastel color schemes. Except for the cell-size accommodations, here's a laudable medium-bracket candidate. The **Residence Liscia di Vacca** is nearby, Second-class, has swimming pool, and said to be pleasant for budget voyagers; we haven't dropped our anchor at its port-als. In the same category, the fresh 70-kip **Cinesta** debuted recently; the 420-guest, First-class **Prvero** ("pear tree") chipped in by the golf links; finally, the **Dolce Sposa** ("sweet wife") makes up more than 100 beds. Additional runners may be found along the shores (perhaps a 1/2-hour drive) and in a dreary town of *Olbia*—but for the full galaxy of happy and/or luxurious resort-style living, we strongly recommend, if you are going and if you can can afford them, that you limit your selection to the established 5 (or possibly 6) stalwarts about which we have written.

For meals, stick to the hotels and order only simple dishes, because all of the cookery we found in them was amazingly (and bafflingly!) substandard for their category. Our best luck was at the **Pitrizza**. If you *must* experiment further, don't drink any of the local wines except Vernaccia or Fundata Olia. Regional culinary specialties are spit-roasted suckling pig and wild boar ham. **El Toulà** in the **Sporting Club** on the half-island of *Punta della Lepre* is the only notable independent restaurant in the entire area. *Porto Cervo* offers the simple **San Marco** (the little brother of the Sporting Club) as its number one candidate and **La Fattoria** as its number two. The main piazza here serves as its central "nightclub."

Finally, 80 miles from **Calgiari** in the south, Trust Houses Forte created the **Forte Hotel Village**. It comprises 600 spacious red-tiled-roofed brick cottages (2 bedrooms) and the attractive 114-unit, air-conditioned **Hotel Castello**. Lighted tennis courts; 18-hole links nearby; 5 pools; Colosseo buffet-style restaurant; seafood-speciality Beachcomber; Torre Steak House; multiple snack and pizza bars; more. Its Piazza Maria Luigia, said to be a fair copy of the Centro in Porto Cervo, has shops, pubs, and nightly entertainment. Reports to us are favorable. We haven't stepped onto this merry-go-round as yet, but it won't be long.

If you can take its snobbish mien in your stride and if your wallet is well-padded, you should find the Costa Smeralda an exquisite vacation dreamland.

SESTRIERE, the modernistic ski vale, boasts the **Principe di Piemonte**, which is well liked for its *joie de vivre* in season. The towering cylindrical **Duchi d'Aosta** offers abundant comfort, excellent cuisine, and reasonable tariffs. Here's the favored winter snuggery of the fashionable Hawes clan of Elstree and Mallorca. **La Torre**, its twin, specializes in singles during the playful months.

SESTRI LEVANTE   (about 30 miles south of Genoa). The far-and-away leader is **Grand Hotel dei Castelli**—3 linked castles which occupy their own high-perched peninsula up a first-gear-only road. Owner Queirolo's gorgeous antiques scattered through its 43 rooms and 6 suites—plus its exquisite panorama and good facilities—merit salutes and salaams. **Vis à Vis** is simple-modern but has a fine bay setting for meditations and quiet pursuits. Pleased reports have come in about the sixteenth-century **Villa Balbi**. One twentieth-century wing; "fine service and food"; "excellent attention."

SIENA   supplies a mesmeric passageway to the Renaissance; it is probably the only city in Italy to retain so much ancient charm. As an illustration, film makers found Verona's complexion had changed so radically over the years that they came here to shoot *Romeo and Juliet.* The **Duomo**, the **Pinacoteca**, and the **Music Academy** are musts; the capper is the spectacular **Palio** ("the world's craziest horse race"), a pageant climaxed by hell-for-leather riding in the huge piazza del Campo; this event is held twice annually on the Festivals of the Madonna, July 2 and August 16.

For peace-lovers, the prime attractions nestle in the surrounding hills. The **Park**, 1 1/2 miles out, is a landed estate beautifully remodeled by the English-based Falcon Inn organization which reputedly spent almost $2,000,000 in updatings. Pool; air conditioning; many more freshets still to come from zealous Manager P. Guarneri. Sixteenth-century furnishings and quiet mien; capacity of 58 rooms, all with private bath. Tranquillizing and very recommendable indeed. Now Park-able the year around. The **Villa Scacciapensieri** ("Scatter Your Cares"), a careless mile or more from the center (but only 5 minutes from the station), was transformed into a hostelry with 19 units in the Villa, 9 in the Villino, and 2 in the poolside Villetta; all accommodations are regaled with loving attention to detail; the dining room reflects the devotion to cuisine and wines of Francesco Pallasini, a connoisseur of heroic stature. (He conducts twice-weekly wine seminars in 4 languages here.) A truly international and discriminating clientele returns with regularity to this country estate. One good reason: Miss Emma Nardi, the owner and a gracious hostess for more than 4 decades, shudders at the mention of mass tourism. She also shutters it tightly when winter winds blow. Enchanting. The **Garden**, in Second-class, won our heart with its magnificent terrace view over the entire city. The spacious grounds are an asset for travelers with children. Just at the fringe of the old section, you'll find the dignified **Palazzo Ravizza**, Pian dei Mantellini 34. Flavorful ambiance punctuated by bookshelves, mounted guns, a concert grand, and similar touches; tearoom-bar that huddles cozily around an enormous fireplace; attractive wooden stools and chairs; 28 tastefully decorated rooms, 10 with bath; #20 is a quaint apartment overlooking the posies, with its own fireplace; demipension compulsory. Handily managed by Sig. DeSanti. The **Excelsior** was revamped but we haven't seen the changes. The **Continental** was icy-cold and uninspired, in our opinion. The **Minerva** is commercial. The 70-room **Moderno**, in the center, is Second-class; it was only so-so.

The local culinary crown belongs to **Guido**, a stone-and-brick vault on the main street of the Old Town. Rugged rusticity lined with photos of opera and theatrical personalities; spitted meats spinning over licking

flames at the entrance; hardy fare that is superb for what it is; friendly service; reasonable tabs. We love it. The most famous tourist meccas are **Al Mangia** and **Alla Speranza**; both have outdoor terraces facing the magnificent piazza del Campo; both are colorful, but oh-so-geared for You Know Who. **Tre Cristi** is next. **La Taverna di Nello** is said to be worthy, but we haven't tried it. **La Campane** is the budget prince of the poor man's peerage.

SIRACUSA If you pause, it's the **Jolly** for well-tempered Yanks or Rebs. The **Grand Hotel Villa Politi** has a marvelous site over an ancient quarry, but we found dismal maintenance, leaky plumbing, and erratic service. The **AGIP** motel, nearby, is one of this chain's better links. The **Park** is a so-so Second-class alternate. We'd suggest pulling on to Catania or even to Taormina for longer sojourns.

Perhaps a meal stop will be enough. If so, **Fratelli Bandiera**, with sidewalk tables, has an eyefilling command of the bay—and the best command of the stove. All others are pretty routine.

SIRMIONE (midway between Milan and Venice). The town juts out into Lake Garda. The First-class **Villa Cortina** overlooks the water from the center of a large park; it's tranquil and pleasant. The **Continental** is runner-up. Everything is seasonal here.

SORRENTO The town itself but *not* the tranquil enclaves established by clever innkeepers is a brassy, artificial tourist trap. Although it has a fine setting and some excellent hotels and restaurants, we'd prefer to spend the night in Coney Island—a community which might be raucous but which doesn't lure the suckers with this particular brand of "quaintness." Perhaps you'll disagree, because this is merely one opinion—but we loathe the village even while we love many of its facilities.

You'll find Manager Osvaldo Coppola of **Acampora Travel**, a CIT affiliate, an extraordinarily resourceful and competent lifesaver in solving any lodgings or similar problems which might arise to plague you. The resort's most renowned stop is the antique, creaky **Excelsior Vittoria**, which stays open year-round. Its Old World furnishings are so quaint they're almost a Bemelmans caricature—but the staff are warm human beings instead of unsmiling robots. Ideal situation; parkland setting with large pool; relaxed atmosphere; excellent food; professional guidance by Ugo Fiorentino. The **Tramontano**, now the largest, creaked up to the big leagues a while back with some renovations. Now, alas, we think it's again fusty, musty, and a bit crusty. Overall, we'd say pretty poor. The **Parco dei Principi** is by the sands, with its entrance at the end of a verdant grove. Perfect setting; air conditioning; 105 good-size rooms with private baths and terraces. The saddening thing here is the pinchpenny attitude displayed in its clashy Formica-clad furnishings, in its frequent absence of pictures, in its stagnant-looking swimming pool on our look, and in its stark, Woolworthy décor. The **Royal**, refitted expensively by Proprietor Renato Scarpato and Manager Antonino Esposito, has been taking giant strides—especially in its public sectors. The swimming pool and gardens are breathtaking. Attractive restaurant; 2 bars. Despite the generous infusions of lira, somehow the living quarters here lack heart, in our opinion—a commod-

ity that money can't buy. The **Europa Palace** impressed us this time as sliding. Oldish entrance and lounge; beach 140 feet down by elevator, with snack bar and sun chairs; large accommodations and baths. Ho-hum. The **President**, governing on a pine-dotted hill overlooking the town, has credentials which include a heavily marbled rotunda lobby, a long lounge warmed by intricate tilework and Persian-style rugs, a sedate dining room adjoining an outside terrace, a woody bar in the mod mode, and a solarium-pool complex. From its contemporarily furnished upstairs precincts there are panoramas of Vesuvius, Ischia, and the azure Tyrrhenian Sea which might catch your breath. We vote a resounding "Yes." The arch-ridden **Hermitage**, far above the town on a pine-draped slope, is aptly named. This haven is about 15 minutes from the action. As quiet as a Trappist abbey; glorious kidney-shape pool; provincial-style dining room; nonascetic furnishings that are also not very aesthetic; bath and spacious terrace with every accommodation. A supersilent retreat. Back in town, the 125-room, fully-balconied **Cesare Augusto** is 100 yards behind piazza Tasso; it's a beauty for modern metropolitan tastes rather than for resort-sort amenities. Management by Sig. Camillo Verga; equally professional and conscientious staff; enormous dining salon with mediocre cookery; woody, almost Scandinavian, Taverna dei Mulini; ice-cool bar. Rooftop pool, plus solarium with snack service. Bid for the 4th or 5th floors, the only ones high enough for a sea view. Excellent, if you don't insist on a waterfront address. The flamingo-colored **Ambasciatori** enfolds 105 nests perched on a cliff over its own stretch of sand. Heavily wooded and tiled lobby in avocado; matching bar with sloping ceiling; airy seaview dining room; lush enclosed garden; rippling pool; alert maintenance throughout. While all of the bedchambers are reasonably proportioned, their bathrooms are almost absurdly cramped; all sport balconies, with the 40% bordering the briny the most choice. Recommended. The **De La Ville** is steered by the Ambasciatori. Dull motor-lodge façade; spritely split-level lobby; green-tiled lounge with modish sink-in chairs and waffled ceiling; somewhat elegant restaurant; sun terrace overlooking the Bay of Naples; pool. All 100 units come with bath or shower; most wear balconies; the front ones peep at the deep. The **Riviera**, another First-class wave watcher with an elevator to the beach, is a plantation-like abode. Spacious lobby and lounge festooned with silver ceiling fixtures and military-postured furniture; dining room warmed with original artwork; diminutive imbibery flanking an alfresco terrace; so-called VIP nightclub-discothèque; seawater swimmery. All cubicles offer full piping and balconies; all are stuffed with straightlaced accouterments; loners with more space per face than the duos. We're told that it's open all year to tour traffic. The **Carlton** makes its bid with a tan and brown restaurant. Chrome bar; swimming pool; total of 70 boxes reachable via a closet-size elevator; pink candy-striped spreads on nonresiliant beds; bathrooms contusive for big-boned North Americans. In neighboring *Santagata*, the **Continental** is petaled with approximately the same level of inn-or-out facilities. The **Aminta**, on the "Green Ribbon Road," has a country mien. Enchanting locale deep in Neapolitan vineyards; modern Italianate lobby; inviting pool and sun terraces; attractive dining room with viewful fresh-air terrace; sparkling, shining, first-rate care. All rooms and baths quite small; private balconies; furnishings adequate but not luxurious; reason-

able rates. A restful haven for the world-weary. Don't bother with the nearby **Metropole**. **La Dania** is our favorite low-cost entry; ask for Signora Delizza. The remainder, in descending order, are the **Plaza** (dead center, with no view), **Regina** (now with restaurant; a favorite among Scandinavians), **Caravel** (70 rooms; swimming pool in garden; many package tours from northern Europe), and **Minerva** (formerly a pension; good cookery in its restaurant; good splashing in its penthouse pool). Both the midtown **Michelangelo** and the neighboring **Flora** provide excellent shelter for moderate tariffs. The former seems more luxurious; the latter boasts a rooftop pool and sundeck. Alternates in this category might include the **Bellevue Syrene** and the more modest **Britannia**. The **Bristol** is a solid Second-class buy. Best position of all, with a terrific scenic scope; handsome floors made with local ceramics; cuisine extra-fine for the category; not plush in any sense, but the money's worth for any budgeteer. Finally, nestling on a mountainside 7 miles out of Sorrento on the Positano highway near *Meta*, the **Nastro Azzurro** offers 74 tiny rooms with bath or shower, a circular 2-part swimming pool, a thrilling command of the bay, and Second-class tariffs and facilities. Too quiet and too isolated for the average U.S. visitor, but sunny and airy for tranquillity seekers who don't mind being vastly outnumbered by Continental sun worshipers.

When it comes to mealtime, this city's accomplished chefs must be in hiding. **Della Favorita o'Parrucchiano** gets the leading vote, and that's in an election among gastronomic gnomes. Two tiers of charming, enclosed, viewless terraces lined with lemon and orange trees; amiable management. Closed Wednesday. **Peppino Francischiello** and the **Tripoli** are gaining more and more attention from other visitors—but certainly not from us. **La Minervetta** (via Capo 21) and a pension called **La Tonnarella** (a few steps away) both offer a cliffside sweep from open terraces on Capo di Sorrento; we think the food is wretched, but the surroundings are lovely. The latter has an elevator down to the sea. At the former, when we asked for a wine list, the waiter brought out the entire *cave* in his 2 hands: 5 half-bottles, all white, all foul, all perfectly in tone with the culinary horrors foisted upon us here. For yachtsmen, the Marina del Cantone at *Nerano* boasts 3 waterfront moorings—pretty rough but fair enough for salty types. The routine **Hotel Residence** is flanked to port by **Lo Scoglio** and to starboard by **Taverna Maria Grazzia**. Be sure to ask prices before ordering at the latter pair.

Shopping   This city is the largest, greatest, and most celebrated center in the world for inlaid furniture and similar artistic accessories. The range of its products is astonishing. Utilizing skills which flowered here ages ago, every single piece from the most modest fruit basket to the most elaborate baroque highboy is 100% inset by hand. To see these displays is a unique shopping experience.

The cornucopia of exquisite, exclusive masterworks in the enormous 3-level showrooms of century-old, 400-employee **A. Gargiulo Jannuzzi** (hub of main square) stops us in our tracks: The monumental collection of everything from dining sets to chests of drawers to ladies' desks to tea carts to 3-table nests to cigarette, music, jewelry, and cigar boxes to a plethora more. Beautiful, moderately priced embroidered table linen, blouses, handkerchieves, and the like, hand made in convents or by orphaned children,

a strong alternate magnet and statues by famous sculptors. Free brochures; worldwide shipment; guaranteed delivery; continuously open 365 days (summers until 10 P.M.). We salute gallantly intrepid Matriarch Gargiulo and sons Peppino and Apollo. Wonderful!

Smaller **Notturno**, nearby, opened its factory in '60 and its retail outlet in '75. Director Pepe Ercolano and Assistant Michele Noturno have much to offer. **Melanie** (Toni DiMaio) and **Cuomo** (father Frederico and son Carlo Cuomo) are dependable but even less versatile establishments which in general seemed to be costlier.

SOVEREIGN MILITARY ORDER OF MALTA   Refer to our comments in the introduction of this chapter.

SPOLETO   Historically, the Second-class **Dei Duchi** usually has been considered the best hotel here. The **Clitunno** near the Teatro Nuovo and the **Ferrovia** in the lower city are the only other acceptable choices we know; we haven't had time to inspect the 18-room **Clarici Commercio**, a Third-category, tranquil abode with a hanging terrace. Most culture buffs drive in from other resort digs because this can be one of the hottest hollers in them thar hills.

STRESA's   pacesetters are **Des Îles Borromées** (operated by CIGA) and the **Regina Palace**. The former, a Gay Nineties holdover, had its heyday about the time the *Titanic* went down; its redone bar looks both brash and apologetic in the bosom of this sprawling, last-century matron; it is spacious, well maintained, and comfortable. The latter, also Victorian down to its tearose toenails, has brilliant gardens, a lakeside terrace-restaurant with dancing, and the ghosts of countless waistcoat-and-bustle memories; here's a pleasant relic, too. The **Bristol**, next to Des Îles Borromées, is newer, clean, and on the small side. Capacity of 114 cramped but nicely turned-out units; 106 with private bath; savory cookery; jarring lobby; better taste upstairs. Not in the class with the 2 leaders. **Villa Aminta**, a converted mansion on the main pike, features a small "beach," a big, sparkling, glassed-in restaurant, an expansive terrace-garden for open-air dining, and an accomplished chef. Total of 35 adequate but diminutive rooms and baths; newer ones infinitely superior. **Astoria** is plunk next door to the Regina Palace—a choice location. Tiresomely modern in tone; 100 accommodations in hair-raising colors; skimpy furnishings. Passable for a single night, if you're stuck. Save for Villa Aminta which runs year round, all the above are open only from April to October.

TAORMINA,   the garden spot of Sicily, caters mainly to the middle-aged sun-seeker. This increasingly tourist-conscious village (and what a pity it's so fast being spoiled!) sits on a headland almost 1000 feet above the outer Straits of Messina (above the bathing beach too, which is good to know in advance). The view of the town and sea from inside the Greco-Roman theater is one of the most inspiring anywhere; the summer concerts draw musicians from as far as Los Angeles. Mount Etna, the volcano of Ulysses, thrusts its snow-capped cone through the clouds to the rear; in '62 this off-again, on-again boiler ("on" in '71, 79, and '80) built a new 120-foot hill beside its crater; CIAT will take

you there on a fascinating all-day excursion. The highlight of the city's social glitter is its annual David di Donatello Film Festival, Italy's most important event in the motion picture industry. It's usually held from the beginning of August for an 8-day period. Here's a great attraction you shouldn't miss if you're anywhere near these waters—but nail down your hotel space well in advance. Highly recommended. Strand-hounds, young and old, prefer to stay at Mazzarò Beach, directly below, to which there is a funicular. Naxus is also popular with coupon clippers (but not with us). Transportation hang-ups? Shoot arrow-straight to the CIT office on the main drag, where Bureau Chief Vicenzo Forestiero will fix you up in a jiffy.

The lodgings parade leads off with the imposing **San Domenico Palace**, once a huge convent. This spectacular sixteenth-century landmark (a hotel since 1880) is perched on the rim of a 1000-foot cliff. Long, white-tiled pool decanted 3 terraces down into the flower-decked garden; Romanesque outdoor bar plus a cluster of changing cabins; fully air-conditioned; almost every suite, bed-chamber, and bath in excellent taste, each different from the next. Spacious rooms with magnificent vistas; extraordinarily fine Sassari tilework and 1984-style fixtures in most baths. Manager Franco Forlano heads what is indisputably the leading house on the island. The year-round **Timèo**, which also nestles in a viewful position, is the only hotel within the town area. Partial recent redecorating has brightened the dining room and bar while retaining a polished Victorian aura elsewhere. Our most recent meal was superb, as was the service by cordial Maître Rocco Bambara and his gracious staff. Many chambers with flowered terraces overlooking (underlooking?) Mt. Etna; venerable antiques including many of the guests.

The **Capotaormina** (its mouthful word springs from the cape of the same name), a large, crescent-shape structure, perches 150 feet high along the edge of the most advanced promontory on the coast, which blesses it with a sweep of the most breathtaking seascape of any major hostelry in the region. Totally contemporary design and ambiance; 200 air-conditioned rooms and baths, all but 12 with balcony; 2 bars; beauty parlor; boutique; sauna; underground garage and parking space above; convention facilities for 350; special elevator to the private beach in its own cove.

The air-conditioned **Diodoro Jolly** claims a sea-and-volcano vista. Ten-minute hike from town; modernistic furnishings; facilities for alfresco dining and drinking; 300-seat inner salon with gold carpet, wooden beams, and green velvet chairs; huge swimming pool for summer and winter dipping; sauna; tennis court; all 102 diminutive units with private bath and big balcony; First-class rating for Deluxe physical standards (this commercially oriented chain bought it after it was built). Recommended. The **Bristol Park** is older in fashion. Similarly breathtaking panorama from a site that is neither in the village nor at the beach (a car would be an asset, but there's free minibus service to the shore); sprightly dining room with pink napery; pleasant terrace for breakfast and apéritifs; 100% air-conditioned; snail-like elevator. Every accommodation with its own attractive balcony; simply but tastefully furnished; demipension required in season. Its warm-hearted family touch is everywhere in evidence. The **Miramare**, pleasantly set at the outer limits, has 60 tastelessly decorated rooms, nearly all with private bath; very clean; heated

pool; good food for the price; a summer house; somewhat under par for its category. If you book here in winter, you might wake up to find your whatsis icicled and navy blue. The **Méditerranée**, in a tranquil urban location, is a solid Second-class candidate. Modern; 70% air-conditioned; rooftop swimming pool; all rooms with bath or shower; most with terrace; good management; panoramic site. Less expensive, naturally. The **Continental**, a few yards away, offers an excellent position, many modern amenities, reportedly good food and service, and extraordinary popularity. No elevator, but full air cooling; 43 units with bath or shower, plus terrace or balcony. Director Renato di Pasquale is a young and personable administrator who keeps his house in good order. We were chilled by the **Imperial Palace**. The year-round **Monte Tauro** vaguely resembles a bunker on its exterior. Top-level reception with outdoor, glassed-in elevator to wisk guests to their rooms on 8 floors below; eager-to-please staff, many quite youthful; comfortable units with Frigobars, TV, and adequate dimensions. Okay for cliff dwellers. While the 33-room **Villa Paradiso** is officially designated a pension, we feel it offers comforts that few First-class hostelries do in this resort. Whitewashed salon divided by arches and gladdened by foliage; penthouse terrace restaurant; uninspired skilletry; extensive use of wrought iron; most perches with vistas of Mt. Etna, the public gardens, and the hamlet of Giardini. **Villa Riis** has been totally refurbished. Now it is open from March to October. This charmer is well liked by just about everybody. **Villa S. Giorgio**, near the town border and the most tranquil haven in its category, does 10 of its 20 rooms handsomely, but the rest are stark. The industrious management here is doing everything possible to bring it up; a homespun sentiment at the entrance reads "The House of Peace." **Arathena** has 45 fully piped pads and sits in a slumberful neighborhood. **Pensione Le Terrazze** is a fine old homestead on the Corso. Appealing vista; economical; a favorite with junior U.S. diplomats. **Pensione Adele**, near the city hospital, is tastefully accommodating in the style of a private home; there are some balconies and garage space, too. **Bel Soggiorno**, 7 minutes from the center through the public gardens, has perked up its 20 rooms and 14 baths; it has one of the most likable staffs in town. The **Sole-Castello**, in Second category, occupies a sensationally dramatic setting up and up and up on a peak overlooking the town, the bay, and the mountains on both sides of the hotel. Modern construction; 80% of accommodations with terrace; handsome dining patio in season; plastic-y furnishings in public rooms, but better taste in bedchambers; 40 units, nearly all with bath or shower. Passable. Down at *Mazzarò Beach*, a lazy 5-minute amble by car, big, Big, B I G things are happening. The **Mazzarò Sea Palace** has swung open its Deluxe portals at a site almost adjoining the funicular terminus (connected to this station by a tunnel). This ultramodern, high-cost entry features a round "superstructure" lounge for 360° pan-o-ramics, a restaurant with tinted glass and white molded tables, a bar to match, a seawater pool, and private beach. Its 120 air-conditioned bedchambers are only a pillow's toss from the breakers. They have expansive terraces, quality twin beds, beige carpeting, and adjustable lighting. **Villa Sant' Andrea** is a sparkling anchorage with a light cargo of wiles. Lovely garden terrace a tier above water level; dining patio and outdoor bar; 40 homey rooms, all with bath; 7-unit annex; nice clientele; open March to October. Just the

retreat for sun-worship, park-strolling, sea-bathing, and lazing up a daydream. The Second-class, 43-room **Lido Méditerranée** and the centrally cited but quiet, 59-unit **Vello d'Oro** are another pair of chicks. We missed them on our latest rounds. A long and expert professional report on the **Holiday Inn** has reached us from a leading engineer of Stone and Webster, one of the world's greatest multinational construction giants. He states that in addition to the infestation of worms and insects in its woodwork and ants, flies, and wasps elsewhere, the overall maintenance of its physical plant and other facilities was so bad during his stay that "The rating should be third or fourth class until (the) deficiencies are corrected. Some rooms should not be rented until (the) insects are exterminated . . ." And that is not all! Hence, we're going to freeze stone-dead on this one until we can again personally inspect it from top to bottom. _Other hotels or pensions in the Taormina area are not recommended._

This center's hoteliers have so mercilessly jammed their Full-Pension needle into the innocent pilgrim that almost no appealing restaurants exist. **Da Angelo** (Corso Umberto 42), a local pacesetter, is reasonably pleasant in aura and viands—but please don't expect to walk away with angelic music in your ears. Closed on Tuesday. **Naumachie** (Corso Umberto 76–80) would be a solid little pasta and pizza parlor in most other centers of this size; here it's another of the leading independent lights. L-shape chamber with brick oven at a right angle; antipasto display near entrance; about 15 tables clothed in light blue or pink. Nine varieties of pizza, plus an equal number of spaghetti variations, are available. **Miosotis** is okay but not outstanding; Mondays are its rest time. **Cyclope** is a tiny dining quarter with so-so vittles for the nonparticular. The rustic-style **Pescatore**, directly in front of _Isola Bella_ on the pike to Messina, is attractive when the sun is shining. The seafood cocktail is a selfish shellfish salad. At nearby _Mazzarò Beach_, **Villa Sant' Andrea** is a charmer for lunch; since it's a hotel restaurant, it's open every day. **La Griglia** resides haughtily and peacefully nearly 2-thousand feet above sea level and more than 1-thousand feet over Taormina at _Castelmola_, perhaps 20 minutes from town by car. Although there are other dining targets in this village, none comes close to matching either the fabulous land- and seascapes or the superb regional cuisine of this one. Here's a dedicated family operation, with matriarch Maria Intelisano and daughter-in-law Angela in the kitchen and sons Giorgio, Giuseppe, and Pancrasio serving clients with sincerity, warmth, and grace. Please be sure to try Bruschetti (crude toast with tomato and oil). It's open all year, all week in summer, and every day except Thursday in winter. A 3-V champ: Verve, vistas, and vittles.

The best shopping target here is **Daneu** (corso Umberto 126) for island handicrafts. Branch in Palermo; versatile and popular. **Giovanni Panorello** (corso Umberto) is worth skimming for antiques. **Giovanni Vadalà** (Corso Umberto 193–195) is an attractive boutique featuring Hermès, Burberry's, Yves St. Laurent, and others. Otherwise, the main street now seems one unbroken string of brassy tourist junk hovels.

TREMEZZO, probably has as its best stop the **Grand Hotel Tremezzo**, with its private little park and pool. We consider it average but not outstanding. The **Bazzoni**, also on the lake, is okay for its lower category.

TRIESTE is a cleaner-than-average town with friendlier-than-average citizens. Although there are some sightseeing attractions, it is much more commercial than touristic.

You'll possibly want to overnight here. If so, the **Excelsior Palace** is an oldtimer which has been somewhat rejuvenated. The **Jolly** evokes only the mildest chuckle of approval from us. The modest **Obelisco**, with its hillside location and nice staff, is rewarding if only for those two features. The **Adriatico**, out at Grignano Bay, can be pleasant in season.

For dining, **Nuovo Dante** holds the title, followed perhaps by **Piccolo**. **Bottega del Vino** is a regional-style establishment inside San Guisto Castle, with music of sorts and dancing; it's open at night only. **Birreria Forst Europa** is the restaurant of the well-known Forst Brewery. The latter 2 are on the down-to-earth side, but newcomers seem to like 'em. We haven't visited this city in too long a time.

TURIN (Torino), a serene metropolis in the Piedmont near the French border (readily discernible in the local dialect), currently rates 4th—but it has passed the million mark and soon might capture Naples' 3rd-place crown. About 30 thousand *Torinesi* work in the Fiat auto works, largest plant in the world outside the Detroit area; the unique **Museum of The Automobile**, containing 370 vintage models, is fascinating. They are equally proud of their city's art treasures, **Egyptology Museum** (second most important in the world), **Cinema Museum**, former **Royal Palace**, and **Palazzo del Lavoro**. With one exception, its mediocre hotels are completely out of key. Despite a couple of excellent restaurants, generally the amenities for welcoming and comforting tourists are 2nd rate. To top this off, air pollution from her industries was so severe on our latest swoop that we could never recommend that any traveler with heart or respiratory ailments drive within even 10 miles of the amber, skyborne doughnut of filth which fouls it when a strong wind is not belting it away. Based on a strong Francophile influence, here is a way of life which, like Milan's, differs from that of the rest of Italy.

The Jolly chain took over and refashioned the famous **Excelsior Grand Hotel Principi di Piemonte**. Director Sergio Cappetta (who also oversees the Jolly Ambasciatori here) shuttered the restaurant, reduced the services, but freshened the décor. Now it is a hostelry appropriate for its targeted client— the businessman who wants simple comfort during a brief stay, with no frills; Telex, telephones that work, and reasonably fast service. The **Jolly Ambasciatori** seems to function on approximately the same principle and, insofar as its audience is chiefly commercial, it serves its purpose very well indeed. Routine cuisine; TV added to bedchambers; some complaints concerning the beds here. Generally acceptable. The **Majestic**, also functional, inclines its decorative taste to its masculine following. Half its 100 units with air conditioning; streetsider with double-glazed windows; radio, Frigobar, and TV on request. Carefully maintained. The air-conditioned **Turin Palace**, opposite the station, has retained its old-fashioned grandeur in the public sections, but modernized its spacious sleepers in a tasteful and practical style. The arresting **City** is proud of its futuristic architecture—and well it should be, because it is an agreeable combination of comfort and imagination that required courage

on the part of the proprietor. Engaging metal structures by Piero Cerato; rouge carpeting; twenty-first-century appointments that are at once soothing and exhilarating. Well done, say we—but *not* for traditionalists. Below these, the **Suisse Terminus** shocks the eye with its glaringly modern façade; regretfully inside we found it drab and charmless. **Grand Fiorina**, while central, certainly did not impress us as grand. **Sitea**? Some halfhearted refreshments, but the clashings of its appurtenances jarred us to our shins. The **Roma** is for emergencies only. If you like the odor of disinfectants, try the **Luxor**, which, incidentally, claims one of the damnedest, chummiest elevators we've just about ever ridden which slaps the fanny *every* time on ingress and egress. Heaven for masochists. **Grande Ligure** has undergone a complete overhauling. **AGIP**, the petroleum interest, has pumped up a sleeping station at the Milan exit of the autostrada. Also away from the city's polluted air, the imposing **Villa Sassi**, 4 miles out on the Genoa approach road, is a stately and tranquil haven for motorists who wish to avoid the industrial hubbub. Only 12 rooms in this 2-century-old mansion overlooking the river; 5-acre park setting; dining room (which needs a refashioning) and terraces which are sometimes commandeered by banquet parties; bedchambers pleasant but not outstanding. A favorite hideaway for many let's-get-away-from-it-all Torinesi.

Food? The metropolis has fine gastronomy and fine vermouths. Our lead-off choice, **Cambio**, is in the Teatro Carignano building—Turin's opera house. Nineteenth-century aura featuring crystal chandeliers and velvet-swathed banquet rooms; good food, friendly staff, and decorous dining. **Tiffany** is intimate; added to its charm, you can count on well prepared cuisine. **Baccarat**, near Valentino Park, is modern in tone and superb in quality. **Muletto** is typical of the First-class establishments in the Piedmont area. **Al Gatto Nero** (corso Unione Sovietica 14), founded in '58, might take you until '88 to track down, but it's certainly well worth the search. Look for the small black cat on the door adjacent to an auto showroom. Entrance through a cozy bar; clublike atmosphere with red brick walls and hanging flora; open 12:30 P.M. to midnight. Reserve in advance. Its 2 owners hustle-and-scussle between the dining room and kitchen, but be patient about the slower-than-average service. Highly recommended. For economizing, **Ferrero**, opposite the station, is a solid choice, as are **Birreria Wuhrer**, **Cerro**, and **Fontana dei Francesi**; you can't go far wrong at **Taste Vin** or **Vecchia Lanterna**. La Cascine operates beside a small lake from June to September; it has a beautiful flower garden and dancing.

VATICAN CITY Standing on the side of a hill on the west bank of the Tiber, it is separated from Rome and Italy only by a wall. The Pope is absolute monarch, with full legislative, executive, and judicial powers. (Please refer to the introduction of this chapter for further comments on this enclave.)

Dominating the City is the **Church of St. Peter**, largest in the world and sited in the smallest independent state in the world. Close by is the Apostolic Palace, home of His Holiness and site of the famous **Vatican Museum** (55-room modern art section). It is the biggest residential castle in existence, with 1400 rooms that cover some 13 1/2-acres. Within are also the City Governor's Palace, a post office, a tribunal, a mosaic factory, a barracks, an observatory,

a railway station, a power plant, a newspaper, a pharmacy, a TV station, and the superradio station over which are broadcast the Pope's messages to 6 continents. A self-service restaurant for visitors is located in the basement in front of the main picture gallery, with a tree-shaded terrace at ground-floor level. *Sampietrini* is the name given to those who maintain the Basilica but do not live here. The ranks of the famed Swiss Guard, a colorful and elite corps whose red, yellow, and blue pantaloons were designed by Michelangelo, is being phased out; their replacements are the plain-blue-uniformed Vatican *gendarmerie.*

St. Peter's is breathtaking. The dome, Michelangelo's work, is almost as high as the tallest Egyptian pyramid; from doorway to altar, you could tuck in the towers of New York's Waldorf-Astoria with room to spare. In the museums, chapels, and libraries of the Vatican you'll find Raphaels, Michelangelos, Peruginos, Botticellis, tapestries, liturgical vessels, priceless manuscripts. An elevator will whisk you to the base of the dome; from there you can climb the winding stairs to the pinnacle for a splendid view of the meandering Tiber and Rome. Then take the walk around the inside upper periphery, put an ear close to the wall, and listen to people talking hundreds of feet away. St. Peter's alone is worth a special trip from America. Please remember that the Sistine Chapel is closed to visitors on Saturday afternoon and Sunday as well as on holidays.

Audience with the Pope: The best way to arrange this is through a letter from your Bishop to Rt. Rev. Msgr. Benjamin Farrell, J.C.D., Casa di S. Maria dell'Umiltà, via dell'Umiltà 30. Small group or individual meetings are becoming more and more difficult to arrange, though His Holiness grants a few almost daily. Apply as soon as you arrive in Rome; the Casa is only 2 blocks from the Trevi Fountain, a bonus to sightseers who are in the area. We're also told that the Paulist Fathers at the Church of St. Susanna are extremely helpful in this respect.

On Wednesdays an enormous audience is held in St. Peter's for which tickets are usually available a day ahead, provided you don't require reserved seats. There are 3 classes: The first 2 permit you to sit in grandstand structures flanking the main altar, while the 3rd is simply admission for standing room. For tickets to this (as well as to the excavations beneath St. Peter's), apply to the same source mentioned above. Short women should don their highest heels, or their view may be completely cut off. Thousands flock to these gatherings, so be sure to get there early! For special audiences *(Baciamano),* ladies should wear black dresses, high necklines, long sleeves, and veils (now optional, but more courteous), while men should appear in dark suits with dark ties. Dress requirements for the Wednesday services are nearly as rigid, although they are constantly violated by scores of unknowing travelers. The Papal address is condensed and translated for the devout in English, French, German, and Spanish. The big assemblages are scheduled from October to July, moving to the summer residence in Castel Gandolfo from July to late September. Transportation to St. Peter's is provided at nominal cost; hotel pickup and round trip are available through SITA (the "coaching" arm of CIT), American Express, and Thomas Cook, also for relatively few lire.

★ TIP   Don't be startled by the collegelike cheers, loud handclapping, and ecstatic cries of "Viva Il Papa!" from European student priests and other

spectators when the Pope is carried into the Basilica by the *uscieri.* It's unlike anything ever heard in America.

VENICE (Venezia) is an absurd and wonderful dream. To protect themselves from the approach of armies by land, a group of staid and somber citizens many centuries ago carved for themselves a slice of sea and proceeded to erect buildings on top of the waves. This fantastic conglomeration of houses, churches, gardens, factories, streets, and squares rests on piles sunk deep into the mud. It has been called "a kind of poem in stone accidentally written by history on the waters." The main boulevard, most of the important arteries, and many of the small streets are paved with *acqua* instead of asphalt—and sometimes this H₂O bears no resemblance whatsoever to *Quelques Fleurs* or *Chanel No. 5.* Warning: Since taxis, buggies, rickshas, bicycles, roller skates, and all types of transportation which can't dance on the water are forbidden, in 48 hours of normal sightseeing the average visitors' backsides will sag to within 2 inches of the ground. He or she can count on the *circolare* (in all other Italian towns a tram or bus, but here a boat), and that, with the vessels of about 600 gondoliers (about a dozen now motorized) plus about 100 launch operators, is IT; the fastest of the *motoscafi* is the *diretto* variety. A special canal pares travel time between the Marco Polo airport and the center of town to 20 minutes. This terminus, built on reclaimed land, can accommodate only jets without full fuel loads at takeoff. **The Lido**, a separate settlement a few minutes away by Chris-Craft, offers a galaxy of summer attractions, capped by its famed Casino. When the white marbles of the roulette tables clatter to a halt at the end of the season, the management tucks them into a velvet case and paddles over to its smaller Cà Vendramin, in Venice proper, where the wheels and dice are set to spinning once again (ironically, in the villa where Richard Wagner died!). Scattered in the lagoon and environs are the smaller islands of Murano (glassware), Burano (lace), Torcello (fine Byzantine church), and Strà (a townlet on the Brenta Canal and site of Villa Pisani with its legendary frescoes). You can also take a summer cruise via the canals over to Padua aboard the riverbark *Il Burchiello* which calls at Strà; for the return, we recommend hopping a bus. Venice's vaunted corruption, racketeering, political chicanery? Yes, but only in the highest circles (well, *mostly* in the highest circles). The city is tightly held in the palms of roughly 700 stalwarts— gondoliers, motor-launch operators, and guides—whose administrative spoils have been accused of outsmelling the Canale Scomenzera at high noon in August. If you're abroad during the right months, it would be a great mistake to miss one of the most unique—if one of the most venal—cities on the globe. Looking ahead to the year 1990—when, it was estimated that this marvel of a metropolis would be 2/3 submerged—an emergency "sinking fund" was established by a concerned Roman Cabinet. The Italian legislature has passed a bill which provides $350,000,000 to fight flooding, pollution, and decay. In addition, Dutch hydraulics experts have teamed up with Italian engineers to seek a lasting solution to the city's permanent wave problem. These specialists have checked the tides by employing removable barriers at the 3 sea entrances plus industrial controls within the lagoon. Many wells have been permanently capped, providing a cushion upon which Venice can "float," the collapse of

the city already has been markedly reduced, and prospects are good that the Venetians will enjoy a new and long lease on life.

Hotels This city is the headquarters of the famous Grand Hotels of Italy Corporation—CIGA. The Koh-i-noor diamond of the chain is the polished little **Gritti Palace** of Ernest Hemingway fame, just Across the River and Into the Trees from the gondola park. Now in the skillful hands of the highly professional Dott. Nico Passante, this house traditionally has been one of the number one stopping places in the world. Now it is operative year-round. First, it is small, gladsome, and almost club-like. Second, nothing has been spared in décor, in staff, in cuisine, or in the attributes of pure luxury. Rooms and apartments on the top floor have been transformed into beautiful "penthouse-studios." The canalside units were later given a puffup; many, incidentally, come with stocked bar-type refrigerators; the entire house, of course, is air-conditioned. If expense is no object, try to reserve Suite #110; it's one of the finest hotel accommodations, in taste and in feeling, that we've seen anywhere. We've carried on a long and devoted love affair with this tiny gem of a hostelry, and are delighted to see that its former chieftain is maintaining all those qualities which have made it a masterpiece of innkeeping in the past.

Almost next door is CIGA's gorgeous **Palazzo del Giglio apartment colony**. It is an exquisite union of bright, joyful colors, modern comfort, carefully selected antiques, and works of art to complement the whole and create an enchanting homey atmosphere. Just 16 suites in varying sizes to accommodate couples or families or friendly migrants; full air conditioning plus TV, radio, beautifully equipped kitchens; the works. Laundry, maid, and other services are available. The cheer, the privacy, the luxury, and the economics of this dandy little enclave make it almost irresistible for travelers who plan to stay a week or more in Venice. Administration is by the Gritti people, who are always at the beck or phone-call of their neighboring apartment clients. We love it and recommend it highly to anyone looking for this particular milieu.

The stalwart, blissfully tranquil, Deluxe-category **Cipriani**, 5 minutes by water from St. Mark's Square, reigns on the island of Giudecca. The chief of operations is Director Natale Rusconi—a master of innkeeping ins-and-outs. Free motor-launch shuttles day and night continuously to St. Mark's, plus daily service to the Golf Club on the Lido; glorious situation overlooking the lagoon; Chef Guiliano's cuisine consistently 5-star; Ristorante Cipriani redone with the renowned Fortuny fabrics; Sala del Gabbiano confrere now in flowers and greenery; pension terms not required. Over 100 air-conditioned, sound-proofed rooms; 11 newly built junior suites, most with their own private garden; 2 additional super-apartments joining "A", "B," and "C" which are fit for any 20th-century doge; large pool (the *only* one at any Venetian hostelry) covered and heated when temperatures drop. Arcade with service facilities, boutiques, and hairdressing salon; car parking service at Piazzale Roma. It is closed part of January, all of February, and most of March. So lovely in every respect that we recommend it with cheers and salutes.

The **Danieli Royal Excelsior** is CIGA's larger Deluxe offering, with greater mass appeal. Entirely air-conditioned; roughly 245 rooms (at least 1/2 of which have been refashioned) in 3 separate structures, coupled by short pas-sageways: The "Palace" building (architecturally gorgeous; double pane win-

dows in front; quietest units on Rio del Vin side); the "New" building (less classic and also appealing); and the "Danielino" building (more in tune with the conventional American viewpoint; use chiefly by groups). Its General Manager is Swiss-trained Pierre Barrelet. Different in concept from the Gritti or the Cipriani, but still fine.

The First-class **Europa e Britannia** offers an extra feature in its sprawling construction; the guest can view the big canal from 4 sides. It is smoothly directed by Dr. Massimo Rosati, who also manages the neighboring Regina (see below). Beautiful garden restaurant ablossom; sweetly color-conditioned on the outside; fully air-conditioned on the inside. Vast changes recently—all of them highly beneficial; same tariff range for a canalside double or a unit facing the Venetian Court. Now highly endorsed.

The **Bauer Grünwald** boasts a houseful of exquisite Medici-style furnishings. Units ending in "52" or "53" cast wonderful glances at the canal; 80% of the building is air-conditioned. Public rooms boast a discreetly modern décor melding softly through a rich antique haze. Splendid Grand Canal terrace; roof garden; Czar-opulent Royal suite; ordinary accommodations "inside" and somewhat cramped; clean, very well run, by Manager Carlo Puppo; expensive, and less lively than most.

The **Luna**, Venice's oldest hotel (dating from 1474, but a religious retreat even prior to *that!*), buffed the finishing touches on its 10-year renovation program a while back. Fully air-conditioned; waterside bar on tiny canal facing the Royal Garden; comfortable bedchambers; most baths replete with marble. There are an attractive rose-toned dining room and open terrace; 1/2-pension is a *must*. If you can, snag #154 for the view or #107 for its huge balcony with table and chairs. Director Carlo Valensin can be rightfully proud of this zenithing "Moon." Unusually good value.

The **Regina**, adjoining the Europa e Britannia and sharing the same kitchen and talented chef, is also under the administrative CIGA-wing. Smaller than its sister, but almost brighter in feeling; fresh lobby plus skylit salon; pleasant outdoor restaurant crowning the waves by the gondola rank; winter dining room with brown-tone bar opposite; uniform standard accommodation; extra-nice terraced nests in #'s 552/554. An equitable buy that is glowing with esteem. The **Metropole** boasts an excellent address a few steps away from the ferry landing, facing the Lagoon. Canal entrance for gondolas and water taxis. Complete air conditioning; sumptuous interior, a modern adaptation of the classic Venetian style; compact restaurant and American bar; generously outfitted bedchambers. For situation and decoration, this rejuvenated house is loaded with appeal. Its service standards are another story. **Monaco**, now reperked with fresh carpets, multichannel radios, air conditioning, and given a handsome bamboo-toned bar, nestles dockside on the Grand Canal just across the walkway from Harry's Bar. The Frenchy accommodations with painted furniture best; moderate tariffs. Not bad at all. **La Fenice** is above the restaurant of the same name, but is not associated with it. Located in the wings of the famous Fenice Theatre; cozy elegant lounge with silk wall coverings; beautiful antique furnishings; no restaurant, but a bar 10-seconds away for thirsting Thespians; 70 rooms, most with bath but some of the "sitz" style. A decent bet within its Second-class ranking. The **Park**, quietly situated across,

from the railway station and city parking garages, has 100 medium-size rooms, the back ones facing Papadopoli Park. We applaud its straightforward comfort, its kind minions, and its homespun hospitality. The 69-room-and-bath **Londra** is beginning to show its will to live. The pulse beat is quickening, we are pleased to report. Although we've changed our minds to conclude that the little **Patria Tre Rose** is somewhat less than a honey for the money, readers' opinions are sharply divided on this one. **Cavalletto**, a property of the charming and brilliant Edward M. Masprone, has been mightily improved. Public rooms refashioned; 96 units, 85 with bath or shower; annex without private plumbing; commercial but worthy for its reasonable tariffs. The **Boston**, near St. Mark's Square, serves breakfast only. Inexpensive and solid. **Ala** has 60 chirpy nests; only breakfast is required. Allah be praised! **Carpaccio**, on the Grand Canal, steps forward with a generous helping of flair for its bracket. Large rooms, generally clean; simply furnished; situation excellent; moderate terms. One of the best *quids* for your *quo* in the city. **Pensione Seguso**, fronting the Canale Della Giudecca, bobs up with 50 units, 1/2 with bath or shower; #23, facing the trees across the water, should double your pleasure. Top value. *Fielding's Low-Cost Europe* lists scads more.

★ **TIP** If you can handle your luggage, do not take a water taxi from the station. Instead of crossing the street, walk toward this hotel, which is visible to the right as you exit. Within 3 minutes by foot you will find a public *motoscafo/vaporetto* stop with convenient transportation to all canalside hostelries. Difference in price? For a taxi you are likely to shell out at least $11.50 to go from the terminal to St Mark's Square. The most you will pay by using public transportation is about 75¢.

Country living near Venice? The grimly fading **Villa Condulmer** (3 miles from *Mogliano* on the A-27 to V. Veneto) is a 250-acre estate set in flat terrain. Big, sparsely furnished halls; 36 antiquated rooms, all with bath or shower; swimming pool lush with tropical greenery. This one is in dire need of a pep-up, in our opinion. If it ever is accomplished, it could be quite agreeable.

In *Asolo*, about 50 minutes out on the main Venice-Verona highway, you'll find the **Hotel Villa Cipriani**, now operated by the exclusive CIGA chain. This town was the celebrated former home of both Eleanora Duse and Robert Browning. Beautifully operated; 35 rooms all with private bath; 4 Deluxe suites; décor similar to the Venice Cipriani; huge garden; full pension—with à la carte menu! Here's a fine stop for lunch or for rest.

In the *Lido*, a few minutes by motorboat from Venice, you'll find the hotel which has made this island a legendary summer resort—the **Excelsior Palace**, guided by Francesco Chiais, who also looks after all of this chain's beach links here. The strand is more beautiful than ever. A pool also is splashing and a waterfront Taverna is sizzling. There are a beach bar and 360 luxury cabanas. Air conditioning murmurs throughout this 380-room house—but not at night during our visit, darn it. (You can't open the windows because of the plague of mosquitoes.) The best units, in our opinion, are the cheerfully modernized ones on the ground level and the 5th and 6th floors. Emphasis is being placed on the creation of a vacation haven for the bright, the vigorous, and the Jet Setters of any age (as long as they're young at heart) in a campaign to wipe away its former image as a hermitage for the creaky in body and spirit. **Hotel**

Quattro Fontane ("Four Fountains"), opposite the Casino, is officially catego-
rized as Second class, but its accommodations (especially in the newer 25-unit
wing) are strictly First-class quality. The owner's wife, who is Danish, has
contributed her taste to the décor. Tennis; live music; garden; open-air restaurant. _Always full, so reserve in advance._ Good within its league for its service,
price, management, and ambiance. We also are reasonably fond of the 75-room
Villa Mabapa, believe it or not a contraction of Mamma, Bambino, and Papa
of the Vianello tribe who run the place. Except for the location, which is far
from the casino and other Lido action, this one competes favorably with the
Four Fountains. **Grand Hotel des Bains**, perhaps due for revamping soon so
check first, is gifted with a warmed seawater pool, 3 tennis courts at its
Sporting Club, a discothèque, a bar, and full air conditioning. The rooms we
saw then, however, were still too old-fashioned and uncozy for us. Maintenance, on this visit, was plummeting. The **Adria Urania** and its neighboring
Villas—**Nora** and **Ada**—are all beautifully managed by Mrs. Biasutti. Back-
street location, 5 minutes from _vapore_ station; fronted by manicured garden;
veranda dining; indoor fish restaurant with shells from Kenya and Mexico,
nets, and Turkish lamps; many homey touches throughout. In the same neighborhood, the **Riviera** also boasts an excellent staff, but the heavy group traffic
slays some of its potential warmth. **Hungaria** is one of the worst stops in the
region, in our opinion—and that's quite a distinction when one considers the
others.

Restaurants   Venice, like Rome, offers everything for the hungry.
Harry's Bar (San Marco 1323), where Mr. Hemingway's Colonel whiled away
so many brooding hours, is a shrine and an apex for visiting firemen. It's a
typical Class AAA, Big City gin mill, U.S.-style—intimate, friendly, sophisticated, and cheerful. Great fun for people-watching; limited but excellent
menu with many stateside delicacies at high prices. Arrigo, the alert and
friendly son of Giuseppe Cipriani, is "Harry"; Roger is the bar maestro.
Harry's *** Restaurant** twinkles happily above the Bar; 60 can be nourished in ***** style at one sitting; we've recently come from another sit-in with
a batch of homemade ravioli and a plate of Scampi Carlina; if we could
untangle our tongue from the carriage of our typewriter, we'd describe it leth
lithp-ingly—but, since we can't, you'd better order it yourself. Always reserve
in Season. Wonderful; getting better, better, and better.

Antico Martini, in the piazza facing the famous Teatro La Fenice, vies for
top honors. Pleasant luxury-leaning interior with French curtains, gilt mirrors,
and crystal fixtures; awning-covered plaza site for outdoor dining; excellent,
kind, and professional service keenly hawk-eyed by Maître Diana. Dinner
only; very costly but good on every score. (Incidentally, for those who wish
to extend the evening, there's a pleasant nightclub in the back.)

Quadri (piazza San Marco 120) is one of the oldest restaurants in Italy and
finally it may be slowing down with age and losing some of its traditional zest.
Elegance and grace; tiny, open dining room at street level and chichi quarters
upstairs; classic Venetian décor at its richest; very expensive indeed; closed
November through March. **Caffè Florian**, across the _piazza,_ began life as far
back as 1720. It offers 6 little rooms, each with its own entrance, plus 7 rows
of outside tables; a 5-piece band gently massages the eardrums of anybody in

the entire square. Shuttered Fridays except in summer. Our pick of the esplanade. **Lavena**, around the corner, is also noteworthy.

For Italian dining and T-bone steaks cut to order, **Taverna La Fenice** (San Marco 1937) gets a blue ribbon, despite a few cavils from travelers. Our latest dinner here revealed a tremendous pickup in service standards. Naturally this judgment is based on watching other tables as well as our own. Handsome, timber highlights; covered terrace in summer; versatile kitchen; tariffs very dear. We are happy to report an improvement. The **Caravella** (calle XXII Marzo) is even higher, but in its way it is more beautiful, too, and the culinary preparations are unusually savory. Bar at entrance with ruby-red chairs at cozy tables; interior room on 2 tiers; wood-lined walls resembling an ancient bark: brass lamps set in velvet-upholstered vitrines imparting a soft glow; gay explosions of flowers everywhere, and all dew-fresh; mock-crystal drinking glasses; calico napkins. The parchment menu—and a big one it is—lists prices for the host only. Specialties include lobster, spaghetti Venetian-style (that's with a mixture of sautéed onions and anchovies which might be too seasoned for many palates), spider crab, and sole. Many concierges in town bad-mouth this establishment, possibly because it does not pay off to attract clients, or possibly because its checks are so steep. We liked it, however, and we think you will as well. **Do Forni** (called Specchiero 468) features young, urbane Proprietor-Chef Paties often at your tableside preparing the dishes for you personally— and mighty lip-smacking good they are. Two of the 3 rooms in medieval Venetian style; tented motif for summer dining; comestibles medium to expensive. Sample his Spaghetti all'Isolana and his Spiedino Do Forni Guarnito (a brochette of 7 meats). Closed Thursday but open every other day of the year. Superb. **A la Vecia Cavana** (Rio Terra SS. Apostoli) borders a canal; in the thirteenth-century gondolas parked under its arches; we moored here recently and loved it. Savoy-trained Alberti Felice is the floorman who speaks perfect London-bred English; his brother Roberto does the cooking. Try their Sardine Saor (a local starter), the antipasto of fish, the Scampi alla Cavana (on a wooden skewer and yumptious), the Eel in Tomato Sauce, the Polenta on a shingle, the Grilled Salad, and the white wine of Verona. Ummmmm! **Trattoria La Colomba** (Frezzeria 1665) and, to a lesser degree, **Al Graspo de Ua** (San Bartolomeo 5094) offer similar attractions at the same level; no terrace at the latter. The former, by the way, is the well-known establishment displaying paintings on its walls and is not to be confused with the newer **Colombo**, which is also lauded for its skilletry. **Antico Locanda Montin** (near the Ca'Rezzonico water-taxi landing at San Trovaso) is a favorite of ours from way back. Picture-lined, raw interior; vine-lined summer garden; simple cookery; basic tariffs; frequented by artists, nobility, and a grateful travel writer or two. **Antica Besseta** (S. Croce 1395) is the "find" of that outstanding food columnist for the *International Herald Tribune*, Naomi Barry. While we have not had an opportunity to don a napkin here, our distinguished colleague awards high praise for the authenticity ("*cucina genuina*") of the cookery. Proprietor Nereo Volpe takes your order while his wife, Mariuccia, pounds the pasta. Sounds true to us. **Al Peoceto Risorto** (called Donzella 249) is not recommended. **Da Nico** (Frezzeria 1702) is also under management that has let it slip; while still okay, it's no longer a rave for bargain hunters. The nearby

Da Gianni is a fair choice for pizza. **Cicci della Salute**, across the Canal from the Gritti Palace, is music to those on a tight budget. **Trattoria Madonna**, near the Rialto Bridge, is very popular, with commendable skilletcraft; one drawback for Americans may be the language barrier; this one is usually so crowded that it's a tough scramble to get in. Don't fall for the shameless photo racket here which comes on as a "gift" but which winds up soaking you for a pocketful of lire. Oh, oh, oh, HOW we hate ourselves for being suckered into this fastie! **Carbonera** didn't seem the same as it used to be, although it's trying hard for a comeback. Although **Trattoria Malamocco Venezia** teems with local residents, we didn't like the noisy atmosphere, the bustle of the waiters, or the house wine—but the bean soup was delicious.

Al Teatro (on piazza Fenice adjoining Teatro La Fenice) still gets star ranking as the top pizzeria in town. The entrance room contains a counter, a bar, an open grill, and a frenzied trade; the second room offers about 15 tables, 24 ceiling lights, celebrity-photo-lined walls, and a cheerful, relaxed atmosphere; between the 2 is an open kitchen with a pizza oven that's home base for 16 types (available only during mealtimes, when the stoves are hot). Super for its category; we tout it heartily.

Ice cream? The silkiest we've discovered is at **Todaro**, near the columns on S. Marco.

Want a wonderful excursion on a bright day? For sophisticated dining at a jewel of a country inn, take a speedboat (35 minutes) to the island of Torcello and its lovely **Locanda ꞏCipriani**. Peaceful terrace; 5 choices of menus of gourmet fare at fixed price in the opulent area; please, please, ask Maître Gianni to bless you with *both* Gnocchis—Gnocchi Torcellano and a Gnocchi Santa Fosca—each featherlight, different in concept, and guaranteed taste treats; they're the finest we've ever savored. For fish dishes and risottos in colorful, cheerful, noisy surroundings, there's the famous **Da Romano** on Burano Island, roughly the same haul; here's a hangout of local card players, artists, and characters.

Al Postiglone, at *Morocco*, is the newest venture of the Cipriani tribe, located 20 minutes from Venice on the Treviso pike. Alfresco terrace with about a dozen cocktail tables; interior salon separated by Moorish arches and glass; décor comprising browns and pale yellow, with splashes of spring colors; excellent staff; fun for a Moroccan adventure.

Dining in the *Lido*? Our dear chum George Prade, worldwide Sales Manager for Mumm champagnes who is even more sparkling and delightful than his noble products, advises us to head straight for the open-air restaurant of **Hotel Quattro Fontane** for its 50-dish antipasti "smörgåsbord" (accompanied by a bottle of Mumm's Cordon Rouge, of course). When this connoisseur labels any cuisine "at the top," *that,* hungry friends, is IT. Otherwise you might like the snackeries at the **Excelsior** or **Les Bains.**

Night Life Four suggestions: (1) the **Casino** at the Lido, with the only real floor show within miles. (2) **Chez Vous** at the Excelsior-Lido, offering all-out competition, (3) a drink, a dance, or a pitch at the **Antico Martini** or (4) go to bed with a good book. Pleasant dinner-dancing on the **Bauer-Grünwald** roof in season only. **Ai Musicanti** gives a first impression of a Bavarian beer hall that has suddenly been dipped in Italian schmalz (if you can imagine

such a metaphor). Happy reception; strolling singers airing their adenoids over such unlikely old chestnuts as *The Colonel Bogey March;* outrageous, funloving flirtations from 9 to 10.30 by ersatz gondoliers who often gently pinch the posteriors of giggling female clients. Ninety percent for tour groups but so obviously contrived that who could care? A hoot. The **King's Club**, hard by the airport, is said to be the only fetching disco in the area. **Antico Pignolo** isn't even mildly recommended for the small hours; it draws a heavy patronage of unhappy sailors who don't know any better.

Shopping   Buyers will find that this lodestone is teeming with guides, concierges, gondoliers, and other fast operators hungry for commissions on their purchases. The usual bite is 20% to 25% on glass and 15% on lace. Don't tell anyone where you're going, inform the shopkeeper immediately that nobody directed you to his establishment (except a guidebook or other disinterested source), that you're paying cash, and that you want the above scale of discounts for yourself.

To counter the fringe operators, the Chamber of Commerce and the legitimate old-line merchants, such as those mentioned below, set up the **Venetian Crafts Association** to attest both product quality and business ethics among its members. Be sure to look for the Association's 4-leaf-clover symbol displayed in all these companies.

Glass: We suggest that you avoid the island of **Murano** and the swindlers or fringe-dealers throughout Venice itself and do 100% of your buying only in the 2 oldest, largest, and soundest houses— ★ ★ ★ ★ ★ **Pauly & Co.** (Ponte dei Consorzi, 3 branches in piazza San Marco) and ★ ★ ★ ★ **Salviati & Co.** (San Gregorio 195, across the Grand Canal from the Gritti Palace plus 2 branches on San Marco). These 2 establishments are impeccably honest and reliable; both are such fairylands of glittering beauty that they're as much a part of the Venetian spectator's scene as the Square, the gondolas, and the cathedral.

We list them in alphabetical order because of their equal ranking.

The venerable **Pauly & Co.** products have won 25 Gold Medals, 16 Notable Award Prizes, 33 Award Diplomas, the French Legion of Honor, the Crown of Leopold, and the Crown of Italy. In their archives, you'll find more than 800-thousand one-of-a-kind sketches of antique, classical and modern patterns. A team of celebrated Glass Masters create exclusively for them. At their Ponte dei Consorzi headquarters there is a demonstration furnace and budget shop on the ground floor; upstairs you may wander through perhaps 20 glorious rooms full of treasures for the table, the home, and the eye.

Salviati, dean of the field, recently captured the celestial "Golden Compasses" award, the biannual "Oscar" presented for Italy's most noble designs in manufactured output. Their pioneering has had a profound influence on the evolution of glass all over the world. Salviati mosaic panels or murals have been commissioned by world-famous institutions. Don't miss a visit to their magnificent display mansion where you will find 2 of the most exciting museum collections of ancient and modern glass in existence. You'll revel in chambers full of objects which shimmer as did the Pleasure Dome of Xanadu.

Both firms guarantee safe arrival to your home of everything they ship—and you can absolutely trust them on this. But have limitless patience about ship-

ment delays (months are par for the course, due to Italian export red tape and
the monumental backlog snarls at U.S. docks)—and be sure to find out approximate delivery costs to your area, because port brokers' fees are sometimes
wicked through no fault of these good artisans. Please remember that nobody
is permitted to pay U.S. Customs duties and handling before our American
officials can evaluate these foreign purchases upon entry, so it is impossible for
these companies to estimate the levy accurately.

Ladies' handbags and stunning boutique items: ★ ★ ★ ★ ★ **Roberta** is the
brilliant, charming Mrs. Giuliana Camerino, who has become one of the top
couture arbiters in dressing The Complete Woman. Her headquarters (Santa
Maria Formosa 6123, down a by-lane) is surely worth a visit—but you will
want to concentrate most of your time in her elegant showplace at Ascensione
1256. Branches in **Rome, Florence, Milan, Naples, Modena, Bari,** and **New
York**; seasonal shops in Lido and Cortina d'Ampezzo. Very, very expensive
but super.

Exquisite Venetian jewelry: In quality, in fame, in the distinction of its
worldwide clientele who seek these treasures, the unchallenged King of this
City of Palaces is ★ ★ ★ ★ ★ **Nardi** (piazza San Marco 68–71). Since 1920 it
has specialized in designing and creating exquisite *bijous* in gold and precious
stones, all handmade and all signed as originals with the famed Nardi name.
Full line of gems, including mouth-watering antiques; new shop adjacent at
No. 68 with exceptionally fine rarities; no purchase tax ever. Ask for the
engaging and knowledgeable Mr. Sergio Nardi, or for Messrs. Menegon or
Zambon. Wonderful!

Lace and beachwear: ★ ★ ★ ★ ★ **Jesurum** (Ponte Canonica 4314) has undergone a glorious revolution. In addition to its famous lace, the lovely old palace
now glows with the incandescent color splashes of a vast, vivid, and strikingly
different assemblage of everything for the beach. Dynamic Mario Levi-
Morenos and Mrs. Eugenia Graziussi will welcome you smilingly. Branch in
Milan. Dramatically exciting.

Leather goods: **Vogini** (4 shops on 4 corners of San Marco-Ascensione) runs
the gamut in fine merchandise in this field.

VERONA, the city of Romeo and Juliet, provides a whirl of ancient byways, tiny piazzas, hill and valley vistas, an open market, superb opera at the
open arena in summer or in its modern hall in winter, and trade fairs galore.
Here's a charmer that you really should visit.

This compact city boasts one of the most unusual hotels in the nation. The
Due Torri is the hobby of a wealthy Italian couple, Dr. and Mrs. Enrico
Wallner. They delegate its day-to-day administration to a professional manager. For more than 1000 years there has been some kind of inn, tavern, or
hostel on this site (Mozart stopped here in 1770); after 80 years of its disuse,
the Wallners have created a showplace. Within its rooms there are 50 different
motifs of exact period-furniture combinations of the eighteenth and early
nineteenth centuries, both Italian and French; a sufficient supply of excess
antiques is in storage to equip 200 additional rooms! Dignity and richness
everywhere; cuisine vastly improved and very well presented; keen-eyed attention from Resident Manager Raimondo Giavarini; rates especially moderate

for such opulence. **Colomba d'Oro** was recently given a shampoo, shower, shave, and massage. First floor, 3rd story, restaurant, and breakfast room renewed; firm-sprung beds throughout; nice perky baths; brass lamps and flowered wallpaper installed; 60% air conditioning sealed-in silence with double windows; garage. Proprietor Tapparini provides a lot for your money. Fresh, clean, and tasteful. The **Grand** has been perked up brightly. Public rooms smartened; lobbyside patio sweet for summer dining; most ceilings so high you'll think you're sleeping in a square silo. Comfortable, nonetheless, and getting better. The **San Pietro** on the Autostrada exit from Venice and Milan, is so-so for go-slow motorists who prefer Verona from afar. Each unit with private balcony; most with bath or shower; clean as shining tile. The **San Luca**, in the Second file, comes up with First-class amenities. Alley situation, which detracts from its status but adds to its tranquillity; cool but appealing lobby with adjoining bar; mezzanine breakfast deck; rooftop solarium; good, modern air conditioning; extra-kind concierge and back-up staff. All 40 smartly appointed contemporary bedchambers with wall-to-wall carpets, muted color blends, and small but efficient baths. For its low rates and relatively high-style rewards, we think it's a sensible buy. **Accademia** now scores about C-minus in this same school by comparison. **Giulietta e Romeo**, as well as **Milano**, are also scholarly Second-class bets. For students, Tanzanian civil servants, or privates in the Yucatan army, the following 3 tag ends may be suitable—but we doubt it. **Europa** is functional; the language spoken here is seldom, if ever, uttered in Buckingham Palace. **Verona** offers less space than the inside of the "o" in its name. **Valverde** is young, but "young" is the only favorable adjective we can muster.

When it comes to dining, **Verona Antica** (via Sottoriva 10) now boasts the most sophisticated tables in town; the proprietors are Onofrio and Romeo Donadel. The mountainside **Re Teodorico** (5 minutes above the city) is tops physically but its kitchen is not outstanding. Approach along a fortress balcony bordered by 80-foot cypress giants; breathtaking outdoor terrace high above the sparkling meanders of the Adige River; peaceful silence broken only by the chiming of chapel bells, far below, from the tile-clad city. Big menu; fair food. You probably won't even notice its simple interior, because here is one of the loveliest perches on the European circuit. Open every day except February's Fridays. The **12 Apostoli** offers a small colorful dining room in the Old City. Named in A.D. 1745 for the 12 friends who advised the founder to turn his butcher shop into a restaurant. The proprietor-chef's family has operated the place continuously since 1904; the cuisine is well served and reasonably appetizing. Our bill was precise, but other correspondents have run up against a different abacus here. **Marconi** (Vicolo Crocioni 6) and **Torcolotti** (via Zambelli 24) are two additional worthy entries for full meals. **Pedayena** (piazza Brà 20, heart of the tourist district), run by a big brewery, sloshes in modern sudsy duds. It has lost its head, in our estimation. **Bragozzo**, near Juliet's Tomb, specializes in fish. Décor composed of the usual flotsam washed through a 5-part room; quite good for what it is. **Tre Corone** (piazza Brá 16), which pulls an international clientele, is not spectacular. It's merely convenient.

VIAREGGIO's   leader is the 250-bed **Grand Hotel et Royal**, between the
sea and pine woods. Open-air and indoor dining areas; American Bar; most
units with bath or shower; weird combination of ultramodern and traditional
décor, akin to finding an astronaut's helmet in a hansom cab. The 80-room-
and-bath **Palace** also faces the waves; here are a lovely terrace, solarium, and
panoramic vistas.

VICENZA   The **Jolly Campo Marzio** and the **Jolly Statione** (no restaurant) probably won't give *you* the jollies, but at least they may keep the
raindrops from falling on your head.

Liechtenstein

Liechtenstein, like Andorra, Luxembourg, Monaco, and San Marino, is a storybook land which frequently seems to get lost by European cartographers. But more Americans are discovering it every year, because this matchbox Principality is one of the last gentle, happy, unspoiled paradises on the face of a tired and cynical continent. Here are some rapid-fire jottings:

Vaguely the shape of Idaho (and about the size of an Idaho potato), this midget Elysium sprawls between the east bank of the Upper Rhine (near Lake Constance) and a towering range of 7000-foot peaks which provide ski slopes for winter sportsmen; it is the historic buffer state, 16 miles long and 4 wide, which separates Switzerland from Austria. St. Gall is only a hop, skip, and jump from the capital; Zürich is an easy morning's drive, and Innsbruck (Austria) isn't much farther by crack train. The main railway line to Vienna, one of central Europe's greatest arteries, cuts across the heartland and then passes on Austrian soil within rods of the bordering river (international transfer points: Sargans or Buchs, both in Switzerland).

Founded in 1719, it has proudly cherished its independence since then; the benevolent and popular Reigning Prince is Franz Joseph II. The national language is German, and the monetary unit is the Swiss franc. Obviously, this miniland is seething with political unrest. Why else would it have put a new government in office—the 3rd change of ruling party in more than 4 decades? There is no standing military might; 40 policemen do the job of the army, navy, air force, and marines. There are no labor unions, no poverty, and practically no taxes (to discourage fugitives and financial-angle guys, however, citizenship papers are almost impossible to obtain). Crime is virtually unknown.

Industries include postage stamps, textiles, tools, sausage casings, space age insulation, false teeth (producing 114-million molars a year, here's a big chomp in the economy!), and optical instruments; agriculture predominates. The postage stamps boast some of the finest engraving in the world; oddly enough, they have the same value to philatelists whether they're canceled or uncanceled.

Vaduz (pronounced Vah-dootz), the capital, crams 4,856 (count 'em!) living human beings (national census: 26,000, composed of 16,900 citizens and 9100 foreigners) into one metropolis, if you can imagine such staggering overpopula-

tion. *Schaan*, the national (not international) railway station, and handsome little *Triesenberg* are the only other villages of importance. In winter almost everyone and his ski partner evacuate the centers for the higher slopes. The isolated hamlet of *Malbun* is the capital of the snowflakes. It's no more than a porcelain-white chalice in a *cul-de-sac* where several hotels and guest houses provide shelter, food, and a fair degree of comfort. If you look carefully, you may recognize the royal sitzmark of Prince Philip, Prince Charles, or Princess Anne, who make this a scheduled winter wonderland.

Hotels Let's consider the ones in *Vaduz* first. More about the Tourotel Gaflei and the Motel Waldeck later. The elfin **Sylva** (said to be cozy) at *Schaan* and the **Engel** (near the Austrian border at *Nendeln*) are somewhat distant alternates.

The **Sonnenhof**, on the mountainside, easily captures top honors not only as the finest hostelry in the land, but also as one of the leading choices in the entire region—in or out of Liechtenstein. This is the happy domain of Emil Real and his beautiful wife, Jutta (pronounced "Utah"). There is a lovely view from its front-facing rooms; the tranquillity is heavenly. This entire plant has been refreshed; there's a splendid woody dining room in 2 tiers which peeks at the Rhine Valley; glass-wrapped swimming pool and wood-wrapped sauna are fully operational; a dozen fine suites, each with color TV, frigo bars, and its own private lawn or terrace—the last word-and-sigh for contentment. Awaiting you are wall-to-wall carpeting, excellent furniture, well-conceived baths, and the feeling that the house is in certain harmony with its peaceful surroundings. Since these warmhearted hoteliers try so hard to create a cozy, friendly "family" atmosphere, all guests are encouraged to enjoy their cups together in the homey main-floor lounge. Its extra-savory cookery is reserved for residents, which keeps the flavor up and the madding crowds down (another Real-istic guarantee of solace). Open all year; tons of bucolic charm; perfect for a rest in every particular. *Wunderbar!*

The tiny perked-up **Real**, the centrally located brother of the Sonnenhof, is the 10-unit (5 singles, 5 doubles) extension of Liechtenstein's most celebrated restaurant. The staff's warmth of hospitality is truly overwhelming. The **Schlössle**, a mock castle in a bluff buff hue, is quite pleasant and homey. The carpeted bedchambers sport painted furniture, TV, and kitchenette. Nice as a miniapartment address. The petite **Adler**, on a bustling site, is carefully managed and provides solid medium-price value. The **Engel** (this one in town) is adequate rather than fancy. Busy-busy location; flower-lined balconies along front; ground-level beer-cellar-type den for dancing, plus Restaurant Français; 19 rooms and 15 baths or showers; fruit in bedchambers for evening snack; sparkling, clean, and appealing. **Vaduzer Hof** of the Winerwald group was recently renovated. Comfortable; many rooms with balconies; reserve away from front of house due to noise; warm, inviting dining room; pleasant woody, open-beamed bar. Good. The 24-room economy-minded **Elite** is in midtown. Clean; breakfast only; nothing special. The ancient **Löwen** offers chiefly its

captivating dining terrace overlooking the vineyards to recommend it. Careful restoration has been rendered to preserve this delightfully antique national trust. **Motel In Liechtenstein**, 3 miles up from the center on an impressive mesa, commands a stunning panorama of the Rhine Valley. New management; wheelborne Americans enjoy its auto-matic convenience. Viewful dining room and terrace; 33 units, all with bath or shower; a cozy stop for ramblers. The revamped **Hotel Meierhof**, closer to town on the same route, has a restaurant downstairs and 21 bedrooms above, including some new suites. Passable for serious budgeteers or summer-izing families who might enjoy the adult and kiddie pools in the back garden. High in the country, the inn in Masecha is ideal for students or hard-driven economy-seekers. Between Vaduz and Schaan, the **Mühle** is a sweet little honeybunch of only 7 rooms which are compact but inviting. The low stucco building resembles a Spanish colonial *hacienda*. Charm-laden restaurants (1 for grills), bar, and polished-rustic lounges. Pert and proper. At *Schaan*, we'd pick the **Schaanerhof**, with the **Dux** waddling up behind. The **Gasthof Samina** in *Triesenberg*, once an enchanting spot, hit the skids for a while, but now that a new owner has grasped the reins and is undertaking a full revision of this house we hope it will resume some of its former glory.

The mile-high, supermodern, 40-room **Tourotel Gaflei** is ideal for splendid isolationists. The scenic paradise is enhanced by a swimming pool, tennis courts, a sauna, and minigolf links. Sweeping panorama of the alps sloping toward Triesenberg and the valley of the capital, ½-hour drive over a curvaceous lane; variable cuisine, good on our several samplings but not always quite up to the mark; handsome, spacious public rooms, but small-gauge bedchambers; all units with private bath or shower, telephone, and radio; bowling alleys; basement bar; yards of terrace space for sun-soaking and oooo-ing and aaaaahhh-ing at the majestic mountains.

Up at *Malbun*, the fully-balconied, 30-room-and-bath **Malbunerhof** leads the small parade. Pool, bowling, and sauna for physical fitness types; tartan dining salon; fireside bar in gray and brown; modernistic paintings; alpine décor tuned to hunting green. Bid for one of the larger units. The same team owns the more group-minded **Gorfion**, which is also a worthy choice for hillbillets. Similar and equally well managed. Both resemble hyperthyroid chalets. The **Alpenhotel** would be our next choice; it is more modest, but it also has an enclosed swimming pool as well as personality and comfort. **Galina** is an attractive, colorful mountain house that oozes value. The sold-and-resold **Hotel Waldeck** at *Gamprin*, near the Austrian border, debuted with 30 streamlined, narrow-dimension bedchambers, all with shower. Captivating setting as viewful as all outdoors. Practically since its outset, this one has been in a serious state of flux. Let's wait some more. A **youth hostel** beckons near *Schaan*, about 100 yards from the bus junction. You can have breakfast here, cook your own food if you wish or get a substantial cheap meal at the nearby Café Forum. About 100 beds with rates close to $5 per noggin. Clean, neat,

and economical. In most hotels and restaurants, you will find very few men on the staffs. The preponderance of female personnel hits the outsider smack in the eye—particularly if he's male. When we pointed this out to a friendly Vaduzer, he admitted with surprise that it was true and that most natives were not aware of it. "Rather nice, though, isn't it?" he commented. As our Irish friends would say, "That it *is*, indeed."

Restaurants The **Hotel-Restaurant Real**, on the main square in **Vaduz**, is definitely first, foremost, and finest in the land—in fact, one of the most consistently sound kitchens in Europe. You'll almost always find the Reigning Family dining here on the cook's night off at the castle. (The Real brothers were decorated for their fantastic catering of the Royal Wedding not long ago.) Small, sweet, not fancy; one of its working family will greet you with a smile and *"Grüss Gott!"* While we could suggest dishes to try, we would urge you to leave it to the Reals to suggest their prides of the season. Here is a genuine master, one of the great traditional-style chefs of our century. Patron Felix Real (brother of the famous hotelier, Emil, of the above mentioned Sonnenhof) brings the best of his Maxim's of Paris experience to the skillets. Our recent feast was a triumph of culinary artistry and joy. Highest recommendation.

Torkel, site of a 3-century-old winepress, is pleasant enough for the rustic-toned flavor of Old Liechtenstein. It belongs to the Prince but is designed for Everyman. Winepress dominating the interior; a few alfresco tables on the edge of a vine-covered slope; moderate prices.

The viewful **Hotel-Restaurant Engel** features a cellar with local musicians; the "Liechtenstein Polka," of which the residents are so proud, is rendered about every 6½ minutes. Here is the trysting place where lonely male may find lonely female when the moon comes over them thar mountains.

The **Löwen**, at **Schellenberg**—only a grapeseed's toss from the Austrian border—is about as old as the historic Liechtenstein Charter. The outside suffers from a severe case of shingles (they are new); the inside is cozy; the menu features such local syllables as KäsKnöpfle, Schwartenmagen, and Sauerkäse. Its quiet, viewful and oh-so-easy on the budget.

The **Waldhof** is no Astoria when it comes to innkeeping, but as a restaurant, it rates commendably with some of Europe's best—the man woman owners having learned their trade at the above Real. The building, located at Schaanwald on the main drag between the frontier and Nendeln, is no great shakes —but you can't tell a book etc. Go inside and dine with the gods.

If you have a car, take the 20-minute ride to wonderful **Schloss Brandis** in **Maienfeld**, a Swiss fortress. The restaurant is in an ancient tower with chevroned shutters; rugged all-wood ceiling; iron chandeliers; stone walls and terracotta floors; leaded windows with etched glass. Delicious Bauernwurst (red sausage); highly ambitious menu that's rich in its selection of international treats; mellow local Maienfeld red wine, our happy choice; friendly, smart service. A very rewarding excursion through beautiful forested terrain.

Chez Fritz, less than 15 minutes by car from Vaduz, is in the Hotel Bahnhof at **Buchs** (Switzerland). This one used to be superb, but our latest dinner was a sad disappointment. It's a 3-minute walk from the main station in case you're planning a rail stopover at this junction. Local friends tell us it has become like the little girl who had a little curl right in the middle of her forehead: very, very good or horrid. Another "foreign" alternate might be **Drei Könige** at **Sevelen**, on the Swiss side, too. Nothing fancy, but substantial.

The **Hotel Lattmann** or the rejuvenated **Grand Hotel Quellenhoff** in **Bad Ragaz**, 30 minutes by car across the Swiss border, are happy targets for a dinner excursion; take your pick. There is a beautiful golf course here, too. Both hostelries offer good cuisine and attention; both are expensive; the latter is closed in winter.

★ **TIP** Just after sunset, cast your eyes up to watch Franz Joseph's mountaintop castle. The kitchen of the fabulous Restaurant Real is 2000 feet directly down the cliff from this Alpine aerie. When the light is right, you can see the Prince reeling down a fishing line with a silver tray balanced at its end, for his evening meal. (We *told* you it's a fairy-tale land!)

Shopping For attractive gifts and artistic handicrafts, visit the ultra-kind Helene DeMarchi at the midvillage **l'Atelier** (Städtle 36). It's a tiny boutique, but the level of taste is tops in town for our value-seeking Swiss Francs. Go to one of the 2 outlets of the wonderful little **Tourist Office Quick** before spending one nickel or investigating one *Schloss* on a lone-wolf basis—because you're almost sure to find what you want at this fountainhead for foreign visitors. The shops are in Vaduz (between the Vaduzer Hof and the Hotel Engel), and on the Liechtenstein-Austrian border opposite Feldkirch. Both are handy for changing currency, and are open routine hours, lunch hours, weekends, *and* holidays. The proprietor, Baron Edward von Falz-Fein, is supercharged with enthusiasm for his work and hospitality for his guests. You'll find postage stamps, cuckoo clocks, silver, all sorts of attractive and cornball local memorabilia, Swiss watches, and cameras and photo accessories at German prices. Or if sightseeing is your interest, the Baron will organize a visit to the Stamp or Art Museums (be sure to view the Rubens paintings at the **Engländerbau**) and other high points, a drive up to Masescha, and later a mountain excursion to the lofty winter-sports resort of Malbun (5000 feet), with 9 hotels, 4 ski tows, and 2 chair lifts which zip up to 7500 feet for a fascinating survey of Austrian real estate to pop your eyes. As a warm-day alternative, he'll recommend a plunge in the ultramodern swimming pool between Vaduz and Schaan or tennis in the brand-new 4-court hall of which the citizens are so proud. Whatever you need during your stay, he either has it, will find it, or will fix it; Americans on tour often suggest that he change his name to "Baron Liechtenstein."

Measure-for-measure, the country may be small, but its pepper-hot **National Tourist Office** director, Berthold Konrad, is a purebred Texan in his vision and wide-angled approach to hospitality. A team of 20 smiling hostesses is

available to arrange museum tours, special interest visits, or guided romps all over the country. If you yearn for anything at all, write to him at Städtle 37, FL-9490, Vaduz. What the principality lacks in girth, it more than makes up for in zeal.

Luxembourg

Luxembourg is a Grand Duchy, a never-never land of castles, turrets, swords, gold braid—a twentieth-century Camelot with toy trimmings. Anno Domini 1963 marked its 1000th anniversary. There's a romantic sort of aimlessness about it, a feeling that nobody works (far from the truth!), that a glittering duke will dash around the next corner on a white charger, velvet cloak flying behind. If a citizen gets mad at his vested officials, he has only to dial 478-1 to hear a voice reply, "Good morning! The Government!" It's a happy, serene, fat little community of 355-thousand people, a quarter of whom are foreign-born; Chicago is said to boast more Luxembourgers than the homeland. It's a prosperous tyke, too—so fond of finance that there is one bank for every 1100 citizens in the Duchy. In the Middle Ages knights and barons controlled the destiny of the nation. Their homes were tremendous strongholds—fortresses the ruins of which dot the countryside at Vianden, Beaufort, Bourscheid, and other locales. They were responsible for dubbing the domain "The Land of Haunted Castles." The country takes its name from the tiny palace of Sigefroi, Count of Ardennes, who 10 centuries ago erected his "Lucilinburhuc" ("Little Castle") where the capital stands today. The mantle of State is worn today by Grand Duc Jean, eldest son of the now retired Grand Duchess Charlotte. After settling the Kammerwald border dispute with Germany, and giving back 1200 acres, Luxembourg again boasts the easily remembered total of 999 square miles. One-third of its inhabitants raise crops or cattle; everybody seems to get rich on the steel mills (7th largest in the world). The army (reduced in size from 2000 conscripts to 600 professionals) is receiving higher pay than ever before. Illiteracy is unknown. The country is 99% Roman Catholic, but there is such freedom of worship that all faiths joined with the Government to help a new rabbi set up his synagogue. There are 130 castles but no full-time university exists. Radio Luxembourg, which broadcasts in 5 languages to 10 countries, claims more than 50-million daily listeners, including 78% of the teen-agers in Great Britain. A national showpiece is the Luxembourg Theater at Limpertsberg, where opera, drama, and ballet reach their peaks; this season may see the completion of a $16-million European Parliament edifice. (This is a scaled-down rush-up of a futuristic plan which was aborted; it featured an

avain form with an angled 35-story rooster tail containing offices and a restaurant perched on top—all for a mere $135 million.) Although the official language is French (parliamentary directives, Government publications, etc.), the *operative* tongue is a jawbreaking dialect called Letzeburgesch. German is also common, but English, despite its recent acceleration, still lags far behind. Womens' Liberationists will be gratified to know that the Burgomaster of its key city is Colette Flesch, a clever gal who received her master's degree at Wellesley. Spend a few days in the capital, untouched by 12 wars, and you'll find yourself living the pages of an Anthony Hope novel.

One of the most striking vistas in the country is the after-dark illumination of the Petrusse Valley bed, which winds its way crookedly through the heart of the once-impregnable, 1000-year-old Luxembourg City, a bastion which covetous generals of yore labeled the "Gibraltar of the North." Clervaux, previously mentioned Vianden with its enormous Hall of the Knights, and several other historic castles in the hinterland are now beautified by the same technique. On many evenings until 11 P.M. in summer (the schedule varies) cleverly placed spotlights and floodlights give the medieval bridges, massive ramparts, towering spires, and greenery the ethereal glow of a Victorian fairytale illustration. Here, in this capsule, is one of the loveliest creations of nature and man.

☑ **TRAVEL INFORMATION**   The U.S. wayfarer in search of further information will be welcomed by the friendly and helpful Anne Bastian of the **Luxembourg Tourist Information Office** at 1 Dag Hammarskjold Plaza, N.Y.C. 10017. The Embassy in Washington now routes all travel inquiries to her. In Luxembourg City there are 2 information offices; your hotel will direct you to either.

☑ **CUSTOMS AND IMMIGRATION**   A glance at your passport, and you're smilingly waved through. If you want it stamped, as a souvenir, you'll have to ask for it!

☑ **HOTELS**   If you wing in by Icelandic Airlines and are booked on to another destination, the "Stopover Program" is a giant-size aspirin for flight-weary travelers who watch their pennies. This package includes pickup service at the airport, delivery to the hotel, all meals, a room with private bath, a citywide sightseeing tour, and transportation back to the airport. Should you nod "yes" to this bonus plan, you may tuck in a good chunk of Luxembourg as a low-cost extra during High Season.

In *Luxembourg City*, the **Cravat** has an overall view of the valley and all-over amenities. The Pétrusse corner boasts 20 spacious, carpeted, twin-bed nests plus 2 suites perched high over the river gorge. Cozy ground-floor café, still the social umbilicus of the city; rôtisserie in the restaurant; lunch and dinner menu includes delicious smörgåsbord-type buffet at bargain tabs; popu-

lar bar at which the good Eddie reigns with his warming smile. This family house is managed by the 3rd-generation Fernand Cravat. Obviously not a Palace or a Ritz, but very pleasant indeed.

The **Kons** (place de la Gare) is an attractive alternative. Many fine oils, prints, tableaux, and friezes in corridors and bedrooms; excellent appointments in French periods; gay, fresh, and uplifting. Inside accommodations surrounding a quiet patio courtyard with murmuring fountain; well-groomed and uniformed staff. The restaurant recently ceased operations and no one seemed certain whether it would reopen. This station hotel has successfully taken advantage of every legitimate engineering and design trick in the book to create an island of calm and midtown tranquillity.

The **Aerogolf Sheraton** is located 4 miles from midtown, flanked by a splendid 18-hole golfcourse and the airport which is 300 yards away. Total of 150 air conditioned rooms all with wall-to-wall carpeting and private bath; grill plus lunch restaurant facing the gardens; 4th-floor cocktail lounge nodding at the treetops. Manager Keller oversees a pleasant rural address.

Holiday Inns has entered its bid opposite the Common Market Center in outlying *Kirchberg*, perhaps 15 minutes from the train station. There's a restaurant, a swimming pool, 250 bedchambers, and ample parking for motorists. Pipes and phones in all single, double, and triple nests; tot-cots provided for a small extra charge; lofty tabs.

The 42-unit **El Dorado** is modern, neat, sparkly-clean, color-toned, spacious, and livable. A fresh restaurant recently was unwrapped. Refrigerators in every room vie with scales in every bathroom. (Management's dark sense of humor?) Highly recommended.

The **Central-Molitor** provides 35 centrally sited kips with bath and shower, plus fresh furnishings, carpets, private safes (we won't say where), double windows and soundproofed walls, bidets ("with hot and cold running water," reminds the administration proudly), automatic door openers, electronically controlled red warning lights that glow "Do Not Disturb" in the corridor, and many other button-poppers. Host Ernest Thill speaks perfect English and couldn't be kinder.

The 4-story **Rix**, with bed and breakfast only, offers 20 bright accommodations which Proprietor Fernand Rix keeps rubbed to a state of immaculate polish. Crusty shell; simple lobby; friendly main-floor bar; well-outfitted rooms with full carpeting; front units with balconies; rear accommodations supersilent for serious snoozers; small baths with excellent ventilation. Clients frequently dine at the Cravat.

The **Alfa** (place de la Gare) has been refashioned; it's 100 units are comfortable and the prices are moderate. The 60-room **International** has perked up somewhat, but we'd prefer to spend $1 or $2 more for one of the previously described hostelries. On the outskirts, the **Euro-Parc**, about 5 minutes along the Route d'Echternach, is a low-octane pit stop for motorists. Chalet-style building; pool, play area, and private lake; camping ground with A-frame

shelters; thatched-roof café-restaurant and dancing on occasion; simple accommodations with curtained-off baths. Not much when compared to the city slickers. The expanding **Novotel** group unveiled 120 units near here (at *Dommeldange*). It is more of a motel than a hotel, but satisfactory as simple shelter.

If it's country life you're after, the **Hôtel du Grand Chef** in *Mondorf-les-Bains* is an Arcadian dream. Situated beside the huge rose-filled Kurpark (state operated, with 40 types of water treatment); back garden along a 3-foot stream, called the Gander River, separating Luxembourg from France. Handsome, imposing structure with modern comforts; 35 units in the old wing and 15 newer ones with private balcony, reputed to serve some of the most satisfactory vittles in the land. A charmer in every respect. Closed in midwinter. The **Heintz Hôtel** in the lovely little town of *Vianden* personifies the gentle charm of Mme. Hansen, its owner. Thirty bedrooms, all with bath and private balcony (you may pay extra for the latter); decorative highlights include vaulted ceilings, timbers, and oodles of antiques. It's about 45 minutes from the capital, and it's the proud possessor of the only chair lift in the Grand Duchy—a low-cost ride to a forest-type chalet where you can have a drink on open-air terraces to spike the already intoxicating view. A former convent, here's one of the nation's oldest and most interesting buildings. Renewed salutes! The **Bel-Air** in *Echternach*, smartly remodeled and expanded, is a garden retreat for weekending. Locals praise the kitchen here. The **Airfield Hotel**, about a 3-minute walk from the terminus, has a country setting, simple amenities, a wide variety of dishes on its menu, a small bar, and a good location for a quick getaway.

Other havens? The **Euro** (not to be confused with the Euro-Parc above) is along the busy Route d'Arlon to Brussels. This one has décor to please any 40-year-old tot: drum stripes, checks, sworls, and animal wallpaper. The **Dany**, on this same road and with an antique carriage out front, is also good basic shelter. Its prize, however, is its charming little restaurant boasting charbroiled steaks, lamb on the spit, and other grills which pop right in front of your popping eyes. Expensive tabs here, but pizza and snacks are available in the Crazy Horse Bar, which adjoins the stables and is ricks of fun. For other rural hostelries, check with the Tourist Bureau or our Embassy.

☑ **FOOD AND RESTAURANTS**   Four of Luxembourg's restaurants are outstanding. The Cravat and Au Gourmet are tops for city dining, and the Hôtel Hiertz's nookery in *Diekirch* plus Bonne Auberge at *Gaichel* (about 25 minutes from the center by car) get our top vote for rural excellence. The neighboring **Reisdorfer** is said to be in the same league.

Full meals in the top establishments should settle at $16 to $23, while the majority of feederies are perhaps $4 less.

We've already mentioned the **Cravat** in our hotel section. It is continental in tone. **Au Gourmet**, a 60-second walk from the Cravat, seems to offer just

a little more color. Two main rooms plus a small nook to the rear, each decorated with wood panels, silk brocade, and pewter highlights; attractive chandelier; comfortable chairs. Versatile menu of game, specialties, and stock dishes comprising perhaps 75 choices; full wine card; somewhat understaffed, but when service finally comes, attentive, friendly, and professional. If the Ostend oysters are in season, please try them for the memory of this happily shellshocked traveler. Excellent. The **Cordial** is still on the comeback trail. Window-wrapped mezzanine in a commercial building, overlooking a routine square; packed at noon with somber businessmen; tops in food but bottoms in service. **Rôtisserie Ardennaise**, not related to the famed Brussels establishment of the same name, has a rustic ambiance. Bar semidivided by greenery; walls partially paneled; cartwheel light fixtures, provincial gimmicks. Despite the obviously touristic outlook, it is chiefly favored by locals who think franc-ly about their vittles. Certainly this is one of the best dining bargain spots in the nation. On one recent swing, when we ordered a simple Châteaubriand for 2, out came a post-office-size chunk of tender-sweet beef AND a colossal platter with side dishes containing French fries, braised endive, asparagus, carrots, peas, sautéed mushrooms, baked tomato au gratin, salad, bread, and a full boat of Béarnaise sauce. All of the extras came at no extra charge! For wholesale calorie shoppers, here's that Big Discount House in the Sky. Unusually rewarding for its type. We've had encouraging reports from local friends on the **Greiveldinger**, but because the believing is in the tasting, we'll soon spoon in.

The **Roma**, featuring an Italian menu, is adequate. Our latest pasta-packing repast here wasn't at all bad for a modest kitchen. The glacially cool restaurant at the **Café du Commerce** is renowned for its *moules;* here's the only place in town that will mollify your appetite after midnight, an innovation which has been well received. Last, and in our opinion least, 2 centrally located **Wimpy** beaneries offer inexpensive, 98-item menus featuring such specialties as eggburgers, fishburgers, and pineappleburgers. Urp.

If you're the type who likes exploring, drive out to the **Hôtel Hiertz** in the sleepy town of *Diekirch* (half-an-hour north on Route 7). The small restaurant in this ultramodest hostelry was awarded a coveted 2-star rating in 1971 by the *Guide Michelin*—an honor almost unknown outside France. Emerald watersilk and wood-paneled walls; flowers and candles on tables; Limoges porcelain supplemented by tiny cloverleaf patterns on salmon-colored napery; smooth, friendly service. Always reserve your table; we saw cars outside from Belgium, Germany, France, and even Japan. Verdict? Five tuneful forks vibrating with happiness for an outstanding dining experience.

Suburban or rural expeditions? The leader is the previously mentioned **Bonne Auberge**, located so close to the border it's almost an immigrant. Rural sophistication; cozy bar; split-level dining room in quarter-circle design with big windows; happy use of colors; Danish-style lamps. Definitely worth the 25-minute excursion, especially when the weather is benign. Now a few bedrooms have been added, if you *really* want to make a night of it. The **Hôtel**

du Grand Chef in *Mondorf-les-Bains*, in the heart of the vineyard country, is convenient and pleasant for a short summertime safari. **Helene Klein's Restaurant** in *Hespérange*, about 15 minutes from the center is reported to offer sound cookery; she's the owner and chef; simple atmosphere; we've never tried it.

Three additional possibilities: Many dining places on the Moselle River are delightful, and king of them all is the **Hotel Simmer** in *Ehnen*. The simple, family-run **Hôtel Hallerbach** in *Haller* (northwest of Echternach) is also special; the *patron* rattles the skillets, and live trout are stored in his little aquarium.

Check these and all other country places before leaving the capital, because most of them close down when business is slow.

Be sure to treat yourself to some wild game in fall and winter. The supply of partridge, pheasant, venison, and wild hare is usually ample. The hare is smaller and sweeter than the Belgian variety. Our favorite is roast saddle of hare; the Luxembourgers seem to like theirs cooked, ears and all, in red wine. But the delight of delights—a dish fit for a palace—is Partridge Canapé—a fat little bird served whole on toast, with baby mushrooms and a sauce of pan juices to crown it. Just flip us that bunch of grapes, Juno, and move over!

If you want a weekend of forests, brooks, trails, peace, and quiet, you might like the aforementioned **Hotel Bel-Air** in *Echternach*. There's stream fishing and hiking for active souls, loafing for others. The building has been extensively renovated in a charming way; the locale is gorgeous and the reception is warmly hospitable. As an overnight stop, it is also highly recommendable.

★ **TIPS** Coffee is inordinately expensive in Luxembourg—often twice the price of a piece of pie.

If you enjoy the tactile sensation of green persimmons, then try Letzburger Kachke'ss (cooked and aged cottage cheese) for breakfast or with cocktails. It's a proud specialty of this ancient land. You may detest it (as we do), or you may love it—but one thing is certain: your breath will never allow you to forget your holiday in Luxembourg, forever and evermore.

☑ **NIGHTCLUBS** Amateur Night at your local Benevolent Order of Snoozing Octogenarians just might be more exhilarating. **Splendid** is doubtless the most sophisticated nightery in the entire Grand Duchy. You've seen its type of acts on any variety show: tricycle-riding chimps, ventriloquists, acrobats, "exotic" dancers (local schoolteachers?), a singing duo, and a quartet. Rouge walls supporting waffled ceiling; mosaic bar with stools so high you'll think you're in the crow's nest of the *USS Enterprise.* It serves honest libations with tariffs nearly as lofty. The **Plaza** is second on this 5-step ladder. Quiet ambiance; attractive décor with awnings and lanterns; 2nd-string show of 3rd-rate strippers and "singles"; similarly bashful barmaids who don't twist your drinking arm. We thought, but were not sure, that we caught the flash of a speck of bathtub enamel once when we tilted our glass. True? **Scorpion** is a disco-

· thèque. As for a gin mill called **Chez Nous**, we dislike this one with a passion. For sipping, snacking, and nuzzling, we much prefer to kick up our hoofs at the **Crazy Horse Bar** at the aforementioned Dany Hotel. Here's *the* spot for stalling around on a loose rein.

Cover these slowly and carefully, savoring each minute—because when you've finished, you've had your whirl. Even though most residents of this little Duchy go to bed with the chickens, so many outlanders from nearby industrial, military, and administrative complexes crawl this circuit that these jernts are sometimes quite lively—particularly on weekends.

☑ **TAXIS** Get them at the station. Standard rate for short hauls is about $4 per mile, but if your journey is a long one, it decreases considerably. Although the jockeys wheel and deal for huge tips at the end of the ride, 15% is ample. Drivers are generally more courteous than they used to be.

☑ **DRINKS** Luxembourg has now thrown the gauntlet at Milwaukee, Munich, and Copenhagen. To keep pace with the output of its 7 local breweries, each Luxembourger—man, woman, and child—downs an average of 33 gallons a year. Brother, *that's* living (with a head on it!). Possibly this deluge of suds has helped to float away memories of the genuine absinthe which used to be available in every bar. The present-day substitute uses anise instead of the banned wormwood elixir as a base. Tops in white wines (reds or rosés are not pressed in this land) for most American tastes is Gewürztraminer. Always ask for the '76 vintage, which is now the choicest year generally available. You might find extra pleasure in a Riesling called Wormeldange Nussbaum. Next comes Riesling Sylvaner (pale, light, and quite dry). The Muscat Othonel is too fruity and too sweet for most U.S. palates. Local gentry seem to prefer the fairly dry Riesling Wormeldange Koeppchen; ask for this one by the grower's name, the best of which bears the Madame Hartmann cachet. For a sparkling wine, either the St. Martin or the Bernard Massard brand is quite drinkable. Additional local production—and it sounds like a tidal wave for such a little land—includes the 100-proof plum brandy (slivovitz-type) known as Quetsch, 2 others made from yellow plums called Prunelle and Mirabelle, and the Swiss-beloved, cherry-pit spirit: Kirsch. The numerous local imitations of French liqueurs are such distant relatives that they'd qualify as 14th stepcousins twice-removed.

★ **TIP** As a guarantee of quality and authenticity in selecting your wines, be sure to ask for those bottles with the "Marque Nationale" sticker. This control device assures you that what you order, you get.

☑ **CAPSULE JUNKETS** Here are suggestions for covering some of the less-known treasures of this little Duchy. You can pick up a map when you get there, and the strange names of these off-trail places will make sense. All of these are one-day junkets, based on residence in Luxembourg City:

Drive to *Clervaux*, take lunch at the Hôtel Koener, continue to *Wiltz*, and backtrack to *Vianden*. From teatime at the Heintz Hôtel you're only 45 minutes from the bright lights.

Or visit the **Hamm Cemetery**, where so many of our soldiers, including General George S. Patton, are at peace—continue to the Moselle River, have lunch at Simmer's in *Ehnen*—and get back to the capital in time for coffee and cakes at Namur's, a ceremony you shouldn't miss.

Or amble out to *Echternach*, where on Whitsun Tuesday there's a renowned **Dancing Procession** which might be called the New York Garment District rumba (3 steps forward and 2 steps back). Splendid basilica, eighth-century tomb of St. Willibrord, and handsome forested surroundings. Then proceed to *Esch-sur-Sûre* (from its amusing pronunciation, known to local wits as "The Seventh Martini Village"), swim, motorboat, or laze above its hydroelectric dam, and return.

For a longer outing, run up to the **Hamm Cemetery** via the road to Saarbrücken. After this stop, continue for 3 miles, turn left at *Sandweiler,* and skip on to *Ehnen* for coffee at the Simmer. As you leave the hotel, turn right along the Moselle and motor on until you reach a stone gate with a huge champagne bottle at the entrance. This is the **St. Martin Cave**, where some of the nation's finest sparkling wine is sleeping—and where, for a trifling sum including a glass of bubbly, you may watch it snooze. It's a fascinating tour into the cliffside cellars; afterward, you can sit on the river terrace (with Germany only 50 yards away) and sip the house product at factory tariffs. Now push on to *Remich* and cut in to *Mondorf-les-Bains*, where you can stroll in the lovely rose gardens of the **Kurpark** or take a hydrotherapy treatment in the modern bathhouse. Have lunch at the Hôtel du Grand Chef (the backyard has a tiny footbridge to the other side of the fairyland stream, which is French soil). Then zip back to the capital by the main pike that passes through *Frisange* and *Hespérange.* It's a full circuit, but not tiring—and most rewarding for all it embraces.

For single-track gustatory excursions: Try for lunch or dinner (1) the **Hôtel Hiertz** at *Diekirch*, (2) the Hôtel du Grand Chef at *Mondorf-les-Bains*, (3) the Hôtellerie de Vieux Moulin near *Septfontaines*, on the Valley of the Seven Castles route, (4) the stops listed above.

At least take a look at *Larochette*, if you can. This lovely village is in the approaches of what is called the "Little Switzerland of Luxembourg," a beautifully wooded and hilly region with striking rock formations, between Consdorf, Echternach, and Beaufort. Here's a perfect example of the toy charm of the Grand Duchy.

Mallorca

If we were asked to select the 2 most stimulating and rewarding targets in Spain for the average U.S. visitor, we'd pick Mallorca (Majorca) and Madrid in one second.

Mallorca, roughly 60 miles by 50 miles at its widest points, is the capital of the Balearic Islands (Menorca, Ibiza, Formentera, and scores of rock-dots; persnickety islanders claim that only the 2 largest bodies form the Balearics, while Ibiza and Formentera should be known as *The Pitiusas*). Lying almost exactly 100 miles southeast of Barcelona, it is accessible from there in 25 minutes by air and from 8 to 9 hours by modern car ferry. The connections to and from every Western European capital and a number of other major cities are fast and frequent. With its 5000-foot mountains, lush plains, magnificent beaches, horses, tennis courts, 4 golf courses, benevolent climate, warmhearted people, colorful background, and moderate (but fast-rising!) prices, it has become one of the most popular resorts on the Mediterranean.

July-August is High Season, with practically flawless weather. Spring and fall are normally lovely in the main; May, June, September, and October have more than enough balmy days to offset gray ones. November-December and March-April are chancy—sometimes glorious, sometimes awful; parts, but only parts, of January and February are very raw, chilly, and unpleasant. The legendary false spring called *Las Calmas de Enero* ("The Calms of January" which sometimes occur in February), like our Indian summer, bring for 2-or-3 weeks heavenly weather and the blossoming of nearly 10-million almond trees attired in petals of pink or white. There's good swimming from late spring to middle fall.

CITIES

Mallorca has the profile of a goat's head: *Palma*, the capital, is at the throat, *Sóller* is near the eye, and *Formentor* is on one of the horns. The heartbeat of the island lies in Palma, its only large center, the population of which has now dizzyingly rocketed up to equal Geneva's. Here is *the* center of the action where you will find most of the good restaurants, hotels, nightclubs, shops, the

nearby new Casino and most of the frenzy. At the peak of the season (not so
noticeably in the spring or fall), the capital is packed so tightly with French,
English, German, and other nationals who are flown or ferried in on bargain
tours like so many cattle that it's grossly tinny and crass; strike out during July
and August for the tiny villages to find the real charm of the Balearics.

☑ **HOTELS**   Mallorca has the highest concentration of hotels and pensions per
capita *of any major resort area in the world*—Florida, Las Vegas, Capri, and
the French Riviera included. Every shoe manufacturer, raffia potentate, and
artichoke entrepreneur seems to have climbed aboard the construction bandwagon with visions of a quick peseta. The isle now has a grand total of
approximately 1700 hostelries. Naturally, the facilities and service in most of
this crop are amateurish in the extreme.

Because our rankings are totally reportorial, we feel no compunction about
downgrading or eliminating numerous "officially rated" top-grade houses
which don't meet our own criteria for inclusion.

In this regard, independent travelers to Mallorca face an extraordinary
situation. Tour-group operators have so engorged various districts by advance
block booking of the vast majority of their hostelries for the entire season that
we are compelled to slice away giant chunks of the island which we think
would disappoint or disillusion North American fun-seekers. As typical examples, *Páguera* is now jammed almost exclusively with German and English
trippers; *Arenal*, *Ca'n Pastilla*, *Ca'n Picafort*, *Cala Ratjada*, *Cala Millor*, and *Porto Cristo* host invasions of Teutonic armies; *Palma Nova* and
Santa Ponsa tan the bleached hides of Scandinavian, Dutch, Belgian, and
other northlandic sun worshipers.

So—with a lynching party on our doorstep bruiting its vociferous objections
—we'll dive into an island summary that will highlight only what we believe,
as professionals and residents, are the most rewarding treasure troves for your
Mallorquin Odyssey.

The **Formentor**, which lit its Golden Anniversary candles in '79, is practically a generic name for holiday relaxation. It is maintained in traditional good
form by don Miguel Buadas, its proprietor. In addition to a lovely nearby
ribbon of golden beach, you'll find 2 exquisite swimming pools (one heated)
tiled in Valencia-style patterns and sited in a palm grove almost at your
doorstep. Fully air-conditioned; wide-angle panoramic lobby; 3 dining rooms;
overexpensive new grill in sterile Art Rétro; strikingly attractive disco; Beach
Bar with buffet lunches; tasteful bedchambers; tennis courts; other alluring
amenities. The setting is a pine mantle along a cliff-lined coast which is 10 times
more beautiful than Capri. London-Savoy-trained Concierge don Francisco
Borrás is a gem; so are Tony and Gabriel, his ever-smiling assistants; so is Chief
Barman Jaime. The taxi ride to or from the capital or the airport takes about
90 minutes and costs around $30. Warmly recommended except for its sub-
standard cuisine.

Son Vida, another threat to dominance in country living, nestles less than 15 minutes from Palma in a breathtaking mountaintop showcase. This totally converted castle had been renowned for centuries for its priceless collection of medieval arms. It is surrounded by an 18-hole golf course which has been carved from this 1400-acre estate. Completely air conditioned; super-lush public rooms; fantastic 250-foot poolside terrace partially awninged for outdoor lunching and supping; spacious main dining salon; 3 bars; muted disco largely patronized by adults; 175 excellent accommodations including its Must-See-To-Be-Believed Presidential Suite; tennis and golf clubs; more. Here will be a serene haven for the wealthy traveler who seeks beauty, peace, and tranquillity IF the administration doesn't cut corners during this slower-than-average year to spoil it.

At the resort harbor which lends its name to the hotel-golfing complex, the **Santa Ponsa** is top tee. Modernistic 18-bedroom clubhouse-hostelry amid the fairways; about a quarter of its space devoted to suites (#s 15 and 16 lead the tourney); 18-hole course; illuminated driving range; pool; neighboring 460-boat yacht basin with additional recreational facilities including tennis. Pro-style administration by José Luis Gaspart, who carries on the family tradition of being a superior host. A long-ball winner, but chiefly for sporting types with youthful tastes.

In *Palma* proper, we continue with enthusiasm to tip our sombrero to the Victoria-Fénix sisterhood. This side-by-side winsome twinsome forms a delightful resort complex within itself. Embraced between the arms of these 2 elegant houses is an aquatic tropical paradise: 2 magnificent sky-blue swimming pools, a spectacular grand patio, plants, flowers, colorful awnings, Palm Springs type bar, snack service for bathers, and nightly cocktail dancing until 1 A.M. The **Victoria Sol** (everything is open to guests of both hotels), parades a pleasantly inviting lobby with glass-enclosed wild-duck pond and fountain; 100% glass-walled stretch commanding the seaside fronts of the wide-girthed lounge, dining room, and leather-and-paneled bar; mammoth open terrace dotted with pine trees and flora, providing warm-weather breakfasters and diners with seagull's-eye view of the swimmers below. All of the 150 smartly outfitted bedchambers with bath, air conditioning, and individual balcony; 115 bayside units and 35 facing the garden; suites that are strictly *ne plus ultra*. Crack Chief Concierge don Miguel and his splendid colleagues Gabriel and Pedro, radiate bottomless warmth, kindness, patience, and savvy; personally, we don't know how we could get along in Palma without their constant succour. This siren stands imposingly over the Mediterranean as one of the more comfortable houses in Europe.

The **Fénix Sol** is excellent, too. Equally well administered by the veteran hotelier, amiable Antonio Pujol, who keeps both of these properties in A–1 order; 100 rooms, all with bath, all air-conditioned, all soundproofed, and all with private balconies which face the bay a hop-and-a-flip below; 6 suites with fireplaces and double balconies also available. The décor is regional modern

in flavor. Light bites in enlarged bar and on tables of beautiful terrace wrapped with greenery; full lunches and dinners served at next-door Victoria Sol. This house may close again in midwinter, so check first if you're traveling then.

For sheer richness or overrichness, nothing here touches the $8,000,000, 150-room **Valparaiso**. Breathtaking view; acres of polished marble floors; extravaganza of costly and showy appurtenances in public precincts; formal dining room plus window-lined grill (where our meals have been costly culinary atrocities); patio for outdoor snacking; 24-hour bar; vast ternate pool area; second pool inside with saunas; handsome discothéque; 3 styles of bedchambers, all with balcony, air conditioning, compartmented baths, TV, and high quality furnishings; stunningly expensive by Spanish standards. Impressive it is; cozy it isn't.

The deluxe, air conditioned **Nixe Palace** is uniformly carpeted and furnished in a contemporary motif. From the peak of a terraced cliff about 10 minutes from the hub of the city, it towers over Cala Mayor beach. Attractive heated pool several levels down the flowered slope with daily buffet for swimmers; handsome main floor, including the English-style dining room with kosher cuisine, the adjoining treetops breakfast patio, the pine-paneled bar, the awning-shaded porch for alfresco sipping, and the richly outfitted nautical lounge. The 35 spacious split-level units are by far the best accommodations in this house. Gracious, hard-trying personnel keynoted by keen-eyed Director Juan Tortella. Now a solid contender.

The **Meliá Mallorca** is a place about which few wayfarers remain neutral; in general, either they love it or they loathe it. Two pleasant pools (one heated); refreshment patio and terraces; vintage hyper-Meliá ambiance and décor; standard rooms either in terra cotta or green motifs, all with bath, balcony, and 3-channel Muzak system and all comparatively cramped. Substandard _residencia_ annex directly across the street, which we'd advise you to avoid. Manager Don Angel A. Palomino de Moral directs most of his efforts toward block bookings made through this chain operation. Verdict? We think it's crassly and brashly institutional, but some travelers don't.

The **De Mar**, about 10 minutes from the center in _Las Illetas_, occupies a lovely suburban hillside which cascades in terraced gardens down to a rocky shore. The pool and palm fringed patios are a design for sunlit days and romantic evenings. This electrifyingly modern contestant—its daring brown ceramic exterior has given it the nickname "Villa Chocolate"—sails extensively in the lanes of bulk commercialism, especially catering to pleasant young British clientele. Active (almost publike) atmosphere in the bar after sunset; excellent presentation of shellfish and other marine fare in its refashioned waterfront restaurant (à la carte is by far the better bet here); peculiar but satisfactory bedroom architecture; nice staff but not enough of 'em when you want 'em. Sleek, viewful, adequate.

The **Maricel**, 15 minutes from the center, has an official 4-star rating (instead of 5), but we like it so much we are including it high in our listings. Extensive

modernizations were made in which its traditional Old Mallorquin flavor has been preserved; there's a stolidness here suggestive of a mansion that was built to stand through eternity. A milieu that might be termed clublike in its dining room and lobby; substantial cookery; tennis court; good swimming pool; 8 bungalows; all baths revamped. Hardworking Director Enrique Cabré radiates true dedication in his supervision of this tasteful little haven. Pert but not elegant. We love it.

The 800-pillow **Bellver Sol**, facing the bay from Palma's Paseo Maritimo, is a hard-bit victim of the touristic boom-bug. All 15 floors air-conditioned; swimming pool; cinema; nightclub; coffee shop; management by Marciano Paredes, a skilled professional. Conventions and mass bookings compose the majority of its roster of registrants, some of whom have complained of *very* impersonal service. Even more heartless, in our opinion, is the newer **Palas Atenea**, with a similar bayfront setting, the same pack-'em-in attitude, and the same administration. If you book one of its 400 look-alike cubicles you may experience how truly boring a hotel can be when—as we feel it is here—human caring is absent. The Hall Porter, however, seemed to be the lone contradiction to this on our incognito sleep-in.

For midtowners, the **Almudaina** is convenient for shophounds and city kittens who can take or leave the sea. Rear perches above the 5th floor offer choice views of the cathedral and harbor; all stalls on the main drag are perfect if you thrill to the sound of clanging gear changes and screeching disc brakes. Savvy and warmly personable Felipe Gaspart II, General Director for the Balearics of the giant HUSA chain, privately owns and operates this friendly and unimposing house.

Saratoga, also for city dwellers, is amiably executed and not expensive. Three lounges and dining room adjacent to heated pool and balconied bedchambers above; another pool and bar topside; colorful contemporary furnishings; doubles with baths and singles with showers; better-than-average cookery. The room card states, "The Management appeals to the guests to use a correct dressing when passing at the dining room"—a hint of their earnest efforts to keep up its tone. Quite goodly indeedly.

The **Jaime III** is sterile by comparison. Muted colors throughout with maroon and black predominating; public areas air-conditioned; 88 twins and only 2 singles; nice balconies overlooking a dry metropolitan gulch. Fair but far from exciting.

The **Capitol**, another candidate just off the main shopping street, is tucked away in a small plaza that echoes the traffic din all day but is reasonably tranquil when the sandman comes. Functional lobby, usually atitter and aclatter with achattering foreign tour groups; tasteless air-conditioned dining room in which the full-pension or half-pension gouge force-feeds every client; bedroom décor anything but capital. Clean, at least.

The **Constelación**, set on a hillside above the city, orbits within a galaxy of other 3-star and lesser planetoids. Extremely helpful and ever-smiling con-

cierge; small pool and bar across a busy byway; glassed-in restaurant opposite reception; 28 twins, 12 singles, and penthouse suite more than adequate but not luxurious. It is so popular among both individual wanderers and tour clusters that it is nearly always filled to capacity.

The **Pensión Armadams**, with 30 rooms and 20 baths, has been moving along admirably. For true peseta-thrifting, most of this next bundle offer simple shelter, cleanliness, reasonable comfort, and 3 meals a day for surprisingly low tariffs: **Infanta** (near the busy Plaza Gomila; nice garden with bar; for the more quiet types), **Yoga** (swimming pool, which can also be used for wise reflection; 40 cells for contemplation; 40 baths and showers for navel rinses; devoted staff of disciples), **Paraiso del Mar**, **Residencia Rosamar**, **La Portassa** (superb situation), and **Pensión Menorquína** (architecture reminiscent of Gaudí; 25 rooms, all with private balcony, but only 3 with bath; Manager Francisco Bonmatí very helpful).

Beach hotels in Palma proper? To reemphasize this important fact, only La Cala and Nixe Palace. For Mediterranean bathing otherwise the visitor must strike out for the boondocks. Here are our choices of the top resort centers and the most appealing hostelries on tap at each one:

Southwest of the metropolis along the rockbound coast, *Cala Mayor*'s runner-up to the just-mentioned Nixe Palace is the **Emperatriz**. Private house converted quite some time ago into a Second-class hostelry; plastics throughout; small chambers; better for its grounds than its interior. The **Bristol** has become a strong challenger. Public zones rezipped; dining salon in old *español* style; lounge with large hearth; restful patio *andaluz;* added furnishings. Coming on well. **Impala** is not recommended to anyone we know or love. Its publicity brochures puff it up as heaven's gift to innkeeping, but all of its many facilities impressed us as being substandard.

In the nearby busy-busy *Las Illetas* suburb, the **Bonanza,** with its neighboring (and cheaper) **Bonanza Playa**, is a sheltering corner. Two pools (one heated), minigolf links, and private beach; garden with ancient cloister décor; evening meals outdoors in summer; bar in bam-bamboo-boo tones; 10 Moorish-mooded "villas" on the grounds. This couplet is big stuff for economy tour packagers, but it's attractive and well maintained. **Gran Albatros**, in the same bracket, is a standout on this part of the coast. It has doubled its nests to 100 and otherwise regilded its cage. A private beach and heated swimmery add to its attractions. Since it is owned and operated by a lady, fetching feminine touches are evident throughout. Best in the area. The Second-class **Bon Sol** is still more suited to European than American tastes, despite improvements and modernizations. The **Illetas** is disrecommended; far, far too amateurish, we think.

The **Bendinat**, 6 miles from the center in the same direction, has deteriorated to such a degree that we can no longer advise this now-seedy old friend which for so many years was a joy. What a romantic setting—if only the proprietor would loosen up with a wheelbarrow full of pesetas for rejuvenation!

The **Son Caliu** takes its name from the cove where it is sited. Adequate beach plus pool; waterside snack bar; maintenance slipping perilously. In danger of overdeveloping, in our opinion.

Not far away, the **Punta Negra** distributes its dual personality of a 40-room hotel and 13 bungalows between the twin beaches at its doorsteps. Sea or pool swimming available; dining room with savory offerings; cozy in tone; a favorite among traveling Yanks and Rebs. Be sure to have confirmed reservations because it is deservedly popular and always jammed. Recommended.

Palma Nova, beyond the Bendinat turnoff on the Paguera highway, offers the **Comodoro** and the **Delfin Playa**, which are neck-and-neck for our number-one local slot. The former boasts a waterfront dining terrace, an indoor-outdoor poolside bar, and warm décor in a maritime theme. Here's a joyful haven in a seedy little baylet. The latter, in sawtooth architecture, displays an intriguing blend of man-made forms and nature. Broad stone staircase tiptoeing directly into the palm-lined swimming pool; greenery married to walls, pillars, and rock terracing; rich rustic Spanish decoration; fine-quality, comfort-conscious furnishings; public rooms air-conditioned; bedrooms that say "welcome," each with its own private balcony plus bath with seahorse towel rings. Thoughtfully masterminded as a good bet for any big fish who washes up on Palma Nova sands. Both First category; both youngsters; both open around the calendar; both recommended. The **Hawaii**, where your Martini may march up in a coconut shell, is passable at best. After our aloha in its depths, we'd prefer to pass it—but the travel agencies obviously don't. The 180-room **Cala Blanca** also woos migrations of package trippers from the graylands of Europe. Very nice physical plant, however, if you can boll-weevil your way in. The **Canaima** lacks aplomb. The basic facilities are here, but when viewed together, they fail to jell; the inclination to cut corners on the housekeeper's budget is noticeable. Some might like it; we're luke. The park-situated **Bermudas** seemed "shorts" on everything—particularly on its badly tailored maintenance; it needs to pull up those knee-length socks. The **Playa** scared us out of our wits. A consortium of blue-ribbon psychiatrists might paw the dust just to meet the chap who painted those corridors. WOW! Go anytime between November 1 and February 28 (or 29th on leap years), because it is operative only from March 1 to October 31. All these hostelries have latched onto the best brochure artist on the island, and his lovely layouts might fool you.

In *Magaluf*, the 15-story, cliff-sited **Coral Playa** is king of the mountain. All 200 sea-seeing bedchambers with terrace and private bath; cooled public rooms and heated swimming pool; dancing nightly in Season; good, sound direction by D. Francisco Capo. Very attractive. **Cala Viñas** usually is booked solid with clients obtained by Great Britain's Trust Houses Forte group which holds the administrative reins here. Not very exciting but passable. The mammoth **Magaluf Park** seems like a skyscraping monument for groupies. It has space for 900 sun-seeking souls, plus 3 bars, 3 pools, and 3 times too many bulk

reservations to suit us. The **Guadalupe** is a 500-room link in the ubiquitous Hoteles Sol chain, which runs the aforementioned **Victoria, Fenix, Bellver, Palas Atenea,** 20 other hostelries on the island, and a few on the mainland. This organization necessarily deals heavily with package tours. The **Flamboyan** caters 99% to pre-booked English clientele. Fully air-conditioned; renovated lobby, restaurant, and lounge; oodles of terraces; 2 bars; 78 units with bath; doubles with individual balcony. Better than average. The 161-room **Pax,** while Second class, offers much more heart and warmth. Not directly on the water but across the road from it; nice heated pool; bar, salon, and dining room; Iberian-tone bedrooms, each with terrace and private bath; plenty of color; quiet and economical for the right traveler. Open April to mid-October. **Atlantic** registers low tide on our chart. Coney Island atmosphere in the Mediterranean sun. **El Caribe,** in the same category as the Pax, comes up with a better seaside situation, but with far less élan than its spiffier competitor. It's okay—but if one doesn't insist on quartering at water's edge, we would choose the Pax. The Meliá-run, gradually expanding **Apartotel** is for long-pausing pilgrims, and its added wing can hold more of them than ever.

At *Camp de Mar*, the First-class **Gran Hotel Camp de Mar** is the juiciest kernel on a rough cob. No-groups policy, a rarity; improved décor throughout; all units with bath and private terrace; swimming pool abubbling. All in all, a corn borer. The **Playa,** one category lower, is more functional but far less appealing aesthetically—quite an achievement. **Villa Real** is even more uninteresting. And so is this entire beach, which is 2nd-rate compared to many other captivating coves, hillocks, and crannies of this romantic isle.

All of these are within about a ½-hour radius of Palma.

Country hotels or hostelries farther out? The ultramodern, medium-price **Molins** at *Cala San Vicente* (2 toy coves near Pollensa, 1-hour from Palma) is a fair bet—especially if you're on an extended diet. (The food totally lacks flair or imagination.) Perched on a hillside facing its little beach, its design is linear-boxlike. Total of 89 rooms, all with bath, radio, and independent terrace fronting the sea; beach bar and American bar; swimming pool and sun terrace with dancing to live music on summer evenings; tennis court; air-conditioned public rooms. Concierge Tony couldn't be more willing. About half the price of the Formentor, and warmly recommended within its comfortable but not luxurious range.

The **Simar** is outfitted with some tiny and some larger accommodations, all of them well maintained. Beautiful pool and recreational apron across the street; staircase to a beach in a charming cove; dining room stretched for sea view. Operative April to October only; coming up perkily. The 35-room **Cala San Vicente,** also seasonal, is routine, with many English tour groups. So-so. The **Niú** is simple, with a pretty fair dining room and low-low tariffs. Accept only the most modern bedchambers in this pension. As a moneysaver, it is quite respectable. The **Hostal Mayol** has matured from its origins as a restaurant and swinging discothèque into a popular little inn. Clean, pleasant, basic

amenities; informal, almost slaphappy atmosphere which can be fun if you're young enough. **Hostal Los Pinos,** on a hillside across from the Molins, is a converted private house which is householded by Anna and Juan Coll. As a former headwaiter, he understands attention to his guests and lavishes it on each one. A happy place. That green-tiled monstrosity is called (among other things) the **Don Pedro**. It caters largely to British trippers. Forget it—if you can.

For fun-and-games at a soothingly reasonable price level, *Puerto de Pollensa* offers the most—especially to unmarrieds and young-marrieds. This is the nearest village to Formentor, with frequent boat service (about a dollar) to the Formentor beaches for swimming (less spectacular but much improved bathing and beautiful maritime surroundings in the Puerto). The outskirting **Illa D'Or**, with its blendfully added wing, has our first slot now. Seaside situation about 10 minutes from town by foot; waterfront patio plus facilities for bay bathing and boating; snack bar for swimmers; tennis court; handsome lounge; fresh dining room with annoyingly small tables; daily outdoor buffet in season; 120 accommodations, many of them new. Recommendable, if you don't mind its distance from the port action. The owner, Sr. Pedro Garau, has just taken over the midtown Daina. **El Montelin,** a block off the seafront, comes up with 32 charming apartments (some with oh-so-handy kitchenettes), a splendid Norseland sauna, and a pool for residents. And not only that: The restaurant, closed Wednesdays, is easily one of the best on the entire island, with delicate offerings home-cooked by charming Lisa, a Danish delight, and served by handsome Jacque ("Yocky"), her German husband. Together they provide a multinational treat which you won't want to miss; Thursdays they offer a sizzling pick-your-own barbeque with a gigantic salad table for botany buffs. The hotel's hosting family, the Reuters, spread their Swedish charm to guests most of the year round. Very comfortable and fun. The little **Sis Pins**, back in the village, has a homey personality. Improved seafront apron for swimming or sunbathing; earplugs suggested if you draw a rear window in summer; open all year; now offering bed and breakfast only in a formula that clients seem to appreciate. Good for its low price. The **Miramar** is a relic of a bygone era. Yet it is very well maintained and sparkles as an island period piece. Elderly travelers or novelists who might wish to insinuate themselves into a quiet colonial setting undoubtedly would preen in its rocking-chair mood. Fading concrete tennis court; elevator service to both old and young wings; large, traditional, and gracious in its fusty tenor. Closed November to March. The whitewashed **Capri** draws a discriminating following within the heart of the village. Total of 33 comfortable rooms, all with bath and 1 with private balcony; amiable bar and terrace fronting the bay; one of the best values on tap. The mammoth **Pollensa Park** is chiefly reserved for registrants on a private charter plan. The **Raf** is a frequent choice of the Yachting Set. Handy situation a short roll from the main quay; genial administration and personnel; informal, basic, and a snug harbor. The **Carotti** specializes in tour groups; you

don't stand a chance of getting in. The **Bellavista** claims 42 rooms and 12 baths. Almost all accommodations with private terrace; tiny dimensions; a staff which speaks Spanish only. Modest. The 32-unit **Marina** is colder than a sea urchin's bottom spine in mid-December. No, thanks. The **Pensión La Torre** doesn't send us either. **Pensión del Luz** is another chipper little budget haven which money-savers seem to enjoy. We like it, too. The 66-room **Uyal**, about a mile along the Alcudia road, continues to deliver the goods for its summer patronage. Seaside swimming and sunning terrace across the highway; swimming pool fringed by the salon and bar; 2 fine tennis courts; large, well-presented annex facing the seaside; now unfreezing commendably. The impersonal **Pollentia** lacks soul. All these houses jump as madly as rabbit warrens during the summer.

In *Puerto Alcudia*, block bookings have now sewn up most of the High Season accommodations, but the area is recommendable because of its lovely, wide, sandy beach.

☑ **CASINO**   The Spanish Government recently lifted the ban on gambling casinos for the first time in 40 years. After occupying a temporary center for several months, in '79 the **Casino Sporting Club of Mallorca** was moved into a stunning new building on the Carretera Cala Figuera at *Mallorca Sol*, about 25 minutes by car east of the capital. This impressive structure is subtly understated in its architecture and décor. Soft illumination, tons of fine marble, a galaxy of paintings by famed artists, tasteful textiles, and gracious furnishings make its ambiance warm and attractive. Among its facilities are full air conditioning, a nightclub, a restaurant, bars, discos, an art gallery, tennis, golf, squash, a gymnasium, 2 swimming pools, a sauna, a bank, a winter garden beach club, a solarium, and alfresco dining in season.

Before our first visit we made the mistake of reserving a table in its 850-seat Gala Mallorca, a hyped-up theater-cabaret which is hangar-like in its dimensions. At the entrance we were asked to pay about $30 per person, which later we found included a prepackaged dinner consisting of one "champagne" cocktail, cream soup, roast chicken, a dessert, the floor show, and the entrance to the gaming rooms ($5 if no meal is consumed). It looked so brassy and mechanical that our party retreated to the deluxe Trebol restaurant opposite the front doors, which is the most elegant public dining setting we have ever seen on this island. Through our long friendship with Maître Antonio Jimenez, he was able to squeeze us in without a booking. The service was impeccable; the level of cuisine was not great but good for Mallorca; the bill was very high.

Later don Antonio escorted us past the barrier to the gambling area. From the ceiling hangs a forest of hundreds of shimmering lights. The 32 tables accommodate a capacity of 600 players. The action is split among American roulette, French roulette, Blackjack, Craps, Punto Banco, Chemin de Fer, and Boule. This area is open daily and Sundays through Thursdays 6 P.M. to 4 A.M.

and Fridays, Saturdays, and holidays 6 P.M. to 5 A.M.; the Trebol and the Gala Mallorca start later and finish earlier. *Please be SURE to take your passport if you wish to try your luck.* Good hunting!

☑ **RESTAURANTS** Today to our dismay we cannot rate even one single establishment on the island as a Great International Restaurant in the classic sense. With a handful of exceptions, instead we find that a selected number of small, relatively simple, family-run operations surpass the culinary standards and gustatory satisfaction of the Big Names at substantially lower prices.

In *Palma*, world-famous **El Patio** (just off Plaza Gomila) has at last climbed out of a long and severe slump to reemerge as unquestionably the leading luxury restaurant in the Balearics. Its cane-lined walls are banked with photos and sketches of royalty, ambassadors, admirals, film stars, tycoons, and other notables who have been nourished here since the 1930's. Spacious bar adjoining; chic clientele; skilletry still uneven, with some choices delectable and others not even debatable; s-m-o-o-t-h staff headed by English-speaking Maître José; very expensive by island standards; closed Sundays plus Monday lunches. Again the best bet for the moneyed traveler—but don't expect a "21."

Club de Mar, nexus of the yacht basin in the *Puerto Pi* section of the capital, today draws by far the largest segment of the illustrious and the Beautiful People. Its strikingly attractive premises, including the luxurious bar, are open the calendar around, but meals are served in its dining room and on its handsome terrace *from July 1 to August 31 only*. When the King and Queen spend their annual holidays in Mallorca, a table is reserved nightly in case they should wish it. Although it is a very exclusive private club, if space is available, for about $2 you may procure a one-time guest courtesy card which would entitle you to all of its copious facilities. Splendid vista overlooking thickets of anchored crafts; stunningly modern, airy décor in blue-and-white nautical rigging; mixed dress from conservative suits and long gowns to seagoing informal wear on the boaters. Due to its ill-conceived reservations system, when its table-count is normal the cookery and service are very good—but when more are added to overtax its kitchen and staff, both are unbelievably atrocious. This expensive sanctuary is *the* place to şee and be seen.

Smaller and less costly is the all-year **Le Relais**, directly across the private street from the entrance to the Club. Through a little garden and up a flight of stairs you'll find a suavely decorated, broad-windowed, L-shape oasis in soothing blues and pastels. The food—not inspired, but not bad either—includes a number of authentic Mallorquin dishes. We especially applaud the atmosphere, the welcome, and the attention. Urbane Captain Cecil Morrison has trimmed up this prized bark so smartly that it now draws aboard impressive segments of the island's Old Landed aristocracy. Reservations at either may be effected through the Club's central number: 236440. Still pricy but outstanding.

Chez Claude (Calle Seis 9) is located in a small, yellow-canopied house of

3 floors. The first is the bar; the second, rather stark, has 4 tables; the third offers 4 with more winsome atmosphere. Created and operated by two Spanish gourmets; limited menu but top-grade cookery by this island's standards; reasonable tabs; reservations mandatory for Friday and Saturday evenings; closed Sundays and all of February. Cozy and charming, with a friendly welcome.

El Coronel (Calle Orilla 14) is sited above the harbor by ancient windmills, with a breathtaking view of the Palma basin. Ground-floor cocktail salon in cool David Hicks tones; dining upstairs at only 8 tables; our local fish very expensive; our grilled steaks not special. Different, sophisticated, and rewarding if you are looking for antiestablishment dining. *Evenings only* and closed Sundays. Owners José Cervera Cris and Paco Munoz Delgado, who look as .if they had stepped out of a bullfight poster, operate the Ski-Club at Palma Nova at lunchtime.

La Caleta, next to the Alcina Hotel, is the ground-floor feedery in the apartment colossus that soars above. Immaculate entrance without any particular decorative motif; long bar leading to swimming-pool deck; huge upper terrace with tables for summer munching; Bagatel-Lo Pub; plate-glassed, seafront interior dining room, with modern red-cushioned chairs, brass globe sconces, and terra-cotta floors. Good reception; improving attention from captains and waiters; better than satisfactory but not exciting. Prices about the same level as those of El Patio.

The ambiance at **Samantha's** (Plaza Mediterráneo) is lovely—not only in the small, discreetly sited bar, but in the diminutive, 25-table dining salon with its softly glowing Tiffany-style lamps. Our only demurrer here is the chef's odd penchant for undermining his own best efforts—as he did, as only 1 of many examples, when our excellent Gigot of Lamb arrived with canned beans. If the costly second-rate skilletry should ever become as organized as the friendly and professional welcome, this chic challenger might be truly worthy. Open from 1 P.M. to 3:30 P.M. and from 8 P.M. to midnight; closed Sunday.

Inviting little **La Broche** (Calle Asprer 3, just off Av. Jaime III) has an intimate, split-level bistro atmosphere. Skilled and hospitable Belgian ownership; kitchen and dark-wood bar at entrance; perhaps 2 dozen tables; redcheckered cloths, candles, and fresh flowers; air conditioning; prompt, smooth, courteous service. Included among our latest choices here were sole smothered in mushrooms and mussels, sea bass in a half-inch of salt and cracked open with a mallet, Boeuf Bourguignonne, Lobster Soufflé Grand Marnier; the latter were as puffy and fluffy as clouds over Paris. Good but not a rave.

Le Bistrot (Teodoro Llorente 4) is a tiny corner of France transplanted into the heart of Palma. Marble-topped tables; Tiffany wall lamps; sizable open kitchen; Nouvelle Epoch chairs; limited menu; excellent food; terrible acoustics. The family of operators doesn't have enough members to provide fast service. We still salivate for their *profiteroles* with chocolate sauce. Closed Sunday.

Plat Pla (Calvo Sotelo 50) has caught on strongly with moneyed Mallorquins—and we simply do not understand why. To us it is a strictly routine oasis in both furnishings and what we consider pretentiously overpriced fare. Perhaps you might disagree.

Among the hotels, at **Son Vida** the enchanting panoramic, shaded bar-restaurant with a buffet at lunch and the open terrace at night—both overlooking the pool—is our number one pick, for ambience. How the quality of its cuisine will fare is open to question at this writing. Be *sure* to order from the à la carte menu here. The big, classic, alfresco terrace at the **Victoria Sol**, also with a glorious sweep, is a close second. The **Maricel**'s cozy, clublike atmosphere and sound viands make it another sturdy bet. The **Nixe Palace**'s installations, while bettering, are not special. Almost all of the rest range from standard to uninspired. At the bottom among the most prominent hostelries, in our opinion, is the fare at the **Valparaiso, Meliá Mallorca**, and **De Mar**.

Now let's get out of the Big Leagues and turn to the more reasonably priced (and often more rewarding) family-type places.

Mac's Cristina (Calle Pursiana 12, a hard-to-find street off Calle Argentina) is one of our top favorites of its category anywhere in Spain. Your hostess Mac Lyons, a beautiful, enchantingly warm ex-film star, insists on personally doing all of the cooking. The menu ranges from super-super fried chicken to steaks to curry to roast Virginia ham to more tempters including 3 of her own beloved Philippine specialties—and each dish is *something*. We have entertained scores of our visiting friends here, including such ranking gourmets as Director Sheldon Tannen of New York's "21" Club and author Harold Robbins, both of whom richly enjoyed it; in fact Mr. Robbins returned later the same week with his own party. *Dinner only;* closed Sundays. What a felicitious find!

The centrally sited **Svarta Pannan** (Calle Brondo 5) is a delightful import from Sweden, smoothly landlorded by Rune Gärdlund, a gentle, thoughtful host. Small library of Swedish books at the entrance; friendly, intimate atmosphere but so busy at lunchtime that advance reservations are urged; variety of dishes from its motherland plus local fish, meats and fowl; moderate prices; closed Sundays. A favorite with the Swedish Consul—it pleases our diplomatic pouch too.

Tirolia (Joan Miró 46 and Teniente Mulet 9, a few steps from Plaza Gomila) is a warmly welcome newcomer. It has 2 entrances to 2 rooms at 2 levels. The front one is its magnet for barflies, while the air-conditioned rear precinct is preferable for meals. Both are pleasant, clean, and airy with their Tyrolean atmosphere and red and white checked cloths. The latter is sufficiently but not disturbingly spacious with paneled-and-stuccoed walls, indirect lighting, soft piped music, a hanging lamp over each table, and flowered dividers. On our several visits the cuisine has been fresh, hot, well cooked, and savory, and the service has been smilingly attentive. As a bonus, it is very inexpensive for the quality of the fare. Charmingly gracious Peter and Hilda Haider, a smoothly

experienced Austrian couple, will welcome you with smiles. Closed Tuesdays and one week in February. Excellent for the outlay.

The **Principado de Asturias** (Avd. Argentina 59) features fare from the mainland Asturias province. Your host, Caesar Martin, hails from that area and apprenticed in London before settling in this capital. One of our particular palate pleasers is the Fabadas Asturiana (white beans, sausage, and pork), but we urge that you indulge in this only at lunchtime because it is rich and h-e-a-v-y. The menu has many other tempters and the prices are right. Do try it!

Rififi (Joan Miró 446) resides in the characteristic Porto Pí district, the earliest harbor settlement of ancient Palma. As you might expect, the specialty is seafood—and it's delicious. Unimposing façade; refrigerated display case with fresh denizens gleaming at incoming patrons; suavely rustic décor highlighted by rims of wine tuns embedded in a wall; a gnarled tree trunk on center stage. A bewildering variety of just about every edible creature that swims, creeps, or hops along the floor of this part of the Mediterranean; other terrestrial selections available but not up to the quality of the marine wares. Closed Tuesdays. Very good by local standards.

La Vileta, 15 minutes out, is another solid, steady, ever-dependable favorite to which we often happily return. It occupies a converted farmhouse which was taken over by Bob Edwardes' English father many years ago and in which this handsome, knowledgeable son is now the highly personable host. He offers a vast variety of British, French, and Spanish staples, from delicious Quiche Lorraine to Roast Lamb in Rosemary to Beef and Kidney Pie to Paella to a number of his own savory inventions. Of equal interest is the fact that the prices are right; the value is delivered for every peseta expended. Often when we're stuck about places in which we can relax and enjoy (incidently, there's an open-air evening dining terrace in season), we'll turn to each other and say, "Let's go THERE!" Unpretentious, comfortable, and warmly friendly.

Ca'n Sophie (better known as Chez Sophie at Apuntadores) is an *enfant de La Belle France*. Shortly after the original Sophie passed on, Odette (of embroidery fame) stitched a sparkling professional partnership with Chef Jean. The premises are still simple, spotlessly clean, and pervaded with the solicitousness which we have always found here. Our twosome repast, including onion soup, snails, sole, and green salad, was as fine an example of French-style home cooking as we've experienced in these parts, and at tabs that are almost a steal. Again very solid and sound. Closed Sunday.

Los Gauchos (San Magin 78) rides in with approximate facsimiles of platters from the South American Chuckwagon. Cultivated pampered-pampas atmosphere spread over 2 small rooms with about 8 tables; savory grills; pseudo-Mexican dishes, flavorful though composed of local ingredients; attentive service with Chief Honcho Ruiz holding the reins. Though of limited authenticity, our grub was quite recommendable.

Next to Mac's Cristina, **La Casita** (Joan Miró 68) is the best American-style

restaurant we've found during our 2-decades-plus residence on the island. Plainly furnished room with 10 tables; service bar and immaculate kitchen to the rear; atmosphere as cheerful as the restaurant's extremely friendly and warmhearted proprietors, New Jerseyite Jim Mangin and his charming French wife Denyse. She supervises the culinary department while he carries out his role as Chief Boniface, Chief Barman, Chief Greeter, and Chief Hawkeye to oversee the comfort of each individual guest. Don't go here for just a hamburger or similar light bite, because it's not a snack bar; the versatile card features specialties of the U.S. and a few savory Gallic dishes snuck in by Madame. The hours are from 1 P.M. to 4 P.M. and 7 P.M. to midnight; it is closed all of July, every Tuesday, and from November through March on Monday nights as well. We will always be grateful to Mrs. Louis Schonciet (the universally beloved "Renée Carroll" of Sardi's fame) for tipping us off to this unostentatious little honey.

Galician fare? We're fond of the rough-and-ready **Casa Gallega** (Pueyo 6) in midcity. The ground-floor counter is always jammed; down here you'll also find a few tables; upstairs is for more formal dining. Some platters are super (such as toasted, seasoned medallions of octopus or the tiny eels called *angulas* in oil and garlic), while others are merely excellent. Rudeness is par for the course in the service here—but for such gastronomy, try to forget it.

The recently enlarged **La Pizzeria** (Calle Bellver 22, in Torreno) tops all local contenders in French-Italian dishes by a dozen leagues. Warm reception by tall, smiling Mme. Monique; sizzling-hot platters by Pierre, her chef-husband. Some of the best-tossed salads in the capital; terrace with checked tablecloths, candlelit jugs, and rustic country-tavern atmosphere; beguiling open courtyard in summer. Except for its so-so *sí-sí* meats, here is a darned good restaurant—not a pizza joint, as its name implies. We go often and enjoy it a lot. If you are in *Palma Nova* you may wish to try its branch there.

Mario's, across the street, is straight Italian—or should we say straight imitation Italian? Despite the facts that this medium-large, pleasantly turned-out establishment always seems to be crowded and that many of our local friends like it, none of us has ever had a good meal here. De gustibus. . . .

Sa Premsa (Plaza Obispo Berenguer de Palou 13, and branch on Joan Miró) is an unfastidious, downright dirty wine cellar which also serves meals. Big, spartan, noisy; 252-gallon wine tuns around the walls; service nonstop during the day and the evening. Burly atmosphere and miserable cookery. Nix. **Fonda de Puerto**, on the palm-lined Port Boulevard, blows both hot and chilly. On our latest try it was the latter; this one has very few pretenses in any case. Sidewalk terrace with perhaps 7 tables; simple dining room now made more chipper with gay ceramics and stucco booths. Fair. For fish only, you might want to hook into the ultrabasic **Lonja del Pescado Cantina** (also known as "Pósito de Pescadores" and "Casa Eduardo"), on the middle wharf. Upstairs location; open kitchen; 10-fathom plainness in furnishings (you must ask for

a tablecloth if you dislike resting your elbows on fancy plastic); viewless terrace for summer customers; homespun service; bargain-basement tabs; little effort made to give it sparkle, élan, or a beatific glow. To get first crack at the daily catches from the boats that dock downstairs, the management offers the crews a special concession of 2 courses, fruit, and wine for about $1. **Celler Ses Rodes** (B. Pinopar 30 near Mare Nostrum), small and also down-to-earth, is one of Palma's few remaining places which serves 100% unadulterated traditional Mallorquin fare. No English spoken; basic and cheap; and it is good.

Ola's (off Plaza Gomila) is okay as a steak joint for medium budgets. The menu contains almost anything that Ola himself enjoys—from Swedish meat-balls to Mexican chili. Kooky but fun. **Penelope** (Progreso 39) is pleasant to the eye, but her cooking wouldn't lure this Odysseus home from any voyage.

The **Horchateria C'an Juan de S'Aigo** (Calle de Sans 10, behind Plaza San Eulalia) was established in 1700. It remains THE place for Mallorquins to drop in for hot chocolate, ensaimadas (a light super-appetizing pastry), or almond ice cream. We applaud the tradition and follow the crowd.

Danish? **El Verd** (Joan Miró 199 near Plaza Gomila) is our leading nominee. This modest but rewarding restaurant-bar is fronted by a friendly English-speaking Spaniard; his Danish wife does all of the cooking. Although the selection is limited, the food is authentic. Among the dozens of Scandinavian establishments in the city, many of them very poor, here's where we most often drop in for a light meal with akvavit and Carlsberg beer.

Chinese? While the day-to-day diet at the **Nanking** (Joan Miró 16-A) is only a cut above average for Spain, when one orders 3 days in advance it is *fabulous.* Retired Senior Editor Dennis McEvoy of the *Reader's Digest*, who has lived in China and speaks the language, did so as a treat for us. The special menu he selected consisted of Shark's Fin Soup, Peking Duck, Mandarin Fantasy, Abalones with 3 delicious sauces, Fried Shrimps and Kidneys, Chicken and Bamboo Shoots, Bean Curds with Almond Sauce, and a fruit dessert. Never in our lives anywhere in the world have 3 of us had a Chinese dinner which surpassed it—and in Palma de Mallorca, of all places! This will be a gastronomic memory which will ever linger joyously. **Madarin** (next to the Victoria), **Chinese Garden** (in the same stable on Plaza Mediterráneo), **Shanghai**, and all the rest are no better than routine.

The **Bar Formentor**, smack in the center of town, used to be *the* local gin mill, social axis, and home-away-from-home for nearly every American on the island. With its complete change of ownership and staff, however, it is fading by delivering less food and less good cheer for more money. Other light-biteries include **Kais** (on the Borne), **Cafeteria Nacar** (on the Jaime III), and **Moby Dick** in Palma Nova. **Yacht Ritz** (Borne) sails in with thin vittles for nickels and dimes. **Cafeteria Marqués** (Marqués de la Cenia 50) flips flavorful Finnish fare.

To review the best possibilities for luncheon or dinner excursions on a sunny day, let's first move out of the city to the west.

The panoramic **Bon Aire d'Illetes**, on the peninsula of Las Illetes, is a short and lovely excursion on a warm and brilliant day. Its warren of small rooms in classic regional décor makes for intimate dining. Fresh fish and seafood are the specialties here—and the chef knows his victuals. We like and recommend this, especially for lunch.

Na Burgesa, atop the mountain which looms over Genova, crowns the turrets of Bellver Castle plus the entire bay and plain of Palma. It is 1 simple room with windows on 3 sides, an open hearth, and a newly opened terrace. The small bill of fare is chalked on a board and consists mostly of hocks of meat, chops, savory toasted bread (_pa amb oil_), and a sturdy red house wine. Inexpensive and crude; visual sweep shared by angels and eagles; no coffee served; closed Wednesday.

At _Palma Nova_ (7 miles), formal **Portanova** is located in an exclusive apartment complex of the same name. Its semicircular dining room affords a stunning bay view from its wide windows; furnishings were chosen in coincident taste with the twenty-first century; the attendance used to be one waiter for every client, but now this ratio has fallen off sharply. The menu is copious; the cookery is, to us at least, no longer spectacular; the price is high. This one is dressy at night and it functions the year around. It is disappointing to find that after such an auspicious start the area cannot properly support such luxury. Near Marineland, **Mesón Son Caliu** bubbles with the delights of the island's regional décor and typical local cuisine, all overseen by Mallorquin Lorenzo Bosch and his British wife, Carol. The setting is sweetly romantic. Closed on Monday except for holidays; always reserve ahead in summer. **Bakara** is also popular in this district.

Near _Santa Ponsa_ (12 miles), the young, strikingly architected **Santa Ponsa** hotel-golfing complex sets an excellent table in a plush milieu. Although the cuisine will never win a trans-Iberian award for top superiority, we have greatly enjoyed our 4 lunches here while ensconced in such attractive surroundings. On the expensive side but worth it. On the inexpensive side and also worth it is **Cán Pau Perdiueta** at nearby _Portals Vells_, which is the next major cove after Magaluf. Hillside situation with poor view. Modern building with 3 walls of glass; kind but sometimes hectic service; specialties borne from the sea. This one is very popular with Palmisano families who pack it to the eaves on Sundays. Go on other days to revel in the sylvan calm of Calvia's mountains. In _Paguera_ (18 miles), the dining facilities at the **Hotel Villamil** are adequate but seem on the dull side. The **Ambassador**, just outside town, can be a pause that refreshes. Extensive selections; prices surprisingly low for such high-key cuisine; bleak setting, but usually (not always) a reward for The Inner Man and Woman. At _Cala Fornells_ (20 miles), the Moorish-styled **Gran Tortuga** ("Great Turtle") overlooks Paguera Bay from its midvillage perch; also below is a pool where on summer nights Mallorquin dancers perform at its apron. Rustic ambiance; hammered-tin lamp lighting; fireplace; indoor-outdoor dining; international dishes plus a few rare local preparations;

service polished under normal conditions but miserably understaffed when at capacity; medium-high levies. In warm weather, book ahead for an outside location. This turtle voices an alluring serenade.

Foc i Fum ("Fire and Smoke") is in the hills backing *Puerto Andraitx*, 24 miles out. Dining on 2 levels, both under the open skies; gas-torch illumination; open kitchen; sun motif on place plates; wine chilled in wooden casks and served from Spanish drinking beakers. The fixed dinner consists of your own selection of self-sliced viands from a huge wooden press draped with sausages and garnished with olives and other tidbits; then comes your choice of cold or hot soup; the main courses are chiefly variations on traditional Mallorquin classic dishes. So far it is open *evenings only* and closed part of the winter. Be sure to reserve in advance. Its adequate but routine-level cuisine is not the inspiration for going here; most definitely its romantic setting is the draw.

One of our favorite pilgrimages on a clear and lovely day—though the food leaves heaps to be desired—is the cliff-high **Es Grau**, teetering 1000 feet above the Mediterranean, about 1 hour from Palma, 9 miles past Andraitx; head for the Mirador Ricardo Roca. Its sunset orientation glories with 35 terrace-sited tables plus 20 more in the interior salon. Service harried but kind; bus tours in profusion. In July and August it's open from 8 A.M. to 10 P.M., closing 2 hours earlier the rest of the year. For eyeful, sighful, my-oh-myful sightseeing, this slice of heaven is tough to top.

Now let's strike out for the most rewarding restaurants for excursions east of Palma. As you will read, they are even more plentiful than those which are westward.

The center of the island offers virtually nothing of special interest in this category. While motoring on the cross-island pike from Palma to the north, you might be tempted to pause at the ersatz castle called **El Foro de Mallorca** between Benisalem and Inca. In our opinions, the eatables here could well be the surplus products from the adjacent wax museum. To us here's a tourist trap of the lowest order which we strenuously disrecommend. In the northeast the first establishment of note is delightful **Ca'n Pacienci-Ye Olde English Inn**, perhaps a 50-minute drive. It is a tiny *finca* (farmhouse) tucked at the end of a short driveway on the left-hand side about 1/3rd of the way from Pollensa to Puerto de Pollensa. Colonel Norman and Phyllis Rose have converted it into an oasis of charm and relaxed friendliness. A tack-room bar features a double-faced fireplace which glows into this nook as well as the cozy dining room which adjoins. There's also an alfresco garden area for sipping. Their personal grace and professional savvy have made it the number one gathering place of the foreign colony who reside within many and many a mile. Cookery? We think it is the best on that entire quadrant of Mallorca, with the versatile price-fixed meal in the $13 range. *Advance reservations are absolutely necessary*; your concierge can make them by calling 53-07-87. Closed for 4 months in winter, and Sundays in summer. Cheers and salutes!

A colorful summertime target in *Cala San Vicente*, terminating a branch-

off 10 minutes farther along, is **Los Encinares**, which features outdoor grilling on a firelit terrace. The simple tables overlook the savage ridge of mountains which clasp a sandstone chapel in their chalice; it is beautifully illuminated at night. A capacious swimming pool with a footbridge arcing above it is available to clients; so is a hard-surface tennis court; both are open day and night. Low prices for unusually high rewards.

In *Pollensa* itself, the best of a poor lot are **Ca'n Juan** and **Sant Jordi**. Both are adequate but not spectacular. P.S.: Parking in this village can generate a size-44 headache.

In *Puerto de Pollensa*, please refer back to our "Hotels" section for our comments on **El Montelin**, one of the best on the island. It's interior walls are painted with flora, the tables are marble-topped antique sewing benches, the bar zings, and the Thursday night outdoor barbecues are yumptious. Remember, it's closed on Wednesdays. Superb, especially for non-Spanish comestibles. Señor Bou's extremely popular **Bec-fi**, along the town shore, specializes in lots of sizzle, steaks, and shishkebobs. Attractive interior; kind service; different from most seasiders. The waterfront terrace, incidentally, is lovely for cocktails. **Stay**, beside the ferryboat landing, is a knockout by night and a buzz of marine activity by day. Until the dinner hour, you'll find a self-service snack bar, a cafeteria, and a lovely awning-clad or open westerly terrace. After dark diners sit inside or on the bayside embankment where sailing dingies tug at their moorings. Helmsman Don Miguel runs a tight ship; his crew is superb; his galley is first class; his prices are appropriate for the quality wares he produces from the earth and the sea. **La Lonja**, on the opposite quay, also is popular. At the end of the same quay, the **Puerto de Pollensa Yacht Club** turns out Mediterranean delights in delightfully fresh surroundings. Super-efficient Juan and his smiling English wife, Ann, labor 25 hours per day (except on Tuesdays) to fit grins of contentment on visiting faces. (His Majesty Juan Carlos's is occasionally among them.) If you dive into a rich lobster stew (called *Caldereta*, a specialty of northern Balearic waters), we'll bet you will agree that it has the capacity to transport the soul to lofty realms; such levitation doesn't come cheap, however. In summer, yachtsmen and their mates keen to get in, so an advance reservation is a certain must. It is open to the public and prices are lower than at either of its harbormates. **Ca Vostra** might please you if you're in the mood for an authentic traditional local feast. The expansive **C'an Pep** earns its share of the year-round traffic. Pepe, the jovial *jefe*, does all of the buying, oversees the cooking, and greets the clients. His fish soup and his full-bodied Paella are especially laudable. **Angelo's** features Latin American guitar music and singing by its quartet of proprietors. Up until 11 P.M. they cook, serve, and scurry, but after that they whip off their aprons and don their *ponchos* to entertain their guests. Fair cookery but delightful music.

If you run up along the western littoral, the mountain town of *Soller* (not its port) offers the dignified **El Guia**, a hotel and restaurant off the central

plaza, near the rail depot. It's immaculate, very Mallorquin, and just the ticket for a lunch break while roaming the crags and vales.

On the opposite coast almost due east from Palma, **Ses Rotges** in *Cala Ratjada* is the talk of this very small town. The garden dining in summer is a romantic treat even though the culinary achievement is something short of grand. While our memories are only pleasant ones, we feel that this restaurant and its small, select hotel are finally making the grade.

Further south at the busy little port of *Cala d'Or* (take the *Santanyi* road for perhaps 90 minutes) is one of the top restaurants on the island —the air-conditioned **La Cuadra**. Expansion is planned from 200 to 500 seats and the construction of an indoor swimming pool with cascades of water is in the works. It is operated by bearded young Geoff, who is the best possible advertisement for his interesting and delicious skilletcrafts. Portions, incidentally, are so excessive that you might imagine yourself as the guest of honor at a lumberjack reunion. Noble assistance by his Mum and Jane, a girlfriend who builds sweet magic into her chocolate cake recipe; expensive tabs which are merited; *reserve in advance* by phoning 65-72-87—especially urged because it is seasonal and closing times are variable. Geoff's major competion comes from the more modest **Ibiza**, in the same area, which purveys Franco-Italian wares at quite a bit less than the preparations at La Cuadra. There's an open kitchen behind the 2 main rooms and bar; red calico spreads cover the tables; meals are presented handsomely on large wooden platters. Low in cost and pleasant, but not as ambitious as Geoff's place. The **Cala d'Or Hotel**, with its attractive downstairs bar, inviting terrace, and winsome Mallorquin flavor, has long been an inviting standby.

Several manor houses (variously prefixed with the word *Son* or *Ca'n* in the island dialect) have been opened to the public with what we'd term, for want of a better word, "barbecue dining" as the feature. The farm fare is simple, but the fun and the food are genuine. Here are a few recommendable manor-isms: The **Moli d'es Compte** ("The Count's Windmill") is situated on the main pike from *Palma* to *Puigpuñent*; **Son Gual** is on the same route; **Son Amar** is a 6-minute drive from the capital on the *Valldemosa* road; **Son Termes** stokes its stoves along the lane to *S'Esglaieta*; **Ses Cullidoras** resides at *Sollerich* on the way toward Orient. At **Orient** itself, at the foot of the western range of mountains, we are extremely fond of the **Hostal de Muntanya**; the Arroz Brut (an island stew) and kid in a special sauce are the satisfaction of any diner's great expectations for regional fare. It usually functions 7 days a week, but Sundays are not recommended because of the crowded conditions. A solid rural bet and an interesting excursion target.

☑ **NIGHTCLUBS**   In *Palma*, until recently **Tito's** was one of the most spectacular after-dark showplaces on the European continent. The 2 long cabarets nightly in season featured some of the top talent in the entertainment world. The vast, magnificent, multi-tiered patio with its transparent roof removable

in season remains the same. Today, however, most of its elegantly dressed clientele has been replaced by tour groups from all over the map. As a consequence, its former peak-star-studded shows have suffered somewhat of a fall-off in the quality of their artists. No entrance fee or minimum charge; first drink very steep, with future libations for much, much less; orchestra continued top-drawer. Despite its lower-quality patronage, this attraction is still definitely worth seeing.

My Own Place is columnist-commentator Riki Lash Lazaar's highly successful investment in warm intimacy and fun—backed by a glorious panoramic sweep of Palma Bay. The irrepressible Riki welcomes all guests and puts many on his radio show—with special speakers beamed into "MOP." Here is a delightful drop-in spot at any time from 7 P.M. to 3 A.M. for handholders, for lonely-spirits who are bored with institutional-style impersonality, and for nightowls who seek relaxed respite in a glorious setting. He is such a gracious host that you should have the feeling you're an honored member of his "club" within 5 minutes.

Kalcutta runs a show plus dancing sequences. **Broadway**, in a basement across from the Victoria Hotel, lights up with strip shows and cabaret — something new for Spaniards but quite a wheeze for most outlanders.

Nightcap: A few steps from the overpass along the Paseo Maritimo, strollers can enjoy a final nip at **New Orleans Bar**. It's one of island's most salubrious drop-in pubs in our view, and just right for friendly persuasions and other nightwork.

Palma has gone discothèque happy—and the throb of ones that we've recently inspected is still ricocheting off our rim-shot eardrums. At the top, **Colapso** seems to be edging out **Alexandra's**. The new **Acron Discothèque-Boîte** is coming along strongly as a contender. All do their zingy thing in the latest mod mood. **La Rueda Numero Uno** has rolled up as a big wheel in town for those on the night trail. **Zhivago** is the loudest. The entrance charge buys your first drink; the pre-Columbian décor *(sic)* has been mutated, but not muted, into a Russian theme. Side dishes of borsch and caviar; occasional appearances by top English recording stars; fresh ventilation, but ambiance hotter than an 8-alarm fire. **Rodeito** is a much cozier swinger. So is **Disco-45**, which glitters with 2 bars and a series of raised and sunken dancing squares (the *décor*, that is). **Kiss** is keener than most on promotion. **Crazy Daisy** and **Bavaria**, down the street from the Hotel Victoria, are back-to-back and belly-to-belly, mass-over-class jernts which we find crass. Entrance chit gets you a drink in either section.

String pickin's? **The Guitar Center**, strums up regular musical evenings, beginning at 9:30, for serious but funloving aficionados of the instrument. We recently enjoyed a concert here by Gene and Francesca Raskin (composer and artists of the smash hits "Those Were The Days" and "Hello Love"). Other equally big-time greats of the musical world also pop in to add their talents to the sessions. Victorian-flea-market atmosphere. Highly recommended for sips and salubrious sounds.

☑ **TAXIS** Ah—_Those_ Were The Days when the drivers used to be sweet-natured, helpful, and honest. Now, unfortunately, the tourist migration has made many of them sour, rude, and dishonest—even to the point, on occasion, of extracting their own tips. _Watch them carefully, and do not pay 1 céntimo more than the metered tariffs_ (plus possibly any supplements which should be printed on a card which the driver can provide). If they object, demand they drive you to the nearest _comisaría._ Tip 5 to 10 pesetas for the average haul. And the prices!?! Within less than 10 months before these words were written, repeated strikes and internecine violence have raised their fares by about 60%. On nights, Sundays, and holidays the cost is substantially more. Give them _nothing_ extra then!

☑ **CAR HIRE** For self-drive autos, 1 and only 1 is recommended in the capital: **Empresa Garaje Vidal** (Rover Motta 11, near the seafront; Tel. 46-17-00); new or nearly new SEATS (Spanish Fiat), Ford Fiestas, or Simcas at moderate tariffs are the specialty. Owners Don Andrès and Don Antonio Darder, cheerful and friendly brothers who speak English, will see you receive conscientious service. You may hire a chauffeur-driven sedan from your hotel for perhaps $50 per day—not too bad if you split it with another couple. On the other side of the island, we are impressed with the kindness and efficiency of **Autos La Parra** (Calle Juan XXIII, Tel. 75, Puerto de Pollensa). It's owned and operated by a local consortium of young mechanics and hotel concierges; it's fleet of more than 80 SEATS is kept in tip-top condition. Please ask for Angel or Gregorio. Recommended.

★ **TIP** If you have any problems concerning car ownership in Spain (or Europe), shipment home of your lizzie, American technical specifications, or retirement abroad and the most economical way to go about licensing your family vehicles, go immediately to the previously mentioned don Antonio Darder who makes an extra-special effort to help readers of this book. This gentleman has gone so far as to provide his personal office telephone number (Palma 46–36–00) for your convenience. His town headquarters, where he is the Ford agent, is **Motor Balear S.A.** at Aragon 2; he also can arrange purchase of other makes of autos. For anything from Spanish tourist plates to a brass ooga-horn, this good friend and brilliant young administrator is the accelerator who will speed you to your destination with the least possible trouble.

☑ **TRAINS** Electric service to Sóller, and Lionel-size miniatures operated on diesel oil to Inca, Manacor, and other points. Both are narrow-guage. The lead coach on the Sóller run is so reminiscent of the original Toonerville Trolley that it's fun, especially if you're bound for a lunch excursion in its port.

☑ **AIR AND SEA TRAVEL** Iberia provides most of the muscle in Mallorca's air bridge, lots of it stretching between Madrid or Barcelona and Palma. British Airways, SAS, Lufthansa, Swissair, KLM, Sabena, Air France, Air

Algeria, and many more offer direct service from their respective capitals to Palma; some are summer only. *Every flight on every airline is nearly always crowded;* nail down your tickets early, or you might be stuck for several frustrating days.

Son San Juan, the island's jet airport, is only 10 minutes from your Palma doorstep via the multimilliondollar speedway. In season, the Saturday and Sunday crush when most charter flights arrive and depart (despite their own detached building) must be seen to be believed. Great balls of lightning, WHAT a human zoo it becomes! The restaurants are wickedly overpriced and wretched. Expect a somewhat disenchanting first impression of Mallorca.

Trasmediterránea, now nationalized, has a sizable fleet of steamers which originate at Barcelona, Alicante, and Valencia and cover the major islands. From Palma to Barcelona in summer there are daily midnight sailings plus noon departures on Mon., Wed., and Sat.; during the winter they go at 11 P.M. every night except Sun. The Barcelona to Palma schedule is roughly the same. From Palma to Alicante they leave at 7 P.M. on Mon., Wed., and Fri. the year around. There are daily connections from Palma to Valencia at 11 A.M. except on Sundays during the colder months. From Alcudia to Minorca you'll also find daily service during high season and on Tues., Thurs., and Sat. when the traffic is reduced. Finally, a more venerable gal plies her way between Palma and the rock-dot of Cabrera each Friday, year round.

Two good ships are in service between Palma and Barcelona. The *Ciudad de Badajoz* and the *Ciudad de Compostela* are the slick chicks on the Balearic beat. Sometimes they alternate with their twins, *Juan March, Santa Cruz de Tenerife*, or *Los Palmas de Gran Canaria,* which normally frequent the Canary Island lanes. These beauties can accommodate as many as 750 passengers and 130 automobiles; they cruise at 21 knots. If you can afford it, book First-class cabins; they're worth the difference; on any of the other older steamers, ask for Deluxe or semi-Deluxe accommodations. The lounges in the younger barks are gracious; the food is ample, badly cooked, well served, and amazingly inexpensive; the bars are friendly. In summer, other ferries such as the new *Cuidad de Sevilla* are brought in to supplement these graceful vessels between Palma–Alicante and Palma–Valencia. Still newer equipment has been tied into the Málaga–Melilla–Almería loop, but these are lighter babies than the fleet's star performers.

Ybarra, the route of the "Blue Kangaroo," offers 7- to 8-hour Barcelona–Palma shuttles aboard a sleek hippity-hopper pouching up to 1000 passengers and 110 autos. It glides in each direction daily from June 15 to September 15, but does not leave Palma on Sat. or Barcelona on Mon. during the rest of the year. The ships of this line are better, in our opinion, than the above ferries; the cost of passage is somewhat higher, too. If you are connecting with Italy, Ybarra steams eastward to Genoa between Palma visits, making the choice of this line even more convenient for motorists. From here Switzerland, Germany, Austria, and France are short drives away over excellent motorways;

Florence, Venice, and Rome are also just down the pike. A smooth professional operation.

Don't, for heaven's sake, take deck passage on *any* overnight sailing, regardless of circumstances. The bigger ships offer airline style chairs (120 to 250 of them!) in enclosed dormitory-like salons; they're clean enough, but when full they're a jungle. The others sleep passengers in open, maritime discomfort. We repeat: Get a stateroom—it will provide you with a delightful cruise, in miniature, on the Mediterranean. For daytime crossings, the cheaper seat ticket is perfectly adequate because a lot of your time will be spent in lounges, pacing the decks, or at poolside.

Finally, a link between Marseille–Palma–Algiers has been forged for summer cruising aboard the French vessels *El Djeizair, Pte. de Cazalet,* and the car ferry *Avenir.* (Caution: Many autos are stripped en route.) Check with your travel agent for last-minute progress on these, as well as exact schedules for the Europe-to-Africa runs.

☑ **DRINKS**   Mallorquin specialties are either sweet or dry *hierbas,* an anise-flavored slugger highly favored by fishermen, laborers, and sophisticates as well; it is absorbed as a pre- or after-dinner nip, neat or served with ice-and-soda in summer. Others are *palo* (originally made from the bark of the Peruvian quina tree), which we prefer presented highball-style, and *anis* (the Tunel brand is marvelous). Try them for size; they cost pennies, and they're mighty interesting. Hunters (probably of dragons and other such perilous game) swallow *meselat* or *canya* on chilly mornings, but how they can find their triggers after a mere whiff of the stuff amazes us. Embalming fluid is kinder to the system. All major international spirits are available on the island.

☑ **THINGS TO SEE**   Our candidate for the number one sightseeing attraction used to be the **Caves of Drach** at *Porto Cristo*, 40 miles on good roads from the capital. Underground music that's now so corny you'll probably have to stifle your giggles; a gimmicky boat ride on an eerie underground lake; worth the time, if you don't get stuck in one of the interminable queues which sometimes stack up at its water section. Bus excursions from Palma at regular intervals. *Artá* also has awesome caves; *Campanet* has them in miniature. Beyond Drach, about 4 miles toward *Cala Millor*, you kiddies from 6 to 96 shouldn't miss the **Auto-Safari**, a 40-acre spread of flamingoes, swans, giraffes, rhinos, and 400 species of bush animals which wander the fields as you drive by to nod good-day. The paved route is almost 2 miles long; top speed is 6 mph.; passengers are prohibited from leaving the protection of their cars. If you are in this region and love God's critters as much as we do, this can be much more fun than a barrel of fleas.

Next most rewarding, in our opinion, is the junket to *Formentor*, with a stop on the return trip to see the Mallorquin dancers at the little hamlet of

Selva. Best scenery and best dancers on the island. Regular excursions Tuesdays and Fridays (other days in summer, too).

A **medieval joust**? You can enjoy it as performed by daredevil stuntmen at the ancient palace of **El Comte Mal**, 7 miles from Palma on a spur that joins the Sóller and Valldemosa roadways. While it may seem unabashedly touristic, this is one of the best performances of Middle Ages theater we have seen in our European travels. While the games of competition, acted out on the earth-covered enclosed court, begin at 9 P.M., you are advised to be present at 8:30. Dinner, served on heaping litters by page boys, consists of consommé, fingerlicken' flambéed chicken, and interesting side dishes plus wine; the meal and show cost approximately $15. After the repast, a large orchestra plays dance music in the adjoining lounge for guests who wish to lengthen the evening. Tickets are available in Palma at major travel agencies, many of which provide bus transportation; otherwise you may have to commission a taxi for the jaunt. It functions all weeknights in summer and 4 days weekly in winter. A socko spectacle which is a splendid value for children and adults.

In the capital, the magnificent, privately financed, multimillion-dollar **Auditorium** is the most impressive cultural magnet of the Balearics. If you're music-hungry, be sure to check the programs and schedules during the time of your visit. Here's a fabulous *coup* for the island—and you!

In the north, the village of *Pollensa* sponsors a **Music Festival** during July and August. Such virtuosi as Segovia, Szeryng, Spierer, Ricci, Rubinstein, Stern, and Richter have given concerts in the charming art-filled cloister of the Santo Domingo Church. Any concierge on the island probably can arrange tickets for you. The prices are laughably low and the rewards are memorably high.

Marineland makes a glorious splash on the Costa den Blanes, a few minutes out of Palma on the Andraitx road. Trained sea lions, dolphins, and parrots, plus a zooful of other critters, are on hand for the splendid shows, the exhibits, or for just strolling around and chatting with the animal kingdom. Within this seaside compound are myriad recreational facilities, rides, play parks, a restaurant, a snack terrace, an aquarium—enough to keep mom, dad, and all the brood engaged for many happy hours. Public Relations Director Roberto Bennett knows very well that the best show on earth is the earth and its residents. Some of our globe's most lovable companions are here just waiting to extend a paw, a claw, or a flipper in everlasting friendship. Recommended.

Petra, about 1½ hours by car from the capital, offers a dot of territory which is an official part of the State of California—the house of the great Junipero Serra, who founded 21 missions on our West Coast and who changed the history of our Pacific area. The home is surprisingly small and sparsely furnished, but it reflects an interesting picture of eighteenth-century Mallorquin living; the nearby Museum Center of Studies contains paintings and books referring to this indomitable pioneer. If you've got time on your hands and adventure in your blood, you may take the aforementioned narrow-gauge

which pokes through the heart of the island to this little village; culture-minded motorists find it a convenient detour en route to the Drach Caves excursion. Especially appealing to Californians.

Valldemosa, the monastery where George Sand and Chopin once wintered, is what we consider a 21-carat tourist trap. While this famous couple were here, there was such mutual antipathy between them and the natives that they left the island under a cloud; now, however, the shrewd locals have "recreated" (to use a kind word) a shrine to these beloved historical characters—almost 100% for foreigners, who swarm through the phonied-up premises by the thousands upon thousands. The view is magnificent; the overcommercial atmosphere isn't. Clever job of "reconstruction," though, so long as the spectator realizes the width of the gap between "legend" (to be kind again) and fact. Only 11 miles from Palma; plenty of bus trips that stop here and continue to Sóller, which is pleasant from a scenic point of view.

The **Krekovic Collection**, devoted to Inca art and culture, is on display at *Son Fusteret*, about a mile from the center of Palma on Calle de Eusebio Estada, or the old road to Buñola. The subjects are monumental and (though the collection is specialized) are so linked to Hispano-American folklore that we think most travelers who have been lured to Iberia would appreciate this fascinating exhibition as much as we do. Open every day but Sunday.

The top **beaches** are at Formentor, Magaluf, Paguera, Cala d'Or, and San Vicente (beware of undertow at the last during certain sea conditions).

☑ **INFORMATION AND ASSISTANCE** The Spanish Tourist Office branch is on Jaime III in *Palma*; the top people there are its warmly congenial Delegado, Matias Mut, and the Office Chief, D. Miguel Sarmiento; you'll find the staff friendly and knowledgeable. Since no bookings or itinerary arrangements can be made here, we always use **Agencia Schembri, Viajes Marsans**, or **Viajes Iberia** (not to be confused with Iberia Airlines; representative of American Express) for tickets or reservations. All three are dependable; see Don Lorenzo Oliver at Schembri, Don Antonio Gómez Serra at Marsans, and Don Luis Linares at Iberia; all speak good English and are cordial in the extreme.

☑ **PERSONAL SERVICES** Sauna, massage, and physical beautification? **Don Abel González**, Spanish Olympic judoist and gymnast, master-muscles the handsomely rebuilt **Therapeutic Institute of Obesity and Aesthetics** (Monserrat 6, tel.: 21-44-52). Wet steam, dry steam, facials, electric or wax depilage, the works—all under medical direction. This engaging and very competent young man is the best masseur we've met anywhere, including Scandinavia; he has pummeled the Fielding ménage and their guests for many years, and we're all very fond of him. A sure cure for tense, weary, or hung-over pilgrims.

Movies in English: Watch the *Daily Bulletin* (see "Shopping") for the pro-

grams at **Cine Regina** (Teniente Mulet, Terreno). More and more first-run films are being shown. On that odd evening when you can't decide between the beach or the bar, see the Late-Late Show (9:30 P.M.) before you begin your night-beat beguine. Closed during part of the summer.

☑ **SHOPPING**   *Palma* is the shopping center; the choicest merchandise is here. Our ★ ★ ★ ★ ★ candidates are individually noted.

La Casa del Hierro (Calle Victoria 22) has striking wrought-iron bric-a-brac.

The ★ ★ ★ ★ ★ **Casa Bonet** (Puigdorfila 3) is to needlework what the Rolls-Royce is to cars—except for its fantastic price values. For nearly a century, Casa Bonet has won consistently every Exposition Gold Medal in sight and has spread the fame of Mallorquin hand embroidery all over the globe. The artistry of its 350 island specialists cannot be duplicated anywhere else today; its museum is an Aladdin's Cave of musical scores, Chinese calligraphy, and intricate etchings exquisitely duplicated by needle. The array of bridge sets, tablecloths, placemats, and the like—every stitch done by hand, in plain or colorful patterns—is (adjective applied literally) sensational. New pride of the house is its even-lower-cost, exclusive, perfectly executed line of machine-made linens of highest quality. For men or for women, one special suggestion: Class AAA linen handkerchiefs, *with your own signature or choice of 200 monogram styles* for one-quarter of U.S. prices. Don Alfredo Bonet, the global King of Embroidery, will be happy to greet you. Lovely branches in Madrid and Marbella (see "Shopping" in chapter on Spain). Super-super.

Pearls: Caution!! There is only one—we repeat, *one*—founder, developer, and leader of this industry: ★ ★ ★ ★ ★ **Perlas Majorica**, with 3000 artisans the largest in the world. Don't confuse it with "Majorca" or "Mallorca"—and be SURE to look for its "Official Agency" seal. Others are rank imitators, but at first sight these inferior ones so closely resemble the originals that it's difficult to tell them apart. Every individual Perla Majorica carries a unique 10-year (!) International Certificate of Guarantee which you may present in the U.S. or 50 other countries. Their sizes, also flawless, run from 4 to 14 millimeters in diameter—offering so many hundreds of combinations that many North American pilgrims end up buying several pieces. And the prices! For *exactly* the same Perlas Majorica exported globally, you'll pay a mere fraction here at the source. If you're making an island excursion to Manacor don't fail to visit the factory at Via Roma 52 or its new shop opposite. But if your sojourn is limited to Palma, its succulent shop is at Av. Jaime III 11, where you should ask for sweet Manageress Antonia Girbau. Buy *only* Perlas Majorica to be safe.

Top jewelers: **Sanz** (Plaza Pio XII 26) is Spain's traditional leader of the Classic School, with gorgeous things; it has branches in all principal Spanish cities. In Palma, you will be welcomed by 2 of the warmest, kindest, most delightfully friendly mortals on this Isle of the Calm—Director don Francisco de la Torre and his sweet English assistant, Mrs. Lesley Thomas. Pablo Fuster of **Relojeria Alemana** (Calle Colón 40) is the youngest man ever to win Spain's

coveted National Handicrafts Award for his unusual custom-made jewelry. He deserves it, think we.

Enchanting Oriental handicrafts and boutiques: The ★ ★ ★ ★ ★ **Manila** chain is the 14-year-old creation of Philippine gentlelady Mrs. Conchita Zethelius, the endearing suzerain of a miniempire of 5 large and successful shops. Twin hubs are the **Manila Import** sisters (Paseo Mallorca 4 and Av. Jaime III 6), proudly featuring exquisite Oriental treasures. **Manila High Selections** (Brossa 2) and ultra-exclusive **Manila Prestigio** (Tous y Maroto) are specialized boutiques. **Rodier** (Av. Jaime III 11) has the complete Spanish-manufactured Rodier sportswear line at 25% to 30% less than elsewhere in Europe. Astonishingly low prices; worldwide shipment; ask for the sparkling "Mrs. Tina" in person. Heavenly!

Outstanding footwear: Ladies' and men's shoes are one of Mallorca's biggest exports, and ★ ★ ★ ★ **Yanko** (General Mola 3) is the pacesetter of this key industry for all of Spain. Don José Albaladejo Pujadas presides over a miniempire of 7 spotless, modern factories which produce a dazzling variety of top-quality, exquisitely finished footwear, plus an 8th called **Coinsa** providing complimentary leather articles which adhere to the same superior standards. As an illustration of Yanko's progressiveness, all of its footwear is made in half-sizes for greater and more comfortable precision in fittings. Its boots for both genders are simply *beautiful*—and their prices are from 35% to 50% less than the best on Fifth Avenue! Among the supplementary items from Coinsa you will find suède and leather jackets and coats for ladies and for men, elegant handbags, business cases, belts, and more. A well-trained staff of specialists who are also multilingual would take friendly care of you. This go-go enterprise is expanding so fast that it has now opened similar branches in Madrid, Barcelona, Alicante, Vigo, and Paris. A reliable and excellent money-saver.

More leather accessories: Chic and glamorous **Loewe** (see the shopping section in Madrid) has an elegant branch at Paseo del Borne 2.

Suède and antelope wearables: After 30 years of searching, we have yet to find one outlet which completely satisfies us. None of the loudly touted factories and shops for antelope or suède in *Inca*, center of this industry, appeals to us much. Incidentally, most of the cheaper lines are so poorly dyed that the color will stain your hands and your body.

Glass: **Gordiola** (Calle Victoria 8) is internationally famous for its regional glassware of all types. Here is the finest quality and most outstanding selection on the island. We do not like the prices, attitudes, or swarms of bus traffic at the much-advertised *Campanet* center.

Antiques: **Linares** (near the Cathedral) rules the roost. It is a branch of the celebrated Madrid pacesetter. Both its stocks and its physical plant are in exquisite taste.

Newspapers: The *International Herald Tribune* is available at better hotels and newsstands. More fun is the English-language-American-idiom *Mallorca Daily Bulletin.* Jammed with island happenings; expert columnizing by gentle, universally esteemed "Benito" and irrepressibly fun-filled Riki Lash Lazaar

(see "My Own Place" in the "Night Life" section). Here's a colorful souvenir of your Mallorquin meanderings.

Dedicated shophounds: Space is too tight here for further listings—so consult this year's vastly expanded and updated pursesize edition of _Fielding's Selective Shopping Guide to Europe_ for more stores, more details, and more lore.

Monaco

Monaco, 12 miles east of Nice, has a higher population density (over 40 thousand per square mile) and a smaller total area (425 acres plus 75 which have been added through land reclamation) than any other nation in the world. It is just about half the size of New York's Central Park. The correct pronunciation is "MON-a-co," not "Mon-AH-co."

Ruled by members of the Grimaldi family since the late thirteenth century, it has been an independent state—almost unbelievable in Europe—since 1415. This remarkable dynasty—"Seigneurs" until 1621, when they became "Princes"—has reigned for more than 5½ centuries. The present sovereign's name is familiar in deepest Idaho, Nepal, and Slavonia—Prince Rainier III. Grace Kelly added further glitter to the royal fairytale that since has produced a prince (Albert) and 2 princesses (Caroline and Stéphanie).

The Principality is divided into 4 distinct sections: Old Monaco (a tiny antiquated village which sits on The Rock), La Condamine (home of many amiable Monégasques), Fontvieille (the industrial complex), and Monte Carlo (named for Charles III in 1866).

Each year 1½-million tourists come to the terraced hills and azure waters of Monaco, to play golf or tennis, to tie up their yachts, or to laze in the gentle sun by day and to dine, drink, dance, or gamble by night. The Monte Carlo Golf Club perches on the 2700-foot cap of neighboring Mont-Agel in France. Its 18 holes are scattered in the mountains in such a spectacular way that if the player carelessly stepped off the fairway to make a niblick shot, he might suddenly find himself doing a slow breast stroke in the sea. The Monte Carlo Country Club offers 20 championship tennis courts, several squash courts and practice courts, an attractive clubhouse, and the fabled Internationaux de Monte-Carlo tennis tournament one of the outstanding sports events of the year. For sailboat, motorboat, water-skiing, fishing, and skin-diving enthusiasts, the Yacht Club de Monaco has major interest. For skeet and electric-target fans, the Shooting Stand Rainier III is so fine that it's the site of the International Championship Meet in February.

In '67, as soon as the Prince Rainier forced Aristotle Onassis to turn over all of his holdings in the mighty *Société des Bains de Mer,* which owns and

operates 5 hotels, 18 restaurants, nightclubs, and the legendary Casino, Monte Carlo was launched on her glorious rebirth. A titanic national modernization plan was inaugurated, backed by the Prince's government and local private capital. Some 50 acres of new construction (1/6th of the country!) has been completed. To start, a great chunk of the 90-thousand square yards of avenue Princesse-Grace, wrung from the sea, is blooming as a flower-lined boulevard. An Olympic-caliber swimming pool has been excavated in front of the quai Albert Ier to supplement the terraced one at the Hôtel Métropole and the turquoise jewel at the Hôtel de Paris. The Spelugues Convention complex is functioning. Drilling crews spent 7 years burrowing a 2½-mile tunnel which now eliminates all surface railroad tracks from the landscape. A spankingly modern station has been unveiled, with a gleaming exposition hall and congress hotel spanning the former rail hub. The present harbor is being enlarged for major vessels, and a new yacht harbor and land site in Fontvieille has been completed. Monaco has a heliport that permits rapid linkage with the Nice International Airport. More than 1-million acres of undersea ground will be converted into a ½-mile bathing beach, part of which will be a costly underwater "dam" to retain the sand for your tootsies. The scope of the SBM's expansion activities, which currently involve 29 separate operations, is breathtaking. On its boards are 2 new hotels; an absolutely enormous new center for galas has been unveiled in the Larvotto area as a part of the reborn $7,000,000 Summer Sporting Club (with its own casino, of course). If you are a guest in an SBM hostelry, you may receive a "passport" admitting you to 5 Monte Carlo sports facilities free of charge. The chief of SBM operations is a U.S. citizen, Bernard Combemale, who recently was recruited by the Prince from his Wall Street precincts. Another satrap is the gifted Fred Laubi, one of the top hoteliers on 2 continents, who oversees SBM properties and tourist facilities. Here is an extraordinarily intelligent, vigorous, competent team which has already accomplished miracles and will soon be accomplishing many more.

The key to this revolutionary renaissance is the philosophy of the Crown. By seeking *selected* mass tourism—and by attracting the high-society group simultaneously—Monaco is having its cake and eating it too. It is superbly intelligent thinking which is bearing fruit in both directions. Prince Rainier and Princess Grace, who labor so tirelessly that they would exhaust the average business tycoon, merit hard-earned congratulations for their extraordinary vision and drive.

The economy has also blossomed into a diversity which old-timers find hard to believe. Chemicals, food products, chocolate, beer, plastics, precision instruments, beauty products, glass, ceramics, and printing now contribute between 25% and 30% of the total state revenue. Tourism and companion trades ante another 30%, stamps 8%, and taxes on tobacco and liquors, plus registration fees, provide the lion's share of the rest. The intake from the gambling concession, contrary to popular belief, makes up only about a 3% share—even when there's a good winning year. Unemployment is nonexistent.

The wheels of the world-famous Monte Carlo Casino, which start at 10 each morning (movie houses don't open until 2 P.M.!), have been spinning since 1856. Of all the gaming operations on the Riviera, this one is the unquestioned aristocrat, far better, in our view, than the American-style extravaganzas that are beginning to appear along this coast. In general, international businessmen (many of them Italian) and the minimum-ante curiosity seekers have replaced the Russian princes and Imperial ladies of the glittering past. Nevertheless, while Middle Eastern oil sheiks have lavished the U.K. casinos with heavy play since the oil embargo, a lot of Arabian Gulf shekels now are finding their way to the Côte d'Azur. In spite of the cycle—nadir or apex—it remains a *must* to every visitor, because in its heyday there was nothing in the world which approached it.

Radio Monte Carlo and Télé Monte Carlo, the local broadcasting and television stations, are powerful voices which are heard or seen throughout the Continent. A huge transmitter—said to be the world's most electronically potent commercial installation—is plugged in; oddly enough, France owns 83% and Monaco the remaining 17%.

Festivals, fireworks, dog shows, opera, ballet, fencing tournaments, international yacht races, swimming championships, lectures, the latest plays from Paris, religious pageants—these are but a few of the many activities and attractions.

Auto trials seem to hold a special fascination for the Monégasques. The *Grand Prix de Monaco,* first sponsored in 1929 by the national Automobile Club, continues to be the topranking race of all the *Courses dans la Cité.* It is run in May, and it counts toward the official world's driving championship. The annual *Rallye,* held around the last of January, is a particular favorite with Americans. Stock U.S. and European cars start from different points—Oslo, Glasgow, Lisbon, Athens, Frankfurt am Main, Paris, Warsaw, Monte Carlo itself—and "rally" along the way. Each has a handicap which brings him into the pack as the finish is approached. It is a contest of delicate timing and precision roadwork, not exclusively of speed. At the barrier in Monaco, climbing contests are then held on the Principality's steepest highways.

☑ **HOTELS** In the **Hôtel de Paris**, one of the 2 or 3 pacesetters within hundreds of miles, the feathers are flying. The client-staff ratio has been reestablished at 1-to-1. In this rambling Edwardian structure are housed sumptuous apartments complete with servants' quarters, the Empire Room restaurant dominated by a colossal Gervais mural painted in 1909, and a cellar of 185-thousand bottles of fine wines (including 35-thousand bottles of vintage champagne). Four additional stories of air-conditioned luxury suites ("La Rotonde"); 8th floor glass-wrapped Grill with nightly dancing; top-drawer boutiques in rear of the lobby. Another stunner is the huge, shell-roofed, oval, heated-seawater swimming pool niched on the cliffside augmented by 9 saunas, opulent dressing rooms, a bar, and a spacious terrace for sipping. Superb

administration headed by the previously mentioned Fred Laubi, famed for his masterly skills at the Ritz Carlton in Montreal and the Gritti in Venice; very, very expensive, but you're almost certain to be wrapped in cotton. There's a wonderful aura of charm about this lively old girl.

The **Hermitage,** owned by SBM, has rejoined the competitive fray with élan. Much to our delight, this weed-gone-to-seed has been totally revitalized in its Belle Époque tradition and is coming up curlicues. Revivified public areas; Princess Wing nobly living up to it Grace-cious name; vastly improved restaurant; 140 spic-and-costly nests radiating newborn glamour; gleaming brass beds; tasteful traditional trappings; modern, functional baths; full air conditioning. A bouquet to Manager Georges Maillet, who also cultivates the Old Beach. Heartily recommended, at long, long last.

The $100-million, 650-unit **Loews** hotel-apartment complex, a small city in itself, dips its toes directly into the Mediterranean at the foot of the cliffs below the Grand Casino adjoining the new congress hall. It contains its own Las Vegas style gaming room, 3 spectacularly outfitted restaurants including the Folie Russe supper club with cabaret, 3 bars, a discothèque, a surprisingly small rooftop pool, sauna, boutiques, and terraces with every accommodation. The décor is almost dazzling in its effort to evoke zip, zest, and pizzazz throughout. To fill it General Manager Maurice Briquet must accommodate many groups. Arresting, to say the least.

Another youngster is the 100-unit **Mirabeau,** which is linked to an even larger apartment complex; both segments here face the sea, but some of the finest waterfronters gaze onto a new freeway overpass which occludes the Med. The hotel is graciously clad in costly raiments, reflecting the excellent taste of Manager Karl Vanis. Cozy dining spread; superb service; just great, if it weren't for that darned pike's peek.

The **Nouvel**, connected by tunnel under the avenue Princesse Alice, might be called a 100-room annex of the Hôtel de Paris—even though this is not officially correct. *Don't let them shuttle you over here;* since the rates are identical, and since guests must make the cross-country hike to the de Paris dining room, Grill, or bar for their sustenance, most American travelers aren't at all happy in this area. There is talk that the SBM might redo it completely soon, but at this writing it is only talk.

The **Metropole** recently moved into Britain's Grand Metropolitan chain. Today this stately dowager's wrinkles are beginning to tattle on her. Nonetheless, while her makeup is peeling and her limbs are creaky, this grande dame retains many of her former charms. Fine restaurant with combo for dancing; summer bar on a tree-canopied patio; Amazon Bar for thirsting sea-gazers; fading pool and sun terrace; 3 communicating villas-in-waiting for long-term suitors. Total of 20 suites; 260 rooms which are comfortably bedded but in various stages of decline. Manager Jacques Simone should spruce up this lady posthaste.

The **Beach Plaza** on Larvotto Beach started life as an American Holiday Inn, but later became a subject of the British Trust House Forte group. Ideal location beside the Sea Club; year-round, heated, saltwater pool; lovely, elegant public rooms; 320 air-chilled doubles with color TV and radio. Its new owners announced plans to introduce a top-floor conference hall plus a new cocktail lounge and bar. Bid for a front room only, since the backs overlook a wall and a highway.

The **Old Beach** has 60 rooms (all with air conditioning and bath or shower), 7 bungalows, 200 dressing cabins, 144 cabanas, 34 private solaria, a restaurant, and 3 snack bars. Guests in all the *Société* hotels may use these facilities, but outsiders must pay an admission fee. Much better than it was.

In town, there's the cold-hearted **Europe** (53 bedchambers with 20 facing or peeking at the sea; pleasant lobby, bar, and remodeled dining salon, but upstairs furnishings scruffy; some baths separated from sleeping areas by curtains only) and the **Alexandra** (noisy, mid-nation perch; no restaurant; gaudy appointments; 60% bath/shower count; clean but achingly small-dimensioned).

The **Balmoral** also boasts a superb vista of the bay and some refashioning, but its rents are considerably higher.

The **Miramar**, on quai John F. Kennedy, comes up with 14 smallish rooms that are almost in the mast riggings of the yachts tied up at its doorstep. The restaurant is 25 steps away. Convenient for docksiders and now very good for its class. **Siècle**, near the station, is ideal for the student exile, but not much for the rest of us; snack bar and terrace restaurant for contemplating the world's problems over an inexpensive Pernod; fun if you're the right age.

☑ **RESTAURANTS** Most spectacular, of course, is the **Black Jack Club**, with its big-name international cabaret; it is downstairs at the **Casino**. Go for dinner or later; the cuisine is just fair; the music (provided by a 16-piece honey-smooth orchestra during a recent repast) is so delightfully danceable you'll forget that anything such as a Rolling Stone ever existed. In the same class is the **International Sporting Club** (winter); the **Summer Sporting Club**, which now is comprised of the Maona, La Salle des Etoiles, Jimmy'z and Parady'z, plus the gaming rooms and recreation facilities is glamorous to look at, but is it ever expensive—and the food we sampled was not at all noteworthy (big notes, too!). The **Winter Sporting Club** (Dec. 20 to Easter) is open only for major events and entertainments; most fashionable is the Easter Bal Paré dinner, with Christmas, New Year's TV Festival, and Rallye evenings the runners-up. Another offering music at least part of the year is **des Ambassadeurs**. Among worthy hotel candidates, the aforementioned Folie Russe in **Loews** generates excitement and rubles with its high-cost cookery and cabaret; the Empire Room and the Grill of the **de Paris** are both outstanding. **Monte Carlo Beach** also has a luxury restaurant with a pleasant atmosphere.

Rampoldi has fine cuisine, but those tabs—wow! Our flea-size lunch for 2 was gargantuanly priced; we're happy we weren't *really* hungry. Small, well-decorated, partitioned room; service that was professionally meticulous but so glacial, mechanical, and disinterested it chilled our gizzards; to us, this establishment seems to reflect a we-love-money-but-not-the-customers attitude. The cookery, however, is excellent.

Bec Rouge is almost as good, but here, too, the tariffs have jumped so high that we wondered if what we last consumed here was worth it. The slightly sterile atmosphere is softened by flowers; 22 tables inside; 15 on avenue St.-Charles for summer alfresco dining. There's a fixed meal and a full carte of more than 30 items. Young, aggressive M. Roux is your pleasant host. He is also the proprietor of **Le Petit Bec** on avenue de Grande Bretagne. On the same Av. St. Charles, **La Calanqueat** is said to be a worthy deluxe contender, but so far we have missed it.

As for others, **Astoria** appealed to us for its quietly sophisticated ambiance and recommendable cuisine. Bar at the portal with a lone cream-color room farther back; our meal was reasonably priced and appetizing; the house Bordeaux was outstanding; we experienced good service, too. Worth a try. The **Vesuvio** is no big puff of smoke. On The Rock, the **Pinocchio** now seems to enjoy a rock-hard reputation. **Rugantino** (2 rue des Iris) is another challenger in Italian kitchen. **La Chaumière**, near the Exotic Gardens, can be marvelous for Mother Nature's scenery but is low on man-made décor; it loads up with so many bus tours in summer that these scenic joys take 30th place. **St. Nicholas**, near the Royal Palace, tried to pass off on us canned paté of wild boar as the fresh variety. Our steak was so thin that it better belonged on a microscope slide in Lab. 32. The **International**, also close to the Regal Residence, is decked out in the rustic mood, highlighted by checkered tablecloths. We enjoyed its skillful skilletry and modest price tags. For Polynesian platters on wax as well as on porcelain, park your outrigger at **Jimmy'z**, next to **Maona** (exotic cookery) on the beach. This sassy **South C's** discothèque, named after New Jimmy's in Paris, has as its guiding coxwain the same swaggering Régine. She also is responsible for **Parady'z** in the same Sporting Club complex. A New Orleans belle rings praise for **Belli**, which she calls "an unusually satisfactory and modestly sealed Italian entry." We'll decipher that semantic plateful on our next session behind the Monégasque napkins. **La Rascasse**, down at the moorings, served us a tongue-twisting lunch in grim surroundings; no English spoken; a favorite of Algerian immigrants; sinking fast. **La Calanque** is any angler's big catch for fish. One of the best of the finny tribe on the coast. L'Escale first changed its cuisine and its name to **Chinatown**, then moved to a modern site at the port while the **Mandarin** took over the original venue. Neither appealed to us one yuan's worth. **Le Dragon d'Or** is a tearoom with extra-tempting pastries—edible variety.

Light bites? The imposing **Café de Paris**, opposite the Hôtel de Paris adjoining the Casino, is your best bet. Its air-conditioned interior is modern and

pleasant; its big alfresco terrace supports perhaps 75 tables; a string ensemble performs here even at *noon,* yet! (Is it the only snack bar in the world with live Bach and Beethoven?) Its specialty is onion soup, but there is a vast choice of hot and cold plates, salads, sandwiches, ice creams, pastries, and the like. Here is the most pleasant stop of its category in the Principality. **Le Drugstore** is the roundup point for the more lively cowboy-and-gal—in an innovation inspired, no doubt, by the fantastic success of its Parisian predecessors— everything from *le hamburger* (ouch!) to *le whisky* to *le parfum* to *les souvenirs corny,* but no pharmaceuticals; open 24 hours daily. Our recent brace of hamburgers à la Holstein and milkshakes totaled more than $22! **Crêperie,** up an alley near the Royal Palace, is a far better snackery, especially for its pizzas, sandwiches, and thin pancakes. Tables and benches; the wide variety of crêpes for very low tabs; pleasant family operation; open late; griddles of fun. **L'Ariston** seems to be stealing the local thunder from **Tip Top**; very "in" at the instant. An alternative is **Le Roxy**, for the pick of the crop. The youthful, tiny, and attractive **Le Louisiane,** near the Bristol, at harborside, features sandwiches, drinks, and youthful romancing à la 1 glass and 2 straws.

Short excursion? The 10-minute run up to the **Hostellerie Jérôme** at *La Turbie* (in France) is a favorite of many Monégasques—and of ours too. Ancient stone house with a 10-table main room and a 4-table dogleg; tiny patio for sipping; ornately painted ceiling; great sprays of flowers and bowls of fruit; menus on huge leather-covered parchment broadsides. Almost no view; open every day in summer; closed in November; between times, be sure to telephone from town first to see if anything's cooking. If you seek panaromantics at higher prices but with lower quality food, the restaurant of the **Hôtel Vistaëro,** at nearby *Roquebrune* (described in the "French Riviera" chapter), may be your candidate.

Pissaladìera, Socca, Pan Bagnat, and Tourta di Ge are among the food specialties. The "blond" Monaco beer, 4-quart steins of which are sold near the Gate of the Royal Palace, is known all over the world for its excellence.

☑ **NIGHT LIFE** The **Monte-Carlo Sporting Club**, on a terrace over the sea, is by far the most chichi oasis during the warm months. During galas, 1200 guests are accommodated in this handsome (and expensive) social center. Now the terraced clubhouse is deftly screened by roof gardens. Its counterpart, the **International Sporting Club**, is opened on December 24, for the winter season only. The **Winter Sporting Club** has been previously mentioned. **Le Black Jack** at the Casino draws the elite of 6 continents. The **Empire Room** of the Hôtel de Paris is also smart, swank, and glittering. **Loews** features its own casino plus the doin's in its supper club and discothèque. The **St. Louis**, done up in American 1890's trappings, is another one. It is small, clean, and recommended. Don't forget the previously mentioned **Jimmy'z.** For an informal beer, it's **l'Ariston**, the **Britannia**, or the **Tip Top**. Finally the **Open Air**

Cinema, miniskirting the Mediterranean, proudly advertises that it shows "100 films in 100 days"—but who wants to go to the movies in Monte Carlo?

☑ **DAY LIFE**   The ubiquitous fêtes, galas, and sports already mentioned; the Prince's Palace (open to the public from July to Oct.; tapestries, art treasures, Napoleonic memorabilia, view of the bay); the National Museum (believe it or not, children will love it); the Oceanographic Museum (one of the world's oldest, finest, and most important, directed by Commandant Cousteau of underwater-exploration fame, with an extraordinary aquarium, a Deep Sea exhibition, and a magnificent collection of nautical wonders and formalde-hideous freaks); the Zoological Acclimatization Center of Monaco (Prince Rainier III founded this project in '54, and it remains his favorite); the Museum of Prehistoric Anthropology (also entered through the Exotic Garden). Big concerts are given in the Court of the Prince's Palace during the summer. Finally, the gardens of the Principality are famous for their beauty—Casino, St. Martin (bordering the Oceanographic Museum), Parc Princesse Antoinette (olive trees millennia old), and the strange Exotic Garden itself (thousands of plants, from semidesert countries, which cling to the slopes of the mountain, flourishing in their new environment). Their climax comes with the Monaco Garden Club's International *Concours* of bouquets in May—a beautiful "do."

☑ **INFORMATION ON MONACO**   This nation's excellent **Direction du Tourisme et des Congrès** couldn't be more cooperative. Experienced Louis Blanchi is its Director. It will give you full information about the Principality, and furnish you with a raft of well-prepared maps, brochures, and booklets about Monaco, its environs, and foreign tourist centers of importance. Location: Smack in the center of Monte Carlo, at 2A boulevard des Moulins. Hours: Mon.-Sat., 9 AM.-7 P.M.; Sun. and holidays, 9 A.M. to noon. If you can't wait, go to 20 E. 49th St. (Telex 42-05-94), and the Monaco Tourist Office will trigger golden Riviera reveries before you leave the sidewalks of Gotham.

☑ **CUSTOMS AND IMMIGRATION**   None. Get a visa only if you want it as a souvenir in your passport; the cost is $1. Bring in a suitcase full of cigars, a barrel of whisky, a fortune in gold, and they're delighted!

Netherlands

Holland is such a tiny country that South Carolina, our fortieth state, covers twice as much ground; multiply the population of Brooklyn roughly by 5, and you'll have every living being within its borders. Yet this microscopic midget has enormous sinews; it is unequivocally a major power today.

The mixup on national terminology is still going on. They've been fighting about it since 1842, and there's still no decision in sight.

The Netherlands covers 11 national provinces, of which Holland is only a segment (this one divided into North and South counties); the Netherlanders are the people-as-a-whole, while the Hollanders, Zeelanders, Brabanders, and other local groups make up the country. "Dutch" is a generic term which means precisely nothing; the Germans are "Dutch" too, and that's why so many local burghers shudder when the word is applied.

Yet—Holland and Dutch are so deeply rooted that "the Netherlands" and "Netherlanders" are applied only by purists and the government. So here's our theory: While it's linguistically incorrect, common usage is a better criterion. Let's call the nation Holland and its people the Dutch or Hollanders.

Nearly ½ the land is below high-tide level. Were it not for her engineers, the nation would be 50% soil and 50% H_2O, twice daily. Water is the everpresent, ever-threatening problem. Since A.D. 1200, an estimated 1,400,000 acres have vanished into Davy Jones's locker. Of this, the Dutch have salvaged almost 1,300,000, acres. They've partially tamed it with fabulous chains of dikes, put it to work on 5000 miles of canals and pushed it back in reclamation projects which make Hoover Dam a merit-badge project for aspiring Boy Scouts. Recovery of the Zuiderzee, 1350 square miles of salt lakes, started in 1928 with the construction of the enclosing dike; many dams (the largest 18½ miles long), giant tidal sluices, huge "polders," 2000 pumping stations, and the latest scientific know-how have changed the face of the countryside. In an area nearly as large as Rhode Island, whole new villages have been created; fertile soil valued at $253,000,000 has been added to the national resources.

The **Dutch climate** is on a par with Ireland's. It's about as unattractive, for year-round living, as London or New York. There is a fair amount of sunshine

—witness the phenomenal growth of a wide variety of plants—but when it's not making honest rain, you can bet a guilder to a dubbeltje that it's foggy from the sea. Average humidity is high; to us (but not to a Dutchman!) the sunbeams seem about as virile as a glass of French beer. Winters are colder than those in Eastern England; Utrecht, roughly in the center, has a January mean of 35°, a July mean of 62°. You'll be thankful for your tweeds about 300 days in the year.

The beloved former Queen Juliana has just turned over the throne to her daughter, Queen Beatrix. Both are direct descendents of William the Silent, the Dutch George Washington. Their House of Orange is one of the oldest and most respected hierarchies in the world.

Holland—as if you didn't know—is famous for its many flowers, which bloom until late fall. The best season is April to June. The village of **Boskoop**, with 700 nurseries, is the largest horticultural center in the world. **Aalsmeer**, 10 miles from Amsterdam, has weekday floral auctions which draw scores of fascinated tourists (see "Other Targets"), plus a vast facility for experimental floristry. Within 20 miles of **The Hague** is the tulip center. Don't miss the **Keukenhof Flower Exhibition** if you're in Holland between about end-March and mid-May (dates subject to weather). It's a comfortable afternoon expedition from Amsterdam.

The finest trip in Holland—one of the most stimulating holidays in Europe —is the circuit of what we'll still call the *Zuiderzee* (the official name is now the "IJsselmeer"), with a stopoff at the wild and beautiful island of *Texel*. The Zuiderzee is a gigantic lake that indents the center of Holland's coastline all the way down to Amsterdam. This body of water is divided into two parts by a 17-mile-long dam from Enkhuizen to Lelystad, which will be dubbed the future capital of the 12th Dutch province (every square inch of it on reclaimed land). The drive along this causeway is a fluidly awesome experience, with nothing but water on either side.

If you're driving your own automobile, you can make the Zuiderzee circle in 1 day of hard pushing—omitting Texel, of course. The short, quick round, however, is not recommended because the pace will knock you out. If you can spare 2 days, you must still skip Texel; in this case, by far the best place to spend the night is the Hotel Wientjes or the Postiljon Motel, both in *Zwolle* (or perhaps at the Stadsherberg in nearby *Kampen*). Though deep in the rural district, their comfort is good. If you can spare 3 or even 4 days, you are in for a junket you'll never forget, for here's the real heart of Holland.

Three points to remember: (1) The Texel ferry accepts automobiles only on a first-come-first-served basis, (2) sailings from Den Helder to Texel depart at least once an hour year round, and (3) waiting times in midsummer can be irksome and long.

At the western flank of this crescent, the once-classic tourist meccas of *Marken* (closed to auto traffic but with parking lots at the fringe) and *Volendam* are not recommended today. We've again returned from a thoroughgoing

tour of both these gimmick hubs, and this admonition, published annually in this book for 3 decades or so, now becomes even stronger. The Dutch Government has been laboring valiantly to knock some manners into these rotten-spoiled villagers and to root out the phony-baloney sham that has flummoxed so many foreign visitors—with some success in Volendam, and less in Marken. Our advice: Skip these traps and go to *Spakenburg* instead; it's in the middle of the crescent heading east out of Amsterdam. Here's a hamlet where the folk dress and charm are far more genuine. Customary hours for wearing these togs is on Sundays around church-meeting time: 9 A.M. to 9:30 A.M. or 6:30 P.M. to 7 P.M. Or. go on from Zwolle to *Giethoorn* (called "The Dutch Venice," but the residents seldom don costumes nowadays), the former island of *Urk*, or *Staphorst*. These are not hammy theatrical displays.

Again, if you have a car, there are bushels of ooohs and aaahs in the more populated zones roughly within the Amsterdam–Rotterdam–Utrecht triangle. Whiz down to *Gouda* (pronounced not as "GOO-da," but as "HOW-da"). On the plaza surrounding the Town Hall, with its contrasting red-and-white shutters and gold trim, dairy farmers sell their famous cheeses every Thursday morning from mid-May to mid- September; a smaller flower sale is held at the same place on Saturday. You can sip a coffee in the 400-year-old **Hotel de Zalm**, on the periphery of the main square, before pushing on to either *Woerden*, another cheese center (by the main highway), or to *Oudewater*. In the latter, ladies, you can be weighed on the town scales. If you register even 1 oz. more than the minimum for a true mortal, you will be given a certificate declaring that you are not a witch (they are presumed to weigh less than normal gals). Personally, we're in love with the tiny, tiny canalside path that ambles through Oudewater and stretches on to *Utrecht*. Should you seek an off-trail adventure that really takes you through the backwash farmlands of the nation, don't miss this sampling of bucolic charm at its pastoral best. Utrecht has her diversions (see "Other Targets"), but we prefer to skim along east to *Soesterberg* for lunch at the 't Zwaantje ("The Little Swan") before viewing the Royal Palace at nearby *Soestdijk*. Then a 1-hour detour to *Muiden*, site of the beautifully preserved thirteenth-century fortress of the same name, is rewarding (but be sure to check on the exact closing time before leaving your hotel, because it varies with the season). You could move further east to *Otterlo* where there are 272 van Gogh paintings and a lovely garden at the **Kröller-Müller Museum**. As for other rambles, *Zandvoort Beach* is passable. Except for the memorabilia of the Pilgrim Fathers, the University, and the ethnological museum, *Leyden* is nothing special. *The Hague* has excellent museums. The lively beach resort of *Scheveningen*, and a fairy-tale wonder for kids and adults alike: **Madurodam**, the most amazing miniature city in existence. This modern-day Lilliput, condensed into approximately 4 acres, employing 2¼ miles of railway track, and illuminated by 44-thousand lights, is a complete community of castles, churches, homes, shops, docks, airport—everything imaginable. And the thousands of details are a perfect

1/25 of their normal scale. More than 1 million visitors promenade its 2-mile circuit annually. It's open from early April to early October, including Sunday; the admission price is peanuts; depending upon the month, closings are 9:30 P.. to 11 P.M.; a restaurant is on the premises; don't miss this unique attraction, whether you're 7, 17, or 70. *Rotterdam*, slightly more than an hour from Amsterdam, has some glorious river views and some excellent harbor installations. Try the **VVV Sightseeing Tour**, leaving at 1:30 P.M. (until 4 P.M.) daily from April through September, which costs about $10 per person, including entrance. It fans out from the VVV office; this is the best. Or try one of the well-known **Spido** cruises of the fabulous docks—1¼ hours on the briny, with frequent departures in both summer and winter, and watertaxi service, all from the Willemsplein Landing Stage. The best canal trips leave from the area near the main station; the ones leaving from in front of the Park Hotel are small beer in comparison. Day excursions to the aforementioned Delta works are also on tap for dedicated polder peepers. As another choice, spins by car to the Mill District have been inaugurated. The **Blijdorp Zoo**, perhaps the most modern in Europe, is also a treat for Bronx Zoo fans—and who isn't? And the new "Lijnbaan" Shopping Center brings cheers from even Texas, California, or Florida gals. Further suggestions for Rotterdam may be found under "Other Targets."

☑ **TRANSPORTATION Taxis** We used to nourish the illusion Dutch cab drivers were more trustworthy than their colleagues in most other European lands. But now, on repeated recent visits, they cheated us blind—or tried to!—at least ¼ of the time. It's disappointing in a nation of such legendary integrity.

As for gratuities, the meter reading now includes the full legal tip. What a boon this is! When you jump in, be sure the flag is pulled down at the beginning—and at the end, be sure he doesn't roll the tabulations back to zero before you have a chance to *see for yourself* what they read. In the larger centers take only cabs with meters; in the villages they may not be so equipped. Then you should always find out the cost before climbing aboard.

You'll find it difficult to hail a street cruiser; head for a taxi rank instead or for the nearest telephone in order to summon a cab.

Trains Fast service, accurate schedules, high frequency. Among the world's most modern rolling stock, 100% electric or diesel—but equipment still isn't sufficient to cope with the enormous traffic demands. During rush hours, you might stand all the way. Always ride First class, because distances are short, the price difference is trivial. (Warning: Both First and Second can be overcrowded during rush hours.)

Electric trains run from Amsterdam to The Hague every quarter hour; some have coffee bars. "D" and "TEE" trains have adequate dining cars. Fares are extremely low. "D" trains charge an inexpensive supplement at the ticket office or on the rods, and they're worth it.

Watch out for the inland 1-day excursion ticket, because the return half expires as soon as the last train on the timetable of that night pulls out. The free publication, "Day Trips

in Holland," available at the sales window of any station, has further information about this.

The best bet for serious riders (unless you have your Eurailpass) is the 8-day season ticket which is valid all over the Netherlands Railways network and on The Hague-Amsterdam bus. Use it until calluses appear on your nether regions—as often and as much as you like—for approximately $45 in First or $28 in Second class. Such money-savers as the Day Rover (24 hours for $14 or less), the Day Multi-Rover or "Meerman's Kaart" (designed for 2-to-6-person groups), and the Weekend or Evening Returns are also available. _Bring a passport photo if you want to be a "Rover" boy or girl._

Porters are found only at the larger stations. A few—not all—possibly could be termed robbers. You must pay a set rate per piece, plus a tip—but don't give them more than a 20% gratuity, even if their bleats can be heard all the way to the Hook-of-Holland. They may be ordered in advance through a special postcard furnished by the railway. As we oafishly stare at the Dutch text and unintelligible blank spaces on the sample before us, however, we've decided we'd rather heft 800-lb. barbells than try to cope with this form.

☑ **FOOD**   The Dutch relish their food; their cuisine, at its best, is delicate, savory, and full of unexpected nuances. At its worst, however, it's torpid, greasy, overrich, and as heavy as U-235.

Under ideal circumstances, breakfast offers a choice of various breads, jelly, butter, cheese (always), tea or coffee, and sometimes a boiled egg or meat. The famous "Dutch Coffee Table" (sometimes a warm dish, then cold meats, cheese, fruits, and beverage) is the national lunch. Many people have a light afternoon tea, and dinner is always the heaviest meal of the day.

Typical Dutch dishes are also typically American: Steak with French fries and salad, asparagus with egg and butter sauce, boiled beef. More exotic are minced beef (rolpens) with fried apples and, in winter, curly cabbage and sausage, hotchpotch (hutspot), and that famous, wonderful pea soup. Oh oh OH, that delight of the last! Let the good local burghers save it for ice-skating time; we like this magnificent erwtensoep about 364 days of the year. It's loaded with spicy sausages and pork fat; it's as thick as diesel oil, as rich as supercondensed cream, as inert as infantry pancakes, and as indigestible as green sawdust—but is it good! Nearly everybody goes for this Polaris of the Lowlands Kitchen.

Some specialties of the Netherlands are herring (try Hollandse Nieuwe—"new" herring—springtime only, as an appetizer), smoked eels (excellent) and other fish; cheese; Deventer gingerbread, currant bread, small sugared fritters (poffertjes); mouth-melting chocolate (Droste and Van Houten are the best); a special caramel candy (Haagse Hopjes), and an unusual egg-flip concoction (Advocaat). Most of them are delicious.

The best bet of all—something no American should miss—is the world-famous rijstta-fel (pronounced rye-staffel, and translated as rice table). This, for want of a more descriptive phrase, was the ceremonial feast of the Dutch colonists in Indonesia. The cuisine is like nothing most of us have ever sampled—vaguely Chinese, but with such major departures that it is unique in the annals of dining. The most recent ones we

staggered through, at the Bali restaurants in both Amsterdam and Scheveningen, consisted of nearly 30 separate platters—platters, not dishes—and, washed down by a couple of steins of good Holland beer, it was worth all the dreams that later plagued us. Starve yourself all day; permit yourself only 1 order of Sateh Babi (spit-roasted pork on a stick in a delicious hot sauce) with your cocktails; when you sit down to face the dizzy array, put 2 spoonfuls of rice in the center of your plate and *limit yourself to 1 small taste of everything.* Otherwise, you're licked from the start. Highest recommendation of all for any visitor.

Skip lobster in Holland; 95% of the supply is imported these days, and it costs up to Rockefeller levels. Fresh or smoked salmon is in the same category.

If you're hungry at an odd hour of the day, try an Uitsmijter sandwich (translated as "Bouncer"). It's one of the 3 national types: Roast beef, ham, or veal (take your choice), with lots of trimmings, and a fried egg on top. A wonderful bedtime snack, if your stomach is a Bessemer converter.

Price tags for dining well in Holland are rising swiftly, but still they're nothing like the costs in Belgium or France. In average places you'll pay $11 for a routine meal, but in the Deluxe restaurants it's easy to triple these minimums, without wine.

For your run-of-the-mill fare, stick to the smaller establishments. A Tourist Menu promotion, in which 700 restaurants have agreed to offer a 3-course meal for a top tariff of about $6, is worth checking into if you're a bargain hunter. First-class hotels are steep; top restaurants are often sky high. There are many snack bars which serve good cafeteria-style food at low prices. You can point at your choice instead of fighting the menu.

☑ **DRINKS** A bonanza in scope. Unknown brands of Scotch can be bought for about $7, with proprietary brands running up to $18.50-or-so; imported ryes, bourbons, gins, rum, Canadian Club, and others are well represented in the better shops, bars, and restaurants, at decent prices. And those good, GOOD Heineken and Amstel beers, bless their soothing souls, are about 55¢ per mug.

Dutch gin (they call it *jenever*) is for taste buds which can flash a college degree. It's colorless, volatile, aromatic, slightly bitter—a flavor you'll find in no other bottle in no other land. The "Oude Klare" is stronger (80 proof) and has greater distinction than the more popular and lighter (70 proof) "Jonge," which compares vaguely to a vodka. Our favorite brand is Bokma, available almost everywhere. Drink it from a shot glass; when you blow out your breath, be careful of that stranger's cigarette 20 feet away. (If proper form is followed, it will be served, instead, in a "tulip" glass—and your first sip must be slurped while the glass rests on the bar!) Never, never attempt to make a martini of it, as we did; the results curled our locks. It simply isn't made for mixing.

The liqueurs, over 40 varieties, are interesting. Ask for Bols or Hoppe products, which are dependable, while some imitations are not.

★ **TIPS** When the drinks are on you, say "Let's have a *borrel!*" It's the universal Dutch invitation; in Americanese, it translates "Got time for a short one, brother?"

The historical national toast is *"Op uw gezondheid,"* which means "To your good health." Most Dutchmen settle for a simple *"Proost"* before the elbow bends and a few use an affected *"Santé,"* derived from the French, *naturellement.*

Since brewers are usually given exclusive contracts, most Dutch restaurants sell only 1 brand of beer.

☑ **TIPPING**   Hotels take 15% automatically on stays less than 6 days (10% for longer visits); this includes bar tabs charged to your room. Waiters get 15% (also always included in your bill). Theater usherettes and washroom attendants deserve the Dutch equivalent of a dime at the most. A law bundles the gratuity into the hairdresser's chit. Give the hall porter in your hotel a few guilders when you check out; he works hard for you, and it's the usual thing to do. Give the maid or other staff people a few guilders, too, if you have had any special services.

In general, the Dutch are far less grabby than the French or Italians but not quite so unmercenary as the Norwegians or Danes. Use your judgment, and you'll get along famously.

☑ **LOCAL RACKETS**   The Dutch are square shooters; 99.99% of them are too dignified and decent to stoop to chicanery. Aside from the occasional larcenous taxi driver, Marken, Volendam, and the Seamen's Quarter in Amsterdam or its equivalent in other cities (even Hollanders ask for trouble when they venture here), you'll encounter honesty and integrity.

☑ **INFORMATION CENTERS**   Spiritually, a huge welcome mat, in neon lights. They want North American tourists, not only for dollars, but for the deep kinship they feel with the American people.

The Netherlands National Tourist Office (NNTO) is one of the best-managed and smoothest-functioning agencies of its type on the Continent. Typical Dutch efficiency, attention to detail, and kindness are reflected by its Director General, Joop Strijkers. This is the fountainhead of Dutch tourism; there are branches in 9 major European centers. In New York, the address is 576 Fifth Avenue, and the Managing Director is J.G. Bertram. In San Francisco, it's 681 Market St., Room 941, with Manageress Mrs. C. Davidson behind the desk and the smile. In Toronto, your Dutch uncle is C. K. Kammeyer at suite 3310, Royal Trust Tower, Dominion Centre.

Working with NNTO are more than 450 local offices scattered throughout the Netherlands, supported mainly by local contributions. These are called **VVV**, and there is 1 for every Dutch hamlet which can show the census takers a population of more than 2 human beings, 3 dogs, and 5 cows. You'll find these offices everywhere, and they are an enormous help to the wanderer. *Amsterdam*'s VVVs are on Rokin 5 and opposite the Central Station—both in the highly capable hands of A. F. Luyken (division on Utrechtseweg); the *Rotterdam* branch is at Stadhuisplein 19 (other booths at the station and Zuidplein); *The Hague* offers one in the center at Groenmarkt, another near Central Station, and a third at *Scheveningen* on the central square.

The interesting program "**Get in Touch with the Dutch**," run by the Amsterdam VVV, is similar to the Scandinavian operations. To meet your opposite number in his or her home and have a cozy look at family life after 8 P.M. in the Lowlands, apply in person for your application at Rokin 5.

The peak tourist season is June and July—but, if you're wise, you'll avoid the crush (and find still greater beauty!) by planning your trip for late spring (April is busier than June) or early fall.

CITIES

AMSTERDAM lighted its 700th anniversary candle in 1975, but it is younger than ever in spirit. The city has much in common with Boston, Massachusetts. It has the same twisting little streets, funny little shops, and Dutch Renaissance or baroque buildings, but most striking of all is its blend of old and new. You can step from the Kalverstraat, the Boylston Street of Holland, and find yourself in sleepy by-lanes a few feet wide; in 3 or 4 seconds you'll lose 3 or 4 centuries. Its main boulevard, Leidsestraat, is a handsome, vital pedestrian mall. Construction of a subway system is currently under way both underground and underwater; a line has just bubbled up connecting Schiphol Airport to Minervalaan Station with departures every 20 minutes. Canals intersect the city at dozens of angles—so don't be surprised if you see a barge or two politely waiting for a traffic light at the local Copley Square. Yet this metropolis is so wide awake that more than 150 American companies have opened offices here during the past several years. The hotel picture has improved considerably. There are plenty of fine restaurants and lively night-clubs, crowded transport, attractions such as the magnificent State Museum (better known as the Rijksmuseum), the Municipal Museum, the awesome van Gogh Museum, the new Historical Museum (housed in a 17th-century orphanage), Rembrandt's House, Royal Palace, the Concertgebouw, the Anne Frank House (having financial troubles), historical maritime and aviation displays, diamond-cutting workshops, pushcarts with raw herring, streamlined department stores, broad *grachten* lined with elms, the House of the Sculptured Heads—a wonderful panorama of color and beauty in majestic old Amsterdam. It's the financial center, the shopping center—and with hundreds of summertime youths huddling wherever the authorities permit, a gradually diminishing hippie epicenter. Don't miss it.

Sightseeing The first thing you should do is to take a boat ride (**rondvaart**) around the city—especially during the Festival (see below), when everything's ablaze with special illumination from 8:30 P.M. to midnight. For about $2.75 you can travel for 1¼ hours, and you'll treasure the barge pilot's view of the most intriguing canals. Along the Rokin, the Nassaukade, and the Damrak you'll find 4 or 5 lines, all controlled by the municipality. (As mentioned, don't bother with the one opposite the Park Hotel; their service on our recent cruise did not include the harbor.) The boats leave at 30-minute intervals; they all have glass roofs. Here is a junket that is really fun. You'll see everything from the Blue Bridge to the Brewer's Canal to the red-light district. Candlelight cruises begin at 9 P.M. and last until 11:45 P.M. from April 13 to October 15 (departure is a half hour later in June and July); there's a ½-hour port-o'-call at a flavorful pub; in this package you'll receive a glass of wine and

no end of wonders in a city where every light is reflected hundreds of times in the rippling canals. The local VVV can get you aboard.

Next, no traveler should *dream* of missing the **Rijksmuseum**, with its unparalleled collection of Old Dutch masters; Rembrandt's "Night Watch" is, of course, its star attraction.

Rijksmuseum Vincent Van Gogh (Paulus Potterstr.) is devoted to the works of the master and to his friends and contemporaries, such as Gaugin, Manet, and Toulouse-Lautrec.

The nearby **Stedelijk** ("Municipal Museum," Paulus Potterstr. 13) offers a modern art panoply from Picasso to Chagall, Monet, Miró, Degas, Cézanne, Braque, Mondrian, Matisse, and Toulouse-Lautrec. The most illustrious American painter represented? Willem de Kooning whose name and heritage bring delight to local connoisseurs. It is operative from 9:30 A.M. to 5 P.M. on weekdays and from 1 P.M. to 5 P.M. on Sunday. The gate toll is $1 for adults, 50¢ for children under 16 and members of groups.

Time out now for a breather? **Heineken Brewery** (Van der Helststr. 30) is the beeline target of battalions of thirsty visitors who are enamored of this zesty Golden Liquid. Go to the Stadhouderskade entrance Monday through Friday; shuttle into the staging area between 9 and 11 A.M. (only during the summer); its delicious beer with niblets of cheese await you at tour's end. Fanciful, filling, fun and also only 40¢.

The 4-story **Anne Frank House** (Prinsengracht 263), in which the martyred child wrote her 2-year diary before being discovered and killed by the Nazis, is in deep financial trouble. The Anne Frank Foundation, launched in '60 to keep the house open as a permanent monument to the dangers of political extremism, now charges $1.50 for adults and 50¢ for those under 18 in order to maintain this cause. We believe that this symbol of courage in the face of inhumanity is worth an hour of your time and as many loose guilders as you can contribute beyond the modest entry fee.

Madame Tussaud's (Kalverstr. 156) is fashioned in the image of the famous London waxery—perhaps not quite as slick, but still engaging on first blush. Open daily from 10 A.M. to 6 P.M. in winter but extended by several hours in summer.

Aspiring architects and perspiring rubbernecks may also find pleasure in one or more of the following: (1) **Royal Palace** (built as the town hall in 1662; perched on exactly 13,659 pilings; famous for van Helt Stockade's allegoric ceiling paintings; open Mon. to Fri. from 10 A.M. to noon and from 1 to 4 P.M. between June 1 and the 3rd week in August, with a 50¢ gate fee for adults and half price for youngsters); (2) **Nieuwe Kerk** (late Gothic Church with wooden vaults and uniquely clustered columns); (3) **Oude Kerk** (consecrated in 1306; Iron Chapel which houses timeworn municipal documents; steeple carillon); (4) the **Waag** (completed in 1488, but previously used as the town gate; contains the Jewish Historical Museum; merchants' weights-and-measures house until 1819; circular floorplan); (5) **Portuguese Synagogue** (early seventeenth-century

structure; a haven for refugees from the Inquisition); and (6) the **Stock Exchange** (built in 1903; the earliest employment of structural iron).

The **Beguinage** (end of Begijnensteeg, off Kalverstraat) is a courtyard quadrangle of seventeenth-and eighteenth-century homes which will shunt you back 300 years. Here's a 3-star stroll that is known and enjoyed by far too few of us outlanders.

Finally, the **Mint Tower** (Muntplein), 3 blocks to the south, draws batteries of foreign-manned Rolleiflexes. The nation's coin presses were hidden in its octagonal base after the French captured Utrecht in 1672. This one is a canal-side charmer.

In June the Holland Festival is an enterprise sponsored by Amsterdam, The Hague, Rotterdam, and Scheveningen; this is a good time to plan to be in Holland. Most of the Festival revolves around music: Alternate or simultaneous dramas, concerts, opera, or ballet in various cities—something big every night—with an occasional film exhibition to change the pace. For reservations, either write or cable Holland Festival, Willemsparkweg 52, 1071 HJ Amsterdam; cables: Festival Amsterdam; Tel. 020-722245; or Haarlemestraat 14, 2587 RA Den Haag; cables: Festival Scheveningen; Tel. 070-558700.

There are many interesting excursions within shooting distance of Amsterdam. *Alkmaar* on a Friday morning between May and late September is a very happy one if the weather is good: The huge **cheese market** is running full blast until noon; it's colorful and surprisingly odorless. If you want to expand this into a fuller loop, start out early for *Monnickendam* and take your morning coffee in the ancient waterside **Stuttenburgh Inn** with its 199 music boxes and antique curiosities. Now move north along the sea route and through *Volendam* (driving straight through is enough), *Edam, Hoorn*, and on to *Enkhuizen* for a visit to the fine little **Zuiderzee Museum**, right at the water's edge. A pleasant lunch can be had at either the next-door **Taveerne in de Meermin** or the **Hotel Het Wapen**, around the corner and across the bridge. After lunch, make your way over to *Alkmaar* (at this hour, of course, you will have missed the busy morning market sales, but it's worth going, anyway) and then down to *Haarlem* for a tour of the small but impressive **Frans Hals Museum**. For a refresher, the tiny Ark pub, down an alley, is a modest, fun-filled, and incredibly old stop for a quick beer. (Engineers may want to continue to *Heemstede* for a look at working models of the fabulous drainage systems employed by Dutch experts since 1860 at the **Pulder Museum**. The drive back to Amsterdam is only 13 miles from this point, so with ease you're back in time for dinner.

AMSTERDAM HOTELS Quick Reference Table

Price categories by national (not U.S.) standards.

EXPENSIVE:

Alexander Prinsengracht 444. Tel. 267.721; Telex 13161; 25 rooms. P. 675
Amstel Prof. Tulpplein 1. Tel. 226.060; Telex 11004; 115 rooms. P. 672

Apollo Apollolaan 2. Tel. 735.922; Telex 14084; 435 rooms. P. 673
de l'Europe Nieuwe Doelenstraat 2. Tel. 234.836; Telex 12081; 87 rooms. P. 672
Doelen Nieuwe Doelenstraat 24. Tel. 220.722; Telex 14399; 90 rooms. P. 675
Hilton Apollolaan 138. Tel. 780.780; Telex 11025; 376 rooms. P. 673
Marriott Stadhouderskade 21. Tel. 835.151; Telex 15087; 395 rooms. P. 672
Memphis Lairessestraat 87. Tel. 733.141; Telex 12450; 90 rooms. P. 674
Okura Ferd. Bolstraat 175. Tel. 787.111; Telex 16182; 411 rooms. P. 673
Sonesta Kattengat 1. Tel. 212.223; Telex 17149; 360 rooms. P. 673

UPPER MODERATE:
American Leidsekade 97. Tel. 245.322; Telex 11379; 185 rooms. P. 674
Amster Centre Herengracht 255. Tel. 221.727; Telex 15424; 99 rooms. P. 674
Caransa Rembrandtsplein 19. Tel. 229.455; Telex 13342; 66 rooms. P. 675
Carlton Vijzelstraat 2. Tel. 222.266; Telex 11670; 150 rooms. P. 675
Dikker en Thijs Garden Hotel Dijsselhofplantsoen 7. Tel. 642121; 100 rooms.
  P. 674
Krasnapolsky Dam. Tel. 263.163; Telex 12262; 254 rooms. P. 675
Parkhotel Stadhouderskade 25. Tel. 717.474; Telex 11412; 184 rooms. P. 674
Port van Cleve Nieuwe Zijds Voorburgwal 178. Tel. 244.860. P. 675
Pulitzer Prinsengracht 315–331. Tel. 228.333; Telex 16508; 176 rooms. P. 674
Victoria Damrak 1–5. Tel. 234.255; Telex 16625; 140 rooms. P. 674

MODERATE:
Arthur Frommer Noorderstraat 46. Tel. 220.328; Telex 14047; 90 rooms. P. 675
Belfort Surinameplein 53. Tel. 174.333; 20 rooms. P. 676
Schiller Rembrandtsplein 26. Tel. 231.660; Telex 14058; 80 rooms. P. 675

LOWER MODERATE:
Owl Roemer Visscherstraat 1. Tel. 189.484; Telex 13360; 31 rooms. P. 676
Van Wehde Korte van Eeghenstraat 8. 10 rooms. P. 676

AIRPORT:
Ibis Schipholweg 181 (Badhoevedorp). Tel. 02968.1234; Telex 16491; 384 rooms. P. 676
Schiphol Hilton Schiphol Centrum. Tel. 511.5911; Telex 15186; 181 rooms. P. 676
Sheraton Inn Kruisweg 495 (Hoofddorp). Tel. 02503.15851; Telex 41646; 168 rooms. P.
  676

ENVIRONS:
Alpha Europaboulevard 10. Tel. 442.851; Telex 13375; 600 rooms. P. 676
Eurocrest Amsterdam De Boelelaan 2. Tel. 429855; Telex 13647; 260 rooms. P. 676
Euromotel Amsterdam Oude Haagseweg 20. Tel. 179005; Telex 15524; 154 rooms. P. 676
Euromotel E9 Joan Muyskenweg 10. Tel. 946.000; Telex 13382; 128 rooms. P. 676
Slotania Slotermeerlaan 133. Tel. 134.568; Telex 17050. P. 676

Hotels In general, Dutch houses are seasonal, clean, and reasonably priced; there's usually plenty of space in winter, but they get tight in warm weather. *Reserve in advance all year round in the capital and principal metropolises; in lesser towns, bulbtime and high summer are the thorniest periods.*

As is the case everywhere, service standards are on the decline. After 4 months of employment a worker can collect 80% of his salary for one year and

60% for the following one. Is it any wonder that staffs are so hard to obtain and retain?

In the less elaborate or smaller houses, baths are at a premium. But you can be almost sure that your room was scrubbed minutes or hours before you got there, because the average Dutch hostelry shines like Mother Hubbard's cupboard.

All of the 30 houses in the nationwide Golden Tulip chain participate in Teleplan, the great alliance which guarantees very reasonable surcharges on all international and intercontinental calls. Save your long distance chats for these, because their competitors will rob you blind with spurious "supplementary" swindles.

This year you'll pay from $26 to $45 for a good single with bath, $38 to $88 for a good double with bath—plus 15% for service if you stay 5 nights or less. Second-class tariffs for the same categories average $22 to $35; breakfast is frequently included.

The **de l'Europe** earns its laurels as one of the Continent's most elegantly sedate havens on the scene today. This patrician achieves the rare status of being stately without being stuffy. It nestles on the bank of one of the capital's busiest and most colorful canals. Main portals welcoming guests with a bright smile; Relais for quick bites, with sky-blue napery at counters and tables, sapphire carpets, and black leather seats; attractive glass-sheathed dining room with separate entrance, just a yardarm from the passing boats; lobby in hues of seafoam green; impressive ½-million-bottle wine cellar. Now 100% of the rooms have been modernized, with the superb beds and excellent baths installed (twin basins; fluffy robes; sleek lines); 10 units with terraces; 10 in English style; many doubles turned into large singles. Manager Pieter Jennen is keeping up the good works.

Marriott introduced its initial European hotel effort by purchasing perhaps the prime piece of property in all of Holland. It then went on to unveil a sparkling (inside, not outside) air-conditioned physical plant that fairly crackles with new innkeeping concepts for the Continent. Personnel—from highly skilled, handsome, and personable General Manager Robert Mul to any bouncy chambermaid to chummy porters—are young, vigorous, and eager to welcome you. Daring color blends evoking exhilaration and warmth simultaneously; cunning illumination throughout; vastly popular public rooms, among the most zestful in Amsterdam; innovative hotel bonuses such as a self-service laundry room for guests and ice-making machines (free) on every other floor. Invitingly nautical Port O' Amsterdam specialty restaurant with novel ideas for the presentation and service of food; Dutch Inn for all-day vittles; below-decks Windjammer Bar for grog between mates (very matey it is); combo for dancing, a big drawing card for townspeople and guests alike. Bedchambers employ similar rich melds of cheerful hues and bold textiles; 5 suites; paltry baths; book on the viewful Leidseplein side. Here is a hostelry that not only does a job and does it well, but is truly fun to stay in.

The world-famous **Amstel** is a mighty link in Britain's Grand Metropolitan chain. The library-mood La Rive restaurant is one of the most attractive intimate salons we've seen anywhere; the piano melodizing lends even more enchantment to its Amstelside setting. High ceilings; classic décor in public

rooms; lobby and corridors restyled; 80 bedchambers rejuvenated; exceptionally warm and friendly staff. Despite increasing competition, this remains one
of the smarter gathering places for sophisticated tourists and socialites. General Manager van Heuveln is trying hard and enjoying a great success.

The Amsterdam Hilton is a bellringer for contemporary-style dwelling and
bright lights. Quiet but somewhat remote location; ground level entrance hall
and public precincts; accommodations from 13th to 22nd floors; Amsterdam
Grill with charcoal-broils and beef flown in from the U.S.; Pâtisserie café;
split-level, natural oak Half Moon Bar with high-backed library chairs; Juliana
Discothèque in cellar. Subdued colors in bedrooms, highlighted with original
Dutch paintings; spacious suites and demisuites; ungenerous twin-bedded doubles but larger studio-twins; tiny, save-that-penny baths throughout, with
awkwardly planned ventilation slots that usurp privacy. Smooth direction by
Manager Rudy Busch. This landmark is an imposing thoroughbred in the
Hilton bloodline.

The Apollo is designed with its lobby fronting the water. Attractive warm-
toned restaurant and adjoining Bodega; Coffee Shop in Scandinavian tones;
underwater Le Poisson Rouge Bar with its fascinating aquarium filled with
21-karat goldfish. As if that weren't sufficient, the adjoining Apollo Sports Hall
complex flexes in with a cinema, its own bar and terrace, and enough gymnastic equipment to weary an Olympic decathlon squad. Older semicircular segment containing single accommodations; some tiny twins; 2 suites that are
enchanting for their waterway panaromantics; all units dressed up with mod-
ern-living design details. Solid British management by the Trust Houses Forte
group.

The young and vigorous Sonesta, beside Amsterdam's oldest canal, is modern in part while incorporating into its structure 13 monument houses from the
seventeenth century plus the ancient circular Lutheran church (a tunnel links
the latter to the hotel and is used for conferences). A garage for 80 cars, a
handicraft center focusing on Dutch talents, a movie theater, and 40 new
accommodations are due shortly. The Rib Room is an enchanting dining
hideaway after dark; the main floor De Serre produces pleasant light fare; there
is a "brown café" (local parlance for a dim tavern) where you can buy a meter
(!) of beer for $7. You'll also find the Patio Bar and the pulsing, throbbing
Boston Club, one of the city's better discothèques. Most units with one brick
wall to add decorative warmth; color TV, radio, wake-up and message services
plus a unique computerized system for security; good-size and well-equipped
baths throughout. Superb suites viewing the church and the city roofs; outstanding Royal Suite with its own penthouse terrace. Very good in its midtown
milieu.

The towering Okura Intercontinental, which reflects its Japanese bloodline,
has undergone a 2-million-dollar renovation that brings it into the first rank
of Amsterdam's contemporary hostelries. Spacious, softly lit lobby brightened
by a tranquilizing interior garden; Yamazato Japanese restaurant; ruggedly
appealing Teppanyaki Steak House; Dutch Corner coffee shop; Canal Bar;
high-in-the-sky Plein Ciel restaurant (piano music at night); sauna. Corridors
are painted in fanciful modern abstracts; all accommodations refreshed; all
with color and cable TV, radio, double-lock doors, refrigerators, and small

baths. Clearly more of an address for businessmen and groups, but nevertheless vastly improved and recommendable.

The **Parkhotel**, once one of our favorites, performed so miserably in every phase except staff courtesy (which was excellent), that we curtailed our week-long reservation and marched off to another hostelry after one utterly wretched night. Even when we were moved from a so-called "freshly redecorated" room to one of the "superior duplex" units we found maintenance execrable. No thanks—and *no* recommendation to any reader of these pages.

The **Memphis**, one of the more intimate and sophisticated members of the Ramada chain, might make you sing the blues when the bill comes, but it's a ragtime band for syncopated comforts and upbeat charm. Its restaurant has a confident air of cosmopolitan dignity; the Sapphire Bar is attractive for nibblers and sippers. Abundant elbowroom; deep-down, rest-provoking furnishings; 5th-floor units with atelier windows. Chic and understandably costly.

The **Pulitzer** is not a front-page headliner, but after our recent week's review we would not hesitate to award it a prize for human interest among hostelries. Fourteen ancient houses have been charmingly joined in a multilevel composite—fine for all but the aged or infirm. Small modish lobby accented by antiques; dining room with open grill and so-so cookery; some units facing a garden court; others on a street; still more on a tiny canal a few blocks from the town's mainstreams. Décor boldly employing open timbers, rough brick walls, rugged textiles and daring colors; friendly but still unpolished personnel during our stay. Here's a refreshing change from the Hilton-Sheraton-Intercontinental versions of Old Glory-fications of which it is a vague copy in Old Dutch dress. Amusing. **Amster Centre** employed the same architectural technique of joining old houses under one roof. The formula is a sound one and these bedrooms are also inviting. If we had our druthers, we'd pick the Pulitzer first in this type of hostelry.

The **Victoria,** opposite the Central Station, fits into the same English-leather portfolio as the Amstel and the American (next paragraph). As we pen these words it is enjoying a Victorian jubilee of fresh raiments and makeup. Lobby and reception redesigned; cozy triplet lounge refashioned in lovely ancient tones, with tapestried walls and lowered oak-timbered ceiling, brown velvet chairs, and animal prints; open-hearth writing nook; 6-table Spanish Room for *comida* and candle beams; side-by-side Grill rebuilt, with air conditioning added; piano music nightly in both dining salons; demipension required. Ambitious reconstruction of nearly all the 150 accommodations; décor mixed; some space limitations. Overall quite good.

The centrally situated **American** recently was revitalized by its generous Grand Metropolitan owners. The exterior, however—a national monument reflecting a distinct period of Dutch architecture—is untouched. Lobby smartly dressed in marble, sandstone, and fresh carpeting; stone reliefs added; ingratiating Europa dining room with a crackling iron hearth; all units resparkled. Some so-called "suitettes" were constructed which feature a sitting area on the lower level and beds on a higher tier. We prefer these for space and the canalside rooms with arched windows for aesthetics. Excellent.

Dikker en Thijs Garden Hotel is the former wing of the neighboring Hilton. Elegant carriage at its canopied entrance; attractive white-brick lobby; hand-

some bar; new restaurant. The studios and twin accommodations impressed us as being somewhat stark but basically sound. Pleasant enough.

The **Amsterdam Arthur Frommer** is an appealing complex of 13 weavers' homes which have been cleverly integrated into a single unit. Breakfast-only restaurant; Golden Age Bar where we found slapdash—nay, screwball!— service plus green "gas" lanterns; 90 Flemish-style rooms with bed vibrators. The only serious drawback we found here was its unremitting flow of U.S. traffic, often youthful and often objectionably raucous. Otherwise, we like this one a lot.

The **Doelen** has been given a perfunctory shakeup. Very central location; restaurant at waterside; Old World bar in true Dutch style with a painting of the hotel in 1896; rooms refashioned in an uninspired way and with far too much plastic to suit our tastes. Fair, in our view.

The **Caransa** is crammed smack into the noisy nucleus of Rembrandtsplein. Parking is a major headache for motorists; even with its double-glaze windows, light sleepers may find it next to impossible successfully to court the sandman. All units are doubles; all splash in with private bath and whoopee color schemes incorporating stripes or florals. The Plaza Restaurant is at street level; please pardon the terrible pun, but we find it totally pedestrian.

The tiny **Alexander** is a luxury dish conjured up by the famous Dikker en Thijs Restaurant, which it adjoins in panhandle fashion. Ultramodern rooms; plastic furnishings; grays and whites as backgrounds for explosions of bright and cheery pigments; phones, radios, and alarm clocks; #'s 502 and 503 our favorite viewful doubles. Pleasant indeed as a blue-ribbon way station.

The **Carlton**? This one keeps rolling along in an unspirited fashion. Upstairs décor in either Louis XV à la Hollandaise, with off-white and cream shadings, or modern tints; original oils and watercolors lend zest. Five suites; smallish twin-bed doubles; midget baths; inadequate luggage space. If you're booked here this season, doublecheck your dates and keep your fingers double-crossed —because legions of readers have complained of careless reservations policies.

The **Port van Cleve**, which occupies 5 floors above the restaurant of the same name, has now passed the century mark. It was once the Haystack Brewery, which became Heineken property in 1863. Midcity location; small lobby; ingratiating oak-panel-and-tile Old Dutch Inn bar. Overall, you'll find a clean, bright atmosphere in cramped dimensions; the singles atop offer excellent scanning of the city through their garret-style windows; suites #131 (with balcony) and #132 are the only nests for stretching in this entire structure, even though the latest 27-room addition features turn-around space. Only fair.

The even more elderly, eternally growing **Krasnapolsky** has paused in its expansion—at least momentarily. It continues to be a mish-mash. Airy, antiseptic lobby and adjoining bar; garage—a vital asset in this midcity enclave. The suspended potted palms in its winter-garden restaurant made us feel like Luther Burbank catching a bite between experiments; cozier interior dining room in gilt and ecru, to offset it; listless cuisine, but top-form drinks, in its American Bar. So-so at best.

The **Schiller**, is still supposed to undergo a thorough revamping. Since the only things that had materialized on our latest visit were new curtains, we'll believe it *if* we see it.

The **Van Wehde**, adjoining hippiedom's Vondel Park, is run by an amiable young couple who do their darndest to provide maximum comfort for economy travelers. Bright dining room; cherry-red central heating; 10 bedchambers and 2 baths. A fat reward for thin wallets. The **Owl**, with breakfast only, is not bad for economizers. Bid for a quiet side if you toss and turn all night.

The **Eurocrest** is in a special category. This 15-story former ESSO hotel is situated at the fringe of the city, about a 15-minute sprint from the Rembrandtsplein and 20 minutes from Schiphol Airport. Within the stalwart edifice are offices, full garage services plus indoor and outdoor covered parking, a boutique, a barbershop,and a beauty salon. Spacious flagstone and wood-ribbed lobby; restaurant; cheery Pot Luck coffee corner; Dracs Bar. Perkily appointed bedchambers with wide windows, balconies, an occasional bouquet of fresh flowers, and small, efficient, "interior" baths. The 18-story **Alpha**, across Europa Boulevard from the Eurocrest in a shopping complex, is now a member of the French Novotel varsity, which also operates hotels in Breda and Schiedam. Lobby now warmed up; intimate café; many nooks for chitchat.

The **Schiphol Airport Hilton** is the only hostelry that is actually sited on the grounds of the flying field's complex—2 minutes from the terminal by shuttle bus. This sleek haven for transients is so convenient to the key highway systems that guests can drive to Amsterdam, the Hague, or Rotterdam in jig time without bucking any big-city traffic. Air-conditioned and soundproofed throughout; exquisite indoor pool affording a scenic grace note to the glass-lined grillroom on a higher tier; sauna; coffee shop; on our test, cuisine beautifully presented, clumsily served, and neck-snappingly expensive; bristling with activity nearly the clock around. You'll pay generously for whatever you get.

The Schiphol Arthur Frommer was sold a while back and is now called the **Ibis**. Its architecture (which to us resembles a sleeping factory) and its heavy patronage by groups dim our enthusiasm for this candidate.

Sheraton Inn is a bit farther from the airport. It reflects an economizing mentality. Dark wood-lined bar; restaurant with leatherette chairs and suspended lamps; poor baths; air conditioning plus basic amenities. Manager Wim van Ingen is trying to do a lot on a low budget. This house and a twin Inn in *Geldrop* (near Eindhoven) both charge modest rates for clean, basic shelter.

The new **Eurotel A-4** is a dark hued building in the airport district; it is large, efficient, and designed for the touring and motoring traffic. The **Slotania** is so far from the center of the city that the ride seems endless; small and unpretentious; definitely not worth the journey for the average U.S. tripper. The **Belfort** is off our list for the very same reasons. The **Euromotel E-9**, in the direction of Schiphol Airport, doesn't thrill us. In this vicinity, **Euromotel Amsterdam** has replaced the old one of the same name. While we disliked the former establishment, we have not judged the latter.

Dedicated budgeteers? Since we're too bottlenecked here for additional entries, please consult this year's edition of our annually revised paperback, *Fielding's Low-Cost Europe.*

Restaurants The leader for elegance today is the **La Rive**, overlooking the canal at the Amstel (see "Hotels"). The gracefulness of this library-style salon, its setting, and the taste manifest in the entire presentation of scene and cuisine, surely make it a water-and-landmark for discriminating travelers. The

Excelsior Room of the Hotel de l'Europe is among the more sophisticated pleasure domes in the city. Less posh, but more animated and colorful, is the maritime-ly **Port O' Amsterdam** in the Marriott Hotel.

One *must* for the average American traveler is the **Bali** restaurant at Leidsestraat 95. We've already reported our enthusiasm for its astonishing multiplate rijsttafel in the section on "Food"; anyone who leaves Holland without enjoying this unique adventure in dining has missed the chance of a lifetime. One-flight up; 100% air-conditioned; modern, pleasant rooms with orange awnings and bay windows; tiny, cozy, ever-jammed Balinese Bar; Javanese waiters in colorful headdresses; 18 female Javanese cooks in the immaculate kitchen; experienced leadership by Proprietor Max Elfring Jr., a friend and admired professional. Ask Max for "the works"; for about $18, they'll give you around 9 weeks' worth of vitamins; lesser choices run as low as $11 or so. And when the meal is finished, order one of their "Bali Mystery" cocktails (iced coconut milk, rum, and secret ingredients)—perfect for cutting and complementing this gargantuan repast. *Reserve in advance* (early the same day); despite its expansion there's almost always a hungry queue in the foyer. Marvelous fare; an unforgettable experience; highest possible recommendation.

De Gravenmolen (Lijnbaanssteeg 5-7) comprises 2 adjoining houses on an enchanting side street in the old center. These were converted into a restaurant-bar-tavern by personable Host Jan Gravendeel. Ground level for liquid refreshment and lighter bites; captivating upstairs linkage of rooms with paisley green walls, vermilion highlights, suspended plum-colored lamps over candlelit tables, brass sconces, comfortable barrelstave chairs, thick sea-blue carpets, and a joy-burst of flowers before each diner. Cuisine somewhat limited in variety; kindhearted service; reasonable tariffs. If they're available, please have a go at the helium-light Quenelles or the delicious Terrine de Ris de Veau.

The most famous restaurant in the Lowlands, the **Five Flies,** is operated by the Krasnapolsky Hotel interests. On our recent sampling, this marvelously decorated landmark—even under its improved management—was as bad as we have ever seen it. The cafeteria-type tableware (stainless utensils and cheap plastic salt-and-pepper shakers) might embarrass a Woolworth's basement; our meal was sad news for the palate; the bill was high for the return; the service was perfunctory when it wasn't entirely absent. Definitely not recommended.

Ile de France, on the other griddle, *is* recommended, but it's about a 15-minute taxi ride from the center in the suburb of Amstelveen. The atmosphere is as sophisticated as the French cookery. Small, select, and recommended if you don't mind the drive.

The upstairs operation of **Dikker en Thijs** (Leidsestraat 82) is traditionally regarded by local burghers as the most distinguished epicurean center in the Netherlands. Although we wouldn't go nearly that far, our latest lunch here was a big improvement over our earlier disappointing experiences. Streetside main room with a small segment facing the canal; blond chairs, gold curtains, and silver candelabra; the general feeling that it requires a yet-to-be-found catalyst to tie together its coolish ingredients for genuine warmth, coziness, and elegance. The service, we concur, is among the finest you'll find in the region, but overall we're only medium-zealous in our praises. The less expen-

sive **Café du Centre**, downstairs, has been enlarged by stretching one section into a long narrow corridor with red-and-white tablecloths and modern touches suitable for a snackery. It's always busy. The subterranean **Prinsenkelder**, part of the complex, shares its chef but not its menu with the alma mater. It's a long, Old-Worldly room with tile flooring, timbered ceiling, and manor-isms of a Pieter de Hoogh painting. Not Princely but a stout vassal nonetheless.

De Boerderij ("The Farm") is conveniently situated on a corner of the Leidseplein—and nearly every American traveler adores it. Intimate ambiance of banquettes, mosaic tiles, fireplace, copper skillets, and piped music; 2 floors, each with 7 tables; small rôtisserie. Medium-high prices and possibly the most savory European-style food in Amsterdam. Reserve a day in advance in High Season; closed Sunday and holidays. Cheers, cheers, and more cheers!

Molen De Dikkert, out on the Amsterdamseweg, is an amusing rural target. It is built into the base of a huge windmill. Tavern atmosphere with weed-fiber blocks set into timbers; Delft theme in linens and china; red rush-bottom chairs; ultramodern bar that is totally out of context. The setting, the occasional music for dancing, and the relaxing candlessence are enough to make an evening. Cornball stuff? You bet, but still. . . .

The fine old-world precincts of the **Port van Cleve** (Nieuwe Zijds Voorburgwal 178) seem to be improving again, we are happy to report. Two floors: Bodega Bar for journalistically inclined visitors on one side of ground floor, opposite a big, barren, cafeteria-like chamber where waiters bawl your order to the counters as loudly as thirsty steers; somber dining room upstairs. The traditional come-on always has been beefsteak—10 separate varieties, from rump steak to double sirloin. They've been individually numbered in sequence since the founding in 1870; yours, if you try one, will probably bear a tag in the neighborhood of 5,500,000—and cross your fingers that it ends in triple zeros, because then all your wine is on the house.

For atmosphere, **La Fontaine** (Kleine Gartmanplantsoen 7) is the masterpiece of Jan Tervoort. Reasonably priced main dishes; distinguished and gentle air; an enjoyable evening out, especially for amatory types.

The **Swarte Schaep** (Black Sheep), Korte Leidsedwarsstraat 24 directly off Leidseplein, is a delight to the eye. Rich atmosphere of polished rusticity, beams, candles, and copper and brassware; comfortable surroundings that enhance a romantic mood; acceptable cuisine which is even improving under its new ownership; rather stately prices; service as soft-spoken as the mood. Distinctly rewarding, especially for ambience.

The next-door **Bistro La Forge** has bellows of style and lower tabs. Managerial headaches, however, still keep it variable in the cookery department. Double-tiered ground-floor restaurant with a grand fireplace commanding one wall; large captain's chairs and trappings that display a generous pocket; upstairs U-shape bar adjoining a second dining room. We hope it can become a high-stepper.

Entrecote (70 P. C. Hoofstraat) follows a successful pattern of independent restaurants that exist in both London and Geneva. Only one main dish is served and that is, of course, its grilled namesake. This comes with a house

wine (only), a delicious salad of lettuce and walnuts, and a luscious display of desserts from which to choose. Structured in 3 tiers, we prefer the middle layer with art deco, blue and silver velour chevrons on its walls and banquettes, and 1920s fixtures. Very pleasant and recommendable.

Claes Claesz (Egelantierstraat 24-26) is one of the more talked about, new-style candidates in the city. Bare wood tables and simple chairs; dim chandelier illumination augmented by candles. Inventive menu that some diners would consider more audacious than ambitious. Our Coquille St. Jacques aux Truffles was delicate and the délices of smoked fish in melon was strangely engaging. Some dishes were given disproportionate ladles of alcoholic spirit which we thought were silly and far too costly for the reward. Reception was poor and service was so incredibly slow that our 2-dish meal consumed more than 3¼ hours—so long that we did not even bother with dessert, cheese, or coffee. If you raise century plants you just might have the patience for this one.

One that's favored by Latin tummies is **Ristorante Mario**, an import from Turin. **Kelderhof** (Prinsengracht 494) puts on a bold, rustic show with brick floors and walls, a fountain in the foyer, a long pine bar plus barrel tables, a larger inner sanctum with wicker chairs, a tavern atmosphere, and cookery that discloses a French pedigree. Tom Fagel's attention-getting **Bistro Klein Paardenburg** at *Ouderkerk*, 10 minutes out beside the Amstel River, is pulsing with enthusiasm these days. It has just been awarded one star in the Michelin guidebook; so has his brother Paul's **Bisro Duurstede** in *Wijk bij Duurstede*. These chaps are big news in the bistro biz!

Amsterdam has a rare seafood purveyor in the **Neptunus** (Rokin 87). It is ironic that in this ocean-born-and-bred capital only modest fish houses (see the one below) existed prior to the arrival of this big catch. Walls of cork and wood; beamed ceiling with lantern beams for lighting; framed reproductions of ships; decorative helm; booths with dark-blue cushions; sky-blue napery; taped soft music. Poseidon's pals handsomely presented and carefully cooked; expert navigation by Skipper Choy and First Mate Gallis; large portions at whitebait prices. Swimmingly recommended for its net profits.

The **Oesterbar**, on the Leidseplein, has long been the favorite fish restaurant in Western Europe of an irreverent Dutch sidekick. He informed us, "I like the hygienic-looking tiled walls and the silly fishes that gaze at you with such tender eyes through the aquarium-windows." We recently returned their gaze and fed our guilt-ridden corpus with ungrateful sole. Perhaps we're just softies, because the food was delicious—but we get the Orwellean feeling that one day *we're* going to be in that tank, with some cocksure mackerel wearing a bib over his starched tucker and waiting for *his* victim. Excellent for any conscienceless palate. If you admire this one as much as we do, you'll also like the **Keyzer,** a sister operation in the wings of the Concertgebouw.

Les Quatres Canetons (IIII Prinsengracht) is sinking, in our view. The plant itself resembles a made-over bunker painted with mud. Sometimes, to us, the cookery seems inclined in the same direction. Anyway, it strikes us as just plain gloomy.

Het Begijntje (Begijnensteeg 6), in a tiny hideaway lane just off Kalverstraat near the Spui, is once again worth the considerable effort to find it. But before

you begin the safari, may we suggest you take a Bokma (gin) or other spirituous drink at the world-famous **Hoppe**, a bar at the corner of Spui and Heisteeg which is the Amsterdam version of New York's P. J. Clarke's? The restaurant features a Spanish guitarist, candle illumination, a U-shape configuration with a bar along one stem, an expensive menu, and a wine list glued around a magnum. Our meal was much better this latest try; we still found the mood pretentious, the former smart waiters replaced by prissy smart alecks, and Owner John Baaker overly familiar with his clients. Some will like it, while others will find the personnel too much to swallow. Count your change here.

The **Lido**, by the canal at the Leidseplein bridgehead, is charming when its beading of lights reflects in the dark waters. Fanciful interior in turn-of-the-century décor; playfully named outdoor terrace called l'Eauberge, on the pier; parasols, tables, and food displays. Attractive for romantic types who consider cuisine to be of lesser importance than sighs.

Staying out late? The **Night Restaurant '66** (26 Reguliersgracht), a short totter from the club-girt Rembrandtsplein, yawns "Good Morning" at 10 P.M. and goes to sleep just before dawn. So-called French cuisine; atmosphere remotely Scandinavian in tone; low tabs. If it's late enough, and if you've imbibed enough, you probably won't even mind the food. The famous **Dorrius** (Nieuwe Zijds Voorburgwal 336) is excellent for guilder-watching pilgrims. It is simple, traditional, and substantial, undoubtedly deserving of being included in every guidebook on Amsterdam since the Year Dot. Its 4-course lunch is more than a bargain. Closed Sunday. **Le Chat Qui Pelote** (Zeedijk 16), in the prostitution lane, is a deep, narrow feedery overlooking from its back windows a quiet waterway. The cuisine is not sensational, but it's adequate for the tariffs and it's fun as a curiosity. **Castell** (Lijnbaansgracht 252-4), next to the famous Continental Bodega, specializes in grills and Indonesian Sates. Open 5 P.M. to 12:30 A.M.; closed Sunday; popular at first but slipping today.

Chow mein, chop suey, and the like? One of the better Chinese restaurants in Holland is **Lotus** (Binnen Bantammerstraat 5), smack in the heart of the colorful red-light district. Open kitchen, half of which is devoted to sino-savories, mainly from Canton; the other half is dedicated to Indonesian dishes. Low prices; immaculate split-level interior of shining metallic finish; interesting clientele. Recommended. Another good one is **Fong-Lie** (P.C. Hooftstraat 80). Cleverly tiered small room for 40, as crowded as a fan-tan game when full; beer and wine only; 12 A.M. to 10 P.M. daily except Sunday and Monday. **Peking** (Vijzelstraat 28) is more costly; it is also more northern in its culinary posture; some excellent gems bubble in its Soo-Gaw pots. Japanese? **Toga** (Weteringschans 128) wraps up nibbles from Nippon which some diners praise and others seem to abhor. We must give it a try personally soon.

Italian? There are dozens now, said to be the result of the increasing Italian influence in the city. **La Capannina** (Korte Leidsedwarsstraat 103) pounds out Neapolitan fare. Every bay-bred device imaginable hangs from the walls or ceiling; the dough is rolled, flung, battered, and kneaded in front of your eyes. This show alone is worth the $7 cost of an ordinary meal. We've had more educated Latin ladles in Düsseldorf. A better bet is **Mirafiori**, across from the Parkhotel; extra-palatable pastas, extra-friendly proprietor. **Roma,** on the Rokin, is modern but sterile in tone. Spanish? **La Cacerola** (Weteringstraat 41)

is currently *en vogue;* you'll drop soothingly few pesetas if you take your *cena* here; the Dutch owner speaks perfect Castilian. Danish? *Skåls* to the **Kopenhagen** (Rokin 84). Low tabs for tiptop snacktime quality. Kosher Kookery? Give **Sandwich Shop Meyer** a flyer; no longer newish but still very Jewish; located by Nieuwmarkt 13. For bigger ruminations of these ethnic nutrients, **Ufaratsta** (Wouwermanstraat 27) has the blessings of the Amsterdam rabbinate—so who are we to argue?

Snacks? **Bodega Continental** (Lijnbaansgracht) is IT for sherry and nibbles between 11 A.M. and 7:30 P.M.; popular among Amsterdamers. **Plein 24** (Leidseplein) is just about perfect for quickie nourishment. Dutch style; very cheap; open until 1 A.M. **Pub O'Henry** (Rokin 89) is right-on for Union Jacks and Jills; it waves the flag from noon to 11 P.M. There's also a Wild West theme: Tossed sawdust on the floor; boar, deer, moose, and a bovinity of heads on the walls; toward dusk an old-fashioned pie-anner player rags out barroom melodies for all and sundry. **Van Dobben** (Korte Reguliersdwarsstraat 5-7-9, near the Rembrandtsplein) specializes in a bewildering variety of tempting sandwiches, plus a few soul-soothing soups. Simple; inexpensive. **Upstairs** (2 Grimburgwal) is a narrow room up a steep flight of stairs that were built in 1536. It serves pancakes (crêpes) only; the prices contradict the staircase; they won't make you puff.

Dedicated budgeteers? Since we're too bottlenecked here for additional entries, please consult this year's vastly revised and updated edition of our annually revised paperback, *Fielding's Low-Cost Europe,* which lists scads more bargain dining spots and money-saving tips for serious economizers.

Night Life Plentiful. Everything from Persian Rooms to Times Square tourist traps to neighborhood taverns to honkytonks—the galaxy. You can sip champagne in your evening clothes at swank membership clubs, or you can drink beer while clutching your wallet in one of the most wide-open bordello districts in Europe. As mentioned earlier, this nation's liberal statutes have attracted some migrants. With the tightening up of legal loopholes in England, France, and Germany, Holland has become a haven and safe harbor for nonconformists. In this freewheeling society, narcotics are sold just in the shadow of a doorway and used openly by many.

Blue Note (Leidseplein area) is miles ahead as the top nightery open to you and me. Very good bands; tiny dance floor; 4 cozy bars; popular with parents and the Younger Set alike. If you're a middle-age smoothie, you've already seen 2 dozen like it; if you're 19 and in love, you'll be in company with plenty of similar couples.

Whisky à Gogo is a jigger-size private club over the Blue Note, with three 14-seat bars and 4 Lilliputian tables. The member or guest-member may select a top brand of any potable, and it will be stored for him in his own locker. All subsequent soda, ice, and service is included in one single bill. If you're well dressed and reasonably sober, you may be invited up when you tap at the door. Operates from 10 P.M. to 4 A.M. (Sat. to 5 A.M.); very pleasant romancing spot (as long as you bring your own romance!).

Le Poisson Rouge, downstairs in the Apollo Hotel also draws moony types. It's not the grooviest, but if you're in that mood and with that someone, it can be a big, big catch.

If you can pry your way in, the **Can-Can** is the city's leading private club. Ask friends to take you or speak to your concierge.

Most fun of all, if you're young in spirit, is to bar-hop through Amsterdam's more typical small bistros. If you're a man and if you're alone, you should particularly enjoy this circuit—although women often get a great kick out of it, too. We are especially fond of the cozy **Auberge Privé** (Leidseplein 8), which is said to be private but still it's easy to get in, the **Bon Mariage** (Herengracht 338) for snuggles, wine, and cheese; then the sea-and-seeworthy **Boekanier,** at the yacht club (toward the airport), where you can sip and linger or even dine in easy chairs drawn up before a crackling fire; or, back in town, the ultra-intimate, ultra-Dutchy **Tapperij Gijsbrecht van Aemstel** (Herengracht 435), where romance is spun from dim light and liquids. **Frascati** (Nes 59) draws most of its following from the theatrical and TV sectors. All of these fall into the loosely classified category of "brown cafés"—lovers' or topers' nooks where *you* provide most of the wattage.

For the "in" crowd a quartet of swingers take the prize: (1) **Voom-Voom,** (2) **Boston Club,** (3) **King's Club,** (4) **Club 67** and (5) **Zzazz.** The first has been rebuilt and now at the bar you can finally hear enough to carry on a conversation with your companion—but *only* at the bar. The second is housed in the Sonesta Hotel, which has endowed it with florins and pep. The third is sheathed with colored plexiglass partitions, mirrors, brass, and crystal; it spotlights an American-style unslipped-disk jockey. The fourth is spacious, modernistic, and loaded with booths; if the policy still holds, you can't enter if you're over 30. (We knew a 12-year-old shill who vouched for us.) The last features black and orange diagonals, a loud atmosphere, cheap drinks, and hot dogs. **Juliana's,** in the nether reaches of the Hilton, seems to host a tired but dapper fraternal assemblage of businessmen who eternally expect to find their ultimate fancy perched on the neighboring barstool, only to discover yet another valve salesman from New Haven after a similar quest. **Boeing** flies by night in the form of a 707 cabin. Odd but hardly jet-propelled. **Toy-Toy** next door, is dressed in vinyl and stocked with little Dutch stenographers. Pretty routine. **Revolution** revolves in fin de siècle moods; it didn't turn us on. **Rasputin** swings in with a zigzag brass-topped bar, molded plastic chairs, a long room, and few long faces.

Jazzland (105 Korte Leidsedwarsstraat) makes wonderful dixieland noises. Band at the entrance; sipping and toe-tapping on 2 levels; most fans stand. Very inexpensive and very good for its fun-loving type.

Zirbelstube has the air of a ski-resort tavern; knotty pine by the kilometer; no tablecloths; whisky on tap, but wine is the usual beverage here; clean, animated, and attractive for a pause, except for its terrible ventilation. Jewish cabaret à la Minsky is available at **Li-La-Lo** (109 de Clercqstraat); services begin at 10 P.M.; we don't know their dishes from their knishes, because we've never said *L'Chayim* here. The **Caliente** (Lijnbaansgracht, just off the Leidseplein) has picked up a blistering batch of BTUs to become a very hot contender. Mild Mexican theme; good spirits in the glass and in the air; routine disrobing every quarter-hour on the belly button. *Saludos, amigos!* The hippie parlor known as the **Paradiso** is back again after a period in limbo. The government advises kids that they can't sleep here, but who can tell the

difference? We were told that pot can be smoked but not sold. True? The **Carrousel** (Thorbeckeplein 20) is a topless bar. **Coupe de Paris** now is said to discourage male customers. We skirted it on our last whirl and from what we hear, we're not panting to get in. Early-to-bedders will probably relish the aforementioned **Continental Bodega**; excellent wines at cave-bottom prices; closing time is 7:30—that's P.M. not A.M.! Another one of this sort but even better is the **Heineken Hoek**, smack on the Leidseplein. It is built around copper brewing kettles. Very atmospheric. **Oosterling** is yet another favorite for sip samplers; shades drawn at 6 P.M. normally, but not until 7 P.M. on Friday. **Courage** stays open later. **Boogaloo** is rather cheap—and we mean this in *every* sense of the word. **Lucky Star,** atwinkle dimly across from Club '67 in the heartbeat of town, has faded slowly. We have a feeling it is an eclipse. The **Moulin Rouge** (5 Thorbeckeplein) puts on one of the splashiest promotions on the nightscape. Frankly, we wouldn't tilt with this red windmill for love or guilders.

Looking for companionship? Try practically any gin mill around the Rembrandtsplein or in the Seamen's Quarter (locally called the Zeedijk district). **Sheherazade** (2 blocks from the Rembrandtsplein at Wagenstraat 5) is currently the pick of the lot; 2 orchestras, dim lights, and Dutch hotshots fad-dancing; whisky which tasted to us as if it never saw the Scottish sunrise; dim, humid, seraglio lighting; no cover or minimum, but drinks run into money. Plenty of hostesses, and some of them fairly cute. The **Casablanca** is a rowdy *boîte:* entertainers, blaring music, crowds of sailors and their girl friends. **Le Maxim,** just off the Leidseplein, is an amusing piano bar for after-dinner revels. Nice people, good drinks, tuneful entertainment by Max Pola. Gentlemanly companionship? The **Bonaparte Club** gave us the impression that it lost some of its attracting power since its redecoration. Ex-prize fighter doorman; long bar for mixing; big pedestal booths for sit-down types; décor in what we'd term Hygienic Twentieth Century Empire. Appears to be popular with those who care. **Incognito** pulls in Jet Setters plus other flighty types of another disposition. More Empire décor; go late if you go-go. The **Privé** is another entry for the inner circle. Very successful as of the instant. Two others are the rage among the foreign elements; membership is required by all comers. They are: **The C.O.C.** (49-A Korte Leidsedwarsstraat) and **The D.O.K.**(460 Singel). We're told that the former is the more "exclusive," and that both welcome the special planeloads of winged weekenders who fly in regularly from London, Berlin, and other more restrictive climes in search of freedom. Apparently they find it in abundance. (A National Tourist Office official disclosed that there are at least 15 such clubs in the city; he added that male mail requests for guidance to these spots are routinely answered.) Heterosexual onlookers are discouraged, of course.

The Seamen's Quarter is as blatant as New Orleans used to be—and, in the same way, an interesting and curious clock-stopper. Along Oude Zijds Voorburgwal and in the neighborhood of Oudekerksplein (ironically, Old Church Place) are low-grade bars adjoining really low-grade cribs. Some of the cribs actually sport red lights. While this area may be relatively safe, if not lusty, please do not wander onto the Oude Zijds Achterburgwal, which can be extremely dangerous. Drugs are marketed openly and rough stuff does occur;

even the police are unable to control the gangsterism that is bred by the narcotics trade. Be careful with your wallet and with what you drink (bottled beer, uncapped before you, is best). It's a wide open district—the last of a social phenomenon that vanished elsewhere in Europe 25 to 50 years ago.

Shopping Bona fide nonresident departing passengers at Schiphol Airport *with destinations outside the Benelux countries* may save up to 60% on a raft of luxury items at its self-service Tax Free Shopping Center, the largest on the Continent. Read its interesting brochure, available on the spot, before you buy. Here is the only enterprise at any airfield in Europe that makes careful distinctions between levied and unlevied merchandise for the benefit of the customers. Sour note: Be prepared for frequent and frustrating disappointments that so many of its stores are chronically out of stock of exactly the item or items upon which the traveler's heart is set.

Our ★ ★ ★ ★ ★ recommendations are individually noted below.

Diamonds: Warning!!!! A quasi-swindle has recently popped up to shear the innocents. The vendor suavely displays boxed or sealed diamonds which he guarantees to buy back any time at the original price IF the seal is unbroken. Although often the gem can be seen through its plastic container, it cannot be examined closely. Should the market rise (which on a long-term basis is virtually inevitable), the customer faces a quandary. If he or she opens it, the contents may not be worth what it cost and the guarantee no longer applies. But if he or she keeps it sealed and returns it for collection, all potential profit is out the window. The only winner is the seller, who happily gives back the original amount and pockets the accrued difference. Here's a legal shell game which is blatantly rigged.

Your local sightseeing guide, operating from a very human desire for a commission, might insist on leading you by the ear to various "factories"— some of which are good, and some of which are fancied-up tourist traps.

For actual buying, we'd far, far prefer to discuss our transaction with gem experts such as the ★ ★ ★ ★ ★ house of **Bonebakker** (Rokin 88), the oldest and most respected gem merchant in the Netherlands. Don't let the elegance of their even more exquisitely redesigned and beautified air-conditioned premises stop you, because their diamond prices aren't a single guilder—or even kwartje —higher than anywhere else. The gentlemanly Adrian Bonebakker or his son Ferdinand (the 6th generation here) lay their almost 200-year-old Bonebakker reputation on the table every time they display a stone to a client. They also carry a complete line of classic and contemporary jewelry, Patek Philippe and Baume & Mercier watches, antique silverware, and other sinfully appealing luxuries. In this world center of this most popular of precious stones, there are still bargains galore—but if you aren't thoroughly conversant with their technical subtleties they can be terribly tricky to buy. For your own protection, it's just simple common sense to do business with the best purveyor. They are exempt from the national 18% B.T.W. tax, too. Tops.

Delft ware has so many perils for the unwary that we always make doubly sure of what we're getting by going to ★ ★ ★ ★ ★ **Focke & Meltzer** (Kalverstraat 176, P.C. Hoofstraat 65, Okura Hotel Shopping Arcade or Stroomarkt 37)—and nowhere else. This treasure house, leader throughout the Lowlands since 1823, stocks a vast choice of genuine pieces, hand-painted under the glaze

in the characteristic blue ware, as well as other Delft articles in rainbow-hued Polychroom plus the famous red, blue, and gold Pijnacker. (Look for the unique pieces signed by Master Craftsmen Saunders, Dessens, or Van Willigen.) In addition you'll find Makkum, the Frisian pottery; Holland's best-known crystal products: Leerdam's hand-blown fluted-style glasses; the most illustrious crystal, china, glass, faience, and earthenware from 22 European countries. These magnates also operate a strikingly handsome, similarly streamlined branch at Hoogstraat 33 in _The Hague,_ a second in neighboring _Scheveningen,_ and a third at _Ryswyk,_ as well as the newest one at _Zandvoort._ In Amsterdam, ask the amicable Mr. Paul Meltzer to be your mentor. This garden of wantables is terrific.

Dutch-style gold, silver miniatures, souvenir items, plus a varied collection of precious stones: ★ ★ ★ ★ ★ **Carel van Pampus b.v.** (Kalverstraat 56 and Nieuwendijk 140) is the perfect problem solver for the wanderer who wants overseas mementos which won't break, won't cost too much, and won't take up too much space or weight in the luggage. Among the most popular features here are the Old Dutch room with handsome silver miniature furniture, colorful enameled silver tulip brooches, gold charms, gold earrings, the attractive Old-Dutch-style silver-tipped line of miniatures; boxes, and similar articles which bear effective reproductions of paintings by Rembrandt, Jan Steen, and other venerated masters, and Quartz Seiko watches. It also specializes in unset "loose" diamonds, van Pampus-imported Japanese cultured pearls, and opals, emeralds, rubies, or sapphires. Mr. van Pampus, the 3rd generation of his family to operate these small, personalized establishments, will greet you at the Kalverstraat headquarters with a warm smile. So will his friendly staff. Traveler's checks, as well as the majority of credit cards, are accepted. Outstanding in its field.

Modern paintings and art objects: **Kunsthandel Ina Broerse** (Nieuwe Spiegelstraat 57) offers triweekly purchase-exhibitions of Dutch graphics, ceramics, wall handings, small sculptures, and some permanent examples of folk art.

Exotic bric-a-brac: **M.L.J. Lemaire** (Prinsengracht 841) sells figures, masks, daggers, old Batik, all sorts of East Indian trophies. **Jan Visser** (Nieuwe Spiegelstraat 58), named for and owned by a cultural anthropologist, accents articles from Oceania and New Guinea and _objets d'art_ from Africa and Indonesia.

Antiques: The **Nieuwe Spiegelstraat** and the adjoining **Spiegelgracht** are famous for their cluster of perhaps 30 dealers, many of them concentrated upon different specialties.

Shopping Center: The variegated **Amstelveen Shopping Center** is 5 minutes from Schiphol Airport.

Please DON'T BUY: Furs, fine gloves, perfumes, or fine wines.

Shopping Hours: Officially the shopkeeper can keep the hours he or she likes. In practice, however, usually department and durables stores are closed until 11 A.M. or noon on Mondays; on Thursday and Fridays many operate at their counters until 9 P.M. Shops featuring consumer goods generally lock their doors on Wednesday afternoons. There's a flock of other variables—so please check before leaving your hotel.

Dedicated shophounds: For shopping elsewhere in Holland, for more stores,

more details, and more lore, please consult the purse-size 25th Anniversary edition of *Fielding's Selective Shopping Guide to Europe.*

Other Targets

AALSMEER (10 miles southwest of Amsterdam) is Holland's permanent flower center, both physically and financially; thousands of blooms from the surrounding countryside pour into this funnel daily, where they are sorted, selected, and sold at auction in 2 gigantic wholesale markets. Exquisite colors and varieties, many new to the U.S. amateur gardener; a lovely spectacle, which must be viewed from 7:30 A.M. to noon any weekday; it is closed on Saturdays and Sundays.

ARNHEM If you are wandering out here near the German border, the **Netherlands Open Air Museum** is the European cousin of the Jamestown and Sturbridge Village projects. As a wise New Jersey friend comments, ". . . if travelers to Holland could see that—and only that—they'd have a true idea of Dutch folklore." Plan on a good 1/2-day to roam this 82-acre park at leisure; superior snack-type food available; open daily from April 1 to November 1; wonderful. *Otterlo*, a few miles to the northwest, offers the splendid **Kröller-Müller Museum**; this alone is worth a day.

EINDHOVEN is proud of its **Cocagne**, a 9-story glass-and-steel showplace erected by the Philips Electric colossus (and what else *is* Eindhoven but Philips?). Completely air-conditioned; large congress hall and 9 conference centers; attractive lounge banked by winter garden and restaurant; commodious Bodega for beer quaffers; 86 functional, decent-size units and 86 baths, but "convertible" singles cramped when they're employed as doubles. A slick operation primarily for the business trade. On the outskirts, the **Motel Eindhoven** is one of the finest motels not only in Holland, but in Europe. If you don't need to be in the town, this stop is a honey. Not far away, at *Geldrop*, a **Sheraton Inn** recently was inn-cubated. Very simple, clean, basic, and economical.

HAARLEM population 165 thousand, has its points for some sightseers —the Frans Hals Museum, which can be seen by candlelight at various intervals, a great cathedral (St. Bavo with its famous organ), pure Dutch architecture, colorful gardens, and the beach resort of Zandvoort where the nation's first legalized casino is located (others at Valkenburg and at Scheveningen.)

HAGUE or DEN HAAG Refer to "The Hague."

LAREN, about 15 miles from Amsterdam, has a wonderful restaurant in **Le Postillon de La Provence**, a rural enchantress. Busy grill; beamed ceiling; moss-green carpet; thick wooden tables; thick steaks, too, and delightful cuisine of all sorts. It is owned by the funloving J.P. De Wijs. In this fellow's hands it has become a red-hot contender.

OEGSTGEEST Genuine "country" atmosphere and charm? The well-known **De Beukenhof** (2 miles from Leyden) is elaborate and expensive in a slick-rustic manner; tap room, gardens, dining room, converted hayloft for larger parties, and the Beech Tree, for which it was named. Close to Amsterdam and now better than ever.

ROTTERDAM, the chief port and undisputedly the world's busiest harbor, used to be as lusty as San Francisco. Hitler's infamous "lesson" to the Dutch people—destruction by bombing of 25 thousand buildings within 20 minutes, without waiting for their answer to his ultimatum—carved it down temporarily to the size of Duluth, Minnesota. But the hardworking burghers, having completed their mammoth reconstruction program, are now expanding at an unbelievable pace. The results are astonishing (and humbling!). Ample accommodations; good restaurants; a splendid zoo; Boymans' van Beuningen Museum (very important collection, with paintings by Bosch, seventeenth-century landscape artists, a few by Rembrandt and van Gogh, and many modernists); Scheepvaart Museum (ship models); outstanding modern statuary, including the prizewinner by U.S. sculptor Naum Gabo. To cap this array, the De Doelen concert hall issues a grace note at the Schouwburgplein; this colossus is the biggest on the Continent; its novel profile rings the audience around the musicians. Groothandelsgebouw, the largest building in Western Europe, with 250 firms (nearly all wholesale companies), a 500-car garage, a 5000-wheel bicycle bin, and a 1-mile air-conditioned interior roadway; the 15-thousand-acre $200,000,000 Europoort project which opened the Nieuwe Waterweg for 250-thousand-ton ships. The pile-driving frenzy of creating too many massive civic projects at once will madden travelers and residents alike for many earsplitting years to come. She has a bustling, busy, clangorous, commercial—and nautical—atmosphere. Not as interesting as Amsterdam, but worth a visit. P.S. to all engineers: There's absolutely no dam excursion like a zip out to the famous Delta Works, the DNA and RNA of the Netherlands. You can climb inside the world's largest sluices, see its engines, witness films, devour snacks, watch boats, and go into hydraulic raptures generally. Fascinating!

Hotels The 11-story, 275-room **Hilton** is a wee shade smaller than its Dutch uncle in Amsterdam. Two-level lobby linked by a white marble, free-form stairway; MacGreggor Bar; woodily outfitted La Côte de Boeuf restaurant; Winter Garden for dining and dancing, with flower-framed pool and lush greenery; freshly perked Coffee Shop, with above-average snacks; Le Bateau discothèque spinning at a mooring beside the hotel. Our first choice by far.

The **Parkhotel** shows laudable managerial effort and expenditures. Every room now redone; despite the inhibiting effects of its vintage structure, some units (but not all) compare favorably with and even outclass the Hilton. There's a very appealing dining room overlooking a 7000-tulip flower patch, and a café. The cane-ceilinged bar and adjoining lounge is beside the narrow Westersingel waterway; the front garden is beautifully terraced and dotted with umbrellas. Hard-driving direction by C. A. van Hout; improving steadily.

The **Atlanta** is a confederation of charms, too. Popular horseshoe bar hung with paintings; 6th-floor units with private balconies. Units on the 4th, 5th, and

6th levels with access to ice-cube machines in the corridors; other bedchambers offer ice buckets; TV available; some modernistic touches, such as leatherette bed headboards here and there. Manager E. F. Sack has at last got this one in the bag.

The **Central** also has done its homework. Paneled café, a stunner; bar in he-man tones; every bedroom immaculately maintained; small baths through-out. Director Philipsen is an ultrawarm and kindly gentleman who exudes friendship; his staff reflects his concern for hospitality.

The conveniently located **Rijnhotel** is only passable. Singles hardly larger than closets, with baths about as cramped as iron lungs; panel-windowed, narrow-bedded doubles that should rightfully be singles. The architect who conceived this gleaming but benumbing dollhouse should be rapped on the knuckles and demoted to designing silos. The **Savoy** impressed us as being studiously spiritless and institutional. Modern as a nose cone and just about as inspiring.

The **Euromotel**, 20 minutes out of town by the apron at the airport, is a sleek contender for motorists, birds in flight, and eremites. Richly decorated restau-rant in the style of a Valais tavern; wonderful bar in subdued tones; modern rusticity in public rooms; full air conditioning. Its 100 units are divided into 60 hotel bedchambers with full bath and 40 motel accommodations with shower. Doubles facing a small canal and lake; singles fronting the jet-ways; soundproofing throughout.

The **Delta**, 6 miles out in the petro-industrial community of *Vlaardin-gen*, is unique. It is not only *on*—but literally *in*—the Maas River; just pour a libation, put your feet up, and view the fascinating restless maritime parade of hundreds of ships that silently slip by every day. Incidentally, here's the only luxury hotel in the world with insurance against ship collision.

Restaurants When mealtime rolls around, please, please don't miss the fabulous tower, the **Euromast**. This 240-ton appendage crowns a 606-foot pylon; the effect is reminiscent of a giant up-ended swizzle stick. About 40-feet up there's a barnacle bulge that contains a working facsimile of a ship's bridge; a bluff, hearty merchant mariner is always on watch to explain its controls, instruments, and gadgets. At the pinnacle are 2 observation platforms from which you can gaze as far as 60 miles, plus an even newer Space Tower that revolves as it ascends. One-flight below are 2 restaurants—the tiered, popular-price mass feedery and the plush Rôtisserie. Suave décor; variable cuisine. The view of the world's busiest harbor and the city is, of course, indescribably beautiful. Unique in the nation.

Coq d'Or (van Vollenhovenstraat 25) has its own cachet, too. We feel, however, that top attention comes only to those who are familiar to the house. In summer there's a serene garden for alfresco repasting. Inside there's a barlike counter where medium-light dishes are offered to clients-in-a-hurry (goulash, chicken stew, tomato soup, and so on); a blackboard lists the choices. Extending from this is the candlelit dining room; formal dining upstairs, with ultrachic clientele and lilting piano melodies which set the exact mood craved by both your digestion and libido. If you pull any strings to be recognized or recommended, we think you might find it very pleasurable indeed. Closed Sunday.

The **Old Dutch Inn** (Rochussenstraat 20)—on the same tack—is the meeting place of Everyone Who Is Anyone in Rotterdam. It's large and exceedingly popular; the décor is very Old and very Dutch. Waiters sweating so hard and running so fast they could be a Keystone Comedy act; atmosphere so frenetic it bursts the pleasure bubble. Go from 9:30 P.M. onward to duck this treadmill pace. The cookery fulfills the yearnings of Hollanders for rich, gooky sauces and zillion-calorie fare. Ground-floor coffee-room and balcony dining; higher-than-average prices. Closed Sunday. Packed for lunch and dinner.

In Den Rust Wat (Honingerdijk 96) is a thatch-roof cottage, vintage 1597. Enchanting single room in ancient rustic motif; careful service; magnificent fare for the region; delicious Snails Provençale and Pepper Steak; quality wines; startlingly cheap for the value. The name means "Bide-a-While" and the invitation couldn't be more sincere.

The **Heineken Hoek** (Coolsingel 65) occupies the Holbein Huis premises and augments other Hoeks in Amsterdam and Antwerp. It was urgently recommended by an especially dear friend, who bursts into lyrical operatic arias whenever he describes the wonder, the beauty, the celestial zest of the beer they serve in this joint. The friend's name? Freddy Heineken, who makes the stuff.

The **Chalet Suisse** (Kievitslaan 31) can be very pleasant if you're in the mood for what it offers. Park surroundings; spacious chalet-style architecture; main floor rimmed by a rectangular balcony replete with scrubbed-wood tables and red-and-white striped curtains; waitresses in regional costume; tiered terrace in front for sunny-day dining or tippling; chummy bar inside. Gigantic 143-item menu; Swiss, French and Italian wines. Packed solid at night; slow but friendly service; closed Sunday. Recommended.

Alpine flavor in both dishes and ambiance can also be found in the **Euro-Motel** Airport restaurant, while an inn-ermost atmosphere is available at the cozy **Herberg** (Kleiweg). **De Pijp** (Gaffelstraat 90) is about as rough as they come. Open kitchen at your elbow; 7 wooden tables pushed together in community fashion; flotsam décor; sawdust on its stone floor; expert cooking. A favorite of true-blue Rotterdamers and often difficult for outsiders to get inside. Not for fainthearts, but highly recommended.

The **Witte Paard** (White Horse), on the outskirts, compares unfavorably with a "country" restaurant in the suburbs of New York or Washington. The exterior blends rusticity, antiquity, and _haut décor_ in properly eye-catching proportions—but the interior, at least to us, is a letdown. Not to our taste.

Night Life Rotterdam's night lights glimmer most invitingly at **El Amra**, a 3-minute toddle from the Hotel Atlanta in midcity. Intimate dimensions cunningly achieved by a hefty stone partition between its twin segments; "showtime" a solo crooner; intimate dancing interspersed with fad-prancing the principal themes. We hope the drinks have improved of late. After that, we'd rate them this way: (2) **Bristol** (glass-lined round-robin nest; superb for late teen-types who don't mind the jam-up on the dance circle; watch your billings here); (3) **Casino de Paris** (2 dimly lighted rooms with candles in bottles; Undersea Bar with huge, garish, fake fish and a few eenie-weenie goldfish with inferiority complexes; expanded Louis XVI Bar; band okay; whisky okay; sandwiches okay; good but not outstanding); (4) **Embassy Club**

(a cozy nest for nighthawks); (5) **La Bonanza** (circular realm under a giant spoked wheel on the ceiling; 2 bars; inner hub for the shortsighted, plus an outer raised ring for tierful gazing; legitimate whisky on our sip; international cabaret; scintillating strip by Mother Nature, despite the ladies' long acquaintance with Father Time); (6) **L'Ambassadeur** (becoming a tough hangout; peepers rank behind a plate-glass barrier; snacks-to-steaks available; show commences at 10:30 P.M., returning every hour until 3 A.M.).

Garden of Eden turned on a membership policy when it began specializing in films about Eve and her sinful progeny. Other less attractive, so-called respectable bars—the take-your-wife types—include **Top Hat, Atlantic, Plaza,** and **Coney Island.**

La Romantica (Witte de Withstraat 14) is a small, clean, coldly decorated room with harsh lighting and a lively neighborhood-tavern-style clientele; don't go out of your way. **La Roulette Bodega-Bar** (Schiedamsevest 146) offers watered-down Reno-type surroundings. Discothèque? **Le Bateau** rocks every night except Monday from 8 P.M. to 4 A.M. at an anchorage beside the Hilton. It's a happy bark. The **Dive Inn** and **De Wieck** compete for the same clientele.

If you're looking for riotous local color, a quick junket to Katendrecht ("The Cape" or Chinatown) is it. In this Seamen's Quarter, you'll find music, lights, and the fastest kind of action—after all, since a whole ship can be unloaded in a couple of hours these days, how much time can a poor sailor and his girl waste on discussions of Aristotelian philosophy? This very instant an effort is being made to dim the red light activity in this precinct, shifting all of the prostitution, saunas, and porn palaces over to the Feyenoord-Noorderland section; during the period of the Great Schism any taxi driver will know where the action is lustier. In the **Brooklyn Bar, Happy Times Bar, Neutral Bar, Pacific Bar, Tsong Kok Low's** chopstick emporium, and dozens of similar old-style saloons or cafés, you'll find dancing, boozing, grass-smoking (possibly), and skylarking in the raw. Lots of harpies on tap for company (some are perfect caricatures of Sadie Thompson). See this before midnight, if you're interested, with the swing through the legitimate nighclubs planned for later. Watch your watch and bankroll, drink bottled beer, and don't act like a tourist who has come to view the animals. They can be very rough indeed if they decide to make trouble.

SCHEVENINGEN (pronounced Skay-vah-ning-uh) is a big resort on the beach, part of The Hague and about 10 minutes by car from the center. Concerts, minigolf, swimming, a jetty with 4 recreational "island" platforms crowned by a 135-foot crow's nest for observation; a brand-new and glittery casino in its rebuilt Kurhaus; riding, nightclubs, soda-pop stands, American bowling alley; seasonal patronage but year-round hotels—the works. In many ways, it is the Atlantic City and the Virginia Beach of Holland.

The hotels here are typically resort style: built for the vacation trade, with an aura of gaiety and an air of nonpermanence about them. The **Kurhaus** seems to attract the most attention, mainly because of the casino, the largest in Northern Europe. (Entrance fee $2.30; no alcohol in the gaming room; winnings over 1000 guilders subject to 25% tax.) This will be the centerpiece of

a vast new recreational enterprise that is scheduled to reach maturity by 1985. The **Europa** offers a swimming pool, sauna, ladies' hairdresser, skittle alley; conference salons; garage and service station with direct elevator connection to your floor. Much improved. The **Badhotel** ("Bad" is Dutch for "bath," in case you're curious about this anomaly) is 1 block off the sea. Attractive cellar restaurant; ground-level feedery; bath-or-bad-tub-size rooms; so-so. The **Eurotel** is composed of apartments, which can be especially commodious for families on the move. Our personal preference in this cluster is the tiny, unostentatious, early-century-Dutch **Bali Hotel**, which is run in conjunction with the celebrated restaurant. Modest rooms; annex; spotless cleanliness; unattractive rococo exterior; fine bar; extremely friendly service; eye-poppingly sumptuous breakfasts only; no public rooms or lobby. Due to design limitations, the original building offers only 1 public bathroom per floor. But the fine newer *dépendance* in the adjoining building brings the room count up to 33, adding 8 doubles (all with bath) and 4 singles. This little haven is so popular it's almost always fully booked weeks ahead.

The **Hoornwijck Motel** parks just outside The Hague at *Rijswijk* on the Rotterdam road. Taverne for cozy fireside and taper-lit meals.

For refined dining, **La Coquille** in the Kurhaus offers recommendable French cuisine. Along the harbor row, **Le Duc d'Alf** and **'t Kokkeltje** both do magical things for fish. Bars and interesting Indonesian eateries also line this walk if you only desire a light bite.

When it's time to strap on the feedbag, the **Paddock** gets our vote for straight fodder; open all year. But if you have time for only 1 meal in this part of Holland, make it a rijsttafel at the aforementioned **Bali**. This is the twin to the Bali in Amsterdam. You'll find more than a score of platters (not plates) of the same exotic delights—bland or pungent, sweet or spicy, light or filling, according to your personal tastes—for a surprisingly modest price. Always crowded; reserve the same day, for sure.

For evening revels, **Tiffany's** offers a necklace of facets, each glittering with an agrestic polish, and each strung cheek-to-cheek by the collection of young gems and their janes beaded with pearls of perspiration. It's in the enormous Palace Gebouw. Low-price tithings and an upbeat spirit that should make most beachcombers glow.

THE HAGUE, with its narrow streets and compact town center, is a jewel of old Dutch architecture. Its museums are myriad and splendid, covering not only art but subjects of specialized interest as well. Here is the seat of the Government; Amsterdam is the capital, but national laws are made in The Hague. As an expense account city, it is rated as one of the world's most expensive hubs. The world-famous Peace Palace (meeting place for the Permanent Court of International Justice), the International Institute of Social Studies, the Palace in the Wood, and a number of royal retreats are all at The Hague. Good hotels, fair restaurants, the U.S. Embassy in its glacial Korte Voorhout building, crowded streetcars, conservative night life, canals, parks, parks, more parks, and century-old elms.

As for its sheltering arms, the leader, a fresh wind off the waves in the hospitality seas, is the **Promenade**. One drawback: It is so far into the outskirts

that the site almost borders the neighboring resort of Scheveningen. We were fascinated to observe how successfully its administrators have blended Old World luxury with twentieth-century modernity while conjoining cold-eyed commercialism with intimacy and warmth—feats of innkeeping legerdemain that are close to impossible. Many fine art works lining the public rooms; grandly patrician glass-lined restaurant; Couperous Bar plus café terrace; attractive snackery; viewful and efficient bedrooms. Most of the staff seem to be fed on happiness pills because of their cheeriness. Your own car is virtually a _must_ if you select this one. Our warmest recommendation.

Nearby, the slabular **Bel Air**, also a youngster, tries to match this local paragon, but to us the strong undertones of group tourism, remote service attitudes, and a less generous budget plainly show through the veneer. That's not to say it isn't comfortable; it is. Still, for approximately the same outlay, we would much prefer the Promenade, providing we had wheels.

In the city itself, the **Hotel des Indes** is the current leader among the Old Guard. In the face of change it has maintained its grace with commendable flair. Its situation, plunk in the middle of Embassy Row, is a B-I-G plus. Its forest-green and red-checked Copper Kettle grill is enticing; its public rooms, while stately, tend toward the fusty; its bedchambers have a dated but spaciously relaxing aura. A midtown winner that is continuing to step up its pace.

The new 144-room **Babylon** resides in a vast shopping complex that shoulders the city's main station. Its French-style restaurant overlooking the Koekamp Park and the adjoining canal is already gaining fame for its excellent cuisine; the banks of hanging flowers and the bar in cherry moiré silk add further touches of color and delight. All singles and 4 doubles with private balcony; rich textiles employed; 2 easy chairs in twin units; individual-control air conditioning, color TV, radio, and wake-up system; small but efficient baths. A welcome addition to the capital and very good indeed.

The **Central**, which may have closed to accommodate a midtown renewal scheme, is the site of the House of Lords Restaurant, formerly the culinary pacesetter of The Hague. The **Park** has undergone a complete renaissance. Rooms much improved by keen-eyed Director William Bergmans. Now there's ample parking space available for clients' cars—a happy coup because of the hotel's narrow-street location, 1-way traffic, and bumper-to-bumper snarl. Try to secure one of its larger abodes when you reserve.

In this cosmopolitan hub, the hotels offer the best cuisine of all. For elegance and smooth service the **Promenade** is the pick of the pack. For intimacy, the Copper Kettle in the **Hotel des Indes** wins a loving cup. The House of Lords in the **Central** is making a sincere effort to rejoin the peerage these days. Among the independents, the midcity, 2-story **Garoeda** (18A Kneuterdijk) spotlights Far Eastern delectations. Indonesian staff; a few European dishes; not expensive but very, very good. The **De Kieviet** (see below) provides sturdy competition in the Deluxe bracket. The **Saur** (Lange Voorhout 51), famous for fish specialties, is a runner-up; less costly, slow service, plain appointments; its snack bar has become _the_ hangout for local Americans—but damned if we know why. **Royal** (Lange Voorhout 44) is rather dull; ultraconservative surroundings, a fine reputation, as giddy as lunching at the Union Club. The **Bistroquet** (same square at

#98) is so popular that you must reserve in advance to enjoy its French preparations. **Chalet Suisse** (Noordeinde 123) is part of a chain; Swiss cookery in the Swiss manner, at medium tariffs. **In den Kleynen Leckerbeck** ("In the Little Gastronome"), Noordwal 1, counts exactly 14 tables. Clean, quaint Old Dutch motif; Lilliputian kitchen; tiny fireplace; they're especially proud of their Poulet Kiëv. A charmer. **Chez Eliza** (Hooikade 14-A) is gaining a following for its French skilletwork. **Roma** (Papestraat 22) wins *salutes* for its Italian creations. **Thousand And One Nights** (Bagijnestraat 24) features a whirling dervish in the kitchen who spins out Middle Eastern culinations. We've never puffed our hookah here. While **Tampat Senang** (Laan van Meerdervoort) is well regarded for its rijsttafel— most locals aver it is the best, in fact—we prefer the creaky sort of authenticity and easy aura of dear old Garoeda. You might disagree.

After sunset, the **Rose & Orange** is a cheerful pub for the Mug Set. **Alexandra** strips on a regular basis; she offers a floor show, too.

The **7 Club**, up 1-flight and operated for adults, recently was reshaped by its new owners. Improved. **L'Etoile's** downstairs hangout for teen-agers has music to suit its clients; fairly good but far from outstanding. **Charlotte Chérie** is a cozy, 25-watt-bulb bar, made to order for hand holding; tiny band, tiny dance floor, nice bartenders, gals, gals, and more gals; pleasant drop-in stop for a quick drink. If none of these turns up anything savory, there are about 25 more hitching posts—mostly small, intimate bars with the omnipresent B-gals.

UTRECHT, fourth ranking in population, is the geographic center; it's one of the oldest cities in the land. As one typical example of its modern thinking, a huge construction program has modernized the rail center, developed a trade-fair site, filled in 2 major canals, and incorporated a new hotel and business buildings into a melded metropolitan scheme. The full project will continue until 1982. Its Hoog Catharijne shopping center is functioning and shouldn't be missed by anyone with an interest in urban planning. Well-maintained hotels, most on the commercial side; busy restaurants; up-to-the-minute facilities. A railway junction, a hub for religious life, science, communications, trade—some Dutch prefer it to its larger sisters. Americans often don't, because many find it somber and dull. Famous industrial Fair in March and September; among museums, (1) one called "From Music Box to Barrel Organ, (2) the Central, with ancient and modern works, and (3) the Railway exhibits are the best-known of its 14 candidates; in addition, 6 castle museums are within Utrecht Province. The cathedral is magnificent; the Vismarkt (fish market) is so unusual no one should miss it. And speaking of sea denizens, there's a wonderful Dolfinarium at *Harderwijk*, where the lovely critters perform tricks; nearby is the 4-H'ers dream at the Flevohof agricultural exhibit. Finally, the Avifauna at *Alphen* is a delight for viewing our feathered friends; swans, rare geese, wood duck, plus other ornamental waterfowl and fluttery fellows occupy a Rhine-side park; fascinating!

For overnighting, the **Des Pays-Bas** has probably reopened after a total renovation. If it hasn't, try the **Figi** or the **'tKerckebosch**, both in *Zeist*, nearby.

VOLENDAM, a tourist oriented hamlet if we ever collided with one, has one redeeming feature, and that is the **Hotel van Diepen**, which is thoroughly honest and legitimate, and which serves the local specialties better than any-place else except perhaps the Spaander. The best thing to order is fried eel, of which they are proudest; it sounds terrible, but you'll be surprised how flavor-some this delicate white meat can be. At the **Spaander Hotel**, our recent "coffee table" consisted of soup, hors d'oeuvres, a variety of meats and cheeses, a some-kind-of croquette, and a pot of coffee; it cost under $4, and it wasn't bad for such a modest snack. At the **Old Dutch**, a Lowlands hamburger with good old native French fries goes for about $2.25. Fair.

WASSENAAR, 3 miles from The Hague, attracts most foreign visitors because of its well-known restaurant, **De Kieviet**, which is still a top favorite with the U.S. Embassy group and American residents. Modern tavern décor, with corner tables placed so awkwardly that Your Waiter automatically becomes Your Friend; glassed-in fireplace rôtisserie; daylight terrace-dining in warm weather. Acceptable fare at neck-snappingly high tabs; always reserve in advance. Some would consider it overrated and overpriced; others would be charmed.

ZANDVOORT (15 miles from Amsterdam, near Haarlem, and venue of the Dutch Grand Prix auto races) is almost everybody's beach—and its wide enough, too, to accommodate any throng. The **Bouwes Palace** boasts 19 stories and the championship among skyscrapers in this very Low Country. The **Bouwes Hotel** houses one of the most active casinos in the north. Total of 100 apartments and 48 rooms about the size of a gnat's eyecup; many of the former preempted by sea-fevered locals; indoor pool; sauna bath; penthouse restaurant somewhat more international under its Austrian direction. If we were to have one meal in the area, however, we'd hop into a car and drive over to *Overveen* where **De Bokkedoorns** dishes out its delights every day but Monday, when it hibernates. This, in our view, is one of the best bets in the district.

Norway

Europe's most northerly country is only the area of New Mexico, but it's so long and thin that distances are amazing. From top to bottom it stretches the same length as from New York to Omaha, Nebraska; from side to side, however, its width varies between 269 miles and 3.9 miles. The famous Skagerrak (same latitude as Scotland) separates it from Denmark; the northern tip rises far beyond the Arctic Circle.

Within its huge, sprawling area of more than 125,000 square miles there are slightly more than 4 million inhabitants—less than one half the population of New York City. Except for Luxembourg and some other tots, this makes it the least populated major nation in Europe—but one of the highest in the world in per capita income. Oslo, the biggest city, has only 475,000 people. Bergen comes second, with 212,000, and Trondheim third, with 140,000. It is so thinly occupied that killingly high taxes are a fact of life. Ethnologically they're dyed-in-the-wool Nordics; 98.7% are of pure local stock, 0.7% are the 25,000 Lapps, and 0.5% are miscellaneous; intermarriage is rare. The typical resident is blond, stocky, muscular, and healthy, with an avid zest for living.

Crook by crook, the coastline measures 12,500 miles—½ the earth's circumference, twisting through a 2 x 4 area—and most of it is islands and fjords. There's wonderful fishing everywhere; you can drop your hook off 150 thousand islands! (Look out! You might strike oil since the continental shelf here seems to be bubbling with petroleum deposits.)

The ideal way to see Norway is to visit all 4 types of terrain: The fjords, the mountains, the valleys, and the plains. The fjords are giant cracks in the earth's crust, where the sea runs along rock-walled corridors which are often a mile deep and a mile high. The big ones are on the west coast, facing Iceland, Greenland, and Canada. The mountains are scattered wherever you go; the valleys nestle peacefully in their shelter and in the depths of the great serrated plateau. The plains run from Oslo up to Lake Mjøsa, but the country is so rugged that only 5% of its land can be cultivated.

King Olav V succeeded the equally beloved King Haakon VII to the Norwegian throne in '57, and, as always, they continue to call this nation, which celebrated the 160th birthday of its constitution in 1974, a constitutional monar-

chy. Realistically, however, it is just about as socialistic as Denmark and Finland—topped only in this aspect by Sweden. Illiteracy is unknown. Transmission of venereal infection is a criminal offense. The endowed state religion is Evangelical Lutheran (96.8%), but all faiths are tolerated.

Don't worry about raccoon coats and red-flannel underwear; the Norwegian climate is duplicated in parts of Massachusetts. The Gulf Stream keeps it warm: In the summer, the means are 60° Fahrenheit at Oslo, 50° on the Arctic Circle; in the winter, they're 24° at Oslo, 10° where Santa Claus comes from. The midnight sun above the 66th parallel makes daylight last for weeks. There's no real darkness, even in the south, from May to August. On the west coast it rains so much you'll think you're in Waterville, Washington. Its flowers and cool green forest are profuse. Oddity: Its golf courses are among the most crowded and heavily played in the world. Why? Exactly 7 exist.

While in Norway, try to see everything you can. Get away from Oslo, which is beautiful but not typical; go west to the fjords or north to either the Peer Gynt Mountain Country (see our separate section) or to Finnmark, because you're not even scratching the surface of a magnificently scenic country if you don't.

If you drive your own car, please remember that Norwegian mountain roads (*e.g.*, Bergen–Oslo) can be hair-raising to vacationers who are timid about heights.

One of the very best bets for the first-time visitor is the exciting, luxury 13-day "**Norwegian Fjord Line Tours**" or 6 days on the "**Fjord Explorer Tours.**" Travel is by motorcoach and fjord steamers; stops are made at the number one mountain and fjord hotels (all offering private bath). In addition to fantastic scenery, there are all sorts of fascinating special events the ordinary traveler misses; on the longer circuit, for example, there's a mush out to the edge of Europe's largest ice field, lunch at an ancient farm, and much more. Route? Between Oslo and Bergen, *or* Bergen and Oslo; itineraries are duplicated, from either point of origin; departures for the 6-day round-robin from Oslo and Bergen on Tuesday and Saturday. The 3-day loops (daily departures in either direction) are extra-fine, of course, but the 6-day junkets include so much more that they're even better.

If you wish to strike out alone, the **Oslo–Flam–Stalheim–Norheimsund–Bergen–Oslo** circuit is possibly even more spectacular and rewarding for unescorted vacationers. This round trip can be done in 4 days, by train, boat, and bus, but extra time in Bergen would make it happier; logical en route stops would be the Fretheim Turisthotell at Flåm and the Stalheim at Stalheim. It's a tour you will never regret. *If you drink, bring your own liquor supplies for weekends and offbeat stops on these itineraries.*

The Gold-Plate Special is a tour of **Finnmark**—the land of Norway's fairy tales, where Kriss Kringle picks up his reindeer, and where the sun shines at midnight during the bountiful, green summer. If we sound like an old-fashioned Rotarian-Baroque illustrated lecture, it is because our enthusiasm for

this particular adventure is boundless. Hammerfest, 944 miles above the Arctic Circle, is the "highest" town in civilization—and the ultimate is reached via a 22-mile highway from the world's most northerly village of Honningsvåg to the North Cape itself. We feel that the vessels that ply these cold waters have considerably lower comfort standards than those ships steaming the more southerly lanes; therefore you might prefer air-and-overland transportation to cruising. Organized package tours have elicited an icy chill-factor from participants in some group plans, so be sure to select your agency with care.

Please note that *everything must be set up long in advance.* Stops can be made at comfortable and charming Guest Houses operated by SAS in the best tradition of the hunting lodge—wines and spirits excepted—with good beds, tempting food, pleasant but simple décor, and efficient plumbing. During the day you can turn the clock back some 200 years; seek out the migrant Sames in their tent villages and watch them lasso reindeer; drive on well-surfaced roads over the treeless Vidda (highlands), the stark beauty of which is matched only by the steppes of Russia. You can drop a line in any stream and hook fresh-water salmon up to 50 lbs., trout up to 25 lbs., and several varieties of game fish which were completely strange to us.

An excellent independent itinerary is **Oslo–Tromsø–Lakselv–Karasjok–Hammerfest**; it may be done in 3 ways. One tour of 6 to 8 days is by SAS plane to Lakselv, by hired car to Karasjok and eventually to Hammerfest, from there by Norwegian coastal steamer (clean, comfortable, cheap) to Bodø or Trondheim, and by SAS plane back to Oslo. (We are especially fond of the Coastal Express vessels, which are practically the only year-round links between the south, the north, and the lovely points in between. Take one of these island-skirting voyages if you can. Apart from the food, which is mediocre, it's a real life dream that you will always remember.) Karasjok is the Lapp capital, a few miles from the Finnish border; if the weather is pleasant, you can hire a colorful river canoe with an outboard motor, as we did, and cruise through the wilderness to this remote frontier. If you have your car with you and enough time, another possibility would be to follow Route 6, the North Cape road, all the 1517 miles; this gets so monotonous toward the end that you'll be crawling up the wall.

With the exception of rented cars, prices in Finnmark are relatively low. The Guest Houses cost about $35 per night. You'll need a warm coat, walking shoes, cap or beret, heavy socks, and (if female) a pair of woollies. The summer weather is generally warm and lovely, but sometimes that wind can be straight from the North Pole. Midwinter can also be surprisingly cheerful, despite the frosty nip. The hours of sunlight are brief, of course.

Do go to Finnmark or see those fjords farther south, no matter what. The Hardangerfjord, Sognefjord (fast boat service available), Sunnfjord, Geirangerfjord, and Nordfjord are so wonderful that any one of them will take your breath away.

☑ **TRANSPORTATION Taxis** Most taxis are modern and comfortable. If you are in a hurry, ask your hotel porter to call one before you come downstairs, and allow 5 to 10 minutes for arrival.

One hackie we met recently lamented, "Prices keep changing so fast that the hackies don't even have time to get their meters adjusted to the new rates!" Indeed this was well said because their tariffs now are stunningly high.

Trains Very good and improving steadily. The Arctic route runs 796 miles straight up to Bodø in the Land of the Midnight Sun. There are about 2000 miles of track, entirely nationalized, in part electrified. The remainder of the main lines are operated with diesel-electrics. Excellent service, streamlined cars, clean compartments, polite conductors on the overnight run to Stockholm; on some of the short local hauls, similarly good-mannered conductors and much better equipment than in the past. On the other hand, virtually all of the diners have been replaced by cafeteria cars (if the traveler is lucky) or by service carts.

★ **TIP** If you're traveling short distances (especially between Oslo and Bergen), pick Tourist class rather than First. Recently, when we booked on the former, we heard a terrific argument between an American lady and a conductor. Her travel agent had selected premium seating for her, but she preferred the economy cars. And she was right! The Tourist units are brightly decorated and divided into smoking and nonsmoking departments; windows are wide; seats are the big airliner type that can be made to recline; you can also reserve one of these chairs at a slight extra cost if you're riding the rods within Norwegian borders. First class offers new coaches with 2 seats on one side of the aisle and a single on the other; they are an improvement, but we'll stick to Second.

As in the rest of Scandinavia, be prepared to lug, lug, and lug ALL of your baggage until your biceps go spastic. Particularly in the hinterlands, this is no area for the physically infirm.

☑ **FOOD** To the traveler's jaded palate, Norwegian food is simple, wholesome, and, in general, well prepared. Although the accent is on fish—hundreds of varieties, hundreds of tricky recipes—that doesn't mean they don't know a good beefsteak when they see one. As a rule, savvy Nordics avoid piscatorial delights on Monday. In a culture where the critter is no longer considered fresh if it is 5 hours out of the sea, any stored fish is regarded as old. Nets, by law, cannot be put down on Sundays; thus, the Saturday catch, while preserved on ice, meets with singular unenthusiasm.

Besides the savory ocean harvests, Norwegian specialties you may like are ptarmigan (mountain grouse), flatbread (crisp cracker thinner than a dime), multer (delicious, all-purpose dessert or jam made from yellow mountain cloudberries with a unique flavor), tyttebaer (known as "lingon" or cowberries to Swedes, this is a small, tart, red berry—a cranberry with a difference), local cheeses of Port du Salut type (not the goat's milk cheese which looks like kitchen soap and tastes like peanut butter), kreps (succulent, 2-inch freshwater crayfish), reindeer steak (dark red, fine flavor), whale steak (ugh!), and the Norwegian "sandwich," which will haunt you pleasantly wherever you go.

The first meal of the day, particularly in rural areas, is rightfully a world-famous institution. It is so extraordinary that elsewhere we have never found anything to match

it. Since only conventional fare is served upstairs during these hours, we suggest—nay, urge!—that you hie yourself to the Breakfast Room to reap its extraordinarily versatile benefits. In addition to such normal staples as coffee, tea, chocolate, juices, hot or cold cereals, eggs, and the like, the buffet table normally displays a bonanza of such comestibles as assorted herring, cheese, cold meats, fruits, jams, jellies, a mini-bakery of breads and much, much more. Whenever it is offered in its correct traditional bounty, it is a joy to behold and to savor.

Norway is a coffee-drinking nation; as in America, the tea is mediocre. It is also the biggest cheese-eating nation in the world; per capita, each Oslo citizen (infants-in-arms included in this statistic) packs away nearly 25 lbs. per year!

In restaurants and nightclubs every voyager should know in advance that ALL food in this nation, no matter where it is purveyed, is disproportionally expensive—with Oslo fare the biggest offender. Universally the prices are flat-out shocking. Just as unfortunately the service standards generally do not match the caliber of its historically fine kitchen. Inflation is beginning to erode quality: lower grades of meat, poorer vegetables, inferior oils and other baser ingredients are now too often being substituted for the exacting specifications of yore. Numerous restauranteurs—all struggling valiantly to hold down the costs—appear to be applying that line from *H.M.S. Pinafore,* "Things are seldom what them seem/Skim milk masquerades as cream." Many of the leading hoteliers, however, still regard their dining rooms as client sweeteners or as loss leaders —the shrewdest advertising they can provide to attract and to retain the loyalties of their followers. Our best meals on this latest trip were consumed in hotels. Most of them were infinitely better than most of those we experienced among independents.

Meal hours are cockeyed to foreigners. The residents eat a heavy New England-style breakfast at 8 A.M.; at noon they munch sandwiches at their office desks, working without interruption; at 5 P.M. they sit down to their big dinner, and from 9 P.M. to 9:30 P.M. they polish off their day with tea and more sandwiches. You can follow your own schedule, of course—but if you should be brave enough to try things the practical local way, hark to that rumble in your stomach until it's adjusted!

☑ **DRINKS** There's a government beverage control in Norway called the Vinmonopolet, and some of the vagaries imposed upon it (and the harried consumer!) by the legislature are the most mysterious in the travel world. John Law tells you how, where, when, and what you can drink; the regulations contradict themselves backward, forward, and sideways. Here are the rules, and please don't ask us to explain them. Over-the-counter drinks are dispensed *only* in Oslo, Bergen, Trondheim, Stavanger, 7 small towns and in the most popular tourist hotels of the hinterland. Spirits may be served only from 3 P.M. to midnight or 1 A.M.; not one drop can be served on Sundays or May 17 (election day) anywhere in the land. The aforementioned tourist hotels are the only establishments allowed to start pouring at 1 P.M. Beer may be consumed all day and all evening except on Sundays, when it is withheld until noon. While the larger establishments are generally fully licensed, almost all of the smaller ones can sell only beer and wine. Bottles up to any number may be obtained in the official Wine Monopoly (Vinmonopolet) stores. In the larger cities they function between 10 A.M. and 5 P.M. on

Mon., Tues., Wed., and Thurs., opening an hour earlier on Fri. On Sat. and days prior to national holidays (if they do not fall on Sun.) their hours are from 9 A.M. to 1 P.M. *Buy all liquor for weekend consumption or for any off-the-beaten-track excursions before leaving Oslo or the key centers.* Should you be forced to do so in the designated tourist houses, you'll be charged up to 50% more than the normal levies.

The prices are intoxicating. By the drink, here are examples per "large" orders (5 centiliters, which is far from generous) in leading establishments. Normal proprietary Scotches, bourbons, good vodkas, and good gins, $3 to $3.50; aquavits, $3; cognacs and other liqueurs, $4 to $5.50. Normally this would not be too rough, but these portions are almost ridiculously elfin in size. In buying bottles at the Wine Monopoly, here are some sample tariffs: proprietary Scotches, $22 to $24; premium Scotches, $32 to $36; vodka and aquavits, $17 to $20; French cognacs, $24 to $50. And the wine—wow! Random quotations when sold in hotels and restaurants: better Bordeaux, $40 to $60; inferior Bordeaux, $20 to $30; fair Burgundies, $24 to $40; champagnes, $44 to $60; sherries, $35. It's a great country for anyone who is on the wagon!

Linje Akevit or aquavit is the pride of Norwegian distillers, and distinctly palatable to most visitors. "Linje" means "line," and every bottle of this brand has been mellowed on a ship that has crossed the Equator. The action of the sea supposedly softens the aquavit. Always drink it with beer; this "keeps away the red nose," Norwegians say. (Danes say the opposite!)

But tie a stout cord to each ear to prevent your head from spinning à la Beechcraft propeller before tackling a brand called Brennevin 60 Per Cent. It has the highest proof of any akevit or aquavit in the world—120. (The strongest proprietary Scotch, in comparison, is a schoolgirlish 86 proof.)

The most popular local liqueur is St. Halvard, a Bénédictine type worth trying. Claret is the national favorite in wines, and the stocks are fairly good. Beer drinkers should order the export type; the lighter ones are thin.

If you are on very good terms with a restaurateur, he may break the law for you by serving aquavit before 3 o'clock—but don't be surprised if it comes up purple. That's just a drop of Dubonnet added to fool the other diners!

For the rites of the Skål ceremony turn back to our "Denmark" chapter.

☑ **TIPPING** One dividend which the sweeping march of socialism has brought to the 3 Scandinavian countries and Finland is the virtual elimination of tipping. The workers are so highly paid as well as cosseted by the governments on the womb-to-tomb cliché, in addition to the fact that their newly instilled sense of pride makes acceptance of gratuities "beneath them," that visitors to these nations now almost get away scot-free from this practice. Although Finland is the most most notable in its absence, today Norway is not far behind.

Two are still mandatory everywhere: Approximately Kr. 2 for each piece of baggage carried by the porter when checking in and checking out of hotels, and a universal charge of Kr. 2 per individual at the checkrooms of restaurants, nightclubs, hotels, or elsewhere.

After lunching or dining, despite the size of the bill it is entirely optional whether the host or hostess wishes to leave a maximum of Kr. 2 on the table to cover the whole group.

The other suggestion is that taxi drivers are never tipped in Finland and seldom tipped in Norway.

☑ **LOCAL RACKETS**   We found none. Norwegians are too proud to be petty.

☑ **INFORMATION CENTERS**   The Norway Travel Association (Landslaget For Reiselivet i Norge) is a large, beautifully managed organization which is visibly and undeservingly suffering from lack of financial support. The government and the commercial companies (hotels, airlines, et seq.) who subsidize it have so blindly and witlessly contained its operating budget that recently it was forced to eliminate its Branch Manager in London. Its chief is the highly efficient Just Muus-Falck. It publishes scores of free posters, booklets, and hotel guides. Here is the top of the umbrella. For the smaller details, check with the **Oslo Tourist Information Office** (at City Hall). Each can either fix it or find it in minutes. These dedicated people want tourists. Despite this shortsighted fiscal bind, they're going all out to get them.

Norwegian Information Service (facts about the country) is at 505 Fifth Avenue in New York, but the **Norwegian National Travel Office** (facts about travel) is on the 11th floor at 75 Rockefeller Plaza, N.Y. 10019.

★ **TIPS**   The Oslo Travel Association set up a **"Know the Norwegians"** program to introduce visitors to English-speaking residents who share their business, cultural, or hobby interests. If you apply to this headquarters in advance, specifying your expected date of arrival, arrangements will be made for you to be taken into the bosom of a Norwegian family. July and August are the leanest months because so many local citizens are away on vacation. No appointments will be made until you show up in person. Free, of course, as a warming example of international brotherhood.

CITIES

OSLO   is the colorful hub of the wheel. It's the capital, chief port (which is saying a lot in this maritime nation), and nexus of society. Despite its aformentioned sparse population density, in area it is one of the largest cities on the globe. Picture Norway as a human finger pointing downward; Oslo is on the inside tip, up from the crook of the first joint. Good hotels, excellent restaurants, 3 major airlines (SAS, Wideróes, and Braathens SAFE), fine trains, mild climate, handsome men, beautiful women.

Sightseeing   Seven-seas' relics range from original Viking ships to the 1895 polar vessel *Fram* to the *Kon-Tiki* raft to the papyrus *Ra II*. The harbor is a sporting sailor's paradise; gunwale to gunwale are the finest ocean racers, sloops, ketches, yawls, schooners, yachts, and other dreamboats with the capacity to turn grown men into boys again. The highly imaginative **Henie-Onstad Museum at Høvikodden** (7 miles west of the city center) was donated by the late ice-skating queen and her shipowner husband, Niels Onstad—both born here but later U.S. residents. The area contains more than 200 contemporary paintings, plus a "pop" gallery in which local pop-ers show their stuff; facilities for ballet, concerts, and selected exhibitions, as well as a congress hall,

a cinema, a restaurant, a cafeteria, an open-air theater-in-the-round, and an esplanade at the base of its fanlike terraces which stair-step down to the lip of tranquil Oslo Fjord. Here you will find Sonja Henie's massive trophy collection. The complex is a proud button-popper for the nation that spent millions of kroner in its creation. Interestingly, this lazily sprawling minimetropolis boasts so much elbowroom that the annual Holmenkollen ski race covers a 35-mile run and 2000 cows graze on tidy farms—all within the city limits! The landscape is gently rolling pasture land and plain—not typical of the terrain as a whole, which is rugged.

OSLO HOTELS Quick Reference Table

Price categories by national (not U.S.) standards.

EXPENSIVE:

Grand Karl Johans Gate 31. Tel. 334.870; Telex 11683; 510 rooms. P. 702
Scandinavia Holbergsgt. 30. Tel. 113.000; Telex 19090; 476 rooms. P. 703
Continental Stortingsgt. 24. Tel. 419.060; Telex 11012; 179 rooms. P. 703

UPPER MODERATE:

Ambassadeur Camilla Collets vei 15. Tel. 441.835; Telex 11446; 50 rooms. P. 704
Bristol Kristian 4's gt. 7. Tel. 415.840; Telex 11668; 143 rooms. P. 703
Stefan Rosenkrantzgt. 1. Tel. 336.290; Telex 19809; 130 rooms. P. 704

MODERATE:

Astoria Akersgt. 21. Tel. 336.700; Telex 18754; 99 rooms. P. 704
Helsfyr Strømsvn. 108. Tel. 672380; Telex 16776; 115 rooms. P. 704
K.N.A. Parkveien 68. Tel. 562.690; Telex 11763; 115 rooms. P. 704
Nobel Karl Johansgt. 33. Tel. 337.190; Telex 11915; 61 rooms. P. 705
Norum Bygdøy Allé 53. Tel. 447.990; 100 rooms. P. 704
Ritz Fr. Stangsgt. 3. Tel. 443.960; Telex 19668; 49 rooms. P. 704
Viking Biskop Gunnerusgt. 3. Tel. 336.470; Telex 11342; 313 rooms. P. 705

LOWER MODERATE:

Carlton Parkveien 78. Tel. 563.090; Telex 11152; 50 rooms. P. 705
Fordbundshotellet Holbergs pl. 1. Tel. 208.855; Telex 19413; 87 rooms. P. 705
Summer Sinsenveien 15. Tel. 377.090; 107 rooms. P. 705
West Skovveien 15. Tel. 562.995. P. 705

ENVIRONS:

Gabelshus Gabelsgate 16. Tel. 562590; 48 rooms. P. 704
Gyldenlöve Bogstadveien 20. Tel. 601.090. P. 705

AIRPORT:

Esso Ramstadsletta 14, Høvik. Tel. 121.740. 54 rooms. P. 705
Globetrotter Fornebuparken, 1324, Lysaker. Tel. 120.220; Telex 18745; 150 rooms. P. 705

Hotels The capital's **Grand** is masterfully directed by General Manager Helge Holgersen. Among its enticements: Captivating Penthouse Restaurant

Étoile with deliciously authentic French specialties; Palmen Restaurant, traditionally one of the captial's most chic gathering places for lunch; celebrated Speilsalen Restaurant ("Mirror Room") with music from 9 P.M. to 12:30 A.M.; 24-hour room service; 160-car underground garage; conference facilities for 1000; baby-sitters on call. A fine indoor heated swimming pool and free sauna disguises its large bomb shelter, which is compulsory by law. Wanderers who seek a smoothly run house with the felicitously executed ambiance and architecture of tomorrow are especially pleased here. Splendid.

The 21-story **Scandinavia** opened in '75 as the tallest hotel building in the land. Spacious, low-ceilinged, pillared lobby is in somewhat sterile tones; gay, cozy, 2-tiered Holberg Grill with piped music and streamlined traditional Rôtisserie décor; 250-seat Café Royal; Gardisten Pub a fancy version of typical Oslo Beer Tavern, but this one combined with Hamburger Shop; strikingly handsome 21st-floor Scanorama Bar with magnificent sweep and jackets required. Intimate, 2-tiered, baby-spot-illuminated discothèque; free indoor heated pool and saunas; 24-hour room service; 160-car underground garage; conference facilities for 1000; baby-sitters; 19 suites; 476 comfortable but not especially exciting soundproofed rooms with latest gadgetry in deluxe, medium, and "standard" categories; mini-mini baths; special desk and staff for group travelers. This addition is indeed meritorious.

The smooth-sailing **Continental**, with its traditional high-tide hospitality, also has been so handsomely refitted that here is one of the proudest rigs in the port city. Dining room attractively panoramic; superb Fortuna Pub Maritime Restaurant; chic hairdressing salon and barbershop; 8 units specifically for early-morning arrivals whose normal accommodations have not yet become available—another convenience provided by the ever thoughtful administrators. You'll find a marble-sheathed entrance, the pleasant "Caroline" breakfast room with a buffet table of tempters, an immaculate Grill, the sidewalk-level Theatercafeen, a ground-floor bar plus another one in marine motif, a first-rate Swiss chef who whips up palate-pleasing vittles, and friendly, capable management by Mathis Berge. Its latest hit is the disco-bar called The Loft, open daily from 8 A.M., except Sundays, is one of the most popular haunts in town. Choicest niche—frankly, our favorite accommodation in Norway— is the 8th-floor, corner-situated Nautical Suite with terrace, TV, and beautifully executed décor; regroomed #807, which nods above the tree-shaded park, is almost as good; 4 less elaborate apartments also with a salty flavor. Solid comfort, superior facilities (in many cases, better than the other leading house), and warmhearted attention provided by the smoothly professional skippering of the perennially personable and gracious Mr. and Mrs. Caspar Brochmann, both of whom are adorable and adored. Beloved by most voyagers—for excellent reasons.

The **Bristol** has been given plenty of sparkle. The lobby is most attractive. Adjoining is the Library Bar, separated only by a wooden grill. Pleasant Trafalgar Bar; somber-paneled Grill, which is the Breakfast Room; crude and sleazy was our opinion of the El Toro cellar restaurant seating 350 to 400; Disco with higher type clientele. Accommodations are a mixed bag, with some quite good and some quite poor; many have splash-everything showers only.

We now rate this oldtimer as a giant step below the Grand, the Scandinavia, and the Continental.

The **Ambassadeur** is something special. Efficient little restaurant and bar; small pool and gym; space for 50 envoys, in its 20 suites and 30 rooms. Reception and lounge area featuring an aquarium and an interesting weapons exhibit; unusually appealing apartments with tiny refrigerators, framed tapestries, dark wood décor, telephone, radio, bathrooms with scales, and many umbrella-clad private balconies. Not really a full-scale hotel, but amply luxurious for anyone who seeks a quiet hideaway without fanfare. Top recommendation for its very particular category.

The recharged **Astoria** offers a modernistic lobby, 99 perky bedchambers, superb single accommodations, bath or shower with almost every unit, radiomusic consoles, lockboxes, double doors, and a lawn of turquoise carpeting. Odd facts department: Every inch of furniture within this entire house was constructed from a single African bibinga tree—so please don't carve your initials in the desk top! A solid utility address.

The clean and attractive **K.N.A.** offers 120 rooms with ultrasmall baths or showers (some old-fashioned); handsome restaurant and bar plus automat snack dispensers in stairwells; special children's menu; radios in every bedchamber. Book into the *older* section, which has better furnishings and a cheerier mien; the newer wing offers less space and beds in tandem. There's a somewhat impersonal, commercial feel to this establishment; many conducted tour groups stop here. The restyled, 115-room **Helsfyr** is now a good buy; Director Arne Haugland has an excellent efficiency-style house. **Gabelshus** completed a massive interior upheaval of it how-dah-like rooms. Converted Norwegian manor house about 5 minutes from the bright lights; residential setting with tiptoe tranquillity; flagstone pathway to its arched portals. Ingratiating ambiance; dining room flanked by a window-walled summer "conservatory" for lunching and snacking; flamed dishes served from a 1911 pram; cellar wine-and-beer rendezvous; kindly personnel reflecting the cheer of Proprietress Agathe Riekeles. Total of 45 rooms, all with bath or shower; our favorites are #206 and #207, which open onto huge balconies. **Ritz Hotell and Pension**, a stately white townhouse, occupies a quiet situation adjoining Embassy Row, 5 minutes by tram from the center. Handsomely turned out lobby; rich wood, leathery glass-bound lounge; lovely dining salon opening to sylvan courtyard; Telex; wine and beer only but set-ups served; friendly service. High on aesthetics and high on value.

Stefan, a Mission Hotel opposite the Bristol, has undergone an immensely thorough top-to-bottom facelift. Inside it has been radically refurbished and new furniture added, plus a children's playroom in the basement; outside it shows a totally fresh facade. Rightfully its biggest boast is the fetchingly redesigned upper-story restaurant, with cuisine and prices which attract knowledgeable locals, especially at lunchtime. There are now ice- and snack-vending machines on every level. The quarters, while somewhat limited in space, show a big improvement.

The **Norum** is especially geared for traveling families. Turreted, vine-covered building about 10 minutes from the center; air-conditioned Bar Bistro which angles out to a tiny popular restaurant with an acoustical ceiling and

ingratiating atmosphere. The serene ambiance of this mellow mansion, directed by Per Mathisen, is homespun; it is heavily patronized by Parliament members and NATO personnel. The **Nobel** has a tiny modern lobby which might put you off right from the start. Norwegian regional furniture—some antiques, some reproductions; a few bedchambers with refrigerator; a breakfast-only policy and indifferent standards of service seem to be the greatest liabilities here. The **Carlton** has zipped up the furnishings and widened the windows; for budgeteers or stoutish snackers, the special lunch table ladles out 16 self-service selections, including 1 hot dish. Still miniature but taking the right hormones. The **Viking,** one of Scandinavia's largest hostelries, is operated by Viking Hotels of Norway, which has appointed Manager Carsten Müller to oversee the extensive upgradings. Fresh facilities include a pub, a dance bar and lounge, a coffee corner, a rotisserie, a reception hall, plus 313 restyled bedrooms, most with private bath or shower. Quite ambitious. The **West** serves breakfast only; a mixture of good to modest accommodations, all with private bath. **Anker Summer Hotel** operates only June through Aug. on a low-tariff basis that should draw waves of budget travelers in season. Cafeteria available; all units with shower and w.c.

Next comes the reshaped and puffed up **Forbundshotellet** featuring quite a number of better accommodations with shower or bath. There are many single units; it's popular because of its fortunate location directly behind the Hotel Scandinavia and hence at the City Airport Bus Terminus.

On the outskirts of the capital, the SAS **Globetrotter** is one of the nation's most efficiently run hostelries. Set in parklike precincts overlooking Oslofjord, it is cozy, attractive, and s-m-o-o-t-h-l-y geared. Fully air-conditioned; Grill with sound food and serene atmosphere; fetching bar and lounge; conference facilities for 4 to 130 participants; well-planned bedrooms with bath, 4-channel radio, and message service. Also near the airport, **ESSO** recently opened a pitstop at *Høvik*, but we haven't rolled in personally. **Gyldenlöve**, in *Bogstadveien* behind the Palace, was given new raiments, but they seem to be heavy enough to be the costumery of an Ibsen play. The suites especially hark back to the Norway of Old even though they are virtually new. Okay for medium-budget historians.

Tariffs vary with the seasons. From May 1 to September 30, the top period, rates for the leading establishments in Oslo—Norway's most expensive city—are roughly $25 to $70 for a single, $50 to $100 for a double, and $75 to $150 for a suite—all accommodations with bath. Most houses now include breakfast in their rates; if they don't, it generally runs from $5 to $7 per person extra. A special discount for children under 12 and a further one for those under 3 are usually offered. We have already noted hotel prices have spiraled flabbergastingly. In the hinterlands, however, your dollars will stretch appreciably further.

Dedicated budgeteers? Since we're too bottlenecked here for additional entries, please consult our this year's edition of our annually revised, heavily updated paperback, *Fielding's Low-Cost Europe,* which lists scads more bargain hotels or pensions and money-saving tips for serious economizers.

Restaurants   Oslo comes up with the greatest culinary variety, with the best values and quality now available in the major hotel dining rooms. Pride

of the **Grand Hotel** is its enchanting Penthouse Étoile, which parades deliciously authentic French specialties in a strikingly urbane, modern milieu. Its **Palmen Restaurant** is a lodestone to the Smart Set at lunchtime, while its sprawling Speilsalen Restaurant ("Mirror Room"), with music from 9 P,M. to 12:30 A.M., is more informal and easier on the pocketbook. The **Continental** is now the only member institute in Norway of *Traditions et Qualité,* the highest-ranking federation anywhere that judges continent-wide international cuisine. The cordially welcoming, window-wrapped main dining room is its star; in addition to its versatile à la carte menu, a superb 3-course table d'hôte dinner may be savored here for $25. Added to this is the more modestly scaled Caroline breakfast room with a sumptuous buffet table. The most elaborate culinary magnet in the **Scandinavia** is its stylish, 2-tiered Holberg Grill with piped music and updated Rôtisserie décor. As additional lures there are: (1) the knockout 21st floor Scanorama Bar with a magnificent panorama and jackets required while snacks are dispensed from 1 P.M. and 3 P.M. and drinks until 11:45 P.M.; (2) the Gardisten Pub, which is a dolled-up application of a typical Beer Tavern and which is combined with the Hamburger Shop; (3) the intimate Hetland's Jubalong, which is a disco with tapes from 8 to 10 and which then switches to live music until 3:30 A.M.; and (4) the excellent, low-priced, 250-seat Café Royal with breakfast buffet until 10:30, lunch buffet to 2:30, à la carte thereafter, and snacks continuously from 7:30 A.M. until 11 P.M. The cookery at the **Bristol** has slid downward, in our opinion. The main Trafalgar Bar with its suave ambiance and the smaller Library Bar (which is in essence part of the lobby) are both hits. As for dining places, we find the quality at the Grill indifferent, at the Disco better than passable, and at the crude El Toro cellar restaurant depressing. The **Stefan**, near the **Bristol**, has attractively redesigned its upper-story restaurant, with servings and prices which appeal to canny residents especially at lunchtime. The **Astoria** is solid, even though it can't turn on much glamour. Both the **Carlton** and the tiny operation at the **Norum** also offer good benefits. Ten minutes from town near the airport, the Grill at the **SAS Globetrotter** is an especially serene and felicitous oasis.

Among the go-it-aloners, **Frascati** (Stortingsgata 20, near the Continental Hotel) has been the traditional leader. Air conditioning in summer; charming little bar; piano-Solovox music for dancing; friendly service; mediocre spiritless cookery. The owner is trying to maintain its venerable name, but we're not yet convinced that he can achieve this goal.

The 30-table interior of **Najaden** (on the island of Bygdøy and in the Ship Museum, 10 minutes by ferry from the Town Hall) oozes with Norwegian maritime décor; the service plates bear a map design from A.D. 1539; picture windows open to the fjord and the legendary Polar ship, *Fram.* The major meal (euphemistically called "lunch" by foreigners), consists mainly of open sandwiches. À la carte service is available; you'll find a trio tootling nightly. Men must wear jackets after 7 P.M. Usually a winner.

Blom (Karl Johansgate 41, 2 blocks from Grand Hotel), a remodeled wine store, caters to artists, writers, and as many tourists as they can pack in. Big sandwich table with 30 varieties daily from 11 A.M. to 2 P.M.; other dishes, including 9 specialties, run an uneven gamut from topflight to poor. Rollicking fun, but not at all cheap; most visitors like its regional flavor.

In the colorful Strøget, a shopping mall, **King George Steakhouse**, with its adjoining Pub, is introduced by an open patio, a fountain, an antique coach, wagon wheels, and a few alfresco tables. Inside, the booths are set into horse stalls, each one honoring a great mount in equine history. The waiters sport nifty tartan waistcoats. Our grilled meat was not from one of the track-bred residents of the paddock, but it was tough enough to suggest it. We haven't yet seen the **Operaklubben**, which opened nearby, but we'll inspect it soon.

Wessels Kro (Stortingsgata 4), near Frascati, is named for the eighteenth-century poet who wrote and imbibed in Oslo. Four interior segments in a row duplicate the pub-crawling haunts of the famous Norwegian literator and toper. Ground-floor back room recreating a street lined with timbered stucco walls and log-end flooring; intimate upstairs nook with tiny dormer windows overlooking the tavern "alley" below; 5 tables under a low ceiling; enormous snack table for self-servers. Our meal was quite respectable for the modest outlay; the service was kind but somewhat fumbling. Open daily from 9:30 A.M. to 11 P.M.; always safer to reserve in advance. Interesting and likable.

Gallagher's Steak House (Karl Johansgate 10) was an authentic reproduction of its famous namesake in Manhattan. After earlier promise, now it is hardly better than routine. The adjoining Pancake House was flipped into a flatter flapjack called the **Sir Winston Pizza House**. The pub-pizzeria personality just doesn't come off, in our opinion.

La P'tite Cuisine (sometimes called Chez Ben Joseph) is a tricolorful entry in midtown. There's a bustling rotisserie plus a night spot upstairs with dancing until 4 A.M. The house boasts "crispy" duckling, pepper steak and such Nordic specialties as steaks of salmon, reindeer, and whale. (They claim the seafood is caught fresh daily; we wonder if that includes the baleen platters.) Smiling team of straw-boater-topped waiters in illustrated aprons to greet incomers with a parley-voo; photos of well-known or well-fed guests; French songs in the air; 3-foot-long breadsticks bristling from 2-foot-high crocks; prices moving up steadily. Funloving Ben Joseph is the key to the cheerful élan of this house. But who eats élan?.

Jaquet's Bagatelle (Bygdøy Allé) costs perhaps two-thirds as much as better-known and fancier places, but its dishes are among the most savory under the Midnight Sun. The service is generally frenetic. Favorites of budgeteers with educated palates are Crevettes à l'Indienne and Volaille à l'Indienne. Exceptional value if you seek food and not frills.

Lanternen, on the Bygdøy waterfront, releases stacks of mouth-watering publicity about its "American" hamburgers and other "U.S." specialties. Unfortunately, however, the PR man isn't the cook. Not for us, after our samples.

If time hangs heavy on a Friday, an entertaining place for lunch is **Tostrup-Kjelleren**, opposite the Parliament Building, where many Ministers dine when the weekly Palace conference is over. Tempting Norwegian sandwiches; also open for dinner.

The open-air **Konge Terrassen**, across from the Royal Palace, beside the Haakon VII Statue, is a kingly setting for princely rewards.

In the mushrooming **Vika area** near the Opera House, a number of small and interesting restaurants are proliferating. **La Popina** (Haakon VII gate 5) is 1 block from the Hotel Continental on the fringe of this section. Upstairs you

will find a low-ceilinged, discreetly lighted, sizeable but cozy sectioned room which comfortably accommodates about 40 tables. At lunch it provides only open sandwiches and other Norwegian midday standards. At dinner, however, it switches entirely to Italian specialties, with a 56-item menu blanketing the field from Pizza to Antipasti to Piccati Milanese to Cassata Siciliana. During our browsing we investigated the **Two Busy Butlers** and the **Cheese House** to examine their milieux and their listings. Both are quite attractive. If you are in a mood for exploring, why not stroll into this small patch to choose which- ever appeals to you?

The restaurant in the **Edvard Munch Museum** serves light and full meals. Big windows opening to the street and park; tiny dimensions; natural wood walls; orange tablecloths and black-leather-covered chairs; reasonable prices. Not at all special, but okay for Munching.

In *good weather only*, there are 4 lovely spots which should be considered. **Dronningen** ("The Queen") is the Royal Norwegian Yacht Club headquarters; it's at the end of a long concrete drive in Oslofjord, 10 minutes from the center. Built on piles; beautifully decorated. Huge-windowed Sextant Bar in the upper reaches done in blues, reds, browns, and white, with a magnificent harbor view; topside Captain's Cabin. Norwegian décor; sea-level Boat Deck restaurant suspended just a bit above the wavelets. After you've had some grog up in the spars, you may choose either galley for dinner. Delightful to the eye and to the seafaring spirit, but—sadly—a dismal shade of its former glories in the culinary department, owing chiefly to its seasonal operation and resultant staff problems. **Frognersaeteren**, 25 minutes by funicular or 20 minutes by car up the mountain (1387 feet), is a municipally owned and privately operated sports- restaurant with a magnificent panorama from 2 tiers of open terraces; if you can tear your eyes loose from the succulent white grouse on your plate, you can see at least 20 miles down the Oslofjord on a clear day. Authentic Norwe- gian log house, interestingly decorated; crowded with skiers in winter and tourists in summer, so be sure to reserve ahead; gorgeous when the sun is shining or the stars are out. The century-old **Holmenkollen** is 20 minutes from the center. Regional stained-wood exterior with wide windows and magnificent vista from its front terrace; cafeteria at one end with 40 tables and large hearth which usually works Sundays only; cozy dining room in the center, charmingly decorated; adjoining dining room at other end for overflow use in summer. The cafeteria begins operations at 11 A.M. and the dining room at noon; both shutter at midnight; snacks, apéritifs, and beverages usually available on request on the outdoor patio. The view alone makes the excursion worthwhile. The **He- nie-Onstad Museum** at Høvikodden can combine a multitude of treasures with your nutrients. When the fjord isn't frozen, summer travelers can wrap up the entire package with a pennies-only cruise from the city on stately ferryboats. There's a cafeteria with excellent inexpensive renderings that can be ruminated inside or on a huge open-air terrace. For the particulars on what's doing when you're in town, check with your Hall Porter. A sightseeing must.

Night Life The after-dark establishments in Oslo encourage the Singles Scene. It is happily accepted by all. The **Telle Complex** tells it best. Except for the aurora borealis, it offers the biggest spectrum in Norway. This opera- tion includes the agreeable Café En Cocotte for French cuisine, the restyled

Rainbow, which is brighter than ever, and the Natt disco with food and drink. For a tough, low-down outing, **Rosekjelleren** (Klingenberg 5; 1 block from the Continental Hotel) might be made to order. Here is the magnet for Norwegian sailors on the loose; they put on their best suits, belt down several quick schnapps, and then stalk through its doors, loaded for bear (or bare?).

Discos? In addition to the aforementioned Natt in the Telle Complex, **Frascati's** entry is also very popular. Hetland's Jubalong at the **Hotel Scandinavia** attracts an older and more conservative audience. **Benyos**, with its North African ambiance, seemed undistinguished in comparison to the rest.

Membership spot? The **Down Town Key Club** (Universitetsgaten 26) is it, if you care to pick the lock. It has been given new tumblers in the shape of the Storyville, a New Orleans style restaurant with appropriate music, the smokey Moke Café, and the enlivened Up Town Bar, all with sharps and flats through the whee-whee hours. The leader of the "in" crowd in naughty old Oslo. The **Leopard Club** in the Bristol Hotel is a handsome cub. A spot worth checking on your next safari. **Château-Neuf** is a student nightclub; proof of this status is required.

Finally, there's a wonderful beer cellar for the Norwegian student trade called **Dovrehallen** (or occasionally Studentkroa) at Storgata 22, 10 minutes from the Grand Hotel. Here the youngsters let off steam, and it's most definitely worth seeing—particularly between mid-May and mid-June, when the "russ" (those who hope to pass their exams) are sporting their striking red caps. See if you can arrange through your hotel director or travel agent (or a friendly sophomore) for admission to this members-only attraction, because it's worth the effort. Beer is the sole beverage; students' orchestra, occasional students' floor show, even students' "police" to keep order; drop in between 7:30 P.M. and 11:30 P.M., if you can work it, and you're in for a treat.

For feminine companionship, the **Ribo Restaurant** (just off City Square, 1 block below the Grand Hotel), the **Rosekjelleren**, and the **Telle Complex** usually offer the best opportunities in winter. Between 7 P.M. and 10 P.M. are the customary hours.

Shopping   Avoid the national Luxury Tax (16.67%) by arranging with the merchant to ship important merchandise direct to your home. You'll need an export license for antiques.

Our ★ ★ ★ ★ recommendations are individually noted.

Jewelry: Norwegian artisans have developed fine enameling to the point where not even Venetian or Florentine craftsmen can successfully compete with them. ★ ★ ★ ★ **David-Andersen** (Karl Johansgate 20), almost universally considered to be the leading house in the country for this work, wrecks our budget every trip to Oslo with their irresistible enameled demitasse spoons, cake forks, and solid-silver salt-and-pepper sets. Another big draw is their original collection of 11th-century Viking jewelry facsimiles—perfect copies of the "Dragon Rampant" ornamentation uncovered in archeological excavations. These exquisitely handworked "Saga" *bijous*—brooches, rings, earrings, pendants, bracelets, cufflinks—are ragingly popular. It carries a full line of hand-crafted sterlingware in exclusive antique and modern Norse patterns, contemporary silver jewelry, and unusual forget-me-nots for gentlemen. For enameling and silver, ask for Miss Dickens, and for jewelry ask for Mrs.

Kjolberg; these extremely nice gals know our Yankee tastes. There's a beautiful branch in Bergen. Tops for gifts—to friends or to yourself.

Tostrup, across the street, also has an enviable reputation and sound merchandise—but we don't have quite the same enthusiasm for their displays as we do for David-Andersen's. Perhaps you'll disagree.

Prize arts, crafts, and industrial design: ★ ★ ★ ★ ★ **Forum** (Rosenkrantzgate 7) is the 20+-year-old Permanent Sales Exhibition of the works of more than 130 of the nation's leading artists and artisans. Ask for the friendly Managing Director Arne Remlov in this nonprofit organization. **Den Norske Husflidsforening,** popularly known as "Husfliden" (Møllergaten 4), has an old name and a large selection of home arts and crafts.

Regional souvenirs: ★ ★ ★ ★ **William Schmidt & Co.** (Karls Johansgate 41 and Fornebu Airport) has everybody licked in wearables and mementos of genuine Nordic flavor. Nothing—repeat, *nothing*—on its shelves is mass-produced. Most sought-after items: Their wonderful sweaters and pullovers in old Norwegian patterns; their famous "Vams" and handwoven silk-lined jackets; their dramatic, long-lasting handbags, gloves, hats, ski boots, and other wearables in genuine seal; their attention-arresting reindeer-skin hats, slippers, or reindeer knives. Collectors of curiosa will find intriguingly sweet woodcut figurines and trolls, as well as dolls in beautiful native costumes to bring sparkle to the eyes of Feminine Small Fry. For the home, you'll see hand-printed place mats, handwoven table runners, pewter in profusion, and scads of other interesting items. American Express and other major credit cards are welcome. Ask for Director T. Fjeld Fretheim or his daughters, Mrs. Ellen Hauge or Mrs. Elizabeth Syberg, the current Family Standard Bearers who are most warmly obliging. Highly recommended.

Exquisite hand-printed lambsfur wearables: ★ ★ ★ ★ **Li Dahl** (Kjeld Stubsgate 1) has revived this almost forgotten Norwegian tradition into a stunning "new" and unique handicraft. Each item, carved as a woodcut, is different and 1-of-a-kind. High-style coats, jackets, rugs, mittens, and other beauties are made in this incredibly suave material at costly tariffs which are merited. Write to Li Skinntrykk for its brochure.

Antiques: **Kaare Berntsen** (Universitetsgata 12) sets the pace, both for quality and price. Smaller **Wangs Kunst** (Kristian IV's Gate 12) and **Hammerlunds Kunsthandel** (Tordenskjoldsgate 3) sometimes offer good rummaging as well. We're particularly fond of **Bergfjerdingen** (Damstredet 5)—2 elves' rooms with copper molds, wood, glass, pottery, and a big fireplace.

Shopping Bazaar: The butchers' stalls in the historic brick firehouse behind the Cathedral have been rebuilt into enchanting little shops which no interested visitor should miss.

Department store: **Steen & Strøm** has a representative cross section of Norwegian retailing.

Shopping hours: In most of the larger cities: Weekdays normally 9 A.M. to 4:30 P.M. in winter, sometimes to 4 P.M. in summer, and 9 A.M. to 1 to 3 P.M. on Saturday, with no noontime closings. Many places stop at 1 P.M. on Saturday, while others do not open before 10 A.M. on Monday. Everything is shuttered tight before Easter for a 7-to-10-day national vacation.

Dedicated shophounds: For shopping in Bergen, for more stores, more

details, and more lore, please consult the purse-size, 25th Anniversary edition of *Fielding's Selective Shopping Guide to Europe.*

Other Targets

(*Refer also to our special section:* Peer Gynt Mountain Country.)

AALESUND is a calling spot for steamers on the Coastal Expressway. It is built on islands; when your ship pauses here for its usual 2 1/2-hour docking, a run up to the summit of Aksla Mountain (only 625 feet high, but with a restaurant affording a breathtaking view of the waterways) is about the only show in town.

AL The Bergsjø is our choice for overnighting.

BERGEN, as jaunty as ever, recently kindled up her 900th birthday candle. She's on the Atlantic side, directly across from Oslo, and her population of 215 thousand makes this sprightly dowager the 2nd largest city in Norway. Don't miss this jovial matron of the seas; her medieval charm will captivate you by day and enchant you by night. A magnificent panorama unfolds from Fløien. There's a fish market where you can select your dinner while it is still swimming; there are turreted bastions, crazy little houses built before 1800, the Edvard Grieg shrine, the aquarium, the intriguing Maritime Museum (don't miss this one if you've got salt in your veins), an upbeat pace to improve a previously indifferent hotel picture, good restaurants, and good comfort. Shipbuilding, trade, and harbor activities keep most of the people busy; don't believe the legend that "it always rains in Bergen"—it is only 99% true, and then only in 10- or 15-minute spells. For local information, call on the Information Office of Tourism, on the square near the Bristol Hotel.

Hotels As for overnighting pleasure, the **Norge** has risen in such a quantum leap that today we rate it in design, décor, appointments, cuisine, and administrative mastery among the 20 greatest major hotels we have seen in the world. Quietly modern lobby in marble tones; remarkable complex of no less than 9 dining and drinking operations ranging from an elegantly deluxe luminary to a sidewalk café, all different and all splendid (see "Restaurants"); Corner Disco Pub; shops; bank. Total of 241 air-conditioned bedrooms; 15 suites, the smaller ones on the lakeside featuring superb views; doubles all with a sitting area; warmly executed furnishings which are timeless; many private balconies; smallish but well-planned baths; 4-channel radio, direct-dial telephones with message lamps. Under the direction of General Manager Fridtjof Thirslund Berge, so outstandingly urbane, sleek, cheerful, and friendly that with delight we give it our all-out recommendation in every way.

Although the banking house which took over the **Bristol** was said to have rapidly planned to unveil a totally new hostelry, little of consequence had been changed on our months-later review of it. While its tariffs are almost as costly as the Norge's, this fusty inn is still obviously in aching need of this large capital infusion. Its cuisine impressed us as being uneven.

Other revamped candidates include the **Ambassador** (30 rooms and a small

restaurant) and the **Abels Hybotel** (18 units in a noiseless part of town; break-fast only).

The **Grand Terminus**, near the station but still surprisingly quiet, has become more and more of a streamliner. For many travelers, however, its ownership by a religious order and consequent lack of alcohol automatically drop it a notch as a holiday haven. We've come from a dry run here and—though parched to the core—we couldn't have been more pleased with the comfort standards, the cleanliness, the flavorful décor, and the gentle goodheartedness and deep-down-warmth of the personnel.

The **Orion** received a genial but not too serious revamping by its Friendship Group owners. Colors have been jazzed up, curtains rehung, spreads freshened, and upholstery redone. The restyled entrance affords a hospitable view of the cozy hearth and the nearby Bistro self-service snack bar with its scrubbed wooden tables. The dining-cum-breakfast salon is on the 3rd floor overlooking the harbor. Moderately good for the outlay.

The **Neptun** splurged on a million-dollar renewal program, adding an extra floor to bring its capacity to 111 rooms. It occupies the 4 top floors of an office building in mid-city. The reception desk is at street level. Its quarters are mid-size and tolerably well equipped. Better attuned to business people than vacation wanderers.

Rosenkrantz has upped the Neptun's remodeling ante to the tune of more than $5 million. Among its many changes, are a new, simply conceived lounge, as well as a new kitchen which make its Triaden Restaurant into a Grill with dancing and live music. Only 3 of its 82 units are without private facilities. In our opinion, with which you may disagree, this very substantial financial infusion is not being invested with the greatest of taste. Our suspicions are strong that this will continue to be basically a commercial hotel.

Restaurants The dining choices in Bergen offer surprising variety, though the emphasis, of course, is on seafood. The **Bellevue** is one of the most outstandingly spectacular restaurants in Scandinavia. Exquisite cuisine; stunning panorama of Bergenfjord and the city; aristocratically suave décor; background music; 16 candlelit tables; fixed-price repasts; à la carte expensive but not prohibitive for its exalted category; superb—repeat, superb—attention by Maître Einer Askeland, the dedicated pivot who has given happiness to uncounted clients during the 25 years of its working existence. New main-floor bar and disco. It, with the Hotel Norge, constitute the *only* truly distinguished dining places in this second city of the nation. Reserve in advance. A rare and true joy.

The parade of dining and drinking operations in the **Norge** is dazzling. They include the crowningly sophisticated gastronomic Main Restaurant, the Rôtisserie; the less-formal, expanded Baldakinen Restaurant on the open mezzanine (continuous service from noon until 11:30 P.M.); the Hjørnet ("Corner") Pub in dark wood highlighted with copper and brass fittings; the cozy Ole Bull (named for a historic local figure) with charcoal grills; the oaken Karjolen Bar with barrel stools active from 3 P.M. until 11:45 P.M. which turns into Norge Dancing to 1:30 P.M.; the glass-enclosed, all-year Pavljongen Sidewalk Café; and the Garden Room Restaurant from mid-June to mid-August, which has dancing. Each exudes its own special character, and each is superbly con-

ceived. It is no wonder that these draw a remarkable 55% of _all_ diners-out in Bergen—an obvious reason being that every one delivers outstanding values for its price range. Although the **Neptun** has a revivified dining room, to our disappointment we found no improvement in its fare. The **Grand Terminus** mutes us in its dreariness. The food we have had at the **Bristol** has always been markedly uneven in its preparation. The **Orion**? No longer would we wish to bother.

Among the independents, the **Holberg Stuen** and the **Wessel Stuen**, under the same ownership, offer low-cost, tavern-style edibles which are appetizing for their category. The maritime-appointed **Show Boat**, opposite the Norge, could be very pleasant at lunch or less so at dinner because—we can't put our fingers on it. Cuisine? Service? Clientele? The reasoning escapes us—but we simply don't like it, while perhaps you might. If you are in this district you might prefer the dine-and-dance **Oscar II**, which is located astern of Show Boat. It's cozy. **Holm's Discosteak** is masterminded by ever-fresh and spar-kling Gunnar and Anna-Karine Holm, whose enthusiasm is pervasive. We haven't seen it, but the idea of combining a grill and discothèque under one rollicking roof sounds fun. Pretty young waitresses in red overalls; stuccoed walls; candlelight; and a limited menu are reported as pluses for these 2 dashing Nordics. We wish them luck both here and at their **Amorine Villa**, located near the Norge Hotel.

Budget dining? The **Gamle Bergen Tracteursted** is situated in an old house 5 minutes north of the center. Its Victorian furnishings and period atmosphere gave us the feeling of walking into an elderly grandma's living room. Time marches backward.

BOLKESJØ   The upgraded 240-pillowed **Bolkesjø** is worthy of bearing this town's fair name.

BREKKE   The amusing **Brekkestranda** comprises split-log construction with rooms and even beds fashioned to scorn rectangular patterns.

EIDFJORD   is a useful speck on the motorist's map because of the scenic drive via Fossli to glory in the waterway and the Vøringsfoss waterfall. Your rooftop here will be the **Vøringsfoss**. Very basic accommodations; its high point is the hand-painted dining room rendered for free drinks by the famous Norwegian artist, Bergslien. Worth a detour for a nip and a peek. For wheel-borne travelers, the **Norheimsund Fjord** is a comfortable stop with a conve-nient motel segment.

ESPEDAL   Refer to Peer Gynt Mountain Country.

FØRDE,   naught but an angler's haven, offers the **Sunnfjord** shining with space for 330 Waltons keenly bent on early-morning fly-casting. Hardy's of London has hooked up a fishing school here with $10,000 in equipment for use by guests, plus experts standing by with baited breath to show how to use it. All units have bath or shower; about $250 buys a week of shelter, food, instruction, and whatever you can catch. You'll find a new wing, a new indoor

pool, a solarium, and more recreation rooms. This one gives our line a mighty big tug.

FREDRIKSTAD is a tale of 2 cities: the New Town (35-thousand modern-minded citizens) and the Old Town (cobbled streets, moats, and surrounding fortress walls, 700 souls, all of whom celebrated its 400th birthday in '67). Here is the site of the famous Plus craft center (its ateliers are open to the public). When it's time for a meal, the best bet in the new town is the **City Hotel** (in the dining room, be sure to wear a coat and tie, gentlemen). If you are searching for a restaurant in the older section, we like (1) **Kongsten Fort** (almost exclusively for groups), (2) **Tamburen** (year round), and (3) either the **Stabbursloftet** or the **Gryta** (both outstanding cafeterias in Scandinavia's largest food center).

GEILO is so special that it is very dear to our travel hearts. On the main railway line halfway between Oslo and Bergen, it offers 1 main street, a handful of cozy hotels snuggling above the valley, excellent food on virtually every table, and an intimate spirit of holiday frolic. Here, for our öre, is one of the most rewarding pockets of vacation cheer on the map of Norway. In the future it may vie with Zermatt, Zürs, Courchevel, and other chummy corners for Europe's upland Jet Set swingers. The ski runs are not as long as they are in the midriff of the Continent, and the cold (yet superdry) air may be too brittle for all except the hardiest outdoor types. But, as a let's-get-away-from-the-rabble resort, this tiny gem is hard to beat. Between Geilo Sport (our favorite) and Intersport, there are 800 pairs of excellent cross-country, down-hill and slalom hickories for rent, plus poles, boots, toboggans, motorized snow scooters, all types of ice skates (the municipal rink is open all winter), and curling equipment. Crowning the peaks and serving as the nexus for winter pioneers or summer hikers is the gloriously panoramic Geilo Toppen. This glassbound restaurant and cafeteria is at the top of the main chair lift, midway between the village and the upper reaches of the mountain range. The local Tourist Office will happily arrange for rental of any tack or gear for any sport in them thar hills—from an adventure-filled hunting trip afoot, aski, or aboard a gasoline-pepped Snow Cat, to pony trekking on the moors, to trout fishing at any of the 40 nearby lakes or streams (license: $1.60 per day, $7 per week, or $13 for the full season). If you prefer your very own wood-lined, ultracomfortable chalet, the Tourist Office can fix *that* too. For a relaxing pause to refresh sagging spirits through unspoiled natural treasures, we'd be hard put to think of any better spot. Please go, if you can; we think you'll fall in love with it, just as we did a long time ago.

If you follow our advice to pause here, the flashy-but-tasteful **Bardøla** now steals the local thunder for travelers with modern tastes. Situation on a hillside glen above the town; private ski lift; spacious; sleekly rustic public rooms and lounges; bar for salubrious slaking; glass-lined dining room with woody touches, cascading greenery; cellar nightclub bouncing mostly for the young and spry; down-in-the-cellar gameroom with minibilliards, minibowling, and a toyland of diversions to keep the Small Fry out of mischief (free supervision, baby-sitting, and scheduled programs for kiddie pastimes); superb His and Hers sauna facilities; beauty salon; large basement hall planned exclusively for

skiers (individual racks for every resident; drying pegs for boots and wet togs;
buckling-on platforms; tools and gimmicks galore); horseback riding available
in summer; health center, gym, and solarium; swimming pool yet another
lovely fluid asset. Proprietors Egil and Elsa Walhovd have spent a treasure
chest of kroner and love to expand this once-modest pension into a First-class
(not Deluxe) enterprise. Traditionalists or family groups historically had opted
for the aging **Holms**, at the fringe of the Geilohøgda (6-minute chair lift, plus
T-bar for the lower ranges). The expanded **Highland** has windows scanning
Lake Ustedalsfjord. Lobby in birchwood, with regional furnishings, 2 working
fireplaces, and rugs on the walls; pleasing touches of a spinning wheel and
antiques hither and thither; dining room in stone and wood; cafeteria to handle
its ever increasing package-tour traffic; updatings in one wing; indoor swimmery; good cookery; small, spare bedchambers with linoleum floor coverings;
poor baths. The **Ro**, on the main drag, is lower in category; ground-floor
cafeteria; pleasant Kro restaurant; not bad. **Geilo Pension** is fun for its Old
Norway atmosphere; Young Norway romps in its downstairs discothèque;
inexpensive gaiety. **Alpin**, on the outskirts, seemed stiff and flairless. The **Geilo
Hotel** offers a modern flavor which we laud. Across the valley on a rocky
plateau, engineers solved an alp's-worth of topographical problems and unveiled the **Sportel**, which has had its agonizing share of teething pains. It has
been taken over by the Bardøla interests, so it has more of a sporting chance.
It accents the antique décor of the region. Also available is the adjoining colony
of chalets. Back in the vale, the **Youth Hostel** is clean, neat, and very cheap;
mostly English-speaking youngsters occupy its bunks.

GOL,   along the general path between Oslo and Bergen, can provide shelter
at **Per's Hotel**, a worthy contender. The surrounding station village is not very
charming.

GOLÅ   Refer to Peer Gynt Mountain Country.

HARPEFOSS   Refer to Peer Gynt Mountain Country.

HARDANGER PLATEAU   Here's a lovely highland perch. The **Hovden**
at **Setesdal** offers good basic accommodation.

KINSARVIK   The 90-bed **Kinsarvik** is a nirvana for nature lovers. New
and especially convenient for ferry passengers crossing the Hardanger to
Kvanndal.

KONGSBERG   The **Grand** offer the tops in accommodation.

KRISTIANSAND   is on the lower tip of the nation; it is a thriving ferry
point for Denmark, England, Germany, and Holland. The leading hotels are
the fresh **Caledonien** or the older **Ernst**. The new **Christian Quart** offers bed
and breakfast only.

KRISTIANSUND   straddles 3 islands with connecting bridges. This center is a fishing port and the striking-out point for climbing tours to the Nordm

øre Alps. Lovely to look at, but not much action. If you stay, check in at the renewed **Grand.**

LILLEHAMMER   This remote mountain setting offers the **Sjusjøen** in the hills above the village or the rebuilt **Nordseter Mountain** with an indoor pool.

LOEN,   in the Nordfjord region, offers the **Alexandra,** with a good kitchen; it has pulled down most of its older limbs and built new ones. The drawback here is its bigness (space for 300 guests), which makes it something of a nordic beehive. For sightseeing, few can top the eagle's-nest **Videseter**, a perch high, high, high, above the Vide Valley. Owner-Manager Erster has razed the former shell and erected a 50-room house, all with private baths. Now he's considering an even newer extension. Excellent for overnighting; an *olé*ing La Jolla reader tells us that "since the tour buses now generally stop here for lunch only, there is blissful quiet after they leave. The food is excellent, the lodgings most comfortable by U.S. standards, the staff attitudes unusually pleasant, the cocktails perfectly mixed—and, as you say, the panorama is fantastic."

LOFTHUS   For overnighting, the **Ullensvang** has undergone a beauty treatment that is a credit to its cosmetician—especially in the pool area. Each room faces the water; the citizens don regional costumes every Sunday. Fun, and now very solid.

MOLDE   is famed for her roses and her panorama of 87 alplike peaks. In the Møre and Romsdal fjord district, the **Viking** at **Ørsta** is the newest hotel, but the older standbys still attract settled vacationers through their smooth-running portals. These are the revamped **Union** at *Geiranger* (*what* a vista!), the updated **Alexandra** at *Molde*, and the **Grand Bellevue** at *Andalsnes*. The area is one of the most striking in Norway.

NORESUND,   nibbling charmingly on the shores of Lake Krøderen, offers pleasant arms at the **Sole**. Modern atmosphere hewn from a former doctor's residence; especially noteworthy for the breathtaking vista. Moving north to the vales of the Valdres district, the **Beito**, in the mountains above *Fagernes*, provides space for 140 guests in 70 rooms; 9 suites; full bath and shower count; air-conditioned; captivating view of Jotunheimen. In the mountains west of this village, the **Sanderstølen** has been colorfully rebuilt from the ashes of a serious fire. Upland gaiety at its sprightly best; 115 units, 1/2 with bath or shower; very sound. To the east, the **Spatind**, boasting 84 accommodations, all with bath, is smoothly operated by Mr. and Mrs. Stig Johansen. In Fagernes itself, **Fagernes** is the king.

ØYSTESE   rolls up with a motel outside the center. The **Gudvangen**, farther up the pike, is better as a coffee stop or excursion target than for overnighting; too modest in mien for most Yankee and Canadian tastes.

RAULAND   The **Rauland** or the **Solfonn** at *Seljestad* are recommendable stops.

RØROS is a historic mining town and a cross-country skier's paradise; miles of rolling slopeland which stay under good powder until the end of April; strictly for sportsmen who love it in winter and antiquarians who love it in summer. The choice stopping place is at the **Røros Tourist Hotel**.

SANDEFJORD, the one-time whaling city (this commerce once made its inhabitants the most affluent citizens per capita in Norway!), proudly boasts of its **Park Hotel**. This monument to Moby Dick and his descendants is so extravagantly constructed, so lavishly outfitted, and so generously maintained that it will never make a dime—and the beauty of it is that it was planned this way! As a result, here is not only one of Scandinavia's finest hostelries, but one of the top oases in all of northern Europe. For physical diversion there are the sliding-roof, saltwater, heated pool (with its very own grill and bar, no less), a gym for fisical fitniks, a solarium, bubble baths for effervescent therapy, keep-your-chin-up underwater massages, 2 saunas, a host of automatic pinsetter bowling alleys, golf links (20 minutes), motorboats (available at the Marina), for sightseeing, fishing, and fjord bathing, and a local hunting and fishing club where you can arrange to hook a salmon from late June through August. The main salon, the Restaurant (dancing nightly year round), the Bistro lounge (snacks, lunch, and sips), and the Jonas (a cellar hideaway where the freshmen-to-postgrad set congregate Sat. evenings). Stay only in the main building. Competent direction by friendly, experienced, Hans Smedsrud. In the environs, the rebuilt **Klubben**, out at _Tønsberg_, is a mod-minded knockout these days. Umbrella-dotted and awning-shaded waterside terrace cracking with the snap of wind-kicked flags; stone-floor reception; window-lined dining spread with schoonerisms on the walls; double rooms with sitting areas; facilities for yachting, golf, congresses, and dancing nightly to combo music. A big plus for the region, so be sure to reserve well in advance.

SKÅBU Refer to Peer Gynt Mountain Country.

SOGNEFJORD REGION We'd pick **Kvikne's** at _Balestrand_ or the 190-bed **Sogndal** at _Sogndal_.

STALHEIM The 100-unit **Stalheim** sweeps the local honors. Attractive lobby gladdened by rich woods and regional antiques; all rooms with bath; some beds in nook-style alcoves. Many amenities, but its brightest feather is the awesome view down the Naerø Valley. Open mid-May to mid-September.

STAVANGER Except for a housing shortage that has rocketed residential rental and sales prices beyond the troposphere, a skyscape dotted by sleek new high-rise buildings, and fatter costs of living, little has been changed in this old, bucolic, and lovely fishing port in its emergence as a key petroleum center. (It remains, in fact, the capital of the national sardine industry.) The normal oil strike pattern of hard-boozing boomers, honky-tonk joints with B-girls, con artists, pitchmen, grifters, and venal merchants does not exist— and never has since the first black gold was discovered off its shores. The same Norwegian orderliness and the same fetchingly open simplicity prevail. Visi-

tors ignorant of its enormous new riches would have to be extraordinarily sharp-eyed to detect them without being told. Nor has it become a resort, despite the fact that 10 of the country's 18 miles of beaches are in this area. It is a characteristically charming town where most of the 88,000 residents (a big recent jump) still go to sleep early, still attend their churches faithfully, and still smile in their encounters with other members of humanity. Incidentally, the people pronounce their town "Stah-VAN-grr." A "Siddiser" is a person from here.

Since this center is experiencing such a petroleum boom, advance reservations here are a must nowadays. The city boasts the handsomely appointed and immaculate **S.A.S. Royal Atlantic;** stay here if you can, because most travelers feel it's worth the price difference from the local competition. Now it has a brand-new lobby, reception, dining room and seafood restaurant, plus a bar-cum-carvery. Indisputably the leader. The 120-unit **K.N.A. Hotel** was built as an apartment house and converted. The Grill is a placidly pleasant room stretched to include an old-fashioned corner that has lots of intimate appeal. Ask for the redone Skapsenger-type doubles with Murphy beds; the rest are uncomfortably small. Although there are obvious limitations, it is immaculate throughout and its management is right on top of the operation. **Esso Motor Hotel** now belongs to a Swedish group. It is the main center for North American residents. Nautical Inn-Spot Bar; 75-place Skipper Worse Grill with bad ventilation; small pool and gym plus sauna; 60 studio accommodations in a new wing. Director Otto A. Emilsen is cheerful and sparky. It is very informal, with no jackets or ties ever required. The hilltop **Alstor** has been partially rebuilt following a serious fire in '75. Routine lobby; exceptionally attractive 100-seat dining room; b-i-g, brassy dance bar; new tiny rooms badly planned; old tiny ones just plain bad. We go here for felicitous dining but never for overnighting. Although the **Victoria** is noted for its outstanding restaurant, its accommodations are so cramped, cheerless, and uninspired, and the rates seem so exorbitant to us for what they yield that here is another in which we would never seek shelter.

Diners will find 5 old wooden wharf houses restored and opened as restaurants.

Currently our vote for leadership is split between 2 establishments. **Restaurationen** ("The Restoration") is a tiny, exclusive charmer which directly adjoins the somewhat mundane main dining room of the SAS Atlantic. It is named for the first ship which carried Norwegian immigrants to North America in 1825. In addition to being cozy, cheerful, and intimate, the provisions are in the superior class for the hinterlands. Since it contains only about 12 tables, advance reservations are mandatory. Patrons are offered the bonus of stepping across its threshold to dance from 8:30 to 12:30 each evening except Sunday in the largest installation. Delightful! The suave restaurant at the Victoria Hotel which is called the **Prinsen** was inaugurated in '76. Capacity of 130; attractive mulberry and darkish-wood décor; open grill at entrance; comfortable banquettes; hanging student lamps; piped music; open continuously from 7 A.M. until 12 P.M., starting with a versatile Breakfast Buffet; Lunch Buffet on weekdays. Both are expensive. The **Alstor** presents an unusually fetching dining room with 100 places, a gold ceiling, baby spotlights, and

a lovely panorama from its hilltop perch. Although its food hasn't much zip, its ambiance is very pleasant. While the Grill at the **K.N.A.** is enticingly furnished (don't miss the antique annex), it is unfortunately situated a half-floor below ground level, with a consequently distorted scene through its windows. The 75-couvert Skipper Worse Grill at the **Esso Motor Hotel** is heavily patronized by north American residents. Informality reigns here. Its ventilation is bad and its cookery could stand considerable improvement, in our opinion. Nonetheless it is merry during the peak hours. The **Blue Sky Cuisine** is owned and operated by non-Norwegian-speaking Chinese. The blend of Sino and Scandinavian accouterments attractively works. But how many travelers wish to fork out $6 for a single order of Spring Rolls? The **Hummeren,** on the ocean about 8 miles from the center, specializes in seafood. This fully licensed old-timer has outdoor service in benign weather. Well-prepared fare may be had at comparatively high prices. Those who order lobster from its pool or smoked salmon pay considerably more. The centrally sited **Ambassador,** owned by the Hotel Victoria, more closely resembles a café than a dining sanctuary. Its pleasant aura makes it an excellent drop-in spot for coffee, beer, or snacks. The sizeable **Columbus** features steaks and other grills. Crinkum-crankum architecture; captains' chairs; teak-type tables; low ceilings; leaden windows; no tablecloths. Its relatively inexpensive comestibles are quite ordinary in quality.

For *nightlife without food,* the Barbella in the **K.N.A.** admits only patrons who are 24 years old or more. Large, lovely, dark-wooded, burnt-orange layout in English style; 340 seats; 6 musicians; dancing and drinks; open 6 P.M. to 12 A.M. Here is a lodestone for more mature singles. It's perhaps the best after-dark rendezvous in the city. The **Alstor** has a b-i-g, brassy dance-bar in its cellar which draws many young singles. Not special.

TRETTEN   Refer to Peer Gynt Mountain Country.

TROMSØ   has a trio of winners: the **Grand Nordic**, the 300-bed **Royal**, which is piloted by SAS, and the more economical 53-room **Saga**. Be sure to reserve in advance before mushing so far north.

TRONDHEIM   third in importance in Norway, is pronounced "Trón-dee-em" by most residents over 40 and to rhyme with Sondheim by the younger ones. It's up the coast from Bergen, nestled in the wrinkles of the skin back of the first joint. Decatur, Illinois, is larger; timber, fish, and shipping are the chief industries. The cathedral is the finest of its kind in Scandinavia. Geographically, you'll find the setting delightful. It's on a fjord; the old name is "Nidaros," which means "Mouth of the River Nid"—and that's just what it is.

The **Britannia** is the only solid, gracious monument of hotellerie in this city. Large, lovely Palm Court in Moorish tones for dining; sizeable and lively adjoining dance-bar with rock band (!); intimate bar; banquet room with sumptuous buffet table; handsome, paneled lounge with creaky floors and Victorian clublike charm; Chief Concierge S.A.A. Berggren a gem. All 120 rooms pleasantly modernized. About 60 come with baths, 52 come with show-

ers, and every one has a private toilet. This 120-year-old family enterprise is extremely well run by delightfully friendly Mr. and Mrs. Stensrud. Head, shoulders, and top hat above all local competition. Next on our roster is the Müller chain's **Astoria**, which has been heavily redecorated in good taste. Intimate Bistro in the modern mood; TV room and lounge on 2nd floor; Disco dance-bar; 42 decent-sized Scandinavian-type units with bath; 10 singles with washbasins only. The best feature of the **NYE Sentrum** is its 6th-floor restaurant with a view of the city and the harbor. At its entrance 3 teak tables with individual plants and hanging lamps form a grace note; its corridors are brick-lined. There are 40 small, undistinguished chambers with bath, as well as 6 without this amenity. Acceptable but not notable. The breakfast-only **Ambassadeur** overlooks the river and a sylvan scene. As exemplified by its lobby, its accommodations are much superior to its public domain. Full count of 34 chambers of which 14 are doubles with separate sitting areas, all with bath, piped muisic, automatic alarm clock, and small refrigerators; 24 with balconies; 31 the choicest twin; wine and beer only. **Larssen** is a charmer for the price. Pleasant dining room lined with paintings up 1 flight; cozy lounges; restaurant and beer tavern on the main level. While the **Neptun** is considerably newer, it is the same type of house. Popular café; beer and wine served in dance-bar; 30 airy but somewhat cramped quarters, all with bath or shower. Not up to the Larssen in our tariff slot. **Trønderheimen**, across from the Prinsen, has chambermaids in regional costume, a honey of a dining room with authentic appointments, and simplicity in its economy-priced bedchambers. Fair **Gildevangen** is still braced intrepidly as a distinctive and imposing mini-fortress. The period 1905 inaugural aura is retained in its old-fashioned high ceilings and elsewhere; its attempts at dispelling this fall flat in heaviness and sadly do not come off. But while it is almost as grim on the inside as on the exterior, this aura is radically countered by the warm friendliness of its staff. An indomitable antithesis to today's sleeping factories. Travelers with cars can find an **Esso Motor Hotel** (just outside of town on E-6). The recently trundled-out 100-bed **Trondheim Youth Hostel**, on a hillock overlooking the sea, is one of the best of its type in Norway; dormitory style, of course, but clean as an Arctic breeze. The 98-room **Singsaker Studenthjem** is an alternate.

For multifaceted dining, go-go Entrepreneur Martin Michaelsen has orchestrated 7 completely different enterprises into a single building on Prinsen's Gate, all playing their individual parts in this lively carousel of entertainment. These include **Naustloftet**, a plain-ish pinewood sail loft with superb seafood; the suave **Rotisseriet "1842"** with tempting viands from its attractive open grill and a sleek décor; the **Kunstner Kroen** ("Artists' Corner"), an intimate disco-bar and restaurant for younger clientele; the **Landlord Pub** for British-style tippling in rather formal paneled surroundings; and the **Baren "Kontoret,"** a handsome, vintage-type bar in which subdued rouge and green predominate. Only the cellar **Grotten Bar** and the **Night Star** for celebrants until 2:30 A.M. are not unusually ingratiating. Except for the last 2, here is a spectacular and rewarding assemblage in cuisine, service, and atmosphere. The **Grenaderen** oozes with charm and urbanity. More than 2 centuries ago the structure was tenanted by a blacksmith; the old forge and other appurtenances are still there. Sophisticated rustic ambiance; about 15 tables; little **King's**

Room to rear with 5 more tables; adjoining bar delightfully reminiscent of an old-fashioned hunter's lodge; mini-attic with stools for imbibers; live music on Wednesdays and Fridays supplemented on other days by taped notes; fine lunch buffet except on Sundays; food service until 11:30 P.M.; high standards of cookery; also expensive. Happily recommended. The **Hotel Britannia's Palm Court** (Palmhaven) is renowned for its dancing, spirits, wine, and one of the leading kitchens in the environs. Its fountain setting with silky-green plants and built-in elegance contradict the northerly latitude in an extremely pleasant way. The **Skansen** is the most popular Disco which is patronized almost exclusively by the Young Set. Sandwiches and light snacks are available at reasonable prices. Typical of its type all over the hemisphere.

ULVIK offers the **Brakanes**—with its emerald lawn nipping at the skirt of the Hardangerfjord. This hostelry is perhaps the most stunning of all. Long, white, fresh-looking building plus a set-back annex (take the former in preference to the latter); lovely waterside terrace; some front units looking straight down the ripples; limited living space; open mid-May to late September. Recommended. The **Hotel Ulvik**, functioning as late as Christmas, is chiefly for passersby rather than for lingerers. The **Strand** is a frostbiter's delight. Step out of bed into a skiff or a sailing dinghy at your doorstep. If your ancestors were penguins, water skiing is also in the ice tap. Brrrrr!

USTAOSET (7 miles west of Geilo) has the **Mountain Hotel**, which was renewed from peak to foothills. Adjoining cafeteria-style **Three Reindeer Inn**; nightclub; grill; bar; 77 rooms with bath or shower; lowish rates.

VINSTRA Refer to Peer Gynt Mountain Country.

VOSS birthplace of Knute Rockne, presented to the University of Notre Dame a handsome memorial honoring this immortal. Pilgrims to this burgeoning village will find a cableway and several ski lifts to haul an ever increasing number of Americans and Britons each snowtime; the trails for walking or slicing down the soft white hills are among the loveliest we've ever seen (be sure to go to the very top first). Fine headquarters for fjord motoring excursions or skiing patrols into the nearby wilderness; après-ski activities for nocturnal upliftings, too.

The 48-room-and-bath **Park Liland** tops our list for dwelling space. Year-round operation; only a 10-minute walk to the aerial cableway (don't miss the view from up there); main-street situation opposite a church built in A.D. 1150; recreational facilities including an orchestra nightly, 2 bars, a TV parlor, a bowling alley, billiards, and Ping-Pong. Unhappily, the bedchambers lack even a smidgen of decorative verve. The gabled **Fleischer's**, so close to the station that every guest should automatically be issued a pocket watch, a fob, and a lantern with his door key, is so old-fashioned in its main building and so modern in its 18-room annex that the contrast is startling. Its "motel" afterthought, across the pike, is targeted for budgeteers, families, and—we suppose —"motorists." The **Jarl**, at the lower end of town, appeals more to Europeans than to Statesiders; its latest wing might provide more State-liness, however;

all rooms have showers. The **Youth Hostel** is another of the splendid Norwegian shelters for bottom-budget undergrads; this one is spanking new and one of the best in the land. The **Motel Voss** is growing; it is now up to 80 beds.

☑**PEER GYNT MOUNTAIN COUNTRY**   Here is one of the few remaining little-known, lightly trodden, breathtakingly beautiful touristic magnets in Western Europe. Scenic glory and celestial tranquillity are the keynotes of what its dwellers have long called "Our Friendly Wilderness." Within this triangle of 2200 square miles, with its apexes at Rondane, Lotunheimen and directly above Lillehammer, you may drive for an hour without encountering another car or seeing a single billboard. It is so pristine, in fact, that you may safely quench your thirst from any pool, brook, stream, lake or other body of water in the entire region!

The name springs from Ibsen's most acclaimed poetic drama, Grieg's opera, and the ballet which followed—one of which, incidentally, is presented hourly somewhere in the world 365 days per year. They evolve around the picaresque international adventures of this mythical Norwegian folk hero. Before starting, the playwright tracked down the grave of farmer Per (one "e") Gynt, the crumbling headstone of which attracts legions of pilgrims to the serene little cemetery in Vinstra.

This grid of diverse ranges and 5 valleys is about 3 1/2 hours north of Oslo by train or car. Bus excursions are made from both of the capital's airports and from landings of ferries from abroad. Because of the shortage of taxis, through prior arrangements hotel cars meet guests at the nearest station.

The winter season from December through April draws the majority of visitors to the slopes for downhill and cross-country skiing. Conversely, the less costly summer season from the end of May to Oct. 1 shows greater popularity in the glades. During the latter you may enjoy the lovely skeins of carefully marked and supervised walking trails, fishing, excursions, various sports including tennis (no golf)—but mostly relaxing to commune with nature at its sublime peak.

Six of the leaders, while operated independently, have loosely banded together to form the Peer Gynt Hotels Groupement. (Telex 18601 to reserve at any.) These are Skeikampen, Dalseter, Golå, Fefor, Wadahl, and Gausdal Mountain hotels (see below). Although full pension is required (reduced rates after 3 days in summer and 5 in winter), clients may lunch, dine or use the facilities of any of the other 5 without extra charge. All offer free entertainment and a resident dance orchestra. While these are fully licensed to serve drinks, some of the less prominent ones aren't.

The **Skeikampen Høyfjellshotell** (2622 *Gausa*, Tel: 28505) is our favorite. This gracious, elegantly sophisticated, impeccably maintained house commands a lovely sweep of lake and countryside. Flowers, candles, paintings, colorful rugs, and antiques abound within its tastefull precincts. Unusually felicitous indoor pool lush with greenery, with adjoining gymnasium and saunas; outdoor pool and sun terrace; tennis court; delightful Spanish-style Bodega, where proprietor Alf-Christian Anderssen gives tasting parties of Bordeaux selected by him in France, with special cheeses offered with his compliments; outstandingly sumptuous Norwegian lunch buffet; international

ski school; black tie 3 times a week in winter; other attractions; closed in May. Since he and his patrician wife collect wines, Haut Brion 1874, Mouton Rothschild 1876, Château La Tour 1907, and several other irreplaceable treasures are on display in the lobby. Accommodations include one suite, 3 junior suites, 50 rooms with bath, and 13 with shower. We rate this expensive but heavenly relaxing home-away-from-home as the pacesetter in the entire region.

The **Golå Høyfjellshotell** (2646 *Golå*, Tel: 1432), owned by the Norwegian-American Line, offers double-barreled amenities. Cozy main building with 30 well-furnished units (try for No. 107); 10-room chalet wing in birch with its own brand of charm; 4 individual yesteryear and 10 new modern double-party guest cottages, each simply and practically equipped for 6 persons with cooking gear, refrigerator, shower, toilet, electric clothes dryer, fireplace and wall-to-wall carpets; riding, tennis, sailboats, fishing, mini-golf, 3 neighboring ski lifts and cross-country ski tracks prepared by machine; closed Oct., Nov., and May. A happy oasis, especially for families in its cottages.

Dalseter Høyfjellshotell (2627 *Svatsum* Tel: 3313), also with a glorious panorama, comes up with a handsome lobby, an intimate Bar-Lounge with fireplace, a 230-seat dining salon, a heated indoor pool, 2 saunas, a well-equipped gym, horses for riding, a children's playground, and more. Its buffet table offers a viking-style breakfast from 8:30 to 10, as well as a versatile cold assortment with selected hot dishes at lunchtime. There are 83 chambers with bath or shower, and 9 with only a private toilet. Try to be lodged on its southern side for the scenery. Elsa and Erik Gillebo run this well. Worthy.

Among the most economical establishments in this group, the **Fefor Høyfjellshotell**, (2640 *Vinstra*, Tel: 35), draws our top ranking. Mountainside site over lake; ski lift, skating rink, curling, tennis, mini-golf, outdoor pool, fishing, saunas, dancing nightly; delicious country-style cuisine with marvelous breakfast buffet; well-maintained 1902 structure with Robert Scott mementos from training here for his South Pole expedition; old-fashioned public rooms with good fireplaces; essentially small bedchambers, some with showers, with the best in the new wing; basic quarters for basic outlays in the rear. Proprietors Aud and John Walter are warm and laudable hosts. Fun.

The **Wadahl Høyfjellshotell**, (2645 *Harpefoss*, Tel: 1446), is a magnet for young and young-in-heart Norwegians, Danes, Germans, and others who seek a folksy vacation. Sprawly public area of no special distinction; large, plastic-y dining room; cigarette, candy, drink and slot machines seemingly everywhere; handsome new indoor pool to supplement the outdoor installation; tennis, riding, fishing, rowboats, ski lift, machine-readied slalom slope; lively atmosphere.

Serious economizers may garner a welcome bonus if they reside at the **Gålåseter Fjellkro**, (2645 *Harpefoss*, Tel. 1562), on the hilltop directly above the gates of the Wadahl. It's only a short walk to the sports, dining and dancing activities at this much more elaborate and expensive hostelry, which quickly can become the seat of the action. The 90-unit pension, with 3 to 5 beds and running water only in each room, is simplistic; there's a reception desk combined with a self-service restaurant and coffee bar, plus a tiny lounge and a bodega-disco. No wonder it is chosen by so many money-saving groups.

Except for the glaringly large and out-of-key Coca-Cola sign plastered at the

entrance, the **Kampesaeter Fjellstue**, (2643 *Skåbu*, Tel: 3325), offers a very plain but ingratiating rustic atmosphere and a panorama which is fantastic. Attractively extended dining room; nighttime stube which r-o-c-k-s in season; 90 rooms and 4 guest cottages; furnishings somewhat tacky; riding in summer. World-famous ski instructor Willy Brandt teaches cross-country during the snow months and correct mountain walking techniques during the green periods. There's a convivial feeling here à la comfortable clothes and old shoes.

The **Sødorp Gjestgivergård** (2640 *Vinstra*, Tel: 1837), architecturally a Norwegian chalet, is almost a straightforward American-style motel in its interior. A pleasant young couple named Austerheim attained their life's dream when they opened it in '76. Large dance hall with live music every day except Monday; 16 rooms with convertible beds, showers, and no frills; lunch stop for bus groups; open all year. Take the full pension plan for $35 per guest, because straight overnight occupancy costs the same. This first meeting place for the small community is a clean and cheerful mixing ground.

Gausdal Høyfjellshotell (2622 *Gausa*, Tel: 28500), is a member of the deluxe groupment with correspondingly deluxe rates. In our opinion, however, it is most certainly not worth its standard investment. Except when the chartered tours pour in for the noontime meal, the ambiance is notably relaxed—but so is the upkeep. The most felicitous feature is its new indoor pool with its adjoining solarium. The accommodations—200 of them and 4 with balconies—are adequately large but very far from inspired. The food makes up in quantity the gap which it lacks in quality. The General Manager and the staff we encountered were the souls of graciousness and kindness—but we had the feeling that here is a hard-used hotel factory which copes impersonally with its large turnover. Perhaps you might disagree.

The **Espedalen Fjellstue**, *Espedal*, Tel: 26127 (65 beds for sportspeople; starting point for the canoe-camping excursion) and the **Ruten Fjellstue**, *Espedal*, Tel: 3357 (stunning sweep of countryside; chalet-type construction; showers or washbasins; steam bath; dancing; ski lessons) were closed when we tried to inspect them.

If you wish to share the majesty, the country-warm hospitality and camaraderie, the special sorcery of spirit which comes in exploring this still virtually untouched pocket of God's world before the tourist mobs inevitably descend to "civilize" it, send all of your queries for brochures, any other information, and/or reservations to dynamic, dedicated **Hans Petter Kleiven** (Nedre Gate 2, 2640 Vinstra), who is the chief of the Tourist Traffic Assn. for the entire area. With great good cheer he would help any prospective traveler in planning or bookings.

Portugal

Here is our Number One choice in 1981 for the North American traveler to Europe.

It is the least spoiled and one of the least expensive nations in the Western Alliance.

We have just returned from an intensive one-month tour during which we inspected almost every site of special interest on its mainland and in Madeira. For space reasons, we will not include a number of minor targets visited or revisited which are notably more attractive to resident vacationers than to overseas wanderers.

Nearly every visible sign of its cataclysmic Communist revolution, its successful counterrevolution, and other concurrent nightmares has been erased. War-damaged buildings are almost impossible to find. The 650,000 refugees from Angola and Mozambique have been absorbed. The hundreds of hotels which were confiscated to shelter them have been turned back to their owners, perhaps 97% of whom have either restored them or improved upon their original facilities. Most of the former millions of potholes on the highways have been eliminated. An immense boom in construction and reconstruction is whirling. Today the land is again a glory in its human, scenic, and enchantingly pristine as well as sophisticated allures.

This historic republic, with fewer inhabitants than the city of Tokyo, measures only 1000 miles in length and 350 miles in width. Yet, first spearheaded by Prince Henry the Navigator, Vasco da Gama, and other epic explorers, during the 15th and 16th centuries it was one of the mightiest powers on the globe.

In the warmth, sincerity, and courtesy of their welcome, the Portuguese people as an entity are at least ten years behind the more hardened and blasé populaces of most of the Continent. What a refreshment it is to be received so cheerfully, openly, and with such friendly dignity virtually everywhere one goes!

Paradox: One of the principal motivations of the more than 34-million foreigners who flocked to Spain in 1980 was "low" prices. But should you stand at any frontier post at any time of day you will observe an endless column of

Spaniards anting both ways through the controls in order to save bundles of money by buying everything from clothes to houseware to groceries to the gamut in the border towns or villages of Portugal. This congestion must be seen to be believed.

The invisible east-west line between **Lisbon** and the Customs point beyond **Elvas** splits the country into two markedly diverse conformations, including a less pronounced cleavage in their California types of climate. The South, which possesses a massive chunk of the overall 500 miles of beaches, has as its matrix the coastal **Algarve** as its crowning playground. In the interior you will find excellent roads with light traffic, tidy, serene, lovely landscapes, and sleepy, charming villages in which most of the dwellings carry their own hue among a large range of soft pastels. The North is far more industrialized and far less colorful, although its inhabitants in general are equally hospitable. Because of their narrowness and caravans of heavy trucks, the main arteries are despairingly overcrowded. However, multitudes of splendid attractions—cultural and for the flesh—await voyagers here.

Following the lead of Spain's *paradors,* in 1942 the State launched its skein of *pousadas* ("places to rest"), most of them country inns off the beaten paths. These were followed by the network of *estalagems* and *albergarias.* Many are located in converted fortresses, monasteries, and ancient mansions. They offer from as few as 4 to a maximum of perhaps 30 accommodations. Their prices are sometimes 50% below the normal commercial scale. The majority are simple but charming. Numerous examples are scattered through this text. The Portuguese National Tourist Office (see later) would be pleased to give you their full rosters.

The national method of listing currency comes as a mild shock to newcomers. The symbol "$" is placed *after* the escudos and *before* the centavos. Thus, at this writing 1 escudo is written 1$00 and is worth about 2¢; an American dollar equals about 48$10 escudos.

Were we to skim on short trips what we consider the richest of its giant national lake of cream, here would be our routes:

(1) Interrupt our European trip in London to take a 1-week charter tour to Madeira and return. See "Madeira," below.

(2) **Lisbon**/day excursion to **Estoril** and **Cascais**, with lunch at the *Hotel Palácio* in Seteais/ fly to **Faro** and lodge where you have chosen on the **Algarve**/ the beautiful small road **Portimão-Monchique-Odemira-Beja**, with lunch at *Pousada dos Loios* in **Evora** and overnight in *Pousada da Rainha Santa Isabel* in Estremoz/ north just before Mora to **Montargil-Chamusca**, lunch at *Estalagen de Santa Iria* in **Tomar-Coimbra-Mealhada**—overnight at **Buçaco**/ **Coimbra-Leiria-Nazare-Caldas de Rainha-Lisbon**.

Further information on all of these high points follows.

☑ **TRANSPORTATION Taxis** All cabs are metered and rates are reasonable for the plethora of free thrills. *Set your price in advance on all out-of-town excursions;*

here you must pay both ways, from cabstand all the way back to cabstand. Tip 5 escudos for the average distance; if longer, 15% will do fine. He cannot legally carry more passengers than the number stipulated over the meter. No supplements or extras after dark, but there is a small one for luggage.

Trains Greatly improved under a generous development program. The ticket costs are so low, the distances are so short, and the differences in comfort are so pronounced that we'd advise you to travel First Class wherever it's available if you can afford it.

There are special deluxe runs both ways between 3 cities daily which levy a peanut supplement for their First Class facilities. They offer club chairs, sofas, a hostess and service for drinks, plus a communal dining car. On the 3½-to-4-hour run from Lisbon to Oporto, for less than $14 you can bask through the countryside on the *Miragaia* (nonstop), *the Foguete* ("Rocket"), and the nonstop *Sete Colinas* ("Seven Hills"). This return journey fields 4 choices. In either direction between Lisbon and Faro, the capital of the Algarve, reservations may be made for about $12 aboard the *Sotavento*. The fixed-price meal is about $5. Since the road arteries between these hubs are the most heavily trafficked in the nation, here are delightfully relaxed escapes.

Car Rentals While self-drive rentals are considerably steeper than in North America, the mileage you will normally cover is relatively so short that their tariffs shouldn't evoke too great pain. Hertz, Avis, and many of the other International Big Boys are active here.

But hired cars with drivers—wow! They work on the principle of the less time consumed the higher the rates. To avoid what might be startling surprises, always check the price before climbing into the vehicle.

Because of the intensive nature of our research work and the necessity for a companion who could take us directly to our hundreds of targets without wasting a second, we have just made a 3-week, 2000-mile tour of the mainland with Luis de Castro (Emintauto, Rua Ferreira Lampa 42-A, Lisbon, tel. 571 254; home tel. 849 536) as our pilot. English-speaking Mr. de Castro is not only a superbly skilled chauffeur and a fountain of knowledge about every worthy touristic attraction in his nation, but he is also so warm, so gentlemanly, so alert, and so eager to be helpful as a delightful comrade that he merits our absolute top recommendation.

Seat belts are required for everyone occupying front seats in Portugal.

☑ FOOD

Nearly 20% of the food for this land must be imported, including large quotas of wheat, corn, oils, meats, and other comestibles.

Portuguese cuisine is not fiery, as one might expect on the Iberian Peninsula neither is it doughy, with the accent on pasta. The French influence is pronounced. The cooking is good, if a bit on the bland side; the variety is bewildering. The wonderful fresh fruits of the sea you will probably find are more appealing than earth's bovinity. Steaks, whether boiled, blow-torched, or pounded, usually turn up as a major challenge to modern dentistry, despite the fact that many of them are from France. Cod is beloved

but becoming quite scarce; sole and all the brotherhood of the crustacean clan are still abundant; lobster (clawed or clawless) is snappingly expensive.

Whenever you go to a restaurant, remember 3 phrases: *sem azeite* ("without oil"), *com manteiga* ("with butter"), and *sem alho* ("without garlic"). You'll need them! You also may require *sem coentros* ("without coriander") which, when chopped and served *fresh* in various stews, seems to our repulsing palates to resemble a fetid first cousin of ipecac. It's bright green—exactly the virescent hue we turn whenever we accidentally run into a sprig.

Since Brazil is a cultural offshoot of Portugal, coffee is the pillar of almost everyone's diet. The local version seems muddy to many neophytes. Actually, the quality is higher than can ordinarily be found in the U.S.; they simply don't blend it, that's all. Some travelers find the "Carioca" style the most acceptable—equal parts of coffee and hot water; others like it *com leite*—coffee and milk, 50-50; after a heavy meal, most of us take it *claro* (plain)—but the wise follow the national custom of filling almost 1/3rd of the cup with sugar before consumption.

Cheese? Serpa, snappy and tangy, is outstanding. Serra is a lighter, creamier version that is pure heaven as a complement to a glass of vintage port. Queijo fresco, a butter substitute with overtones of cottage cheese, is liked by many foreign visitors.

Agua de Luso is the best-known bottled water. To us somehow it tastes "wetter" and is more thirst-quenching than any other H_2O on the Continent. Darned if we know why!

☑ **DRINKS**   Port is the major national wine, of course. Economic conditions have forced the export of virtually all of the most superior class. Your best chance of securing fine vintage stock will be at some outlet that caters chiefly to foreigners. There are 5 kinds. Vintage, which takes 20 years to reach its prime, is the best; Crusted, never dated, is excellent; Ruby and Tawny (favorite of most travelers) are blends of up to 40 separate wines; White, light and pleasant, is the only type served before a meal. (The rest are consumed at the end, with the cheese).

. Madeira is the minor national wine—not as fashionable as it was when the clipper ships were sailing, but still as kind to the taste. It has the longest life of any. The 3 best types are Bual (our preference), Sercial (dry, characteristic flavor), and Malmsey (on the sweet side).

To us and to many others, Portugal's stars for just about every second meal are the unique *Vinhos Verdes* from the old Minho region in the far north. Although they are called *verde* ("green") because their grapes are picked when young, most are white or straw-yellow and some are deep red. All of these light, dry, delicate, inexpensive bottlings, each with its official seal which guarantees the contents as genuine, must be drunk cold. With virtually everything from meat to shellfish, the amber Gato and Logosta are among the most popular brands. A traditional exception is the service of a red variety with freshly caught sardines. Literally dozens of vintners produce this different and delicious treat.

Among the standards, our candidates for leadership are Clarete, Ferreirinha (a very fine red), Quinta da Aguieira (excellent in red and white), Reserva Sografe (another mellow red), Monopole and Ermida (both exceptional whites), and Buçaco (supply

rather severely restricted). The reds from the Dão, the second largest area of growth, are full-bodied and strong, with a translucent ruby hue and a taste closer to burgundy than claret. It is especially useful to ascertain their age before ordering these; between 7 and 10 years is normally their peak. Rosés? Most of them, including the famed Lancers and Mateus, are noticeably effervescent—a far cry from their confrères in the Provençe or Côte de Rhone. All of the still versions we've tried have been undistinguished. As for the naturally sparkling choices, we think you might find Caves da Raposeira "Bruto" to be the most acceptable local substitute for champagne. Be warned, however, that most Portuguese bubbly is cloying and unpalatable. Last, there's always the wine of the country, in "open" servings; order this as *vinho da casa,* and remember that the law requires they furnish it with every table d'hôte (not à la carte) meal.

Brandy? Quite a few poor ones. The best we've sampled (and we confess that our experience in this area is limited) is Antigua, in a lovely tall, green fluted bottle. We're also fond of Macieira Five Stars, a splendid black-label entry. A brand named Constantino is seen frequently, but we now prefer the former two.

All major Western spirits except American whiskey are available at very high prices due to heavy import duties. As an example, a bottle of proprietary scotch (White Label, Walker Red, Ballantine, et seq.) costs perhaps $23. Imitations from Tangier have almost entirely vanished.

Ginginha, the cherry liqueur first invented and distilled by local monks, couldn't be more Portuguese. Characteristic, curious, and worth a try.

Sagres and Skol have become the ranking beers. On recent tours, for some strange reason, we had repeated troubles with Imperial. At one hotel, for example, we had to ask for 3 bottles before finding one that was drinkable; at another, it took 2. Perhaps it's the fault of innkeepers who keep their supplies either too cold or for too long a period. When right, however, all these brews are excellent.

Cola-based beverages are now widely available and the prejudice against the quinine content in tonic water has finally been beaten down; gin-and-tonic lovers are no longer parched for Schweppes, Canada Dry, Ideal, or Hall. If you're a soft-drink fan, stick to those wonderful orangeades which are at their peak in winter (harder to find in summer).

☑ **TIPPING** In Portugal, as elsewhere, Americans are far more lavish than others. The current level is well below American standards.

Give taxi drivers 15% on top of the meter reading; hairdressers, 10%; washroom attendants, 5 escudos; station porters should get their fixed charge only; and theater ushers, 5 escudos. For waiters, add only 5% inasmuch as service and a tourist tax are already included.

In general, the Portuguese themselves tip in mini amounts, but as many are so strained economically, you will win their hearts and gratitude if you tip normally—which will seem generous to them.

☑ **LOCAL RACKETS** As a whole, the Portuguese are a simple, independent people, unversed in most of the slick and shady arts; while it's good business to have a resident along whenever you go shopping, don't worry about being fleeced if you go

alone. Count your change, of course; there's always the occasional chiseler who gives back a handful of small coins in order to filch a few extras for himself. Don't buy a "swizs" (sic) watch from a street vendor. (You hardly need being warned of this old flimflam.) Most merchants will respect you as an American, just as you will respect their birthright—and chicanery is the very rare exception rather than the rule.

Women should walk with the latches of their pocketbooks turned toward themselves not outward. Purse snatching is not uncommon nowadays.

☑ **INFORMATION CENTERS**   *Please come!* That's the clarion call from official sources. To make it easier, this year you can even receive "Portugal on a Silver Platter" —a program in which 130 hotels on the mainland and on Madeira are participating. If Lisbon is used as a gateway by air or sea, you will be gifted with one free night for every four at a 5-star hotel which bears the bonus emblem. Other goodies include wine, gifts, handicrafts, free meals, shopping discounts, sightseeing, and slashed car rental fees.

The **Directorate-General for Tourism** (executive offices at Av. Antonio Augusto de Aguiar 86, with travel information facilities at Praça dos Restauradores 27) is the government tourism organization. This alert and go-go agency, under the hardworking directorship of Dr. Cristiano de Freitas, publishes voluminous travel literature, maintains a string of Information Offices, and assists the visitor in all possible ways. Because it's open every day of the week (Sun. 10 A.M. to 5 P.M.), and because English is spoken by nearly everyone, it makes an excellent mail delivery point. One of its major triumphs —and responsibilities—is the construction and maintenance of the aforementioned, splendid chain of Portuguese *pousadas;* these are the simple, plain, inexpensive, strategically located resthouse hotels especially designed for foreign traffic. The average tariff is an astonishing $28-or-so for 2 persons nightly with breakfasts. (The tiptop rate per couple at the exceptional Pousada dos Loios or at the extraordinary Pousada da Raínha Santa Isabel at Estremoz is all of $38, inclusive of breakfasts, service, and taxes); 5 days is the maximum permissible stay. They are scattered in such a manner that travelers on normal routes may usually sleep at one, take lunch at another, and spend the night at still another, thus avoiding the rigors of routine back-country lodgings; all are clean and comfortable. If you need help with an industrial problem, the efficient Pedro de Vasconcelos, Secretary General of the **Portuguese Industrial Association** (F.I.L. in Alcântara) will cheerfully advise you. The **Portuguese National Tourist Office**, at 548 Fifth Ave., N.Y. 10036, is the national representative. And the head of this administration is the everhelpful Nuno Almeida. Branches also are located at 3250 Wilshire Blvd. in Los Angeles and at The Palmer House in Chicago.

CITIES

LISBON   (Lisboa, pronounced "LISH-boa") is the capital and heartbeat of the Republic. Except for the blitzkrieg of political wall posters which have been ubiquitous throughout the nation since the start of its latest tumult, normalcy has returned. Again here is one of the most international and charming metropolises in the world. It's relatively small for its importance—only about 1-million people—and there's a small-town air about it, particularly in the

winding little streets of its Old Quarters. The contrasts are striking: Luxurious hotels, an overcrowded airport, epicurian food, shops overflowing with opulent goods from 5 continents—and centuries-old poverty between the cracks in the plush façade. Historic treasures and cultural arts abound. The jewel in its crown is the 752-foot figure of "Christ the King," with arms outstretched, which rises on the opposite bank of the Tagus facing the city. As its nexus, here *is* Portugal—because this land has room for only 1 nerve center.

Sightseeing In our opinion, the most beautiful tourist sights in Lisbon and the suburbs are the Coach Museum (a unique collection of vehicles; usually functioning 10 A.M. to 6:30 P.M. in June, July, Aug., and Sept. and to 5 P.M. during other months), the Old Moorish Castle (Castelo de S. Jorge), and that part of the Old City adjoining the Castle. Go escorted to the latter, and in daylight; see the Popular Museum and a slice of life left over from the days of Columbus; the Gulbenkian Museum offers Rembrandt, Rubens, and superb Middle Eastern artifacts; the Tower of Belém (the sixteenth century starting block on the Tagus for many of the ancient explorers); Jerónimos Monastery (burial place of Vasco da Gama, kings, poets, and Portuguese heroes); the neighboring Naval Museum, which has many beautifully restored vessels as well as early aircraft; Sé Cathedral (a Romanesque resident of Lisbon since the middle fifteenth century; a trove of gold and silver objects can be viewed upon request). Museums rest in the capital on Mondays, while Queluz and Sintra Palaces are shuttered on Tuesdays.

For a holiday in Portugal involving sun, swimming, dancing, all sports, old-fashioned loafing and/or big-league gaiety, Lisbon isn't your dish of tea. The experienced traveler, particularly during the hot months, splits his or her time between the capital and escapes to such neighboring resorts as **Estoril**, **Cascais**, **Guincho**, and **Sintra**. These areas are described later.

LISBON HOTELS Quick Reference Table
Price categories by national (not U.S.) standards.

EXPENSIVE:
Alfa Av. C. Bordalo Pinheiro. Tel. 775876; Telex 18478; 544 rooms. P. 734
Intercontinental Ritz R. R. da Fonseca 88. Tel. 684131; Telex 12589; 300 rooms. P. 732
Lisboa-Sheraton R. Latino Coelho I. Tel. 575757; Telex 12774; 400 rooms. P. 733
Tivoli Av. da Liberdade 2. Tel. 4II0I; Telex 1588; 320 rooms. P. 733
Altis R. Castilho II. Tel. 560071; Telex 13314; 219 rooms. P. 733

UPPER MODERATE:
Avenida Palace R. Pr. Dezembro 123. Tel. 360154; 100 rooms. P. 734
Lisboa Plaza Av. da Liberdade. Tel. 370331; Telex 16402; 100 rooms; P. 734

MODERATE:
Capitol Rua Eça de Queiroz. Tel. 53681I/5; Telex 13701; 58 rooms. P. 735
Diplomatico R. Castilho 74. Tel. 562041; 90 rooms. P. 735
Embaixador Av. Duque de Loule 73. Tel. 530171; 96 rooms. P. 734

Fenix Praca M. de Pombal 8. Tel. 736161; Telex 12170; 125 rooms. P. 735
Florida R. Duque de Palmela 32. Tel. 554171; Telex 12256; 120 rooms. P. 735
Lutecia Av. F. Miguel Contreiras. Tel. 897021; Telex 12457; 151 rooms. P. 735
Mundial R. D. Duarte 4. Tel. 863101; Telex 12308; 150 rooms. P. 735
Penta Av. dos Combatentes. Tel. 740141; 592 rooms. P. 736
Principe Real R. dal Alegria 53. Tel. 360116; 24 rooms. P. 735
Rex Rua Castilho 169. Tel. 682161; 77 rooms. P. 735
Roma Av. de Roma 33. Tel. 767761/3; Telex 16586. P. 734
York House R. das Janelas Verdes 32. Tel. 662435; 48 rooms. P. 736

LOWER MODERATE:
Dom Carlos Av. Duque de Loule 121. Tel. 539071; Telex 16468; 73 rooms. P. 735
Eduardo VII Av. Fontes P. de Melo 5. Tel. 530141; 100 rooms.
Europa Praca L. de Camoes 6. Tel. 361371; 61 rooms. P. 735
Excelsior R. Rodrigues Sampaio 172. Tel. 537151; 90 rooms. P. 735
Flamingo R. Castilho 41. Tel. 532191; 35 rooms. P. 735
Impala R. Filipe Folque 49. Tel. 58914; 35 rooms. P. 735
Jorge V R. Mouzinho da Silveria 3. Tel. 562525; 56 rooms. P. 735
Metropole Praca Dom Pedro IV 30. Tel. 369164; 57 rooms. P. 735
Miraparque Av. Sidonio Pais 12. Tel. 54181; 100 rooms. P. 735
Praia Mar 143 rooms. P. 736
Presidente R. A. Herculano 13. Tel. 539501; 59 rooms. P. 735
Principe Av. Duque D'Avila 199. Tel. 536151; 55 rooms. P. 735
Reno Av. Duque D'Avila 195. Tel. 48181; 50 rooms. P. 735
Residencia América. Rua Tomaz Ribeiro 47. Tel. 531178/9; Telex 13701; 61 rooms. P. 736
Suburban hotels often associated with Lisbon are covered separately under our alphabetical listings for "Cascais", "Estoril," "Guincho" and "Sintra."

Hotels Enormous—almost miraculous—changes have been wrought since the Government turned back to their owners virtually all of the lion's share of the nation's major hotels after confiscating them to lodge the hundreds of thousands of Portuguese refugees from its warring African colonies. Not only have nearly all of them been restored, but many of their prior facilities have been upgraded. Further, new hostelries are popping up by the score. In sum, the innkeepers across this land are both eager and *ready* to welcome you!

Broadly their room tariffs are appreciably below those of their North American counterparts—and dramatically below the scales in the hubs of England, France, Germany, Belgium, Netherlands, Switzerland, Italy, Scandinavia, and others, even including Spain. Meals, on the other hand, are higher than one might expect—particularly in 5-star establishments—partially because so much food has to be imported. On balance, however, your wallet or pocketbook will come out as a winner.

Try to have your reservations confirmed in writing anywhere you go. This might (only *might*) avoid the overbooking practice which has become so common on the Continent.

In the capital, the **Intercontinental Ritz** is unquestionably the Queen of

Portugal's hotellerie. After this American-based chain moved in, this hostelry had again become one of the most beautiful, elegant, and prestigious in the world. Architecturally, its 300 air-conditioned, soundproofed rooms and 300 baths are sweeping in dimensions. Technically, it is a miracle of engineering. In décor, it is a sumptuous contrast of old and new which you'll almost never find in any modern hotel today except London's Berkeley and perhaps 4 or 5 others. The owners, praises be, are seriously determined to add to its luster rather than to spoil its unique existing character and ambiance. Urbane, vastly experienced General Manager Peter Birchall is installing its first swimming pool, bringing music to its bedchambers plus pianos to its Grill and Bar, and redoing all of its accommodations in exactly the same styles. Veteran Chief Concierge António Domingos has assembled a super-helpful team of assistants. Everyone seems to be working to retain it as the flagship house of this huge organization. Let's hope that they do so with colors flying!

The **Lisboa-Sheraton** is a sound choice for devotees of American-type living. In 1979, $1.5-million was poured into a renovation blitz. Rooftop restaurant totally redecorated for warmer aura; each of its 400 nests refurbished; soigné Taverna Bar doubled in size; multiple other fresh administrations. For meetings and/or banquets, a ballroom and 4 satellites now hold from 20 to 630 clients. General Manager H.K. Schaefer, with 10 years of American and 12 years of European experience in this profession, should (but doesn't have time to) bust his buttons about one of the best planned and most attractive Sheraton links abroad.

The **Tivoli**, booming with well-earned success, remains a showcase of professional innkeeping. This Portuguese version of an American operation is commercial in tone, but its airy, freshly revamped, and totally refurnished public rooms and its conservatively modern and well-maintained accommodations are so attractively done that impersonality is minimized. Carpark and garage part of the Tivoli-Jardim complex (see below); All units clean, with bath, radio, TV outlet, and air-conditioning; varied color schemes from soothing to aggressively extroverted; many handsome marble baths. There's a beautifully viewful rooftop terrace-grill-nightclub combination which overlooks the slope to the river, with a cheery fireplace for cool months and a patio for summer tippling. The service is keen and friendly. The courtly and amiable veteran Director Alfredo Coelho Fernandes merits bows for his upgrading of facilities. Very good.

The modernistic **Altis**, which gives us the impression of a Scandinavian hotel transplanted intact to Iberia, is in the process of tripling itself. This corner-sited establishment has purchased 2 equal-sized adjoining parcels to shape it as an L. When converted these buildings will add 200 more accommodations to its original count of 225. General Manager João Mendes Leal, formerly of the Sheraton, also hopes that a sliding-roof pool, a 1200-seat convention hall, a 400-seat auditorium, a health club, and a shopping center will be functioning by early this year. Dark marble lobby dominated by a colossal metal Christus; window-lined penthouse Grill; appealing Girassol restaurant at treetop level; Herald Bar; some chambers adequate in size and

others narrow-gauged. This is a substantial address that can be enthusiastically recommended to the avant garde.

The **Avenida Palace** in midcity is struggling against so much antiquity that we have our doubts that any New World voyagers can yet appreciate its creaky status. The excellent staff is so kind and well-meaning in both the living sectors as well as in the Old World restaurant that we are obliged to voice our commendation. Nevertheless, the few patches of modernity, such as the entrance, lobby, and several other areas, are not enough to warrant a position with the other 2 in its price grouping.

The **Alfa**, last member of the Big 5, opened the portals to its 24-floor tower after our latest Portuguese inspection. It is located in the direction of the zoological gardens. Rooms divided into 181 singles, 21 doubles with large beds, 377 twins of varying types, 4 suites and one vast Presidential Suite, which has half the square footage of a normal private home. Ground floor with 18th-century Pombalino restaurant plus the rustic A Pousada room, the Labirinto bar, a shopping arcade and garden; barber and beauty parlor; garage; second floor with open air swimming pool, 2 squash courts, sauna, gym, physical therapy, snack service. While the expansive congress facilities will attract many conventioneers and business travelers, perhaps its scope is broad enough to encompass the full range of tourism. We wish it luck.

The cozy **Lisboa Plaza** has been urbanely reborn. Ingratiatingly subdued lobby; attractive adjoining Grill; soothing Bar in soft greens and whites; Coffee Shop; 100 small, simple, but well-done rooms; private car parking. Excellent use of colors is the highlight here; the decorator merits kudos for this and for the furnishing arrangements. We like it.

Just behind its *alma mater*, the Tivoli, you'll find the **Tivoli-Jardim**, which some loyalists even prefer to the mother patch. Set-back construction insuring extraquiet and insulation; independent reception desk; easy parking; orange and blue lounge; woody snack bar with a magnificent Lurçat tapestry; cozy dining room with white bricks; mezzanine bar; rooftop solarium; full air conditioning. All bedchambers equipped with comfortable beds, radios and piped music, bright, well-designed baths, full-length mirrors, and ample storage space; front units featuring wide balcony; a few accommodations overlooking the lovely garden for which it was named. Very good for its category.

The centrally situated **Embaixador** ("Ambassador"), also air conditioned and also replete with traffic sounds, has widely reworked its interior. Bandbox lobby; tasteful, quiet lounge up 1 flight with happy little bar; 9th-floor, L-shaped, self-service restaurant pleasant in appearance but with its cookery untested by us; hairdresser and barber; 96 rather cramped accommodations without special character. Its general maintenance is fair to middling. Routine.

Despite the unusual range of its facilities, we regard the **Roma** as a rather crass sleeping factory. Very noisy location; uninhibitively commercial lobby with glass-lined boutiques, neon signs, and jazzed-up appurtenances; panoramic 10th-floor restaurant, bar, and solarium its best feature; impersonal main

bar-lounge, Coffee Shop, Brasserie, self-service Barbecue-Beer Hall, Pizzeria-Snack Bar, and Laundromat on lower floors or in basement. This entry has 82 units with "sitting room" (curtained-off beds) and 265 twins, all with tiny baths and all plain but efficient within their dimensions. At least it is air conditioned, which is needed.

The **Principe Real** seems worthy again. We commend its aplomb and durability. It comes up with a tranquil address in midcity, an unimpressive entrance and façade, and better public rooms than bedchambers. Charming ground floor composed of a hearth-brightened lounge, a red-rooted bar and 3-table cocktail cranny, and—happiest of all—the warmhearted welcome of Sra. José Rezende, lavishes love on this peaceful little hideaway. Viewful 5th-floor breakfast room with 10 tables—a knockout; A-plus maintenance from cellar to rooftop; 24 units, each with private plumbing, wall-to-wall carpeting, odd-shape configurations, and bolts of clashing cretonnes; no radios, TV, or piped music. Except for the letdown in the sleeping segments, this one has a unique allure.

Although the fully restored, clean **Miraparque** is agreeable enough in other respects, to us the feeling of choppiness in its layout is such that everything seems distressingly squeezed to those who like s-p-a-c-e. A Claustrophobe's Bad Dream.

The **Flórida** has taken on a commercial tone, but it is passable in our opinion. Portuguese textiles and regional hues throughout; lobby in gray, red, and blue, with adjoining wood-paneled bar; cool dining room facing plaza; Grill serving à la carte selections from 9 P.M. to 3 A.M.; umbrella-dotted terrace for breakfasting or imbibing now buffeted by more and more traffic noises. Fair.

The **Dom Carlos**, a semicircular house, nestles at the edge of a small park. It has rebounded and welcomes outlanders with reasonable amenities.

The **Fénix** offers full air conditioning, a Spanish-style Bodegón (taproom), a commercial patina, inadequate elevator service, and tiny, tiny rooms in jocular colors with equally small baths. Okay, except for its mercantile feel and overcramped design.

The **Mundial** is much in the middle of things—too much so, from the standpoint of noise. This house caters to tours, to journalists, and to business people; it is well adapted for these specialized types of clientele. Its 146 rooms, all with bath, are better than cramped. Pleasant roof-garden restaurant.

The **Presidente**, the **Jorge V**, the **Flamingo**, and the **Impala** are all poor value for this year's visitor, in our view.

The **Príncipe**, **Reno** (adjoining), and **Excelsior** (best of the lot) are typical representatives of the flock of smaller havens that sprang up a few years ago to lure the mass influx of bygone holidaymakers. May they thrive again, because basically they do their jobs quite well. The older **Europa**, **Lutecia**, **Metrópole**, **Diplomático**, and **Rex** are all adequate; the cookery is often their weakest point. The **Capitol**, with fair rates, draws many older clients; book on its air-conditioned 7th floor. It is sited on a cacophonous corner.

The **Praia Mar**, pried away from the water by a superhighway, suffers from its off-the-sea location, but boasts compensatory comforts and amenities. Subdued ambiance; public rooms air-conditioned; splashworthy pool; large 8th-floor glass-bound restaurant with a wonderful vista; 2 bars; lounges; small nightclub. Handful of little suites in its overall complement of 143 accommodations with confined dimensions; sparse furnishings. Except for its unfortunate situation, this one's basically sound.

Budgeteers? The **York House** (Rua das Janelas Verdes 32), a converted seventeenth-century monastery plus a much newer annex, is very, very special. Homelike atmosphere within its cloistered confines; inconvenient suburban situation; hard-to-find, inconspicuous gate; tiny reception area; intimate, half-tiled main dining room; cozy bar. Reputedly excellent Portuguese specialties with French overtones; menu otherwise chiefly international in scope. Its delightful French-speaking proprietress, Madame Andrée Goldstein, is assisted by her French nephew and her American niece. As an informal and friendly hideaway, here is one of the best "pension" bets (if we can call this establishment a "pension") we have seen in a long time. Caution: Make reservations long, long, *long* in advance. Our highest recommendation in every respect, within its low-price league.

The **Residéncia América** is another outstanding bet in this price group. Across the street from the Sheraton Shopping Center; 7-floor operation with lounge, bar, restaurant, TV room, and visual sweep; 56 nests with 1 to 3 beds and 54 baths ample-sized but not spacious; dirty rug in elevator but clean and tidy upstairs. Worthy for the outlay.

Finally, the ultramodern, 18-story, 592-room **Lisboa Penta**, 2 miles from both the city and the airport, is partially owned by Air Portugal, British Airways, Lufthansa, TWA, and Swissair. This busy-busy bee is essentially patronized by a multinational transient trade. Air conditioned; massive lobby; dramatic Passarola Grill; 2 bars; partially self-service Coffee Shop; heated pool; shopping arcade; accommodations well planned, comfortable, and impersonal. In purpose and in tone it is reminiscent of the better houses that cluster around London's Heathrow.

Restaurants   In Lisbon, there's a big choice of restaurants. While few establishments merit Great or near-Great cuisine classification, the general standard is fair and prices are still agreeably low to metropolitan North American pocketbooks. For extra-special short excursions from the capital, please note further along our reports on the Hotel do Guincho at *Guincho* and the Palácio de Seteais near *Sintra*.

Among the city's hotels, the beautiful Grill at the **Intercontinental Ritz** is far and away the most elegant in its aura and the most savory in its cuisine. Proper dress is *de rigueur*. Costly by local standards but a joy in its suavity and urbanity. The **Tivoli** penthouse is also outstanding. Woody, clublike atmosphere with huge windows viewing the town and the Tagus; excellent on every count. The also altitudinal Panorama at the **Lisboa-Sheraton** has just been 100% redecorated to bring warmth into this formerly stiff oasis; although we haven't dined here since this physical transformation, doubtless its cookery remains at the same praiseworthy level. The rooftop grillroom of the **Altis** offers a sweeping vista and comestibles which, in our opinions, do not quite

equal those of these rivals. All others we have tried in this category have ranged from fairly good to indifferent in comparison.

Among the independents, the legendary **Aviz** (Rua Serpa Pinto, off Rua Garrett) remains the brightest and shiniest gemstone. Premises 1-flight up; handsome oak-and-quilted-leather bar with globe sconces, velvet upholstered chairs, green brocade wall-coverings, and a small vitrine displaying a novel pocket-watch collection; 3 dining rooms, 1 in beryl and 2 in gold; sophisticated atmosphere and fashionable clientele; flawless service throughout our visits covering decades. Since Proprietor Rugeroni is seldom on the premises during mealtimes, ask for courtly, kindly, English-speaking Maître Espirito Silva, who is an extra-charming host. For Portugal it is very expensive—but it's tops.

The **Travessa das Amoreiras** (no. 1 same street, 5 minutes from Ritz) gets our enthusiastic runner-up vote. Three of its glass-lined walls border a lovely interior patio with a blue-and-white pool and greenery. Down a few steps is its lush, richly decorated bar-lounge segment with the polished intimacy of a fine private club. The 13 tables make an L directly on the fringes of this central oasis. Our Paté Ovas of red fish roe was unusual and very, very good; our turbot was super-delicious—and its almond cake, WOW! Charming, English-speaking Senhora Maria Isabel is your attentive hostess. Closed Sun. and 2 weeks in August. Pricey but outstanding in every regard.

The highly popular **Escorial** (Rua das Portas de Santo Antao 47–49) is modern in concept. One room with a counter and quick service; the other with wood walls, vertical metal strips, globe lamps on polished steel brackets, and fireman-red tablecloths. Drinks cart for premeal sippers; shellfish specialties; attractive and clever presentation; fairly respectable steaks; rushed but smooth service. Reserve ahead, but still expect to wait in a cramped corridor until a table is cleared. Recommended for cuisine but not for that quiet, low-cost evening out.

The nearby **Gambrinus** (Rua das Portas de Santo Antao 25) is an old-timer that remains right up at the front of the pack. Entry to a seafood display; long bar leading to a split-level, arch-ceilinged dining room. Handsomely brightened; principal wall featuring a colorful Portuguese abstract painting; 23 tables; extraordinarily agile service by Lisbon standards; well-prepared cuisine. This stalwart and costly veteran is not in the Aviz or Travessa class, naturally —but it is one of the better independents.

Chester (68 Rodrigo Fonseca, in the neighborhood of the Ritz) is a steakhouse which appeals to the chic Young Executive Set. Cellar bar with bold, diagonally striped carpets; fresh airy lounge; ground-floor restaurant with wooden coffers and paneled walls; placemats recalling scenes from the U.K.; engaging touches such as candles floating in vases surrounded by flowers. The service was superb, but alas, our meat was tougher than a buffalo shank. In the same district, **Numero Um** ("Number One") has, in our opinions, slid well down the numerical scale through its radical changes. Now the former owner who repurchased it has switched to fondue, homemade cakes, and lighter fare. Completely different—and to us unsuccessfully so.

Up in the charming, ancient Castelo S. Jorge district, **Michel** (Largo de S. Cruz do Castelo 5) is one of the "in" places today. It is a converted artist's studio with white walls, terracotta floors, and piped classical music playing

through its several rooms and bar-lounge. Interesting, ambitious menu; very low prices for the superior cuisine; friendly. We enjoyed our meal and strolling through this hilltop area.

Tavares (Rua da Misericórdia 24) claims to be trying to recoup its former reputation as the leader, but it still has a long, long way to go. Why so many loyal Portuguese continue to speak in such rapturous tones about this one is a mystery to us. Even at its Old World best, we can find little excuse for the drab presentation of its rather ordinary pretentions toward elaborate cookery. Not at all revered by these evaluators—but a local landmark.

Faz Figura (Rua do Paraiso 15-B) resides high in the Alfama district over-looking the harbor cranes and shipping channels of the Tagus River. Two rooms with leather Chesterfield banquettes, large windows, air conditioning, and a wonderfully posh clublike atmosphere; expansive 14-table open terrace with an awning for summer diners; exceptionally kind reception; attentive service. Our shrimp cocktail was delicious; the Steak Portuguese is cooked in a casserole with boiled potatoes and smoked ham; the tiny Squids Gratiné were lovely. Our enthusiastic recommendation for viewing and dining in the medi-um-budget category.

Pabe (Rua Duque de Palmela, 27-A) means "Pub"; decoratively, it is one of the most stylish establishments you'll find in the land. Half-timber exterior with stained-glass leaded windows; first room with open beams, pewter plates, rich woodwork. We made the mistake of going to the rear chamber through the saloon doors, where the atmosphere oppressively suggests an Edwardian parlor. Our crêpes were leaden and our partner's Sole was burned. We have a feeling that this could be one of the nicest spots in the capital if tiptop management took the helm—but now, we rate it as just another Pabe.

The **Algarve** is a constituent of the massive new shopping center in the midtown railway terminal near the Avenida Palace. It is 1 flight up the main escalator. Comfortably overstuffed bar; dining room with 2-story-high windows; Moorish décor; piped music; medium high tariffs; cookery good but not distinguished. We feel that this has greater appeal to upper-level local business executives than to foreign pilgrims—though friendliness prevails throughout.

António (Rua Tomás Ribeiro 63), in the shadow of the Sheraton, is a corner site with two rooms; this time we prefer the one further back. Ink-block molded ceiling in blue and white; inset planter boxes; always busy with schools of hungry Portuguese who swim in for its excellent piscatorial preparations. You might appreciate the house specialty called Acorda, an airy pasta which resembles a marriage of a fallen soufflé and a damp omelette; it is made with whipped bread, egg, clams, shrimp, and black olives. A huge lunch for two with wine should hardly dent your budget for more than $25. Sound.

La Gondola (Avenida de Berna 60) serves a savory selection, with emphasis on Italian dishes. Agreeable little summer garden; adequate cellar; glum wai-tresses; choice for a tranquil, unhurried lunch in serene surroundings, provided the nearby air traffic is using the east-west runway pattern not the north-south. In general, we're fond of this one.

Frascati (Padre Antonio Vieira) is where a former Chef, Maître, and 2 Captains of the Ritz decided to create their own restaurant only 2 blocks from their hotel. Although initially it was designed in Norwegian motif with Scandi-

navian vittles, Came The Revolution to an Italian kitchen. Only about 30 seats; almost always a queue; moderate tabs; skillfully productive skillets. It fully merits its high popularity.

Taj Mahal (Av. S. João de Deus 31-B) is a sweet and tiny Indian effort run by a charming lady who welcomes many U.S. diplomats to her small restaurant. Try her onion-and-flour *bojes* or the patties called *samosas* as first dishes. The chicken Tandoori is delicious and for dessert, sample the 7-layered *Bebinka* or the *Saviya,* which is composed of milk, ice cream, almonds, and raisins. A nice change of diet and of pace.

~ **A Quintá** ("The Farm"), atop the Santa Justa outdoor elevator in the heart of the city, serves small portions; if you're intensely hungry, a refill costs practically nothing. Selections including Hungarian goulash, steak-and-kidney pie, home-cured corned beef, and fluffy omelets; no pretensions, not the best ventilation, no crystal chandeliers, no heel-clicking headwaiters—just a friendly reception and a simple atmosphere. Closed Sunday.

Belcanto (Largo S. Carlos) comes up with 11 tables, red velvet banquettes, wood paneling, and a comfortable, unglamorous air. The bar is very popular with menfolk. Through the course of our meal we watched many lone ladies come in, sit down, and smoothly find companionship. The edibles are nothing to rave about, but some of the 2-legged dishes that sauntered in did indeed look appetizing.

Cortador ("Butcher shop"), also known as "Oh Lacerda!," used to be one of our chops—but no longer, emphatically. On our last look at this steak house in which the clients pick their own cuts of meat, the atmosphere reeked of such contrived touristy "quaintness" and our meal was so substandard for the price that we're not going back.

Budget dining? **A Primavera** (Travessa da Espera 34) is tiny, tiny, tiny. This one has 2 long tables and 1 small table, tiled walls, an open kitchen, and stools for seats. Closed Sunday; a whopping meal (including wine and service) in down-to-earth surroundings for a song; excellent for the type. **As Velhas** (Praça da Alegria 19) and **Oriental** (Rua São Julião 132), lunch only, also bat high in this league.

Night Life Fado. No lively traveler should leave Lisbon without visiting one of the world-famous *fado* restaurants—birthplace and home of the heart-rending folk music so beloved by the people. These are the "taverns" (for want of a better word) where women in aprons or potbellied characters in sweaters will suddenly burst forth in these stylized, haunting, provocative laments. Informal atmosphere; adequate food; songs which will never leave you. *Reserve early everywhere.*

Lisboa à Noite (Rua das Gáveas 69) is a solid candidate that is (as of this writing) patronized almost exclusively by Lisbonites—but the key is to go late; after midnight is best. It gets better every *noite* ("night"). Whitewashed den under arches; open tile-lined kitchen at one end; guitars and copperware on the walls. Solid local fare; pure *fado* renditions every 30 minutes after 11 P.M. (our only carp is that one waits too long between sessions); the soul-buffeting voice of Fernanda Maria. We still prefer it to any in the city. **Painel do Fado** (Rua S. Pedro de Alcantara 65/69), high in the town, is a long downstairs room with a bar at a still lower level. The handsomely pillared sanctum displays oil

paintings, carpets, colorful table settings, candles in pewter, and rose-toned lighting. Well-dressed waiters; excellent *fado,* with interludes of organ, guitar, or piano music. **Parreirinha d'Alfama** (Largo Chafariz de Dentro) is much lower on our musical scale although many tourists roll in here. Overcrowding and poor ventilation seem to be its chief drawbacks. A **Severa**, on the same street as Lisboa à Noite, is the monotonously insistent choice of almost every concierge and taxi driver in town. They've got a point, at least concerning the musical renditions. **O Faia** (Rua da Barroca) is where you will hear everything from "My Bonnie Lies Over the Ocean" in Danish to very beautiful native songs to the latest mod-*fado.* Don't eat here; we've already made this sacrifice for you. Our bill was incorrectly figured, so be careful. **Taverna del Rey**, at the base of the Alfama and near the waterfront, evokes a flavor of neighborhood pub—if it is still functioning when you arrive. (Check before going.) Both male and female musicians with excellent instrumentalists; low prices; authentic, though rawboned. **Adega Mesquita** (Rua do Diário de Noticias 107) pans out favorable food and very occasional portions of *fado.* **Timpanas** (Rua Gilberto Rola 22–24), offers dances, songs, and piano melodizing; not bad. **Herminia** (Rua da Misericórdia) belongs to a popular artist named Herminia Silva; local folk love her, but we're personally not so enamored. **Luso** (Travessa da Queimada), crawling with rubberneckers, not only leaves us prodigiously unenthusiastic, but it gives us the miseries. **O Forcado** (Rua da Rosa 221) is yet another in the something-for-everybody category. The music is professional, but the gimmickry is overwhelming. Group pilgrimages seem to have sapped its viability. As for **Machado** (Rua do Norte 91), the most famous of all, we now consider it completely unacceptable. What a pity they felt it necessary to add all the cornball yocks to such fundamentally enchanting music. Folk dancing forms a large part of the evening here.

When it comes to night life, apart from the *fado* haunts, for that elegant evening out, the **Carrousel** in the Hotel Ritz is not only the pacesetter, but it's also *the* lone entry in the thoroughbred class—smartly decorated in tasteful Ritz style. Street entrance only, with no direct hotel access; comfortable elegance; no show; dancing, tops, but expect to pay the piper handsomely.

Porao da Nau (Rua Pinheiro Chagas 1-D) has dancing as its big drawing card. **Cova da Onça** (Liberdad 248) means "The Bear's Cave"; it's popular for hugs and romantics, but there's no show. There is an *espectáculo* at the **Frou-Frou** (Av. General N. de Matos 2), where *art nouveau* is the decorative theme. Dinner at 11 P.M.; dancing until 4 A.M., with folklore and music-hall entertainment interspersed.

Nina (Rua Paiva de Andrada 11) is going stronger than ever. Bar with 2 friendly cats freeloading from the customers; cavernous main room with free lancers who can leave at your bidding, plus about a dozen B-babes who probably are house property; small international cabaret (matinée from 6:30 P.M. to 7:30 P.M.; small show at 8 P.M.; reopens at 10 P.M.; more shows at 2 A.M. and 3:30 A.M.; closing 5 A.M.); untampered whisky and fair prices; don't trek there before 12:30 A.M. at the earliest. Above average for its type.

Maxime (Praça da Alegria 58) comes up with tatty surroundings, plenty of solo gals for solo gents, wheezy shows, seminudes (1:30 A.M. and 3:30 A.M.),

souvenirs, and drinks that might sharpen your choppers to needles. In 1 word, run!

Á Cave (Avenida Antonio Augusto de Aguiar 88) is *the* quick turnover den in the city. Instead of having to build up the boy-meets-girl rapport by the usual routine of soaking up a ½-dozen drinks, here the lone fox can strom in, sip 1 quickie, and toddle off with a vixen 5 minutes later. Cellar setup; peppery combo; no show; restaurant service if desired; tiny quaffs of questionable origin; packed with distaff opportunities; animated and worthy; go after midnight.

Fontória (across the square from Maxime) teems with "hostesses" who could easily be entered in the Westminster Dog Show; all of them are *very* hungry; during our short visit we were approached for that "Cigarette, please?" no less than 5 times. Hardly worth it, unless you're a titanium prospector fresh from the volcanic craters of Zambia.

Barracuda (Rua da Misericórdia 12) changed its name and management a while back—but not, unfortunately, its dreary, dismal, drab mien.

Hipopótamo (adjoining Hotel Eduardo VII) herds in the Student Set by their leather-lined eardrums. Combination snack bar (open all day) and dancing oasis (functioning until 2 A.M. *if* the traffic warrants it); records only; noise level only 3 bels lower than the amalgamated decibels of New York's subway. Closed Sunday; very inexpensive. The small Ponderosa (Avenida dos Estados Unidos da América) is now popular with teen types and the young-at-heart elders; again disks only. Other disco precincts include the modernistic Mundial (Rua M. Ferrão 12-B), where the tone is proper for visitors of any age, Stone's (Rua do Olival 1), where you'll pay about $3 minimum, the Beat Club (Rua Conde de Sabugosa 11F), where you can beat it up daily, even on Sunday, Charlie Brown (Av. S. Cabral 39), which we haven't sampled, and Archote (Rua D. Filipe de Vilhena 6D), which is the lowest in cost and in value, too, in our opinions.

Lisbon-in-the-raw? The rough joints proliferate at the docks, but readers are advised 3 serious notes of caution: (1) always keep a weather-eye open in every direction to protect yourself, (2) never be provoked into a fight, no matter how great the temptation, and (3) unescorted female curiosity seekers should stay the hell at home. Texas Bar is the "best" of the lot—if charity can stretch the adjective that far. Grimy, raucous, turn-of-the-century atmosphere with a wincingly ridiculous 3-piece combo; mixed mob from sailors to tramps to jetsam to the occasional pop-eyed tourist.

The Ritz (NO relation to the hotel) rates somewhere between 11th and 12th class, in our estimation. Merchant mariners in profusion; frequent brawls; stay away, or you might be paying the dentist for new bicuspids. Others for the brass-knuckled adventurer, all within a block or 2 of the Texas bar, are Filadelfia, Arizona, Europa, Atlantic, and California. The same cautionary measures apply in all of these.

Shopping Our ★ ★ ★ ★ ★ recommendations are individually noted.

Gold is the best bet in the country. The law says that 18 or 19 carats is the minimum weight that can be sold over the counter. Of the many purveyors here, the nation's oldest and most respected specialist is ★ ★ ★ ★ ★ W.A.

Sarmento (Rua do Ouro 251). If your budget is limited, there is an almost bottomless display of alluring, intricately filigreed earrings, brooches, cuff links, 19¼-gold charms, and natural sterling "costume" creations, many of them in handworked, gold-plated silver—a huge variety of subjects and designs in a very inexpensive price range. For the beauty lover who can afford to spend more, Sarmento points with pride to its very important collection of sterling silver copies of masterpieces in the Portuguese Art Museum, its rare collection of antique gold jewelry copies, its largest stocks of flatware and other house silver on the Peninsula, its dazzling gems, and its carefully selected array of artistic bric-a-brac. Be sure to ask for the Senhores Sarmento personally. As solid as the Beira mountains.

Boutique ★ ★ ★ ★ **Sereira** (Rua S. Bernardo 108, 2nd floor) is a joy to the clothes-conscious gal, to the fabric-happy hunter, and to the pilgrim in · search of unusual lovely touches for the home. Captivatingly gracious Senhora Sereira Amzalak reflects her flawless taste in every item in her chic apartment-showroom. Just telephone 66-68-52 and she will open the door to welcome you.

Madeira embroideries, organdies, and tapestries: ★ ★ ★ ★ **Madeira Superbia** *(Lisbon*'s Av. Duque de Loule 75A and Hotel Intercontinental Ritz; in *Estoril,* Hotel Estoril Sol; also in *Faro)* is THE house, in our unqualified opinions. Every piece of its richly wrought stocks comes direct from its venerable studios and "factory" in the island capital of Funchal. This progressive enterprise has expanded its vast range of tableware to include full lines of linen dresses, silk and linen blouses, fine handkerchiefs for both genders, and daintily designed children's wearables. Also waiting your inspection are floral needlepoint chair covers, and both petit and gros point evening bags. Colorful regional tapestries, into which every thread is hand-embroidered, have long been one of Madeira Superbia's most famous specialties. Art Connoisseurs will find rugs and wall hangings which are remarkably duplicated tapestry copies of the paintings of classic and contemporary masters. Splendid! **Pavilhão da Madeira** (Ave. da Liberdade 15) is also dependable, but to us not in the same class.

Ceramics and porcelains: Lovely, lovely stocks at **Vista Alegre** (Largo do Chiado 18 and Hotel Intercontinental Ritz). They're worth the attention of any shophound. **Sant' Anna** (Rua do Alecrim 91A) is equally fetching in another way; more and better antique tiles are featured; at your instructions, the borders on shades will be painted to match the design on any lamps which catch your fancy. **Fabrica de Loiça de Sacaven** (Av. da Liberdade 49–57) offers handsome big tile pieces, and **Ana** (Hotel Intercontinental Ritz, 2nd floor) has an enchanting selection of pottery.

Portuguese handicrafts: **Casa Quintão** (Rua Ivens 30) is known for its Beiriz and Arraiolos rugs. The latter come ready-made or in weave-it-yourself kits. Other centers are **Casa Regional da Ilha Verde** (Rua Paiva de Andrada 4), **Centro de Artesanato** (Rua Castilho 61) and **Avendiarte** (Av. da Liberdade 224). The last two have the largest abundance of wares.

Exquisite antique furniture copies and leatherwork: ★ ★ ★ ★ For a unique experience, tour the magnificent **Fundaçao Ricardo do Espírito Santo Silva** ("Decorative Arts School Museum" at Largo das Portas do Sol 2), a glorious

treasure house of perfect reproductions of 17th- and 19th-century European furniture plus Portuguese silver, tiles, Arriolos rugs, and other masterpieces. (It has been whispered that most of the copies in Versailles were manufactured here.) Deliveries take months; please be prepared for high-key hustle and bustle. Here's a landmark!

Antiques: The flight of scores upon scores of landed rich families during the revolution plus the inflationary squeeze has brought an Aladdin's cave of beautiful antiques to the market. The only sad note is that the prices are skyrocketing. **Solar** (Rua D. Pedro V 68–70) is normally a fruitful first stop for the aficionado. **Xairel** (Rua D. Pedro V III) could be another winner. If you don't find what you're after in either of these, browse up and down the same street through a number of interesting alternates.

At least two so-called commercial centers have recently sprung up. They stay open from 9 A.M. to 12 P.M. during 7 days a week the year round, including holidays. One is the **Terminal Market** in the central railway station, but its superior is the **Limaviz Shopping Center**, across from the Hotel Sheraton. In both of these you will find a complex of about 50 different stores, restaurants, and boutiques.

Things NOT to buy: Fabrics, perfumes, and any imports.

Shopping Hours: These vary slightly. You may be sure of 2 practices, though: Everything is now closed on Saturday afternoons and everybody puts up the shutters for lunch during the week—with the exception of the aforementioned shopping centers.

Dedicated shophounds? Space is too tight here for further listings—so consult this year's purse-sized, _25th Anniversary Fielding's Selective Shopping Guide to Europe_ for more stores, more details, and more lore.

Other Targets

ALCOBAÇA , on the Lisbon-Oporto road about 87 miles from the capital, with overtones of the classic French abbey. This huge Gothic monastery-church-cloister complex, begun in A.D. 1178, bears the architectural characteristics of the twelfth to fourteenth centuries.

ALGARVE This glorious maritime province, which forms the extreme southwest of the European Continent, is Portugal's lushest garden and principal playpen. It is a narrow ribbon 96 miles long which occupies the nation's entire southern coast and which is geographically separated by a barrier of hills. Summer never really finishes in this subtropical Hesperides. It is always ablaze with flowers, familiar and unfamiliar, for it basks in more sunshine than Mallorca, the French Riviera, or California. Spectacular rock formations of strangely eroded shapes enfold many of its golden sand beaches. The scenery is hauntingly serene when you escape from the occasional pockets of high-rise architecture. The only industries of importance are fishing and tourism. Over centuries its people have been known for their simplicity, their openness, and their great capacity for making friends.

Faro, the capital and site of its only commercial airport, is close to the center of the fine trunk road which runs from _Sagres_ on the Atlantic tip to _Vila Real de St. Antonio_ at the Spanish border. Its fortunate location almost halves the

travel distances to the resorts both to the east and west of this most popular gateway.

Virtually every conceivable summer recreational facility abounds—swimming (because of fitful undertows, go only where there is a lifeguard), all water sports, tennis, riding, 6 golf courses (3 with 27 holes and 3 with 18), fado singing, folk dancing, 3 casinos, nightclubs, discos, hang-gliding, festivals, carnivals, name it and it's there.

Our favorite pastime whenever we drive in this region is the "Chimney Game"—to be the first to spot the winner for that day. These beguilingly charming structures, most of them individually and uniquely designed, are a joy to behold and to compare.

This reporter and his Nancy have just inspected or reinspected 52 hotels from end to end along the corridor—not to mention hosts of restaurants, after-dark spots, and other attractions. Our reports follow.

Albuferia This major resort is widely known as "The St. Tropez of Portugal." While here is a colorful, hilly settlement with a good but crowded beach teeming with holidaymakers, its best quarters are in its environs. In the luxury category, **da Balaia** has employed strikingly interesting and advanced architectural concepts in both its exterior and interior. Sextagonal lobby ascending to 7th-story skylight; urbane, viewful Grill and restaurant; big heated pool; adjoining "bungalows" in customary solid-block building; 186 air-conditioned accommodations somewhat sterile but facing the ocean; longish hike to splendid strand. Our Number One local choice. The 250-room, 7-flight **Alfa Mar** also features the same straight-up lobby. Its less fetching units look down to a basement-level patio-garden. Parade of recreational facilities; total of 120 "bungalows" with sitting room, kitchenette, tiny bath, and either 1, 2, or 3 bedchambers; wonderful beach quite a haul by foot. Okay but not outstanding. **Montechoro**, one of the newest Big Boys, is down 1 notch in official classification. White, white, white entrance hall; blue, blue, blue lounge; dining room another extension of its Moorish theme; 2 pools; 2 tennis courts; 4 bars; 362 spacious, well-furnished, wall-to-wall glass-fronted chambers; 45 suites, some of which are lovely. An excellent buy. **Aparthotel Auramarcomes** comes up with 282 pleasant but rather cramped double studio-type nests with kitchenette and terrace. Cheerfully decorated; superior pool en route to expansive sands; no room service. Worthy for the prices. **Aldeia das Acotelas**, with 300 studio apartments sited on its 100-plus acres, is not only bare-boned, but it struck us as haphazard in its operations. Maybe we're wrong. **Clube Praia da Oura** seemed much too squeezed and commercial for most North American pilgrims.

In town, the veteran **Sol e Mar** has lost its once-famous luster, in our opinions. Cheesy reception on top floor; lounge with b-i-g circular bar in center; at the bottom, huge sun terrace with self-service cafeteria and steps to beach; overstuffed, old-hat furnishings with shabbiness evident while we were there. It disappointed us sorely to see that it has deteriorated into what we consider a production-belt touristic machine. **Rocamar**, near the city limits, sits above the same strand. This cubistic, 91-unit haven is quiet and convenient. Restaurant and bar at entrance level; lounge and reception on 3rd tier; adorn-

ments not distinctive; family ambiance. The **Baltrum**, in a lower bracket, is small but passable for short-stopping budgeteers. **Cerro Grande** offers apartments, villas, and "bungalows" for sale only.

Among the independent restaurants, **Panorama** (Albufeira-Jardim complex) is said to be the most elegant and comfortable. There's an outdoor terrace which overlooks a swimming pool and the sea. It was closed during our latest rounds. We had the same bad luck with **La Cigale**, rated by residents as the runner-up. It is on Olhos de Aqua beach, and reservations are recommended. **Horda d'Aqua**, about 2 miles from the center at Praia da Oura beach, is keyed to the foreign mobs. Seafood the specialty; main establishment with sizable bar; self-service section with its own bar in lower areas. Ho hum. **O Cabaz da Praia** ("The Beach Basket"), operated by Englishman David Shean, has a bar beyond its entrance and an outside, 2-level, unshaded sun terrace with 12 rather battered tables for 2 and a lovely sweep of the shoreline below. Light fare—chicken pie, salads, soufflés, delicious fresh fried sardines, and the like—is featured. Closed Sundays. Fun. German-run **Cafe Doris** is a modest oasis for apple and cheese cake, waffles, assorted ice creams, other snacks, coffee, and various drinks. You may lunch but not dine here. The **Funky Chicken** opened just after our departure. Don't set you sights too high for the vittles in this region.

The shopping is also largely tourist-oriented. **Vinda** has a bountiful stock of handcrafts as well as clothes designed from Portuguese fabrics. **Joalharia das Naus** (Rua 5 de Outubro 30) is the leading jeweler. Antique hunters may have the best fortune at **a Tralha** (Rua João de Deus 1). Save your important purchases for Lisbon.

Alvor   The opulent, high-rise **Alvor Praia**, which commands a heavenly cliff-site panorama above a rock-and-sand beach, offers just about every imaginable provision for vacationers who seek comfort and recreational activities. Handsome white linear structure; full air conditioning; spacious and gracious lobby; split-level dining room with maritime vista plus candlelit Grill; heated pool the best on the whole coast, we opine; elevator to strand; 400-seat Convention Hall; 241 smallish balconied units and 16 very large suites. Reserve on the ocean side to escape the busy road in front. A pacesetter in the Algarve. **Aviz** is the newest project of brilliant tycoon John Stilwell, who owns and operates the above-mentioned Alvor Praia and the equally luxurious Penina Golf (see later). He is hoping to inaugurate a portion of it by late spring and then to have it fully opened by Easter of '82. This 18-story, 325-bedchamber giant will doubtless conform to his impeccable standards. The less-costly **D. João II** boasts fabulous golden sands and a huge pool—but very little else to us. We regard it as a blatantly overcommercial pleasure palace. In the same vein and with the same tariffs, the 24-floor **Tarik** and the run-of-the-mill **Jupiter** also do not earn our praises.

Armação de Pera   lays claim to the largest beach on this entire coast. The **de Garbe** is immaculate again. Glorious clifftop situation; airy dining room; chalet-style nightclub; open terrace for seaside dancing; 54 cheerful sancta. This beehive has become a family target for many British trippers. First class. **Do Levante** dominates a lovely promontory. Soothing lounge; nice restaurant; 2 pools with bar and sun terrace; 41 smallish quarters; 90 steps to

excellent strand. Same tariff ranges but less action and much cozier than the de Garbe. The avant garde **Viking**, 2 miles from the settlement, operates only from March to November. This 400-bed house, with its stamped-out modern aura of impersonality, is typical of its type all over the map. It gave us the chills. The **Vilalara Holiday Village** is a 1 mile out. Although its setting is spectacular and its sports amenities are versatile, we don't think that this would hold strong appeal to the average North American vacationer. Restaurants? A **Grelha** (rustic and simple), **O Forno** (over the sea with outdoor barbecue), and **Panorama Grill** (clifftop) make just about it.

Faro, the capital of the Algarve and its principal gateway, should be bestowed only a fleeting glimpse, in our conclusions. It does not possess what the vacationer to this coast seeks. There are only 3 first-class lodgings—both the **Eva** (commercial but well-operated) and the **Apartments Garantia** (23 penthouse units fully furnished) in its center, as well as the **Estalagem Aeromar** (18 rooms) on Faro Beach. The **Adão** ("Adam") **Restaurant** in the Eva is the best for conventional fare. **Al Faghar** (up one flight at Rua Tenente Valadim 30) is so unusual that it's fun. The 6-table bar in Portuguese Victorian with a high ceiling, a creaky floor, and pink-and-white kerosene lamps on each table, is straight from Roland Searle. Smaller, more modern dining room adjoining; prix-fixe, 3-course lunch-dinner about $9; cookery unexpectedly and rewardingly savory in this milieu. Recommended. Their nearest competitors—**Doris Irmaos**, **Caracoles**, and **Kappra**—are plain, regional, and routine. The **Pousada de São Bras** in **Alportel**, about a 30-minute drive in the hills, is a happy excursion for the noontime repast. We urge that you skip this hub and hie to the resort of your choice.

Lagos, toe to heel with **Praia da Rocha**, means "lakes"—but there's nary a pond to be seen. The **de Lagos**, centrally situated facing the harbor promenade, is officially classified as First Class instead of Deluxe only because a small segment of its rear rooms are too cramped to qualify. Sited on a 3-acre hilltop; 100% air conditioned; spacious arched lobby; verdant interior courtyard; dining room, Grill, and Coffee Shop; comfortable, relaxing bar; 6 cozy lounges tucked at different levels; heated pool; English direction. Large expanses of white combined with orange, cooling blue, and vibrant green form its outstandingly attractive theme throughout. All clients are extended free privileges of its Duna Beach Club, 5 minutes by shuttle, with its clubhouse, sands, pool, and daily buffets. Here is a sleeper—the best of its class we've seen on the Algarve. The 5-story, 259-room **Golfinho** is typical of the hurry-built hostelries in this area. Appealing vista from Penthouse Grill; ground-level restaurant crammed with 350 seats; clam-size space concepts which are far too spare for longstaying holidaymaking. Not bad, but far from exciting. In comparison to this we prefer the eensy **Pensão D. Ana** around the curve of the coast, about 100 yards above a bathing cove. It has a mere dozen clean accommodations at lean tariffs. The Second Class **da Meia Praia** and **São Cristovão** are both too far from the action and not worth the bother, in our opinions. Forget about the jerry-built "motel" beside the road to Sagres; we erroneously took it at first sight for a gypsy campsite. Restaurants? **O Alpendre** ("The Shed") is one of the most sophisticated along the entire coast. Handsome paneled-stuccoed décor with clever touches which add richness and intimacy; about 20 tables

in L-shaped main section and nook at rear; strikingly lavish food display in center; bar downstairs; fine tiled, stainless-steel, open kitchen with white-capped chef; all of our dishes excellently cooked and presented. Although the average meal with wine is $20 to $25 per person, it should be worth this investment to moneyed voyagers. Owner-Host Mattos merits pride. **Os Arcos** and **Dom Sebastian** are next in line. While the shopping in general is routine here, **Porches**, on the main Faro-Portimão road, stocks a large, unusual assortment of handmade, hand-painted pottery in the traditional regional style, most of which is spun from the local red clay.

Penina   The **Penina Golf** remains one of the most famous and illustrious golfing resort havens in Europe. This great estate, on which more than 400,000 trees have been planted since '64, is 2½ miles from the sea—an advantage for players who shun the wicked Atlantic-borne winds. Magnificent championship 27-hole links designed by Henry Cotton; fully outfitted clubhouse downstairs in main building a few steps from 1st tee; practice ground and putting greens; caddies, golf cars, caddy carts, and clubs available for hire; Olympic-size swimming pool in the garden; 2 tennis courts; sauna. Attractive interior appointments set amid modern Algarve architecture; clean-lined lobby with sumptuous adjoining lounges; spacious dining room; chic, intimate Monchique Grill with brass lanterns, touches of timber and glass-covered rôtisserie; dancing nightly; total of 214 air-conditioned rooms, many with their own balcony. Hotel King John Stilwell and Director Adriano Bento spare nothing to keep this great landmark in the forefront. The plush **Alvor Casino**, only a 5-minute walk, is open every day from 5 P.M. to 3 A.M. Good restaurant with dancing and 2 floor shows where Penina guests on full pension terms may dine for a small supplement when they present a voucher; 3 bars; the normal games of chance. Don't forget your passport if you wish to play!

Portimão is the second largest and second busiest settlement in the province. During its days and evenings it is constantly a-bustle with residents and visitors. Despite its numerous high-rise buildings and its public market which covers the central plaza with racks of clothing, textiles, and other products—all sold to the strains of screeching rock music—a substantial portion of its traditional color remains. Curiously, the Second Class **Globo**, with a crisp lobby, panoramic 7th-floor restaurant, and 80 mini-mini-mini abodes, is the only hotel above the bottom-budget level. Its small, family-operated restaurants, however, are numerous. We understand with watering mouths why **A Lanterna**, near the harbor bridge with no view, is the most popular eating place within many a mile. Modern in tone; open kitchen; 17 tables split by arched partition; midget greenhouse bar; blackboard menus on the walls. Fresh, fresh seafood is the staple of its delicious fare. Their delicate small clams steeped with mild onions in a white sauce were the greatest of this bivalve we have ever enjoyed anywhere. Dynamic and sympathetic Celestino and Isaura Batista, who have lived in America, are its owners and operators. Closed Dec.-Jan. and Sundays. Super within its category. The **Old Tavern** is charming in a British way. Pub-style interior; light, airy, enclosed garden with tables to rear; curries, spareribs, clam chowder, turkey à la crème and vol au vent are typical standards. Closed Saturdays. This English-run house is a comfortable and clubby oasis. **Humphrey's**, a newish entry, occupies a century-old man-

sion. Key Largo Lounge with live music; generous drinks in the African Queen Bar; dependable skilletry in the Casablanca Room. We think that the legendary Mr. Bogart, from whose activities all of these names spring, might have shared our liking for this place. **Veneza** has been expanded to 120 seats. Bar and snack bar on ground floor; dining room on mezzanine; passable but not notable. The **Dennis Inn** features a fetching bar and a snack-tea-coffee shop. Favored by the foreign trade. Shopping? Tourist junk abounds. Well above this in quality are **Vinda** (branch in *Albufeira*) for boutique items, celebrated **Vista Alegre** (see "Lisbon") for porcelains, and **Galeria Portimão** for Portuguese paintings, tapestries, and sculptures.

Praia da Luz   Luz Bay Club Villas is a colony of about 200 individual attached "villas" with 2 swimming pools and 2 restaurants in the garden area. These quarters are basically constructed with 2, 3, or 4 bedrooms with bath at ground level, plus sitting room, dining nook, kitchen, and terrace upstairs. Your happiness here depends on your reaction to the owner's taste in decoration and her thoughtfulness as a hostess. Minimum of one week's reservation; open all year. The only restaurant of note in this pleasant little village is **Fortalza**, which has a glorious panorama from directly over a wonderful beach and the sea. It is operated by an English husband and his American wife. Reportedly it is open for lunch (about $9) and 3-course dinner (about $12) in season, but in winter it is closed except in the evening and Sunday at midday. Our timing was so unlucky that we had to peek through its windows but couldn't try it.

Praia da Rocha   This center is too zestless and mundane for many holidaymakers—especially since other top-quality oases have sprung up in the near vicinity. Its pride is the famous 7-story, 210-room, white-and-blue, luxury **Algarve**. Although a king's ransom has been poured into this landmark, somehow we feel the truly discriminating traveler would find it overshowy, overboisterous, and overspectacularly Las Vegas in its concept. Almost every conceivable warm-weather amenity has been crammed into its imposing hulk for the sustenance and recreation of its guests. While the effort, the tremendous investment, and the extraordinarily high quality of the construction and appointments must surely be commended, personally we would rather pay the same high tariffs elsewhere. You might strongly disagree. The lower-category **Jupiter**, which orbits a few hundred yards away, is another attraction in this hamlet. Groupy in feeling and more commercial in general; heated swimming pool (covered in cooler months) at its entrance, too close to the traffic for comfort; aloof-minioned restaurant; nightclub; disco; 144 appealingly decorated bedchambers with bath. Satisfactory for its bracket. The new 21-floor **Tarik**, 5 minutes from the sands, is firmly in the modern mood. V-ended pool; tennis; 2 restaurants; tiny "supermarket"; 120 doubles and 63 very small suites, plus 36 studio-type "suites" and 77 single-chamber "studios," both of the last with kitchenettes. Although for the humdrum Torralta chain it's a star, we rate it as only fair. The Plaza-sited **Rocha** is still resting after its renewal and expansion program a while ago. **Bellavista**, just above a beach, does have a lovely view—but the conditions in this former private mansion must be seen to be believed. This creaky plant, 103 years old, gave us the impression that it hadn't been changed since its inauguration—literally speaking, an overstate-

ment, of course. Yet we would not recommend this relic to any traveler for all of the port in the Douro Valley.

Sagres is a small harbor on the lee side of _Cape St. Vincent_, the magnificent harsh promontory which is the most southwesterly point of Europe and which for centuries has been called "O Fim do Mundo"—the End of the World. Because the Continent first meets the onslaught of the Atlantic here, nimrods will find the best fishing grounds in Portugal and scuba divers can glide through a virtually unrivaled aquarium. The drive to its famous fortress and lighthouse is a _must_ for every visitor. Whenever this road takes you close to the edge of its all-embracing cliffs, there are thrilling views of the sea pounding away hundreds of feet below. Many human flies with poles sit nonchalantly on its rim and play out their amazingly long lines into the swirling waters.

Pousada do Infante, with its stunning maritime panorama, is so popular that it is wise to book reservations at least 4 months ahead. Its cellar-to-garret reconstruction and renovation in '80 jumped its room count from 15 to 60 chambers with bath and balcony. Simple modern building; 2 sweet dining places with 200 capacity; garden terrace; pool; barbecue; reasonable tariffs as in all these government-operated _pousadas;_ open all year. Director Alfredo Maria França de Azevedo has TRULY shaken up this unostentatious but heavily-trafficked target. **Da Baleeira** is sited directly above a good sandy beach. This poorly maintained house caters frequently to German tour groups. Our judgment? Strictly routine, despite its viewful location. The little **Residencia Dom Henrique**, in town, is a mixed bag. Some of its limited number of abodes have private bath and some offer a small sitting room. So-so. The modest **A Tasca**, a typical fishermen's bar-restaurant with a lovely sweep of the bay, is the only independent eating spot of consequence which we found in these environs.

Vale do Lobo is a completely self-sufficient world of its own. The Reception Center at its main entrance, operated 24 hours per day, has a pleasant but smoothly alert and protective multilingual staff. On arrival, passports or identification cards are required to be presented. In addition to its hotels and villas, you'll find a splendid 27-hole golf course designed by Henry Cotton, 6 independent restaurants, 6 independent bars or coffee shops, beach and water activities, 2 swimming pools, 12 all-weather tennis courts, beauty shops, medical attention, 4 nightclubs, a drugstore, physiotherapy and just about everything needed in resort community living. The luxurious **Dona Filipa**, one of Trust House Forte's prize showcases, is a gem. Superb location close to 9 miles of golden sands; outstandingly tasteful décor; air conditioning that automatically shuts off when doors or windows are opened; Rotonda and Bistro its 2 new gracious dining rooms; Kasbah nightclub with show just inaugurated; tennis, pool, and many other amenities. Here's a teed-up winner in our Tournament of Champions which we recommend especially to the mashie set—not to city slickers in search of metropolitan pastimes. Adjoining are the 125 domiciles and 123 baths of Village Villas (attached in clusters) and Garden Villas (separated). Each has a sitting room, kitchen, direct access to a pool (and in the latter case to a garden). A minimum stay of one week is the rule during High Season. They are very good for traveling families. The **Toca**

do Coelho, down by the waves, is more modest and less costly. All clients in this upper-drawer complex are furnished with a list of its multifarious facilities.

Vilamoura will soon be Europe's largest and most complete privately owned vacation center. Its 1615 acres of beach and gently rolling hills—1200 of which are set aside as green zones—make it bigger than Monaco. If all goes on schedule, it will be completed in 1988.

The facilities here are already vast. In addition to hostelries, apartments, and Holiday Villages, there are manmade lakes, 2 excellent 18-hole golf courses designed by Frank Penninck, a new casino, a private airport, a riding center, tennis courts, swimming pools, a 2-mile strand, and much, much more. The Marina, which now berths 615 boats, will eventually shelter 2800 craft. In its area there are a number of private homes, rentable villas, a sizable shopping center, the moored floating **O Vapor** restaurant, and a pub. The Tourist Villages (**Aldeia do Golf, Golfeiras, Aldeia do Mar, Aldeia do Campo, Le Clube, Monte da Vinha, Prado do Golf**, et seq.) consist of apartment blocks, "bungalows" in communal buildings, and small groups of villas, all clustered around their central clubhouse with their restaurant, bar, pool, and shared public precincts. Among the stopping places, The **Vilamoura Golf Hotel** is the most sophisticated. Each of its 52 nests has a full bath, a terrace, and a subterranean parking area; airy suites are available. The international restaurant, bars, boutiques, and dining terrace are built around a handsome swimming pool. It is too somnolent for anyone but golf buffs, in our opinions. The 9-story **Dom Pedro**, 300 yards from the Casino and 2 miles from the Atlantic, has recently been inaugurated. Curvilinear structure; modern, rather cluttered lobby with overloud piped music; Grill with limited choices; simple, crowded Buffet; lovely sun area with pool and jumbo Gazebo Bar; 2 tennis courts. Not bad but far from special. **Aldela do Golf** comes up with 150 quarters all built in attached groups of 3, 4, and 5. These range from single-level villas with 2 chambers to 2-level villas with 3 chambers to the so-called Golférias of 2-story "apartments." Unexciting. **Golf Hotel** jams 52 rooms in villas to its rear. The furnishings are well kept but cheezy in design and quality. Not very good, but its people were amiable. Among others on the drawing boards, **Sheraton** will launch a five-star house here in '83. Restaurants? In general they are routine to date. **Casa Velha** bodes no competition for opulence except the neighboring Dona Filipa. Spacious, impressive, urbane establishment atop hill; suave main segment leading to glassed-in terrace which opens to patio. Its ambiance has the panache but the sterility of an illustration in a glossy interior decorator's magazine. While our cuisine was good, it was not especially memorable. Expect to spend at least $25 per appetite. Despite these drawbacks, it is still delightful for a sunny day's or balmy evening's excursion. Closed Sunday plus Monday lunch.

ALBUFERIA, ALVOR, and **ARMAÇAO DE PERA** See "Algarve."

ARRAIOLOS This village—not too far from Estremoz—is famed for its distinctive carpets. We feel this center is a waste of time as a sightseeing target. It is almost totally in the hands of communists, there is no place to eat (not

even a bar clean enough where you would want to sip a cup of coffee or a soft drink), and the town is certainly one of the most run-down we have ever seen in our travel experience. What a pity!

AZEITAO   This settlement gazes at the capital from across the Tagus. Its nicest target is the romantic little **Quinta das Torres**, a seventeenth-century palace. Some modern comforts, but the management scorns electricity in favor of petroleum lamps and open fireplaces, for authentic Old World atmosphere. Lovely park, courtyard, and lake swimming pool; 11 units, mostly suites, in different styles.

BRAGA, an inland city 44 miles from the northern frontier, is one of Portugal's most historic shrines. Ancient monuments, churches, paintings, and tombs abound; it is also the seat of a small university. The First Class, 132-unit, air-conditioned **Turismo** offers just about the only comfortable lodgings here. Sterile, commercial lobby; Golden Bar as garish as a pinball machine; pleasant dining room and extensive lounge with terrace up 1-flight; probably the best cuisine and service in the region; some bedchambers merry with color. **Pensão Grande Residência Avenida**, next on the roster, is a giant step downward; only 9 of its 22 billets have private plumbing. The other 8 houses are strictly for bottom budgeteers. If your interests are cultural, it is worth exploring— but if they aren't, we suggest a bypass.

BUÇACO   (pronounced "Boo-CASH-oh") tops our list as the single most enchanting attraction on the Portuguese mainland. Its spacious, ultrarococo **Hotel Palácio**, crowning a huge forest-park, is straight from the pages of a fairytale book. This splendid palace in Manueline style—originally the hunting lodge of a Portuguese king—is adorned with a galaxy of works by notable artists and artisans, finely furnished, and embraced by extraordinary gardens. Its public rooms are so regal that they must be seen to be believed. There are 70 abodes, 8 of which are suites; the best is the Queen's Apartment—with a reception room, dining room, bedroom, dressing room and bath—which costs about $180 for 2 persons including breakfasts. The excellent cuisine is matched by a cellar where reportedly 80,000 bottles of wine sleep. Tennis and 2 pools (1 thermal) are at hand. Gentle Director José Rodrigues Dos Santos has devoted more than 40 years of his life to this marvel. If time permits, and if you have a rented car, all of our reportorial team urgently suggest that you make an excursion from Lisbon to this gem for at least 1 overnight. Start at about 10 A.M. on the heavily traveled inland main highway north; stop for a leisurely lunch at the charming **Estalagem Do Mestre Alfonso Domingues** in **Batalha** and please don't miss the fantastic next-door 14th-century Gothic Cathedral; head for **Coimbra** and turn off at **Mealhada** to conclude this 145-mile jaunt. (To save money you could lodge at the Estalagem and visit the Palácio for the noon meal only—but your departure would have to be earlier.) Because both of these places are so popular, be certain to nail down your room reservations in advance. In our judgments, this foray can be one of the most delightful highlights on anyone's journey through Western Europe.

CASCAIS This resort is 14 miles from Lisbon. It is dominated by the colossal, 19-story, 400-room **Estoril Sol**. Towering mightily near Cascais Bay, it dominates the skyline for miles around. For youngbloods, group leaders, and modernists, it also dominates the social life of the area. Its vast skein of entertainment or pastime facilities include a terraced Olympic-size pool, kiddy pond, artificial beach with tunnel access under the road, bowling lanes, Turkish bath, sauna, discothèque, 5 bars, a beauty parlor, barbership, and 2 banquet-conference rooms for 1200. Lobby and reception are effectively redone in Moorish style; 10th floor nerve center with spacious lounge, panoramic restaurant with atrocious cuisine (on our sampling), bar, card nook, and ballroom; each level hued in different color schemes. The best accommodations for the money, in our opinion, are the penthouse suites on the 16th floor—exceptional values when split among 4 to 6 occupants. Book away from the "front," because of the railroad and auto traffic noises. Service? Impersonal and institutional, with a long climb ahead. The **Albatroz** is a tranquil retreat. A happy-family atmosphere (almost slaphappy really when the service is off) pervades the cliff-high 16-room manse, the lawn, the tear terrace, the fireside lounge, the breathtakingly situated dining salon, the bar, and every cranny of this amiable home. All units have a sea view, full bath, and individual décor; we prefer #1, #6, or #14. Quite good. **Cidadela** is unusual in concept and, we think, fair in execution. You may choose between hotel-style living or private apartment-style living with connecting-door units stretchable from 1-to7 person occupancy. (A small but well-stocked downstairs supermarket can furnish the comestibles for your fully equipped kitchenette.) Inside-outside dining area; glass-fronted and poolside bars; large terrace adjoining main floor; beauty salon; 2 boutiques; garage and parking space. For the wayfarer in search of Portuguese P. & Q., this haven probably will be suitable to most trippers. On this latest round, the 59-kip **Baia** seemed so commercial, so clangorous, and so well used that it's not for us—or for you either, we opine. **Residencial Solar Dom Carlos** is a sweet, elfin haven in the town itself. Grand roster of 15 bedchambers, all with bath; new breakfast room and kitchen; chapel renovated; striking 18th-century dining room. We like this one for what it is. **Estalagem Na. Sra. Das Preces**, with the same ownership and prices but different management, is a converted mansion in the most elegant local residential area. The furnishings in its 17 nests, all with private plumbing, are also simple and practical. *Fado* is performed here nightly from 10 P.M. up to dawn, depending upon the clientele and the outside groups which come to listen. If you don't like these haunting refrains, stay away, because this house is not large enough to get away from it! **Estalagem Do Farol** is another gabled old home with low tariffs, but without much taste.

Food? **Baluarte** is a haunt of monied sophisticates. Promenade-sited with sweep of harbor; avant-garde, semicircular bar at ground level; gracious, window-wrapped dining room with small terrace up 1-flight; music nightly, with dancing thrice weekly; versatile menu with costly tabs; closed all day Monday and Tuesday for lunch. A smoothly professional, upper-bracket operation. **Pescador**, a 2-minute stroll from the port behind the fish market, is also superior. Trappings of rough nautical life cover the walls; the atmosphere is refined but almost sporting in its informality; the attention can't be faulted for

a place of its type; and the cuisine—both in preparation and volume—is savory. Outstanding value in an outstanding fisherman's hut. On the same mall, **O Pipas**, a few doors further into town, is perhaps even more attractive in a gimmicky fashion, but we found the cookery fourth-rate by comparison —and at very little difference in outlay. The garlands of garlic, the false wine tuns on the walls, and the maritime come-ons somehow seemed artificial here. Quite popular, but not with the Fielding tribe. Also in the port area we would choose **João Padeiro** over O Pipas. It doesn't give off the same fireworks, but it served us much better Atlantic harvests on our recent swing. **Retiro** is in the same family as João Padeiro, which in itself is a recommendation. **O Batel** (Travessa das Flores, opposite the fish market) is situated in a tiny courtlike square, also away from the sea. Two immaculate rooms (18 tables) divided by arches and colorful Portuguese draperies; beaming staff who fairly bust to please in their friendly but fractured English. **Jardim Visconde da Luz** was recommended to us by our old friend Shr. Pereira, the crackerjack Chief Concierge at the Hotel Palácio in Estoril, as new and very, very good. We couldn't find time to try its Portuguese kitchen specialties or shellfish, but we trust his judgment implicitly. **John Bull**, at the rear of the Baia Hotel, comes up with an authentic British pub atmosphere, but it is 100% Portuguese piloted, despite its name and ambiance. Two small rooms at ground level with paneling in such mellowed brown that it appears black; front segment carpeted and appointed with 2 or 3 overstuffed chairs and a sofa; back portion with a 3-stool-or-standup bar. Here is a friendly intimate pop-in spot for a cool drink and a chat. We're told that **Os Doze** is excellent. **Reijos** struck us as second rate in gastronomy, too. noisy, too Americanized, and the waiters were too inattentive. **Santini's Ice Cream Bar** has just moved in. Immaculate precincts; 10 flavors, all creamy.

Tiny excursion? **Restaurante da Marinha**, in a pine grove a skip up the shore road (about 800 yards inland, via a secondary lane), is peacefully situated but noisy when crowded. Handsome swimming pool to one side; 3 walls of windows enfolding rough timbers, a farmhouse hearth, and colorful trimmings; seafood specialties, with a plentitude of other selections available; droves of yowling tots on Sundays and feast days. Out on the coastal pike toward Guincho, there are open stands where all types of fresh sea fare are grilled before you. Benches for seats, planks for tables; simplicity itself, but usually delicious. Take a sweater if you motor out in the evenings. A pocketful of small change should buy a feast.

For evening revels, **Palm Beach**, on the water, has 2 faces. After sundown, this mecca for swimming is transformed into a nightclub. Outdoor terrace with colored lights and flowers; when this section is closed at 2 A.M., the clientele is moved en masse into the building for more dancing and a floor show. Recommended. **Borsalino** has funny art deco outfittings, but it was sleepy and dull on our peep-in. **Van-Gogo** is the go-goingest pop-stop in town for (Dutch?) bop-hoppers. Typical, but good for its type. **Juliana's** is another which, by name alone, might appeal to Lowlanders. Fun and not expensive. **Pickwick** is a solid pub. The **Rodrigo Bar** specializes in *fado;* the walls are decorated in coats of arms; Rodrigo does the tonsilwork. His place is at *Birre,* on the fringe of Cascais.

COIMBRA the fourth city, is ancient, beautiful, and serene. It spreads itself lazily over one big hill, rising from the banks of the Mondego River to a dominant clock tower at its cap. The nation's largest University, with more than 12,000 students, is here; its library alone is worth a special trip for bibliophiles. The famous *fado* "April in Portugal" was composed as a tribute to this two-tiered town. It is unfortunate that its facilities for visitors range from mediocre to wretched. For lodgings they are offered 3 second-class hotels, 3 fourth-class hotels, and 16 pensions. None of us has ever been able to find a single interesting restaurant. Therefore, we do not recommend a stop in this venerable center.

ESTORIL We think it beats the Riviera during the summer (not in other seasons)—less crowded, less frenetic, friendlier reception, and cheaper tariffs. Gambling, swimming, yachting, golf, horseback riding, trapshooting, tennis, fishing, thermal baths, dancing—the works. Less than ½-hour by car or 45 minutes by Toonerville-type train from the center of Lisbon; dead in winter, spring, or fall.

The **Estoril Palacio** is being reborn in magnificent fashion—a credit to brilliant Owner Antonio de Figueriero and handsome, dynamic General Manager Manuel Quintas, who virtually brought this house back from the other side of the Styx. Not only do its traditional glamour and fine antique furnishings glisten again, but in July 1979, on its centennial year, a $2-million, 24-month renovation and expansion program was inaugurated. Its room count will be upped by 50% to a total of 300 bedchambers. A new heated indoor pool will complement the outside one. A sophisticated Grill, a Coffee Shop, a solarium and a mineral-water spa will be erected from scratch. This legendary house is immaculate. So is concierge Mario da Silva Pereira, one of the best in the nation. Our salutes and highest recommendations.

The **Lennox Country Club** is a hotel—not a club, as its title implies. Here is a perfect little gem for golfers and tranquillity-seekers. It is just a chip shot from the center, on a narrow, peaceful uphill lie. Two buildings resembling a private-mansion complex (10 bedrooms in the main structure, 7 in the annex); glassed-in dining room opening to a swimming pool with its own ranch-style imbibery; lounge with small bar (pour-your-own-drinks and write-your-own-bills policies); all but one unit with private bath. No tour groups ever; only residents and their guests permitted use of the public rooms, bars, pool, or cinema; complimentary shuttle services to airport, golf course, and docks; free, unlimited supply of house wines, bottled water, fruit, midmorning coffee, afternoon tea, and a welter of other kindnesses. Write to Mr. or Mrs. D. C. Reid, the proprietors, or to personable Manager José Capitao *long* in advance, because the clientele consists chiefly of well-contented repeaters.

The inland **Sintra Estoril**, a short hop from the center, is the second largest hostelry in this resort. Avant-garde, semicircular, 3-story structure; fascinating metal collage stretching across entire long wall opposite reception; large public areas with a chill factor; dining room with small tables almost lost; 2 bars; 192 air-conditioned lairs; pool, tennis, mini-golf, and more. A Superior First-class house which is striking but stark and impersonal.

The lower First-class **Lido**, in a quiet residential zone, offers a pool, a bar

and bright topside restaurant, and 55 accommodations (7 of them 2-bedroom suites). Nice relaxed family feeling here.

Atlántico is scissored from the sea by railway tracks. The formerly disgraceful maintenance standards here have been somewhat tightened at last. _Comme si, comme ça._

Paris, which for at least 20 years we regarded as hopelessly frozen in the Calvin Coolidge era, exudes a brand-new persona throughout. Energetic Director A. Teixeira Murta, formerly of Lisbon's Avenida Palace, has not only radically sparked up its plant but the morale of its staff as well. Reconstructions, renovations, and repaintings galore; 2 pools (1 heated); disco; gym and sauna. Our hats are off to this innkeeping tiger.

The little **Hotel Das Arcadas** is under the same ownership and management as the Palácio and consequently was restored in a thorough-going fashion. Today it has come back smartly and is recommendable again.

The 84-room **Monte Estoril**, on a hillside overlooking the sea, must wait a while before we can wax enthusiastic. The **Zenith** and the **Londres** are off our list.

Food? The **Casino** and the mammoth **Hotel Estoril Sol** are flawed' by cookery which, in our opinion, ranges from miserable to execerable. The **Palácio** is now our first choice for patrician dining. **Tamariz**, on the beach, is pleasant on a sunny day—especially since the installation of the pool and locker rooms. Attractive dining terrace, plain interior; seemingly slightly on the grimy side, but not enough to throw you. The **Estoril Country Club**, open to Palácio Hotel guests, is the luncheon favorite of golfers. Wonderful view, lovely surroundings, fair food, waiters who often vex us with their surliness. The cliff-dwelling **A Choupana** in São João do Estoril presents wide windows for coastscape vistas, courteous service, gentle-to-the-tummy but not outstanding cookery, and moderate tabs. This one gives us the impression of an upper-grade seaside roadhouse, if we may be permitted to mangle our language so liberally.

Big-time entertainment and gaming regularly are dealt out in the **Casino**— the world's largest without sleeping accommodations. Within this massive, modernistic, park-fronted structure, you will find: (1) A Las Vegas-type night-club-restaurant with a surprisingly inexpensive (albeit mediocre) dinner from 9 P.M. to 1 A.M., featuring a floor show at 11:30 P.M., a prairie-size stage which ebbs and flows in independent segments, and a sizzling orchestra, (2) a small nightclub, (3) a cinema, (4) 2 bars, (5) a snack bar, and (6) the gambling rooms. There are separate salons for baccarat, U.S.-style craps, boule, and a regiment of one-arm bandits for lovers of levers. Other pastimes include roulette, chemin de fer, blackjack, and French Bank. Limits vary; $3 minimum play at blackjack is one example. Your passport is required (no exceptions!) for admission to the gaming rooms; the entrance fee is a dollar (plus a quarter more for the slot-machine salon) per person for a 2-day ticket. Whether you bet $100 or nothing makes not a whit of difference.

ESTREMOZ This fascinating city is easily accessible from Lisbon by car over new highways (which will also enable you to see Evora in the same day's excursion). _Please_ take time for at least a meal or night at the

palatial **Pousada da Rainha Santa Isabel** (Tel. 22618). It overlooks the whitewashed stucco houses amid awesome beauty of an era that will never return to Portugal. The building is a living museum of aristocratic antiques, furnishings, paintings, and art. Directly adjoining are a glorious ancient chapel and the medieval apartment of a long-ago Queen; ask Reception to arrange a quick visit to both, because they are fascinating. To those who sleep here twice or more, we also urge a 24-mile excursion to the **Pousada Santa Luzia** in **Elvas**, near the Spanish frontier, for its famous 4-course lunch. This is by far the leading gastronomic center in the entire region. The prix fixe is about $10 per person.

ÉVORA   This one's a sleepy little town near the Spanish border, with the Temple of Diana, quaint monasteries, all sorts of things dating back to the Romans. Here is one of the keystones in the development of Portuguese history. The **Pousada dos Loios** (Tel. 24051) is not only a sightseeing must but a great reward if you have time to spend the night. It is composed of ancient courts, thick walls, arches, and vaults—the former convent of Lioios. A number of the rooms were cells in the fifteenth century. Some units with painted walls and ceilings, some with terrace, all with bath. The cuisine places its accent on dishes of the immediate region—very interesting, but not the platters for anyone without a sense of culinary adventure.

FARO   See "Algarve."

FÁTIMA   Atop a mountain range called Serra d'Aire, this is the scene of the celebrated religious miracle—where the Virgin Mary appeared before 3 peasant children on repeated occasions during 1917. The site is 107 miles from Lisbon, a strenuous 1-day round trip. A new express highway is in operation. Or if you don't have a private car and don't like the frequent and easily available bus excursions (ask your hotel concierge about these), you may take the train which will deposit you within 15 miles of your goal, at a station named Fátima, and run up the rest of the way by taxi. The *Sud-Express* (Paris-Lisbon) also stops daily at this point and is met by shuttle buses. If traveling locally by rail, it's wise to pack a lunch and thirst-quenchers. You may stay at the **Estalagem Os Três Pastorinhos** or the **Hotel Santa Maria** (we've not yet seen these, but readers tell us they're the choicest), the **Pensão Zeca** (also untested by us), the **Beato Nuno** (operated by the Carmelite Fathers; 8 rooms with bath, 60 with shower, 65 roomettes; many altars; English-speaking priest always on duty), or the 20 small pensions. It distresses and dismays us to observe the increased parasitic commercialism that thrives at the outer fringes of this wondrous monument to faith. As in Lourdes and Montserrat, this aspect has grown so crass that some of the visitor's reverence is inevitably tempered. There's a magnificent new church and mammoth esplanade which will ultimately resemble the great plaza of Rome's St. Peter's; spectacular healing miracles have occurred at the Shrine. It's Catholic, of course, but travelers of Protestant, Jewish, and other faiths flock here, too. Despite its tinny, shoddy, mercantile edges, this should be seen by everybody, regardless of denomination.

FIGUEIRA DA FOZ, a major seaside resort, is 123 miles north of Lisbon. Splendid beach; imposing promenade; facilities include a gambling casino, a big open-air swimming pool, scads of hotels (the **Grande Hotel da Figueira** is the leader, followed by **Estalagen da Piscina, da Praia**, and **Albergaria Nicola**), pensions, and restaurants (mostly modest), a theater, and the usual summer attractions. Cheap, informal, and animated in season.

FUNCHAL See "Madeira."

GUINCHO is 20 miles from Lisbon and 4 miles beyond Cascais. Please don't miss the exquisite **Hotel do Guincho**, which commands one of the most glorious settings of any hostelry in the land. Its cliff-high perch is flanked on either side by bowls of golden sand rising from the breakers up into the gorse-covered dunes. It was restored in the sixteen-hundreds, but the latest updatings to comfortize this sparkling antique gem were effected without altering the original tone or structure to any appreciable degree. At a cost of more than $6,000,000 in redecoration, the 38-room *fortaleza* probably will never make money—but profit was never the intention here. Each room different—most with balcony, some large suites with fireplaces (pick #309, 310 or 312), all with air conditioning, many with carved vaulted stone ceilings. Some furnishings dating back 350 years. Our very recent lunch in its elegant seafront dining room was nothing short of superb (see below), at a surprisingly reasonable price. Be certain to reserve long in advance *summer or winter*. Our top recommendation for coastal navigators. The neighboring **Muchaxo** has 24 modest bedchambers. The **Estalagem** has 13 simple, clean rooms and the same view but far less color.

As we said above, for dining we are fond of the **Hotel do Guincho**. Elegance is the word. Very highly recommended for discriminating voyagers. Much more informal, the nearby combined **Muchaxo Restaurant** and **A Barraca Bar** are drawing knowledgeable excurionists from miles around. Vastly expanded facilities now seating 400 guests of all descriptions, economic brackets, nationalities, and sizes; swimming pool adjoining; service excellent and friendly; food also excellent for its inexpensive category. It is packed to the scuppers when the weather is right. As for **Faroleiro**, it stank—literally—at the time we inspected it. No, with ringing sincerity. **Arriba**, on the seaside cliffs before you reach Guincho, is nice for sunning and poolside lounging, but for little else, we think.

LAGOS See "Algarve."

MADEIRA As sweet as her wines, as soft as her sea zephyrs, as colorful as her bower-banked cliffs, she is one of Europe's last unspoiled outposts. Here, to us, is the uncontested Queen of the West Atlantic islands (there are 8)— far more ingratiating than the spoiled Canaries and the more starkly primitive Azores.

On "boat days," when the cruise ships anchor, she is overbustling and overexcited. But the moment they pull away, she reverts magically to her natural, easy-paced, utterly delightful enchantment and charm.

Now for some capsule facts to pinpoint this ocean fairyland: *Situation?* About 1½ hour's flight by jet from Lisbon, north of the Canaries and 300 miles off the coast. *Inhabitants?* The 280-thousand *Madeirense* are virtually always gentle, kind, warm, outgiving, generally with ripe-olive eyes that reflect their sunlight and inner tranquility. *Climate?* Benign almost year round. The mid-winter sweater-weather is only 15 degrees lower than the 78-degree mean of high summer. Early November to mid-December is supposed to be Off Season, but we love it then (good sun, a few scattered showers and frequent winds to freshen the foliage, and no tourist mobs). Dark clouds are most likely to linger in February. No other European region—the Greek islands, Mallorca, Sicily, or elsewhere—offers such a salubrious aura and tempered clime. *Topography?* A bastion of rocky cliffs, soaring hills, and lustrous vales which burst with fruits and gay flowers. Mountains peak at well over 6000 feet. Ridges crisscross her 35 miles of length and 14 miles of breadth. The coastal loop contains 2300 curves, with its longest straightaway exactly ¾ths of a mile. (If car-sickness afflicts you, sit in the front seat, stop at *miradors* to break the trip and take extra fresh air.) The profusion of wild and cultivated flora is breathtaking. Bananas, sugarcane, grains, blossoms, and tropical fruits blanket the rich earth near the coast. Thick forests mat and tint the higher reaches of the slopes. *Language?* Officially Portuguese, of course—but enough English is spoken in hotels, restaurants, and shops to ease your fears. *Connections?* All by air, because passenger ships beyond those to neighboring Porto Santo are no longer operated. The heaviest traffic is from and to England (see following "Tip") and Lisbon; Air Portugal also maintains a lesser route between Las Palmas (Canaries) and Funchal. The touchdown at the Santa Catarina Airport, 15 miles from the capital, often seems to newcomers a white-knuckle experience which is provoked by the unavoidable shortness of the single airstrip; while pilots must pancake their birds as if they were coming down on a carrier, all of them, specially qualified to land here, are such experts that in reality nobody should worry. *Food?* Pretty limited. Scabbard fish, often misnamed "black swordfish," is the most renowned and most exotic specialty. This extraordinarily long and narrow critter is brought up from 3000-feet on drag lines. It is beautifully delicate and savory. The *caldeirada* is a piscatorial stew with dark minestrone undertones. *Espetata* is a local variation of a shishkebab with a maniacal affinity for salt and olive oil. *Lepas* are limpets which are grilled with butter and served in their mossy shells. Excellent! Especially delicious silver bananas are indigenous here. *Bolo de Mel* is the mouth-melting regional honey cake which will keep for a year. Cod, a dietary mainstay throughout this nation, now comes principally from Norway. Vegetables are magnificent in the market, but somehow they seldom seem to find their way to public tables. Why? We can't tell you. *Social note?* One of the holdovers from British Colonial days is that upper-bracket Madeira is quite dressy. In *all* of the leading hotels, gentlemen *always* wear a tie and coat after nightfall; normally you will find almost as many dinner jackets as business suits at Reid's. For ladies in these establishments, cocktail dresses are a virtual must. Go to Madeira for relaxation, natural beauty and calm. Go elsewhere for "action."

★ **TIP**   As mentioned earlier, one of the most felicitous suggestions we can make to today's independent overseas travelers is to break the trip in London and

to take a one-week charter tour to Madeira. Under normal circumstances, this adventure is worth far more than its very reasonable price. Thomas Cook (587 Fifth Ave., N.Y., NY 10017) or Kunoni (11 E. 44 St., N.Y., NY 10017) would make your arrangements.

Cities? **Funchal** is the heart and capital. To us, here is one of the world's most beautiful metropolises. Magnificent bay; home base for ⅓rd of the populace; houses stair-stepping up, up, up, up the mountainside. Its dwellings accent the Portuguese addiction for vivid shadings and hues. The sidewalks are surfaced with intricately patterned small cobblestones—charming to the eye, but hell on ladies' high heels. The world-famous fireworks display every New Year's Eve illuminates the great crescent of the bay in stunning and awesome cascades of flame. For many weeks beforehand nearly every householder plots his own pyrotechnic wizardry for this thunderous 15-minute climax of his year. Prizes are awarded by the Municipality for the best presentations in various categories. Many cruise ships target their arrival for this time—and so should you, if at all possible.

Hotels This is the only area abroad we know where the regional Tourist Board exercises such rigidly stringent control of its accommodations for vacationers. Its administrators are scared to pieces of following Greece, Spain, and so many other nations in their grossly deplorable overbuilding. The location, architectural plans, and erection of every new hotel must be approved by them every step of the way. By limiting their number and monitoring their operation, the standards within their categories remain unusually high. In nearly every case except Reid's they have allotted between 90% and 95% of the rooms to tour groups and between 5% and 10% to independent trippers. Although this seems an anomaly, the great disbalance in mass traffic has not spoiled the capital or the outlands to any notable degree. Almost all of the hostelries require demi-pension, with full pension as a moneysaving alternate. Hence, we repeat our above fervent advice to GO!

The king of kings remains century-old **Reid's**, one of the last of the fabled Great Hotels of character, tradition, and élan. Its General Manager is the prestigious Georges Hangartner, who has wrought the same wonders here as he did in reshaping Zürich's super-lux Dolder Grand. Commanding position crowning a promontory; ornate dining room; exquisite glass-walled Garden Restaurant gazing at 1 of its 2 pools and the sea; absolutely *superb* cuisine; glass-lined dance floor with wonderfully romantic view; tennis court; elevator to private beach. While the Old Wing in this fully air-conditioned edifice has been totally redecorated, the New Wing seems to hold the edge; avoid streetside units, which can be noisy despite the soundproof windows. With the added ministrations of the "Hangartner Touch," this flower-girt Eden has reached even greater heights as a resort-style pastoral paradise for the voyager. Marvelous!

The massive **Sheraton** belies its almost offensive façade with a warm and ingratiating interior. The Churrasco Grill, in terracotta tones, has the mien of an ancient tavern. A larger restaurant in 17th-century décor is well designed but seemingly swollen with group traffic. A new tearoom seating 80 has been launched. Lobby on 6th floor; bathing plus 2 pools (one heated); sauna; massage facilities; free movies; amusing little indoor-outdoor pub facing the port;

active night life in the Farol, a glass-lined drum-shaped rookery above the water. Three categories of bedrooms, all with balconies; gothic doors with wrought-iron hinges set into lava-stone arches; rich furnishings; baths with stall showers and tubs; superb illumination. Though bulk traffic seems to predominate, the basic facilities of this modernistic house give it appeal.

The spectacular **Casino Park** is a creation of the renowned architect Oscar Niemeyer, the genius behind every brick and pebble of Brasilia. Vast glass-fronted linear building on stilts with literally acres of lobby and lounge fast-nesses; restaurant so expansive it seems a part of the sea—and as cold; spacious greensward by the heated pool; 2 tennis courts; solarium and gym; 400 clean-lined, comfortable, and sterile units. Impressive it is; warm it is not. Our dinner for 4 in its most costly, supposedly elegant but odiferous Grill was the greatest culinary calamity we had suffered in many months; our cuisine could have been compared to swill and our service was wretched almost beyond belief. Here is a personification of the mammoth, immaculate, soulless Sleeping Factory. The adjoining new gambling casino is an architectural wow.

The **Savoy** is a huge rambling establishment turned out in a mélange of decorative styles that range between Adam effects and neoclassical Grand Rapids. There is a certain regal warmth which seems to please the British migrations. Glass-bound 7th-floor restaurant—only slightly smaller than the state of Montana—eye-boggling in its *nouveau richesse;* lavish rooftop Fleur-de-Lis Grill with terrace; better skilletry than in many competitors; airy abodes; 2 heated pools; pontoon to island for Atlantic bathing and water-skiing; 2 tennis courts; more. If flamboyant is your bag, this one has it.

Madeira Palácio, formerly the Madeira Hilton, has been taken over by the group that owns and operates the Estoril Palacio on the mainland. This 9-level, twin-winged giant is shielded in front by a restaurant and a heated pool. The décor and furnishings throughout are attractively executed in a tastefully modern mood. Within its deluxe precincts you will find a whopping list of amenities for its guests of all ages, from the hand-holding atmosphere of its Viceroy Grill, to its 3 bars, to its horseshoe-shaped pool, to its cheerful, air-conditioned accommodations, to its tennis courts, to more than a dozen other places. Although it is sited on a headland perhaps 1 mile from the center (free shuttle buses are provided), we prefer this fetching house to the Sheraton, Casino Park, and Savoy.

Quinta do Sol, a block up the hillside from Reid's, is the flagship of the 4-hostelry Ramos chain. This First-class entry comes up with an attractive ground-level restaurant, an intimate bar, a panoramic rooftop "Garden" solar-ium with snackery and café for light fare, a pool and 107 domiciles which include 2 suites on every floor. Good for its tariffs.

Second in this quartet is the altitudinous **Villa Ramos**. Pleasantly subdued lobby; tasteful corridors with brown "leather" walls; amiable split-level dining room; heated pool with terrace and bar; full air conditioning. Among its 107 lodgings, the front ones are excellent except for their tiny baths and the rear ones are somewhat cramped. It has been officially demoted down one step from the Deluxe category. We wonder why.

Third is the unorthodox **Hotel Apartamentos do Mar**, which is down a steep road overlooking the ocean but not beachside. Little L-shaped lobby adjoining

heated saltwater pool, solarium and bar; chipper all-glass-fronted restaurant; 141 super-compact apartments with seaview, sitting room, balcony, kitchenette, Frigobar, and elfin bath; mini-supermarket for your own casual meals. We think that it holds much greater appeal to Europeans than to North Americans.

Finally, the **Raga** is markedly inferior to the rest of this groupment, in our opinions. Mishmash lobby with cheap overtones; rock music pervasive and inescapable in its public rooms; Henry VIII restaurant overjammed with tables; cozy Pub the only thing we truly liked. Perhaps you'll disagree.

The well-scrubbed **Cirassol**, with a disastrously close-quartered dining room, heated pool, 12th-floor terrace, 136 squeezed billets, and inadequate elevators, seems barely passable—if that. The neighboring **Gorgulho**, in a curiously architected building with a façade of tiles intersticed with burly chunks of wood, seems to hold considerably more allure for young folk than for their seniors. Our evaluation is lukewarm or colder. At the entrance of the **Santa Isabel** we counted 22 stickers of tour organizations. Its facilities reflected the same hodgepodge to our eyes. The **Miramar** is adequate but in no way outstanding. **Monte Carlo** is British Old School, with very high ceilings, drab furnishings, a small pool, and a 6-room annex. Although its vista is magnificent, we opine that it is only for the elderly and sedate who are devotees of this fusty ambiance. All of the hotels within the capital are noisy and second- or third-rate. **Nova Avenida**, with its grand sweep of the cityscape and the ocean, used to exude Victorian charm. Now we feel that it has faded beyond the pale. **Monte Rosa**, **Golden Gate**, and **Santa Maria**, all in cacophonious locations, are too bare-boned for praise; the first is frequently the choice of overly hard-driven budgeteers.

The 18-story, richly accoutered **Atlantis**, 1 hour from Funchal beyond the airport at *Discovery Bay,* impresses us as being a gorgeous but fiscally hopeless White Elephant. It was built as a Holiday Inn—almost as amazing a contrast to this chain's normal establishments as a smaller Fountainebleau of Miami Beach. Fully air conditioned; suave, spacious, elegant lobby separated by glass from stunning indoor heated pool and to one side from b-i-g Z-shaped outdoor pool, Copacabana Bar, buffet lunch apex and saunas; attractive Madeira Grill; gaily colored Restaurant Algarve; Bar Madeira and more formal Bar Estoril; disco; tennis; nautical sports; much more. Its 300 comfortable, cheerful accommodations come with 2 king-size double beds, bath, balcony, and majestic views of the sea and surrounding mountains. Next to Reid's, unquestionably we rate this as the best luxury hostelry on the island—but we strongly suspect that the selection of the site so isolated from outside action kills it for many visitors and brings grave traffic problems to its operators. The First-class **Dom Pedro** is directly below the Atlantis at the edge of the village of **Machico**. While this house is pleasant enough, it suffers the same difficulty of location. Not worth the distance to most North Americans, in our opinions.

Restaurants   Agreement is virtually universal that the Grill Room and the Garden Restaurant of **Reid's** remain the most elegant dining establishments within 500 miles. Their level of cuisine and service can't be touched elsewhere on the island. The Viceroy Grill of the **Madeira Palácio** plays upon charming intimacy. Its motif reflects contemporary stylings, with flowers on

tables, nibbles of crisp salad, and embroidered overcloths. The attention is also superb. As for other hotel dining rooms, please refer back to the previous section for those descriptions.

The *independent restaurants* in the center of the capital range from fairly good to poor, probably because so many of the hotels require full pension. **Caravela** offers a bonus with its up-1-flight, glassed-in "terrace" and fine span of the harbor. Menu in 5 languages; Aveleda *vino verde* excellent; service brisk and attentive; solid but not outstanding. Our solo lunch, including the wine, was $10.70. **Estrela do Mar** resides smack in the nexus of the traffic ebb and flow. Dark hole-in-the-wall lined with seaborne flotsam; candles by day and night; menu on a dried fish hide; seating at community tables; passable for nutrients. The nextdoor **Romana** is also pleasant. Its dishes are more international than local. **Boa Vista** is run-of-the-grinder. **Kon Tiki**, with a nice aura but routine vittles, just about makes it to us.

Taverna Real is a 15th-century wine cellar that was once owned by Henry the Navigator and frequented by Columbus. You can nod along through a lively evening here listening to *fado* singing, guitar, and mandolin music—at a cost so low it will surprise you. Our sirloin steak with onions was good as was our partner's sausage served in a flaming ceramic cradle. A very enjoyable and inexpensive evening.

The **British Country Club**, where the cooking was nothing short of grotesque on our recent try, is interesting because of its colonial setting, its fine large palm-fringed swimming pool, its chipping greens for casual golfers, and its breathtaking gardens with all of the flora labeled—many species from tropical Asia. Go for sport, for drinks, or for strolling in the park, but please not to swallow anything solid.

The best independent dining places are outside the city. Our favorite is **O Boieiro**, a 20-minute ride up, up, up the mountainside at **Caniço**.Its name means "Driver of the Sleigh"—the world-famous carriage-body vehicle on skids described in "Sightseeing." No view; 7 sleds with tables, cushioned basketweave seats, canopies, curtains and individual lights very comfortable for 4; 15 additional tables down a step at floor level; menus presented inside shallow straw hats; unusually warm and interested staff; pleasant complimentary cocktail of mango, rum, and milk; reservations normally necessary. In our 3-course lunch, the fresh tuna salad opener, the delicately baked Scabbard fish with light breading, and the spiced house butter were outstandingly delicious. With wine we spent about $8 per appetite, including service. It is open the year around 7 days per week except for the month of June or July. So delightfully rewarding that it was very much worth the trip. **Espadarte** ("Sword"), on a high road in the outskirts, is gloomy at noon but attractive at dinner. Urbane rustic ambiance; semi-open kitchen; handsome gray-and-white mural along entire rear wall; about 15 tables for 4 with wicker mats, candles, and flowers; *fado* and folk dancing twice weekly and lone singer other nights; closed Wednesday noons; book in advance. A good bet, with better than average fare and smiling minions. For regional fare without luxury, **A Seta** (Estrada do Livramento, 15 minutes out toward Monte) is a fun-filled little sweetie. Canary cages by entrance; about 2 dozen sparkling-clean wooden tables place mats; open-air rooftop perch with umbrellas and meal service. Our house-style

shashlik *(espedata)* was placed on a contraption unique to the island which actually *hung* straight down over us; we were instructed to serve ourselves. Although it's not fancy, we fancy it very much indeed. **Club de Turismo da Madeira** (Estrada Monumental 179, about 10 minutes out) is more sophisticated. Cliff-hanging site, with sheer drop to the sea; gorgeous vista; partially open-air dining terrace by the pool, plus 10-table indoor dining room; lounges upstairs. The cookery is a far cry from Reid's, but quite good for the region; it's not expensive either. Amiable for quiet lunching on a sunny day. No club membership is necessary. **Jardem do Sol**, about a 20-minute haul, is large, rambling and often loaded to its eaves with busloads of tourists who come for its *fado* and folk dancing. A commercial mass operation.

Sightseeing If you'll forgive Madeira for its total lack of decent beaches (but not of water sports, which are listed below), a rapturous parade of other attractions is at your command. Most visitors give highest priority to trying the aforementioned sleigh ride over the cobblestones of *Funchal*. Take a taxi for the l-o-n-g climb to Terreiro da Luta. After drinking in the glorious panorama of the capital at your feet, climb aboard the wood-runnered sledge and bump down, down, down—2 miles of "tobogganing"—through the narrow and pictorial streets. There is absolutely no danger, because 2 or 3 men race alongside, guiding the clumsy vehicle in the proper direction (or pushing it whenever the going gets too slow). The price is about $5 per person. While it would never offer a thrill to a Cresta Run driver from St. Moritz—or even more than a mild tingle to an elderly spinster—it's fun, and it shouldn't be missed. If this isn't sufficient in the Curious Transportation Department, you may also hire bullock carts in the Avenida de Mar, near the pier, or mobile hammocks in such villages as Camacha, Santo da Serra, and Curral das Freiras. For motorboating along the coast, the Tourist Bureau's *Altair* and the craft belonging to the Golfinhos do Mar are available for charter. Within the hub there are 4 more traditional lures: (1) The tiny Aquarium (in the Municipal Museum at Rua da Mouraria), (2) the Municipal Museum itself (regional and natural history), (3) Cruzes (antique art, with a fine orchid house adjoining), and (4) Arte Sacra (religious art). Whether you play or not, you'll certainly want to see the new Casino, a wonder of modern architecture soaring stunningly beside the Casino Park Hotel. Open every day in the year except Christmas from 8:30 P.M. to 3 A.M. or 4 A.M.; French and U.S. roulette, blackjack, craps, chemin de fer, French Bank, baccarat, and 120 slots (20¢ and 50¢); penthouse Panorama Restaurant with show; Boite-Nightclub Zodiaco with late cabaret for night owls. *Don't forget your passport!* Then there's the Public Market, which is a ball if you see it sufficiently early in the day. Now —and please note this carefully—for any fortunate soul who is not subject to car sickness from the plethora of curves everywhere, it would be just as heinous a crime to limit his or her wanderings to Funchal as it would be for any visitor to Switzerland to see Geneva only. Our fervent recommendation would be to hie to Avis, the leading car-rental agency in the capital, and ask for Manager Miguel Diniz, who is located in front of the Sheraton (Largo António Nobre 164, Tel. 25495). Should he be out at the moment, one of his kindly English-speaking colleagues would take good care of you. Be certain to request a *small* model; we had perfect luck as an illustration, with a Morris Mini with road-

gripping front-wheel drive. Then simply head in any direction with a picnic lunch. So most of the roads on this 35-X-14-mile island are narrow and rough? Begone, dull care! Personally, one of our most delightful excursions was to **Porto Moniz** on the extreme northwest corner of the island—a *gorgeous* ½-day drive to a small, sleepy fishing village with the most spectacular natural pool that we have ever seen. Here you can lunch among the fjords and cliffs at the **Cachalote**, a breathtaking extraterrestrial setting where whales frolic in the deep sea. Take bathing attire and swim in the other-worldly chalices of rock —an experience of a lifetime! Hall porters often recommend a meal stop at the **Aquário** in *Seixal*, but we found it a dull and overpriced roadside rest. Another awesome target is *Curral das Freiras*, a tiny, primitive, fascinating hamlet cradled in a valley of towering peaks, where the vivid impression persisted that we were 3 days' journey from Lima, Peru, in the heart of the Andes; it was almost impossible to believe that this sanctuary from another century is less than 45 MINUTES from the bright lights of the Big City. Never will we forget our basket lunch in these incredible surroundings! **Caniçal** is promoted as a whaling port. 'T'ain't so, and it ain't the least bit interesting either. If you take a round-the-island drive, a pleasant stop for a coffee is the **Cabana** at *S. Jorge*, way up in the hills of the north coast. (The thatch-roofed huts also serve as individual hotel cottages.) Then a dash back to Funchal takes about an hour.

Shopping   The very best shop in all of Madeira is **Casa do Turista** (Av. do Mar), where you will find a cross section of Portuguese handicrafts which is unequalled even on the mainland—ceramics, porcelain, pewter, brass, copper, embroidery, wickerware, and lots, lots more. There are a wine-tasting room, reproductions of a country shop ("venda") and an old-fashioned rural living room, plus a thatched shed in the basket-weavers' tradition. Safe shipment to any part of the world is guaranteed. Founder-Director Ramos is an aristocratic gentleman with exquisite taste and immense personal charm; ask for him or for Mrs. Maria-Luisa or Mrs. Gregoria. Here is an absolute *must* which NO traveler should miss!

The embroidery and organdy studios and "factory" of **Madeira Superbia** (Rua do Carmo 27-1, up 1-flight) make a serene, venerable complex of large, plainly decorated rooms in which are displayed for sale the hosts of beautiful products made by this ranking establishment. For further information, please turn back to the Madeira Superbia write-up in the "Lisbon" section.

Charming Sra. Farra at **G. Farra & Co. Ltda.** (Rua da Ponte S. Lazaro 8, with branches in most of the top hotels) has also a fine selection—different from the Superbia creations.

A call at the famous **Madeira Wine Association Ltda.** is again rewarding for wine lovers.

Department store? The Victorian **Maison Blanche** is smalltownish in tone, quality, and styling. Its personnel couldn't be sweeter.

At the town of **Camacha** (about a half-hour drive from Funchal), virtually all of its 3600 inhabitants seem to busy weaving wickerware for the store-factory in the main square. Surely somewhere in these sprawling premises you should find what you were looking for in this fantastic assemblage.

Shopping hours? Same as Lisbon.

Go to Madeira if you can. Here is a still-unspoiled paradise (except on "boat days"), made by the Creator for lazing, sunning, strolling, browsing, and more lazing. To repeat, expect no fireworks of any description—except on New Year's Eve. Simply pause in its crystal air, amid its banks of flowers, so that your soul may soak up the tranquil contentment that will recharge your world-weary batteries. How we adore this Magic Isle!

MONTE GORDO   See "Algarve."

NAZARÉ (pronounced Nah-zar-ay), about 3 hours from Lisbon, is a colorful little fishing village and Portuguese summer resort of whitewashed houses, tourist-conscious fisherfolk, and narrow streets which all run down to the sea. Unfortunately, it is fast being ruined by the tidal flood of foreign rubberneckers. Legend ties the famous local tartan costumes to a crew of Scotsmen shipwrecked here centuries ago; you may buy this unique hand-woven cloth along the beach. Wonderful swimming; fishing from sardine to fighting *carapau;* boats at reasonable rates. There's a funicular (when it works!) to the Sitio, or Upper Town, where you'll find a lighthouse, a church, and a glorious view. Lodgings? The **Hotel Nazaré** is the best of a routine lot, followed by **Da Praia**, the very plain **Dom Fuas**, and 9 pensions. Go in spring or fall if you can, because it's so jammed during the hot months that lots of the fun is lost. Highly recommended—*if* you mind your calendar.

ÓBIDOS This totally walled city is an easy excursion hop up from Lisbon or a worthwhile overnighting point if you can secure accommodation in the **Pousada do Castelo** (Tel. 95105). The hostelry contains a mere 6 rooms, half of them with private bath, but it is so overwhelming in its beauty that we urge you to spend some time here if you can. This installation is built into the fortress tower—at the same time both intimate and grand. A visitor has the feeling that he is part of the court of a noble household. In the lower village, also within the crenellated walls, is the **Estalagem do Convento** for an emergency pit stop—and other poor entries. A mildly athletic tourist can circumnavigate the entire village walking on the wide tops of the walls. In the hamlet itself there are numerous bars, a restaurant and tearoom on the main street, several churches, and, of course, the inevitable sourvenir shops vending just what you always wanted from the Republic of Korea. As a possible alternative to the above stopping places, you might find space in the **Mansão da Torre-Motel**, 2 miles out of town towards Santarem. Try not to miss this fascinating jewel.

OPORTO, through a curious twist, has long been the accepted name applied by *foreigners* to this nation's second city—possibly a relic of its heavy early British influence. The Portuguese, on the other hand, always call it **Porto**. This massively industrial gateway to the ocean, larger than El Paso and Jersey City, bustles with determined activity. It is built from top to bottom on a dome-shaped hill; exits of its famous 2-tier bridge hit the riverbank both high and low. Business is its consuming dedication. Architecturally, culturally, hedonistically, in charm and in joie de vivre it lags strikingly behind softer and

infinitely more interesting Lisbon—so much so, in fact, that we have always found its frenetic commercial aura unattractive from the vacationer's point of view. Its hotels are almost universally undistinguished, most of its restaurants are rough-and-ready, and the quality and quantity of its sightseeing lures suffer markedly in comparison. However, its residents are delightfully warm and hospitable.

Were we driving north on holiday and stopping in this area, we would not lodge in this metropolis. Instead we would proceed a half-hour further to the **Vermar dom Pedro** in the beach resort of *Povoa de Varzim*—a First-class, modern, 13-story, air-conditioned hostelry bordering a splendid strand which offers blessèd tranquillity and bracing, unpolluted sea air away from the hurly-burly. This would be our base for exploring the municipality. Although it is no great shakes, here is one of the leading houses on the long *Costa Verde* ("Green Coast") strip which starts 6 miles below Oporto and runs all the way up to the Spanish border. As a sidenote, while this ribbon is highly popular among Portuguese escapists, the Algarve and Madeira are so much more beguiling that, in our opinions, overseas visitors should skip the clusters of the first and find their sun and their beauty in the other two.

For overnighting in town, far-and-away our first choice is the new, contemporary **Porto Atlântico** in the Boa Vista residential district. Full air conditioning; 3 floors; décor vaguely Scandinavian; adjoining Galeria restaurant; popular avant-garde bar; 2 pools (1 covered); 2nd- and 3rd-level rooms with their own balconies. In this mercantile hub it normally has 80% occupancy from Monday to Friday and 40% on weekends. Despite its distance from the center, we like its freshness, friendliness, and sparkle. Next comes the antique **Infante de Sagres**, a fixture that has seemed to resist any major changes since '51. Now we are told that the owner has launched a $1.4-million, top-to-bottom renovation program to modernize this sad, old-hat structure. We'll believe it when we see it. **Sheraton** plans to inaugurate a third officially deluxe plant here by '83. In the First-class Superior groupment, the 16-story, air-conditioned **Dom Henrique**, planted on stilts, towers over its centroid precincts. Lobby practically nonexistent; 102 progressive but not very comfortable bedchambers to 13th floor; Breakfast Room on 14th; viewful O Navegador Grill-Restaurant on 15th; Bar 16 and oh-so-weird disco (wow!) on 16th. Mechanical. **Castor**? Darned if we know what to say about this one, because it's different from any shelter we've ever visited. It is a riot of colors, with most of its furnishings 18th-century reproductions. Air conditioned; large salon adjoining lobby in old style; bar and dining room which to us don't come off; basement spaceship disco with elaborate dummy controls and airline seats. We think you'd either love it or loathe it. **Albergaria Miradouro**, on the 10th to 12th floors of a yellow-tiled office building, is an adjunct to the Restaurante Portucale, one of the nation's most distinguished dining places (surprise, surprise for Oporto!). It calls itself a "Private Hotel," reportedly because the owner packs it with friends and associates. Small, happy, and hue-filled nests; baths Lilliputian. A pleasant novelty. **Grande Hotel da Batalha**, **Grande Hotel do Porto**, and **Do Império** are all routine and listless.

Food? Nothing north of Lisbon touches the aforementioned **Restaurante Portucale** in its 13th-floor penthouse. Three walls of v-a-s-t windows to down-

nose the city and river; décor striking but charmingly intime in deluxe suavity, from sculptured walnut ceiling with buried spotlights to center service area to sage carpeting; silken attention; management by gentle, kind Ernesto Azevedo; open every day in the year. Our full lunch for 2, including wines, was about $60. So sophisticated that it qualifies among the top rank anywhere in Europe. Next, we would choose the Galeria in the **Hotel Porto Atlântico**. The chairs here are fitted with boxing-glove leather. Well-above-average cookery. Nearby, in the same Boa Vista area, you will find the **Steak House**, which specializes in you-know-whats. It is pretty good. Finally, **O Esconbidinho** is a solidly established, no-nonsense local institution. Gay little façade between double doors; L-shaped dining room with blue-and-white tiles around walls to waist level; perhaps 20 tables with high, comfortable chairs; service outstandingly fast, attentive, and courteous. Slip by a muddle-headed author: When he ordered a treat of an unfamiliar smoked fish (sturgeon-like?) listed as "Presunto Fumado," up came an excellent prosciutto! Deservedly approved, especially by businessmen at lunchtime.

PENINA, PORTIMÃO, PRAIA DE LUZ, PRAIA DE ROCHA, and **SAGRES** See "Algarve."

SESIMBRA is located only 45 minutes from Lisbon via the gloriously panoramic bridge. The **Hotel Do Mar** nestles 75 yards above the sea and this still-unspoiled fishing village. Vaguely Hawaiian-style construction, with buildings staggered up a hillside for successively better vistas of the bay; entrance at top, with access to 4 tiers of rooms and terraces; glassy crown composed of a 2-section restaurant with a sweeping view. Bar at lobby level; patio adjoining; sun roof; small nightclub. Sea-level dining pavilion (season only), backed by 3 crescents of rooms; lovely circular swimming pool here. Highly recommended (1) to sunbathers who want serenity in comfort, and (2) for a lunch excursion from Lisbon (be *sure* to reserve your table in advance). Ask your driver to go about ¼-mile past the hotel on the shore road for a peek at the beach and the fleet of typically colorful and interesting fishing boats.) Full, full, full from June 1 to late September.

SETÚBAL fifth in size, is a sardine-factory center which is a half-hour ride from the capital on the new express highway. The Church of Jesus, in which the pillars are twisted to resemble fishermen's ropes, is so curious it shouldn't be missed. Above the town is the **Pousada de São Filipe** (Tel. 23844). It is built into a glorious, 16th-century mountaintop fort with a magnificent view of the sea and surrounding hills. Only 15 small but pleasant rooms, 8 with Atlantic vistas; fine little tile-lined restaurant overlooking the port; bar under vaulted ceiling; covered terrace for tea and evening libations. Inspirational for observing, but simple in creature comforts. Down in the city, the **Esperança** is about the only other choice—and we disrecommend that one. Somewhat better would be the **Tróia** in the burgeoning Torralta project, which contains several hotels on the adjoining peninsula; this can be reached in 5 minutes by Hovercraft, 20 minutes by normal ferry or in several hours of driving by the roadways. By far the leading alternate in this immediate area is the **Pousada**

Palmela in *Palmela*, about a 10-minute run from the municipality. It is in a 1000-year-old castle with its own fabulous panorama which incorporates Lisbon. The furnishings in its 27 abodes, all with private plumbing, are plain but modern and effective. A nice stop, particularly in September when the muscatel wine festival is held in the public square.

SINTRA This one you must see; it's about an hour from the capital. Drive out through Estoril and lead through the spectacularly beautiful mountain road through a national forest preserve. (For the longer seaside route, go out to Guincho). When you near your goal, climb up and up through gardens and flowering camellia trees to the mammoth castle (closed on Tuesdays), straight from an illustrated fairy tale, perched on a peak. This was the summer home of the last kings of Portugal, and its medieval splendor is stunning. The road leads down past the old Moorish castle atop a neighboring crest to the little town in the valley. Some of the finest *quintas* (country estates) of Portugal are here, and they are a dream. Sintra also can be reached by train from Rossio Station in the capital which runs to and fro about every 30 minutes.

The **Hotel Palácio de Seteais** has a wonderful setting, gorgeous gardens, lavish furnishings, and superb çuisine. Here without question is our Number One lunch choice for excursions from Lisbon to the Estoril-Cascais-Guincho-Sintra circuit. This former summer residence of a king was converted into a classically luxurious country inn with elegant public chambers and 18 dwellings. Gentle Director Alberto de Carvalho, a quarter-century veteran, and *Chefe de Mesa* Estefanio Pereira take such warm personal care of their clients that advance reservations are almost always obligatory. Recommended with cheers and salutes.

The 7-floor, 77-unit, air-conditioned **Tivoli Sintra**—a new protégé of the excellent Hotel Tivoli in the capital—will be inaugurated this spring to the rear of the Castle. Reports indicate that this First-class house will come in strong.

On the road to Sintra, the historic **Queluz** (pronounced "Kayloosh") **Palace** is a peanut-size replica of Versailles. In its ancient, enormous scullery, the owners have built a full-scale restaurant called the "Cozinha Velha" ("Old Kitchen")—and that's exactly what it is. You'll see the original spits used for hundreds of years to roast whole oxen—plus enough utensils and gizmos in fine old copper to arouse larceny in the soul. Interesting and unusual; *Cozinha*-work adequate rather than exceptional.

TOMAR This area is likely to draw motorists because of its lovely situation overlooking a dam and because of the euphemistic **Castelo do Bode**. Unfortunately we find the **Pousada de São Pedro** to be a disgrace to the government-run system. On our recent overnight we found smelly accommodations, broken faucets that gushed forth brown water—none of it too hot—and rickety furnishings. It is shameful, in our opinions, that such a potential attraction is in the hands of such administrators. Happily, there is a solution. Go back to the charming town itself and find accommodation at either the bucolic **Estalagen de Santa Iria**, which is located in a romantic willow grove beside a stream, or at the well-run **Dos Templários** which resides in its own park and gardens.

While here you must visit the overwhelming Church of Christ, the ornate, Emmanuelene headquarters of the Knights Templar for approximately 9 centuries and one of the most powerful seats of riches, intellect, and politics in Christendom. Seldom have we been so stunned by architecture as we have at this shrine. The town also offers a famous synagogue and additional attractions that make it one of the chief drawing cards in Portugal.

VALE DO LOBO See "Algarve."

VALENÇA DO MONDO, 9 miles from the ocean along the northern frontier, is an ancient walled town with narrow, crazily winding streets jam-packed with perhaps 150 small, variegated shops for the mass Spanish trade which floods across the border to buy Portuguese merchandise at substantially lower prices than those in their homeland. The crush of cars, buses, and pedestrians in the center is eye-popping. In majestic tranquillity above the madding crowd sits the lovely **Pousada de São Teotónio** on the crown of a hill, with a beautiful vista over the Minho River, its long bridge ever choked with vehicles and walkers during the daylight hours and a sweep of the foreign countryside. Warm lobby leading to 2 small lounges, 1 with fireplace and TV and the other with a cozy bar and a 2nd chimney; 2 gracious panoramic dining rooms with tempting arrays handsomely displayed, professionally deft service and good food. (Try the unique local cheese.) Upstairs are 16 diminutive, modern, comfortably decorated accommodations; #11 is the choicest. In July and August and during the Easter and Christmas holidays, reservations must normally be booked 2 months ahead. This unusually well-run haven is truly a delight. **Pensão Rio Minho** and **Pensão Valenciana**, the only other lodgings here, are quite basic; each has 2 private baths. If you are interested in driving 4 miles to the **Albergaria Atlântico** in Monção for one of the best regional lunches in this part of the country, please refer to the Viana do Castelo section which directly follows.

VIANA DO CASTELO, 13 miles from the nation's northern frontier, is often called the Resort Capital of the Costa Verde. (For further information on this seaside ribbon, please turn to the 2nd paragraph of the Oporto section.) This attractive port, facing an estuary, booms in season and lazes during the cold months. Although it contains a Municipal Museum in the Palace of the Barbosa Macieis which is especially noted for its collection of national pottery, the 16th-century Palace of the Távoras, the Castle of S. Tiago, a number of churches, and other cultural features, its typical visitor comes for sun and relaxation. The **Hotel de Santa Luzia**, 3 miles up a winding road from the center, caps a mountain. The sweep of its views in all directions is magnificent. Old-fashioned structure; pool; tennis court; conference facilities for 200; fuddy-duddy "modernized" bedchambers; cuisine no better than routine. During our off-season stay, when this house was almost deserted, our so-called service was so aggravatingly bad that it finally became ludicrous; we hope that it is better when the action is there. Despite these inadequacies, the quiet and the glory of its panorama makes this our first pick. **Do Parque** is sited over the

estuary on the edge of the settlement. The architecture and the accouterments are typical of the '71 style at the time of its opening. Low-ceilinged lobby with brown overstuffed chairs; window-wrapped penthouse dining room; 2 nice pools; 16 suites; 70 decent domiciles with terrace; very clean and well maintained. A good bet. **Alfonso III**, located in the same area and also launched in '71, is a palette of gayer colors. Air conditioned; vivid lounge in burnt orange and green with clever seating areas in alcoves; 7th-floor restaurant with heavy Portuguese mien which smelled to us as if lunch lingered; outdoor pool with bar facing the River Lima (a 300-yard walk); ample-size dwellings with simple décor but an attempt at brightness. The upkeep is much better in Do Parque but the aura is livelier in this entry. We rate these 2 about even. **Rali** and **Aliança** are respectively 2nd-class and 3rd-class—and they look it. In addition there are 11 pensions, the best of which are the **Laranjeira** and the **Residencîa Terra Linda**.

Food? With 2 exceptions all of the local independent establishments we tried were mediocre. **Os 3 Potes** ("3 Pots") is one of the brightest and most charming regional-type dining places we've found in the nation. While its atmosphere was nakedly contrived with all of the stops pulled out, it is smoothly executed. Housed in a former public bakery of unknown age; rectangular square in heavy stone with tables surrounding center block; intermittent folk dancing; lanterns from raftered ceiling; prix-fixe 4-course menu at about $10; inexpensive wine; cookery not notable but better than average in its category; closed Mondays. The 2 English and 2 Portuguese owners who have created this cozy, fetching oasis are pros; sweet Mrs. Barbara Andrews will welcome you. In neighboring *Darque*, the **Quinta do Santoinho** also schedules folk dancing. To us it is not at all up to Os 3 Potes in its lure or performance. Special delight: If you have a car and sufficient time for a short lunch excursion, we urge that you drive 20 miles further north along the frontier to the **Albergaria Atlântico** in *Monç ão*—one of the most famous gastronomic stars above Oporto. Its international clientele comes from far and near. Simple, pleasant, L-shaped, 4th-floor room with wide glass windows and vista of the river and village; tranquil and comfortable; super-fresh salmon in May and June; other delicious specialties; closed Christmas Eve only. Start with Dom Fernando chilled white port; move along to a numbered bottle of Alvarinho Palazo de Brejoeria which is reversed by many oenologists as the best *vino verde* in the world—and, golly, is it to us! (Only about 100,000 liters of the latter are produced annually in this limited local area.) Then, if you'd like a liqueur, wind up with Aguardinte Alvhine. Our huge and superb meal for 3, including wines and spirits, was about $39. Proprietor Manuel Moscoso and his lovely, English-speaking daughter Maria Helena will take regal care of you. Highest recommendation.

Shopping? The residents of Viana do Castelo boast that it is one of the country's leading headquarters for handicrafts. Our agreement is dubiously partial. When you stroll along the main promenade you will find a welter of family establishments which purvey good-looking, inexpensive fishermen's sweaters for both genders and a few other products which might be of interest. The disappointment is that most of their stocks are virtually identical—but it's worth the outing. Finally, please avoid a large, supermarket-type warehouse on the outskirts—the name of which we have gratefully forgotten—where the

merchandise is tons of pure shlock. This is a scheduled stop on numerous bus tours.

VILAMOURA　See "Algarve."

VILA REAL　See "Algarve."

Scotland

S cotland—despite the listless "devolution" movement which seeks a higher degree of autonomy at home—remains the second largest stockholder in the mighty business partnership of Great Britain Unlimited. It combines so many contrasts on a single patch of earth that sometimes its visitors get the feeling they're touring a Hollywood movie lot. Within an area roughly the size of West Virginia, fjords, glens, moors, mountains, prairies, heaths, bogs, woodlands, rills, alpine lakes, and even Gulf Stream-nourished palm trees on its island of Arran—just about everything in the geography book except Himalayan ice bridges and Amazonian rain forests.

This scenic kaleidoscope, only 275 miles long and 150 miles wide, breaks down naturally into 3 divisions and several clusters of islands. The *Southern Uplands,* a brain-shape wedge between the English border and the Edinburgh-Glasgow line, stretch in a number of moorlike ranges from south to north—the Lowthers (or Leadhills), Moorfoots, Cheviots, and others. Sheep-rearing and woolens keep these hardworking folk out of mischief; the fishing is extra-fine, because the Clyde, Tweed, and other rivers rise here. The *Central Lowlands,* that narrow band which belts the waist of the nation, contains ¾ths of Scotland's 5-million inhabitants and nearly all its heavy industries. Edinburgh, certain Clyde lochs and resorts, and the handful of its better attractions shouldn't be missed. Otherwise, this crowded ribbon, ravished by factories, is generally joyless for the tourist. The *Highlands,* on the other hand, are among the most glorious holiday areas in the world. These granite mountains and plains, split across the center by Loch Ness and Loch Lochy, sprawl over more than half the country's terrain. Grouse, deer, salmon, trout, ptarmigan, and hare abound in their purple moors, flashing streams, turquoise lakes, and cool forests. They're as different from the Central Lowlands as the lovely Pennsylvania Alleghenies are from the drab New Jersey industrial salt marshes. The once sleepy Shetland and Orkney island groups are growing richer by the instant as petroleum investments wash ashore from U.S. and other sources. A boom town character is replacing their former somnolence. The Hebrides,

Skye, Arran, Bute, and other tranquil isles—each different, each fascinating to the off-trail explorer—round out the picture.

Halifax visitors please note: "Scotland" springs from "Scotia," as in "Nova Scotia"—literally, "the land of a tribe of Scots." When the Romans tried to rename the nation "Caledonia," there was almost another Battle of Cannai. These proud, stubborn, tough-fibered northerners have always worshiped liberty; their history flames with impassioned patriots of the stamp of William Wallace, Robert Bruce, and John Knox. In 1603, when Scottish King James VI succeeded Good Queen Bess on the throne of England, a Union of the Crowns was effected, which later gave the smaller nation a voice in the London government—but even today, many wearers of the plaid consider this a disaster ranking somewhere between the Great Whisky Famine of 1854 and Armageddon.

The Church of Scotland and the United Free Church (Presbyterian) joined hands in 1929, and their rigidly moral doctrines penetrate nearly every parlor from Lerwick in the Shetlands to Gretna Green in the south. You won't find nightclubs, bordellos, B-girls, or tolerated licentiousness in any form. On Sundays and religious holidays, you might as well be in Great Coco, Adaman Islands, as in Edinburgh, Glasgow, or any city here, because all that stirs is the electric current and dripping faucets. It's a constant source of amazement to Americans that the Scots can be brought up under such a bluenose code, in such a hard climate and in such cheerless, austere buildings—and still be among the warmest, wittiest, and sweetest people ever to walk on 2 legs.

Shipbuilding (down seriously in recent times), oil-rig manufacture for offshore discoveries, textiles, brewing, pottery, marmalade, computers, bottled dew-of-the-heather—these are mere samples of this nation's powerful industrial complex. About 100-thousand men are employed in coal mines. Herring, prawns, cod, and whiting engage a flotilla of fishermen. Scottish beef comes from the famous Aberdeen Angus, Galloway, and Short Horn strains. (Sadly, as with premium grades of most commodities, the export market snatches so much that what remains for the local table often resembles filet of flintstone). Although Clydesdale draft horses and Shetlands, Highland, and Cheriot sheep are the traditional moneymakers, the country is gradually entering a bright new era of productivity and development. It's a working country, this one; from Ayr to Uyea, you'll find few loafers.

Finally, if you persist in referring to people, landscape, architecture, and local attractions as "Scotch," don't be surprised if your kilted companions lick their lips and rush away on "forgotten" appointments. It's "Scot," "Scotsman," "Scotswoman," or "Scottish," unless you're talking about (1) the whisky, or (2) a few oddball expressions such as "Scotch broth" that combine with a second word. Say "Scotch" only if you're thirsty!

☑ **SIGHTSEEING**   *Edinburgh* is the traditional base for the traveler's Scotland. Nearly every visitor starts or finishes his Scottish explorations here. If you wish to begin looking into your own family past, this is also the touchstone for genealogical discovery. **Register House** in Charlotte Square probably has a record of every Scottish skeleton in every closet of your illustrious heritage. Anyway, here's the spot to commence digging up your ancestry. Turn ahead to "Cities" for more details on this wonderful metropolis of calm and culture.

The lower end of *Loch Lomond* buzzes like a flytrap with excursion buses, trailers, campers, and a zillion tourists in season. *Balloch*, at the southern tip, is euphemistically called the "Henley of Scotland." During the milder months, twice-daily steamer sailings across the loch originate from here; it's a 2½-to 3-hour trip each way, and a lovely one. This region shouldn't be missed—but we strongly urge you to overnight elsewhere.

Provincial Scotland breaks down into 5 main areas: (1) the Trossachs, called the "Rob Roy" and "Lady-of-the-Lake Country" (which, like Lower Loch Lomond, is fast being spoiled by hordes of sightseers), (2) the "Burns Country," dominated by Ayr and Dumfries, (3) The Highlands, lord and master of Scottish grandeur, (4) the "Sir Walter Scott Country," from Edinburgh to the English border, and (5) the Isle of Skye and the Hebrides.

Since most American visitors to the Land of the Heather follow jet-propelled itineraries, we recommend this 2-day trip, with 1-day optional extension. We believe it encompasses the greatest cross section of landscape, history, beauty, and charm on the Scottish map. This 48-hour itinerary allows you to sample every type of terrain and view such major sights as Gleneagles, Loch Ness, Loch Lomond, Ben Nevis, and a score of others. Thousands of pilgrims undertake the bone-wearying haul by motor coach to *Inverness*, back to *Fort William* (3 hours), and then on to *Glasgow* (5 hours), a journey that would make misanthropes of Messrs. M. Polo and F. Magellan. So here's our compact tour that packs in ample scenery, great variety, and easy convenience:

Edinburgh is the beginning and end of your loop, and *Inverness*, capital of The Highlands, is your midway stop. One day before departure, if you've never tried a real Scottish Haggis (see "Food"), ask your porter to telephone the Station Hotel in Inverness and arrange that this traditional treat be waiting in place of the fish course of your dinner here; 24-hour notice is generally required. Then on the following morning, leave *Edinburgh* at 8:30 A.M., point the nose of your car toward *Stirling*, and get the lowlands along the Firth of Forth behind you as briskly as you can. At nearby *Doune*, there's an unthinkably ancient fortress-castle, if you're interested, plus a sports- and racing-car collection of the 1920's and '30's—but perhaps you'd rather push on to Gleneagles, Scotland's most fabulous hotel (closed Oct. to mid-Apr.) for a coffee break; this baronial country estate is something special. Then proceed to the Dewar's White Label town, *Perth*, for a friendly apéritif with Joe in the American Bar of the Station Hotel, followed by lunch in the dining room here (the food is the best in the area). Now cut northwest along the river valley

through *Pitlochry*, *Blair Atholl*, along glorious *Glengarry*, through *Dru-mochter Pass* and the *Forest of Atholl* down to *Dalwhinnie*, and onward. (Mid-Apr. to early-Oct., the Pitlochry Festival Theatre draws culture-hungry crowds to its competent performances. Six plays ranging, say, from Shakes-peare to Chekhov to Jean Anouilh to Noël Coward are presented Mon. through Sat.) By teatime, *Carrbridge* should loom up, and the simple, fishing-and-sporting Carrbridge Hotel should break out homemade dainties—high tea for about $5 per person. You might want to take in the **Landmark Visitors Center** which capsulizes Highland history and lore. It has its own restaurant plus shops. One hour after you're roadbound again, you'll be in *Inver-ness*, where the austere but adequate Station Hotel—and your Haggis, we hope!—is waiting.

The second day you take a different, even more spectacular, route. Start no later than 8 A.M. After leaving the "Ceud Mile Failté!" sign (Gaelic for "ioo,-ooo Welcomes!") behind at the city limits of Inverness, you loaf along the *Caledonian Canal* until it opens into *Loch Ness*—and as you parallel the 29 miles of this landmark, keep every eye in the car peeled for "Nessie," the fabled Loch Ness Monster! *Loch Lochy* is next—and then, 2 miles before *Spean Bridge*, you'll pass the famed **Commando Monument**, a stirring sight in a stirring location. Now it's time for coffee in the Milton Hotel in *Fort Wil-liam*. Refreshed, stretching your legs almost in the shadow of Scotland's highest peak, *Ben Nevis*, you next take the bridge crossing at *Ballachu-lish*, then swoop across the magnificent *Rannoch Moor* and *Black Mount* to stop for lunch at the Royal Hotel in *Tyndrum*—again unimaginative food, but the only spot worth considering in the region. After the turnoff at *Crian-larich*, there's an interesting ride down *Glen Falloch* to the northern tip of *Loch Lomond*, and you now view this loch of song and story in its entirety all the way down to its termination at *Balloch*. Tea at the Buchanan Arms at *Drymen* will then be yours for the asking—and home you go to *Edin-burgh*, in time for a well-earned dinner. Less than 400 miles, round trip—with about 4000 miles' worth of scenery!

For the 1-day extension, on the second morning of the trip, instead of driving to the Caledonian Canal, continue west and north from *Inverness* to *Beauly*, *Muir of Ord*, *Garve*, and *Braemore Forest*; turn off on A-832 around *Braemore Lodge*, go through *Dundonnell*, follow along the south shore of *Little Loch Broom* (not to be confused with Loch Broom and Ul-lapool to the north), and then sweep in a U-shape hook through *Aultbea, Poolewe*, *Gairloch*, and back along the lovely shores of *Loch Maree* to *Kinlochewe*. Turn southwest on A-890 at *Achnasheen*, and follow it to the turnoff for *Kyle of Lochalsh*, your destination. This is the ferry point for the *Isle of Skye* and its capital, *Portree*. (Fair warning: this routing is well off the beaten tourist-path, and a good part of the roads are secondary and small. But if you want unspoiled rural flavor and untouched scenic magnificence, this is it.) Round-trip bus excursions from *Inverness*, encompassing the enchant-

ing *Isle of Skye*, operate selected days between May and September. On these we flatly guarantee a splendid case of fatigue.

On the third morning, take off early for the *Kyle of Lochalsh* ferry and continue along A-87 through *Dornie*, *Invershiel*, *Cluanie Br. Inn* and *Tomdoun* to *Invergarry*. At *Invergarry*, pick up the route down *Loch Lochy* described in our 2-day tour (to *Spean Bridge*, *Fort William*, *Loch Lomond*, and eventually to *Edinburgh*). The only thing you'll miss is Loch Ness, but honest to goodness, you'll never miss it.

These are fairly stiff hauls—but in 48 or 72 hours, you'll have a better cross section of the real Scotland than most travelers can get in a week.

Oban, a lovely little port, is one of the most convenient jumping-off points for scouting the Hebrides. Day excursions may be made to the islands of *Mull*, *Lismore*, and *Iona*. (The last is the birthplace of Scottish Christianity, where St. Columba preached, and where the first abbey has been restored.) Aboard the *RMS Columbia* you can take 3-day mini-cruises or hop on a car-ferry for a visit to the islands. Even shorter skims aboard 12-passenger motor launches leave at scheduled intervals from the *Oban Times* slip and glide out to *Seil Island*. There you may stroll the beach and actually pet the animals for which the isle was named. Caledonian MacBraynes' Steamer Services also run a comfortable year-round short cruise through both Inner and Outer Hebridean points with the comfortable and cozy *Claymore*. Departures are at 7 A.M. on Monday, Wednesday, and Friday to *Tobermory* (where there's a sunken treasure ship) and then to *Coll*, *Tiree*, and *Barra* (the "Tight Little Island"), arriving in the evening at Loch Boisdale on *South Uist*. You may sleep aboard on the night before casting off. Since this craft accommodates as many as 50 automobiles, it is possible to drive off here (or take a bus) to *North Uist*, *Skye*, and *Kyle*, or to make your return along the same route, arriving at Oban before noon the next day. We think this is a well-rounded, economical, scenic composite for any wayfarer who does not wish to concentrate much time in any one area. The vessel is solid; the comfort is sound (her Deluxe cabins even have showers); the food is hardy and substantial; the price is right. Local wags who thirst for a sea voyage remark that MacBrayne's steamers are all beautifully equipped "with quite a few engines" (local parlance for "bars")—and that they are, mon!

☑ **TRANSPORTATION Taxis** When you first climb aboard one of Edinburgh's high-button-shoe-era Oxford taxis and see the driver pick up a microphone for broadcasting, it's about as unexpected as stumbling across a color TV on The Ark.

These Oxfords and most other cabs seat 5. You'll pay about $4 for the first mile, and there's no supplement for baggage *unless it rides in front with the chauffeur.* If the fare is $1 tip 15¢; if it's from $1 to $2, make it 25¢.

Drivers are generally courteous, friendly, and honest.

Trains Since Scotland is crosshatched by branches of the British Railways network, see "Trains" in the section on England. All facilities and equipment are pooled

throughout the U.K. The popular Thrift-Tour Tickets and other bargains include the noted Circular Tours of Scotland, and Caledonian MacBrayne's Steamer Services in the West Highlands and Western Isles. *Most of these are sold only in North America.*

☑ **FOOD**   Never let misguided cookbook editors tell you (1) Scottish fare is heavy and coarse, or (2) Scottish specialties of gourmet rank are sparse. The Scots love the table, and their approach to it bears little resemblance to that of the English. It's a separate food culture—and to us, a more stimulating one.

Although few would deny their vegetables are often lumpy and sodden, the Scots are pastry-mad—and any nation famous for such scrumptious goodies must surely carry this delicate touch into other fields of cookery.

Specialties? No aspiring epicure should miss any of the following Scottish staples— and these are only a few: Haggis (see below); Scotch broth; Cock-a-leekie (chicken and leek soup); roasted or stewed grouse or ptarmigan; fresh trout, salmon, haddock, cod, or sole; Arbroath Smokies; kippers; fried herring in oatmeal batter, or grilled herring with mustard sauce; Findon Haddock (finnan haddie) with poached egg; scones; pancakes; oatcake; shortbread; heather honey; Black Pudding (oatmeal, blood, and seasonings); White Pudding (oatmeal base); Black Bun (chewy with raisins and ginger); marmalade; many, many more.

Meal hours: lunch, 12:30 P.M. to 2 P.M.; tea, 3:30 P.M. to 5 P.M.; dinner, 7 P.M. to 9 P.M. or later in summer, but 6 P.M. to 8 P.M. in winter. Chinese restaurants plus a few occidental ones (you'll find 2 or 3 in almost every city today) usually operate until or shortly after midnight, providing the only late-hour fare on any Main Street.

★ **TIP**   No visitor can say he knows the real Scotland until he has gone through the Haggis Ceremony—a little gustatory adventure that is an ironclad requisite for every traveler of spirit. This national festival dish of oatmeal, assorted chopped meats, and spices must be specially prepared, but that's easy; just call any good hotel on your itinerary 1 day before you plan to arrive, and ask them to give you a Haggis with your dinner in place of the fish course. Be sure to order hot mashed turnips on the side, and be doubly careful not to forget what the Scots call the "gravy"—straight Scotch whisky sipped between bites, the *only* liquid that complements this fascinating dish. Maybe you'll love it (as we happen to), or maybe you'll loathe it—but we'll guarantee you'll find it sufficiently intriguing for that low-cost gamble of buying it.

Nearly every important independent dining place is a member of the British Hotel and Restaurant Association. Thus, it's revealing that accredited restaurants, tearooms, cafés, pubs, oyster bars; and snack bars in the country's 30,405 square miles cover a mere 8½ pages in this organization's directory.

By way of compensation for this, tabs are among the lowest in Britain (with the exception being the petroleum boom towns facing the North Sea fields). Full repasts in the finest establishments seldom exceed $18, with the majority charging tariffs in the $12 range.

When a Scot eats out, he almost automatically heads for a hotel. As a consequence, the Scottish restaurant, while blossoming notably, is still a foot-of-the-table institution. To fill the gap in a labor-short economy, you may find your kilted waiter purring in the purest Castilian, Sicilian, or even—as we discovered on our recent visit—in *Turkish!*

☑ **DRINKS** For nearly 500 years, distillers all over the civilized world have tried to imitate Scotch whisky. But even with identical ingredients and methods—for reasons which are unclear—no foreign-produced product has ever come within hat-tipping distance of the original.

This Most Seraphic of Solaces of Gentlemen, as Samuel Johnson put it, is classified into 5 types—4 geographical (Highland, Lowland, Islays, and Campbeltowns) and the 5th chemical (grain spirits for processing). Each is as different in flavor as U.S. rye from Canadian rye. North Americans overwhelmingly prefer the Highland category, because its peat-fire-dried malt adds the distinctive smoky tang to which they are accustomed.

After it is matured in casks for at least 3 years (usually 4 or 5), top-secret blending formulae are applied by each producer. When we last toted 'em up, there were about 3000 blends—until we lost count. The Scotch we drink in the States usually contains from 17 to 45 different whiskies.

The Royal Family of this kingdom are the pure Pot Still Malt runs which are *not* blended but remain in their virgin glow. Of these there are fewer than 100. Many Scots sip theirs with water; personally, we prefer it neat on a cold day; soda is universally considered to be a sacrilege, and ice is also not quite cricket. If you appreciate superb whisky, don't leave Scotland without sampling this extraordinary potable. It's fit for the Gods. Tullmore is our favorite. Islay (pronounced Eye-lay) is mysteriously rich in peat, lacking in sweetness, and firmly in a class by itself; so is the smoky two-fisted 10-year-old Laphroaig; Glenmorangie, at the other end of the scale, is one of the smoothest, softest, and most delightful elixirs we know. Glenlivet, Glen Grant, and Glengarry are all better known and fine.

Ironically, it's sometimes a chore to find your familiar proprietary brand in the nation of its birth. Too much is exported.

Drambuie, that Isle of Skye nectar, is the national liqueur—proudly. Its base, of course, is Scotch, but the rest, except for mountains of sugar, is a secret. For saving his life during his attempt to regain the throne, Bonnie Prince Charlie gave the Laird of Mackinnon the recipe, and it's been guarded as carefully as the crown jewels since 1745. Don't miss this one either. (Incidentally, we put a bottle in our freezer at home—and it's *twice* as delicious at this cold, cold temperature.) Glayva, the second-string national liqueur, doesn't please our palate as warmly.

Scottish brewers build brass knuckles into many of their products. "Prestonpan's 12-Guinea Ale" (delicately referred to, when ordered, as "a wee heavy" or "a dump") is one of the strongest ales made; it's dark, thinnish, sweetish, and loaded with rubber truncheons as well. Be sure your hat is on tight!

Finally, in the States a socko TV advertising campaign persuaded us to buy a Caledonian bottled aperitif called Scotsmac which bears the subheading of "Wham's Dram." While we found the taste of this bizarre concoction tolerable but not sufficient to allure us for a second round, a description on its label made us sit straight up in amazement. Boldly it states "(You are drinking) a blend of Scotch malt and Scottish wine." Scottish *wine*? Whazzat again?

McEwan's, the most popular export ale, and Younger's, the leading beer, are on draft

in the better pubs. Many Scots prefer mixing various types ("mild and heavy," etc.) rather than drinking them straight.

They love their dram and their glass in this land—and why shouldn't they, considering what they put in them?

* **TIP** When you drink with a Scotsman, say "Slans-Jevah!" (phonetic spelling) instead of "Cheers!"—and watch his eyes sparkle with surprise at hearing his traditional Gaelic toast from the lips of a stranger.

☑ **LOCAL RACKETS** So startlingly unusual in this honest, decent, God-fearing land that when even a mild one pops up the citizenry explode. Some years ago, for instance, a red-hot newspaper hassle raged about (we quote) the "revolting spectacle" of certain "disreputable-looking characters" along the Trossachs highways, who were fast-talking tourists out of an occasional buck. "Dressed in a caricature of Highland clothing," one horrified critic stormed, "and playing the bagpipes badly, these individuals behave like Eastern mendicants!" This violent reaction against such minor chiseling is any traveler's guarantee of the high moral integrity he'll find among these wonderful Scots.

☑ **INFORMATION CENTERS** The **Scottish Tourist Board**, with headquarters at 23 Ravelston Terrace, Edinburgh, does a phenomenal job for the traveler, in view of its limited size and budget. This Board of eminent Scots from all fields and walks of life minister to the nation's welfare.

The Board has completed various ambitious programs; now it's attacking new ones. Its main targets are the increase or betterment of accommodations for the traveler and the lengthening of the tourist season. It also encourages planners in other up-and-coming areas or in crowded established centers. Crofters and cottagers, as well, have been urged to make rooms available for visitors. Road improvement; new car ferries; natural resources further developed; ski lifts, additional fishing and shooting facilities, and other projects are being spotlighted.

For pamphlets or off-the-cuff information on anything from Edinburgh's Royal Mile to Sule Skerry to salmon fishing in Loch Lonachan, write, phone, or drop in at the **Information Centre**, 5 Waverley Bridge, in Edinburgh (Tel. 031-3322433).

* **TIPS** If you require any hard-to-get reservations or savvy guidance for places to hunt, golf, fish, ride, sail, or sightsee anywhere in this land, get in touch with our dear friend Bill Nicholson, **Tourist Promotion (Scotland)**, 36 Castle St., in Edinburgh (Tel. 031-2266692, Telex 72372). This brilliant gentleman almost single-handedly gave the country a tourist industry after he initiated Scotland's early promotional projects. Having retired, Bill just can't sit still when there are people to help, so he continues his genial services under the umbrella of his own personal company. He has a special warmth for our readers and no one knows Scotland more intimately or more comprehensively than this top-flight professional. His annual edition of "Scotland Wonderland" (free!) lists an exciting selection of tours throughout the land and contains a roster of castles and country homes which welcome guests.

By phoning Edinburgh (031-) 246-8041 between May 1 and September 30, you'll get up-to-the-minute details on what to see and do—thanks to the STB-sponsored "Teletourist Service."

A plan whereby visitors may receive a 20% discount on many facilities during certain off-peak months may be offered again this year. Ask the STB about the "Highlands Holiday Ticket." Readers have not been too enthusiastic about it, but if you are still interested, the lookin' ain't much.

☑ **GOLFING GUIDELINES**   If you yearn to win a passel of Scottish pounds bet some patsy that Edinburgh is farther north than Moscow. Then if you need a follow-up, challenge your opponent to guess within 50% of accuracy how many golf courses there are in the capital area. There are eighteen 18-hole circuits *within the city limits* (located no farther than 5 miles from Holyrood Castle) plus five 9-hole rounds. And if that doesn't zap them hard enough, you can open the Edinburgh phone book and rattle off at least threescore more just for the record.

There are few things that can make you feel quite so "foreign" as teeing up on Scottish turf and not knowing the lore of the links. Soon enough you'll learn that Scots play golf with quite another style. In this windswept country, the high arc of a beautifully lofted ball is seldom observed—it might land behind you on a breezy day. We've entertained a notion that entire tournaments could be played with only a two iron and a putter!

For a wealth of tips on the fairways and the oddways of the Scots, we've turned to our dear friend and golfing companion the Honorable Richard Funkhouser, who has hung up his American-made ambassadorial pouch and picked up a Scottish golf bag as a joy for retired life. Here are His Excellency's excellent tips:

- Only use eight or nine clubs stuck into a pencil bag. You probably won't find carts and there are all too few caddies nowadays.
- Be prepared for the worst weather and pack along rain gear even on the brightest days.
- Don't display colorful sartorial fashions appropriate for Palm Springs. Dress like a grouse—in drab shades, tweeds, or wearing plus-twos. Un-chic is proper.
- On those blustery courses, don't speak loudly—unless you want to be answered by someone at the next downwind hole.
- Don't believe Scottish handicaps; they're either too high or too low. (Only 3 scores are turned in each year!)
- Play with dispatch; 2½ hours is par for 18 holes.
- There are no "Mulligans" in Scotland. That's an Irish term. Instead, ask for a free drive on the first hole.
- In Scotland a "foursome" means two balls and four players. To convey the American concept of a quartet of players teeing off together, you should refer to "four-ball" play.
- A "scratch" player is one who regularly makes par. Par and scratch are used almost interchangeably.
- Here are some don'ts at the 19th hole: No ice with your malt—and no soda either.

• Never display cash for bets at private clubs. Resist any urge ever to discuss business at the clubhouse.

And now that you are armed with those helpful hints, here is the Funkhouser Private List of golf courses—his picks of patch for maximum enjoyment in each category:

Public courses: Gleneagles, Turnberry, Gullane, Carnoustie, Dornoch, Cruden Bay, and St. Andrews.

Private courses: Muirfield, Prestwick, Troon, Blairgowrie, Bruntsfield, Burgess, and Western Gailes.

Quaint golfing (all public): Braids, Boat of Garden, Macrinshish, Stonehaven.

CITIES

EDINBURGH combines the old and the fresh—one of the most ingratiating cities on the travel map. Here's the political, judicial, and cultural capital of the nation. Two-thirds of its history is tied up in the **"Royal Mile"**—nearly a straight line from world-famous **Edinburgh Castle** to **Holyrood Palace,** incorporating such landmarks as the **Shrine,** the **High Kirk** (St. Giles's Cathedral), **John Knox's House,** the **Canongate Tolbooth, Queen Mary's Bath,** and a half-dozen of similar interest. **Sir Walter Scott's "Dear 39"** and the **University of Edinburgh** are musts. **Princes Street,** with its **Scott Monument, National Gallery, Royal Scottish Academy, Scottish-American War Memorial,** and smart shops is one of the handsomest thoroughfares in the world. Quiet atmosphere, except at Festival time every August; hotel situation adequate-to-poor (which may perk up now that Hilton plans to launch a 300-room house late this year; the Mercury and the Centre also plan to open fresh new portals soon). Excellent sports and spectator facilities, so-so restaurants, additional nightclubs, 2 modest gambling casinos that operate about as sheepishly as a Lothian herder; matronly, serene, beguiling. Cut your time in other metropolises to the bone and base yourself here.

EDINBURGH HOTELS Quick Reference Table

Price categories by national (not U.S.) standards.

EXPENSIVE:
Caledonian Princes St. Tel. 2252433; Telex 72179; 213 rooms. P. 783
George George St. Tel. 2251251; Telex 72570; 196 rooms. P. 782
N.B. Princes St. Tel. 5562414; Telex 72332; 195 rooms. P. 782

UPPER MODERATE:
Carlton North Bridge Tel. 5567277; 92 rooms. P. 784
King James St. James Centre, Leith St. Tel. 5560111; Telex 727200; 146 rooms. P. 783
Post House Corstorphine Rd. Tel. 3348221; Telex 727103; 208 rooms. P. 783
Roxburghe Charlotte Square. Tel. 2253921; 75 rooms. P. 783
Royal Scot Tel. 3349181; Telex 53168. P. 783

MODERATE:

County Abercromby Place 8. Tel. 5562333; 60 rooms. P. 784
Howard Great King St. 32. Tel. 5561393; 40 rooms. P. 784
Mt. Royal Princess St. 53. Tel. 2257161; Telex 727641; 154 rooms. P. 784
Rutland Rutland St. 3. Tel. 2293402; 19 rooms. P. 784
Scotia Great King St. Tel. 5563266; 48 rooms. P. 784

ENVIRONS:

Borthwick Castle Gorebridge. P. 785
Braid Hills Braid Rd. 134. Tel. 4478888; 51 rooms. P. 785
Dalhousie Castle Bonnyrigg, Midlothian. Tel. 0875.20153; Telex 727396; 24 rooms.
   P. 784
Ellersly House Ellersly Rd. Tel. 3376888; Telex 76357; 58 rooms. P. 785
Forth Bridges Forth Rd. Bridge. Tel. 3311199; 98 rooms. P. 785
Hawes Inn South Queensferry. Tel. 3311990; Telex 53168; 8 rooms. P. 785
Houstoun House Uphall. Tel. (Broxburn) 853831; 21 rooms. P. 785

Hotels Dramatic improvements have been made in key localities, particularly among the top-liners—but, speaking in general, too many are still too stiff, stark, and down-to-earth. The entry of breweries into mass-market innkeeping is adding new yeast to the volume keg but little sparkle to the individual mug. In all too many cases, these malt-masters are neglecting their bedchambers and service standards to pull more traffic into their taprooms. You'll find no nonsense about the average Scottish hostelry (not the front runners, however): It's a place to eat and sleep, just that.

You'll pay from $30 to $45 per person for bed-and-breakfast in the better group, and up to double this price in the Gleneagles league. Simple accommodations, especially in rural areas, can be had for as little as $16 per day.

★ **TIP** About breakfast: (1) Be sure to order it *before* 9:30 A.M.; otherwise you won't be able to coax a nibble until noontime, even if you starve. (2) Either gobble it down pronto or set all your plates on the night table. The shortage of serving trays throughout the British Isles invariably results in a visitation from your waiter about 10 minutes after his initial delivery. (3) Be prepared to shell out 20 New Pence supplement for munching in your room, instead of in the breakfast nook. Now—Good Morning to you!

The **George**, under the management of John Acton, is a dramatically improved example of Victoriana made up-to-snuff with the present-day pamperings of a prosperous petroleum-producing nation. The full-scale rehabilitation not only includes revisions in the current facilities, but the grafting of 116 extra bedchambers which join the main building, bringing the overall house count to 202 units; yet another wing is due before long. Excellent Buttery for light meals; 2 salubrious bars, one devoted to the lore of whisky distilling; Restaurant des Ambassadeurs, featuring its traditionally-hearty roast-beef specialty and extra-smooth kindhearted service; dancing nightly; typical Scottish entertainment in High Season (see our "P.S." below). All-in-all an ingratiating house in classic good taste.

The 200-unit **"N.B."** (North British Station Hotel) is a teammate of the faded Caledonian which once topped our Edinburgh list. Ably directed by Jack Maguire; bright touches everywhere; extensive steam blasting to remove soot

from its imposing facade; Cleikum Restaurant and Bannatyne Bar; tiptop cuisine for tiptop tabs; Happy Sam's Bar for off-lobby chuckles and toping. Comfortable sleeping quarters; pastel suites; gardenside units the best; a truly outstanding Hall Porter in Mr. J. J. Petrie; mixture of commercial and touristic clientele.

The Railways-operated **Caledonian**, opposite Edinburgh Castle, seems to be chugging along on a reduced head of steam, in this engineer's opinion. From the exterior, this fortress-like landmark might be mistaken for a Scottish House of Usher; inside, however, the welcome is warmer if still a bit pedestrian. Plenty of private baths; some units stately (the quietest face the abandoned station, not the Castle), some only so-so. There is dancing nightly (except Sun.) in the popular Pompadour; light meals are served in the Laird's Lodge Coffee House. In our view, it is time that the railroad moguls consider giving this property a roundhouse renewal.

P.S.: The Caledonian, the George, and the "N.B." have "Scottish Nights" between May and September—national food specialties served up with generous helpings of piping-hot bagpipings and regional dancing by experts in authentic costume. These evenings are expensive by local standards, but the spirit, the fun, and the performance secure your investment.

If you have transportation, the outlying **Post House** is one of the most appealing modern addresses in the nation. It's a 10-minute drive from the center on the Corstorphine Road to Glasgow, raised above the highway and looking across rolling meadows toward the Pentland Hills. Excellent Ravelston Room restaurant festooned with local tapestries; inviting Honey Bear Buttery (that colossal statue is the beloved Wotjek, mascot of the Polish regiment that once was billeted in Edinburgh) bar and public quarters recalling the region's Celtic heritage; superb comfort in its well-appointed bedchambers. We are very fond of this Post House.

A little farther out on the same pike and only 5 minutes from the airport, the **Royal Scot** is physically more daring in concept. Wood has been handsomely melded into the free-form concrete structure providing warmth; tan-and beige-toned textiles enhance the humanizing process. The food is said to be noteworthy in its restaurant, but the German maître who took our order so bungled every aspect that we had to flee to catch a plane before we could sample a bite. (Dishes for other clients looked tempting, however.) Service probably will always be a problem at this remote site, but perhaps Manager Barry Shatwell has the answers.

Back in town, the **King James**, yet another recent addition, is packing 'em in. The commercial atmosphere is softened by the richly adorned Stuart Restaurant, by the Queen's Lounge, and by the King's House for light lunching. The Coffee Pot adjoins a busy shopping mall. K.J.'s discothèque pulses Monday through Saturday. The smallish accommodations are thoughtfully outfitted. Okay as an up-to-date midtowner, but do yourself a favor and miss the Scottish Dinner Show which, on our visit possessed an extraordinary talent for generating yawns.

The tranquilly situated, 69-room **Roxburghe** retains far more of a family air than its busy-busy colleagues. We like it from the cozy top-floor singles in garret style to the jousting-tent Consort Restaurant in the cellar (so-so cuisine

and orchestra-dancing); traditional tones with Adam highlights lovingly preserved; top-form maintenance; first-rate attention by Willy, the hyperfriendly
concierge; light, airy, flower-dotted dining room; captivating ground-floor
cocktail bar (which we prefer for light dining as well as for sipping) in Victorianisms; self-serve luncheon buffet; cramped inside baths or shower compartments; some units perfectly designed for a mother-in-law with the sharpest
tongue in the world. This one has been the favorite of many visiting performers, musicians, and gentle folk of the arts. Comfortable, homey, and recommendable for its warmhearted personnel.

The 87-room **Carlton**, a Scottish Highland Hotel Group homestead across
the bridge from the N.B., has sited its reception desk up 1-flight from the
hurly-burly street. Entrance, lounge, and bar redecorated, with the entire
remainder of the hotel due for a pep-up (no guarantees by us, because we've
heard only promises, promises for the past several years); every unit with
private bath; most with double-pane windows; corner bedchambers ending in
"15" the largest. Now well run, comfortable, and worth the price.

The **County**, more quietly situated, commanding the point of Abercromby
Place and Dublin St., has furrowed a neater row in a hoedown revamping of
its public rooms and most of its sleeping segments. Attractive entrance, reception, cocktail bar, dining room, and lounge; 50 so-so units; only 12 baths; #40
is our choice of doubles. Fair, if you can alight in one of its better nests.

The **Mount Royal** is fair, but it is time for a general revamping, in our
opinions.

The partially redecorated **Scotia**, on Great King Street within 5 minutes' walk of the George, consists of 5 Georgian houses comprising 50
rooms with a quotient of 14 private baths. Guidance by brethren Reginald
and Cyril Elliott; many young staffers, pleasant and forgivably amateurish.
Modern, perked-up lounge and bar; good restaurant adorned with fine old
paintings and gay red tableclothes; modest appointments including electric
heaters; (try #33 for a pleasant back unit). We hope it continues to render
top value for top dollars.

On the same street, the **Howard** now glows with renewed vigor. All 40 units
pepped up and provided with private baths. Quite recommendable.

The **Rutland**, across from the Caledonian, offers viewful accommodations
at 30% less than the outlay at the County. Proprietors Mr. and Mrs. Richmond are trying to convert its mercantile character into more of a family
haven. Total of 19 rooms; no baths; bar and grill noisy after nightfall. Strictly
for dedicated penny-watchers.

Several splendid havens have opened for travelers with special tastes or
needs. Our personal favorite is **Dalhousie Castle**. The neighboring Jacobean
Feast (at Dalhousie Courte, a few miles distant; see "Restaurants") is a highly
bruited publicity come-on, but its soft-spoken luxury accommodations in the
quiet isolation of the fortress are absolute charmers. Henry IV held the castle
in siege for 6 months and we could happily bivouac here for a lifetime—or at
least a fortnight. All 24 units truly superb, but we are especially fond of
Dalhousie Suite in the Tower or #22 up on the battlements (no elevator).
Something unique and spectacularly rewarding for twentieth-century day-and-
knighthood. The official address is Bonnyrigg, Midlothian, a short haul from

Edinburgh. Another winner is **Houstoun House** at _Uphall,_ about 20 minutes by car from the bright lights. What a tranquil dreamland it is, too! This one is a converted mansion embraced with green lawn, guarded by a rolling 18-hole golf course. Proprietors Mr. and Mrs. Keith Knight are known for their fine gastronomy, the best we've lately enjoyed in Scotland and high in the culinary rankings of Europe. Only set meals are offered. Virtually every dish is prepared by the owner-chef. Handsome, refined dining salons on the 1st floor; glass-lined, linkside lounge; vaulted whitewashed bar with deep soft divans and crackling fire in the chimney; 19 bedchambers with private bath (or one immediately adjoining); added wing with modern conventional décor. For reservations, write to the Knights, Houstoun House, Uphall, West Lothian, or if you want to telephone to book a table, the number is Broxburn 3831. One of the warmest recommendations in this book, but not at all for seekers of the fancy, the ritzy, or the pretentious. **Borthwick Castle**, 20 minutes from the capital at _Gorebridge_, is a cozy snuggery from which Mary Queen of Scots once escaped custody. Had she waited until it was refashioned, she would have changed her mind. From minstrel gallery to turrets, here's a tidy tower of taste and comfort. **Prestonfield House**, out on Priestfield Rd., is mentioned under "Restaurants," the category on which its esteem is more properly based. The **Forth Bridges Lodge**, at the headland of the famous firth, casts a commanding sweep over the wind-chafed waters. The views are breathtaking, but the whiffs from the Vat-69 distillery just below can be breathalizing when _those_ cups runneth over. Efficiency-style bedchambers; 40 doubles; 20 more which can be stretched into trios; all with bath; some with TV (who could watch it with that magnificent sea outside your window?); each unit with its own teamaker set and all the fixin's. For motorists and wide-eyed wanderlusters. **Hawes Inn**, nearby at _South Queensferry_, is down by the water opposite the old pier. Here is where (room #13 to be exact) Robert Louis Stevenson blocked out the plot for _Kidnapped_ and began writing the novel; it is also where Sir Walter Scott penned his _Balfour_. Only 7 bedchambers, 2 private baths, a darned good dining room, and a cozy cocktail lounge and bar nestle within the white walls and black enamel trim of this tiny hideaway. For nostalgics, excursionists, and overnight adventurers, but not for long stopovers—or Norman Mailers. The **Esso Hotel** is out in the same direction. Six floors of 120 lookalike cells; 6 so-called suites; 2 levels of public rooms; wide windows that don't allay the narrowness of the dimensions. Sheltering arms, but sterile ones. **Braid Hills**, south of town on Braid Road, weaves much more braided flair. Total of 70 units split equally between singles and twins; reasonable rewards; pleasant as a suburban address. **Ellersly House**, about 2 miles from the center on Ellersly Road, is under the aegis of the Mount Royal, which gave it a complement of bedchambers, all with private bath. Garden situation and croquet green enhancing the converted private home; elevator; large carpark; hotel shuttle to town available and inexpensive.

    Restaurants   At long last Edinburgh's dining establishments are beginning to recognize that the 20th century is hard upon us. Young and daring entrepreneurs are making a noble effort to enliven the tablescape of their capital town, but it remains to be seen whether the crusted Old Guard will support those gallant whippersnappers. Perhaps the tourist traffic alone will

be enough to keep them alive—and indeed they do merit the outlanders' attentions. Let's hope they keep up their inspired kitchenwork.

Cousteau's (109 Hanover St.) is—as if you hadn't guessed—a breath of sea-fresh air. Outside hang colossal iron swimfins and a giant diving mask suggesting a link with the great French naturalist (which doesn't exist except for the proprietor's esteem for the deep). Come down several steps to a clean, well-lighted place—a cozy bar to the right and a comfortable lounge nook to the left. Well-made cane furniture with leaf-green upholstery; aquarium with tropical fish, coral trees, and shimmering bubbles; Philippine fans employed as wall sconces; tables of white-grain pine held together with shaved copper rivets. Main dishes in the $8 to $9.50 range; excellent mussels; splendid grilled fish. But the show-stopper is the spectacularly attractive cold seafood platter served in a rugged scoop of cork bark almost a foot long and radiant with marine critters. There were a few service glitches on our try but the reception was warmhearted and every effort was made with eagerness to make each guest feel special. Closed Sundays and Mondays. Very good and trying hard.

Charlie Parker's, a few steps down the street from the George Hotel, is another youngster to watch. The façade of simple glass and neon is a tip to trend followers that this spot is "with it." Ground-floor dining area with white furniture and a ceiling of undulating white gauze-covered light fixtures. While there are no surprises on the menu, downstairs there is a jumping and vibrant bar with a large clothed statue of the house's namesake seated at the keyboard of a piano. The people are nice, the mood is fashionable, and we suspect the spot will catch on.

Vito's (55A Frederick St.) is a bright touch of Tuscany in the heart of the city. (We prefer this Vito to the original one at 109 Fountainbridge, which is hued in gray and brown.) Down a few steps to a bewitchingly colorful cellar; unusual heavy white-pine tables and chairs with red backing; terra-cotta floors; gaily painted tiles; front wall composed of beehive wine racks; two small rooms plus a bar and lounge. Amiable Italian waiters; muscular seasonings in the ample selection of Latin dishes; sweets rolled out on an amusing trolley carved as a wooden horse. Different and uplifting.

Flappers (8 West Maitland St.) is one of the new breed, not unlike the previously mentioned Charlie Parker's in concept. In execution it won a British guidebook's "Most Exciting" award during its inaugural year. That's a fair peg for its black and red raiments, but you've probably been more stimulated by culinary adventures in your travels. The chef's favorite platters come from France and Italy. Closed Saturdays at lunchtime and all day Sunday.

The previously described "**N.B.**" Grill (dancing on Sat. night) and the Pompadour (dancing nightly except Sun.) at the **Caledonian** are known for their excellent standards of cookery. The Ambassadeurs at the **George** turns droves of visiting Americans into calorie-counters. A gargantuan portion of Aberdeen Angus roast beef, baked potato, Yorkshire pudding, and a large tossed salad will set you back surprisingly little per gastronomic ton (our latest tonnage for 2 couldn't have been better). Uncomfortable banquettes; swinging dance band nightly, rendering such hip tunes as "Nola" and "Glowworm". All of these serve lunch, but dinner is livelier. The **Café Royal & Oyster Bar** (17 W. Register St.) prides itself on its seafood. Upstairs still inviting for its dated

elegance; public bar updated (shoving it reluctantly into the modern world of the nineteenth century); exquisite cream, rouge, and gold Crown Room; lower-cost Paddock for lunch and evening grills; revamped Oyster Bar still a bivalve treat—best for informal meals; overall capacity of 200 munchers; reservations a must before 10 P.M.; big à la carte menu; medium-high prices. Traditional and worthy. **Howtowdie** (27A Stafford St.), somewhat more expensive, is also appealing, especially for game, steaks, and salmon. About a dozen tables aflutter at lunch and dinner with well-presented table d'hôte and à la carte creations. Closed Sundays; costly but rewarding. The **Cavalier** (20 Abercromby Place) parries and thrusts with an elegant French businessman's club atmosphere. Burgundy-canopied bar and lounge; diminutive dining den with more private quarters farther back; bay windows; gold patterned wallpaper; moss carpeting; royal-blue ceiling trimmed with carved white wood; discreetly placed dueling swords; rolled parchment menus; adept, unobtrusive service. Closed Sunday. **Le Caveau** turns out French cuisine—usually at about $16 per *tête. Bon!* The **Doric Tavern** (15-16 Market St.) is on the Left Bank and might be a bit difficult to find; 12 tables with black-and-white-checked cloths; cozy, informal, "family" aura; food superior. **Hunter's Tryst** (Oxgangs Rd.), a delightfully cozy former coaching inn, once hosted Scott and Stevenson—and if their roast beef was as good as ours, they must have been regular customers. The name aptly embodies its romantic candlelit mien. A lover's tryst, too. For snacks or medium-price casual dining in bright-hued, cheerful surroundings, the little La Caravelle in the **"N.B."** Hotel is just the choice—especially the tempting "Scottish specialties" menu. The Consort in the **Roxburghe** has an attractive theatrical ambiance with tented ceiling, striped textiles, and antlers for lighting fixtures. It offers a splendid value in its cold buffet. We've had good reports on the **Beehive**. The 2 top-floor dining rooms of the popular late-hour **Royale Chimes Casino** (3 Royale Terrace) furnish limited warm nutrients plus an assortment of snacks. The emphasis here is on what's on those groaning boards downstairs—namely, blackjack, chemin de fer, and roulette (service also by a pair of one-armed bandits). If you're looking for further action, check in at the **Carriage Club**. Ask your concierge for introductions. **MacVitties** (6 S. Charlotte St.) is largely devoted to self-service ingestion.

For elegant dining in the suburbs, please look at our "Hotels" section for the description of **Houstoun House** at Uphall, which wins our bid as one of the top tables in the British Isles. After this, **Prestonfield House**, 10 minutes from your midtown doorstep, has been the prestige oasis. Here's a beautiful converted estate gentled by somnolent grace, fanning peacocks, and grazing lambs. Fireside bar for friendly persuasions; a few bedrooms for visitors with lingering ambitions; large menu and generally excellent cuisine; chic clientele who find it wiser to reserve in advance. Hostess-Owner Mrs. Cunningham is a perfect delight, and Ernest, her earnest maître d'hôtel, will fly to meet your every whim. Open all year for lunch and dinner. Another little gem we've long favored is **Cramond Inn**, 5 miles (20 minutes by #41 bus) from the center, where the River Almond meets the Firth of Forth at *Cramond.* This 300-year-old village tavern and adjoining pub, winner of the nation's Pub of the Year Award in '72 (*1972,* that is!), is the hobby of one of Scotland's best-liked and most cosmopolitan tycoons, Lindsay Gumley; with loving attention he has

restored every speck of its charm. Peat fireplace, low beams, dark oak, gay paintings; sweet bar with 12 seats; handsome lounge; cozy atmosphere. Specialties include Steak & Kidney Pie, Chicken & Ham Pie, Welsh Rarebit, lobster, crab, duck, goose, and Gumley-smoked salmon. plain country-style cookery; low tabs; Cramond bottled-and-labeled Burgundies, Bordeaux, and Champagnes imported direct from French vineyards; outstanding wine list. Caution: *8 tables and 25 persons are the dining limit here, so be sure to book your reservation before you go.* La Potiniere, at Gullane near Muirfield, has only about a half-dozen tables, but its fame goes well beyond its capacity. The French cuisine is served only at lunchtime and it shutters on Saturday, so be sure to book if you're going this way. It's about a 45-minute drive from Edinburgh, along the coast and overlooking the course which hosted the 1979 Walker Cup. The tiny Scandinavian-minded **Howgate Inn** (30 minutes out of the center) is another winner; rich dining on copper service; medium tabs for superior rewards. If you tire of Scots fare, the **House of Chow** is the local mandarin. The service is superb; the surroundings are decidedly untartanesque; the cookery is good by European Oriental standards; the prices are modest. **Sik-Tek-Fok** also rates as a tong leader among Chinese feederies. **Babar's**, which we haven't tried, is said to be best for Indian dishes.

Don't forget the previously mentioned Jacobean Feast out at **Dalhousie Courte** (3 miles from the Castle) in *Bonnyrigg*. Eat with your fingers or a hunting knife; lusty singing by medieval troubadours; free double-decker bus service from Edinburgh Monday through Thursday; find your own way out and back Friday and Saturday; always book ahead. Inclusive banquet, serving about 170 vassals, for about $25, and no tipping. These robust spectacles have become pretty popular all over—but not with gastronomes.

A dinner afloat? Try **Pride of the Union**, a 60-foot barge which ambles along the Union Canal, leaving Bridge Inn jetty at Ratho (near the airport) before (7:30) sunset and returning around 11 P.M. An accordionist adds a few more notes of charm. The mini-cruise and galley works cost about $20 per passenger. No sailings on the Lord's Day; reserve by phoning 333 1320 and allow about 15 minutes (and $6 or so) for the taxi run from midtown.

★ **TIP** Laws now sanction public drinking in Scotland on Sundays. Bar hours throughout the nation's 7000 taprooms have been extended to 11 P.M.

Night Life Zero. Weeknight dancing at some of the better hotels, but no strip or girlie cabarets, B-girls, hostesses, or ordinary after-dark action. Pickups must stay on the streets; they're not tolerated in even the less respectable bars. Folk singing and dancing are pervasive as family entertainment.

When the sun goes down in Scotland, you've got your choice of hotel dancing, pub crawling, the handful of casinos in Edinburgh and Glasgow, or washing your drip-drys 5 or 6 times. At last Edinburgh offers a real live discothèque: **Buster Brown's**, which is open Mon.-Thurs. until 2 A.M. and Fri.-Sat. unitl 3. A spot called **Pipers** (which is a disco in the winter) specializes in Highland folk shows beloved by tour leaders; it also features dinner dancing.

Pubs As in London and Dublin, the pub of yore is rapidly being replaced here by a hybrid that is part saloon and part discothèque. Today it's rare to find a thoroughbred stall where hairy-chested males gather for purposeful drinking. The oldest and best examples, physically unchanged for decades (when you can find one today), are rich with color, flavor, and charm. Routine

neighborhood-corner-tavern examples, on the other hand, are often painfully plain and colorless.

Edinburgh offers several enchanting establishments. For the authentic feel of the Old City, the canopied rectangular bar and ornate woodwork of **The Abbotsford** (3 Rose St.) will transport you to mellow Victorian days. You may lunch here or nibble its snacks; noon to 2:30 P.M. and 5 P.M. to 10 P.M., jam-packed on Saturday night; delightful. Equally beguiling is **The Volunteer Arms** ("Canny Man"), about a 15-minute taxi ride from the center at 237 Morningside Road. Its Public Bar is stuffed with mementos accumulated over nearly a century; on the sides are 3 small lounges, including 1 modernized that clashes with the venerable mood. Go between 7 A.M. (if your liver functions at that hour) and 8 P.M.; Saturdays are best. The **Jolly Carter's** (Thistle St.) has a roughshod appearance in a studied way. **Tankard Lounge** (Rose St.) is a noisy playpen in which we saw many of the Gay Set. The **Chain Pier** (out at Newhaven docks) is pleasantly filled with the flotsam and jetsam of many a long voyage. **Scott's** (202 Rose St.) is a family institution with a loyal following. Drinks only; an exceptionally amiable spot. The **Golf Tavern**, 10 minutes out at Brunstfield Links, faces the pitch-and-putt course of one of the world's oldest golfing centers. Sporting clientele; friendly Public Bar and higher-toned Cocktail Bar; separate entrance to the multi-storied "Restaurant the 19th" upstairs, where you'll find 2 small rooms with 5 or 6 tables and passable fare. Lunch or beverages from noon to 2:15 P.M.; evenings from 5 P.M. to 11 P.M.; go Saturday, if possible. The **Victoria and Albert** (Frederick St.) harks back to the good old days. There's a flavor we like a lot here; we hope it won't be destroyed by the encroachment of modernisms. **Bere & Byte** (across from the Caledonian) is a lodge-style snackery which, in our opinion, has matching food, furnishings, and flavor—all blah. The **Laughing Duck** specializes in German beer and atmosbeer.

Shopping   Mild caution: Avoid the phony "white heather" peddled as a "rarity" and shun the typical tourist claptrap worth about half what is asked for it.

Our ★ ★ ★ ★ ★ recommendations are individually noted.

Fine jewelry, gold and silver plus knockout traditional Scottish accessories: To informed travelers a visit to ★ ★ ★ ★ ★ **Hamilton & Inches** (87 George St.) is a *must.* For more than a century this has been the country's leading jeweler and purveyor of fascinatingly unique Scottish creations (sken dhus, clan brooches, kilt pins, et seq.). In addition to its comprehensive array of "Thistle" and "Star of Edinburgh" crystal are the illustrious Laird Sets, exquisite sterling quaichs, gold and silver Luckenbooth articles, a huge collection of antique military badges and lots, lots more. Ask for 4th-generation Ian Inches or his charming daughter Deirdre. Marvelous!

Scottish handicrafts: 2 leaders: **Scottish Crafts Centre** (Acheson House, Canongate) for the whole regional gamut (you may even have your family crest woven in tapestry here) and the nonprofit **Highland Home Industries** (94 George St., plus 11 branches throughout the nation) for the typical handicrafts created by artisans from the Highlands and the Islands.

Kilts and men's clothing: **Kinlock Anderson & Son** (16 George St.), are the Kilt Makers for the Royal Family and tailors of international fame.

Antiques: In Scotland, most zealots look first for Portobello pottery jugs and

copper or brass candlesticks. **Henry's** (High St.) is the best establishment for these and other treasures. **Wildman Brothers** (54 Hanover St.), operated by Syndey and Jack Wildman, is dependable for silver, jewelry, china, and the like.

Department stores: **R.W. Forsyth Ltd.** (Princes St.) has a fine cross section of merchandise. The Export Department is 1 flight up.

Shopping Hours: Weekdays, 9 A.M. to 5:30 P.M., except Saturdays; 9 A.M. to 1 P.M. in the higher-class places. Second-line merchants stay open on Saturday afternoon.

Bonus shopping tip: The ★ ★ ★ ★ **St. Andrews Woolen Mill**, adjoining the Old Course Pilmour Links at St. Andrews, is *the* knitwear outlet for us. Manager Jimmy Stuart is so in love with the business that visitors are warmly encouraged to watch their 13-stage process of knitting Shetland or Fair Island sweaters or their creation of other articles. Among their additional tempters are top-name cashmeres, tartan travel blankets, sheepskins, mohair throws, stoles, and yard goods (including cut-priced ends-of-batches, factory seconds, discontinued lines) and a category amusingly dubbed "Frustrated Exports." Coffee for guests is a ritual; packing and mailing are flawlessly provided. Please don't miss it!

Dedicated shophounds: For a comprehensive list of other shops throughout this land, please consult the purse-size 25th Anniversary edition of *Fielding's Selective Shopping Guide to Europe.*

Other Targets

ABERDEEN successfully blends medieval mellowness with the gaiety of a modern seaside resort. There is also a new fever of prosperity as the region enjoys what might be termed a black-gold rush. One result of this is that the city's thoughts have turned away from tourism more and more and now incline chiefly toward commerce. Hotels are jammed with business visitors and petrodollars have caused local prices to skyrocket. The expanding limits spread along the banks of the Don and the Dee rivers and not far from the off-shore oil fields that are being developed by the nation. Between the mouths of these streams, a 2-mile sandy beach has been dedicated to any remaining holiday-makers—perfect for Polar Club bathers who sprout walrus hair on limbs, back, and shoulders. Outstanding university, 8 lovely parks, spectacular Rubislaw granite quarry, venerable St. Machar's Cathedral; don't miss the Fish Market (with guides), one of the most interesting in the United Kingdom.

Among its hostelries, the **Station,** traditionally the doyenne of the dowager division, was again a sad disappointment to us on our latest swing. Since then, however, a thoroughgoing face-lift was scheduled, so it may be much better by your arrival. The 113-room **Treetops,** on Springfield Road in the west end, has been linked to the Centre Hotels chain, so we can't report its status until we visit it anew. Tranquil situation 5 minutes from the traffic nucleus; handsome dining room overseen by the former maître of the famous Royal Athenaeum; enormous menu and better-than-average cuisine for the region; long, inviting, lantern-lit bar sided by intimate tables; fire-crackling lounge and TV nook. The **Royal Darroch** has a country address and country solace. Superb comfort. The cuisine is tiptop, too. The 100-unit **Sheraton Inn** exchanges waves

with the North Sea at its doorstep (innstep?) on Oldmeldrum Rd. Binnacle restaurant recalling clipper-ship times; 2 bars; extensive use of wood and dark timber tones; indoor swimming pool; 2 suites plus a clutch of simple but adequate accommodations. Its goal is not luxury and it achieves its more limited aims rather well. The **Caledonian**'s antiquated aura may be the headache of a new director. Its previous owners liquidated it, and the fresh team has moved in. Complete carpeting has been installed, and the entire plant refurnished. The **Dee Motel**, 1 mile out on the river and opposite the greyhound stadium, deserves mention along about here. A steady construction program now puts the overall count at 46 plain but bright bedchambers, each with shower and toilet. Three bars, including a snack corner; pine and brick décor; comfortable lounge; carport beneath every accommodation. The massminded **Gloucester** has bashfully perked up with a few meek improvements. Redecorated dining room and lounges; some twins cheerful; dreary, perfectly horrid corridors lined with a maze of public toilet cabins. Total of 86 units and 27 private baths. Basic shelter *only* at times of dire distress. The **Imperial** offers 100 updated bedchambers, each with private bath. Its neighborhood seemed grim to us. The commercially oriented **Douglas,** run by the Gloucester people, has redone some of the arthritic bedrooms; they still seem zipless. Friendly Manager Gordon is its chief asset. If you're driving, the 40-room **Northern,** 10 minutes from the center and 5 from the airport, might fill the budgeteer's bill; cramped but chipper bedrooms in pastels with white furniture; only 4 baths; Lilliputian restaurant; jigger-size bar. A good little bet at the price. Northwest of here, 2 miles out of *Meldrum,* Robin Duff, the Laird of **Meldrum House,** is as respectful of his skillets as of his guests. Space for only 8 overnight couples, but 72 couverts for diners. Imposing graystone castle structure at the end of a drive lined with towering oaks and rhododendron shrubs; wide greensward at its door; a deluxe target for which you should certainly reserve in advance. Finally, the $8.2-million **Aberdeen Airport Inn**, a 160-chamber house constructed around Scotland's first climate-controlled mall for year-round recreational activities, has just been inaugurated. We haven't yet inspected it.

In the restaurant review, a tuneful contender is the **Fiddlers** in Old English style; fish and steaks are their double stops. **Ledodo** is French owned and so inclined gastronomically. **Gerrard's** boasts the former chef of the Station Hotel. The garden is nice in summer. For local culinary achievement, it would be hard to match the consistently high-quality fare at both the **Station** and the aforementioned **Treetops** hotels. The former, a traditional front-runner, comes up with wood-paneled dining room and clean-lined decorator touches. The latter offers far more flair, modernity, and color; there's a vast menu of international favorites, fish, crustaceans, roasts, and grills. The **Chivas,** operated by the Chivas Regal whisky people, also draws praise from most customers. Once-fresh décor that could use another shake or 2; indirect lighting; huge map of Aberdeen to reorient you after that Scotch Mist; superskilled and extra-nice barman. From sip-to-sup, here's a First-class winner. The highly touted **Lengsteng** was a dismal disappointment to us on our incognito try—especially since seemingly every cab driver, concierge, and elevator operator we met in the city grew almost breathless at the sound of its name. Hard-to-find alley location on Bon-Accord Terrace, off Union St.; single wood-lined room with bar at one

end; Swedish light fixtures; rushed service by an insufficient team of waiters; noisy atmosphere; poor wine list. Respectfully, therefore, a "no"—but perhaps it's better now. The **Egg & Bacon,** across from the Douglas Hotel, gets our vote for snacks and budget fare. A quartet of Chinese kitchens also have noodled in; the **Bamboo** on Union St. wasn't bad—but it wasn't good, either. Pub? **King's Highway** is an old inn partially and unconvincingly restored in pseudo-Tudor. Ask directions from the hotel porter to this hard-to-find, drinking-for-drinking's sake establishment.

ADVIE   A hedonistic entry called **Tulchan Lodge** is writing a deluxe chapter in the Spey River anthology. Shooting and angling rights plus all the comfort and convenience that humanity can divine will cost you close to $1700 per week per person. It is so special that we cannot devote more space to it except to recommend it to the sporting set.

AIRTH   This uninspiring village about 28 miles west of Edinburgh is proud of its pre-Victorian **Airth Castle Hotel,** which resides handsomely in its own sylvan park. The well-worn restaurant bar and chambers have undergone a beauty treatment of brushes and paints. Ambitious they are; comfort they provide; cookery's fair enough, considering. What's more, it doesn't cost the Airth. Not bad in a pinch.

APPIN   Casual, homespun **Ardsheal House** is the quiet domain of Resident-proprietors Jane and Bob Taylor, young and eager Americans who open their 12 rooms (3 with private bath) and their great hearts to tranquillity seekers. It's on the shores of Loch Linnhe and has roots reaching back to the 16th century. Clearly, the greenhouse dining salon is one of its most arresting blossoms; the cuisine is interesting in choice and wins orchids locally for execution; rooms are simple and fair; a put-your-feet-up atmosphere pervades the Old World coziness of this very private realm. There's nothing fancy about it—unless, of course, you fancy P&Q. For more information, write for a Taylor-made holiday at Kentallen, Appin, Argyll PA 38 4BX. The hills of Morvern may kidnap you forever.

ARROCHAR   **Ardmay House** in Dunbartonshire (75 minutes from Glasgow, on Loch Long) is a small Scottish country mansion. Heated, indoor seawater (not freshwater) swimming pool—a genuine button-popper; home atmosphere with now aging lochside cabin accommodations; beautiful setting; garden-fresh food from Ardmay Farm; special house blend of Ardmay Heritage whisky; viewful dining room overlooking the torpedo testing range (they're unarmed, of course); 18 bedchambers. Write early for space. The **Arrochar,** with 65 rooms and baths, may be a worthy alternative, but we don't know it personally.

ARGYLL AND ENVIRONS   This region lies slightly west of Dunbartonshire. At **Kilchrenan**, sitting on a small bluff beside Loch Awe amid one of the great informal gardens of the West Coast of Scotland, is the graceful **Ardanaiseig**. All of the main public rooms are viewful, and the bedrooms for

its 32 guests, each with its own bath and telephone, are comfort-oriented. The hotel supplies boats for fishing in the Loch—both rainbow or brown trout—and a picnic hamper, if desired. Also on the grounds are facilities for tennis, croquet, clay pigeon shooting; a liaison has been made in the neighborhood for golf, rough-shooting or deer stalking. We like this charming manor house, built in 1834, for its serenity and its solace. The **Bridge of Orchy Hotel**, 20 miles from *Loch Lomond*, is much better now, according to a helpful Canadian reader. He reports friendly service and appealing cuisine. We haven't looked in for a while, so we are grateful for the tip. In the same county and just outside of *Strachur,* we stumbled across a cutie called **Creggans Inn**—and fell in love with its modest country charms. Its proprietor, Sir Fitzroy Maclean, Bt., is operating this honey of a haven for tranquillity seekers. Situation just across the shore road on Loch Fyne; panoramic lounge; public rooms cloaked in chintz; pleasant flower-papered dining salon; adjoining woody cocktail lounge; exceptional cuisine (Mrs. Maclean is the author of 2 best-selling cookbooks); ingratiating summer veranda; cozy little bar in a rustic corner in the back of the house. Of its 24 rooms and 5 private baths, we're especially fond of #22, a garret-style double. At *Inveraray,* the **Argyll Arms,** with its pier and grassy beach in front, is recommended for summer sojourns. The **George** is tops in winter, followed by **McBrides** at waterside. The **Taynuilt** is famous for its table, but the scenery is niggling and so are the accouterments. At the end of the Crinan Canal beyond Inverary in *Lochgilphead,* the **Cairnbaan** is a chalet-type port of call with small dimensions but comfortable milieu; excellent beds; oil-fired central heating. The crowning glory here is the kitchen. In very few places throughout the British Isles have we witnessed such a vast and varied menu. The wine *carte* is also thoughtfully prepared and generous. Its management is by G.F.D. MacKay, who sports a kilt; the Polish chef is named Mr. Kluger. (Incidentally, the same company also owns the Crinan Hotel at the other end of the Canal; a meal interchange is possible.) Yet another member in this same clan, and said to be a finer address, is the larger and attractive **Stonefield Castle,** a few miles away at *Tarbert.* All 32 rooms boast private bath; early visitors have praised the cuisine and been tickled by the house policy of piping guests to the dinner table.

AVIEMORE   This Inverness-shire ski town scratched out from bare foothills, is blossoming with Cairngorm candidates. This phenomenal site, a bustling, ice-ribbed center of winter sport, might be a worthwhile skiing target for Britain's Union Jackrabbits and their snow bunnies who can't travel to the Continent for their muscle strain; for North Americans, however, we think it is not rewarding enough to warrant the transatlantic costs involved. Chairlifts, T-bars, and rope tows web the 4000-foot range; bowling, indoor bathing, curling, trout fishing, and dry-skiing facilities (nylon hills) are on tap; there's a community center complex with a restaurant and a huge theater. King of the mountain remains the **Coylumbridge Hotel**. Overall accommodations for 250 in "normal" bedchambers and 8-bunk double-decker "lodges"; mock-Swedish décor; restaurant, cafeteria, cocktail lounge, bar, snack corner, and nightclub; game room with slot-car racing; ski shop (rentals available); frequent movies; enclosed covered swimming pool, ice rink; private fishing lake; horses and golf

nearby; supervised nursery for the kiddies. Here's a fascinating experiment. The **High Range** has thrust up with 24 individual cedar-sided chalets and 8 private baths. Attractive sporting lounge with copper-hooded hearth; ski boutique; hairdresser; well maintained and recommendable. The rambling 100-room **Post House** is a handsome offspring of the Trust Houses Forte group. It is sporting and familial, just the niche for informal fun seekers. The **Freedom Inn,** nearly the same size, is worthy, too. The **Strathspey,** with curiously boxlike "tower" architecture, is completely out of harmony with the surrounding landscape, but so much in harmony with the times it has already had to build extra bedchambers. Rooms generally very small; cuisine above average for the region; service extra-kind; future bright and unlimited. The central **Badenoch** is a close carbon-copybook example of success breeding success. We're not so fond of it, but others seem to be. The nearby Spey Valley urbanization contains more dwelling space, but since we are not too fond of the entire range, the above represent what we consider to be the pick of the crop. All plan to remain open year round. Please don't even *think* of scaling these peaks in search of a St. Moritz or Sugarbush, because Aviemore is definitely still a raw, untried towhead among today's winter resorts. Praiseworthy for its valor, but so-so for its value.

BALLACHULISH   Refer to "Fort William."

BALLATER   This captivating townlet might be called the gemstone of the castle belt. Down the pike a few miles is the Queen's own **Balmoral**, where the gardens are open to public inspection (when she is not in residence). A bit farther is magnificent **Craigievar**, which was lived in until very recently and was left totally intact and furnished when the owners shifted to other digs so that everyone could share the beauty of their ancestral estate. Of course, **Braemar Castle** is next door (see our separate comments) and is viewable; the lecture tour here is superb. In the same region are **Crathes Castle and Gardens, Drum Castle**, and engaging **Banchory Museum**. There's the Z-plan **Castle Fraser** with its extensive **Castles of Mar** exhibition. This area is so sylvan and so enchanting that unless you had compelling reasons for settling in nearby busy, dusty Aberdeen, we would overwhelmingly urge you to bunk here. Our own recent stay at **Tullich Lodge** was fit for a baron. This 10-bedroom noble mansion sits tall in its own park overlooking the rushing Dee. Antiques and fine furnishings fill the twin first-floor lounges and spaciously comfortable accommodations. Young and alert resident proprietors Hector Macdonald and Neil Bannister create an atmosphere of cheerful bonhommie; they also are responsible for producing some of the finest cuisine in Scotland and presenting it in one of the loveliest salons in Aberdeenshire. A beguiling retreat. Not too distant is **Kildrummy Castle** surrounded by 15 acres of manicured nature and water gardens. In fact, the hotel has its name on all the fish along a 3-mile stretch of the River Don. Game for the table also frequently wears the Castle's name tag. Across the greensward is the original fortress dating from AD 1245. Your own comfort standards, however, are purely 20th century. **Raemoir House** is backed by the 1500-foot Hill of Fare plus legions

of supporters who sing its praise from all quarters of the globe. The landscape around this hostelry is a chapter from *Field & Stream*. Excellent. **Mar Lodge** is a former royal hunting manse and judging from the clientele we observed on our visit, its chief appeal is still for nimrods and anglers. If these are not your primary interests, we think you might be happier in one of the above establishments.

BALLOCH   **Lomond Castle**, on 18 acres of Loch Lomond's shore (30 minutes from Glasgow), is a former private manor house—not a "castle." It's more of a restaurant (and a good one, too) than a hotel. Lovely garden parking-apron and entrance; ivy-sheathed stonework exterior; homey public nookeries; 14 pleasant but unspectacular rooms, with dressing tables cunningly arranged to block the views; only 3 baths. Small, semicircular dining room overlooks the water; the modernized bar shares its pastoral panorama; there's a wildly exciting bowling green for outdoor sportsmen plus water skiing facilities for residents of polar ice caps. Mildly recommended. Closed end-October to the first week in April. As for the **Loch Lomond Hotel,** it strikes our professional soul as a Chamber of Horrors; personally, we'd rather bed down in a canoe.

BANFF   The 30-room **Banff Springs** is on a lonely bluff overlooking a magnificent stretch of sea and coast. The modern lines remind us of a suburban grade school; nevertheless its comfort is abundant. A car is a necessity, of course. Farther on, at *Cullen,* the **Seafield Arms** is a cozy nook in a cozy hamlet.

BRAEMAR   The leading house here is the 60-room **Invercauld Arms.** Cheery appointments; cozy lounges; many updatings; top dining spot in town; amusing Colonel's Bed buffet, with food displayed on the soldier's bunk. One of the worthier stops in the area. The **Fife Arms** pipes in next. Open all year; migrations of bus tours pause here. Creaky. The modern **Spittal** is an amiable lunch stop if you're running south through the *Satan's Slide* (formerly called Devil's Elbow; the crookedness has been removed and now it is wickedly slippery at icy periods). Inexpensive; tailored for budget ski buffs.

Near Braemar, the **Dalmunzie Hotel** on the 6500-acre Spittal O'Glenshee estate has an altitude of 1200 feet, making it Great Britain's highest hostelry. Rather bleak secluded location; facilities for tennis, golf, fishing, mountaineering, skiing, grouse shooting, and deerstalking. The **Spittal Hotel** is on the main route through Satan's Slide. Very satisfactory; no luxury.

CALLANDER   The turreted **Roman Camp Hotel** is on a 30-acre estate which is 38 miles due north of Glasgow, above Stirling. Formerly it was the seventeenth-century hunting lodge of the Dukes of Perth. Library, lounge, magnificent gardens, fascinating tiny Gothic chapel; 15 bedrooms, nearly all with private or connecting bath; 1 eminently relaxable suite. The shocking-pink annex across the drive is less luxurious. Locals love it for its famous tea and scones. Closed in winter. Now under English ownership and hopefully maintained in its traditional fashion.

CUPAR This is the closest (4 miles) hamlet to **Fernie Castle** is a fresh, appealing, whitewashed fortress dating back to the 14th century. It is generally considered to be in the St. Andrews area; thus, 45 golf courses are located within its county. Lovely approach along a fir-treed lane; circular dining salon overlooking a small private loch; the Keep Bar in its own stone vault; 11 large bedrooms with TV and tea-making units; dancing on Saturday nights. The Scottish menu and the international à la carte selections are well regarded locally. Refined and warmly recommended, but more for short stops rather than for longer holidays.

DIRLETON Refer to "North Berwick."

DORNOCH The **Dornoch Hotel**, in oddly named Sutherland (odd because Sutherland, with Caithness, is the most northerly tip of the mainland), gorges itself with tour packages. Now it is closed in winter. When we last rattled this doorknob, it was a stark building with many amenities; how long they will endure is a puzzle to us. **Dornoch Castle**, the former palace of the Bishops of Caithness, overlooking the Firth, is said to have been attractively converted. Both offer the celebrated facilities of the Royal Dornoch Golf Club, plus loch-or-sea fishing, cold-water swimming, shooting, and deerstalking. Except during Highland Week (mid-May), when they buzz with activity, these are attuned to the nature lover. We hear praiseworthy lip-service concerning the nearby **Tongue**, in the townlet of the same name. A London reader recommends it as a Victorian hunting and fishing retreat.

DRYMEN The **Buchanan Arms**, Stirlingshire, is 5 miles from Loch Lomond, 36 miles from Glasgow, and 50 miles from Edinburgh. Country-house style; tartan carpets, colorful lounge, charming enclosed dining terrace; glass-sheathed rooftop cocktail lounge; 23 spotless rooms, 18 with private bath; cuisine inoffensive to mediocre to downright poor; management by French-born Pierre Bretenoux. Except for the unskilled skillet-work, our only other serious demurrer is the bedchamber décor, in which each piece of furniture seems locked in mortal aesthetic combat with the next. Okay, but no rave.

DUNBLANE **Cromlix House**, in the same Eden family for more than 4 centuries, resides on a hunting estate of some 5000 wooded acres about 4 miles north of this picture-postcard town. We have seldom experienced such warm, gentle, and refined hospitality as we received in this Garden of Eden—the lord himself as host and the lady who sees to the manor-grown food and its gracious presentation. The Victorian mansion, with a heritage reaching to the dawn of Scottish history, has its own private chapel, antiques of museum quality, and heraldic needlepoint for which enthusiasts cross the Atlantic just to view. Meals—and superb they are in their home-spun way—are served at the family round table overlooking a greensward and the forest verge. The 10 bedrooms (with private baths) are in the grand tradition of a great country house. Rates are high, but so is the quality for the rare privilege of visiting such a home.

DUNDEE, the jam and jute center, frowns down from a majestic site over the Firth of Tay; the bay-spanning bridge puts St. Andrews almost within a chip shot of this hub; it's industrial. The local hotel champ is the **Angus**, a long, rectangular, glass-and-concrete heavyweight agraze in the city's blossoming shopping complex. Statleresque in tone; mezzanine restaurant with well-presented but institutional fare; handsome snack bar below lobby. A godsend for such a dismal town. After this, and far below, there's the **Queens** (somber, stern, and dull) or the **Royal** (commercial, and bustling with marmalade moguls). Both of these are Trust Houses Forte entries; both, at last, are receiving a smattering of color, Clorox, and cheer.

DUNKELD   **Dunkeld House** (Perthshire) resides on one of the most romantic Tay-side stretches you're likely to find in all of Scotia. Entrance via an arched stone gate; a mile's drive through forest and garden to the ocher-hued mansion; lawns of Karastan neatness and lush vegetation; pitch-and-putt golf course; all facilities for fishing in that glorious river. Our recent meal was pleasant but not outstanding. Sport is the theme and that it has. **Cardney House**, about 3 miles away, is a charmer in its more personal fashion. It is the love of Naval Cmdr. Finandus MacGregor, his talented and ingratiating wife Mariquita, a singer of considerable note, and their daughter, Una, who is a budding hostess. The atmosphere evokes more that of a Scottish house party rather than the cool austerity of hotel living. Everyone sits at a common table dining on farm-fresh pickin's and viewing the dales and glens of the estate. Fresh appointments; very nice accommodation with cheery color blends. A whacky sort of place that we happen to like, but not so eccentric that any traveler with a sense of adventure wouldn't love on first sight. Special and fun.

ERISKA   This is a flat water-girt island about 15 minutes by car from Oban. It is dominated by the distinguished and costly **Isle of Eriska**, a stately home which has stood above the Firth of Lorn since 1884 and which is reachable via a modern bridge today. The personable, hard-working couple Robin (he) and Sheena (she) Buchanan-Smith have wrought wonders in providing such a discriminating panoply of enticements in so remote a clime. Crackling fires, oak panels, deep snooze-away chairs, a well-stocked bar, restful vistas, books, books, and more books all conspire to giving up thoughts of ever wearing a wristwatch again. The exceptions are just before mealtimes when telltale cooking fragrances hint of grand things to come. Our salmon pâté was so delectable that we'd dub the chef a Scottish lochsmith for revealing the mysteries of the deep. Some of the best repasts of our recent Scottish rounds were enjoyed behind an Eriska napkin. Rooms are named for Hebridean Islands and our own favorite twin mooring is "Skye" with its vast vaulted wooden roof, its rich antique appointments, its color-keyed linens, its excellent carpeted bath, and its own large Skye-light in the ceiling. Here is one of the happiest spots in all Caledonia for nourishing both body and spirit. Highly recommended on every count.

FORT WILLIAM   is an important junction for motorists that is 2/3 of the way between Inverness and Oban. The imposing **Inverlochy Castle** steals not

only all the local innkeeping thunder but, to an ever-growing number of devotées, it is now considered one of the brightest lightning bolts in the national welkin. Exquisitely appointed baronial estate surrounded by 50 acres of garden within 500 acres of farmland; only a dozen supersumptuous luxury accommodations; skilled skilletry with predinner drinks in the richly outfitted salon; coffee and libations in the lounge; billiards (if you take the cue) in the trophy room; blue-ribbon price tags; open May through October normally, but they will welcome special parties throughout the year if requests are made. Please reserve way, way, w-a-y in advance with personable young Director Michael Leonard. Wonderful. The First-class **Milton** is a solid bet—but not for the victuals say several trippers. We hear the expanded (40 rooms, 40 baths), ranch-style **Croit Anna Motel,** 3 miles out, has become a close contender, with solid comfort and cookery—but we haven't wheeled in since the revampings. The **Alexandra** is much improved since it spent a packet on modernizations. These are followed by the **Imperial** (for bareback riders only) and the busy-busy **Highland.** Down the pike at *Ballachulish* (new bridge completed and ferry discontinued), the **Ballachulish** comes up with home-style comfort, waterside dining, and year-round availability. Convenient, but not posh. The **Onich,** a few minutes away, offers lochs more color and charm. Stone-and-stucco house that grew, g-r-e-w, and G-R-E-W; 2 cheery bars; tartan-toned dining room with a reputation for savor; 20 well-appointed bedrooms, with hot and cold running water. Not bad. The **Creagdhu Hotel** at *Onich* has a remarkable location overseeing Loch Linnhe; 8 of its 18 rooms have been modernized. At nearby *Glencoe* (scene of the massacre of Macdonalds by Campbells), the **Kingshouse** is a pleasantly updated coaching inn at the edge of Rannoch Moor. The dining room is outstanding for the vicinity —that is, if the chef isn't a Campbell and you are a Macdonald.

GLASGOW With nearly 1 million inhabitants, here is the commercial capital of Scotland and the 3rd largest metropolis in Great Britain. Shipbuilding and engineering make her wheels turn; her famous cathedral dates back to 1197 and her University to 1450. The Kelvingrove Art Gallery, City Chambers, Hunterian Museum, Provand's Lordship 1471 house, Botanic Gardens, and Zoo are among her attractions; she has 50 public parks and 5 newspapers. The center of the city is currently undergoing a revolutionary face-lifting which will replace uninhabitable slums with longitudinal or skyscraping apartment dwellings and office buildings. These are laced nimbly through a skein of projects which include a hostelry sited at Anderston. For the time being, avoid a district known as the Gorbals, one of the roughest areas of Europe, especially after dark. Abbotsinch domestic airport is now second only to London's Heathrow in its traffic of British skywaymen. The hotels, drab and mercantile until recently, are improving; a tough, rigidly enforced antismoke campaign is fast dispelling her one-time grim, grimy, and forbidden franchise on smog; its newly scrubbed face as well as the city's beautiful antiquities are at last being revealed in a more flattering light. Convenient jump-off point for many interesting excursions.

The modern, 9-story, 250-nest **Albany** is the top hotel in town, in our view. Its Four Seasons dining room is a delight for formality while the red-and-black

Carvery sizzles with open banks of grills; a trapper's cabin hides in the cellar for light biting; accommodations throughout are well conceived and smartly attired. The century-old **Central** is a property of British Railways. Scads of improvements, including vast technical revampings behind the scenes; fearful street noises in some of its units. The high-style Malmaison Restaurant, in the Versailles mode, completes handily for local gastronomic honors. The " **N.B.**" (another "North British" operated by the Railways) also has taken vanity pills. Chipper white façade; perky lobby carpets and curtains; bedrooms from top-to-bottom fluffed up; many baths modernized. Smarter in every respect. The **Pond**, with 137 rooms, has been refashioned, while the 90-chamber **Ingram** has joined the fray and soon plans further restylings—which it vitally needs. The 116-unit **Royal Stuart**, opened in '65, dedicates 2/3rds of its accommodations to the lone traveler. Shamefully compact cells with tiny intercommunicating baths; air-conditioned and centrally heated; rooftop restaurant in prospect when funds appear. It is very popular, however. The small but tastefully contemporary **Tinto Firs** is a worthy stop for a brief layover. The Copper Grill is especially inviting; so are its 4 bars if you have an overwhelming thirst. For budgeteers, the **Lorne**, 15 minutes out of town, is sleek, and okay if you have wheels; the omnipresent Scottish brewers tapped this one.

The **Excelsior** (sometimes called the "Airport Hotel") at Abbotsinch domestic terminal renders topflight shelter and service. The **Silver Thread**, at nearby _Paisley,_ is just fair.

The **Macdonald**, in Giffnock suburb about 10 minutes from midtown, is a favorite of wayfaring executives. Jumbled entrance; small lounge; paneled pub; simple, adequate, but showing wear.

The **Campsie Glen**, in the settlement of the same name about 12 miles from Glasgow, roots in the country coombs. Quiet as the inside of a chinchilla muff and almost as pretentious; venerable country mansion with up-to-date décor; appalling concrete dining salon that reminds us of a beachhead bunker. Otherwise, the creature comforts are plentiful and satisfying.

For self-drivers, the **Newlands** (15 minutes from the center) is a honey for Scotland, despite its dearth of double accommodations. Tartan lobby; plasticy bar; all 34 rooms have sprightly décor and bath or shower; only 6 lodge 2 occupants; Dennis Lynch its young and winningly personable manager.

As for restaurants, the previously mentioned Malmaison at the **Central Hotel** is decorated à la Versailles. Separate entrance; 30 tables in 3 sections; high ceilings; suave ambiance; food on the upgrade. Also for hotel dining, the Four Seasons in the **Albany** is tops for style and grace. The Carvery here is also worthy for hungry beefeaters. **Casino-Restaurant Chevalier** (244 Buchanan St.) takes top dollar for late dining among the independents. Handsome grill up 1-flight; nightly dancing on illuminated glass-paneled floor; active bar. Gaming rooms on the 3rd tier with "21," boule, and roulette; friendly atmosphere (the _croupiers_ are on a first-name basis with the regulars); rendezvous of Glasgow's Young Executive Set. **Piccadilly,** another casino, is also a jackpot in the pots and pans department. The "**101**" (Hope St., directly across from the Central) and the **Grosvenor** (Gordon St.) are also popular favorites among the city's gentry; both recommended. We prefer the former for food and the latter for décor. **Guy's** is liked by business and professional people. **Rogano**

Restaurant & Sea Food Bar (11 South Exchange Place) is internationally renowned for its fish, crustaceans, and bivalves; not bad. **Ferrari** (10 Sauchiehall St.) offers continental-style dishes in a vaguely Bohemian atmosphere; sorry, but we feel this one has slipped. Finally, the **Whitehall** (51 West Regent St.) has a happily agreeable dining room upstairs and a pub and lunch bar (cold snacks only) below; pleasant, popular, and reasonable. A half-dozen Oriental flowers have blossomed but we were just too occupied rechecking the older haunts to pick up a chopstick on our latest round; all stay open late-ish. Outside of town (15 minutes by taxi), the **Lansdown Crescent** shines for the Bentley-Jaguar Set. Stable ambiance around a paving-stone courtyard; à la carte only. Although costly, it has thoroughbred tack and feed. Be sure to reserve your stall.

In this city, most pubs are so rough and rugged that you're liable to leave your front teeth with the sweepers. In **Lauder's** on Renfield St., though, you'll not only be safe but you'll probably enjoy it. Ladies shouldn't try it alone.

GLENCOE   Refer to "Fort William."

GLENEAGLES Gleneagles Hotel Perthshire, 1 1/2 hours from Edinburgh, is undoubtedly one of the top stopping places in the nation. Wonderful pastoral setting and lovely gardens; splendid golf facilities including three 18-hole championship courses (and a fourth on the way), one pitch-and-putt 9-hole course, and one 18-hole putting run; tennis, riding (arranged), and fishing; croquet; flat green bowls; heated swimming pool and indoor games room; saunas; squash courts; air-conditioned French Restaurant (High Season only); dancing nightly; bar, massage parlor, the works. Central heating; color TV in every room for lonely golf-widder-ladies; new conference center. Its manager is J. K. S. Bannatyne, an able administrator whom we admire greatly. Open April to end-October only. Highest recommendation. If you are out this way, for a change of pace you might try a meal at the highly respected **Nivingstone House** at *Cleish*. Be sure to ask for directions and since it is so small, be certain to reserve in advance.

GRANTOWN-ON-SPEY   The 57-unit **Grant Arms** has marched smartly to the fore. It's an easy hour's drive south from Inverness or Nairn. Boniface Barry Rosier runs a splendid rest haven. White-leather furniture commanding attention in the parade-ground-size lounge. Winter-garden restaurant reconnoitering the Cromdale Hills; elaborate menu forecasting superior fare; expert service by Maître Rolf. You'll also discover a licensed snackbar, a sauna, and a beauty parlor. Most of the private quarters are color-keyed in matching curtains, bedspreads, tablecloths, and wallpaper. Queen Victoria summed up her visit in 1860 with the notation "Dinner very fair, all very clean." More than a century later, we can't top it for candid commentary. Down the pike a way is the **Craiglynne Hotel**—pure Walden for the nature lover, the sportsman, or the world-weary. Tumbling, salmon-full Spey only a toddle from your doorstep; daily (or overnight, if you wish) pony trekking across fells and mountain slopes; shooting parties arranged by Manager David Small; handy to golf courses and Cairngorm ski slopes (special instructress for

tots). Comfortable, eye-appealing public rooms; regional food among the most savory in Scotland (our latest Haggis and malt "gravy" were heavenly); hardy tartan bar with peat fire usually smoldering; friendly, home-style service. **Nethybridge Hotel,** 15 minutes south along the river at the hamlet of the same name, offers less zing in its more ancient amenities. But fishermen go into ecstasies over its 6-mile reach of private Spey. Strictly for dedicated anglers.

INVERNESS Here is the capital and one of the key touring centers of the Highlands. It's typical of a tranquil provincial town. The **Caledonian** offers 100 units with private bath. Modern rather than traditional tone. Peppy, fun-filled atmosphere. The **Mercury Inn** provides 84 latchkeys to contemporary dwelling space. The linkside and youthful **Kingsmills** is a mile from the center and only 10 minutes from the home of the Loch Ness Monster. Its ways are traditional while its amenities are modern. We recommend it if you have a car. The generously recharmed **Culloden House,** 6 miles out, is where Bonnie Prince Charlie was defeated in his attempt to capture the British throne for the Stuart kings. Never mind. We'll bet it will capture your heart and soul more than 2 centuries later. Everything about it bespeaks the easy comfort of Country Life. Back in town, the **Station** was old-maidenly when we saw her, yet her service standards are those of a hostess of breeding. Two dining rooms (we prefer the one in rouge tones); almost 1/3 of its 71 units now with private plumbing; general upkeep fair. The **Glen Mhor** overlooks the River Ness. It rambles in houselike fashion, employs chenille and cretonne by the square mile, and creaks and squeaks from its welcoming floorboards. Call us addled, but we like it even for its faults. The Scottish Highland group have put Jack Galloway in charge of their latest acquisition here, the **Glenmoriston.** All of its 23 bedrooms have been refurnished and redecorated. It should be suitable. The **Royal** may never live up to its promising moniker; it's a noble choice, however, for economizing vassals. A helpful Claremont, Calif., reader praised the **Palace,** with its quiet location on the Ness. We paddled up to its greystone portals and found a stately, old-timey, Establishmentarian establishment with 2 tall towers and tariffs not too steep for the ample comforts. The **Cummings,** with a fresh white façade and windows outlined in brown, is moving up in quality. Many private baths have been added, too. Now quite recommendable.

The **Station Hotel** garners top honors for gastronomy. Now that it is refreshed and new baths have been added, it might be worthy for overnighting, too. The **Caledonian** is a keen competitor in the pots-and-pans department. The **Carlton** heads the independent pack. Restaurant and adjoining bar 1-flight above street level; not too inspiring. **Full Moon,** a Chinese contender, seemed in partial eclipse to us.

IONA A short cruise in the Inner Hebrides? Here, facing the New World, is the rockdot where St. Columba landed and began to christianize the north of Britain in the 6th century. It is a 1¾-hour whisk via hydrofoil from Oban, skirting the vast, lonely and hauntingly beautiful island of Mull. (You also can hop to Mull on a ferry, take an overland transfer, and cross to Iona at the western extremity.) Within easy walking distance of the small dock is the ancient Abbey, the Nunnery, a coffee shop and, naturally, a golf course. Of the

2 tiny hotels, we prefer the **Columba** to the **Argyle**, but both afford reasonable comfort and restful vistas of the Sound and Fionphort on the Ross banks. Shoppers can visit charming "Fiona of Iona," mistress of **Iona Scottish Crafts** where woolens, jewelry, and pottery of the isles are purveyed. Time ashore is 2 hours (if you took the speedy *Sea Bird*), the time it takes for other navigators to zip up (nonstop) to *Staffa*, round the island of Fingal's Cave, and pick up passengers for the homeward journey at 5 P.M. Arrival at Oban is 6:45 P.M., and due to the northern latitude, the light is as clear as noontime. The cost is minimal for a mini-cruise you'll always cherish for its natural beauty.

KINROSS   The engaging **Windlestrae House** is the effort-of-love by the Quinn family—she as the smiling hostess, he as the unseen but able chef. Only 4 bedrooms, but they are pleasant; attractive dining salon where you shouldn't miss a try at the Duckling Seychelloise or the Chicken Jan van Riebeck. A pause that refreshes.

KIRRIEMUIR   This is the nearest pocket of civilization to the remote and lonely and bitingly costly Rottal Lodge, which is stitched to a blanket of heather a few miles from Glen Cova. Some go for deer stalking, bird shooting, or just plain lazing. (Indeed, a platoon of staffers tried vainly numerous times to scatter us away from the fireside where we were reading and off to beddy-bye before 8:30 P.M.) The lounge, we concluded, is all-important in this wistful retreat because there was hardly space enough to open a suitcase in our so-called double bedroom. Our food was routine—a charitable view. And please don't expect to find cold white wine for your fish choice, because the kilted host will level you with a crusty lecture on how chilling destroys the bouquet. (We couldn't even arrange for a beer that was lower than skin temperature, so we requested iced water and got it—with one lump, period.)

A perfect place for grouse—and that's what we did.

By the way, if you wander this far to the Earl of Airlie's fief, be sure to drive over to nearby *Strathmore* to the **Castle of Glamis** for a peek. That almost makes everything worthwhile.

KYLE OF LOCHALSH   The **Lochalsh Hotel,** 80 miles west of Inverness at the ferry point to the Isle of Skye, features an admirable view across the strait, modern appointments, and genuine Scottish flavor and color. Well supplied bar; 45 rooms, about 1/3 with bath (we nabbed #20, on a corner); cookery reported to have fallen off alarmingly, but we can't say from personal experience; service also spare, according to other howls; book long, long, long in advance, because this mini-house is always crowded. And speaking of "mini," a veteran Park Ridge, Illinois, friend of the book wryly comments, "With the exception of a YMCA room, I have never seen a smaller accommodation than the one we drew." While it is open all year, the biggest crush comes during High Season when visitors are heading Skye-ward. Here is the most important way station en route. A doctor from Oneonta, N.Y., praises the viewful **Balmacara**, 6 miles south of *Kyle.*

MELROSE   The **George & Abbotsford**, near Galashiels (Roxburgh), drops its lure to fishermen and to scholars hooked on Sir Walter Scott. (He's buried

at nearby Dryburgh Abbey.) Rights on the River Tweed to 4 private pools; groups never sheltered; 22 rooms and 13 baths; solid comfort with abundant touches of grace and charm; room #19, with 4 windows and a view of the ancient abbey, is our favorite. Very Scottish; recommended. We're happy to hear that new owners are putting life into the **Waverley Castle Hotel**, at which we'll stop by soon.

NAIRN The **Newton**, 30 minutes northeast of Inverness on the Moray Firth, was described to us by a good Scotsman as "a civilized place"—and that it is. Here is a favorite quiet hideaway of prime ministers, industrial colossi, and Very Old Families. Vintage 1850 structure surrounded by 35-acre parkland; castle architecture; 2 championship golf courses; tennis courts; trout and salmon fishing; central heating and open peat hearths; numerous lounges; cocktail bar oriented (or is it "occidented"?) toward the most glorious sunsets in the Highlands. The cuisine is above average for Scotland. Not posh, but deeply satisfying. We like it. The 57-room **Golf View** is bigger, more modest, and less expensive. Waterside situation; also with tennis facilities, also near the links; commendable cookery; attentive service; the best corner units are #106, 207, and 307. Both of these are seasonal only. The **Royal Marine**, with 47 kips, most with private plumbing, is kept in fine trim. Recommended.

NORTH BERWICK The internationally famous **Marine Hotel,** 20 miles from Edinburgh, is on the march again. This disciplined, taut, bright-eyed Marine—which stood so long at parade rest—is now snapping smartly to attention. **Blenheim House** is so tiny it's almost an afterthought; pleasant décor; savory à la carte selections; perky. The **Open Arms** at _Dirleton,_ 3 miles from North Berwick, is well regarded for its kitchen; the cookery certainly opened our arms in a gesture of thanks.

OBAN The traditionally front-running **Caledonian** has been enjoying a pep-up party of late. Waterfront situation just a toot from the Hebridean ferry slips; old exterior; spacious public rooms; vista-oriented dining salon. Coming up with gratifying speed. The **Great Western**, beautifully perched on the Esplanade, is an imposing gray-and-white Georgian building with a viewful lochside command. Glass-fronted terrace and adjoining bar; excellent position, in our personal opinion. **Manor House** has fewer than a dozen rooms, but we like it most for its reliable kitchen. The **Park** is satisfactory in its amenities. The **Alexandra**, less appealing for comfort, in our view, boasts a better down-the-loch panorama; it is older in tone, despite recent refurbishings. The **Lancaster**, on the Esplanade, offers a magnificent vista! It operates all year. So does the **King's Knoll**. The **Columba** and the **Regent**, back at dockside, are for budget voyagers. Here is the springboard for cruises out to the Hebrides. There is a zippy hydrofoil service to _Iona_ (see separate comments) and _Staffa_ (**Fingal's Cave**) plus steamer runs in the general island hopper. For 5-star elegant country living, please check our report on _Eriska_.

PEEBLES If you're dead set on staying in "Sir Walter Scott Country," the **Peebles Hydropathic** is the logical selection. Sprawling structure with many recent redecorations; vast dining room, in which you're asked to use the same

napkin for several successive meals; à la carte restaurant; cool, uninspired bar; dancing nightly. Recreational or health facilities include steam baths, massage parlor, swimming pool, 8 tennis courts, badminton, a pitch-and-putt course, Tweed River fishing, and nearby golf and horseback riding. Manager Pieter van Dijk is trying hard to renovate this unwieldy and cumbersome plant. Recommended. The sprightlier **Tontine** is younger in spirit. Fresh block of studio-style accommodations facing the river and Newby Uplands; older bed-chambers more spacious; cozy, clean, and filled with warmhearted cheer. Manager Brian Scott gives you a heaping handful for your Pence. The **Park** is now colorful and inviting. Both inexpensive, both for travelers younger than typical Hydrophiles, and both very pleasant indeed.

PERTH's berths are cozy in the **Royal George**, a riverbank Trust Houses Forte member that was once the local haven of Queen Victoria. Nice views of the Tay and Perth Bridge; especially tempting grills in its restaurant; engaging Black Watch Bar; handsome lounges; 43 bedchambers; 43 baths; considerate service; solid in comfort; appealing in concept. Now a frontrunner in this city. The sparkling clean **Station Hotel**—ironic because both its exterior and the adjoining terminal buildings are still dismally gray from the coal-smoke era— is also a sound bet. Midcity garden with lime-treed border; ambiance so cheerful you'll immediately feel your spirits lifting; lounge with plenty of Perthshire perk. Not as nicely situated as the Royal George, but very recom-mendable, indeed. The commercial, ultrabasic **Salutation**, in midtown, greets its guests with traffic noises about the level of a 3-gun salute. Routine. The **Isle of Skye**, at the bridgehead across the Tay, is an excellent nest for money-saving pilgrims. White stucco and wood façade; captivating Iron Hinges Cock-tail Bar; Glenshee Ski Bar for buffet and snacks; Tudor dining room; firelit parlor; added wing with best accommodations. The **Waverley** (next to the market) and the **Hunting Tower** (on the Crieff Road, 4 miles out) are other inexpensive stops.

PITLOCHRY, Perthshire, offers 6 hotel choices—all routine—but this jump-off point for the annual Games and for exploring the central Highlands can't be ignored because of its key geographical position. We'd pick the **Green Park**, 1/2-mile out of the center, as number one. Bankside situation nuzzling the Tummel River and man-made loch; lovely view of footbridge and majestic soaring mountains; first-rate management the courtly Graham Brown; yellow mansion with carved green eaves; comfortable but nonpalatial ambiance; cheerful waterfront dining salon; parkside wing with spacious rooms (we like #7, a corner double with a romantic vista). A tranquil slumberer which shutters from late October to the New Year. Baronial **Atholl Palace**, a colossal graystone eminence set in a hillside park, is a *pur sang* aristocrat. Since this is one of the Great Houses of Scotland, we were delighted to see that it is now being given the maintenance it deserves by its Trust Houses-Forte proprietors. Most rooms with private bath; many changes for the good. Everything is on the grand scale, including the tariffs. The next few years will be decisive for this noble blueblood. The now-sprinting **Hydro**, with 68 rooms but only 44 baths, has been making the waves crest in recent months. Enlarged dining

salon; lounges redecorated; Saturday night dancing; fresh carpets everywhere; gay wallpaper and brightness sprinkled throughout. We like the corner turret accommodations the most. This Hydro is bubbling with sometimes-misplaced enthusiasm. The midvillage **Fisher's** used to be better for food than for sleeping. **Scotland's**, another bustle-bustle hive, also plays host to the mass market. The **Pine Trees** is more of a converted estate than an inn-and-out hotel. It pines away on a lovely 14-acre sweep of Perthshire. Please don't miss the chance to dip your hook in Pitlochry's legendary stream—Killiecrankie. Gear and license for the day may be obtained locally. And who knows?—you may end up with a 40-lb. salmon! **Atholl Arms**, 7 miles north at *Blair Atholl*, is reportedly a worthy stop; we haven't seen it. The **Tilt**, another one on our futures list, is reported to be even better and more cheerful. **Crieff Hydropathic**, near *Crieff*—also in Perthshire—is said to be good for teen-agers, especially on holidays; inexpensive rates; many activities on tap, including horseback riding, Scottish dancing lessons, and a full program to keep them out of the shrubbery. Popular with oldsters, too.

PRESTWICK AND ENVIRONS   This, of course, is the location of the large international airport on Scotland's west coast. Since you may land or take off from here, we include some overnight suggestions in the region. The seaside **Queen's** now rules the waves. Extensive redecorations and additions; nice stone-and-brick dining room, snug cocktail lounge; units #8 and #9 are good waterfront doubles. Improving. **Towans** (adjacent to the airport) can be recommended only for its main-building accommodations; the newer wing is so basic and shoddy it is downright depressing. The **Golden Eagle,** on the noisy main thoroughfare in town, was razed and then rebuilt. Fair. **Sundrum Castle Hotel,** 4 miles outside of *Ayr*, has been lightly spruced up to the point where its old and newer elements combine for the barest of comforts. Walls 3 yards thick; shooting, riding, and fishing available; 26 rooms; low bath count; open April to October. A sundrum that's the least humdrum of a sorry lot unless the city-cited **Caledonian** lives up to its advance publicity. This should be a 130-nest haven for modernists and a vitally needed breath of fresh Ayr for the region. The **Station Hotel** in town is adequately managed by the Reo Stakis group. All 36 units come with private bath. This is a reliable chain. The **Savoy Park**, about the same size as Sundrum, boasts a residential situation, similar rents, and passable amenities.

The **Marine Hotel** at *Troon*, a quick skip from Prestwick Airport and 26 miles from Glasgow, offers an unprecedented 20 miles of golf courses in a row (whereon the British Open took place in '73). Almost 2-dozen units beautifully refashioned; lounge renewed; extended dining room with sea-and-links panorama; handsome cocktail bar; 70 rooms, 3 suites and 46 private baths. Heaven for golf bugs, but becoming a frequent target for short-stay excursionists and package trippers. *Turnberry*, further south along the coast, is listed separately.

RANNOCH   This lochside haven is west of Pitlochry at the foot of Schiehallion Mountain. The **Rannoch Apartments** here are said to be fine examples of luxury dwellingspace. If you wish to pause for more than just a day or two, it might be worth a look.

ST. ANDREWS tees off smartly with the **Old Course**, a member of the British Transport Hotels group which blankets the British Isles with top-grade oases. The handsome, sandstone-and-concrete, 74-room candidate is easily a master in this tourney. The modernistic house, bristling with balconies for lovely vistas, nuzzles only a pitch-and-putt from the 17th hole on its namesake, best-known of the 4 circuits at The Royal and Ancient Club; the back units overlook the flatter landscape of the Eden Course. Ground-level restaurant and bar, plus main dining room with balcony on the viewful 4th floor scanning the links, the bay, the seal islands, and the North Sea; wee Jigger Inn pub, in ancient style, adjoining the hotel for open-hearth merriment. Our recent rounds of golf and the tables couldn't have been more satisfying. Golf Clubs, even shoes, for rent; parking for 100 cars; most units in twin configuration; 6 singles and twice as many suites; full bath count. A straight-down-the-fairway winner on every score. Next, we would venture that the choice of most far-sighted swatters will be the tiny **Rufflets**—"farsighted," because its 20 bed-chambers (4 singles and 14 doubles) are almost always booked way, way in advance. Outskirts situation about 10 minutes by car to the tee; substantial cuisine; solid homespun comforts. The well-known **Scores**, on a hillock over-looking the course, is ideally situated. After seeming eons of lassitude, it is showing progress toward broad-spectrum improvement. Fresh entrance, re-ception foyer, and main-floor seafront lounge; redesigned bar; expanded mu-ral-clad dining room; carpeting replaced throughout; bath count upped to 20 for 38 bedrooms. We prefer front units with their white furnishings and club-swinging spaciousness. Although its score is better, here is still a duffer in resort hotel circles. The 50-room **Rusack's**, bordering the links, has been updated smartly by Proprietor John MacLaurin. Attractive lounge; agreeable dining room; 50-private baths. Twosomes, threesomes, foursomes, and vaster sums of North Americans are now finding this to be a delightful 19th hole. Easter to end-October only. Excellent location. The Imperial has been re-named the **Argyle**; its okay for budget-minded sportsmen. Three miles out, the aristocratic **Kincaple House** can be reserved only by special arrangement, but it offers a bonus in its 9 log cabins, which are always available to 4-person parties—ideal for families or golfing foursomes. Rates run around $320 per duffer for a week, and shorter holidays can be had here if bookings are slack. Facilities are excellent if you don't expect the Ritz. The ancient **Kinburn**, which functions all year, is drably rickety. The **St. Andrews**, with the same sea-and-course view as Scores, has renewed its entrance and brightened its interior. The **Star** also has leaped up in magnitude very recently.

When the golfing is done and evening light lingers in these northern skies, the penthouse bar and dining rooms of the **Old Course Hotel** are su-perb for views, service, and masterly cuisine. The upstairs spread of the **Niblick** often chips in with even better cookery; still, we're hooked on the panorama at our first choice. The **Grange**, an outskirts cottage, is better for atmosphere than for cookery. The **Commodore** is our runner-up. **Cross Keys** is a student pub.

ST. FILLANS The **Four Seasons** certainly must occupy one of the most eye-catching patches of Perthshire open to the tourist. Loch Earn, worthy of

a volume of poetry, is at your doorstep. Vaguely Scandinavain in tone; nice people; good food; moderate prices. What more could one ask?

SKYE   **Skeabost House**, 5 miles out of *Portree*, is a lochside country estate converted into a restful nook for sporting or lazy types. Rough shooting, river salmon fishing, trout angling or sea fishing as easily arranged as that soothing whisky and soda in the firelit lounge. Total of 28 rooms and 11 baths; private; lovely dining salon; inexpensive but tasteful furnishings; some handsome antiques. We suspect 3-day (or longer) stayers are preferred to overnighters. Soooooooo nice if you aren't looking for fireworks. The **Royal** now seems to be thriving and deserving of its great popularity. We must have a look soon. **Coolin Hills**, also in Portree, has 21 rooms, 9 private baths, and an unhappy mixture of genuine charm and crass modernisms. The **Sligachan** in *Sligachan* is renowned among mountain climbers. Since we spied flocks of slippers under the chairs by the entrance, we guessed most of the guests were high up in the heather. Of its 23 units, 9 come with a private bath; #41 is especially appealing for its sea and mountain view; though we've had only coffee here, we're told the food is the tip of local culinary peaks. Owner Ian Campbell and Manageress Hunter do their competent best to maintain the comfortable air of informality and the homey flavor for which it is so well known. The **Marine Trident** at *Kyleakin* (ferry stop on Inner Sound) is a simple, clean port-o'-call with 25 units. Bright dining-sitting room; no central heating; no private baths; Mr. MacKenzie is the owner. The **Dunvegan**, across the island, is a charmer. Its décor is simplicity itself, but somehow there's plenty of heart, which we hope its new owners will preserve faithfully. Attractions have included pony trekking, fishing, sailing, sketching, painting, pottery instruction, and angling courses. Good food; autumnal color everywhere; 16 rooms and 3 private baths; #11 is a viewful double; end-September is the local festival period. The 24-unit **Uig**, in a hamlet called *Uig*, is said to evoke utterances of delight that resemble its name. We'll fly by this Skyeway soon. All these houses operate chiefly during the April-to-October season. *Be sure to have reservations confirmed before going off on a Skye-lark,* since available beds on the island probably total no more than 500.

STIRLING   The **Golden Lion**, 1 hour from Edinburgh, has long been one of the most popular centers for excursionists to Loch Lomond, the Trossachs, and the Southern Highlands. This old and famous house now enjoys an 18-karat, $500,000 replating which includes a 58-room wing, renewed reception area, restyled dining room, excellent reports now on its cookery, Rose Bar and Thistle Lounge, revamped entrance, 1 late model elevator, and a carpark. Recommended. The **Sword**, on the outskirts caters more to diners than overnighters. 'Tain't much. About 20 minutes southwest, the 33-room efficiency-modern **Falkirk Metropolitan** also is available as an en route stopping point. Chiefly commercial, but suitable for the holiday trade.

TURNBERRY   The **Turnberry Hotel**, Ayrshire, 50 miles south of Glasgow and 15 miles from Ayr, is the favorite of the "Burns Country" excursionist, as well as many dyed-in-the-Shetland golfers. Each and every one of its 121 units

now with private bath or shower plus TV sets throughout; entire structure renewed; color-matched textiles to offset the stark-white walls; fresh bar; complete revamping of lounges, dining room, heating system, virtually everything from cellar to eaves. The selected grounds sanctified for British Open Golf Championships; tennis courts; indoor pool; dancing and movies; snooker room; minibus service to Prestwick and other getaway points; smoothly operated from check-in to *adios*. (The **Cairndale** at *Dumfries*, less expensive, also draws heavily among the Bobbie Burns pilgrims.)

Spain

S pain is California, Arizona, and Mexico on a huge canvas—with Colorado's towering mountains, Virginia's September sun, and Florida's dazzling blue waters thrown in for good measure. There's a balm, a warmth, a caress to Spain—a special *peace,* somehow; there's a feeling of being in a never-never land, where worry is part of the world left behind.

The country today is experiencing its first democracy in more than 4 decades, with a bicameral legislature and elected officials. The cautious guidance of King Juan Carlos I is manifest in every aspect of social change. He is definitely at the helm of this ship of state—the charming Queen Sofia at his side—successfully navigating between the shoals of absolutism on the right and the agitated waters of socialism on the left. There remain pockets of discord, to be sure, but in most of the centers and resorts that you will visit, the only unrest you are likely to experience will come from staying up too late and partying too much.

Catholicism is the primary religion, but others are practiced openly and in complete freedom. Education is free and compulsory between the ages of 8 and 14; women have the right to vote. Limited military service is mandatory for able-bodied men. In today's liberated atmosphere, individual provinces have a high degree of political autonomy, gambling in state-approved casinos flourishes, pornography is now sold openly on the streets, and new magazines voice fresh ideas with uninhibited zeal.

Though Spaniards are more and more devoted to soccer these days, the age-old blood sport of bullfighting still draws a throng. This occurs despite the falloff in strength and quality of the fighting *toros.* Outlanders often are not so discerning and with tourism soaring and the number of *corridas* more than quadrupled over these boom years, breeders are no longer able to turn out sound, sure-footed animals. April to mid-October is the season; if you go, be sure to sit on the *sombra* (the shady side of the ring), or *sol y sombra* (half and half), not on the *sol* (sunny side), unless you want an inexpensive seat and plan to leave after only one or two of the six kills. Ticket prices vary according to where you sit in relation to the sun, how close you are to the action, and who's fighting. They *cannot* be purchased far in advance; you'll have to wait

until you're there, and then ask your hotel concierge the week of the *corrida*. The better placements are quite expensive.

King Alfonso the Learned summed up his domain most lucidly and ably. Here's what you'll find today, just as he wrote in the thirteenth century:

"Spain has an overflowing abundance of every good thing . . . fruitful in crops, delicious with fruits, abounding in fish, rich in milk . . . plenteous in deer, well-stocked with horses, securely protected by castles, made glad by good wines, rejoicing in an abundance of bread . . . great wealth of minerals, silver and gold, precious stones and all kinds of marble, salt from land and sea and rock . . . lapis lazuli, ochre, clay, alum . . . sweet with honey and sugar, lighted with wax, seasoned with oil, and gay with saffron . . ."

☑ **TRANSPORTATION Taxis** Fares inching up far too frequently and fast, but still relatively cheap. Avarice seems to be the inevitable handmaiden of upward economic movement nationwide. As a typical illustration of their endless exploitation, just before going to press again we were cheated by still another crook. He asked Pts. 600 ($9) to drive us to Barcelona from the airport—a flat rate. When we said "Wow!", he shrugged and said the tariff had just doubled. Returning, we found the correct amount from one of the too-rare honest cabbies. Many cars now have fancy digital meters on which there are 4 buttons the driver presses: #3 is used within the major city limits. As soon as these are passed he presses #2, which ups the rate; #1 is for Sundays and holidays only, and #4, at this writing, is a dummy. Result: Exactly the same distance cost us 25% more. If you should ever run into trouble with any cabbies, don't pay a cent more than you should. Just demand that he drive you to the nearest *comisaría* (police station)—an order that will *always* settle his bleats.

Subways In the capital, you can often avoid the hassle with hacks by opting for this fast, clean and efficient public transport. It will set you back all of 10 pesetas per ride weekdays, swelling to 15 pesetas on Sunday. A timesaver and a moneysaver in an increasingly traffic choked metropolis.

Trains Improving notably. We've recently sampled the sleeper from Madrid–Cadiz–Madrid, and we were pleasantly surprised that the Wagons-lits' comfort standards have been boosted to match those in almost any European country today. Our 2 dinners in the restaurant cars were well prepared and served with deftness and grace.

Border-to-major-city and major-city-to-major-city schedules are quite comfortable—but be sure to pick the best expresses only. The *Talgo,* which formerly ran only from Irún to Madrid, now has another section which makes the Barcelona–Madrid connection in 9 hours, a cut of 4 hours in travel time; on the Barcelona half of the run, the tracks are still so mismated that you'll sympathize with the ice cubes of a cocktail shaker.

Passenger fares, though boosted by 22%, are still very modest by U.S. standards.

You can save 15% buying a pass called *chequetrén* for approximately $180, which can be used by a maximum of 6 people with no time restrictions or validation period. The value of the coupons also applies to Talgo or sleeping surcharges. Passengers over 65 receive a 50% reduction. The Eurailpass is a better bet—if you're traveling in other countries as well.

An enormous reconstruction program will eventually eliminate washboard roadbeds and replace the chicken-coop passenger coaches. More than half the steam-engine fleet has already been retired.By this year *in theory,* all locomotives are supposed to be electric or diesel-electric, with 1400 miles of trackage powered by current. But as a precaution, we repeat: Take most long-distance trains and carefully selected excursions with impunity; otherwise go by private car, hand-picked bus, or airplane.

☑ **FOOD**   Regional specialties are surprisingly good, and their varieties are enormous. But the manner of preparation is so stereotyped throughout the land (*e.g.,* whenever you order *Entremeses,* literally "between several dishes" or hors d'oeuvres, you'll get the identical portion of a lonely sardine, ham, cheese, tuna, olives, etc.), that the food tends to pall on American palates as soon as the novelty has worn off.

Except in a handful of international establishments, all cooking is done in strong olive oil—one full serving of which is guaranteed to entwine the stomach and gullet into a perfect clove hitch. To avoid Traveler's Complaint, insist that everything be *preparado en mantequilla* ("cooked in butter"). Salads, fruits, and fresh vegetables are safe wherever you go. Incidentally, it's *always* wiser to pass up milk and ice cream in smaller towns and hamlets.

The *nouvelle cuisine* has its practitioners here, as well. The movement began among Basque chefs and is spreading slowly throughout the nation.

Aside from straight meat and poultry, here are some of the favorites of visiting Yankees: langosta (the clawless local "lobster" which now puts a helluva bite on your wallet or purse), Paella (world-famous Valenciana specialty of rice, peppers, shellfish, chicken, saffron served in a huge frying pan), lenguado (sole, brother!), perdiz (small whole partridge, rich and savory), and centollo (tender, flavorful crab from the Bay of Biscay).

Roast lamb (cordero asado) and roast suckling pig (cochinillo) are generally the finest meats. Steaks? They're getting better. The quality of your meat nowadays often depends on the standard of restaurant you select.

Poultry? Also improving, but in some places, chickens and turkeys are athletic and stringy, with muscles like Larry Holme's. In the better restaurants, however, they range from good to delicious.

Exquisite fruit of all varieties, including the world's best oranges (winter only); honey with the fragrance of rosemary, marjoram, and orange blossoms; almond, nougat, marzipan, and tons of confections. As for cheeses, the better types include the Tetilla (soft and greasy), Cabrales (fermented and piquant), Burgos (all cream), Asturias (smoked-cured), and Manchego. Try the last, which has been molded in matting and preserved in oil; it's our favorite. Your friends might avoid you for 2 weeks afterward, but it's worth the gamble.

Officialdom also has taken steps to nip mounting inflationary trends by guaranteeing foreigners a full meal for much lower prices than the normal ones. This so-called Tourist Menu is also available in Deluxe establishments, but in these the maximum tariff has been set at about $8. Restaurants must indicate their category on their menus and other printed material: 5 forks for top-ranking houses straight down to 1 fork for Fourth-class

feederies. Cafeterias are distinguished by cups: 3 for Special grade ($3.50 for a Tourist Menu), 2 for First class, and 1 for Second class ($2.25 meals). Don't expect nectar and froufrou, because your limited choices obviously won't be the most savory on the griddle (and it also won't endear you to the restaurateur). But it is an ironbound warranty from the Chief of State that you can visit this land and be fed for very close to these amounts. What you'll be asked to swallow, however, is another matter. If your tastes hover above ground level, you can expect to shell out about $15 per meal in most good feederies and $25 to $40 in the classiest calorie castles.

★ **TIPS** Drink bottled water always, even though the tap water of the major cities is sweet and potable. If you like it without bubbles, ask for Solares; if you wish bubbles, any *agua mineral con gas* such as Lanjaron or Vichy Catalán will do.

If it's late spring (May or June), don't miss the wild Aranjuez strawberries and orange juice, a dessert for the gods—or the equally Olympian Aranjuez asparagus.

Spanish meal hours call for heroic belt-tightening and self-discipline on the part of the visitor. By the time most Americans finally sit down to tackle the groceries, they're so faint from hunger that an O'Sullivan's Heel Belle Hélène would be gratefully welcomed.

Breakfast is at your option, generally as early as or late as you choose—and 99½% of the time, it will be served on a tray or cart in your bedroom (although buffet breakfasts on the ground floor are more frequent now that staffs are being reduced in order to economize, most downstairs food services are closed until noon). Lunch is from about 2 P.M. to 3:30 P.M.—so it might be 4:30 P.M. before you stagger away from the table to your siesta. Dinner usually starts at about 9:30 P.M. at the earliest—which often brings the dessert and demitasse swinging down the aisle after midnight.

★ **TIP** In many of the typically Spanish, medium-priced establishments, strolling musicians festooned in colorful capes, ribbons, pantaloons and high stockings may enter to serenade you. While they purport to be graduate students picking up extra money for their studies, some of them seem to have been around since the invention of the lute. And though their musicianship is hardly up to the level of Andrés Segovia or Narciso Yepes, they often liberally seed their tambourines, which they pass around after a few numbers, with 100-peseta notes or even larger bills. Dropping in a few small coins is sufficient.

☑ **DRINKS** Sherry, the national wine, comes in 7 major types, some with a number of subclassifications; like port (Portugal), it is always bottled blended rather than "straight." Call it Jerez (pronounced Hair-eth), and drink it whenever you'd normally reach for a Coke at home. Through the revolving *solera* system of mixing, the old and the new vintages are combined to produce a product which is always standard. Years ago, a small inner circle of British pukka sahibs made superdry sherry a mark of social elegance in England; this foible, based on snobbism far more than on actual taste, quickly spread to America. During our residence in Spain, not only have we been weaned away from the Manzanillas, Finos, and other salty, acrid varieties, but we've also converted a number of our overseas house guests through a simple 2-glass experiment. If you'd like to try this for yourself, line up an order of Tio Pepe next to an order of Long Life (or

Dry Sack, in a Pinch)—and your palate will instantly decide which pleases you more. Tío Pepe ("Uncle Joe" in Spanish) has the big reputation and international markets, but it's too saline and puckery for our maximum enjoyment; Long Life (or any similar Oloroso blend) is old, soft, and golden, with just enough dryness and richness of body to give true delight. Perhaps you'll disagree.

Spanish red table wines are perhaps the most underrated of any in Europe. Countless gallons flow over the border each year to be sold as "French" types in France and elsewhere. Most of these reds resemble Burgundies rather than Bordeaux in their heaviness and fullness; the whites, not as fine, are most often too sweet. Some of the rosés (_rosadas_ such as Marquis de Riscal or Señorio de Sarria) are now surprisingly dry and crisp.

If we were forced to pick out 1-of-a-kind for comparatively expensive daily consumption, we'd take Marqués de Riscal for our red, Monopole for our white, Cepa de Oro for our Chablis, and Codorniu N.P.U. for our Spanish "champagne." Viña Pomal and Federico Paternina "Ollauri" also used to be superior rubies in their "Reserva" class, but their quality has fallen off shockingly since the flood of well-heeled tourists inundated Spain. All the "Reserva" and "Gran Reserva" types have deteriorated, in fact. Since there is no official _Appellation Contrôlée_ (as in France) to police the producers, any Juan Doe or John Smith can fill a bottle with 1964 rotgut, label it impressively as "Gran Reserva 1929," and place it on public sale! We make no specific accusations against any specific companies in this text—but we _do_ wish to point out this very curious anomaly. Monopole is our favorite dry white. Aside from N.P.U., the "champagnes" range from sweet to cloying to sick-making. You'll pay from $2 to $5 for all of these save the N.P.U., which runs perhaps $10.50 per bottle.

During the summer, be sure to sample the cooling, refreshing wine punch called Sangría. Choose your own base (red, white, or champagne); it will be served in a pitcher with orange slices, lemon slices, seltzer, sugar, and usually a tiny glass of cognac for flavor. Available anywhere at any mealtime; light, delicate, and much more delicious than the bottled junk which is sold in U.S.A.

Bourbon is available in many of the larger and better hotels, restaurants, and bars in the major cities. Rye drinkers too, have found adequate stocks in better pubs; Canadian Club, Seagram's, and other such nectars are now raising their noble hats behind Spanish bars. Prices nip up from about $20 to $25 per bottle in the marketplace.

Scotch? So many Spaniards are now drinking it that there is a surplus in various locally produced beverages. Most of it is genuine, but in nightclubs and other places you might still run into counterfeits—filthy tasting!—smuggled in from Tangier. Even a small pouring of either the honest or dishonest product will cost you plenty. Some years ago, Iberian highlanders from Segovia succeeded in producing a first-cousin facsimile of the barley brew. It is called DYC (pronounced as in Tracy). A fifth costs around $15. If DYC doesn't please you (and quite possibly it won't), switch to Fundador _coñac_ for your highball; Fundador is by far the leading choice among visiting Americans, because it's the only truly dry, champagne-type brandy on the local market. You'll pay perhaps 75¢ per glass or about $5 per bottle in the average bar or grocery shop. (It's around $14 in the States, now that it is sold on our side of the Atlantic.) Spaniards like Carlos I,

Gonzalez Byass Lepanto, Larios 1866, and similar distillates, but they're much too rich and too heavy for the typical stranger.

Liqueurs? Just name your favorite, and chances are good that they'll have it. Any big bar stocks at least 30 or 40 varieties.

Beer? All of the leading brands on the Continent are now imported Guinness and Pripps (Swedish) have set up their own Iberian plants. There are now 40 breweries spread over 25 of Spain's provinces. Almost everyone agrees that San Miguel has taken over the leadership among domestic labels.

For soft drinks, Coca-Cola, Pepsi-Cola and Fanta are omnipresent, even in the smallest villages; ginger ale and Schweppes tonic water and bitter lemon (other brands are fierce) can be had from place to place; lemonade *(limonada)* and orangeade *(naranjada)* are wonderful in winter and spring during and after the harvests, but poor in other seasons. *Horchata,* a milky beverage made from a native root, has an almondy flavor which is highly pleasing.

★ **TIP** Cuba Libre (rum and cola) fans will blanch at this tipple here, because the mixer is always compounded for the infinitely sweeter tooth of the Spaniard. Thus, if you're North American, be sure that the barman adds at least 10 drops of tart Rose's Lime Juice (or a similar product) to create the balance to which you're accustomed. Otherwise, it's sickening.

☑ **TIPPING** Give your taxi driver from 10% to 15% of the fares. (For more on this manifestation of highway robbery refer to Taxis under "Transportation.") Hotels extract their own service charge, usually 15%; to this, add the following: Baggage porter, 25 pesetas per person per suitcase; maid, 60 pesetas per day; room waiter, if used, 100 pesetas per day; concierge, minimum of 100 pesetas per day, not exceeding $10 per week, unless special services have been rendered; valet, if used, 50 pesetas per call. Restaurant waiters should be given 5% to 10% over and above the check, depending upon the quality of the attention. Theater ushers get 5 or 10 pesetas—or 15 pesetas if you are generous.

The people aren't as grabby as the Italians or the French; you'll like their independence and their effort to do a good job without the tip as the primary consideration.

☑ **CASINOS** Spain has given the nod to more than a dozen provinces to build casinos with up to 3 in each region. The restrictions include the stipulation that they not be located in the major cities. Naturally, tourist zones are favored, so if you are gamboling around Iberia this year and are looking for games of chance, be sure to check with your hotel concierge to learn where the nearest one is. As the government monitors all activities related to gambling, you can be pretty sure you will get a fair shake or shuffle.

☑ **THINGS NOT TO BUY** Spanish shawls. The only real Spanish shawls are antiques from China. This has become a tourist racket; prices have skyrocketed to heights that only a naïve visitor would pay. Handkerchiefs are often sleazy and expensive except in wonderful Bonet (see "Madrid" and "Mallorca" sections, and please remember that it has a gorgeous branch in Marbella). Beware also of the metal of the cheaper varieties of handbags or costume jewelry; it might tarnish all too soon.

☑ **LOCAL RACKETS**   The Barcelona docks are one of the rare places in Spain where the traveler must be wary. Porters sometimes overcharge; local ship's personnel, especially stevedores who load tourist automobiles aboard steamers, sometimes demand fantastic tips; certain cartage companies who transfer heavy baggage to hotels or connecting transportation centers run up enormous charges. Make your deal first, and be careful.

Watch *any* transaction *anywhere* with a gypsy. You can count on magnificent honesty from most Spaniards, but the gypsy lives by trickery.

"Ronson" and "Omega" lighters (asking price: $5), "Parker" pens (asking price: $9), and other "branded" merchandise are hawked by sidewalk sharpies in the cafés of the larger cities. It's all sucker bait, counterfeited in illicit Italian factories—and it's guaranteed not to work.

Keep an eye peeled for pickpockets in streetcars, buses, and crowded areas in Madrid, Barcelona, and the tourist centers. They and motorized bandits have sharply increased during the past few seasons. Many of them, naturally, are gypsies.

Forbid the shoeshine boys on the street to apply any kind of dye (not wax polish) or to change your heels. If you don't, you'll be sorry later.

Spanish integrity is 99.99% universal; as a nation and a people, you'll find far less thievery, far less cheating, and far less chicanery than in Italy, France, or most of the world—sad to say, even than in America. Discounting the gypsies, the moral standards are not only admirable but splendid.

☑ **INFORMATION CENTERS**   *Come*—in ones, twos, or tens of millions! The economy is now so highly geared toward visitors that it would be in serious trouble without them. To preserve the environment, there is chat that when Spain hits the 40-million mark (in fact it did, last year), it will begin discouraging callers at her portals. The taste of honey is so addictive, however, that we have serious doubts that this will *ever* occur. The Secretary of State for Tourism, Sr. Ignacio Aguirre Borrell, is one of Europe's most active and competent specialists in this lucrative market. Minister of Commerce and Tourism, the dynamic Sr. D. Juan Antonio Garcia Diez, also is handling an enormous responsibility with splendid results both for his nation and you.

The **Spanish National Tourist Office** (Dirección General de Empresas y Actividades Turísticas) has its headquarters at Alcala 44 in Madrid.

The outstanding triumph has been the construction and operation of approximately 83 government-sponsored inns (*paradores,* hostels, mountain lodges, etc.)—one of the most farsighted touristic ventures in Europe. Their popularity is so enormous that the expansion program had to be pepped up. As a result, this year's adventurer will have a bevy of new ones at his disposal. These are practical, plain, clean hotels (not Deluxe), uniquely Spanish in design and furnishings, set up noncompetitively with private industry to open virgin tourist areas. Some of them are remodeled castles. The basic rate runs from about $8 to $20 per person, exclusive of meals, service, taxes, and extras. Visit or write to the Tourist office for a list of these colorful and reasonably priced vacation centers; they will handle your arrangements. This chain now has an American repre-

sentative: Marketing Ahead, Inc., 515 Madison Ave., N.Y., which handles its reservations. Some travel agents dislike them because they pay no commissions.

In the United States, there are official information branches in New York, (Sr. D. Enrique Garcia-Herraiz is the chief), Chicago, San Francisco, St. Augustine, plus San Juan (P.R.). They are also in most European capitals, in Latin America, and in North Africa.

CITIES

MADRID This capital of more than 3 million people is right smack in the middle of the country. It's the perfect hub of the wheel, with spokes radiating in every direction—physically, politically, and socially. In size it ranks just under Philadelphia; in temperature, hotels, food, and gracious living, it's hard to find an equal in Europe. May and October are the best months; midwinter is sometimes surprisingly cold, due to the city's situation and altitude. It's uncomfortably hot for only about 2 weeks per annum—and many hotels are now fully or at least partially air-conditioned. Increasing air pollution, however, is a menace that authorities are now trying to control. On a muggy afternoon your eyes may smart, but when the wind blows and the morning skies are a cornflower blue, they might tear in awe at Spain's glittering metropolitan diadem. We like Madrid at *any* time; it's a constant wonder and delight. To bypass it would be like visiting France without seeing Paris.

Sightseeing One of the first stops for any art lover is, quite naturally, **El Prado** (closed Mon. but open every other day of the week and from 10 A.M. to 1:30 P.M. Sun.). With its staggering treasures of El Greco, Velázquez, Goya, Murillo, Botticelli, da Vinci, Tintoretto, Rubens, Van Dyck, and dozens of others, we consider this, as a matter of personal taste only, the number one art gallery of the world—despite its bad hanging and poor lighting. The increasing pollution of the capital's air and the oral and skin emissions of up to 10-thousand visitors per day were making its 2500 paintings "ill," according to Curator Xavier de Salas who has at last won the battle to install air conditioning plus a brand-new security system. The project, costing $15 million, also includes a conference room, a research center, and a café. In addition to this there's the **Royal Palace** (open mornings and afternoons), the suburban **Pardo Palace**, the not-to-be-missed **Museo de Lázaro Galdeano**, the fascinating **Rastro** ("Thieves' Market"—try it on Sunday morning, bargain for everything, and be careful about pickpockets!), **University City** with its **Museum of Contemporary Art** (or another one at Calvo Sotelo 20), the **National Archaeological Museum**—all the Baedeker wonders rolled into one, for which local guidebooks are available at hotels or the Tourist Office. The **Wax Museum** in the Central Colón delights kiddies and parents alike. Cortés, the Conquistadores, Cervantes, Romeo and Juliet, El Cordobés, Louis Armstrong, Einstein, Rasputin, Wild West movie sets, and scores more, all backgrounded with appropriate music, are represented. Hours are 10:30 to 1:30 and 4 to 10: open Sundays without that midday siesta.

Surroundings of Madrid? Bus excursions are operated on various days of the week to 5 popular suburban targets; check with your concierge for schedules and details. **Toledo**, 44 miles to the south, has often been called "the most perfect and brilliant record of genuine Spanish civilization." Most unfortunately, however, it has become one of Europe's biggest and worst tourist traps. The setting is magnificent, the **Cathedral** is a treasure house of art, **El Greco's** house is routinely interesting (his best works have gone elsewhere)—but so many souvenir hawkers and curbstone promoters greet the swarming armies of sightseers that the atmosphere is increasingly tinny, mechanical, and cheap. *Don't buy a single piece of merchandise in this city;* the sharks who run some of the supposedly most respectable shops charge up to 40% more than you'll pay in Madrid for the identical item. (We must interject a personal note here: Since we first published this admonition in '56, the excursion guides have lost so many commissions from these Toledo sharpies that they've launched a major campaign against this book, our personal integrity, and once, with an anonymous death threat sent by some hotheaded paranoid, against our life. Some of them, for example, have "stood there and watched with their own eyes" while Madrid shopkeepers "bribed" me with "$5000 in cash" to "keep the business from leaving the capital." Because the Spanish State Tourist Office and I are eager to crack down on these vipers, any reports of this type of incident—date, time, name of bus company, and name or description of the guide, forwarded to me personally at Formentor, Mallorca, Spain—will help us a lot.) **El Escorial**, 31 miles out, has Philip II's famous castle-monastery filled with paintings, books, royal tombs, and royal antiquities. **Valle de los Caidos** ("Valley of the Fallen"), Generalísimo Franco's tombsite and monument to casualties on *both* sides of the Spanish Civil War, is so breathtaking in concept and so colossal in scope that it might be straight from the time of the Pharaohs. A mountain of rock, topped by a cross 500-feet high and 300 feet across the arms (elevator inside), has been converted into a gigantic basilica and great nave large enough to hold 4 good-size churches with space to spare; you'll find the 8 magnificent Tapestries of the Apocalypse, an 800-foot crypt, an exquisitely carved transept, a cloister, a monastery, a novitiate, an ecclesiastical study center, and a hostel. Approximately 30 miles from the capital; ATESA buses cover both Los Caidos and neighboring Escorial for honest fares that include the usual third-rate lunch. But don't let the quality of any meal interfere with your journey here, because to miss it would be like going to Rome and skipping St. Peter's or the Colosseum. **Avila**, 70 miles to the northwest of El Escorial, is a fairy-tale city from a distance, with 86 towers and a medieval wall rising starkly from the landscape; when you've seen this, however, you've had the frosting and top 2 layers of the cake—because there's nothing especially spectacular inside.

Our enthusiastic preference goes to the **Segovia–La Granja** tour—by far the most rewarding itinerary of this group, in our opinion. If you're on your own, you can easily pause for an inspection of the "Valley of the Fallen," which

is en route. Then continue on via the road that tunnels 1½ miles under the Guadarrama Mountain Range; the small toll is negligible for a look at this engineering marvel. Segovia, 60 miles from the capital, couldn't be more Castilian in flavor, with moats, castles, a marvelous **Roman aqueduct** (now in need of structural muscle), the renowned **Zuloaga Museum of Ceramics** (which most travelers especially enjoy), and the internationally famous **Mesón de Cándido** restaurant. On the return trip, an alternate routing that is not far out of the way will put you in storybook La Granja, the "Spanish Versailles," with its fountains, gardens, summer palace, and the nation's finest tapestry collection.

Festivals? Nearly every city, town, and village has its own *fiesta.* The majority are in summer, but there are also spectacular celebrations in spring and fall. Far, far too many even to begin to list in these pages—but drop a line to your nearest official Spanish outlet for their free booklet, *Festivales de España.*

The Spanish National Tourist Office can also furnish you with more than 70 gratis publications covering the principal sights of every region.

MADRID HOTELS Quick Reference Table

Price categories by national (not U.S.) standards.

EXPENSIVE:

Luz Palacio Paseo de la Castellana 67. Tel. 4425100; Telex 27207; 200 rooms. P. 821
Meliá Madrid Princesa 27. Tel. 2418200; Telex 22537; 248 rooms. P. 820
Miguel Angel Miguel Angel 29. Tel. 4420022; Telex 54134; 307 rooms. P. 819
Palace Plaza de las Cortes 7. Tel. 2211100; Telex 22272; 526 rooms. P. 820
Princesa Plaza Princesa 40. Tel. 2422100; Telex 44377 P. 820
Ritz Paseo del Prado 5. Tel. 2212857; Telex 22272; 175 rooms. P. 820
Villa Magna Paseo de la Castellana 22. Tel. 2614900; Telex 22914; 200 rooms. P. 819

UPPER MODERATE:

Castellana Castellana 57. Tel. 4100200; Telex 27686; 378 rooms. P. 821
Eurobuilding Padre Damián 23. Tel. 4577800; Telex 22548; 570 rooms. P. 822
Plaza Plaza de España 8. Tel. 2471200; Telex 27383; 354 rooms. P. 822
Sideral Casado del Alisal 14. Tel. 4671200; 50 rooms. P. 822
Wellington Velazquez 8. Tel. 2754400; Telex 22700; 325 rooms. P. 821

MODERATE:

Carlton Paseo de las Delicias 26. Tel. 2397100; 150 rooms. P. 824
Claridge Plaza de Conde Valle Suchil 5. Tel. 257300; Telex 22058; 150 rooms. P. 823
Colón Doctor Esquerdo 117. Tel. 2730800; Telex 22984; 350 rooms. P. 824
Don Quijote Av. Federico Rubio y Gali 145. Tel. 4592100; 101 rooms. P. 823
Meliá Castilla Capitán Haya 43. Tel. 2708003; Telex 23142; 1000 rooms. P. 821
Mindanao S. Francisco de Sales 15. Tel. 4495500; Telex 22631; 300 rooms. P. 822
Pintor Goya Goya 79. Tel. 2254521; 170 rooms. P. 823
R. Marquina Prim 11. Tel. 2229010; 17 rooms. P. 824
Residencia Florida Norte P°. de la Florida 5. Tel. 2416190; Telex 23675; 338 rooms. P. 823

Sanvy Goya 3. Tel. 2760800; 109 rooms. P. 823
Serrano Marqués de Villamejor 8. Tel. 2257564; 36 rooms. P. 824
Suecia Marqués de Casa Riera 4. Tel. 2316900; Telex 22313; 64 rooms. P. 823

LOWER MODERATE:
Alcalá Alcalá 66. Tel. 2251650; 153 rooms. P. 824
Apartamentos Quintana Quintana 22; 56 rooms. P. 825
Cuzco Av. Generalísimo 55. Tel. 4560600; Telex 22464; 331 rooms. P. 825
Ecuestre Zurbano 79. Tel. 2539400; Telex 27578; 126 rooms. P. 825
Gurtubay Gurtubay 6. Tel. 2258692. P. 825
Hostal Amaya Av. José Antonio 12. Tel. 2222151. P. 825
Mayorazgo Flor Baja 3. Tel. 2472600; 204 rooms. P. 824
Pensión Claris Plaza de las Cortes 4. P. 825
Pensión Easo Plaza de las Cortes 3. Tel. 2212888; 10 rooms. P. 825
Pensión Embajada Joaquín García Morato 5. Tel. 4473300; 67 rooms. P. 825
Pensión Ferrer Ferrer del Río 6. P. 825
Pensión Galiano Alcalá Galiano 6. 19 rooms. P. 825
Pensión Gaos Mesonero Romano 14. Tel. 2316305. P. 825
Pensión Mori Plaza de las Cortes 3. Tel. 2219925. P. 825
Pensión Rosalía de Castro Campomanes 6. Tel. 2479204. P. 825
Residencia Bretón Bretón de los Herreros 29. Tel. 2547400; 57 rooms. P. 824

ENVIRONS:
Monte Real Arroyo Fresno 17. Tel. 2162140; Telex 22089; 80 rooms. P. 821
Victoria Palace Juan de Toledo 4. Tel. 2961200; 90 rooms. P. 826

AIRPORT:
Alameda Ctra. de Ajalvir, Km 12. Tel. 2055040; 150 rooms. P. 825
Barajas Aeropuesto. Tel. 2054296; Telex 22255; 230 rooms. P. 825
Motel Osuna Luis de la Mata 30. Tel. 7418100; 175 rooms. P. 825

Hotels In the Spanish capital, they're wonderful: Plush, luxurious, clean, and with superb facilities and service.

The sparkling midcity **Villa Magna** is our *número uno* choice. Extravagant garden fronting its set-back entrance; balconied 9-story structure of polished marble, glass, and stainless steel; breathtaking Carlos IV lobby by world-famous Jansen of Paris; opulent dining salon and Rue Royale restaurant; Mayfair Bar in English motif plus burgundy-banquetted Bonbonierre imbibery; aristocratic lounge; shops, hairdresser, and secretarial services; sauna; subterranean garage. All feathernests amply proportioned; 2 large easy chairs; double-glazed windows; individual thermostats; radio and TV; compartmented baths with twin basins. Concierges Ovejero and Pacheco are tops in their trade. A bouquet to Director Antonio Lopera, always a friend to the traveler. A pearl that we recommend with cheers.

The **Miguel Angel** (Spanish, of course for "Michelangelo") is, indeed, a masterpiece of the luxury hotel arts—traditional values supplemented by modern materials and thoughtful techniques. The lounges are vast, with icelands of chandeliers—even with crystal balustrades; the Farnesio bar pulses quietly under a smoked-mirror ceiling; the Zacarias restaurant-cum-discothèque is down a few steps off the lobby; a garden court offers apéritif tables and stone

sculpture by Assler (reminiscent of Lipchitz); the indoor pool is airy, with cheerful white furniture on its apron; there's a Finnish sauna, a Turkish bath, hairdresser, and a shopper's lane. Upstairs, the corridors are sedate, but too dark for our tastes; the spacious bedrooms feature silk spreads and textiled walls, brass sconces, silent valets, deep carpeting, TV-music consoles, huge closets, air conditioning, and superb furnishings. A broad canvas for a rich and colorful palette. We hope that its new management will maintain its vital spirit.

The patrician **Ritz** is quiet, elegant, smallish, and in a major state of flux as we write these words. A new administration came to bat here and at the Palace club (see immediately below); so far we have not been impressed with the overall performance between these two. We hope that some of the dated baths and furnishings as well as some of the poor color blends will be exorcised in the promised rejuvenation. Basically, it's a fine little establishment when in form. You'll find one of the most willing staffs on the Continent. Veteran Director Pablo Kessler, whose warmth and gentle courtliness match the quiet urbanity of his landmark, remains at its helm. The highly competent Chief Concierge Jesus Sarrionandia typifies the topflight personnel—people who have served loyal clients for more than a quarter-century.

The **Palace** is one of Europe's largest hotels; the entire house is air-conditioned; most of the bathrooms have individual telephone, shower, and tub. The public rooms are spacious; the bar is famous as the most popular meeting place in the capital. What concerns us at this juncture is whether the new owner may be allowing this once-proud house to slide downwards while paying too much attention to the bottom line. Many floors are now without room service, requiring the client to slog to the restaurant and sometimes wait in line up to an hour for his or her wake-up coffee—a sad demonstration of cost-cutting management and we hope not illustrative of the general policy. Handsome entrance and baggage area; gorgeous handwoven carpeting; richly attractive Grill; dining room cuisine fair; garage; telephone service still spotty but improving (this headache is due largely to the city exchange, not so much to the hotel). Let's keep an eye on this former favorite and see how it progresses.

The gleaming white, 14-story, **Meliá Madrid** is the evolutionary zenith of Spain's most ubiquitous tour tycoon, bus operator, and private innkeeper, don José Melia. Spacious lobby cleverly architected to kindle warmth in an essentially cool milieu; Don Pepe Grill up 1-flight, bigger, impersonal, less ingratiating Princesa Restaurant in the same level; Ebano ("Ebony") Bar with dimensions too open for intimacy; adjoining lounge; Bing-Bong Night Club with discothèque. Rooms comparatively commodious and air-conditioned, all with TV, refrigerator, piped music, wall-to-wall carpeting, and handsome fabrics; baths small but efficient; showers over nonskid tubs. The 3rd floor is devoted to a quintet of Deluxe suites, with a hand-picked staff to coddle their occupants. The cuisine is fair to middling; the welcome is friendly; the concierge and his staff are affable and willing. Although its mass appeal has left a patina of commercial chill, for standardized convenience, modern urbanity, and luxurious amenities in surroundings of contemporary good taste, this metropolitan stalwart is good.

The **Princesa Plaza** makes a dignified bow to modernity, nicely blended with an amplitude of well-chosen deluxe amenities. Vast, stalwart edifice;

spacious lobby and lounges; yellow-toned Margarita restaurant; Triángulo cafetería; Bar Chic; hairdresser; saunas and massage facilities; underground parking. The large number of suites are exceptionally plush, and even normal bedrooms reflect excellent taste. We find it restful and efficient—in the better traditions of the 21st century.

The **Wellington** is fashionably moored on the fringes of sylvan Retiro Park. Recently, 140 bedchambers were rebuilt and 7 suites with kitchenette added; all units now have air conditioning, taped music, TV, hand-stitched broadlooms, and attractive _seregrafía_ tiles in the baths; dive into one facing the pool if you can. Dining room plus wood-paneled El Fogón grill; banquet hall; efficient phone exchange; garage. A sound plant, but on our last inspection we wondered if the inspired zeal of earlier days was not wearing thin.

The 15-story **Meliá Castilla**, one of the most massive shelters abroad, is an "aparthotel" run as a concession for a multitude of investors. Vast convention facilities for assembly of 2500 at a single roundup; kitchen capacity of 10-thousand hot meals per day (well, _warm_ anyway); 3-level brick-toned Hidalgo Grill plus a cafeteria; attractive La Marisquería seafood nook; everything under the sun for the wanderer, especially if he and she are business oriented. Despite efforts to the contrary, the lobby, the public rooms, and the ambiance are as _intime_ as Grand Central Station. Upstairs, the pinched "efficiency" bedchambers each offer radio, TV, and an elfin bath. This monster is frankly designed and operated more and more for the conventioneer—and not the lavishly open-pursed one, either. With it has come a high chill factor.

The sumptuous **Monte Real** is in a special category because of its outskirts situation at Calle Arroyo del Fresno 1—15 minutes out by taxi and just a potent mashie shot from Generalísimo Franco's country estate, El Pardo. Tennis courts; crescent-shape swimming pool; summer bar in Philippine motif; garden-bowered with bouquets of color; nearby golf course. Within, you'll find a pale-blue Frenchy dining room, a downstairs Grill with Signac and Matisse paintings (other oils by Murillo, Dalí, and a trove of Impressionists displayed elsewhere), a nightclub, and other appurtenances. Pleasant accommodations; duplex units with 2 bathrooms the premium retreats. The cuisine on our stopover was average, not extraordinary. For any well-capitalized traveler who wishes to avoid the cacophonous throb of big-city jitters, this is an elegant answer.

The **Castellana** offers one of the capital's friendliest staffs, for our pesetas. Shopping promenade with plaza effect; taper-lit restaurant with king-size buffet Saturday nights; adjoining Coffee Shop; grill merged with ballroom; Patio Jardin, with its guitar strummings nightly. It boasts the La Ronda bar, the rather high-priced Oxeito nook for _marisco_ (seafood) niblets from noon to midnight, a Turkish bath, some impressively viewful double suites, management by Miguel Ordinas, who trained at London's Savoy, and a competent concierge in Chief Alfredo Molero or his Assistant Jose de la Pompa. You'll also find an 80-car garage and other supplementary facilities. If the chambermaids, carpenters, and painters were only a smidgen more enthusiastic about their trades, this house would rate still higher in our rankings.

The suave, stainless-steel-and-marble-fronted **Luz Palacio** stands 9 proud stories above a residential block of the Paseo de la Castellana. Totally air-

conditioned, effective, gracious entrance and lobby; cleverly illuminated adjoining bar; attractive food displays; evening dancing in the spacious yellow-
hued dining room; careful maintenance; a pervading atmosphere of soft, modern luxury befitting its Deluxe station. Ample garage space and normal
conveniences. All units with bath, shower, and radio, plus TV on request;
predominance of smallish doubles, which they prefer to rent even to lone
clients; tasteful appointments which make courageous use of unusual color
combinations. Management by Manuel Alvarez. *Saludos* for its physical
amenities.

The air-conditioned **Mindanao** makes its Deluxe headquarters in the University District. We'd score it B-plus. L-shape lobby; coolish Domayo restaurant; evenings-only Club Mindanao; adjoining Coffee Shop; dimly lighted,
lazy-S-form bar; somewhat uninviting P-shape swimming pool in the basement. Predominance of twin units; a few suites and singles available; small
bedchambers for stout rates. Except for a few aesthetic and spatial drawbacks,
here's one which we like.

The fully air-conditioned **Plaza**, One of Europe's tallest hotels, has a wonderful penthouse. On its 25th and 26th floors, you'll find dancing, a swimming
pool, and roof-garden dining, plus an unparalleled view of the city; at teatime
(7 P.M. to 9:30 P.M.), when 2 orchestras play, it is particularly popular. Spanish
flavors both in décor and in its all à la carte cuisine; huge panoramic windows;
an urbane bar with a small lounge; no groups ever accepted in this area.
Swarms in sterile lobby; boutiques, a drugstore, and travel agency on mezzanine; downstairs Coffee Shop; big dining room; brightened corridors. Motorists
have access to the underground garage across from the entrance. The king-size
frame contains 90 suites (29 duplex, featuring a tiny refrigerator and bar); none
is elaborate, but for their layout, comfort, and garniture, they are among the
better buys in town. Increasingly commercial but still acceptable.

The **Eurobuilding** is composed of 2 attractive, angular edifices of laminated
white marble. While the 8-story wing contains the posher pads, another 15-floor
segment is devoted to more cost-conscious voyagers and convention groups.
A quartet of restaurants, with the Balthasar, in Arabian reds, offering the most
elegance; 4 distinctive bars; massive congress quarters; concourse of shops;
sauna and garden-sited pools; barber and hairdresser; 700-car garage. Generous spread of 150 suites in the high-priced plush section; 450 bedchambers in
the other block. Full air conditioning; balconettes; TV and piped music; pastel
color schemes; modern furnishings; good baths. General Manager Mateo
Bosch keeps this swing-wing sizzler on its course. We'd buy a billet here
anytime.

The 4-star **Sideral** is located 50 yards from Retiro Park and 50 yards from
the Prado. Air-conditioned; conventional lobby with dimly illuminated snack
bar to its rear; colorful but routine restaurant; large, attractive, gaily decorated,
especially pleasant Bodega Castellana with roast lamb and suckling pig its
specialties; garage for 50 cars; piped music. In general, we are even more
enthusiastic about its 45 doubles and 5 singles upstairs than about its public
precincts; in addition to a comfortable marble bath with 2 washbasins as
adjuncts to the former, each boasts a small but cozy separate sitting room as
well as a balcony done with charm.

Pintor-Goya, named, of course, for the great Spanish artist, makes its address appropriately at Goya 79, a brushstroke from picturesque Retiro Park and the Serrano shops. A tableau of tourist comforts fills its 9-story canvas. Lobby verdant with cascading flora; glass-hemmed garden; restful peacock-blue salon; small dining room that seems an afterthought; good barber; partly submerged garage. All quarters are tastefully blessed with pleasing pastels, chilled air, and commodious baths. A sound and artfully conceived composition.

The **Suecia** ("Sweden"), conveniently sited behind the Cortes, is now only fair in our judgment. Except for the ground-level lobby, the first 4 floors of its building are occupied by Swedish offices (a bonus in silence for the upper tiers of bedchambers). Entrance on a tiny street; maintenance falling off, we think; sauna (men only); 66 small rooms, all with old-fashioned baths, all air-conditioned, and all with Swedish-style furnishings; Bellman Restaurant. Here's a nonfancy operation.

Hotel Residencia Florida Norte greets you with a handsome high-ceilinged lobby lined with light gray marble. Strikingly lighted salon to right with coffee-brown wall-to-wall carpeting; harmonious furnishings, and huge Gobelins; Bar Goya on open mezzanine communicating with cafeteria; world-of-tomorrow subterranean restaurant; TV lounge; gift shop; hairdresser and barbershop; 100-slot garage. All units come with air conditioning, taped melodies, and a Hiltonish brand of appeal; all but the smallest singles have an independent seating area and ample dimensions. Director Luis Peiró has created one of the happiest recent additions to the Madrid hotellerie circle.

The **Emperatriz** was a total disappointment to us on our latest reinspection. We can't recommend it personally.

Don Quijote tilts in the bucolic meadows of the Cuidad Universiteria district. Aluminum and glass micro-Hilton concept with a pseudo-Spanish flavor; indoor and outdoor swimming areas; sunken lounge dotted with brown and black overstuffed chairs; paneled bar in tasteful pastels; spotless 25-table restaurant opposite. The corridors linking the 8 singles, 84 doubles, and 8 suites on 4 floors are punctuated with artistic interpretations of you-know-who; the reading lamps are good; the firm beds are inscribed with quotations from . . . right, again.

The **Principe Pío** is too routine to inspire much enthusiasm from us.

The **Sanvy** features an English Club (attractive as an extra residents' lounge), an American-style cafeteria with Spanish-slanted vittles, a ballroom, the violet-and-white Victor Bar-Discothèque, a beauty salon, and a barbershop. While few of these featherings appeal to our personal taste (we found them garish), we must commend the dedication of its proprietor. Pool still a popular puddle for Madrid's summer heatnicks; every unit with private plumbing; 4 suites on each of its 6 floors; no singles, but doubles rented at lower rates to lone wanderers. In general, not our pick.

The **Claridge**, a 3-star hostelry under the same administration as the Wellington, stands at Calle Conde de Casal 6, across Retiro Park. It's a long haul from the city's heartbeat. Corner situation rising 15 floors above the portals; 180 rooms, all with bath, shower, and air-conditioning; modern dogleg lobby with a coffee shop, a small food stall, and a cocktail lounge at the paw's end;

noise level heightened by bar music; unfancy but adequate cellar dining room with open kitchen; dimensions inclined to be dwarfish. Director José Navarro serves as boniface to many groups; some readers like it, others aren't so keen on the staff attitudes. A bit remote geographically, but a worthwhile hideaway for the price.

The **Menfis** seems to us to be slipping.

The 50-room **Serrano** is only a hop from the U.S. Embassy and around the corner from one of the most fashionable shopping avenues in the city. Small, 1970-vintage structure with no restaurant, but a cozy pub with snacks; spotless chambers in contemporary Iberian motif; all doubles with Frigobar; administration by young, shy, and competent Don José Prados; extra-careful maintenance; eager and kindly staff.

The **Carlton**, in a noisy, unattractive situation beyond the railway station, is gradually becoming fuddy-duddy and spiritless. Small dimensions with onionskin-paper-thin walls; plain, uninspired décor. Tolerable only.

The **Velázquez** was in sore need of a major restoration on our latest study. Not recommended.

The **Colón** issues oodles of charm but is handicapped by its location across Retiro Park from the main shopping district. Monolithic construction with balconied façade shedding tiers from the 10th-floor down; main restaurant, grill, and a cluster of boutiques directly below; penthouse dining room, bar, and pool. All units with air conditioning, bath, and radio; simple, fresh, functional décor that is kept sparkling clean; ample living space for the bracket. Except for its distance, normally a sound value for your peseta.

Residencia Marquina is operated by the owners of an adjoining movie theater (Calle Prim 11, off the Castellana near Av. José Antonio), in which the clients will find their hotel restaurant and cafeteria. Less than 2-dozen accommodations, but each with bedchamber, sitting room, and bath, plus space for a proposed kitchenette; full air chilling; sufficient luggage storage areas; slim elbowroom, in keeping with its reasonable tabs. Reserve ahead, and don't expect cosmopolitan fireworks, because—like its address—it's Prim but not posh.

The **Alcalá**, near Retiro Park, is a quiet retreat with a small lobby-lounge and circular iron hearth, a better-than-average restaurant (under outside concession and with Basque specialties), cheerful halls, discreet lighting, and a kindly staff. Air conditioning throughout; dual-glaze windows on the front to blunt the din of the busy street; TV and piped music for further soothing. Narrow bedchambers with dark furniture, full-length mirrors, and walnut-paneled walls. Getting better each season and deserving of its higher turnover.

The **Mayorazgo** welcomes visitors with a Castilian lobby. It is soothingly and conveniently set back from the street. A fresh lounge, replete with fireplace and stained-glass windows, also offers a warm welcome. Units here are sized on the small side and range in ambiance from adequate to pleasant. Moving up.

The still-youthful, 6-floor **Residencia Bretón** has a pleasantly modern lobby from which a booze bar, snack bar, and breakfast nook are separated by screens. Among its 56 nests with bath, 10 of the singles contain limited plumbing. While this compact hostelry does not sparkle with much character or personality, we like it and hope you might too.

At the **Hotel Ecuestre** a vast palette of browns from sand to chocolate prevails from the lobby to the dining room to the upstairs corridors to the furniture and textiles of the accommodations and probably to the house cat (if there is one). Most of its 126 retreats (6 singles) are not only decent in size but present the *rara avis* of 2 closets; each has its viable bath which, even without the ring around the tubs, is brown.

The **Cuzco**, quite a stretch from the center, wings in with 310 accommodations, none of which are singles. Large characterless lobby; no restaurant; brightly lit snack bar and café; clean and efficiently executed, but sterile and impersonal in tone and atmosphere.

El Coloso, **Emperador**, and **Zurbano** are all off our list.

Pensions? Zillions, ranging in quality from superior to stinky. **Gurtubay** (Calle Gurtubay 6) is fair enough. **Apartamentos Quintana** (Quintana 22) caters only to visitors who will bide for a week or more. Its 56 small modern flats are neat; all offer a tiny kitchen, fireplace, terrace, bath, shower, private safe, and bookcases. Not bad. For older folk, **Pensión Galiano** (Alcalá Galiano 6) is a quietly charming and dignified pension. Each of its 19 rooms (17 of them doubles and all on 1 floor) with bath; spacious and well maintained; only Spanish is spoken. Reserve well in advance. The once-praised **Pensión Ferrer** (Ferrer del Río 6–8) has sunk so far down on our charts that we can no longer recommend it. Sorry. There are other pensions on other flights of the same building where you might find better pickin's. Also reported to be worth a try are Pensións **Claris** (Plaza de las Cortes 4), **Easo** and **Mori** (both at Plaza de las Cortes 3), **Embajada** (Joaquín García Morato 5), **Gaos** (Mesonero Romanos 14), and **Rosalía de Castro** (Campomanes 6). **Hostal Amaya** (Av. José Antonio 12) seems to be going down for the count; 1—2—3—4—. Since sparse savings accrue with fewer meals or units without private plumbing, order the works.

The **Barajas**, on a hillock overlooking Madrid's busy airport, is a spacious perch for your capital fly-over. Its director is veteran hotelier José María Carbó Jr. The 4-level, red-brick, linear structure contains 230 air-conditioned and jet-proof bedchambers, all with bath—and many with private balcony too. The wide-angle suites are extraordinarily appealing; these nests are equipped with TV sets, full dressing rooms, circular tubs, and bars. It also boasts the Toledo and El Porche restaurants (the latter is alfresco), El Patio Coffee Shop, Las Brisas Club (by the pool), Discothèque 747, a shaker of bars, a beauty salon, a sauna, a gymnasium, and convention facilities; a heated pool also gushes an invitation to relax. As a ★ ★ ★ ★ ★-Deluxe springboard, this one is a vitally needed addition on the touristic circuit. Our only cavils are the smotheringly awful air conditioning in our latest double bedroom which in the morning made us feel as if we'd slept in a World War I submarine (the windows are sealed for soundproofing)—plus the fact it is so overbusy that its maintenance had aged and crumbled notably since our latest prior overnight. How we hope that that this once-super house will correct these deficiencies! Although we've often inspected but never courted the Sandman in the neighboring **Alameda**, newer and with the same ownership, next time we'll see if we can awaken without CO_2 turning us temporarily into zombies.

Closer to town, the **Motel Osuna** is a vastly more modest but cheery operation. Its restaurant, lobby, lounge, and double tier of rooms overlook a

lovely garden and swimming pool. A cutie for budgeteers in search of peace.

P.S. For Excursionists From Madrid: **Victoria Palace** is practically the only show in *El Escorial*—aside from the basilica, of course. Though it boasts a pool, it still doesn't make much of a splash with us.

Restaurants   There are 2 leading restaurants in Madrid, both extraordinarily fine.

Sharing the head of the list is **Horcher** (Alfonso XII 6)—superb, intimate, and, of course, expensive. The late Otto Horcher, its founder and a legend in his own time, turned over full reins to his son, Moppi, who with Maître Cristóbal forms a gracious hosting team. With a staff-to-client ratio of 2-to-1, your attendance is absolute perfection—among the superstars of Europe! Its hours (starting at noon for lunch and at 8 P.M. for dinner) enable U.S. pilgrims to eat at their accustomed times, to avoid the later rush, and thus to benefit from superior service. Try the magnificent roast baby lamb (spring and early summer); if this isn't available, there's a galaxy of specialties which range from pressed duck and Chicken Salad Fielding (sic) to Turkey Xavier to liver dumplings to Pineapple-Lobster Titus to goodness knows what—each with a masterful touch. And please, please cap your meal with a Horcher creation called Crêpes Sir Holten; here's one of *the* prize taste-sensations in Spain. Closed Sunday. Highest recommendation.

In exactly the same tip-of-the-top bracket is the **Jockey Club** (Amador de los Ríos 6), one of the Great Restaurants of the world. It is small (18 tables only), highly exclusive, and expensive; it is not a private club, as the name implies. Don Carlos Cortés, the proprietor, runs it with a velvet hand. Each dish—possibly, and ironically, with the lone exception of Crêpes Toledo—is a masterpiece of culinary art (note the presentation of each platter to the diner!), and the service is most often but not always wonderfully smooth. The menu is printed in English, Spanish, and French. *Always crowded,* so arrange with your hotel concierge to book in advance. Closed all of August; open daily. and Sunday, otherwise. Ask for Maître Gerardo (Herardo) or Manager Felix, both of whom speak English; Mr. Cortés himself knows the Latin languages only. The only demurrer here is that sometimes the "regulars" get too much good attention, while the newcomers are given the impression they're out in left field; when no table reservations are made at peak times, the neophyte almost surely will be shunted into the listless lofts upstairs, without even a hope of experiencing the Jockey that booted home such fame and fortune for its proprietor. Be that as it is, this establishment has the feel of New York's "21" with the intimacy of the Laurent. Go late (2:30 P.M. or 10:30 P.M.) to be fashionable. Highest recommendation, as well.

The 4-chambered **Zalacain** (Alvarez de Baena 4) is currently one of the most sought-after dining meccas in the capital. It is approached via an illuminated lawn off the Castellana. Rust-tone bar; textile walls, some hung with game paintings; rich woodwork; beautiful floral arrangements; Basque kitchen in the *nouvelle cuisine* style; elegant appointments in concord with its 5-star classification. Our platters have always been truly outstanding—even to the bread, which is baked in its own ovens. It is also at rest on Sunday plus all of August. We consider this 2nd only to the celestial twins above and certainly a serious candidate for the finest penultimate bet in Madrid's roster.

O'Pazo (Reina Mercedes 20), the nostalgic heartbeat of romantic Galicia in the capital, offers an elegant greeting with its dressed-stone façade, coach lamps, and Georgian windows. Marblesque English bar to the right of entrance foyer with green banquettes, hunting prints, and shelves of Toby mugs; L-shaped, 3-segment, large dining room pleasantly outfitted with homeland paintings, patterned carpet, and moss and coral tablecloths; intimate seating despite the spaciousness of the salon. Our party's seafood cocktail, medallions of octopus, croquettes, and grilled whitefish were uniformly succulent, revealing careful preparation; Rio Femar, an earthy, sparkling white wine, provided a spirited counterpoint to our nauticalories. The Albariño de Fefiñane also is a regional treat. Closed Sat. noons, Sundays, and August. Delightful.

Charlot (Serrano 70) is in the tenderloin of the chic shopping district, attracting The Smart Set of the city. It was kindly brought to our attention by a savvy Golden Gate couple, Bill and Helen Taylor, who travel the globe from Carmel to Chu Shan and who know their calories intimately. Superb *fin-de-siècle* menu; specialties such as quail eggs and caviar, quenelles of lobster, and tantalizing baked sea bass in a pastry shell bathed with a maritime sauce. The ocean harvest seems more inventive than the bovine and other 4-footed creations, but this may only be a matter of personal preference; in season wild game is available, both imported and local. A full repast with wine might dent $70, but surely the extravagance has its rewards. Exceptional.

Las Cortes (Madrazo 24) is sited in an ambitiously reformed 300-year-old building which is perhaps 5 minutes by foot from the Hotel Palace. Small bar beyond its portals; 5 separate rooms with 4 to 8 tables in each; graceless accouterments and tableware; disturbingly noisy when full. Though it has received isolated praise in American publications, our own experience was extremely disappointing. Very poor for the classification.

Clara's (Arrieta 2), another pretentious newcomer near the Puerta del Sol, was equally grim to our tastes. Severe rectangularity provoking a sensation of claustrophobia, in our view; heavy expense account trade at lunch; recessed banquettes lining its walls plus 14 individual tables; good taste in appointments. Costly but agreeable culinary preparations (Our bill included a $4 mistake a while back which could have been accidental). We rate this as borderline for its values.

Escuadrón (Tamayo y Baus 8) marches proudly on the Madrid battlefront. It has recruited a camp following of the local Social Set. Delightfully elegant mien punctuated with paper-white napery, ink-black armchairs, ruby-hued paisley carpet, partially canopied ceiling, high cottage windows, and a rouge leather bar where the Squadron halts. About 14 tables plus 1 small private dining room; our meal was truly superb on a recent mess call; closed in August. We have a feeling this bivouac will make the troops happy for a long time to come. 'Ten-SHUN!

Bajamar (Av. José Antonio 78), a few steps from the Plaza Hotel, is regarded as one of the better seafood restaurants in town—though not up to O'Pazo, in our opinions. It is also one of the most expensive candidates on the Continent. Entrance beside a trout tank to a modernistic downstairs complex; counter backed by a legion of smoked hams and drying meats; refrigerated display of shell shockers of enormous size and tantalizing freshness. (Madrid,

though the most inland of Spanish metropolises, is also one of the best for seafood, since the best catches arrive in less than 60 minutes by air from both the Mediterranean and Atlantic coasts.) Prices vary with the individual selections—depending upon weight, time of year, scarcity, and other variables. **La Trainera** (Calle Lagasca) is another nook for nautical niceties; it's not as expensive as Bajamar, but not, we think, as good, either. *You* aren't the one getting hooked here.

Old-world dining? Try **Lhardi** (San Jerónimo 8), which is sequestered atop an antique bar and takeout shop. Dark interior; embossed leather walls; parquet floors; heavy framed mirrors, burgundy velure banquettes; globe lighting, ancient waiters in tails. The cuisine is less important than the distinctive atmosphere. Here is a unique holdover from a graceful era that we believe conservative diners will relish. Always reserve at least 24 hours ahead. A touch of Victoriana that we love.

The **Puerta de Moros** (Don Pedro 10) used to be a dining champion of the capital, but now, with its eye shifting toward group trade, we feel it may be slipping somewhat. Guests in this converted Conde de Riudom Palace ascend vía an elevator or tread the massive ancestral staircase to one of the 4 salons—each with its own décor. Large, high-borne bar, plus 2-wheel rig to dispense beverages at your elbow; extensive Iberian menu on parchment broadside; pushy service; lambent piano melodies for evening meals, which we much prefer to the midday munching. Totally appealing to 4 of our 5 senses, but for our *taste*, its gastronomy did not match up to the other levels of success.

Breda (Castellana 78, directly opposite Hotel Luz Palacio), a spear carrier in the Las Lanzas group (see below), is usually packed tighter than a peperoni. Even so, we find it more relaxing than its older Lance-mate, where one sits funnybone-to-funnybone with the other patrons. Down the steps to a subdued and pleasant milieu; about 20 tables with blue-and-white napery; wooden garniture; acoustic-tile ceiling to hush the rush; leather chairs; too-frequent appearance of chipped china and our latest trial was marred by indifferent service. Careless attention can spoil some aspects of a meal, but now we feel that the sins of omission go deeper here. Disappointing.

La Mesa Redonda (Nuncio 17), not far from Madrid's impressive Plaza Mayor, is a joint effort by Connecticut Yankee Bob Pecka and San Dominican Pedro Lluberes. Immaculate premises restored from the former stables of the Nunciatura Palace; dual-sectioned room divided by beams; spotlighted greenery in bar and 10-table dining area; periodically changed art exhibits on its white-stucco walls. Fish, grills, and stews seem to preoccupy the chef, with the accent on the best available products in the Madrid market each day. Many North Americans find their way here and seem to be as satisfied as we were on our very recent foray. Dinner served all year; closed Sundays and lunchtime in August.

Mayte Hostal (General Mola 285, a longish ride), named for its highly talented proprietress, marches on, but we thought it was growing weary on our latest look. Candlelit atmosphere in L-shape configuration; stand-up and sit-down bars; ubiquitous sketches, caricatures, and oils (that's Mayte herself on the back wall); furnishings now due for a freshening. Every platter we've ever

sampled here ranks as a masterpiece of gastronomy. Its 15 specialties include goose with raspberries, lobster, Clams Meunière, steaks, smoked cheese, and Torron ice cream. A capital bet in the Spanish capital.

Another **Mayte**, this one in the **Commodore Hotel** (Plaza de la República. Argentina) offers twin dining segments, one for resident guests only and the other for the general public. During the colder months you'll find a rôtisserie offering sportsman's targets of so-so quality (wild boar, partridge, venison, and the like in season), plus broiled steaks, flaming turbot, and similar passing-fare. In summer, the tables are moved directly onto the lawn of the large patio, illuminated by treetop lights and the open sky. Air conditioning; 2-level bar; swimming pool. Fair on a fair day, but here, too, a dash of inspiration would help.

Club 31 (Alcalá 58) was launched back yonder in '59 as a less formal, less expensive sister of the famed Jockey Club (see above). The décor of wood-paneled walls and wood ceilings, with recessed soft illumination, is almost Swedish or Finnish in tone. Tiny, chic bar in front; main room with a cluster of good-size tables for expansionists. The range of its menu is prodigious. Open continuously from noon to 2 A.M. daily and Sunday; after-theater onion soup and grilled chicken a popular feature. Be sure to reserve in advance, because normally it is jammed. Usually—not always—excellent for its category and tariffs.

The **Medinacelli** (del Prado 27, near Palace Hotel), a 4-fork venture, bordered the maximum 5 forks in ambiance, substance, and tariffs. Bar; L-shape dining room in subdued tones with suspended red Tiffany-style lamps over its 20-plus tables; good Iberian-international menu belying its name; 2 upstairs banquet settings convertable for overflow. If the eagerness of service and the chef's enthusiasm continue, here indeed willl be a medium-high-cost enterprise which delivers on every invested peseta.

Bellman, the _intime_ restaurant of the Hotel Suecia, has been relocated within the same building—and somehow, sad to say, it seems to have lost something in the shift. Perhaps the paucity of the staff revealed it in a poorer light.

Las Lanzas (Espalter 10), previously mentioned as a more frenetic sister to the Breda, is still dear to the hearts of both resident Americans and Smart Set Spaniards. Steaks and chops spotlighted on the charbroiler; native selections also featured; well-intentioned but poorly trained waiters; service plates grossly chipped (as at the Breda; both must hire gorillas as dishwashers); other operating touches amateurish; prices now moving bullishly. While the management still has a lot to learn, it is trying hard—so we must rate this armory of "The Lances" a solid value in overcrowded surroundings.

Principe de Viana (Calle Doctor Fleming 7) is actually around the corner from its street address—a few steps from where your taxi stops. Ground-level lair divided by a stairwell; longer upstairs salon with green stained-glass windows; wooden walls and polished ceiling beams; blue and forest-tone carpeting. Our waitress, outfitted to resemble a secretary bird, for some unfathomable reason changed our silverware 3 times before a single calorie was brought to the table. How's _that_ for service? Loved by locals, but our expensive meal did not warrant a return visit, unless to figure out that caper with the cutlery.

Poncio Pilato (Almirante 5) schemes its black-on-white theme around 4 Latin columns, flowers on 18 tables, gray-toned artwork, and a loyal conclave of satisfied legionnaires. We were impressed by the menu of international dishes, the versatility of the chef, and the moderate prices for its imperial rank.

Casa Botín (Cuchilleros 17) is a tried-and-true standby, famous all over the world for its bullfighting guests and its roast suckling pig. This is the restaurant where Jake Barnes, hero of _The Sun Also Rises,_ plays his last scene; Hemingway gave the place considerable attention in _Death in the Afternoon_ as well. Cooking is still done in the original oven, dating from A.D. 1725. Be sure to order the Cordero Asado or the Cochinillo Asado because this baby lamb and this juicy little piglet are too good to miss. Little English is spoken; ask for Don Antonio, the hospitable son of the owner (and the 4th generation to be represented here), to translate your needs. Crowded by fellow tourists; reservations gladly accepted even though every table has been sold out ages ago; expect to wait (standing in a jammed passageway) for at least 45 minutes beyond the time of your booking unless you get there around 8-ish; the air conditioners dating from A.D. 1971 help in summer. Very reasonable; very Spanish; very plain. Definitely worth a visit if you're in the mood for atmosphere. This authentic landmark we _do_ recommend—highly.

Alkalde (Jorge Juan 10) splits its multiple personality and waiters between upper and lower dining alcoves and brick-walled basement grottos. Chummy service; classical regional fare plus Basque and Chilean specialties; unique fish soup, a dream; many local patrons. Sound.

El Bodegón (Pinar 15) remains a solid contender. The staff is professional but friendly; the food is substantial; high segments of Madrid society often may be found within its precincts. Certainly no Horcher or Jockey Club, but pleasant. Closed in summer.

José Luis (Rafael Salgado 11), hard by the football stadium, draws athletes, aficionados, Babbitts, and a mixed clan. Originally a neighborhood pub, it grew faster than Jack's beanstalk. Bar and 8 tables at entrance; main dining room down a few steps, clublike with paintings, diplomas, and a large bookcase; relaxed atmosphere brightened by mulberry touches; urbane food and attention; separate bar next door on mezzanine level; small glass-wrapped sidewalk restaurant; closed Sundays and August. Don José Luis loves to present little souvenirs to the ladies. Prices high but not exorbitant. Very, very good.

Other colorful worthies? Here's a triumvirate of amiable examples: **Casa Valentín** (headquartered at Calle San Alberto 3, just off Puerta del Sol) has opened 2 newer havens, each boasting the same belt-bruising fare. Its original entry has long been a bullfighters' favorite. Ground-floor, L-shape, standup bar (not set up for ladies), where the local gentry gorge themselves from the copious array of tidbits on display, trading jokes and tossing discarded shrimp husks on the floor; narrow stairway to the delightfully regional dining accommodations upstairs; medium-priced and especially beloved by first-timers. The second entry **Los Porches** (Paseo del Pintor Rosales 1), is active in summer only (June 1 to Sept. 30); appealing surroundings, happy ambiance, and excellent service. The last, **Nuevo Valentín** (Concha Espina, opposite the football stadium), is the most chic of the trio. Sidewalk dining at about 40 tables when old Sol is benign; small, intimate, red-leather bar to the right of the entrance;

spacious dining room to the left with hunt-and-harvest scenes; leaded windows and walnut panels. Our incognito reception, our meal, and our service were all excellent. Same eager and sympathetic attention at each address; same prices; same praise. All recommended—especially the *Nuevo,* which we found unusually rewarding.

Ruperto de Nola, topping the unusual Torres Blancas apartment building, occupies a circular free-form room finished in a glazed white porcelain-like surface. Basket-handle arched windows affording a splendid view of the city; perfect acoustics for a music hall but so reverberative for human voices that it is uncommonly (and uncomfortably) loud; posh red upholstery; massive food displays sometimes requiring 2 busboys to carry a single platter; better than average cuisine for higher than average tabs. The clamor inside this mod-lined chatterbox and the theatrical performances in bringing out the food put us off. Perhaps you'll disagree and be more favorably impressed than we were.

Casa Paco (Puerta Cerrada 11), in the old part of town, zings with color for the eyes, peasant-style flavor for the tummy, and noise for the ears. Two floors (we prefer upstairs); always busy, if not hectic; steak's the main thing and it's usually ordered by weight; Cebón de Buey is also delicious, as are some of the seafood platters. Don't worry if the meat is not done quite well enough for you; the plates are literally oven-hot, so simply slice off a slab, touch it to your heavy porcelain platter, and it will be brown in a jiffy! We enjoyed it on our several recent eat-ins, but some travelers find its ambiance too, too "authentic" to suit them. Not for the squeamish.

Julián Rojo (Ventura de la Vega 5, a short hike from the Palace) is another tavern-type temple of taurine trauma. Again 2 stories; bright with bullfight pictures; skilletcraft not as skilled as of yore, on our recent test.

Sixto Gran Mesón (Cervantes 28), behind the Palace Hotel, offers a busy, yeomanlike ground floor bar plus tables, an upstairs restaurant, and additional rooms for private parties. Rugged open rafters; Castilian shutters; antique plates on whitewashed walls; moorish tiles as baseboards surrounding the terracotta floors. The most attractive segment, in our opinions, is the section near the hearth in the end of the main room. Popular; rush-rush service; food acceptable, as are the prices. Very Spanish in flavor.

Both **La Corralada** (Villanueva 21) and **Aroca** (Plaza de los Carros 3) impressed us as being as routine as a gaggle of other small, basic Iberian-style feederies in the city. Neither is as easy on the bankroll as it physically appears. The former is a favorite of the younger set. The fish in the latter is exceptionally fresh and savory, but its starkness and its slambang but well-meaning service detract from our desire to return.

La Fragua (Ortega y Gasset 6) belongs to the same armory as the aforementioned Breda and Las Lanzas. Small, intimate, with sound service; similar fare to that of "The Lances." Recommended.

Mesón de San Javier (Calle del Conde, 3) is a typical, lively, somewhat ingratiating *bodega* on a tiny, hard-to-find street which is extremely popular among North American explorers. No cocktails, no whiskey, no gin; Spanish brandy-and-soda, sherry or a pitcher of house wine at a song; warm and friendly welcome and attention by unpolished staff. Strangely enough, the whole baby fowl roasted in butter has been renamed Chicken Fielding; we

wonder why. Its somewhat drear air of shabbiness is normally overcome by
the merriment of its guests. Simple, rough-and-ready tavern for the down-to-
earth traveler.

La Quinta del Sordo or "The Home of the Deaf One" (Sacramento 10), once
the Goya residence, is named for this great artist who lived in a sad world of
silence. Ownership by Patrón Miguel Jimenes, formerly the spark behind the
abovementioned Mesón de San Javier; rustic cottage surroundings with snack
bar in front, a wider expanse farther in, and 2 intimate 6-table quarters to the
left; stone, timber, and hearthside atmosphere; soothingly low outlays for
simple inlays. Lunchtime is quieter; dinner is livelier.

El Ultimo Cuplé (Palma 51) means "The Last Tune," and it certainly seemed
to be croaking a swan song on our visit. Kind, hard-working staff in dismal
surroundings; tatterdemalion menus; geriatric combo wheezing out a caco-
phony of melodies; more examples and more's the pity since the personnel
seemed to be trying so hard. It's hymn time, we think.

La Grillade (Calle de Calatrava 32) is still striving to squeeze into the
sophisticated inner circle. Downstairs site with speckled emerald carpet,
acoustic ceiling (trying in vain to absorb the overly loud recorded music),
candles, paintings, and an assortment of decorative effects that didn't jell to
our aesthetic senses. Smooth service by waiters in red jackets; better than
average cuisine; reasonable prices. A more intimate feeling suffuses the room
after 10 P.M., when 2 guitarists begin to strum. Worth a try.

The **Gure-Etxea** (Plaza de la Paja 12), if you hadn't already guessed from
the distinctive spelling of its name, is a serious Basque bailiwick. Diminutive
working bar near entrance; tastefully decorated with lore of the northern
province; varied menu; amiable service by waitresses from 1:30 P.M. to 4 and
from 9 to midnight; closed Sundays. A beret-clad old-timer here told us that
guests receive special attention if they address the proprietor by name—which
just happens to be Ignacio Loinaz Echániz Galarraga Arrizabalaga Garmendia
Alcorta Leunda Joaristi Zalacain Landa Mendizábal Aranguren Guruceta
Elorza Elola Gurruchaga Egaña Soraluce Izaguirre Galdós Oyarzábal. Got
that? If not, go anyway. It's fun.

Pazo de Monterrey (Alcalá 4), a *"restaurante-marisquería,"* gives a lot
for the money. This bustling, modern, down-to-earth enterprise, with its
bar and paper-littered floor-rail area (a Spanish custom where open appetizers are offered stand-up drinkers) separated by a partition from the tables, is proud of its fine variety of shellfish (*mariscos*) and well it should
be; the special trencher-eater's platter (½ lobster, ½ giant crab, oysters,
shrimp, and more), at about $20, alone cost more than everything con-
sumed by my 2 other companions. Generous choice of briny and nonbriny
dishes; h-u-g-e portions; unpolished but smiling attention; very popular, especially for lunch. If you're not seeking atmosphere, here's one hell of a
good bargain in regional type fare.

Las Reses (Orfila 3) tucks its cookstoves into the crook of its L-shape
configuration. Neo-Andalucian in atmosphere, employing Moor-or-less North
African overtones; Spanish skilletry; well-prepared beef and lamb. We've nevir
boasted over hour spelling abilities, but git a lode of there menyou entrees:
"Yearling Cutler Mother-in-law Dish, Rib Steak Holher-in-law Dish, Pour-

tuguese Chiken, Scrambled Eegs with Mush-rooms, Mixeed Salid, Chees as Ordered, Whippes Creem and particulary Iris Coffee." Clozed Sundae. Purdy gut.

Hogar Gallego (Plaza Comandante las Morenas 3), on the other fin, long one of Madrid's leading exponents of seafood, has been surfeited by its success —in our opinion, at least. Its charmless, overcrowded summer garden seems to go further to seed every year. We liked our latest fish soup, but the rest was for the sandcrabs. Typical fare of Galicia is also offered. Sorry, no longer for us.

Balthasar, in the basement of the Eurobuilding, draws mostly businessmen at midday. Cozy entry bar plus buffet on show; 28 tables divided into 2 segments by a beaded wooden screen; ample attention. The cuisine seemed more suited to satisfying the hungry diner rather than the discerning gourmet. Fair enough, however, if you're out at this neighborhood at mealtime. In the same district, **Las Cumbres** (corner of Alberto Alcocer and Condes del Val) is the choice of one of Madrid's top female executives, Victoria Escribano. She particularly praises the maritime dishes and the grand assortment of predinner nibbles. See our separate section below: "Tascas for Tapas.".

El Invernadero (Jorge Juan 39), belies the elegance of its proud address in the stately Salamanca suburb by displaying a façade of no special distinction. Inside, it's totally another story. Honoring its namesake ("the greenhouse"), the three-tiered room is a leafy study of botanical charm—even the pictures portray green motifs. The menu is short but with many succulent choices. Our Besugo à la bilbaína (baked sea bream with red peppers), veal brochette, and Crema Invernadero (custard with chopped almonds) provided a garden of culinary delights. Moreover, the service couldn't have been kinder and more attentive. Can a chef have a green thumb? If so, here's the place where you'll probably hit paydirt.

El Púlpito (Plaza Mayor 9) is pleasant. Total of 28 tables on 2 floors; open kitchen where you can watch the chefs at work; small bar and chilled food display at entrance. Our salad was crisp and our thick steak was topped with smoked ham and an egg! A bow to owner José Luis—plus a mild recommendation to you.

An identical ailment seems to have hit both **La Barraca** (Reina 29) and the refashioned **Caves of Luis Candelas** (just off Plaza Mayor, below El Púlpito) —namely, Too Many Tourists. Their authentic flavor, once so appealing, has been lost. Neither is recommended to any reader of this year's book.

Riscal (Marqués de Riscal 11) is also for the birds, not for us. The **Urogallo** (Calle Gavina 23) seemed to be a molting rooster on our latest peck around the Madrid henhouse.

American and pseudo-American? **Hollywood** (Magallanes 1) flashes back to a Silver Screen fantasyland which never was. It was installed and mechanically institutionalized by shrewd Los Angeles entrepeneurs. General impression of cheesiness; bar and quick-lunch facilities at entrance; spiritless Art Deco dining room; menu mainstays 7 varieties of ½-lb. and 8 varieties of ¼-lb. hamburger platters; these and other U.S. junk foods outstanding for Spain. Open 365 days per year from 1.30 P.M. to 3 A.M. Its piped rock music is horribly loud; during this latest visit, we didn't see one customer who looked over 25. Very

expensive in comparison to competition, but superior to all in authenticity. We have not yet sampled its new branch at Apolonio Morales in the Dr. Fleming area.

The **California** chain has 7 links, the largest and best at Goya 47. It is far plainer, noisier, busier, and cheaper than Hollywood. Curious parodies of U.S. quick-service fare; only 14 sandwiches (no hamburgers or hot dogs), but 146-plate galaxy in an astonishing mélange of Iberian offerings; superfast personnel; masterfully organized. High-quality vittles for low outlays; well-mixed drinks; normally mobbed day and night by locals; open 7 A.M. to 1:30 A.M. the calendar around. You'll save a bundle, but you'll eat *a la Española.*

The self-service **Burger King** operations (Orense 4 and Princesa 3) dispense Whoppers, Yumbos, Whalers, hamburgers, and apple pie which taste to us as barely passable counterfeits of their originals. **Lums** (Alcalá 202), **Kentucky Fried Chicken**, and **Helen's** (Generalísimo 90) should be rapped on the knuckles, in our opinion, for purveying what we regard as such punk imitations of our national kitchen. **Dolar** and the scads of others which now pepper the city shouldn't, because they just don't know any better.

The **Drugstore**, a 3-minute walk from Kreisler's fine emporium on Serrano, is a mod-mooded lunch stop, discothèque, boutique center, and—well, drugstore sans drugs. Counter or table service; fair hamburgers, sundaes, milk shakes, or other flip-siders. Fun, in a teenie-bopper way.

French? **Le Bistroquet** (Calle del Conde 4) resembles an MGM bistro right down to its checkered tablecloths and wax-dripped wine bottles with candles. Perhaps 20 tables, almost rim-to-rim; disturbingly loud piped music ("The Last Time I Saw Paris"?); limited *carte* featuring grilled meats and fish; Maître Pierre—er, Pedro—the soul of kindness. *Comme ci, comme ça.* **El Galeón** (Calle Velázquez 80) is another Frenchie.

German? **Edelweiss** (Jovellanos 7) serves a skimpy meal with fine German-type beer for matching tariffs. Herring in sour cream and onions (Arenque Crema); bratwurst with potato salad and sauerkraut; pumpernickel bread; Camembert; also many other non-Teutonic selections. Depressingly stark décor; harassed service; go very early or very late, because it's *always* overfull at meal hours, and they won't accept reservations. Branch in the country (see below).

Italian? **Rocco** (Jardines 3) occupies the spot once held by the Tranquilino steakhouse. The small restaurant is downstairs with a hopping little snack bar above. **Alduccio Pizzeria** (Av. del Generalísimo Franco 38) is more of a *trattoria* than a full-scale restaurant. Simple surroundings on street level; 9 tables; bilious green ceiling and cotton-cloth wall coverings emblazoned with blue and gold churches; inexpensive; we licked our chops over its Tagliatelle and Lasagne. *Bene* for *pasta* hounds. **La Trattoria** (Plaza del Alamillo 8) is in a quiet sector of the Old Town. Nothing too special about it, in our opinion.

Chinese? Because many of the key vegetables which are necessities in classic Chinese cookery are not grown in the area, and because other standard ingredients are either too high priced or unobtainable in Spain, **El Buda Feliz** (Tudescos 6), **Chino Kowloon** (Travesía del Conte Duque 15), **House of Ming** (Castellana 74), **Mandarin** (Brasil 16), **Mei Ling** (Generalísimo 74), **Pagoda** (Leganitos 22), **Shanghai** (Leganitos 26) and a couple of others are forced to

improvise combinations—some of them billed under familiar names—which are weird and occasionally unpleasant to these travelers' palates. It is virtually a culinary school of its own. House of Ming and Mandarin are especially well established. While we don't happen to enjoy them at all, scads of customers —especially residents—do.

Japanese? The **Mikado** (Calle Huesca 71) struts in with honors that would be a compliment to anyone's ancestors, considering its Iberian address. Excellent reception from its kind doorman, to the waitresses in the raiments of Nippon, to the courtly Manager Suzuki-San; Malacca lighting fixtures; extractor fans over several tables to draw off the cooking aromas; good fish-based soup; savory Tempura; fair Sukiyaki, within the limits possible with Spanish beef as the base. Its location on the edge of town is its only major drawback. Our courteous bow of respect.

Philippine? **Sulú** (Av. Generalísimo 58) bills itself as a "steak house," but wait until you taste the delicious Misono, a specialty of the archipelago that is prepared not only *at* your table but *in* your table! What a delight—your exquisitely costumed chef-waitress melding the ingredients on a fire-hot grill around which you dine, the aromas drifting up into individual ventilator hoods. A ½-dozen such installations are here plus conventional settings for more continental cravings. Entrance through a shimmering, tinkling curtain of nacre medallions; additional mother-of-pearl decorative touches behind the handsome Malayan bar; sinfully appetizing curried niblets, *satés* (kebabs), and island delicacies; relaxing cane-back chairs augmenting the forest of malacca separators and rattan screens. Here's something exotic for the eye, ear, nose, and throat. A touch of joy to all the senses. **Casa Anselmo** (Plaza de las Salesas 7) is a newer, smaller, and lower-priced example of the same origin. How satisfactory it is we do not know.

Mexican? ¡¡**A Todo Mexico**!! (San Bernardino 4) is a segment in a group of 3 outlets which also include **Mexico Lindo** (a long, costly taxi ride out to Plaza de Ecuador 4) and **El Charro** (San Leonardo 3). The 3-language menu is 100% alike throughout. Bar; dining room in vivid colors against white stucco; amiable attention; open every day. Watery Margaritas; 10 set meals at painless prices; echiladas with the firepower of the *USS Enterprise*; Special Mexican Combination Platter with Guacamole on the side. Fun, for a change of diet.

Swiss? **Chalet Suizo** (Fernández de la Hoz 80) is an alpine facsimile where inordinate amounts of garlic and oil are foisted on fine Helvetian cuisine. An American and his Puerto Rican wife landlord this chalet-style venture; unfortunately, they've matched the Swiss décor far, far better than they've duplicated the fodder. Attentive, tidily groomed staff; not expensive. Too bad, but our reaction to this one is nix.

Kosher? The **Sinai** (Príncipe 33, 1 flight up, and another at Av. José Antonio 29) answers the Diaspora with Sephardic cookery (based on the creations of the Jews who fled to Spain and Portugal), rather than the more familiar recipes of the Ashkenazim (those who went farther up into Europe, and who predominate in North America). The former will find *eppis essen*, but the latter should go only on *Donnershtick*, when the specialty is Couscous with chicken or lamb. Even more startling is the kosher Paella (mamma would faint at the very *thought*). There's an excellent take-away service—just right for a snack.

Moroccan? **Al Mounia** (Calle Recoletos 5) is the most authentic Maghrebian eatery we've seen since making the rounds of Casablanca's better spots a while back (the Shari family, your hosts, have another Eastern-Oriented oasis there). Finely detailed and exquisitely tiled Arabesque salon; 14 bright tables; waiters in ethnic habit; piped Middle Eastern melodies; excellent couscous, shish kebab, and other specialties from the lands of the Atlas; minaret-high, but worthy tabs. Salaams to the Chef, who labors with Allah's hand.

Further East? **Vihara** (Plaza Santa Bárbara 8) brings Hindu atmospherics from the hinterland of India. Curries form only a chapter, because its cookbook is fat and varied. Of its 3 segments, we prefer the downstairs "grotto." Quite good for its specialties. Recommended.

Tea? **Embassy Club** (Paseo de la Castellana 12) is a fashionable rendezvous for upper-bracket *Madrileñas;* delicious watercress sandwiches, petits fours, and the like; go about 6 P.M.

The best hotel surroundings for lunching or dining in Madrid are found (in season) at the lovely garden of the **Ritz**, expensive as the devil. The Rue Royale of the **Villa Magna** is trying to bring blue-ribbon French cuisine to the Spanish capital. Our inspection most assuredly disclosed that the décor will aid any digestion—Iberian or Gallic. Prices are close to those of Horcher or the Jockey Club. We wish it, and you, *bonne chance.*

During the summer, the one place not to overlook is **Pavilion**, in Retiro Park. Open-air dining and dancing in a lovely setting; smooth, fast floor shows, which generally come up with excellent talent. Now tops in the city. The **Florida**, also in Retiro Park and also alfresco, takes second honors; same features and same prices; excellent as well. Nearby, the **Pinto** (Montalbán 9) trots out 14 tables, a bar, and Spanish home cooking by the friendly family that fills its feedbag. Nice and neighborly. **Villa Rosa**, 20 minutes out in the suburb of *Ciudad Lineal,* used to have a dreamy physical plant, stately trees, a swimming pool, and other lures to the eye. Then, through inept management, it hit the skids and deservedly dropped out of vogue. Now we hear that Sr. Luis Hernando Olives has remodeled it into shades of its former self.

Excellent reports have reached us about the new **Horcher-Ascot**, also less than a 30-minute ride, on the Plaza de la Morale ja in *Alcobendas*. It was instituted and is operated by the extraordinarily savvy management of the original Horcher in midtown. As an informal retreat principally for a 35-or-younger clientele, under this aegis it should be fine. We're mighty anxious to try it.

La Casa Grande (Torrejón de Ardoz), not far from Madrid Airport at Barajas, is an impressive establishment which in antiquity housed the San Isidro Jesuit School and several noble families all of whom left traces of their sumptuous, ascetic, or agrarian lives. You dine—rather simply—among colossal earthenware wine vats and granary bins, with vaults above, open bricks, and huge timbers abounding. Parts of this expansive enterprise, which often is given over to groups, reveal the splendid refinement of Old Castille. Ambitious as a project. More curious as a sightseeing target than as a choice for pure gastronomy.

Beyond Barajas Airport, in the classically beautiful university town of *Alcalá de Henares*, the State-Tourist-Office-operated **Hostería del Estudiante**

is a charming target for lunch or dinner when the weather is halcyon. Ancient, rustic baronial hall remodeled; typical Spanish fare; tabs so inexpensive your eyes will pop. This one is inside, with no garden facilities—but the settlement itself is delightful sightseeing bait.

Tascas for Tapas For a Spanish-style Care package to prevent early-evening atrophy of hungry U.S. tummies, be absolutely certain to try the **tascas** (taverns) on or near the Calle de Echegaray—just an olive-pit's throw from the Palace Hotel. Here's where Madrid's lively hordes huddle for snacks and apéritifs from 7 P.M. to 10 P.M. The word _tapas_ literally means "covers" and the gentle art of creating and serving them began in Andalusia where it was simply too hot to face a full meal. Today tasca-hopping is practiced all over Spain, usually in stand-up bars where heated trays or display counters afford you an opportunity to glimpse the wares before you buy them.

Each stop banners its own specialties. **La Casona**, which can pack in 400 nibblers, is noted for its potatoes and mushrooms. **La Chuleta** draws ham and _mariscos_ (shellfish) fans. **Gayango** is renowned for its _bacalao_ (cod), steaming casseroles of baby shrimp, oysters, and hot tamales. **Posada del Enano** comes up with a trove of _boquerones_ (a very special anchovy); **O'Pote** serves delicious _vieiras_ (scallops); **Motivos** offers _chanquetes_ (oh-so-good sea minnows); **Espuela** purveys _pinchos morunos_ (barbecues); **La Trucha** is good for heavier fare, and **Taverna Toscana** has other palate tempters. **Los Corsarios** (Calle de Barbieri 7) projects a swinging atmosphere beloved by the Younger Set; cellar-sited **Sésamo**, where the Fielding gypsies usually throw in the towel, features the reviving _Sol y Sombra_ ("Sun and Shade," half anis and half Spanish _coñac_). Drink either the house wines or common sherry; beer is too filling, but some prefer its cooling effect (tiny bottles called "cervecitas" are available, as are small drafts). Scads more places may be explored in these Tidbit Alleys. They are very, very inexpensive, and they provide a scrumptious experience for travelers in ALL economic brackets. But please remember that dinner is still coming up!

Night Life Since most neophytes to Madrid usually want to see the world-famous and historic flamenco dancers, let's open the curtain with a sampling of the most prominent names currently on stage.

Corral de la Morería (Morería 17) means "Corral of the Moorish Quarter." L-shape main room with small stage occupied by shapely ladies and handsome, swarthy male dancers; about 10 performers on our night, all much more attractive than those in other flamenco parlors; corner bar; capacity for about 80 show-viewers; popular for dinner; food miles from great, but edible; your first libation painfully high and your later ones less; untampered spirits in our glasses. It's best to go late to avoid the bus excursions. Tops for its type for zing and fire, although sometimes short on artistry and polish.

Café de Chinitas (Torija 7), a long room with green textiled walls and a stage at one end, today resembles an elegant Spanish salon, but the original café was a far more modest Malaguenian _tablao_ of the 1850's. Red-framed portraits of renowned matadors; tomato- and avocado-colored bar; chairs, tables, and other trimmings carrying out the Andalucian motif. Smaller flamenco ensemble than at the Corral; performances better conceived but far less spontaneous; excellent costumery; top guitarists and singers; honest drinks; no groups.

Eminently rewarding for a sophisticated evening, but we prefer the Corral's spirit-of-the-moment.

Las Brujas ("The Witches") is situated at Calle Norte 165 in the Old Town, a narrow street that's hard to find and virtually impossible for parking. Dogleg bar at entrance facing a huge blue-and-white mural; l-o-o-o-n-g arched main room to the rear resembling a Quonset hut and recalling the tunnel from Grand Central to 125th Street; 200-seat capacity at 40 tables; small stage way up front with about 20 wee (if you're in the back) performers; intermittent shows from 11:30 P.M. to 3:30 A.M. Don't go for dinner, even though it's served. Drinks in the Corral price league, but our so-called White Label tasted suspiciously gray. As in the above establishments, there are no B-girls. Don't go out of your way for this one.

Torres Bermejas (Mesonero Romanos 15), formerly the Taberna Gitana, has perhaps the most attractive setup of all. The ceiling is coffered in gold; the walls are brightened by Moorish tiles; a sweet little loggia bedecks a corner beside the raised stage; numerous small package-groups tumble in; our drinks were legitimate. The service matches the artistry of the performers—enthusiastic but not too professional. (Strangely enough, flamenco dancing can be enhanced by this ironic fault, since its essence is spontaneity.) You may see grime, traces of amateurism, and undercurrents of organized tourism here, but basically we think it is rewarding if only to absorb the fundamental richness of the Arabic décor. Recommended.

Villa Rosa (Plaza Santa Ana 15), on our swing, was being bruited by nearly every concierge and hackie we met in the city as being the hottest stomper in town. To us, its *belle époque* interior and hyper-theatrical stagings simply didn't ring true. Dining commencing at 9:30 P.M.; main show at 11; operative until 3:30 A.M. We don't mean it unfairly when we say that we don't like it, but that's the way we call it when that's the way we see it. Perhaps you'll be more indulgent than we are.

Madrid's nightscape is now pulsing with the beat of discothèques. **La Boîte** is tonight's chichi panjandrum. White-brick façade with globe sconces; green paisley textiled walls; gilded mirrors; *fin-de-siècle* paintings; danceable music; steepish tabs. Sophisticated as a cool perch for night owls and their fine-feathered birdies. Don't, incidentally, confuse this with the "Boite-Theatre" rage now sweeping Madrid. **Ales** (Veneras 6) is one example of these softly lit dens where music, drink, and light drama are offered—of course, *only in Spanish*. These are a far cry from the disco-scene with which we now continue. **Bocaccio** is owned by the 2 brothers who run its solid namesake in Barcelona. Huge, even for a big city discothèque; turn-of-the-century thematics on ground level; more "with it" substrata for dancing (just follow the decibels); attractive patrons; good live bands; expensive but unadulterated libations. This one is deservedly popular. **Tartufo** is becoming one of our faithful standbys. Clubby upstairs atmosphere exuded by only 3 intimate tables flanking a working fireplace; lower-level rectangular den with smallish dance floor; couples-only admission policy. In a word: tasteful. **Long Play,** which had been spinning along famously prior to our visit, seemed to have slowed to about 15 rpm when we inspected it for labeling purposes. **Carnaby St.** and the **Royal Bus** traffic in miniskirted and hot-pantsed twisters. **J&J** is a challenger that comes on

strong if the crowd is right. As always with this type of establishment, it might be in one minute and out the next.

Among the "respectable" places in Madrid which are fun for everybody, the leader tonight is **El Biombo Chino** (Isabel La Católica 6), a former movie house which was converted into a fairly attractive reeler without cinematics. Alluring entrance, with flowers and plants and running water bordering the stairs; balcony with handsome bar and a few tables at street level; main seating area and dance floor 1-flight down; grade-B B-girls on our night. Sizzling orchestra of 14 to 16 musicians; cabaret not an extravaganza but excellent in quality; libations priced at levels similar to those in New York and Los Angeles ginmills. Clean, pleasant, and decent.

Flamingo (Av. José Antonio 34) draws a lively young clientele, well-dressed, well-mannered, and nonbeatnik. Good Italian band and soignée gal vocalist.

Bali Hai (Flora Alta 8) is a South Sea-soned cellar specializing in Polynesian nutrients, both in the glass and on the plate. Some exotic beverages sipped out of distinctive containers through 2-foot-long straws; décor suggesting a Malayan longhouse; high-backed Malacca chairs; waiters in glossy dinner jackets; enough flotsam and jetsam on the walls, hanging from the ceilings, and stuffed into vitrines to evoke the envy of Old Vic—Old *Trader* Vic, that is. Superb combo on our visit. We also were pleased with the samplings of Oceanic, Chinese, Japanese, and Indian tidbits that we exchanged among the members of our party who dined and danced here. Highly recommended for romancers.

In winter, **Cubaclu** (Virgen de la Alegría 9, near the bullring) swings best to a Latin beat; dancing; low tabs; weekends are the jumpingest if you love humanity. **Camagüey** (Desengaño 16, just off the Gran Vía) does not extend invitations to the ball, but the atmosphere is nice, the music is excellent, the cookery is recommendable, and the drinks are good; go late. **Alazán** (in the Castellana) impressed us as being a fleecing corral. Many young people prefer **Club Castelló** (Castelló 24), which is open from 6 P.M. to 9 P.M. and from midnight to 2:30 A.M. Many older ones prefer **Larré** (in the Castellana). The latter is more of a convivial drinking spot. **Canesteros** (Calle Barbieri 3) is recommended by a kindly Palo Alto lady who opines that "the dancing and singing were rendered with grace and spirit." Thanks for the tip.

In summer, fly straight as a swallow to **Pavi** (Retiro Park). When the climate is benign, no other place in the capital can touch it. Garden dining-and-dancing under the stars; high-class floor show; cuisine far below the Jockey Club-Horcher bracket. Worth the fairly steep outlay, if only as a Madrid memory to take home and nurse during those bleak nights in January. **Florida** (Paseo de Coches del Retiro) also hits the cash register with a firm finger; newish décor; almost as fine.

For Men Only, **Micheleta** (Costanilla de Los Angeles 20) is well stocked with B-girls. It offered on our visit a small band, a good singer, and what one chum called "a totally nude young couple doing some sort of mating dance." The rest of the cabaret was also aimed at masculine interests rather than family entertainment. For pickups, both the **Aladin** and the **Kokett**, two interesting bars on Calle Dr. Fleming, seem peopled by very attractive young ladies of a willing nature. Strictly for amorous gents with well-lined wallets—and, for

heaven's sake, DON'T make the stupid blunder of taking your wife here or to the others mentioned below, because somebody might spit on her for brashness.

Casablanca (Plaza del Rey 7, across from the Circus) is still popular. Stage show of 20 performers; 10-piece orchestra; ballroom layout with a slide-away stage; sleazy; dismal, cornball in its overall personality. We encountered a big-change gouge by the cigarette girl. No admission charge, but sobering tariff for The Cup That Cheers; go about 12:30 A.M. Hostesses galore, both at the balcony bar and at the downstairs tables—many of them in wool sweaters that cry for a strong deodorant. Open all year, except Holy Week. This one, we'd guess, is a prime target for hicks happily down from the Asturian hills.

Another candidate in this men-only group is the big, impressive **Pasapoga** (Av. José Antonio 37), which is more lavish than Micheleta or Casablanca. The "hostesses" are now back, after being banned in an effort to raise its tone. Good cabaret; the usual nightclub junk sold from table to table; closed August.

Down the list about a dozen pegs is the **Folies** (Paz 11-13), a busy, barnlike mecca of starry-eyed lassies fresh from the farms. Unsophisticated and not very interesting. Entertainment 2nd-string. The **Lido** has been renewed.

Stay away from a joint called **York Club**. Its B-girls are the brassiest vultures I've ever seen in the capital; they're all honor students in How To Take The Visiting Sucker. Although our party emerged unscathed, we wouldn't have been surprised if they'd tried to slip us Mickey Finns. **Moulin Rouge**, **Las Palmeras**, and **Congo Club** are traps which are also firmly *not* advised.

Sipping and friendly persuasions? **Hermitage Bar,** in the Eurobuilding, lights up a warm, living-room ambiance in which to heal the day's wounds or seal more positive alliances. Sumptuous divans; unusual silver lamps with smoked shades; soft-spoken gentlemanly staff; a soothing mood. The nearby **San Francisco,** another hospitable haven, comes on with 3 whole floors, English-speaking personnel, many Yanks at the brass rail or at tables, and drinks mixed in the back-home fashion. The **Wahine** (Serrano 80) whistles up Polynesian tempters à la Trader Vic's, but that's where the comparison falls out of its long boat. The bar in the center is low tide on our plumbline; the backwater atoll behind it is a more in-tune lagoon for your paddling.

Shopping Visitors do not need export licenses if their purchases total 25,000 pesetas or less. This applies to goods which are carried at departure or subsequently shipped. If this amount is exceeded, however, a license is mandatory. The dealers will make the arrangements.

Warning: Wherever you wander in today's Iberia, please be extremely leery of any of the stores or so-called "factories" where tour guides might lead you. The commissions they collect on *your* purchases with *your* money normally average 25%; in such notorious traps as Toledo, the bus guide, the local guide, and the driver skim off up to a total of 50% (!). You'd be wise to comparison shop and then to patronize ONLY reliable independent merchants.

Our ★ ★ ★ ★ ★ recommendations are individually noted.

Embroidered linens and needlework: ★ ★ ★ ★ ★ **Casa Bonet** (Nuñez de Balboa 76; see "Mallorca") is the world's mightiest name and greatest exponent in this field. Its exquisite handworked pieces are sold at prices still so low that you won't believe them. All its glorious Palma stocks are available. Make this your first stop, ask for Miss Soledad, and don't miss it!

Clothes: Spain is still a paradise for the affluent clothes-conscious gal. Only the wealthy, however, can now afford to patronize the Big League houses— **Pertegaz, Herrera y Ollero, Pedro Rodríguez, Miguel Rueda, Lino,** and a few others.

Well known and respected men's tailors are **Ongard** (Av. José Antonio 34), **Cutuli** (San Jerónimo 29), **González y García** (Barquillo 9), **Gregorio Ruiz** (Zorrilla 23), **Marcelo** (San Jerónimo 5), and **G. Cristóbal** (Castellana 53).

Handcrafted silk blouses and lingerie: **Srta. Emilia de Valeiras** (Diego de León 39), whose mother was the official seamstress to the Royal Court, continues the tradition with her carefully fashioned things. Lacework and other items are available. Warmly recommended since 1951.

Galleries: Despite the tremendous renaissance in Spanish art, it is still much less costly than French, Italian, American, and other *oeuvres.* Nowhere in existence is there anything comparable to this school.

American-operated ★ ★ ★ ★ ★ **Galería Kreisler** (Serrano 19) displays and sells the best of the nation's figurative ("representational") art in its regal, spacious, and beautiful edifice. Every 20 days one of Spain's most illustrious painters is honored with a 1-man show which occupies its entire main floor. The basement level contains graphics and a striking galaxy of oils of other top luminaries. On the 2nd floor, you will find the finest assemblage of Lladró porcelain available anywhere, including limited editions and other selected handicrafts, many of which are made exclusively for this house. (Without its special connections with Lladró the store would frequently run out of these extraordinarily high-demand stocks.) It's worth dropping into this fascinating complex to say hello to Ohio fireball Edward Kreisler, its delightfully friendly founder. Ignore the pack of crooked tour guides who lie that it's "more expensive"; he won't pay them any under-the-counter commissions. Here is an internationally famous treasure trove.

★ ★ ★ ★ ★ **Galeria Kreisler Dos** (Hermosilla 8, about 75 yards away) fills out the spectrum by exhibiting on a regular basis the avant-garde creations of these leading Spanish artists. They range from the oils, graphics, and sculptures of such masters as Miró, Picasso, and Juan Gris, to those of virtually all talents of special note within the nation, to those of the younger group who show exceptional promise for later dividends. Most are permanently represented in Madrid's National Museum of Contemporary Art and in prodigious foreign showcases.

Next best known are **Tartessos** (Serrano 63) and **Biosca** (Génova 11). Although scads of new ones continue to pop up, we have yet to find any true notables among them.

Shoes: Spain's finest shoes for both genders (and *what* boots at *what* prices for ladies!), with other wearables as a bonus, are found in ★ ★ ★ ★ ★ **Yanko** (Avda. José Antonio 40; see "Mallorca"). Manager Miguel Angel will indeed be pleased to take personal care of you. These are unrivaled from border to border.

Furniture, fabrics, and decorative items for the home: ★ ★ ★ ★ ★ **Artespaña** (Hermosilla 14, plus several branches) has a stunning range. Chic? Indeed. Expensive? And how! Worth it? Yes.

Leather accessories: Far and away the No. 1 house in the nation is ★ ★ ★ ★ ★ **Loewe** (main stores: Av. José Antonio 8 and Serrano 26). Since its founding

in 1846, it has earned gold medals in more than a score of international expositions, as well as the 24-carat reputation for producing some of the most striking works of art in the industry today. Handbags, luggage, jewel boxes, suède and leather jackets and coats, frames, shoes, flasks, gaming sets, a galaxy of executive-type gifts—all are here, and all are so carefully fashioned that each piece has the style, flair, and finish of a fine jewel. Write to its central offices (Barquillo 13, Madrid) for specific information concerning its network or its articles; your query would be welcomed. It has other dazzling shops in *England* (see "London"), *Barcelona* (see "Barcelona"), *San Sebastián* (Miramar 2 & 3), *Granada* (Hotel Alhambra Palace), *Bilbao* (Gran Vía 39), *Sevilla* (Plaza Nueva 12), *Valencia* (Av. Poeta Querol 7), *Las Palmas* (Santa Catalina Hotel) and *Palma* (see "Mallorca"), plus a golden net further afield. Legendary!

Colognes and cosmetics: **Aleixandre** (Av. José Antonio 23 and Pl. Canalejas 5) offers some exciting bargains—particularly in French colognes which are made in Spain without import taxes. **H. Alvarez Gómez** (Generalísimo 41, Sevilla 2 and Serrano 14), also long-established local landmarks, have equally large and versatile stocks. The prices are aromatic to many visitors' noses.

Books: **Miessner Libreros** (José Ortega y Gasset 14) probably contains this city's largest selections.

Flea Market: **El Rastro** ("The Thieves' Market") is an interesting jumble of junk—some good, some dreadful. Haggle hard; go from 10 A.M. to 2 P.M. on Sunday, and leave all your valuables (including passport!) in your hotel. Its so-called antique stores are also open on weekdays. Pickpockets are rife; trust *nobody.*

Department stores: **Sears Roebuck** (Serrano and Ortega & Gasset) has a reservoir of Yankee-Doodle sections. **Celso García** (Serrano 52) is definitely the highest-class Iberian entry. **Galerías Preciados** is stuffed with merchandise at lower-cost levels. **El Corte Inglés** is extremely popular with the Madrileños. **Woolworth's** (Juan Hurtado de Mendoza) offers a wide range, including Spanish souvenirs (mostly claptrap), and a cafeteria-cum-soda fountain. These are open during the usual siesta hours.

Please DON'T buy: Spanish shawls. The only real ones are antiques from China. This has become a tourist racket.

Shopping hours: Most shops selling anything but food: From 9:30 A.M. to 1:30 P.M. and 4:30 to 7:30 or 8 P.M. weekdays, with Saturday afternoon closings. Public markets: From 7:30 A.M. to 1 P.M.

Dedicated shophounds: Space is too tight here for further listings—so consult the purse-size, 25th Anniversary edition of *Fielding's Selective Shopping Guide to Europe* for more stores, more details, and more lore.

Other Targets

ALGECIRAS, traditional gateway to troubled Gibraltar, has grown to a city of 100,000 souls; it is Spain's 2nd fishing port and a tie-up for many passenger liners as well as container ships. Festivals and fairs occupy her time in June and August; there's a sleepy old town and a bustling new metropolis. In its environs, no fewer than 3 major tourist centers are either already perking or are preparing to lure merrymakers with sun, sea, sand, and salubrious

saludos. As the chief springboard to North Africa, Algeciras has hydrofoil (1 hour) and ferry (2¼ hours) links to Tangier which further enhance holiday rewards.

The **Reina Cristina** is the traditional choice for traditional living—a graceful morsel of yesteryear. Gardens, tennis, minigolf, seabathing, beautiful heated pool, in blue and gold mosaics, dancing, shopping, elbow-bending in its Patio Bar—all are on the premises or within easy reach. Cuisine which vies with the finest hotel fare in Spain; British ownership; well-trained Spanish staff as kind as ever on our recent stopover. We were especially fond of suites #246 and #346, which face the pool; both have working fireplaces. Keen professional attention by Manager Miguel Ares Lafuente. Highly recommended as a haven of tranquility if you are booked into any of its better accommodations. **Octavio**, which debuted its 80 units in late '73, seems eager to please—and except for its urban situation facing the bus depot, we think it achieves that end pretty well. Airy mezzanine restaurant; classic furnishings with marble highlighting; soundproofed accommodations; eye-soothing blues, reds, greens, or gold predominating on each floor. A reasonable value. Nearby, **Las Yucas**, one year older, boasts a more recessed location but not quite the same élan. All 33 rooms with bath or shower, piped music, and air conditioning, and a few of them (such as the "01" and "09" series) with terraces. Groups win the restaurant while independent explorers are shunted over to the cafeteria—so how's *that* for revealing its priorities? **Guadacorte** resides at *Los Barrios*, on Algeciras Bay about 12 miles toward Sotogrande. It still has many God-given assets in its favor. Man, however, has managed to infect the placid scene with a busy highway and a noxious petroleum cracking tower crowning the crest of a nearby knoll.

For dining in the region, the only sensible choice is the **Reina Cristina**, with its lovely summer garden and soothing music, or the independent romantic siren on neighboring Getares Beach, with its fish so fresh they'll practically leap off the plate to insult you, its sardines grilled on an open fireplace, its big steaks, and its view of "The Rock" (Gibraltar) across the bay. Full pension guests of the hotel may dine at the first without extra charge. **La Langosta**, with steaks, clawless lobster, other denizens of the sea, and good wine, is agreeable for its class. **La Cazuela**, cooks up open beams, nautical paintings, rugged country-textured flooring, and specialties of the briny. Not too bad when one really considers the alternatives. **La Sirena Dorada**, on the beach, happens to be one such alternative, in our book. **Mesón de Sancho** (20 minutes toward Cádiz) has sunk below sea level in our tide chart. Nix.

ALICANTE   **Apartotel Meliá Alicante** is a massive semiresidential promotion containing 800 apartments. A lease-out arrangement permits the renting of these private cliff dwellings to the general public. Its sawtooth eminence fairly dominates the sprawling metropolis. Within its society are 2 heated pools, 3 restaurants (we like the scenic El Postiquet with its buffet), the bar El Acuario, hairdresser, newsstand, souvenir shop, and nightclub. Accommodations break down into 7 decorative styles. When reserving pick an odd-numbered key for a sea view; we also recommend the "61" type. Massive in concept—as Meliá's projects usually are. Then we'd select either the **Gran Sol**

or the **Maya**. The former, in mid-city, offers a quiet lobby as a retreat from the frenetic street, a snack bar on the 26th floor, a sparkling and viewful bar-lounge, and pleasant, splendidly maintained kips, some of which proffer kitchenettes in their studio enclaves. The Maya, a 200-room, 10-story, chocolate-brown edifice overlooking Santa Barbara Castle, tilts heavily to an Aztec motif and tribal migrations from heap-big travel agencies. Ample facilities; 3 pools, tennis court, solarium; basement cafeteria; restaurant on first floor. Fatigue seems to be settling in at the **Carlton**. The staff remains one of the most graceful and helpful in the region, but the plant itself could use a shot of rejuvenation. At the newish **Residencia Covadonga** your happiness will very likely depend upon your luck in drawing an acceptable bedroom. If you snag a spacious one facing the plaza and the Lucerios fountain, your stay might be delightful. Otherwise, we're not too sure. Next we'd pick the 108-room, air-conditioned **Leuka**, perched up the hill and away from the worst effects of the madding crowd. This would be followed by the **Cristal**, which, appropriately, is sheathed in "cristal" and reflects a fair amount of commercial chill. Like many glass houses, it's pretty colorless and brittle. The **Bernia**, on the other end of the synthetic ladder, leans decidedly toward plastics. Of the front-desk personnel whom we encountered, we doubt if one was older than 14. With normal luck, a few may have aged by the time you check in. The **Residencia Palas** and the **Hotel Palas** have more in common than name and management. Both also share our lack of enthusiasm as oases for weary camel drivers. In brief: A last resort.

For diners, the leading choice, apart from the hotels which are not choice at all, is out at *La Albufereta*, a longish taxi jaunt from the center. It's called **Pizzeria Romana**, located on the Finca Las Palmeras, a private residence of the Decouty family, who have opened their ground floor as a 3-room Italian restaurant. The décor is just what you'd expect—right down to the red-checked curtains—and the cookery is a delight. Even though it's not Italian, please try the Mouclade Charentaise, which is heavenly. Tiptop, in any language. **Ranchito Vera Cruz**, at Playa San Juan, blows hot and cold, depending on the pair of proprietors who also blow hot and cold. Can be fun.

Strangely, this town seems to specialize in after-darkness ennui. **El Duende**, in the Hotel Carlos, and **Taifa**, in the Mélia, try, but, oh my, how we yawn! The **Albany** is less of a wheeze than the **Chamonix**; both could heal the woes of chronic insomiacs. Outside the city limits, **Playboy** and **Paraiso** knit up the ravell'd sleave of care with stunning efficiency. If you're like these reporters, you'll yearn for the sunrise.

ALMERIA   Refer to "Costa del Sol."

BARCELONA   This second most densely populated city in the world, is second in importance—a point which any good Catalan will heatedly challenge. It's on the Mediterranean coast, northeast of Madrid, about 100 miles from the Pyrenees, sitting on a rich plain between 2 rivers and 2 towering mountains. Catalans feel a very special identity with their metropolis, which proudly produces so much of the nation's wealth; since 1980, it has had its own provincial government called "La Generalitat." Artistic activities abound;

although its cultural attractions are numerous, it conducts business in American style and is a huge commercial port. One detriment is the throat-rasping smog from its booming industries that occasionally blankets the metropolis. The sudden and welcome proliferation of new hotels, restaurants, and other up-to-date facilities to shove into the background the generally weary and worn ones has already totally changed its complexion vis-a-vis the comforts of the visitor. Now it has become a dramatically more desirable touristic target.

★ **TIP** A new shuttle train runs between the Airport and the metropolis. By rail it's about 90¢ versus around $9 by taxi. The entrance in the flight terminus, well-marked, is up an escalator.

Sightseeing You may choose from the **Fine Arts Museum** (Medieval, Renaissance, Baroque Paintings and Sculpture), **Archeological Museum** (prehistory of the Moorish invasion), the **Natural History Museum** (stuffed animals and specializded 7000-volume library), the **Scenic Art Museum** (theatrical memorabilia in a Gaudí-designed building), the **Numismatic Museum** (coins of all periods), the **Municipal Museum of Music** (musical instruments, manuscripts, and effects of celebrated composers), the **Maritime Museum** (ship models and nautical lore), and other displays. The **Modern Art Gallery** features collections of nineteenth- and twentieth-century paintings, sculpture, and drawings; even more timely, the expanding **Picasso Gallery** was inaugurated in a fifteenth-century palace; it houses early paintings and sketches, later experiments in ceramics, plus the artist's 2 gifts of his assembled personal collection totaling more than 2000 works done between the ages of 9 and 22, plus a set of canvases finished when he was 36. Antiquary hounds may visit, under the street, the excavations of the original city as it stood from Christ's time to A.D. 400. Antonio Gaudí's **Templo Expiatorio de la Sagrada Familia,** a colossal, 1/5-completed (it was started in 1882) cathedral which resembles a 300-foot tall tower of gingerbread, is a must. Architecture buffs have been arguing about this edifice for nearly a century; you'll find it wondrous or a nightmare, but certainly you won't be apathetic. There are a fairly good **Zoo,** a **Terrarium,** and an **Aquarium.** The Young and the Brave have great fun riding the aerial railway and the Ferris wheel on **Mount Tibidabo.** As for the world-famous Monastery of **Montserrat,** about 30 miles out, you'll find a glorious vista—but like Lourdes, it is now so rotten spoiled by fringe commercialism that it is a disgrace. Our advice is to stay away.

Hotels Our leading choice is the sleekly modern **Princesa Sofia.** Totally air-conditioned; today-style marblesque lobby illuminated with baby-spots; commodious lounge up 1 flight; Le Gourmet restaurant in rust and black; rustic Bavaria room for more informal dining (a peculiar selection of Spanish rather than Teutonic dishes which were not impressive on our sampling); relaxing Mayfair Bar; Top City penthouse rendezvous for dinner dancing; light biting in the Snack 2002. To burn off some of the built-in calories there's a glass-fronted interior pool, a sauna, and a small gymnasium; there's also a hairdresser plus massage facilities. Bedrooms limited in space concepts but efficiently executed; all with TV, multichannel sonics, a Frigobar, and luxurious accoutrements; tariffs rather high for Iberia. Its location, about 15 minutes from midcity, may be a disadvantage to travelers who seek urbanity at their

doorstep; but if you don't mind the taxi ride, here, indeed, is a pleasant twenty-first-century address.

The **Ritz** boasts a loyal following from all over the globe. It is in the hands of Don Salvador Palmada, who made the Hostal de la Gavina at S'Agaro (70 miles up the coast) world famous as virtually the only gem along the otherwise squalid Costa Brava. He was also instrumental in polishing the facets of Mallorca's prestigious Son Vida. Gracious, ever-helpful Director Agustin Calonge boasts one of the most dedicated and efficient staffs in Europe. What this house vitally needs just now is a generous infusion of pesetas to exorcise the increasing creakiness which seems to be collecting like Spanish moss in a cypress garden. Most rooms are spacious, and all have private bath; Concierges Pablo and Pasqual are splendid professionals and human beings. Be sure to shop for your room here to secure top-grade lodgings. Hope your luck of the draw is good!

The 250-room **Diplomatic**, also in the center, may have more appeal for modernists. Handsome Los Borrachos Grill with a full, rich menu, a wine bin, and piano music nightly; Restaurant Chez Diplomatic; snack plus drinking bar; The Scotch disco hub; writing room and sumptuous lounges; TV nook; barber and beauty salon; garage; travel agency; news kiosk; Telex hookup. The 10-story, setback structure contains a Tom Thumb swimming pool and solarium on the 8th level with beverage and light-bite service; office facilities available for businessmen who live out of a briefcase. The bedchambers are not a smidgen of the Ritz's size, but most are well appointed and thoughtfully conceived; we're especially fond of #1026, a clean-lined suite. Carrier heating and cooling system with individual controls; phones in rooms and baths; AM-FM radio consoles; double windows; TV in suites and in the excellent double units ending in "5". Manager J. Mercadal, former chief at the Manila (see below) and a retired blue-water skipper (sea below), has a sound ship to command; we hope he holds a steady course and a happy crew.

Gran Hotel Calderon is a recent and welcome addition to the Barcelona innscape. Rooftop swimming pool with small bar and separate solarium affording a magnificent view of the city; hypermodernistic entrance and lobby; extremely handsome, spacious mirrored lounge; cocktail nookery with comfortable upholstered chairs; calm, tasteful dining room; piped music wafting through the public sancta; 100% air-conditioned. All 244 rooms with bath, double basins, and your own TV; varying arrangements for its smallish accommodations; 20 nice but routine suites; rather dark décor. Not quite up to the Diplomatic in its newest wing, but nevertheless good for the price and category.

For business reasons we recently spent about 3 weeks at the **Avenida Palace.** We think the best way we can describe it is to liken it to that proverbial well-shined and comfortable old shoe. Suave, genial Don Juan Gaspart is its experienced, energetic, and watchful majesty. Concierge Luis Romeu and his colleagues are outstandingly courteous and efficient; most of the floor personnel are adept; every minion we met here was sweet and kind. Busy lobby in marble, glass, brass, and wood; listless dining room with glassed-in fountain and better than adequate cuisine; plain bar; air conditioning; immaculately maintained; blond-wood furnishings and white chenille spreads in all the bed-

chambers. Good solid solace without glamour at a purse-satisfying price. The **Presidente** is in a very noisy locale. Unfortunately, its modern-day construction techniques are already disclosing such telltale signs of severe overstrain and extensive "settling" that they alarm and distress us. This 15-story structure, off the main traffic lanes, is of white stone, steel, and glass; a small hook-shape swimming pool-terrace on the 9th floor overlooks another outdoor sipping patio at the 4th-floor level. Simple but smart glass-lined restaurant with ebony leather chairs, globe illumination, and a maritime mural; wood and tartan bar adjoining the spacious mezzanine lounge; tiny Concierge's desk which results in client logjams during rush hours; management by Miguel Cabré, who did a sparkling job with the more modest Manila. All of its 150 doubles and 8 suites come with individually controlled Carrier air conditioning. Ample dimensions (except in the expensive and inexcusably cramped suites); wide, wide windows commanding romantic vistas of townscape and bay; burgundy wall-to-wall carpeting, bright prints, and twin beds throughout; every bath with twin basins, separate toilet-bidet compartment, and frosted louvered window. This Presidente is fast losing our vote.

The 200-room **Colón** is scenically sited face-to-face with the ancient Cathedral in the Old City. Management by young and alert Sr. Oritz; all units claim air conditioning and private bath or shower; pleasant subterranean Carabela Restaurant; smartly renewed corridors with brass lamplights of low wattage; demisuites ending in #06 are among the best buys in the province. We are also fond of the quintet of 6th-floor units with wide-open terraces; they'll put you eyeball-to-eyeball with one of the oldest churches in Christendom. Handsome décor highlighted with velvet furnishings, gold-leaf mirrors, and lovely prints; maintenance could be picked up a bit in some quarters. Many European travelers of taste choose this one for its tranquility, grace, and homey atmosphere. Here's a "Columbus" worth discovering.

The **Derby** tipped its brimful of British mannerisms onto a residential location near Sears, a 5-minute taxi ride from the Paseo de Gracia; marble-floored lobby with crimson-carpeted staircase; Epsom restaurant; wood-hued hideaway bar. All 115 units with chilled air and warm baths; all in soothing tones. Not in the top winner's circle, but a dependable "place."

The **Manila** continues to climb. Now air-cooled for summer sufferers; Telex; rustic rooftop Grill with marvelous view; expanded Nautical Bar, plus opera-lounge nook displaying portraits of famous singing stars; reasonably spacious rooms with woody touches; Lilliputian baths boasting sterile-seal guarantees; reasonable return for a reasonable outlay. Helmsman Francisco Carbonell, former Assistant Manager at the Avenida Palace, has taken over with flair and enthusiasm. As Barcelona stogies go, here's a pretty good local-Manila wrapper.

The **Arycasa** offers many Deluxe features in keeping with its category, but the universally tiny dimensions of the physical plant are its most forbidding detractions. All units with radio, private safe, and air conditioning; a handful of suites with private terraces; décor vaguely in the Chippendale manner. Trying hard, but it still leaves us cold.

Among the flock of lesser chicks, the **Barcelona** used to be one of the slickest. Now we find it molting pretty noticeably. The 60-unit **Regencia**

Colón, near the Colón and with the same ownership, offers bare shelter at greatly reduced tariffs. Poor for view, but passable for peseta watchers. The **Majestic** is passable as a midtowner; it has a small rooftop pool and sun deck; the newest wing is best. The **Cristal** is now so clouded, in our view, that we can't recommend it. The 76-room **Regente** offers better maintenance. Panoramic rooftop solarium, plus open terrace, restaurant, and tub-size swimming pool; newish restaurant at salon level; 2 floors with private balconies; well-outfitted bedchambers with individual air conditioners, 2 phones, door chimes, night bins for shoeshining, wall-to-wall carpeting, and cleverly designed bedlamps that won't disturb the other snoozer. Modern, functional, but too small in its twins for long-staying visitors; the singles, however, are ample. Director Rafael Bela gives a lot for the money; very pleasant for its type. The youthful **Balmoral** is more of a residential stop than a full-blown hotel; parking facilities for motorists; passable as a midtown hitching post. The **Gaudi** had sunk to such abysmal depths on our latest inspection that under no circumstances is it now recommended. The **Dante** kindles no inferno in our enthusiasm. Fair, but somewhat expensive for its unimaginative lodgings. The **Astoria,** the **Zenit,** the **Roma,** and the **Rallye** provoke only yawns in our moments of reflection.

Tibidabo Mountain rears its head over the city with 3 alternate entries. The **Florida**, with 54 rooms and baths, is near the top. Lovely view of the metropolis and the sea, but shoddy resort-style furnishings and poor upkeep; closed Off Season. **La Masía**, same ownership and crowning the peak, is category 1-B. Cretonne-y décor and bargain-basement fittings in its 29 units, all of which are located over its mass-production restaurant; simple and noisy. The **San Jerónimo**, at the Halfway mark, is fourth rate; not recommended to Yankee trippers. None of these, in our opinion, is worth the long haul from the doin's.

Restaurants This city's culinary pickin's are not as slim as they have been. Several notable additions within the past few seasons have perked up its table considerably. The Catalans—perhaps the most traveled Executive Set in all Spain—are demanding their due at last.

The Old World dining room in the **Hotel Ritz,** long a bell ringer for international kitchen craft, is the leading exponent of French *haute cuisine* though the rest of the hotel is not so *haute* anymore. High ceiling; classic mirrored walls; soothing piano lilts; faultless service reminiscent of bygone days; extensive (but not overextended) menu of traditional favorites; bountiful wine cellar. Our most recent repast here, set in the gentle and low-keyed ambiance often preferred by serious gastronomes, was perfect on all counts. Heartily recommended to any educated palate.

Atalaya (Av. Generalísimo Franco 523), in the penthouse of Catalonia's tallest building, turns on a spellbinding view of the metropolis and particularly of Antonio Gaudi's unfinished Sagrada Familia Cathedral. Stunning decorative complexions of purple, cyclamen pink, and white; attentive, knowledgeable staff; prices to match the sky-high locale; commensurate level of fare supervised by Chef Juan Méndez Raja. Although the menu, again, is not ponderous, it incorporates selected Spanish and French choices, focusing especially on fresh pickin's from local, Galician and Madrid markets. Both the restaurant and its underground bar and snackery are closed Sundays and

during August, as are many restaurants in this city. Splendid management by Director Manuel Giménez. Head and shoulders above any other independent groundling. The same group operates the novel **Zacarias** (Av. Gen. Franco 477) which is sort of an Executive Set discothèque with calories added. Small menu, but well selected; suave presentation; dressy, expensive, and recommended to young marrieds who jingle and swing.

Via Veneto (Ganduxer 10-12) is the gemstone of the young and keen Sr. Don Oriol Regas, who, with his brother, has also cornered the chichi trade at their equally luxurious Bocaccio discothèque. Professional greeting by a liveried doorman who also parks your cars (rare in this country); small cocktail nook at entrance with a standup minibar; main dining room on 2 tiers; flowered carpets, *fin de siècle* décor lavender-hued globe fixtures; plum leather chairs and banquettes; about 20 tables and several back rooms for satellite service; flower-embraced silver candelabra. Imperial attention from a sharp-eyed battery of carefully trained waiters; staff sometimes inclined to affect snobbish airs now that its success with Catalonia's nabobbery is assured; general supervision by Director Juan Carlos Lopez, Maître Roberto, and Sr. Quenó. Grand presentation from merlon-cut melons, to stuffed feathered pheasants, to flaming crêpes. Our wishes for luck and prosperity here appear to have been answered with cornucopias of good fortune and pesetas. *Muchos saludos!*

Hostal del Sol (Paseo de Gracia 44), formerly Olivero's, consumed $1-million from its previous owners before they cried "Uncle." It's a 2-story complex with a poor-ish snackbar on street level and a lavish, beautifully decorated, luxury restaurant up one flight, Outstandingly comfortable ambiance; piano after dark; good service by waiters in blazers; extensive menu. On-the-house extras include before-meal hor d'oeuvres and after-meal coffee, pastries plus a glass of sparkling wine. To our surprise and keen disappointment, however, dish after dish presented us were so loaded—*saturated*—with grease that after 1 taste of each we rejected them as inedible. Will it be "Uncle" again soon?

El Gran Gatopardo (Aribau 115) is a muscular "Great Leopard" that stalks a fashionable younger clientele. Though interesting in spots, overall we found it a bit pretentious. Burnt-orange terrycloth wall covering; comfortable black barrel chairs; lighting from cleverly conceived beige sconces; 12 tables on ground zero; 8 more on the mezzanine; electric humidors puffing up 9 varieties of stogies (4 from Havana); no music; adept waiters. Our only demurrer in the skilletry department concerns the chef's cloyingly apparent sweet tooth; everything—even the vegetables—seemed to have been dusted with a dose of Jack Frost. A high-priced sweetie, but not for diabetics.

Reno (Tuset 27) is another member of the silk-stocking bracket. Air-conditioned heptagonal room, with suave décor highlighted by comfortable black banquettes, paneled walls, and oversize windows; 15 tables inside, plus 10 smaller ones on glassed-in sidewalk terrace; deft, discreet service which oh-so-smoothly tends toward the "hard sell" approach. We happen to prefer it at lunchtime, because it's more crowded at nightfall. Better every year.

Quo Vadis (Calle Carmen 7) is simple but often very good. On other occasions, however, the chef goes wild with his salt shaker and condiment shelf. You'll find a decorative scheme employing stonework and bright tones;

a host of fast-paced waiters; meats and regional dishes, mostly. Patron Martin Forcada and his handsome son demand staff perfection; spotlessly clean. Tip: The smooth verbal pitch here to order the costliest items (*French* oysters, crab, and the like) is an irritant. Closed Monday.

Orotava (Consejo de Ciento 335) has been a favorite of loyal Catalonians for decades—so much so, in fact, that many regard it as their private club in Barcelona. The beaten-copper façade graphically depicts the wild game specialties that are featured inside. The service is swift and kind; the cuisine and the presentation are highly laudable. A topflight bag, but bring along your money belt loaded with ammo.

Guría (Casa Nova 99), one of the most highly praised havens in its niche of the sky, is a complete enigma to us. Close friends swear their affection for us will dissolve unless we pronounce it the finest gastronomic center in Europe. Other knowledgeable Barceloneses wink and say that the owner's technique is a masterpiece of artifice. "Insiders" maintain that the luscious young waitresses are so craftily trained in coquettish wiles that the diner could stuff himself with bedsprings and not know the difference. Our recent incognito tests were a total shambles, from service to cookery. Basque specialties are predominant. It's dealer's choice on this one.

Agut d'Avignon (Trinidad 3), tucked away in an obscure cul-de-sac off Calle Aviñó in the Old Town, is another regional bell ringer. Ramon Cabau, its mustachioed, energetic owner, carefully supervises the belfry of belles, including his daughter, who swing to your wishes in black uniforms and pink aprons. Romantic 3-story residence divided into quintet of working segments; clean surroundings; simple interior highlighted by huge turn-of-the-century murals. Our party's Sopa al ¼ hora (fish soup), Pulpitos (infant squid), Tortilla de Trufas (truffle omelette), Habas a la Catalana (broadbean stew), and Anec amb Figues (duck with figs) were fit for a feast. Lunchtime jammed with businessmen (and occasionally Salvador Dalí); dinner hours crowded with legions of society settlers; functioning 1 P.M. to 5 and 9 P.M. to 1 A.M.; closed Sundays, Christmas, and *Semana Santa* (Holy Week). *Saludos y olés!*

Epsom, in the lower paddock of the Hotel Derby (Loreto 25) is a worthy mount in the local sweepstakes. Wreath-like food display greeting hungry stallions and mares at the bottom of the stairs. Very sound tip sheet touting, Catalan and French entries, all of which are well groomed and priced to stay in the running. Proud silks, every one.

Carballeira (Reina Cristina 3) faces the port, unloading a cargo of similar nibblings in far more modest precincts. Possibly $5 have been invested in fancying up the joint, but the fins in the pan receive primary concern in this coaster. The long lines of happily anxious clients waiting to dine here vouch for the values. Kind, considerate service (daily Spanish stock-market report on each luncheon table); hosting by Sr. Ribas; extremely busy from 1:30 P.M.

Casa Bofarull-Los Caracoles Bodega (Escudillers 14) is colorful and charming, with so much regional flavor that many less hardy clients consider it unsavory. Not so at *all!* Caracoles means "snails"; this is the specialty, but everything under the sun is available! The entrance looks discouraging, but once inside, you pass the huge woodstove to find yourself in a small backroom,

one of 3, with a balcony above. The walls are lined with wine casks, peppers, garlic clusters, and drying spices; the snail pattern is followed in the shape of the special bread. Daily recommendations of the chef are written on the back window, in bright chalk; all tables are generally full during the rush hours. The roast-chicken-on-a-spit is worthy of an award—which it once received in Paris (order *pechuga* if you want white meat). Menus are in 4 languages, including English—and their listed prices are still simple for this simple type of place. Use a cab instead of your own car, because the streets are too narrow. Beloved Founder-Owner Antonio Bofarull has passed to his reward, but his spirit remains to reward the customer—and so does his experienced and personable son, Don Feli. In our opinion, this down-to-earth oasis which has pleased hundreds of celebrities gives the most and the best for the money in the city. Open from 1:30 P.M. to 1:30 A.M. every day of the year.

Hogar Gallego (Layetana 5) is another no-nonsense vendor of very variegated victuals, the galaxy flavored with Galician gusto and none pegged to pop the top off your piggybank. Shellfish, which are the specialty here, have their own small stall near the door; the main dining room, mezzanine, and back area hold perhaps 60 tables; service is rushed but capable; our sea-fresh Centollos (spider crabs) were sheer gifts from the cool Atlantic. Open every day; reservations recommended for Sundays and holidays. YUMMY.

The **Hostal del Dimoni** (Antico Ampurdanes Herzegovino) is on our list for an upcoming trial. It's said to be amusing in a crackpot way.

Koldobika, behind the Ritz, spotlights Basque cookery. Conglomerate decorative themes. Heavy use of tiles; adroit waitresses; spotlessly scoured. The cuisine here has picked up so markedly that it's left us almost speechless (but *not* wordless!). Now basking in its well-earned glory.

Udala (Sicilia 202) provides yet another bow to the gastronomy of the Pyrenees—and even less expensively than the above. Lobby entrance to the main chamber; upper sanctum with 8 more tables; bar with guayana wood stools; simple, clean décor; unobtrusive piped music. Our Pisto a la Bilbaína (scrambled eggs, tomatoes, and red and green peppers) was an unusual treat; so were the accompanying *sidra* (cider) and the follow-up glass of Karpy, the Basque version of Cointreau.

La Pérgola (Av. María Cristina near Plaza España) faces Europe's largest colored fountain—an impressive display which, unfortunately, splashes only on Saturday and Sunday evenings during the colder months. Commodious premises with capacity of 500 noisy munchers or sippers, split 50-50 between ground floor and spacious terrace 1-flight up; popular with the masses (and the Iberian equivalent of our own drugstore cowboys) for lunch, tea, dinner, dancing, and nipping; cozy for its size; well illuminated; no cabaret. Never bother at teatime, because you'll think you are fighting your way through a January white sale at Macy's. So crowded on weekends that advance reservations are urged. Fair enough for the price bracket.

A la Menta (Plaza Manuel Girona 50, behind the Royal Palace) opened in this essentially residential area in '70. Long, narrow *marisco* (shellfish) bar on street level; downstairs segment of 3 rooms and perhaps 15 tables, plus an arresting display of raw vegetables, seafood, and fruit; rustic national décor; l-o-w tariffs for such hearty fare; smooth, cordial service. Open from 1:30 P.M.

to 4:30 and from 8:30 to 1 A.M. every day except Christmas. More than worth the long taxi trot from the center.

La Bruixa Borracha, or "The Drunken Witch" (Sarria 15), is every bit as off-beat as its name, décor, and menu suggest. Three diminutive dens conjured with painted ceilings, red velvet, Tiffany lamps, old heavy portraits, pale-purple linen, and antiques in abundance, all of which meld into a savory brew. The recipes of the spirit world bear such titles as "Garlic Soup Which Makes The Man Handsome" and "Feast of the Wizards" (a nineteenth-century con-coction of snails in rabbit sauce); finish off with "The Cup of the Drunken Witch," combining pineapple, peach, flan, ice creams, sherbert, whipped cream, and rum cake served in a mortar bowl the size of Bela Lugosi's skull. Please ask that your wine be decanted into one of the 15 exquisite champagne glasses found in a Gerona convent *(convent???)*. Open from 1 P.M. to 4 and from 9 to, well, to the bewitching hour; closed Sunday from June to September. This bubble's definitely worth the toil and trouble.

Finesterre (Av. Gen. Franco 469) had perhaps the greatest fame, but to us it sadly lacks consistency. Some dinners we've eaten here have been quite good; at other times, the plates have been stone cold, the potatoes limp with cold grease, and the table service about as sloppy as that of a Tenth Avenue Coffee Pot. Good when good, but very poor when bad.

Petit Soley (Plaza Villa de Madrid 5) is a young and tiny entry; ample parking, for a change; open grill in center; roving guitar players at intervals; hot in summer; busy, noisy, and gay. The cookery is recommendable but not exciting. The only surprises are on the bills—unhappy ones.

For finny denizens in more characteristic surroundings, **Casa Costa**, in nearby *Barceloneta*, is a Catalan-style picnic pavilion that opens directly onto the beach. There's a baker's dozen of similar establishments along this row. Cheap prices; rough but friendly service; enormous kitchens with hefty blue-clad Mammas rattling the pans; savory preparations in the plebeian manner.

Restaurant de l'Ast, on Miramar, offers a lovely view of the Barcelona Port, fine rôtisserie chicken *(Ast* means "Spit"), a charming terrace, soothing prices —and now its welcome has improved vastly.

In this same general vicinity, **La Torre de San Sebastián**, a cableway tower overlooking the harbor, comes up with crude seafare, low prices, an abundance of litter on the floor—but one of the most magnificent panoramas in the region. Go for the view only.

Casa Jordi (Passatge Marimón 18), an inexpensive family eatery, romps in with *porróns* of red wine on the tables and plates of fried whitings, Pa Torrat amb Oli i Domática (toasted peasant bread with olive oil and sliced tomatoes), local olives and other such nibblings delivered as soon as you are seated. We like this honest house and its owner, who trained at the fabulous Gleneagles in Scotland and scored a double birdie when he married a bonnie lassie and brought her home to open this braw *casa.*

Niu-Guerrer (Plaza de Tetuán 6, about 4 blocks from the Ritz), is a long narrow establishment reached through a jumble of bars and checkrooms. Ceramic plates and pitchers on a dado under the ceiling; Catalan offerings on an expansive but not expensive menu; okay in an oddball way. **El Canario de la Garriga** (directly opposite the Ritz) is another comfortable, family-style

nest. About 30 tables; another decorative collection of kilned platters, pots, and pitchers; happy waiters in plaid shirts; a gratis offering of *boquerones* (white-bait marinated in brine) to encourage your appetite. Although the prices are low and the food is substantial, we can't get too enthused over this one.

Tinell (Freneria 8–10), in the Gothic quarter, is convenient for visitors to the Cathedral. Small, simple bistro; 3 weensy dining dens; clean; economical; sound, wholesome cookery featuring game in season.

Italian? **Peppone** (Maestro Nicolau 2), a block-wide combination snackery and deluxe smackery, loses something in the Catalan translation. Both sections are large, effectively fitted with autumn-hue tablecloths, white chairs, black ceilings, and planter boxes; you'll also reflect on a mirrored wall, a tiered antipasto board fringed with fresh fruit, and rush-covered wine bottles. Attractive presentation dimmed somewhat by the rock music. Fair, but not too authentic in flavor—at least to our palate.

Spanish-style "American" hot dogs, hamburgers, griddle cakes, and the like? Dozens of cafeterias have begun to sprout in the city. Catalonian attempts to imitate our light bites can sometimes be lauded for effort but almost never for results. Although the **Atalaya Cafeteria** is removed from the shopping area (Avenida Generalísimo Franco 523), it is worth the longer ride because here is by worlds and worlds the most attractive of the rather sorry lot we have inspected. This is sited in the basement of the city's tallest skyscraper and is under the same management as the ultrachic Atalaya Restaurant in the penthouse. The surroundings are rich and soothing; the fare is so far from what mother used to make that it won't even give you nostalgia for your corner drugstore. Nonetheless, if you play the Pretending Game here, you might like it. Sit at the bar area for reduced rates, because the dining area on the side has boosted prices by perhaps 10¢ or 15¢ on each item. **Kok d' Or** (Calle Balmes 149) is also physically attractive—but oh, that chef! Never again for us. **Le Pub** (Paseo de Gracia 44) does, indeed, show the trappings of Albion. However, its multinational combination of Spanish-made Yankee-style burgers in an English aura filled with a faintly French-sounding name adds up to a rather pale copy of the letters U-S-A. **Comedia Club** (next to the Avenida Palace Hotel), on the other griddle, pans out passable but far from memorable skilletry on its ground level. All breads and pastries baked on the premises. Upstairs restaurant not worth the climb, in our opinion. The **Treno** (in the Cristal Hotel) is also better than average for small appetites, but please remember that the average around here is pretty darned low. **Moka** (on the Rambla, opposite the flower market) perks out a snack area with steeper-tariffed grillroom beyond. Our beef was overseasoned; don't order vichyssoise unless you're accustomed to having it served hot. To our cup, this Moka is a weak blend. **La Luna, Samoa,** and **Kansas** huddle under the same managerial wing. We now skip the lot. **Salón Rosa** (Paseo de Gracia) is popular with Spanish *señoras* for tea. We walked into **Navarra** (Paseo de Gracia 2), pivoted on our first step, and walked right out. **Glaciar** (Plaza Real) is well catered and cheap, but hyper-Iberian in its notions on light-biting.

Out at the airport, **San Jorge** is an almost hidden nook beside the main restaurant. A dozen tables in Deluxe surroundings; charming décor; polished, attentive service. Although its prices are virtually double those of the main

establishment, in our view it's worth the difference to the tired traveler in transit who seeks blessed quiet and who doesn't mind the higher costs. *Open noon to 4 P.M. only 7 days per week*.

Night Life In this nocturnal city, the Smart Set highsteps smartly out to the **Bocaccio** (Muntaner 505), which is owned by the Regas tribe of Via Veneto fame. Chic clientele of well-dressed discothèque-niks; crimson color scheme with Art Nouveau trimmings; Tiffany lamps and glasses in a bamboo pattern; well-paced music that even permits fuddy-duddy fox-trotters such as us to get in an occassional jog. Here's an elegant entry that vies with this brand of night spot almost anywhere on the Continent. Top recommendation for its type. Next is **Los Tres Molinos** (end of Av. Gen. Franco). This "Three Windmills" offers interior, patio, and teatime dancing; poor cookery; same ownership as La Pérgola; highish prices; flamenco entertainment at times; no bar girls (as such); open year round. These are followed by—*at this instant only* —**Baccara, Ciro's, Snob,** and **Le Clochard**; way, way up at Fun Fair, a peer titled **Lord Black** turns on unusual flicks on midsummery eves.

The hottest corner for *winter* play is the sophisticated, modern **Papagayo**, a subterranean living room (or Junior Executive Suite). Mustard-colored easy chairs; gaming-table bar; superb orchestra during our Bar-ce-lone-rangerings; no show; reasonable tabs. Elegant, suave, and pleasant for this mercantile city. **Las Vegas**, where local socialites gambol, sip, jiggle, and yak, places second in this hierarchy. *Nouvelle vague* singer, usually French; fairly expensive; no pickups. Closed during the *caliente* months. **Shangri-La** (Muntaner 492) is an infant sired by the Las Vegas owners. Dancing but no cabaret. The **Planeta 2001** is a novelty. The highlight here is in your highball—an illuminated drinking glass that is now blinking in several other Iberian darkspots. After you've closed this one (*if* you're single that evening), down your nightcap at **Chez Charley** while sizing up the battalions of distaff talent.

Next, here's a rundown, starting at the top, of the hustle-for-bustle gin mills: The air-conditioned **Emporium** (Muntaner 4) has improved—but, although it now offers the best show and draws the nicest clientele in its league, we always expect to be greeted at the portal by Texas Guinan or P. T. Barnum. This one's for the big-spending butter-and-olive trade; too rich for our blood. **Jardines Granada** is supremely uninteresting, as is **Andalucía de Noche** (Rambla). The **Kit-Kat** (Escudillers, in the Old Quarter) is a nightclub-cum-discothèque-cum-cafeteria-cum-snack-bar, with sterile furnishings, and limp atmosphere; forget it. The nearby **New York** is reported to be far, far better; we haven't yet commuted to this Gotham. **El Brindis** (Plaza Real) is a sailors' favorite; routine dancing spot, apparently not clip (but don't bank on it). **Pan Am's** is about the same; it has nothing to do with the airline of the same name; allegedly, from reports, a fly-by-night operation. **Barcelona de Noche**, **La Macarena**, and **Venta Eritaña** are not, repeat not, recommended; the customer has about as much of a break in these as he would get on an old-fashioned carnival midway.

Jamboree (Plaza Real) is a rock-em-and-sock-em jazz joint for listening and jam sessions. Here's where nearly every visiting big-name musician jumps when he's in town.

Flamenco? The best we've found is at **Los Tarantos**, next to the Jamboree

and under the same ownership. V-shape room with a raised platform at the bottom of the V; ambiance that tries valiantly to resemble a gypsy camp; lantern illumination; continuous shows from 10 P.M. to 3 A.M.; every performer a serious artist in this ethnic specialty. To us, certainly worth the outlay.

Bodega del Toro (Conde del Asalto 103) also can be a delight to lovers of this form of Iberian art—as long as they (1) have flaps on their pockets, and (2) learn the Spanish word for "no" (it is "NO!"). Attractive mien; small stage; no food; terrific musicians and performers; painfully expensive for the Catalan league. Watch out for this smoothly executed swindle here: after 10 or 12 gypsies have come to your table to show their stuff, they'll coolly invite themselves to 1 or 2 rounds of drinks at your expense—and suddenly you'll wake up with a $100 tab clutched in your moist palm. To avoid this slick charade, your best protection is to glue yourself to the bar from the time you enter; you can see and hear all the doin's from there. Gaiety and excitement if you hit it right—but don't trust even your own brother here or in *any* of the gypsy joints in the Old Quarter, because they're expert in flimflam. Closed Monday.

Straight discing? They are, in descending order: **Metamorfosis** (Calle Beethoven—*sic*!), **Mix** (Urgel 10), **La Lechuza** (Tuset 1), **Le Clochard** (Muntaner 492), and **Lord Black** (Parque Montjuich).

Nightlife perks along the Calle Tuset. Among the candidates is the downstairs **La Cova del Drac**, the upstairs **El Drug Store** with music and entertainment at stiffish tabs, **El Doblón**, **Runner's Club**, and **Club Gotarda** (opposite the José Antonio monument). **Baccarra** and **Bori y Fontesta** are said to be fun places. Catalan friends recommend each for its respective character—but more we cannot tell you.

For cocktails (8 P.M. to 10:30 P.M.), there's the **Marfil**, where just about everybody goes for that casual drink—or to meet that "model." In conformance with many other establishments, it's divided into 2 sections; one bar is for men only (in the Spanish sense), and the other is for "respectable" clients. Ho-hum. On our recent round, we were again told that even better-looking babes inhabit the **Bar Club**. When we investigated, the clientele consisted of 1 lone, toad-faced inebriate who was heaving his hulk away from the sauce counter; we had another look later—almost exactly the same scene.

In the shank of the evening, **La Masia** really rocks. It's a few minutes out of town (Av. Gen. Franco at Esplugas); from the outside, it looks like a country house, but the inside has tables, a dance floor, a bar, hard-working musicians, a serious-minded chef, and 86-proof clients. Just the place to go after that 3rd or 4th brandy-and-soda, when the world is encased in a gentle rosy glow. Your wife might lap up this one, too. No show.

Tropical and **Capri**, summer entries at nearby *Gavá* (9 miles out), are so 2nd-string in quality that your drive would be wasted. Starseekers, however, enjoy them for the swimming.

Something very special? **Salòn García Ramos** (San Elias 42 bis; be *sure* to get directions from your concierge, because few cabbies know it) is a rare "find." The entrance is via a garden gate, basement staircase, and then through a narrow passage to a simple cellar vault. Here is Don García's shrine to Spanish folk and classical music—to poetry from Lorca to unknowns, to study

by worshipful students (who bring their instruments and are permitted to play), to nonbeatnik respect for sentiment and art. Although he may pour the drinks, turn the lights up and down, and greet incoming guests, the Master is not a nightclub operator. While he recites in his native tongue only, you will learn his meanings through his eyes and his gestures, even if you don't understand a spoken word. Plain, plain room; paintings, rosaries, and guitars on the walls; creaky to outright broken chairs; a simple but honest atmosphere, with low-price drinks to match. If you are at the door and hear him performing, please enter quietly and wait for him to seat you. (He also respects his neighbors, even to the point of asking that you speak softly on the streets surrounding his haven.) This we promise: If you approach this gentleman's studio with respect and in seriousness, you might be rewarded with one of the deeply spiritual experiences of your life. Highest recommendation.

Shopping Barcelona's **Paseo de Gracia** between Plaza Cataluña and the Diagonal has the best shops; if you stroll along each side in turn, you'll probably find what you're after, in the highest quality. For local color, try the U-shape walk from **Plaza de Pino** through **Calle Petritxol**, around the corner of **Puerta Ferrisa** to **Galerias Malda**, and back again to Plaza de Pino. This street offers a gaggle of shoes, watches, candy, and staple items. **Loewe** (Paseo de Gracia 35) has no rivals for handbags and traditional Spanish leather goods. Neither has **Yanko** (Paseo de Gracia 100) for the finest ladies' and men's shoes in the nation.

BENIDORM seems to cater solely to German tourists. The wide sandy beach is a dream—one of the best on the Mediterranean—but, on every day during High Season here, it is just like Coney Island on the Fourth of July. The **Delfin** is the Deluxe catch of the school. Quiet waterside situation with a sleek residential ambiance; excellent pool; appealing restaurant; winsome cafeteria for light bites; simple furnishings; bid only for a room facing the sea. Recommended chiefly for being away from the hurly-burly. The **Corregidor Real** is in the same bracket. It's 1 block from the sea, in the center of town. This youngster opened all the stops and valves in its Spanish décor—so overdone, in our opinion, that it is touristy-gimmicky. Extensive use of wood, bricks, rough textiles, and colored glass; tiny pool with adjoining bar; nightclub; 35 rooms and 35 baths. All right if you go for *mucho, mucho, mucho* flash. Operative from March 1 to October 30. The triangular-shape **Glasor** is efficient but coldish; snag a seaside unit, because the others can be deafeningly noisy. **Los Alamos** is also in the front line. **Les Dunes** has become so careworn its sparkle has gone, we're sad to say. Excellent midbeach situation; grimly pedestrian in taste. The **Brisa** also has become winded in the race. Now spavined, to our eyes. **Planesia**, on the mountain slope, provides a warm welcome from Reception Chief Andreas Guerrero, brother of our friend at Valencia's Royal. Although the remainder of the Benidormitories are not recommended at this writing, changes occur so rapidly here that it would be wise to make an up-to-the-instant check with your travel agent immediately before departure from the U.S.

BILBAO's most up-to-date comfort salesman is the centrally sited, 4-star **Ercilla**, which complements its 350 fully bathed bedchambers with a restau-

rant and cafeteria, discothèque, sauna and massage facilities, beauty parlor, travel agency, souvenir shop, and car-hire service. Next comes the riverfront **Nervion**, with enough of a parking problem to unnerve arriving motorists. (Once you unload, however, it does have a garage.) Dark lounge; airy cafeteria; dining room with gracious bar; thoughtful space concepts which make this a sound buy for overnighting. The **Aranzazu** (meaning "Holly") is a fair tuck-inn, with ample-size bedchambers and an ingratiating staff. Its sister operation, the **Avenida**, doesn't tick over quite so well in our opinion. Perhaps this chain is concentrating on the deluxe star on the Gran Via, the **Villa de Bilbao**. We haven't yet seen it, but we hear that it could become the local pacesetter. Down the scale come the **Conde Duque**, facing the river near the Nervion, with small, clean, yet uninspired cubicles, the old-fashioned **Carlton** which has seen better days and nights, and, finally, the **Almirante**—a creaky bark that to us no longer has bite.

When you're hungry, fly arrow-straight to **El Txangurro** (Alda, Urquijo 74) with its fishnet trappings, paintings framed in portholes, waitresses in sailor's garb, friendly service, and daily harvest of fresh, fresh fish. We loved every nibble of the bait and urge you to take its hook, too. After this one, we like **Luciano** (Barrencalle 38 and 40, in the Old Town). When you strut down the alley, peek in at all the frenzied culinary commotion in the kitchen and be prepared to lick your chops. Polished timbers, brass chandeliers, and brick fireplace; well-groomed clientele; kindly welcome. And don't let war, depression, or lockjaw keep you from trying the fresh anchovies, the palate-cheering Changurro (Basques spell it as in the above restaurant; it's chopped crabmeat in its giant shell), the piping-hot stuffed red peppers, or the home-grown Tarta (cake). You'll gobble for hours and then float away light as a fine soufflé.

If it's summer, join the stream of pilgrims to *Santurce*, 3 miles out. Then follow the tradition by buying sardines direct from the fishing boats and taking them to the little *tascas* where they'll fry them for you in a special way. Order Chacolí (apple wine) and bread, roll up your sleeves—and you're already 50% a *Vasco!* A famous ritual.

Bilbao is big on bars (about 125 in its Bario Chino district, which is perfectly safe and fun to see). **Trana, El 7, Gaucho, San Remo**, and **New York** are a few better examples. **Guria, Lasa, Machimbenta**, and **Changurro** are the leading nightclubs.

BURGOS, the home of El Cid and the early capital of Spain, comes up with the colorfully rustic **Hostal Landa**, 2 miles south of town on N-1, and the less attractive **Hostal del Cid**, north of the city limits on the same highway.

CÁDIZ has the drab commercialism of a port town. Its citizens spring from such mixed stock that they hardly look Spanish, as a group; the physical and psychological contrasts with neighboring Seville couldn't be broader or more striking.

This harbor will never be remembered for its hotels—or perhaps it will. They're miserable—so bad, in fact, that unless you *must* stop here, we sincerely recommend you pass it up and whip around the bay to overnight at the Hotel Fuentebravía in Puerto Santa María (description directly follows). The **Atlántico** is coming up, we're told, but we haven't seen it lately ourselves.

What's left is the 65-kip **Francia y Paris**, which never thrilled us. Shelter can be found at the **Isecotel**, which turns on 120 apartments year round—mostly for French package tourists who don't seem to mind its abundant gloom.

Now, here's how we'd rate the local restaurants: (1) **El Telescopio** (casks of local flavor), (2) **El Anteojo** (simple, dirt-cheap, with some of the most savory prawns and filet of sole in the nation), (3) **El Sardinero** (spotless, unpretentious, and centrally located, with friendly staff), and (4) **Comedor Vasco** (*bodega*-type décor with U.S.-Greek-restaurant overtones, for winter dining). **Pasaje Andaluz** is getting better and better.

CANARY ISLANDS   The climate, though windy, is gloriously benign; most of the handsome population offer hearts and smiles of rare warmth and beauty; some of the scenic vignettes are magnificently spectacular. It so distresses us to see these lovely isles despoiled by mass, crass tourism that we never wish to return. Therefore, please accept our apologies that further information about this erstwhile semitropical paradise must be sought elsewhere. To us, these islands have slid so far down the drain in terms of travel pleasure that today we do not consider them worth reporting in these pages.

CARTAGENA   offers the sea-girt sporting paradise of **La Manga** with its 36 holes for golf, 15 clay or lawn tennis courts, marina and cove, clubhouse, and facilities for brief or extended holidays as well as for resident settlers. Late reports to us state that is has slipped as a dream zone for sporting types. True? We don't know, but we'll trek there soon.

CASTELLÓN DE LA PLANA   (Mediterranean coast, 39 miles north of Valencia): The beachside **Golf** features Seville-style architecture, with its modern accommodations embracing a wide open patio. We are told that the service is now poor—contrary to our prior findings. The smaller **Turcosa** is said to provide better client attention, possibly because, as a year-round operation, the staff is more stable.

CÓRDOBA   beguiles us more on each successive visit—and we're darned if we can figure out why, because it's practically changeless. Its colossal Mezquita (1000-year-old mosque which is now the Cathedral) is one of the show places of the nation; its Romero de Torres collection (the twentieth-century eccentric who painted prostitutes as saints) is intriguing; its narrow streets in the Old Town and ghetto have color and charm. About 5 miles out, the fabulous ruins of the Medina Azahara are breathtaking; this palace (almost a mile long and more than a ½-mile wide) was built at the same time as the Mezquita, by the Caliph of Córdoba. The nearby Monasterio San Jerónimo (vintage 1405), with its enchanting primitive cloister, is also worth a visit; try to talk your way into its privately owned precincts. We did—and we loved it.

Locally, the **Parador Nacional de la Arruzafa** comes as a tonic to trippers who count their greenbacks. This up-to-date link in the Spanish State Tourist Department's chain is startlingly deluxe for its rates. Gorgeous ambiance with sweeping plains of polished marble; 56 doubles; air conditioning and central heating; highly dunkable pool; telephone in every room *and* bath; private

terraces overlooking the city and Guadalquivir Valley; kiddie-corner for children's dining. Here's a king-size value for anyone's money. A passable choice in the independent league is the **Meliá Córdoba**. Though its physique is handsome, its grooming looked slack to us. Enclosed dance terrace overlooking the swimming-pool patio; dining salons getting oldish; TV lounge; every suite with a refrigerator; cunning desk-table tops which disguise the air-conditioning ducts. Only fair. Facing La Mezquita, the town's chief tourist attraction, **Residencia Maimonides** welcomes pilgrims with gracious arms, clean appointments, and a friendly míen. The Caballo Rojo snack stall subs for a fuller restaurant. All 1973-vintage chambers with private bath; plenty of living space; good taste on display from cranny to cranny. In short, a *mitzvah*. **Los Gallos** crows about its rooftop pool, terrace, and bar; a viewful patio; an attractive, somewhat spare lounge; a red and white diner in the cellar; 97 doubles, 6 singles. The **Gran Capitan** offers the finest view imaginable of the railroad yard. Five-tiered structure enfolding 100 look-alike units; commercialized 2nd-floor reception; limp garlic-spiced restaurant; bar-lounge. Maintenance overall seemed pauce to us. That aside, our main demurrer here is the roundhouse location. The **Zahira** also excites us—to beat a retreat! Possible alternates include the **Selu**, the **Colón** and the **Marisa**, none of which we've carefully inspected.

Among the restaurants, for color, **El Zoco**, owned by the Melía interests, is a stunner. This was an authentic Moorish market situated in the very heart of the ancient ghetto. In the basement (now a *bodega*), a nucleus of Jews kept their forbidden religion alive during the Inquisition; across the alley, in a state of wonderful preservation, is the oldest (only one small room) synagogue in Europe. In addition, this structure also houses the Museum of Bulls (Museo Taurino) for Córdoba. Several rooms strung throughout numerous levels of the complex; open patio for summer dining and viewing the evening flamenco dancing; lovely fountain bubbling throughout the performance. Not a gustatory shrine—very poor, in fact, for cookery—but a memorable experience for any holidaymaker's circuit. Tops in town as a touristic drawing card. For simple nutrients without as much theatrical and/or historical flair, the **Mesón El Caballo Rojo** ("House of the Red Horse"), with its viewful summer terrace, and the **Mesón del Conde** ("House of the Count") are recommendable; both are typical regional taverns. For a sunny-day excursion, **Castillo de la Albaida** is a modest but deserving choice. One mile out of town, on the road toward Trasierra; tranquilizing 270° vista of the plains and distant mountains; country manse atmosphere, with the best feature its open terrace for viewful munching; homespun service that can become over-busy-busy on weekends or holidays; steaks cooked "well done" unless you specify otherwise; our garlic soup was the best we had on that circuit (but it lingered for days, our friends tell us). No great fireworks, but it can kindle a cheerful ambiance if you're in the mood. For hotel fare, we hear that the **Córdoba Palace** has improved significantly in its skillet skills. In fact, the only flies in the *gazpacho* come from readers who complain that swarms of winged critters attack at mealtimes on the open poolside terrace. Otherwise, this hotel seems to be taking giant strides in all directions. On our latest try, the dining room in the **Gran Capitan** combined fumbling service with sludgelike Stuffed Bull's Tail Cordoba.

COSTA BLANCA ("White Coast"): This fancy name for the coastline between Almeria and Alicante is being popularized to handle the overflow from the overcrowded Costa Brava. Still primitive in general, but the building spree has already added dramatically to its aspirations to carbon-copy its neighbor. To its credit, it has not quite achieved this goal—but another few seasons of gigantismic growth should make the mutation complete.

COSTA BRAVA ("Rugged Coast"): This stretch of mountains, cliffs, and bays between Barcelona and the French border, has undergone a shocking transition. Here is today's story, and it is grim: (1) Thundering herds flood across its borders in bargain-basement charter groups to despoil its beautiful landscape. (2) Generally speaking, the hotels are miserable. In addition, only a handful are situated on scenic sites. Some sections of the "Rugged Coast" are more panoramic and breathtaking than the Amalfi Drive, but there are no lodgings on them. (3) Although a number of fine new trunk highways have materialized, the vast majority of the roads are still very narrow and serpentine. Loaded with buses, cars, trailers, motorbikes, scooters, campers, and heaven knows what else, they remain a single gigantic traffic snarl during the holiday months. Personally, we find so little of true value here that we have decided to peel this Spanish onion right off our research lists.

Our lone exception remains the world-famous **Hostal de la Gavina** at **S'Agaro**, about 70 miles from Barcelona. Almost 100% reconstructed or refurbished; the features receiving most of the beauty treatment include the entrance, elevators, Japanese garden, snack bar, Candlelight Room (elegant, intimate dining to piano lilts), and oak-paneled, gold-leafed Louis XV Royal Suite. Beautiful lounges with antique furnishings; terrace-dining in season; high cuisine; 100 rooms and 16 suites, most with plush décor and bath; a few accommodations still small and simple; tennis courts and fair beaches. Its pool with cabanas and Snack Bar rivals any similar installation on the Mediterranean coast. The jewel of jewels in Catalonia; top rates and top quality. Splendid —as long as you don't mind the man-made horrors along its approach roads which spoil the area for us.

COSTA DEL SOL ("Sunny Coast"), with Torremolinos, Marbella, El Rodeo and other resort settlements strung along the 106-mile strip of seacoast on the Algeciras–Estepona–Málaga road, is geared to package tourism as well as to independent voyagers. The streets of Torremolinos and neighboring Málaga swarm in High Season with nonwriting writers, nonpainting painters, everyday sun-and-funseekers, and expatriates of a dozen nationalities. Contrary to her neighbors, Marbella is much more select and sedate; the sea bathing is excellent, the golf courses are perfect, and the atmosphere is sportingly chic. Rampant new construction in all categories from Deluxe to budget level has transformed hamlets, villages, and entire areas into an Iberian version of a Florida land boom. With so many hostelries writhing for attention, the newest trend is the low-cost apartment dwelling for 1-week-or-longer residence. Even some of the established houses have converted to this format, since taxes are lower and service standards are minimal. For do-it-yourself holidaymakers, however, this householding gimmick can represent a sizable saving in the

Peseta Department. The region's nonstop activity will provide for the traveler a mélange of smart-to-poor hotels, restaurants, and other attractions. Definitely worth a visit provided you don't buck the mob from June to mid-September.

Hotels *Almería*: Known as the "Hollywood of Spain" because of its pure light, this has become the focal point of film folk from all over the celluloid world. And to coin showbiz terminology, the **Gran Hotel** is practically the only show in town. The modern edifice stands at the junction of the port's 2 main streets, offering a pool and, on our visit, a hefty ration of smugness from the pompous critters behind the desk. Not much else to recommend it. The **Costasol** didn't send us, either—except, perhaps, in the opposite direction. This could be followed by a tag-along list of hostelries such as the **Indalico**, the clean 40-room **Residencia Hairán, Hostal Guerry**, the **Embajador** (ugh!), and the unpolished **La Perla**. Good-bye, "Hollywood."

Málaga, during the summer, is hot, crowded, and unimpressive—but the winter temperatures are so mild, comparatively speaking, that many sunworshipers flock down from the North to bask (or sometimes to shiver!) in its suburbs along the Costa del Sol or to hop the luxury *Ibn Batouta* ferry for a 5¼-hour trip to Tangier in Morocco. Its aeronautical welcome includes a modern building and control tower. There's also a slightly sunnier note in the hotel and restaurant scene. Nice setting at the foot of the mountain range, on the sea—but that's about all, touristically.

The 230-room, Deluxe **Málaga Palacio**, about which we have mixed sentiments, established a new and rather expensive standard of innkeeping in this coastal nexus—traditionally a 2nd-string watering hole compared to many other tourist centers in Spain. Surprisingly expensive and frequently kooky construction that scrimped on nothing—from woodwork to textiles, glassware, and linens; attractive lobby and lounges, more French than Iberian in tone; shopping bazaar; disco-cellar for all age groups; popular dark-paneled, brass-highlighted bar; coolish but urbane glass-lined, marble-pillared dining room, with now faltering cuisine; stunning rooftop swimming pool, with an apron for food service and a marvelous vista of the port, the sea, and the cathedral; fully air-conditioned. Parking remains a headache despite an 80-car garage nearby. The best (if only) Palacio in town. (Out of the center we much prefer the Parador Nacional Gibralfaro, but more about that later.) The 44-unit **Residencia Bahía Málaga** is slipping; moreover we were unable to find a view of that famous *bahía* from any corner of the house that we inspected. Situation anchored on a busy street of commerce; ample space; all staterooms with baths. **Casa Curro** fits into the next slot in our today's rankings. Scruffy plant with rustic Spanish (what else?) dining room, plus another in simpler motif; complete air conditioning; all 49 sun-shy doubles with private bath. Routine but passable. **Los Naranjos** smiles at its namesake fruit trees (oranges) in its front garden. Cheerful, clean, and certainly adequate within its 3-star bracket. It serves only breakfast—and guess what juice? **Gaviota**, up a mile in the hills overlooking a verdant valley and the sea, is a winner for seekers of informality. Dining room kind of slaphappy, as everything here tends to be; outdoor mealtime terrace with one table sited under a vine-covered cupola; 27 rooms, mostly doubles, with baths; swimming pools; slopeside gardens; bar; a haven

for flocks of French tourists in the hot months and for battalions of British in winter. **Hostal El Peñón** now seems to be sinking; too bad, because we had liked it. **Hostal Carlos V**, hard by the cathedral, offers sheltering arms, but not a smidgen more—no meals, no breakfast, not even coffee. It answers one need only—sleep. And that it can provide in pleasant surroundings. From A-to-ZZZZzzzzzzz, A-okay. Inexpensive, too. The **Maestranza Apartotel**, on the other hand, puts its accent on its bar trade and cafeteria traffic. Somehow the accommodations wobble in 2nd best, in our opinion. Now we come to the **Las Vegas**. Now we leave the Las Vegas. That was quite enough, thank you. Let's scat back to that aforementioned government-run parador: For motorists, oooolala! There's a heavenly choice just 2 steps below the welkin and 10 minutes from the center of Málaga. This is the **Parador** section of the Gibralfaro complex. Only a dozen rooms, but each features a special panoramic slice of Earth, Sea, and Sky; rustic décor; huge double accommodations; wide-angled terraces with folding louvered doors. So superior a value, with such a rewarding billion-dollar vista, that it's even worth renting a little car just to take advantage of this dreamland.

Marbella, in our opinion, leads the pack of Costa del Sol resorts. Like all the others, it has skyrocketed in growth and popularity, but its maturity seems to have arrived more gracefully and its following seems more tasteful to us than the elbow-to-elbow mob scenes associated with many of the throng centers. For one thing, it is more spread out. For another, it now boasts a gambling casino which enhances its tone as a playground of sophisticates. The innkeeping aristocrat of this peerage, for instance, **Los Monteros**, is a delightfully ingratiating suburbanite which beckons only a ½-mile from the first tee of the famous Río Real course; free private bus to the greens; original stucco-and-wood structure surrounded by 3 lovely pools (one heated); it has Pavillon Mediterraneo complex with 50 hyperdeluxe units plus 7 suites; Abanico section in duplex form with splendid vistas (#'s 178, 278, and 378 are our choices); 7 superb tennis courts, and informal gardens; thatched-roof beach club, one of the loveliest in Southern Europe; 5 excellent horses and acres of cantering space; pleasantly rustic feeling with twentieth-century comforts. Dining at either the beach haven, the Sportsmen's Clubhouse, the Grill Room (open all year with piano music nightly), or the salon; the lavishly redecorated English Bar (orchestra every night) and a 2nd one in the hotel, plus another at the banks of the Med; management and staff fairly bubbling with kindhearted efficiency; friendly clubby atmosphere. Incidentally, if you require even more pampering, this same organization operates the interesting and luxurious **Incosol** medical institute with a capacity for 375 registrants in 193 rooms. Almost every physiotherapeutic device, dunk, shower, massage, heat, or cold treatment imaginable is here. Doctors, dentists, technicians, nurses, radiologists, caddies,—you name it, and Incosol probably can provide it. A private hospital also will provide face-lifts, plastic surgery, and obesity regimens. It looked so good, in fact, that we can hardly wait to come down with something. *What* a holiday! Returning to the normal vacation diet, the **Don Carlos** is a fast 15-minute drive from Marbella itself. It was the Hilton chain's first venture into a purely seasonal European beach atmosphere; recently it changed relatives and appelatives. This 150-foot-tall, 17-story, 270-room slab of eye-shocking

architecture is beset with drawbacks and blessed with advantages. Assets: Fantastic coastal vistas, especially from the upper levels; a beautifully designed swimming pool and covered terrace with snack service and a marine theme; a handsome interior court surrounded by boutiques, a hairdresser, a cosmetics corner, and a newsstand; a charming Moorish fountain in the center of the main patio; 3 tennis courts; 21 acres of estate with a vast palm and cypress grove spreading to a thatched-roof beach hut offering bar and nibble wares. Debits: An ill-planned, tunnel-like entrance that often leaves several cars choked up in a long waiting line; dinky bathrooms; the to us stupidly conceived, viewless, interior Los Naranjos Restaurant with grim colors. We've long maintained that its greatest need is strong competition. Perhaps it will have it now in the Deluxe **Puente Romano** ("Roman Bridge"), a 200-room entry that's not far from our next contestant, just short hop from the town center. Its zealous manager is highly skilled Norbert Frank, the former chief at the splendid coastal Sotogrande and at the successful Plaza in Madrid. He may have the best show going before long. Anyway, we'd bet on it, sight unseen. The **Marbella Club Hotel** is composed of 2 parts—the "New" and the original one. The promoter behind this enterprise is a certain Prince Alfonso Hohenlohe, an innkeeper who has spent a large portion of his career on the Costa del Sol and elsewhere in Spain. We prefer the "New" M.C.H. with its 120 rooms, its handsome beach baskery, and its myriad recreational facilities both on the premises and nearby. Décor varies between modern simplicity and mock Andalucian; 80% of all units with private terraces; ample space; better, in our opinion, as a lingering base than as an overnight stop. The original Marbella Club, further up the pike, stands on 11 acres of outskirts terrain. Our recent incognito stay here proved to be a mixed bag. Personnel in its tiny, drab reception area had progressed (?) from smartalecky attitudes to indifferent ones. The attractive but expensive grill, with its large windows, central hearth, clubby atmosphere, and canine corps of clients' pets on our visit, served us a savory smoked salmon and a wretched Chinese Fondue (were we not dog lovers, we might have slipped the latter under our table). Veranda Bar; a trophy room for more loving cupfuls; a beach retreat; a small pool plus aviary in a molting garden. The newer suites are modernistic; the older cottages reflect Iberian traditions; rooms vary from spacious to cramped; all were clean; all seemed overpriced to us for the value returned. **Golf Hotel Nueva Andalucia** is the leading handicapper of a trio which also comprises the groupy **Andalucia Plaza** and the charmless **Torré de Andalucia**, which caters almost exclusively to golfers. Our choice in this threesome boasts only 14 doubles and 7 singles —plus 2 golf courses, the Las Naranjas Golf Club, a handsome pool, and such a loyal following of links buffs that advance reservations are an absolute must. Director Antonio Larrad is the man to write before you start to pack your tees. The remaining pair didn't excite us chiefly because their larger size and mass tourism concepts have usurped so much of their personality. The **Golf Hotel Guadalmina**, near the hamlet of *San Pedro de Alcántara*, also is such a mecca for the mashie set that links addicts are often required to book as far ahead as 1 year. Two courses at your doorstep plus the clubhouse; riding; tennis; 3 pools (one heated) and cabanas; restyled lobby; 100 rooms, each given a personality course and now very inviting indeed; each with its own bath and

balcony; 6 bungalows plus another privately owned cluster which is rapidly becoming a subdivider's paradise; varied cuisine in its restaurant; Grill air-conditioned; more informal than Los Monteros. Tee-rrific for players who can also enjoy exchange privileges with the Los Monteros and Atalaya courses. Dramatic changes occur so swiftly on the coast that this one appears to be standing still in comparison with its golfing partners. No longer a champion, but very much in the playoffs. The massive **Don Pepe** is almost *forced* to be popular. This 250-room titan is a landmark in the Meliá mass-construction mania. Aside from the nearby mountains, it's the tallest thing around—and to us, it gives a vivid impression of being architecturally out of joint. Vast list of resort amenities, including a nice private beach, circular, all-weather pool, water sports, gardens, seasoned Almirante Bar, El Farola grill in green and mocha, sauna bath, nursery, hairdresser, shops, and scores of terraces for sunning by day or murmurs by moonlight; 2 tennis courts, and a movie theater. While the staff remains tiptop, we now feel that its very massiveness steals away the fun. We still haven't inspected the youthful **Marbella Inn**, adjoining *Puerto Banus* with its tennis, golf (by bus shuttle), and bathing facilities on tap. We see, however, that reservations can be made through the Holiday Inns organization, so you might check with them. Facilities include the El Morocco restaurant, the King Kong Klub, with live entertainment, and the Jet Set bar. One thing about this Puerto Banus area: It is thunderingly expensive, far out of line for the values but so "in" with the Spanish *nuevos ricos* that an attitude of "anything goes" seems to prevail. The mass-minded **Atalaya Park,** 9 miles toward *Algeciras*, used to be a quiet suburban choice, but it is now growing so rapidly that we've lost all our enthusiasm. A Frankfurt management team has just taken the reins, so it plans to expand even further. It has tacked on a 7-story, 300-room addition in the immediate vicinity—the dual segments romantically referred to as "No. I" and "No. II." Lap-of-the-sea location, beauty and health farm pamperings available; 18-hole golf circuit teed up; handsome Clubhouse with a timber-lined restaurant, a snack bar at the first tee, lovely lounges, and free bus service to and from the hotel; billiard room; bowling alleys, swimming pool and bathers' restaurant; riding and water-ski facilities; plus catamaran sailing and windsurfing; 11 tennis courts; snack bar, grill, and nightclub; shops; full air conditioning. All 200 rooms with bath and terrace; 25 bungalows for quieter vacationers or families. This one seems to be losing its administrative grip while growing too big for its beaches. Not for us. The homely **Skol** is slanted more toward apartment than conventional hotel-room construction. **Estrella Del Mar** has a modern aura sprinkled with antiques, antique reproductions, and scads of genuine Teutonic reproductions in human form who are not quite antiques—yet. Handsome rustic mien; kitchen noises rattling across the neighboring pool area (we could smell the *Kraut* stewing all the way out on the highway); all sleeping units with decorative fireplaces. Reasonably good choice if you *sprechen Deutsch.* **Cortijo Blanco** is a 107-room, patio-dappled, Andalusian structure. Ground-floor accommodations with a superb view of sun-soaking guests—*and* vice versa; demand upper storied units unless you're a chest-beating exhibitionist, because no goldfish ever commanded less privacy. Handsomer for landscape than for innscape. The **Pueblo Andaluz**, next door, has gobbled up the cottage concept spurned

by Cortijo Blanco. Miniature village of about 100 tiny houses, all with private terraces and tiny baths; swimming pool and cabanas; Teheran Room for Middle Eastern vittles; managed by a deposed Persian prince who is also an art collector. A fairly amusing beat-the-heat stopover. It is shuttered in winter. **Las Chapas**, on the main highway in the settlement of *Las Chapas*, is a startler: The restaurant, bar, and some of its living quarters semienclose a tiny bull ring instead of the conventional patio. Some rough spots polished smooth by Manager Manolo Ramos Podadera; plain but passable décor; swimming pool; tennis courts; minigolf; on many Sundays, small but jet-powered cows are released for the *tienta,* and YOU can be the matador for free. Loews, the American innkeeper, plans to unveil 500 deluxe units and a beachfront golf course, so keep your eyes open and your clubs polished. **El Fuerte** and **Bellamar**, the only 2 major candidates in *Marbella*, itself, are simple and adequate. The former has had many renewals; pool; tennis court; mini-golf; cool dining hall; comfortable but not inspired; open all year. The latter offers bareboned public rooms, dismal bedchambers and a pool; open March to October only. The Second-class **Artola**, in *Artola*, also bubbles up with a water hole (it looked about as clean as one), a tennis court, and a 7-hole (yes, 7!) golf course for abbreviated or lazy sportsmen. No frills, no thrills. The **Alhamar**, at *Calahonda*, is in the luxury bracket. Park setting with superb outdoor facilities and grounds; weary, gloomy, hangdog hutches as bedrooms; lovely, book-and-fireplace lounge with thick rug and stained-glass windows; listless dining room. Improving too slowly. The nearby **Calahonda** is newer, but too raw for U.S. wanderers. The **Guadalpin** and the **Río Verde**, both outside *Marbella* on the main pike to *Algeciras*, are emergency stops when everything else is jammed. Passable and inexpensive, but not for the long-term holidaymaker. **Santa Marta**, open April 1 to October 31, boasts horses, a private beach, a host of large, rebuilt bungalows—and solitude by the carload. Cheery lounge; excellent dining room; air conditioning throughout; big bathrooms. Now a 4-star hermitage that we recommend to the welkin. Along the path to *Estepona,* the flowering **Golf El Paraiso**, in the Patio El Alcornocal development, is a knockout. Gary Player played a major part in the sporting side. Situation a ½-mile from the beach; heated pool plus children's paddler; 2 tennis courts; playground; revolving rooftop restaurant; discothèque; beauty center; space for nearly 400 guests in air-conditioned luxury. Otherwise in this vicinity, **El Mero** wiggles in with a fish-shape pool and an irregular-shape façade. Two minutes from the breakers; pleasant glass-lined dining room air-conditioned; reasonable tariffs; open March to October. The nearby **Patricia** is. Its corridors remind us of the tunnel network in the heart of Gibraltar. At *Fuengirola*, the 243-room **Mare Nostrum** is a lifeless mass operation which conjures in our minds the image of an ogre's castle. Three turrets; naked light bulbs; crumbling plaster; pool, tennis, and jai alai. So grim it gives us the willies. Never our Nostrum, but ever our night-Mare. **Las Piramides**, unearthed in A.D. 1970, certainly gives this archaeologist pause to reconsider the follies of our time. Its twin middens are 10 stories tall; 4 apartment digs surround these; all feature pyramidal roofs in such incongruous pigments as to suggest mutiny among the painters of Ramses II. Lounge gaudied up with modish overhead lighting and Bell Époque ice-cream-parlor furniture—all in

absolute disharmony to our peepers; blue-and-white candy-stripe feedery glazed with all the sticky charm of a half-spent lollipop; cutesy beige bar with glazed flowers, glazed shells, and our glazed eyes peeled upon them; gooey corridors lined with white slatted doors; baths blossoming with floral-patterned toilet-seat covers. **Somió** and **El Cid**, flanking the village on opposite approaches, are modest. We prefer the former. We don't like the **Florida** at all—too big, rambling, and unkempt.

Excursion point? If you're on wheels, try **El Campanario**, in the budding Sitio de Calahonda development near Mijas. Travel-weary appetites might be stimulated by a swim in its pool, a riding lesson, or a few sets of tennis on the subdivision's sparkling spread of Andalucia. Although the 15-table restaurant is stronger on gastronomy than it is on aesthetics, the versatile facility makes this a worthwhile target for Costa-hoppers. Splendid.

Last (but light years from least), the sumptuous **Sotogrande del Guadiaro** complex, a sportsman's paradise, has taken root. For physical attributes, almost nothing in the nation can touch it. Huge holdings of 3200 acres in view of the Rock of Gibraltar; magnificently manicured, cork-and-olive-tree studded, 18-hole championship course, plus smaller 9-hole circuit, both linkscaped by Trent Jones, the well-known American golf architect; eligibility to tee off becoming easier every season, according to old linksmen; ruggedly handsome membership-only Clubhouse with restaurant; 3 bars, pro shop, 2 boutiques, and L-shape heated pool; 200-yard-wide sandy beach sweeping for ½-mile along the private shoreline. The 46-room Tennis Club Hotel, open to the general public, with very comfortable inn-type atmosphere; pool, stable, a bull ring, tennis, its own 18-tee links, Frontón Club by the shore, shops, restaurant, and discothèque; movies in English; children (14 years and older) accepted here, but not in the other residential or recreational facilities. Total of 12 superdeluxe bungalows for members or for holders of cards to other recognized clubs throughout the world; charming décor; each spaciously designed with a working fireplace, a bath with flowered tiles, a comfortable sitting room, and a refrigerator but no kitchen. The main hotel, which now accepts small groups, provides a mesmeric golf-course situation; 120 rooms and every conceivable resort amenity.

Torremolinos? Vast changes in this boom-boom-BOOM town. Both in the hamlet itself and along its coastal approaches, new hostelries until very recently were popping up as rapidly as bubbles in a pitch-pot. So many in this roiling caldron are house-of-cards affairs that the older generation of leaders, which gave way to these bright-and-shiny buttons for a while, have now come back into their own glory. Others that could not keep up with the double-time pace have converted to apartment dwellings. Many of the giant new structures, too, trend toward the residential concept—either renting their space, or leasing or selling it under a cooperative arrangement. For the tourist who plans to spend a week or longer, this can be a big money-saver, because (1) they are cheaper to run, (2) building codes are more relaxed than for hotels per se, and (3) service standards are low to nil. Typical rates in these can range from $95 per person per month (winter) including breakfast and house cleaning, to $250 for the same renderings in High Season. The very best we saw—and it stacked up well against any luxury hotel accommodation in the vicinity—drew $650

per month for a 3-bedroom spread (6 beds, no service). Within its living complex were 2 swimming pools, shops, gardens, and a minigolf course; the apartments all had telephones and were efficiently air-conditioned. Some of the leaders in this bracket are: (1) **Playamar** (our pick of this type on the coast; 21 15-floor buildings with 1000 units overall; a metropolis of fun, recreation, and relaxation at village-size price tags), (2) **La Nogalera** (excellent furnishings; accommodations of all sorts), (3) **Eurosol** (more metropolitan in concept), (4) **UTO Ring** (acquired from the Meliá stable but retaining the hyper-Español décor, cramped space, and lofty tariffs of yore), (5) **Alay** (smartly clean-lined; a refreshing production by José Sendra, one of the most likable and skillful innkeepers on the coast; the best buy around), (6) **Las Cascadas,** (7) **Aloha**, and (8) **El Congresso** (eventually to be a stack of 3500 units in 8 edifices looking like columns of Paul Bunyan's poker chips; a good bet, providing you get a map with your key). Since hotels are our chief concern, we did not overnight in any of these. But we did check their facilities, and all seemed to be more than satisfactory in their respective categories. For details, go further into these with your travel agent.

At the city's airport gateway, **Holiday Inn** greets flyway inn-comers with 200 nests spread over 8 floors of white stucco. Spacious dining terrace overlooking pool complex and gardens (the beach here is rather punk); restful Andalusian décor with all-American undertones; cozy green-clad Retiro cafeteria; grill plus La Bodega restaurant; Corrida Bar in black and red. Accommodations featuring 2 double beds, wall-to-wall warp-and-woof, twin-sinked baths, and a generous cargo of U.S. comfort standards; the "16" series of suites is especially inviting. Service was sluggish on our investigation, but otherwise it passed every test as a recommendable Holiday stop.

The **Pez Espada** ("Swordfish") is a game fish with spirit for any holiday angler. It has been taken over by new people who have spent huge sums to improve its facilities and augment its services. Structurally, it is in the modern tower concept. Precisely 100% of its 150 refurnished double accommodations offer an angular sea view. It is big, with full air conditioning, large terraces. Grill Room with dancing, a nightclub, 4 bars, inviting pools (summer and winter), sauna bath, private beach (one of the best on the shore), tennis court, minigolf, water-skiing, and a garden with a tropical bar. Everyone is working hard to give it more personality and zest. They seem have it zinging already.

The 106-room **Carihuela Palace** has a historic place in the sweepstakes record book. As it stood on our recent scouting, this was a crossbreed between a holiday retreat and a Westchester shopping mall. On one hand, you'll find a cafeteria, a movie theater, and souvenir counters in a split-level Spanish bazaar. On the other, are 2 pools (the beach is poor), surrounding gardens, a tennis court, an alfresco summer nightclub on weekends, a dining room, and amenities that are generally comfortable but are now in need of some sparkle. The cottage-style units at lawnside are particularly attractive; bid for a seaside unit (a little less noisy than those facing the road).

The **Tritón**, with a touch of romantic euphemism, claims to be in Benalmadena-Costa, but for practical purposes we still consider it a part of the main town. Director Eloy Durán is polishing up the prongs, snapping the whip, and

setting fires under staffers who had grown too complacent after its initial success. He has changed all of the mattresses, updated baths, improved the gallery between the 2 buildings, and enlarged the barbecue patio at poolside. Many resort fillips including 2 tennis courts and 2 saunas. Try for a garden room, not one facing the fortress of apartments.

The 9-story **Riviera**, where your key is linked to a miniature anchor, comes up with a beach and seawater pool with overlooking dining room While the maintenance generally is grim, you'll also find a terraced summer grill, cunning use of rocks, cactus, and fountains for landscaping and decoration. Cool public facilities; sauna; beauty salon and barbershop; parking lot plus covered garage; all 190 units and 8 suites with bath, private terrace, and air conditioning. It's a house yearning for inspiration, in our opinion.

The **Meliá Torremolinos** is another barque in the Meliá fleet. It is also the largest structure on the coast—and you may *just* be able to see it if the buses which herd in front to deposit tour groups happen to move. Of its weakly air-conditioned rooms, 70% face the sea and 30% curl around the pool. The lower deck is thickly larded with anchors, bottles, fishnets, and other maritime flotsam; gigantic 250-seat dining hall; 3 bars; 2 nightclubs. Sleeping accommodations are disturbingly cramped. As a space-and-money-saving device, the bathroom is separated from the bedroom by a wooden partition which starts 7 inches from the floor and rises 7 feet straight up—fascinating if you're either 6 inches or 8 feet tall.

The **Al-Andalus** now seems to be fading into the pack. Since it is located across the highway from the sea, we believe this is a better choice for winter than for summer. Red Room for à la carte meals and terpsichore; ground-level, mural-clad dining salon (where you may be seated with strangers if you don't insist on your own table); garden dancing; rustic trappings and handwrought touches predominant in the décor; L-shape pool; tennis courts; balky central air conditioning that can be maddening when the highway racket grows particularly bothersome. Total of 8 suites, 18 singles, and 80 doubles, all with bath, private balcony, and sea view; 66-room annex; full pension required in High Season; cuisine so-so.

The pity about the massive 400-unit **Cervantes** is that it could be so much better if its decorators had turned on more aesthetic éclat. As it stands, the halfhearted sprinkling of armor in its lounges suggests to us that a patrol of medieval mercenaries might have discarded a few pieces of hardware under the broiling Spanish sun and marched on. All of the recreational pluses are here, the rooms are of good size and have balconies, the public areas are well engineered, but the minuses in drab color schemes, enfeebled flair, and unenthusiastic maintenance counterweigh against the overall impression. Sorry, but it gives us a grand case of yawns.

The **Gran Hotel Nautilus** is beginning to surface from the depths. Glass-enclosed heated pool; tastefully redecorated seaview bar and lounge; indifferent cookery and dining-room service on our sampling; clean but cheerless marble corridors; billiard parlor, kiddy nook, tennis court, boutiques. Most of its accommodations have been revamped; these now sparkle. Assistant Manager Nicholas Beck's serious professionalism belies his years.

The 300-coop **Las Palomas**, a crescent-shape structure across from Al An-

daluz, is functionally modern but chillingly sterile, in our view. The septagonal pool is nice for dunks; otherwise it doesn't raise a ripple from us.

In First-class, the 260-room **Alay** is a peach, but it is very costly for the bracket. It is attached to both the 1000-capacity congress hall and the similarly styled Alay Apartments, mentioned earlier. Clean, modernistic lines blending with colorful adaptations of Moorish design; tropical dining room overlooking 1 of 2 swimming pools; cafeteria; Arabic bar; game room; boutiques, flower shop, and news kiosk; Rendez-vous nightclub under a crimson tent, with whimsical décor and paintings from the flea market; charming colonial lounge beneath a cascade of greenery. Some pads on the narrow side; we prefer the accommodations facing Málaga to those peeping at Torrebermeja.

In the next less-costly category, we are very fond of the inviting, 86-room **Tropicana**. Here is an informal atmosphere that is homey and cheerful. Its brightest baubles are the Trader Victorian dining room and the romantic pool that suggests an attractive Seminole campsite. The kindness of the staff and the warmth of their attention show the epitome of Spanish hospitality. Adequate (but not sparkling) maintenance; comfortable rooms with good-looking rustic touches; appetizing meals. Recommended as a happy house with lots of heart. The **Torremora** is a fairway from the golf course along the Málaga highway. Private bus service to the links and nearby beach; 105 accommodations with bath and terrace; some units with wide awnings; colorful décor employing brick, tile-work, copper, and rough textiles; lovely willow-side pool, plus children's pond in the garden. Pleasant, despite its distance from the action. The **Siroco**, in a still lower tariff group, is an economy link for the same chain that operates the Tritón, the Emperatriz in Málaga, and the Las Chapas in Marbella. All 121 bedrooms with private bath; only 16 without individual balconies; swimming pool; tennis now lobbing. Though it lacks flair, here's certainly a bargain buy.

The ruggedly charming **Parador del Golf**, sponsored by the Spanish Tourist Office, is a better-than-par challenger to the top group for out-and-out living comfort (especially for golfers who don't mind taking a few extra swings at the sparrow-size mosquitos that strafe in from the neighboring swamp; now there's air conditioning, so they no longer attack by night); low, low tariff for a handsome double lodging. This 40-unit project, architected in the rustic *ranchero* style, occupies the center of an 18-hole golf course 5 miles out on the main road toward Málaga and beneath the Airport's approach lanes. Impressive circular swimming pool; attractive public rooms; outdoor dining May to September; private beach 100 yards from the doin's; rough-hewn wooden planking in the bedchambers; motel atmosphere with do-it-yourself-dammit service standards. Here's a perfect hitching post for motorists, links buffs, or wayfaring families. A value for the price—if you remember the citronella.

El Pinar, a 100-room First-category candidate a little closer to town, is slipping, in our opinion. Little English spoken; perversely inviting public rooms with rampant plastics, batteries of fireplaces, and a rabbit's warren of facilities in aimless disarray. Glassed-in dining room, topped by splendid circular terrace; swimming pool across the road. Its big drawback is the unappetizing pastiche of bedchambers.

The **Isabel** reclines gracefully behind the high-tide line, a short stroll south

of the action. Rectangular 7-story mountainous structure; teardrop pool with garden; placid Moorish-tone lobby with brick and tile hearth; leather-padded bar; adjoining equestrian lounge. Cheerful restaurant with terra-cotta floor, iron chandeliers, and other Iberian touches; alfresco dining terrace; discothèque. A mere 40 units, mostly doubles with seaview terraces; some corner triples; North African garniture; heavy wooden furnishings, Frigobars; large twin-basin bathrooms. A spacious ultra-clean haven; exceptional in its category.

The totally revamped **La Roca** was a pleasant rediscovery. Attractive garden with swimming pool; private beach across the highway; a handful of bungalows for rent; hunting-lodge lounge and bar; 28 doubles with bath and terrace; 4 suites and 4 singles. Nice for its bracket. The 270-unit **Los Patos** and the neighboring **Aloha Playa** are a pair of production belt sleeping factories that might be placed on your "alternates" list. Fair but cool is our weather report. **Lloyd's** has been in a state of flux. Careworn semicircular building; a few added chambers, but that's about all; tasteless trappings. **Los Nidos**, in our estimation, is tolerable only to specialists in abnormal psychology who could be driven loco by trying to figure out that startling, multigadgeted, bangle-clad, spiral, elliptical, vertical, tangential, metallic gismo in the lobby. Now it is expanding in a village concept. The **Amaragua** is a part of its scheme. West of town toward Algeciras, the **Delfín** seemed amateurish and overrun by tour groups; a quick-buck-turnover setup, if we ever saw one. The **Costa del Sol**, opposite, reflects a similar personality; it attracts many British guests. Also disenchanting is the **Mar Y Sol**, which is a weirdy in its excruciating color-clashes in public rooms and gingerbready construction. Magnificent sea view, one of the best in the region; mediocre sleeping quarters with 10 more tacked on in 10 brand-new hues; angry reader reports about rude clerks. Not recommended, not if your eyes aren't écru-heliotrope-henna-periwinkle-sensitive. The **Jorge V** should abdicate, in our judgments.

The **Blasón** greets incomers with a reception arsenal stocked with armaments. Further along we found halls reeking with disinfectants, water-stained walls, exposed electrical wires over mirrors, and renditions of the Symphony for Horn, Brake, and Gear emanating from the street. Students of the bizarre may enhance their repertoire by checking into one of its triangular rooms or wriggling into a tub which can be entered only from one end (such is the structure of the bathroom).

Restaurants Let's start with *Almería*, where gastronomy certainly was not born, but where it is given a modest foothold at **El Rincón de Juan Pedro**. The décor makes no pretensions; it is purely and simply regional, clean, attractive, and relaxing. You could say exactly the same for the food.

Estepona turns up quite a variety of restaurants, the **Yellow Book** being the top choice on the bestseller list. It is located at Km. 167 on the Malaga-Cádiz pike. Taped music and décor of the twenties; baby lamb carved at tableside and quiche lead the gustatory parade; reserve ahead by phoning Maître Robbie (Tel. 800484); closed Mondays. **Mesón Arni** (Calle Mondejar 16) is also strong on atmosphere, created by the American chef-owner-guitarist who is a virtual Adam to the ribs trade. It is closed Wednesdays. **La Cacerola**, in Edificio Victoria, is more conventional, designed for the family,

and serving simple, moderately priced vittles—except on Thursdays when it shutters. Just between ourselves, we have a hunch that the budding *Puerto de Estepona* complex will one day knock the spots off its Banus competitor. The **Club Nautico** is quite good too for fish and grills.

In *Fuengirola*, **Don Bigote** (½-mile out at Los Boliches) is the choice (except for the nearby **La Langosta**, where the food's fair, but the service kills it for us). Century-old-former sardine-packing factory; Spanish-style bar and small hearthside lounge near entrance; 3 dining nooks seating a total of 250; the first, our favorite, lined with cozy raised alcoves on one side plus textured walls, ceiling beams, Mexican curtains, and Moorish lamps; 2-tiered alfresco terrace brimming with flowers. Roy Wykes, the mustachioed proprietor (Don Bigote means "Sir Mustache"), is your amiable host, while Vera, his whisker-less better half, cruises among the guests to see to their comfort and satisfaction. Our richly endowed Andalucian fish soup, perfectly spiced, was delightful; so was our guest's beef casserole, an honest, hearty dish well suited to the cool evening. We like this friendly and cheerful domain. Heading toward *Estepona*, **El Molino** is more culinary grist for your mill. The miller, incidentally, is Belgian—and do *those* folks know how to cook!

Marbella's waves have rolled up a crester on a hill named **La Hacienda Las Chapas**, at kilometer stone 200. It's a white adobe structure composed of a small bar at its entrance leading to a T-shape room with a fireplace where the T is crossed. Beamed ceiling; bleached walls; terra-cotta floor; wooden tables; cushioned chairs; elegant place settings with gargantuan wineglasses. Our Roquefort Salad and veal baked in aluminum foil were superb, as were the Roast Partridge in Vine Leaves and Quail Flambé enjoyed by others in our party. Belgian Owner Paul Schiff has composed a melodious Suite for Gastronomes. Phone ahead (831 267 or 831 116) for reservations. Closed Mondays. Recommended. One of Madrid's leading restaurateurs, Horcher, has opened **La Fonda** at Plaza de Cristo 9-10, a former hotel that is said to have been lavishly redesigned with the sleeping portions removed. Nouvelle Époque interior with 16 tables and twice as many on its summer patio; lush botanical décor; menu featuring many original Horcher creations plus some regional homestyle dishes; average meal around $25 without wine. Dinner only; closed Sundays. **La Tricicletta** (Buitrago 16) bounces in with baskets of atmosphere and eye appeal. Don't go for lunch, because it is never served. Your taxi will deposit you at the edge of a small plaza; follow the arrows through the shoulder-hugging alley and up to its low iron gate; enter a peaceful courtyard; to your immediate right, in a separate adjunct, is the bar. Wooden staircase leading to an L-shaped dining room; timbered gambrel roof, with windows in the treetops; taper illumination; check-patterned and gay solid-shaded tablecloths; rush-bottomed, black-lacquered chairs; simple décor oozing with charm. Extensive and daring menu (for Spain); joint ownership by an Irishman, an Englishman, another Belgian, and an American, who keep this 4-wheeler free-wheeling at a happy clip. Very good, indeed. **La Bonne Auberge**, on a residential street overlooking the lighthouse, boasts 2 dining rooms, a waterside terrace, and artillery barrages of kitchen noises. Stucco-and-beam interior; so-so cookery; French management. Better for viewing than for chewing. **Grillon** is another entry from Gaul; it's said to be better in Low Season,

when service is a reality. **Charlemagne** tries to be French, too. **Las Picas is** not noteworthy. Hotel dining everywhere is not too inspiring.

Out at fashionable *Puerto Banus*, Madrid's doge of dining, the remarkable Don Cárlos Cortés of Clubs Jockey and "31" fame, has extended his capital gains to this coastal venue. The **Club 31** hosts 200 guests in the main establishment with seating for 26 more in a private salon. Décor similar to the Madrid "31"; cuisine and its cost also following suit; functioning 7 days per week save in November, when it hibernates. Very chic; another triumph for Sr. Cortés, who remains one of Spain's most illustrious arbiters of gastronomy. Frankly, we feel that so many entrepreneurs in this yacht basin scalp their clients so unmercifully for the mediocre values received that we would rename the region the *Costa Tu Much.*

San Pedro de Alcantara, midway 'twixt Estepona and Marbella, can be proud of **Los Duendes**, which offers a cool terrace in summer, a crackling fire in winter, and chilling price tags the year round for its refined French-inspired cuisine. Service, cookery and atmosphere are all deluxe calibre.

Sotogrande, of course, has the various dining and snack facilities of the 2 hotels, but if you are in quest of simple Spanish fish dishes and no-frills platters, then hop in a car and roll up the road toward Estepona. A few miles out you'll discover **Bernardo's**, then **Pepe's**, then the inevitable **Antonio's**—each reliable, plain, and easy on the budget.

Torremolinos has an indifferent lot. **Chez Lucien**, a few minutes out toward Málaga, is the most rewarding choice. French specialties on the menu; almost French prices too; service slipping on our latest tryout; if you don't order ahead, you're in for a long wait, sans bar or garden in which to sip your apéritif. Expensive but still a standard bearer. **Tortuga** (Calle San Miguel) is a popular novelty. Lobster bisque and sirloin steak are the best bets, we found. Ground-floor bar with fireplace and barrel chairs; 11-table upstairs dining room; babbling pool with rocks and greenery; aquarium with curious angelfish to envy your nibbling; rooftop kitchen, plus space for a small complement of alfresco diners. Rather high tabs, but the general quality is there. Even higher prices and much lower quality? Our advice is to miss the **Seven Seas** in the Eurosol apartment complex. Indoor orientation overlooking gardens; grim atmosphere that tries to be clubby. On our visit, the service was fumbling; the cooking was strictly 2nd-rate to our tastes. **La Brocherie** (No. 704 in the La Nogelera apartotel) allegedly is Gay Liberation, South, according to an amused reader who said his party's Fruta del Mar, onion soup, roast lamb, and filet mignon were sssscrumptious. **Kings Club**, also in the Nogalera, seemed doomed to us. Almost empty almost every night—and we understand why. **La Grenouille** serves only light bites and beverages. The Moroccan patroness can often be found at the corner table, elegantly smoking a king-size cigarette held in her ringed fingers by an 8-inch-long ebony holder—and studiously reading a comic book. The **Napoli** dishes up typical Italian Cous-cous, not to mention North-African-style pizza. **Hong Kong** sounds the gong from 1 to 4 in the afternoon and from 7 to 12 in the evening, with you-know-what. Recommended. The **Canton** can, too, but not nearly so well. **Mandarin** stokes up a 4-course Indonesian dinner that's not too bad. **Bali** (Plaza Andulucía) spotlights the

same cuisine with a second focus on Chinese fare. Tolerable. The **Bodegón** (Calle Cauce), with scarlet pillars, white walls, and bench seats, seems to be a happier hunting ground for rabbits than for carnivora. **El Cacique** waves a welcome with a surfside alfresco hut and a *pampas*-pampered inner sanctum. Argentine specialties such as Empanadas (meat pies), Berenjenas (cold pickled eggplant), and sirloin steak draw gastronomic gauchos from miles around. Inexpensive and different. **Antonio's** (Calle Bulto) stokes up a 9-candle holder producing enough molten wax to dwarf Mont Blanc. Packed to distraction in season, with the result that service can be appalling. Branches in Málaga and Nueva Andalucía. **Pedro's,** a complex on the main drag, is *the* haven for vagabonds who thrive on a fish-and-chips diet. Low prices and lower quality. The neighboring **V.I.P.** and **Bar Central** cater to similar patronage; go for drinks only, if that. **El Porrón** may cluck proudly over its spitted chickens and grilled steaks, but we don't crow at all. **Pogo's** serves snacks on the square. **Caballo Blanco** (4 miles out) is serene, rustic, and simple. **Chez Mas**, a hut on the seaside across the highway, served us a delicious Shrimp Bisque and a Dorade with herbs for a reasonable price. Max Fognon, its proprietor, is French. Very raw in ambiance. **Torremuelle** (a few minutes toward Fuengirola) surrounds an ancient fort; a magnificent view surrounds you. The **Bar Manolo,** just off the main plaza, is good for seafood and *tapas* but dreadful for meat and eggs. **Victor**, on the midtown drag, is a shadow of its former self. For late afternoon snacks, **La Vina P.**, next door, offers a grimy counter loaded with grilled tidbits and shellfish goodies. Until after midnight, **El Goloso** (down an alley off the main square) flips up Crêpes Grand Marnier; hamburgers and hot dogs also on order for more plebian tastes. One *must* in this 90-proof hamlet is a predinner snort at a tiny Spanish pub called **Casa Quitapenas** (San Miguel 34), where potables are tapped from giant Ali Baba crocks; along about sundown, every second Iberian south of Bilbao pops in here for a quickie. Don't miss it. **Casa Prudencio** (Calle Carmen 43) has a better location than its chef deserves, at least in our view. Moonlight dancing by the sea during our visit; beamed ceiling; nautical dry-mounts; plain red tablecloths; decent service. At least the bill here won't give your wallet lesions.

In *Málaga*, the State-operated **Hostería de Gibralfaro** (see "Hotels") offers one of the most stunning panoramas of any restaurant in Spain. It's atop Monte de Gibralfaro, 10 minutes out (about $3 each way, by taxi); heavenly terrace, especially at night; cuisine tasteless but prices reasonable; don't miss a trip up here. For excellent cookery and sophistication, on the other hand, the dining room of the **Palacio Hotel** is the patrician choice. Superb in every way on our recent trial runs. The French-owned **Le Gourmet** now functions chiefly as a bar. *C'est la vie.* **La Algería** (Marín García 18) is busy, smoky, noisy, and animated; large standup bar at entrance and twin dining rooms to rear. One shocked diner once reported that he watched his waiter mix a salad—with his hands! (We're anxious to see how he prepares scrambled eggs.) For a sunny-day lunch, the seaside, pueblo-style **Antonio Martín**, near the bullring, is a relaxing noontime choice. Here you'll find the best general level of cookery in the town; sit only in the waterfront patio; its inside dining room seemed a mite less inviting and is always packed. Finny fare is best (especially the *chanquetes,*

if they are running—inch-long white fish that resemble fat needles and are kissin' cousins to anemic eels); tabs are low; go early or reserve in advance. Very popular.

Night Life *Málaga*'s nightscape is unusually dreary, since most of the action is siphoned off by the insomniacs farther along the Costa del Sol. The bar of the **Malaga Palacio** is the top spot for sipping before dinner. **El Troubador,** under Canadian proprietorship, is best for later libations. The **Pigalle** dishes out a modern ambiance; pepper-hot band and cabaret, and a bevy of placid B-girls. **La Taverna de Gitanas** is another challenger; typical mien; medium prices; well ventilated; the city's best flamenco.

In *Marbella*, El Serrallo, in the **Hotel Don Pepe**, gets the biggest after dark play from the tourist traffic. Far-out Far Eastern motif dimly illuminated by 3 giant snowflakes; Mediterranean-blue carpeting, matching velvet settees; and cream-colored leather hassocks; brass tables; dance floor, but no cabaret. Best of an almost nonexistent lot. **Playboy,** near San Pedro de Alcántara, is a routine beach discothèque. **Platero** now takes 2nd honors from the **Pagoda** for flamenco performances. An experiment called the **Crazy Gambas** was operating sporadically, so it may have folded by the time you pull in. Be sure to check locally, if you are handicapped with masochistic tendencies. You'll also have to ask about the **Régine's** discothèque, which may be open by the time of your arrival in the developing deluxe Puente Romano Hotel. She, of course, is the vital organ behind eleven such high-priced nocturnal rookeries which bear her name from Paris, to Gotham, to South America. One thing we can promise: It won't be cheap!

Torremolinos lives for sunset. Its nocturnal pastimes come in all classes, sizes, shapes, colors, genders, and nongenders. **Long Play** is the suave émir of the disco set. Brown velour walls; oval dance pad; L-shape bar; discreet lighting shining on discreet clientele. A quality roost for birds and roosters. **El Madrigal,** in the Sol y Mar urbanization (main pike toward Algeciras), is luring droves of merrymakers from the city lights. International shows; 2 orchestras which seem to own more microphones and electronic assists than Radio City Music Hall; regularly scheduled flamenco presentations. Well respected. The **Blue Note** seems to be fading. **Jaleo** goes in for groups, flamenco, and organized fun. Routine but always packed. **Piper's** is a subterranean, multilevel monument to Pandemonium. It's dotted with 3 bars and a seemingly endless number of tiny dance floors, all connected by twisting, graded aisles and decorated with used auto parts and other geegaws screwed into its vibrating walls. **Tabu** is for a more mature and better-heeled crowd. Modest door bite includes the first drink; effective racing-past-the-stars videonics; comfortable copper-clad bar at rear; lively yet thoughtfully modulated music. **Cleopatra,** almost next door, is another contender in the sophisti-category. Rectangular chamber with small square for gyrators; revolving, reflecting-"eye" chandelier; paneled and padded libations counter stacked with all-purpose champagne glasses, flanked by a huge sun disk; waiters in Egyptian tunics. Hieroglyphics, sphinxes, and other pharaoh-panalia are set amid these sands of time and run through the hourglass as follows: dance music from 9:30 to 11:30, floor show ending at midnight, rock rhythms and a Charlie Chaplin film until 1:15, second floor show, food service from 2 to 3 A.M., followed by

psychedelic melodies until the 4:30 closing. **Tiffany's** keeps a cote of doves within its pounding walls. Oh, how we mourn for these sleepless feathered creatures! **Pedro's**, mentioned under "Restaurants", attracts the most informal sartorial getups anywhere. Swinging, blues-y modern music in the downstairs lair; 3 tiers of banquettes suggesting padded baseball bleachers; our generous drinks of politely termed "Scotch" never saw the Highlands. The chairs at the next door **VIP** are more comfortable; ditto for everything else. **Top-Ten** is now a better tieup for teen types. **El Dorado**, with medium prices, has throngs of jeans-clad whippersnappers undulating to the tattoo of the lastest record hits. **Betty's Club** usurped 15 minutes of our lives; we begrudge each of them. Ditto for the dark, dingy **Bier Keller**.

Other drinking spots? Plenty. But first a word of caution. Many of the watering holes in this tourist-glutted town have succumbed to the very un-Spanish practices of fleecing customers and stocking bathtub booze, not to mention more nefarious misdemeanors. We therefore urge you to be on your guard in any questionable nook and to be doubly watchful around the Begoña area. A buxom barmaid at the **Jockey Club** offered us a filly as a groom's companion for the evening. Lots more were seemingly available in this paddock. The **Galloping Major** apparently plays host to seafarers judging by the *USS Nathan Hale, Andrew Jackson,* and other Sixth Fleet plaques on its whitewashed walls. Small stuccoed and beamed room; stone floor; large bar; Spy prints; crossed cavalry swords; clashing chairs with floral jackets; pubby atmosphere. Tranquil, cozy, clean, and honest. **Don Quijote, Chocolate Café, La Province, Moulin Rouge, Di Do, El Ancle, Samba, Corazón, El Refugio, Sportsman,** and **Ye-Ye,** all within tooting range of a police whistle from Begoña Passage, were still ladling out the sauces when we tiptoed through the seedy *begoñas,* but there's no guarantee in this weed patch as to how many will be pruned away by the time you test your green thumb. A final suggestion: In all but the top-line hotels, pay for your drinks and snacks the moment they are served to you.

GANDÍA   This expanded whistle stop between Alicante and Valencia offers the **Bayren** (2½ miles from the village; front rooms overlooking the swimming pool and the sea; quiet in Off Season; friendly personnel), the young **Residencia San Luis** (clean-lined and sound), the **Safari** (even younger), and the **Recati** (small, quiet, on the dunes; coming up once again)—plus a gaggle of alternates.

GRANADA   is lovely. In addition to the world-famous Alhambra and the Generalife, here's the International Command Post of the gypsies—many of whom live in comfortably furnished, electrically lit caves. (At least they do during "working hours"; then they hop into their cars and cruise out to their estates in the country.) Be careful of your money and personal possessions in this center; Spaniards won't touch 'em, but gypsies are among the most light-fingered gentry in the world.

Hotels   Our first choice for overnighting is easily the state-operated **Parador San Francisco** up in the Alhambra complex itself. The building was originally an Arab palace and mosque; lately it was converted into a Francis-can convent and finally into a parador. ("Lately" in the Granadino's mind

means circa 1492!) This officially declared National Monument is a unique repository for many of the region's greatest artists and artisans. It is literally crammed with rare iron and copper pieces, rugs, tiles, mosaics, and embroideries. Its 32 air-conditioned nests are always booked 6 months in advance. Just plain wonderful.

Among the privately owned hostelries, the **Luz de Granada** provides by far the best accommodations and service we've experienced around this hub. The problem is that it's not in the city proper. This one is sited in a dreary outskirts locale that is okay for weary motorists but absolute zero for sightseers unless they want to roar in and out by taxi. Clean modern structure; spacious lobby with tentacles of lounges radiating from one side; masculine bar and wide-angle dining room up 2 flights; delicious cuisine on our belly-busting luncheon; perfect attention from a well-trained squadron of maîtres and waiters; different ownership El Cadi disco on the premises. Bedrooms not too big, but thick in comforts and thin in price. If you can accept the transportation hang-up, we'd call this the tiptop independent buy in town and the most rewarding as well. Recommended for everything but its address. Then there's the much improved 250-room **Meliá Granada** in midtown. Public rooms renewed and painted in soothing hues; full air conditioning (a welcome noise muffler); plastics added everywhere possible; mediocre food; popular snack bar; ultrakind staff; some bedchambers cramped (if you're bad humored) or cozy (if you're amorous). Very central and convenient for midtowners. The 133-unit **Alhambra Palace**, with perhaps the best position of all for sightseeing, seems to be responding at long last to the enthusiasm of its new management. Gervasio Elorza has wrought wonders in sweeping away cobwebs for the Chavarri brothers who originally owned this house; they dropped it for a dismal spell, and now have resumed ownership. Rooms perked up; full air cooling now; fresh facade. Portions remain dreary, but if they continue at the present rate, we predict that it will once again be a gem in the Andalusian diadem. No promises but lots of hopes. **Residencia Macia**, at the foot of the Alhambra, offers fresh, clean, attractive kips in the low-priced category. Splendid for money-savers. (The owners, incidentally, probably will have opened a 3-star competitor next to the Luz Granada by the time you alight.) **Brasilia** turns on its greatest appeal at the 7th floor, where the front accommodations boast Sierra-view balconies. Midcity situation, sparkly, air-conditioned, and worthy for the outlay. The **Guadalupe** welcomes numerous groups to its Alhambra arms. If you can snag either #407 or #426 we think you will dance a *jota*. The **Los Angeles** seems so mass oriented and overpriced, in our opinion, that we say ho-hum to this one. While the personnel were cordial and this hostelry is one of the 2 which has a pool, we think most pilgrims will share our boredom. French patrons predominate at the **Kenia**. They know a bargain when they see one. The unpretentious **Rallye** nudges bumpers with the Renault showroom. Lots of polish on this mini; compact prices too. Our kudos diminish respectively for the 60-room-and-bath **Sacromonte**, the older but similarly outfitted **Sudan**, and the chill-blown commercial **Monte-carlo**. For budget-watchers, the youthful **Hostal Internacional** provides basic shelter. The location, however, put us off. Further down our list, the **Victoria** is noisy and the **Washington Irving** seems to have lost its muse. Both, at best, are just passable. **Hostal**

Carlos V might serve in an emergency. But we pray one never occurs. Finally, the **Anacapri** and **Los Faisanes** are not recommended.

Restaurants The dining room or the rooftop grill of the **Luz Granada Hotel** runs away with every trophy in town among private entrepreneurs. The service is suave; the cuisine is tops in the region; the prices are fair. Highest recommendation. The Moorish Grill at the **Alhambra Palace** has picked up a bit, but there's still a long way to go. Arched windows, pastel filigrees, hanging brass, trick mirrors; beguiling décor which, to us, is still wasted. The upstairs dining room seems even more faltering by comparison. The garden at **Parador San Francisco** is lovely in good weather. The inside is pleasant, too. Since it is a Government-run kitchen, it is almost phenomenal that the quality is so lofty. Not a trace of institutionalism. Actually, we even prefer it to the privately operated competitors. For shellfish and finned fare, nothing tops reliable old **Cunini**, behind the flower market. As usual in these harbors, the *marisco* bar is at ground level and the full restaurant is up in the spars. Fresh catches? Look at 'em wigglin! For similar nettings in more fancy surroundings, try **Mesón de las Vidrerias**, where Granada shines through every stained-glass window. If you're trying to slim down, please don't peek into the open kitchen. You'll gain 3 pounds just on a glance. Very popular. **Casa Salvador** whips up family atmospherics, simple cookery, simple surroundings, simple prices. Pure and simply, a winner—except on Fridays when it rests. **Los Manueles** occupies one entire street—every inch of Zaragoza 2 to 4, one of the shortest lanes in Iberia. Cheerful, basic, and busy. When you pay the reasonable tab, it will then be rubbed off the marble bar top where your waiter has chalked the summing up. We meticulously studied the menu at the **Mogambo** and were tempted to order the "Grab Custard." Our unshaven waiter, however, pointed to the "Han With Broad Beans", so we took that plus some "Roval Soup" and a slice of "Breand". For day-in-dine-out consistency, we always keep coming back to the **Sevilla,** where you'll see nothing spectacular and you'll swallow nothing spectacular. Nevertheless, for this city, it's darned good—and it seems to stay that way year after happy year. **Los Leones** couldn't be less colorful or less costly. **Alcaicería**, supposedly in the same category as the Sevilla, has spruced itself up, but its noisy, hurly-burly pace and upsie-downsie quality still turn us off.

Night Life The gypsy dancing has become a disgusting racket. The sucker is levied the fixed price for a package deal, and the tour operator then selects the cave which will yield the most profit for the least effort. Average performance less than 30 minutes; "artists" so untalented no top operation would hire them (the best migrate to Madrid, Barcelona, or Seville); 1 free eyedropper of rotgut *manzanilla* for "refreshments"; spectators packed in too tight for anyone to escape before completion of the show. You'll be sorry if you don't avoid this travesty; it's a cosmic low in tourist-racketeering. Satisfy that yen at **Zincale** (Sacromonte 19), which is one of the notable exceptions to the otherwise sorry scene. Private audiences may watch Mario Maya's artistry in cozy studio surroundings from 7 P.M. to 3 A.M. any day but Sunday. This one we *do* recommend. Away from the city, there are the nightly 2-hour performances at the poolside **Jardines Neptuno**, where the entrance fee of around $10 includes one quaff and the show. The flamenco sessions in **Las**

Cuevas de las Golondrinas (advance notice necessary) have been sterilized, dehumanized, and left bereft of any cultural significance. As a curiosity, however, they still may be worth a jaunt. **Rey Chico** (in Alhambra) turned on an embarrassingly miserable show during our night beat. Not recommended. The **Granada Night Tour** offers an amusing cross section of this slice of Andalusia. Unfortunately, the quality of its folkways was so low as to be termed pathetic by us. We are reminded regretfully that the derivation of the word *gyp* comes from *gypsy.*

HUELVA The **Luz Huelva** might very well be the best in town. The fresh-faced **Residencia Tartessos** would be our next choice in a more modest category. The **Victoria** has a kind staff, good kitchen, and poor amenities. The **Motel Ferreira**, on the route to Portugal, is now barely passable for folk on the move; pool, restaurant, and bar; so poorly maintained that we've lost all enthusiasm.

IRÚN **Alcázar** or **San Sebastián**. It's almost a tossup.

JÁVEA The **Parador Costa Blanca** is about the only grace note in this otherwise humdrum backwater—well, actually it's a beachfront settlement about 25 miles from Gandia. The palm garden is nice, but the facilities for travelers are routine.

JEREZ DE LA FRONTERA, home of sherry and Iberian-style "cognac" (in Spanish, *coñac),* revolves around these palatable products to the exclusion of all other interests. Make the fascinating tour of one of the major *bodegas* (Gonzalez Byass, Terry, Pedro Domecq, Harvey's, Sandemann, Martin, or Williams) which extend all the way down to the oceanside village of *Puerto de Santa María* to see how these potables are produced; all are open from 11 A.M. to 2 P.M. daily, all are free, and all will load you with such samples of their wares that you'll be as stiff as a board by high noon. Charming little country town, with lots of color.

This center historically has been the absolute lees of the innkeeping cup. However, the '71 vintage, 103-room **Jerez** banged out the bung to become the unquestioned area leader. Spanking-white 3-story structure; cool, steel-blue-carpeted reception and sunken lounge; clean, airy dining den (with uninspired fare) abutting an alfresco terrace and pool; chummy equestrian bar. Management seems to us to be riding on its laurels rather than high in the saddle. Stirrup-linked keys unlock pads with rust broadloom, stucco walls, Brobding-nagian twin beds sheathed in avocado spreads, and spacious bathrooms with long fluorescent lights, magnifying mirrors, lake-size tubs; most chambers with balconies. The newer, 2-star, 30-room **Hostal Residencia Mica** might be a worthy alternative if this one is fully booked. The 27-room **Imar** impressed us as ranging from depressing to downright sickening. Except for the Jerez, we'd prefer to curl up in a barrel at one of the local wine cellars than to sleep in any of the other public offerings here. Finally, there is a parador at **Arcos de la Frontera**, about 18 miles from Jerez, that's a good option.

But what this sherryland lacks in hotels, it more than equals in its absence

of good restaurants. Jerez, for some strange reason, seems almost a gastronomic desert. The **Hotel Jerez** is the exception, particularly in the steak department. The area leader, indoors or on the sunny terrace. **El Bosque**, 1 km from the center along the Seville highway, remains the most famous candidate, but it was again a big disappointment to us on our latest trial. With sorrow, not recommended except for a drink in the garden. On a later recheck of Jerez, we were so desperate to find a good meal that we fell back upon a creaky old procedure which has worked well for us in the past: to stop 5 locals at random on the street and politely to ask, "Where can we find the best food in town?" To our surprise, each was vehement in his selection of a little midtown spot named **Joaquín** (Calle Ramón y Cajal 10). Only 8 tables; bar occupying ¼ of the room; spotlessly clean until the standup patrons begin dropping *marisco* shells, in the Iberian tradition. The fish soup was one of the best balanced, most delicate, most delicious that we have had of this nationally popular brew during our long residence in this nation. Please don't miss this masterpiece which is made *especially* for you, not laddled out of a mammoth cauldron. Stick to the sea-ways; the meats are strictly routine in quality; avoid the house wine. **La Vega** is fair as a cafeteria. The **San Francisco** is so-so. Others are worse.

LA CORUÑA's   prize is the recently renovated, portside **Finisterre**. The restaurant is so appealing that you will probably feel grateful for the 3 pools, gym, saunas, Turkish baths, tennis courts, basketball spread, skating rink, and playground. When you've completed the workout, the bedrooms are restful and sparkling clean. Warmly recommended. The **Atlantico** views the harbor through one eye and a lovely garden through the other. Modern tone in its 7 floors containing 200 bedchambers; 50% with Frigobars; cooler than our leading choice but certainly adequate. The beachfront **Riazor**'s sharpest feature is its excellent staff. Go here if you want a close-up of the ocean and kindhearted attention. Back in town, **Residencia España** seems more fit for traveling rope and hemp salesmen than for carefree holiday makers. Not exactly our splice of life.

As for dining, among the independents, we'd choose **Pornos** (*sic!*), **El Rápido, Abrego, Duna**, in that order—or a picnic shopped at **Aniceto Rodrigues**, at Cantón Pequeño 23, if you want to enjoy the countryside.

LA MANGA DEL MAR MENOR   This spit of seashore, located approximately 15 miles from Cartagena, is now slipping badly after having experienced a mammoth low-cost tourist boom. Today it fails to raise a pimple of excitement on our flesh. Of the 100 or so hotels, our preferences are for the **Luz Cavanna**, the **Galua**, and the **Entremares**, in that order. If you'd rather overnight at *Cartagena*, our choice for the moment is the **Cartagonova** with the **Mediterraneo** next; a newcomer, however, may change our ratings as soon as it becomes fully functional.

LEÓN   **Hostal de San Marcos** (building begun in 1530 and constructed for 2 centuries; now totally made over for Deluxe patronage; exquisite marriage of glass and stone; superb management; A-plus comfort; baronial interior; 258

rooms, each with private bath, telephone, and air conditioning; glorious melding of the life of the cloistered era with the comforts of the twentieth century. The main restaurant is open in summer only; the flamenco nightclub functions on fiestas and weekends. Director Enrique Gonzalez is a pro who knows his innkeeping P's and Q's from A to Z. The Spanish National Tourist authorities have every right to be superproud of this gemstone. The commercial **Conde de Luna** would have to rank next in our poll. All of the amenities are here; there's even a bit of flair from the decorators, but in comparison with the San Marcos, it is decidedly number two. **Quindos** is smaller and more modest with a corresponding drop in price tags. Adequate. Across the Bernesga River, the **Riosol** represents—to us, at least—a port only in times of raging storm.

LÉRIDA   The **Hostal de los Condes de Urgel** (34 rooms with baths, 2 suites; 2 dining rooms; bars, terraces, and some units with balcony; swimming pool; air conditioning; very recommendable en route stopover). The **Nacional** isn't a worthwhile tie-up, in our opinion.

MÁLAGA   Refer to "Costa del Sol."

MALLORCA (or MAJORCA)   See our separate chapter on this big little island.

MARBELLA   Refer to "Costa del Sol."

MOJÁCAR   Down on the coast about 50 miles from Almeria, this shoreliner boasts the **Parador de Los Reyes Catolicos**, not to be confused with the Hostal of the same name in northwestern Santiago de Compostela. The white modern complex may have expanded to 100 seafront units. Enormous pool; broad vistas; superb comfort; interesting textures—a common feature of the parador system. The neo-Moorish, 145-room **El Moresco** hangs on a cliff higher up toward the whitewashed town. The octagonal rooftop pool is a marvel; the bedchambers, however, were somewhat disappointing.

MURCIA   Our rating reads this way: (1) **Siete Coronas Meliá**, (2) **Conde de Floridablanca**, (3) **Fontoria**, and (4) **Rincón de Pepe**.

NERJA   The **Parador** is tops for seaside lazing. The **Balcón de Europa** is also friendly and comfy. Both are for seekers of absolute tranquillity.

OVIEDO   boasts the majestic **Hotel de la Reconquista**, which incorporates within a *hospicio* (children's refuge) built by Carlos III a restored ancient chapel, a restaurant, grill, coffee shop, tearoom, and a host of hospitable nests for today's wayfaring pilgrims of any age. Fully air-conditioned for the heirs of yesteryear. Splendid. Halfway to León, the **Parador Nacional Puerto de Pajares** offers only 15 rooms (#9 is our favorite) plus a breathtaking balcony view of the Peña Uviña mountain range. Charming regional restaurant; no private baths; bedrock tariffs for solid rewards.

This town, by the way, is not exactly overrun with gastronomical shrines.

After possibly the **Reconquista Hotel**, you might try the **Pelayo, Marchica, Ronda**, or a sliced apple and local cheese.

PAMPLONA   The 8-story, curvilinear **Hotel de los Tres Reyes**, with its 3 crowns shining over the fringes of the city, is a godsend in this shelter-poor community. Total of 176 units including 8 suites, each with private terrace, bath, telephone, and radio; all public rooms and bedchambers air-conditioned; summer swimming pool plus patio dancing; good food in its modern-tone restaurant; 3 bars; barbershop and beauty salon; garage for 125 cars. Also worthy is **Nuevo Hotel Maisonnave**, near to the Plaza del Ayuntamiento and Estafeta St., where the running of the bulls occurs. **La Perla** remains barely adequate as the sentimental host of Hemingway *aficionados*. **Yoldi**, with about 50 units, must have been designed for Spanish anvil salesmen. Sorry, but it doesn't qualify—and neither do the rest of the ragged lot.

When it comes time to eat, Pamplona's pride and joy (and all of Spain can take a bow for this one) is **El Mesón del Caballo Blanco**. This "House of the White Horse" was built by the city itself, with absolutely no reservations on the purse strings. Although only an architectural youngster, it is a perfect duplicate—sensitively rendered—of a fifteenth-century stone homestead. Ground floor Chacoli Bar offering rock-lined arches, smoked hams and sausages, bottle-glass windows, and a massive wine press; upstairs restaurant wrapped in timber and granite, with L-shape conformation in a split-level layout; inviting hearth with wrought-iron fixtures and coats of arms of ancient Navarra; floors of brick and solid planking. The attentive waitresses are tricked out in polkadot blouses and velvet jerkins. Our meal of Trucha Navarra (local-style trout), Cordero en Chilindrón (heavenly roasted lamb), Cardo (a celery-like vegetable) and Cuajada de Urdiain (sugared-and-iced sheep's milk yoghurt which, unlikely as it might sound, is a taste treat) was superb. Very inexpensive for what one receives. Under the administrative aegis of the Hotel de los Tres Reyes, it is beautifully managed as a regional oasis. **Hostal del Rey Noble**, also known as "Las Pocholas," takes the midtown honors. More cosmopolitan ambiance; 2 dining rooms; beamed ceilings; pleasant but not visually exciting in the same way as the Caballo Blanco; broad menu selection; high prices for the district. A solid second. **Iruña**, also central and very nearby, is next. Highly touted by locals, but we've never lifted our fork here.

PUERTO SANTA MARÍA-ROTA   Driving north from (or south to) Tangier, Gibraltar, or Algeciras via the coastal route? The **Hotel Fuentebravía** is near Puerto Santa María at the Rota border, a skip-and-a-jump from Jerez. Situated on a knoll commanding a beach, with Atlantic rollers for lullabies; lovely main building with a fresh dining room, bar, administrative section, modern-as-tomorrow kitchen, Papagallo Night Club, and a scattering of lodgings 1 level down; adjoining edifice with 90 comfortable doubles, each with bath and bay view; perfumed by 3 acres of flower gardens; 40 bathing cabins with shower; beauty salon; children's playroom; cluster of shops; 200-car garage; swimming pool. The friendly staff is on the youthful and inexperienced side, but normally it is eager and kind; the cuisine is interesting and varied, thanks to regularly imported chefs from other lands for "culinary months," when each

specializes in his own national cookery. Our favorite accommodation is number 201, a double. We like this stop for its simple yet comfortable charm, and for the purebred, put-your-feet-up atmosphere which is evoked by Director José Luis Kutz and his delightful French wife, Monica. The barnlike **Playa de la Luz**, at *Rota*, on the other hand, is not recommended at all by this book. Mammoth production-belt-style dining room; huge courtyard walled in on 3 sides by single-story sleeping cells which were cramped and unattractive to us. Nix. Away from the sea, the stucco **Motel El Caballo Blanco** ("White Horse"), 1-mile south of Puerto Santa María on the Cádiz-Jerez highway, is a good-looking nag in the rapidly expanding Meliá stable. In bathing season, guests ride by horse and carriage to the beach, a 300-yard haul through groves of whispering pines. Whale-size swimming pool for the stay-at-homes; jungle gym for the tots; outdoor bar for the thirsting. Of its numerous individual bungalows with carports, a bevy are studio doubles, and the rest expand to accommodate 4 to 8. A reasonable alternative when the Fuentebravía is jammed.

RONDA   The **Victoria** is much better now, and the food is surprisingly savory—but the road up from the coast, while improved, is still a motorist's trial.

SALAMANCA **Gran**, **Monterrey** (both so-so only). **Residencia Universitaria Gran Vía** at Rosa 4, has been urgently recommended by one of our readers (a U.S. university professor) who lived there all summer; it is budget level.

SAN SEBASTIÁN, formerly the summer capital and presently an important center of Basque political sentiment, is an Iberian Coney Island. Originally the Roman port of Easo, it has been Spain's most jam-packed bathing resort for centuries. When the mood for separatism is quiescent, tourism still booms in as regularly as the Atlantic rollers, but when local agitators rumble there is a marked decrease in the number of visitors. Officially, the Basques have made peace with the government by being given a degree of autonomy, but the minority E.T.A. separatist movement at this writing is still assassinating State policemen and prominent civilians who oppose it at the rate of at least 1 killing per week. (To date, no foreign vacationers have been harmed.)

Winning setting, with its semicircular bay flanked by twin mountains and backed by green hills; hotels numerous and restaurants outstanding for their sea-rooted recipes and Basque regionalism; practically no ancient buildings or antiquities of note. Golf and horse racing at Lasarte; tennis at Ondarreta; plenty of jai alai, yachting, motor racing, and other sports; site of one of Europe's 4 most important annual Film Festivals. Now that gambling has been approved, City Fathers have unveiled a casino which rivals the installation at neighboring Biarritz. The 66-foot-wide bridge between the respective Spanish and French border stations of Irún and Hendzye eases the formerly tortuous access from the north. La Concha ("The Seashell"), the world-famous beach, is imposingly attractive in its natural state—but from July to September it's worse than Sunday afternoon at Blackpool. Although its people are hospitable and ingratiating, it's such a disappointing travel target for most Americans that we'd advise skipping it.

If you do overnight here, however, the spectacular topper is the cliff-high
Monte Igueldo—so high up on that Monte, in fact, that it smiles down upon
the lighthouse. It's a blessing to let's-get-away-from-it-all holiday-hounds who,
like us, are unnerved by the din of the city. Ocean-wide lobby; glass-fronted
lounge looking seaward; coolish bar nookery; starkly marblesque dining room
with appealing vittles; 4th-floor pool; small shop; 121 rooms; corner units
peering at the summer capital, the bay, and the unbelievably enchanting
Basque coastline; full carpeting; full bath count. Service much improved by
Manager José-María Casado. Access is via a private road (a sticker is put on
your windshield so that you won't have to pay a toll each time) or on the
funicular (also free for hotel guests). Open year round. It must be as windy
as Dover, however, on a wintry day. Truly a wonder of architecture; sky-highly
recommended as a stunning achievement.

The **Londres** should have moved its casino to the Gran Kursaal. This
hostelry is one of the slicker havens along La Concha (the bayside beach),
despite the coldly institutional fastnesses of plastic and Formica in its older
bedchambers. Ask for one of the refashioned units, which are miles better, in
our opinion. Now we do admire its overall atmosphere, brightened corridors,
freshened and attractive wood-lined and flower-dotted dining room, and open
seafront terrace for summer sipping. The staff attitudes seem to have soared,
too, of late. Very worthy, indeed.

Also down at sea level, the old-fashioned **Maria Cristina** is in a special class.
Five minutes from the beach; spacious and serene; creaky yet spotlessly clean;
expansive grounds; traditional furnishings; in general, standing still. Its view
of the once-lovely Urumea River has alas been disgracefully despoiled by
paper-mill deposits that drift by in giant malodorous wads. Taut management;
the people in attendance are fine. Youngbloods probably won't like this *grande
dame,* but older pilgrims should find solace here.

The **San Sebastián** earns onions from us. In our notebook we've penned,
"Blah on the outside; blah on the inside." The glass-and-marble **Orly**, a
First-class entry diagonally across from the Biarritz, offers better accommodations. Lobby at ground zero, 60 terraced units on floors 8 to 12, and private
apartments (occasionally available) sandwiched between. Private garage;
Snack Bar; utilitarian furnishings and claustrophobic dimensions. **Hispano-
Americano** offers a flower-lined river-terrace for summer dining, a solarium,
carpets, improved bathrooms, and relatively fresh paint everywhere. All 82
units with showers; full pension obligatory; now open the year around.

The **Biarritz** is always remembered by us for its almost frighteningly antique
lobby. Razing plans were scotched in favor of a wait-a-while policy that was
still waiting on our latest check. Sixth floor the newest of an old lot; all levels
retouched; plastic chairs and low beds; full pension required. Pretty dreary to
us. The 12-unit **Chomin**, above the restaurant of the same name, is a resident-
style stop which might be ideal for families. Despite its association with the
feedery below, it scorns the full-pension-required gouge. Two blocks from the
sea; all bedchambers with bath; so-so maintenance, which is pitiful considering
its potential. The **Codina**? This used to be absolutely wretched. Our latest
investigation, however, notes a considerable swing toward better housekeeping
standards. If you must stop here, pick the "9" series of rooms, which leads the
grim parade. The 21-room **Parma** is bare-boned, but fair enough in a pinch.

Along the pike at *Fuenterrabía*, the **Parador El Emperador** lights up 16 cells in the ancient fortress of Carlos V. Though the total number of accommodations is small, the rustic enchantment of the Middle Ages pervades the atmosphere. Also near the San Sebastián Airport, you'll discover the **Hostal Provincial de Jaizkibel**, a mountainside retreat which we found excellent for lunch; we prefer the parador for sleeping, however. At nearby *Rentería*, **Hostal Lintzirin** reverberates from the growl of highway traffic. Better than adequate facilities, but far from restful, unfortunately.

At mealtimes, **Salduba** (long a fishermen-district favorite) is a delightfully rustic siren who beckons to hungry wayfarers of all callings. It also rates as our number one restaurant in this seaside city. The 2 floors contain stalwart beams of timber, wagon-wheel chandeliers, fat pigtails of plaited garlic, copperware, red-checked linens, and giant candles in wrought-iron braces. The young waitresses seem to find the recipes for foreign cocktails a bit mysterious —but ooooolala-di-da-di-da, when they toted out that repast of Sopa de Pescado (fish soup), Sole Meunière, Changurro al Horno (baked deep-water crab), and Crema de Espinacas (creamed spinach)! Our taste buds took off. It is superb in the honest manner of a native feedery. If you *must* dine deluxe style, you might not like it, but if you let your palate master your aesthetics, we think you will find this a nutritious and enriching experience in every way. Recommended as one of the tops of its type in Iberia. The **Chomin** (downstairs in the inn of the same name, near the Codina Hotel) is a more sophisticated offering, despite its Basque chalet exterior. Nondescript international interior with polished wood and marble trimmings; about 25 tables plus a working bar; open terrace for summer; medium-to-high tariffs; Neptune's dishes far more savory than the meats on our visit; professional service. Not as good as it was, in our opinion, but still worth a try. Devotees of *nouvelle cuisine* (here referred to as *nueva cocina*) speak in hushed tones when they mention **Arzak** (Alto de Miracruz, 21) and **Akelare** (Barrio de Igueldo). We are told that this pair are on the way to becoming gastronomic shrines. True? There's no time left to check them for this edition, but we'll have a full report in the next one. Sorry! **Azaldegui** (Miraconcha 23), we are sad to observe, has slipped dangerously into a tideless backwater. Hillside situation with unspectacular ocean view; decoration that has gone zipless; terrace in summer; main dining room in 3 sections, with tiny bar at one end. Its service is now more frenzied than a Le Mans pit stop. Regrettably, our Lobster Thermidor tasted almost *au gratin,* while our partner's Sole Au Gratin seemed to have been baked in a Thermidor sauce. Prices higher than ever; to us, no longer a value for those rich, rich tabs. **Casa Nicolasa** (Aldamar 4) still commands the greatest fame locally. On our round, the cookery was still coming up commendably. Sidestreet location; 3 small, austere rooms; well-dressed diners as busily achatter as monkeys. Expensive for the region, but worth the outlay.

For 3 rough-and-ready seafood dens, try **Aita Mari** ("Father Mari" in Basque), just 50 yards from the fishing boats at Calle Puerto 23 and **Juanito Kojua** (pronounced "Coo-ow") at #14 on the same street. The former has 3 levels with stone walls, wooden dados, tile floors, and lip-smacking specialties. The latter has 2 dining areas in a sterile, brightly lit, wardroom atmosphere. **Restaurante Eguía**, just a sardine's leap away, works both sides of its narrow

street from the same kitchen. Bar, snack room, and perspiring chef in the economy division.

On your first balmy day, don't miss **Cumbre Monte Ulía** (10-minute ride to the top of Monte Ulía) for a glorious panorama of the city, bays, and La Concha at your feet; immaculate dining room with mirror-sheen floor, pink and yellow linens, and waitresses in regional costumes; 50-table hedge-ringed terrace with low stone wall slopeside, so that you can soak up the view. Better-than-average culinary standards. A *must* in good weather. The *Monte Igueldo* complex is a fortresslike structural mélange, with an enormous ballroom, movie theater, children's playground, zoo, restaurant, and bar. Funicular for pedestrians and toll road for motorists: 40 tables for cocktails; promenade-terrace; unfancy dining room with limited menu; we haven't tried the food. Here's an alpine Yankee Stadium that is glutted with every form, shape, and manner of humanity during the Travel World Series from May to October. Worth a look, but take your Louisville Slugger to beat your path through the throng. The deluxe **Monte Igueldo Hotel** is tranquil, of course. We never found time to sample its cuisine. The vista is enchanting, so for this alone it is recommendable. The **Club Gudamendi** on Carretera del Barrio de Igueldo is perched around the shoulder of the same mountain. Terrace-dining in local country-club atmosphere; splendid position, but routine heavy-on-oil kitchen. In *Pueblo de Igueldo*, the family-style **Recondo** leads with a strong challenge from **Mendi Sorotz**, in the town square.

Back at sea level again, the **Royal Club Náutico**, at the apex of the Concha, is a ferryboat-shape building that doubles as a restaurant and nightclub. Park outlook from the "stern"; 2 "decks" with inside and outside tables; roofed, open-sided "sundeck" for floor show and dancing; cool and pleasant in summer, as long as your gastronomy isn't too choosy at the moment. For bistro-type nourishment in the Old City, **Casa Rodil** (Esterline 8) is a worthy excursion. Bright yellow, coral, and natural-wood décor; menu in Spanish and French; crustacean specialties of Langostinos (prawns), Bisque de Cigalas (lobster-type soup first enriched by the shells and then strained), and Centolla (crab—a Biscay Bay delight). Pleasant but not exceptional. **España** is more colorful, typical, and earthy. Tiny, covered patio in season; nakedly stark furnishings; local workers happily tilting its Spanish-version pinball machines or intent on card games at its marble bar-tables. As authentic and flavorful as a cask of pungent sherry. **La Cueva** (plaza de la Trinidad) boasts a scenic niche in the Old Quarter. It's a bar that grew up to become a specialty corner. Fun.

Outside of town about 4 miles, *Rentería* offers the **Panier Fleuri**, where the Fombellida family has been stoking the ovens since 1920. Its shaded garden is inviting in summer. The interior, with its turn-of-the-century décor, sheds 2 tiers of delight in winter. Happily recommended. About 6 miles from the airport and a ½-mile off the main pike, you may find the **Atamitx**, in the Barrio Ugaldetxo of *Oyarzun*. Split-log construction; communal bench seating; 2 separate grills (fish and meats); rough and ready and lots of fun. Finally, at *Orio*, **José Marí** is the pick of the local sweets. A couple of other chocolate covered Orios reside in the main plaza, but we always dunk with José Marí.

The nighteries of San Sebastián are the epitome of boredom. Rated from V to Z, they run (1) **La Perla** (on the beach and only a summer operation), (2)

Tennis Club (closed in winter), (3) **Royal Club Náutico**, (4) **Trinquete** (converted country house with flat music and flatter pickups), (5) **Igueldo** (mountain ballroom for mass entertainment).

SANTANDER   now has the **Real** as its leader among hostelries. You' find deluxe accoutrements plus 124 comfortable bedchambers. Tops. Next comes the ultracommercial **Bahía**. It counts 250 tiny cubicles with baths, but we can't wax enthusiastic over any of 'em. At the beach sector, **Sardinero** is a renewed old-timer. **Maria Isabel** would be our next choice followed by the **Rhin**. Further out, at *Santillana del Mar*, the **Parador Gil Blas** is a sweet medieval complex in a wonderfully intimate dairying hamlet. Don't miss this touch of arcadia if you are within 100 miles of the village. **Los Infantes** is in the same settlement, blending old-world décor with modern times. Simple but nice. At *Fuente Dé*, along the route of the Picos de Europa mountains, there's the 4-star **Parador Nacional del Río Deva**.

Santander is composed of 3 gastronomic syllables: The prefix is **Puerto;** the middle-fix is **Vivero**; the suffix is **Casa Valentin**. And that spells *San-tan-der*. But if you want to go tilting at windmills try **El Molino** (Puente Arce). We hear it is another bastion of the new cuisine in the north.

SANTIAGO DE COMPOSTELA   The multimillion-dollar **Hostal de los Reyes Católicos** ("Hostel of the Catholic Kings") is a fantastic architectural and decorative monument—so opulent, so grandiose, and so extravagantly conceived that it's a wonder to the eyes. Commercially, however, this all-season retreat must always remain, through this very lavishness, a Taj Mahal-size white elephant. Spacious public rooms, 4 dining salons, concert hall, auditorium, bar, and hairdresser; dancing nightly in both the nightclub and the grill. There are 150 units with bath; three 1-room suites that are slightly smaller than Candlestick Park; the doubles are regal; the cuisine is expensive and appealing. Worth a special detour to overnight here, because there's nothing else like it in Spain.

SANTIAGO DE LA RIBERA   (Murcia): **Los Arcos**, on the Mar Menor, probably remains a leading light, but we're not sure.

SEGOVIA   **Las Sirenas** is the main hotel in town. Noisy and so-so.

As a lunch excursion from Madrid, the **Mesón de Cándido** (on the main plaza) is practically a national institution. Even the enthusiastic local police —if they see a hungry look in your eye—will automatically steer you to this address before you can say "boo." Several room levels; stupendous roast piglet and roast lamb; colorful, not too expensive, and fine. A number of travelers have squawked about higher lunch tabs for their drivers than for themselves. Service is fast, if not abrupt. *Phone for your table in advance.* **El Abuelo** ("The Grandfather") is a characteristic cellar, unspoiled, with a cobblestone floor, low ceilings, and poor old "Grandpa" in a cage in one corner; its suckling pig is just worth oinking about. Basic.

SEVILLE   is glorious, with its wealth of archeology and art. There are churches, convents, tombs, museums, and galleries on practically every block;

orange trees line the winding streets, and in the parks are snow-white pigeons which will light on the head, shoulders, and arms of any traveler who'll spend 2¢ for birdseed. The *Feria,* held soon after Holy Week, is the biggest, most frenzied, most colorful traditional celebration in Spain. Every soul in town pulls out his regional dress from the mothballs, and for 144 dizzy hours all work is forgotten. This event alone is worth a special trip to Europe—but reserve your space months in advance, because every pallet in the district is sought after by the hordes of outside visitors.

Hotels   We are happy with the sweet little **Doña Maria**. We also suspect that discriminating readers will even compare it favorably with the prestigious dowagers of Seville. Midtown situation squinting at the Cathedral from the narrow Calle don Ramondo; vaulted lobby with brick pillars; restaurant in Moorish décor; rooftop swimming pool with bar and snack tables; 100% air-conditioned. Total of 50 doubles and 12 singles—and no 2 alike; full carpeting; 12 units with canopied beds; Simmons mattresses for all snoozers; attractive paintings; many baths with double basins; some with French doors leading to balconettes. The proprietor is the artfully motivated Marquis de San Joaquín; Manager Miguel Villegas, formerly of the Colón, runs the day-to-day show. Very tasteful; very comfortable; very highly recommended.

The youthful, 82-room, gaily terraced **Pasarela** exudes good taste, modern tones, expensive garniture (marble trim in baths, as one small example), a garage (which is a blessing in this town), and such highlights as potted gardens hanging in front of your picture window. You'll also find a cafeteria for putting on weight and a sauna for taking it off. Well conceived by Santander Proprietor Don Manuel Peña. We like this entry. *Saludos!*

The 8-story, fully air-conditioned **Luz Sevilla** also is tuned to the tastes of modernists and Jet Settlers. This one boasts a collection of up-to-date international hotel amenities fused with undertones of Spanish flavor. Attractive soft-hued décor throughout; viewful rooftop summertime Grill, with dancing on weekends; alfresco apron for panaromantics; orchestra nightly; leathery bar with handsome wooden panels and tartan carpet; hearthside library; marblesque dining room, also with open terrace adjoining; solarium and children's pool. A boutique, an Avis car rental agency, barbershop, beauty parlor, and basement garage make up the panoply of fringe benefits. All bedchambers with piped music, bedside and bathroom phones; wall-to-wall carpeting; first-quality appointments; frigobars in all suites; units ending in "02" the most spacious. Highly recommended for its type, but impressively expensive by national standards.

The historic **Alfonso XIII** ("thirteen" is pronounced "TRAY-thay") is almost a shrine for nostalgic visitors to Andalusia. As we write these words, it is completing an exhaustive restoration program, so we are not able to comment fairly on the hotel as it will appear by the time of your arrival. The lobby had been a museum of Spanish and Moorish art; the lavish workmanship, the specially baked tiles, the tapestries, and the priceless gold service for royalty will never be duplicated. Let's hope it retains some of the antique flavor. **Nuevo Lar** offers 139 units with most of the necessary mod-cons. Marble lobby cheered by a small aquarium; restaurant for intimate dining near entrance; larger banquet hall up a flight; staff on the cool side but well trained. The bedchambers are meticulously maintained; patterns are at war with each other

but the colors overall formed an amnesty pact; book units ending in "18" because they are much more spacious than others.

The slightly larger **Maria Luisa Park** resides on a scenic avenue across the river. One peek will assure you that it is very much in the twentieth century. If you want to cash in on a splendid view, bid for a frontside address with terrace. The rust-toned **La Macarena** blushes incarnadine beside the old wall of the city—a nice touristic touch that later seems merely tedious when you are saddled with the effort of getting to or from midtown. The glassed-in patio is a plus as is the rooftop, L-shape swimming pool. In sum, however, we think you can do better closer to the doin's than way out in the ruins.

The **Colón** has charged in with many spectacular gains recently. Cleverly conceived Burladero Restaurant in *torero* style (even the plates bear a bullring design); huge dining room overlooking a lane of orange trees; masculine bar untouched; 100% air-conditioned; 261 bedrooms; some baths with double basins and bright floral patterns; well-equipped living space with huge wardrobes and silent valets; 7th-floor accommodations with private balconies (especially desirable in balmy winter weather, when they are in sunshine all day long). Director Don Pedro de Torres Gracía provides as much as any of the luxury-category innkeepers at half their blue-ribbon tariffs. This house has the feeling of a back-home Statler—cool, commercial, but efficient. Now a solid favorite of wayfaring Americans—for excellent reason. Superb for the money.

Many of the architectural features in the '73-vintage **Becquer** were salvaged from the razed *palacio* that stood on this site. Marble portal leading to an open lobby divided by wrought-iron screens; English bar; breakfast-only service; garage; Andalusian patio on first floor; 126 air-conditioned bedrooms. Sound returns in the medium-price range.

The **Cristina**, directly across the plaza from the Alfonso XIII, evokes an air of somber commercialism. Appealing roof garden in summer, plus Bodega nightclub in basement, offering some of the best flamenco dancing and other entertainment in town; friendly personnel. Its chef, however, is in howling need of a refresher course in cooking school, poor fellow. In our personal judgment the beds are small and the furnishings tasteless; moreover we found the maintenance dragging. Lackluster to us. The off-beat **Murillo** is sited on a charming, lamplit, hard-to-find, pedestrian-only street (Lope de Rueda 3, 5, and 7) in the Old Town. Slaphappy, informal administration, overseen by funloving Proprietor Miguel Linares, a brother in the family that operates Spain's largest chain of art and antique shops. Colorfully decorated with pieces of his Linares collection; 64 small rooms with bath or shower; all front units with private balcony; best buys in the 14-suite annex. Cheerfully amusing; for the young-in-heart. To our distress, the **Inglaterra** is turning into one of those "big bustling establishments." It delivers 120 now-worn accommodations, the last installment looking onto a quiet interior garden. Sleek glassy entrance warmed somewhat by wood; 200-year-old tiles decorating the lobby and public areas; richly framed oil paintings; window-fronted dining room facing the active plaza; leathery bar stamped with the seals of 8 colleges of Oxford; a boutique. Curiously, this house features the most comfortable telephone booths we've ever dialed in our travel snoopings—2 easy chairs, artwork, glass doors, and antique phones. One decorative theme in all bedrooms: brownish-gold carpets,

yellow-to-beige chenille spreads, carved wood headboards, black chairs, twin basins in baths plus a shower cap for milady. The suites, except for corner-sited #508, were unimpressive to us; all 5th floor units sport terraces, by the way. Fatigue seems to be setting in here.

Now let's round up our budget shelters: The **Reyes Católicos** would be our pick of the low-cost havens; dining for registrants is at the Montecarlo. Then comes the unpretentious, Spanishy **Ducal**, followed by the aesthetically surprising **Don Paco**, which is a paean to pigments. Nice facilities and extra-sweet staffers, but why it hues its ode-ious path we'll never know. **Alcazar** also leans to passionate pink, salmon rouge, khaki brown, and pistachio green. Clean it is, however. The **Venecia** and the previously mentioned **Montecarlo** (dining room) are emergency hole-ups only. The **America** was discovered by a savvy friend who tells us it's well located, modern, and kind to the wallet. We'll be exploring it soon. Incidentally, unless you're willing to take potluck as a boarder in a private house, *do not go for* Semana Santa *(Holy Week) or the* Feria *without a confirmed reservation from one of the above;* any other hotels are not, repeat *not,* recommended. Since you'll be forced illegally to pay double the normal rates wherever you stay during these jam-packed weeks, you might as well do so with a degree of cleanliness and comfort.

Restaurants   Seville will never exactly outdazzle Paris as a Temple of Gastronomy; there's an old Spanish saying that the people of Andalusia think too much about living to waste time on food, and it couldn't be truer. The number-one restaurant of the city—and a notable exception to the Andalusian adage—is the **Burladero** in **Hotel Colón**. Attractive décor designed to pique the interest of bullfight aficionados; comfortable, handsome appointments, extensive menu, outstanding viands, stiff prices for the region. Locally unrivaled. By tradition, next in line has been the **Hostería del Prado**, on the Prado de San Sebastián; we like it for regional cookery and *tapas.* Then flows the **Rio Grande**, perched on the far bank of the Guadalquivir beside the San Telmo Bridge. Intimate maroon-tone cocktail area near entrance effectively ruined by a cold food display; elegant dining room divided by glass and wrought iron, accented with globe lamps, oil portraits, and potted plants; massive windows abutting a summer-only alfresco terrace; adroit service. Our recent repast here turned up a mixed bag: garlic soup that couldn't have been better and a sirloin that tasted as if it had once lined Larry Holme's punching bag; the accompanying potatoes, tomatoes, and carrots were not tepid—they were downright cold and so, at that point, were we. **La Muralla**, in La Macarena Hotel, jams its tables too much together. The chef's hand was heavy on our sampling. So-so. **Casa Senra** (Becquer 25, a 15-minute taxi hop from the center), formerly the sloppiest, grubbiest, dirtiest, most dreadful dump that ever delighted Sevillanos, their guests, and us with superb culinations—has cleaned itself up. Entrance bar for premeal libations and mariscos; stucco dining alcoves; beamed ceiling; polished marble floor; wooden tables covered with clean tartan cloths; comfortable chairs replacing old stools and benches; waiters in white jackets; air conditioning. The cookery is still as scrumptuous as ever, particularly the seafood specialties flown in daily. The grills are also prime—so is our Grade-A recommendation. **Los Alcazares** (Miguel Manara 10) is an unpretentious eatery dividing its 11 tables between 2 floors. Seascape murals and

bullfight posters decorating the upstairs segment; chummy service; student minstrels sometime roll in after 10. The hot garlic soup and partridge in sherry casserole are inexpensive but worthy selections. Next down the stepladder is **La Raza**, at the entrance to María Luisa Park—but unfortunately facing the traffic rather than the greenery. Identical menus, tariffs, and ownership as Hostería del Prado; appetizing steaks—for Spain, that is. In summer, this one has the edge on its harness mate. **Luna Parque**, across the street, also stares obsessively at the thoroughfare rather than at Mother Nature. (*You* figure 'em out.) Décor jarringly disjointed by a cold-box placed in the dining room; professional service; fair cuisine. Open all 4 seasons—as if anyone here cared about blossom time. **Bodegón Torre del Oro** (Calle Santander 29, a 3-minute stroll from the Alfonso XIII), has a noisy beerhall ambiance, savory Pechuga Villeroi (a chicken-breast specialty), fairly reasonable tariffs, and a no-nonsense approach to skilletry. Fun, if you're in a rollicking mood. **Los Corales** (Sierpes 102) draws almost as many tourists as flies; there were plenty of both during our last visit. Central location; friendly reception and service; food and drink so-so; seafood is best; medium-to-high prices; colorful décor, in a contrived way. Just fair. **Manolo Bar** (Pasaje del Duque) offers good cookery and good service; covered terrace; medium-to-low price bracket; popular. **Casa Luis** (Paseo de Colón 6) is very plain, very cheap, and very characteristic; service standards sinking radically with its too-easy success; sidewalk terrace, hideous artwork in dining room, beautifully tiled bar adjoining. **Pescadería Málaga** (Calle O'Donnell) specializes in fried fish; typical. So does the **Bar Colón**, but it's exceptionally raw in character. **Restaurant los Monos** or **Juliá** (Plaza de México) has an attractive but overbusy garden. Inside, its 1000-seat dining fastness reminds us of a cheap snack-stop on the old U.S. No. 1. Locals are attracted by its *feria*-type décor and regional fare. Nothing special. The newish **El Fogon** (Habana 8) turned us off with its window display of dead fish and meat. Somehow it all looked ready for Madame Tussaud's.

Night Life   The city's leading exponent of flamenco is the **Patio Andaluz** (Plaza del Duque 4) which is keenly challenged by the **Patio Sevillano** (Paseo de C. Colón 11a) both owned by the enterprising Juan Cortés and Matías Garrado. Both offer excellent *tablao,* clean surroundings, and a polka-dot nebula of whirling Andalusian atmospherics for the $10 entry fee. A duo that we have no hesitation in recommending. **La Cochera** (Av. de Menéndez Villajos) dances close on the heels of the first pair—it might even have fractionally more chic. Highest marks to the flamen-corps; rustic bar and restaurant in front serving regional fare; 3-alcove back room under a beamed ceiling; raised platform for the excellent young dancers and singers; honest drinks. The management was so grateful for the business that it gave the 2nd drink gratis to his appreciative guests. But don't count on that every time. For crisp, authentic flamenco and a full evening's entertainment (albeit somewhat tourist-oriented), we give orchids to this one. **Turin** (Asunción 21), reputedly, is very popular; so is **La Trocha**. For economy night-owling, **Garbanzo Palace** (Menéndez Pelayo 18), which means "Chick Pea Palace" is a sweet pea, as far as we're concerned. A lot of locals seem to agree. Fun and folksy. Among the discothèques, the well-run **Petrarca** (M. Carmelo 10) is the fastest spinner. **El Dragon Rojo** (Betis 60) is also near the top of the pops. We are fond of its

fireplace lounge and the small illuminated fountain which provide a modicum of relaxation. The **Melody**, near Petrarca, is not recommended. Neither is **Los Gallos**. As for bars, the **Siete Puertas** ("Seven Doors") is now only a drinking parlor; gentlemen of the old school are advised to don a suit of armor before venturing inside, in order to protect themselves from the harpies who, if still there—we're quite serious—will grasp them in a startlingly indecent manner as soon as they step up to the bar. In our travels, we've never come across such openly and persistently predatory trollops. (If you *do* go look out for that blonde with the hangnail.) Across the pike, are the **Ta-Ca-Ta** and **La Vaquita**, which are routine, followed by **Maxime** and **Desirée**. **La Marina** sometimes zings for that lonely forlorn male who gets his kicks by holding hands with a gold-toothed wench. (You *know* the cost of gold these days!) **Valentíno**? Forget it.

SITGES   is a charming little fishing port 45 minutes down the coast from Barcelona's airport. It's packed in high summer with trippers from all lands. In fringe seasons, however, it is an ingratiating rest stop with good food, fair hotels, and seaside golfing. Within the town, the **Calípolis** is the leader. Amiable staff; reasonable cuisine; spacious rooms with balconies; simple suites; moderate tariffs. Clients may use the municipal pool and receive a 50% greens fees discount at the links. The **Terramar**, by the golf club and overlooking a ringlet harbor with private beach, is seasonal but good. Wedding-cake construction with flower-girt terraces for all seafront rooms; inner court with a decorative pond; tennis courts; horses available; water sports facilities; swimming pool and adjoining outdoor bar; institutional dining salon as big and cold as the Avalon Ballroom; large bedchambers; oddly shaped suites; mélange of furniture from Iberian Provincial to Grand Rapids Seconds. Not bad in a sprawling, multischematic way. The Scandinavian-style **Los Pinos** is modest and not without its charms. The 40-unit **Platjador** is amateurish; it's strictly for econ-o-misers. The **Subur** is zipless; this one caters heavily to European migrants. The enchanting **Vallpineda** development is designed chiefly for householders, but perhaps a chalet can be rented for a holiday respite. Excellent swimming pool in an enclave of gardens; deluxe restaurant; fine bar; the peace of the country, broken only by the sound of tennis balls plopping on its 7 championship courts. A pleasant clublike hideaway, but not by the sea.

As for restaurants, the town boasts the superb little **Mare Nostrum**, one of our favorite fair-weather choices in the province. Awning-topped, umbrella-dotted apron across from the seaside promenade; interior units split into a bar and a dining nook lined with paintings; delicious shrimp cocktail served on an open plate, with the sauce mixed before your eyes; carefully and intelligently prepared filets of sole, done either in simple butter or with an almond garnish; Crema de Mariscos soup that is just out of this glittering world; good meats, too—but we inevitably come back for the piscatorial delights. These, with a cold bottle of Las Campanas *rosado* (the best Spanish rosé), should put the glow of romance into any cheeks. Courteous service by the same staff year after happy year; tabs slightly higher than most medium-range candidates in the nation. We love it day or night. **El Greco**, also on the front, provides an extensive menu of well-treated comestibles. It, too, is best for outdoor dining

when the climate is benign. **Fragata**, near the lovely seaside chapel and the fishermen's wharf, serves decent drinks and culinations, but the prices knocked us for a loup (if you'll pardon our finny pun). The service is often careless and care-less. The Brasa, downstairs in the **Hotel Calípolis**, is an amusing stop for snacks, club-platters, and light meals late in the evening; it swings in season. The **Baxeroe** in nearby *Villa Nueva* gave us sole food fit for the gods. Always filled with loyalists. **El Velero** is so unattractive you'd never believe that its array of pastries could mutilate your diet with second helpings. A sweetie for sweets, but a misery for main courses. The previously mentioned **Vallpineda** complex is pleasant by sunlight or by moonbeams. Inland valley situation; modern, clubby atmosphere; outdoor-indoor dining. If you scoot down here from Barcelona, try to make it during the fringe seasons, because it's a colossal hassle in midsummer.

For night life, the leader is **Monaco**. Dancing from 10 P.M. until your sandals need resoling; entrance fee pays for first drink; peppery 6-piece band; fun atmosphere for young folk. **Mi Borito-Jo** ("My Donkey And I") clops up next. The **Brasa**, below the Hotel Calípolis, is the late-night gathering spot for that final nuzzle and sip. This town is jammed with a zillion bars—none of which will remind you of New York's Algonquin.

TARRAGONA's Imperial Tarraco stands above the main crossroads as tall as a modern, flag-decked fortress—but it is not imposing, except in its massiveness. Although easily the leader for accommodations, it seems such a tasteless a vacation stop that we can't imagine ourself in a merry mood choosing it as a holiday house. The **Lauria** is next, followed far down the list by the **Paris**. None is really exciting.

TOLEDO has skyrocketed in its hospitality offerings of late. The duet of national paradors make it unique in Spain, for nowhere else to our knowledge are there 2 in such a small area. The **Conde de Orgaz** affords the most glorious view of Toledo possible—especially from its summer terrace where you may also take lunch. Boosted room count of 100 doubles, all with balcony. The **Parador del Virrey Toledo** actually resides within the fourteenth-century Oropesa Castle—one of the most impressive we've seen in all of our travels. It's about an hour's drive, incidentally, from midcity. If you can snag some digs high in the older section, we think you will have found your castle in the Spanish sky. Fabulous—and that's a word we seldom employ. Among the privately operated houses, the **Hostal del Cardenal**, within the ramparts, stands turret and parapet above any other independent inn in sight. Fountains, hearths, flowers, elegant staircases, and a salon sheathed with intricately carved wood form a proud cloak of refinement for this newish but cleverly antiqued house. Two-tier restaurant; suite, 3 singles, and 2-dozen doubles whisper their Castilian heritage. **Carlos V** leads the also-rans; if you should hear strange sounds as you walk through the Tombs of the Spanish Kings in the Escorial, they might be wails of protest from this great Emperor for this calumny on his name. **Alfonso VI**, with its updated interior and kind personnel, is a sounder bet today.

When you're ready for a meal, the **Hostal del Cardenal** has an enchanting

garden, a marvelous arbor-covered dining-terrace, a cleverly "aged" 2-story restaurant (we prefer the upper level), and a score of attractive features—but the food we ate, course by course, and the so-called service we experienced could only be termed appalling by us. Above the Cardenal about 200 yards, there's the viewful **Chirón**, which can turn out sound regional fare for very reasonable tabs. A delight. **Casa Amelio** is the suggestion of friendly Palm Beach readers who call it a "tiny, crowded local bistro patronized by Spaniards." They praise the cookery and the atmosphere. It's on Calle Sinagoga, an offshoot of Calle Hombre de Palo. **Venta del Aire** has very little charm, no view to speak of, and service which we'd hardly call the world's most agreeable; in addition, so many flies appeared to enjoy its full-pension plan on our last visit that it seemed a pity to interfere with their feeding. Both establishments are loaded, but loaded, with tourists in season. Try the parador; it's bound to be better.

TORREMOLINOS   Refer to "Costa del Sol."

VALDEPEÑAS   Point your headlights straight for **Motel del Hidalgo**, now under the crack direction of José María Mateu of Palma's Meliá Mallorca fame, because the next-ranked **Paris** is for lumberjacks.

VALENCIA   has a special charm—but it's also not a favorite with most foreign travelers. Like Barcelona, it's so busy and so bustling that the atmosphere is more impersonal than in various cities of the interior. The city prefers to be an agricultural and shipping center. Its lifeline, water, is held in such reverence that the 1000-year-old Arab ceremony of electing a tribunal to regulate the flow to the orchards is still practiced and still recognized under the Spanish legal system. (You can see the judges in session every Thursday outside the Cathedral door.) There's a low-grade beach resort, 2 good hotels, 1 good nightclub, and a few points of antiquarian interest. But the twin high spots of the year—the famous _Fallas_ fiesta on St. Joseph's Day (mid-Mar.) and the magnificent Battle of the Flowers (early Aug.)—shouldn't be missed by any U.S. vacationer who is footloose in Spain during these times; they both make the Carnival of Nice a tawdry, tinny, mechanical show in comparison. Be sure to arrange sleeping accommodations beforehand, however.

Hotels   A late addition is the 320-room **Rey Don Jaime**, pleasantly out of the center and fringed by its own park, gardens, and swimming pool. Full air-chilling; marble lobby in beige and brown with highlights of polished wood and crystal; English-style bar, darkly handsome; cheerful dining facilities; nightclub with circular brass dance floor; comfortable suites but smallish doubles, all equipped with TV and direct-dial phones. A welcome newcomer ably managed by the talented José (Pepe) Sendra. Top billing. The **Astoria Palace** presents 208 spacious but stark rooms; La Bruja nightclub; terrace dining-and-dancing; a chilly marblesque lobbyette, an uncozy lounge, an unattractive restaurant, and all of its accommodations air-conditioned. Improving staff attitudes; warming up nicely; better than ever. The ubiquitous Meliá group recently unveiled a challenger here. The 4-star, 129-room **Azafata** is its name, but we haven't had an opportunity to check it out as yet. The **Excelsior**

is coming up once again—but there's still a long climb ahead. Fully air-conditioned with individual controls; American Bar with adjoining summer-winter terrace; 65 rooms and baths; 12 corner suites; fresh wall coverings and paint make it much brighter than it was, but nicks, chips, and sticking hardware still turn up with disturbing frequency. The ancient and seedy **Reina Victoria** has had a piecemeal renovation job that still lacks flair. Full bath count for its 92 units; some Charles Addams doubles at dwarfish tabs; traffic-choked location. Fair, but uninspired, in our opinion. Except for the **Renasa**'s situation at the edge of town near the soccer stadium, we think it is one of the better and newest hotel buys in Valencia. Fresh, Scandinavian, clean-lined personality that we can recommend cheeringly. The **Sorolla** is smack in the middle of the bright lights. It's pretty perky too, so if you prefer midtown to the suburbs, this should fill the bill for a modest outlay. The **Oltra** is basic; you can't go too far wrong, but we wish the housekeeper would swallow more vitamin B. The **Llar** specializes in heavy group patronage. Bustling, genial staff; clean modest surroundings. The starkness at the **Ingles** tingles our nerves. Bah. The **Alhambra** shouldn't fool you with its attractive lobby, because here the beauty is only skin deep, in our beady-eyed view. "Give a man a landscape and a passion," said Jesús Gómez Escardó, "and you give him everything!" That last word nicely sums up what this master host and his charming wife Doña Alicia provide the fortunate guests of the **Hotel Monte Picayo.** This hostelry is not actually within the city limits of Valencia, but 14 miles down the pike in *Puzol-Sagunto.* Sprawled over a large hill are the central building, 10 cottages, swimming pools, and 2 championship tennis courts. The lobby is stunning in concept, unusual in design, and flawless in execution: It consists of 4 descending tiers, housing respectively the reception area, the library, the bar, and the lounge overlooking the cascading main pool. Within easy strolling distance are the Grill, the sauna, the shopping gallery, the discothèque, and the 46 hypersumptuous chambers in the principal edifice. More? Much, much, much more. Suffice it to say that what the extremely talented Gómez team has done with their landscape has become our passion too. Fabulous!

Out at *El Saler*, the **Parador Luis Vives** provides peaceful duals in the sun. All 40 accommodations doubles; clinical taste; pool fringing the golf links. Fair-ways. In *Torrente*, 14 miles from the port up a difficult 3rd-class road, the **Lido** is better as a dinner-and-dance stop than as an overnight hitch. For motorists, **La Pinada**, at kilometer stone 28 on the Zaragoza highway, has a pleasant pool, a routine restaurant, and so-so sleeping quarters. One thing to be said for this one: it's on the way *out* of town.

Restaurants Viveros (Jardines del Real), our first choice, has unglamorous but substantial cookery and slow service. The same company operates the newer **Les Graelles** (Paseo de la Alameda), where we dined very, very well in lovely surroundings. The offspring, in fact, now seems even better—and certainly it's more attractive than the alma mater. **Ateneo**, on Plaza Caudillo, probably turns on better cookery more consistently. Cafeteria plus a rather overwhelming old-world restaurant. Stuffy in its mood, but reliable in its quality. For dinner only, **Casa de Lee** includes a few Oriental dishes among

its Iberian selections. Whacky but fun. Across the street, **Mesón de Maris-
quero** specializes in fruit of the sea, cleanliness, good value, and friendly
service. What else could one ask? **Lara** (Calle Paz 46) comes up with a small
dance floor, intimate corners, and palate-tickling atmosphere; not bad. **Lionel,**
facing the Plaza Caudillo, is genteel, discreet, and chicly intimate. The cuisine
is French, _mais oui!_ Closed Sunday. **Mesón del Conde** (Calle de José Iturbi
18) has 2 brick-and tile-lined rooms and 15 blue-and-white-robed tables. Waiters in tartans and waistcoats; attentive service; low tabs; many Italian selections have slipped onto its Spanish menu. **La Gran Parrilla** (Calle Marqués
del Turia 10) features an open kitchen and a respectable menu. **Palas Fesol**
(Hernán Cortés 9) is plain and inexpensive; budgeteers like this one, but we
feel that it has been slipping lately. **O'Lano's Basque** (Calle San Martín) boasts
a bar, restaurant, and O'Lano's élan; amusing at night because O'Lano is such
a character; this one gets better every visit. If you're restless, if the day is lovely,
and if you don't mind participating in a mob scene, **La Pepica** (Playa Levante)
is right on the beach (10 minutes by taxi from the center). It's simple, cheap,
Spanish, and busy as a minny in a minnow hatch. Lunch is preferable; so
popular that a hotel has recently been added; the food—well. . . . **Las
Arenas**, farther down the street, has better fare but less character; same management as **Café Noel** (Calle Ruzafa). **La Marcelina**, also by the water, is
pleasant for a lazy daytime, maritime meal. The **Club Náutico** is directly on
the wharf overlooking the port entrance. From your table you can toss a line
to that passing boatswain. Outdoor terrace and glassed-in, flower-lined dining
salon; separate bar; wonderful seafood, especially shellfish; courteous service;
physically raw in appearance; teeming with local folk in season; inexpensive.
A happy choice if you wish to flee the bustling city. Finally, if you are outward
bound from the airport, we think that the **Azafata Hotel Grill**, off Route 111,
is better than any terminal cookery (that phrase is almost 100% accurate) you
are likely to ingest before you fly.

Night Life   **Club Internacional** (Ribera 4) now wins the cup. Vaguely
oval zinc bar; sophisticated inner sanctum with single acts twice nightly;
professional service; pleasant bar girls who are not too aggressive. Okay. **Sala
Stop** (F. Esteve 4), a red-lit, barn-like dance hall, charges $6 for entry. Some
B-gals on "reserve." Pretty routine. Number three is **La Bruja**, in the **Astoria
Hotel**; best band for dancing, cold ambiance, but popular. **Mocambo** (Sangre
9), in midtown, is open year round. Air conditioning; bar to the right of its
arcade entrance; one main salon in tearoom disguise, frosted with a baker's
dozen of tarts; legitimate drinks; much improved. Festivities begin at 11:45 P.M.;
main show at 1:15 A.M.; mock flamenco that is more Holyoke, Mass., than
Andalusia. Lone males may enjoy it here. As for the rest, **Club Simun** (Sta.
Clara 5) is a pale carbon copy of our first choice; in the shank of the evening
it's a disco hub, later it's a routine night roost; **Brunos** (Riberas 8) and **Zambra**
(Ribero 16) are ho and hum, respectively.

VIGO   This is Spain's salty old girl of the north. Among its hotels, the **Bahía
de Vigo** leads the convoy. It's on the waterfront a few steps from the docks;
there's a modern commercial atmosphere throughout; we liked the ocean-wide

restaurant on the 2nd floor as well as the Corsair's Bar; all 106 staterooms come fully plumbed. Shipshape. The fresh **Niza** would rank next in the Vigo regatta, followed by the **Ensenada** and the beachfront **Samil Playa**.

In the Vigo vicinity, the environs almost bristle with those wonderful Government-run paradors. Our pick of the neighboring trio is the **Conde de Gondomar** at *Bayona*. It nests in an L-shape fortress bathed by the same winds that drove the ships of Sir Francis Drake along these shores. Infinite variety of pastimes, sports, recreation—even a genuine dungeon in which to drop the kids when they get cantankerous. Then there's the 50-room **Parador Casa del Baron** in the town of *Pontevedra* (20 miles from Vigo). The situation is not so maritime, but the regional cuisine is seasoned by the sea and the comfort and aesthetic standards are high. Finally, there's the **Parador de San Telmo** at *Túy* (17 miles from Vigo) which gazes at Portugal across the Rio Miño. It's a nice stop if you wish to dawdle a while longer in Spain before hopping the frontier.

VITORIA   Canciller Ayala (Deluxe category; 200 rooms; by far the most imposing in the region). Avoid the **Frontón** (ouch!).

ZARAGOZA   The 10-story **Corona de Aragón** was the scene a swiftly spreading kitchen fire in 1979 which swept through air ducts and finally was responsible for the deaths of approximately 80 guests, many of them overcome by smoke. The tragedy was one of Europe's worst building disasters in more than a decade, though the edifice itself was not extensively damaged. Now fully functional, it provides space for 520 guests in Deluxe surroundings; 2 restaurants featuring American, French, and Spanish cuisine; excellent and colorful grill; active bar; patio, solarium, sippery, and swimming pool on the roof; dark but spacious bedchambers. A grim memory for one of Spain's proudest houses. Then come a covey of question marks: **Alfonso I** (120 rooms; reportedly nicely furnished), **Ramiro I**er (60 units in Deluxe quality), and **Don Yo** (170 door keys). Bringing up the wagon train, we have **Goya** (Statleresque in atmosphere; 100 newer rooms, all air-conditioned; 60 older units revamped; 100% bath count; clean, fresh ambiance; garage), **Gran Vía** (31 cubicles, each with private shower; okay for peseta-pinchers), **Conde Blanco** (chiefly for motorists), **Centenario** (seemed downright scabrous to us; recommended for mouth-breathers who never hope to smell again), and **Oriente**.

This city has dozens of bars for tidbits—but a paucity of full-fledged restaurants. The **Savoy** (good service, clashing décor, fair prices) and the **Laguna** (we prefer this one) are the only candidates serving international cuisine. For strictly regional cookery in colorful Aragón surroundings, the **Mesón del Carmen** is tops. Busy-beehive atmosphere; U-shape room with nibbler-and-sipper's bar down one side and tables down the other; smoky; full of rich Spanish life and vitality; excellent skilletcraft in the manner they know best; reasonable tariffs. Recommended as your first shot in this way station. The nutrition complex at the **Hotel Corona de Aragón** includes the Moorish-striped Albarracín Grill for spit roastings, the Bearn Restaurant on the mezzanine for international fare, the modernistic Formigal for coffee-shop wares

(plus take-away service), and Piccadilly's Bar for sips and snacks. We are especially fond of the grillroom here.

The after-dark candidates include (1) **Cancela** (3 sections: bar, cabaret, and flamenco stage), (2) **Cosmos** (routine), and (3) **Venus** (summer terrace; shows; 1 mile outside the city). All require a moderate minimum.

Sweden

Most of us picture Sweden—especially Lapland—as a rugged, rocky, wind-swept country, where the good-natured, fair-haired stalwarts milk reindeer, drink Swedish Punch, battle the cruel elements, and never take off their red-flannel underwear.

Not on your life! It's a land of lakes and streams; much of it is flatter than Ohio. Thousands of pools and rivulets glitter on the placid, green landscape of the south; the summer sun there is warm, fields burst with ripe, golden wheat, and gentle pastures are brilliant with flowers. One-tenth of the population tills the dark soil on these plains, the coastal terraces, the lake shores, and the northern valleys; in this balmy bottomland climate, warmed by the Gulf Stream, everything flourishes from peas to sugar beets to long-stemmed roses. The mountains, sentinels shared with Norway, rise in the north and west.

Until very recently Swedish stock was almost as undiluted as Kentucky's best thoroughbreds, with about 8 million pure Nordics against 500,000 Finns, Lapps, and others. In what seems a twinkling, however, its influx of refugees and assorted outlanders have now brought its foreign population to 5%. Lutheran Protestantism is far and away the dominant religion, but the 98% national participation is a loaded statistic; unless you declare yourself otherwise, you're automatically a member of the Church of Sweden. There's complete freedom of worship; education and military service are compulsory and universal.

Democracy and socialization have far outstripped America. This northern wonderland also happens to be one of the most "capitalistic" nations on the globe (above the per capita income in the U.S.)—while still being the most civic-conscious of major free-world countries. To support this, taxes are now so murderous that someone with a salary of $16,000 takes home only $7890 while the upper brackets pay out more than 85% to Uncle Svend. Some by-products of this State paternalism are startling or amusing to the stranger. Few jails in Sweden have iron bars. Smoking is relatively low on a per-capita basis, but legislation has gone through to virtually create a nonsmoking nation over the next decade or so. Labor is extremely strong—yet management relations are so enlightened that there have been only a handful of strikes since World War II. Any Swede under 20 who has a job but doesn't behave himself

is required to pay room and board at home, upon his parents' request. Except for expense, no country in Europe is better suited for tourists—as holidaymakers are beginning to discover more and more.

☑ **SIGHTSEEING** In the suburbs of Stockholm, dozens of resorts and maritime beachscapes afford the visitor fascinating glimpses of coastal Sweden. You may charter a fishing boat and crew to poke at your whimsy through Stockholm's archipelago of 25-thousand islands and skerries. Anglers must have fishing licenses before they are allowed to wet a line. Green shores, smiling beaches, pastures and groves, sunbaked isles, and foaming bays; a delight.

Should you proceed independently, go by commercial steamer and return by rail or bus. *Saltsjöbaden*, a short ride from the city, is the best known beach; take your bathing suit and plan on luncheon at the local Grand Hotel. If you are young, rugged, and want to get away from the crowds of this popular resort, get off the Saltsjöbaden train at the station nearest *Erstaviksbadet*, a wooded beach with fewer people and wonderful swimming. You used to have to undress behind a tree, a matter that was supremely unimportant to everybody but yourself. Now cabins have been provided for the modest.

Sandhamn, the largest yachting center, has perhaps the best bathing of all; the ride takes 3½ hours each way—a long haul but definitely worth it. *Vaxholm* is a pretty trip and excellent for a quiet lunch. Swimmers can take a dip at nearby *Eriksö*.

Away from Stockholm, there are dozens of organized expeditions that range far afield. The 7-day Lapland Tour mushes from June 19 to August 7. Also available is the 6-day junket to Copenhagen and Oslo from Stockholm's home plate; on this there's a special reduction for Eurailpass holders. Reso sponsors any number of treks from 2 to 21 days to fit almost any wanderer's whims or budget, including visions of Scandinavian coastal areas, Norwegian fjords and mountains, lake districts, the Isle of Gotland, Western Scandinavia, capital cities, and many other tempters. Your travel agent has details on all of these —and more.

If these don't appeal to you, a quick tour of *Östergötland* might. About 3 hours by train from Stockholm, on the main line to Copenhagen, it's Sweden in a capsule, with rolling fields, sweeping forests, lovely lakes, and miniature mountains. High point to most visitors here is the excursion on the Göta, or Kinda, canal—charming at first but quite dull after the novelty has worn off. You can also play golf, sail on the lakes, fish for salmon or char, go to horse races or county fairs, or do practically anything you like. This is rural living, but it is usually busy and always urbane.

Farther down in *Skåne* Sweden's southernmost province, the late Dag Hammarskjöld's farm near Löderup is open to visitors during summer months. The lovely white farmhouse, with its enclosed cobbled courtyard, reflects this great mediator's wide cultural interests and world travels. All of his personal possessions are here. It is a fascinating stop—one well worth a detour.

Sharing the same bucolic enticements, but much more familiar to Americans, is *Dalarna* province. This round requires at least 2 days, and preferably 4. Here, too, there's not much excitement, but you'll get a glimpse of a way of life different from anything else in Scandinavia. Go first to *Rättvik* (4 to 5 hours from Stockholm)—and then proceed, if you like, to the entrancing little village of *Tällberg*, beloved of so many of Sweden's overseas guests.

From Rättvik it is 3 hours by car or hotel bus to the strikingly different terrain around *Sälen*. Here are the high mountains and deep valleys of the West. *Sälens Högfjällshotellet*, the best mountain-resort hotel in the nation, is open to the public only in winter. Skiing conditions are nearly perfect. You'll find good food, magnificent scenery, bus excursions to Norway, and every convenience to which you are accustomed. Of the 110 rooms, 74 have private bath—a high percentage for rural Sweden. An alternative is Hotel Högfjället at *Storlien*, situated on an Alpine plateau near the Norwegian border. Its 246 rooms and 41 baths make it Scandinavia's largest resort hostelry; tiny accommodations; modern décor; unusually happy for children.

Want a full day's excursion to keep the tykes out of mischief? Drive east to *Lake Storsjön* and search for the Swedish brother of the Loch Ness Monster, which was sighted again recently by 4 workmen. King Oscar I long ago commissioned an official hunting party, and his ancient beast-snaring equipment can be seen in the Östersund City Museum. Accounts vary about this uncaught but oft-seen fellow. Some say he's black, others say he's brown. Some measure his length at 15 feet, some swear he's not an inch under 70 feet. But they ALL agree on one observation: He wears a *very* sinister smile.

Or how about a cruise? Steamers depart from Stockholm bound for the semi-autonomous *Åland Islands*, halfway to Finland. The 8-hour round trip costs under $10 and you can fill up on tax-free stores aboard, sights galore, and a pretty fair smörgåsbord on some of the ferries. Inquire locally for details.

The world-famous glass center of *Orrefors*, just off the main east-coast highway between Denmark and Stockholm (220 miles north of Helsingborg), is an especially interesting little detour for motorists. Here you may watch master glassblowers turn out exquisite products. Alternate choices might be at Kosta, Boda, or Strömbergshyttan in the same district.

Skokloster, which dominates a large lake about ¾ of the way toward Uppsala from Stockholm, is one of the most magnificent palaces in the hemisphere. It was built in the mid-seventeenth century for Field Marshal Carl Gustaf Wrangel—and the gorgeous interiors bear witness to the splendor of Sweden's Golden Age as a major power. If you're wheeling toward the University City, this one is more than worth the short turnoff to any rover who appreciates its special type of beauty and magnificence.

No tourist should miss *Visby*. This insular capital, the only walled town in northern Europe, is one of the most worthy sights in Scandinavia. You'll find Viking remains such as you have never seen before; occasionally you'll see traces of Minoan, Greek, and Roman cultures. The wall is about 2 miles in

circumference; there are 100 churches which stood before Shakespeare donned his first pair of long trousers. Now Visby is a vacation center. Broad beaches, good bicycling, good tennis, gorgeous scenery; impressive musical drama, *Petrus de Dacia,* presented during July and August in the medieval cathedral ruin of St. Nicholas. One night from Stockholm by boat, or about 50 minutes by SAS (5 flights daily from June through Aug.; more on the weekends).

☑ **TRANSPORTATION Taxis** Gone are the days when taxis were plentiful. Now they are too often excruciatingly difficult to obtain. The wisest method is to ask your concierge, restaurateur, or shopkeeper to telephone 15-00-00 for one—and plead for the help of your personal shepherd while this is being done. If it doesn't work, then you are forced to other means of transport such as buses, trains, or your own legs. This acute shortage is a disaster. Although the minimum rate is fairly low, the meter goes up like a missile. A trip across the city can cost you $6 or more. "Ledig" means "For Hire." If you can spot this on his car flag and wave with appropriate vigor, it's yours.

As in many other countries, scores of jockeys "don't happen to have change"— trusting you'll let them pocket the difference. Watch this racket.

For Stockholm sightseers: For about $8 you can buy a 3-day, unlimited-travel ticket valid on all buses and subways, including the lines to Drottningholm Castle and Lidingö Island.

Trains Superior. There's a continuous program to hitch up new "comfort" cars with double-deck domes and posh up-to-date amenities. First-class smoking compartments often come equipped with twin banquettes of 3 seats each, plus a table flanked by 2 sink-in adjustable armchairs—all in the same roomy, handsome, and practical salon area. Other compartments (always including Second class) are conventional but also relaxing and well designed. Many trains feature half-coach snack bars instead of full-fledged dining cars. They're immaculately clean; limited menus in 4 languages; soft drinks, wine, export beer, tea, and coffee are the only beverages; the food attracts the eye but is lackluster to the palate.

The Swedish Railways, known as "SJ" (Statens Järnvägar), operates 95% of the nation's railroads, 22% of its buses, and 5% of its highway freight, plus a network of travel offices. For the visitor who wants to see a lot and whose funds are limited, SJ and its Danish, Norwegian, and Finnish counterparts offer (1) train "circular tours" around Scandinavia (interrupt your journey wherever you wish, and save 10%-25%), (2) a sliding scale of prices which decrease as the distance increases (if you buy all your tickets at once, this arrangement will earn dollars for you), and (3) a 50% discount during summer—regardless of nationality—for anyone older than 65. Fares are low; sleepers are very cheap. A low-price card is available, valid for 1 year, which cuts the cost by 30% to 50% on all days of the week except Friday and Sunday. This is well worth the investment of $2.50 for First class or $1.50 for Second class.

☑ **FOOD** A black and white picture. When restaurant fare is good, it's superb—but when it's not good, it's often heavy, tasteless, larded with grease, and unimaginative. Top cooks use sensitive fingers and palates as delicately as angels; routine cooks use muscle-

bound thumbs and fists. We've never found a land where the contrast between fine eating places and greasy spoons is so apparent.

Until a few seasons ago, smörgåsbord was nearly extinct in its own homeland, mostly because restaurateurs found they could heap up bigger piles of kronor from straight dining. At that time, thanks to a crusade led by one of the nation's leading restaurateurs, these oh-so-heavenly, delightfully groaning banquet boards then began reappearing.

As far as we can tell, the finest manifestation of this feast is offered upon the "Miracle Table." This oval masterpiece eliminates all the fancy folded napkins, floral patterns, doodads, and gimmicks which clutter up working efficiency. Its 40 trays and bowls of varying sizes, all beautifully inset and rigidly controlled from freezing to simmering temperatures, permit the diner to peruse the *full* display at a glance and then to dive into his choices. It is topped by a crockery decanter built to dispense 6 varieties of snaps. This smörgåsbord goes full blast at the Operakällaren and the Stallmästaregarden restaurants (see following section), weekdays from noon to 3 P.M. and Sundays and holidays (if no change occurs by the time of your arrival) from noon to 8 P.M. Don't miss it! Elsewhere in the capital, this type of service can be found at the Grand Hotel (on the Veranda), at Ulriksdals Wärdshus, at Solliden in **Skansen** (11:30 A.M. to 3 P.M.), at the Grand Hotel in **Saltsjöbaden**, and at several scattered oases—and *remember, it's always lunch, never dinner.* Some city restaurants offer its items individually on small plates, tailored to the customer's girth and pocketbook; these are known as *assietter.*

Cardinal rule with smörgåsbord: Eat all fish on the 1st plate, meats on the 2nd, and hot appetizers on the 3rd (optional). Never mix fish and meat.

As a curiosity, try the delicious tiny crayfish called *kräftor*—a freshwater toyland lobster. It's expensive but you'd be wrong to miss this important ceremonial dish; the season is most of August. Odd facts department: Since a disease recently killed many of them, a fresh crop is being bred from those of our own Lake Tahoe.

Then there are—or should we say were—copious quantities of *strömming*, the dwarf Baltic herring. For centuries the Swedish cook boiled, fried, pickled, pounded, and minced it, made croquettes, fishburgers, and canapes of it, serving it in every conceivable fashion except raw, at which the good housewives drew the line. Now there has been such calamitous overfishing by a number of nations that ultra-tight restrictions have been imposed by the European Economic Community Commission. Hence, you will find a paucity of this former staple during your current visit. Fortunately, however, there is still plenty of smoked eel, which we think is extra-delicious when served with c-r-e-a-m-y scrambled eggs. But the very best, in our opinions, is the juicy, delicately sweet salmon trout.

Sweden has no special meal hours. Most people lunch from 12 to 2 P.M., dine from 5 P.M. to 8 P.M. (afternoon tea is not popular), and later "sup" on snacks—but restaurants are open continuously during the day and evening.

☑ **DRINKS** Package sales today are unrestricted. The Swede is the world's 2nd-thirstiest tippler, lining up at the counter right behind the Yugoslav. You may buy unlimited amounts of whatever you choose at any State liquor store from 9 A.M. to 6 P.M. on weekdays and from 9 A.M. to 1 P.M. on Saturdays. Restaurants keep the corks out of the bottles from noon until closing time.

Scotch, Canadian Club, English gin, French cognac—you'll find a variety at the official dispensaries. An 18% surtax has raised the cost of a bottle of routine Scotch to $25.

Aquavit, the national drink, is also called "snaps," "brännvin," and "aqua vitae." But no matter by what name it slides down the gullet, there's enough heat in 1 glass to turn all the radiators in the Empire State Building cherry red. The base is potatoes, grain, or an extraction of _wood_ alcohol! It is flavored with berries, seeds, leaves, herbs, flowers, and spices. Drink it well chilled with smörgåsbord (not with the entrée or by itself), gulp the potion in 2 or 3 swallows (don't sip!), and chase it quickly with 5 or 10 gallons of beer. The best brand, to our taste, is Åhus, which is closest to that King of Scandinavian Good Cheer, Denmark's Aalborg. Swedes prefer others, such as Överste (slightly spiced, slightly sweet) or O.P. (aroma of cumin).

Swedish Punch is a happy beverage. The ingredients are Java arrack and a special rum; float Remy Martin or another good French cognac on top of the glass; you'll find a drink fit for the gods. Expensive but worth it.

Beer comes in the following grades (based on their alcohol content): _Starköl_ (4.5%), _Folköl_ (2.8%), and _Lättöl_ (1.8%). One Swedish wag quips that the first leaves you in no doubt as to whether you are drinking beer and the last in some doubt as to whether you're drinking water. Pripps and Skål are the most popular brands for middle-of-the-road drinkers (not drivers). Now that the government controls the nation's largest brewery, it is curbing the outlets of the stronger types and limiting many of their former ones to only the weakest variety.

★ **TIP**   Beware of inferior Swedish gins or aquavits; some of the less reputable brands are distilled from cellulose. It's always wise to insist on Gordon's for your martinis, because 2 or 3 of these innocent little wood-alcohol cocktails—believe me!—will jar you into a state which only a qualified physician or mortician can distinguish from rigor mortis.

☑ **SKOL** (or **SKÅL**)   See under "Denmark." The same applies here, only more so; the formalities are far more rigidly observed.

☑ **TIPPING**   Due to socialization and high salaries, this custom has almost disappeared here. Since most restaurants automatically add 13% to the bills, leave small change on the table only if you desire to do so. In hotels, a 15% service charge appears when it has not already been included in the room rate (virtually all the prestige houses now bury it in your bill). Give hatcheck girls 2 kronor and taxi drivers 10% of the fare. The hall porter in the hotel gets a separate bite on top of your automatic service charge; it's not customary locally to tip him when you check out unless he has given special service to you. Railway porters (identified by _Stadsbud_ on their caps) in Stockholm's Central Station charge about $1 to $2 to tote 1 or 2 bags between the train and the taxi stand; each additional piece is around 30¢.

☑ **LOCAL RACKETS**   None that we could ever find of more than microscopic importance which were tourist-oriented. You'll leave with strong admiration for Swedish ethics. With amazingly few exceptions, Swedes are an honest, reliable, decent people.

☑ **INFORMATION CENTERS** Five separate organizations fly the banners of welcome for foreign visitors, and each tackles its special phase with earnestness, intelligence, and efficiency.

The **Stockholm Tourist Association**, directed by Fritz Alm, operates inquiry bureaus at Hamngatan 27, the headquarters in Sweden House, at Värtahamnen (landing stage of Finland steamers), and at the Stockholm City Hall, plus a mobile unit Tourist Center. Enough? Its hotel booking office functions year-round in the Central Railway Station. Finally, it sponsors the intriguing "Sweden at Home" program for the benefit of overseas guests: You are invited for an evening with a local family which shares your professional interests, hobbies, or other mutual bonds—in their house, without fees or considerations of any kind. Merely fill out the form at the Tourist Center with your personal particulars, and they'll cross-check their files for exactly the right host. It's the kind of hospitality —and heartwarming contact—which money can't buy.

The **Swedish Tourist Board**, also in Sweden House, is the master organization and moving force in the promotion of international understanding through travel. It maintains 10 branch offices in foreign capitals, publishes many useful pamphlets and brochures, and coordinates all official activities in the field. If you're a journalist, radio commentator, television producer, author, photographer, movie cameraman—anything to do with any aspect of the press—go to this enterprise for sound advice and invaluable local assistance.

The **Swedish Institute for Cultural Relations** handles foreign-study groups (labor, management, religious, farmers, teachers, social workers, professional associations, and similar units); **Reso** (Travel and Holiday Organization of the Popular Movements) not only operates 1 First-class and 4 budget-price hotels in the capital, major oases in Malmö, Jönköping, and Göteborg, and about a dozen bottom-price resort centers in the hinterland, but it also makes available a whopping number of private homes in Stockholm for workers, students, and low-income vacationers, Swedes or foreigners.

In America, **Scandinavian National Tourist Offices** are at 75 Rockefeller Plaza, N.Y. 10019 and at 3600 Wilshire Blvd., Los Angeles, Calif. 90010. They will plan your trip, answer your questions, do everything but make your actual reservations. Here are the places, too, for further information on Reso, study-group facilities, and other special data.

Make certain you have advance reservations before venturing to Sweden.

The **Stockholm Convention Bureau** (Jakobstorg 3), sponsored by trade and industry in the capital, is one of the most live-wire organizations of its type that we have ever encountered. Handsome, charming, extraordinarily alert Managing Director Donald M. Hellstedt eagerly and with utmost efficiency projects his special talents in endeavoring to make every assembly an outstanding success. In addition to other facilities, the dramatically and efficiently architected **Folkets Hus Congress Hall**, which boasts a plethora of the very latest equipment, can be subdivided into 3 independent units. A wide selection of additional meeting rooms is available for smaller sessions.

The Stockholm Tourist Association sponsors "Miss Tourist," a telephone voice in the capital to give you fresh-off-the-griddle facts on local events of interest. Just dial 22-18-40.

The daily newspapers also print a section summarizing the international scoop in English. It's darned good, too.

Youth Hostels are in operation between June 1 and September 1; of these 185 shelters ranging from farmhouses to historic buildings, only 21 are open year round (exception: Dec. 23 to Jan. 2). Rates are about $3.50 to $5 per night for members during the summer, with a 40¢ supplement from September to June; meals are $2 to $4 Little English is spoken in this circuit. Hitchhiking is sternly discouraged in Sweden. For information write to **Svenska Turistföreningen** (Swedish Touring Club), Fack, S-10380, Stockholm 7.

CITIES

STOCKHOLM is a miniature New York, Washington, Chicago, Los Angeles, and Podunk rolled into one and transported to Scandinavia. Somewhat larger than Washington, it has 800-thousand people, 3 railroad stations, a subway system that is practically a museum of contemporary artistic endeavor, an excellent hotel picture, plenty of restaurants and shops, wonderful relics; and the Rotary Club meets on Tuesdays! The 5-block, glass-and-concrete, "New Manhattan" business complex, with small skyscrapers, terraced gardens, and garages (6 floors underground), has risen on the site of outmoded houses in the Klara District. The paralyzing shortage of adequate housing has been given A-1 priority by the government. Suburban apartments at last are becoming available—and at *what* a cost! This 700-year-old city of islands is spick-and-span, modern, efficient and beautiful to the eye.

Sightseeing Drottningholm Palace is particularly impressive. This used to be the favorite royal winter residence of the king, the most beautiful of royal homes, with Gobelin tapestries scattered around like bathroom rugs. The adjoining **Court Theater**, untouched since 1766, is still very much in use; several times per week beginning in May performances "De l'Époque" are featured. See it if you can.

In **Östermalmstorg**, the public market in the center of the city, you'll find vegetables, flowers, practically every kind of fish—the works.

Djurgården (Deer Park) shouldn't be missed. It's the island home of world-famous Skansen: A magnificent open-air museum with authentic farms, a zoo, a Lapp camp, Nordic antiquities, and great natural beauty. Speaking of pulchritude, a young lovely named "Miss Skansen" will meet you at the information booth (inside at Bollnästorget) in regional costume any day in June, July, or August at 11 A.M., 1 P.M., 3 P.M., or 5 P.M. to give you up-to-the-minute developments on everything from the concerts to the folk dancing to the performances by international artists to the teen-age dance fests to the feeding time of the 4-footed critters. Free, too! It is 7 minutes from the city by Bus No. 47 or No. 67. If possible (and if the weather is benign), plan to have lunch at either Stallmästaregården (a short drive), Djurgårdsbrunns Wärdshus (behind Skansen), Solliden (in the Park) or Ulriksdals Wärdshus; see "Restaurants" for details.

Social Tours, in-depth study programs in the arts, sciences, business, and social welfare, offer the foreign visitor a rare opportunity to see how the Scandinavian people live. Highlights might include a visit to a family in a suburban housing project, a lakeside children's camp, or an ultramodern home for the aged. Operated between June 25 and August 31; programs range from several days to several weeks; stimulating, educational, and different. Just telephone Stockholm 247425, and the Tourist Sightseeing Organization will set up a swing through 2 apartments (one for retired people), a church, and 2 suburban shopping centers.

Packaged **motorcoach excursions** include the 2 "Grand City" Tours, the nonstop City Tour, an Evening loop, and a day-long trip to Uppsala and Sigtuna. Motorboat outings include the Grand Scenic Tour Under the Bridges, the Royal Canal Tour, the Archipelago Tour, and a waterborne version of the Evening Tour. Prices vary from $4 to $10 for the capital sightseeing to around $30 for the all-day Uppsala-Sigtuna circuit. Most operate in summer only. Tickets may be purchased at any travel bureau or leading hotel.

A marvel that is a *must* for every visitor is the seventeenth-century warship *Wasa,* which was salvaged intact from the 110-foot depths of Stockholm Harbor in '61. Divers with powerful water-jets pumped 6 tunnels beneath her hull, through which several thousand feet of 6-inch cable were threaded to hoist her out of the mud and face up to the surface—one of the most complicated undersea salvage projects ever undertaken. She occupies a site of honor in a provisional building near the Nordic Museum and Skansen. She's in a remarkable state of preservation for her 3½ centuries—mostly due to the cold, cold waters in which she lay.

The **Stockholm Student Reception Service** welcomes foreign undergraduates with dances, movies, lectures, sightseeing tours, picnics, and other events during 2 months of the summer vacations. It also puts out a revised pamphlet listing activities available to foreign students.

New, large, beautiful **Silja** and **Viking Lines'** ships ply between Stockholm and Helsinki or Germany. There are also overnight runs to Turku (Finland). These voyages are comfortable and reasonably priced, with a myriad of amenities available. Their reduced fares are especially appealing to people over 65, who reap substantial benefits during weekdays.

STOCKHOLM HOTELS Quick Reference Table

Price categories by national (not U.S.) standards.

EXPENSIVE:
Diplomat Strandvägen 7-C. Tel. 635800; Telex 17119; 120 rooms. P. 908
Grand S. Blasiehomshamnen 8. Tel. 221020; Telex 19500; 355 rooms. P. 907
Sheraton Tegelbacken 6. Tel. 142600; Telex 17750; 476 rooms. P. 908
Strand Nybrokajen 9. Tel. 222820; Telex 10504; 100 rooms. P. 908

UPPER MODERATE:

Anglais Humlegardsgatan 23. Tel. 249900; Telex 19475; 206 rooms. P. 908

Carlton A. Kungsgatan 57. Tel. 223400; Telex 13400; 150 rooms. P. 909

Continental Vasagatan. Tel. 244020; Telex 10100; 250 rooms. P. 909

Esplanade Strandv. 7. Tel. 630740; 32 rooms. P. 911

Park Karlavägen 43. Tel. 229620; Telex 10666; 240 rooms. P. 909

Reisen Skeppsbron 12. Tel. 223260; Telex 17494; 126 rooms. P. 909

MODERATE:

Alexandra M. Ladulåsgatan 42. Tel. 840320; 80 rooms. P. 910

Amaranten Kungsholmsgatan 31. Tel. 541060; Telex 17498; 363 rooms. P. 909

Birger Jarl Tulegatan 8. Tel. 151020; Telex 11843; 259 rooms. P. 910

Kom Döbelnsgaten 17. Tel. 235630. P. 911

Malmen Götgatan 49. Tel. 226080; Telex 19489; 254 rooms. P. 910

Mornington Nybrogatan 53. Tel. 631240; Telex 10145; 115 rooms. P. 910

Palace S:t Erikgatan 115. Tel. 241220; Telex 19877; 225 rooms. P. 910

Wellington Storg. 6. Tel. 670910; Telex 17963; 52 rooms. P. 910

LOWER MODERATE:

Domus Körsbärsvägen 1. Tel. 150510; 200 rooms. P. 911

Flamingo Hotellgatan 11. Tel. 830800. P. 911

Frälsningsarméns Drottninggatan 66. Tel. 222240; 147 rooms. P. 911

Jerum Studentbacken 21. Tel. 635380; 136 rooms. P. 911

Sjofarstshotellet Katarinavägen 26. Tel. 226960; Telex 19020; 184 rooms. P. 911

ENVIRONS:

Esso Ekgardsvägen, Kungens Kurva. Tel. 7100460; Telex 11326; 153 rooms. P. 911

Grand Salsjobaden. Tel. 7170020; Telex 10210; 100 rooms. P. 911

Gyllene Rattan Vantorsvagen 285. Tel. 462660; 109 rooms. P. 911

Kristineberg Soderbgs v. 10. Tel. 130300; 146 rooms. P. 911

Star 105 rooms. P. 911

AIRPORT:

Bromma Bromma 1. Tel. 252920; Telex 13125; 139 rooms. P. 910

Flyghotellet Bromma. Tel. 262620. P. 911

Hotels The Swedes (and Finns) promote the bonanzarific **Hotel Cheque** plan that can save up to 30% of your holiday expenses. It works this way: Your cheque is valid at any time during June, July, and August. There are no restrictions on your itinerary or your time spent in any of the participating hostelries; bed-and-breakfast is included; a number of independent restaurants have also climbed aboard this budgeteer's bandwagon. For its pamphlet and other details, consult your travel agent or the Swedish National Tourist Office. Hotel Cheque, as well as the money-saving Air Cheque plan, must be bought outside Sweden.

The **Grand** is the Stately Noble Dowager among the capital's hotels. Beautiful location on the water; enviable physical plant, most of which has been redecorated and refurnished; enlarged lobby area with drugstore, gift shop, and SAS ticket office; bedchambers modernized and expensively comfortized. Its famous front verandas, one of which is now serving the city's best reasonably

priced smörgasbord at lunchtime, has been glassed in and air-conditioned for all-year operation. Restaurant and cozy British-style bar felicitous; Spegelsalen ("Hall of Mirrors"); dancing every weeknight except Monday; all rooms and baths with radio and TV and most with refrigerators; 3 large and 6 junior suites of which our favorites are #338/339 and #340; sauna installed. Our verdict? An aristocrat throughout.

The Diplomat, housed within a classic downtown structure, presents elegant and charming credentials. The prevailing decorative schemes range from Swedish-birch freshets to English open warmth. Since it completed its expansion into the former Iranian Embassy, this addition gives it 10 new rooms, 2 of its plushest suites, and a private sauna. Although this totally converted building has no restaurant, it offers an inviting green-tinted bar with snacks and the only tearoom among the local hostelries. During our most recent visit to this metropolis, we pampered ourselves by paying a relatively small additional sum for one of its larger corner rooms over the inlet—and it was more than worth the extra outlay. The staff is warm and the aura is delightfully friendly. We are extremely fond of this distinguished, comfortable, and homey house. Highly recommended.

The Sheraton is a 9-story, 13-million-dollar midcity slicker. Banquet and convention facilities for 425 big dealers; chilly lobby in contrast to its welcoming accommodations; telex; on-the-spot banking; expense-accounter room tariffs; high quota of attaché cases among its luggage check-ins. Its stunning 220-seat Royal Blue Restaurant has a line of brass-rail-topped, semicircular banquettes which hold up to 8; it also features big, low-hanging, movable lamps, and a Captain's Table limited to diners who come alone. All walls and fabrics in an especially lovely shade of blue brilliantly blending with its orange-and-brown carpeting; sauna; top-floored balconied units its premier spreads; 6 lakefront suites; many twins with 2 double beds surrounded by teal, rouge, and other rich colors in modern themes; TV plus superb music console; small but well-equipped baths. In sum, here is a fine example of the American mood.

The youthful **Anglais** overlooks Humlegården Park. Façade dotted by flaming gas lamps; Swedish-modern lobby in ceramic tones; candle-brightened Grill Room with forest-green furnishings; attractive cocktail bar with red leather chairs and sofas in today's ambiance; enclosed court accessible to first-level guests. Every unit with bath, an alarm-clock/radio, an individual thermostat control, a centigrade thermometer for readings of the outside weather, foldaway luggage racks, and 3-way vanity mirrors; the poorest 41 units in the basement. Competent Chris Folker is its helmsman; Reception Chief Tajani and Chief Concierge Eriksson man their desks smilingly and efficiently. In physical appearance, handsome indeed—but the client attention as nearly everywhere in this highly welfared state is occasionally slack. A good bet.

Ever since the **Strand** was constructed for the Olympic Games in 1912 it has had a highly checkered history. Its recently completed beauty treatment has made it inviting to behold and as fresh as a breeze from the Norse. Soothing lobby in white marble; renowned Maritim Seafood Restaurant especially noted for its Salmon Trout au Bleu and Salmon-on-Skewer from its Rôtisserie; Roof Terrace Restaurant with one of Stockholm's finest views plus twilight dancing; Hip-Pocket Bar with versatile drinks and a variety of high-type light bites.

Most of the 110 quarters, the majority of them touched up, come with 2 types of showers plus a full bath. It is our sincere hope that the management is having increasing success in lighting rockets under its sloppy and couldn't-care-less minions.

The **Park** greets its guests with a lemon-colored lobby which adjoins a salty maritime restaurant and a merry-time bar. Excellent sauna; kitchenettes available; General Manager Ernst Wallerström has upgraded staff attitudes commendably. If you can snag a sleeper overlooking the lovely Humlegården you will be rewarded with a majestic sylvan tableau smack in the center of the city.

The 11-story **Continental** is a Reso chain-link forged close by the main station in midtown. Air-conditioned; handsome lobby; large-but-cozy, low-ceilinged; wraparound Café on the mezzanine overlooking the entrance hall; quick-service cafeteria in the cellar by the subway exit; Steak House; gorgeous split-level, split-personality dining room in blacks, golds, and reds, ingeniously highlighted by striking use of Orrefors glass insets on pillars and lamps for decorative effect; bank, travel agency, beauty parlor, underground station, and garage. Seven types of rooms, all with wood floor-to-ceiling panels backing the beds, and offbeat employment of textiles and colors; sliding partitions to separate sitting and sleeping areas in the demi-suites; all baths supermicroscopic; baggage stowage adequate for business travelers but far too small for overseas voyagers. Commercial and solid.

The **Amaranten** is one of the largest hostelries in Sweden—and one of the best investments for your travel dollar that we've found in this city if you can weather its tempest of convention and other groups. Noncentral but not inconvenient location (subway station in the block); spacious lobby; adjoining Brasserie with room dividers, hanging lamps, and excellent cafeteria-type food service; sumptuous restaurant with both tables and booths. Spacious 200-seat nightclub for dining, dancing, and live shows decorated in burnt orange, dark brown, and brass trimmings, and serving international-type cuisine; Jolly Bob Grill for steaks; Traveller's Piano Bar with English music hall entertainment and photo blowups depicting curvaceous beauties from all over the world; battery of saunas with plunge pool. All of the studio-type accommodations have now been converted into conventional bedchambers. For a hostelry which is classified as Superior First Class, we continue to be impressed by facilities and attention which equal if not better many of the deluxe entries in this city. General Manager Jörgen Brandt is a fireball who continues to interject electric vigor here. Very highly recommended for its category.

A sister candidate, the **Reisen** is a pert, fresh-faced charmer refitted from the linkage of 5 homes and 3 warehouses which date back to A.D. 1639. From topmast to keel, the milieu here is nautical. The lobby exudes warmth. Both the Piano-Bar (theme song "As Time Goes By") and the 13-table Clipper Club Restaurant, separated from each other by an artistic brass grill, have been redecorated in matching décor with paneling, comfortable leather armchairs, indirect illumination, and softly piped music. As a grand illustration of its specialty of 1-dish meals, its steaks are flown in directly from America. Guestrooms incorporating the rugged brick walls of the original structures; cellar with 2 saunas; swimming pool; vaulted clubroom. Director Olle Asp is doing a splendid job of milling maximum value into your travel dollars.

The **Carlton**, heavily patronized by traveling businessmen, is radically im-

proved. At least 90% of its rooms have been entirely rebuilt and refurnished under the discerning eye of Manager Jakob Jonker. The balance, plus the corridors, have been spruced up in varying degrees. A total of 115 offer private bath, and the remainder have private toilet but no tub or shower. Three suites with TV and 2 baths each; entrance and lobby fully modernized; ground-floor lounge enlarged and redecorated; cocktail bar. There's a beauty parlor at your disposal and the British-overtoned Carlton Inn for quick meals. Accommodations on the cramped side, all offering simple but practical Swedish furniture, radio, and TV-for-hire. Now less expensive than the Strand, but still not as cheery, in our opinion. Much better than ever before, however.

The **Birger Jarl** was inaugurated in '74. Lounge somewhat cluttered by vitrines and TV; self-service cafeteria with homey fare from 7 A.M. to 3 P.M. converts into Coffee Shop from 3 P.M. to 9:30 P.M.; small gymnasium, sauna, and plunge pool; compact but reasonably comfortable studio-type rooms, all with bath, shower, and alarm-radio unit; ice machines and 2 shoeshiners on each floor; 200-car garage with elevator to ground floor. Since this house is owned by a Baptist organization, beer is its only alcoholic beverage. Lars Fellke is the Director. Well maintained on a no-nonsense basis.

The **Wellington** and the **Mornington** are sister houses. Interestingly, a night porter and a bellboy are the only men on their payrolls; the rest of their staffs are women, most of them under thirty. Each offers simple but colorful amenities, dining rooms which are continously open between 11:30 A.M. and midnight, and saunas. Some of their chambers are conventional in design while others are studio-style. The 7-floor Wellington has 6 suites and 46 units, some of them with a fine view. The Mornington occupies the 3rd, 4th, 5th, and 6th floors of a structure otherwise occupied by members of the Swedish Dentists Association. Here you will find 115 rooms with 95 baths and 20 showers. Although neither is in the deluxe category, they are proud of the personal touches which are reminiscent of a small-town rather than of a metropolitan hostelry.

In number of beds but not of rooms, the refashioned **Palace** is one of the larger hotels in the city. It occupies 4 floors of a fringe-area commercial building (the premises of a local automobile dealer); with such ample garage space, its main occupancy target is the motorist. There are 220 rooms with bath or shower, plus color TV; these include the so-called Motel Rooms, which are triumphs of architectural planning for children, elves, or midgets. Restaurant, self-service cafeteria, cocktail bar, Finnish bath, beauty parlor, barbershop, garage, and other facilities; clean, utilitarian décor.

The **Malmen**, owned by the municipality and operated by Reso, is a streamlined, starkly modern factory of mass-production tourism. Dining salon refurnished; Club Malmen for night owls; 265 minuscule rooms; service for minimum essentials only. This time we were disappointed to see how much it had run down since our prior visit. The **Stockholm** occupies the 6th and 7th floors of an office building; lovely view; some bedchambers agreeable and some shoebox-size; breakfast room but no restaurant. Manager Wally Frisack is pleasant, competent, and hard-toiling. More a sleeping convenience than a full-blown hotel. The **Alexandra** (75 singles and 25 twins) and the **Bromma** (near the domestic airport with 143 chambers) are both truly basic. Close to

the latter, the **Flyghotellet** is reasonable enough as a medium-priced landing field. The **Esplanade**, in a courtyard next to the Diplomat, advertises itself as "an informal hotel for diplomats, businessmen, and tourists." After viewing this two-story plant of 32 bedrooms, 3 baths, 26 showers and no restaurant, we found only two accommodations which were amply big and to our taste. Yet because of its official rating, its tariffs come close to those of its plush and handsomely equipped neighbor. Nix. The centrally sited, breakfast-only **Kom** is open all year. Fully air-conditioned; sauna; conference rooms; parking facilities; somewhat cramped quarters including mini-pantry with refrigerators and all with shower but no tub. Routine. The **Flamingo** might be termed a supermarket hostelry. No porters, so you load your luggage into a grocery cart provided in the lobby and wheel your cargo to your bin; no reception minions even to show you to your address. Restaurant, grill, bar, and cocktail lounge similarly impersonal; clean, ultramodern, and oh-so-sterile. The **Sjöfartshotellet** waddles in with a quick-frozen lobby, a nautical dining room, and monotonous corridors. Within the 6 stories are 183 modern, utilitarian rooms with glass-front masks; efficient for group bookings, but not recommended to independent voyagers. The **Jerum** (June-Aug.) and the **Domus** (open all year), are students' dormitories in winter and equally sterile, institutional-style hotels in summer. The **Frälsningsarmén's (Salvation Army's) Hotell** is open to both genders; very cheap, and better than most YMCA's or YWCA's in the States. Dry, of course. The 146-room **Kristineberg**, about 10 minutes out in a residential district, lacks zip, zest, or zing, in our opinion. Too dowdy for most merrymakers. **Esso** has dropped the checkered flag on a 153-cylinder competitor at **Ulriksdal**, north of the city, and yet a newer one on the route to Arlanda Airport. Both are located inconveniently in very unattractive surroundings. The **Star** was born out of the former Holiday Inn; its 105 units are quite good for the outlay. Finally, there's the **OK Motor Hotel** at Årsta south of the center and **Gyllene Ratten Motell**, 4 miles south, as well as a covey of new entries farther out.

Dedicated budgeteers? Since we're too bottlenecked here for additional entries in Stockholm, please consult this year's vastly updated edition of our annually revised paperback, *Fielding's Low-Cost Europe,* which lists more bargain places to stay and money-saving tips for serious economizers.

Saltsjöbaden, the renowned beach resort now only 15 minutes from the capital via the expressway, is proud of its venerable **Grand**. Administration by the same Stockholm Grand Masters who also own the Strand and Carlton; waterfront situation; now redone almost from the ground up in excellent taste; cookery reportedly improving; often frequented by Golden Age clients. There are 2 bars, a TV room, table tennis, so-called casino roulette, a sauna, and nearby facilities for swimming, yachting, tennis, golf, and water-skiing, plus winter sports. A swimming pool and medical bath facilities should be operating by the time of your arrival; plans probably have been realized too for the addition of another 100 bedchambers. Under the strong driving force of Arthur Wahlstedt, Executive Supervisor of the whole group, it is beginning to become a contender as the star of the Marcus Wallenberg chain.

Restaurants   The best values can often be found in your own hotel. The **Grand**'s elegant Winter Garden is unique during the cold months. It has candlelight dinners from 6 P.M. to 10 P.M. every Wednesday. With its 6-string ensemble melodizing for diners or dancers, its rich, soft, Andalusian atmosphere, its lovely pods of greenery growing in strategic corners, and its suave, well-dressed clientele, here is a truly civilized and sophisticated isle of calm. We love it. The excellent but less opulent Red Room here operates every night except Sundays. For information on what we find the greatest money-saving lunchtime smörgåsbord in the capital, further along you will find a review of the spread on its Bar-Terrace veranda. While the cuisine at the Sheraton's **Royal Blue Restaurant** does not offer such high-level gastronomy, it is worthy and its ambiance is absolutely stunning. The Maritim Seafood Restaurant and the Roof Terrace Restaurant at the **Strand** have long been famous for what they purvey; the atmosphere is especially winning. The 13-table Clipper Club at the **Reisen**, noted for its 1-dish meals including American steaks, is a honey. The **Amaranten** offers a galaxy of facilities for the Inner Man and Woman, including a 200-seat nightclub for dining, dancing, and live shows. The fare at all of the capital's other hostelries, in our opinion, is cut-and-dried.

For dining without dancing, the city's most celebrated and distinguished institution is **Restaurant Riche**. Enclosed sidewalk dining terrace with big windows and flower boxes; eighteenth-century French-influenced décor, plush and opulent; superelegant Riche Bar at entrance, where gold-leaf frescoes go mad; service notably fast and deft. Our number one candidate within the city. Its intimate Theatre Grill, with a separate entrance, has been refashioned with apple-red upholstery, glass-and-gold partitions in a window-box effect, and with synthetic marble pillars and matching tables. Our meal was served much more professionally on our latest curtain raiser, but $112 for a very light 4-person dinner with 2 bottles of routine German wine strikes us as simply too much—even as good as it was.

Another *must* for the affluent food (and interior-decoration) lover is **Stallmästaregården** ("Royal Stablemaster's House"), 15 minutes by taxi from the center. Enchanting patio garden, made glad by cool pools, tiny waterfalls, and flowers; dining pavilion on lake (view blocked by the SAS terminal); previously described (see "Food") 40-dish smörgåsbord at lunch only on weekdays but up to 8 P.M. on Sunday (again, if still open on the Sabbath; presentation not as imposing as that in the Operakällaren; excellent flame-lit Grill for conventional dining); lovely atmosphere and urbane fare. Open all year, but a sunny day in summer is happiest. A gustatory and aesthetic *must*.

The landmark **Operakällaren** is part of the Royal Opera House. An *opus magnum* it is—and seldom have we viewed such an impressive and awesomely efficient complex. *Fin de siècle* décor; Grill, American bars, sidewalk café; tiny Snack Bar adjoining the traditional Opera Bar; glass-enclosed, 400-seat banquet hall; from May 1 to August 1, the most magnificent smörgåbord table in the land (see "Food"); beautiful firelight effect from gas flares surrounding the 2nd floor; fantastic wine cellars. The *pièce de résistance* is an ultraplush oasis facing the sea, complete with rainproof terrace for the warmer months. The tariffs, are also 21-carat. Swiss Chef Werner Vögeli's hands are famed for their delicate touch. Technically and aesthetically, this one is a marvel.

Djurgårdsbrunns Wärdshus, behind Skansen in the famous Deer Park (15 minutes from the center), continues to show splendid improvements. This converted 18th-century, Gustavian-style mansion, over verdant greenery and a lovely canal, has been refreshened. It has a graceful, soft-pastel, spacious-but-intimate dining room with comfortable round tables elegantly set off by fine napery, needlepoint chairs, candles, and flowers. Toward the declivity there is a lovely veranda with perhaps 15 units, glassed in when it is cold and open when it is warm. Opposite is a charming bar which is equally fetching. Its cuisine is superb. In summer a self-service open-air cafeteria operates at lunchtime and is so popular that it attracts up to 1000 persons per day. Beautiful and distinguished.

In the Old Town there are also 2 winners. **Källaren Aurora** (Munkbron 11), sited beneath the vaulted ceilings of a 300-year-old cellar, interweaves historical and culinary traditions. Italianate entrance; collection of hideaways including Gustafva's Salmon Cellar, The Cadet Corner, The Little Society, and other intimate nooks; fowl suspended from ceiling rods; charcoal rôtisserie grills; the Table of Plenty with a bountiful display; wine from Patron Herman's *cave*; somewhat dull bar. Normally it is jammed with the Younger Executive Set and their chic lovelies. Costly but agreeable.

The second is **Latona** (Västerlånggatan 79) with a like but somewhat simpler ambiance. The 4 floors of this 17th-century assemblage of houses, including a subbasement, are so crinkum-crankum in architecture that we wonder how its food is served so efficiently. Several small rooms; brick-lined walls; slate stairs; birch tables, banquettes, chairs and benches; effective appurtenances; large menus in Swedish and English with American-style explanations and puff-ups of the dishes. Manager Gunnar Enström offers good Swedish and French food for the prices. Very pleasant.

Another pair that are gaining appropriate attention are the expensive, suave and elegant **Coq Roti** (corner of Sturegatan and Östermalmsgatan) and the amusing **Hedvig** (Storgatan 6), near the Hedvig Eleonora Church. The former was formed by Maestro Hedman. It's in the dining aristocracy of this noble city. The latter, also international in flavor but less costly, draws its hostesses from Stockholm's finer families—certainly an attraction in this male's eyes. Both are recommendable in their respective respects.

Except for furnishings, colors, subterranean site and other features, the **Fem Små Hus** ("Five Small Houses") is strongly reminiscent of the Aurora and Latona. Our meal was satisfactory, but we were overcharged $3 on our bill. The bar, quite naturally, is utilized to encourage drinking while the guests are waiting to be seated; during this lag, however, we saw numerous tables which were too obviously ready inside. We wonder, therefore, if this isn't a ploy— if so, a clumsy one—to extract a few extra kronor from its innocent trade. Extremely engaging atmosphere but the attitude toward the client just might border on being naughty.

Berns, in the heart of the capital, is one of Europe's most vast and imposing feederies; 1200 customers can be served simultaneously. After entering through the Red Room (designed by illustrious Yngve Gamlin), decorated with memorabilia of Swedish Literary Immortal August Strindberg, you're given the choice of the Roulette Room for penny-ante gaming (once the Chinese

Restaurant, which has now moved to Kornhamnstorg in the Old Town) or the main dining room (music, balconies, high ceilings, barn-size). Always booked tight for major shows, so please reserve well in advance for opening nights or when headliners are in town. Usually closed June through August. The atmosphere is surprisingly quiet, the cookery is surprisingly appetizing, and the tariffs are surprisingly moderate for what it offers.

Östergök (Kommedörsgatan 46) comes up with a fine net of fish. Side by side are two completely separated restaurants. The piscatorial segment on a street corner is the quintessence of simplicity, with unadorned marble tables and utilitarian furnishings. Directly adjoining is his cozy, tavern-y establishment for grills and other meats. The price levels in this duet are virtually identical. The steakhouse is closed in July. Be certain to reserve in advance.

Concerning the **Sturehof** (center of town), which for more than 80 years had an exalted reputation for its finny preparations, on our latest try we felt that it was in a downward slide. An English Pub has been added which closes at midnight. Still very popular, but to us not what it used to be.

Recently, an urbane and cosmopolitan Swedish friend implored us to try **La Brochette** (Storgatan 27), informing us that it had become the number one star in the capital's restaurant firmament. Within its colorful long room banked by large windows we found a profusion of cheerful but calculated pretensions and gimmicks. Among the items we consumed were watery Quiche Lorraine, almost inedible oysters which apparently had been shipped in rocksalt and ice, inexcusably limp and soggy Sole Belle Meunière, prerefrigerated, badly traveled Tavel Rosé—enough. Another type of pain came with our bill for 3 persons—an "inexpensive" $66.40. At the aforementioned Östergök we enjoyed such higher quality at so much lower prices that we regard this as a jazzed-up orange juice stand compared to a Tour d'Argent. To us, here is an overpriced culinary dramatic performance without requisite accompanying back-up substance which under no circumstances do we recommend.

Le Gourmet is becoming more attractive by the moment. Mirror Room with rich woods and smoked and etched glass; main quadrant recently given the warm-up treatment; superb gourmet menus at startlingly low tariffs; quick lunches and snackery nibbles also available. This one is a bargain in almost any category for discriminating ingestion. Firmly recommended.

The famous old Bacchi Wapen finally bit the dust and phoenixed as the **New Bacchi**. Reportedly it has a different owner and milieu. Unfortunately, we missed it on our latest rounds, so we can't tell you more. Sorry. **Adam and Mari**, on a small island in the heart of the city, has a warm-weather terrace, somber accouterments, and a sturdy French kitchen; 2 orchestras; no cabaret; singles abound; currently open all year, for a change. The **Alexandra** has become second-rate on our scale; the clientele seemed to be slipping, too; open every day on the calendar.

The ultramod **Royal Garden**, in midcity opposite the N.K. Department Store, whips out exceptional value for moderate to medium-high tariffs. Handsome place-settings reflecting the finest national skills—from beautiful wine goblets, to handloomed textiles, to the leather chairs on which you sit. Superb presentation that is not luxury category, but is certainly appealing; delicious cuisine (our plate of warm garnished *gravadlax* was heavenly); rushed service

that tries to please. And please don't miss a peek or a nibble or a sip in the lower-tariffed downstairs wine restaurant. Waiters wear black smocks, smoke curls from the cigarettes of lingering newspaper readers, and the quality is tops for tavern-type snacks. We're very fond of every department in this cosmopolitan candidate.

In the somewhat more moderate category, **Cattelin** is a traditional standby. Simple, friendly atmosphere, not chichi; full of socialites, artists, students, civil servants, and assorted Characters; rôtisserie grill to rear; seafood annex; open all year. **Stortorgskällaren** ("Cellar by the Market") is located, quite naturally, on the Great Square in Old Town. It offers a cozy ambiance with 24 candlelit tables; at the street-level entrance, you'll find a bar and 2 small dining rooms for overflow trade. Unelaborate and agreeable. **Promenade** is central, opposite Humlegården Park. Help-yourself selections; now rekindled after a sputtering spell. The **Bill & Bull** offers an interesting combination: a restaurant with a sauna. This one is divided into 2 operations. Downstairs it contains a complex which not only caters to individuals but which business people, families, clubs, and other groups rent first to sweat off weight and then to put it back on in its dining room. This 50-table IKA-chain enterprise, subdued in tone, is split into a number of small nooks. It is open daily and continuously from noon and 11 P.M. Upstairs is the fast-service **Bull Steak House** in which you order from 25 items (including 3 types and 6 weights of steak) entirely by number. Although the prices are reasonable, it is run-of-the-corral. **Pizzeria Capri** is cheery for peninsular pickin's. **Piazza Opera,** formerly the Tessin, now rivals this one as a pizza parlor. The **Victoria,** a chameleon which is a somber rendezvous for businessmen at lunchtime and a swinging Fun Fair mostly for the Younger Set when darkness falls, is further described under "Night Life." The **Stekhuset Falstaff,** a 10-minute taxi jaunt to Tegeluddsvägen 90, is the latest rage among local beefeaters. Low-ceilinged room with 2 adjacent annexes; terra-cotta tile flooring; highly polished enamel-red chairs; blue, green, and black placemats; black-handled utensils; azure paper napkins; busy, gas-flame rôtisserie sizzling sirloins, T-bones, chops, and filets. The menu is a do-it-yourself multiple-choice ticket on which you note the type, weight, and preparation of your cut. Our sampling was only fair.

Two pet bargains? **Brända Tomten** (Stureplan 13) is a 50-year-old colorful drop-in landmark. The ground floor has 2 rooms with dark paneling, small tables with flowered cloths, dimly lit hanging lanterns, big copper bowls bright with seasonal posies, pewter molds, a piano, and the aura of a comfortable family-style haven. On warm evenings you may sup under a French canopy in its sidewalk restaurant. In its basement, lunch is served to the public and dinner to private parties. Here are samples of its choice of 41 dishes, all of which come in huge portions: Large shrimp salad with local "caviar" and fixings; 3-type herring Clover plate; blueberry ice cream. Service 13% extra; open during the week continuously from 10 A.M. to 12 P.M.; no beer or spirits before noon; very good culinary standards. Here is a delightful answer to travelers who are weary of rich cookery and who seek even coffee and cake only as a respite from overfeeding. The other is the lavish smörgåsbord featured at lunch on the glass-wrapped bar-terrace of the **Grand Hotel.** The ambiance is elegant; the vista of the harbor is beautiful; the variety is eye-popping; the preparation

is delicious; the tariff is low for all you can eat, be it seconds, thirds, or fourths. How this world-famous institution manages to offer such a large and mouth-melting spread at today's costs is a mystery to us. Advance bookings here are strongly urged.

Pubs? Two are unusually inviting. **Player's Inn** crackles with a hearth in the middle one of its 3 adjoining salons. The ceiling is oak, and so is the atmosphere. The food is incidental. **Tudor Arms**, slightly less refined, is turned out in half-timber and white stucco. A young throng parades through every evening for steak-and-kidney pie, roast beef, and other publican pamperings. Neither is for purposeful dining, but both are fun.

Now for a pair of highflying, low-value novelties: The enchanting aerial vista from **Gondolen**, an altitudinal barque above the Old Town, will almost make you forget that miserable fodder on your plate. Our good friend, Swedish gourmet and world traveler Georg Sylwander, claims this panorama has synthesized his personal rule: "Never eat seriously at any spot where there is a magnificent view!" Mr. Sylwander couldn't be more right—at least about this one. Book a window table on a sunny day; go only when you're not hungry. The next is the **Kaknästornet**, 360 feet up in the TV tower which looms above the Djurgarden. Entrance costs peanuts per adult; it's free for young tots accompanied by oldsters. Indoor and outdoor sightseeing terraces for oooohing and ahhhing from 9 A.M. to midnight; glass-lined restaurant functioning from 11:45 A.M. to the bewitching hour; topographical maps, a telescope, and a tape-recorded guide service on tap on top; an ultrascenic, multilingual hostess to orient your hawk-eyeing. If that basement-level cuisine served way up in the stratosphere doesn't get you, then surely the elevators will. They rocket aloft and plummet down at more than 15 feet per second (among the speediest in Europe). Here is certainly a tourist attraction that's popular—but we wish that the food were better. Oh—let's not forget the spotless, efficient **I.C.A. "Ringbaren"** chain, while we're up; moderate-price cafeterias plus table-service outlets; excellent value for budgeteers. What we saw of **Conti** didn't impress us very much—but we got there too late to make a fair judgment. For Mexican crafts, you might want to try **El Sombrero**, which has recently been freshly blocked and pressed. The cookery is top-hat, too, for South-of-the-Border specialities.

In addition to the previously mentioned Stallmästaregården, there are other likely targets in the suburbs. **Solliden**, nearby, is medium-cost and caters to a mass trade. Enormous recent improvement, thanks to the perspiration, plasma, and lachrymal outpourings of Manager Lennart Lindgren; now a delightful choice for a sunny day; recommended with salutes. The aforementioned **Grand Hotel** in *Saltsjöbaden* serves a splendid smörgåsbord on Sunday noons. **Ulriksdals Wärdshus** at *Solna* (10 minutes from Stockholm), a lacy filigreed wood and window-paned country mansion built in 1868, is popular summer and winter. Small porch at entrance for cocktails and chitchat; glass-sided 25-table dining room in gay pastels; enchanting bucolic view; appealing upstairs for private parties and banquets. Our recent sampling of the Swedish national feast was nothing more than smörgåsboredom; it's served weekdays between noon and 3 P.M. and Sundays from noon to 7 P.M. More for eye appeal and sylvan leisure than for palate satisfaction.

In the miscellaneous category, that 1713-vintage cellar called **Den Gyldene Freden** ("The Golden Peace") has color galore—*and* now there's a lot more quality mixed into the pigments. Different helmsman who has it sailing even more smoothly than before; ground-floor salon in tavern style; cellar portions cozier for evenings; one segment bisected from end to end by a single community table; excellent service from staffers in regional costumes; prices very reasonable and eatables improving; for those who want a fashionable place to dine and sane value-packed billings; closed in July. For shoppers, the summer-only, high-up terrace at the **NK Department Store** has one of the finest views in midtown, plus a self-service cafeteria; very popular and very good; winter lunchrooms, too. The **Lille Köbenhavn**, across the street, specializes in Danish goodies; moderate tabs; a hit at midday. For students, **Minerva** has a Parisian bistro décor, a Swiss chef, and great élan; closed mid-June to mid-August; hot as Hades, but lots of laughs. A Big Mac? **McDonald's** has a farmed-out version of its U.S. hamburgers at the Kunsgaten, a perfect central location and an impressive establishment. This has stirred up a griddle of sizzling competitors. **Clock** is one. **Floyd's** (named for Pugilist Patterson) is one more. There are others. In a land famed for its delicious meatballs and smörgåsbord, we can't get too enthusiastic over this feverish bun-fest.

For sky travelers, the **Flygrestaurangen Restaurant** at Arlanda International Airport can accommodate 185 guests at a single sitting. There is also a cafeteria for 425 and a cocktail bar for 45.

Night Life On special application, licensed restaurants may stay open until the wicked hour of 3 A.M.; alcohol must cease to flow at 2:30 A.M. And that's that!

The **Bolaget** is bowling 'em over in the capital aisles these nights. It was recommended to us by our dear friend, the ever-keen, highly perceptive Gordon McLendon, who has tipped us (and you) off on a number of superb entries in this guidebook. This versatile swinger's haven spins from 7 P.M. to 3 A.M. every day of the week; the midnight show spotlights local and international artists; tinklings in the Pianobar ripple from 8 P.M. till closing; dancing trips in from 10 P.M. to 2 A.M. While the normal restaurant dinner chomps standard bites out of your wallet, the segment called The Wreck provides simple nutrients for becalming tariffs. Its go-getting Bonifaces are Gun and Sten Holmquist, a double-barreled Sten-Gun combination of blond pulchritude, intelligence, hospitality, and youthful vigor. With that magical McLendon backing, we give this one enthusiastic huzzahs of praise. We wish it continuing success.

The **Hamburger Börs** is a hot contender, presenting such headline relish as Sammy Davis, Jr., and other top bananas of show biz. **Berns** gets its share of big spenders too. This house still pours out first-class gin-mill talent. Mini-Lido type atmosphere; nominal cover charge; food improving. Some semblance of movement might be found in the **Strand Hotel** and perhaps at the previously mentioned **New Bacchi**. **Club Opera** is popular for dancing. The Royal in the **Grand Hotel** is consistently dependable. **Golden Days** throbs with British piano and banjo pickin's on the merry mock-stern of a ship. **Konstnärshuset** and **Alexandra's** (a discoperation) plus a molting covey of pipits, warble for a woeful wayworn welter of night hunters. **Baldakinen**, **Aladdin**, and **Hasselbacken** also draw an array of thwarted insomniacs. **Engelen**, a converted

pharmacy, stirs out beer only with a dash of jazz for members—but you probably can wiggle in. **Bobbadilla**, an Old Town cellar haunt for youngsters, was wheeling gaily on our latest spin of the platters, followed by the **Manzanilla**. The **Gazell** isn't worth the leap. The **Berzeliiterrassen** offers invitations to the dance every night except Monday year round; meals and wines added; good orchestra; college-age travelers can usually find partners here. **Stampen** is great fun for Dixieland rebs like us'ns. The ceiling and walls are hung with whimsical junk items: an upside-down Christmas tree, a bib-and-tucker, a baby carriage, and one of the most forlorn sights we've ever seen—a stuffed dog. Only beer is served along with some of the happiest sounds in the North. Top recommendation for the carriage trade to toe-tapping tailgaters.

Singles a speciality? **Victoria** (Kungsträdgården) is a startling paradox: conservative, quiet, solid businessmen's restaurant at lunch which turns into the most raucous, crowded, merry Singles center in Sweden from 5 P.M. onward. Its 3 good-sized rooms plus warm-weather terrace are so jammed with celebrants (or would-bes) that to be certain of entry, reservations are usually mandatory to pass the waiting line at the door. All sexual tastes and persuasions might find exactly the partner they seek virtually up to its 3 A.M. closing. Snacks to full meals are always available. The fastest action is at the bar. **Adam & Mari**, operative only a few days each week, was jovially termed "a meat market" by a local friend before we rechecked it. Its dinner with dancing is fair. Actually, for singles of either gender who are on the prowl, at least one-half of the niteries in the city can be a happy hunting grounds if language difficulties can be overcome.

Sex shows? It is a basic fact that normally these are presented in grubby, grimy surroundings to furtive people who are in constant fear of being recognized. **Chat Noir** is the only major exception that we have ever come across in our travel lives. It is a small, clean, comfortable, plushly-furnished theater which is attended by many matrons with their husbands and older children as well as by singles and younger couples. Everyone we saw behaved as if they were watching a Strindberg play. The attendants are pretty girls dressed pertly in the Bunny style. The broad armrests of each seat are designed to hold beer mugs, the only beverage served. The performers, most of them lovely or handsome, are skillfully and impeccably costumed when they appear. The stagecraft and lighting are completely professional. A total of 45 different skits are presented nonstop nightly from 9 P.M. to 3 A.M., and the ticketholders may stay as long as they like. Each hour there is a cycle which includes striptease, petting, lesbian performances, and actual intercourse; male homosexuality and sadomasochism are barred. In what otherwise would virtually always be a dirty, smutty netherworld, we found this establishment unique. None of us has ever been to the 4 places which follow. **Sexorama** advertises "Shows on your own table and even just under the ceiling. Posing in private rooms. All-sexy chicks with enormous busts . . . topless—bottomless. They'll do anything for you . . . Welcome." Its open from noon to 3 A.M. **La Madelaine** states "Pssst! How much do you pay when you experience the Swedish sin?" Pay 60 Kr. to avoid the typical tourist club, and you will experience more. Intercourse, petting with the audience, striptease, pornofilms. On top of this we can offer

you our exciting Sex-Cave, where entirely naked girls do almost everything you want. Sexy Topless Bar—WELCOME!" This one operates nonstop from 8 P.M. to 3 A.M. From what we gather, both the **City Sex-Shop-Show** (Kungsgatan 70) and **Soho Sex** (Birgerjarlsgatan 15) have magazines, slides, books, sex kits, and continuous porno films from 10 A.M. to midnight. Naturally there must be others.

Shopping Swedish quality is renowned. In integrity of merchandise, you won't get stung. Price is the major consideration.

Be careful about delivery *within* Sweden of gold or silver articles, chocolate, carpets, liquor, or furs. Arrange for airport, ship, or home delivery to save the 17.1% V.A.T.—and keep your sales slip to show at departure.

Our ★ ★ ★ ★ recommendations are individually noted.

Swedish glass: The outstanding specialist for Orrefors, Kosta, and other producers is named exactly that— ★ ★ ★ ★ ★ **Svenskt Glas** (Birger Jarlsgatan 8), which has supplied the Royal Families of Sweden, Denmark, and the United Kingdom for more than 40 years, as well as armies of foreign guests such as you and us. The dazzling advantage here for Yankee and Reb shoppers is that with ALL costs included—purchase price, shipping, insurance, and U.S. Customs duties—you'll still pay about half the American retail price for precisely, identically the same articles. What fantastic bargains!! The most popular categories among pilgrims are their tableware (monogrammed if you wish), engraved art crystals, and barware. In collaboration with the World Wildlife Fund, this fine house is creating a limited line of animal sculptures of endangered species—and a substantial portion of each purchase price is being contributed to that cause. Mail Order Department; expert export shipping with 17.1% discount. Ask for the gentlemanly, kindly Owner-Manager, Anders Borg, or for Miss Martensson. Here is *the* target for *the* discerning shopper.

Ceramics and china: **Gustavsbergs Utställning** (Birger Jarlsgatan 2) is a charmer, with grace and gladness in its gorgeous table and decorative pieces.

Swedish silver and gold in all price ranges: Our respect for—and fondness for!— ★ ★ ★ ★ ★ **Kurt Decker AB** (Biblioteksgatan 12) flame brighter on our every return to this Garden of Wantables. Among his treasures are a b-i-g assortment of silver or gold charms, unique flatware, the largest Georgian silver collection in the nation, and for gifts its best-selling wine-bottle drip stoppers—plus a handsome display of rare gems and bibelots spun from plate, sterling, yellow or white gold, and platinum. For genial Director Decker, an English and German diplomate in gemology, this is his joy, his fun, and his occupational passion. Wonderful!

"Bits and Pieces": This is the translation of **Slumpen Tyger-Ting** (Köpmang 1)—and it's amusing to buy from its widely assorted stocks which are scattered willy-nilly. The category which particularly delighted our childlike eyes was the handmade models of stores—a complete flower shop with teeny, teeny blooms, a butcher shop with minuscule cold cuts hanging from hooks, and others. Fetching and different.

Furniture: **Möbel-Shop** (Roslagsgatan 8) has a full and handsome line of Swedish furniture which is hand-fashioned from old pine. Because they only work on logs which have been lying in the forests for a long time, the wood

takes on a lovely sheen in the Nordic 16th-to-18th-century manner. Write to Mr. Kai Durchman for brochures; they ship throughout the world.

Handicrafts: **Svensk Hemslöjd** (Sveavägen 44) is the marketing center for many of the nation's best artisans of their genre. **Nordkalottshopen** (Birger Jarlsgatan 35) offers wares from Lapland. **Panduro Hobby** (Kungsgatan 32) sells the raw materials from which you can create your own Scandinavian arts and crafts.

Swedish-modern potpourri: 2-storied **Svenskt Tenn** (Strandvägen 5A) is a beautiful establishment. Here you will find original pewter, furniture and a mélange of curiosa—most with their own colorfully tasteful touch. **Konsthant-verkaran** (Mäster Samuelsgatan 2) belongs to 70 freelance artisans and artists for a permanent exhibition of their creations. Ceramics, jewelry, paintings, wall plaques, beads, tapestries, and much more are on display.

Department stores: **NK** is one of the world's greatest department stores. **PUB**, a cooperative, is lower-level and not so interesting. Very modern **Ahléns** (Klarabergsgatan/Drottninggatan), less central, is one of the largest. **MEA** has almost no appeal to most outlanders, including us.

Shopping Centers: The 5-block **Galleria** and the 3-tiered **PK**, across the street, have now become the most important, with **Hötorgscity** following right behind. The **Hötorget Station** (subway) and **Central Station** (basement) feature a cluster of merchandisers which stay open until 10 P.M. daily as well as Sunday afternoon and evening.

Please DON'T buy: Perfumes, cigarettes, and similar luxury imports, because heavy duties make them prohibitively expensive.

Shopping hours: Standard shops are normally open from 9 or 9:30 A.M. to 6 P.M. from Monday through Friday and from 9 or 9:30 A.M. to 1 or 2 P.M. on Saturday.

Dedicated shophounds: Space is too tight here for further listings in Stockholm, Malmö, and Göteborg. For information on these, more stores, more details, and more lore, please consult the purse-size, 25th Anniversary edition of *Fielding's Selective Shopping Guide to Europe.*

Other Targets

ÅRE   First, are you ready for a delightful off-beat expedition? The **Grand-Åregården**, 425 miles north of Stockholm, is very special in its deep-heart-of-Sweden atmosphere and beautifully selected deluxe facilities. It is divided into 3 sections: The Diplomat (14 singles, 23 doubles), the Åregården (18 singles and 25 doubles), and the Sporthotel (40 doubles). In summer there is skiing, white-water canoeing, mountain hiking with guide, water-skiing, fishing, swimming, sauna, tennis, table tennis, dancing, riding, boating, and film shows. In winter there is downhill skiing (13 different lifts), cross-country skiing with teacher, a ski school, curling, fishing, sauna, table tennis, dancing, disco, film show—and even gliding. Highly recommended to the adventurous traveler who seeks sport in beautifully pampering tranquillity.

BÅSTAD, SOUTHWEST COAST   This region has recently enjoyed a touristic boom period. *Tylösand* (the seaside resort on a cape facing Denmark, 5 miles from Halmstad on the Malmö-Göteborg road) comes up with a cluster

of summery hotel buildings, several bungalows for transients, 1 restaurant seating 550, 2 smaller dining establishments, Finnish steam baths, a wonderful beach (cold water—brrr!), and 27-hole golf courses, tennis courts, dancing, and many other attractions. Main plant open mid-June to mid-August; stay at the **Tylösands Haysbad**, best in the community. At _Halmstad_, the **Hallandia** is new-ish; said to be quite good. For pilgrims from Denmark, the _Europafergen_ makes the daily ferry run between Grenå and Varberg. At neighboring _Falkenberg_, the seafront **Strandbaden** is dramatically avant-garde in architectural concept.

DALARNA AND LAKE SILJAN   In the Dalarna province of central Sweden, not far from the Norwegian mountains, there are 3 prime regional targets. _Tällberg_ has by far the most color and charm with its mountainside spread, lake view, pine groves, and scattering of turkey-red cottages in the lap of Siljan forests. Its silent mystique is periodically upset in High Season by reindeer-like herds of tourists. _Rättvik_ also radiates lure, but it is more urban and physically less enticing. The outskirts should not be overlooked. _Leksand_ is relatively commercial and dull; not worth the transatlantic fare to see it, but if you are in the area it has its points. As for hotels in this birch-and-pine heartland, here's our detailed town-by-town breakdown: In _Tällberg_, the **Greens** boasts lovely buildings and an enchanting situation. In many respects —especially physical allures—it reeks with Dalecarlian appeal from its gables to its tables; dozens of nooks for cozy chats; Rumpus Room; tiny Picasso lounge; seventeenth-century library with a twentieth-century TV set; brass place settings in its viewful woody dining room; sweet young hostesses; indoor-outdoor swimming pool with temperature control; minigolf and badminton. All rooms (named, not numbered) now have tub or shower and fresh furnishings; "Gesunda," with its arched ceiling, sublime little balcony, warming hearth, and gay colors, is our personal pick; open all year except 1 week before Christmas. The **Dalecarlia Turisthotell** offers 80 rooms, only 28 baths, and a nearby annex with 50 additional units. Its tiny sixteenth-century reception hall is engaging; very large glass-fronted dining room with a heavenly command; earthly dancing once or twice weekly throughout the year; casino; bar; mini-bowling. This one demonstrates a certain flair for mass appeal, suburban-style —but it is spectrums below the Greens for sheer color. The **Långbergså rden**, a farmstead occupying 10 hilltop acres of ancient cattle-grazing land, boasts 55 rooms—25 in the main building and 30 in sleepy little cottages dotting the rumpled terrain. Poma-type ski lift for winter sports; 3 chalets, which Americans seem to love for their peaceful seclusion. Our recent visit convinced us it is indeed making progress, but we'd be happier—and so would you—if the pace were quicker. _Rättvik_'s leader is now the **Lerdalshöjden**, which is out of the hurly-burly above the lake. As soon as the Siljansborg, its former superior, was closed, a major renovation program was activated. Among other improvements, construction on an additional 20 chalets was initiated and more baths or showers were added to its then existing 13. Its rambling main structure contains 38 rooms; supplementing are 3 annexes with 13, 4, and 17 units. All bedchambers, while tight-dimensioned, are ultra-clean and somewhat more attractively furnished than before; those with plumbing

have the tiniest baths outside of Lilliput; the friendly personnel are headed by Manager Birgitta Nogeman. Very pleasant. The **MHF Motel's** 36 doubles are woefully weensy. *Leksand* (about 6 miles from Tällberg) has as its leader the ancient 40-room **Trekullor**. The **Furuliden** might come next, but we must review the scene again to be sure. The **Siljansnäs** (on the lake, 9 miles west) lists a pool, sauna, curling, and scenery, plus 30 rooms, 22 baths, and 20 balconies. At *Mora*, the **Mora Hotel** deserves mention; 75 moorings; 25 baths. We haven't yet seen the **Siljan**; 37 units with toilet and TV; 9 with shower; sauna. The celebrated **Sälens Högfjällshotell** at *Sälen* has an annex that functions during the summer. The main house will operate only in the winter season and will be rented to private sources during the warm months.

GÖTEBORG (Gothenburg), pronounced "YOTE-ah-borg," celebrates its 36oth anniversary next year. This ancient seat, Sweden's busiest port, is second in importance—about the size of Newark, N.J. It's on the west coast, seaward. There are many historic canals here, and the Göta River ends the famous Göta inland waterway which winds cross-country to Stockholm. Circulation in the city itself has been improved through new traffic controls. (It's the home of Volvo, you know.) Several hotels are available. Dining spots are now more engaging than before. There are ample tourist facilities. The city is an interesting one, and the inland boat ride across the peninsula is a relaxing and pleasant journey. It now boasts a new international airport; you can fly back to Stockholm by fast, frequent SAS service. A new private airport has relieved pressure on the main commercial terminus.

The **Park Avenue** is our candidate as one of the leading hotels of the nation. Modern, fresh, attractive décor; wonderful Lorensberg Restaurant with top-talent floor show and dancing every evening but Sunday; delightfully cozy, beguiling Belle Avenue Grill; anchovy-size Tidbit Room with light fare for budgeteers; mezzanine bar and snack loggia; self-service breakfasts at rates that won't curdle your café au lait. Vast opulent new wing; new sauna and pool; new sky bar and Panorama tearoom; of all the twins, 1/4 have private verandas; top floor (10th) is entirely in elegant balconied large suites; 9 small suites are one of the best values in Sweden. All accommodations are newly furnished and appointed, with a keen eye toward comfort and convenience. Our only nitpick is the dismal lobby décor, which remains the same year after year. We haven't yet seen the 323-room **Scandinavia**, a link in the SARA chain, but we hear that it leans heavily toward the convention trade. For modernists, the newish Reso-owned, 10-story, crescent-shape **Opalen** is as fresh as a fjord breeze. The designers, thank goodness, did not make the same boudoir design bumbles here that were made in the Stockholm Continental (see earlier comments). Careful planning of the bedchambers, in fact, gives these comfortable and tasteful accommodations the edge over the cool-tempered public rooms. Clerestory restaurant that has been given a warmup treatment (dancing except Sun.); popular Bodega Cafeteria with trencherman servings; quick-lunch den converting to a roulette rank at nightfall; hairdressing and barber facilities. All 230 rooms with well-equipped baths (good ventilation, soap flakes, peignoirs, Kleenex, bidets). There are artful touches in the displays of twentieth-century tapestries and the handicraft vitrines in the corridors. Here's a thoughtfully

conceived and clean-lined haven that the young-in-spirit should undoubtedly enjoy. Somewhat commercial, but a sound and solid second; highly recommended. The **Rubinen**, under the same Reso proprietorship, stands a few doors away from the Park Avenue. Although its prices are higher, it is Swedish miles below the leader in quality and performance, in our opinion. The 400-room **Europa** is a recent major addition to the city. Two dining quadrants; a bar; gym, sauna, and pool; pedestrian passage connecting it to the Ostra Nordstan shopping mall. **Three Crowns** proffers 172 accommodations all with faucets (in bath or shower), a restaurant, cafeteria, a sauna, a garage, and bedchambers textiled in blue hues—royal, no doubt. We'll be anxious to seek our first audience here next swing. **Eggers** is next—but it may not be for long. Its proposed renovation has been scuttled; hopes of moving to an entirely new site are now troubling the owner's slumber. Current total of 88 rooms and only 16 baths; friendly, cheery personnel; well maintained and sprightly, despite its century-plus of wear. Lodge *only* in the more modern bedchambers here, because the others are scrambled Eggers. The **Ritz,** across from the railway switchyard but nevertheless quiet, is run by the Salvation Army. They keep it brighter than a Christmas glockenspiel. Restaurant unveiled a while back; very, very good, clean shelter for the bargain hunter who rolls in thirstless. The **Carl Johan Hotel,** plus the **OK** and the **Hallarna,** are new ones on us. The last has 92 units; from the brochure before us, it seems to be a reasonably appealing efficiency camp for motorists who tire at the E3-E6 junction. The **Excelsior** is a fair bet for budget-conscious families; a handful of baths on tap; also sparkling. **Ramada** has opened a sleeper here; normally they are pretty plain outside but comfortable inside. There's one **Esso** at the entrance from the Malmö highway and a newer one on the Oslo highway. Cozy restaurants; modern comforts; better-than-average pitstops for traffic shunners. In *Kungälv,* 13 miles north of Göteborg, the 130-room **Fars Hatt** wears the sylvan crown. Two comfortable wings and a swimming pool; 2 saunas, tennis, bowling, and a golf course nearby; 2 popular restaurants and an active bar. Very solid accommodations, as a motel-type stop, we love it.

For dining in this city, the **Park Avenue Hotel** is a knockout. Fashionable clientele; attentive courtesy but staffing insufficient; chic, lively, and delightful. Among the independents, traditionally the best known is **Henriksberg,** 10 minutes from the center. Glorious view of the harbor and busy cargo cranes; further expansion onto the veranda; dancing downstairs in the nautical Kajutan Room in season; friendly, fast, and deft service. Our chief objection is the tariffs, which, in our opinion, are plainly rapacious. The now-famous **Johanna** has shot up not only to rival but to better it. Actually we would classify this contender as 1 of the 5 leading restaurants in the nation. It is so dedicated to *haute cuisine* that 80% of its menu are house specialties. From its creations to the ambiance to the napery to the tableware to the personnel, it is top quality in every regard. Manager Leif Mannerström frequently visits France to follow new developments and to create new items. He insists on advance table reservations. It operates from 11:30 A.M. to 3 P.M. and 6 P.M. to midnight. Also terribly expensive but superb. Although the big **Trägårn** can handle 500 diners, Manager Pelle Lundberg is similarly adamant that all reservations be made ahead of time. Its cabarets are excellent and its food is good but not remarkable.

Normally it operates from 7 P.M. to 2 A.M. In summer there is outdoor service, as well as a nightclub which closes at 3 A.M. Like its other 2 competitors, again its prices seem excessively high. While eminent, we would rate it in third place. The **White Corner**, a 2-minute walk from the Rubinen, is much less costly. Ground-level snack center, bar, and popular-price restaurant; ruggedly handsome downstairs Grill with steaks the feature; crackling rôtisserie and hearth at one end; comfortable armchairs and booths; blue- and gray-checked tablecloths; pewter place plates; illumination by candles; excellent service by waiters who present the meat choices on plaques. Highly recommended—especially downstairs. The **Masthugget** is another good buy. Self-service and table attention; modernistic décor; decent tabs. A treasure island for budgeteers in this Land of the Disappearing Kronor. The **Opalen's** restaurant-nightclub swings with Junior Executive Suiteniks and nice lone ladies hoping for action. Our meal was grim, but the animated atmosphere makes up for almost any kitchen sins. Okay—if you're just learning to handle a Gillette, and if you've just grabbed a snack somewhere else. The **Valand** is comprised of a series of rooms that includes the main dining salon, the Little London, a congenial bar, the Club Alexander, and a small upstairs Casino (where you can risk your own in its penny-ante play). We are told that the **Belle Avenue Grill** and the **Europakällaren** in the Europa enjoy sound reputations; both of them are untested by us.

In summer only (May to mid-Sept.), there are 2 popular choices. The **Liseberg**, in Liseberg Amusement Park, is lively; good food and band, top artistic attractions; medium tariffs. **Långedrag**, in the Yacht Harbor 15 minutes by taxi, offers a glorious view of the Göteborg Inlet and its heavy ship traffic; spacious in size; production-belt vittles and reasonable prices; worth trying if the day is sunny.

For night life, the **Ambassador** seats 750 celebrants. There are dancing and entertainment every night except possibly Sunday. We haven't visited it. The **Mirabelle** in the Park Avenue Hotel is among the best in the North. Don't miss it. The **Opalen** also swings for the Younger Set. The previously mentioned **Valand** is next in line. Our favorite night-galloping Göteborger tells us that **Krokodil** is now very "in," but we haven't checked it personally as yet.

GRÄNNA   For honeymooners, the favorite is **Gyllene Uttern**, 1 1/2 miles south of the village on the Stockholm-Jönköping-Malmö route. Two hotels (1 First class, 1 for country living); Tudor-style architecture; grass growing on the roofs; lake view; guest cottages with 1-or-more bedrooms, a bath, and a sitting room; exquisite Wedding Chapel to make it legal; lovely setting and enchanting décor; not overexpensive. May to September only. Just the dish for lovebirds who want bucolic scenery and less-than-zero chatter from anybody.

JÖNKÖPING   as a town, is pretty industrial-minded. To counteract that tone, the waterside **Stora Hotellet** rules the wavelets. Dining room facing Vättern Lake; newer wing with more comfort but less vista than the older portion; total of 130 rooms and 82 private baths. The better choice for traditionalists. The Reso-built **Portalen**, in the middle of town, is for pilgrims who prefer sleek modern lines and strict functionality. Restaurant with giant

chunks of carved wood (we ate lunch here, so we'd guess the food _must_ be better at the Stora); summer garden and dining patio; Bodega Cafeteria; full Reso panoply of gadgets, including TV, radio, piped music, clock, phone, and an ingenious window-blind system (set inside Thermopane glass for controlling light to any desired gradient). Its cramped layout is its chief drawback. Still fair for overnighting, but not longer. The **Esso** and **MHF** motels might even be better for wayfarers on the go. Adequate space in the latter is MHF— Mighty Hard to Find. We don't know about the **Ramada** entry here.

LINKÖPING (pronounced "Lin-shoe-ping") produces the delightful little **Frimurarehotellet,** provincial but comfortable. Its newer section is best;-there's a bath provided with every unit. Good dining room under a slat roof; ancient Grill with hunting scenes in stained-glass windows; chef laboring happily under a copper hood; off-lobby bar. Inviting in a clubby fashion. The 100-room **Rally Motel** is just a fair bet for motorists. We've recently Rallied here again and found it now basic-to-skimpy, but entirely suitable for what it is. Squash court, Finnish bath, barbershop, grill-restaurant, and 24-hour coffee shop with help-yourself snack bar; all but the loners have bath. **Esso** is also on the scene with 96 gleaming reasons to pause for the night. In the center, the **Stora Hotellet** is adequate for emergency shelter if all else is filled.

LULEÅ is far up north. A regional sensation was caused by the inauguration of the **SAS Globetrotter.** General Manager Kurt Ritter is said to be young, vibrant, and very competent. Reports have it that this 219-room hostelry, the eleventh affiliated with this airline, is closely similar in facilities and service standards to its predecessors. If so, this is a virtual guarantee that this house is an exceptionally pleasant lodging.

LYSEKIL, 2 hours north of Göteborg just off the trunk road to Oslo (Norway), has the well-known seaside **Lysekil.** Travelers tell us this merry little house has 50 rooms, some with bath and all with private toilet; 3 restaurants, a nightclub, a bar, and a gaming room adjoin. Facilities are amiable without being plush. In this very Swedish summer mecca, you'll find fishing (no licenses or restrictions), an open-air cafeteria on the beach, an Aqualung Diving School, an International Youth Club, teen-agers dancing nightly at the Al Fresco restaurant, a Carnival in mid-August, and other drawing cards. It sounds like fun.

MALMÖ, Sweden's third city, resides down on the southwestern tip, closest to Germany and Denmark. This is the jumping-off point for excursions to the Swedish châteaux country; there are at least 200 fine ones from the sixteenth and seventeenth centuries. Five major hotels, 1 outstanding restaurant in a restored ancient house, plenty of shops, and plenty of bustle; 6 miles of quays, Sweden's biggest man-made harbor, and one of Scandinavia's largest and most modern theaters are here. Immaculate and comfortable ferryboats make the crossing to Copenhagen in 1 1/2 hours, and 36 hydrofoil services per day in both directions nip the time to a mere 35 minutes.

The modern architectural syndromes of spacelessness and iceberg-chill in

functionality result from this city's greater interest in businessmen than in tourists. The **Savoy,** mellow, charming, and carefully maintained, has an enviable location overlooking the canal and maritime docks. Cozy, popular Grill and gracious dining room, both noteworthy for cuisine; biggest banquet facilities in South Sweden (again for its heavy business clientele); more suites added; hodgepodge building pattern containing 100 bedchambers and 65 baths, all with hip-pocket closet dimensions. Director Lars Lendrop and his live-wire art-collecting wife do a fine job here. The Reso-run, mercantile **St. Jörgen** is a sterling example of the modern crop. Centrally situated and thoughtfully planned; built-in tranquillity surrounding 2 garden courts, effectively designed restaurant and cafeterias, cocktail lounge, and coffee bar; dancing every night but Monday in the Tavernan, which doubles in daytime as a breakfast den and quick-lunch snackery; roulette room where you can play for your meal chits; sauna and gymnasium. Total of 304 accommodations, including 23 singles and 5 doubles with shower only (1 day is the maximum permissible stay in the former, due to a health ordinance governing windowless rooms), 5 suites, and doubles with a full array of convenience features. Very good for jet-age tastes. The **Kramer** carries on as a traditional Malmö address. Pleasant lounge; Ambassador room for dinner and dance; 2 nightclubs; handsome bar in mahogany tones plus the Pub. A penthouse lords over 4 suites plus 100 lesser pads with 64 baths; each floor features a different shade of linens. Newly renovated and better. The 180-unit, supermodernistic, privately owned **Scandinavia** provides a surprising amount of elbowroom for a contemporary north-country enterprise. Beguiling roof garden; cheery restaurant, bar, and casino; sauna and gymnasium; billiard parlor; 44 bowling lanes (site of a World Championship); all bedchambers with 2 windows, alarm clock, radio, telephone, silent valet, and full bath, plus telephone-style shower in each; soothing color schemes. Some 30 apartments rent cheaply by the week or month. Especially recommendable for families, athletes on holiday, or ten-pin addicts. The centrally sited, 175-room **Garden** flowers on 2 floors atop an office building. New restaurant plus enclosed tea and breakfast room surrounded by flora; small modernistic units; dull colors; commercial but economically priced; adequate for brief stays. **Teaterhotellet,** across from the National Theater, and the **Plaza** are both pretty routine. Adjoining the racetrack is the ultrabasic **Jägersro Motell.**

Malmö's best bet in restaurants is the **Kockska Krogen,** the vaulted cellar of Jörgen Kock's palace. (He was the city's powerful mayor in the fifteenth century, when the port was Danish.) As an example of authentic period architecture, we'd call it an *absolute sightseeing must;* it's a happy haven for gastronomy as well. One main sanctum with several radiating brick-arched rooms; wonderful cheese bar at the entrance for munching with beer or wine while you wait for your table; shipment-home service for anything on the 28-item dairy tempter; benches with stuffed coffee bags for cushions; interior units with comfortable banquettes; leather-backed armchairs with brass studs; wooden place platters and bread plates; candles in wrought-iron bases; rich brown carpet to warm away the basement chill. The menu is in Swedish, but a maître in chef's costume helps with the translations; food bills—presented in a music box—are very reasonable for the quality. An extraordinary tourist

attraction that rings true, without the slightest spoilage by gimmicks. Highest recommendation for this city. Another worthwhile eye-pleaser, providing a panoramic view of the town and of Copenhagen (across the sparkling strait), is the penthouse **Kronprinsen,** a Top-of-the-Mark spellbinder crowning a residential structure. This is South Sweden's space platform. It contains a garage, a 2nd-floor nightclub, and enough ground-level shops to keep your wife busy until you're hungry again. Heavy food odors; cuisine not special; clientele drawn from every quarter; go for the vista and the relaxing ambiance, not for the cookery. The **Primeur** wins cheers for its ambitious presentations of *nouvelle cuisine,* derived largely from local produce and the fish market in Copenhagen. (The chef commutes daily by hydrofoil.) Airy, conservatory atmosphere that hints at the freshness on the plates; salads, terrines, and a few star attractions of the day. Simplicity almost reaches the exquisite proportions of the Orient here. Closed Sat., Sun., and holidays, plus all of July; otherwise functioning for lunch and dinner. Among the hotels, it's the **Savoy,** the **Kramer,** the **St. Jörgen,** and the **Scandinavia,** in that order. In nearby *Skanör* a few minutes from Falsterbo, **Gästgifvaregard** offers the perfect village diversion for city-tired travelers. Cozy old house converted into a restaurant in 1910; 3 rooms inside a flag-lined building; geese by the gaggle greet the guests; white-hatted chef doing wonders with each and every goose. Try this and the smoked eel (the latter cut with sheep shears and presented on a special server with scrambled eggs and rye crisp). Another treat is a delicious bitters called Malört, extracted from a local plant. Same Lendrop administration that sails the Malmö Savoy; lovely for a fair-weather excursion.

NORRKÖPING   The **Standard** has been completely rebuilt around 182 fresh rooms, making it the local banner entry. The **Ritz,** with its revamped façade and lobby, dates back to '35 in one wing and to '65 in the other; book into the "other" only; no restaurant. **Mobilen,** 1 mile out of the center, is U-shape, with the reception desk and a cafeteria at one end and a restaurant on the second flank; textiles in rich burnt colors; interior brick walls; 2 beds and a folding divan in each of its 42 accommodations; efficiency baths. Fine as a motel-type stop. **Esso** is another, of course; it pumps up 150 units.

VISBY's leaders are (1) **Snäckgärdsbaden,** and (2) **Visby,** rebuilt and enlarged some years ago. The former has a pool, minigolf, badminton, and dancing during the evening; its big drawback is its paucity of private baths; June 1 to August 31 only. The latter comes up with a considerably higher bath count; open June through August.

☑ **MOTELS**   Touring by car? U.S.-style motels are springing up like crocuses, all over Sweden. Ten examples, plus a bumper crop of unknowns that we hear are worth a gambol: (1) **Fleninge Motell,** 6 miles from the Elsinore (Denmark) —Helsingborg ferry, offers every room with bath, radio, and waking alarm; restaurant and cafeteria; adjoining service station; no tipping permitted; sponsorship of the Union of Temperance Drivers of Sweden. (2) **MHF Motel,** 1 1/2 miles north of *Helsingborg*'s Central Station, has 45 rooms, each with shower, toilet, TV, and radio. (3) **Stadshotellet** at *Värnamo,* about halfway between

Stockholm and Malmö on National Highway E-4, features superadvanced Swedish décor and furnishings; TV, radio, waking alarm, and bath or shower in every room; spacious, fully licensed restaurant with smörgåsbord; breakfast room, bar, and hairdresser; starkly modern in tone. (4) *Stockholm*'s entry is the **Gyllene Ratten** ("Golden Steering Wheel"), 4 miles south of the city at the intersection of the Södertäljevägen and Vantörsvägen highways; commercial enough to be a Seventh Avenue Community Center; 109 rooms (some twins, some studios, some bunks); 98 baths; grill, bar, and dining room; carservicing facilities. (5) **Rally Hotel** in *Linköping* has been previously described. (6) So has **Jägersro**, near *Malmö*. (7) And so has the **Mobilen** at *Norrköping*. (8) **Stad** at *Karlstad,* while not technically a motel, is a perfect rest point for motorists rolling between Stockholm and Göteborg or Oslo. One reader raves about his Louis XVI suite, huge bath, and Deluxe appointments. "Our daughter," he writes, "had a double room the size of a tennis court, beautifully furnished . . ." (9) Going north from Göteborg to Fredrikstad (Norway), the **Carlia Gästis** at *Uddevalla* has chilblains; still, it's reasonable. (10) Further up near the frontier, in *Strömstad*, **Stadshotell** is almost the only winter choice; not much.

Now for that bevy of question marks: The **Esso** petroleum interests (the name was not changed to Exxon in Europe) have pumped up 30 roadsiders strung out across the nation, 28 of which are owned by Standard Oil. Ask at any filling station in its Swedish fraternity for brochures on the rest stops. Most that we have inspected have been excellent in facilities, but often lacking in service and culinary polish. **Vätterleden,** 11 miles north of Jönköping, has 52 units, most with shower and TV, and low tariffs which include breakfast and service. **Stadt Ljungby,** at *Ljungby,* features 20 bedchambers all with bath or shower. **Terraza,** also at *Ljungby,* boasts 75 rooms, some with full bath and some with only shower and toilet. At *Sandviken,* the **Eos** is reported to be a pleasant budget stop by a reader from Haifa who paused here. Up in the far north, **Blå Aveny,** in the university town of *Umeå,* has 80 rooms with bath; restaurant seating 220 munchers; nightclub, casino, sauna, gymnasium, and garage. Sounds excellent for this north port. In *Kiruna,* 90 miles north of the Polar Circle, the **Ferrum** provides shelter plus drinks in the Midnight Sun Lounge. P.S.: Since the sun doesn't set here in June and July, don't try to anticipate the cocktail hour by watching the shadows.

For information on hotels or motels in other parts of Sweden, consult your travel agent or the Swedish National Tourist Office.

Practically every small town and resort has comfortable pensions with reasonable charges, all meals included. To get pension terms you must stay a minimum of 3 days. The **Swedish Tourist Board** can send you a folder and fill you in on details. *What* a buy in contrast with the costly general level here!

Switzerland

I f a group of scientists were given 50-trillion dollars, atomic power, and instructions to carve from the earth's surface a tourists' paradise, they'd probably just point to Switzerland, shrug their shoulders, and say, "Why build another?"

Switzerland has everything. It's got mountains, lakes, snow, the sort of thing you've been taught to expect, of course—but it's also got electric trains, castles, old-age pensions, fondue, wild ibex, and, with few exceptions, one of the most honorable collections of human beings on the globe.

This country, almost twice the size of Massachusetts, has often been called "a nation of hotelkeepers"; if said without scorn, there's truth in it. The tourist industry is a key business which occupies more than 190-thousand citizens. Over 20-million foreign visitors are registered in hotels each year. Yet Swiss travelers are so peripatetic that foreign nations retrieve more than half of the total income spent in Switzerland by all of us outlanders!

In religious division, there are 48% Reformed Protestants, 49% Roman Catholics, and 3% in other denominations—with freedom of worship for all sects. Military training is compulsory for all males at the age of 20; paradoxically, you'll probably see more and better soldiers here and in Sweden than in most other tourist lands in Europe. If the alarm is sounded, more than 600-thousand troops can be mobilized within a mere 48 hours. As mod-minded Minutemen, the alert Swiss stock their guns and field gear in their own homes. Unemployment is almost nil. Quite a few of the residents still are from abroad. The recent referendum to expel ⅓ rd of the foreigners living in the nation was rejected by the cautious electorate—but only narrowly.

Amazing people: To the eye, there are enormous regional differences, but at the core there is a stubborn and admirable sameness. The Italian Swiss in the South (Lugano, Locarno) seem the softest, gayest, and merriest; the French Swiss in the West (Geneva, Lausanne) seem the liveliest, most urbane, and most volatile; the Alamannic Swiss in the East (Zürich, Berne, Basel, Lucerne, St. Gall) seem the most wooden and humorless in social relationships. Yet under the surface they all share one characteristic that dominates everything: they are *Swiss*, down to their toenails.

☑ **SIGHTSEEING**   If you're after a region which few U.S. vacationers know and which hasn't been "civilized" beyond repair, the 2-day or 3-day circuit from *Zürich* through the Principality of *Liechtenstein* and *La Suisse Orientale* (Eastern Switzerland) is an enchanting choice. Spend your first night in *Vaduz*, the capital of this rustic little border state on the Rhine (see separate section); the second night might be spent in *St. Gallen*, where the hotel situation has improved. If you stop here, there will be time for a look at neighboring *Appenzell*, the Abbey Library, and other points of interest. And the return to Zürich should be made around the other leg of the loop, through *Romanshorn*, *Kreuzlingen*, *Stein am Rhein*, *Schaffhausen*, *Winterthur*, and *Effretikon*—with a pause at *Neuhausen*'s Rhine Falls if you're not in too much of a hurry. Full information on this off-trail territory can be obtained from any Swiss National Tourist Office branch (there's one in St. Gall at Bahnhofplatz 1a) or at the Vaduz HQ on Stätle 37. Quiet rather than spectacular beauty; recommended to old-timers rather than first-trippers.

From *Zürich*, should time be too pressing for such extensive coverage; a junket to the aforementioned Rhine Falls makes an interesting 1-day safari; you may lunch comfortably in the ancient Sonne Restaurant at *Stein am Rhein* —or take the repast at the Fischerzunft in *Schaffhausen* (excellent cuisine), with tea at Stein.

There are 23 well-equipped mineral spas in the country. *St. Moritz* is the highest in altitude—and possibly in price. *Baden, Bad-Ragaz, Rheinfelden*, and *Tarasp-Vulpera* are characteristic. Each is a center for particular types of illness; some are purely for rest and relaxation. The Swiss National Tourist Office publishes a free Pocket Guide about them.

August 1 is the big Swiss national holiday—the Bundesfeiertag—with bonfires and dancing all over the country. Annual folk festivals include Good Friday at *Mendrisio*, Camellia at *Locarno*, Blessing of the Alpine Pastures at *Lötschental* (a great folklore experience; you'll also see the grotesque carved masks of the region), and Escalade at *Geneva*. *Zürich* pops its fuses twice: once during the traditional Spring Festival of Sechseläuten, when Old Man Winter (a mammoth dummy stuffed with fireworks) is publicly burned at the stake, and again during the June Festival weeks, with concerts, opera, exhibitions, theater, and other gala events. *Lucerne* toots its whistle from mid-August to early September, with enough concerts, choirs, plays, and cultural exhibits to make you positively unlivable to your friends, neighbors, and even casual acquaintances at home. *St. Gallen* also blows off the lid at the end of June *every third year,* when 9000 children march through the streets in the triennial Children's Festival, consuming as they go the legendary 29 miles of Bratwurst; check during the spring of your particular journey.

The **Jungfrau** and *Interlaken*; the **Schilthorn** and the high surrounding triad corona seen from *Mürren*; the **Lake of Constance** with its castles, orchards, and quaint villages; the **Grisons**, land of 150 valleys; **Bürgenstock;** the **Bernese Oberland**, with its lakes, glacial valleys, and high-Alpine land-

scape; the **Jura** (which just became the nation's 23rd self-governing canton with Delemont as its capital); the glorious French-and-German **Valais**— everywhere in Switzerland you'll find something quaint and beautiful.

☑ **TRANSPORTATION Taxis** Rather expensive. Both the full-size cabs and the smaller *Kleintaxis* charge at the same rate. Limousines are more, of course.

Geneva has opened a **Taxi Telephone Center**. Simply dial 141, and one of a fleet of 150 cars will be at your disposal. In *Berne*, it's 24-24-24; in *Zürich*, it's 44-44-41.

After many disappointments by chiselers in big cities, at airports, and in chic resorts, we make it a habit to count our change and to check into any supplements before paying them. We're especially watchful when we take a cab from the vicinity of Zürich station. Intercity fares are also inexcusably rigged, by common consent.

There's no need to tip since your bill already includes a 15% service chomp.

It's smart to use buses for short hauls in any Swiss city; conductors, usually English-speaking, will steer you to your destination in a friendly way—and you'll save plenty.

Trains Excellent. The SBB's (or CFF's, if you prefer the French initials to the German) national network is 100% electrified; they run like Swiss watches. They usually keep their split-second schedules; they are usually clean; they usually go like a bat out of Helvetia. One of the fastest runs is made by the noon flier from Geneva to Zürich.

A total of 260 First-class and 230 Second-class coaches, all of a radically improved design, have been placed in service. Fifty *couchette* coaches (6 daytime seats converting to 6 sleep-in-your-clothes berths in each unit) have been added to the Basel–Vienna, Zürich–Rome and other hauls. These are on the unfancy side; while they used to save money, you now probably can fly for about the same outlay.

The food in the dining cars (many modernized, with air conditioning and nonsmoking sections added) is both inexpensive and excellent. Breakfast (ham and eggs—the works) costs $4-or-so; lunch and dinner are about $7. Service is polite, fast, and efficient except on crowded mainliners (*e.g.*, Zürich–Geneva), when they'll sometimes make you stand up for your sandwich and drink instead of deigning to disturb an empty table that has been set up for a full meal.

Ticket prices are quite reasonable considering the value received for your franc. (Those francs, incidentally, can be dropped directly into automatic ticket dispensing machines—a timesaving innovation that is beginning to blanket the nation.)

There are 5 classifications—and knowing what each does is important. First is the **ordinary** variety, full fare for 1-way trips. Validity lasts up to 2 days.

Second is the **round-trip** ("Return Rail") class, a 15% saving on the cost of 2 single rides. Good for 10 days; validity may be extended for another 7 or 14 days for a slight extra charge.

Third is the **Holiday Card**. It can be issued only outside of Switzerland in 4-day, 8-day, 15-day, or 1-month versions which allow you to travel at will around the country on rails, by steamer, on postal motor-coaches, or up and down numerous cableways. The savings can be tremendous for anyone who plans to move around a lot. Check with your travel agent or any branch of the Swiss National Tourist Office.

Fourth is the combination of **Half-Fare Season Ticket** and Supplementary Vouchers.

The basic unit here costs only in the vicinity of a dollar a day; it will take you to most of the principal tourist targets. For off-trail points, mostly in the mountain areas, you may purchase as many Supplementary Vouchers as your itinerary requires. These are sold in "days"—5 for $30 (First class) or $20 (Second class), or 10 on a prorated scale. Once equipped with both of these, you can ride for unlimited mileage at 50% of the standard fare on 3125 miles of Federal trackage and lake routes, 144 private railways, 9 private steamship lines, and unlimited postal motor coaches (this sentence has made us reach for our vitamins). They're obtainable only at railway stations (2-to-24 hours' notice) or through travel agents *within Switzerland.* Please remember that your passport photo must be submitted with your application. For further details, see the man at the window.

Fifth is the **Party type**. Groups of 10 to 24 persons get a 25% reduction. If most of your in-laws are with you, take advantage of the 35% discount for parties of 25 or more. Validity is for 2 months, and if more than 15 adults travel together, the tour conductor may ride free.

But don't forget first to look into the Eurailpass if you are touring other countries as well.

An interesting statistic: If the 5000 bridges and 700 tunnels of the Swiss Federal Railways were stretched out in a line, they would reach over 275 miles.

★ **TIPS** An excellent time-, sweat-, profanity-, and worry-saver is to arrange with your hotel concierge (give him at least 1 hour's advance notice) for your luggage to be shipped separately in the baggage car of the train—usually the same one or ones that you ride. This is a *wonderful* help, particularly if you must make changes (Geneva to St. Moritz, for example, involves 2). Very inexpensive and 99½% dependable.

Old trick: Buy a Second-class ticket and waltz over the landscape in deluxe style, highball in hand—by riding all the way in the dining car.

Children under 6 years of age ride as guests of the conductor and engineer; children from 6 to 16(!) pay ½-fare. For extensive traveling, men of 65 or over and women who will confess to 62 years of age may buy ½-fare tickets valid for 12 months; the "pass" for this status costs 80 francs. When applying for the Senior Citizens' privilege ask for the "Season Ticket for the Aged"—and we wonder who the 14-year old public relations stripling was who gave it *that* name!

☑ **FOOD** Switzerland has a superb cuisine; and unfailingly cosmopolitan service standards in the major cities or resorts. In fact, there are today many, many restaurants which outshine the one- two- and three-star firmaments of France. Countless times we have seen *grands chefs de cuisine* of neighboring Gaul seated at Swiss tables on their days off—and often taking notes surreptitiously. (Later when we are testing *their own* praiseworthy creations we are amused to discover fragments of Helvetia in those splendid "French recipes.") It's not all chocolate and cheese, as many visitors suppose. Being a crossroads nation, it offers a tremendous variety of international fare—plus culinary masterworks of its own, of course. Some hotels don't serve hot meals after 9 P.M., so check up on yours if you plan to be late.

Fondue is as local as baked beans in America; don't miss it, if you like cheese. It's

a vague Welsh rarebit made with white wine, into which you dunk (and swab) chunks of bread. When the opposite sex shares this dish, Swiss tradition dictates that the one who loses the bread off the fork owes the others a kiss; offenders beyond kissing age must buy the company a bottle of wine (no instances recorded). From Valais comes raclette, another melted cheese dish even more delicious than fondue.

As for straight cheeses, our favorites are Alpenzieger (Glarus), a sharp, tangy blend seasoned with green herbs; Vacherin du Mont d'Or, a winter product with the viscosity of Liederkranz—and that fine Gruyère..

Sausage is a national specialty, and each region has its own types. The big, fat Zürich version, a bologna with a Napoleonic complex, is one of the most succulent. Even more famous is the St. Gall Bratwurst. Order *any* kind of sausage—*any* time—with the fluffy, hashed-brown potatoes called Rösti, and you are in for a deeeeee-licious treat. Other typical offerings of this region include Geschnetzeltes nach Zürcher Art (thin-sliced veal with a cream sauce). Zürcher Leberspiessli (liver strips with sage seasoning, spit-roasted and served with beans), or Ratsherrentopf (mixed grill on a bed of rice or noodles). If you're only mildly hungry, order *Tellerservice,* which are snacks or hot items on one plate. .

Dinner in top places runs perhaps $35 without wine; prepared blue-plate specials can be had for about $8.50. At the other end of the scale, both the tearooms and the Mövenpick restaurants (an interesting combination of drugstore and cosmopolitan cookery, with branches in key cities) offer snacks and light meals for $5.50 or so. It's simply a matter of choosing your own category and spending what you please, because the range is ample. Prices are generally lowest in small villages or at train-depot eateries.

☑ **DRINKS** Everything is available including absinthe (illegal), at neck-snapping prices. Popular brands of Scotch cost about $17 per fifth; Canadian Club sells for about the same; imported gins and ryes are less. Supplies are ample. Highballs run from $2.25 to $3.50, and most of the bartenders could do just as well with a medicine dropper as they do with their jigger glasses.

Swiss wines? If you want to economize, order a glass of white wine instead of harder stuff; you'll find it refreshing. Almost any wine lover can instantly set them apart from good French, Spanish, or Italian vintages, even when blindfolded. They have a unique character of their own: A slight effervescence, a distinct tang to the tongue which is missing from all others. They take learning before true enjoyment can come. Most should be ordered young. (But even a mature character such as your humble author enjoys a glass or two.) The weather conditions, incidentally, in 1978 rendered Vaudois pressings scarce and expensive; hence you may detect a flavor of neighboring Valaisan grape which was added to take up the slack due to evaporation (about 8%) during the bottling process.

The majority of visiting Americans seem to prefer Johannisberg as their white and Dôle as their red. You'll always be reasonably safe if you order either of these sound old standbys. Personally, we happen to prefer the Cortaillod of Neuchâtel to the Dôle, but that's merely a matter of taste. Other satisfactory types, at random, are Oeil de Perdrix (Geneva area), Maienfelder, Altstätter, and Churer-Schiller (St. Gall and the

Grisons), Crépy, Mont d'Or, Dézaley, and St. Saphorin (Lavaux), Fendant and Tor-
renté-Château la Tour (Valais), and Cru de Champréveyres or the sparkling whites of
Bienne or Neuchâtel. If you can find it, Heida-Gletscherwein from near Visp's glacier
zones comes from Europe's highest vines. Here are the best of the land.

Swiss beer is cheap and plentiful. Swiss brewers seem to make an ideal potion for
invalids, old ladies, and nursing mothers. All brands we've tried share a watery, Mil-
quetoast spinelessness. The Cardinal brand seems to embody the most zing. Dixie
drinkers, however, may draw a draught of southern comfort from a brew called Beauregard. The label slogan reads "SPECIALE BLONDE, SPEZIAL HELL." Saddleup,
Genruhl! Dat South's gonna rise agin'!

For teetotalers, the noncarbonated, natural white or red grape juice called Grapillon
is wonderfully uplifting, if you like a sweet drink; about 75¢, but be sure it's served icy
cold. Apfelsaft is a pleasant and soft apple cider; the milk-based Rivella product is still
taking the country by storm. Domestic cola types are preferred to U.S. colas by many
Swiss, mainly for reasons of thrift.

Kirsch, made from the juice of compressed cherry pits, is the national hard drink. It
is to fondue what an embrace is to a lover. Don't miss a sample of this fiery, rather bitter
spirit, especially with cheese or fruit.

Pear liqueur is equally characteristic and even more delicious. Pear brandy (Eau de
Vie de Poire Pure) has oversize vertebrae and bulging biceps. Shut your eyes, take a sip,
and then blow—IF you can (but not near a lighted candle, please).

The most astonishing Swiss liqueur is Appenzeller Alpenbitter. Appenzell is the town
and Alpenbitter is the product—"Alpine Bitters," made up of the essences of 67 different
flowers and roots. In taste it is vaguely reminiscent of gin-and-tonic consumed in a
perfume factory, but don't let this stop you from sampling a genuine curiosity among
potables.

Another flag-waving oddity is the so-called Marmot Chocolat Suisse—in taste a kissin'
cousin of Crème de Cacao, with tiny cubes of extrasuave milk chocolate floating in the
upper half of the bottle. All it needs is cheese and a wristwatch in the bottom half to
make it 200% Swiss.

Absinthe, long banned by the Government, is bootlegged all over the land. The base
is wormwood elixirs; Pernod, as most travelers know it, is the watered-down version.
You'll find it in almost every rural inn or tavern—but the proprietor must trust you
before he'll serve you, just as in the U.S. speakeasy days. Ask for it with sugar and water;
it will probably be dispensed in a porcelain beer mug to fool the police. The price is about
$2.50 per glass; treat it with utmost respect, because the "proof" is sometimes 120 or
136 against the 100 proof of the strongest ryes and bourbons in the States.

☑ **TIPPING** An automatic service charge of 15% across-the-board in all cafés, restaurants, and hotels is in operation. This means you can greatly reduce your individual
gratuities. Even taxis now include a 15% supplement automatically, so the tab alone is
what you should pay.

☑ **LOCAL RACKETS** Solely among a scattering of Swiss taxi drivers have we ever
found any dishonesty in this nation. The only other reader-complaints we've ever had

about Swiss ethical patterns were on a similar minor subject: the Kurtax (at Interlaken, for example, you're given a little shopping brochure issued by the merchants in return for this extra tax which is automatically slapped on your hotel bill). These are trifles. Switzerland is one of the most honest and upright communities on the globe today.

Curious sidelight: The integrity of the famous "Swiss Made" stamp on wristwatches was recently subjected to a crass indignity with the discovery of floods of Italian-wrought phonies on the *Swiss* market—each one bearing proud Helvetian trademarks. These fakes, worth $2.30 apiece, were peddled for between $34.50 and $46! Italian authorities have now cracked down on the bogus workshop and its *tempus fugitives.* Nevertheless, avoid all street-hawkers' "bargains" in timepieces, no matter how tempting.

☑ **INFORMATION CENTERS**   Since ¼th of the national investment is tied up in tourism, the Swiss are all-out to cater to the visitor. The **Swiss National Tourist Office** is a whopping enterprise; no country in the world can match it for size or spread. They have the most voluminous, most readable collection of free guidebooks we've ever seen. Their architects are studying 44 vacation centers street by street, hotel by hotel, and room by room, planning new partitions and bathrooms as far ahead as A.D. 2001.

General Manager of the worldwide SNTO network is Walter Leu. While this gentleman's mind, body, and soul are totally devoted to visitors to his land, please don't hoist your troubles onto this busy executive's doorstep. Instead, if any extraordinary situation should arise while you are in Switzerland, communicate with the young and dynamic Press and Public Relations Director Peter Kuhn at the headquarters at Bellariastr. 38, CH-8027, in a residential part of Zürich (Billoweg tram stop)—but, for heaven's sake, don't bother him either about inconsequentials. For everyday travel questions go to the Tourist Office at 15 Bahnhofplatz, which is a member of the master network.

By all means visit one of their branches before or during your trip. The *New York* office, at 608 Fifth Ave, is under the aegis of Helmut Klee; in the *San Francisco* bureau at 250 Stockton St. that Golden Gate-way is swung by Willy Isler; a modest subagency also functions with Beat Bächler manning the deck at 106 S. Michigan Ave. in *Chicago*; Max Lehmann is Switzerland's man in *Toronto*. Many cities in Latin America have SNTO representatives; so does practically every capital of Europe. And every Swiss town, no matter how small, has its "**Verkehrsverein**," Tourist Promotion, or Official Enquiry Office. They'll give you free expert advice.

CITIES

BERNE, the capital, is one of the few undestroyed medieval cities of Europe, and it's charming. The Aare River divides it twice, in a horseshoe, and the turreted buildings on its banks look like an illustration from *Grimm's Fairy Tales.* The world's oldest and largest horological puppet show every hour in its historic Clock Tower; famous fifteenth-century Bear Pits, housing the city's traditional mascots; excellent hotels, fine little shops, covered sidewalks, winding streets (many of them now experiencing an experimental traffic ban), an almost rural atmosphere; 18-hole golf course 11 miles out, with clubhouse, restaurant, and pool. Here is certainly one of the most historically and architecturally engaging seats of government in the world, but as with many

administrative hubs, when the sun sets it concentrates more on decorous repose rather than on fun and frivolity.

BERNE HOTELS Quick Reference Table

Price categories by national (not U.S.) standards.

EXPENSIVE:

Bellevue Palace Kochergasse 3. Tel. 224581; Telex 32124; 221 rooms. P. 937
Schweizerhof Schweizerhoflaube. Tel. 224501; Telex 32188; 120 rooms. P. 937

UPPER MODERATE:

Metropole Zeughausgasse 28. Tel. 225021; Telex 33144; 110 rooms. P. 937
Savoy Neuengasse 26. Tel. 224405; Telex 32445; 60 rooms. P. 937

MODERATE:

Alfa Laupenstrasse 15. Tel. 253866; Telex 32480; 40 rooms. P. 937
Bären Schauplatzgasse 4. Tel. 223367; Telex 33199; 56 rooms. P. 937
Bristol Schauplatzgasse 10. Tel. 220101; Telex 33199; 76 rooms. P. 938
City Bubenbergplatz 7. Tel. 225377; 55 rooms. P. 938
Krebs Genfergasse 8. Tel. 224942; 42 rooms. P. 938
Nydeck Gerechtigkeitsgasse 1. Tel. 228686; 18 rooms. P. 937
Regina Mittelstr. 6. Tel. 230305; 45 rooms. P. 938
Stadthof Speichergasse 27. Tel. 227727; 30 rooms. P. 938
Wächter Mövenpick Gentergasse 4. Tel. 220866; 45 rooms. P. 938

LOWER MODERATE:

Arca Gerechtigkeitsgasse 18. Tel. 223711; 22 rooms. P. 938
Continental Zeughausgasse 27. Tel. 222626; Telex 33055; 35 rooms. P. 938

ENVIRONS:

Goldenes Kreuz Gerzensee. Tel. 980836; 28 rooms. P. 938
Le Vieux Manoir au Lac Morat. P. 938

Hotels You'd expect to find outstanding accommodations in this "nation of hotelkeepers" (said again without derision), and you most certainly do. Most of Switzerland's 8000-plus stopping places for transients are models of comfort, cleanliness, and efficiency; elevators work, maids don't talk your ear off, breakfast comes so hot it burns your gullet. Not only is the Swiss hotel manager an institution from Buenos Aires to Birmingham, but the Swiss concierge is such a fixture that many of the current crop are the 4th or 5th generation in the trade.

Prices vary considerably, but they've been frozen by law for the past few years. Perhaps 30% of Swiss hotels feature a modified American plan (room, 2 meals, and basic tips included in the bill). On this arrangement (3 meals plus lodging), you'll pay around $50 per person per day. Deluxe metropolitan hotels and resorts such as St. Moritz double, triple, or even quadruple these figures. As a median guideline, however, we'd peg a twin accommodation with bath in a substantial Swiss address at around $75, plus service and taxes but usually inclusive of continental breakfast.

In this capital we're always deeply fond of the ever-luxurious, 130-room **Schweizerhof**, with the most convenient location for shoppers. It is far, far ahead of anything else in the city proper—but do look at our comments on the out-of-towners further down. This house blends the fabulous Gauer-family antique collection with up-to-the-minute streamlining in living facilities; each hallway, for example, offers almost priceless collections from different periods (3rd floor in seventeenth century, 4th all-Swiss floor with ancient rifles, harness, a sleigh, *et al.*)—while each of the staff carries a short-wave "Walkie-Talkie" locator. When you pick up the direct-dial phone in your room it automatically switches off the radio, turning it on again when you put down the receiver! One of the most captivating innovations is the Simmental Stube, a dining salon of a fine old house that was dismantled and reassembled to the last splinter as a cozy restaurant; moreover, there's a brand-new ultra-posh nightclub featuring live orchestra music, the Arcady Snack-Bar, with entrances to both the hotel and the appendant Gübelin jewelry arcadia, and an underground tunnel to the Berne station where there is ample covered parking space for motorized clients. The outstanding Horseshoe Grill adjoins. General Manager Jean-Jacques Gauer, personable son of the founders; Concierge Louis Achermann surely one of the best in Europe; a few suites with 2 tubs and 2 showers in the same bathroom. If you're a wealthy Easterner or a poverty-stricken Texan, cross your fingers for one of the trio of apartments (#110, #210, #310); all windows have now been soundproofed. The favorite hotel abroad of scores of travelers. The 200-room **Bellevue-Palace**, high on the riverbank, has a beautiful view of the Alps and a décor which is being updated now that Swiss banking interests are involved. New Manager Fritz Maeder and his wife, Lotti, are adding 50 rooms on the fifth floor for this season; restaurants have been revamped and moved within the older shell; the grill now holds hands with a nightclub and expanded bar plus lounge—the dust is really flying and good things are happening. Big sun-front dining terrace, commanding the valley; suave and friendly concierge and service; scads of thoughtfully executed amenities. The majority of bedchambers are spacious, in Old World taste throughout. A steadily improving picture of traditional grace and modern comfort.

The **Metropole** may be short on bedroom space, but its public sancta are a cheering delight. Colorful, woody Brasserie with beer-wagon theme, Vieux Moulin grill with a working waterwheel, gaily decorated President-Club bar. Lots of fun in an altogether odd-ball fashion—which we'll bet foreign visitors will love. The midtown **Savoy**, oh-so-handily located, cooks up the corner Burgunderstube as the most appealing unit of its 5-part dining setup. Of its 71 bedrooms, 25 have full-tub baths, 25 have showers, and all have essential plumbing and radios; just a few attractive accommodations are available (#230 is an example). Heavy South American trade in summer. Talk was rife that it may be renewed very soon. The **Alfa** has a snack bar and a restaurant within its poured-concrete hull. Efficiency is the word, but this gets dressed up nicely in the bedchambers. Book the larger doubles for comfort and away from the busy Seilerstrasse for peaceful slumber. The **Nydeck** is an inexpensive choice in the city's antique district. Very nice people running it; spare but prim; especially good for singles. **Bären** romps in with 60 rooms, 30 baths, and 30

showers; bright décor; its only fancy quarters are #215, #315, and #415. Adequate. The **Krebs** is sprightly and very clean; 42 rooms, many with bath or shower—and these are the better bets; breakfast only; a value for the price. The **Wächter Mövenpick** is in the same bracket; #209 is a pleasant wood-lined twin. The **Regina**, 10 minutes from the center in a residential section, is also petite; breakfast is the only meal; good bet when the kids are along. The centrally sited **Bristol** is colorful in a modern plaid-and-plastic fashion. Not bad for modest budgets and breakfast-only overnighters. (If it's a rather special night, room #10 is the honeymoon suite; it comes with its own swimming pool in the apartment!) The **City** has experienced an urban renewal program; it is moderate in cost and useful for short stopovers. The **Stadthof** claims no lobby at all. But it *does* boast a Swiss-style Grill with rôtisseries and a mini-mini-mini-bar that are cute. The many mini rooms might be okay for elves, but not for our personal full fathom of flesh. The **Continental** can easily be missed. The **Arca** is a good bet for skinny-pursed-and-bodied budgeteers; very small cells.

About 20 minutes by car from Berne on the route to Lausanne, there is a small paradise known as **Le Vieux Manoir au Lac** just outside of *Morat* (or *Murten* in German). It sprawls lazily across a greensward that slopes to the lake and peeps through the trees at the Jura Range. Structure of wood, stone, and stucco; tiny boat harbor at the garden's edge; dining salon with brocade panels, paned windows, and an aristocratic yet cozy bearing; comfortably updated and tastefully accoutred bedchambers in a manorhouse style. Our cuisine was outstanding as was the ultra-friendly service. Try the perch from the lake, also the local wine which is distinctive and, we think, extraordinary. Young, amiable Director Hans Scherrer is a highly skilled, warmhearted host. For a meal, a holiday, or a lifetime, this one is recommended.

Another inviting country house outside the capital is the **Goldenes Kreuz** at *Gerzensee* which also studies a lake scene, meadows, and vine lands in the Bernese valleys. The neat, 28-room hotel is separated from the restaurant section. The latter is composed of a popular-priced hunting segment on road level where locals sip wine and spin yarns; down a handsome flight is the luxury category grill with elegant décor, wood panels, and explosions of flowers in season; flowing from this is an open terrace commanding a vista that will make you think you've been transported to your Maker. A marvelous experience for tranquillity seekers.

Restaurants The Simmental Stube and the famous Horseshoe Grill of the **Schweizerhof** are unquestionably above everything else in the city limits. The former is the dining room of an old mansion, transplanted intact. The Horseshoe Grill has *gemütlich* dimensions, versatile menu, wine list so staggering that the printing probably costs a bottle per copy, and artful drink blending; huge, juicy steaks with corn-on-the-cob (!) year round. The tip of the top. For a taste of old Berne, we love an ancient tavern called **Zum Löwen** ("Inn of the Lion") at the nearby suburb of *Worb* where this establishment has been in continuous operation for more than 600 years. Patinated stucco walls; tile *Kachelofen* (oven); cozy alcoves; delicious simple regional cookery at modest prices. Try it. **Charley's Beef Corner** slices into you-know-what on its main floor, which resembles a woody sort of brasserie. Excellent grills, steak sandwiches, and huge bowls of mixed salad for surprisingly moderate tabs. Our

service could have been better, but the atmosphere doesn't seem to require highly trained minions. Downstairs is the Cadillac discothèque in upbeat modern tones, a den for young executives and their cuties. A successful package. So is the popular priced **Churrasco**, an Argentinian chain-bred hoofer that appears with frequency in German grazing grounds these days. At the **Rossli** in *Säriswil* (15 minutes by car) you can grill your own meat in the rustic farmhouse. For *cous-cous,* you might like **Ali Baba**. **Frohsinn** near the cathedral, is small but good. **Pomodoro** has frolicsome décor and inexpensive pizzas; it's not bad for a quick meal. The **Galaxy**, rigged out as a ship, nets a fair catch of water-bred denizens. **Mistral** blows in with the cuisine of Provence served in an ancient cellar. Vaulted brick ceiling, stone walls, terra-cotta floors, hanging lanterns plus fat spluttery candles on polished dark-wood tables. The ground floor breezes in with a nice bar and lounge for lighter refreshments and freshets of conversation. Even more antique is the 400-year-old **Klötzlikeller**, a typical subterranean student hangout. **Harmonie** captures a similar choir of warblers. **Della-Casa** (Schauplatzgasse 16) presents a listless café at street level, but an ingratiating, low-ceiling, wood-lined restaurant above. Soft lights; leaded windows; planter boxes; menu with selections ranging from Zarzuella to Calf's Knuckles; wine card covering the slopes of the Valais (Switzerland) to the flats of Benisalem (Mallorca). Closed Sunday. For Swiss specialties, the rustic, simple, inexpensive Taverne Valaisanne of the **Hotel Hirschen**, a few steps from the above-mentioned Schweizerhof, has come up under Leo Wellig's care and is fun again. **Restaurant Räblus** (Zeughausgasse 3, near the Clock Tower) is Gallic in accent. Upstairs dining room; simple décor with wine bottles; downstairs bar with pianist; flaming specialties are featured. Cleverly merchandised atmosphere that is more cconvincing than the cuisine. Fun and—happily—open until 1 A.M. Monday through Saturday; closed Sunday. **Ratskeller** (Gerechtigkeitsgasse 81) is about as Ratskellery as the Eiffel Tower—which isn't situated in a cellar, either. Cuisine basically French, with a few Italian dishes (Pappagallo Bolognese, Fritto Misto, and the like) thrown in for spice; extra-creditable wine list; menu available in English; waiters amiably accommodating. The décor is undistinguished Swiss-modern, with the only notable departure the stuffed beaver which greets you at the door with paws outstretched. They try hard—but a good French bistro does exactly the same thing better. Closed Mondays. **Le Dézaley** is the budget choice of a Helvetian friend who knows his calories; we've never set tongue to fondue here, but we accept his verdict with alacrity. **Kornhauskeller** is a baronial German-type beer cellar, dominated by a massive wine barrel and made glad (evenings only) with an oomp-pah band; trendcherman's fare, substantial cookery, horrible service, moderate tariffs; try the home-grown Berner Platte; recommended to sausage-and-sauerkraut fans. **Du Théâtre** is celebrated for its kitchen—especially since Chef Schlegel performs here; he is a guarantee of fine viands and practiced attention. The famous **Mövenpick** chain now boasts 4 capital branches, and "capital" they are, as drop-in feederies. They all sport the usual handsome décor and the characteristically huge range of prices. The one with the Gade Restaurant is tops, in our opinion. The **Café Rudolf** is routine but agreeable. The **Commerce**, a bistro that serves Spanish fare, is noted locally for its Paella, its Arroz Marinera (fish soup), and other Iberian

exports cooked up by Enrique Ros. The 10-table room is about as sullen as a squid's glare, but the cuisine sparkles if you hanker for Spanish calories. If you ride the rods this season, you may want to sample the wares at any of the **Railway Station Restaurants** in midtown; they chug up with variety, savor, and boilers of steam. There's a self-service snackery at track level; the conventional dining platforms are upstairs.

Night Life This city is now glutted with cheapy, boring dance bars that cropped up to allay the loneliness of its thousands of foreign workers. American tourists would feel decidedly out of place in them. Outside of these, the town's hottest burner is the **Mocambo**. Its Scotch Bar is at street level; reasonably attractive and very busy on Saturday night. Main enterprise in the cellar; spacious, multitiered sanctum, wrapped on 3 sides by tables at the balcony stratum; small bar in one corner. Dramatic Braille-provoking cell with 1-watt illumination and blue-and-white paneling; 5-piece band, with organ-inspired music straight off the corncob; dance floor more jammed than a Virginia turkey farm in early November. Hour-long cabaret at 10 P.M. and midnight. **Chikito** (within a block of Mocambo geographically, but perhaps 10 blocks down in quality) draws a younger crowd; in its slightly lighter gloom, we glimmed only 2 or 3 old men of 27 or 28. The **Babalu** bounced in after our night-beat along the Gurtengasse. Two bars adjoin, including the local **Playboy Club**. The **Happy Light**, a disco-spinner in the Casino, also was switched on recently. **Cadillac** shifts nightly into a dine-and-dancery. The Schweizerhof's new night-club, **Jaylin's**, should be open by the time you arrive.

Other Targets

AROSA is a spellbinder for looks, but not a lass with quite the same patrician panache as St. Moritz, a chic competitor that resides 68 miles to the north. Her surrounding hills are peopled by funloving Swiss and by a seeming flood of prosperous German visitors. Numerous woodland trails, ski slopes, ski lifts, aerial cableway, and chair hoists; a cross-country ski school at Maran; glorious 2-hour excursion up to 7600 feet over the famous Arlenwald Circle by horse-drawn sleigh; summer 9-hole golf course, horseback riding, tennis, fishing, rowing, Alpine bathing "beach"; superb sport accommodation; all varieties of cookery, from refined hotel cuisine, to a good selection of restaurants in the town, to tavern meals high up on the slopes. If you should need any help here, the hardworking, alert local Tourist Chief, H.R. Zünd, is a mighty good man to see or to know; he does his job with utmost efficiency, and he's always ready with expert assistance.

In the upper crust of hotel circles, 3 houses—each with its own personality and appeal—are outstanding. The **Tschuggen** is stunning if your taste chooses the slalom run for modernity. Proprietors Julie and Armin Wyssmann have invested a shah's ransom in creating a holiday nucleus that glitters almost as brightly as any contender in the Swiss Alps. The public rooms are vast and handsomely outfitted; there's a pool on the roof, plus a sauna, massage parlor, and panoramic snackery; there's a full ski shop in the basement, a zinging discothèque, a bowling center, and a sweet little *Stübli* where a warning on a gigantic cowbell advises "Whoever rings buys a round!" The dining room is airy; the grill adjoining the ballroom-bar is inviting; there's dancing to an

orchestra every night. The twentieth-century bedchambers—replete with every conceivable comfort while providing hectares of space—focus their wide-angle windows on a Kodak kingdom of natural beauty. Instead of the snow-flake emblems worn by its staffers, you might just as well imagine buttons proclaiming that "We Try Harder"—because they truly do! The **Kulm** now appears in fresh modernistic raiments that blend glass, wood, and happiness into one effervescent cocktail. Finally, the accommodations match the quality of its general allure—a winner now in all respects, especially for sporting types. There's enough whoop-de-do per hour here to make a Catskill social director hide in terror. Sparkplug of this jovial case of internal combustion is the debonair Hans Leu (rightfully rhymes with "joy"), an alumnus of Zürich's fabulous Dolder Grand (and, we suspect, also a graduate of Barnum & Bailey, Disneyland, and Tinker Toys Inc.). Here, too, the tireless holidaymaker will find the supercharged range of recreational facilities as well as a "fitness and beauty" program—probably developed to help revelers recover from all of the other excitements. Glass-sheathed swimming pool with tickling water jets; sauna; solarium; bowling; old bar moved to the "entertainment area"; most major ski runs at your doorstep; ice rink; an American-style grill with yumptious beef imported from the U.S.; lounges, games and events galore. For high-stepping gaiety, throw away your Miltowns and check in here. Exhaustedly recommended. The **Park** captures the crown for pure alpine esthetics. The woodwork, the carefully hewn polite rusticity, the costumed staffers, the mandate on coziness—all conspire to give this house a mellow glow of a deluxe Arcadia. Unfortunately, however, its situation in a viewless bottomland makes this the least appealing of the Big Three. Perhaps you'll disagree. The **Savoy** —lovingly renewed—seems to have a mandate on charm. Rich open timbers counterpoint the white stucco walls; antiques dot the lounges; new sparkle is everywhere—from bright textiles to smiling faces. Newest wing of 20 doubles; swimming pool; sauna; dancing, bowling, high living at reasonable prices. The **Prätschli**, product of a successful architect turned hotelier, is away from the center in its own hillside domain. Proprietor Graessly, a well-intentioned hobbyist, seems to extend greetings to more Teutonic clients than to any other nationality, so we think that wayfarers who speak only English might not find it as convivial as the multinational enclaves of the Tschuggen and the Kulm. The **Hof Maran**, also on the Prätschli slopes, turns on 85 rooms, most of which claim private baths. The vivacious will find a 9-hole golf course, ice skating, tennis, children's recreation, skiing, and curling. Dining room, grill, cafeteria, and separate restaurant; comfortable bedchambers with ample space and good baths. Proprietor Traber has a warm affection for Americans. Recommended. The **Bellevue** is an excellent bet—franc-ly speaking. Keen administration by friendly, hard-driving Fredy Hold; attractive Arven Restaurant downstairs; cozy bar-lounge; orchestra for après-ski terpsichore; 75 balconied rooms and 66 baths. Try for its corner units. Very good. The **Valsana** draws a lively young set; its bar glows with robust revelers when the snowflakes fall; there's a pool to add to the splash. Fun, but don't sleep here. The totally refashioned **Alexandra** offers space for 200 sleepyheads, but we've not yet snoozed among them. The **Seehof** has 78 rooms and 40 baths; it's okay. For the economy-minded, the **Merkur** might be just the thing. **Des Alpes** is a foothill of its former self.

Excelsior has begun to come up again since its restyling. All 80 units with bath; swimming pool. Showing promise. The **Central** is also very worthy, now that it has repaneled its bedchambers; it is noted for its kitchen. Many Arosa hotels are closed during part of April, all of May, part of June, and all of November; exceptions are 10 Second-class hostelries and 15 boardinghouses which operate throughout the year, most of which are simple, clean, and comfortable.

As for restaurants, the **Central**, bound neatly in Arven wood, features regional dishes from the Grisons. The **Kursaal** (Casino) comes up with 3 bars, 2 orchestras, and vittles. Most appetites are shackled to their hotel pension plans. While the **Tschuggen** and other major hotels don't require registrants to dine in the house, most smaller ones do. The **Kulm**, more informal in the hotel or at its amusing tavern by the ice rink, has the top cuisine, in our franc opinion. Its steaks are prime. The **Park** is handsome; now the cookery and service are superior, too. The bars of the **Posthotel** and the **Carmenna** hop to lively lilts in season. The grill of the **Savoy** is a gem for eye appeal, as is the Relais de Champagne in the **Valsana**.

ASCONA   Here's how we rate the hotels locally: (1) The youthful and scenic **Sasso Boretto** (a beaut with pool and sauna; directed by Mr. and Mrs. Nötzli), (2) **Europe au Lac** (modern Italian motif; 2 sides of triangular construction face lake; private beach and swimming pool; closed Nov. through mid-Mar.; excellent cuisine; happy resort choice).

BAD RAGAZ   (1) **Grand Hotel Quellenhof** (indoor thermal swimming pool for hotel residents only; 18-hole golf course; rambling, classic spa style; closed in winter; setting and region reminiscent of Interlaken; lovely for serenity), (2) **Grand Hotel Hof Ragaz** (also with an indoor splasher). (3) **Touring Mot-Hotel Schloss Ragaz** (conventional hotel, with motel in gardens; good but not luxurious).

BASEL   Here's a cultured dowager who is so cosmopolitan that she shares her roots with both France and Germany; she is also a major financial center. The confluence of these social and economic wellsprings provides the city with a unique richness that discriminating voyagers appreciate. The Kunstmuseum, as one outstanding example, offers such variety, not to mention quality, that it alone warrants a visit to this riverbank town; its many antiquities, its Holbein collection plus 22 other museums, its university (which was in operation before Columbus weighed anchor), its zoo, its extraordinary chemical plants, and its skyline on the Rhine are additional lures for adventurers. The Carnival in February is so spectacular for costumery and revels that it daunts the imagination, if not the stamina; the music and festivities are literally nonstop; the atmosphere is merry; the air is spiked with jovial toasts night and day. Most of the gaiety occurs in the Old Town where auto traffic is prohibited. The Swiss Industries Fair in April is said to be interesting; we've not yet seen it.

Hotels   We continue to lead off with the veteran **Euler**, near the station. While always tip-top, we expect it to climb another several rungs up the quality ladder now that it is being administered by the Gauer team, which headquarters at Berne's glorious Schweizerhof. Its massive redecoration program has

been enormously successful, providing banquet facilities, an underground passage connected to the new subway, a basement cafeteria, a spacious carpark
and the rear courtyard. For traditionalists, this house remains the pacesetter.
For modernists, the **Hilton** occupies a pleasant residential situation and functions efficiently—albeit without much personality. Lobby so small that it really
should be termed a foyer; dignified, darkwood Wettstein Grill with candle
illumination, orange textiles, brass-trimmed dividers, friendly service and fair
cuisine; Bora Bora Bar and Polynesian-style discothèque; poorly executed Café
de la Marine Suisse, which labors to achieve a lakefront theme; pool facing
inner court; sauna; ample parking. We'd classify the bedchambers as Internationally Nondescript, yet they are well outfitted and colorful, with narrow
dimensions and inside baths. The staff reflect the courtesy and cheer of their
Basle homeland. Our recent stay here was satisfactory. The **Drei Könige**
("Three Kings"), founded in A.D. 1026, is Switzerland's oldest hotel. It used
to be our favorite (yep, far more recently than in the eleventh century). Sadly,
the antique touches which gave it its particular charm have now been almost
totally erased; its now-modernized units seem flat and uninteresting by comparison, although the refreshened riverfront units still offer a wondrous view.
Streetside rooms air-conditioned, with triple-plate glass installed to ssssssh the
traffic din, but still so far from adequate that earplugs are provided by every
bed. Our recent meal in its viewfull dining salon was a grim disappointment.
This venerable house impresses us as being overpriced for land-view locations
—but, for its better offerings overlooking the Rhine, it is acceptable. **Alban-
Ambassador** is moving up steadily due to the keen ministrations of Jürg
Aenishänslin. Air-conditioned public rooms; modernistic rôtisserie and grillroom; with better-than-average culinary production; bar; sauna; hairdresser
and barber; minigolf; automated parking facility with slots keyed to the
driver's room number. Airy units, each with stocked refrigerator; radios and
alarm clocks throughout; small baths; better and better every season. The
200-room **International** has been taking pep pills; it has become a much higher
octane operation. Plenty of color in the Modern Convention Hotel approach;
especially cheerful pool, sauna, and gymnastic facilities very well architected
and maintained; main dining room, with rich timbers, stone, and wrought iron;
appetizing rôtisserie and chummy tavern; full air conditioning; a few viewless
cubicles; others crackling with flair. Dynamic Director R. F. Gasteyger is
doing a first-rate job here. Very good in the medium-to-high bracket. The
175-room **Europe** is divided with 4 floors in the main building and 3 in the
annex; an uncovered walk through a garden joins the independent units.
Decorative highlights include toy planes, old fire-fighting equipment (don't
worry), antique mirrors, a lee-boarded ship's model, and the whimsical
Bajazzo restaurant which features a harlequin theme. Rooms are compact, but
overall it boasts an upbeat package of hotel wares. The rose-colored **Basel** is
in the old quarter; it generally carries out the antique motif with modern
comfortizing touches. The age-old impression is rendered immediately by the
façade with its covered promenade, wood, and theatrical lighting. Stone-lined
restaurant with crackling grill; amusing bars and cozy corners; historic corridors; fitness room; space limited in bedchambers, with the most imaginative
ones on the fifth floor. A mixture that's a good one. The **Schweizerhof**, more

than a century old, has been updated recently. Rates hover in the welkin zones for the earthy rewards; #36 is one of its best maximum twins. Okay, but a bit steep. **Victoria-National** welcomes guests with an artful lobby depicting scenes from the local zoo, the fish market, the festival, and the tower. Limited in space but very clean; 40% with bath and shower; double-glazed windows on the noisier front; 5th-floor units with balconies on the façade. Warming up. The youthful, cozily conceived **Alexander** boasts many winning charms. Each floor has its rooms named for cities; town maps of their individual namesakes are in each bedchamber—an inexpensive but clever means of smashing institutionality to smithereens. The restaurant has been outfitted in weathered timber impacted in white stucco and dressed with farm implements; the cooking focuses on provincial recipes. Space limitations are a problem, but they are so cloaked in attractiveness that for brief stopovers we don't think you'll mind. We like it for its type. The **Jura** is interesting from an artistic point of view. It is almost a museum first and a hotel second, with works of Braque, Matisse, Léger, Rouault, Poliakoff abounding and a vast Etruscan collection of artifacts dominating the dining area. Simple, clean, cheap accommodation. A reward, in our opinion. Also inexpensive are the modern 60-room **Merian** with its riverside Café Spitz and breathtaking Old Town vistas, and the waterfront **Kraft**, also with a charming Rhine-lapped restaurant. Good buys for good living. **Drachen** is a candidate in the contemporary crop of functional houses. Its 40 narrow-dimension rooms are skillfully planned. All have air conditioning, radio, rental TV outlet, private strongbox built into the floor of the wardrobe, and courtside situation for added quiet; tiny baths. **Excelsior** added 2 dining salons and completed a total overhaul of the structure a while back. Busy-busy-busy, with a Shell gas pump at the front door. The **Bernina** has 30 chambers and a modest mien. The **Alfa** is adequate for autoists shunting between Germany and Zürich; for others, it is too far out.

Restaurants Basel can feel pride for its **Bruderholz**, one of the finest practioners of traditional cooking arts in the nation but still not so set in its ways that Owner-Chef Hans Stucki does not venture occasionally into fresh fields of gastronomy. The house (a mansion really) occupies a residential address with several salons providing different moods—all of them distinguished, rich, and exquisite. Immaculate reception; perfect service; deluxe accoutrements featuring polished crystal, brass chandeliers, candles, flowers set in vitrines; décor chiefly derived from 19-century furnishings and paintings. For summer there is a cheerful terrace through French doors for sipping and chatting. Menus at 3 prices or à la carte. It was a galvanic joy to experience such extraordinary quality for such reasonable tariffs. This one is a *must* for any traveling disciple of *haute cuisine*. **Donati** garners a loyal following, many of whom are fond of its varied and select Italian preparations. Our Lasagne was so blissful that we think it should serve as the definition for all Lasagnes. The Saltimbocca also was superb—and Parma ham just doesn't come better. Kooky (almost Dada-ist) theme drawn from the 1930's; highlighted with works by Chagall and Calder plus some rather ornate sculpture; one section with wood paneling and another suggestive of a brasserie; prices as easy to swallow as the excellent cookery. An experience that any follower of the arts should not miss if he ever claims to have visited Basel. Next comes the watch-ful

Rôtisserie de l'Horloge in the main Swiss Industries Fair Building (Mustermesse); this one ticks only during exhibition periods. It's a bit more jubilant than its neighboring horological exhibit. Expensive and fun. **Mediterranée** (next to Drei Könige) has a fresh appearance; the **Schützenhaus** ("Ranger's House") has color, good skilletry, and highish tabs; **Resslirytti** produced cookery on our try which seemed to come from a House of Horrors kitchen; the **Walliser-Kanne** is rustic and attractive; the **Casino** deals out so-so fodder. On a benign day, you might try the extremely variable but eye-appealing **Schloss Binningen**, in a park setting a few minutes from the center. It's a renovated thirteenth-century castle (Junior Prince size), with a small Wine Garden at its entrance, a *Gaststube* in its front room, an enchanting medieval-style *Trinkstube* upstairs (private parties only), a quiet and intimate dining room, and a knockout of a terrace for warm-weather dining (lunch or dinner). The cookery could be improved, but the atmosphere makes it worth the short ride. Medium expensive. In hotel circles, the **Euler** still walks off easily with the epicurean honors, while the **Drei Könige** ("Three Kings") still draws complaints from travelers. We had a nice bale of roast beef at the **Hilton's** quietly chic Wettstein Grill. The service was friendly and skilled; the atmosphere was elegant; the dark wood panels and polished brass added to the executive suiteness. Avoid the Caesar Salad—surely contrived by a Brutus. The **Alexander** is a reliable dining bet. **Red Ox Grill** and the **Golden Dragon Chinese Restaurant** are delightfully cozy and charming, and their cookery is delicious. **Goldenen Sternen** is only fair.

Basel folk know how to dine, but if you tire of fancy fare then try to sample two regional dishes that are typical of their cottage cooking: pea soup and liver-*rösti*.

BÜRGENSTOCK There's no place like it in the world. This 500-acre sky empire over the Lake of Lucerne (25 minutes from Lucerne proper) must be seen to be believed. A bronzed, good-looking magnate named Fritz Frey would need an alpenstock to count the Swiss francs spent to blast, carve, and whittle the top of his private Alp into a Deluxe resort. The result is eyepopping—the mountain vacationist's dream. Three hotels (the palatial **Grand,** the plush **Palace**—with every suite and bedroom now beautifully redecorated—and the more moderate **Park**), all hung with Van Dycks, Brueghels, Tintorettos, and the like, and all with a magnificent view; Mountain Inn for light refreshments at the 3000-foot peak, reached by one of Europe's fastest and highest elevators; 6-minute funicular to lakeshore bathing and quay for the 100-passenger Bürgenstock yacht; Guest Club entertainment center; nightclub; the world's most exclusive 9-hole Golf Club (Mr. Frey is its ONLY member, but he'll permit you to play); championship tennis courts; fine heated Alpine swimming pool with dancing at Poolside Café; and Underwater Bar for oglers; Golf Grill, Sporting Club, 2 orchestras, gala evenings, concerts, shopping center, beauty parlor, fashion shows, private chapel—this cloud-kissed community offers just about everything but harp solos by the neighboring angels. The latest baubles include an athletic club with an indoor pool (white marble set amid black marble terraces), a sauna, massage facilities (dry as well as underwater types), and a restaurant—all reached via a tunnel leading to a cliffside elevator. An

ancient Tavern has been remodeled and turned on for Burgenstock-brokers. Season: May to October for the Grand Park, and June to October for the Palace; everything shut tight in winter. As always, recommended with cheers.

CRANS-MONTANA is experiencing a boom. From a resident population of around 3500 in the sleepy Off Season, the crescent of hills which has lengthened on both ends of town can accommodate some 25-thousand sun-worshippers or snow-bunnies—many of them luscious weekday widows whose husbands join them for weekend frolics. If you don't mind alpine traffic jams, Crans, with its environs, can be a jovial swinger for a highland fling. This recently "discovered" Valais perch, 5000 feet above sea level in a glittering chalice, deserves a ranking a few rungs below St. Moritz and Gstaad. Virtually every major resort amenity is available: a championship golf course, heated swimming pools, horses, a casino, a theater, helicopter service, curling, and enough ski lifts (32 on our latest count, capable of hauling up 16-thousand people an hour) and runs to befuddle an athletic centipede. Costs are high, now that the spark of fashion has been kindled.

Among its hotels, the sleekly rustic **Royal,** overlooking a fir-flecked 9-hole golf course, offers the greatest rewards, in our opinions. Viewful, hearth-warmed main-floor lounges, bar, and dining room lined with glass; charming, lodgelike Caveau du Roy for Valais cheese specialties; cordial administration by Manager Gédéon Barras. All 80 havens with bath or shower; 50 bedchambers facing south, each with sunny balcony. Very sound. The **Golf** chips in with a tranquil setting at the edge of the major links. From your doorstep it's a putt to the first tee, a 5-minute hike to the ski lift, a totter for a splash in the covered swimming pool, and an hourly wait between bus shuttles to the village. This one is the social heartbeat of the hillfolk, but to us it looks as if it will soon need some spiffing up up in them thar hills, folks. The extensively remodeled **Excelsior** is managed by André Barras, cousin of the Royal's emperor. Modern lounge; nice bar; convenient playroom; balconies on the southern exposure; fresh-to-the-eye but cramped dimensions in the latest segment. Not bad. **Des Mélèzes,** an 8-iron shot from the Golf Club, is also on par. Here's an eagle in comfort for budgeteers. The **Rhodania** and **Richelieu** offer similar amenities in big sprawling houses at higher basic rates. Okay, but not raves. The former has the better chef, not to mention the sweet-toothed barman who dumped 6 (!) cherries into our Old Fashioned. The **Etoile** is agreeable for accommodations. The modern little **City** provides one of the best hotel kitchens in the region, for our money. The **Robinson** and the **Mont Blanc** are the best of the year-round operations. **De l'Etrier,** a good-looking A-frame structure in wood, comes up with 150 door keys for rentals on a monthly (perhaps on a weekly) basis. Tiny bar; no lounge; pool; superior for its type of apartment-hotel complex. The **Beau Séjour** and the **Eurotel** are adequate; many check into these because of their swimmeries. There are 3-dozen additional hotels or pensions on this mountain perch, plus a throng of guesthouses and apartment dwellings which are available. Most of the bigger ones are strictly seasonal. At *Montana* itself, the most impressive edifice for miles around is called **Supercrans**—and as an apartment citadel with a swimming moat that is just what it is. Super! The **Ambassador,** also with an aquatic

spread, is a chalet-style beaut. *Anzère,* a budding resort nearby, can provide additional kips in its tiny but ultracozy **Hôtel de Masque.** It remains a quiet village that is bound to wake up and roar very soon.

Crans-Montana nourishes most of its visitors either in its hotel dining rooms or in private chalets. Among the independents, only one really shines: the **Channe Valaisanne.** Typical foodstuffs and preparation of the Valais (as the name implies); raclette and fondue always steaming invitingly; functioning year round. As stolid as the mountains which surround it. **Rôtisserie de la Reine** offers an impressive international table ably lorded by Max Léonard. We enjoyed our meal; our eyes enjoyed the surroundings. In hotel circles, we'd pick the **Royal** if we were trying to impress Ursula Andress or the **City** if we were interested in cookery; the latter is modest. The **Sporting** is THE spot for dancing and for displaying the creations of the Paris fashion command. Rustic Upper Rhône décor; food mediocre but stunningly expensive; ties and jackets required on gentlemen. Chic as can be, but much, much better for *after*-dinner persuasions, in our opinion. **Le Français,** more informal, is usually more fun for the uninhibited. Other night stops include **The Club,** the **Pub, 400 Coups,** and **Whisky-A-Gogo,** which hop according to the season and the crowd on that particular evening.

CULLY The **Auberge du Raisin,** 6 miles from Lausanne, is a story-village hostelry run by the Gauer interests of Berne. The 10 rooms, individually decorated in French provincial style, nod "hello" to vine-covered slopes rising from Lac Léman; Chef Blokbergen brings his big city talents to these inviting country tables. If you desire tranquillity, try on the cuddles at Cully.

DAVOS Here is one of Europe's leading centers for winter sport. Its visitors are often youthful and purposeful on the slopes rather than fashion-oriented and idle. Among its hostelries, the **Belvedere,** just purchased by Germany's Steigenberger chain, is one of the brightest lights of the Alps. Many-balconied, block-long building; fresco-walled dining salon with carved wood ceiling and brick arcade; 2-level peasant-style Grill; play lounge for tots; 200 units and 120 baths. Now that the new owners have poured more than $3-million into improvement, it ought to be more glittering than ever. Most American ski buffs are as happy as seal pups here. The **Derby** also gleams with an inviting warmth. Approximately the same tariff level; chic clientele; atmospheric Palüda Grill; sauna and health center; its 145 bedrooms and 68 baths have been given a thorough renovation. Also recommended. The **Schweizerhof** recently was given a total renovation, plus addition of a Bel-Étage, balconies for its southern façade, and an indoor pool. The **Flüela,** next to the railway terminal, has effected many bedroom improvements, with additional goodies in the shape of uplifted public areas, a sizzling grill, a pool, a gym, and other recreational facilities. The **Post,** another in the Belvedere stable, swings with fun and frolic. There's a pool and a dapper 25-apartment wing called the Pöstli. We hear praise for the ever-expanding **Sunstar-Park** and for the renewed and scenically sited **Waldhotel Bellevue,** which is aptly named. Both sound mighty inviting. The **Europe** is a popular action station with the Young Set, who frolic in the Cabanna and

Grischa Cava night spots. Glass-lined swimming pool; sauna and massage; good basic comforts with few pretentions. **Seehof,** with its La Bohème club, also is a good bet for the spry. The **Des Alpes,** a young entry on the main drag, has small accommodations; breakfast only. One reader who did not enjoy her stay at the Belvedere highly recommends the **National,** which we've not seen recently. We'll pop in on our next hillclimb.

If you are not bound to your hotel vittles, try chicken curry and other Oriental specialties at **Meierhof.** The **Waldhotel-Bellevue** cops the honors for scenery; the kitchen is notable, too.

FLIMS   For overnighting, we'd pick the **Parkhotel Waldhaus** (with swimmery), followed by the **Adula** (also with pool) and the **Schweizerhof** (covered tennis and curling halls).

FRIBOURG   Here are our choices: (1) **De la Rose** (nightclub; 80 rooms, all with bath). (2) **Duc Bertold** (outstanding architecture; lovely appointments; top cuisine). (3) **Elite** (small and, well, elite).

GENEVA   is beautiful—and full of tourists. The lake is fantastically blue (except for the sparkling white plume of the world's tallest fountain—the Jet d'Eau). The atmosphere is French, the buildings are handsome, the gardens are bursting with color, and the streets are a blaze of Ferrari-red, Porsche-silver, DB-green and other hues of the international Sporting Set. If you want gaiety, action, and familiar faces, it's a fine place as a base for western operations.

Hotels   The century-old **Richemond** is a prizewinning nominee in fine hotel circles. There are an informality and warmth here which do not exist in other top-category hotels in formal, correct Switzerland. Direct credit for this can be traced to Jean Armleder, the supercharged proprietor, of the 3rd successive family generation to hold this post. Almost 90% of the establishment is furnished with traditional Continental softness and appeal; the spacious lobby has just been broadened still further and a day-bar added. Some units lately redone in Directoire style; a bevy of accommodations in sleek-rustic moods for more masculine tastes; a handful of less elaborate, small billets with daybeds, radio, wall-safe, additional telephone in the bathroom, and other twentieth-century innovations which are cheerful, utilitarian, and slightly sterile in aura. The Presidential Suite #407, with gold-silk walls, lovely blending colors, and refrigerator, is the chief-of-the-stately ticket; suite #510 is the largest in the house. One brand-new hyper-modern suite is a bow to the 21st century: number 610, with futuristic furnishings, brown walls, glossy turquoise ceiling, beige carpeting, and a circular marble bathtub in the center of the bedroom. We are especially fond of the belle époch Le Jardin and adjoining sidewalk café, both bursting with flowers. Le Gentilhomme grill-bar bubbles with its music and sophisticated clientele. Parking space has been obtained for 350 cars within 100 yards of the hotel. A superduper Phantom V Rolls Royce and a Mercedes Pullman limousine are at guests' disposal for airport or station pickup and excursions—a unique, silk-stocking fillip in this city. Highly recommended.

Hilton has just joined the stately homes of the Quai du Mont Blanc, reflecting handsomely beside Lake Geneva—one of the most ambitious and costly
links in the worldwide chain. There's an indoor-outdoor pool, a fitness center
with sauna and massage, plus ample dining facilities for putting back any
weight you might lose. You'll find a shopping lane, dancing, a modest casino,
and grand suites, smaller apartments, and well-appointed bedchambers with
color TV, frigo-bar, and the new Uniqey security system on a housewide basis.
It opened just after our latest Swiss research rounds so we did not stay here,
but early indications were promising indeed.

The lakeside **Beau Rivage** is sparkling as brightly as Leman's waters under
the dynamic direction of young Proprietor Jacques Mayer and his exquisite
wife Snuggi. Its fine rustic-toned Chat-Botté (Puss-in-Boots) rôtisserie, already
respected for its outstanding cuisine and admired for its Louis XIII décor, has
now taken another step forward by training all of its staff at the world famous
l'Oasis of La Napoule on the French Riviera. In addition, the hotel dining
room has been reopened as well as a flowered terrace on an upper level. New
conference facilities; English-style piano-bar; grand suite in which dwelled the
Empress of Austria (the bath is the last word in luxury); a host of bright front
rooms; all back units—many of them the most attractive in Switzerland—are
preening proudly this year; the lakefronters are the latest gems to be polished.
Coming up and up and up, with good taste and carloads of flair.

Du Rhône, with an excellent riverside situation, comes on stronger and
stronger as a zesty cosmopolitan address for globe-trotters. On our recent
incognito stay, we could only find reasons to commend Director R.A. Lendi
and his go-getting team of administrators; day-to-day operations are in the
capable hands of personable Eric Glattfelder, one of the most admired hosts
in all Helvetia. The cork-and-wood lined Le Neptune has become one of the
top dining spots in the nation; the adjoining salon is airy, cheerful, and richly
rewarding (see "Restaurants"). Now the entire accommodation skein has been
updated, a fresh wing fluffed up, carpets spread to add warmth, old baths
modernized with phones in each, all suites renewed, the telephone system given
direct dialing, TV put into all rooms, and a parking lot opened for 6o cars. We
were highly impressed by the good taste and excellent comfort standards
currently employed here. There's a busy-busy atmosphere with lounges a-
chatter with clients from all 4 corners of the earth. Now strongly recommended to readers who seek action, comfort, and modernity.

The 4oo-room **Intercontinental** is a 16-story giant located about 5 minutes
along the Lausanne Speedway. Immense marble-ized commercial lobby, 1-
flight up by escalator; rich, cunningly decorated Les Continents Restaurant
with nearby Les Palmiers Bar; coffee shop; rooftop Le Carnaval Supper Club
redone after a recent fire which caused no harm to any guests. You will also
find a galaxy of shops, a swimming pool with summer barbecue for lunch and
candlelight dining, a 17o-car underground garage, and full air conditioning.
Extensive bedroom revamping with colors and styles varying by the floor; 8
suites include separate dining salons. Management by Georges Desbaillets is
skilled, but providing warmth in such a massive institution must be his everpresent endeavor.

The **des Bergues** functions smoothly under the sharp-eyed guidance of

Manager Hubert Marquot. Updated reception area and uplifted lobby; old wing entirely refashioned to provide uniform quality throughout; 2 bars; main dining room with balconied tables overlooking the lake spillway; Amphitryon restaurant, very popular with the Diplomatic Set; bustling Snack Bar; superb Concierge in Léon Wellinger and his assistant, Paul. Traditional gathering place of Swiss bankers, couponclippers, and The Oldest Families.

The **de la Paix** is one of the most distinguished smaller hotels in the nation. Lakefront situation; dignified lobby; restaurant *à la français;* TV now in every haven; gay touches splashed throughout; colored tiles, up-to-the-minute fixtures, and scales added to practically all bathrooms. While some of its lodgings are small, others are so spacious that Prince Rainier and Princess Grace chose de la Paix on one state visit. Worldwide reputation meriting every iota of its fame.

The **President** never seems too busy to us though it has achieved a certain status in the opulence circuit; it now accepts a limited number of group tours. Lakeside setting in an unhappy location for shoppers or sightseers; dazzling white marble façade; French Restaurant, with adjoining bar, Grill, Tearoom, and cocktail retreat; rich, rich downstairs décor a startling contrast of Gobelin tapestries, showy period pieces, and Lunar Missile modernity; lounge with sliding roof; 100-car garage. The handful of apartments, 20 suites, and 270 rooms all have bath, radio, 2 or 3 telephones, and floor-to-ceiling windows. Bedroom rates as well as food prices are shockingly high. Very costly, but appealing to many nabobs.

The Deluxe **La Réserve** is under the management aegis of the Richemond, which gives it a double bonus in travelers' rewards. This ultra-quiet rural beauty dominates a spruce-dotted, 8-acre domain near the outskirting hamlet of Bellevue; it is pedestaled upon a setback garden hummock severed from the lake by the Lausanne autoroute. Open-space-concept lobby livened by ceramic butterflies; window-lined split-level dining room with a glorious view of lawn and trees. A new chef is justifiably stirring jealousy in many Geneva kitchens; his domain has been refashioned, given the name La Closerie, and an orchestra adds to the harmonious whole. (La Réserve also has an enviable Chinese restaurant which is independently operated); wide terrace adjoining for summer pastimes; richly outfitted, ruby-toned bar; ocher-hued coffee shop; beauty parlor; heated swimming pool and 4 tennis courts (one enclosed); private harbor and beach for water sports. All bedchambers with private loggia, bath, shower, radio and TV; color-keys in blue, green, and orange; some 3-person units available in its 60-room total. Both cuisine and dwelling space come at premium rates. From what we could see, this sylvan *réserve* boasts many alluring features that the city slickers can never provide. (Indeed, in summer it almost gives the impression of being a country club rather than a hotel.) The Armleder clan has put together an enchanting package which Manager Roland Klinger maintains in high polish.

Back in town, **La Résidence** has been perking up. There's a rejuvenated lobby plus an enlarged restaurant and bar, all brightened sparklingly by lots of plate glass and mirrors. Its 140 bedrooms are being refashioned at a rate of about 20 per season; the contrast between the renewed and the older units is vivid. Recommended *if* you draw one of the better lodgings. The American-

bred **Ramada** is a happy surprise. It traveled well. Color, zest, and tasteful vitality are its stock in trade. The Rive Droite, the main restaurant, provides an excellent open buffet plus live music for fixed prices; the smaller Swiss Chalet is a charming rustic nook for informal meals; there are 2 inviting bars and a cache of cozy corners for idle conversation. We think you will like the cheer and efficiency of this delightful newcomer. The **Bristol** offers many deluxe amenities—the primary one being its excellent gold-toned restaurant, which is becoming *the* place to go at lunchtime. A conference room plus 50 top-line bedchambers also have just been added; existing units are being upgraded. If you sleep lightly, avoid any kip near the elevator shaft. Manager Roland Cirafici grooms his house as if it were his very own dwelling. There is an appealing meld of tradition and modernity here. The **Royal** devotes most of its 145 accommodations to group bookings, which usually means that guests only pause here for brief stints. Some of the units we saw, however, incorporate kichenettes, which make them ideal for longer stays—especially in a city where food costs in restaurants are so high. Pleasant décor, quality carpeting; a few cork walls; ample shelf and desk space; full-house air conditioning. Refreshment available in the evenings-only Swiss Corner, the King's Bar, or the Old Geneva. Very sound and recommendable. The **d'Angleterre,** boasting a restyled entrance, lobby, and reception area, offers 66 soundproofed rooms, all with private bath, most of them amply dimensioned. Pleasant setting, with its excellent dining sections fronting the waterside; keen management by Robert O. Bucher; friendly people; vague plans for further updatings; heartily endorsed as one of the best candidates in its medium-price category. The **Balzac** is youthful and First-class; its restaurant, bar, and brasserie are independent; there's private parking in the adjoining Gulf station. All 40 unusually large bedrooms with efficiency bath or shower; comfortable armchairs or divans in some units; a few dressing alcoves; night tables with radios and telephones; TV on request; wide-angle windows affording townscape vistas. This Balzac pens out an entertaining *Human Comedy.* The **Cornavin** has added garage facilities near its portals and numerous modernizations inside. Warmhearted Concierge Gottfried Rudisuhli always finds time to chat with his guests and make them feel welcome to his city. Prices very reasonable; not bad if you say "okay" to the station area. The 95-unit PLM **Rotary** welcomes guests with a gustily ornate Empire lobby; the elaborate motif is carried throughout the house, with each accommodation different and each well presented as a period piece. Le Sporting bar and restaurant is more subdued; rooms are thoughtfully equipped with color TV, radio wake-up consoles, frigo-bars, and automatic telephone. Management of this Deluxe gem is in the capable hands of George Hangartner Jr., a family well-revered for professional innkeeping. The stripped and attractively naked **Metropole** is due for total renewal soon. Perhaps you will see her fitters at work this season. The Rhone-sited **Ambassador,** on the quai des Bergues, was somewhat of a disappointment to us. Woody lounge with modernistic padded easy chairs; corner restaurant and bar; 90 contemporary-style bedrooms, all fully carpeted but extremely small and with virtually no baggage space; tiny baths, and 28 units with only w.c.'s. The brochure looks better than the real thing.

The pert little **Grand-Pré** is the economy-class triumph of the resourceful

Armleder family of Richemond fame. All 85 units tiny but tastefully outfitted; singles in front and doubles in back; only 6 singles without bath or shower; no restaurant. There's a crisp, happy atmosphere here, generated and maintained by Resident Manager Graff. Excellent for budgeteers. The **Century** impressed our Judy as a house designed almost exclusively for male patronage. All sizes, shapes, and lines for mascu-linear appeal are here, without a single dainty frill. Large, gracious lobby with comfortable chairs functionally arranged; 140 rooms with 120 baths or showers; 50% of the accommodations with he-man kitchenettes. Deservedly popular. The **California** has a chummy cellar bar and a roof-garden snackery. All 67 units with bath or shower; good desk space for working types; 7 with kitchen facilities plus dining counter; 25 others with kitchenettes only (we saw no ventilators); lovely, delicious, noble combination of colors that would warm and gladden any Princeton Tiger's heart (orange and black, *mais oui*). But so Many, Many, Many groups thunder through it that we felt lost as footloose independents. The **Du Midi** boasts an excellent central address, a spiral entrance stairway beside a gurgling fountain, the cellar Carnotzet for fondue, a sidewalk terrace, a breakfast room, and 82 accommodations, all with bath or shower, a refrigerator, radio, telephone, alarm clock, scales, and an air of no-nonsense functionality. Very solid for the modest outlay; highly favored by us. The 165-room, marble-fronted **Méditerranée** provides an efficient modernistic concept. French-style les Quatre Saisons restaurant with abundant salad choices and seasonal accent on vegetables; cellar Taverna Ticinese with its focus on Italian dishes; sun-dappled breakfast nook; coffee shop; bar; sauna; nearby carpark; well-outfitted chambers (with refrigerators) with back views of Lac Léman and the Jet d'Eau. It is clean, smooth, and on the hop. The **De Berne** was initially planned as a haven for tour groups. Expansive lobby with acres of space for luggage; full air conditioning; dining room in mustard tones; small bar; improved hallways; peanut-shell quarters, each packed with telephone, radio, red and white furniture, and private bath. Better, but still groupy. The **Windsor**, across the street, offers 56 bedchambers. Small lounge, small bar, small cells, small recommendation. The **Excelsior**, a station hotel, has space for 75 snoozers with very thin wallets. Fair shelter. The **Rivoli's** sleeping quarters are even more minuscule. The youngish **Phenicia** offers 56 cubicles with garish décor, bath or shower, radio, and just enough space to stretch out. Clean but lean. The **Époque**, which faces it, is 2 years older and 2 well worn. Weensie restaurant off the lobby; 60 functional units with showers. **La Tourelle**, at *Vésenaz* nestles in a homey parkland setting; with its lake view, it can be just the ticket for thrift-minded tranquillity seekers of taste. Skip the **Lido**; an all-night bakery next door might knead your dollars into doughnuts as far as sleeping is concerned. **Penta**, largely held by a consortium of airlines, is sited in the vicinity of the airport. Artfully conceived grill room; coffee shop; cocktail lounge; bedchambers resembling studio design. Excellent value. Both the **Hotel 33** and **Air Escale** are heavily boarded by airline crews. Out at neighboring *Petit-Lancy* we hear fond praise for the comforts and cuisine of the tiny **Hostellerie de la Vendée**, but personally we haven't tried it.

Only 11 miles across the border from Geneva (20 minutes by the Speedway), *Divonne-les-Bains* offers resort thermal-spa facilities, 3 aging but adequate

hotels, an 18-hole golf course, a racetrack, occasional polo matches, and the richest gambling facilities in Gaul. The Casino—with roulette, baccarat, American games (including craps), boule, and chemin de fer—is the town's main attraction and almost its reason for being. Both the Hôtel du Golf and the Parc (formerly called Chicago) now come under the escutcheon of the Rothschilds. The du Golf has a lovely garden situation, a barnlike ambiance brightened with sparkly hues of fresh paint, and a number of fainthearted, cost-conscious renovations. All 100 bedrooms come with private bath; 50% have been renewed. We felt a notable lack of warmth throughout. Be sure to have confirmed reservations here; also check your bills carefully. The pool, shared with the Parc, is large and very handsome. The Parc is really an antique annex of the former. Its unretouched mien has more charm than that of the principal house, but wherever it is old (going on its 13th decade), it is downright decrepit. No restaurant; 50 of its 100 units with private bath; June through September only; rumors rife that it may be razed for an apartment site. The 3rd possibility, Château de Divonne, is just outside of town on a commanding perch. It is a beautifully maintained structure dating from the second half of the eighteenth century. Captivating terrace for settin', starin', and rockin' those blues away; 40 period rooms; 25 baths; open June to September. This Divonne world is as tranquil as the inside of a bubble, so don't expect fireworks. Recommended only for lazing, gazing, and gaming.

Restaurants   Geneva does much of its finest dining these days in exclusive hotel restaurants. The Neptune segment of the **Du Rhône** currently is a bellringer. If it is in season, try the Croûte Landais (warm fresh goose liver with a blanket of chafed cream sauce); the Sole Grand Véfour also is superb; even simple grilled chicken is delicious done on the open flames behind thick glass panels. This unit is closed on weeekends, but the adjoining dining salon is equally appealing and it remains open the week through. The Chat-Botté of the **Beau Rivage** is the hottest item in town among gastronomes. (We've already mentioned its association with l'Oasis in La Napoule.) There is an air of refined rusticity here and a friendly professional manner in the way its outstanding cuisine is served. Incidentally, the oversized plates are the latest rage among the ranking chefs of Europe. Le Gentilhomme at the **Richemond** continues to draw fashionable clientele, many of whom arrive early to listen to the first-rate trio that strums and tinkles in the adjacent bar. As an alternative, Le Jardin terrace-restaurant here, with its connected sidewalk café, comes up with thousands of flowers, skillful after-dark illumination, and music piped from Le Gentilhomme; a happy focal point for visitors and residents alike, from breakfast to after-theater snacks; U.S.-styled table d'hôte lunch (consommé, hamburger-steak platter, ice cream) for hurried trippers, plus self-service hors d'oeuvres table. The Amphitryon Room at the **Hôtel des Bergues** now draws heavily from the diplomatic corps to sample its pleasant ambiance, deft service, and good food. The view from the **La Réserve** dining room is enchanting. Our lunch was pleasant, too, but it wasn't cheap. Down one flight, **Tse Fung** is the best Chinese restaurant we have ever found in Switzerland—and it vies for our top ranking in all Europe. Elegant setting, furnishings, and tableware; large selection of Cantonese, Peking, and Shanghai specialties, beautifully prepared; open 365 days for lunch and dinner. More expensive than

average Cathay establishments, but infinitely better in its suavity and quality. The open table at the **Ramada** is just the ticket if you are hungry but don't know what you want to eat. A treasure of tempters; all you can swallow for a fixed price; live music at dinner. Varied, colorful, and fun. As for straight restaurants, our happiest stop in the city is **Le Béarn** (quai de la Poste 4); it remains as good as ever. *Fin-de-siècle* décor; paneled walls with red "silk" that is actually plaster; 9 tables in front; larger room to the rear for overflow traffic. All-out recommendation for this little gem; *don't miss it!* Next in line is **L'Or du Rhône** (place du Cirque 1). Here's a rôtisserie-type establishment with an open fireplace where steaks and chicken-on-the-spit are broiled by white-capped Patron Fiechter, in full view of the guest; the bar in front, as impersonal as an airport waiting room, is neither fish nor fowl. Old Tavern authenticity, not Olde Taverne phoniness; advance reservations mandatory for dinner. **Au Fin Bec** (rue de Berne 55) is an unpretentious old-timer to which Genevois flock, especially in game season. Enclosed-garden entrance; begonia-bowered, arch-lined, tree-covered patio for fair-weather meals, plus 3 inside dining rooms; neighborhood drop-in atmosphere; warm attention dispensed by Hostess Mme. Janet and her staff of aproned waitresses. Our substantial dinner for 4 (hors d'oeuvres, woodcock, kidneys in white wine, and Blanc de Blancs '61) was a treat at around $18 per tummy. Around October (or later, if in season), order as a curiosity the large celerylike vegetable called "cardon," which is a house specialty. No patrons received after 2 P.M. or 10 P.M.—a rigid rule—so plan accordingly. Plain but beckoning. The **Parc de Budé**, near the Interconti-nental, is an aquarian entry nurtured by the Armleder interests. Entrance alcove with easy chairs for premeal libations; up a 1/2-story to the sail-loft where a dozen tables complete the picture; marine décor theme; superb fish; perfect service on our boarding. The same family oversees the many facets of the **La Coupole** complex, a linkage of several sprightly feederies within a midtown office building. Its 22 backgammon tables (free) along with frequent tournaments are its backbone. These are fleshed out so enticingly that it is just as alluring for nonplayers. Striped bar at entrance packed during peak hours with a mélange from the ultrachic to the semidemimonde; suave Backgammon bar where the dice quietly roll and where clients relax in comfortable chairs to sip their perfectly blended drinks; reasonably priced Swiss-rustic dining room with temptingly prepared vittles and a business clientele at lunch; swing-ingest action in both bars from 5 to 8, continuing in the gaming areas from 10 to 1; closed Sunday and Christmas week. A merry and meritorious fun spot which we highly recommend. **Auberge Communale de Confignon** (10 minutes by taxi in the Confignon suburb served us the best steak of our entire Swiss loop not too long ago. Simple, long building on a hillock overlooking town; huge delicious cuts of steer; fast service; outstanding quality for medium-to-low tariffs. Highly recommended for purposeful beefeaters. **Lion d'Or**, about the same distance to Cologny, is bouncing back smartly under the inspired direction of Henri Large. It's again worth a visit if you feel like a short excursion from mid city. The **Mère Royaume** (rue Corps-Saints 4), dating back to 1602, seems to be bouncing back to life under the Doldi leadership. Our *omble* (lake fish) in butter sauce was not good, *it was fantastic!* More *nouvelle cuisine* dishes being added to up the quality without up-ing the price tags.

Chummy brick and timber personality enhanced by kind, efficient service, and splendid value in the culinary output. **La Perle du Lac**, on the lake, has a lovely terrace, and an impressively agreeable alfresco atmosphere. Manager Kyburz is aiming at gastronomic recognition—and, happily, he's achieving it. The prices, of course, are astronomic, too. Closed when winter winds blow. The **Port Gitana Grill**, 1 mile farther along, has a shorefront setting and satisfactory viands; small cabaret; numbingly expensive, in our opinion. **Le Mazot** (Hôtel d'Alleves, near American Express) features flambeaux and chafing dishes galore; piano player and genial aura; the lovely bar upstairs is knee-deep in Persian rugs, and from here you can gaze down at the diners. Our service was quick, firm, and proper, but lacking in warmth; the cuisine was passable (except for the fish, which was notably poor). It might kindle some glow if (1) your lucky star is with you, and (2) you wrap your beard in a wet napkin to prevent starting a holocaust.

The **Bar Américain and Grill** (in the Cornavin Station) offers 7 interesting regional menus from 11 A.M. to 1 A.M. The restaurant proper, with heavy yellow curtains and fetching mien, is faintly reminiscent of a small, smart East Side New York bistro. **Café-Crémerie La Clémence** (Bourg-de-Four 20) is a tumultuous churn of male students, newspaper snoopers, and soapbox orators; worth seeing if you take your earmuffs. **Café-Restaurant de la Pointe** (rue Jargonnant 3) is known for its Steak au Poivre; inexpensive and amusing. The well-known **Mövenpick** has one of its ubiquitous superrestaurants on place de la Fusterie. Another, on the right bank, is proclaimed to be the biggest and most modern in Switzerland; the cookery has become routine. Incidentally, the payment system at the production-line stand-up snack bar defies the most exquisite brand of Soviet bureaucracy; its complicatedness borders on the comic (if you're not hungry or in a rush to eat). **À l'Olivier de Provence** (rue Jacques-Dauphin 13) offers 14 tables, paper napery, candle illumination, and fanny-firmer kitchen chairs; calves' liver and big-casseroled Potatoes au Gratin are better bets. **La Pescaille** (15 av. Henri Dunant) is a bit out of the center, but our seafood adventure here was well worth the taxi hop. Warm reception; careful attention by waiters in waist-coats; cheerful décor in its one-room precinct. Prices float up to the higher tide levels of Geneva dining, but we'd say it's top value for top dollar. **Roberto's** (10 rue Pierre Fatio) invites you to grow more and more Fatio on its Italian flavors mainly. From the Land of the Rising Sun? **Yamakawa** (rue Henri Blanvalet 3) is simplicity itself, in the finest traditions of the Orient. The Japanese chef provides about 6-dozen dishes of superb quality for an audience that is at least 80% Nipponese. Our meal of 2 portions of raw fish appetizers, Sukiyaki, and Sake totaled around $40. Chinese? Our first choice would be, of course, the aforementioned **Tse Fung**, but after it would come **Fleur de Ming** (rue de Port) followed by the less dandy **Celeste Empire** (rue Tour-Maîtresse). We haven't had an opportunity to research **Auberge des Trois Bonheurs** which very recently moved to 14 rue Crespin and, according to a Geneva pal who knows the dining scene worldwide, "it went very fancy, jacked up its prices, and now produces noteworthy cuisine." **McDonald's** does its American-bred convenience thing on the rue du Mont Blanc. **Wimpy** has rolled out several stations in the city for budget biters. Finally, this book must continue to withhold its endorsement of **Le Chan-**

delier; to our distress (and perhaps we are again partially responsible), this once-charming little haven impressed us on our latest visit as a slick, commercial, tourist-motivated operation; now heartily disrecommended, despite murmurs it may be trending upward again.

Outskirts dining? There's a tiny bistro at *Chambésy s/Genève*, about 15 minutes from the center of Geneva (start along the Lausanne highway and turn off up the mountain). The name is **Relais de Chambésy**; it's at the hub of the village; there's a tree-shaded terrace with 7 or 8 tables; the atmosphere is bustling and friendly. Don't fail to try their 2 specialties, Entrecôte (steak) with a mustard sauce and the light, mouth-watering Sabayon to settle the meat. (The sliced ham is also delicious.) **L'Auberge du Grand-Lancy**, 2 miles from the center, is utilitarian rather than social; game and fish specialties; quite expensive; closed Mondays and most of July; also agreeable when skies are clear. The **Restaurant du Parc des Eaux-Vives**, across the far waters on the lake bank opposite the Richemond Hôtel, is an impressive graystone château which the city owns. Iron gate entrance; lovely landscaping with the Geneva Tennis Club courts behind; portal canopied with a blue- and white-striped baldachin; umbrella-lined terrace for tea or apéritif sippers, without food service; 6 huge windows in the main dining room with magnificent views of the water and the distant UN enclave. The quality of the gastronomy is now spiraling upward, so that it stands today as one of the city's more sophisticated and worthwhile dining targets. Try the Soufflé d'Omble and see why. Closed Mon. **Pavillon de Ruth**, a lakefront venture at the previously mentioned *Cologny* (2 miles), works continuously from March to December 15; we wish the cookery was as satisfying as the scenery. Pity. **Carnotzet** (Lausanne road) is a sprawling outdoor-indoor establishment with a perfectly wonderful spread of Lake Léman and Geneva; delightful as a drop-in spot for coffee or refreshments when the air is balmy. **Rôtisserie du Lac** at *Coppet* (also Lausanne road) has been entirely renovated. Indoor dining room with fireplace and beamed ceiling, lakeside terrace; rôtisserie in summer; horseshoe-shape, Scottish tartan bar upstairs, with piano background music; 8 bedchambers and 4 baths; Chef-Owner René Gottraux speaks no English, but his daughter is a linguist. Very fashionable these days among the smart set of the metropolis who swarm in by car or boat; if your gastronomy isn't fussy and your wallet is verdant with greenbacks, you'll find this a beguiling retreat. Variable. **Auberge des Grands Bois** at *Buchillon* (2 exits short of Lausanne on the auto route, near Ste. Sulpice) turns out some of the best lake-fish cookery in the nation. The trout, perch, and *omble* (deep-water critters) are heavenly, the prices are relatively low, and the drive into the country is lovely. Typically rustic atmosphere with no pretensions; the proprietress is the mother of André, the world-famous bar chief of the Palace Hotel in Gstaad. Very popular, so do call ahead to reserve. A food-savvy friend, David Blum, the famous conductor who adds a grace note to this book from time-to-time, recommends the **Gothard** in *Chêne Bourg*. We so frequently concur with this gentleman on matters of cuisine that we can suggest it to you without a personal trial. Another solid contender is **La Belotte**, a mile or so from town, where the Quenelles and filet of beef are outstanding. If you have your own transportation, please refer to the "Lausanne" section because it is not far away and offers many additional choices which are excellent.

Night Life   The **Velvet Club** mixes modernity with Rétro art forms through several comfortable tiers of delight. High ceilings, warm velvety tones, dance music, late dinner available. Say you read about it in this book and you should have no trouble getting in. Another gathering place for the socialite and sophisticate is the **Le Gentilhomme** at the **Hôtel Richemond**; no show, cocktails, gourmet dining, and Diors the main attractions. **Le Club 58** and **The Pussy Cat Saloon** share a common entrance; turn left for the former, right for the latter. Admission chomp on weekends; Edwardian interior with patterned carpeting on walls; rouge and black color scheme; excellent strips, similar to the Crazy Horse in Paris. Better for Him than for Her. The **Griffin's** is one of the most fashionable discothèques in the land. It's private, but membership can be purchased; frequently, generous Proprietor Bernard Grobet or Maître Joe Panarinfo invite newcomers to join on a gratis basis. Highly stylized, modernistic downstairs retreat; adjoining rustic dining room serving from 8 P.M. to dawnish (meats are best); very comfortable surroundings; music in the twentieth-century mood, but hardly reminiscent of Glen Miller. For its type, one of the better examples on the Continent. **La Tour**, a split-level cave with alternating combos, draws a similar clientele of youngbloods and nonacidhead hippies. Crowded dance floor; good ventilation; attentive service. Worth a Tour. **Ba-Ta-Clan**, wickedly fashioned in Frenchy tones, grinds out set after set of seminude shows, strange sort of sexy ambiance; Tom Thumb tables in music-hall arrangement; weekend admission bite; whisky legitimate on our latest sip. **Maxim's** swings in with an ornate glass, brass, and iron entrance; wood and burgundy tones in its cellar salon; multilevel seating for better views of the jugglers, strippers, and crooners; standard tariff. **Moulin Rouge** made our party see red; here's one windmill we'd like to tilt without pulling a single punch. Never again for us. **Le Grillon** is agreeable for dancing; perky combos; small cabaret at 11 P.M. **Le Baladin**, nearby, is chiefly for terpsichore; there's no show. **Piccadilly** is smaller, more *intimo,* and okay for avoiding that certain someone. A bit of strip; everything closed (and clothed) Sunday. **Mylord** is a disco-haunt for youngsters. **Chez Monique** is 4th-rate. Finally, **rue des Étuves**, 200 yards east of Hôtel du Midi, is lined with amusing workmen's cafés.

Shopping   Quality is the byword here. You may be sure that anything you buy will stand up, if you can afford it.

Our ★ ★ ★ ★ ★ recommendations are individually noted.

Appenzell needlework: **Au Chalet Suisse** (place du Lac 1) specializes in this lovely embroidery, as well as in organdy and lace table settings, children's dresses, and dozens of inexpensive textile oddments. Very good.

Ladies', men's, and children's fashions and accessories: We most strongly urge that every visitor set his or her comparative bearings for ★ ★ ★ ★ **Bon Génie** (rue de Marché 34, with branch in Lausanne), the 5-story headquarters of the celebrated luxury specialty store which markets close to 100-thousand different manifestations of the latest styles and designs, both original and Swiss creations, plus glamorous boutiques and departments of the greatest names in the industry. Tycoons Jean-Jacques and Michel Brunschwig faithfully expand on the dictum established by their grandfather in 1891: "Mode, Quality, and Price." Long one of Switzerland's undisputed vogue setters.

Chocolates: Always our first and last errand is to load up on what we

consider the finest chocolates in the world—**Lindt's**, which are traditionally the number one craftsmen of their art in this land. Sadly, *no candies containing alcohol are passed by U.S. Customs.*

Watches: Because space is too limited here to attempt to tackle this complex and lengthy subject, those who wish to buy a watch might be interested in consulting our purse-size, 25th Anniversary edition of *Fielding's Selective Shopping Guide to Europe,* where we have delineated our ratings of the 31 leading Swiss manufacturers and what we term the *"25 Musts"* which we believe every potential customer should know before making any purchase in this special field. Where to buy a watch? Please turn to "Lucerne." Also for more stores, more details, and more lore throughout this nation for dedicated shophounds, you may also refer to this pilot.

The biggest drugstore in the world: **Pharmacie Principale** now surpasses Rexall's in Los Angeles as the record-breaker. It stocks everything from dried pimpernel flowers to maternity garments to neon-lit bikinis—you name it. If you look hard enough, you'll also find toiletries and medicines.

Stunningly chic Greek gold jewelry: Legendary tastemaker ★ ★ ★ ★ **Ilias Lalaounis** has launched a dazzling display of his masterpieces at **Bon Génie** (see above) and at **Grieder's** in *Zürich.* Please turn back to "Greece" for details which should make your mouth water.

Antiques: Stroll along rue de la Cité, Grand Rue, and rue Hôtel-de-Ville. The quality is generally good, but oh—those prices!

Shopping hours: They vary wildly throughout the nation. During the tourist influx there's no usable rule-of-thumb. They open from 7 to 8:30 A.M.; some fold up for lunch anywhere from 12-or-12:30 to 1:30-or-2 P.M., while others stay open all day; most (not all) close at 6:30 P.M. on weekdays and midday or 5 P.M. on Saturdays; some are open evenings and Sunday mornings in the summer. In winter, however, nearly every merchant goes home between noon and 2 P.M. on Saturday.

GRINDELWALD, 13 miles up the valley from Interlaken, is a tiny toenail on the foothills of the magnificent Bernese Oberland. Europe's longest chair lift will set you atop the point called First for a fantastic First-hand view of the spires above and the Lilliput below. A rack-railway scrambles up the 2-mile-high Jungfraujoch to the loftiest station in the Alps. Flanking this is the infamous "North Wall," that formidable barrier of stone and ice that has taken the lives of so many climbers. The Eiger and Jungfrau are next door. Three transportation hookups now link the most important round-the-valley slopes into a skier's dream-come-true. The usual accounterments are thoughtfully provided by The Lord and His angels for hiking, skiing, fishing (the last in the glacially formed Lütschinen River); man-made facilities for heated-pool swimming, tennis, and sleigh-riding; 35 hotels or pensions. Her granitebound people often seem as closed and forbidding as a snow-sealed crevasse—extremely reserved, ingrown, and of a suspicious nature. Once they know someone, they are warm and cordial. But at first sight they impress many travelers as among the least outgoing, least personally attractive regional groups in the nation.

For those who stay, unquestionably the queenly choice is the **Grand Hotel Regina**, rejuvenated by Fred Krebs and his hotelier clan on a cost-is-no-object

basis. New annex—a luxury chalet-style edifice with 9 luxury suites, open fireplaces, color TV, and even some baths with tubs for twosomes and a view of the Eiger. His 300-piece collection of antique local prints (on display throughout) alone has consumed a small Alp of francs. The exterior remains gingerbready—but inside there has been a revolution. Numerous standard units restyled with built-in furniture and hip-deep wall-to-wall carpets; plenty of flowers around; big, open-air, heated pool with colorful umbrellas on lawn, against one of the most glorious Alpine backdrops imaginable; adjoining Health Pavilion with a covered pool, sauna, massage parlor, and clubroom. Folklore Fondue Dinner Parties every Monday featuring a yodeling quartet (delightful in winter after a community sleigh ride); Candlelit Dinner Dances every Thursday night in summer, with occasional floor shows; Sunday Tea Dances in winter. "La Ferme" ("The Farm") nightclub with huge open *Alphütte* fireplace, charcoal grill, and the sizzling sounds of a discothèque; Sports Bar. Hats off to this talented, hardworking host! The 80-room **Adler**, also teetering above the deep valley, is a chalet-style structure. Garden, tennis, Ping-Pong; glorious vistas from the dining room-lounge-bar combination and the open terrace. Its modernistic and tasteless furnishings are a handicap to the warm, wood-lined rooms; 45 very minuscule baths; amiable personnel. Very sound. **Belvedere** has the usual resort appurtenances without a speck of unusual flair. The indoor pool and sauna are welcome splashes. **Parkhotel Schönegg** offers cozy public rooms—especially the rustic down-1-flight Gydis Bar—but bedchambers that are much too snug. Many caressing touches including those (dictated by the dimensions) that you're bound to get constantly from your snoozing companion. Too tiny but sweet. **Schweizerhof** (like the Schönegg, on the "wrong" side of the road) is an inn that grew "out." Moderate renovations begun, but ho-hum except for its interior natatorium and sauna facilities. For budgeteers, **Bel-Air Eden**, next to the Regina, is spic, span, and snappy. We consider it superior for the modest outlay. **Bernerhof Garni**, adjoining the Central Wolter, is also a tidy choice for tidy, uncluttered wallets. Noisy, but a pretty good buy.

Among restaurants, the **Gasthof Steinbock**, opposite the Hotel Adler, takes top honors in our survey. Bustling, no-nonsense, bare-floored, Swiss-modern eatery with a 3-language menu and close ventilation; drinks served at your table; no bar; portions so H-U-G-E they might daunt a grizzly bear. When we first boggled over the platters set before other diners, we shuddered—but, to our surprise, our Wiener Schnitzel and its trimmings were light and well cooked. Piano and accordion in evening; occasional yodeling and regional entertainment. Best in the village for its category; recommended. The adjoining **Alkoholfreies Restaurant Zur Alten Post** is a mountain-style T-room for T-totalers. You'll never get that alpenglow here, but if it is tidbits you fancy, this teeny tapless tavern should suit you to that T. **Rendez-vous** offers the Hungry Man a starvation menu: sandwiches and pastries only. But the Thirsty Man or Dancing Man will leave replete. Lovely small open terrace with sweeping panorama for sunny-day sipping; a cute little spot. The **Regina** wears the undisputed crown in the hotel regency; it offers *haute cuisine* at prices that don't bite back. **Spinne** is the evening mecca of teen-agers. One combo upstairs challenges another downstairs. At **"First,"** the last stop on the 7220-foot-high

chair lift, there's a simple restaurant and terrace for plain fare and fantastic viewing. Never mind the provisions; you'll never see what's on your plate, anyway.

GSTAAD   Here, the international set does most of its dining, dancing, drinking, gossiping, and wife-swapping in the merry surroundings of the famed Palace Hotel—but it retreats to privately owned or rented chalets for its beauty sleep, indoor acrobatics, and repairs. Beautiful setting in an open valley which absorbs more hours of sunlight than many of its competitors; slick-rustic atmosphere with everything from Karl Brunner ski pants to bargain-basement chinos and rummage-sale caps on its crowded main artery; golf course, riding academy, and 50 mountain lifts; helicopter service to the higher grounds; annual Yehudi Menuhin Festival in August; Roy Emerson tennis weeks in summer; special ski bargains in January and March. If you stay within its moneyed precincts, allegro, expensive, and chichi. Seasons: mid-December to March, and mid-June to mid-October.

The **Palace** is a traditional attraction. This castle-style hotel, Swiss flags flying from its truncated ramparts, dominates the village. It draws an ultrachic, sophisticated, international clientele, which is bolstered by fashionable residents of opulent chalets who make it their social fulcrum; many guests wear black tie every night at dinner. (But for those who don't wish to, the generous owner has just unveiled a new restaurant adjoining the grill playfully named Le Sans Cravatte, where the dining is cozy and, of course *sans cravatte*. The lobby and many of its public rooms are conservative rather than high-borne. Exceptions include: (1) The *wonderful* Maxim's Room, which blooms on Saturday nights only. The world's greatest headliners are either on the stage or in the audience. (2) The suave Grill-Bar with dancing nightly, presided over by André, one of Europe's most famous and beloved dispensers. (3) The pleasant, charming, well-executed dining salon. Veteran-Proprietor-Director Ernest Scherz keeps these running as smoothly, as quietly, and as sumptuously as a Rolls-Royce Mulliner-Park Ward convertible. Hi-Fi Club in basement for teen-agers or young marrieds, jumping from 4 to 6:30 P.M. and from 8 P.M. to 1 A.M.; large skating rink, curling, 2-lane "automatic" bowling, tennis, heated pool, beauty parlor, and table tennis room; instructors for all sports; sauna and massage; Cable TV (over a 20-mile line!); within call (off premises), everything from golf to riding to ski lifts to mumblety-peg. This season every accommodation is dressed afresh and glittering—that's 150 units in Swiss baroque, 13 new suites or junior suites, and 5 twins with 2 baths. Here certainly is one of this globe's finest mountain hotels, suavely and savvily run by Herr Scherz, his delightful wife Silvia, and their 2 stalwart sons. Top recommendation. As a P.S. to its indomitable dynamism and farsightedness, the Scherz treasury has cascaded almost $10 million into its neighboring new **Résidence Palace**, a complex of privately owned apartments (many of celebs) who rent them out under hotel supervision. Hence, these sumptously grand suites also can be obtained as part of the Palace's ever-expanding services with all guest privileges included and many additional conviences as well.

The **Parkhotel** occupies its own hilltop. Somewhat stuffy public rooms;

natural-wood bar-grill in the cellar (athwart a slope); the 2-table Cave Romande is the dividing hyphen between the latter units. Well maintained, with
pots of new cosmetics applied—but, except for its situation and the cellar
installation we have described, it's so fuddy-duddy that here is a Giant Step
down from the Palace in elegance, quality, and flair (but not in tariffs). Open
mid-December to late March, and early June to late September. The **Bellevue**, at the approach to the village and structurally similar to the Parkhotel,
is set in its own garden just off the main highway. We have the feeling this one
caters heavily and somewhat impersonally to mass tourism. Also seasonal. The
Alpina, near the Palace but on higher ground, has been refurbished and
scrubbed up of late. A 70-bed wing and a few baths recently added; run-of-the-
mill décor with spare provincial zest. In season the **Olden** is appealing more
as a merry perch for night owls than for its lodgings. Attractive café and
restaurant; popular La Cave night life activities; 25 simple bedchambers and
4 baths that are no better than routine in any regard—but here's the 5th-
ranking house in Gstaad. **Post-Rössli** offers a total of 50 rooms, 7 of which
are in an annex; good cuisine; homey atmosphere. The location is noisy but
handy (no taxi required to get to the doin's), and the price is right. The little
Chalet Christiania is breakfast-only; clean, well situated, and inexpensive.
Bernerhof, near the railroad station, is, in our opinion, a gloomy mass-production sleeping factory. Not recommended. In a special category, the **Chesery**, expertly managed by the Gauer group of Berne, is an exquisitely executed
chalet-style building with 3 handsome dining areas—but with a total of only
1 suite and 3 double rooms for overnighting. Its 4 accommodations are tastefully and imaginatively done in what might be punned as late Cantonese.
During months of winter sport, live concerts by big-name jazzmen are a
regular feature. Although it is chic, expensive, and fine—albeit with a high
decibel level at night—we'd still be far, far happier parking our tired tootsies
at the Palace. If this one had more door keys, however, it would definitely rate
as #2 in the region. A friendly M.D. from Philadelphia sent us a brotherly
Rx for the **Sporthotel Rütti**, operated by the Villiger family. It's a couple of
minutes out of the center and sounds just the medicine for quieting jangled
nerves and face-lifting sagging spirits into robust smiles. Thank you, Doctor!
At *Château-d'Oex*, 8 miles away, we hear mighty alluring reports about the
Chalet du Bon Accueil.

For dining pleasure, we've already mentioned the **Palace Hotel** and the
Chesery, our 2 top choices in their respective ways. The hilltop-high **Parkhotel**
features its own intimate Bar-Grill in natural wood and regional fixin's, plus
the Cave Romande. The **Olden** is a swinger—chiefly because of the attractive
Englishspeaking proprietress, Miss Hedy, known far and wide as "the Dinah
Shore of the piano."

INTERLAKEN is the most fun if you hanker for nostalgia. The real-life
clock seems to have stopped back when this century was in diapers. Speaking
of timepieces, it has a noteworthy Flower Clock; the legendary view of the
Jungfrau from the hotels lining the Höheweg, the annual Mozart Festival, and
medieval Unterseen are other reasons to be here. Hop the funicular up the

Harder Kulm, go to the Ibex Preserve, and take the circle trip to the Jung-fraujoch (Lauterbrunnen and Kleine Scheidegg, returning via Grindelwald)—marvelous! As one gateway to the hauntingly beautiful Bernese Oberland, pause only briefly here while reserving most of your time for the majesty of the hills. The drive from Berne to Grindelwald and Lucerne via Interlaken threads along the shores of 5 lakes and through innumerable Alpine vistas. The environs are what count, not the town. Major efforts, such as the addition of a community swimming pool, the teeing up of a golf course, and the inaugura-tion of open-air plays in summer, are being made to change this Victorian dowager's spots and to promote her as a convention center—an operation involving the same basic problems, it seems to us, as transforming a Boy Scout camp into an Alpine Las Vegas.

Most of the accommodations are strictly Swiss-Resort-Traditional: Gables, cupolas, crystal chandeliers, terraces, red plush, Louis Quinze via Basle or Grand Rapids. Along hotel row, which fronts the main park for several blocks, the Splendid, Victoria-Jungfrau, Schweizerhof (razed by fire while in the pro-cess of renovation), Belvedere, Royal St. Georges, Beau-Rivage (bus parties by the scores), and Du Lac line up stiffly, primly, and austerely, almost tippet-to-tippet. Shades of Grandma's day! To us, the sight is like viewing a bikini-clad beauty contest of octogenarians. The 180-pillow **Métropole** was renewed and given an indoor pool, a sauna, heaps of entertainment facilities, oodles of drinking and snacking corners, plus the welcome hint of fresh innkeeping ideas. Kind personnel and a splendid house. The **Victoria-Jungfrau**, partially redecorated back yonder in '58, has the weightiest reputation. Typical of its style; many groups, but these served in a separate dining salon; some com-plaints of staff high-handedness and of lumpy beds. We'll look in soon. The **Beau-Rivage**, near the Interlaken-Ost station, is painfully plain in some of its accommodations and painlessly fine in some of its others; savory à la carte temptations and excellent dining-room service; bitter howls from readers who tell us that the bed-and-bathroom linens aren't changed often enough and that it is time for the fumigators to pay a call here. The family-style **Krebs** has a variety of rooms, and a friendly welcome; complaints have been received concerning the limitations of its menu. The mother and sister of the renowned Krebs clan operate an 80-room, 20-bath companion called the **Bellevue**, in the old part of town; travelers report identically excellent cuisine, a lovely garden, good service, plenty of towels, taut management. The **Belvedere**, however, is not recommended; reports of surly desk personnel would keep us away. The **Bernerhof** and **Eurotel** top our agenda for our next go-around. The former, however, is on the bottom of the list of a kindly Clearfield, Pa., traveler who wails that she could find "more amenities in a railroad station than in room #48." Perfect holiday community for travelers between 80 and 120 years of age.

At mealtimes, this town is interlocked with hotel dining rooms almost exclusively. If you're a renegade like us (and many local residents), you'll break step and hop over to the little **Hotel Bären**, near the post office. Our recent Bratwurst, Rösti (Swiss-style hashed-brown potatoes), and draft beer were all superior in preparation and quality. A new fillip for filling up is its Swiss meal consisting of Fondue, Brienzlig (fried lake fish), Bratwurst mit Rösti or some

other main course, salad, and a dessert of ice cream and cake topped with hot chocolate sauce—just the thing for dieters. Exceptionally fine service, too! Ask for either of the Proprietors Frei. Yum-yum.

KLOSTERS   In the hotel sweepstakes, the **Silvretta** and the Vereina race ahead of local competition with the newer Pardenn challenging hard. At the former, under progressive-thinking Alfred Egli, all rooms are stylish, modern, and comfort-plus in rendition; fire-prevention systems exist throughout; the cuisine remains tip-top, with special emphasis on the Charcoal Grill Rôtisserie, the Farmer's Buffet with Swiss folklore every Saturday, and a Chäs Teilet of fondue and raclette every Tuesday. The charming, split-level Five-to-Five club and the bar are always hopping after dark. Hotel now operating in winter only; current total of 105 rooms and 85 baths; elastic pension plan to suit the appetite of either the robust athlete or the relaxed lounge lizard. Better every year— but expensive. The 100-room **Vereina** is operated by the father-and-son team of Anton and Stephan Diethelm who fret personally over the needs of every client. Baronial atmosphere in public rooms and lounges; dancing in season (live orchestra) in the Grisons-style Caveau; adjoining dining room; warm-hearted pub-grill with live lobsters and other seafood; Scotch Bar in tartan, with a piano tinkling during the busy hours; tennis courts; ski school at the back doorstep. Most of the accommodations come with private bath; about 1/3 have their own balcony (the views overlooking the slopes are superb); the southwestern units, with wood paneling, are excellent; #23 is a double with a single annex—a perfect combo for a couple with a small child. Most units extra-spacious and comfortable; swimming pool. All-in-all, a happy feeling pervades this wholesome family retreat. The **Pardenn** indisputably steals the local thunder for modernistic good looks. Long, balconied, 5-story building bordered by slate walks, 2 1/2 acres of south-side lawns, and luxurious flower beds; broad terraces; copper-hooded open grill; open or glass-bound heated swimming pool, depending on the season; sauna plus beauty and health facilities; bar-lounge; sumptuous suites; spacious twin units with seating alcoves; same Graessly proprietorship as the Prätschli in Arosa and the Elite in Geneva. Excellent for physical assets—and definitely among the frontrunners. Hans Guler's **Chesa Grischuna**, another highland jewel, exudes a rustic-style ambiance so delightful it would mellow the crustiest of Philadelphia lawyers. Total of 30 accommodations in knotty-pine *arvenholz* style (8 with bath and 3 with shower), including a 14-room (6 with bath) annex with larger bedchambers—and that's all! But if you'll search the premises, you'll also uncover a restaurant, subterranean bowling lanes, a sportsman's bar, music, and barrels of animation. Here indeed is a pint-size prodigy. The 30-room **Alpina**, a short glide from the station, offers cozy shelter. Old-fashioned lounge-bar; ground-floor restaurants where Proprietor-Chef Hermann Bolliger pans out masterly vittles; small dining salon à la Louis XV; attractive, well-maintained units, all with radio and telephone; warmhearted staff. Good value. **Guler's Weisskreuz** is chiefly for groups; it's a white-hot money-saver for budget pilgrims, however.

KREUZLINGEN   is at the junction of Rhine and Boden See The very modern **Schweizerland** draws high praise from a merry Sarasota couple. Front

rooms with fine lake view; worthy restaurant; 3 bowling alleys; sounds delightful.

LAC CHAMPEX (above Orsières). It offers the **Alpes et Lac**, (which a Cleveland reader calls "the best spot of our trip"; this refurbished house has been in the same family since 1888, and it is now run by young Mme. Meilland).

LAUSANNE, quieter and smaller than neighboring Geneva, is another popular center for holidays in French Switzerland. On the south slopes of hills which gradually fall away to Lake Leman, it is sheltered. The climate is unusually beguiling, with a record of 1912 hours of sunshine per year. Its university and schools are world-famous. It offers good sports, entertainment, and food, along with the world's shortest subway, the new and queer Musée de l'Art Brut, a generally well-ordered aura, and the homes of many international celebrities.

The **Beau Rivage** in the Ouchy district (5 minutes from the center) continues to soar. You'll discover more than a million dollars in new treasure—from a swimming pool (heated and in the shape of a grand piano; in winter it is wrapped in sliding glass walls) to a health club to saunas to a snack bar clad in California redwood (low prices, too!) to a huge oval lakeside terrace that converts into a winter garden to some new suites that are the last *mot* in luxury. Manager Bodo G. von Alvensleben, assisted by his modelesque wife Marie, come to these fresh happenings from Manhattan's Waldorf Towers, so perhaps a few Yankee seasonings will be stirred into the Swiss fondue. Its 3 wings have been melded into one smoothly functioning composite. One superdeluxe duplex apartment (sitting room, 2 double bedrooms, 2 baths, maid's room, and private stairway) is operative; enchanting Grill (closed Mon. and for lunch) with one of Europe's top chefs; expanded bar with delightful live trio melodizing; corridors beautified. Lovely gardens which require 5 full-time gardeners and 2 year-round flower arrangers; tennis courts; automatic laundry; 80-car garage. One of the crown jewels of Switzerland.

The **Lausanne Palace**, born an aristocrat many decades ago, continues to reveal its *pur sang* breeding under proprietors who are endowing it with an amplitude of *francs*. All accommodations in the Palace Building have been refurbished; the Grill is one of the 2 most fashionable hotel restaurants in the city; there's an attractive bar off lobby with pianist. The Brummell Night Club is operated by an independent company. The connecting Beau Site Building adds 50 rooms to the overall total plus shops by Pucci, Ferragamo, Saint Laurent, and Gerard, plus a sleekly modern barber and beauty salon, plus a sauna and massage parlor, plus a garden court, plus, plus, . . . plus! Many accommodations feature shadowless reading lamps, pillow-side command consoles for adjusting everything in the room except your bedfellow (wanna try?), electric blinds, infra red bathroom heating and piped music as you bathe, Frigobars, thermal taps, and—wow!—we're breathless. You might be, too, when you see this palatial Palace. Management by André Hauri; Concierge Ernest is the perfect Answerman for your Lausanne needs. Highly recommended.

We also have a high regard for the **Royal Savoy**, which, after it came under

recent new management, closed it doors for a thoroughgoing revamping and will appear this spring in entirely new royal raiments. Modernized entrance to this old-fashioned baronial establishment; well-respected restaurant overlooking garden; bar; 2 conference quadrants; swimming pool plus skating rink and tennis courts 200 yards away. The staffers are especially warm and kind here. We look forward to reporting on this born-again and stately *grande dame*. At long last the **Mirabeau** is clean and comfortable; central location and traditional in tone. Ask for a waterside room on the 4th floor; these are the quietest and most viewful. At the **Hôtel de la Navigation** 15 of its 39 bedrooms face the lake, the pleasure-boat harbor, and the distant mountains. Attractive grill and café; mustard-color velvet wall in its small lobby; carpeted corridors with doors of wood planking; double-glaze windows. The flexibility of having 3 beds in some rooms makes it an excellent choice for traveling families. The **Aulac**, also in Ouchy, conjures up a delightfully nautical theme in Le Pirate, an amusing restaurant that resembles an old sailing ship; waiters are dressed in black trousers, white shirts, red cummerbunds, and ascots. All-in-all a comfortable and whimsical package.

The 60-room **La Résidence** adjoins the estate of the luxurious Beau Rivage, its richer Kith. The rooms have been so handsomely refreshed that here is certainly one of the best buys in suburban living. There is also an excellent restaurant in its spacious lakeside garden for summer dining. A reasonably priced and intimate sylvan domain. Excellent for its category. The **Carlton** boasts 55 face-lifted units, all with private bath; try for #310–11, a corner suite; its refurbished Le Richelieu Grill is a favorite of peripatetic royalty; the Ascot Bar is spirited; friendly, ever-helpful Concierge Peter is a BIG plus for keen-eyed Director André L. Chollet. Sound in a cozy way. The **Victoria** greets incomers with a lovely Lurçat tapestry behind the reception desk. Attractive Le Paddock nightclub; snack bar; 65 units, most with bath and some with rubber executive chairs and padded headboards that smelled to us like gymnasium wrestling mats on a hot day; #311 is a pleasant garden-sited double in traditional style. We like this one—except for a few of those isolated appurtenances. The **de la Paix** has undergone a *paix*ful revolution and it sure does glow with pride. Though conveniently located in midcity, the upper floors offer a magnificent command of the lake. The restaurant and bar are added pluses. The **Continental**, hard by the station, chugs in with 123 pleasantly modern bedchambers. Within its slick core are the renewed Le Beaujolais Restaurant for French cuisine and grills, a refreshed snack center, and the updated Natacha bar with dinner and music. There are also a downstairs shooting gallery and a bowling alley, plus the Basement Brasserie. Front units air-conditioned; 5th-floor attic rooms spun up as demisuites; décor highlighted with paneling or stonework in soft brown, yellow, or orange tones. Convenient, comfortable, and functional; better for Hiltonites than for Old Worlders. The **City**, a Georges Fassbind holding, is plain, stark, and distressingly plastic-ridden. Bare lobby; narrow but fresh-looking corridors; bright accommodations with new furniture; 70 bedchambers with only 18 full baths and 4 showers. Popular among students and the parsimonious. The **Alpha**, a clean, 270-bed house, is also a Fassbind interest. Glazed-concrete lobby; cellar-situated Carnotzet for raclette, fondue, and other Alpine specialties; ground-level Calèche restaurant

for more conventional dining; extensive bedroom revampings with wide windows, colorful linens, radios (which we like) and nonclosing closets, low beds, and eensie baths (which we don't like). A fair bet for tolerant trippers. **Parking**, yet another Fassbinder, officially is rated as First-class. Space for more than 200 parkers, about 300 yards from the main station. Its 2 restaurants serve up French cuisine plus specialties such as Fondue Bacchus and Malayan Curry. The **Bellerive**, a converted apartment house, offers a micro-lobby, a black-red-blue-yellow-brown-white miniature bar, and 38 tiny, cramped, functional, sterile bedchambers; not the nest for tall, rangy, or long-shanked Americans. The 104-room **Novotel** boasts a grill and a swimming pool, but more we cannot tell you. The revamped **Château d'Ouchy** is a bulky antique whose site dates back to the twelfth century. Today all bedchambers come with shower and private bath; some accommodations only slightly smaller than Burning Tree Golf Course. Tourist-oriented, but different.

When dinner time rolls around do try the Grill (known also as the **Wellingtonia**, named for California redwoods) at the **Beau Rivage**; it boasts a mighty reputation—and backs it up with truly splendid cuisine by Chef Louis Pelletier, from traditional to simple meats imported from the U.S.A. to the latest fashions from the advanced European kitchen. What amazed us was the very reasonable cost for such magnificent quality. Decorated in Florentine style; maximum of 75 clients; combo music from the delightful adjoining bar; genial, urbane attention; perfect for gentle people; *evenings only and closed on Mondays.* The **Lausanne Palace** Grill is also good, but the mood is cooler. A favorite of the local establishment. **Rôtisserie de la Grappe d'Or** maintains a dubious lead in the city itself among the independent restaurants. Enormous open grill, from which come some of the tiniest servings outside of a Harz Mountain aviary; beamed ceilings, and sophisticated rustic ambiance. *Entre-nous* atmosphere; well-schooled, attentive staff who prefer to perform for the clients whom they know best; many of the choicest selections limited to 2-person portions; priced for guests with big fat, unnumbered accounts in those big, fat Swiss banks. The presentation of the cuisine—as evidenced by the clever rolling apéritif cart, for example—is far more eye-appealing than that of many of France's greatest gastronomic shrines; its quality, however, suffers somewhat by comparison. M. Girardet's **Hôtel de Ville** in the tiny hamlet of *Crissier* is now one of the most talked about shrines on the continent—certainly a recommendation, but so much in demand that you must book at least a week in advance. It is worth it, however, if you've got $140 to spend on a monumental twin meal with a decent wine. You may choose from a set repast or à la carte, but either way you will be transported to gastronomy's heaven. Modern single room with brown textile panels, sleek lighting, beige-cloaked tables with fresh flowers, service on vast floral-etched platters. A no-fault experience, so if you want to give it a whirl, dial Crissier 34•15•14 and hope for the best—which you'll surely receive if you do get in. Closed Sun. and Mon. The **Voile d'Or** ("Golden Sail"), formerly the Centre de l'Hôtellerie, is a unique jammer beginning to heed the helm. Beautiful reed-lined lakeshore situation; pleasant split-level lounge, bar, and restaurant in stonework and Douglas fir, with icicle-thin ceiling fixtures in serpentine pattern; rope carpets, and scatter rugs; orange-and-white-fringed umbrellas dotting the snack ter-

race. It's highly variable, according to local friends who go more frequently than we do. The chef at the **Royal Savoy** is earning his numerous orchids. Croix d'Ouchy, in the **Hôtel Orient**, does delightful things with its choice of Italian dishes and bovine specialties. One room with burgundy carpets, scenes of Siena, blue and mustard textiles, and fresh-cut flowers to add to the cheer. For a medium charge the reward is high. Le Beaujolais in the **Continental Hotel** turns on a reasonable meal for the outlay. The uninterested, slow service, however, reduces the pleasure of the overall experience, according to one cosmopolite who has been several times. La Calèche, ground floor in the **Alpha Hotel**, is fun for rusticity in the city. Steaks of all dimensions and cuts; cafeteria-style service; downstairs Carnotzet for cheese-whizzing. Fair returns for the outlay; very popular. Down the line comes the more modest **Pomme de Pin** (Cité Derrière 15), with its renowned chicken specialties, also good, but far from cheap. **Aux Trois Tonneaux** ("3 Barrels") is taverny, with intimate dimensions and limited menu; we enjoyed our recent meal of stuffed mushrooms and steak. Proprietor Huguin, we're happy to say, is rolling out the barrels again. Pleasant for lodge-type dining. **Chez Charles**, (rue des Mousquines) is a simple family diner; low-cost for substantial quality. Ironically our podiatric plates were alive with frogs' legs and pig's feet. **Café du Jorat** (place de l'Ours 1) is famed for fabulous fondue-fondling. **Mandarin** (avenue du Théâtre 7) wins our fortune cookie for Chinese delights. **Kwong Ming** (av. de Cour 74) is a worthy alternate. **La Cravache**, a pub next to the Palace Hotel, is simple and cozy for a nip 'n sip. For a surprisingly low-cost snack in delightful surroundings, don't forget the pool bar at the **Beau Rivage** in _Ouchy_. The menu costs $10 or less, with cheeseburgers for half as much; salads, grills, and other tempters are on tap. The Sunday Brunch ($15) pipes out a colorful cornucopian buffet from 10:30 A.M. to 2 P.M., which should fill any pilgrim's calorie requirements for the entire sabbath.

Sunny day or starlit evening? The Gauer interests of Berne's Schweizerhof manage the **Hotel du Raisin** at _Cully_, between Lausanne and Montreux. It's a small-town tavern furnished with covered wooden banquettes and touched up appealingly in other respects. Worth a visit for its hearthside dining, but a bit expensive. The **Major Davel Restaurant**, down the slope at water's edge —a combination of café, bar, and restaurant—seems even better. Fish specialties, with Filet de Poisson Belle Meunière and Truite du Lac Poché Hollandaise both delicious; Chicken Curry for 2 is a piquant alternative. **Sauvabelin** is the choice of savvy locals, but we haven't yet had the luck to try it. Other stops of interest along the shore are **Auberge de l'Onde** at _St.-Saphorin_ (rendezvous of artists and authors), **Restaurant Le Monde** at _Grandvaux_ (vineyards and a glorious view; RESERVE IN ADVANCE), **Chez Pitch Restaurant** at _Pully_ (open all year, with reservations also a _must_ in season), and the simple **Les Chevrenils** at _Jorat_, a country house viewing the hills and serving family-style meals that are delicious in flavor and modest in price. Finally, the celebrated **Swiss Chalet** of the Brussels World's Fair was reassembled at _Signal de Sauvabelin_, 1800 feet above the city. It presents a magnificent Alpine panorama, with the blue Léman waters at its feet.

Near _Morges_, on the road to St. Sulpice, be sure to navigate to a converted house known as the **Auberge du Chasseur** (Preverenges), which certainly

qualifies as one of the unsung gastronomic shrines of Switzerland. The owner trained at the previously mentioned Girardet establishment in Crissier, so many of the creations reflect the immaculate standards of the famous Hôtel de Ville. We were particularly betaken by the oysters baked in a light pastry and garnished with thinly shaved vegetables; the fresh duck liver, the escalope de saumon in the Chef's sauce, and the carré d'agneau were also evoked by the divinities. The dessert trolley is so colorful that it would make any self-respecting rainbow blush with shame. This delightful spot and the **Restaurant du Cerf** at *Cossonay* (20 minutes west of Lausanne) are from the private list of our dear friend and former Princeton classmate Bill Jadden, who lives in this region, travels the world, and knows his vittles. This candidate is more attractive to the eye, residing in a single room with arches of stone and a heavy timbered ceiling; a candelabrum provides soft luminescence while candles and roses decorate the 10 glittering tables. Our party of 4 exchanged nibbles from the following platters: mousseline of salmon, ris de veau, julienne de truffe, raw marinated salmon with lemon, and Savarin de loup; desserts were chocolate mousse in a cake form as well as mocha tart. Every bite, swallow, and sigh was blissful. Both of these Jadden "finds" are highly recommended to you with grateful thanks to the friend who pointed us in their directions.

After dark, Lausanne offers nightowls the lavish **Tabaris**, which is on the rise again after a few slack seasons. Rich furnishings, good-size cabaret, yummy B-girls, the usual. **Metropole** and **Paradou** are less plush enterprises, with floor shows and routine appurtenances—some of whom might accept an invitation to the prance. **Brummell**, the nightery in the cellar of the Lausanne Palace, has no affiliation with the hotel. The management is enjoined from using "Lausanne Palace" in any of its publicity. Independent entrance from the street; art-theater-type foyer; textiled walls in lavender and blends; L-shape, softly illuminated, split-level room; striptease agrinding. The **Scotch** provides individual lockers for its loyal patrons' bottles; Young Marrieds like this one for hand-holding. **Bagatelle** attracts the Young Unmarrieds. Name bands always; operated by the Tabaris people. **Johnnie's** comes up with black leather furniture, a mosaic floor, canned music, and fairly reasonable tabs; we saw no B-girls. **Le Paddock** is for side-saddle hand-holding, loose reins, and informal prancing. The **Château d'Ouchy** offers darkling revels indoors only now that the garden has been pruned from its vine. For action along different lines, go to *Divonne-les-Bains* or across the lake to the casino at *Évian* (France); steamer service to the latter all 4 seasons.

LENZERHEIDE-VALBELLA Here are 2 toy villages snuggling together in a mile-high Grisons' valley. There are almost 100 miles of ski runs obtainable via 33 skilifts and cableways; in summer it is a leaf-green dimension of paradise with a multitude of activities for sporty types. Its 2500 beds are divided among 8 top-grade hotels, 11 of medium class, and 9 which offer only bed and breakfast. Our picks locally? (1) **Kurhaus**, (2) **Schweizerhof**. The new **Post-Hotel** (Valbella) might well knock the spots off the traditional leaders here. Cozy rustic appointments; handsome Grill, lounges, and terraces; indoor glass-wrapped swimming pool; all units with bath or shower; southside ones with private balcony. We also hear fond words about the nearby **Guarda Val**, which

some consider to be Switzerland's most unusual country inn. It's a First-class hotel by official standards, uniquely composed of 7 renovated farmhouses, each room individually decorated. The **Valbella Inn**, the **Sporthotel La Riva**, and **Sunstar** all win orchids from ski buffs, too. Each bubbles up with its own swimming pool.

LEYSIN Here's a fast-developing winter sports mecca for budgeteers that is 13 miles by road or 4 by rail from the lake-level junction of Aigle. Admirable location on sun-catching slopes, with a glorious panorama below; téléféric to the tip of the Oldenhorn; a score of simple, not very attractive hotels; restaurants equally plainly adorned but offering solid Swiss quality; heavy patronage by families.

For our francs, the **Grand Hôtel** is biggest and best—and probably one of the only hostelries in the world with its very own railway station. Game room, indoor pool, tennis, bar with dancing. Its Carnotzet, _the_ local hangout, is often merry. Sleeping space for 250 clients; furnishings too spartanlike for some. The undisputed local leader—but a poor relative to the number one houses in scores of other Swiss resorts. **Central-Résidence** turns on an indoor swimmin' hole, a loggia-terrace with every room, a kitchenette, and a full bath count. A youngster with plenty of pepper. **La Mésange** offers a colorful, chipper lobby; an extremely cozy dining room with wide windows framing its L-shape; very small bedrooms, and 2 private baths. Imaginative despite its structural limitations. **Les Orchidées** is a small, sharply angled, pastel-hued edifice dropping downhill from the main road. Bland, zingless furnishings and décor in its public rooms and 25 bedchambers. So-so. The **Eden** we don't know from overnighting, but its view is lovely. **Mont-Riant** nestles by the edge of the forest. All front units with balconies; outstanding cuisine; otherwise routine. **La Paix**, with its trim chalet exterior, is in a somewhat noisy location; friendly staff and atmosphere; tiny, tiny bedchambers. **La Primevère** is simple; it does have a good kitchen. **Relais**, in First class, is comfortable. The remainder are so bareboned that most North American visitors would probably be happier spending the night under a spruce.

Among the non-hotel restaurants, **Prafandaz** for fondue is the big cheese in the local pot, followed by **L'Horizon** and perhaps **Le Leysin**.

LOCARNO, the lowest city in Switzerland (with only a 600-foot elevation), is an ideal stop for the traveler to or from Italy. It has a lovely setting on the shores of Lake Maggiore; the Ticinese here are among the most warmhearted and hospitable people in Europe. Reasonably good accommodations and fine restaurants; one of the scariest (absolutely safe!) cable-car ascents in the Alps; several swimming pools down by the Lido plus one covered dippery; plenty of good shops; International Film Festival in August; the Flower Festival each Whitsunday; friendly atmosphere.

The **Palma au Lac** celebrates more than a century of gracious living, growing mellower every year. Its _haute cuisine_ is internationally famous—for excellent reason. Byronic setting; focal point for high-life and action; terrace dining by the shore in season; friendly bar with piano lilts nightly; attractive French-style restaurant; elegant Coq d'Or Grill with gold flatware, candelabra, and a

14-karat ambiance; courteous reception and staff attitudes. Proprietors Bolli and Frey, aided by Assistant Manager Füry Thommen, are devoted hoteliers; our friend Mr. Bolli's avuncular cheer seems to permeate his house. He has lately waved his magic wallet to make it even more radiant. There's an indoor heated pool, a private strip of lakeside beach, a sauna, a barbershop and beauty salon; many new suites have been unveiled. (Those we've inspected are gorgeous.) All front units with full bath and balcony; back units now about 50% with full plumbing; most rooms are adequate to spacious. Concierge Guiseppe Bass will sort out most any problem. Top recommendation. The spacious **Esplanade** (Aubonne Section) offers a lovely lake view, open-air dining, dancing, a heated pool, tennis court, a restyled lobby, vans of new furniture, and a rekindled spirit that has it glowing radiantly. Here is a bucolic country address to keep in mind, especially if you are on a lazy trip by car to or from Italy. The **Park** is another restful stop. Its turquoise pool is a perfect color meld with the stately braces of peacocks which strut in iridescent splendor at its brim. If you are an avid naturalist who seeks Edwardian amenities in twentieth-century Europe, you might enjoy unpacking your trowel, hoop-skirts, and spats here. For tranquillity seekers, it's an Eden, but it's decidedly not for high-spirited youngbloods accustomed to more razzmatazz. The **Reber**, along the promenade where the Palma au Lac also resides, seems to have grown cooler on our charts. Swimming pool a-bubbling; tennis courts; nightclub next to the Grill; 3rd and 4th floors featuring private refrigerators, safes, and furnishings that are a cross between classic and avant-garde; balconies jutting from each waterside unit; corridors sheathed in mock-wood; baths cramped and poorly executed. When you register, try to snag #208, a wide-angled older type double which is 10% cheaper than the latest wingers—and we think better. The rates are in the same general bracket as our top choice, but the rewards are not so high, in our opinion. The adjoining **Pavilion Reber** offers 14 rooms and 14 baths—a pleasant outbuilding with motel privacy but hotel-room service. Better every year. The **Orselina**, at the top of the funicular winking down at the slope, the town, and Maggiore, is a honey. Kips for 100 relaxers who can probably be heard zzzzz-ing on any quiet afternoon. The modernistic **Muralto**, close to the station, overlooks the lake from midcity. Within its shell is a snack center, a terrace restaurant, a heated pool, a metropolitan post office, a newsstand, 2 levels of shops, and an arcade. The décor is a blend of twentieth-century and earlier themes which, paradoxically, meld well. Spankingly clean and eye-stimulating; bar and refrigerator in lakefront units; good baths with twin basins; huge towels; service primarily for do-it-yourselfers. For what it is, we like it. The **Quisisana**'s best feature is its waterside dining room. Much better dwelling space now, too. The **Rondinella** proudly boasts a covered swimming pool; it has pleasant bedchambers, but a rawboned and unappetizing restaurant is somehow quite popular; we've never sampled the skilletcraft. The **Remorino**, also with a swimming pool, provides space for 44 sleepers; full bath ratio; breakfast only. The **Beau Rivage** has been refashioned under the experienced guidance of Hans Hollenstein. It is functional. The **Excelsior**, next to the Tennis Club, serves up 25 rooms with bath or shower, clean, unadorned simplicity, amateurish management, and budget-bracket tariffs; sun worshipers will revel in its roof-garden solarium. The

Belvédère impresses us as a potentially desirable way-stop which is going to seed—and we wish it were otherwise. The tiny **Alexia Garni**, on the Station Square at Locarno-Muralto, offers breakfast only; Ticino-style lobby, about a dozen rooms in a private house, economy prices. **Zücherhof** is even more simple. The **Motel Losone**, 5 minutes' drive from the center toward Ascona, doesn't send us—except, perhaps, farther down the pike.

Want a real adventure in this region? Try the **Cardada Hotel**, 4500 feet up the Cardada Alp via one of the most hair-raising rides by suspension railway ever sweated by the acrophobic traveler. The view is unbelievable from this little hostelry; if you're not a sissy about cliff-hanging, a night or even a meal here will be an experience you'll never forget.

Locarno's Feed Box Special is **I Due Gatti-Los Gatos**, lashed at 1400 feet to a mountainside just past the hamlet of Brione, 15 or 20 minutes from your hotel. To get up to it, be sure to use the Orselina route, and be sure to take a bug-size Fiat instead of a Cadillac, because the road is narrow. Open terrace with breath-catching panorama; Spanish specialties (including a Catalonian-speaking cat named Muchacho), plus French and Italian dishes; excellent cookery. The setting alone is worth the price of admission.

In town, the **Campagna Ristorante & Grotto** has 4 rooms, 2 fireplaces, and a tavernish architecture; terrace with stone tables for summer dining; modest prices and simple furnishings; typical Ticinese atmosphere. The **Oldrati**, on the main square, has a masculine, ground-floor, "modernistic" tavern and an upper-level, tea-roomy restaurant. Glorious view. Among the hotels, **La Palma au Lac** draws highest kudos from many leading epicurean societies (14 in 1 swoop recently!)—and we most heartily concur. Try to make it when a buffet is scheduled if you also want to give your eyes a feast (usually once a week in Season). The **Esplanade** is agreeable. Both feature alfresco dining in season. **Du Lac** is amply rewarding for the moderate tabs. **Caverna degli Dei** has more of a cave-born nightclub atmosphere than that of a full-blown restaurant. Maritime specialties; dancing nightly; a few hotel rooms for weary revelers. Routine, but it's almost the only late stop in town. The Grotto Grill in the **Grand** is said to be amusing, but we haven't crept in. At *Brissago* (beyond Ascona), the **Giardino**, in an ancient town house, came up with a loftier reputation than foodstuffs on our recent sampling. Perhaps you'll have better luck.

LUCERNE, with the deserved slogan of *"Living* Lucerne," has the greatest influx of Americans of any Swiss city, town, or hamlet. Its traditional star attractions are the Lion Monument, the year-round Glacier Gardens with its museum, the covered bridge, and the famous August-September International Music Festival. Its 2 pet mountains are supplemented by a scenic 18-hole golf course, a fascinating Transport Museum (historic and/or modern locomotives, cars, airplanes, plus a steamer; a star-bright planetarium has twinkled on the scene and there's a restaurant) and a suspension cable-car system to the top of Mt. Pilatus. In town, the sparklingly refreshed Kursaal-Casino spins for penny-ante gamesters (boule only), dancers, and diners. The Casino Chalet stirs in a dash of local flavor with fondue, local color with flag-throwers, and local sounds with yodelers. As in Florence, tourism makes 99% of its wheels

go around; into this center of 70-thousand inhabitants, from 10 to 30 thousand foreigners pour *daily* off the boats, trains, and cars; there are now at least 65 hotels with 5500 beds. If you're a first-tripper, naturally you won't want to miss the landmark. But hit it in the spring or fall, if you can—because in peak season it's so jammed with sightseers that its atmosphere, normally so alluring, becomes tinny, mechanical, and production-belt in feeling.

Hotels The fresh-faced **Grand National** ranks among the key stopping places of the nation for appointments, luxury, and attention to the guest. Its philosophy reflects a dedication to providing the finest in these changing times. Hence the number of rooms have been reduced to 75 and vastly improved; a *Résidence* has been created with 30 lakefront apartments for longer stays; there's a new swimming pool, the swinging San Francisco night club, barber and beauty salon, travel agency, and boutiques. There are also the Promenade (a quayside tearoom), the Pfyffer Stube (a grill), the Viennese Café, and the Carousel Bar with 100-year-old wooden horses leading the way to drink. All-in-all big, BIG changes—and all of them praiseworthy. The **Palace** also has rebounded dramatically from its earlier listlessness; young-in-heart deluxe wayfarers might enjoy it just as much as Grand National. Swinging Intimo nightclub in split-level with ruby and sapphire tones, *belle époque* fixtures, Lautrec prints, and the ambiance of a soft-spoken discothèque; aristocratic public rooms; Mignon-Grill and bar; nearly every bedchamber and bath spiffed up, most of them boasting fabric wall coverings underlined with foam-rubber matting for silent nights; raw-silk curtains usually mated to upholstered headboards; a handful of mother-in-law rooms. A modern-style wing plus a pool and a sauna are on the future list. With its enviable setting on the lakeside promenade, we think more and more Americans of taste will flock to its doorstep. Also open year round. The **Schweizerhof** claims an excellent lakefront location. Fuddy-duddy features, fossilized furnishings, and flagrant fustiness are strategically offset by up-to-date trappings and occasional revisions. In the younger wing, every accommodation is air-conditioned, double doors are installed, and all appurtenances have been reupholstered or replaced. The older wing still suffers from geriatric miseries. Why in heaven's name doesn't it perk up its bar and throw out the cheap carney-show candy game machine in its lobby? We are still hoping that the dust will begin to fly, now that the Hauser family proprietors are—after disgracefully shameless years of delay—speaking franc-ly. The **Carlton-Tivoli** is still being extensively remodeled by Director Fritz Furler, who is aided in the day-to-day operations by Robert and Silvia Westermaier, an experienced young couple. Entire façade modernized; roof-garden restaurant with lakeside dining in addition; Grill and expanded terrace recently unveiled; kitchen recooked not long ago; oodles of bedrooms refashioned; 3 luxury suites, 120 rooms, and a full bath count; high incidence of refurnishings and updatings including the addition of TV and refrigerators for many units. Private bathing and water skiing; 4 tennis courts; dancing in 1 of its 2 popular bars. Now youthfully zesty; a very good bet at the price—*if* you hit the right location. The **Astoria** an 8-story establishment on the main Pilatusstrasse thoroughfare, has been renovated and given a lobby on the street level. (Previously guests signed in near the roof line.) A much better arrangement in a much better house. The midcity **Monopol & Metropole** has been

completely revamped in a spiffy way. Good medium-price dining room; busy bar; 5th-floor units never given to groups; #314 especially pleasant twin in Tirolean theme. Solid value. The **Montana**, 250 feet above the Palace, is reached by funicular or road. Glass-and-aluminum entrance tacked onto a period piece; 75 rooms and 45 baths; most units with balcony; 80% of them face the lake; we're fond of #114; closed in winter. Fair. The sweet little **Luzernerhof** has cozy rooms and picture windows with Venetian blinds; improved lobby, reception, and bar; 12-room annex; good dining salon consistently serving up some of the yummiest cuisine in the region; all accommodations so clean and bright that they cheer the soul. The **Wilden Mann** also offers one of the leading restaurants in the city; fresh-as-Swiss-cream kitchen and modernized dining facilities; meal-exchange program with the Carlton-Tivoli and the Gütsch (see below); 2 small, quiet penthouse suites with terraces overlooking a charming crazy quilt of roofs; 46 rooms with bath; antique-style décor in this architectural joining of 7 tiny houses. Now under the management of Walter Arndt with his wife Susi at reception. We've never stayed at the **Royal**, but it looks adequate for its category; closed November to Easter. The **Hermitage**, 5 minutes out at Seeburg, impressed us as quite an investment for the noise, the discomfort, and the inconvenience that one might encounter for even the very low rates; creaky old section; loud, road-sited, modern annex. Not recommended by this book under any circumstances. The twelfth-century **Balances & Bellevue** is in a special category. Pilgrims with a penchant for antiquity might feel they're stepping right into a Brueghel landscape here (or, if they're lodged facing the street, into a boiler factory which clangs until 1 A.M. or 2 A.M.). Romantic painted façade commanding the Weinmarkt (Wine Market Square) and the River Reuss, on the more tranquil postern side; décor predictably flounced in velvets, tapestries, and similarly fussy froufrou; warm, attractive Zur Ratslaube dining room with abundant art work, red curtains, and chain-held chandeliers; enchanting vine-lined terrace that will level you, eyeball-to-eyeball, with inquisitive swans. When Zur Ratslaube overflows its capacity, clients may take their meals in the mural-clad Rotes Gatter, in which hangs a portrait of this very room painted 8 centuries ago. If your beard measures 9 feet, and if you can tolerate the correct but sometimes disagreeable-to-wayfarers current management, we think you might adore this gentle, venerable escape from the Missile Era. The comfortably revamped **Gütsch** is also in a singular bracket in our reporter's notebook. This intersting castle-like structure is located 5 minutes above the city, with an enchanting vista of the lake and the huddle of pitched roofs below. Authentic iron battle masks flanking the entrance, plus such decorative carry-overs inside as lances, suits of armor, and mounted deer heads; swimming pool in the forest garden; open patio with terrace-nibbling in summer; 2 dining rooms; dancing nightly in the rustic hall; wine cellar with Fondue service. Its 45 gaily recast rooms include 4 extra-charming duplex apartments in split-level arrangement for intimate hideaways, some units with four-poster beds, open ceiling beams, soft carpeting, and the atmosphere of a medieval fortress; now ther's an excellent private bath with every accommodation. Taking giant strides under Manager Pius Wallimann, who is assisted by his personable wife, Carla. Here's a manorial haven for the right type of overnighter. Down by the lake again, the **See-**

burg, with space for about 100 Seeburgers, opened its portals recently, then added an annex to augment its capacity. All units canted toward the water; all with bath or shower and balcony; 3 restaurants. The **de la Paix** has undergone a peaceful revolution. It still doesn't suffer from aggressive tendencies, but the pool is a cool fillip.

Restaurants **Old Swiss House** remains the first choice for a refined and colorful repast, thanks to the tireless hard work of urbane Proprietor Willy Buholzer and his equally indomitable wife, Hanny. Its décor and ambiance are still Overdone Swiss, with too much aimed toward the tourist trade (waitresses in costume, antique crucifixes, and the like)—but here is such a tight ship that the cuisine is excellent, the service kind, and the welcome warm. The price scale is substantial by national standards. It gives us great pleasure to recommend this one as the best independent dining place of the city. Reservations mandatory in season. Lonesome for home? Try the delicious, unfancy wares at the **Luzernerhof.** The Dittli family can fill our bill any morning, noon, or night with their honest creations. Here vegetables taste like vegetables; food tastes like food; there's no trickery. The service is so sweet that the waitresses urge you to finish the huge portions; the dining room is attractive; the prices are very reasonable. What traveler could ask for more? Highly recommended. Next, the **Wilden Mann** features Châteaubriand steaks and similar belt-busting fare. Tavern motif in one segment; sleeker, more international lines in another; slipping a bit on our scales. **Schwanen** is schwimmin' handsomely under the aegis of Director Urs Lauper. We must get back for another sampling at the **Stadtkeller,** which a local friend stoutly avows is one of the better attractions in the city. Swiss music, Swiss food, Swiss alpenhorn tooting from special stage—almost more Swiss than the Swiss, to please its big foreign trade. This city lives for the tourist in season and here is one of its magnets. Other entrys for sampling include the **Hofbräuhaus** and the **Braukeller.** The Lapin Restaurant hops in the **Hôtel de la Paix.** Split-level dining room in sleek rustic-modern; waitresses in provincial costumes; moving-color-slide gismo for selecting your dishes; some counter service; choice of 7 types of sausage, the house specialty; our Bratwurst and Rösti were delicious. The owner's wife is a sister in the Real family who conjure up such culinary magic in Liechtenstein's leading gastronomic haven. The **Li Tai Pe Chinese Restaurant** (Furrengasse 14), has been converted into a Jade Pavilion of the Orient by hardworking Robert and Margaret Chi Tsun. (He was the former number one diplomatic aide to Gen. Chiang Kai-shek.) Breathtaking collection of rare Cathay artworks; 5 Far Eastern cooks mind the Soo-Gaw pots; savory cuisine and lovely presentation. If you're a party of 4, be sure to order the Peking specialty variously called Chrysanthemum Pot or Chue Hua Kuo or Steamboat; this cauldron of Oriental treasures is, as far as we know, unequalled in Europe. It must be ordered 1 day ahead; we venture this would be one of the memorable feasts of a lifetime. Top recommendation. **Raben** (in the old part of town) is an upstairs rôtisserie with 9 tables, beamed ceilings, tapestries, crossbows, and leather casements; worth a try. **Galliker's** is redolent of an English pub atmosphere. Hardy fare for these hardy Alpine rancheros; Pot au Feu seems to be the favorite choice. Bully for it. For light but full meals, **Café Arcade** is just the ticket; inside tables, plus a ringlet of alfresco *couverts* bordering the water-

side and the Open Market; excellent pastries; Mrs. Helfenstein speaks English. Colorful as a ham-and-eggery. **Da Peppino** works up Italian specialties. _Buono!_ Calories afloat? Try the good ship **William Tell,** moored in front of the American Express office. It carries a cargo of tea, snacks, and full repasts. _Bon voyage!_

Night Life   Lucerne isn't the wildest town. The expansively modernized **Kursaal-Casino** may provide a mild tingle, if you like to bet nickels; you'll find more things to do and nicer places to do them here today or tonight; now it's operative year round. The **Dupont** is slightly better than it was, which still isn't saying much. **Kakadu,** when we peeked in, was _really_ rocking. The flashier set were getting their kicks by blowing the paper envelopes off the drinking straws. Yipes! The Palace Hotel offers the **Intimo** which we've already described. The **Adler** is a disco hub.

Shopping   Now for watches in this center-of-centers. After comparing the stocks and prices of probably all the major dealers in the land, we have settled upon the obviously outstanding pair—one for the Ford-Oldsmobile type of buyer, and the other for the Rolls-Cadillac league.

No American or Japanese watch can meet the quality of the best creations of these Swiss master workmen. Because standards are so high and costs are comparatively so low, the traveler who goes home without a good Swiss timepiece on his wrist and 2 or 3 inexpensive ones in his or her bag for gifts hasn't made the most of this fine opportunity. The U.S. Customs has no limit on the number you may bring in for personal use, but there are restrictions on the number of certain brand names allowable. So please check before stocking up. Don't bargain. Prices are rigid.

With the widest variety from dependable low-cost to precision luxury horo-loges and a globewide guarantee service, ★ ★ ★ ★ **Bucherer** is the largest and best-known watch retailer in the world. No other establishment in the industry can offer so much to so many, buyer and browser alike. The headquarters are in _Lucerne,_ where you will find a choice of 50-thousand different items. One of the primary reasons they give such enormous values is that they manufac-ture their own watches from the movement up. The Gift and Souvenir Depart-ments are packed with goodies; the jewelry range spans from the inexpensive Charms Department to all price categories in their eye-popping yellow-and-white gold articles. New styles are constantly being added by their maestros, who specialize in creating diamond solitaires and in manipulating such gems as emeralds, sapphires, and rubies. There are 4 branches in the _Zürich_ area, plus others in _Geneva, Lausanne, Basel, Locarno, Lugano, Interlaken, Burgen-stock, St. Moritz, Davos,_ and _New York._ Tops for the budget, normal and fatter pocketbooks.

Since 1854, ★ ★ ★ ★ **Gübelin's** dynamic spirit of creation has inspired the industry as it has continued to add to its reputation as Europe's most honored citadel for quality in its field. For more than a century cosmopolites have basked in the innovations given them by the advanced design coups of these magicians. "The House of Time" is their enticing headquarters here, with elegant, impressive branches in _Zürich, Geneva, Lugarno, Bern, Basel, St. Moritz, Bürgenstock,_ and _New York._ Holding the all-time record for thinness is their latest triumph: The "1.98 mm. Quartz," the Rolls-Royce of Eterna.

Another super-distinguished success is the Gübelin Duo-Quartz watch for Him and for Her. They are equally renowned wizards with precious gems—diamonds, emeralds, rubies, sapphires and all. Prices? Nary a worry! Just walk straight in; their stocks cater to almost every budget. This institution is owned and directed by the world-famous virtuoso, Walter Gübelin and his two sons, Marco and Thomas. You'll never find another treasure house displaying the same masterworks as at Gübelin!

This city is also the apex of Switzerland's most lively, prominent, and dynamic photographic enterprise, which also happens to be the most popular with the U.S. shutterbug—the ★ ★ ★ ★ ★ **Weber Group**. If you seek honesty and reliability, quality and versatility, top-drawer advice, and top-drawer service, here's your perfect answer. For the largest and best selection of all leading cameras (worldwide service certificate with every purchase), try **Weber b. Bahnhof** (opposite station); for the pacesetter in high-quality Zeiss sunglasses and general optical aids, go to **Central Photo & Optics** (Hertersteinstrasse 47) or **Weber Victoria Ltd.** (Pilatusstrasse 18); for electric or electronic equipment, souvenirs, and the like, proceed to the large, modern **Tefora Ltd.** (Grendel 8). If your problem is an especially puzzling one, Paul Weber himself is usually on tap, so do not hesitate to ask for this ranking expert in person. The best part is that you can totally depend upon the renowned Weber service, just as have so many other thousands upon thousands of its delighted North American clients, among so many others. Absolutely unrivaled.

LUGANO is on the lakeside not far from Locarno, backstopped by the mountains. It has been taking giant strides recently to improve its hospitality facilities. The bustling modern Congress Center herds conventioneers from all over the world. One of its biggest drawing cards is the gambling casino at Campione d'Italia ("Sample of Italy"), almost directly across the lake by frequent ferry service—an isolated chunk of Italian territory, 1.8 square miles in area; apart from the gaming, it's pretty dull. The steamer excursion to Gandria is mobbed in summer. About 160 hotels or pensions, almost all of them on the jump; funiculars, chair lifts, and cable cars galore. One thing which shouldn't be missed is the fabulous Thyssen collection of Goya, El Greco, Holbein, Dutch masters, and Italian Renaissance artists which is housed in a private museum adjoining this family's villa; it is open to the public from April to October on Fri. and Sat. from 10 A.M. to noon and from 2 P.M. to 5 P.M., also Sun. afternoons. A waterside hub that's becoming increasingly popular with Americans; it's best seen around the Easter holiday period, in our opinion.

Near Lugano at Melide (lake bridge on main highway from Italy), a unique exhibition called Swissminiatur has already wooed more than a million spectators. Towns, hamlets, castles, mountains, automatic railways, remote-control steamers, and other real-life things are reproduced in exact dimensions and detail, on a scale of 1 to 25. Surely worth a stop if you're staying in Lugano or driving the southern route—or if you're an elf. The sport centers of _Carona_ and _Bedano,_ both nearby, are now catching on, too.

Lugano's 150-plus hotels and pensions have changed radically over the past few seasons. In the town, the lakeside **Eden** has been given a shower of

delights. It is now vivaciously colorful and modernistic. Sunbursts, arcs, glowing beads, bangles, painted rainbows, dyed leather, cheery textiles, sprightly
plastics, and other gladsome inspirations of fanciful artistry give this house a
decorative character unmatched anywhere in contemporary Europe. Totally
upbeat lobby in cool, whimsical tones; fairytale lounge with coral sink-in seats
matching the carpets; canary-yellow breakfast room dolloped by orbital disks;
grill ringed by circular patterns; ultra-hip turquoise snack bar; adjoining waterside terrace for dining, sipping, or dancing; heated pool plus another one filled
with salt *(sic)* water—in landlocked Switzerland. Bedchambers also flairfully
attired, with balcony, radio consoles, TV, and refrigerator; predominating
schemes of olive, blue, or red. This one now stays open year round. In the
nearby shoreside village of **Morcote,** the **Olivella Au Lac** scoops clean-lined
luxury into a parfait of tranquillity. Viewful French restaurant; tavern-style
snackery; amusing nightclub (watch out for those chairs that resemble a
shark's mouth); glass-fronted indoor swimmery plus garden-sited pool; massage and beauty parlors; nursery. The bedchambers are smart but not spectacular; comfort standards range nearer to superior First class than to Deluxe. Very
worthy as a hideaway, if you don't mind the distance from the center. Back
in the city, the **Splendide-Royal** now has been given a spiffing up and a
watering down—the latter via an indoor domed and skylighted natatorium.
Classic resort mien, with all the traditional appurtenances; location on main
boulevard facing lake (a disadvantage shared by all other major hostelries
except the Arizona); waterfront bar. Try to get accommodations on the 3rd
or 4th floors, which are the most modern in mood. Open all year. The **Europa**
has also been on the jump. Very recently restyled and updated; modernized
dining room; adjoining outdoor patio with bubbling fountain and awning
arcade; heated covered pool with hanging garden and bar; service occasionally
rankling; parking for 50 cars; street-level shops and Café Boulevard where
snack-meals appear. Sleeping accommodations are pleasant; front corner doubles are best; well liked by upper-echelon tour groups. The **Bellevue au Lac**
offers the following: a fresh lobby; tasteful dining salon plus open-air grill; bar;
most rooms converted to modern tone; color TV on request (but we prefer the
lake view from the balconies); extra-efficient kitchen; all units now with private
bath. Much improved and now staying open for all seasons. The 60-room
Arizona, high on a hill overlooking the town and the water, is a friendly and
comfortable oasis for the weary motorist. Total revamping just completed; all
rooms with bath or shower, balcony, and angular walls in irregular directions.
It was purchased by the bright-eyed and bright-idea-ed Eden gardeners. Off-
beat but surprisingly pleasing. The **Du Lac,** hard by the water, also has been
totally revivified. Swimming pool in attractive setting; managed smoothly by
Mr. Corrado Kneschaurek. Very pleasant. The modernistic, efficiency-minded
La Residenza, a tawny youngster, serves breakfast only. The **Holiday-Select,**
also recently hatched, is best from its upper floors, which provide a view of
the lake; there's a sauna, but otherwise too many extras of note. The cream-
colored **Motel Vezia,** 10 minutes along the St. Gothard highway, is a steadily
improving possibility for the roadbound. Adjoining restaurant; heated pool—
red-hot sauna, too; low rates; 150 beds; most units with bath or shower. Tip-top
administration by Roland and Rosemarie Wilke, formerly of the Arizona. The

Excelsior shelters 100 souls per night—not with much inspiration, either, in our view. The **Plaza** is a bargain, considering its competition. About 2 blocks from the lake; 33 small, functional rooms, all with radio and bath or shower; bed-and-breakfast only; open year round. The **Schmid**, a white-balconied old-fashioned house midvillage in *Paradiso* (foot of the San Salvatore funicular), is clean, quiet, and comfortable; rates are low for its full-pension rewards. In the district, the **Admiral** sails in as an imposing member of the local flotilla. Handsome dining, sipping, and snacking areas; indoor and outdoor pools; good and fresh comfort standards. Very trim indeed. The **De la Paix** also seems to be a relaxing medium-price oasis in this suburb; it was given a full refitting plus airconditioning and sound proofing. The **Commodore** sails under the burgee of Manager Giuseppe Bazzani, a Hilton alumnus. This one has a fine situation and many up-to-date riggings to recommend it. A sister operation, the **De la Paix** in *Lugano Paradiso,* provides a heated open-air pool around which meals are sometimes served if the weatherman is kind. Both are very nice for their category. We must soon size up the park-bound **Villa Castagnola** in outlying *Cassarate* and the restyled **Lago di Lugano** aparthotel in neighboring *Bissone;* both boast swimming facilities; the former seems to offer numerous baronial touches.

The city's best kitchen used to be the **Hôtel Splendide-Royal,** but it has been colorfully upstaged by the flairfully renewed **Eden**. Full meals or snacks are available at the latter. The **Capo San Martino,** on the main highway to Italy, is on a promontory which is medium-high over the water; vast terrace service; clean; cheaper and quieter; very popular for lunching and gazing.

Within the city, **Bianchi** now brooks no pretenders to its independent crown. It is old-fashioned and solid, with gold-silk walls, high ceilings, a fireplace, and no-nonsense fare. Recommended to the hungry Inner Man, if not to the Glamor Seeker. **Galleria,** in an arcade off via Vegezzi, comes up with reasonably good vittles at fair prices. **Orologio** is beginning to tick again; okay if you're a VIP or known to the management, so be sure to have your concierge shovel it on before strutting in. (This irks us, but that's the way of the *monde.*) **Grotto del Renzo,** 3 miles into the hills toward *Sorengo,* is pleasant for typical fare.

MARTIGNY, a short 35 minutes from Lausanne, is a pleasant little place, but it is so undistinguished that it wouldn't be worth mentioning were it not the headquarters of **Tidstrand of Sweden**. Most observers find it unchallenged as the greatest designer and manufacturer of blankets and allied products in existence, with worldwide distribution limited only to the most illustrious specialty shops and department stores. Because of tax difficulties in its home-land, it has opened a warehouse at rue de Léman 33, where you can also purchase its exquisitely hued blankets, throws, shawls, skirts, ensembles, and more. A visit here should definitely be to your advantage. Hours: 8 A.M. to noon and 1:30 P.M. to 5 P.M. If you are running up to *Verbier*, Tidstrand has a small showroom in this ski resort.

MERLIGEN **Beatus** (on Lake Thun midway between Thun and Inter-laken; modern in concept; indoor pool; 140 rooms with baths and balconies;

private beach; this one's an absolute peach; definitely worth a detour to pause here).

MONTREUX, in grandma's day a Main Station on the Grand Tour and later an unwitting victim of overpopularity by the Follow-the-Leader Set, is bouncing back through her forward-looking and lively luring of the big-fish traveler. With the opening of the conference and exhibition center, conventions inevitably headquarter here in winter, fall, and early spring. The Casino includes a stunning array of restaurants, night spots, a movie house, and a recording studio. You should also take in the dramatically medieval Castle of Chillon, the lakeside promenades and roads, the heated pool, tennis, golf, the International Television Symposium (biannually), the Jazz Festival (July), and the Classical Music Festival each September. The Great St. Bernard Tunnel (coupling Germany's autobahn and Italy's Autostrada) is nearby, so in high season there's a certain funnel effect; at other times the town snoozes peacefully.

Hotels   Among its hotels, the **Palace**, under the wing of Director Alfred Frei, is worth the francs in value. Brighter entry and lobby; informal dining salon; *Salle de spectacles;* bar, shopping arcade, and glass-lined elevators to the restaurant level; kitchen rebuilt; virtually all of its 270 rooms totally freshened, with the best facing the lake and with balcony; lovely pool with Bather's Bar and cabanas. Commendable on every score. The new lakeside **Continental** is the next-door neighbor to the Convention Center. Space for 400 conventional visitors. **Eden au Lac** nods by the waterfront promenade, another Victorian dowager of excellent grooming; the small restaurant at terrace level is justly proud of its fish specialties; the lobby and another dining spread are one flight up. The 170-room-and-bath, chain-operated **Eurotel** makes a vigorous splash with an indoor-outdoor pool plus sauna and massage facilities; 2 handsome dining areas; many units with kitchenette; rooms ending with "5" featuring lakefront balcony. For modernists who prefer sleekness and dash in their architecture to strict conventionality, here's the lone choice in town. The **Excelsior**, on the lake, is blessed by blissful vistas and the lively ownership of Mr. and Mrs. Fritz Liechti. Every room has been cunningly redone; additional major works also have been wrapped up, including a lobby, bar, expansion of the Grill and terrace, redecoration of the dining room (with delicious food as a standard bonus), a new wing of apartments with its own pool, sauna, and sporting club. The southwest corner doubles (rooms #136, 156, 176: 196) are extra-beguiling in taste, brightness, charm, livability, and space. The **National** has also been given the works in its beauty treatment. Lobby and public sections agreeably redone; appetizing à la carte Restaurant Français plus the Panoramic dining salon; fresh-as-droplets garden-sited pool. Long-stayers should be sure to order the units with the big baths; the small ones are passable only for overnighters. Now creditably on the ball. The **Golf** doesn't shoot its par; uninspired and lackluster, despite some earnest perkup touches such as the repainting of its façade. Other worthy choices include the smallish **Bonivard**, the somewhat larger **Europe** (different from the Eurotel), the 100-pillowed **Helvétie**, a little pearl if you are looking for a charming family-run Swiss shelter. The refashioned **Splendid** is well regarded for its ground-level

pub. **Pension Masson** is a neighbor of Chillon castle, which means it's a long, long hike into town; the house is fresh and worthy, as is the **Pension Wilhelm** (rue du Marchè), which is immaculate but has a low bath count. **Bon Port**, with 2 dining rooms, and **Bon Accueil** are both modern in taste. **Victoria**, at *Glion*, row has its own swimmery. The **Alpes Vaudoises** is for traditionalists cheifly; we like it.

Restaurants Le Montagnard ("The Mountain Man") is our top choice. About 15 minutes up by taxi you'll find this former old stable, hand-transformed by Hans Odermatt personally, who did most of the carpentry, the masonry, and the perspiring. The main hall is a split-level woody area with a slate-roofed bar to one side (note especially the all-wood clock at the door). Lights in brass bells, old-fashioned farm implements, chamois pelts, waiters in regional costumes, a mural, a loft, and several tables outside for warm-weather dining complete the picture. Don't fail to try "riz montagnard," the big specialty of the house; it's superdelicious. Herr Odermatt, with beard, a huge chef's cap, mountain knickers, and perfect English with a strong Australian accent (!), is a charmer. Liveliest in the evening; very good. **Manoire**, another Alpine alternate about 4500 feet up on the Col de Jaman (a normal 40-minute ride from Montreux) is another typical highland nest. Open-air rôtisserie; simple fare-of-the-country well prepared. Now back to the town itself: The recently and lavishly redecorated Grill of the **Casino** is extra-pleasant for elegant dining. If your tastes run to the *nouvelle cuisine,* try the above average **Le Pont de Brent**, which lately has been refashioned. The **Museum Club** harks back to the 13th century when it was a wine cellar. Entry via an antique arch to subterranean nooks for atmospheric sipping and dining; old pots and pans decorate the walls; music and dance available in one segment. Fun and different. Other fair bets include the **Richemont**, **Du Soleil**, and the **Chamossaire**. La Vieille Ferme is a rustic farmhouse panning out Swiss and French platters; don't fail to sample the Chef's own homebaked ryebread. Yum. Don't bother with Chillon Castle. Ugh!

MORAT (or **MURTEN** in German): **Le Vieux Manoir** is now excellent, so please refer to our full report under the hotel listings for Berne.

ʹORGES Hotel du Lac (and it's smack on the *lac*). Other choices: **Mont Blanc au Lac** or La Couronne. Usually, we stop here only for a meal while en route to another bedroom. The somewhat overrated Chez Felicie rôtisserie will stuff you happily with grilled chickens. The **Mésange**, the **Union**, and the **Léman** are recommendable.

NEUCHÂTEL Our hotel choices run this way: (1) **Beaulac** (efficiency type, built on wonderful lakeside position; 40 small rooms with tiny baths, showers, and radio, plus 6 with toilet only; open-air-terrace dining, private jetty "beach"; coolly efficient). (2) **Terminus** has an excellent chief conductor who is pouring on the steam; it's now chugging along happily. (3) **Touring** has a café but no restaurant. We haven't seen the 240-bed **Eurotel**, but we'd bet on it anyway since things are so spare hereabouts. The **City** and **Beaux-Arts** are

clean but routine. This town's blue-ribbon bet for dining is **Des Halles**. It has a classic French personality in one portion, a brasserie in another. The steamship, **Le Vieux Vapeur**, docked in the harbor, is a cargo of delights for nautical nibblers. **Du Théâtre, Beau-Rivage**, and **St. Honoré** are substantial; on a sunny day, the lakeside terrace of the ultramodern **Beaulac Hotel** offers a lovely setting. **Buffet de la Gare**, believe it or not, is darned good for your francs. And so is the restaurant of the **Hôtel Beaux-Arts**. **Le Jura** takes pride in the manufacture and production of Neuchâtel specialties; try them; they're good. We're told that **La Grappa** and the **Hôtel Auvent** out at *Boudevilliers* are okay, but we've tried neither. In *Saint-Blaise*, **Au Boccalino** does nice things for Italian cookery; it is 3 miles out of town.

NYON   For overnighting, we'd first choose the **Hostellerie of the XVI Century**. Also **Du Clos de Sadex** or possibly the **Des Alpes**. For dining, *Corsino* is a lakeside wonder.

PONTRESINA   The famous **Schlosshotel** skis away with the crown in this winter wonderland, but since the Club Méditeranée took it over, alas, membership is now the price of admission. There's an indoor pool, one of the finest in Europe, with a fully mirrored wall reflecting the snow-draped Alps through floor-to-ceiling windows; it's a sapphire gem. Panorama Bar with mountain view. If you are a club person, very good indeed. The nearby **Kronenhof-Bellavista** seems tacky compared to its elegant peer—especially when you first see that huge, ridiculous illuminated crown on top of its domed rotunda. Swimming pool its greatest pride; bowling, minigolf, children's playroom; adjoining skating and curling rinks; lovely open terrace for lunch and sunbathing, with separate bar; Rustic Tavern and Fondue Grill for regional or seasonal specialties. About 175 rooms; low bath count; furnishings generally not very attractive; one of the best kitchens in the valley. The Swiss-rustic **Schweizerhof** appears totally modernized. Cheery, hardy-fare restaurant with cheese specialties; greater variety of nationalities on its register than many other houses in the district; kind service. Solid, stolid, and recommendable. The **Sport Hotel** has polished off an extensive renovation program, adding the Nordiska bar in the process. Big doubles; we like #11, #45, #82, and #122 as extra-spacious twins. Coming up rapidly. The **Walther** has finally been spruced up. We like the spruce in the Clubhütte nightclub, too. **Engadinerhof** is trying to make improvements. Bedrooms still so-so on our inspection; restaurant going strong. The **Atlas** reformed its world; it now stays open winter and summer. For budgeteers, the village-edge **Steinbock**, owned by the Walther, is now very pleasant. **Bernina**, also outlying, has an amiable ambiance. No rave. The **Palü** is so modern in tone that it seems almost Scandinavian. Small bedrooms but appealing public corners; now offering half-board instead of breakfast only. Not bad for its type.

RAPPERSWIL   (1) **Schwanen** (up-to-date rooms overlooking the Lake of Zürich; food, service, and bar above average; medium prices; unruffled and good); (2) **Du Lac**, (3) **Speer**, and (4) **Hirschen**—all 3 routine.

RIGI KALTBAD   A sport center called the **Hostellerie Rigi** has replaced the Grand Hotel which burned down several years ago. Indoor pool for winter paddlers; spacious "dispersal" construction rather than "compressed" architecture of conventional hostelries; sounds revolutionary.

ROSSINIÈRE   The living antique, **Grand Chalet**, steals the Vaudois thunder locally.

ST. GALLEN   This mountainous pocket is a lovely piece of Switzerland. Here's how we rate the hotels locally: (1) **Walhalla** (opposite railroad station; commercial but well run by the Leu-Waldis team; clean as a moon rocket; entrance to ground floor, popular, café-style Stadtrestaurant). (2) **Hecht** (management by Roland Studer; rooms modernized; 50% with bath or shower; excellent ground-floor restaurant; appealing downstairs bar with pianist). (3) the refashioned **Metropol** (across from the terminal; 36 rooms, all with full bath or shower; Peter Musa, the chief). (4) **Im Portner** (café on ground floor; rooms neat and clean; Mr. and Mrs. H. U. Egli-Moser are trying hard; we hear that their labors are paying dividends). At neighboring *Gossau*, the modernized **Ochsen** is tops. The tiny **Rössli Flawil**, 8 1/2 miles from St. Gall, offers a pleasant restaurant, public rooms, and extra-basic bedchambers; operated by the chef-owner; 8 rooms and 3 baths; 20 minutes by secondary road; a little country inn that you might adore, but don't expect a Schweizerhof. In *Wil*, chug straight into the futuristic-styled **Derby Bahnhof**.

The stucco-and-timber **Walliserkeller** is tops for regional dishes such as fondues, raclette, and other cheese-whizzes. Taverny atmosphere with plates as wall-sconce reflectors, hanging lanterns, a charcoal grill, and a smoky air; extensive menu. Good, as long as you know what it is. The previously mentioned **Hecht Hotel** offers superb cuisine. **Baratella** is an Italian *trattoria* that many wanderers like. **Seeger Bar-Tea Room** (plus discothèque on the first floor) is busy and amiable around the Lipton's hour—but stay away on Saturday nights, because so many customers are in the pot that they jam its spout.

Swiss embroideries and handworked appliqués have been famous for centuries; so have the St. Gallen linens and organdies, the most distinguished in Europe. For the best values and most tasteful stocks, try the nearest **Sturzenegger** store. Headquarters are in *St. Gallen* (St. Léonhardstr. 12); home base for the mills that make those gorgeous materials; branches are located in *Zürich, Geneva, Lucerne, Berne, Basel, Crans sur Sierre, Davos, Gstaad, Interlaken, Montreux, St. Moritz*, and *Zermatt*.

ST. MORITZ,   roughly 6000 feet high, is the most celebrated winter resort —and a delightful summer resort, too. It is a cluster of 4 small communities strung along a mountain valley like glistening pearls on a green or white string; the Village, the Spa, St. Moritz-Suvretta, and St. Moritz-Champfèr are its components. Winter traditionally has been very elegant and sophisticated, while summer, more sedate (and ideal for children). St. Moritz remains The Queen of Swiss Resorts, despite its accelerating influx of packaged tours and clubmanship festivities. If any gems have toppled out of her crown of late, it surely is the result of the hardness of the Swiss franc and the softness of the

economies of the other nations. Train, bus, and air-taxi connections with most principal cities; nearly 60 hotels, from super-plush to simple, clean and amply confortable pensions; scores of restaurants, from chichi, black-tie establishments to holes-in-the-wall; probably the most fabulous winter sports facilities of the world, from the Cresta toboggan run to the Olympic bobsled run to Olympic ski jumps to 18 ice rinks to almost 3-score ski routes to curling lanes; helicopter service for skiers or sightseers, plus ski-plane airport on a glacier, plus an aerial cableway extension to 11-thousand feet which combine to hustle a capacity of 19-thousand snow-bunnies up the slopes every hour; championship regattas for summer sailors; tennis; dancing, fashion shows, bridge tournaments (plus lessons in 4 of the top hotels), lectures, concerts, horse races on frozen lake surfaces, ice parades, "skeleton" races, every imaginable type of social activity; handsome terrain, not as breathtaking as Zermatt or even Arosa, but more pruned and polished.

Go between December 1 and April 15 or mid-June to end-September, because these are the seasons; at other times, however, you'll be rewarded with healthy discounts on your hotel bill and might even be able to bargain down to the price you yourself suggest. For the lively sophisticate, there is only a single pacesetter, the **Palace**—to us, one of the finest resort hotels of its type we have seen in the world. The building is Wedding Cake, with nothing left off in the way of spires, V-shape gimmicks, and architectural frosting which could possibly be glued or screwed on. Inside, however, it is a triumph of urbanity which brings sunlight to the soul. Direction by the Badrutt brothers, Andrea and Hansjurg, whose family practically founded St. Moritz as a holiday center. The swimming pool, glassbound and set among rocks and a waterfall, might qualify as the 8th wonder of the hotel world. A marine bar overlooks it from the mezzanine. "Regular" bar with dancing and nonstop zip; elegant little Renaissance Bar, a hideaway for quiet cocktailing and gossiping late at night; "Grand" bar always with the swingingest bands in Europe; Engadiner *Stübli* for more easygoing merriment; *intime* à la carte Grill; regular restaurant; King's Club discothèque full, full, FULL (reserve in the morning); superb service throughout, with client-staff ratio at 1-to-1. Total of 300 rooms, most with bath and all furnished in classic-style comfort and livability; extra-sumptuous suites; south side completely balconied; sauna and masseuse; gymnastics and swimming instruction, plus a tennis coach; organized bridge games and tournaments; every plush facility imaginable. An annex beckons across the street with a shopping arcade, a floor of "sports type" rooms for youngsters on limited allowances, and a top tier with 3 large apartments for longer lingerers; copious staff and garage space also are tucked into this new petit palace. Sparkling, bright, chichi, social, and usually full. Highest recommendation.

Suvretta-House, a short bus ride (or longish hike) from the center, has been moving alps with its multi-million-franc Suvretta-House-party. She is becoming one of the loveliest ladies of the Engadin. This now-glamorous landmark occupies its own distinguished niche as the ideal family-type hotel; it also seems to be favored by many prosperous German guests. The huge, sprawling structure, perched on its own mountainside with its own spectacular vista, is a totally self-sustaining resort community. Everything is here: The Suvretta ski

runs, the Suvretta ski lifts, the Suvretta ski school (40 instructors), the Suvretta skating rinks, the Suvretta stables, and Suvretta nursery, the Suvretta curling rinks—a complete plant for every holiday need, including a glass-lined swimming pool, brightly facing the sunny south. Free bus service to the village every 30 minutes. Handsome wood-lined entrance hall; arched corridors; exquisite nightclub in rouge hue with gold trim; bars everywhere you tipple. Attractive dining room with topflight skilletry, lovely dining-terrace, tennis courts, bowling, private club for regional residents, splendiferous boutiques by Céline of Paris and Pucci, playgrounds, orchestras, many social events and galas; garage; vast staff quarters; 325 rooms and 250 baths. Manager Müller pilots this jumbo with skill and grace.

The **Kulm**, a mainstay of tradition and fun, is managed by friendly and energetic Heinz Hunkeler with the aid of his sparkling wife Erika. Extensive revampings totaling more than 9 million dollars over the past several seasons; new lobby; many new bedrooms; totally modernized Hauptkulm wing with 75 fresh units. An Olympic-size heated pool has made its splash in affiliation with the Carlton-Kulm Sporting Club; it's *lovely* for lunch on a warm sunny day; a covered pool and sauna also have added a further dash of merriment. Ballroom; baronial Rôtisserie des Chevaliers; gloriously restyled French restaurant; Sunny-Bar nightclub with live music in winter; snack-bar; sun terrace. Superb in every way and easily one of Switzerland's top resort hotels.

The **Carlton** recently underwent a change in management and ownership by the same people who back the excellent Lausanne Palace. Such a fact alone is recommendation enough, in our opinion. Entire lobby in modernistic tones; Grill-Bar refreshed as well; attractive lounge for dancing. Many works already completed and more on the way. Splendid professional direction that can only keep pushing it ever higher in the rankings.

The **Monopol** is a midtowner that has been zooming up dramatically. It is smoothly managed by Mr. and Mrs. Hans Strässle. Woody Grischuna Grill, filled with animated couples dancing nightly to its peppery combo; adjoining Bärengraben room for specialties, fondues, and other hippy dips; rustic bar popular with chattering bench-sitters; 1 floor plus a covered rooftop pool; solid comfort, pleasant décor, ample space in most accommodations; some units too cramped, however. Concierge Lorenz is so pro-Yankee you'd think he was a presidential candidate. Tariffs hovering between those of the middle bracket and the luxury entries; excellent for the outlay; getting better every year.

In medium-price stops, the strikingly modern **Cristallo** crystallizes all of the dramatic splashes of color, New Wave furnishings, and production-belt concepts that might be found in any equally soulless counterpart in Santiago, Stockholm, or Syracuse. Central location; standard hotel amenities plus hydrotherapy facilities and Finnish mud baths; small bedrooms and tiny baths. Overall, to us at least, it seems as cool as *cristallo.* The **Schweizerhof** was revamped not long ago and is maintained in smart and snappy style. Attractive top floor; restyled dining room; handsome Stübli offering Swiss dishes that vary daily; Sunday night buffet; Scotch Bar; picnic club on the Suvretta slope; wood-lined Grill. Good space, and getting better every season. The newer midcity **Hauser** features a restaurant-tearoom at ground level and 50 woodtoned, brightly decorated bedchambers above. Pert, reasonable, and fun. Mme.

Spiess, for half-a-century active in the **Post** (1 block from the Palace) and its owner for 3 decades, has posted all of her dedication to her beloved house. Caution: Between seasons, when the Big Four are closed, quotations are jacked up to the Deluxe category. If you can promote one of these choice accommodations for yourself, you should be both snug and satisfied. Then there's the rather expensive **Chantarella**, halfway up Corviglia in lofty isolation; full of terraces, sports chatter, gaggles of easygoing old-timers taking their ease in easy chairs, and hot buttered rum; 110 units, many facing south; open-air restaurant; skating and curling rinks; principally for ski enthusiasts and dedicated relaxers. The **Calonder**, at the edge of the village, offers about 70 rooms and 24 baths; most have recently been redone, and 30 have radio. Cozy, appealing Caprice Grill; pleasant bar and lounge; not operated during the dead months; amiable—and we hope it stays that way under its new owners. The **Steffani**, in Class 1-B, has its amusing modernized Malibu discothèque; self-service cafeteria; cozy Cresta Bar; bowling, terrace-dining, other features. There's a new penthouse level; most other nests have been refluffed; a garage adjoins; very central and swinging in its youthful way. The **La Margna** is small and economy-level. **Languard**, our choice of the *garni* bets, is where we once spent 2 weeks of a delightful ski holiday. Same view as the Palace; a family-run and family-feeling hideaway which we loved. The **Bernina** is in the same league; it's very economical and well situated for moving about. Finally, the old-style but well-outfitted and well-situated **Belvédère** also serves only breakfast; solid bedchamber comforts; small indoor pool; reasonable tariffs. Not at all bad as a respectable money-saver.

Dining can be costly in this chic mountain paradise. The local "21" is **Chesa Veglia**, owned by the Palace Hotel. Here's a glorified Engadine chalet with a marvelous (yet low-price) pizzeria, 2 bowling alleys, and a perfectly delightful life-size wooden horse. Heart of the enterprise is the vastly more exclusive, dressy, and expensive Chadafö Grill. Aside from the tariffs, the only difference between this room and the others seems to be the use of charcoal here, while the adjoining nooks utilize electric ovens and grills; the vegetables are given identical treatment throughout; there is piano melodizing in the Chadafö, with dancing featured elsewhere. All couverts must be reserved at least 24 hours in advance (48 hours on High Season weekends). Even for an après-ski Neapolitan nibble in the cellar, it is almost impossible to snag a table between 4 P.M. and 7 P.M. Our blue-ribbon meal was only fair—not memorable. (Our accountant remembers it, however, and never fails to remind us.) On the other hand, the Grill at the **Palace Hotel** (advance reservations advised) was infinitely more rewarding on our recent tries. Outstandingly superb cuisine, suave service, and good cheer; highest recommendation in every regard. The Grischuna in the **Hotel Monopole** is fun. Separate niche for Swiss cheese specialties; bench bar; dancing nightly; prices medium-high; cookery satisfactory but not startling. The Caprice Grill in the **Calonder** is more *intime* and less costly. The **Calèche Cafe**, in the center, left this reporter stone cold when it was last checked. **Salastrains** is halfway up the slope. Snacks for skiers; packed tightly on sunny days. Stem in at noon for lunch and begin schussing earlier for maximum pleasure. **Acla Clavadatsch** is the nearby alpside hut for Schweizerhof guests. Outdoor grills; piano player by the hearth; noontime only; meal

chits in lieu of francs; a chummy bonus if you are staying in this hotel.
Corviglia Club, mecca of society sportsmen, is restricted to members and their
guests; uncrackable, unless you're invited. Lunch expedition on a balmy day?
The trip up the **Diavolezza aerial railway** to 8800 feet can be enormous fun,
if your company is as nice as ours was. It's a leap-and-a-skip past Pontresina,
a drive which takes perhaps 20 minutes. At the top, the panorama from the
terrace of the mountain restaurant called **Abeba** is fabulous. You'll eat locomo-
tive-size hot dogs and typical farmer fare—and love it. In *Pontresina* itself,
the **Sarazena** tries to be the chief of the chic clique; the effort was in vain, on
our peek.

SAMEDAN Bernina (cozy; good for families; superior cuisine; home-style
service; reasonable prices), possibly followed by **Clubhotel Quadratscha Des
Alpes**, the **Sport Hotel**, or the **Terminus**.

SEENGEN Schlosshotel Brestenberg (on a hummock overlooking the
peaceful Hallwilersee, a lake that's an hour's drive from Zürich; lovely woodland castle; comfortable for rural lazing).

SIERRE Either the **Europe** or the **Atlantic**; both newish.

SILS MARIA Waldhaus, then maybe **La Magna**, **Maria Sereina**,
Edelweiss, or the **Pension Privata**.

SION is one of the Valais's most attractive springboards. Europe's highest
lake is nearby, so are many fine ski slopes. It provides everything from sixth-
century castles and churches to glacier landings by mountain pilots.

SOLOTHURN The well-appointed, pension-priced **La Couronne**.

TARASP Kurhaus Tarasp first, then the **Hotel Tarasp**, the **Waldhaus** the
Schweizerhof, or the **Vulpera**.

UNTERWASSER The **Sternen** shines brightest for the sporting crowd.

VEVEY (1) **Les Trois-Couronnes** (million-dollar modernization program
finished; 100 rooms and 100 baths; handsome, ample-sized, and luxurious in
parts; big dining-terrace and redesigned entrance; ask for #66 if you're splurging; great character and charm in this veteran). (2) **Du Lac** has been bought
by the same interests; a modernization program has been wrapped up. At
Mont Pèlerin, above Vevey, **Le Mirador** is a viewful repose for peaceful
wayfarers—not too many of 'em because it has kept its room count down to
116, which even includes its new East Wing. Twins in the latter sport 2 large
beds and 2 bathrooms; the accommodations can be linked to a parlor so that
5-room suites are now a possibility. The Cloud 9 discothèque provides a
magnificent view of Montreux, Vevey, and Evian. Luxurious glass-domed
swimming pool plus sauna, gymnasium, massage, tennis, and recreation galore. Reportedly fine cuisine in the grill or Fontainebleau Room (**reserve**

ahead); superlative accoutrements for high life in the outer stratosphere of society. Price tags when we last looked in (but subject to revision—and probably upward) ranged from $57 to $91 for singles, $100 to $181 for doubles, and from $225 to $450 for suites. A major stamping from the founder of Pennsylvania's Franklin Mint who took it over not long ago. Though relatively young, already becoming known to discriminating travelers, so be sure to book well in advance. (As an interesting fillip in these volatile economoic times, tarriffs here are set on April 1 and October 1 and do not fluctuate with the day-to-day vagaries of the money markets.)

VILLARS, near Montreux, is just off the main artery to Italy. You'll find plenty to do in both seasons. During the summer, this mile-high vale offers golf, minigolf, tennis, swimming (one pool with salt water, no less!), horseback riding, bowling, and curling or skating on artificial rinks. Winter pastimes including skiing over 25 miles of runs made accessible by 12 miles of mechanical aids, an ice center, hockey, and the other usual snowtime pursuits. French tourists (and their language) predominate, followed by Belgians, and a handful of British twice a year—with just a few Americans so far. Impressive Sports Center where you can order a snack or a pair of skates or a bowling ball or a slot to park your car. Prices within the complex are very reasonable. All categories of hotels for all categories of wallets.

The **Sporting** was totally renewed not long ago. The **Eurotel** is also a youngster. **Grand Hôtel du Parc** boasts a woodland setting and a 1932 exterior. Lobby and public rooms warmly inviting; cute minibar; cheerful, airy dining room; intimate nightclub downstairs; indoor pool; 2 ski lifts. Good taste; skimpy portions sometimes in the cookery; the same parsimonious trait is carried into its 100 pastel-shaded bedrooms. **La Renardière** is composed of 4 separate chalets; heavy French and Belgian patronage who praise its table; fair enough. The viewful **Montesano**, across the Arveyes line on the main road outside the village, resembles the top 2 strata of a 6-layer wedding cake. Entrance via the second coating of icing; clean, sound, and somewhat refashioned by the funloving son of its late proprietor. Developing an upbeat flair. The **Curling** has been updated. We like the dining room; the bar is a bit overdone and corny. Very sporting. **Marie-Louise** is due for another check by us now that it has new management. In the budget bracket, **Garni Ecureuil** is a honey for its category. Help-yourself-to-your-own-key policy in both its main building (vintage '62) and its older chalet; charmingly cozy dining room with highland specialties; 19 housekeeping "apartments" which are a wonderful buy for 2 people (perfect for long do-it-yourself ski holidays). Genial, enterprising Owner-Manager Charles Seeholzer speaks some English. Closed May and November. Highest recommendation for its type; here is a true "find." The **Chalet Henriette** wiggles in with a polished-rustic exterior that is trim and attractive. Many interior improvements; baths and showers recently tapped on; skillets attended by Proprietor Huguet, who is reported to be a deft chef. A cutie if intimacy is your bag.

In general, this town offers scant facilities for the gastronome. There are few restaurants as such—most vittles are swallowed in the dining rooms of the leading hostelries or the pubs. Of the latter group, **Sporting** is the champ. Its

Tisonier segment turns on the most *haute* cuisine, while there are nooks for grills, pizzas, and wines, and even a nightclub for the strong in spirit. Fine open terrace for snacks; terpsichorean frivolities at teatime and from 9 P.M. to 1 A.M.; many big-name performers engaged from time to time; occasional cabaret. Here's a real swinger. **Alpe-Fleurie**, opposite the station and adjoining the hotel of the same moniker, occupies a laggard's 2nd place. Ground floor divided between its ordinary feedery (paper "tablecloths") and an equally simple nightclub (cloth tablecloths). For chalet fixin's, the **Chez-Gollut** at **Frience** and the **Refuge** at **Solalex** raise the roofs of most discerning mouths —with pleasure, that is. **Mon Repos** in **Arveyes** does a commendable job with its Italian cookery.

VILLENEUVE **Byron** (big villa-esque mansion overlooking the garden, the swimming pool, and the lake; grill-restaurant; only 5 minutes from Montreux).

VITZNAU **Parkhotel** is invitingly parked beside the Lake of Lucerne, only a hoot from the sedately passing steamers. There's a private beach, waterskiing, indoor and outdoor pool, 2 tennis courts, sauna, solarium, mini-golf, 18-hole links (nearby), and, whew, thank goodness!—The Rocking Chair Bar for relaxing. There's also an appealing poolside grill and an intimate restaurant for restoring lost calories. Spacious and gracious.

WENGEN **Hirschen** is rather commercial; it has a pool, nightclub, and shopping center. The **Schnöegg** is a moneysaver. Splendid view of the Jungfrau; lots of space for singles. At **Wildhaus**, the **Acker** is perhaps the leader of the Toggenburg Valley; the panorama restaurant, Alphütten bar, and sporting comfort draw many repeaters to its door.

WINTERTHUR (1) **Garten** (much improved recently). (2) **Krone** (not what it was).

ZERMATT Here, a full mile above sea level and 2 miles below the tips of towering Monte Rosa, you will find one of the most breathtaking creations of Providence. For snow-buffs, it is Paradise on Skis: 30 slopes ranging up to more than 6 1/2 miles, with an altitude differential of over 7000 feet; 33 lifts totaling nearly 33 miles in length in 6 varieties of transport; almost 75 miles of officially maintained ski courses, plus oodles of deep-powder zones for off-trail adventurers; skating and curling facilities; seasonal trails to the rooftop of the world; a Hollywood director's Elysium of photographic possibilities (don't forget your ultraviolet or skylight filter, Cecil). A new system of skyhooks pulls skiers up to the lofty Klein Matterhorn, which scratches the belly of Heaven at almost 12,000 feet! Meanwhile, a tunnel is being reamed for a new funicular (perhaps for this season's inauguration) to increase capacity to Sunnega on the Blauherd. (There are 3 systems of interconnecting mountains: Blauherd, Gornergrat, and Theodul Glacier, plus a link from the last over to Italy [Cervinia] via the Testa Grigia run.) All of this welkin world is watched over by the avuncular Constant Cachin, the town's amiable tourist director. Narrow-

gauge trains pull from Visp to Zermatt in 65 minutes with 14 hauls a day each way. An auto route from Visp stops at Täsch (maintaining the traditional no-motor-driven-vehicle policy within town limits; expansive parking facilities are now at Täsch, 4 miles below Zermatt a rather expensive taxi, a minibus, or the cheaper train service, running every 15 minutes, provide the final leg). The Vergers have wound up a fine modern multi-plane chopper service as an aid to mountain rescue and as a lure to well-heeled go-it-alone skiers. Since local medical facilities are limited, we'd recommend chartering it should a serious injury occur; it's well worth the outlay as an airborne ambulance. (Our team knows this very well because the heli-pilots plucked Joe Raff, our president, off a Matterhorn glacier and whisked him to the excellent Visp hospital in minutes following a serious leg fracture in high, remote drifts. If you need medical help, call Dr. Betti Huhnholz in Visp, Tel. 464443; this amiable professional is as fluent in English as she is in kindness. For heavy injuries, we have confidence in Dr. Peter Z'Brun, Chief of the Visp hospital and one of Europe's most experienced and leading orthopedic surgeons.) Summer is a lovely time to come, too, because it turns into an arcadian upland garden of wildflowers, rippling streams, and clear blue light. Here at the top of the world is The Great Architect at His most majestic.

Among the hotels, we'd call it a 3-way tie at the top among the classical Mont Cervin the chalet-style Alex, and the big traditional Zermatterhof—the choice of house depending upon your own tastes rather than on any notable differences in quality.

The sweetly running **Alex** is a charmer—and _what_ a buy! It is sited on a viewful but hard-to-find perch down a narrow lane, 1 block from the railroad station. Overgrown chalet-motif building; captivating rustic lounge with crackling fire, snack service and cozy corners in 3 separate sectors; 10 luxury suites that are beauts, which have their own working fireplaces and artistic doors of cast Italian bronze; sumptuous Presidential Suite, formerly the owner's private apartment; vast, variform indoor swimming pool with waterside service of snacks and beverages; saunas (both of these and the pool are free for hotel guests); tennis hall for year-round volleys plus one scheduled for outdoor play; 2 squash courts. Main-level breakfast room in the timbered motif of the house; exceptional Tavern Chez Alex in cellar, delightfully regional in dress, with old beams and all the trimmings. The rooms are outstandingly good for the price bracket: bright, well conceived, immaculate, and larger than those of many more costly houses. Sweater-clad Alex Perren, a 4th-generation mountain guide who lost a foot in a rockslide in '59, is the cheerful, smiling, attractive personality who will go all out for your welcome and comfort. His delightful wife and helpmate, smiling Gisela, is another sugar-coated bonus in personality. Sometimes they get so enthusiastic that they overbook; so be sure, sure, sure your reservation has cast-iron confirmation spikes nailed into it. To us, here is the number-one money-saving value in Zermatt.

The freshly painted **Mont Cervin** (French for "Matterhorn") for decades has been the most famous hotel of the Canton. Not long ago it instituted big changes which include a refreshed reception zone, lobby, a fashion boutique, a watch and jewelry store, a new ski room, expanded bank facilities, lounge, an exquisite residents' bar, conference zones, injections of cheer and color

everywhere, a six-pack of new units in the main building, and a clutch of "romantic" rooms in the original Villa Margharita section (now connected to the main building). Manager Wolfgang Pinkwart is doing a commendable job in every respect. It boasts a covered swimming pool plus sauna and massage facilities—a proud feather in its alpine cap. There's a special supervised area for children aged 2 to 10 with a nurse from 9 A.M. to 6 P.M each day. Bubbling Rendez-Vous bar, jammed to the scuppers after nightfall; expanded and vastly improved adjoining Matterhornstube, in attractive bleached timbers, with dancing to a live orchestra—also so packed in season that even a midget peri without a table reservation couldn't be shoe-horned in (a coke or a highball costs $5). The skillet-work is good in the main, but the High Season Friday night buffets are nothing short of spectacular—among the finest seen anywhere in Europe today. The spirit, flair, and overall sense of renaissance in this house are thrilling. Better and better.

The **Zermatterhof**, owned by the town's citizens, presents as its face the most professional hotel exterior of all. Handsome, modern entrance into an immaculately pruned lobby; split-level lounge a casebook example of period gentility; L-shape dining room with one leg old-fashioned and the other brightly blended (a curious combination which comes off). This season there's an indoor swimming pool partially glass-lined, a fitness center, and 2 saunas (extra fee for use). All viewful fifth-floor units were lately renewed. The redesigned ground-floor U-shape section, fronting lawn and street, contains (1) the cozy, glass-wrapped, exquisitely executed Grill with an open rôtisserie in its far corner, (2) an ultramodern café with live and discothèque music and eye-jiggling raspberry banquettes, divided from the Grill by yellow and green curtains, (3) an urbane dining salon, and (4) a sterile, brassy rotunda bar. The 100 rooms come with 60 full-tub baths; 2/3 of them sport appealing Swiss-rustic décor, with burnished and slightly darkened natural wood ceilings, doors, bedboards, wardrobes, and trim; 1/3rd have a pleasant classic mien; all offer the identical yardsticks of quality and upkeep. General Manager German (pronounced "Gurman") is the efficient and instantly likable Boniface.

The **Tenne**, behind the station and connected to the restaurant of the same name, maintains its quiet flair. Lobby with coffered ceilings (painted in scenes of Zermatt's history), ruby velvets, emerald-green divans, and sapphire carpet; dining in the restaurant if desired; 28 superbly comfortable, spotless, and sumptuous bedrooms—all with bath and radio, except for 2 singles with showers only; 14 units with balcony facing the Matterhorn (beyond the railroad tracks); top-floor accommodations cozied-up with lots of wood; baths chippered with flowered tiles; some 4-person spreads. Shuttered October and November. Highly recommended.

The **Walliserhof**, a Zermatt landmark, today has full regained that old zing of yore. Recently it renewed its public sancta and every one of its bedchambers in a mood of upland rusticity. All now come with bath (many of 'em new, too) or shower, phone, radio, and Frigobar; many feature wooden ceilings. Guests are admitted gratis to the Christiania swimmery. The grill has been resizzled and the Weinstube remains one of the most popular social hubs of the Valais —making this truly a *Walliser-hof.* The weekly buffet during ski season is mighty alluring—and its flavor lives up to its stunning eye appeal. Proprietor

Theo Welschen and Manager Arnold Frei turn on a zesty fry of highland nutrition for any plainsman's soul. Always abuzz with frolicsome holiday-makers.

The **Monte Rosa**, an antebellum period piece, was born in 1853 and very recently was given its latest major remodeling, affording it nearly a full private bath count and new balconies on its south side. Today it flowers with bouquets of appeal without any serious loss of character. Smallish lobby and 3 lounges; sweet, sweet 4-table, 7-stool bar; low-ceilinged 100-seat dining room. Manager Urs Keller continues to coddle this lady of classic breeding. A lovely rejuvenation.

The **Seilerhaus** is a mixture of modern and traditional values. Now the façade has been brightened and top and back units refashioned. The ground floor is occupied by a post office, independent shops, a tiny lobby, a small sun terrace, and a clean-lined but unexciting 140-seat dining room offering a 4-course menu (wide choices), plus snacks. The Otto Furrer-Stube, a basement nook, is described in "Restaurants."

The **Schweizerhof**, to us at least, evokes a coldly commercial aura. Coolish foyer; dining room and bar markedly on the arctic side; 30-room annex (simple, no private baths) connected to main building; 49 units, 43 baths, all cramped, and all utterly without character or charm, in our opinion, despite some very recent updatings. No resort ambiance, except in the garb of the guests; so humdrum in appointments and tone that the traveling salesman of legend would feel at home. Same ownership as the National-Bellevue.

The well-concieved, smoothly running midvillage **Nicoletta** is operated by Werner Seeholzer, a pleasant, softspoken professional. Lovely view-bound rôtisserie; coolish dining room; happy Carnotzet; recommendable cuisine and much improved staff attitudes in all dining sectors; game segment; ideal location for skiers—equidistant from all major lifts. It adjoins a midtown super-market and popular-price cafeteria; it turns on a solarium, a pool, and a sauna; the rooms are large and superbly furnished; the colors add vim; the baths are carpeted. Pretty good for a modern hotel.

The **Beau-Site** is a Grand Old Warrior, which has been made a speck more youthful through an outside cleaning, an interior pep-up, and the addition of a swimming pool. Its adjoining chalet has been sold to become the not-unpleasant **Garni Christen**. Half of the **National-Bellevue** has been razed to become a shop; the new Bellevue portion which replaces it is now better than the National segment. While the director tries hard, his staff seems to us to be one of the least disciplined clubs in the majors.

Alpenblick, closest to the Matterhorn, is at the extreme edge of the settlement about 10 minutes by Shank's Mare from the hub. Lovely open terrace to one side (20 tables; drinks, snacks, or full meals), with a magnificent unbroken sweep of this mountain whenever weather smiles; glassed-in terrace facing the street; large dining room without distinction; 25 cramped and characterless rooms with dwarf-size baths; overall raw-new air that doesn't send us. Cuisine very poor at our lunch-for-1. For the difference from the leaders, not worth it to us—except for that glorious view on the Matterhorn side.

The 59-room **Bristol** features dancing in its neo-gothic cellar grill, a favorite

spot for après-ski romancers. Minisize cells, most with bath or shower. Fair pickin's for small-boned clients. **La Couronne**, with a good situation at the end of the river bridge across from the Zermatterhof, is a '61 chalet-style candidate. Old Zermatt Restaurant-Bar-Grill and hairdressing salon in front (count your change extra-carefully in the former); so-so accommodations; fair but hardly a rave. The **Christiania**, important because of the chair lift at its doorstep, seemed too slaphappy in its administration to suit us. Adequate plant and a proper kitchen for its expanded dining facilities, but we simply didn't tune into its wavelength. Adjoining swimming pool, sauna, fitness center, and an apart-ment-hotel. The **Perren** is neither new nor old—except for its fresh-as-spring *garni* wing. On the river; routine furnishings and rooms. The small, bland **Rhodania** is, in our opinion, much, much too tall in the Pocketbook Depart-ment to worry its competition. Not recommended.

In the budget category, all of the following are *Garni* (breakfast only), but full meals can be arranged in most of them, on separate terms. In this group, the side-by-side **Eden & Rex** form a twin combo under the same administra-tion. They are joined in the middle and share an excellent indoor pool. Unusu-ally large accommodations, many with balcony and all with breathtaking Alpine vista; public rooms and corridors highlighted with copperware, spin-ning wheels, and regional touches; new chalet-annex nearby plus sauna. Nice. The **Jägerhof** is run by Victor Perren, one of the most popular young ski instructors on hickories. Clean, airy, informal, and recommendable for the sweet people who operate it. The mid-village **Darioli** has no lobby, but its tiny grill and *Stübli* weave a gypsy spell. Peasant-style furniture in bedrooms; attic units without bath; simple, but winsome. **De la Poste** is globally noted for its discothèque complex in the cellar. We prefer the nonsleeping quarters to the kips. Overall, however, the operation strikes us as slaphappy, if not downright amateurish. But that's just our personal impression. The **Derby**, on the main street next to the Walliserhof, sprouts typical upland architecture. Sizable restaurant on ground floor that is intimate, low-ceilinged, and pleasant; open-air terrace service a few steps above the milling throng on the road; bedrooms tiny, tidy, and cheerful, with baggage space sufficient for 1 small attaché case; appealing, nevertheless, in their fully paneled walls, small streetside balconies, and color touches. Noisy in front, of course. The **Biner** is okay. Chummy staff here. The **Chesa Valese** is a warm, cozy 30-room villa with 6 baths, 6 showers, many balconies, and a feeling of "Welcome Home." Very ingratiating in its quiet fashion. The **Excelsior** and the **Aristella** are newish production-line plants à la Chalet School of architecture and appointments; these are also passable for their category. The barnlike **Bahnhof**, a summer bunker for rough-and-ready climbers, is as raw as they come. The prices are ultrabasic, too. Shelter here often means 6 to a room and "Everybody up at dawn!" Way, way up the Gornergrat Rail, the **Riffelberg** is for total isolationists. The views, of course, are magnificent, the rates are low, but we prefer it chiefly at meal-times since our preferences are not so solitary.

Finally, down at the neighboring hamlet of *Täsch*, there are several entries which have come to flower or are budding. Travelers with cars sometimes prefer to live here because of the enormous parking lot. We think it is decidedly 5th-rate by comparison with Zermatt. We imply no scare tactic whatsoever

when we report that avalanches have tumbled into this region in years gone by.

Among Zermatt dining spots the Taverne Chez Alex, the cellar of the **Hôtel Alex**, is a cutie. Rusticity by the carload, with old beams, Alpine architecture, and the flavor of the hills; menu selections are small but choice. For day-in-night-out dining, nothing in the valley can touch it with a 10-foot slalom pole. The tip of the topmost peak for its category. **Tenne** steals some of the local thunder for decorative allure; and—happily, at last—our latest dinner was excellent from warm reception, to polite service, to attractive presentation of the dishes, to the culinary performance itself. Main 11-table dining room in miniature medieval court-and-cloister architecture; alcove seating; casement windows; central covered atrium, 2 stories high, with zodiacal mural on the ceiling and an organist's perch 3/4 of the way up; adjoining bar cunningly carrying out the same motif, with inverted-V roof, walls in ancient timbers. Upstairs, via a rope-banister staircase, are 2 more rooms—a grill with blue-and-white textile touches and a weathered-and-woody den that is strikingly attractive. If they have it, try the lamb in a jacket of mustard and herbs—Ummmm! If you are a hotel guest you must enter through the steamy kitchen unless you wish to walk outside and around. The slick-rustic Otto Furrer-Stube—named for the famous mountain guide who was killed—is the popular cellar haunt of the **Seilerhaus**. Entrance from the street or from the hotel; its scant 16 tables nearly always packed to the scuppers; small bar behind arches; glasswrapped terrace; air-conditioned, but still hot; redolent with food smells; a severely overworked staff; cookery that impressed us as too costly for the so-so rewards. **Chez Gaby** is strong on eye-appeal, but Gaby's place is a witch to date. Miserable reservations policy on every one of our numerous tries; poor reception when you finally do make it. Ground-floor dining room dominated by a green tile-topped table; open rôtisserie; upstairs bar with more settings; an earnest chef (Gaby himself) who often apologizes for the staff shortcomings in a hospitable way. Okay for grills, but _what_ a production to get in. The back-o-town **Spycher** features a tiny intimate quadrant in the back of a multisection room. Lodge décor; typically overheated, as only the Swiss can overheat a restaurant. We found our platters too heavily sprinkled with Aromat, a flavor accenter. The **Bambi**, at the lower end of town, is not only attractive to the aesthetic senses, but here we've repeatedly had one of the best shish kebabs we've ever savored anywhere in Europe. Add to that its comparatively low prices and the sweet family service, and Bambi becomes a teriffic buy. Personally, we go back frequently and love it. The **Stockhorn**, near the Eden & Rex, is quite a warm and cozy nook today. Ski instructor Émile Julen is the owner, and his taste for winter sport, climbing, and good solid cookery is reflected on its walls and tables. Ropes, crampons, picks and other lore of the mountains for décor; intimate ground-level dining room plus a charming dark raclette _Stube_ in the cellar. Now definitely recommendable for its type. **Le Chalet**, at riverside near the rail bridge, offers one room fetchingly decorated with carvings of Old Zermatt. Taped music; attentive kind service; several excellent Indonesian dishes plus regional selections and grills; reasonable price tags. We enjoyed this flavorful hideaway. The **Couronne** is best for après-ski _Glühwein_ and snacks when the slopes have been retired for the day. The **Walliserkanne**, next to the

Walliserhof, is in no way associated with Theo Welschen's hotel interests. Not at all special. The **Mont Cervin** whets your appetite with predinner libations in the Rendez-Vous Bar. Handsome, nonaggressive dining room with wholesome well-cooked fare. Very pleasant, indeed. The Grill of the **Zermatterhof** is an exquisitely polished oasis. Intimate, elegant, glass-wrapped; open rôtisserie crackling in one far corner; yumptious cuisine. A café with live and recorded music is partitioned from this high-style aristocrat by green and yellow curtains; in this section are banquettes of raspberry hue and a more informal air. Sound, solid and recommendable. The **Walliserhof** boasts both its locally popular *Gaststube* up front (regional décor and dishes to match) and its sprightly modern, glass-bound restaurant to the rear, where the weekly buffet is truly splendid. Each has its appeal, depending upon your mood. The **Alpenblick**, a 10-minute hike toward the Matterhorn, unveils a perfectly splendid panoramic terrace, but perfectly atrocious victuals. Don't forget the high-flown, viewful **Riffelberg Hotel** dining room up the Gornergrat rail trail. Order a bratwurst or a *käseschnitte* and savor the glory of the Alps.

Finally, you might try **Elsie's place**, a few steps from the Hotel Zermatterhof. In this very ancient house you'll find 6 tables, a small semicircular bar, knotty walls, casement windows, and a friendly atmosphere. Elsie's prides: Irish coffee (very costly but *delicious*), ham and eggs, hot dogs, other light snacks, and all beverages (which can sometimes taste foreign indeed to U.S.-bred sippers). Closed May, October, and November; otherwise it goes full blast from 10 A.M. to midnight, 7 days a week.

ZUG   In this delightful medieval town a local friend and doctor, Betti Huhnholz, once praised the cozy little **Aklin am Zytturm** to the high blue-Swiss heavens. If this food-savvy gastronome said it was good, well, we were jumping to give it a try. We made a special foray out here one Thursday only to discover that this is the exact day it closes for a rest. Instead, we lumbered down to the **Hecht**, at lakeside, and pouted until we were presented with a marvelous fish platter, a glorious waterfront panorama, and a delightful wedge of Kirschtorte (a Zug specialty which was invented by the gods) that melted away the last vestiges of regret. What the Hecht!—we'll recommend both. The **Rathaus** is okay for light bites and atmosphere and the **Ochsen** leads the hotel herd.

ZÜRICH   is the largest and most business oriented metropolis in Helvetia; commerce, industry, and culture are centered here. You'll find the leading banks and insurance companies; biggest shops, factories, markets; excellent hotels, restaurants, and amusements. From the tops of the encircling hills, the city is a stunning sight: Villas and gardens stretch down to the silvery inland sea, with snowcapped mountains always in the background. The people here are supposed to be the greatest boasters in the country—and why not, when 1 out of 275 residents is a millionaire (so who sneezes at millionaires in Swiss francs)? Actually, they prefer to be called the "superrich." Make Zürich and Geneva your excursion centers, for everything worth seeing in the nation can be covered from these 2 bases. If you can, plan to be in Zürich in June; the month-long Festival here is one of the most famous on the Continent.

Hotels   The **Dolder Grand** has a mountainside location, 10 minutes by car from the heart of the city. Breathtaking panorama; entire façade refash-

ioned; balconies extended; entrance restyled; the last word in elegance today; viewful crescent-shape La Rotonde restaurant with excellent cuisine; occasional gastronomic weeks supervised by great chefs from elsewhere in Europe; lilting piano bar; 200 rooms and 200 baths; volume-governed radios; free newspaper with breakfast; tiptop concierges in Mr. Soliva and Mr. Follonier. Hotel limousine service to town is much cheaper than ordinary taxi, incidentally; you also can ride down or back on the inexpensive funicular. While suite #315–316 is outstanding, #368–369 in one Tower is our favorite among favorites, one of the snuggest nests we've inspected in many a palace. A splendid Royal Suite which is nearly the size of Wyoming is ready for this year's noble • voyager, too. Excellent and costly simultaneous translation facilities in the convention center headquarters; spacious gardens and woods; 9-hole golf course and tennis courts nearby in private club. We are favorably impressed by soft-spoken Manager Raoul de Gendre, who in his quiet professional way is successfully injecting a more youthful tone that loses nothing to the fine Dolder traditionalism.

The **Baur au Lac** boasts a superb downtown lakeside setting and slightly higher tariffs than the above entry. The lobby and lounges are gathering places of wealth, nobility, and chic; there's an impressive Men's Club (where captains of industry can indulge their fancies with everything from the latest stock market quotations to a private secretary; women guests are admitted after 6 P.M.); in its cellar is the Petit Palais discothèque; there's an excellent telephone system throughout, a boutique plus barbering and hairdressing salons, air conditioning for the public rooms, and a panoply of posh accommodations. You'll snooze in a velour-upholstered bed, park your luggage on slide-out shelves, and use an improved bathroom (still smallish, but equipped with dressing tables and illuminated mirrors for the ladies). The Grill-Bar remains one of Zürich's top spots. Now resplendent in sheen and glitter.

Down a notch to First-class, the air-conditioned **Eden au Lac** is a splendid house. It turns out the imaginative fare in its intimate restaurant. The aura, bathed in a Trianon gray, is on the old-fashioned side, in a nostalgically serene way; the 53 rooms, all with bath or shower, are comfortable, but you mustn't expect luxury; many have been repowdered and some have been given air conditioning. Young, friendly Rudi and Hanni Bärtschi comprise the managerial team and they are delightful. Service unusually attentive; upper-case clientele who return with migratory regularity. Not for mods; those who seek a tranquil niche will find a home-sweet-home-away-from-home. The **Carlton-Elite** is smack in the center. Its Pub, decorated with saddles, bridles, and raw bricks, is more popular than ever even though we found the service in it worse than ever. It is sited in a charming little cul-de-sac. Colorful Locanda Ticinese Italian-Swiss tavern; attractive Flower Terrace for open-air summer meals; communal plus private bar for guests; 10 split-level accommodations in natural wood and textile motif, with color TV, refrigerator, "silent valets," twin washbasins, and up-to-the-minute gadgetry; other units on the smallish side, with wall-to-wall carpeting and modernistic tone. The restaurant ideas, as sired by Mövenpick and as evinced by the Pub, are a good show but are wanting in quality, in our opinion. The **Waldhaus Dolder** splits its structure between apartments and rooms for transients while sharing its mountain address with its neighboring alma mater, the Dolder Grand. It is a 10-story _éminence grise_

(gray concrete) which is First class, not Deluxe. Engagingly decorated restaurant and dining sectors; grill under iron hood with leaded glass and outfitted with woodsman's tools; Dolderbahn Bar for nostalgics; glass-lined pool area that can be opened in summer; sauna. Bedchambers as well as the longer-rental apartments rely heavily on formica and other coolish effects. Space is ample; comfort is abundant; tranquility is assured; flair seems to be in short supply within the dwelling areas. We suspect families will find it perfect for their needs. **Zum Storchen**, which occupies one of the better midcity situations, offers a timber-lined waterside rôtisserie, a dining terrace over the water, a soulless bar with piano-tations, and an alp of aid from Chief Concierge Roth. Total of 80 refashioned rooms, all with radio, TV minibar, direct-dial telephone, and most with bath or shower; singles facing the town; the choicest streamside doubles #323 and #423, (often held for loyal clients); demipension required in summer. Unless you snag one of its prime accommodations, we think you can do better elsewhere. Out of midcity, the all-*nova* **Nova Park** is emphatically for mods. Wild color combinations in the lobby; public rooms jazzy with paintings and sculpture. Music (some piped, some live) filtering everywhere—from busy lounges, to the woody self-service restaurant, to its backgammon club, to another nook where a piano player tickles the keys, to any of several feederies, one of which contains executive chairs and individual TV sets tuned into the stock-market quotations. Of its 360 accommodations all seemed cramped to us, but the so-called "Executive Doubles" provide the highest dividend in space per dollar. The "Dreamland Suites" truly must be seen to be believed. Shag carpeting covers the floor, walls, ceiling, and much of the built-in furniture (2 come in burgundy and 2 in blue); they feature dozens of pinpoint lights glinting romantically through the textiles à la El Morocco; the bed (in repose) is sunken, but can be made to rise, fall, or angle at a button's touch; a huge 2- (maybe 3-) person bathtub—also sunken and unseparated from the bedroom—beckons Dreamlanders to roll out of their mechanized bunk and into their own azure Mediterranean (or Red Sea, if you pick one of the wine-dark suites); overall the space is rather limited (not that a lot will be required by clients who bid for these) and the prices are almost out of sight. Our lunch was fair but not better; the cocktails were good; the service was poor. Later we saw a client carrying his own dirty laundry to the front desk and were told that this was SOP, as no valet pickup existed. Some travelers might extract a giggle out of the whole experience, but at the blue-ribbon price tags it demands we would feel as if the joke were on us. The **Zurich**, on the other hand, impressed us as being just as commercial but much more artfully so. Handy, scenic location overlooking the river and a magnificent townscape; waterfront restaurant with cyclopean ceiling lights; inviting Tourne Broche Grill; bar, pool, gym, shops, garage; handsomely furnished bedchambers, again with a heavy inclination toward white formica surfaces; color-brightened baths. Somehow this brand of subdued modernity appeals to us much more than that espoused by the N-P. Also costly by local standards. The railbird's **Ascot** is near one of the train stations. Tastefully refashioned; front rooms with balconies and deck chairs; 2nd floor Bel Étage with special flavor; 6 suites (2 with kitchens) in velvet, silk, and flowered décor; 60 rooms, all with bath, radio, and most with picture windows; many with color TV; enlarged lobby;

high-in-the-stirrups, rouge-toned, intimate Jockey Club restaurant (microwave kitchen); sidewalk café; busy Turf Bar. Nobel Prize on the Bel Étage is #215 with rust carpets, gold curtains and a button beside the bed to raise or lower him or her (or both) to any desired position; if *this* becomes boring, another button lowers a mirrored panel across the room to disclose a TV set. The rather costly **Bellerive au Lac** is proud of its attractive but somewhat commercial lobby, dining room, and bar. Handsome wildlife paintings by Hug throughout the house; all baths restyled, remaining small but efficient. Singles are the best values; the twins seemed high to us. The **Atlantis Sheraton**, 15 minutes by taxi from the center, is sited in a suburban office complex. The American hotel chain recently linked this one into its management program. Spacious lobby in Scandinavian motif; 2-tier rôtisserie plus intimate pinewood *Stübli;* bar toned up in green leather; adjoining nightclub; glass-fronted swimming pool covered by a sail; sauna with snoozzzzable easy chairs; hair dressing salon; fine Grieder boutique; Avis agency plus garage. The well-furnished rooms are efficient in the modern theme, highlighted by photomurals and generously outfitted with phones at bedside and in the bath; radios and TV (some in color and all with remote-control switches), refrigerators, infrared heat lamps; ample space; individual terraces. The penthouse units are especially laudable. There's plenty of zing per cubic foot here. But despite the fact that a hotel bus goes to and from the city 12 times per day, we believe that many independent travelers will find it unhappily remote as a holiday headquarters. How we'd like to be wrong! For a homelike nest, the **Im Park** (Billoweg stop on the tram) is a quiet, viewful suburban house with 100 beds, lots of renewing, a charming restaurant, and a sedately relaxed atmosphere. If you want to avoid hubbub and high prices, this one is a honey. Back in town, the **Europe** glows with Old World charm and crackles with twentieth-century convenience. Winningly attractive French-provincial lobby; beverage salon under cystal, embraced by ruby velour walls; patterned corridors; delightful accommodations with such touches as rheostat lighting, humidifiers, refrigerators, electric bed controls plus radio-TV consoles, air conditioning, wall safes, silent valets, shaving mirrors, drying racks in baths and much more—even to bowls of fruit placed in the rooms. Number 52 is a superb corner double; we also like #46 or any unit ending in "6." Excellent as an intimate hideaway. The nearby **Opera**, behind its namesake, offers rooms but no meals; it closes in winter. **St. Gotthard**, 1 block from the main station, is in a district that is now a pedestrian zone. This landmark is best known for its Hummer ("Lobster") Bar, its cosmopolitan sidewalk café on the Bahnhofstrasse, and its rebasted Rôtisserie; its 110 rooms and 8 charming luxury suites show commendable improvement plus a notable trend toward gaiety and decorative flair. The newer wing of 28 bedchambers twinkles with white brick, rustic textiles, rich wood, and floral patterns; all units now with color TV and frigobar. Much better, in our judgement. The neighboring **Glockenhof** isn't bad as a family stop. The **Continental**, a glass-and-steel edifice that started life as an office building, exorcises its commercial origins with a cunning use of lovely Valais antiques. Accommodations with radio, bath or shower, and makeshift closets; full air conditioning; attractive restaurants (especially the Diff) serving unusually high-grade cuisine. The **Savoy**, oldest in town, has just reappeared—its ancient façade intact—after a

hypercostly reconstruction jamboree by its banking proprietors. Midcity location in the eye of the shopping hurricane; modern but sedate lobby highlighted by plants and crystal fixtures; lounge/bar; simple Café Baur plus more ornate Savoy, Grill and Bel Étage dining rooms; a few units with balcony; substantial comfort; restful color scheme leaning toward golds, beige, and buff tones. A fresh deluxe traditionalism pervades this born-again contender. The 56-room **Rigihof**, en route to the Dolder, is a converted apartment house on a clangorous street. Full bath count; homey atmosphere; excellent kitchen for reasonable outlays; for budgeteers and travelers with children superb for its special type. The **Kindli**, with no views from its inner-canyon site in midtown, is, in our evaluation, a conglomeration of good and bad. You pays your money and you takes your choice. **Chesa Rustica**, at Limmatquai 70, is as cute as they come for tiny inn-type hostelries. The cookery in the restaurant, grill, or bar is lip-smacking, too. The **Krone**, originally built on the Limmat Quai in A.D. 1599, had total refitting not long ago. The management and staff also were keelhauled and we think this ship is much for the better because of it. Small, intimate, and vaguely French in tone. The **Adler**, with 50 rooms and 18 baths, is fair. The **Schweizerhof** has made some heroic attempts at restylings. We admire Manager Straessle's efforts to reclaim it from dreariness—a task in which he has met with reasonable success. The **Alexander**, across the lake in *Thalwil* and not to be confused with one of the same name in Zürich proper, has gone into a such a slump that the charm is gone for us. The **Ermitage**, 10 minutes by car (or 30 by boat) at the lakeside suburb of Küsnacht, has been in a state of flux since Manager Baumgartner took over and is seeking to add new sparkle to his haven. Here's the residential wing of the well-known restaurant of the same name, with 28 rooms and 28 baths; tranquil and agreeable setting; inconvenient location for the traveler-in-a-hurry. We like this house and wish it well. We suspect that earlier complaints from diners here came at the lowest period of its recent transition. Finally, the 50-room **Waldorf**—with astorian tabs for double occupancy—did not seem worth the outlay. Not recommended. For weatherbound air travelers, the youthful **Airport Hilton** roars in with topflight public quarters, a viewful swimming pool and sun deck, and a newer wing of 125 rooms. Fabulous Sutter's Grill that's a gold mine for beef-hungry U.S. prospectors; honky-tonk piano music nightly; salubrious dark-toned Bonanza Bar; Coffee Shop maintaining a spur of Old West flavor; bedchambers adequate but not up to the flair of the lobby and restaurant décor. The manager may sincerely believe that the gold-tinted plate-glass bedroom windows are see-through *only* from the inside out, but after we'd paraded through the parking lot one night, we can advise more than a dozen female registrants that he is delightfully wrong. Recommended. Across the highway, the fortress-like **Holiday Inn** is linked in gray concrete massiveness to the Mövenpick complex, its Swiss dining partner. The sister **Inn** at neighboring *Regensdorf* has somewhat more architectural style, but both are intended to be only functional flyway-stations. Our recent meal in the Appenzeller Stube of the airport entry was quite tasty and lots of fun. Well done for what they are, but somehow both give us the feeling of being in a Las Vegas "Strip" hotel rather than on European soil. **Hotel Airport** (5 minutes from the jet blast and 20 minutes from the city) offers 47 adequately appointed units for one-nighters.

All accommodations with bath or shower; attractive 9-tabled Grill Room plus Japanese restaurant; pleasing main-floor bar; ask for Manager Gehrig. Good for its purpose.

At **Horgen**, on the south side of Zürich Lake 10 miles from the city, there's the gleaming **Seehotel Meierhof**. Sleek lines; viewful rooftop La Rôtisserie l'Horizon adjoining the cocktail lounge; public restaurant and snack bar; lovely no-extra-cost indoor pool, with slide-away glass panels, agurgling round the calendar (open until 10 P.M.); infrared ready room for palefaced pilgrims, plus open-air solarium for the genuine article; beauty parlor and barbershop; gift center, bank, and 90-car garage on the preserve. Total of 140 smallish doubles and suites, each with private bath, TV, radio, 2 phones, and your own stocked refrigerator—everything from a fifth of Ballantine's to a magnum of Pommery. Management by Hans Zürcher. One novel convenience is its very own speedboat, which shuttles to and from Zürich's principal piers. Say *sí-sí* for the Zürichsee-side (despite the rail line in front), because it's the most see-worthy at this See-hotel.

Out at **Oerlikon**, a suburb in the direction of the airport, we found the vast **International** about as institutional as they can come. The pool and sauna on the top floor and the Panorama Grill on the penultimate level are its highest points in every sense.

Restaurants   Zürich's most fashionable gourmet oasis is **La Rotonde**, the dining room of the **Dolder Grand**. The Grill of the **Baur au Lac** also has a fine reputation, but lately we've felt it is a shade less than it was in its kitchen skills.

Among the independents, **Chez Max** (also called **Chesa**) not long ago shifted headquarters to the suburb of **Zollikon** (Seestrasse 53). Proprietor-Chef Max Kehl is assuredly one of the young luminaries of European gastronomy. First, the atmosphere: It's brown-toned sanctum is darkly intimate, lovely, and joyfully relaxing—with contemporary paintings mixed with polished copper, flowers, and a delicate easygoing theme woven into every feature. Next, the cuisine: It might have been prepared in the kitchens of Kingdom Come, but Max is so ultra-particular about what he serves that frequently he arrives gloomily at tableside to report that what you have chosen doesn't quite measure up to the standard he prefers. He pouts with ill-concealed annoyance. Then he consults with you in a friendly manner over the quality of this meat or the freshness of that vegetable and finally out comes unadulterated bliss. Even if you don't fancy sweets, ask to see the artistic dessert trolley. Wines span the best of Swiss hillsides to extraordinary French vintages. Prices are the only items that are hard to swallow, often giving hosts from soft-currency nations a permanent wince. The rewards otherwise, however, are indeed memorable. Always reserve in advance.

Kronenhalle (Ramistrasse 4) varies a lot in cookery, but the service remains staunchly consistent—always rotten, at least on our repeated tries. It remains popular possibly because of its unusually fine and vast assemblage of paintings in every cranny. Two floors; old-fashioned ambiance, enlivened by the Picassos, Dalis, and Matisses on the walls; rendezvous of journalists, authors, painters, and people in the arts; miserably rushed attention that nearly always borders on negligence; go early for dining or later for tippling, because more

and more stern (and justified!) complaints are reaching us from discriminating travelers.

Ermitage, once our favorite, suffered a seizure of doldrums for many months —but, as we've already stated, we hope its new management can revive it. Lovely lakeside country-house situation at Küsnacht-Zürich, 10 minutes by car or 30 minutes by motorboat from the center; graduated terraces for fair-weather dining, and picture-windowed interior for inclement days or evenings. Now open all year.

Haus zum Rüden (Limmatquai), built in 1295 and restored in 1936, preserves the charm of the traditional Guild House. Proprietor Peter Halter and his lovely wife offer a friendly welcome. Handsome furnishings, fair cooking, and adequate service. Still solid, but lately we've developed a fondness for the ancient guild of the hat weavers; **Zunfthaus zur Waag** (Münsterhof 8) which is in a more colorful antique square. Upstairs dining rooms with leaded windows, cream-colored panels, thick carpeting, candles and flowers on tables, and ultrakind attention by staffers who have a limited facility with English. The grilled meats are hewn from rancher's dreams. If you like these, then **Schmiden Zunft** and **Kaiser's Reblaube** (Goethe Stübli) are more names to jot down in your Zurich notebook. The **Kropf**, just off Paradeplatz, goes back before the turn of the century—as perhaps do some of its big buxom waitresses who bellow orders across the hall to its kitchen. Wooden floors, wonderful no-nonsense cooking, low prices, jovial in the best tradition of an honest tavern-type hideaway. Filled with Swiss. (Privately, one of our favorite corners in Zurich.) For beef served in a more North American manner, steer yourself directly to **Jacky's Stapferstube** (Culmanstrasse 43); it's nothing fancy for the peepers. Stucco walls; low-timbered ceiling; electrified "gas" lamps plus candles; a beautiful shrimp cocktail, an oh-so-succulent entrecôte for 2, herb-tinged spinach, garlic-flavored pasta (spätzle), and tiptop service. Reserving ahead is a *must* in this simple steakery. **Casa Ferlin** (Stampfenbachstrasse 38), sometimes called Chiantiquelle, has the biggest name among Italian restaurants. Wall panels of red damask; ceiling decorated with ceramic denizens of the Mediterranean; delicious Fettuccine; adept service. The owner sometimes plays the organ—sometimes too loudly. To us, the chief demurrer with this *casa* is its price scale. Also *buono* is the more modest **Piccoli** (Rotwandstrasse 48). The Veronese proprietor is the host, as well as the hunter who often shoots the game which is served; his wife commands the skillets with exquisite grace. **Trattoria Toscana** (Fraumünsterstrasse 14, a 5-minute stroll from the Baur au Lac) could be a winner if some of its cocky personnel were held under water for 30 minutes and a new chef were employed. As is, not for us. **Osteria Fiorentina** dishes out more attractiveness in its *osteria* corner than it does in its big, coolish café. The ravioli was good but our other commestibles seemed pedestrian. The **Silver Ranch** (245 Letzigraben), is not a favorite of ours. Vegetarian munching? **Gleich** (9 Seefeldstrasse) is as slick as a polished tomato. It is very attractive, modern in manner, and fully soundproofed to tone down the clack of healthy teeth crunching crispy-krinkly carrot steaks. The service is superb; our very recent meal here was so surprisingly delectable that we returned on a later day to enjoy an even better one. It has become extremely popular, especially at noon. Highly recommended. Closed Sunday. **Hiltl** (Sihlstrasse 26–28) is another leaf in this botanical brotherhood. Its fashion is also

modern now that it has been restyled and the cuisine is top-of-the-stalk. Ground-floor for groundling cookery; upstairs featuring an Indian plate, but in either place please finish your graze with the delicious mango ice cream. **Investor's Club**, across from the Carlton-Elite, markets light refreshment (rolls and coffee) along with ticker-tape replay of the stock market report. Savvy hostesses help you with your share selections, give advice, and answer your bids. Please don't step on a gnome, however. **Huguenin**, offers nibbly meals only, in a "grand-café" setting. The ancient **Veltliner Keller**, now operated by Mr. Jonkmanns, seems to be even better than before. **Töndury's Widder** spreads over several separate rooms on 4 floors of a venerable residence; intimate dimensions, excellent cuisine, routine tariffs; book in advance; praiseworthy for the bracket. Go to **Walliser-Keller** only for fondue; very Swiss. We're not especially fond of the **Schiffstube**, but the people are nice and the piano music is tranquillizing. **Hong Kong** rings our gong for Oriental skills. Ueli Prager's remarkable **Mövenpick** chain now has 6 outlets in Zürich (others in Geneva, Lausanne, Berne, and Lucerne). The most elaborate example is in Dreikönighaus ("Three Kings' House") on Beethovenstrasse; here, as in the previously described Geneva operations, you'll find everything from standup facilities to the Deluxe Baron de la Mouette Rôtisserie-Grill. **Old Fashion** (Fraumünsterstrasse 15) is under the aegis of Olga Hefti; comfortable, friendly, Swiss-pub style; for lunching, dining, or quaffing. Finally, no sweet-toothed traveler should miss the wonderful **Sprüngli Confiserie** on Paradeplatz; as in Demel in Vienna, here's sugar, spice, and everything *extra* nice in pastries, snacks, beverages, and candies; retail shop on one side and refreshments on the other; main outlet of the celebrated Lindt chocolates, to us the best in the world; yum, YUM, YUM!

Dedicated budgeteers? Since we're too bottlenecked here for additional entries, please consult our annually revised paperback, *Fielding's Low-Cost Europe*, which lists scads more bargain dining spots and money-saving tips for serious economizers.

Night Life In Zürich, the night spots can stay open until the wicked hour of 2 A.M.

Until the nocturnal wheels really start rolling and new challengers enter the nightscape, your most lively choices (partners often available, if desired) are (1) **Mascotte**, (2) **Café de la Terrasse**, and (3) **Hazyland**, for a barn-dance atmosphere. **Birdwatcher's Club** in the Simplon Hotel is a quiet, elegant lounge where nighthawks preen for their well-feathered chicks. **Red House** and **La Puce** also are colorful contenders. **Downtown** incorporates a Mexican restaurant called Santa Fe at ground level. Discothèques? The **Queen Anne Club** (Kreuzstrasse) is the first public offering in the region. It's only a few steps from the Eden au Lac and Bellerive au Lac hotels, and it's amazingly fancy for Zürich. The **Boîte de Nuit** is the spinner of Jo Roland, the famous chansonnier. Musical shows nightly; elegant clientele; very à la mode. **La Ferme**, a rustic disco-very owned by the Trattoria Toscana, can be barns of fun. **Golden Life** also glitters for the same lifestylists. **Blackout** blinks near the airport.

Shopping *Handicrafts:* If you seek honest-to-goodness regional craftsmanship instead of souvenir-stand junk, ★ ★ ★ ★ **Schweizer Heimatwerk** might warm your shopping soul. There are 5 of them. The headquarters is at

Rudolf Brun-Brücke (ask for Manageress Miss Hagenbuch); branches are at the National Bank Building (see Manageress Miss Steiger), the *Zürich* Airport, Hinterlabuen in *St. Gall,* and Hauptgass in *Stein am Rhein.* In all you will encounter only the finest handwrought products from Alpine farm families and small artisans all over the national map—original costumes of the Swiss cantons, colorful Toggenburger wooden articles, ceramics, woodcarvings, dolls, handloomed textiles in gay patterns, fondue dishes, Swiss Army knives, basketware, Swiss semiprecious stones—and these are only the beginning. When you have examined this most exciting harvest of exclusively Helvetian rural treasures in any shops anywhere today, will you have finished your adventures in this particular field? For your sake we hope not, and here's why:

Remarkable Director Wettstein has applied his decades of specialized expertise to purchase, to expand, and masterfully to streamline his second related creation, ★ ★ ★ ★ **Spindel** (St. Peterstrasse 11). His taste and professionalism have converted this 3-story structure into one of the best commercial assemblages of *international* hand-wrought arts and crafts from every European nation in existence. Your oracle here is Manageress Mrs. Akhrif-Hartung. Here's again a fascinating crossroads of far-flung cultural triumphs which pops the eyes!

Leather goods: ★ ★ ★ ★ **Mädler AG** (Bahnhofstrasse 26) is the Swiss and Austrian (see "Vienna") headquarters of this illustrious, historic, and widely renowned chain. This fine old house, launched in Leipzig by gifted patriarch Mortiz Mädler in 1850, has maintained its priceless name, traditions, and skills ever since. Awaiting you in these precincts is a sumptuous scope of strikingly beautiful, hard-to-find originals. The workmanship is exquisite, the styles have their distinctly illustrious cachet, the quality is superlative, and the cost range for the artistry is appealing. Patrician and chic Ms. Stephanie Mädler would bring geysers of pride to Founder Herr Moritz. Superb!

Sublime Chinese art objects: ★ ★ ★ ★ **The Jade Dragon Ltd**. (Talstrasse 16) is a connoisseurs' treasure trove. While part of the prize harvest of individual glories in this smallish haven is at the dedicated collectors' level, it also offers a variety of enchanting selections at prices which thou and we, as average acolytes, can afford. Delightful Manageress Miss Rosemary Spring will welcome you warmly. P-l-e-a-s-e make this breathtaking pilgrimage, if only to look and yearn!

High fashion and accessories: The ★ ★ ★ ★ **Grieder** department-specialty stores (Paradeplatz, and many branches) have often been called "the Neiman-Marcus of Europe." They are emphatically the trend setter in eastern Switzerland. Exceptional in every particular.

Antiques: The center of the action is on Schulüsselgasse around St. Peter's Church.

Air Travel

I n 1981, there's something in the wind—and it just may be the airline discount you've been searching for.

Airlines and clients alike are scrambling for a piece of the gold rush. The savings to the customer have produced new migrations of hopefuls who are seeking to climb aboard a cheap flight to Europe. And finally after a season of blatantly bruited bargain basement avaition promotions, some welcomed order has appeared to relieve the previous chaos. Lines are not so long, advance purchase programs have developed, and fewer panicky trippers have been driven to spur-of-the-moment takeoffs. In spite of increased fuel costs and worldwide inflation, the money-savers in the transportation skies are myriad and exciting. Moreover they are more assured for you the traveler.

☑ **SCHEDULED FARES** As you well remember, Sir Freddie Laker is the supercharged Englishman who pioneered the no-frills "Skytrain" concept which raked down the tariffs for transatlantic passage. (For details on how to buy a ticket and get aboard, refer to the individual airline later in this chapter.) He is going stronger than ever and now has added Los Angeles to his earlier New York port-of-call. Then, quite naturally, everybody else clambered to get onto the low-cost bandwagon. Predictably, this produced a snowball effect. When we last counted, 23 cities had become U.S. gateways for cut-rate flights —and the number is rising.

Domestically, in order to link up with airports that service foreign destinations, a rash of new low fares are being displayed on the shelves. Names such as Super Saver, Super Coach, Twosome, Liberty, Peanut, and many more are now beckoning customers to become airborne-again travelers.

Internationally, Skytrain passage between London and New York can be picked up for as little as $120 one way or $178 between Great Britain and Los Angeles (eastbound flights run slightly higher.) Major airlines such as TWA, Pan Am, British Airways, Air India, and El Al rushed in with Standby fares that averaged close to $280 roundtrip on the New York–London loop. (This ticketing puts passengers on first-line aircraft, provides them with hot meals at no extra cost, and sets them down at primary airport.) Under the Super

Apex plan which costs perhaps 30% more, the ticket must be purchased 21 days before departure and the passenger must spend from 7 to 180 days abroad —and *you* specify the flight and dates. Standard Excursion outlays require 14 to 60 days at your destination and it levies more than twice the standby rate, while Economy (isn't *that* a laugh?) is set at nearly 20% more. Then you can almost double that sum to arrive at the First-class total.

The above should serve only as the broadest guidelines when you begin to plan your itinerary because as we write these words mighty forces are at work to create even further bargains in the travel market. Restrictions are constantly being reduced on charter flights, affording new opportunities and broader programs involving land arrangements, local transportation, and accommodation; these you should consider when you plan your overall trip. As the fever of competition reaches a higher pitch, new destinations will be rolled out for lower fares in order to lure travelers away from conventional airports. If you are not too finicky about landing at one of the major cities, then this tack may realize considerable economies for you. *The main thing is to shop, shop, and shop* for the ticketing that brings you the greatest scheduled airline rewards for the lowest price. Keep an eye on the news and advertising media for the bonanza that awaits you.

☑ **CHARTERS**   Here too the skies are rumbling with new and thrilling and money-saving innovations. In fact, today it is becoming more and more difficult to distinguish between a charter and a standard fare—except that somehow the former is cheaper. Now that the CAB is allowing airlines to sell individual charter tickets directly to the public rather than having to go through middlemen, a whole new marketing approach is being formed—in which *you* gain most of the benefits and the savings.

Discounts are appearing for every imaginable category: preferential dates of departure, children, families, one-way travel, where you sit in the airplane, the color of your eyes, or the flatness of your feet. There are still charters that incorporate land arrangements, that is, packages including your hotel, a car rental, or other goodies tossed into the bundle. These, of course, will vary with the quality and character of the holiday you desire. The most dramatic change is that the new CAB-approved Public Charter no longer stipulates that the customer must buy any kind of accommodation, or tour, or even pay in advance for the ticket. Darned if we can understand how this varies from standard ticketing, but ours is not to reason why; it is only to outline to you the tremendous bargains unleashed when Washington decided to celebrate its red-tape-cutting jamboree. For more information be sure to browbeat your travel agent or refer to our LIVING GUIDE service mentioned in the business reply card in the center of this book.

In conjunction with charter and low-cost transatlantic ticketing, a thicket of **ancillary benefits** is beginning to appear on our side of the Atlantic for use

on the Continent. Europeans have long profited from the tantalizing jackpots cooked up by British packagers. The idea was to snatch the most economical transatlantic hop you could find and then sign up for a variety of tours departing from England. Now however, so many routes to so many continental destinations are being okayed by the governments involved that it is no longer necessary to funnel through Great Britain in order to take advantage of the proliferating bargains. Now that the flood gates have opened, everyone is seeking a piece of the action.

Space doesn't permit us here to spell out in further detail the many options that are available, but the chock-filled *How to Fly for Less* ($3.75 postpaid) is a splendid compendium assembled masterfully by travel expert Jens Jurgen. It is the clearest publication we've ever studied on this convoluted topic. Write to him at P.O. Box 105, Kings Park, N.Y. 11754. It will be money well spent to assure greater savings.

☑ **THE SUPERSONIC CONCORDE**   Here, unquestionably, is a bird for disciples of flight—graceful *pur sang* aviation from lift-off to landing. We strongly and sincerely aver, moreover, that this pioneering speedliner is as important to the field of aeronautics as the first commercial jets were when they were introduced to the public back in 1954. As they revolutionized not only an industry but also a way of thinking about travel, so too will Concorde establish its distinguished mark as a trailblazer.

Though necessarily expensive and not designed to provide the same wide-angle comforts you'll find aboard larger aircraft, the benefits of alighting absolutely fresh at your destination and in half the time expended on subsonic jets are puissant, joyful, and incontestable. At present, the Concordes of Air France and British Airways take off and land at JFK in New York and Dulles in Washington, D.C. A Braniff Concorde flies subsonically from Dallas to New York and then makes the transatlantic trip supersonically (see Braniff, below).

Our own transatlantic dash between Paris and Washington was an escape into the future. During 3 hours and 43 minutes of jetting, 2 hours and 52 minutes were at supersonic levels. All slower readings were necessitated by passage over populated areas where Air France and British Airways throttle back to reduce the risk of sonic showers below.

Strictly speaking, the Concorde is selling speed. Confident that this is the warranted commodity that droop-snoots assuredly provide while airborne, every erg is expended on terra firma to shave milliseconds off check-in time, baggage handling, customs, processing, and boarding. These have become so ultra-efficient and so smoothly coordinated, we'd wager that no chief of state could be transferred from throne room to gangway with greater swiftness than that accorded any ordinary ticketholder darting from midcity to tarmac. V-V-VIP lounges are available, where friends or clients may enter—and become

appropriately impressed; there are phones, seas of beverages, magazines and smiles by the heavenful; bulky coats are hung on racks and loaded neatly into cabin stowage; there's a special tax-rebate desk for travelers who have made purchases abroad. For the hurry-up voyager, in other words, all systems are "go."

☑ **BAGGAGE** Yes, now it is size, not weight! IATA rules allow First-class passengers on flights of U.S. origin 2 free bags, but the length, width, and height of each bag must total no more than 62 inches. Economy-class travelers are permitted 2 bags, one with dimensions that total no more than 62 inches, and both bags totaling a maximum of 106 inches. Also given the nod is a regulation that you may carry aboard as many pieces of hand luggage you like as long as their combined lengths, widths, and heights do not exceed 45 inches. Beyond this you are charged by the piece according to a scale of flat amounts determined by the distance you are flying. Returning from Europe to the USA you might be in for an ugly surprise since few of the overseas carriers have adopted the American 2-piece plan and still weigh everything but your pocket change—which they often extract from you at check-in time.

☑ **LOST BAGGAGE** Don't start worrying—not yet. Most luggage is recovered by the owner within 24 hours of loss. While airlines permit 7 days for notification, you should report your misfortune while you are still at the airport. If you are with a tour, then collar your group leader as soon as you are aware that your bindle has not followed you to your hotel. Some airlines, when they know they cannot retrieve the pieces quickly, provide emergency overnight kits to defrocked travelers; others hand out modest sums of money for basic necessities.

A "property irregularity" form must be filled in describing all the particulars of your loss. If you put some identification inside your suitcase, it will help tremendously should the outside tag have been ripped off. You are required nowadays to have your own personal luggage card on every piece. (All airlines, incidentally, have keys to every sort of luggage; rest assured that Customs also will be having a look inside; this is also why you should be absolutely candid in reporting that extra bottle of Scotch or perfume that you may have tucked in among your sweaters.) If it finds your baggage, the carrier will deliver it to you promptly.

After a week has passed and your caboodle still hasn't been located, you should then begin the process of extracting a settlement. Our experience has been that you won't get anything near like the value of your carryall or wardrobe (not to mention valuables such as cameras or jewelry—which should have been among hand luggage anyway). We were once offered $25

for a suitcase and contents worth nearly $650 and after going to the top of the executive ladder managed to pry only $50 out of the company!

The best protection, in other words, is your own insurance policy.

☑ **BUMPING OR BOUNCING**   These are the names of an increasingly widespread game played by airlines which use you as the ball. It goes like this: The 747 that's supposed to wing you to, say, Paris has 352 seats. Because Carrier X knows from experience that a number of people with reservations will be "no-shows," it covers itself when its loads reach capacity by overselling perhaps 20 extra passages. (Usually airline officials figure that 10% of the registrants on the computer won't arrive at the airport.) Sure enough, 19 inconsiderate individuals fail to appear—but what if you are customer number 353? "Sorry," says the clerk, "no more room." You have been bumped, bounced, and flounced.

What to do?

Know your "fly-rights" and use them.

The CAB has ruled that provided you hold a confirmed reservation plus a properly validated ticket and have shown up on schedule, the airline must deliver you to your overseas destination by other means *within 4 hours* of your planned arrival time. If unable to do so, it is required to give you at least partial compensation, depending upon the distance, of not less than $37.50 or more than $200, plus free passage on the next available flight. If they don't get you to your destination within 2 hours of the scheduled time, their apology must be doubled, to a maximum of $400. This is *in addition* to the price of your original ticket, which you can turn in for a 100% refund. Moreover, you must be paid this "denied boarding compensation" within 24 hours; if you aren't, you have 90 days in which to file a claim. So if you get the bounce, for heaven's sake don't stamp off muttering darkly about seeing your lawyer. Stay right there and insist that you be given the CAB's printed regulation on the subject as well as the necessary forms you must fill out to collect this penalty. (This applies, of course, only within the USA, before or after international flights.)

As you may recall, public troubleshooter Ralph Nader once got bumped, sued the airline for damages, took the shindy to Federal Court, and won the day—a decision which suggests that even the CAB provisions to guarantee your privileges are perhaps insufficient. If this juridical stance is current, then we suppose bumping per se might be considered a fraudulent misrepresentation. In either case, if you *do* get bumped and you do display defiance plus a knowledge of the portentous intimidations at your disposal, we'll bet our wings that any wise airline official will quickly break into a righteous and gelid sweat, yielding mercurially to almost any of your demands for comfort and coddling. For more information on bouncing and

other helpful hints for the airborne pilgrim, write to the Office of Consumer Affairs, Civil Aeronautics Board, Washington, D.C. 20428, and ask for the pamphlet, "Air Travelers' Fly-Rights." It could reward you with justifiable dividends and save you from jumbo-size headaches. Complaints about carriers also should be addressed to the CAB. (And possibly Mr. Nader?)

THE LINE YOU ARE FLYING

Here are some quick facts about the international airlines you're likely to use. The European carriers come later listed alphabetically according to their parent nations.

NORTH AMERICA   **Trans World Airlines (TWA)**: TWA's far-flung network spans 36 U.S. cities and 20 overseas centers. From its U.S. gateways, it carries more transatlantic traffic than any of its competitors.

The superstars of TWA's international fleet are the giant Boeing 747, the wide-body Lockeed 1011, and the Boeing 707. Coming soon will be a squadron of Boeing 767s.

Keen-minded L. Edwin Smart, is the wing commander; he's the line's Board Chairman and Chief Executive Officer. President and Chief Airline Executive is C. E. Meyer, Jr.

TWA's landed-gentry subsidiary, Hilton International, totes up 72 hotels in 43 foreign countries, thus assuring travelers of down-to-earth comfort almost anywhere they alight.

The Trans World Flight Center at Kennedy is a study in convenience and efficiency. Flight Wing One handily accommodates the jumbo jets. It also boasts integrated health, immigration, and Customs inspection facilities, allowing international passengers direct access to continuing domestic flights. Each gate has its own comfortable waiting room in which ticketholders may relax before entering the planes via telescopic Jetways which protect them from exposure to the weather. TWA's fleet of 707s is equipped with carry-on-luggage compartments for international flights, an innovation that TWA pioneered earlier domestically.

TWA's plush Trans World Service on 747s includes an upper deck lounge for First-class passengers with economy sections on most aircraft boasting the cleverly designed "Twin" Seat, a TWA "first." When the center seat is not occupied, its back drops down, its armrests go up, and the occupant can rest and relax in dimensions approaching those for First-class passage. Extra consideration is given to disabled passengers; the line publishes an excellent pamphlet titled "Air Travel for the Handicapped".

Dining choices include 5 entrées in First-class, with a choice of 3 meals in economy. A salute to the carrier's culinary capabilities was recently received in the form of the coveted Golden Plate Award of the International Foodservice Manufacturers Association. The award, presented for out-

standing contributions to the U.S. food service industry, marks yet another "first" for TWA.

In-flight entertainment aboard TWA includes a choice of 2 top-quality films, either "mature" or "general." Special audio/stereo entertainment is provided by way of 9 channels with choices ranging from contemporary music to timely topics on the special "Executive Report" channel.

No-smoking areas are located in the First-class and economy sections of the aircraft. The airline was first to configure its entire fleet in such fashion. A special "Business Zone," located in the forward part of the economy section, has been set aside, load permitting, on transatlantic 747 flights primarily for the business traveler who wishes to work or sleep uninterrupted, in a quiet, relaxed atmosphere.

Safety record? When you climb aboard that painstakingly maintained TWA job, you're riding one of the planes which won award after award from the National Safety Council. And it should reassure you even more to know that the jet pilots who fly the President of the United States are given their refresher courses at the TWA Training Center.

Recommendation: Here's one of the best-equipped, best-maintained, and best-experienced carriers. To most international travelers this trio of star qualities shows up vividly.

Pan American World Airways, Inc. (Pan Am): The big news is the merger between Pan Am and National Airlines, which provides the parent carrier with a U.S. domestic network to meld into its international skein—a Pan Am quest for the past 3 decades. This colossus of commercial aviation has an unparalleled record for pioneering new routes, planes, technical advances, and legislation. Starting as a Caribbean and Latin American trailblazer in the '20s, its flying boats were the first scheduled aircraft to bridge the Pacific and later the Atlantic.

Today Pan Am's Clippers wing along on many of their familiar routes as well as on some that TWA handled previously—all part of a cooperative program to reduce operating costs and to conserve aviation fuel. While the pathways of modern flight may be changing, Pan Am still concentrates heavily on passenger comfort. On long-haul 747s a Sleeperette seat has been introduced which stretches out and reclines to a 60° angle. (Conventional First-class chairs tilt only 45°.) A more capacious table-type tray comes swinging down the aisle at mealtimes if two travelers are seated and dining side-by-side; this conforms with Pan Am's broadened First-class menu and more extentsive beverage selections. Our own experiences aboard Pan Am's 747-airships embodied the epitome of travel's more graceful moments. The cabin crews were alert and kind, the culinary preparations and presentations were superb by airline standards, and our particular flight was a joy in every thoughtful detail. We relished every mile. Our very recent hops in and out of West Berlin, however, were another story. This shuttle service is about as perfunctory as a cattle march. Efficient it is; appealing it isn't.

Economy-class, no longer standardized by IATA since Pan Am checked out of that body, is more varied, too. There's a choice of 3 meals, with some unusual creations such as Chicken Alfredo, a pasta platter, beef and mushroom pie, the Kabejaufilet (cod in dill sauce) and Sauerbraten.

Pan Am's elliptical 16-gate "Worldport" terminal "brings the plane to the passenger" at Kennedy International Airport. Luggage can be checked in at curbside and Customs matters dispatched within the very same building. Voyagers board at fuselage level beneath a cantilever roof. It is a $150,000,000 architectural marvel, the most beautiful and efficient structure of its type we've seen. It has recently been enlarged to 5 times its original size, with 52 check-in positions and rooftop parking (short-term) for 400 cars.

Pan Am can provide many other services in addition to air transportation. Its Inter-Continental Hotels Corporation is one of the world's largest hotel chains—totalling some 79 properties in 48 countries. "Panamac 2," the reservations system, can book hotel rooms and make car rentals globally. Pan Am has its own passenger check-in center at La Guardia where passengers are bussed, gratis, to Kennedy.

Recommendation: The quality of the aircraft, the soundness of the maintenance, the skill of the pilots, and the competence on the mechanical side can't be topped by any airline in the world. Its First-class service holds its own with just about anything in the Atlantic skies.

National Airlines: As we've already mentioned, this carrier is now married to Pan Am. To expand its grid which started in 1934 between St. Petersburg and Daytona Beach and proliferated to encompass 41 cities on the East, Gulf, and Pacific Coasts, as well as international destinations, National became the 3rd U.S. transatlantic flag bearer in '70 by inaugurating a daily flight in both directions—now exclusively with DC-10s—between Miami and London. It also now flies nonstop to and from Paris and Frankfurt. Personally, we haven't crossed the Atlantic aboard National.

Braniff: This newcomer to the transatlantic lanes boasts gateways in both Boston and Dallas/Fort Worth with same-line service to 53 U.S. cities, plus links on to Mexico, South America, and the Far East. The colorful 747 and DC-8 birds call into London, Paris, Frankfurt, Amsterdam, and Brussels. Here's an innovative go-getter with a splendid domestic network, years of experience, and the dash of pioneering spirit which has always been a chief ingredient of great airlines. PS: Be sure to ask whether standby or budget-fare ticketing is available on your itinerary since Braniff has applied for such low-cost proposals. If you are a European resident, the company's Airpass will save you a bundle should you want to wing around the New World.

Air Canada (AC): This carrier, formerly known as Trans Canada Air Lines or TCA, started in '37 with two 10-passenger monoplanes, 71 employees, 122 air miles to service, and nothing in its pockets. Now it employs 25,000 people, wings over 87,000 unduplicated miles, and jingles with more than 1½ billion

dollars in operating revenue. Last year it carried 11-million customers to 31 destinations in Canada, 10 in the U.S., 7 in Europe, and 11 in the Caribbean. The all-jet fleet counts 115 modern aircraft of various sizes, the latest including Boeing 767s and Lockheed 1011-500s.

We've had the pleasure of riding AC only once in our lives (Montreal to New York), but plenty of readers report that its long-haul Atlantic service is splendid in every detail.

Canadian Pacific Air (CP Air): This air arm of the world's mightiest independent transportation body was energized in 1942, by the amalgamation of 10 "bush" services in western and northern Canada.

In 3 decades it has mushroomed almost unbelievably. Today it boasts a 64-thousand-mile route pattern which links all major cities in Canada with 5 continents. CP Air has 4 daily round trips in each direction between Vancouver, Toronto and Montreal—serving intermediate cities en route. It also boasts 2 hops per day between Vancouver and San Francisco.

Its DC-8 and Boeing 747 jetliners whoosh all over the world, while Boeing 737–200 short/medium jets zip to and fro. You may also hear a duet of Boeing 727s in the crisp Canadian air. In addition, a $24,000,000 overhaul to the Vancouver base has been completed. The overseas routes extend through Hong Kong and Tokyo; Sydney, Fiji, and Honolulu; Mexico City and Acapulco; Lima, Santiago, and Buenos Aires; Amsterdam, via the polar route and North Atlantic, Lisbon, Rome, and Milan, plus Athens.

We first hopped CP Air up to Great Slave Lake in Northwest Territories many, many moons ago, and ever since, our admiration has been profound. Our Good Neighbors up North can fly like angels. They should, because they're among the most experienced, most careful, most reliable air experts around.

Delta: Though we've never flown this line internationally, its domestic services are well known and well respected. It has built an airbridge between Gatwick (in London) and Atlanta and New Orleans. Delta's "Medallion" treatment is aboard a Wide-Ride (their own term for it) TriStar L-1011 with first-run movies and 7-channel entertainment plugged into your $2.50 headset. One big advantage is Delta's broad coverage below the Mason-Dixon Line; hence a linkup transoceanically is undiluted southern comfort.

Others: Let's start with **Transamerica**, formerly called Trans International. This one-time charter line now joins Amsterdam with East and West Coast U.S. gateways plus forging links to Paris and Frankfurt. The rates indeed look attractive. Check with your travel agent for late developments. You might also inquire about **USAir** (previously known as Allegheny) which is now moving into the transatlantic skyways. **Air Florida**, too, is in on the transoceanic jamboree, seeking permanent CAB approval for the temporary routes it forged between Miami and Amsterdam, Zürich, and Brussels—the same Dutch and Swiss services, by the way, that Pan Am and National recently suspended.

EUROPEAN Austria Austrian Airlines (AUA) builds domestic air bridges daily between the capital and Graz and 3 times per week between Vienna and Salzburg. The fleet of DC-9s, with each plane named after a famous composer, fans out to 34 cities in 22 European, Middle Eastern, and North African countries. We recently stepped off another AUA loop as hotter converts to this company than we'd ever been before. Its highly skilled administrators have custom-built superb service, kindness, and s-m-o-o-t-h thoroughness into just about every aspect which affects the passenger. For airborne cookery, the cuisine was so beautifully presented that we could scarcely believe our eyes —and it tasted even better than it looked!

AUA's slogan is "The Friendly Airline." This strikes us as being far too modest a claim for what such legions of admiring travelers, including us, regard as one of the finest smaller carriers flying today.

Belgium With a sleek fleet of 26 aircraft and 140 thousand miles of far-flung routes, Sabena is one of the more important and most respected carriers in the industry, with an annual average of more than 2 million ticketholders.

The glittering fleet of Boeing 707 and 747 and Douglas DC-10 jets is employed on the Brussels—America (New York, Detroit, Chicago, Atlanta, Montreal, Mexico City, Brussels—Africa, and Brussels—Orient (to Tokyo, Jakarta, and Singapore via the North Pole or via Southeast Asia) links, while Boeing 737s serve the shorter-haul destinations.

From Brussels, Sabena planes fan out to 75 cities on 4 continents. Brussels International Airport is the base airport and headquarters. At check-in time here, you can register for the seat of your choice on your outgoing aircraft. Ask at the counter for this thoughtful service.

Recommendation: On our recent Sabena rides we were again delighted in every particular. The aircraft were comfortable, beautifully appointed, and beautifully flown; food was superb; service was exceptionally suave and pleasant. Sabena is an efficient, well-established carrier with an excellent record and a progressive attitude. We find it outstanding and recommend it heartily.

★ **TIP** At the Brussels International Airport, tax-free shops offer tobacco, liquor, liqueur, camera, watches, perfumes, and selected manufactured goods.

If you're going to town and loathe the abominable taxi drivers as heartily as we do, there are superb electric train connections; low tariffs; follow the signs from the disembarking ramps; only 15 minutes to the city.

Denmark For general information, see "Scandinavian Airlines System."

SAS reins for Denmark are in the hands of dynamic and personable Frede Ahlgren-Eriksen; if this executive is out of town, take your problems to the SAS City Terminal Manager Erlander.

Air service to the Faeroe Islands, the group of 21 islands between Iceland and the Shetlands belonging to Denmark, was inaugurated by Faeroe Airways

some time back and is now under the SAS burgee. Fokker Friendships do all
the flapping to and fro.

Danair recently lifted off as a domestic carrier. It services all home territories
except the routes between Copenhagen and Greenland, Aarhus, Aalborg, and
Rønne, which SAS continues to visit. We've not yet had an opportunity to
climb aboard.

It is infuriating that the government-owned and SAS-operated Kastrup
Airport has no porters for the luggage of arriving passengers. A spare few
pushcarts are available occasionally, but for the elderly or the infirm the
carrying and fetching—not to mention the agonizingly long walk to the bus
or taxi ranks—are inconvenient and, moreover, very possibly dangerous. This
negligent, pinchpenny thinking is a national disgrace which SAS or the authorities should correct immediately.

England **Laker Airways**, of course, continues to steal most of thunder
from the skies—that heaven-sent noise actually being the rumble of Skytrains
(DC-10s, Boeing 707s, or A-300s) roaring along with their low-cost fares.

Since we've already described Sir Freddie's bargain prices, let's get some
other practical questions answered next.

Many travelers are still confused about how to obtain passage. You can
buy your ticket and check in any time from 4 AM to 9:30 PM at the Laker
Travel Center, 95-25 Queens Boulevard in Rego Park, Queens, New York.
The entrance is on Junction Boulevard. Other satellite bureaus are at 1 E.
59th St. and Number One World Trade Center; another is at the Airlines
Center, 751 Broad St. in Newark, N.J. (In Los Angeles the ticket office is
at the Los Angeles International Airport, at the Ambassador Hotel, and at
3 other sites.) Passengers buying their ducats earlier in the day may return
to the Center before flight time to enter buses which will transport them to
the United Airlines Terminal at JFK where they board the flight. If they
prefer, they may proceed directly to the UAL Terminal at JFK on their
own, making sure to be there at least one hour before departure. (The gate
will be indicated on the information screen at the terminal.) All luggage
must be checked in at the time the ticket is purchased. With the exception
of the Kennedy interline passengers, no luggage can be accepted at United
Airlines. Each passenger is allowed 2 pieces, according to international
standards, and one small cabin bag. Payment may be made by cash, travelers checks, or credit card (American Express, Diners Club, Master Charge,
or Visa-BankAmericard).

Two wrinkles of convenience are the Reservaseat program, which provides
a no-strings advance round-trip booking for roughly $600 and a $420 Excursion fare requiring purchase 21 days in advance and a minimum stay abroad
of one week. (This represents a saving of about $170 and $75 respectively over
two similar plans under the IATA fare structure.) A person may purchase the
ticket for an accompanying friend. One representative of a family may do the
buying for his immediate family and for one friend. The accompanying people

need not be present, but the purchaser must have everyone's passport and baggage.

Next, you then may select and pay for any food service you'll want aloft—or you may bring your own picnic. Continental breakfast costs $1.50; lunch or dinner goes for $4. Movie and stereo headsets are paid for on board. Duty-free purchases of liquor, cigarettes, perfume, and the like also may be made aloft.

Seat availability can be determined by telephoning (212) 459-7323 in New York on the day of departure. (In Los Angeles the number is (213) 646-9650). These reports are updated every hour. General information about Skytrain service may be obtained by calling (212) 995-2113. Laker's "live" number if further help is needed is (212) 459-6092 in New York or (213) 646-9600 in Los Angeles. And, as we go to press, we hear that Laker has just added flights from Miami.

The BMT-N subway line stops at the 63rd Drive–Queens Boulevard–Rego Park station, on the street adjacent to the Center, or passengers from Manhattan may also take the IND E and F trains to Roosevelt Avenue in Queens, where they change to the local and go to the same 63rd Drive station. The #60 Green Bus departs from Second Avenue and 60th Street in Manhattan. Transportation is also available from LaGuardia Airport by taking the Junction Boulevard bus from opposite the Traveler's Hotel.

How about in London? On arrival at Gatwick Airport you can hop over to the train depot in the same terminal and be at London's Victoria Station in about 40 minutes. This is express train service operating every 15 minutes from 6:00 AM to midnight in both directions, and hourly from midnight on. One way fare is about $3.50. The sale of tickets for the westbound London to New York or Los Angeles flights are at Gatwick Airport beginning at 4:00 AM on the day of departure, or tickets may also be purchased at Victoria Station in London (the Laker Travel Center), open from 8:00 AM to 4:00 PM. All baggage, however, is to be checked at Gatwick. The latest information on westbound Skytrain service may be obtained by telephoning London 828-7766 or (0293) 517-777.

In short, fly Laker and save a bundle.

With the exception of British Caledonian Airways and several independent operators who exist upon charters, cargo, and a wee ration of passenger trade, the British Government owns and controls (in practical effect) virtually all important scheduled air service within the United Kingdom. In 1974, its 2 huge fleets—BOAC (British Overseas Airways Corporation) and BEA (British European Airways)—were merged into one giant national flag carrier: **British Airways**, circling the globe through a 1/2-million-mile network that now calls at 149 airports in 80 countries. Its flock of more than 200 planes is among the world's largest; moreover, 4 years ago it introduced the 1350-mph Concorde on regular supersonic runs. For a detailed report on this speedster, turn to our earlier comments.

Air Anglia is well worth sampling if you are flying out of or into Scottish fields. The work is done by Fokker Friendship turboprops and an F28 pure jet. It ranges over to the Continent and to several British ports. This is a small, smiling, try-harder airline that we recommend with enthusiasm.

British Caledonian was hatched in 1970. Its fleet now consists of shiny DC-10-30s, Boeing 707s, and BAC III's, based at Gatwick (near London). Today it flies to Houston, Dallas/Fort Worth, and Atlanta, with hopes to call on Denver, St. Louis, and New Orleans. Internally, it stirs the air all over the U.K. We wouldn't turn a hair if this outfit's Golden Lion emblem were to appear on a moon shuttle before long, thanks to hard-driving Chairman Adam Thomson, whose imagination encompasses everything from ordering multimillion-dollar jets to plaid kilts for the line's pretty, polite, and highly polished hostesses. He is pushing Scottish-type hospitality and amenities with full force and enormous success. Our intra-European jaunts have ranged from excellent to superb.

British Airways fairly blankets the U.K., with hookups throughout the Continent, the Middle East, and North Africa. Its international equipment consists of TriStar air buses, Tridents, which are gradually being replaced by Boeing 737s, BAC III's and Super-III's. A regular helicopter service chops a swath between Penzance and the Scilly Islands.

The short-haul and European links have never evoked much enthusiasm from us, but perhaps the new Club Class for businessmen (replacing First Class) will perk things up for those other than Robert Morley. Be sure to ask about a proposed "channel hopper" fare which it was hoped would cut the old cost of getting to Paris by half.

The intercontinental service provides in-flight comforts so pleasant that we're happy to ride it any day to any destination. This enterprise was first with jet propulsion in commercial service (1952), first with propjets on transatlantic schedules (1957), first to fly the paying passenger over the ocean on pure jets (1958), and first (in conjunction with Air France) to launch commercial aviation into the supersonic era via the Concorde (1976).

The welkin buzzes with its own Boeing 747 hummings-and-goings. It also takes pride in its fleet of Lockheed TriStars and Vickers Super VC-10s (137 passengers). We deplaned from the latter after hightailing it across the Atlantic —and what honeys these babies are! The cuisine is superb in *both* classes; despite IATA's chokes on what operators can offer budget travelers, these crafty chefs present food so masterfully it seems a Lucullan feast. The service is best-British in attentiveness, friendliness, and watchfulness—in step with the nation's centuries of heartwarming good manners.

★ **TIPS** For wander-woes, a lady who will receive you cordially is BA's Customer Relations Manager, Mrs. Marion Porter, at the British Airways Terminal, Buckingham Palace Road, London, S.W.1.

Unfortunately, for regional and European flights you can no longer check in either yourself or your luggage at the West London Terminal. (Transoceanic

passengers can register at the Buckingham Palace Road Air Terminal in town.)
Now the traveler is responsible for getting himself to the airport on time, so
be sure to allow for this; flights to some politically sensitive areas require as
much as 95 minutes advance check-in. Buses leave the West London terminal
for Heathrow every 20 minutes, but a flight will not be held if your bus is
delayed. Also there is the new "Piccadilly Tube," a subway from central
London to Heathrow Central that departs every 4 minutes and costs peanuts.
Walkway travelators further ease the burden of carrying luggage over long
distances.

Finland   No country is more custom tailored to air travel than Finland.
And few nations can provide such a handsome welcome in their primary air
terminals. Helsinki's reflects the sylvan forestlands of birch and other timber
which convert cold institutionality into graceful intimacy. Striking it is—and
convenient, too.

Finnair, the lion's share of which is nationally owned, is its perfect answer.
This half-century-old carrier offers the second densest domestic network (next
to Iceland) in Europe—plus the lowest domestic flying rates.

In its ground and in-flight passenger service, Finnair strongly and repeatedly
—on flight after flight—continues to impress us as a well-meaning but unsophisticated SAS. (As one amusing example, domestic aircraft sport advertising
cards on the cabin interiors à la bus and subway ads in our country.) But its
personnel couldn't be more friendly, kindly, or obliging.

If you should have any special Finnair problems, dump them into the
capable and kind hands of Usko Määttä. He may be reached at the Finnair
Building in the capital.

In 1966, Finnair broke new ground in the European aviation industry by
abolishing baggage weigh-in on *domestic routes;* 3 pieces of luggage are carried
free of charge regardless of weight on flights within Finland, with a minimal
charge for any additional bags. (For passengers to or from international flights,
these liberalized regulations apply *only* on the domestic leg of the journey, and
only if a stopover is made in Helsinki.)

Recommendation: Finnair adds up to a crackerjack feeder airline which
we like, respect, and would fly any day. But, for its ticketholders' comfort,
it still has much to learn from the more savvy, world-experienced Big
Boys.

★ **TIPS**   Don't grab a cab for town; the cost is lethal and bus shuttles run every
half hour to the town terminus just behind the Intercontinental Hotel.

If the signs of your zodiac are favorable, this is one airport where you might
find a baggage porter—but don't count on it.

Finnair offers a $135 **Holiday Ticket** to non-Scandinavian tourists, permit-
ting 15 days of unlimited use of all domestic airlanes. Be sure to check with
your travel agent, because this bargain, if it is still cooking by your arrival, is
much too good to miss.

Smoking is prohibited on Finnish domestic flights, part of a national program to discourage the use and promotion of tobacco.

France　Air France bridges all 5 continents with more than 369 thousand miles of unduplicated routes; it ranks 2nd in Europe and 9th in the world; it carries among the highest number of passengers transported by international carriers—some of them aboard the swift, supersleek Mach II Concorde (read our special report on this pioneer earlier in this chapter). Every 2 1/2 minutes a modern, up-to-date Air France liner arrives or departs somewhere in the world.

At Air France destinations all over the map, "Welcome Service" desks have been staffed with multilingual personnel especially trained to lend advice and assistance to travelers. At Kennedy, Charles de Gaulle, and Orly airports, nursery facilities are available; at the Paris airports, there are First-class and VIP lounges plus an extra-sumptuous Concorde compound at Charles de Gaulle. Most transatlantic flights (including the Concorde) and many connecting ones depart and arrive at Charles de Gaulle; however, there are several each day which still utilize Orly, so be sure to note whether you have to make an airport transfer (about $8 twixt CDG and ORY). CDG is 14 miles north of Paris; it offers drive-in-check-in services (as well as check-in positions at entryways); the 30-minute ride leaving for Porte Maillot every 15 minutes costs about $4. Buses to Orly gear up at Les Invalides every 15 minutes; they take usually less than one hour. Both city terminals are equipped with shops, restaurants, bars, car rentals, ticket bureaus for theater and sightseeing, barber and beauty parlors. Aloft, among the Air France cachets for the customers' comforts are kosher and special diet meals, infant hammocks, baby foods, and disposable diapers. In addition, the company is following the in-flight entertainment trend by providing first-run color movies in 2 languages and 10-channel musical offerings for transatlantic and other long-distance jetters. Screens are the giant overhead type, with audio portions transmitted through earphones.

Board Chairman Pierre Giraudet has long been a guiding light in the French transportation industry; Gilbert Pérol is the line's president; Roland Hawkins, an American from Iowa, ably oversees his realm of the North and Central American Division; and Antoine Girot now is the General Manager within the USA.

French cabin service is traditionally excellent. On all of our recent hops, the crews in both First class and Economy class were absolutely outstanding in every regard in seeming to *care* about the welfare and happiness of their charges. Our latest transoceanic crossing was a study in hedonism—from the actual comfort of the aircraft itself, to entertainment aloft, to meal-and-snack-timing, to the courtesy of the crew when a "stack" over JFK delayed our landing. Without exception, the *Chefs de Cabine* and the stewards were amiable yet proper and extra-thoughtful.

In food Air France flies a course that befits a nation of gastronomes. While the cuisine on board Concorde, of course, is regulated by space limitations, the offerings on bigger aircraft are the equal of grand chefs who reign in grand kitchens. On both long-range or intercontinental flights the dishes are tiptop in quality and presentation too.

If scheduling difficulties or other special problems should plague you, take them at once to American-born Ed Tourtellotte at Air France, 1350 Avenue of the Americas, New York, N.Y. He is the airline's Manager of Public Relations, USA. In our years as travel reporters, we have never met a faster thinking, more dependable, more patient, and more cheerful PR executive anywhere.

In summary, we like Air France more than ever. What's more, we predict you will, too.

★ **TIPS**   Be sure to inquire about the "Vacances" service, a peak-season special rate which looks like an important moneysaver; last year there were 4 crossings per week aboard 747s.

At Orly blue-uniformed baggage handlers of the Elan company tried to extract tips from us on several separate arrivals for loading our luggage into the airport-town bus. Don't fall for it because they're already paid very well for operating this concession. But *do* be sure that they put your suitcase inside the bus before it grinds into first gear.

Germany   **Lufthansa**, the German National Airline, boasts an all-jet fleet of Boeing 747s, 707s, 727s, and 737s, plus the DC-10 and the Airbus.

Stewardesses are generally pleasant; all speak English. Some stewards, however, can turn into snippy, officious smart-alecks at times. On one Hamburg-London passage, nothing could have been more important to our pair than their own wisecracks (aimed at ladies as well as gentlemen) and their incessant peddling of tax-free booty; the comfort of their ticketholders appeared to come last. The First-class "Senator," which we've never ridden, flies between German terminals and American points. Special "sleeper chairs" have been installed in the upper lounge of the 747s; a supplemental charge is asked for this extra fillip, however. An aura of *Gemütlichkeit* is allegedly added by beer service from a freshly tapped keg called *Dämmerschoppen* ("dusk-pint"). The barrel is rolled down the aisle on a cart also laden with smoked ham and pumpernickel. You may also sit in the *no-smoke* zone; on all Lufthansa flights, the left side is reserved for nonpuffers, the right for smokers.

Greece   **Olympic Airways** is the sole domestic carrier. The current fleet consists of Boeing 707-384s, 727s, 720-B's, plus a pair of 747s, a twin-turbo prop Japanese YS-II, and an increasing hopper of choppers and lighter birds to lift travelers to the islands. There's a transatlantic link between New York and Athens nonstop. This is augmented by a terminus in Montreal. We haven't yet had a chance to climb aboard the transoceanic leg. Other international services, besides the European skein, run down through Africa. Olympic operates its own reception and booking center, of course, but a fine new $10 million

terminal eases some of the congestion at peak season. Traffic to Rhodes had become so massive that, even with several dozen shuttles per week being operated, these harassed citizens would not ordinarily carry any passenger to the island who could not show a confirmed return ticket before his departure from Athens. In an effort to ease this situation, even more flights have been added.

We've used this line on numerous recent European or domestic flights. The earliest ones were superb, but the latest hops were fraught with rudeness from ground personnel, high-handed treatment from overburdened officials, or inexcusable neglect on land or aloft.

Ireland Aer Lingus-Irish International Airlines is the promotional name of 2 operational divisions which share common management: Aerlinte Eireann for transatlantic service, and Aer Lingus for British and European runs.

These highborne Hibernians fly the Boeing-747 jumbo on long runs—and they fill them with more seats than most any other carrier; 4 Boeing 707 pure jets do the work for 133 passengers per cabin. During the summer season these shuttle to London, making the run in 50 minutes. We've recently hopped off a New York–Dublin spin and our First-class physical facilities (*not* the wonderfully kind crew) did not impress us as favorably as on some more luxury-minded fleets. The Economy section is vast, absolutely enormous. The Deluxe segment, however, contained a mere 8 seats plus a galley; a forward cargo hold totally consumed the lounge (practically a standard offering on other intercontinental jets). We understand, furthermore, that there is no First Class whatever on the Montreal loop. Here's an operator that is frankly after the Economy trade; it does beautifully in this category. But it does not shoot for the higher-paying passenger; the cuisine suffers in variety and quality (and why not, with an incentive to feed a maximum of only 8 mouths per flight?); its leg-stretching areas were designed for leprechauns, not for long-boned North Americans (the seat itself is comfortable). But the service! Oh, those warm, kind, lovely, friendly, generous-hearted colleens!!! They are *marvelous*—and so is Aerlinte Eireann, IF you hold an Economy-class billet. Irish hospitality is renowned—and shure they don't be calling it "The Friendly Airline" as a mere bit of blarney!

The Aer Lingus leg is one of the most efficient feeder companies in modern aviation. Their passenger load factor is almost habitually the highest in commercial aviation—both domestically and between other nations. They just don't come safer, more wide-awake, or better.

Italy Alitalia Italian Airlines, as you undoubtedly know, is an official transportation arm of the nation. As such, it reflects much of the havoc of a government that has endured nearly 40 changes of administration during the past 3 decades or so. When it is functioning smoothly it likewise radiates a Latin grace and charm that can only bring passengers back again for more high-flying adventure.

Harnessing a fleet of Boeing 747s and DC-8s (mostly over the North Atlantic), Caravelles and DC-9s (for important European runs), Alitalia soars along as one of the largest commercial carriers in the world.

In the Italian chapter we have already delineated with agonizing detail the disruptive effects of Italy's rampant strike situation. The diabolical result of this all too often carries over into the aeronautical realm as well. Within the skein that is Alitalia, more than 20 separate unions are involved, and even when one of these syndicates decides to go out on a "wildcat," a "flash," or a "hiccup" protest, very frequently the entire line shuts down. Aviation being what it is, there is so much interdependence among the specialized divisions that one often cannot function safely without the others.

As so many of these paralyzing issues are referred back to political paper-shufflers and assorted bumbling martinets, there's little that Alitalia can do to resolve its deeper problems until the administration in Rome itself is functioning properly.

In spite of this, however, Alitalia's administrative pilots at last seem to be climbing over the turbulence of a storm-bound government and operating more independently of the crippling bureaucrats. Studies are underway and programs are being implemented that we hope will unravel many of these earthborne glitches. The carrier again is recognizing that the passenger comes first.

Luxembourg Luxair sprouted its wings in '62 with one Fokker "Friendship." The "Friendship" must have taken, because now there's another little Fokker plus a few Boeings. These zip to-and-fro daily between the capital and Amsterdam (via Brussels) and Paris, twice a day over to London, 5 times a week to Frankfurt am Main, and twice a week to Nice and Palma de Mallorca, plus darts to Athens, Málaga and Tunis. Icelandair provides daily service between New York, Chicago, Reykjavik, and Luxembourg at prices below IATA rates; an associated carrier which could be called "Sunlandic" but is actually International Air Bahama dashes 6 times a week between Nassau and Luxembourg at similar bargain tariffs.

Netherlands KLM is a colossus of aviation, with a sterling reputation and a magnificent overall record. It earns such respect from its colleagues, in fact, that 26 other airlines send their established (not new) pilots to KLM for training.

The company flies 15 Boeing 747 Jumbos, 7 DC-10-30s, and 14 DC-8 jetliners of various types to 118 cities in 73 countries residing at all points of the compass, with 20 DC-9s earmarked for the European network. KLM's subsidiary, NLM City Hopper, operates a largely domestic network using 9 Fokker-27 Friendship turboprops and 4 F-28 Fellowship jets to link Amsterdam, Eindhoven, Enschede, Groningen, and Maastricht. It also has taken over a few hops to German, French, Belgian, and English destinations.

Schiphol Airport, 7 miles from the center of Amsterdam, is home base for the KLM fleet. It's name, which means "Hell For Ships," may be switched to

Amsterdam Airport because a recent poll pronounced Schiphol too difficult to pronounce by the traveling public. It's a monument to Dutch drainage skills that on this very spot in 1573 the navies of Spain and the Netherlands fought a sea battle! Should you approach the field via the Ringcanal dike road, you will see ships riding higher than your ground level—and before you take off on the runway, you'll be 14 feet below the adjoining canal.

In addition to being aesthetically pleasing in a sleek way, it is perhaps the best-planned and most efficient airline passenger facility in Europe today. Conveyor belts for luggage, rolling sidewalks, an ingenious message system for travelers, all types of restaurants, and a self-service tax-free shop are only a part of its twenty-first-century picture. Its First-class Van Gogh Lounge is indeed a masterpiece, one of the finest we've seen in all of our global flying—a pair of adjoining rooms, deeply comfortable armchairs, stunning softspoken décor, and a copious bar-buffet from which Flying Dutchmen or visitors may select caviar, smoked salmon, foie gras, and other delicacies to accompany the wide array of beverages. Here is a remarkable spread—indicative of the caring and deluxe attitude this airline applies to every one of its premium passengers.

Recommendation: We recently stepped off our latest of at least 10 transatlantic crossings with Dutch wings and wonder how KLM can continue to better itself every flight. It does so without fail. Here is a magnificent carrier. KLM (located at 437 Madison Ave., KLM Plaza, in New York) has our complete respect, confidence, and admiration.

Norway See "Scandinavian Airlines System."

Braathens SAFE is independent and flies mostly within Norway. Equipment consists of a feathering of Fokker Fellowships.

Main airports of Norway are Fornebu (15 minutes from the center of Oslo; now, at last, with baggage porters; fine SAS-catered Caravelle Restaurant), Gardermoen (now used chiefly for charters; far out of the capital), Flesland (25 minutes from Bergen), Sola at Stavanger, Vaernes (modern and well equipped; good cafeteria; too-damned-long 45-minute ride from Trondheim), Bodø (north of the Arctic circle), Vigra off Aalesund, Bardufoss, and Tromsø. The Far North route has been extended to Alta, Lakselv, and Kirkenes.

If you run into any SAS problems in this land, take them to Oslo and the line's efficient, energetic Norwegian Director of Public Relations, Odd Medboe, or his charming, patient colleague, Mrs. Signe Siebke. They're the perfect answer for any troubled voyager.

★ **TIPS** The shocking dearth of baggage porters in Norway and the rest of Scandinavia is not only a tribulation to you, but presents a very real danger to heart patients and others with handicaps.

Portugal Air Portugal (AP), the official airline of the Department of Civil Aviation, formerly known as TAP, rules the local skies unchallenged and wings to many other nations as well. Along with its brand-new logo, AP

hostesses have also flung off their old wrappers and donned new rig from French designer Louis Féraud. The airline's new motif is green and red, the national colors.

Bonus: U.S.-Lisbon round trippers on a 14-to-21-day excursion fare may fly to-and-from glorious Funchal, Madeira, for an extra $13 from the Portuguese capital! (For our comments on Funchal Airport, please refer to "Madeira" in the Portuguese chapter.)

In New York, AP's address is 601 Fifth Ave.; the North American Director is the experienced António Parreira Pinto; Chicago, Los Angeles, San Francisco, Philadelphia, Washington, Boston, Newark, Cleveland, and Montreal also have reservations centers.

In the Azores, there's an interisland network covered by SATA, which operates 2 DH Doves. We've never flown it—but, for these short hauls, it is probably quite adequate.

Curiously, there are only 3 commercial (and very poor) airports on the whole mainland of this nation—Lisbon, Oporto, and Faro. Yet its international skein embraces more than half the globe. This is the only carrier we have flown which after dark dictates that all passenger lights be extinguished on all domestic or island takeoffs and landings.

Recommendation: AP has an excellent record in the air. (The pair of Madeira crashes—one a AP plane and the other a charter flight—relate more to the shortness of the island's single airstrip rather than to flying inadequacies or equipment.) If we can fault it at all it is on the ground, where personnel don't seem to care a whit for their customers. We recently climbed aboard AP on 7 different runs. Not only were we happily impressed by the knowhow of the pilots and cockpit crews, but our meals were delicious and the cabin service in each case was the ultimate in courtesy and kindness.

Scandinavian Airlines System In 1346, Denmark, Norway, and Sweden got together to discuss a Scandinavian Union. Six hundred years later they did something about it when, in 1946, they joined hands in the Scandinavian Airlines System—and it's just as remarkable as if Gimbel's said to B. Altman and Lord & Taylor, "Let's plunk all our merchandise on the same counter and sell it together!"

Credit is shared so scrupulously that 3 urchins couldn't divide a Hershey bar with greater solemnity or exactitude. The corporation chairmanship is revolved at yearly intervals; all crews represent 3 nationalities. The letterhead lists the partners in alphabetical order; the fuselage of each plane is emblazoned with 3 flags. And as the supreme Solomon's decision, *English* became the compromise official language!

The line now has 79 aircraft flying to 102 cities in 53 countries on 5 continents. Wide-body DC10 and 747B jet service cuts the sky time between New York and Copenhagen to slightly more than 7 hours, and between Los Angeles and the Danish capital to under 11 hours (about 9 from Seattle). The Chicago-Montreal-Copenhagen hookup has totaled only about 10 hours, while the

nonstop Chicago speedster cuts off about 2 hours from that. SAS has the largest fleet of spunky DC-9's outside the USA to zip around the Nordic lands, and elsewhere in Europe. Moreover, it recently put the A-300 Airbus on line for high-capacity short hauls. In all, the inventory of American-made aircraft and equipment on hand or on order is over the $1,000,000,000 mark—for 3 tiny countries who can muster only 17 million people among them!

Trunk routes fan out directly from the 3 Scandinavian capitals to (1) New York (also via Bergen and Göteborg), (2) Montreal and the Midwest, (3) Seattle and Los Angeles, (4) South America (all the way down to Santiago), (5) Monrovia and Abidjan, (6) South Africa, (7) Tokyo, over the Pole and via Anchorage or along the speedy trans-Siberian route through Moscow, (8) Tokyo, along the southern route via India, (9) the spectacular Trans-Asian Express, on a straight line across the USSR to Bangkok, Singapore, and Jakarta, (10) the West Indies, (11) Kuwait, Dhahran, Abu Dhabi, and (12) the world's most northerly service—to Spitsbergen. Coupled with Thai International, SAS also delivers through service to Sydney via Bangkok. With combined equipment, every capital of Free Europe is now reached; so are various satellite countries, Moscow, and Leningrad. And by the time you pack your chopsticks, the line's "Dragon Fleet" probably will be calling into Peking. The pilots, predominantly Scandinavian (one of them a woman), are crackerjacks —or crackerjackies; in looks some of the hostesses are wholesomely rustic, while others beat Anita Ekberg to a frazzle.

The remarkable growth of SAS is based on service, more service, and still more service to its ticket holders—the brand of personal attention which makes the traveler come back on his next trip for another helping. It's just the right size—big enough to handle big things, but not too big to stop caring about its individual ticket holders. This interest in the passenger can't be touched, in our opinion, by any transatlantic competitor—consistently one of the finest we've found among the 43 international companies we've flown. Its Economy-class schedules are also just about unbeatable in the standard budget category. Its kitchens still boast that no food is ever frozen, that every item is market fresh, and that diners are given the unique privilege of savoring such rare northern delights as Baltic salmon, Greenland shrimp, frikadeller, reindeer steak, and similar delicacies. For domestic hops, latecomers now can jump aboard and fork over the fare after they are seated. Within Scandinavia, incidentally, there are several special deals relating to family plans, senior citizens, business travelers, or sightseeing adventurers. You can check on these through SAS once you alight in the northlands.

The President of SAS is Carl-Olov Munkberg, who moved up from a wholly owned SAS subsidiary. Other members of top management include Frede Eriksen (Danish), Kai Sotorp (Norwegian), and Yngve Wessman (Swedish).

The present General Manager of North American Operations is B. John Heistein, a Norwegian with vast experience as an American Express executive and SAS Veepee. If any special SAS problems or puzzles should befuddle you,

drop a line to the able, scholarly, and graciously personable Sven Ralph Cohen, North American Director of Public Relations, who was lured from a similar role in the International Air Transport Association.

Safety record: Practically perfect. Minimum-safety standards set by SAS are, in our opinion, maximum-safety standards on several other well-known carriers. They seem to miss nothing, overlook nothing.

Recommendation: Complete. We continue to consider SAS virtually unbeatable—and, just as we've reported for many years in this book, its passenger service remains to us consistently among the most comfortable of the American or European carriers we fly.

Spain There are nominally 2: (1) **Iberia**, the state-owned carrier, and (2) Aviación y Comercio S.A., called **Aviaco**. The first controls the second, but they will continue to fly under separate burgees. They exchange aircraft, however, on certain routes. Two other independents, **Spantax** and **Aerlype**, are employed solely in charter and cargo work.

Aviaco plies partly on a nonscheduled basis to Nice, Tangier, Algiers, Oran, Mallorca, Menorca, various points on the Spanish mainland, and up to Brussels.

Iberia is a small colossus—and a haughty one, due solely to the fact that they've got just too damned much business. They employ the most modern aircraft internationally; locally, most of the time you'll find good equipment too. Maintenance, from a technical standpoint, is first-rate, but the fleet does work hard.

Service? Oh, *how* it varies! On several earlier transatlantic loops we've experienced sun-drenched Spanish charm both on the ground and while aloft. On one recent round-trip between Palma de Mallorca and New York, however, we could easily understand why our desk is spread with complaints from travelers who seem to have shared our bad luck on their overocean flights. Our food in Tourist Class was plainly inedible; the hostesses were kind but inept (even with no more than 18 passengers aboard); frequently the cocky stewards were too busy flirting with the stewardesses to attend to their passengers; the ground staff at Kennedy couldn't be bothered to offer us the smallest courtesies. (All of the terminal's baggage lockers were occupied or broken, but Iberia would not watch over our hand luggage for us while we ran some errands at the airport. Swissair, a few doors away, gladly volunteered to keep an eye on it.) When our flight was delayed for more than 3 hours for mechanical reasons, we had to *demand* a meal ticket as midnight approached. Any progress reports or announcements made to the waiting travelers had to be sought by the passengers themselves and passed on to their colleagues, prompting one wag to dub the line *"Siberia."* Never was a drink offered us nor was there an apology for all of the inconveniences from the ground supervisor, the desk staff, or the pilot or crew. In addition, one of our pieces of luggage—in such a meager cargo—was lost (but subsequently recovered; since then Iberia has lost 3 other peices, all finally returned intact). From our latest circuit, we'd venture that

segments of Iberia are beginning to take their customers too much for granted. This is so untypical of the Spanish personality that we hope its directors will cast a stern eye on the few negligent staffers who need their knuckles rapped.

Some of the metropolitan ticket offices (not flight crews) still have some of the most boorish, peremptory personnel we have ever come across in the aviation industry. In many cases, it seems to be a "don't-care-and-don't-bother-us" attitude—and this is a pity, because these people are Spain's ambassadors to thousands of visiting foreigners, and their lack of courtesy is totally un-Spanish. To be fair, however, not all Iberia's office employees fall into the indifferent category. The chiefs of the ground staffs at the airports in Palma de Mallorca, Barcelona, and Madrid, as 3 shining examples, always seem to go beyond the line of duty in kindness and consideration for the passenger. They are wonderful. If the overworked desk clerks can't give you satisfaction, just ask for the *jefe* and chances are he will smooth your flight path admirably.

Recommendation: Iberia will get you there, with efficient, safe flying. International services vary widely, with transatlantic flights largely in need of better, sharper administration and much more carefully trained, much less lazy hostesses. In sum, we think it's shake-up time at the Spanish national carrier.

Sweden For information on Swedish air service, please turn to Scandinavian Airlines System. **Arlanda International Airport** stands virtually alone far, far out in the boondocks. Since it is a 45-to-60 minute drive from the city on a fast highway, only if you are rich should you hire a taxi. For a reasonable sum, frequent and comfortable shuttle buses will whisk you to the center almost as quickly. Its terminal, thank goodness, is well equipped to cope with its heavy travel flow. Although it has the aforementioned luxury Flygrestaurangen Restaurant, the cafeteria, and the bar, contrary to common belief there are absolutely no hotels in its vicinity.

Switzerland Always a favorite of ours, this carrier seems to get even better as time goes on. Very recently we again boarded **Swissair** from Zürich to N.Y. (we've stopped counting our air crossings over 38 years). When we stepped off the DC-10 at JFK, we concluded that here was the most perfect transatlantic flight we'd ever enjoyed—and we knew it was good not just because we are travel writers, but because of our painstaking research to learn the reactions of other passengers aboard. The nonstop vitality and friendliness of the cabin crew, the superb First-class cuisine (which also looked mighty appetizing in Economy class), the felicitous surprise touches, the superb behind-the-scenes organization—all seemed so excessively good to be true that we promptly booked our return with this same company to reassure ourselves that this hadn't been a freak. It wasn't. Our eastbound trip aboard a 747 was again equally outstanding in every fine detail. Any carrier in the world, no matter how good, inevitably must come up with one sour flight now and then. But it is our belief that Swissair, like a luxury Swiss watch, almost consistently is in the top of the pack in giving to its customers extra comfort and happiness.

"Quality, not quantity" is the motto it lives by—and that's why, in our most

thoughtful opinion, here is indeed one of the finest carriers in the air. With such peak standards in passenger and technical operations, it's small wonder most of its customers are "repeaters" or "regulars."

This year's fleet consists of Boeing 747Bs and DC-10s which service the North Atlantic between New York, Chicago, Boston, Montreal, Toronto, and 2 Swiss gateways—Geneva and Zürich. The DC-10 and the DC-8 are employed on many North and South Atlantic passages plus routings to the Far East and Africa. Spin the globe and pick a destination. Unless your finger lands on Central America, New Zealand or Australia, Swissair can fly you there on a Jumbo, a DC-10 or -9 or -8, or a carrier pigeon.

Within the country, the skies are always busy with shuttles from and to Zürich, Geneva, and Basle.

The Swissair Director for North America is now Reynold Schwab. (He replaces our long-term chum on this beat, Dr. Hugo Mayr, who has moved up to the position of Delegate to the President.) If any special (not routine) problems involving the organization should arise, take them straight to Mr. Schwab at the Swiss Center, 608 Fifth Ave., N.Y. 10020. You may count upon his most interested and helpful personal attention.

Recommendation: We recommend Swissair unreservedly as a careful, efficient airline, with fine equipment, superservice within IATA limits, superior food, and pilots who know how to fly. We love it, and we hope you will too.

There are 3 major international airports—Kloten (6 miles from Zürich), Cointrin (3 miles from Geneva), and Basle-Mulhouse (4 miles from Basle). The fourth, near Berne, has been phased out by Swissair and replaced by an airline bus service between Zürich and the capital. As a spicy point of interest, the Kloten terminus was named for a neighboring village; sturdy Swiss burghers fainted like flies when an amused Hollander told them the startlingly vulgar Dutch translation of this word—but it wasn't changed to "Helvetia Airport," as planned, because too many announcement pamphlets had already been printed!

MISCELLANEOUS Icelandair (formerly Icelandic Airlines): This is the airline which *really* pioneered low fares to Europe 28 years ago when it resisted joining IATA. It has consistently maintained that policy. In '81, with an open rate war being waged over the Atlantic (because IATA was unable to agree on uniform tariffs among its members), every carrier wants to get into the bargain act. Icelandair makes its tempting bid with a $399 round-trip ticket between the U.S. and Luxemborg—a single-fare policy with no restrictions on advance purchase or length of stay abroad. Icelandair and International Air Bahama have joined in a unique "marriage of the Arctic and Tropics," representing each other worldwide and offering low fares and big savings to Luxembourg, whether you fly from Icelandair's New York and Chicago gateways or IAB's Nassau port.

Don't get the notion that here is a slapdash, 1-horse operation that flies tattered old candidates for the boneyard. It's a substantial, serious venture, with carefully maintained equipment, multimillion-dollar annual revenue, a nearly 700-million annual passenger mileage, U.S.-trained pilots, a high proportion of American personnel, and 2 ultramodern 218-room hotels in Reykjavik.

In safety standards it has the full approval of the U.S. Civil Aeronautics Board. Up to this writing its safety record is flawless.

Icelandair celebrates its 30th anniversary of regularly scheduled transatlantic service next year. It flies an all-jet fleet of DC-8s, with 250-seat "stretched" versions on the New York-, Los Angeles-, or Chicago-Luxembourg routes. A number of new flights now operate non-stop to Luxemborg.

Low-fare bus and rail service link Luxembourg with Paris, Frankfurt, Cologne, and other major cities—but if you want to linger in the Grand Duchy for 1–3 days, Icelandic provides bargain stopover tours. It also flies Oslo-Copenhagen-Stockholm and London-Glasgow from New York (some linking into Chicago), with one-hour stopovers in Iceland. You also can book the European hops aboard 727s operated out of Keflavik by the European division of Icelandair. Fares on the Scandinavian and British legs are identical to those of IATA lines, but with an important extra fillip. Passengers on these routes can enjoy one of the world's great travel bargains—layovers in Iceland, for 1 to 3 days, at a *maximum* of $20 a day including double room with bath in a First-class hotel, 2 meals daily (including delicious smörgåsbord luncheons) the first 2 days, breakfast on the 3rd day, sightseeing trips on the first 2 days, and transfers between airport and hotel. Children aged 2 to 12 pay half price. Regular summer rates (at press time) on these stopovers, for Luxembourg-bound passengers, are $53 for 24 hours, $95 for twice as long, and $122 for 3 days as of our press time, but can be expected to rise slightly by the time you wing in. Adventurous ski buffs can take advantage of the bargain winter hickory runs in the homeland. Additional offerings include youth fares (through age 23), group packages allowing different return dates, 1- and 2-week ski runs via Luxembourg; summer escorted motorcoach romps of 2 and 3 weeks to countries in western and eastern Europe; and Saga Discovery escorted summer loops which include Norway, Sweden, Denmark, and Iceland. Also popular are the winter weekend hops from New York to Iceland, and a series of Iceland Adventure summer tours—more than 20 packages to Iceland (pony treks, camping, geology and nature expeditions, salmon fishing), Greenland, and the Faroe Islands (about as off-the-beaten-path as you can get).

You won't find pink orchids aboard Icelandair, although the airline does serve complimentary wines and cognac with its full-course meals—but you will find a real value for the price—and please visit Iceland on one of the stopover plans or longer tours.

International Air Bahama: Since '68 this carrier has been affiliated with Icelandic as another big money-saver. Its DC-8 fan-jets, piloted by American million-mile captains and serviced by expertly trained multilingual hostesses, soar 6 times per week between Nassau (capital of the Bahamas) and Luxembourg, on 8-hour schedules. Since Nassau is only 30 minutes by air from Miami, here is an especially attractive bargain for residents of the southern states—as well as an exciting routing. IAB's year-round tariffs from Nassau to Luxembourg are roughly the same as Icelandair's, but there is no surcharge for weekend departures. Kids from 2 to 12 are charged 1/2-fare, and infants under 2 get aboard for 10%; a Golden Youth Fare has been launched for striplings of 55 or older. The free baggage allowance for everyone except babies is the same as IATA's. All meals, cocktails, champagne and other wines are gratis. If connections should snarl you up in Luxembourg for an overnight, the company will give you good hotel accommodations without charge, provided you make your request when you buy your ticket. IAB offers the same low-cost tours from Luxembourg as does Icelandair: 2- and 3-week car-and-rail packages all year and 1-week packages in winter, escorted 2- and 3-week summer motor-coach tours to countries in western and eastern Europe, and 1- and 2-week ski tours to Austria, France, and Switzerland. For further details, consult your travel agent or write direct to International Air Bahama, 25 S.E. Second Ave., Miami, Fla. 33131, or to any office of Icelandic Airlines.

Air India: Having learned to pamper maharajas in its pioneer days, this soundly managed and reliable long-line carrier tries to offer (with fair but not outstanding success, in our judgment) the transatlantic tripper an extra measure of plushiness. Its Boeing jetliners ply between (1) New York and London, Paris, Prague, Geneva, Frankfurt, Beirut, Cairo, Nairobi, and (2) Moscow, Singapore, and Sydney. A twice-weekly "express" links New York and New Delhi, via London and Moscow. Delhi, Bombay, and Calcutta are the company's Asian focal points. Its multimillion-mile pilots are U.S.- and British-trained. All Air India's jet skippers have had several months of tutelage in America.

Aircraft interiors reflect the rich coloring of the nation. Multilingual stewards, stewardesses, and sari-clad hostesses dispense exotic hors d'oeuvres and sweetmeats. Gourmet-class continental cuisine and a range of beverages are offered.

We recommend it highly for technical competence.

Ethiopian Airlines (EAL): We did our East African teething on this carrier, and it is impossible to express our delight in witnessing, as we did recently between 3 European cities, a safari-cum-Indian-Ocean cruise, a flying tour of East Africa, and an every-day-in-the-air 2-week domestic network romp aboard DC-6s and DC-3s, the fantastic growth and sophistication it has undergone. As a reporter for *Reader's Digest, Saturday Evening Post,* and other U.S.

media, we bounced with its Texas pilots over the exotic terrain of Ethiopia, Eritrea, and the Somalilands when the line was lucky if it could snag 2 other paying passengers. (Once, in stocking feet, we even crawled over a cargo of $1,000,000 of Maria Theresa thalers before flying with them to Aden, Arabia.)

Today, this stalwart is beautifully equipped and skillfully manned—flamboyantly attired outside, gorgeously decorated inside, and hospitalityenriched by attractive English-speaking hostesses in native *shamas*. Its pride of *simbas* consists of Boeing 707 jets, Boeing 720-Bs, DC-6Bs, DC-3s, 3 Bell helicopters, and 6 training planes. TWA boosted it into the air during its early days, but now, except for occasional consultations, it runs its own show smoothly and very nearly independently. As a sample, Ethiopian provides service that is simply out of this world. Incidentally, it has the only aircraft maintenance center on African soil which has been certified by the U.S. Federal Aviation Authority as meeting or surpassing 100% of its demanding standards. From its European termini of Paris, Frankfurt, Rome, and Athens, you may be whisked over 27-thousand miles of awesome scenery—all the way to Shanghai in the East, to Nairobi and Dar es Salaam in the South, and to Lagos (across the Sahara) and Accra in the West. Africa is its specialty—and it is strictly à la mode all the way. Grab EAL wherever you can—on any of 3 continents —because here is the best small airline that we have ever enjoyed in our travel lives, globally, and certainly the Vanguard of birds over Africa.

El Al Israel Airlines: Here's one, regrettably, which we've still missed to date—but reports from all sources (except the Syrians) also couldn't be better.

Like Ethiopian, El Al is said to concentrate extra-heavily on passenger comfort and service, which may account for its having the highest load factor of all North Atlantic carriers.

Nonstop Boeing 747 and 707 jets, between New York and Tel Aviv—the longest scheduled commercial haul offered by any international carrier—fly 2 Atlantic-European crossings daily in peak season. Flight time is an amazing 10 hours and 20 minutes. It is the only carrier zipping nonstop both to and from Israel.

These blue-and-white birds also cover such ports-o'-call as London, Amsterdam, Brussels, Munich, Frankfurt, Geneva, Copenhagen, Vienna, Zürich, Lisbon, Paris, Marseille, Rome, Athens, Istanbul, Mexico City, Bucharest, Nairobi, and Johannesburg.

El Al is also pushing for reduced air fares. *Mazel tov!*

Obviously these Israelis are doing a big job.

Aeroflot: The Russians hop the Atlantic once a week with 120-passenger IL-62 between Moscow and New York, via Montreal. We haven't sampled its caviar—not *nyet*. **CSA** (its Czech mate) has twice-weekly probes to Prague with New York en passant. Bratislava and Amsterdam can also be ports-o'-call for the IL-62's, plus more than 50 cities on 4 continents. **Japan Air Lines**

jumps daily from either London or Paris springboards to New York. Mexico's **Aero Mexico** says *sí-sí* to Miami 3 times a week from Paris and Madrid. These 3, too, are new on us.

This year there will be a lot of new burgees fluttering over the Atlantic due to the liberalized charter codes which put supplemental and scheduled carriers effectively on an equal footing as far as ticketing is concerned. Our best advice is to watch the ads and look for the great new bargains in air travel.

Index

NOTES

NOTES

NOTES

NOTES

NOTES

NOTES

NOTES